Chemistry in focus

Chemistry
in focus

JOHN ANDREW AND PAUL RISPOLI

Hodder & Stoughton

LONDON SYDNEY AUCKLAND TORONTO

© 1991 John Andrew and Paul Rispoli

First published in Great Britain 1991

British Library Cataloguing in Publication Data
Andrew, John, *1944–*
    Chemistry in focus.
    1. Chemistry. – For schools
    I. Title II. Rispoli, Paul
    540

ISBN 0 7131 7742 X

Typeset in Ehrhardt and illustrated by Gecko Limited, Bicester
Printed and bound in Great Britain for the educational publishing
division of Hodder and Stoughton Limited, Mill Road, Dunton Green,
Sevenoaks, Kent by Thomson Litho, East Kilbride.

Contents

Acknowledgements

The authors are grateful to the following persons for their contributions in the production of this book.

All those at Edward Arnold and Hodder & Stoughton, especially Joan Angelbeck who first brought us together and gave us unstinting encouragement and support in the early stages; the reviewers of our earlier manuscript drafts, especially Carolyn Davies for constructive criticism and helpful suggestions; students and colleagues who worked through parts of the text pointing out errors and omissions, especially Nigel Mason and Andrew Graydon for their patience in meticulously checking the original manuscript; our long-suffering wives and families who cheerfully (for the most part) accepted the long hours spent at the wordprocessor during the gestation of this book, and many others too numerous to mention individually who have contributed towards the final version.

Any errors or omissions which remain are, of course, entirely our own responsibility.

John Andrew and Paul Rispoli

The following companies, institutions and individuals have given permission to reproduce photographs in this book:

A Shell photograph (48, 141 top, 431 top, 432, 450 bottom, 450 middle, 450 top, 454 top left), All-Sport UK Ltd (567), Anglian Water Authority (422 bottom), Barnaby's Picture Library (38 left, 38 top right, 39 top left, 72, 117 bottom, 279 middle, 304 bottom, 358 left, 363 bottom right, 566 bottom), British Alcan Aluminium PLC (111 right, 292 top, 292 bottom right, 301 top, 301 bottom), British Coal Corporation (160 right, 422 top right), Bubbles Photo Library (566 top), By permission of the Syndics of the Cambridge University Library (4 top left), C W E Ltd (494 top left, top right, bottom right, bottom left, Calor Gas Ltd (430), Chris Nicoll, Kingfisher Studios (8, 78 right, 279 right, 517 top, 530, 517 top, 554), Corning (141 bottom), Courtesy of Marie Curie Cancer Care (12 left), Courtesy of STEAM (407, 555), Crown Paints (363 bottom left), Department of Medical Illustration, St Bartholomew's Hospital, London (78 far right, 519, 577), Dr Alan Beaumont (410 top), Dr Arthur Lesk, Laboratory for Molecular Biology/Science Photo Library (85), Dr B Booth, G. S. F. Picture Library (293 top left, 293 bottom left), Dr Jeremy Burgess/Science Photo Library (303 bottom left), Dunlop Ltd (454 right), Equal Opportunities Commission (441), Evostick Information Services (498), Ford Motor Company (161 top right), Frank Lane Picture Agency (261), Friends of the Earth (337), GeoScience Features Picture Library (293), Greenpeace Communications Ltd (429 top, 429 bottom), Griffin & George (410 bottom), Harrogate Resort Services Department (171), I C I (202, 240, 270 bottom right, 315 bottom left, 326, 340, 517 bottom), Imperial War Museum (4 right, 17, 470 top, 470 bottom), International Stock Exchange Photo Library (452), J Allan Cash Ltd, Worldwide Photographic Library (342 top left, 342 top right), James Holmes, Hays Chemicals/Science Photo Library (21 bottom, 355 bottom), Jerome Yeats/Science Photo Library (217 bottom), Malcolm Fielding, Johnson Matthey PLC/Science Photo Library (78 far left, 166), Manchester City Council (2), Martin Bond/Science Photo Library (340), Mary Evans Picture Library (111 left), N A S A (270 bottom left), National Grid, a division of the C E G B (292 bottom middle), National Power, a division of the C E G B (39 top right, 424 top, 424 bottom), Nursing Standard (471, 566 middle), Philippe Plailly/Science Photo Library (142 bottom, 499), Popperfoto (20 middle, 20 top, 95 bottom left, 117 top, 401), Roddy Paine (39 bottom left, 279 left, 303 bottom right, 345 right, 431 bottom, 504), Sefton Photo Library (198), St Bartholomew's Hospital, London/Science Photo Library (10 right), The Hulton Picture Company (161 bottom), The Metropolitan Police (330, 495), The Yorkshire Museum (363 top middle), Topham Picture Source (315 top), Trustees of the Science Museum (1, 10 left, 161 top left, 461), U K A E A (12 right, 18, 19, 20 bottom, 21 top), Vandenbergh & Jurgens Ltd (449), West Kent Coal Store (160 left), Z E F A Picture Library (UK) Ltd (355 top, 355 middle, 329 top, 329 bottom, 363 top left).

CHAPTER 1

Evidence for the Modern View of Atomic Structure

Contents

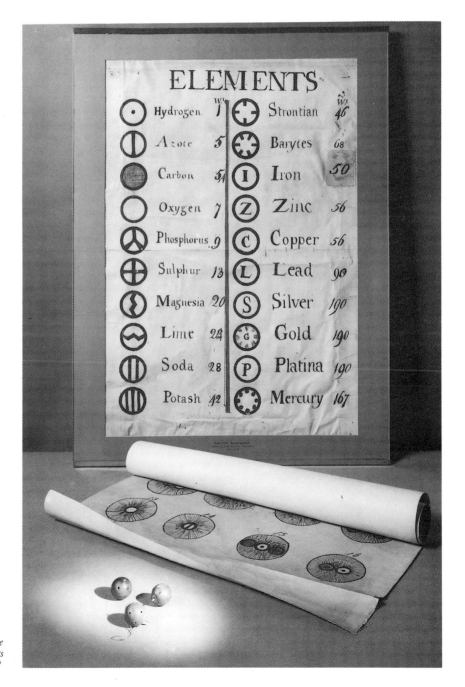

In 1807, John Dalton (1766–1844) published his Atomic Theory. These are the symbols he used to denote the elements. Do you agree with each of the main points in Dalton's Atomic Theory, as described over the page?

Well over 2000 years ago, the Greek philosopher Democritus proposed that all matter was made of tiny indivisible particles, which he called **atoms**. Unfortunately, he had no evidence to support his theory and the Ancient Greeks preferred the idea that matter resulted from some mystical combination of Four Elements: Fire, Earth, Water and Air. Indeed, it was not until the 18th century that chemists began to explain their results in terms of atoms.

In this chapter, we shall briefly look at the evidence which has led, over the last 200 years, to the development of the **nuclear model of the atom**.

1.1 Dalton's Atomic Theory

Between 1774 and 1802, chemists proposed a number of laws concerning the ratios by mass of the elements in pure compounds. In 1807, Dalton published an Atomic Theory which explained these laws and his own experiments. The main points of the theory are:

▶ All elements are made of very small particles called atoms (from the Greek word *atomos*, meaning indivisible).
▶ Atoms cannot be created, destroyed or divided.
▶ Atoms of the same element are identical but differ in mass from those of other elements.
▶ Atoms form compounds by combining chemically in simple whole number ratios.

During the 19th century, the idea of an indivisible atom gradually lost favour. It was finally discredited in 1897 when Thomson proved the existence of a sub-atomic particle, the **electron**. Furthermore, *atoms of the same element but with different masses*, called **isotopes**, were discovered by Thomson in 1913. Even with these inaccuracies, though, Dalton's theory allows chemists to define an atom as the smallest part of an element which can possess the chemical properties of that element.

1.2 The discovery of the electron

Experimental evidence for the existence of the electron came from research into the conduction of electricity by gases. In one of these experiments, first performed by Crookes in 1875, a high voltage is passed through a gas at low pressure and invisible radiation is emitted from the cathode. Like light, these **cathode rays** move in a straight line and this enables them to cast a shadow of objects in their path.

John Dalton engaged in one of his experiments – collecting marsh gas which is mainly methane. This painting, by Ford Madox Brown, hangs in the Town Hall, Manchester

Figure 1.1   *The theory behind Millikan's oil-drop experiment. When the oil drop is stationary, the gravitational force downwards will equal the electrical force upwards*

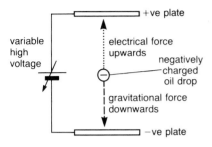

By studying their deflections in electric and magnetic fields, Thomson, in 1897, showed that *cathode rays were negatively charged*. He also found that:

▶ the charge/mass ratio (e/m) for cathode rays was 1.76×10^{11} coulombs kg^{-1} (a coulomb is a small unit of electrical charge); and,

▶ e/m remained constant whatever cathode material or gas were used.

From these results, Thomson concluded that *cathode rays were beams of very small negatively charged particles*, which he called **electrons**. Since e/m did not depend on the gas used, he suggested that electrons were present in all chemical elements.

Accurate values for the charge on the electron and its mass were obtained by Millikan in 1909. He prevented the fall under gravity of a charged oil drop by applying an electric field (figure 1.1). By equating gravitational and electrical forces, he measured the charge on a stationary drop. After many experiments, *Millikan found that the charge on any drop was always a multiple of 1.60×10^{-19} coulombs*. Thus, he concluded that this must be the basic quantity of electricity due to the charge on one electron.

Now, by using Thomson's value for e/m (1.76×10^{11} coulombs kg^{-1}), and Millikan's value for e (1.60×10^{-19} coulombs), we can estimate the mass of an electron, m:

$$m \;=\; e \div e/m \;=\; \frac{1.60 \times 10^{-19} \text{ coulombs}}{1.76 \times 10^{11} \text{ coulombs kg}^{-1}}$$

$$\Rightarrow \text{mass of an electron, } m \;=\; 9.1 \times 10^{-31} \text{kg}$$

1.3   Positive rays and protons

Positive rays were first observed by Goldstein in 1886. Using a discharge tube fitted with a perforated cathode, he detected a glow at each end of the tube (figure 1.2). As expected, the fluorescence at A was caused by cathode rays. However, the radiation at B was found to be attracted towards a negative charge, which meant that it must be positively charged.

In 1911, Thomson measured the charge/mass ratio of positive rays by studying their deflection in a combined electric and magnetic field. He found that the masses of positive ions produced by various gases were usually multiples of the mass of the hydrogen ion, H^+ (e.g. He^+ was found to be four times heavier than H^+). Thus, *the hydrogen ion was adopted as the atom's basic unit of positive charge* and it became known as the **proton**. The proton has a mass of 1.67×10^{-27} kg, that is, about 1850 times heavier than an electron. Since an electron has such a low mass, an ion will always have virtually the same mass as the parent atom.

Figure 1.2   *Goldstein's experiment for the detection of positive rays. At points X, a rapidly moving electron strikes a gas molecule or atom to form a positive ion. This moves towards and then through the perforated cathode*

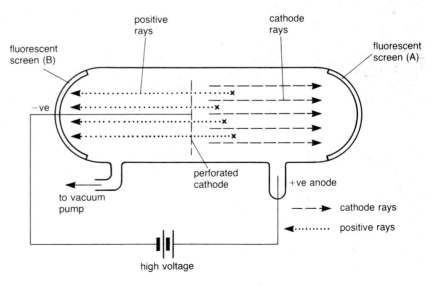

Ernest Rutherford (1871–1937) received the Nobel Prize for Chemistry in 1907 for his work on radioactivity. He proposed the nuclear model of the atom in 1911

1.4 Rutherford's concept of the atomic nucleus

Since atoms were known to be electrically neutral, Thomson proposed that they must contain the same number of protons and electrons. Thus, he pictured the atom as a solid sphere of the positive charge (i.e. made of protons), with a large number of electrons embedded in it. Thomson's model was accepted for about ten years and it became known as the 'plum pudding' model of the atom.

A major step forward in the investigation of atomic structure came from work at Manchester University in 1909. Under the supervision of Professor Rutherford, Geiger and Marsden studied the scattering of alpha (α) particles by thin sheets of metal foil. α-**particles** *are helium nuclei, $He^{2+}(g)$, produced by the decay of certain radioactive elements such as radium.*

The fifteen inch forward guns and bridge of HMS Queen Elizabeth photographed circa 1917. These guns had a range of sixteen miles

Figure 1.3   *The apparatus used by Geiger and Marsden*

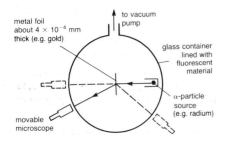

Figure 1.4   *An illustration of Geiger and Marsden's results*

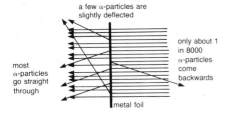

Using the apparatus shown in figure 1.3, Geiger and Marsden showed that *most of the α-particles passed straight through the foil or were very slightly deflected* (figure 1.4). However, to their amazement, about *1 in 8000 of the α-particles came backwards off the foil.* Rutherford's own account of the discovery is worth noting:

'I remember two or three days later Geiger coming to me in great excitement and saying, "We have been able to get some α-particles coming backwards . . .".

It was quite the most incredible event that had ever happened to me in my life. It was almost as incredible as if you fired a 15-inch shell at a piece of tissue paper and it came back and hit you.'

Rutherford's explanation of Geiger and Marsden's results is described in figure 1.5.

Following these experiments, Rutherford introduced the **nuclear model of the atom** in 1911. *This viewed the atom as a very small, dense nucleus of positive charge with negatively charged electrons arranged around it.* Indeed, modern techniques show that the radius of the nucleus is only about one ten-thousandth of the radius of the atom. Also, the particularly low mass of the electron means that the nucleus can be taken as the sole contributor to the atomic mass.

At first, Rutherford thought that the positively-charged nucleus must be made of protons held together by massive attractive forces. However, further study of the α-particle scattering patterns showed that the mass of the protons in the nucleus was only about half the atomic mass. Consequently, Rutherford suggested that the *nucleus must also contain neutral particles having the same mass as the proton.* These neutral particles were termed **neutrons**.

Figure 1.5 *Rutherford's interpretation of Geiger and Marsden's results*

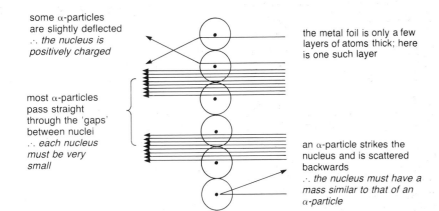

some α-particles are slightly deflected
∴ *the nucleus is positively charged*

the metal foil is only a few layers of atoms thick; here is one such layer

most α-particles pass straight through the 'gaps' between nuclei
∴ *each nucleus must be very small*

an α-particle strikes the nucleus and is scattered backwards
∴ *the nucleus must have a mass similar to that of an α-particle*

• the very small nucleus

○ the much larger arrangement of electrons

1.5 Atomic number

In 1869, Mendeleev showed that when the elements were arranged in order of increasing atomic mass, elements with similar chemical properties were found at regular intervals. His arrangement became known as the **Periodic Table of the Elements** (discussed later in section 19.1).

There were, however, some problems. To fit in with the overall pattern, certain elements had to be placed out of 'atomic mass' order. For example, tellurium had to be put before iodine, a slightly lighter atom. Mendeleev got round this by saying that atomic masses could not be measured accurately enough at that time. When more accurate methods of mass determination were discovered, he expected his order to be proved correct. Well, he was wrong, modern methods show that tellurium **is** heavier than iodine! By the start of the 20th century, scientists were seriously questioning whether the Periodic Table should be based on the order of atomic masses. But what other order might be used?

This debate was resolved in 1914. Firstly, van der Broek noted the similarity between the number of positive charges on the nucleus and the atomic number (i.e. the ordinal number of the element in the Periodic Table). For example, oxygen has a nuclear charge of $+8$ and its atomic number is 8 (i.e. it is the eighth element in the Periodic Table).

Shortly afterwards, Moseley found that X-rays were released when metals were bombarded with electrons. He measured the frequencies of these X-rays and tried to relate them to (i) the atomic numbers and (ii) the atomic masses of the metals used. After drawing various graphs, he eventually obtained an excellent straight line by plotting $\sqrt{(\text{X-ray frequency})}$ against atomic number (figure 1.6(a)). However, a graph of $\sqrt{(\text{X-ray frequency})}$ against atomic mass was not linear (figure 1.6(b)). Moseley's impressive evidence confirmed that atomic number, not atomic mass, is the fundamental property upon which we should base our periodic arrangement of the elements.

The **atomic number** *of an element is defined as the number of protons in an atomic nucleus*. It also tells us:

▶ the number of electrons in a neutral atom;
▶ the numbered position of the element in the Periodic Table.

When we need to state the atomic number of an element, we write it as a subscript in front of the element symbol. Thus, $_{46}\text{Pd}$ means that palladium, atomic number $= 46$, has 46 protons and 46 electrons in a neutral atom. It is the 46th element in the Periodic Table.

Moseley's research enabled chemists to (i) *identify elements* from the frequency of the X-rays they emitted and (ii) *calculate atomic numbers* from experimental results. Moseley's results also acted as a signpost to the discovery of unknown elements (e.g. scandium, $_{21}\text{Sc}$).

Figure 1.6 *Some of Moseley's results for the X-ray spectra of various metals. (a) an excellent straight line graph for $\sqrt{(\text{X-ray frequency})}$ against atomic number; (b) plotting $\sqrt{(\text{X-ray frequency})}$ against atomic mass gives a poor straight line graph.*

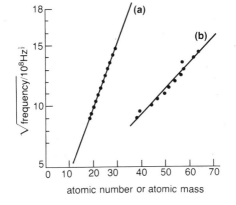

atomic number or atomic mass

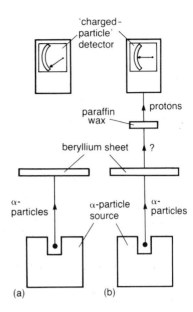

Figure 1.7   *Chadwick's experiment to prove the existence of the neutron*

1.6 The neutron and mass number

The existence of the neutron was first proved by Chadwick in 1932. When he bombarded a thin sheet of beryllium metal with α-particles, no charged particles were detected (figure 1.7a). However, when a film of paraffin wax was placed between the metal and the detector, there was a reading on the 'charged-particle' detector (figure 1.7b). From their charge/mass ratio, these particles were identified as protons. Chadwick proved that these protons must have been dislodged by particles of similar mass. Since the first experiment showed these particles were uncharged, Chadwick had detected neutrons. His work confirmed Rutherford's idea of twenty years earlier, that the atomic nucleus contained neutral particles.

With the exception of hydrogen which is a single proton, all atomic nuclei contain neutrons. The number of neutrons in the nucleus can be worked out from its atomic number and **mass number**. The mass number of an atom is the *number of protons plus neutrons in the nucleus*. When we need to state the mass number of an atom, we write it as a superscript in front of the element's symbol. Thus, ^{18}O represents an atom of oxygen for which the total of protons plus neutrons is 18. (Protons and neutrons are sometimes termed **nucleons**; thus, an ^{18}O atom contains 18 nucleons.)

We saw in section 1.5 that the atomic number is written as a subscript before the element's symbol. Thus, an atom of $^{19}_{9}F$ has 9 protons, 9 electrons and 10 neutrons; it contains 19 nucleons.

Activity 1.1

A $^{35}_{17}Cl$ atom contains 18 neutrons.

A $^{57}_{26}Fe$ atom contains 31 neutrons.

A $^{257}_{103}Lr$ atom contains 154 neutrons.

1   How is the number of neutrons calculated from the mass and atomic numbers?

2   List the numbers of protons, electrons and neutrons in the following atoms:

$$^{228}_{89}Ac, \ ^{133}_{55}Cs, \ ^{127}_{53}I, \ ^{204}_{82}Pb, \ ^{15}_{7}N, \ ^{100}_{44}Ru, \ ^{126}_{52}Te, \ ^{238}_{92}U, \ ^{68}_{30}Zn.$$

1.7 Comments on activity 1.1

1   number of neutrons = mass number − atomic number.

2

	Ac	Cs	I	Pb	N	Ru	Te	U	Zn
protons	89	55	53	82	7	44	52	92	30
electrons	89	55	53	82	7	44	52	92	30
neutrons	139	78	74	122	8	56	74	146	38

1.8 Summary and Revision Plan

1   An **atom** is the smallest part of an element that can possess the chemical properties of that element.

2   **Cathode rays** are produced when a high voltage is passed through a gas at low pressure. Thomson proved that cathode rays were beams of **electrons**.

3   From experiments involving the scattering of α-particles by thin sheets of metal foil, Rutherford concluded that the atom consisted of a very small **nucleus** of positive charge surrounded by the negatively charged electrons. The nuclear radius is about one ten-thousandth the size of the atomic radius.

4   Rutherford proposed that the nucleus contained positive and neutral particles called **protons** and **neutrons**, respectively.

5   The properties of the fundamental sub-atomic particles are summarised in table 1.1.

Table 1.1   *Properties of the fundamental sub-atomic particles*

Particle	PROTON	NEUTRON	ELECTRON
charge	+1	0	−1
mass/kg	1.67×10^{-27}	1.67×10^{-27}	9.10×10^{-31}
location	nucleus	nucleus	around the nucleus
effect of an electric or magnetic field	deflected	no effect	deflected
discovered by	Rutherford (1911)	Chadwick (1932)	Thomson (1897)

6   The **atomic number** of an element is defined as the number of protons in the nucleus of an atom. It also tells us: (i) the number of electrons in a neutral atom, and (ii) the element's numbered position in the Periodic Table.

7   The **mass number** of an element = number of protons + neutrons in the nucleus.

8   Mass number and atomic number are written as super- and sub-script, respectively, in front of the element's symbol.

9   **Isotopes** are atoms with the same atomic number but different mass numbers, that is, they contain a different number of neutrons. Whilst they have different physical properties, isotopes show identical chemical behaviour (because they have the same number of electrons).

CHAPTER 2

The Atomic Nucleus and Radioactivity

An analysis of an unknown hydrocarbon shows that it contains 84.0% carbon and 16.0% hydrogen. Which element do you think has the most atoms in the hydrocarbon molecule? Well, to a new student of chemistry an obvious, yet incorrect, answer would be carbon! In fact, the hydrocarbon is heptane, C_7H_{16}. Although they make up only 16% of the molecular mass, the hydrogen atoms easily outnumber the carbon atoms. The reason for this is that, in terms of their relative atomic masses, each carbon atom is *about twelve times heavier* than a hydrogen atom.

2.1 Relative atomic mass

In 1961, it was agreed internationally that

$$\text{relative atomic mass of an element, } A_r = \frac{\text{average mass of one atom of the element}}{\text{1/12th the mass of one atom of carbon-12}}$$

An **atomic mass unit, u** was taken as 1/12 of the mass of the carbon-12 atom (i.e. 1.66×10^{-27} kg). Thus, one atom of carbon-12 weighs 12 u and its relative atomic mass is 12; one atom of hydrogen weighs 1 u and its relative atomic mass is 1.

For chemical studies, relative atomic masses are usually taken as whole numbers e.g. $A_r(\text{Ne}) = 20$, not 20.183; chlorine is an exception, having $A_r = 35.5$. A table of relative atomic masses is given on page 245.

This bank cashier is counting money by weighing coins. He knows, for instance, that £5 in ten pence coins weighs 567 grams. In the same way, chemists can work out the number of atoms, molecules or ions in a sample of pure substance by weighing it

2.2 The Avogadro constant

Any sample that we weigh out will contain many billions of particles, whether these be atoms, ions or molecules. But how many?

We need to measure them by using a 'standard' number of particles, just as, for example, we buy eggs by the dozen (12) or test-tubes by the gross (144). Thus, we define the **mole** as *the amount of any substance which contains the same number of particles as there are atoms in 12 grams of carbon-12*. These particles may be atoms, molecules, ions, neutrons and so on.

The actual number of particles in a mole, known as the **Avogadro constant** (**L**), can be determined using X-ray diffraction (section 6.4). Its value is found to be 6.023×10^{23} mol^{-1}. Looking at table 2.1, you can see that by weighing out the relative atomic or molecular or ionic mass in grams, we will always be working with one mole of those particles.

Using simple ratio, we find that for pure substances

$$\text{number of moles present in a sample} = \frac{\text{mass of the sample}}{\text{mass of one mole of the sample}}$$

For example, 8.05 g of sodium ($A_r = 23$) contains $8.05/23 = 0.35$ moles of sodium atoms.

Table 2.1 *The relationship between the mass of one particle and the mass of one mole of particles (1 u = 1.66 × 10^{-24} g)*

Particle	boron atom (B)	chlorine molecule (Cl$_2$)	lithium ion (Li$^+$)
Mass of one particle/u	10.8	70.9	6.9
$\Downarrow$ × 1.66 × 10^{-24}	$\Downarrow$	$\Downarrow$	$\Downarrow$
Mass of one particle/g	1.79×10^{-23}	11.76×10^{-23}	1.15×10^{-23}
$\Downarrow$ × 6.023 × 10^{23}	$\Downarrow$	$\Downarrow$	$\Downarrow$
Mass of one mole of particles/g	10.8	70.9	6.9

Activity 2.1

Using the table of relative atomic masses on page 245 answer the following questions.

1   List the atomic masses of: cerium, iodine, palladium and titanium.
2   What is the mass of one mole of: (a) potassium chloride, KCl; (b) iron; (c) hydrated sodium thiosulphate, Na$_2$S$_2$O$_3$.5H$_2$O; (d) silica, SiO$_2$?
3   Calculate the mass of the following:
    (a) 0.5 moles of ammonia molecules, NH$_3$;
    (b) 0.375 moles of caesium atoms, Cs;
    (c) 1.50 moles of fluorine molecules, F$_2$;
    (d) 0.275 moles of hydrated sodium carbonate, Na$_2$CO$_3$.10H$_2$O.
4   How many moles are there in:
    (a) 14 g of magnesium atoms, Mg;
    (b) 8 g of carbon dioxide molecules, CO$_2$;
    (c) 0.5 g of copper(II) chloride, CuCl$_2$;
    (d) 38 g of hydrated copper(II) sulphate, CuSO$_4$.5H$_2$O?

2.3 The mass spectrometer

First introduced by Aston in 1919, the **mass spectrometer** provides the most accurate method of measuring relative atomic, or molecular, masses. The operation of a simple mass spectrometer, figure 2.1, is described below.

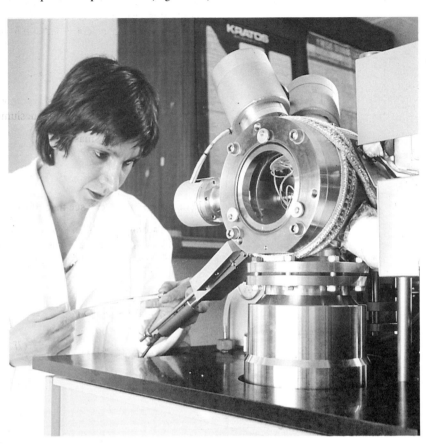

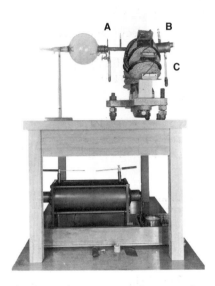

A scientist loading a sample into the mass spectrometer at St Bartholomew's Hospital in London. This instrument is used to identify compounds by exploring their behaviour in a strong magnetic field

Aston's original mass spectograph. Gaseous particles pass at high speed from A to B and, in the process, they are deflected by the magnetic field from the electromagnet at C

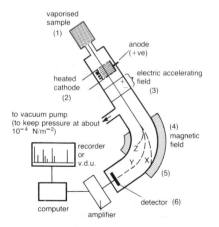

Figure 2.1 *A mass spectrometer*

1   The sample is vaporised and flows into the main chamber which is kept at very low pressure.
2   High energy electrons are released by the hot cathode. These strike the gas particles, forming positive ions most of which are singly charged:

$$e^- \quad + \quad X(g) \quad \rightarrow \quad e^- + e^- \quad + \quad X^+(g)$$

| 'bombarding' electron of high energy | low energy electrons | positive ion |

3   An electric field is used to accelerate the positive ions up to the same velocity . . . .
4   . . . . and then they enter a magnetic field. While in this field, the ions suffer a deflection, the size of which depends on their charge/mass ratio. *Providing that they have the same charge, we find that ions of lowest mass experience the greatest deflection.* Thus, in figure 2.1, the mass of the ions shown is $X^+ > Y^+ > Z^+$.
5   By varying the magnetic field strength, then, each of the ions can be deflected so that it strikes the detector.
6   The detector measures the percentage abundance of each ion in the sample. After computer analysis, the results are reproduced on a chart or visual display unit.

By skilful variation of electric and magnetic fields, the operator can produce a mass spectrum. Figure 2.2, for example, gives the mass spectrum for magnesium. It shows that there are three **isotopes** (i.e. *atoms of the same element but containing different number of neutrons*). This data can be used to calculate the relative atomic mass of magnesium (section 2.4).

The existence of isotopes, first suggested by Thomson in 1913, was confirmed by Aston using his original mass spectrograph. Nowadays, the mass spectrometer is most often used in the determination of a compound's molecular mass and structural formula (sections 6.2 and 6.3).

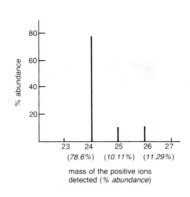

Figure 2.2   *The mass spectrum of naturally occurring magnesium*

2.4 Calculating atomic masses from mass spectra

The atomic mass of an element can be worked out from the percentage abundances of its isotopes. For example, magnesium has the isotopic composition:

Isotopic mass/u	% relative abundance
24	78.60
25	10.11
26	11.29

From this data, we can see that 100 atoms of the Mg will contain:

78.60 atoms of mass 24 giving a combined mass of (78.60×24) u
10.11 atoms of mass 25 giving a combined mass of (10.11×25) u
11.29 atoms of mass 26 giving a combined mass of (11.29×26) u

Now,

$$\text{average atomic mass} = \frac{\text{mass of 100 atoms in the isotopic mixture}}{100}$$

$$\text{average mass of 1 Mg atom} = \frac{(78.60 \times 24) + (10.11 \times 25) + (11.29 \times 26)}{100}$$

$$= \frac{1886.4 + 252.75 + 293.54}{100}$$

$$= \frac{2432.69}{100}$$

$$= 24.3 \text{ u}$$

Thus, the average mass of a magnesium atom is 24.3 u and the relative atomic mass of magnesium is 24.3. One mole of magnesium atoms will weigh 24.3 g.

Activity 2.2

The mass numbers and percentage abundances (in brackets) of xenon isotopes are given below. Calculate the relative atomic mass of xenon.

124 (0.13), 126 (0.09), 128 (1.92), 129 (26.44), 130 (4.08), 131 (21.18), 132 (26.89), 134 (10.40), 136 (8.87).

2.5 Radioactivity

In 1896, the French scientist Henri Becquerel noticed the darkening of photographic plates stored in the same drawer as a uranium salt. He showed that the salt emitted radiation, spontaneously, irrespective of the temperature and the chemical nature of the uranium salt. Becquerel used the term **radioactivity** to describe this *spontaneous emission of radiation by an atom*. Such atoms are said to undergo **radioactive decay** or **radioactive disintegration**. Following its discovery, scientists questioned whether radioactivity was a unique property of uranium, and this sparked off a search for other radioactive elements.

a *Marie and Pierre Curie (1867–1934 and 1859–1906) at work in their laboratory. Marie Curie began studying the radioactive emissions of uranium shortly after their discovery by Becquerel in 1896. She discovered that thorium was radioactive and by the end of 1898 Curie, working with her husband, detected two further radioactive elements. which they named polonium and radium. The Curies were awarded the Nobel Prizes in both physics and chemistry for their work*

b *Radioactivity is now known to be a danger to health, and strict monitoring and safety procedures must be followed by those exposed to it. Here both a Geiger counter and a safety badge are being used to keep a check on the radiation dose received*

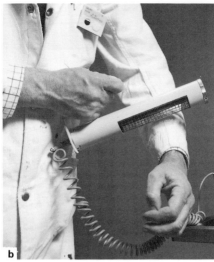

A major discovery was made by Marie and Pierre Curie in 1898. They found that the intense radioactivity of pitchblende, a uranium ore (U_3O_8), could not result just from the uranium in the mineral. Using fractional crystallisation, their dedicated research led to the separation from the mineral of two more radioactive elements, polonium and radium. These elements are extremely radioactive. Radium, for example, is many millions of times more active than the same amount of uranium.

Over the years many other radioactive elements, of widely varying activity, have been identified. Some of these are naturally occurring (e.g. francium, ^{223}Fr). Many more are produced artificially by **nuclear transmutations**. In these processes, an atomic nucleus is bombarded with small, highly energetic, particles such as protons or neutrons, e.g.

$$^{23}_{11}\text{Na} \quad + \quad ^{1}_{0}\text{n} \quad \rightarrow \quad ^{24}_{11}\text{Na}$$
sodium-23   neutron   sodium-24   (radioactive)

This is an example of a **nuclear equation**; *note that the mass and atomic numbers must balance on each side.*

Some uses of artificially produced radioactive isotopes are described in section 2.13.

2.6 Types of radiation and their properties

Radioactive substances can emit three types of radiation: **alpha (α) particles, beta (β) particles** and **gamma (γ)-rays**. When they pass through a magnetic or an electric field, these behave differently, as shown in figure 2.3.

α-particles

Alpha particles are fast-moving helium nuclei, $^{4}_{2}\text{He}^{2+}$. However, in nuclear equations, an α-particle is given the symbol $^{4}_{2}\textbf{He}$, not $^{4}_{2}\text{He}^{2+}$, e.g.

$$^{225}_{89}\text{Ac} \quad \rightarrow \quad ^{221}_{87}\text{Fr} \quad + \quad ^{4}_{2}\text{He}$$
actinium-225   francium-221   α-particle

It is understood that, on forming the α-particle, the $^{4}_{2}\text{He}$ atom releases two extranuclear electrons.

β-particles

β-*particles are electrons which have been ejected from the nucleus*. They move extremely rapidly, with the fastest travelling at almost the speed of light.

Figure 2.3   *The effect of an electric field on the radiation emitted by bismuth-210*

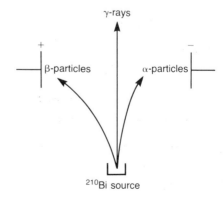

Beta particles may be represented by the symbol for an electron, $_{-1}^{0}e$ (i.e. mass number = 0, charge = -1), e.g.

$$\underset{\text{bismuth-213}}{_{83}^{213}\text{Bi}} \rightarrow \underset{\text{polonium-213}}{_{84}^{213}\text{Po}} + \underset{\beta\text{-particle}}{_{-1}^{0}e}$$

γ-rays

γ-rays are highly energetic electromagnetic waves, having a wavelength about a million times shorter than that of visible light (section 6.3).

Emission of γ-rays nearly always accompanies the loss of a β-particle. Research has shown that when an atomic nucleus ejects an electron, it finds itself in an excited state. By releasing this excess energy as γ-radiation, the nucleus is able to return to a more stable energy level.

The properties of α, β and γ-radiation are summarised in table 2.2.

Table 2.2 *Properties of the types of radiation emitted by radioactive isotopes*

Property	type		
	α-particles	β-particles	γ-rays
nature	helium nuclei, He^{2+}	electrons ejected from the nucleus, moving almost at the speed of light	electromagnetic radiation of very high frequency (like high energy X-rays)
mass/u	4	$\simeq \frac{1}{1850}$; negligible compared to that of the nucleus	none
charge	$+2$	-1	none
range	several cm	several m	several km
relative penetration	1	100	10 000
absorbed by . . .	paper, air	aluminium sheet	several cm of lead, several m of concrete
deflected by an electric or magnetic field	yes	yes	no

2.7 Radioactive decay series

During radioactive decay, radiation is emitted and a different, smaller atom is formed:

$$\underset{\text{larger atom}}{_{90}^{232}\text{Th}} \rightarrow \underset{\text{smaller atom}}{_{88}^{228}\text{Ra}} + \underset{\alpha\text{-particle}}{_{2}^{4}\text{He}}$$

If the nucleus of the new atom is also unstable, it will decay further:

$$_{88}^{228}\text{Ra} \rightarrow {_{89}^{228}\text{Ac}} + \underset{\beta\text{-particle}}{_{-1}^{0}e}$$

Sometimes, **a series of disintegrations** can occur:

$$_{89}^{228}\text{Ac} \xrightarrow{\beta} {_{90}^{228}\text{Th}} \xrightarrow{\alpha} {_{88}^{224}\text{Ra}} \xrightarrow{\alpha} {_{86}^{220}\text{Rn}}$$

Eventually, the series is ended by the formation of an atom with a stable nucleus (in this case $_{82}^{208}\text{Pb}$). There are five main radioactive decay series, the sequence above being part of the **thorium series**.

Once again, note that the mass and atomic numbers balance for each step in the series, e.g.

$$_{86}^{220}\text{Ra} \rightarrow {_{84}^{216}\text{Po}} + {_{2}^{4}\text{He}}$$

Table 2.3 *Data for activity 2.4. Atomic numbers and relative atomic masses of some stable isotopes*

Atomic number	relative atomic mass
1	1, 2
6	12, 14
12	24, 25, 26
17	35, 37
21	45
25	55
26	54, 57, 58
30	66, 67, 68
33	79, 81
41	96
44	102, 104
45	103

Activity 2.3

The **actinium** radioactive series is shown below. For each nuclear change, fill in the missing atomic and mass numbers and state which type(s) of radiation is emitted.

$$^{235}_{92}U \xrightarrow{\alpha} Th \rightarrow \ ^{231}_{91}Pa \xrightarrow{\alpha} Ac \rightarrow \ ^{227}_{90}Th$$
$$\downarrow \alpha$$
$$Pb \xleftarrow{\beta} \ ^{207}_{81}Tl \leftarrow Bi \xleftarrow{\beta} \ ^{211}_{82}Pb \leftarrow Po \xleftarrow{\alpha} \ ^{219}_{86}Rn \leftarrow Ra$$

2.8 The stability of isotopes

An atom of polonium-202 exists for a fraction of a second, whereas the beryllium-9 atom is indefinitely stable. What factors determine the stability of the atomic nucleus? Activity 2.4 will help you to answer this question.

Activity 2.4

Table 2.3 gives the atomic numbers of various elements together with the relative atomic masses of their stable isotopes.

1   Plot a graph of number of neutrons (vertical axis) against number of protons (horizontal axis).
2   Does the shape of your graph suggest that there is a relationship between the numbers of neutrons and protons in stable isotopes?
3   The artificially produced isotopes, $^{42}_{18}Ar$, $^{56}_{28}Ni$, $^{66}_{28}Ni$, $^{76}_{36}Kr$, are unstable (i.e. radioactive). Do the positions of these species on your graph suggest that this should be the case?
4   Use your graph to predict which of the following isotopes will be radioactive:

$$^{18}_{7}N \quad ^{27}_{13}Al \quad ^{59}_{27}Co \quad ^{96}_{40}Zr$$

For stable nuclei, plotting the number of protons against the number of neutrons produces a **band of stability** (figure 2.4). Nuclei within the shaded region are stable, i.e. not radioactive. Unstable nuclei will decay so as to form a nucleus nearer the stability band.

Activity 2.5

Use your graph from activity 2.4 and figure 2.4 to predict what type(s) of radiation might be emitted by the following isotopes:

$$^{56}_{28}Ni \quad ^{76}_{36}Kr \quad ^{96}_{40}Zr \quad ^{232}_{90}Th \quad ^{8}_{2}He \quad ^{18}_{7}N \quad ^{72}_{34}Se \quad ^{224}_{88}Ra$$

2.9 Mass defect and binding energy

Consider an atom of deuterium, $^{2}_{1}H$. This is an isotope of hydrogen whose nucleus contains 1 proton and 1 neutron. Now, accurate measurements show that

$$\text{mass of a proton} = 1.67208 \times 10^{-27} \text{kg}$$
$$\text{mass of a neutron} = 1.67438 \times 10^{-27} \text{kg}$$

thus, in theory,

$$\text{mass of the } ^{2}_{1}H \text{ nucleus} = \text{combined mass of 1 proton + 1 neutron}$$
$$= 1.67208 \times 10^{-27} + 1.67438 \times 10^{-27} \text{kg}$$
$$= 3.34646 \times 10^{-27} \text{kg}$$

Figure 2.4 *An unstable nucleus moves towards the 'band' of stability (shaded) by decaying usually as follows:*

① *emits α-particles ($^{4}_{2}He$), ∴ n/p ratio increases, e.g.*

$$^{212}_{84}Po \longrightarrow ^{208}_{82}Pb + ^{4}_{2}He$$
$$^{n}/_{p} = 1.52 \qquad ^{n}/_{p} = 1.54$$

② *captures an orbiting electron, ∴ n/p ratio increases, e.g.*

$$^{119}_{52}Te \xrightarrow{+(^{0}_{-1}e)} ^{119}_{51}Sb + (^{0}_{-1}e) \ ^{119}_{50}Sn$$
$$^{n}/_{p} = 1.29 \qquad ^{n}/_{p} = 1.33 \qquad ^{n}/_{p} = 1.38$$

③ *emits γ-rays and β-particles ($^{0}_{-1}e$), ∴ n/p ratio decreases, e.g.*

$$^{14}_{6}C \longrightarrow ^{14}_{7}N + ^{0}_{-1}e$$
$$^{n}/_{p} = 1.33 \qquad ^{n}/_{p} = 1.00$$

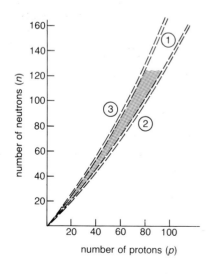

Now, using a mass spectrometer, the actual mass of the deuterium nucleus is found to be 3.34250×10^{-27} kg. Although the real and theoretical values only disagree by about 0.1%, this difference is too big to be explained by experimental error. In fact, for all nuclei except ^1_1H, the nuclear mass is always very slightly less than the combined mass of its protons and neutrons. This loss of mass is known as the **mass defect**.

Einstein, in his Theory of Relativity (1905), proposed that mass (m) and energy (E) are linked by the equation:

$$E = mc^2,$$

where c = the velocity of light, 3×10^8 ms^{-1}. Calculations show that the *mass defect corresponds to an enormous release of energy*, known as the **binding energy**, *which occurs when protons and neutrons are brought together in the nucleus.* For deuterium, then,

$$\text{mass defect} = (3.34646 - 3.34250) \times 10^{-27} \text{ kg}$$
$$= 0.00396 \times 10^{-27} \text{ kg}$$

By substituting the mass defect into Einstein's equation, we find that binding energy per ^2_1H nucleus $= 0.00396 \times 10^{-27} \times (3 \times 10^8)^2$
$$= 3.56 \times 10^{-13} \text{ J}$$

Although, in itself, this is a small amount of energy, it is over 200 000 times greater than that released when one molecule of methane is burnt! Clearly, chemical bond strengths are minute in comparison to the massive forces which bind the nucleons together in the nucleus.

We can compare the stability of different atomic nuclei by working out their **binding energy per nucleon**. Thus, for deuterium, ^2_1H,

$$\frac{\text{binding energy}}{\text{per nucleon}} = \frac{\text{binding energy per nucleus}}{\text{number of nucleons}}$$

$$= \frac{3.56 \times 10^{-13}}{2}$$

$$= 1.78 \times 10^{-13} \text{ J}$$

A graph of binding energy per nucleon plotted against mass number (figure 2.5) has some interesting features:
▶ Since they have the highest binding energies, atomic nuclei of mass number about 50–60 are the most stable.
▶ In theory, less stable nuclei should decay to give nuclei having greater binding energies, i.e.

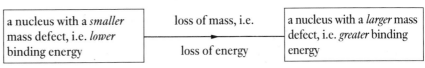

| a nucleus with a *smaller* mass defect, i.e. *lower* binding energy | loss of mass, i.e. ⟶ loss of energy | a nucleus with a *larger* mass defect, i.e. *greater* binding energy |

Energy will be released in the process. This can happen in two ways:
▶ *A heavy nucleus can split into lighter, more stable, nuclei e.g.*

$$^{235}_{92}U + ^1_0n \rightarrow ^{95}_{42}Mo + ^{139}_{57}La + 2^1_0n + 7^{\,0}_{-1}e$$

This process is known as **nuclear fission** (see section 2.11).
▶ *Nuclei of low mass can join together to form a larger, more stable nucleus*, e.g.

$$^2_1H + ^3_1H \rightarrow ^4_2He + ^1_0n$$

This process is known as **nuclear fusion** (see section 2.12).

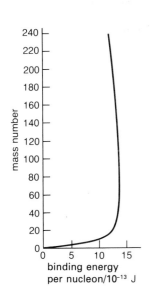

Figure 2.5   *A graph of binding energy per nucleon plotted against mass number*

2.10 Rate of radioactive decay

Radioactive atoms decay at different rates. For example, iodine-131 emits β-particles about a million times faster than nitrogen-18. The **rate of radioactive decay** *is defined as the decrease in the number of unstable nuclei in a given time.* In activity 2.6, we shall investigate the rates of decay of two nuclei, caesium-130 and xenon-138.

Activity 2.6

The following data were obtained from the decay of caesium-130 and xenon-138.

Time/s	activity of ^{130}Cs /disintegrations s^{-1}	activity of ^{138}Xe /disintegrations s^{-1}
0	200	100
500	165	72
1500	113	36
2500	79	19
3500	54	9
4500	38	4
5500	26	2

The activity of the sample is a measure of the amount of the radioactive isotope that is left (i.e. high activity means many unstable nuclei still remain).

1 For each isotope, plot a graph of activity against time.
2 From your graphs, determine the time it takes for the activity of each sample to drop
   (a) to one half of its initial value;
   (b) from one half to one quarter; and
   (c) from one quarter to one eighth of its initial value.
What do you notice about the values in (a), (b) and (c) for each decay?

This activity shows that:
▶ *The time it takes for half of the initial number of radioactive atoms to decay, known as the* **half-life** ($t_\frac{1}{2}$), *is a characteristic property of the isotope.* For example, radium-224 and radium-226 both give α-decay but with very different half-lives of 3.64 days and 1622 years, respectively. Radioactive elements, then, can have widely different half-lives (see table 2.4).

▶ For a given element, *successive half-lives are constant*, as shown in figure 2.6. (Later on, we shall see that radioactive decay follows first order reaction kinetics, sections 11.4 and 11.8.)
Unlike chemical reactions, the *rate of radioactive decay is not affected by physical conditions* (such as temperature, pressure).

2.11 Nuclear fission: reactors and 'atomic bombs'

In 1939, Hahn and Strassman bombarded uranium-235 with low-energy neutrons. They found that, instead of emitting a small particle, the nucleus splits into two large fragments of similar mass. Simultaneously, at least two rapidly moving neutrons are released. On slowing down, these secondary neutrons can cause the splitting, or **fission**, of other uranium-235 nuclei (figure 2.7a). A wide variety of fission products are formed, with masses varying from 70 to 160 u. A typical fission reaction is:

Table 2.4 *Half-lives of some radioactive isotopes*

Isotope	half-life
uranium-238	4.51×10^9 years
carbon-14	5730 years
radium-228	6.7 years
phosphorus-32	14.3 days
lead-214	26.8 minutes
radon-220	55.5 seconds
polonium-212	3×10^{-7} seconds

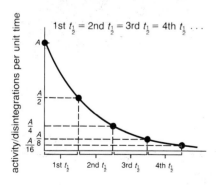

Figure 2.6 *Successive half-lives, $t_\frac{1}{2}$ are constant during radioactive decay*

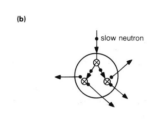

$$^{235}_{92}\text{U} + ^{1}_{0}\text{n} \rightarrow ^{94}_{38}\text{Sr} + ^{140}_{54}\text{Xe} + 2^{1}_{0}\text{n} + \gamma$$

low energy
neutron

these decay until a
stable nucleus is formed

secondary
neutrons

Every fission is accompanied by a loss of mass of about 0.2 u, and this is converted into energy. Incredibly, this mass defect leads to a massive energy release of 75 million kJ per gram of uranium-235. To obtain the same amount of energy from petrol, we would have to burn about 500 gallons of fuel!

Now, by using a large enough mass of uranium-235, the secondary neutrons can cause a **nuclear chain reaction** to be set up (figure 2.7b). Such a reaction, if uncontrolled, will release a massive amount of energy in a very short time. In other words, there would be a nuclear explosion, and this is just what happens in an **atomic bomb**.

Atomic bombs work by violently bringing together two small pieces of a fissionable isotope (uranium-235 or plutonium-239), to form one piece larger than the **critical mass** (6–8 kg). Uncontrolled fission takes place and we get a violent explosion during which enormously high temperatures and pressures are generated in a fraction of a second.

Figure 2.7 *(a) Nuclear fission in uranium-235 . . .*
(b) . . . can cause a chain reaction if the sample is above the critical mass

(a)

slow neutron

$^{235}_{92}\text{U}$

$^{144}_{56}\text{Ba}$ $^{90}_{36}\text{Kr}$

$^{90}_{36}\text{Kr}$ $^{235}_{92}\text{U}$ $^{235}_{92}\text{U}$ $^{124}_{56}\text{Ba}$

$^{144}_{56}\text{Ba}$ $^{90}_{36}\text{Kr}$

4 secondary neutrons cause
further fission of ^{235}U atoms

(b)

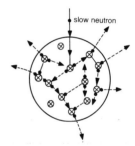

slow neutron

slow neutron

A small piece of ^{235}U is safe because secondary neutrons escape before the chain reaction is set up

In large samples above the critical mass (about 8 kg) the chain reaction is set up. This may be controlled in a **nuclear reactor** or uncontrolled in an **atomic bomb**

The horrific effects of such conditions were all too apparent after the dropping of the atomic bombs on the Japanese cities of Hiroshima and Nagasaki in 1945. Of the 130 000 people killed by these bombs, some were vaporised where they fell while others were buried in the ruins of buildings flattened by the blast. About a fifth of the fatalities were caused by the intense radiation, mainly γ-rays, released on explosion. Many survivors received radiation burns; others were made sterile or, over the years, have developed cancers.

The mushroom cloud of smoke and dust sent up into the atmosphere by a nuclear explosion. This one took place at Bikini Attoll in 1947

Of course, atomic fission also has a less sinister application: in **nuclear reactors**. These function by carefully controlling the speed of the fission chain reaction, so that the 'nuclear' energy can be converted into electricity. There are two main types of nuclear reactor, **thermal** and **fast breeder**.

The main components of a thermal reactor are shown in figure 2.8.

Figure 2.8   *The main components of a thermal nuclear reactor*

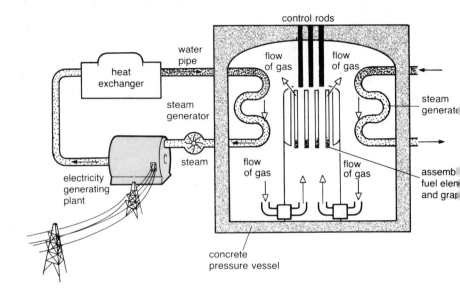

Nuclear fuel rods being handled. The technician works from behind a thick plate glass window using robotic arms. At present, about 5% of the UK's energy comes from nuclear reactors

1   Thousands of uranium-235 fuel rods, each covered with magnesium alloy or stainless steel, are held in holes in a large graphite block. The metal coating prevents oxidation of the uranium and also helps to keep the fission products within the fuel 'cans'.

2   *Uranium-235 will only undergo fission with thermal (i.e. low-energy) neutrons.* Thus, a graphite moderator is used to slow down the secondary neutrons, so that they can cause further fission of uranium-235 nuclei. In this way, a fission chain reaction is set up. Eventually, the neutrons escape from the pile or are absorbed by the non-fissionable uranium-238.

3   As the chain reaction proceeds the fuel rods become very hot. So a coolant (carbon dioxide or water) is pumped around the rods and out to a heat

This 250 megawatt prototype fast reactor at Dounreay in Scotland has been producing energy since 1975

exchanger. This uses the energy in the hot coolant to convert water into steam. The steam drives a turbine and electricity is produced.

4 Rods made of boron, a very efficient neutron-absorber, are used to control the rate of the fission chain reaction. As they are lowered deeper into the pile, the control rods absorb more and more neutrons and the reaction gradually slows down. By carefully varying the position of the control rods, the rate of fission, and hence, the energy output of the reactor, can be held constant. In an emergency, the control rods would automatically drop into the core and the reactor would be shut down.

5 *Nuclear fission produces highly dangerous radioactive waste.* To prevent the leakage of any radiation, the core is encased in steel and concrete shields, some five metres thick. As well as fission products, thermal reactors also yield plutonium-239 which, as we shall see, is another fissionable isotope.

Since naturally occurring uranium only contains about 0.7% uranium-235, it is very costly to extract. To make use of the more abundant, but non-fissionable, uranium-238 isotope, nuclear scientists and engineers have developed the fast breeder reactor.

In a fast breeder reactor, fission of a small amount of uranium-235 produces high-energy neutrons. These strike the non-fissionable nuclei or uranium-238, producing (or 'breeding') plutonium-239:

$$\underset{\text{high-energy}}{{}^{238}_{92}\text{U} + {}^{1}_{0}\text{n}} \rightarrow {}^{239}_{92}\text{U} \xrightarrow{\beta} {}^{239}_{93}\text{Np} \xrightarrow{\beta} {}^{239}_{94}\text{Pu}$$

When a plutonium-239 nucleus is struck by a high-energy neutron, fission occurs. *By breeding a quantity of plutonium-239 greater than its critical mass, we can set up a controlled chain reaction.*

The locations of nuclear reactors in the UK are shown in figure 2.9.

Figure 2.9 *The location of nuclear reactors in the UK*
What is the common feature of each location?
Why is this important?

On 26th April 1986, there was an explosion in the Chernobyl nuclear power plant near Kiev in the USSR. There was a serious leak of radioactive gases, with increased levels of radioactivity detected as far away as the Scottish Highlands. The reason for the explosion was not reactor design but a series of human errors

With fifty times the efficiency of their thermal counterparts, fast breeder reactors can liberate from 1 tonne of uranium the same energy as we would get by burning 1 million tonnes of coal.

After operating for some time, the nuclear fuel rods become contaminated with large amounts of fission products, many of which are highly radioactive. If these are not removed, they may absorb the secondary neutrons, thereby slowing down the nuclear chain reaction. Consequently, automatic *reprocessing* techniques are used to extract the fission products, and the pure unused fuel is returned to the reactor. At present, highly radioactive waste is stored in stainless steel tanks which are embedded in thick concrete 'jackets'. However, research is being focused on the possibility of making the most dangerous waste into very durable glass blocks which can then be safely buried deep underground.

There is enough uranium on earth to meet the world's energy needs for many hundreds of years. However, the merits of nuclear energy must be balanced against the dangers of an explosion or a radiation leak. Whatever our views on nuclear energy, though, we can hardly fail to marvel at the awesome power which is generated from such small amounts of material.

2.12 Nuclear fusion

Looking back to figure 2.5, you will recall that *if nuclei of low mass join together to form a heavier, more stable, nucleus, a lot of energy is released.* This process, called **nuclear fusion** is the source of the sun's energy. A typical 'fusion' reaction would be:

$$^2_1H + {}^2_1H \rightarrow {}^3_2He + {}^1_0n$$

Weight for weight, this reaction liberates about 100 million times more energy than we obtain by exploding TNT (trinitrotoluene).

Not only does nuclear fusion offer us a massive source of energy but, unlike fission, the products are not radioactive. Moreover, the amount of deuterium in the earth's oceans would give us enough fuel to last for millions of years. *So, why aren't there any fusion reactors?*

Well, unfortunately, an enormous amount of energy is needed to overcome the repulsion between the positively charged nuclei. Thus, *nuclear fusions only occur at very high temperatures of about 10 million degrees Celsius.* At present, a fission bomb is the only way of getting such high temperatures. Regrettably, though, the destructive power of nuclear fusion has already been realised in the design of the 'hydrogen bomb'. In this device, the fusion of deuterium nuclei is initiated by a small fission bomb. Such weapons are many thousands of times more powerful than the atomic bombs dropped on Hiroshima and Nagasaki.

German firemen washing down a truck after discovering radioactive contamination resulting from the accident at Chernobyl

2.13 Use of radioactive isotopes

Carbon-14 dating

This log boat was found in 1984 near Holme on Spalding Moor. Samples of wood were radiocarbon dated by the Isotope Measurements Laboratory at Harwell and the boat was found to be well over 2000 years old

Carbon-14 is formed in the atmosphere when a nitrogen atom collides with a high-energy neutron:

$$^{14}_7N + {}^1_0n \rightarrow {}^{14}_6C + {}^1_1H$$

The carbon-14 reacts with oxygen to form carbon-14 dioxide, some of which gets absorbed by plants during photosynthesis. A food chain is set up and, eventually, all living material reaches a constant level of radioactivity. Of course, when an organism dies no more carbon-14 is taken in by it. However, the carbon-14 already present in the dead plant or animal continues to decay at a well-known rate ($t_{\frac{1}{2}} = 5700$ years), Thus, by comparing the amount of carbon-14 in the sample with that known to be present in living tissue, the age of the plant or animal remains can be estimated.

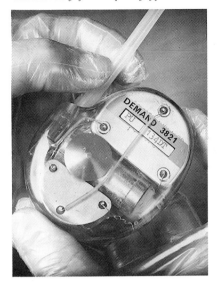

The miniature nuclear battery in this heart pacemaker is about 35 mm long and 15 mm across. The battery has a design life of 20 years. Electricity is generated by the radioactive decay of a small quantity of plutonium–238

Medical applications

Radiation destroys cancer cells more rapidly than it does healthy cells. Thus, γ-rays from a cobalt-60 source can be used to destroy inaccessible tumours.

A small quantity of plutonium-238 is used as an energy source in some heart pacemakers.

'Heatless sterilisation'

An exposure to intense γ-rays will sterilise medical supplies which would otherwise burn or decompose during 'heat-sterilisation'. The ability of radiation to kill micro-organisms has also been extended to food preservation. For example, exposure to radiation slows down the moulding of strawberries and it also prevents the sprouting of stored potatoes.

Measurement of thickness

The thickness of a variety of materials (e.g. plastics, metal sheet, paper) can be accurately monitored by measuring the level of radiation which can pass through the sample.

Radioactive tracers

By 'labelling' a molecule with a radioactive atom, we can trace its movement within a given system. This technique has many applications, e.g. (i) monitoring the movement of river waste; (ii) investigating the function of biological phosphates; (iii) studying reaction mechanisms (see section 40.5.3); (iv) following the passage of a substance around the human body.

This worker is checking one of the external radioactive sensors used to monitor the level of liquid chlorine in the tanks

2.14 Comments on the activities

Activity 2.1

1   $A_r(Ce) = 140; A_r(I) = 127; A_r(Pd) = 106; A_r(Ti) = 48.$
2   The molar masses, in grams, are: (a) 74.5; (b) 56; (c) 248; (d) 60.
3   mass of the sample = number of moles $\times A_r$ (or M_r)

    (a) mass of NH_3 molecules = 0.5 $\times$ 17 = 8.50 g

    (b) mass of Cs atoms = 0.375 $\times$ 133 = 49.87 g

    (c) mass of F_2 molecules = 1.5 $\times$ 38 = 57.00 g

    (d) mass of hydrated sodium carbonate = 0.275 $\times$ 286 = 78.65 g

4   number of moles $= \dfrac{\text{mass of the sample}}{A_r \text{ (or } M_r)}$

    (a) number of moles of Mg atoms $= \dfrac{14}{24} = 0.58$

    (b) number of moles of CO_2 molecules $= \dfrac{8}{44} = 0.18$

    (c) number of moles of $CuCl_2$ molecules $= \dfrac{0.5}{135} = 3.70 \times 10^{-3}$

    (d) number of moles of $CuSO_4.5H_2O$ molecules $= \dfrac{38}{250} = 0.15$

Activity 2.2

mass of 100 atoms of the mixture of Xe isotopes	$= (0.13 \times 124) + (0.09 \times 126) + (1.92 \times 128)$

$$
\begin{aligned}
\text{mass of 100 atoms of the mixture of Xe isotopes} \quad &= (0.13 \times 124) + (0.09 \times 126) + (1.92 \times 128) \\
&\quad + (26.44 \times 129) + (4.08 \times 130) + (21.18 \times 131) \\
&\quad + (26.89 \times 132) + (10.40 \times 134) + (8.87 \times 136)
\end{aligned}
$$

$$
\begin{aligned}
&= 16.12 + 11.34 + 245.76 + 3410.76 + 530.4 + 2774.58 \\
&\quad + 3549.48 + 1393.6 + 1206.32
\end{aligned}
$$

$$= 13\ 138.36$$

$$\text{average atomic mass} \quad = \frac{\text{mass of 100 atoms in the isotopic mixture}}{100}$$

$$= \frac{13138.36}{100} = 131.3836 \text{ u}$$

Thus, relative atomic mass of xenon $= 131.4$

Activity 2.3

$$
{}^{235}_{92}\text{U} \xrightarrow{\alpha} {}^{231}_{90}\text{Th} \xrightarrow{\beta} {}^{231}_{91}\text{Pa} \xrightarrow{\alpha} {}^{227}_{89}\text{Ac} \xrightarrow{\beta} {}^{227}_{90}\text{Th} \xrightarrow{\alpha} {}^{223}_{88}\text{Ra}
$$
$$\downarrow \alpha$$
$$
{}^{207}_{82}\text{Pb} \xleftarrow{\beta} {}^{207}_{81}\text{Tl} \xleftarrow{\alpha} {}^{211}_{83}\text{Bi} \xleftarrow{\beta} {}^{211}_{82}\text{Pb} \xleftarrow{\alpha} {}^{215}_{84}\text{Po} \xleftarrow{\alpha} {}^{219}_{86}\text{Rn}
$$

Activity 2.4

1   The graph is shown in figure 2.10.

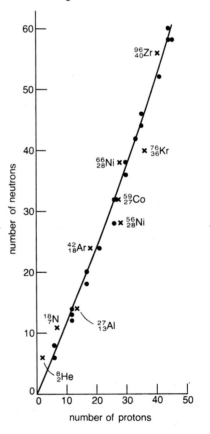

Figure 2.10   *Graph from question 1 of activity 2.4*

2   Yes. For stable isotopes, n/p steadily increases as n gets larger. The plot of neutrons against protons for the stable isotopes gives a reasonable curve (figure 2.10). Thus, we would expect other stable isotopes to provide points which lie on, or close to, this curve, and this is usually the case.

3   When plotted on the graph, it is clear that $^{42}_{18}Ar$, $^{56}_{28}Ni$, $^{66}_{28}Ni$ and $^{76}_{36}Kr$ do not lie on, or very near, the stability curve. Thus, we would expect these isotopes to be unstable.

4   From the graph we can see that $^{27}_{13}Al$, $^{59}_{27}Co$ give points on the curve and are stable. On the other hand, $^{18}_{7}N$ and $^{96}_{40}Zr$ give points well off the curve and these isotopes are unstable.

Activity 2.5

$^{232}_{90}Th$, $^{224}_{88}Ra$ are heavy nuclei giving α-decay.

$^{56}_{28}Ni$, $^{76}_{36}Kr$, $^{72}_{34}Se$ give electron capture + γ-rays.

$^{96}_{40}Zr$, $^{8}_{2}He$, $^{18}_{7}N$ give β-decay + γ-rays.

Activity 2.6

1   The graphs are shown in figure 2.11.
2   *Results* (in s)

	^{130}Cs	^{138}Xe
(a)	1840	1000
(b)	1860	1030
(c)	1855	1020

(d) They are constant within experimental error.
The time taken for half the radioactive substance to decay is known as the *half-life*. During radioactive decay then, *successive half-lives are constant.*

2.15 Summary and Revision Plan

1   **Relative atomic mass of an element** A_r $= \dfrac{\text{average mass of one atom of the element}}{\frac{1}{12}\text{th mass of a }^{12}C\text{ atom}}$

An **atomic mass unit**, u, is $\frac{1}{12}$ of the mass of the ^{12}C atom (i.e. 1.661×10^{-27} kg).

2   The **mole** is the amount of substance which contains the same number of particles as there are atoms in 12 grams of carbon-12.
The number of particles in a mole is known as the **Avogadro constant** (L). X-ray diffraction gives $L = 6.023 \times 10^{23}$ mol^{-1}.

3   If the mass of one particle is X u, then the mass of one mole of particles will be X grams.

4   **Relative atomic masses** can be accurately determined using the **mass spectrometer**. The sample is converted into gaseous positive ions and these are deflected in a magnetic field. A computer calculates the mass of the atom from the size of the deflection.

5   The relative atomic mass can be calculated from the isotopic masses by taking the weighted average (section 2.4).

6   **Radioactivity** is the spontaneous emission of radiation by an atom. It results from nuclear disintegration and the **rate of decay** is independent of temperature and the chemical environment of the atom.

7   Naturally occurring radioactive isotopes may emit:
α-**particles** (helium nuclei $^{4}_{2}He$) with short range and low penetration;
β-**particles** (electrons, $^{0}_{-1}e$) with medium range and penetration;
γ-**rays** (electromagnetic radiation) with long range and high penetration.

8   Plotting the number of neutrons against number of protons for stable nuclei gives a **band of stability** (figure 2.4). Radioactive nuclei decay so as to form isotopes which are on, or closer to, the stability band.

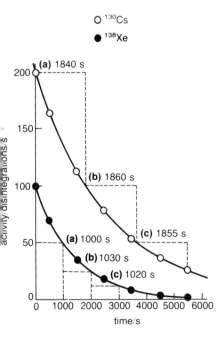

Figure 2.11   *Graph from question 1 of activity 2.6*

9   Hydrogen apart, all nuclei have a slightly lower mass than that of the protons and neutrons which are present. This loss of mass, called the **mass defect**, corresponds to the **binding energy** released when the protons and neutrons are tightly bound together in the nucleus.

10   The forces binding the protons and neutrons together operate over minute distances. However, they are massive in comparison to chemical bond strengths.

11   The rate of radioactive decay is directly proportional to the number of radioactive atoms which remain in the sample. The decay follows first order kinetics (section 11.4).

12   The time it takes for half the original number of radioactive atoms to decay is known as the **half-life**. For a given element, successive half-lives are constant.

13   Some radioactive isotopes can be produced artificially by bombarding a stable nucleus with high-energy particles (e.g. protons, neutrons or α-particles).

14   **Nuclear fission** occurs when a nucleus splits into two large fragments. An increase in mass defect results in an enormous release of energy. Fission reactors harness the energy released by the fission of $^{235}_{92}U$ or $^{239}_{94}Pu$.

15   During **nuclear fusion** , nuclei of low mass join together to form a heavier, more stable, nucleus. In doing so, a massive amount of energy is released.

16   Radioactive isotopes can be used to date archaeological specimens, measure thickness, study reaction mechanisms and sterilise medical supplies.

3

The Arrangement of Electrons in Atoms

When an unstable atom emits radiation, a nuclear change take place. For example,

$$\underset{(6p,\ 8n)}{^{14}_{6}C} \quad \rightarrow \quad \underset{(7p,\ 7n)}{^{14}_{7}N} \quad + \quad \underset{\beta\text{-particle}}{^{0}_{-1}e}$$

Radioactivity is a property of the atomic nucleus. During a chemical reaction, though, the atom's nuclear structure is unaltered. The chemical behaviour of an atom, then, depends solely on the way its electrons are arranged. Carbon-12 and carbon-14, for example, have the same chemical properties because they have identical electron arrangements.

A knowledge of the electron arrangements in atoms, and molecules, often allows us to make accurate predictions about their chemical reactivity. In this chapter we shall use experimental data to explain how the electrons are arranged in atoms. Then we show how these **electron arrangements**, or **configurations**, are represented on paper.

3.1   Atomic emission spectra and electron energy levels

Certain atoms and molecules emit light when they are supplied with heat or electrical energy (see table 3.1). When this light is viewed through a **spectroscope** (figure 3.1), we see a number of coloured lines, called an **emission spectrum**.

Table 3.1   Some examples of atomic emission and their uses

Substance	energy supply	colour of light emitted	use
sodium vapour mercury vapour	electricity	yellow white	street lamps
lithium salts potassium salts barium salts	heat	crimson lilac light green	flame tests for the identification of metal cations (see section 6.1)

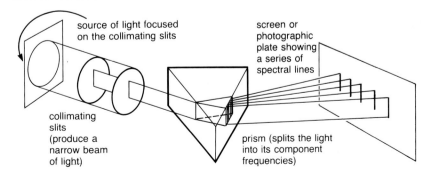

Figure 3.1   Obtaining an emission spectrum

Atomic emission spectra have provided us with valuable information about the electron arrangement in atoms. In 1913, Bohr explained emission spectra by suggesting that electrons move around the nucleus in stable orbits without emitting energy. When the atom absorbs energy, electrons jump from a lower energy orbit to a higher energy orbit in which they are less stable and cannot remain (figure 3.2(a)). Thus, the electrons return to a lower energy orbit and release their excess energy as light. *Each spectral line is caused by electrons falling back from a certain higher energy orbit to a certain lower energy orbit* (figure 3.2(b)). The greater the energy difference between these orbits, or energy levels, the higher will be the frequency of the corresponding spectral line (figure 3.2(c)).

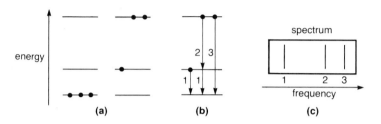

Figure 3.2 *Explaining atomic emission spectra*

3.2 How many electron energy levels are there in atoms?

The visible region of the emission spectrum for hydrogen was first recorded by Balmer. The more prominent lines in the Balmer Series for hydrogen are shown in figure 3.3.

Figure 3.3 *The more prominent lines in the Balmer Series for hydrogen*

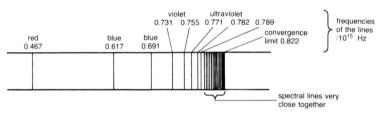

As they move towards higher frequencies, the lines get closer together. Eventually, the lines merge at a frequency known as the **convergence limit**.

Since the spectral lines are getting closer and closer together, there must be an infinite number of energy levels. Each energy level is given a **principal quantum number**, $n = 1$, $n = 2$, $n = 3$ and so on up to $n = \infty$. So, the *higher* the energy level the *greater* its principal quantum number and the *further* its distance from the nucleus. In fact, we find that all known atoms, in their lowest energy state, can only hold electrons in energy levels $n = 1$ to 7.

A photograph of the complete hydrogen emission spectrum shows that there are *five* series of spectral lines (figure 3.4). Each series corresponds to the energies released by electrons falling back to a given energy level:

Series	Lyman	Balmer	Paschen	Brackett	Pfund
Electrons fall back to $n = ..$	1	2	3	4	5

Notice the overlap of the Paschen, Brackett and Pfund series.

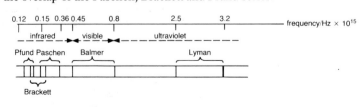

Streetlamps make use of the light emitted when a high voltage is passed through sodium or mercury vapour

Figure 3.4 *Relative positions of the five series of lines in the hydrogen emission spectrum*

A closer look at the Lyman, Balmer and Paschen series shows how each spectral line results from a particular electronic transition (figure 3.5). *Each series of lines converge as they move towards higher frequencies*. This happens because the energy differences between neighbouring energy levels get progressively smaller.

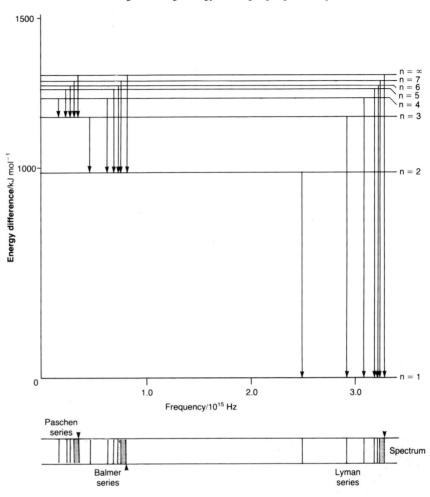

Figure 3.5 *Each line in an atomic emission spectrum is caused by a particular electronic transition*

3.3 Energy differences between electron energy levels

The energy difference, ΔE, between two energy levels can be calculated from the frequency, ν, of the corresponding spectral line, measured in Hz i.e. waves per second. To do this, we use **Planck's equation**:

$$\Delta E = h\nu$$

where h = Planck's constant, $6.626 \times 10^{-37}\ \text{kJ Hz}^{-1}$. For a mole of atoms,

$$\Delta E = Lh\nu$$

where L = Avogadro's constant, $6.023 \times 10^{23}\ \text{mol}^{-1}$.

As an example, let us calculate the energy difference between the electron energy levels $n = 1$ and $n = 2$ in one mole of hydrogen atoms. This electronic transition gives a line in the Lyman Series at 2.47×10^{15} Hz. So,

$$\Delta E_{1,2} = 6.023 \times 10^{23}\ \text{mol}^{-1} \times 6.626 \times 10^{-37}\ \text{kJ Hz}^{-1} \times 2.47 \times 10^{15}\ \text{Hz}$$
$$= 986\ \text{kJ mol}^{-1}\ \text{of H atoms}$$

Table 3.2 *The frequencies of the prominent lines in the Lyman Series for hydrogen*

Frequency, ν /10^{15} Hz	corresponding electronic transition
2.466	$n = 2$ to $n = 1$
2.923	$n = 3$ to $n = 1$
3.083	$n = 4$ to $n = 1$
3.157	$n = 5$ to $n = 1$
3.197	$n = 6$ to $n = 1$
3.221	$n = 7$ to $n = 1$
3.237	$n = 8$ to $n = 1$

Activity 3.1

1   For one mole of hydrogen atoms, calculate $\Delta E_{1,n}$ where $n = 3, 4, 5, 6,$ or 7 (Use the above method and the frequencies of the lines in the Lyman Series, table 3.2).

2   A mole of hydrogen atoms absorb, in turn, the following amounts of energy (in kJ):
(a) 1167   (b) 1197   (c) 1260   (d) 1280   (e) 1300
In each case, use the answers to question 1 to work out the energy level to which the electrons may be promoted.

Activity 3.1 illustrates the way in which *definite amounts of energy, called **quanta**, are absorbed or emitted when an electron changes energy levels. The size of the quantum must always be exactly equal to the energy difference between the two energy levels.*

3.4 Ionisation energies and their measurement

We saw earlier that electrons in higher energy levels are further from the nucleus. If the atom absorbs enough energy, an electron can be promoted just beyond the highest energy level, i.e. $n = \infty$. In this case, the electron escapes from the atom and a positive ion is formed:

$$M(g) \rightarrow M^+(g) + e^-.$$

The **first ionisation energy, $\Delta H_i(1)$,** *is the minimum energy needed to remove one mole of electrons from one mole of gas atoms to form one mole of gaseous positive ions, each of which has a single charge.* For example:

$$K(g) \rightarrow K^+(g) + e^- \qquad \Delta H_i(1) = +420 \text{ kJ mol}^{-1}$$

First ionisation energies can be obtained from atomic emission spectra, and hydrogen is a good example.

A hydrogen atom has only one electron. If no heat or electrical energy is absorbed, this electron will occupy the lowest energy level, $n = 1$. Thus, the difference in energy between $n = 1$ and $n = \infty$ will be the ionisation energy. Since results from electrons returning to $n = 1$, the Lyman Series can be used to calculate $\Delta E_{1,\infty}$. Activity 3.2 shows you how this is done.

Activity 3.2

In this method, we shall find the frequency of the convergence limit, ν^*. This corresponds to the energy needed to ionise a hydrogen atom (i.e. promote an electron from $n = 1$ to $n = \infty$).

1   Copy and complete the table of values (all/10^{15} Hz) given below.

(i) ν, the frequency of the lines in the Lyman Series	2.466	2.923	3.083	3.157	3.197	3.221	3.23
(ii) the frequency of the previous line	–	2.466	.....	3.083	.....	.....	....
(iii) $\Delta\nu$, the difference in frequency between neighbouring lines (i.e. subtract (ii) from (i))	–	0.457	.....	0.074	.....	....	....

2   Plot a graph of Δv (vertical axis) against v (horizontal axis), i.e. row (iii) against row (i).   Note: use $2\,cm = 0.1$ Hz on the vertical axis and $4\,cm = 0.1$ Hz on the horizontal axis.

3   *When the lines converge, Δv will be zero.* Thus, read off the frequency of the convergence limit, v^*. Since we are using the Lyman Series, v^* corresponds to the energy difference between energy levels $n = 1$ and $n = \infty$. So, by using Planck's equation,

$$\Delta H_i(1) = \Delta E_{1,\infty} = hv^*,$$

you can calculate $\Delta H_i(1)$ for hydrogen.

3.5 How many electrons can occupy an energy level?

When one mole of gaseous magnesium atoms absorb 736 kJ of energy, one mole of electrons will be released:

$$Mg\,(g) \rightarrow Mg^+(g) + e^- \qquad\qquad \Delta H_i(1) = +736 \text{ kJ mol}^{-1}$$

If enough energy is supplied, successive ionisations will occur and more highly charged magnesium ions will be formed. Thus, the **second ionisation energy of an element, $\Delta H_i(2)$,** *is the energy needed to remove one mole of electrons from one mole of gaseous unipositive ions.* For magnesium, the equation is

$$Mg^+(g) \rightarrow Mg^{2+}(g) + e^- \qquad\qquad \Delta H_i(2) = +1448 \text{ kJ mol}^{-1}$$

Similar definitions and equations can be written for successive ionisation, e.g.

$$Mg^{2+}(g) \rightarrow Mg^{3+}(g) + e^- \qquad\qquad \Delta H_i(3) = +7740 \text{ kJ mol}^{-1}$$

Successive ionisation energies, which can be determined from atomic spectra, provide much information about the arrangement of electrons in atoms.

As electrons are successively removed from an atom, the protons increasingly outnumber the remaining electrons, e.g.

$$\begin{array}{ccccccccc}
Mg(g) & \xrightarrow{-e^-} & Mg^+(g) & \xrightarrow{-e^-} & Mg^{2+}(g) & \xrightarrow{-e^-} & Mg^{3+}(g) & \xrightarrow{-e^-} & Mg^{4+}(g) \\
12p,\,12e & & 12p,\,11e & & 12p,\,10e & & 12p,\,9e & & 12p,\,8e
\end{array} \cdots$$

Consequently, the remaining electrons 'feel' a greater nuclear pull, and this makes them more difficult to remove. For all atoms, then, *successive ionisation energies get larger.*

The successive ionisation energies for magnesium are listed in table 3.3. These can be shown as a graph of $\log_{10} \Delta H_i(N)$ against the number of the electron which is being removed (N) (figure 3.6). As you can see, the $\log_{10}\Delta H_i(N)$ values do not increase steadily; thus, the electrons cannot be equivalent (i.e. in the same energy level). In fact, this graph suggests that the 12 electrons in the magnesium atom are grouped into *three* electron energy levels, $n = 1$, 2 and 3. Patterns in the successive ionisation energies of other atoms confirm this 'grouping' of electrons. Overall, we find that a given energy level, n, can hold a maximum of $2n^2$ electrons. Thus,

Table 3.3 *Successive ionisation energies for magnesium*

Number of the electron removed, N	$\Delta H_i(N)/\text{kJ mol}^{-1}$
1	736
2	1448
3	7740
4	10470
5	13490
6	18200
7	21880
8	25700
9	31620
10	35480
11	158300
12	199500

$$energy\ level \left\{ \begin{array}{l} n = 1 \text{ can hold a maximum of } 2(1)^2 = 2 \\ n = 2 \text{ can hold a maximum of } 2(2)^2 = 8 \\ n = 3 \text{ can hold a maximum of } 2(3)^2 = 18 \\ n = 4 \text{ can hold a maximum of } 2(4)^2 = 32 \end{array} \right\} electrons$$

Multiple occupation by electrons is also a property of the higher energy levels $n = 5$ to $n = \infty$.

Electron energy levels are often called **electron shells**. In an atom of silicon (atomic number $= 14$), then, electrons occupy the following energy levels or shells: 2 in $n = 1$, 8 in $n = 2$ and 4 in $n = 3$. This arrangement of electrons may be written 2.8.4. What are the atomic electron arrangements for beryllium, carbon and argon?

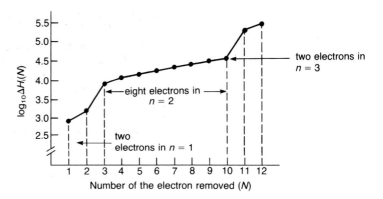

Figure 3.6 *A graph of log$_{10}$ (successive ionisation energies) plotted against the number of the electron removed. As the 'n' value increases, the electrons get further from the nucleus*

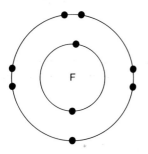

Figure 3.7 *A 'dot and cross' diagram for fluorine*

'*Dot and cross' diagrams* are a useful way of representing the electrons in energy levels, e.g. fluorine in figure 3.7. (These diagrams are fully explained in most GCSE chemistry textbooks.)

3.6 The arrangement of electrons in energy levels

Figure 3.8 shows some *'big jumps'* in the values of the successive ionisation energies. *These occur whenever the first electron is removed from a full energy level.* For magnesium, the 'big jumps' occur for:

▶ $\Delta H_i(3)$ when an electron is removed from the full $n = 2$ energy level;
▶ $\Delta H_i(11)$ when an electron is removed from the full $n = 1$ energy level.

Since it is more difficult to remove an electron from them, *electron arrangements having only full energy levels (shells) must be particularly stable.* Further evidence for this comes from the chemical inertness of noble gases helium and neon. These gases have stable electron configurations made up only of full electron energy levels – hence their lack of chemical reactivity.

By comparing successive ionisation energies, we can often work out the **Periodic Group** (section 19.1) in which the atom is found. For example, the first eight ionisation energies of an element X are

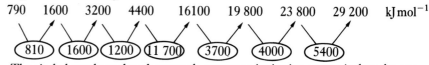

The circled numbers show how much greater an ionisation energy is than the one before. Clearly, four electrons can be removed before the 'big jump' in ΔH_i values. Since the 'big jump' occurs when the first electron is removed from a full energy level, an atom of X must have four electrons in its outermost, or valence, shell. Thus, element X is in Group IV of the Periodic Table; in fact, X is silicon, electron arrangement 2.8.4.

Activity 3.3

Elements A, B and C have the successive ionisation energies shown below:

	successive ionisation energies/kJ mol^{-1}								
Element	1st	2nd	3rd	4th	5th	6th	7th	8th	9th
A	500	4600	6900	9500	13400	16600	20100		
B	1680	3400	6000	8400	11000	15200	17900	92000	
C	1520	2700	3900	5800	7200	8800	12000	13800	40800

In which Periodic Group will these elements be found?

3.7 Electron energy sub-levels or sub-shells

In section 3.2, we looked at the most prominent lines in the Balmer Series for hydrogen (figure 3.3). However, in the spectra of other atoms, there are many other lines in the Balmer series. These *less intense spectral lines, termed* **fine structure,** *are due to the existence of* **electron energy sub-levels** *or* **sub-levels.** *By studying the fine structure of atomic spectra, scientists have shown that:*

▶ *the* n = 1 *level can hold a maximum of 2 electrons, both in a 1s sub-level*
▶ *the* n = 2 *level can hold a maximum of 8 electrons,   2 in a 2s sub-level*
6 in a 2p sub-level
▶ *the* n = 3 *level can hold a maximum of 18 electrons,   2 in a 3s sub-level*
6 in a 3p sub-level
10 in a 3d sub-level.

The energies of these sub-levels increase in the order:

$$1s < 2s < 2p < 3s < 3p < 3d.$$

Further evidence for sub-levels comes from the **periodicity** (i.e. regular pattern) of the first ionisation energies of the first 54 elements (figure 3.8). This graph has several interesting features.

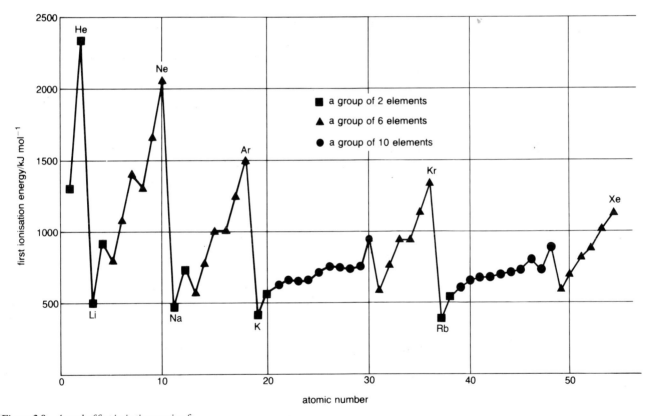

Figure 3.8 *A graph of first ionisation energies of the elements plotted against atomic number*

▶ *Noble gases have the highest ionisation energies*. The removal of an electron is so difficult because their electron configurations are extremely stable (section 3.6).
▶ In between the noble gases, the points on the graph can be gathered into groups of 2, 6 or 10 elements, depending on whether the ionisable electron is in an s, p or d sub-level.

▶ *Electrons enter the 4s sub-level before the 3d sub-level* (i.e. potassium has the electron configuration $1s^2\,2s^2\,2p^6\,3s^2\,3p^6\,4s^1$ and not $1s^2\,2s^2\,2p^6\,3s^2\,3p^6\,3d^1$). Since it fills first, the 4s sub-level must be at slightly lower energy than the 3d sub-level. Figure 3.9(a) shows the relative energies of sub-levels in atoms (up to the 4p). *Electrons always occupy the lowest energy sub-level that is available* (e.g. 3s before the 3p, 3p before the 3d, and so on); this is known as the **Aufbau Principle**. Thus, fluorine (atomic number 9) will have 2 electrons in the 1s sub-level, 2 electrons in the 2s sub-level and 5 electrons in the 2p sub-level (figure 3.9(b)). The periodicity in first ionisation energies is further discussed in section 19.4. Usually, atomic electron arrangements, termed **configurations**, are written across the page, e.g.

fluorine, F (atomic number 9): $1s^2\,2s^2\,2p^5$

The superscripts indicate the number of electrons in each sub-level. Two other examples are:

carbon, C (atomic number 6): $1s^2\,2s^2\,2p^2$
titanium, Ti (atomic number 22): $1s^2\,2s^2\,2p^6\,3s^2\,3p^6\,3d^2\,4s^2$

Even though it fills first, the 4s sub-level is written after the 3d. We also use the symbols [Ne] and [Ar] to simplify electronic configurations, e.g. Ti would be [Ar] $3d^2\,4s^2$.

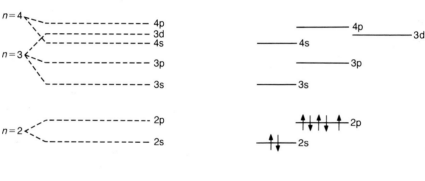

Figure 3.9 *(a) Relative energies of the electron sub-shells in atoms (up to the 4p); (b) the electronic structure of fluorine*

(a)   (b)

Activity 3.4

Give electron configurations for the following elements (atomic numbers in brackets): H(1), N(7), O(8), Al(13), Ar(18), Ti(22), Cr(24), Fe(26), Cu(29), Ge(32), Br(35).

3.8 Electrons: particles or waves?

So far we have described the electron as a very small, negatively charged particle which moves rapidly around the nucleus. Certainly, the work of Thomson (1897) and Millikan (1909) would support this theory (section 1.2). However, in 1924 de Broglie suggested that very small particles should have measurable wave properties (i.e. like visible light). This theory was confirmed by Davisson and Germer in 1927, when they showed that electrons, like light, could be diffracted. (Diffraction is explained in most advanced physics textbooks.)

From this experimental evidence, therefore, we know that *electrons can behave either as particles or as waves, depending on the type of experiment.* Thus, we say that electrons have a **dual 'wave–particle' nature**.

3.9 Orbitals, sub-levels and quantum numbers

If you play a ball-game, such as tennis, your success will depend largely on your ability to judge the position and speed of the ball at any given time. Compared to the tennis-ball, though, an electron is very small, moves extremely fast and has wave properties. Even using the most sensitive equipment, we cannot measure both the exact speed and the exact position of the electron at the same time. This was proved mathematically by Heisenberg in 1927, and it is known as the **Uncertainty Principle**. Clearly, the behaviour of atomic electrons cannot be explained by the 'exactness' of the classical laws of motion.

To solve this problem, Schrödinger (1928) adopted a different approach, called **wave mechanics**. Instead of trying to define the 'exact' position of an atomic electron, *he worked out the probability of finding it in a given place*. In this way, Schrödinger proved that:

▶ each atomic electron is most likely to be found in *a certain volume of space around the nucleus;* this is known as an **atomic orbital**. Two types of atomic orbital are shown in figure 3.10. An **s** orbital is spherical, whilst a **p** orbital is said to be 'dumb-bell' shaped.

▶ each atomic orbital can hold one electron or a 'pair' of electrons;

▶ 'paired' electrons spin in opposite directions;

▶ an electron in a particular sub-level can occupy certain atomic orbitals. For example,

an s sub-level can hold up to   2 electrons in one s orbital
a p sub-level can hold up to   6 electrons in three p orbitals (figure 3.11)
a d sub-level can hold up to 10 electrons in five d orbitals.

Atomic electrons form a cloud of negative charge around the nucleus. Schrödinger used three **quantum numbers** to define the portion of the charge cloud in which a given electron is most likely to be found. A fourth quantum number tells us that when electrons are paired in an atomic orbital, they spin in opposite directions. *Since no two electrons can have the same set of quantum number values* (this is called the **Pauli Exclusion Principle**), each electron will make its own unique contribution to the size, shape and density of this charge cloud. Thus, an electron in either the 1s or the 6s sub-level will give rise to a spherical charge cloud but that due to the 6s will be much larger.

3.10 'Electrons-in-boxes' diagrams

An atom's electronic configuration can be represented using **'electrons-in-boxes'** diagrams. In these diagrams, we use the following symbols:

↑   is one electron,

↑↓   is a pair of electrons, having opposite spins, and

☐   is an orbital, which can hold one electron or a pair of electrons.

The s sub-level can hold a maximum of two electrons. Therefore, it has only one orbital, i.e. one box. So,

☐   means an s sub-level.

The p sub-level can hold up to six electrons in three 'dumb-bell' shaped orbitals. So,

☐☐☐   means a p sub-level.

The d sub-level can hold up to ten electrons in five orbitals. So,

☐☐☐☐☐   means a d sub-level.

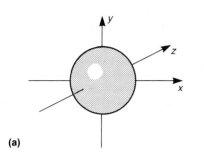

(a)

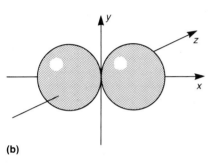

(b)

Figure 3.10 *The electron cloud of an s orbital is spherical, (**a**), whilst that of a p orbital is 'dumb-bell' shaped, (**b**)*

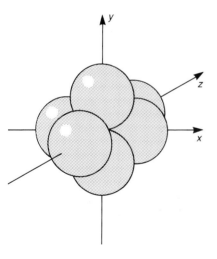

Figure 3.11 *A p sub-shell is made up of three 'dumb-bell' shaped orbitals mutually at right angles*

We can now draw the sub-levels in order of increasing 'n' value:

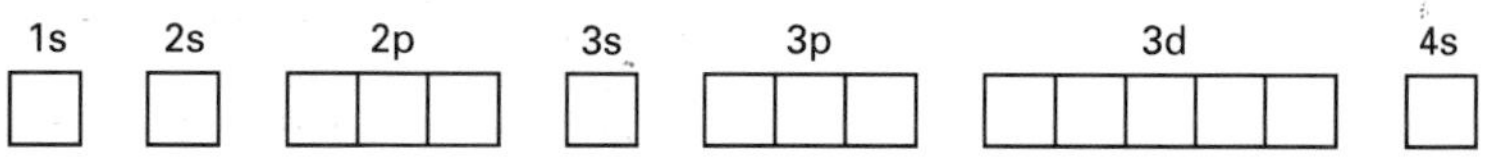

Notice that the 3d sub-level is written before the 4s sub-level, even though the latter begins to fill first (section 3.7).

Next, we place the required number of electrons in each sub-level. For example, an atom of sodium (atomic number 11) has the electron configuration $1s^2$ $2s^2$ $2p^6$ $3s^1$. Thus, the 'electrons-in-boxes' diagram for sodium is

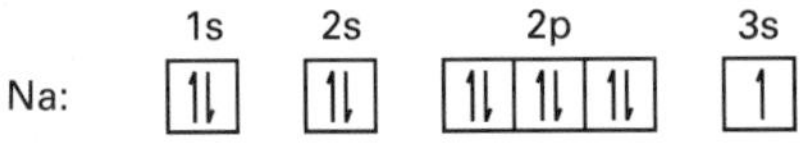

Another example is nitrogen (atomic number 7), electron configuration $1s^2$ $2s^2$ $2p^3$:

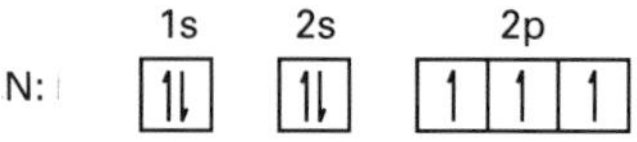

In this example, we have used **Hund's Rule**. This says that 'electrons-in-boxes' diagrams must be drawn so that sub-levels contain the *maximum number of unpaired electrons*. Thus, iron (atomic number 26) is written as

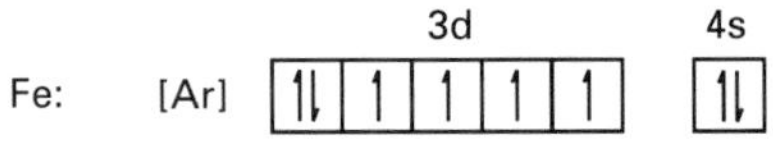

and not

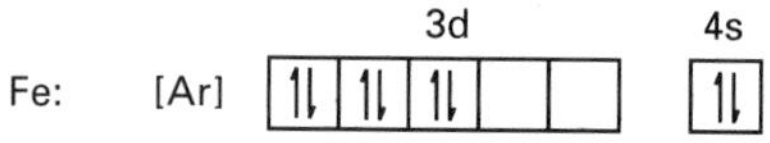

Notice the shorthand use of [noble gas] to represent the configuration of electrons in that atom (i.e. [Ar] $= 1s^2$ $2s^2$ $2p^6$ $3s^2$ $3p^6$).

A final example, then, is sulphur (atomic number 16):

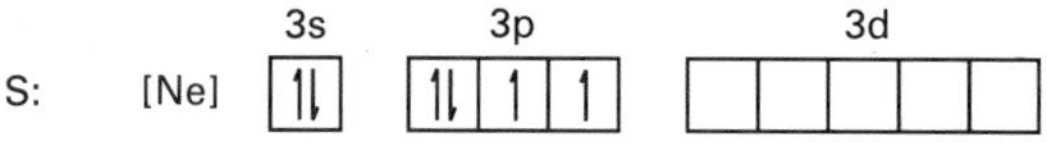

Empty sub-levels need not be drawn but, as we shall see later, they are often useful when explaining chemical bonding.

Activity 3.5

Draw 'electrons-in-boxes' diagrams for the following atoms (atomic numbers in brackets): H(1), C(6), O(8), Ne(10), Al(13), Cl(17), Sc(21), Cr(24), Cu(29), As(33) and Kr(36).

In this chapter, we have seen how 'dot and cross' and 'electrons-in-boxes' diagrams provide a simple way of describing the complex 'real-life' nature of atomic electron configurations. As long as we accept their limitations, these diagrams can help us to describe how the electron clouds in atoms move around during a chemical reaction.

3.11 Comments on the activities

Activity 3.1

1 Using Planck's equation, $\Delta E = Lh\nu$, we get

$$\Delta E_{1,3} = 6.023 \times 10^{23} \times 6.626 \times 10^{-37} \times 2.923 \times 10^{15} \text{ kJ mol}^{-1}$$
$$= 1167 \text{ kJ mol}^{-1}$$

Similar calculations give the following answers:

$$\Delta E_{1,4} = 1230, \ \Delta E_{1,5} = 1260, \ \Delta E_{1,6} = 1276 \text{ and } \Delta E_{1,7} = 1285 \text{ kJ mol}^{-1}.$$

2 The electron in $n = 1$ will:
(a) be promoted to $n = 3$; (c) be promoted to $n = 5$;
(b) , (d) and (e) remain in $n = 1$.
For answers to parts (b), (d) and (e), you may have thought that enough energy was supplied to promote the electron to $n = 3, 5$ and 6, respectively. In fact, Bohr proved that when an electron changes energy levels, energy is absorbed, or emitted, in definite amounts called **quanta**. Only in (a) and (c) is the electron supplied with the exact quantum of energy needed to promote it to the higher energy level.

Activity 3.2

1 The complete table is

(i) ν, the frequency of the lines in the Lyman Series/10^{15} Hz	2.466	2.923	3.083	3.157	3.197	3.221	3.237
(ii) the frequency of the previous line	–	2.466	2.923	3.083	3.157	3.197	3.221
(iii) $\Delta\nu$, the difference in frequency between neighbouring lines, (ii) − (i)	.....	0.457	0.160	0.074	0.040	0.024	0.016

2 The graph of $\Delta\nu$ against ν is shown in figure 3.12. From the graph, ν^* is found to be 3.27×10^{15} Hz.

3 Using Planck's equation,

$$\Delta H_i(1) = Lh\nu = 6.023 \times 10^{23} \times 6.626 \times 10^{-37} \times 3.27 \times 10^{15} \text{ kJ mol}^{-1}$$

$$\therefore \Delta H_i(1) = 1305 \text{ kJ mol}^{-1}$$

Emission spectra can also be used to measure the first ionisation energies of other atoms.

Figure 3.12 *A graph of $\Delta\nu$ plotted against ν for the Lyman Series for hydrogen: ν^* is the frequency of the convergence limit.*

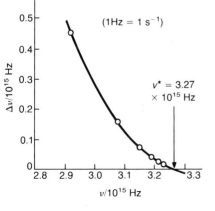

Activity 3.3

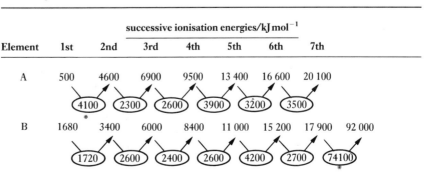

Element	1st	2nd	3rd	4th	5th	6th	7th
A	500	4600	6900	9500	13 400	16 600	20 100
B	1680	3400	6000	8400	11 000	15 200	17 900	92 000

successive ionisation energies/kJ mol^{-1}

A: 4100* 2300 2600 3900 3200 3500

B: 1720 2600 2400 2600 4200 2700 74100*

Element	1st	2nd	successive ionisation energies/kJ mol^{-1} 3rd	4th	5th	6th	7th		
C	1520	2700	3900	5800	7200	8800	12 000	13 800	40 800

(1180) (1200) (1900) (1400) (1600) (3200) (1800) (27 000)*

Element A has the 'big jump' after its 1st ionisation. Therefore, A has one electron in its valence shell and it is probably in Group I.

Element B has the 'big jump' after its 7th ionisation. Therefore, B has seven electrons in its valence shell and it is probably in Group VII.

Element C has the 'big jump' after its 8th ionisation. Therefore, C has eight electrons in its valence shell and it is probably in Group 0, the noble gases.

Activity 3.4

H $1s^1$
O $1s^2 2s^2 2p^4$
Ar [Ne] $3s^2 3p^6$
Cr [Ar] $3d^5 4s^1$ (not $3d^4 4s^2$!)
Cu [Ar] $3d^{10} 4s^1$ (not $3d^9 4s^2$!)
Br [Ar] $3d^{10} 4s^2 4p^5$

N $1s^2 2s^2 2p^3$
Al [Ne] $3s^2 3p^1$
Ti [Ar] $3d^2 4s^2$
Fe [Ar] $3d^6 4s^2$
Ge [Ar] $3d^{10} 4s^2 4p^2$

You will probably have incorrect answers (in brackets), for Cr and Cu. In fact, the electron configuration is *stabilised* when the 3d sub-level is *half-full* or *full* (i.e. $3d^5$ or $3d^{10}$). Thus, Cr and Cu adopt the configurations $3d^5 4s^1$ and $3d^{10} 4s^2$, these being more stable than $3d^4 4s^2$ and $3d^9 4s^2$, respectively. Try to remember this anomaly.

Activity 3.5

The 'electrons-in-boxes' diagrams are shown below:

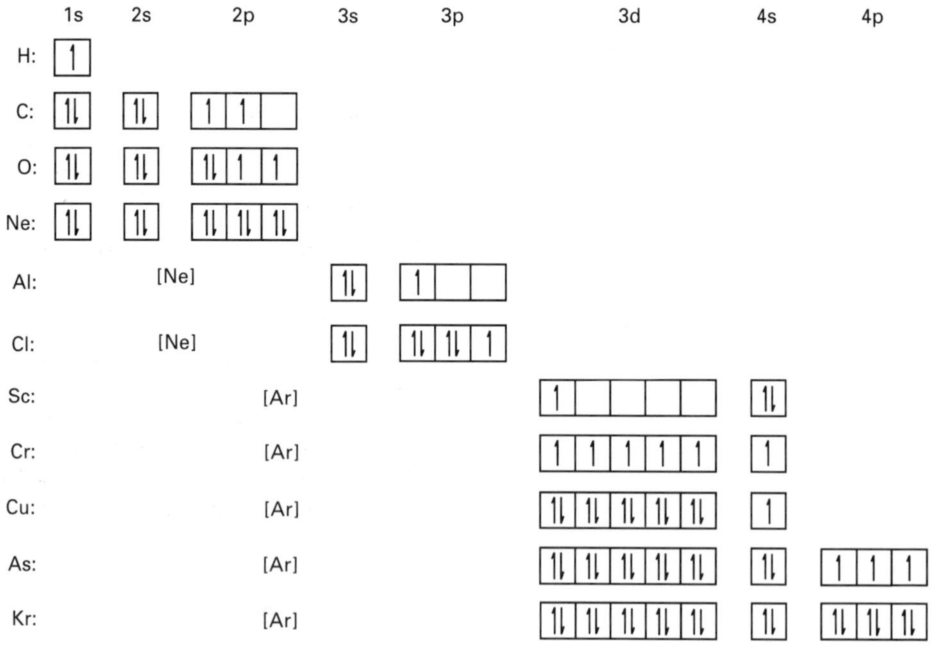

[Ne] = $1s^2 2s^2 2p^6$; [Ar] = $1s^2 2s^2 2p^6 3s^2 3p^6$

3.12 Summary and revision plan

1   For certain atoms, an input of heat or electrical energy leads to an **emission spectrum** as follows:

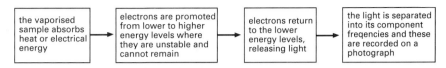

2   Emission spectra consist of series of discrete lines. In each series the lines **converge** as their frequencies increase, e.g. the Balmer Series for hydrogen.

3   Emission spectra show that, for known atoms in their ground state, electrons may occupy up to seven **energy levels** denoted by their **principal quantum number**, $n = 1, 2, \ldots \ldots 7$. An electron in a higher 'n' level is more likely to be found further from the nucleus than an electron in a lower 'n' level.

4   Since each element has its own unique emission spectrum, these can also be used to (i) identify the element and (ii) measure ionisation energies (section 3.4).

5   The **first ionisation energy**, $\Delta H_i(1)$, of an atom is the minimum energy needed to remove one mole of electrons from one mole of gaseous atoms to form one mole of gaseous positive ions, each of which has a single charge.

6   Trends in successive ionisation energies indicate that there is multiple occupation, by electrons, of energy levels (shells). We find that the 'nth' energy level can hold a maximum of $2n^2$ electrons.

7   The fine structure in atomic emission spectra and the pattern in the values of $\Delta H_i(1)$ for the elements proves the existence of electron **sub-levels** or **sub-shells**. Our main interest is in the **s, p** and **d** sub-levels which can hold a maximum of **2, 6** and **10** electrons, respectively.

8   Since electrons are so small and move very rapidly, we cannot be sure of both their speed and location at any given time. Thus, we talk of the **probability** of finding the electron in a particular volume of space called an **orbital**.

9   **s, p, d** and **f** sub-levels consist of **1, 3, 5** and **7** orbitals, respectively. Schrödinger proved that for energy levels $n = 1$ to 4, sub-levels are available as follows:

	1s	2s	2p	3s	3p	3d	4s	4p	4d	4f
$n=1$ can hold a maximum of 2 electrons,	2									
$n=2$ can hold a maximum of 8 electrons,		2	6							
$n=3$ can hold a maximum of 18 electrons,				2	6	10				
$n=4$ can hold a maximum of 32 electrons,							2	6	10	14

10   Electron sub-levels (up to the 4s) increase in energy, thus;

$$\underrightarrow{\text{1s} \quad \text{2s} \quad \text{2p} \quad \text{3s} \quad \text{3p} \quad \text{4s} \quad \text{3d}} \text{ increasing energy}$$

In stable atoms, electrons first occupy the lowest energy sub-levels, (the **Aufbau Principle**).

11   s sub-levels are **spherical**, p sub-levels are made up of three **'dumb-bell' shaped** orbitals at right angles (figures 3.10 and 3.11).

12   **'Electrons-in-boxes'** diagrams are used to represent electronic configurations in atoms (see section 3.10).

CHAPTER 4

Energy Changes During Chemical Reactions

Contents

The chemical energy in glucose molecules can be converted into heat, mechanical and electrical energy

Almost all chemical reactions involve energy changes, and a number of these play a vital role in our everyday lives. For example, by absorbing the sun's energy, plants can convert carbon dioxide and water into glucose:

$$6CO_2(g) + 6H_2O(l) \rightarrow C_6H_{12}O_6(aq) + 6O_2(g)$$

In this process, called **photosynthesis**, light energy is converted into chemical energy, which is stored in the bonds of the glucose molecule. If the plant is now eaten, this chemical energy is converted into

▶ heat energy, which keeps us warm,

▶ mechanical energy, which operates our muscles, and

▶ small impulses of electrical energy, by which messages are passed around our nervous system.

This is how photosynthesis helps us to store up energy from the sun. It is a reaction in which energy is absorbed.

Over the years, our lifestyle has become more and more dependent on the interconversion of chemical energy and other forms of energy. For example, imagine what life would be like without the heat, mechanical and electrical energy which is obtained from the chemical energy in fossil fuels. These are all reactions in which energy is released.

By measuring the energy change during a reaction, we can get some idea of the relative stabilities of the reactant and product molecules (section 4.13). In industry, chemists often study energy changes because it can help them to minimise production costs.

The study of energy changes during chemical reactions is known as **chemical thermodynamics** or **thermochemistry**. In this chapter, we shall:
- ▶ explain which energy changes are of most interest to chemists;
- ▶ outline some experimental methods for determining these energy changes; and
- ▶ describe the use of these energy changes in thermochemical calculations.

Fossil fuels in use: a pneumatic drill which relies on a petrol-driven air compressor, coal being delivered to a power station, a stir-fry being prepared using natural gas, and a diesel-driven canal boat

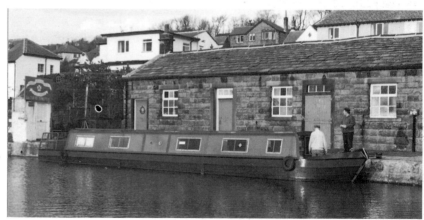

4.1 The first law of thermodynamics

The first law of thermodynamics states that energy cannot be created or destroyed but it can be converted from one form to another. We want to apply this law to a chemical reaction. Thus,

energy lost (or gained) when reactant molecules form product molecules   =   *energy gained (or lost) by the surroundings (e.g. the solvent, reaction flask or the atmosphere)*

4.2 Which energy changes do we measure?

In thermochemistry, we say that all substances possess a **heat content** or **enthalpy, H**. Many chemical reactions involve an **enthalpy change, ΔH**, where

$$\Delta H = \underset{\text{(enthalpy of the products)}}{H_p} - \underset{\text{(enthalpy of the reactants)}}{H_r}$$

Enthalpy changes can be described by **enthalpy level diagrams**, as shown in figure 4.1.

Figure 4.1 *Enthalpy level diagrams for (a) an exothermic reaction and (b) an endothermic reaction*

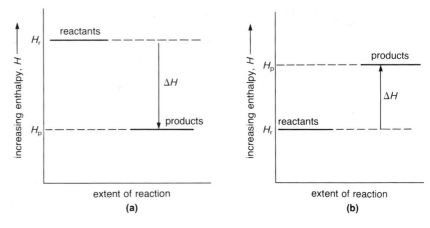

(a)   (b)

If $H_p < H_r$, ΔH is negative and the reaction will be **exothermic**, *that is, enthalpy is released during the reaction e.g.*

$$C(\text{graphite}) + O_2(g) \rightarrow CO_2(g) \quad \Delta H = -394\,\text{kJ}$$

If $H_p > H_r$, ΔH is positive and the reaction will be **endothermic**, *that is, enthalpy is absorbed during the reaction e.g.*

$$N_2(g) + O_2(g) \rightarrow 2NO(g) \qquad \Delta H = +180\,\text{kJ}$$

Bear in mind that $-$ and $+$ signs tell us whether enthalpy flows out of ($-$) or into ($+$) the reacting molecules.

4.3 What do we observe during an enthalpy change?

Consider the exothermic reaction of magnesium with dilute hydrochloric acid:

$$Mg(s) + 2HCl(aq) \rightarrow MgCl_2(aq) + H_2(g)$$

If the system is kept in a sealed vessel at constant volume, then energy can only be released to the surroundings as heat. If, however, the reaction is performed at constant pressure, then part of the total energy released must be used to overcome atmospheric pressure as the hydrogen gas expands. Thus, when a gas is formed (or used up), the heat released at constant pressure is slightly different from that measured at constant volume.

Enthalpy change is defined as the heat change under constant pressure and can be measured directly for chemical reactions carried out in apparatus open to the atmosphere.

4.4 Standard enthalpy changes

In order to compare enthalpy changes, the amounts of material used, their physical states and the reaction conditions must be standardised. Thus, we define the **standard enthalpy change for a reaction, $\Delta H^{\ominus}$**, as the *enthalpy change when the mole quantities shown in the balanced chemical reaction completely react together at 298 K*

A small piece of magnesium is added to about 2 cm³ of dilute hydrochloric acid at 20°C. Hydrogen gas is rapidly evolved and the temperature rises to 59°C

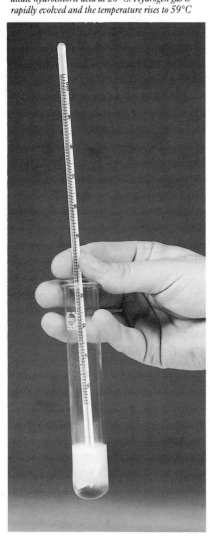

and a pressure of 1 atmosphere. All the substances involved must be in their normal physical states under these conditions. Two other points to note: (i) the most stable allotrope at 298 K and 1 atm is taken as standard, (e.g. P_{red} not P_{white}), and (ii) all solutions have a concentration of 1 mole of solute per dm^3 of solution.

Of course, many reactions do not occur under standard conditions (e.g. petrol will not burn without the high temperature caused by an electrical spark or a flame). In these cases, the standard enthalpy change is either (i) calculated from a ΔH value for the direct reaction under non-standard conditions or (ii) obtained using an indirect method, (discussed in section 4.12).

Activity 4.1

Which of the following equations do not represent standard enthalpy changes? All ΔH values are in kJ.

1 $C_3H_7OH(l) + \frac{9}{2}O_2(g) \xrightarrow[1\,atm]{298\,K} 3CO_2(g) + 4H_2O(l)$ $\Delta H = -2010$

2 $CH_4(g) + 2O_2(g) \xrightarrow[1\,atm]{298\,K} CO_2(g) + 2H_2O(g)$ $\Delta H = -809$

3 $H_2(g) + CO_2(g) \xrightarrow[1\,atm]{900\,K} H_2O(g) + CO(g)$ $\Delta H = +39$

4 $NH_3(g) + HCl(g) \xrightarrow[1\,atm]{298\,K} NH_4Cl(s)$ $\Delta H = -177$

5 $C_6H_6(l) + O_2(g) \xrightarrow[1\,atm]{298\,K} 6CO_2(g) + 3H_2O(l)$ $\Delta H = -3268$

6 $2C(g) + 6H(g) \xrightarrow[1\,atm]{298\,K} C_2H_6(g)$ $\Delta H = -2844$

4.5 Standard enthalpy of combustion

The **standard enthalpy of combustion, $\Delta H_c^{\ominus}$**, *is the enthalpy change when one mole of a pure substance is completely burnt in oxygen under standard conditions (298 K, 1 atmosphere).*

Complete combustion is essential. For example, rhombic sulphur can react with oxygen to form sulphur dioxide, SO_2, or sulphur trioxide, SO_3:

$S(rhombic) + O_2(g) \rightarrow SO_2(g)$ $\Delta H^{\ominus} = -297\,kJ$

$S(rhombic) + \frac{3}{2}O_2(g) \rightarrow SO_3(g)$ $\Delta H^{\ominus} = -395\,kJ$

Since complete combustion of sulphur gives sulphur trioxide, it is the second equation which respresents the standard enthalpy of combustion of sulphur, $\Delta H_c^{\ominus}[S(rhombic)] = -395\,kJ\,mol^{-1}$.

Often, we have to write chemical equations which correspond to the standard enthalpy change on combustion, e.g.

$\Delta H_c^{\ominus}[C_2H_6(g)] = -1560\,kJ\,mol^{-1}$ means

$C_2H_6(g) + \frac{7}{2}O_2(g) \rightarrow 2CO_2(g) + 3H_2O(l)$ $\Delta H^{\ominus} = -1560\,kJ$

and $\Delta H_c^{\ominus}[CH_3OH(l)] = -726\,kJ\,mol^{-1}$ means

$CH_3OH(l) + \frac{3}{2}O_2(g) \rightarrow CO_2(g) + 2H_2O(l)$ $\Delta H^{\ominus} = -726\,kJ$

Table 4.1 *Approximate energy values for foods and fuels*

Substance	energy value/kJ per 100g
pickled beetroot	115
skimmed milk	145
apple	196
semi-skimmed milk	210
full cream milk	290
baked beans	315
wholemeal bread	885
corn flakes	1560
sugar	1650
cheese	1700
alcohol (beer)	2900
butter	3050
octane	4835
methane	5560

On average, the energy requirements of men and women are about 11 000 and 7500 kJ per day, respectively. Any excess energy intake is converted into fat. Which of the following snacks is the more 'fattening': (a) a cheese sandwich (50 g wholemeal bread, 50 g cheese, 15 g butter) + a pint of beer (18 g alcohol) or (b) baked beans on toast (25 g wholemeal bread, 200 g baked beans, 10 g butter) + a pint of full-cream milk (500 g)?

Figure 4.2 *A bomb calorimeter*

Figure 4.3 *A graph of temperature plotted against time for a typical bomb calorimeter experiment*

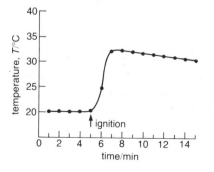

Activity 4.2

Write thermochemical equations from the following data (all in kJ mol^{-1}):

1. $\Delta H_c^{\ominus}$ [CO(g)] = −283
2. $\Delta H_c^{\ominus}$ [C$_6$H$_{14}$(l)] = −4195
3. $\Delta H_c^{\ominus}$ [C$_2$H$_5$OH(l)] = −1367
4. $\Delta H_c^{\ominus}$ [C$_6$H$_5$CO$_2$H(s)] = −3228
5. $\Delta H_c^{\ominus}$ [H$_2$(g)] = −286
6. $\Delta H_c^{\ominus}$ [Zn(s)] = −348

Standard enthalpies of combustion are often used by scientists to compare the energy values of fuels and foods (table 4.1).

4.6 Measuring a standard enthalpy of combustion

Standard enthalpies of combustion are accurately measured using a **bomb calorimeter** (figure 4.2). A known mass of the sample and excess oxygen are ignited electrically. Heat is released and the temperature of the calorimeter and its contents is noted at one-minute intervals. A graph of temperature against time is plotted (figure 4.3). The reactants are then replaced by an electric heating coil and the current adjusted so as to reproduce exactly figure 4.3. Then we calculate the electrical energy used, this being exactly equal to the energy change during the chemical reaction.

A bomb calorimeter measures an energy change under 'non-standard' conditions (i.e. constant volume and high temperature). Thus, the value must then be adjusted to give the enthalpy of combustion under standard conditions.

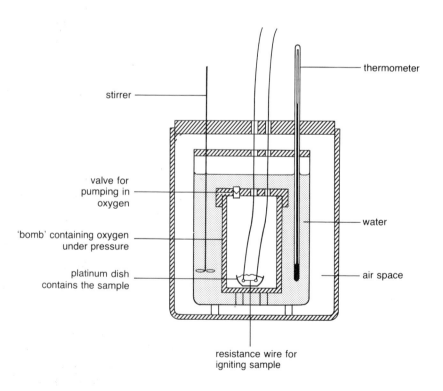

The photograph overleaf shows a simple apparatus for measuring an approximate $\Delta H_c^{\ominus}$ value of a liquid fuel, such as ethanol.

4.7 Standard enthalpy of formation

The **standard enthalpy of formation, $\Delta H_f^\ominus$,** is the enthalpy change when one mole of a pure substance is formed from its elements in their normal physical states, under standard conditions (298 K, 1 atmosphere).

These enthalpy changes can be represented by thermochemical equations:

$\Delta H_f^\ominus [C_2H_5OH(l)] = -277 \text{ kJ mol}^{-1}$ means

$$2C(\text{graphite}) + 3H_2(g) + \tfrac{1}{2}O_2(g) \rightarrow C_2H_5OH(l) \qquad \Delta H^\ominus = -277 \text{ kJ}$$

and $\Delta H_f^\ominus [NH_4I(s)] = -201 \text{ kJ mol}^{-1}$ means

$$\tfrac{1}{2}N_2(g) + 2H_2(g) + \tfrac{1}{2}I_2(s) \rightarrow NH_4I(s) \qquad \Delta H^\ominus = -201 \text{ kJ}$$

Another point to note is that, from the definition above, *the standard enthalpy of formation of an element in its standard state is zero.* For example,

$$H_2(g) \rightarrow H_2(g) \quad \Delta H_f^\ominus = 0 \text{ kJ mol}^{-1}$$

$$Na(s) \rightarrow Na(s) \quad \Delta H_f^\ominus = 0 \text{ kJ mol}^{-1}$$

A simple 'heat of combustion' apparatus being used to estimate the enthalpy of combustion of ethanol. A known mass of ethanol is burnt and the rise in temperature ($\triangle T$) of a calorimeter containing water is measured. Then the enthalpy change ($\triangle H$) is given by:

$\triangle H = $ *mass of the calorimeter $\times$ heat capacity of the $\times \triangle T$*
+ contents   calorimeter + contents

Activity 4.3 ─────────────────────────────

Write thermochemical equations from the following data (all in kJ mol^{-1}):

1 $\Delta H_f^\ominus [CH_3Cl(l)] = -81$ 2 $\Delta H_f^\ominus [CH_3COCH_3(l)] = -248$

3 $\Delta H_f^\ominus [CH_3OH(l)] = -239$ 4 $\Delta H_f^\ominus [Mg_3N_2(s)] = -461$

5 $\Delta H_f^\ominus [HI(g)] = +26$ 6 $\Delta H_f^\ominus [H_2SO_4(l)] = -814$

7 $\Delta H_f^\ominus [CH_3NH_2(g)] = -23$ 8 $\Delta H_f^\ominus [MgCl_2.6H_2O(s)] = -2500$

Standard enthalpies of formation can sometimes be measured *directly* (e.g. by using a bomb calorimeter). In many cases, though, the elements will not combine under experimental conditions. For example, $\Delta H_f^\ominus [CH_4(g)]$ cannot be obtained directly because graphite and hydrogen will not react together in a calorimeter. Fortunately, standard enthalpies of formation can also be measured *indirectly* (section 4.12).

Standard enthalpies of formation provide useful information about the stabilities of compounds (section 4.13).

4.8 Standard enthalpy of atomisation

The **standard enthalpy of atomisation, $\Delta H_a^\ominus$**, *is the enthalpy change when one mole of gas atoms is formed from the element under standard conditions (298 K, 1 atmosphere).*
An example would be

$$\tfrac{1}{2}Cl_2(g) \rightarrow Cl(g) \quad \Delta H_a^\ominus = +121\,kJ$$

and this may be abbreviated to $\Delta H_a^\ominus\,[Cl_2(g)] = +121\ kJ\,mol^{-1}$.

Note that atomisation is always an endothermic process. Also, *beware the common error of incorrectly defining $\Delta H_a^\ominus$ as the enthalpy change when 1 mole of the element is atomised.* For example, to atomise one mole of chlorine, (i.e. $Cl_2(g) \rightarrow 2Cl(g)$), we would need $2 \times \Delta H_a^\ominus\,[Cl_2(g)] = 2 \times (+121) = +242\,kJ$.

Activity 4.4

Write thermochemical equations from the following data (all in $kJ\,mol^{-1}$):

1   $\Delta H_a^\ominus[C\ (graphite)] = +717$ 2 $\Delta H_a^\ominus\,[Ca(s)] = +178$

3   $\Delta H_a^\ominus\,[Br_2(l)] = +112$ 4 $\Delta H_a^\ominus\,[N_2(g)] = +473$

5   $\Delta H_a^\ominus\,[K(s)] = +89$ 6 $\Delta H_a^\ominus\,[P_4\ (white, s)] = +315$

Standard enthalpies of atomisation are often obtained from absorption spectra of gases or from the heat capacities of solids and liquids. We shall make use of $\Delta H_a^\ominus$ values when we discuss the energetics of chemical bonding (sections 5.2 and 5.7).

4.9 Standard enthalpy of neutralisation

The **standard enthalpy of neutralisation, $\Delta H_n^\ominus$**, *is the enthalpy change when an acid reacts with a base to form one mole of water, under standard conditions (298 K, 1 atmosphere).* Thus, $\Delta H_n^\ominus\,[HCl/NaOH(aq)] = -57.9\,kJ$ is the abbreviated form of the equation

$$HCl(aq) + NaOH(aq) \rightarrow NaCl(aq) + H_2O(l) \quad \Delta H^\ominus = -57.9\,kJ$$

However, for the reaction

$$2HNO_3(aq) + Ca(OH)_2(aq) \rightarrow Ca(NO_3)_2(aq) + 2H_2O(l)$$

the standard enthalpy change is found to be $-114.8\,kJ$ because *two* moles of water are being formed. The correct thermochemical equation for $\Delta H_n^\ominus\,[HNO_3/Ca(OH)_2(aq)]$ is

$$HNO_3(aq) + \tfrac{1}{2}Ca(OH)_2(aq) \rightarrow \tfrac{1}{2}Ca(NO_3)_2(aq) + H_2O(l) \quad \Delta H^\ominus = -57.4\,kJ$$

4.10 Measuring a standard enthalpy of neutralisation

Standard enthalpies of neutralisation are one of the easiest enthalpy changes to measure. Known volumes of standard acid and base solution are mixed together in a simple calorimeter (e.g. an expanded polystyrene beaker). The measurement of $\Delta H_n^\ominus\,[H_2SO_4/NaOH(aq)]$ is described below.

When aqueous sulphuric acid and sodium hydroxide react together, the equation is

$$H_2SO_4(aq) + 2NaOH(aq) \rightarrow Na_2SO_4(aq) + 2H_2O(l)$$

From this equation, you can see that the reactants must be mixed together in the mole ratio: **$H_2SO_4(aq): NaOH(aq) = 1 : 2$**. Consequently, we put $25\,cm^3$ of $1\,M$

H_2SO_4(aq) (i.e. 0.025 moles) in the polystyrene beaker and note its temperature every minute for four minutes. On the fifth minute, $25\,cm^3$ of 2 M NaOH(aq) (0.050 moles) are added and the mixture is stirred. The temperature of the reaction mixture is taken every minute for a further ten minutes.

These results are used to plot a graph of temperature against time, as shown in figure 4.4. After making a cooling correction (by extending the line AB to C), the temperature rise during the reaction, ΔT, is found to be 13.9 K.

Since the beaker has a negligible heat capacity, the enthalpy change, ΔH, is given by

$$\Delta H = \begin{array}{c}\text{mass of aqueous}\\ \text{solution}\end{array} \times \begin{array}{c}\text{its specific heat}\\ \text{capacity}\end{array} \times \text{temperature change}$$

$$= \quad 50\,g \quad \times \quad 4.2\,J\,g^{-1}K^{-1} \quad \times \quad 13.9\,K$$

$$= 2919\,J$$

$$= 2.919\,kJ$$

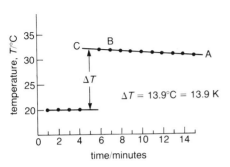

Figure 4.4 *A graph of temperature plotted against time for an experiment to measure the enthalpy of neutralisation of sulphuric acid by sodium hydroxide*

(Notes: we have assumed that (i) like pure water, $50\,cm^3$ of aqueous solution weighs 50 g; (ii) an aqueous solution has the same heat capacity as water, namely, $4.2\,J\,g^{-1}K^{-1}$.)

In our experiment, 0.025 moles of acid reacted with 0.05 moles of base to form 0.05 moles of water. Thus,

when 0.05 moles of water are formed 2.919 kJ of enthalpy is released;

when 1 mole of water is formed $2.919 \times \dfrac{1}{0.05} = 58.4\,kJ$ are released.

From this experiment, the enthalpy of neutralisation of sulphuric acid by sodium hydroxide is found to be $-58.4\,kJ\,mol^{-1}$ of water formed (the value is negative because the reaction is exothermic). More accurate calorimetry gives $\Delta H_n^{\ominus}[H_2SO_4/NaOH(aq)] = -57.6\,kJ\,mol^{-1}$.

4.11   Hess's Law of Constant Heat Summation

The neutralisation of sulphuric acid by sodium hydroxide can be performed in two steps, via sodium hydrogen sulphate:

step 1: H_2SO_4(aq) + NaOH(aq) $\rightarrow$ $NaHSO_4$(aq) + H_2O(l)

step 2: $NaHSO_4$(aq) + NaOH(aq) $\rightarrow$ Na_2SO_4(aq) + H_2O(l)

To do this, we use the method in section 4.10 but add the aqueous sodium hydroxide in two separate portions of $12.5\,cm^3$. A student obtained the following enthalpy changes: $\Delta H_{step\ 1} = -1.54\,kJ$ and $\Delta H_{step\ 2} = -1.45\,kJ$. Both steps are exothermic and combining their enthalpy changes we get $\Delta H_{total} = -1.54 + (-1.45) = -2.99\,kJ$. As we saw in section 4.10, these quantities of reagents will form 0.05 moles of water. For the formation of *one mole of water*, then, the enthalpy released will be $-2.99 \times 1/0.05 = -59.8\,kJ$. Within experimental error, this enthalpy change agrees with that we obtained for the 'one-step' route:

$$H_2SO_4\text{(aq)} + 2NaOH\text{(aq)} \rightarrow Na_2SO_4\text{(aq)} + 2H_2O\text{(l)}$$

namely, $-58.4\,kJ$ per mole of water formed.

In fact, these values illustrate the **Law of Constant Heat Summation**, proposed by **Hess** in 1840. This law states that *the enthalpy change during a chemical reaction depends only on the nature of the reactants and the products, no matter what reaction route is followed.*

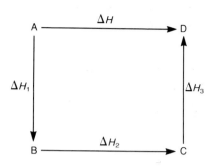

Figure 4.5 *An enthalpy cycle showing the conversion of A into D via the intermediate compounds B and C*

4.12 Using Hess's Law to calculate enthalpy changes

Hess's Law can be represented using an **enthalpy cycle** (figure 4.5). This enthalpy cycle links the enthalpy changes which occur when the reactants A form products D either directly or indirectly via the compounds B and C. Using Hess's Law, we can equate the enthalpy changes:

$$\Delta H = \Delta H_1 + \Delta H_2 + \Delta H_3$$

(A useful 'rule of thumb':
enthalpy changes for the clockwise arrows = those for the anticlockwise arrows.)

When drawing an enthalpy cycle, we must decide which intermediate reactions can be used. Very often, *this choice will depend on which standard enthalpy changes are available.* Consider the following example.

Example 1

Calculate the standard enthalpy of formation of methanol, using the following data:

$$\Delta H_c^{\ominus} [C(graphite)] = -393 \text{ kJ mol}^{-1}$$
$$\Delta H_c^{\ominus} [H_2(g)] = -286 \text{ kJ mol}^{-1}$$
$$\Delta H_c^{\ominus} [CH_3OH(l)] = -726 \text{ kJ mol}^{-1}$$

1 An enthalpy cycle is needed. Write the chemical equation for the required enthalpy change i.e. $\Delta H_f^{\ominus}$ [CH$_3$OH(l)] ▶

2 Look at the data given; these are $\Delta H_c^{\ominus}$ values ∴ suggesting that the combustion products complete the enthalpy cycle ▶

$$C(graphite) + 2H_2(g) + \tfrac{1}{2}O_2(g) \xrightarrow{\Delta H_f^{\ominus}} CH_3OH(l)$$

$(+\tfrac{3}{2}O_2(g)) \quad \searrow^{\Delta H_1} \qquad \quad {}^{\Delta H_2}\searrow \; (+\tfrac{3}{2}O_2(g))$

$$CO_2(g) + 2H_2O(l)$$

◀ **3** Label the enthalpy changes ΔH_1 and ΔH_2

According to Hess's Law of Constant Heat Summation:

$$\Delta H_f^{\ominus} + \Delta H_2 = \Delta H_1$$

$$\therefore \Delta H_f^{\ominus} = \Delta H_1 - \Delta H_2$$

◀ **4** Equate the ΔH terms, according to Hess's Law.

5 Consider which ΔH terms make up ΔH_1 (Note: it is 2 × $\Delta H_c^{\ominus}$[H$_2$(g)] because 2 moles of hydrogen are burnt) ▶

$$\Delta H_1 = \Delta H_c^{\ominus} [C(graphite)] + 2(\Delta H_c^{\ominus}[H_2(g)])$$
$$= \quad -393 \quad\quad + 2(-286)$$
$$= \quad -393 \quad\quad + (-572)$$
$$\therefore \Delta H_1 = -965 \text{ kJ}$$

◀ **6** Substitute values (don't rush here)

7 Consider which ΔH terms make up ΔH_2 ▶

$$\Delta H_2 = \Delta H_c^{\ominus} [CH_3OH(l)]$$
$$\therefore \Delta H_2 = -726 \text{ kJ}$$

◀ **8** Substitute values

9 Substitute the ΔH terms into the Hess's Law equation ▶

$$\Delta H_f^{\ominus} = \Delta H_1 - \Delta H_2$$
$$= -965 - (-726)$$
$$= -965 + 726$$
$$\Delta H_f^{\ominus}[CH_3OH(l)] = -239 \text{ kJ mol}^{-1}$$

(Notice how the enthalpy changes given in the question guide us towards the structure of the enthalpy cycle.)

Activity 4.5

Use the above method to:

1   Find the standard enthalpy of formation of ethane, C_2H_6, given

$\Delta H_c^\ominus$ [C(graphite)]   = -393 kJ mol^{-1}

$\Delta H_c^\ominus$ [H_2(g)]   = -286 kJ mol^{-1}

$\Delta H_c^\ominus$ [C_2H_6(g)]   = -1560 kJ mol^{-1}.

2   Find the standard enthalpy of combustion of propan-2-ol, given

$\Delta H_c^\ominus$ [C(graphite)]   = -393 kJ mol^{-1}

$\Delta H_c^\ominus$ [H_2(g)]   = -286 kJ mol^{-1}

$\Delta H_f^\ominus$ [$CH_3CH(OH)CH_3$(l)] = -318 kJ mol^{-1}.

4.13 Chemical stability

Quite often, a chemical substance is rather loosely described as being stable or unstable. *But what exactly do we mean by chemical stability?*

As a chemical reaction proceeds, the change in the enthalpy of the system can be described by an **enthalpy profile**. Two simple enthalpy profiles are drawn in figure 4.6. Compared to the reaction products, the reactants are said to be

▶   *energetically unstable* if the reaction is exothermic (ΔH is negative);

▶   *energetically stable* if the reaction is endothermic (ΔH is positive).

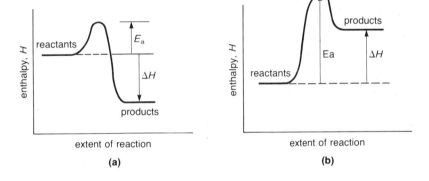

(a)   **(b)**

Figure 4.6   *Enthalpy profiles for **(a)** an exothermic reaction (ΔH is $-ve$), and **(b)** an endothermic reaction (ΔH is $+ve$). The activation energy, E_a is always an endothermic quantity*

A fruit stone stuck in a jar of jelly is energetically unstable since it would tend to fall under gravity to the bottom of the container, a position of lower potential energy. The stone is kinetically stable though, since it is unable to move through the 'set' jelly

Whether the reaction is exothermic or endothermic, it will not occur in the absence of a certain minimum amount of energy, known as the **activation energy, E_a**. The reactants will be *kinetically stable*, therefore, if the activation energy is very high. For example, the decomposition of ammonia,

$$2NH_3(g) \rightarrow N_2(g) + 3H_2(g) \qquad E_a = +335 \text{ kJ mol}^{-1} \text{ (very high)}$$

will not occur at room temperature. On the other hand, reactants which have a low activation will be *kinetically unstable*. For example, in the presence of sunlight hydrogen and chlorine will explode at room temperature:

$$H_2(g) + Cl_2(g) \rightarrow 2HCl(g) \qquad E_a = +25 \text{ kJ mol}^{-1} \text{ (very low)}$$

Let us apply these ideas to the combustion of petrol in a car's engine. When the petrol–air mixture is ignited, there is a considerable release of enthalpy. One of the reactions involved is the combustion of **octane**:

$$C_8H_{18}(l) + \tfrac{25}{2}O_2(g) \rightarrow 8CO_2(g) + 9H_2O(l) \qquad \Delta H^\ominus = -3498 \text{ kJ}$$

Clearly, octane is energetically unstable relative to its combustion products, carbon dioxide and water. However, as long as the safety procedure is followed, motorists can fill up their petrol tanks without fear of an explosion. The activation energy for the combustion is quite high, and octane is said to be kinetically stable, relative to its combustion products.

Predicting the feasibility of a chemical reaction is an important, and complex, aspect of chemical thermodynamics[*]. Generally speaking, *a reaction is more likely to occur if the reactants are both energetically and kinetically unstable relative to the products*.

As we have seen, activation energies give us some idea of the kinetic stability of the reactants. But what thermochemical quantity reflects the energetic stability of a compound?

A vast number of chemical changes occur without heating because the activation energy is obtained from the enthalpies of the reactants. Theory suggests that a substance will have zero enthalpy only at absolute zero (i.e. 0 K, $-273\,°\text{C}$). However, in practice *we assume that an element in its standard state has zero enthalpy*. This assumption is reasonable because we do not measure actual enthalpies but enthalpy changes (see figure 4.7).

Since all standard enthalpies of formation refer to this assumed 'zero' enthalpy level, the $\Delta H_f^\ominus$ value should be a measure of a compound's energetic stability. For example, the equation

$$\tfrac{1}{2}N_2(g) + \tfrac{1}{2}O_2(g) \rightarrow NO(g) \quad \Delta H_f^\ominus = +90 \text{ kJ mol}^{-1}$$

means that the elements (assumed to be at zero enthalpy) take in 90 kJ of enthalpy in forming one mole of nitrogen monoxide. This oxide is an example of an **endothermic compound**, that is, *enthalpy is absorbed on its formation*. On the other hand, the enthalpy of formation of dinitrogen pentoxide, $N_2O_5(s)$, is -43 kJ mol^{-1}:

$$N_2(g) + \tfrac{5}{2}O_2(g) \rightarrow N_2O_5(s) \qquad \Delta H_f^\ominus = -43 \text{ kJ mol}^{-1}$$

Dinitrogen pentoxide is an example of an **exothermic compound**, that is, *enthalpy is lost on its formation*. The two enthalpies of formation can be compared on an enthalpy level diagram (figure 4.8), Clearly, nitrogen pentoxide, and not nitrogen monoxide, is the more energetically stable of the oxides.

Later in this book, we shall use standard enthalpies of formation to compare the energetic stabilities of the chlorides, oxides and hydrides of the elements lithium to argon. You might find it useful to have a quick look at tables 20.1 to 20.3.

Petrol being delivered to a service station. The petrol is energetically unstable with respect to its combustion products, carbon dioxide and water. Since the activation energy from the combustion reaction is very high, however, the petrol is kinetically stable and does not ignite spontaneously. Notice the hazard warning sign on the side of tanker which indicates the load being carried, the dangers in handling it and the form of extinguisher that should be used in the event of a fire

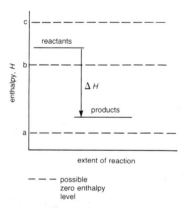

Figure 4.7 *The definition of a zero enthalpy state, for example at a, b or c, does not affect the size of the enthalpy change, ΔH*

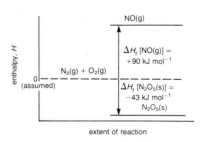

Figure 4.8 *Comparing the standard enthalpies of formation of nitrogen monoxide, NO, and dinitrogen pentoxide, N_2O_5*

---

[*] To find out more about this subject, look up the topics entropy and free energy in a more advanced physical chemistry textbook.

4.14 Using $\Delta H_f^{\ominus}$ values to calculate enthalpy changes on reaction

Like earlier calculations, these involve the use of enthalpy cycles. Work through the following example.

Example

Ethanol reacts with the halogenating agent phosphorus pentachloride according to the reaction:

$$C_2H_5OH(l) + PCl_5(s) \rightarrow C_2H_5Cl(l) + POCl_3(l) + HCl(g)$$

Calculate the standard enthalpy of reaction, using the following data (all in $kJ\,mol^{-1}$):

$$\Delta H_f^{\ominus} [C_2H_5OH(l)] = -277$$
$$\Delta H_f^{\ominus} [PCl_5(s)] = -443$$
$$\Delta H_f^{\ominus} [C_2H_5Cl(l)] = -136$$
$$\Delta H_f^{\ominus} [POCl_3(l)] = -597$$
$$\Delta H_f^{\ominus} [HCl\,(g)] = -92$$

1 An enthalpy cycle is needed. Write the chemical equation for the required enthalpy change ▶

2 Look at the data given; these are $\Delta H_f^{\ominus}$ values ∴ suggesting that the elements must complete the enthalpy cycle ▶

$$C_2H_5OH(l) + PCl_5(s) \xrightarrow{\Delta H^{\ominus}} C_2H_5Cl(l) + POCl_3(l) + HCl(g)$$

$\Delta H_1 \nwarrow \qquad \Delta H_2 \nearrow$

$$2C(graphite) + 3H_2(g) + \tfrac{1}{2}O_2(g) + P(red) + \tfrac{5}{2}Cl_2(g)$$

◀ **3** Label the enthalpy changes ΔH_1 and ΔH_2

By Hess's Law of Constant Heat Summation:

$$\Delta H_1 + \Delta H^{\ominus} = \Delta H_2$$
$$\text{(clockwise arrows)} \quad \text{(anticlockwise arrow)}$$

$$\therefore \Delta H^{\ominus} = \Delta H_2 - \Delta H_1$$

◀ **4** Equate the ΔH terms according to Hess's Law

5 Consider which $\Delta H_f^{\ominus}$ terms make up ΔH_1 ▶

$$\Delta H_1 = \Delta H_f^{\ominus} [C_2H_5OH(l)] + \Delta H_f^{\ominus} [PCl_5(s)]$$
$$= -277 + (-443)$$
$$\therefore \Delta H_1 = -720\,kJ$$

◀ **6** Substitute values (don't rush here)

7 Consider which $\Delta H_f^{\ominus}$ terms make up ΔH_2 ▶

$$\Delta H_2 = \Delta H_f^{\ominus} [C_2H_5Cl(l)] + \Delta H_f^{\ominus} [POCl_3(l)] + \Delta H_f^{\ominus} [HCl(g)]$$
$$= -136 + (-597) + (-92)$$
$$\therefore \Delta H_2 = -825\,kJ$$

◀ **8** Substitute values

9 Substitute the ΔH terms in the Hess's Law equation ▶

$$\Delta H^{\ominus} = \Delta H_2 - \Delta H_1$$
$$= -825 - (-720)$$
$$= -825 + 720$$
$$\therefore \Delta H^{\ominus} = -105\,kJ$$

This type of calculation is very useful for determining the enthalpy changes which cannot be measured directly.

Use the same method in the following activity.

Activity 4.6

The platinum-catalysed oxidation of ammonia,

$$4NH_3(g) + 5O_2(g) \rightarrow 4NO(g) + 6H_2O(l)$$

is used in the manufacture of nitric acid. Calculate the enthalpy of reaction using the following data (all in kJ mol^{-1}):

$$\Delta H_f^{\ominus} [NH_3(g)] = -46$$
$$\Delta H_f^{\ominus} [NO(g)] = +90$$
$$\Delta H_f^{\ominus} [H_2O(l)] = -286$$
$$\Delta H_f^{\ominus} [O_2(g)] = 0 \text{ (see section 4.7)}$$

4.15 Comments on the activities

Activity 4.1

1 and 4 These equations do represent standard enthalpy changes for the reactions. All the reactants and products are in their standard states and the reaction conditions are also standard (i.e. 298 K and 1 atm pressure).

The other equations do not represent standard enthalpy changes for the following reasons:

2 one of the products, water, is not in its standard state;
3 the temperature (900 K) is not standard;
5 the equation is not balanced (it should be $\frac{15}{2}O_2(g)$);
6 the reactants are not in their standard states.

Activity 4.2

1 CO(g)	$+ \frac{1}{2}O_2$	$\rightarrow CO_2(g)$	$\Delta H = -283\,kJ$
2 $C_6H_{14}(l)$	$+ \frac{19}{2}O_2(g)$	$\rightarrow 6CO_2(g) + 7H_2O(l)$	$\Delta H = -4195\,kJ$
3 $C_2H_5OH(l)$	$+ 3O_2(g)$	$\rightarrow 2CO_2(g) + 3H_2O(l)$	$\Delta H = -1367\,kJ$
4 $C_6H_5CO_2H(s)$	$+ \frac{15}{2}O_2(g)$	$\rightarrow 7CO_2(g) + 3H_2O(l)$	$\Delta H = -3228\,kJ$
5 $H_2(g)$	$+ \frac{1}{2}O_2(g)$	$\rightarrow H_2O(l)$	$\Delta H = -286\,kJ$
6 Zn(s)	$+ \frac{1}{2}O_2(g)$	$\rightarrow ZnO(s)$	$\Delta H = -348\,kJ$

Activity 4.3

1 C(graphite)	$+ \frac{3}{2}H_2(g) + \frac{1}{2}Cl_2(g) \rightarrow CH_3Cl(l)$		$\Delta H = -81\,kJ$
2 3C(graphite)	$+ 3H_2(g) + \frac{1}{2}O_2(g) \rightarrow CH_3COCH_3(l)$		$\Delta H = -248\,kJ$
3 C(graphite)	$+ 2H_2(g) + \frac{1}{2}O_2(g) \rightarrow CH_3OH(l)$		$\Delta H = -239\,kJ$
4 3Mg(s)	$+ N_2(g) \rightarrow Mg_3N_2(s)$		$\Delta H = -461\,kJ$
5 $\frac{1}{2}H_2(g)$	$+ \frac{1}{2}I_2(s) \rightarrow HI(g)$		$\Delta H = +26\,kJ$
6 $H_2(g)$	$+ S(s) + 2O_2(g) \rightarrow H_2SO_4(l)$		$\Delta H = -814\,kJ$
7 C(graphite)	$+ \frac{1}{2}N_2(g) + \frac{5}{2}H_2(g) \rightarrow CH_3NH_2(g)$		$\Delta H = -23\,kJ$
8 Mg(s) + Cl_2(g)	$+ 6H_2(g) + 3O_2(g) \rightarrow MgCl_2.6H_2O(s)$		$\Delta H = -2500\,kJ$

Activity 4.4

1 C(graphite)	$\rightarrow C(g)$	$\Delta H = +717\,kJ$
2 Ca(s)	$\rightarrow Ca(g)$	$\Delta H = +178\,kJ$
3 $\frac{1}{2}Br_2(l)$	$\rightarrow Br(g)$	$\Delta H = +112\,kJ$
4 $\frac{1}{2}N_2(g)$	$\rightarrow N(g)$	$\Delta H = +473\,kJ$
5 K(s)	$\rightarrow K(g)$	$\Delta H = +89\,kJ$
6 $\frac{1}{4}P_4(s)$	$\rightarrow P(g)$	$\Delta H = +315\,kJ$

Activity 4.5

1 The notes □ refer to the example in section 4.12.

$$\boxed{1} \qquad 2C(graphite) + 3H_2(g) \xrightarrow{\Delta H_f^{\ominus}} C_2H_6(g)$$

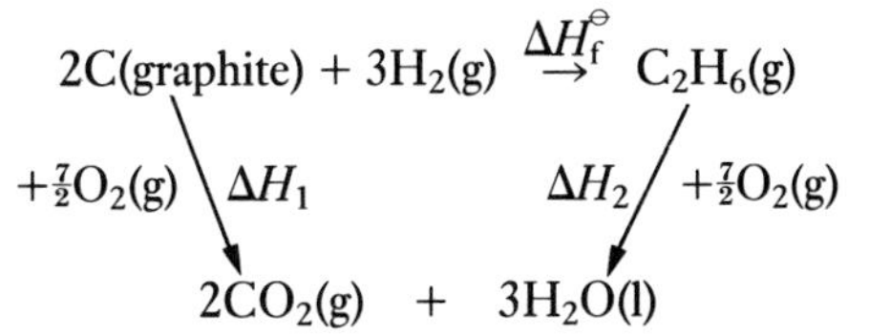

$$+\tfrac{7}{2}O_2(g) \searrow \Delta H_1 \qquad \Delta H_2 \swarrow +\tfrac{7}{2}O_2(g) \qquad \boxed{3}$$

$$2CO_2(g) \ + \ 3H_2O(l)$$

2 Note: enthalpies of combustion ▶

By Hess's Law of Constant Heat Summation:

$$\Delta H_f^{\ominus} + \Delta H_2 = \Delta H_1 \qquad \boxed{4}$$
$$\text{(clockwise arrows)} \quad \text{(anticlockwise arrow)}$$

5 Note: that we burn 2 and 3 moles of graphite and hydrogen respectively ▶

$$\therefore \Delta H_f^{\ominus} = \Delta H_1 - \Delta H_2$$

$$\Delta H_1 = 2(\Delta H_c^{\ominus} [C(graphite)]) + 3(\Delta H_c^{\ominus} [H_2(g)])$$
$$= 2(-393) + 3(-286) \qquad \boxed{6}$$
$$= -786 - 858$$
$$\therefore \Delta H_1 = -1644\,kJ$$

$$\boxed{7} \qquad \Delta H_2 = \Delta H_c^{\ominus} [C_2H_6(g)]$$
$$\therefore \Delta H_2 = -1560$$
$$\boxed{8}$$

$$\boxed{9} \qquad \Delta H_f^{\ominus} = \Delta H_1 - \Delta H_2$$
$$= -1644 - (-1560)$$
$$= -1644 + 1560$$
$$\therefore \Delta H_f^{\ominus} [C_2H_6(g)] = -84\,kJ\,mol^{-1}$$

2 The notes □ refer to the example in section 4.12.

$$\boxed{1} \qquad CH_3CH(OH)CH_3(l) \xrightarrow{\Delta H_c^{\ominus}} 3CO_2(g) + 4H_2O(l)$$
$$+ \tfrac{9}{2}O_2(g)$$

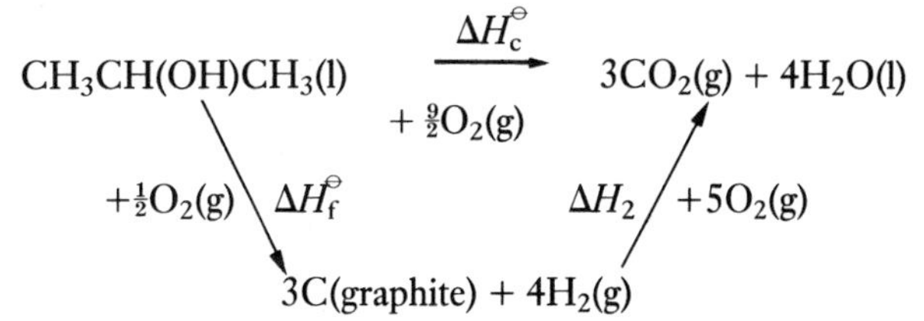

$$+\tfrac{1}{2}O_2(g) \searrow \Delta H_f^{\ominus} \qquad \Delta H_2 \swarrow +5O_2(g) \qquad \boxed{3}$$

$$3C(graphite) + 4H_2(g)$$

2 Data: includes enthalpy of formation ∴ elements complete the enthalpy cycle ▶

By Hess's Law of Constant Heat Summation:

$$\Delta H_c^{\ominus} + \Delta H_1 = \Delta H_2 \qquad \boxed{4}$$
$$\text{(clockwise arrows)} \quad \text{(anticlockwise arrow)}$$

$$\therefore \Delta H_c^{\ominus} = \Delta H_2 - \Delta H_1$$

$$\boxed{5} \qquad \Delta H_1 = \Delta H_f^{\ominus} [CH_3CH(OH)CH_3(l)]$$
$$\boxed{6} \qquad \therefore \Delta H_1 = -318\,kJ$$

$$\Delta H_2 = 3(\Delta H_c^{\ominus} [C(graphite)]) + 4(\Delta H_c^{\ominus} [H_2(g)])$$
$$= 3(-393) + 4(-286) \qquad \boxed{8}$$
$$= -1179 + (-1144)$$
$$= -1179 - 1144$$
$$\therefore \Delta H_2 = -2323\,kJ$$

7 Note: we are burning 3 and 4 moles of graphite and hydrogen respectively ▶

$$\boxed{9} \quad \Delta H_c^{\ominus} [CH_3CH(OH)CH_3(l)] = \Delta H_2 - \Delta H_1$$
$$= -2323 - (-318)$$
$$= -2323 + 318$$

$$\therefore \Delta H_c^{\ominus} [CH_3CH(OH)CH_3(l)] = -2005\,kJ\,mol^{-1}$$

Activity 4.6

The notes ☐ refer to the example in section 4.14.

$\boxed{1}$

$$4NH_3(g) + 5O_2(g) \xrightarrow{\Delta H^{\ominus}} 4NO(g) + 6H_2O(l)$$

$\Delta H_1 \qquad \Delta H_2$

$\boxed{3}$

$$2N_2(g) + 6H_2(g) + 5O_2(g)$$

By Hess's Law of Constant Heat Summation:

$$\Delta H^{\ominus} + \Delta H_1 = \Delta H_2 \qquad \boxed{4}$$
(clockwise arrows)   (anticlockwise arrows)

$$\therefore \Delta H^{\ominus} = \Delta H_2 - \Delta H_1$$

$$\Delta H_1 = 4(\Delta H_f^{\ominus} [NH_3(g)]) + 5(\Delta H_f^{\ominus} [O_2(g)])$$

$$= 4(-46) + 5(0) \qquad \boxed{6}$$

$$\therefore \Delta H_1 = -184 \text{ kJ}$$

$$\Delta H_2 = 4(\Delta H_f^{\ominus} [NO(g)]) + 6(\Delta H_f^{\ominus} [H_2O(l)])$$

$$= 4(90) + 6(-286) \qquad \boxed{8}$$

$$= 360 + (-1716)$$

$$\therefore \Delta H_2 = -1356 \text{ kJ}$$

$\boxed{9}$

$$\Delta H^{\ominus} = \Delta H_2 - \Delta H_1$$

$$= -1356 - (-184)$$

$$= -1356 + 184$$

$$\therefore \Delta H^{\ominus} = -1172 \text{ kJ}$$

2 Data: ΔH_f values $\therefore$ elements needed to complete enthalpy cycle ▶

5 Note: 4 moles of NH_3 formed $\therefore$ $4 \times \Delta H_f^{\ominus}$ Also, $\Delta H_f^{\ominus}$ (element) = 0, by definition ▶

7 Note: 4 moles of NO(g) and 6 moles $H_2O(l)$ formed ▶

4.16 Summary and revision plan

1   Nearly all chemical reactions have an associated energy change.
2   All substances have a heat content or **enthalpy**, *H*. We are interested in the enthalpy change, ΔH, which accompanies the reaction where

$$\Delta H = H_{\text{products}} - H_{\text{reactants}}$$

If ΔH is negative, the reaction is **exothermic**. If ΔH is positive, the reaction is **endothermic**.

3   To compare ΔH values, we must measure them under standard conditions. Thus, we define the **standard enthalpy change on reaction, $\Delta H^{\ominus}$**, as the enthalpy change when the mole quantities shown in the balanced chemical equation react under standard conditions of 298 K and 1 atmosphere pressure.

4   Often $\Delta H^{\ominus}$ is calculated from an enthalpy change measured under non-standard conditions.

5   Enthalpy changes do not depend on the choice of 'zero' enthalpy level (see figure 4.7). Thus, we make the assumption that an element in its standard state (i.e. 298 K and 1 atm pressure) contains zero enthalpy.

6   The **standard enthalpy of combustion, $\Delta H_c^{\ominus}$**, is the enthalpy change when one mole of a substance is completely burnt in oxygen under standard conditions (298 K and 1 atm).

7   The **standard enthalpy of formation, $\Delta H_f^{\ominus}$**, is the enthalpy change when one mole of a pure substance is formed from its elements in their normal physical states under standard conditions (298 K and 1 atm).

8 Calorimetry is used to measure an enthalpy change, ΔH, where a direct reaction is feasible. This technique involves the measurement of the temperature change, ΔT, experienced by a mass, m, of specific heat capacity, C_p. Then,

$$\Delta H = m \times C_p \times \Delta T$$

Don't forget to state whether the enthalpy change is exothermic ($-$ve) or endothermic ($+$ve).

9 The **standard enthalpy of atomisation, $\Delta H_a^{\ominus}$**, is the enthalpy needed to form one mole of gas atoms from the element under standard conditions (298 K and 1 atm).

10 The **standard enthalpy of neutralisation, $\Delta H_n^{\ominus}$**, is the enthalpy change when an acid reacts with a base to form one mole of water under standard conditions (298 K and 1 atm).

11 **Hess's Law of Constant Heat Summation** states that the enthalpy change during a chemical reaction depends only on the nature of the reactants and the products, no matter which reaction route is followed.

12 Enthalpy cycles based on Hess's Law can be used to calculate enthalpy changes for reactions (see section 4.12 and 4.14).

13 Compared to the reaction products, the reactants will be:
(a) energetically stable if $\Delta H_f^{\ominus}$ is positive, but energetically unstable if $\Delta H_f^{\ominus}$ is negative;
(b) kinetically stable if the activation energy, E_a, is high, but kinetically unstable if E_a is low.

14 A reaction is more likely to occur if the reactants are energetically and kinetically unstable.

15 A compound's $\Delta H_f^{\ominus}$ value reflects its energetic stability relative both to its constituent elements and to other compounds. Thus, **exothermic compounds** ($\Delta H_f^{\ominus}$ is negative) are energetically more stable than **endothermic compounds** ($\Delta H_f^{\ominus}$ positive).

□ C H A P T E R □

CHAPTER

CHAPTER

5

CHAPTER

CHAPTER

□ CHAPTER □

Electron Rearrangements and Chemical Bonding

Contents

In nature, separate atoms are very rare. Of the 92 natural elements, only a handful (the 'noble' gases–chapter 28) exist as separate atoms and even some of these have been 'persuaded' to combine with other elements to form compounds. In this chapter we shall survey the nature of various types of bond and investigate the energy changes which accompany their formation.

Electron density maps obtained by the X-ray and electron diffraction techniques outlined in section 6.4 show that the formation of a chemical bond involves *redistribution of the outer electron clouds* of the atoms concerned. Electrons may be completely *transferred* from one atom to another or be *shared* between two or more atoms, as sketched in figure 5.1.

The electron theory of chemical bonding forms one of the main foundations of modern chemistry. It enables us not only to predict which elements will combine together, but also to forecast what the properties of the resulting compounds are likely to be. Rather than trusting to 'trial and error', chemists are now able to 'design' substances to particular 'specifications'.

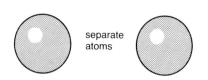

separate atoms

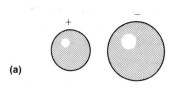

(a)

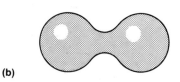

(b)

Figure 5.1 *Electron rearrangement during chemical bonding*

5.1 Ionic bonding: the complete transfer of electrons

The noble gases of Group 0 in the Periodic Table are most reluctant to form chemical bonds. Their outer electron configuration, i.e. full s and p sub-levels (s only for helium) must therefore be very stable. Atoms which can lose or gain electrons to achieve this arrangement form positive and negative ions respectively.

$$\begin{array}{ccccc} Na & + & Cl & \rightarrow & Na^+ & + & Cl^- \\ 1s^22s^22p^63s^1 & & 1s^22s^22p^63s^23p^5 & & 1s^22s^22p^6 & & 1s^22s^22p^63s^23p^6 \end{array}$$

i.e. $\quad$ [Ne]$3s^1$ $\qquad$ [Ne]$3s^23p^5$ $\qquad$ [Ne] $\qquad$ [Ar]

$$\begin{array}{ccccc} Mg & + & 2F & \rightarrow & Mg^{2+} & + & 2F^- \\ 1s^22s^22p^63s^2 & & 1s^22s^22p^5 & & 1s^22s^22p^6 & & 1s^22s^22p^6 \end{array}$$

i.e. $\quad$ [Ne]$3s^2$ $\qquad$ [He]$2s^22p^5$ $\qquad$ [Ne] $\qquad$ [Ne]

The electron density map in figure 5.1a shows that the electron density between the ions falls to zero. *The mutual attraction of the oppositely charged ions constitutes an* **ionic bond**, but it must be stressed that the crystal structure is a 3-dimensional lattice and that each ion is attracted equally to several surrounding ions of opposite charge. A detailed discussion of the structure of ionic crystals may be found in section 9.5.

Whilst extremely common, the noble gas electronic structure is not the only stable configuration found in ions. Other examples include:

H^+ $\quad$ no electrons $\quad$ not found in isolation (see chapter 21);

Pb^{2+} $\quad$ [Xe]$5d^{10}6s^2$ $\quad$ 'inert pair' effect (see chapter 24);

Fe^{3+} $\quad$ [Ar]$3d^5$ $\quad$ transition metal type (see chapter 29).

Activity 5.1

Using a copy of the Periodic Table, write the electron configuration of the cation in each of the following compounds. Give the 'noble gas' core in square brackets followed by any additional electrons as shown in the examples in section 5.1.

$$LiF \qquad CaO \qquad SnF_4 \qquad SnF_2 \qquad Sc_2O_3$$

5.2 Energetics of ionic bond formation: the Born–Haber cycle

In the preceding section we have used the idea of a 'stable' electron configuration as the driving force for ionic bond formation. Although this is a very useful model for working out the formula of an ionic compound and the electronic structure of the ions, it should not be interpreted too literally. For example, energy must be *supplied* to remove the outer electron from a sodium atom, so the resulting Na^+ ion must be energetically *less* stable.

Consideration of the energy changes involved in forming an ionic solid gives much greater insight into the tendency of elements to form such compounds. The standard enthalpy of formation of sodium chloride may be represented as follows:

$$Na(s) + \tfrac{1}{2}Cl_2(g) \rightarrow NaCl(s) \qquad \Delta H_f^\ominus = -411\,kJ$$

Using the standard enthalpy changes introduced in chapter 4, we may calculate the energy required to convert one mole of sodium metal into gaseous ions:

$Na(s)$	$\rightarrow$	$Na(g)$	ΔH_a	$= +109\,kJ$ (atomisation energy)
$Na(g)$	$\rightarrow$	$Na^+(g)$	$\Delta H_i(1)$	$= +494\,kJ$ (first ionisation energy)
			total	$+603\,kJ$

Similarly, for the formation of one mole of gaseous chloride ions from chlorine gas,

$\tfrac{1}{2}Cl_2(g)$	$\rightarrow$	$Cl(g)$	ΔH_a	$= +121\,kJ$ (atomisation energy)
$Cl(g)$	$\rightarrow$	$Cl^-(g)$	ΔH_e	$= -364\,kJ$ (first electron affinity)
			total	$-243\,kJ$

where the **first electron affinity** is *the enthalpy change on forming one mole of gaseous singly charged negative ions from separate gaseous atoms.*

Overall, $\Delta H = +603 - 243 = +360\,kJ$.

Since in total 360 kJ of energy must be *supplied* to convert both elements into their isolated gaseous ions, the latter are energetically *less stable*. We have already seen, however, that the enthalpy of formation of sodium chloride is exothermic, i.e. solid sodium chloride is energetically *more* stable than the elements. Using Hess's Law (section 4.11) to construct an enthalpy cycle, known as the **Born–Haber** cycle, we can see from figure 5.2 that 771 kJ of energy must be released when one mole of *solid* sodium chloride is formed from its separate *gaseous* ions.

i.e. $\qquad Na^+(g) + Cl^-(g) \rightarrow NaCl(s) \qquad \Delta H_1 = -771\,kJ$

*The enthalpy change on forming one mole of an ionic solid from its isolated gaseous ions is known as the **lattice energy** ΔH_1 and originates from the mutual attraction of the oppositely charged ions. Ionic bonding is only likely to take place if the lattice energy is sufficiently large to make the overall enthalpy of formation exothermic, i.e. make the ionic crystal energetically more stable than the elements.*

Lattice energy is a measure of interionic attraction and will *increase* as the size of the ions *decreases* and as their charge *increases*. Why then is the formula of sodium chloride not $NaCl_2$, or even $NaCl_3$, since the lattice energy of these compounds would be much higher than that of $NaCl$? The answer lies in the values of *successive ionisation energies* of the sodium atom. These are usually the biggest *endothermic* term in the Born–Haber cycle and there is a very large increase in ionisation energy when the 'noble gas' configuration of Na^+ is broken. You can see from the energy cycles in figure 5.3 that this outweighs the increase in lattice energy, making $NaCl_2$ and $NaCl_3$ energetically much *less* stable than the elements.

The tendency of elements to form simple cations decreases on passing across the Periodic Table and increases on passing down any group. Conversely, *elements towards the right and top of the Periodic Table are more likely to form simple anions. There are no simple ions with a charge greater than + 3.* In sections 19.4 and 19.5 we shall study the trends in ionisation energies and electron affinities which explain this.

Figure 5.2   *Born–Haber cycle for the formation of NaCl$_{(s)}$*

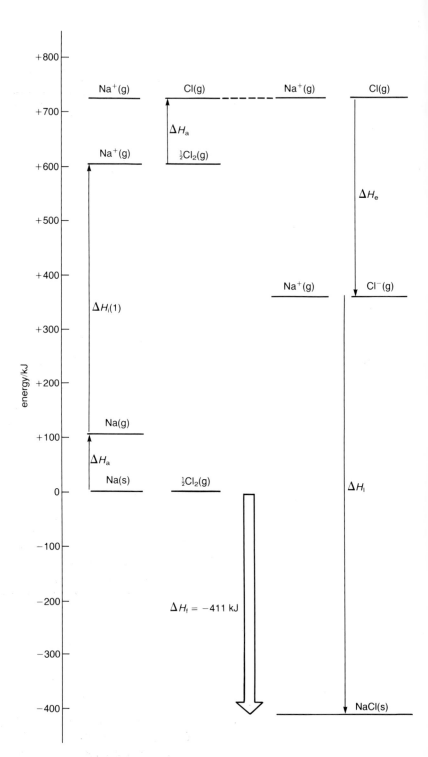

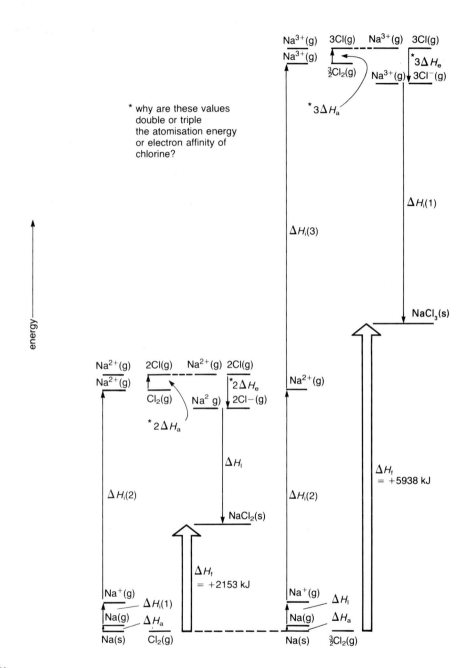

Figure 5.3   *Theoretical Born–Haber cycles for the formation of NaCl₂ and NaCl₃ (approximately to scale)*

Activity 5.2

This activity concerns the feasibility of forming the compounds MgCl, MgCl₂ and MgCl₃ from the elements.

    1   Construct a Born–Haber cycle, similar to that given for sodium chloride in

figure 5.2, for each of the above chlorides. Use the following data, all in kJ mol^{-1}, to estimate their enthalpies of formation. You may find it helpful to draw the cycle to scale on graph paper.

atomisation energies:	magnesium		+150
	chlorine		+121
ionisation energies of magnesium:	1st		+736
	2nd		+1450
	3rd		+7740
electron affinity of chlorine			−364
theoretical lattice energies:	MgCl		−753
	MgCl$_2$		−2502
	MgCl$_3$		−5440

Now consider the following questions.

2 Which of the three chlorides is energetically less stable than the elements?

3 Which single energy change above is largely responsible for the instability of this compound?

4 Since the remaining chlorides have negative enthalpies of formation, we might expect to be able to form them both by combining the elements in the required molar ratio. What explanation can you offer for the fact that magnesium forms only one chloride?

5.3 Covalent bonding: electron sharing

Again, the idea of atoms achieving 'stable' electron configurations such as those of the noble gases is a useful model. In the case of **covalent bonding**, however, *outer electrons are shared rather than transferred from one atom to another*. As shown in figure 5.1b, there is a considerable concentration of electron density in the region between the nuclei of the atoms concerned. Such bonding may simply be illustrated by 'dot and cross' diagrams showing the arrangement of the outer, valency electrons. For example, two chlorine atoms, each having seven outer electrons, may form a diatomic molecule by sharing one electron each in a single covalent bond, thus achieving a stable outer octet.

In the case of oxygen and nitrogen, two and three pairs of electrons, respectively, must be shared between the two atoms to achieve a stable structure. The oxygen molecule is said to contain a **double bond** and the nitrogen molecule a **triple bond**.

Pairs of electrons in the outer shells of an atom which are not used in bonding are called **lone pairs**. As we shall see in chapter 7, they are important in deciding the shapes of molecules.

Dissimilar atoms may also share electrons, e.g. hydrogen chloride, carbon dioxide.

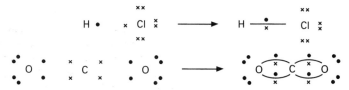

It should be noted that the noble gas configurations are not the only stable electronic arrangements found in covalent molecules. *The third and subsequent principal shells may contain more than eight electrons.* Thus sulphur forms three fluorides, SF_2, SF_4 and SF_6, where the central sulphur atom has totals of 8, 10 and 12 electrons respectively in its outer (third) principal shell.

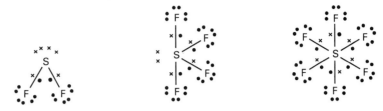

Oxygen on the other hand, although in the same group of the Periodic Table as sulphur, only forms a difluoride, OF_2, since *the oxygen atom can only accommodate a maximum of eight electrons in its outer (second) principal shell.*

Some covalent molecules contain atoms with fewer outer electrons than the corresponding noble gas. In boron trichloride, for example, the valency shell of the boron atom contains a total of just 6 electrons and is sometimes described as **electron deficient**.

5.4 Dative covalent bonding

In some cases, *both of the electrons to be shared come from the same atom, forming a* **dative covalent bond**. Since all electrons are identical, such a bond, once formed, is indistinguishable from an ordinary covalent bond. In 'dot and cross' diagrams it is customary to denote a dative bond by an arrow pointing from the atom which donates the lone pair to the atom which receives it. Thus, for example, carbon monoxide, CO, may be drawn as shown.

Other instances of dative bonding may be found in some **molecular addition compounds**, e.g. boron trifluoride ammonia $BF_3.NH_3$, and in **transition metal complexes**, e.g. $[Fe(H_2O)_6]^{2+}$, covered in more detail in chapter 30.

In all such cases one of the species must possess a lone pair of electrons which may be shared with an electron deficient species. The **lone pair donor** is known as a **Lewis base** and the **acceptor** is referred to as a **Lewis acid**. The importance of dative bond formation as the first step in the mechanism of many reactions in organic chemistry is dealt with in chapter 33.

5.5   An orbital view of covalent bonding

In sections 5.3 and 5.4 we have assumed the sharing of electrons between atoms without giving any indication of how this is achieved. The theory developed in chapter 3 requires that we consider electrons to occupy certain regions of space known as **atomic orbitals**. In the case of a hydrogen atom, the electron occupies a spherical 1s orbital. Overlap between the half-filled orbitals on two such atoms gives a **molecular orbital** containing two electrons.

atomic orbitals   overlap gives a 'molecular' orbital

This molecular orbital treatment may also be applied to more complex systems. Simply speaking, *a strong covalent bond may be formed by the overlap of two suitably placed atomic orbitals that contain between them two electrons.*

For example, the oxygen molecule, O_2. Each O atom has the electron configuration [He] $2s^2 2p^4$:

A strong bond is formed by *end-on overlap* of a half-filled p orbital on each of the atoms. This is known as, a σ **bond**:

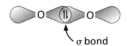

Here maximum overlap occurs *directly between* the two *nuclei* and this is known as a σ **bond**. The second bond results from *sideways overlap* of the remaining half full p orbitals *above and below* a line joining a nuclei. This is referred to as a π **bond**.

In the nitrogen molecule, N_2, each atom possesses three singly occupied p orbitals. Overlap of one pair of these orbitals gives a σ bond and overlap of the remaining two sets of p orbitals gives rise to two π bonds.

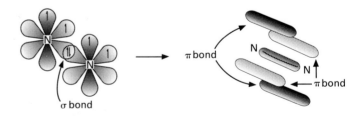

5.6   Electron promotion and hybridisation

All the examples in section 5.5 contain covalent bonds formed by the overlap of simple atomic orbitals available in the lowest energy or **ground states** of the atoms concerned. There are, however, many molecules for which such a simple model is unsatisfactory.

A carbon atom may achieve a noble gas electron configuration by sharing four electrons, i.e. by forming four covalent bonds. Since in its ground state a carbon atom contains only *two* unpaired electrons, it must **promote** an electron from the 2s orbital into the empty 2p orbital.

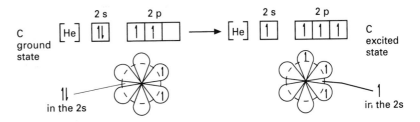

Some or all of these pure atomic orbitals are **hybridised** or **mixed** before bonding occurs. The number of carbon orbitals which are hybridised corresponds to the number of atoms to which it is to be bonded. These **hybrid** orbitals are used to create a σ **bonded** molecular skeleton with any electrons remaining in **pure p atomic orbitals** overlapping to produce π **bonds**. We shall now examine examples of the three different ways in which the atomic orbitals on the carbon atom may be hybridised.

sp³ hybridisation

This is found in molecules where the *carbon atom is singly bonded to four other atoms.* The 2s and all three of the 2p orbitals are mixed to produce four equivalent sp³ hybrid atomic orbitals. These overlap with suitable half-filled orbitals on other atoms, forming σ bonds, e.g. as in methane, CH_4, shown in figure 5.4a.

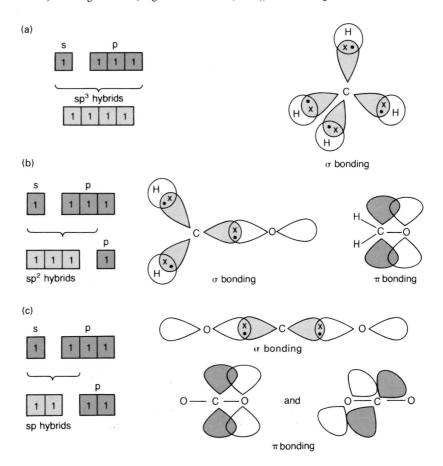

Figure 5.4   *Orbital hybridisation in carbon compounds*

sp^2 hybridisation

This occurs when *a carbon atom is bonded to three other atoms*. The 2s and two of the 2p orbitals mix to give three equivalent sp^2 hybrid orbitals in a triangular arrangement. σ bonds are formed by overlap of these hybrids with suitable orbitals on the other atoms. The remaining electron in the carbon pure p orbital remains available for π overlap giving a double bond to one of the other atoms as shown in figure 5.4b for methanal, H_2CO.

sp hybridisation

In carbon dioxide, CO_2, mixing of the 2s with one of the 2p orbitals gives two sp hybrids. These overlap with half-full 2p orbitals on each of the oxygen atoms giving a linear σ bonded skeleton. The remaining two electrons in pure p orbitals on the carbon atom then form π bonds by overlap with other half-full oxygen p orbitals as illustrated in figure 5.4c. Identical hybridisation takes place when the carbon atom forms one single and one triple bond, instead of two double bonds.

Activity 5.3

1   Draw 'dot and cross' diagrams showing the arrangement of outer electrons in each of the following covalent molecules:
    (a) hydrogen chloride, HCl; (b) ethene, C_2H_4; (c) ethyne, C_2H_2.
2   What type of hybridisation occurs in the carbon atoms of molecules (b) and (c) above?

5.7 Energetics of covalent bond formation

In the case of an ionic compound, the lattice energy released when the separate gaseous ions form the crystal is a measure of the bond strength, i.e the magnitude of interionic attraction. *The strength of the bond in a diatomic covalent molecule is given by the* **bond dissociation energy (BDE)**, *defined as the enthalpy change on converting one mole of gaseous molecules into its constituent gaseous atoms.* (Note that this term is *endothermic* since it involves *breaking* bonds, whereas lattice energy is always *exothermic* since bonds are being *formed*.)

e.g.
$$HCl(g) \rightarrow H(g) + Cl(g) \quad BDE = +431\,kJ$$
$$H_2(g) \rightarrow 2H(g) \quad\quad\quad\quad BDE = +436\,kJ$$
$$Cl_2(g) \rightarrow 2Cl(g) \quad\quad\quad\quad BDE = +242\,kJ$$

For hydrogen and chlorine the BDE is exactly twice the atomisation energies of these elements.

In the case of a polyatomic molecule the situation is a little more complex, even if the bonds present are identical. Methane, the simplest hydrocarbon CH_4, has four C—H bonds, each with a different BDE:

$$CH_4(g) \rightarrow CH_3(g) + H(g) \quad BDE1 = +461\,kJ$$
$$CH_3(g) \rightarrow CH_2(g) + H(g) \quad BDE2 = +403\,kJ$$
$$CH_2(g) \rightarrow CH(g) + H(g) \quad BDE3 = +424\,kJ$$
$$CH(g) \rightarrow C(g) + H(g) \quad BDE4 = +374\,kJ$$

The individual BDEs vary because the electronic environment is changing, thus affecting the strength of the remaining bonds. However, we may define the **bond energy term (BET)** as the *average* of the separate BDEs for each of the four C—H bonds.

$$BET\ (C—H) = \frac{BDE1 + BDE2 + BDE3 + BDE4}{4}$$

It is important not to confuse BDE, the enthalpy change on breaking a specific bond, with BET which is an average value.

To a good approximation the strength of a particular kind of bond is *independent* of the nature of the rest of the molecule. Thus for example, the BET for the C—H single bond is very similar in a whole range of compounds, including

Table 5.1 lists average BETs for a range of covalent bonds. Since these values are of the same order as the lattice energies encountered in section 5.2, we may assume that ionic and covalent bonds are of roughly comparable strength.

Since BETs may be considered to be largely independent of molecular environment, we may treat them as being roughly *additive* and this makes them very useful in estimating enthalpy changes for reactions involving covalent substances. As an example we shall estimate the enthalpy of hydrogenation of a simple alkene:

$$> C{=}C< + H_2(g) \rightarrow >CH{-}CH<$$

We must determine which bonds are *broken* and which new bonds are *formed* during the reaction and then find the corresponding enthalpy changes from the list of BETs in table 5.1.

$$>C{=}C< \quad + \quad H{-}H \quad \rightarrow \quad >C \ C< \quad + \quad H \ H \quad \rightarrow \quad >CH{-}CH<$$

bonds broken	enthalpy change (endothermic) kJ	bonds formed	enthalpy change (exothermic) kJ
C=C	+612	C—C	−348
H—H	+436	2 C—H	−824
	+1048		−1172

overall $\Delta H = +1048 - 1172 = -124\,\text{kJ}$

This estimated enthalpy change is generally in quite good agreement with the following experimentally determined enthalpies of hydrogenation:

ethene	propene	but-1-ene	but-2-ene	cyclohexene
−157 kJ	−126 kJ	−127 kJ	−120 kJ	−120 kJ

The variation in these values shows the extent to which *molecular environment* does affect covalent bond strength.

Table 5.1 *Average bond energy terms*

Bond	$\Delta H/$ kJ mol^{-1}	bond	$\Delta H/$ kJ mol^{-1}
H—H	436	C—H	412
D—D	442	Si—H	318
C—C	348	N—H	388
C=C	612	P—H	322
C≡C	837	O—H	463
C⋯C	518	S—H	338
(benzene)			
Si—Si	176	F—H	562
N—N	163	Cl—H	431
N=N	409	Br—H	366
N≡N	944	I—H	299
P—P	172		
O—O	146	C—O	360
O=O	496	C=O	743
S—S	264	C—N	305
F—F	158	C=N	613
Cl—Cl	242	C≡N	890
Br—Br	193	C—F	484
I—I	151	C—Cl	338
		C—Br	276
		C—I	238
		Si—O	374
		S=O	435

Activity 5.4

The equation representing the standard enthalpy of formation of methylamine is

$$C(graphite) + \tfrac{5}{2}H_2(g) + \tfrac{1}{2}N_2(g) \rightarrow CH_3NH_2(g)$$

This process may be considered to take place in two theoretical stages.

1 Atomisation of the elements:
$$C(graphite) \rightarrow C(g)$$
$$\tfrac{5}{2}H_2(g) \rightarrow 5H(g)$$
$$\tfrac{1}{2}N_2(g) \rightarrow N(g)$$

If the atomisation energies of graphite, hydrogen and nitrogen are $+715\,\text{kJ}$, $+218\,\text{kJ}$ and $+473\,\text{kJ}$ respectively, calculate the total enthalpy change for this atomisation stage.

2 Combination of the isolated atoms to give the product:

Use the BET values in table 5.1 to estimate the total enthalpy change involved in forming the bonds in the methylamine molecule and hence predict the enthalpy of formation of this compound.

5.8 Electron delocalisation

A simple 'dot and cross' diagram of the benzene molecule, C_6H_6, might suggest that it contained alternate C—C single and C=C double bonds:

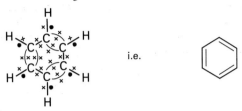

i.e.

This does not correspond, however, with the reluctance of benzene to undergo electrophilic addition reactions which are typical of the C=C bond in alkenes (see chapters 35 and 36). In addition, if benzene were a normal 'triene' we should expect the enthalpy change for its complete hydrogenation to cyclohexane to be approximately *three times* that for the hydrogenation of cyclohexene. Actually the experimentally determined enthalpy change for benzene is much *less* exothermic then predicted.

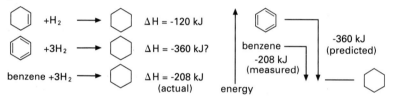

This suggests that benzene is some $152\,\text{kJ mol}^{-1}$ *more stable* than the cyclic triene structure. In other words, on average the bonds between the carbon atoms in benzene are *stronger* than the BET values in table 5.1 predict.

If we consider the structure of benzene from the point of view of orbital overlap, then the true situation becomes apparent. Three sp^2 hybrid orbitals on each carbon atom overlap to form a σ bonded flat hexagonal ring:

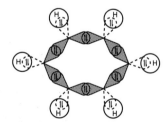

The remaining unpaired electron on each carbon atom occupies a pure p orbital perpendicular to the plane of the ring. Each of these overlaps with its neighbours on both sides, forming a circular π molecular orbital which contains six electrons and extends over all the carbon atoms in the ring:

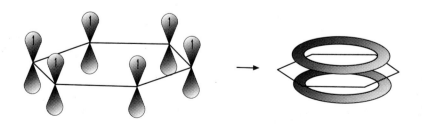

Figure 5.5 *Extended electron delocalisation in (a) graphite and (b) metals*

a) graphite

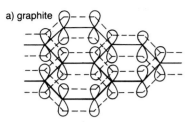

broken lines show π orbitals which extend over the whole molecular plane

b) metals

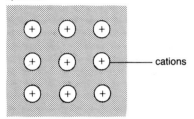

cations

sea of valency electrons, mobile in all directions

Further evidence in support of this structure comes from the measurement of carbon–carbon bond lengths obtained from X-ray diffraction studies. Double bonds are usually shorter than single bonds between the same atoms: the normal C—C bond length is 0.154 nm whereas the C═C bond length is 0.134 nm. In the benzene molecule all the carbon–carbon bond lengths are *equal* and at 0.139 nm are intermediate between a single and a double bond.

Such **electron delocalisation** is quite common and may even extend over many atoms. Graphite, for example, consists of essentially separate macromolecular sheets of carbon atoms. As in benzene, three valency electrons on each carbon atom are used in σ bonding but the fourth electron in a pure p orbital undergoes π overlap as shown in figure 5.5a. Since movement of electrons is only possible through the π molecular orbital, graphite will only conduct electricity in the plane of the 'sheets'.

One of the characteristics of a metal is that it will readily conduct electricity in any direction in the solid state. Since the ionisation energies of metals are generally low, the valency electrons are easily separated from the atoms and may be considered to occupy molecular orbitals delocalised over the lattice as a whole. In simple terms, *the metal cations are held in place by a 'sea' of mobile electrons* as shown in figure 5.5b. This model also explains the malleability and ductility of metals, since the binding electrons may readily move to accommodate any distortion of the lattice.

Further examples of molecules and ions which exhibit electron delocalisation may be found in chapter 7.

5.9 Polarisation of covalent bonds and hydrogen bonding

The electrons in a covalent bond joining two identical atoms are *equally shared*. On average, they will be midway between the two nuclei and neither atom will develop a permanent charge, e.g. for the chlorine molecule, Cl_2.

If, however, the two atoms are dissimilar then the bonding electrons will not be equally shared. *The relative attraction of an atom for a pair of bonding electrons is given by the* **electronegativity** *of the element.* Values on an arbitrary scale suggested by Pauling are listed in table 5.2. As we might expect, electronegativity generally *increases* on passing across a period, owing to increasing nuclear charge and decreasing atomic radius, and *decreases* on passing down a group since both increasing atomic size and the screening effect of inner electrons reduce the attraction of the nucleus for electrons.

In any covalent compound the atom with the greater electronegativity will clearly attract the bonding electrons closer to itself, thus creating a **permanent dipole**, e.g. in hydrogen chloride and water:

where δ indicates a partial charge

Table 5.2 *Electronegativities of the elements (according to Pauling)*

														H	He			
														2.1				

Li	Be											B	C	N	O	F	Ne
1.0	1.5											2.0	2.5	3.0	3.5	4.0	

Na	Mg											Al	Si	P	S	Cl	Ar
0.9	1.2											1.5	1.8	2.1	2.5	3.0	

K	Ca	Sc	Ti	V	Cr	Mn	Fe	Co	Ni	Cu	Zn	Ga	Ge	As	Se	Br	Kr
0.8	1.0	1.3	1.5	1.6	1.6	1.5	1.8	1.8	1.8	1.9	1.6	1.6	1.8	2.0	2.4	2.8	

Rb	Sr	Y	Zr	Nb	Mo	Tc	Ru	Rh	Pd	Ag	Cd	In	Sn	Sb	Te	I	Xe
0.8	1.0	1.2	1.4	1.6	1.8	1.9	2.2	2.2	2.2	1.9	1.7	1.7	1.8	1.9	2.1	2.5	

Cs	Ba	La	Hf	Ta	W	Re	Os	Ir	Pt	Au	Hg	Tl	Pb	Bi	Po	At	Rn
0.7	0.9	1.1	1.3	1.5	1.7	1.9	2.2	2.2	2.2	2.4	1.9	1.8	1.8	1.9	2.0	2.2	

Fr	Ra	Ac
0.7	0.9	1.1

Ce	Pr	Nd	Pm	Sm	Eu	Gd	Tb	Dy	Ho	Er	Tm	Yb	Lu
1.1	1.1	1.2	1.2	1.2	1.1	1.1	1.2	1.1	1.2	1.2	1.2	1.1	1.2

Th	Pa	U	Np	Pu	Am	Cm	Bk	Cf	Es	Fm	Md	No	Lr
1.3	1.5	1.7	1.3	1.3	1.3	1.3	1.3	1.3	1.3	1.3	1.3	1.3	

Why don't He and Ne have electronegativity values?

Activity 5.5

1 The polar nature of the water molecule may be demonstrated by the following simple experiment.

Produce the thinnest possible continuous stream of water from a tap. Vigorously rub a dry plastic comb or plastic ballpoint pen on some polyester fabric to produce a static electric charge and hold it as close as possible to the stream of water, without actually touching it.

What you see and how do you explain it?

2 Try repeating the experiment with other covalent liquids, including the following:

hexane   ethanol   propanone

trichloromethane   tetrachloromethane

In this case use a burette to create the thin stream. Use your observations to class each compound as polar or non-polar and explain your results in terms of the structures of the molecules shown above.

Effectively, this introduces **partial ionic character** into an essentially covalent bond. Where it occurs, it will result in some degree of **intermolecular attraction**, e.g. in hydrogen chloride:

Table 5.3 *Percentage of ionic character in bonding expressed in terms of the electronegativity difference between the elements*

Electronegativity difference	Percentage ionic character
0.1	0.5
0.2	1
0.3	2
0.4	4
0.5	6
0.6	9
0.7	12
0.8	15
0.9	19
1.0	22
1.1	26
1.2	30
1.3	34
1.4	39
1.5	43
1.6	47
1.7	51
1.8	55
1.9	59
2.0	63
2.1	67
2.2	70
2.3	74
2.4	76
2.5	79
2.6	82
2.7	84
2.8	86
2.9	88
3.0	89
3.1	91
3.2	92

What is the % of ionic character in the bonds formed between the following pairs of atoms?

K,F
Mg,O
C,Cl
P,H

(Hint: use table 5.2)

The extent of the attraction between such molecules will depend upon the size of the dipole, which in turn is governed by the differences in electronegativity between the atoms concerned. Pauling estimated the percentage of ionic character introduced into the bond by various electronegativity differences – see table 5.3.

Such intermolecular attraction and its associated effects on physical properties such as melting and boiling points are discussed more fully in chapter 8. In most cases, however, the magnitude of such interaction is very much less than that found in a true ionic or covalent bonding. *The greatest effect is found when a hydrogen atom is covalently bonded to a very electronegative atom, e.g. as in hydrogen fluoride, HF.*

Appreciable **hydrogen bonding,** *as this is known, occurs only when a hydrogen atom is bonded directly to a nitrogen, oxygen or fluorine atom.* In such cases, the strength of the hydrogen bond is up to about 20% of that of a covalent bond.

Further reference to hydrogen bonding and its associated effects is made in sections 21.5, 25.6, 26.4, 27.5, 38.2 and 40.2.

5.10 Polarisation of ions: introduction of partial covalent nature

In section 5.9 we explained how covalent bonds may develop partial ionic character. Pure ionic or covalent bonding is really the exception rather than the rule and most chemical bonds may be considered to be *intermediate* between these two extremes. Let us now reflect upon how an ionic bond may develop some covalent character.

We have so far regarded the electron distribution around the ions in the lattice as being spherically symmetrical:

It should be clear, however, that the cation will *attract* the outer electrons on the anion, deforming or **polarising** it to some extent:

This polarisation shifts electron density from the anion towards the cation. If the deformation is sufficient, the bonding electrons may be considered to be partially 'shared' between the ions, i.e. the bond develops some *covalent* nature:

The extent to which this process occurs depends both upon the polarising power of the cation and the ease with which the anion may be distorted. **Fajan's Rules**, summarising the factors which *favour* the introduction of covalent character, may be stated as follows.

CATION	ANION
high positive charge	*high* negative charge
small size	*large* size
i.e. *high* charge density	i.e. electrons more *loosely* held

Introduction of appreciable covalent character into essentially ionic bonding is often demonstrated by abnormally low melting and boiling points and by solubility in covalent solvents such as ethanol. Comparison of experimentally determined lattice energy with the theoretical value calculated assuming no anion polarisation provides further evidence. In table 5.4, whilst there is good agreement between these figures for the iodides of sodium to caesium in Group 1, the large discrepancies found in the case of lithium iodide indicates considerable covalent character in the bonding.

Table 5.4 *Comparison of experimentally determined lattice energies with theoretical values for the iodides of Group I metals. Good agreement indicates 'pure' ionic bonding*

Compound	lattice energy/kJ mol^{-1}			cation radius/nm
	experimental	theoretical	difference	
LiI	-744	-728	16*	0.060
NaI	-684	-686	2	0.095
KI	-629	-632	3	0.133
RbI	-609	-607	2	0.148
CsI	-585	-582	3	0.169

* Indicates considerable covalent character owing to polarisation of iodide ions by the small Li$^+$ cation

5.11 Comments on the activities

Activity 5.1

LiF	contains	Li$^+$	[He]
CaO	contains	Ca^{2+}	[Ar]
SnF$_4$	contains	Sn^{4+}	[Kr] 4d^{10}
SnF$_2$	contains	Sn^{2+}	[Kr] 4d^{10} 5s^2
Sc$_2$O$_3$	contains	Sc^{3+}	[Ar]

Activity 5.2

1 See figure 5.6.
2 MgCl$_3$ is the only one of these chlorides which is less stable than the elements. Figure 5.6 shows that it alone has a positive (i.e. endothermic) enthalpy of formation.
3 The largest single endothermic energy change in the Born–Haber cycle for this compound is the *3rd ionisation energy* of magnesium, $+7740$ kJ. The very big jump in ionisation energy on breaking the 'noble gas' electronic configuration of the Mg^{2+} ion is not compensated by the increase in lattice energy.
4 MgCl$_2$ has the greatest exothermic enthalpy of formation and, as expected, may be prepared by direct combination of the elements.

$$Mg(s) + Cl_2(g) \rightarrow MgCl_2(s) \qquad \Delta H_f^{\ominus} = -652\,kJ$$

If we reduce the amount of chlorine used, then we might expect to obtain the monochloride.

$$Mg(s) + \tfrac{1}{2}Cl_2(g) \rightarrow MgCl(s) \qquad \Delta H_f^{\ominus} = -110\,kJ$$

However, it is energetically more favourable to form the dichloride, leaving half of the magnesium unreacted.

$$\tfrac{1}{2}Mg(s) + \tfrac{1}{2}Cl_2(g) \rightarrow \tfrac{1}{2}MgCl_2(s) \qquad \Delta H_f^{\ominus} = -326\,kJ$$

Figure 5.6 *Enthalpies of formation of magnesium chlorides*

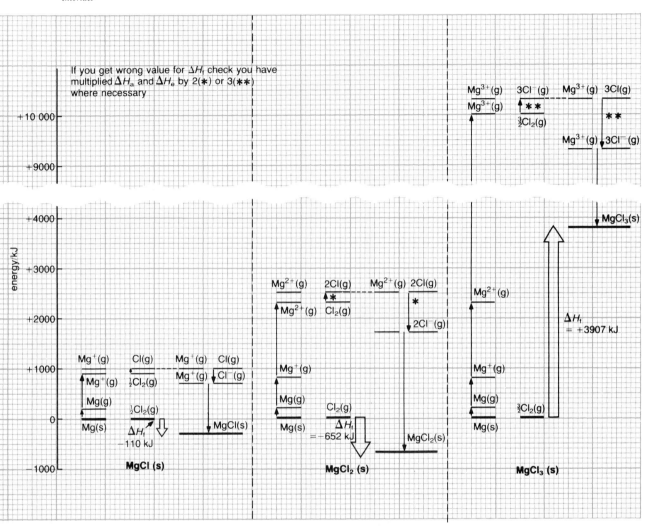

Activity 5.3

Compare your answers with figure 5.7.

Figure 5.7 *Bonding in the molecules dealt with in activity 5.3 ('dot and cross' diagrams)*

Activity 5.4

1   Enthalpies of atomisation:

$$C(gr) \quad \rightarrow C(g) \quad 1 \times 715 = +715\,kJ$$
$$\tfrac{5}{2}H_2(g) \quad \rightarrow 5H(g) \quad 5 \times 218 = +1090\,kJ$$
$$\tfrac{1}{2}N_2(g) \quad \rightarrow N(g) \quad 1 \times 473 = \underline{+473\,kJ}$$
$$+2278\,kJ \text{ total}$$

2   Enthalpies of bond formation:

$$3\;C\!-\!H \quad 3 \times -412 = -1236\,kJ$$
$$1\;C\!-\!N \quad 1 \times -305 = -\;305\,kJ$$
$$2\;N\!-\!H \quad 2 \times -388 = -\;776\,kJ$$
$$-2317\,kJ \text{ total}$$

The enthalpy of formation of methylamine is given by the sum of those for the atomisation and bond formation stages, i.e.

enthalpy of formation of methylamine $= +2278 - 2317 = -39\,kJ\,mol^{-1}$.

This is in reasonable agreement with the experimental value of $-28\,kJ\,mol^{-1}$. The discrepancy results from using bond energy terms which are average values and not specific to the molecules we are considering.

Activity 5.5

1   You should find that the stream of water is attracted towards the charged plastic comb or pen. This is because each 'end' of the water molecule carries an opposite electrical charge.

$$\delta- $$
$$O \quad \text{electron drift}$$
$$\delta+ \; H \qquad H \; \delta+$$

Testing the polarity of a liquid. Why is the stream of water attracted by the charged comb?

2   Ethanol, propanone and trichloromethane are all **polar liquids** which are attracted to a static electric charge. Like water, opposite ends of their molecules carry different electric charges.

ethanol   propanone   trichloromethane

Neither hexane nor tetracholoromethane are deflected by an electric charge. They are both **non-polar liquids** but for different reasons. In hydrocarbons, such as hexane, carbon and hydrogen have similar electronegativity values and the bonds are effectively non-polar. Unlike trichloromethane, tetrachloromethane is non-polar, even though the partial charges on the chlorine and carbon atoms in each molecule are similar. The reason lies in the highly *symmetrical* shape of the CCl_4 molecule. Even though each individual C—Cl bond is polar, the molecule as a whole is non-polar because the partial charges do not occur on the 'ends' of the molecule. The positive charge on the carbon is located exactly at the centre of the molecule with the negatively charged chlorine atoms equally spread around it. Other compounds which are non-polar as a result of the symmetry of their molecules include carbon dioxide and boron trichloride.

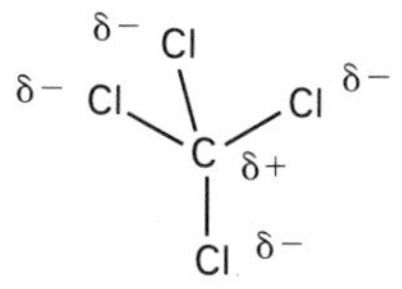

$$\delta - \quad \begin{array}{c} \delta - \;\; Cl \\ Cl \diagdown \;\;\; | \;\;\; Cl \;\; \delta - \\ C \;\; \delta + \\ | \\ Cl \;\; \delta - \end{array}$$

$$\delta - \quad \delta + \quad \delta - \\ O = C = O$$

$$\delta - \;\; Cl \diagdown \;\; \delta + \;\; Cl \;\; \delta - \\ B \\ | \\ Cl \;\; \delta -$$

tetrachloromethane 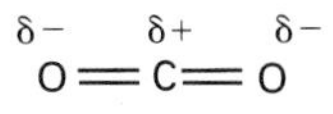   carbon dioxide 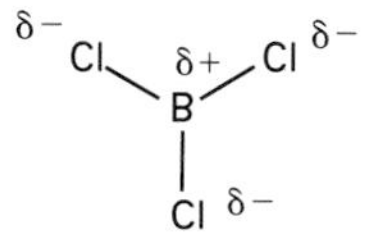   boron trichloride

5.12 Summary and revision plan

1 Chemical bonding involves the redistribution of valency electrons:
   (a) **ionic** – complete transfer (usually of up to three electrons);
   (b) **covalent** (and **dative**) – sharing;
   (c) **metallic** – delocalisation.

2 By bonding, atoms frequently (but not always) achieve a 'noble gas' or 'octet' electron configuration, i.e. completely full outer s and p sub-levels.

3 The energetics of bond formation may be explored by constructing appropriate energy cycle diagrams.

4 **Lattice energy** may be used to estimate the 'strength' of ionic bonding, and **bond energy terms** give a measure of covalent bond strength.

5 Covalent bonding may be explained in terms of the overlap of suitably placed half-full '**atomic' orbitals** producing '**molecular' orbitals**. In some cases this may involve:
   (a) '**promoting**' electrons from their ground states to higher energies;
   (b) '**hybridising**', or mixing, atomic orbitals prior to covalent bonding.

6 In σ **covalent bonds**, maximum orbital overlap occurs on a line directly between the two nuclei. These are generally stronger than π **bonds** in which overlap occurs above and below such a line.

7 **Multi-centre** π bonding can lead to '**delocalisation**' of electrons, e.g. in benzene and graphite, and generally leads to a more stable structure.

8 Most bonds are intermediate in type between pure ionic and pure covalent.
   (a) Deformation of the electron cloud on an ion introduces covalent character into ionic bonding. The extent of this may be estimated using **Fajan's Rules**.
   (b) **Electronegativity differences** introduce some polar nature into covalent bonds formed between dissimilar atoms.

9 **Hydrogen bonding** may be regarded as strong 'intermolecular' attraction which arises when hydrogen is directly bonded to either nitrogen, oxygen or fluorine.

Determining the Structure of Compounds

Contents

A biological chemical factory! Penicillin, the first antibiotic drug, was first isolated in a food mould

In 1928 when Fleming accidentally discovered the first antibiotic drug, penicillin, in a bread 'mould', he had little, if any, idea why it was so effective. Before large quantities of this material could be made 'synthetically', its detailed chemical structure had to be established. Although this task was not completed until the 1940s, it has led to the wide range of structurally similar drugs in use today.

$$C_6H_5CH_2 - CONH - CH - CH - S \underset{\begin{array}{c} | \\ CO - N - CH \end{array}}{\overset{}{}} \overset{CH_3}{\underset{CH_3}{C}}$$

structure of penicillin G

First let us consider what we mean by 'structure'. The term 'chemical formula' is rather imprecise. We may identify at least three main types of formula which give various amounts of information about the substance concerned.

Empirical formula

This shows only the *simplest whole number atomic ratio of the various elements present.* Many substances, particularly organic compounds, may share the same empirical formula. For example, all the alkenes contain carbon and hydrogen only in the atomic ratio 1:2. Their empirical formula is therefore CH_2.

Molecular formula

This gives the actual *number of each type of atom present in one molecule of the compound*. Although the alkenes all have the same empirical formula, their molecular formulae differ; for example, C_2H_4 ethene, C_3H_6 propene, C_4H_8 butene(s). *Different compounds which share the same molecular formula are known as* **isomers**. Ethanol and methoxymethane are *isomeric* since they both have the molecular formula C_2H_6O.

Structural formula

This shows exactly *how the various atoms present in the molecule are bonded together*. Thus the structural formulae of the isomers ethanol and methoxymethane may be drawn

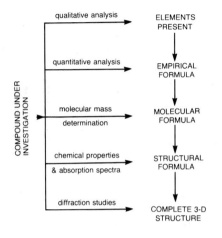

This is an example of **structural isomerism** *since the atoms are actually joined up in different ways*. Mention should also be made of **stereoisomerism** *where molecules have an identical bonding pattern but a different spatial arrangement of atoms*. A detailed discussion of isomerism may be found in chapter 10.

Investigation of the detailed structure of any compound generally takes place by a series of steps in which the empirical and molecular formulae are first established. We shall examine such a sequence, illustrated in figure 6.1. In the course of the chapter we shall outline some modern instrumental techniques which now supplement, or even replace, classical chemical methods.

Figure 6.1   *A typical sequence for structure determination*

COMPOUND UNDER INVESTIGATION

qualitative analysis → ELEMENTS PRESENT

quantitative analysis → EMPIRICAL FORMULA

molecular mass determination → MOLECULAR FORMULA

chemical properties & absorption spectra → STRUCTURAL FORMULA

diffraction studies → COMPLETE 3-D STRUCTURE

6.1 Determination of empirical formula

The first step must be to establish which elements are present in the compound. Clearly, this will be much easier if the source of the material, for example the materials and methods used to prepare it, is known. Techniques vary widely but each element may be detected by certain unique tests. Systematic schemes for both organic and inorganic compounds may be found in most standard texts dealing with qualitative analysis and here we shall only consider a few examples.

Many inorganic compounds are ionic in nature, and analysis of these simply involves identifying the ions present. Certain metals may be detected by observing their characteristic flame colours or emission spectra, table 6.1. Other ions may be

Table 6.1   *Characteristic flame colorations of some metal ions*

	Metal	flame coloration
Group I	lithium	crimson
	sodium	golden-yellow
	potassium	lilac
	rubidium	red
	caesium	blue
Group II	calcium	brick-red
	strontium	crimson
	barium	apple-green
	lead	blue
	copper	green

identified by reactions in aqueous solution. For example, the formation of a white precipitate on addition of barium nitrate solution indicates the formation of an insoluble barium salt. There are several possible anions which give such a reaction, including fluoride, carbonate and sulphate.

$$Ba^{2+}(aq) + 2F^-(aq) \rightarrow BaF_2(s)$$
$$Ba^{2+}(aq) + CO_3^{2-}(aq) \rightarrow BaCO_3(s)$$
$$Ba^{2+}(aq) + SO_4^{2-}(aq) \rightarrow BaSO_4(s)$$

If, however, the precipitate is found to be insoluble in dilute nitric acid then it must be barium sulphate.

If an ammonium salt is warmed with an alkali, then the characteristic smell of ammonia gas is detected:

$$NH_4^+(aq) + OH^-(aq) \rightarrow NH_3(g) + H_2O(l)$$

Reactions which involve colour changes are also useful. Potassium thiocyanate, for example, gives a deep 'blood-red' colouration with solutions containing iron(III),

$$Fe^{3+}(aq) + SCN^-(aq) \rightarrow [FeSCN]^{2+}(aq)$$
$$\text{blood-red}$$

In the case of organic compounds, carbon and hydrogen may be detected by oxidation with hot dry copper(II) oxide. Any hydrogen is converted into water which will turn anhydrous cobalt(II) chloride from blue to pink, and carbon gives carbon dioxide which will form a white precipitate with calcium hydroxide solution ('limewater'). Fusion with sodium metal will convert any nitrogen into cyanide (providing carbon is present), sulphur into sulphide ions, and halogens into halide ions, each of which may be detected by standard tests.

As with inorganic compounds, test-tube reactions are often able to 'spot' the presence of specific groups or atoms, termed **functional groups**, as well as individual elements. Thus the carboxyl group, —COOH, shows typical acidic properties, e.g. it will liberate carbon dioxide from a carbonate:

$$2\text{—}\square\text{—}COOH(aq) + CO_3^{2-}(aq) \rightarrow 2\text{—}\square\text{—}COO^-(aq) + H_2O(l) + CO_2(g)$$

where $\square$—is a hydrocarbon skeleton. Detailed reactions of some common organic 'functional groups' may be found in chapters 34 to 41.

In order to give some idea of the progress of a typical structure determination we shall now concentrate on a specific example, a white solid which we shall call X. Selected experimental results will be given at each stage and you will be invited to compare your conclusions with those listed at the end of the chapter.

Activity 6.1

What conclusions can you draw concerning the elements present in compound X from the following observations?

1 On heating, X first melts readily then ignites leaving no residue.
2 When heated with copper(II) oxide it produces a gaseous mixture which turns blue cobalt chloride paper pink and gives a white precipitate with calcium hydroxide solution.
3 No elements are detectable by sodium fusion.
4 Addition of X to sodium carbonate solution gives a colourless gas which gives a white precipitate with calcium hydroxide solution.

Once the elements present in the substance have been identified, the next step is to determine their *proportions by mass*. Conversion to **molar** composition will then lead to the empirical formula. In many cases the methods used are similar to those involved in qualitative analysis, but now accurate measurements must be made. In the case of an organic compound, such as our example X, complete combustion will convert all the carbon into carbon dioxide, and all the hydrogen into water. The products are passed through concentrated sulphuric acid, which absorbs the water vapour, and then potassium hydroxide solution, which absorbs the carbon dioxide. The mass of each of the products equals the increase in mass of the relevant absorption tube.

$$C_xH_y + (x + y/4)O_2(g) \xrightarrow{\text{burn}} xCO_2(g) + (y/2)H_2O(g)$$

$$\underset{\substack{\text{absorbed by} \\ \text{KOH(aq)}}}{} \quad \underset{\substack{\text{absorbed by} \\ \text{conc. } H_2SO_4(l)}}{}$$

Activity 6.2

On complete combustion, 0.340 g of X gave 0.880 g of carbon dioxide and 0.180 g of water.

1   How many moles of carbon dioxide and water were formed?
2   How many moles of carbon and hydrogen atoms must the sample of X have contained?
    (Note that 2 moles of H atoms are needed to make 1 mole of water.)
3   Assuming only oxygen to be present as well as carbon and hydrogen, find what mass of oxygen the sample contained and hence the number of moles of oxygen atoms.
4   What is the empirical formula of X?
    (Relative atomic masses: C = 12, H = 1, O = 16.)

6.2 Determination of molecular formula

Although we now know the simplest whole number atomic ratio of the elements in X, we do not know how many atoms of each element are present in one molecule of X. *The molecular formula may be any whole number multiple of the empirical formula.* Thus, the following are all possible molecular formulae for X:

$$C_4H_4O, \quad C_8H_8O_2, \quad C_{12}H_{12}O_3, \quad C_{16}H_{16}O_4, \quad \text{etc.}$$

In order to decide the molecular formula we need to know the **relative molecular mass** (M_r) of the compound. There are several ways in which this may be determined. Classical chemical methods rely upon the measurement of some **colligative** property. These properties, discussed in chapter 16, depend only upon the number of molecules present and not upon their type. Table 6.2 lists some common methods, together with the types of compound to which they are most suited.

Table 6.2   *Methods for relative molecular mass determination*

Technique	most suitable for
gas density	gases and volatile liquids
lowering of vapour pressure	non-volatile solutes
elevation of boiling point	non-volatile solutes
depression of freezing point	solutes which are appreciably soluble near the freezing point of the solvent
osmotic pressure	particularly useful for solutes with very high molecular mass, i.e. polymers and macromolecules

Activity 6.3

You will need to be familiar with the theory of boiling point elevation, described in section 16.4, in order to attempt this activity.

In an experiment, addition of 6.70 g of X to 200 g of water was found to increase the boiling point by 0.130 °C. The boiling point elevation constant for water is 0.52 °C per 1000 g of solvent. Use this data to determine:

1 the concentration of X in g per 1000 g of water;
2 the concentration of X in moles per 1000 g of water.

Hence deduce:

3 the mass of one mole of X;
4 the molecular formula of X.

Mass spectrometry, described in section 2.3, provides a very accurate alternative method of determining relative molecular mass. The **mass spectrum** of our compound X is shown in figure 6.2. The peak with the highest mass/charge ratio corresponds to the **molecular ion**, i.e. *the molecule which has lost only a single electron*. This gives the relative molecular mass of X directly as 136 (compare this with the figure you calculated in activity 6.3).

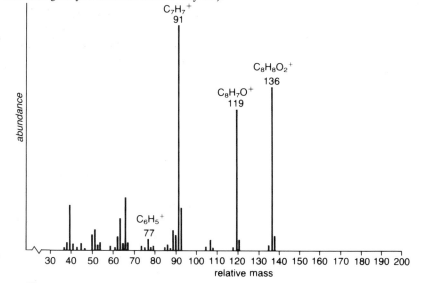

Figure 6.2 *Low resolution mass spectrum of X with suggested assignments for some peaks*

Very precise measurement of relative molecular mass using 'high resolution' mass spectrometry may give the molecular formula directly, without the need to first establish the empirical formula. Although there are various combinations of carbon, hydrogen and oxygen atoms which have a relative mass of approximately 136, each will give a slightly different result.

Relative atomic masses of the most abundant isotopes:

$$C = 12.0000 \quad H = 1.0078 \quad O = 15.9949$$

Thus relative masses of:

$C_7H_4O_3 = 136.0159$
$C_8H_8O_2 = 136.0522$ } may be distinguished by accurate 'high resolution' mass spectrometry.
$C_9H_{12}O = 136.0885$

The remaining peaks in the mass spectrum of X are due to breakdown of the molecule in the mass spectrometer. Such **fragmentation patterns** may be of great use in establishing the structural formula of the compound, and the mass spectrum of X will be considered in greater detail in the next section.

6.3 Determination of structural formula

Knowing the molecular formula of a compound, the only remaining task is to determine exactly how the atoms present are bonded together. A wide variety of chemical and spectroscopic methods may prove helpful and both chemical intuition and luck may save considerable time and effort at this stage.

Let us review the information we already have on our compound X. Its molecular formula is $C_8H_8O_2$, and, since it gives carbon dioxide with sodium carbonate solution, it must contain the carboxyl group, —COOH. This is confirmed by the fragmentation pattern in the mass spectrum of X (figure 6.2) which contains strong peaks at relative masses 17 and 45 less than the molecular ion. These correspond to loss of an —OH and a —COOH group respectively.

That leaves C_7H_7 to be accounted for.

$$C_7H_7 \!-\! C \!\!\!\begin{array}{c} O \\ \diagdown \\ O\!-\!H \end{array}$$

structure unknown
as yet

X shows little tendency to undergo addition reactions, e.g. it will not decolorise bromine at room temperature and this, together with an ability to undergo substitution reactions and the high carbon to hydrogen ratio, suggests the presence of a **benzene ring** (see section 5.8). X is therefore an **aromatic carboxylic acid** (section 40.1), but, in order to match the known molecular formula, a methyl group, CH_3 must be attached directly to the benzene ring.

$$CH_3 \!-\!\!\!\!\bigcirc\!\!\!\!-\! C\begin{array}{c} O \\ \diagdown \\ O\!-\!H \end{array}$$

CH₃ attached to the
ring at some point

At this stage of a structure determination, **absorption spectra** may also be of great value. Whilst a detailed treatment of such techniques is beyond the scope of this book, you may find it interesting to examine the ultraviolet (UV), infrared (IR) and nuclear magnetic resonance (NMR) spectra of X, illustrated in figures 6.5, 6.6 and 6.8, and try your hand at extracting structural information from them in the accompanying activities.

Electromagnetic radiation, which includes visible light, is characterised by its wavelength or its frequency. These quantities are related by the equation

$$c = f\lambda$$

where c is the speed of light in $m\,s^{-1}$

λ is the wavelength of the radiation in m
and f is the frequency of the radiation in Hz (i.e. waves s^{-1}).

The whole range of such radiations, known as the **electromagnetic spectrum**, is shown in figure 6.3. Such radiation is emitted as fixed 'packets' of energy known as **quanta**. The size of these quanta depends directly upon the **frequency** of the radiation. Thus from figure 6.3 we can see that a quantum of ultraviolet radiation has *more* energy than a quantum of radio waves.

Molecules have several types of energy associated with them, e.g. the energy states of the individual particles in the structure and vibrational and rotational energy of the molecule as a whole (figure 6.4). The values which each of these different types of energy may take is limited, i.e. *only certain fixed quantities are allowed.*

Molecules will absorb electromagnetic radiation of a particular frequency if, and only if, the size of the quantum involved is exactly that needed to promote the molecule to a higher permitted energy level. The various absorption spectra in figures 6.5, 6.6 and 6.8 show which frequencies our compound X absorbs in various regions of the electromagnetic spectrum. Since the energy states of a molecule depend upon its structure, interpretation of this data can give much useful information.

We shall look at each of the different spectra in turn, examine the type of molecular energy change involved, and outline how structural information may be obtained from it.

Figure 6.3 *The electromagnetic spectrum – its applications in chemistry and everyday life*

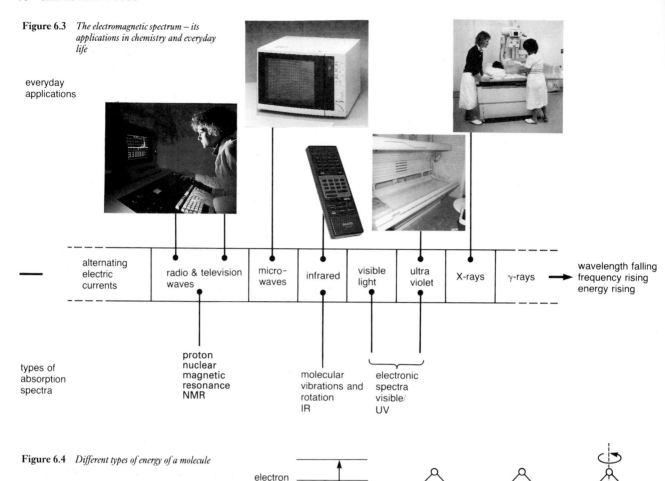

everyday applications

alternating electric currents | radio & television waves | micro-waves | infrared | visible light | ultra violet | X-rays | γ-rays

wavelength falling frequency rising energy rising

types of absorption spectra

proton nuclear magnetic resonance NMR

molecular vibrations and rotation IR

electronic spectra visible/ UV

Figure 6.4 *Different types of energy of a molecule*

electron energy levels

stretching   bending

vibrational energy

rotational energy

Figure 6.5 *UV absorption spectrum of compound X and absorption peaks of some common organic compounds*

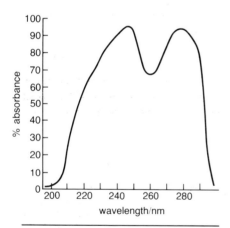

Reference compound		main absorption peaks
Propanone	$\begin{array}{c}CH_3\\CH_3\end{array}$>C=O	188 nm, 278 nm
Benzene	⬡	184 nm, 203 nm, 255 nm
Nitrobenzene	⬡ NO₂	260 nm
Phenylamine	⬡ NH₂	234 nm, 286 nm
Benzoic acid	⬡ COOH	228 nm, 273 nm

Ultraviolet spectra

Here the quanta of radiation are relatively large and may cause an electron within the molecule to be promoted to a higher energy level. This is particularly likely if the structure contains 'delocalised' electrons or multiple bonds. Certain organic functional groups absorb at the characteristic wavelengths shown in the table with the UV spectrum of our compound X in figure 6.5.

Activity 6.4

What support does the UV spectrum of X give to the structural information we have already established?

Infrared spectra

Radiation in this region may be absorbed by molecules gaining **vibrational** energy, i.e. bending or stretching of the covalent bonds. Since molecules with different structures cannot vibrate in exactly the same way they will absorb radiation at different wavelengths, providing a **'fingerprint'** of the compound. Under certain

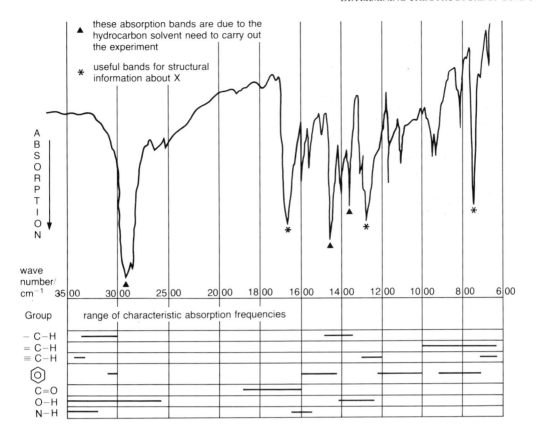

Figure 6.6 *IR spectrum of compound X in nujol (a hydrocarbon) and the characteristic absorption bands of some organic groups*

conditions, absorption by a particular type of bond occurs within quite a narrow wavelength range, irrespective of the rest of the structure. Such 'characteristic' absorption bands may be used to identify specific functional groups within the molecule. The IR spectrum of compound X is shown in figure 6.6, together with a table showing some characteristic absorption wavelengths for certain groups.

Activity 6.5

Could any of the absorption bands marked with an asterisk in this IR spectrum support the structural evidence so far accumulated for X?

Nuclear magnetic resonance spectra (NMR)

Like unpaired electrons, certain nuclei, including ^1H, have the property of **spin** and can occupy different energy states in a magnetic field. **Radio waves** of the correct frequency may be absorbed to promote such nuclei from the low energy state to the higher one (figure 6.7).

Figure 6.7 *Radio waves can promote nuclei to a higher energy level in a magnetic field*

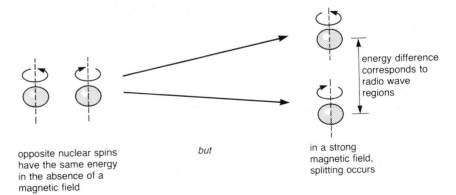

This absorption of energy gives rise to an NMR spectrum, often referred to as a PMR spectrum when the nucleus involved is hydrogen (i.e. the proton!).

In practice, the sample is exposed to radio waves of a fixed frequency and the applied magnetic field is varied until absorption occurs. The actual magnetic field which a particular proton experiences is actually less than the applied field, since it is **screened** somewhat by the bonding electrons around it. This means that protons in different environments will absorb the radio waves at slightly different values of the applied magnetic field. The position of an absorption is usually given as the field difference in parts per million (δ) relative to tetramethylsilane, $(CH_3)_4Si$, which is included as an internal standard in the sample. The *area* under a particular peak or set of peaks in the PMR spectrum also gives a measure of the relative *number of protons* of a particular type and can be most useful in a structure determination.

Activity 6.6

The PMR spectrum of compound X is shown in figure 6.8, together with the absorption positions of protons in different organic groups. What information regarding the structure of X can you deduce from this spectrum?

Figure 6.8   *NMR spectrum of compound X in D₂O solution and the absorption ranges of some protons*

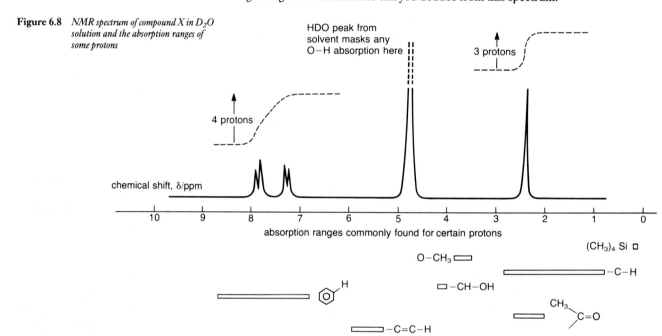

6.4 Determination of the 3-dimensional structure

Expert analysis of the various absorption spectra of X might enable us to establish the structure unambiguously but, at present, we are left with three possible structures for the molecule, corresponding to different positions for the methyl group relative to the carboxyl group on the benzene ring,

2-methyl benzoic acid   3-methyl benzoic acid   4-methyl benzoic acid

We shall now turn to **diffraction** methods which, although laborious and time consuming, may be used to build up a 'scale model' of the actual molecule.

A crystal consists of a regular 3-dimensional arrangement of atoms, molecules or ions. The wavelength of X-rays is of the same order as the distances between the particles, and the crystal lattice acts as a **diffraction grating** for X-rays. The pattern of X-rays diffracted from a crystal may be used to determine the positions of the atoms within the lattice quite precisely. A simple explanation of the effect may be given in terms of the 'reflection' of X-rays from sets of atomic planes within the crystal, as shown in figure 6.9.

Mathematical considerations show that a strong 'reflection' is only obtained for certain glancing angles, given by the **Bragg equation**,

$$n\lambda = 2d.\sin\theta$$

where n is a whole number known as the order of the reflection,

λ is the wavelength of the X-rays,

d is the distance between successive atomic 'planes',

θ is the angle between the atomic planes and the X-ray beam.

If the spacing between a sufficient number of different sets of atomic planes can be determined, then the positions of the atoms within the lattice may be established (figure 6.10).

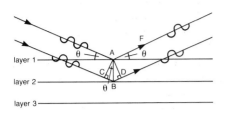

Figure 6.9 *Conditions for 'strong' X-ray reflection from a set of crystal planes*

Figure 6.10 *Crystal planes*

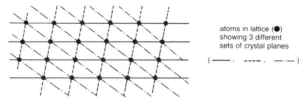

atoms in lattice (●)
showing 3 different
sets of crystal planes

(—— , ---- , —·—)

Modern methods use a **monochromatic** X-ray beam (a single wavelength) with different techniques being used to bring crystal planes into 'reflecting' positions. Bragg examined the 'reflection' positions for various sets of crystal planes individually but the methods shown in figure 6.11 allow 'reflections' from many sets of planes to be detected *simultaneously*.

Figure 6.11 *The 'rotating crystal' method of X-ray diffraction which allows 'reflections' from many different crystal planes to be measured simultaneously. When the crystal is rotated about one of its axes, many sets of crystal planes will eventually come into strong reflection positions. All the reflected X-ray beams may be detected photographically using either a flat film placed behind the crystal or a cylindrical film placed around it. If the experiment is repeated, but rotating the crystal about its other two axes, then all possible reflections will be observed*

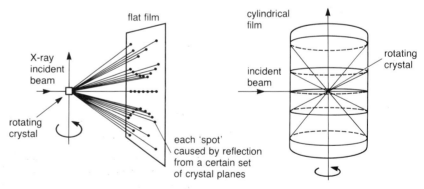

flat film

X-ray incident beam

rotating crystal

each 'spot' caused by reflection from a certain set of crystal planes

cylindrical film

incident beam

rotating crystal

Structure determination involves finding a model of the crystal lattice which will account for the observed diffraction pattern. While for relatively simple structures this may be done by 'trial and error', advanced computer analysis of the results is required for more complex crystals. By such methods it is possible to produce a 3-dimensional **electron density map** of the lattice, from which the positions of the atoms and hence the bond lengths and bond angles in the molecule may be established. Since the ability of an atom to 'scatter' X-rays depends on its atomic number, it is difficult to place light atoms, particularly hydrogen, with any accuracy.

X-ray diffraction studies on a crystal of our substance X gave the electron density map shown in figure 6.12.

Figure 6.12   *Electron density map for a molecule of compound X*

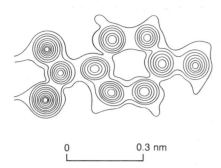

0   0.3 nm

Activity 6.7

Bearing in mind what we have already discovered about our substance X, use the electron density map, figure 6.12, prepared from X-ray diffraction studies, to draw the structure of the molecule. What is its systematic name?

    X-ray diffraction experiments are suitable only for *crystalline solids*. However, electrons also have associated 'wave properties' and may be used in a similar manner to X-rays to obtain diffraction patterns from gaseous samples. The apparatus and a typical **electron diffraction** pattern are shown in figure 6.13. Diffraction occurs for all interatomic distances in the sample. Since gas molecules are in constant random motion, the distances between non-bonded atoms will vary and produce general background scattering. However, within a molecule, the interatomic distances will be *fixed* and these will produce circular diffraction patterns on the photographic plate. Since the diameter of each of these circles is a measure of an interatomic separation within the molecule, a structural model may be proposed which fits the data. Electron diffraction is capable of locating light atoms, especially hydrogen, with much greater precision than X-ray diffraction, but its use is generally restricted to quite simple structures.

    Although the spectroscopic techniques outlined in section 6.3 may not give such detailed and unambiguous structural information as diffraction methods, they usually yield results much more rapidly and more conveniently.

Figure 6.13   *Electron diffraction: the gas sample introduced at C is bombarded by electrons from A which are diffracted into a series of conical beams which register as circles on the photographic plate D*

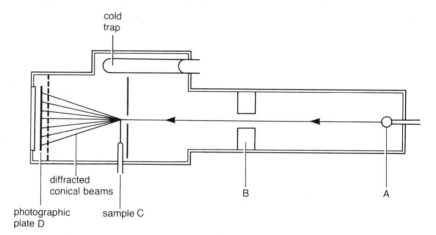

cold trap

diffracted conical beams

photographic plate D

sample C

B

A

6.5   Comments on the activities

Activity 6.1

1   Since X melts easily it is probably a simple covalent compound. As it does not leave a residue on burning, it is very unlikely to contain a metallic element.

2   X contains both hydrogen and carbon, since complete oxidation gives both water and carbon dioxide.

3   The sodium fusion result indicates that X does not contain nitrogen, sulphur or halogens.

4   X is an acid, since it liberates carbon dioxide from sodium carbonate solution. It probably contains the carboxyl group, —COOH.

Activity 6.2

1   moles of carbon dioxide $0.880/44 = 0.020$
    moles of water $= 0.180/18 = 0.010$

2   moles of C in 0.20 moles $CO_2 = 0.20$
    moles of H in 0.010 moles $H_2O = 0.020$

3   mass of carbon in X $= 0.020 \times 12 = 0.240\,g$
mass of hydrogen in X $= 0.020 \times\ \ 1 = 0.020\,g$
therefore, mass of oxygen $= 0.340 - 0.0240 - 0.020 = 0.080\,g$
moles of O $= 0.080/16 = 0.005$
4   molar ratio is 0.020(C): 0.020(H): 0.005(O)
simplest whole number ratio of atoms 4(C) : 4(H) : 1(O) gives the empirical
formula C_4H_4O

Activity 6.3

1   6.70 g of X in   200 g water
therefore $5 \times 6.70\,g$ of X in 1000 g water
Concentration of X in solution is 33.5 g per 1000 g of water.
2   1 mole of any solute in 1000 g water raises b.p. by 0.52 °C
1/0.52 moles of any solute in 1000 g water raises b.p. by 1.00 °C
0.13/0.52 moles of any solute in 1000 g water raises b.p. by 0.13 °C
Concentration of X in solution is 0.25 moles per 1000 g of water.
3   0.25 moles of X weighs 33.5 g
1 mole of X weighs 33.5/0.25 = 134 g
4   The empirical formula of X is C_4H_4O, which has a relative mass of 68.
The actual relative molecular mass determined above by elevation of
boiling point is almost exactly double this, so the molecular formula of X
must be $C_8H_8O_2$.

Activity 6.4

The UV absorption spectrum of X, figure 6.5, shows two principal absorption peaks
at approximately 248 nm and 280 nm. Our conclusion from activity 6.1, that X
contains a carboxylic acid group —COOH, is supported by the similarity of these
absorptions to those of **benzoic acid** at 228 nm and 280 nm. The only other
reference spectrum in figure 6.4 that might apply to X is a primary aromatic amine
(phenylamine). However, elemental analysis and chemical evidence rule out this
possibility.

Activity 6.5

Unfortunately, the IR spectrum of X was carried out with the sample in a
suspension of 'nujol', which is a saturated liquid hydrocarbon. This gives strong
peaks (marked ▲ on figure 6.6) which would mask similar absorptions from X.
However, the peaks marked * are consistent with our proposed structure of a methyl
substituted benzoic acid and might be assigned as follows:

wave number	group
1670	C=O carbonyl
1280	O—H hydroxyl
750	C—H aromatic

Figure 6.14   *Structural interpretation of the
electron density map of a molecule of
compound X*

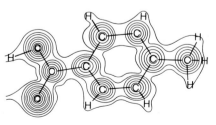

4-methyl benzoic acid

Activity 6.6

The NMR spectrum of X shown in figure 6.8 shows a set of peaks around $\delta = 8$
which are probably due to *aromatic C—H* and a single peak at about $\delta = 2.4$ which
could be assigned to a *methyl group —CH$_3$*. The areas under these absorptions are
4:3, i.e. exactly what we would expect from a methyl substituted benzoic acid.
No signal is obtained from the —O—H proton, since this undergoes rapid
exchange with the deuterium atoms in the D_2O which is used as the solvent in the
NMR investigation.

Activity 6.7

The structure of the molecule is drawn superimposed upon the electron density
map in figure 6.14. The substance is 4-methyl benzoic acid.

6.6 Summary and revision plan

1   There are several 'kinds' of chemical formula:
   (a) **empirical** showing the simplest whole number atomic ratio of the elements present;
   (b) **molecular** indicating the actual number of each kind of atom in one molecule of the compound;
   (c) **structural** showing exactly how the atoms are bonded together in the molecule.

2   An empirical formula may be established by finding the percentage by mass of each element present. In organic compounds, hydrogen and carbon are estimated by complete combustion to water and carbon dioxide respectively.

3   Determination of **relative molecular mass**, either by use of **'colligative'** properties, or directly by **mass spectrometry**, will then give the molecular formula.

4   Much 'indirect' structural information may be obtained from:
   (a) the chemical reactions which the compound shows;
   (b) instrumental methods such as **infrared, ultraviolet**, and **nuclear magnetic resonance** spectroscopy. These all rely on absorption of electromagnetic radiation by specific structural features of the compound.

5   Molecular structures act as 3-dimensional 'diffraction' gratings for either **X-rays** or **electrons**. Study of **diffraction** patterns can give a detailed, unambiguous scale model of the structure, but such methods are usually much more time-consuming than those above.

Shapes of Molecules and Ions

Contents

As long ago as 1894, when Fisher proposed the **lock and key** mechanism to account for enzyme action, it was suggested that molecular shape might be an important factor in the chemistry of some compounds. Enzymes are large protein molecules which act as catalysts in particular biochemical reactions. Without enzymes, life as we know it would be impossible. Fisher reasoned that each enzyme had **active sites** on its surface in the form of specially shaped holes (or locks). Only molecules of the correct shape to fit these holes (keys) would be acted upon by the enzyme (figure 7.1).

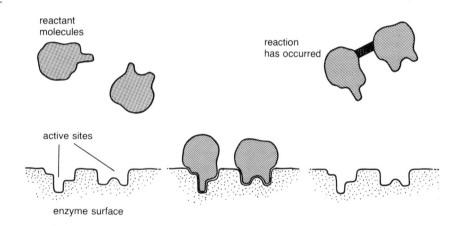

reactant molecules

reaction has occurred

active sites

enzyme surface

Figure 7.1   *The 'lock and key' mechanism of enzyme action*

The 3-dimensional structure of an enzyme

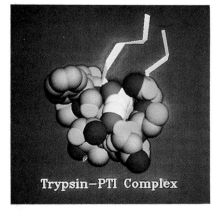

Trypsin–PTI Complex

Results of X-ray diffraction experiments (see chapter 6) have helped to confirm Fisher's idea but these methods are still very time consuming and laborious. Fortunately, from such experimental results it has been possible to develop a simple theory which enables us to accurately predict the shapes of simple molecules or parts of molecules.

At first glance, there seems to be little pattern to the variety of molecular shapes. Even some molecules of the same general formula, e.g. boron trichloride, BCl_3 and nitrogen trichloride, NCl_3, have different shapes.

Note: To show 3-dimensional shape, bonds in the plane of the paper are drawn, —, those coming up out of the plane are drawn / , and those going below this plane are drawn - - - - -.

It is only when we look at the electronic structures of the molecules in more detail that we can explain such differences.

Using balloons to model molecular shapes

7.1 The relationship between basic shape and electronic structure

In 1940 Sidgwick and Powell proposed that *molecular shape is determined largely by the number of different sets of electrons in the valency shell of the central atom. Since electrons are negatively charged, they will repel each other and arrange themselves in space so as to minimise the repulsive forces.*

Activity 7.1

The following simple experiment will help you to visualise the arrangement in space of electron sets around a central atom. You will need six balloons of the same size and shape, either round ones or the long thin type.

▶ First blow up two balloons, not quite fully, and join them by knotting the open ends together.

▶ Repeat this step with the other balloons so that you have three such pairs.

▶ Join the balloons by twisting their knotted centres around each other a number of times. You should now have a model with six balloons pointing roughly at right angles to each other. This represents the way in which six sets of valency electrons will arrange themselves in space so as to minimise the repulsive forces between them. If you try bending the balloons towards each other, you will find they spring back to their original position when released. This shape is referred to as *octahedral*, since it just fits inside a regular octahedron.

Table 7.1 *Molecular shapes in terms of outer electron sets*

total number of outer electron sets	spatial arrangements		
2	linear		
3	triangular	V-shaped	
4	tetrahedral	triangular pyramid	V-shaped
5	triangular bipyramid	distorted tetrahedral	T-shaped
6	octahedral	square pyramidal	square planar
7	pentagonal bipyramid		

▶ If you now burst one of the balloons with a pin you should have the arrangement for five sets of valency electrons. If it doesn't look like the *triangular bipyramid* shape shown in table 7.1 then hold one of the balloons and gently shake the model.

▶ Burst the other balloons in turn, at each stage comparing the shape with that given in table 7.1.

The basic shapes resulting from different numbers of electron sets on the central atom can be found in table 7.1. Examples of each type are discussed below.

2 sets of electrons

Mutual repulsion gives a **linear** arrangement as in beryllium chloride, $BeCl_2$:

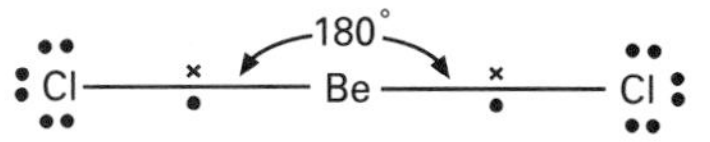

A set of electrons need not be a single pair. Atoms commonly achieve a 'noble gas' outer octet of electrons by covalent bonding. If these eight electrons are divided into two sets, i.e. two double bonds or a single and a triple bond, then again the shape of the molecule will be a straight line.

3 sets of electrons

This gives a **plane triangular shape** as in boron trichloride:

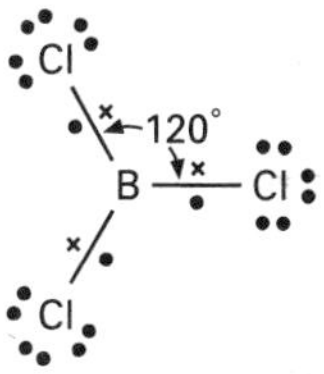

Again, the common 'octet' electron arrangement must include a double bond, as in carbonyl chloride, $COCl_2$:

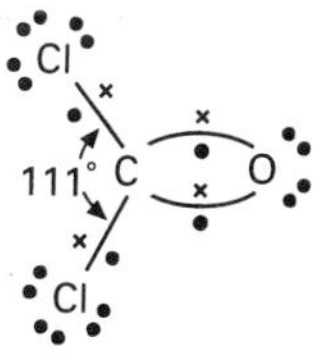

Note, however, that in this case, although the molecule is still planar, the bonds' angles are *not* identical. Since the double bond consists of four electrons, it repels *more strongly* than the single bonds. As a result, the chlorine atoms are squeezed together slightly, reducing the Cl—C—Cl angle to less than 120°.

4 sets of electrons

This is a very common arrangement, where the outer 'octet' of electrons is divided into four pairs, giving a **tetrahedral** shape as in methane, CH_4:

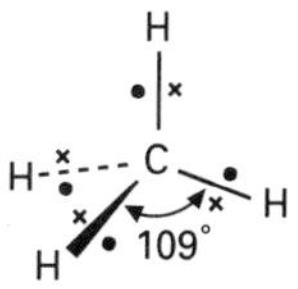

One or more of the sets of electrons on the central atom may not be involved in bonding, as for example, in ammonia and water:

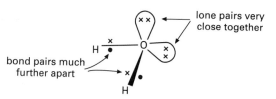

These are called **lone pairs** of electrons.

Whilst the presence of lone pairs must be taken into account when deciding upon the basic structure and 3-dimensional arrangement of the sets of electrons in space, the molecular shape describes the atomic arrangement only. Thus although the arrangement of electron *sets* is tetrahedral in each case, the ammonia molecule is described as **pyramidal** whilst the water molecule is **angular** or **V-shaped**.

The decrease in the bond angle on going from methane to ammonia to water is caused by the progressive replacement of bonding pairs on the central atom by non-bonding lone pairs of electrons. *Lone pairs repel more strongly and 'squeeze' the bonds closer together.* Whereas bond pairs are shared between two atoms, lone pairs occupy orbitals on a single atom. Two lone pairs on an atom are therefore much closer together than sets of bonding electrons and the relative strengths of the repulsive forces are as follows:

lone pair–lone pair > lone pair–bond pair > bond pair–bond pair

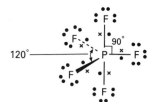

Atoms in the Period lithium to fluorine can only accommodate a maximum of eight electrons in their valency shell. This is equivalent to four sets of electrons at most. Molecules with such atoms at their centre are therefore restricted to the shapes covered so far.

5 sets of electrons

These are arranged in a **triangular bipyramid**, as in PF_5:

Again, one or more of the sets of electrons may be a lone pair and this gives rise to the following molecular shapes.

Note that in this case the sets of electrons may be divided into two distinct types, the three in the triangular plane and the two at right angles to this. At first glance it might seem equally possible to place lone pairs in either set, but in practice they always seem to occupy positions in the triangular plane.

Activity 7.2

What explanations can you offer for the following observations?
1. Lone pairs always occupy positions in the plane of the triangle in structures based on the triangular bipyramid.
2. The F—Cl—F bond angle in ClF_3 is about $87°$.
3. The ICl_2^- ion is linear. (Hint: the iodine atom contains five sets of electrons in its valency shell.)

Each of these questions may be answered using arguments similar to those already given in this section.

6 sets of electrons

These are arranged **octahedrally** around the central atom, as in SF_6:

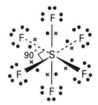

All the positions in this structure are equivalent. Inclusion of lone pairs gives the following molecular shapes.

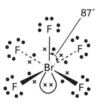

square pyramidal

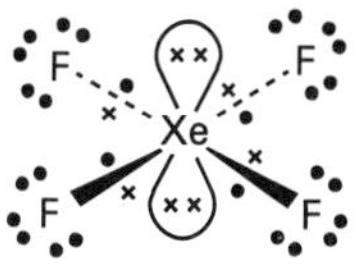

square planar

7 sets of electrons

This results in a **pentagonal bipyramid** arrangement:

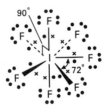

Activity 7.3

If you are familiar with the construction of 'dot and cross' electron diagrams showing covalent bonding (chapter 5), you should now be able to work out the shape of any simple molecule or ion.

Draw diagrams clearly indicating the arrangement of *outer* electrons and the overall shape of the following species:

HCN $TeCl_4$ $COCl_2$ PCl_6^- ICl_3 BrF_5 SO_3^{2-} NH_4^+ ICl_4^- SO_2

7.2 Effect of electron delocalisation on molecular shape

There are several structures which cannot be fully explained using the simple approach developed in section 7.1. Consider the nitrate ion, NO_3^-. A simple 'dot and cross' representation correctly predicts a **plane triangular** shape.

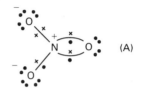

(A)

However, although double bonds are usually *shorter* than single bonds and would be expected to repel more strongly, all bond lengths and angles in the nitrate ion are *identical*. The difficulty lies in placing the double bond. Equally acceptable 'dot and cross' diagrams may be drawn with the double bond connecting the nitrogen to each of the other two oxygen atoms.

(B)   (C)

A much better representation of the actual structure, illustrated in figure 7.2, is given in terms of **orbital overlap** (see sections 5.5 and 5.6). A triangular σ bond skeleton is formed by overlap of sp^2 hybrid orbitals on the nitrogen with p orbitals on the oxygen atoms (figure 7.2a). The remaining two electrons occupy a π orbital formed by overlap of the remaining pure p nitrogen orbital with other p orbitals on the oxygen atoms (figure 7.2b).

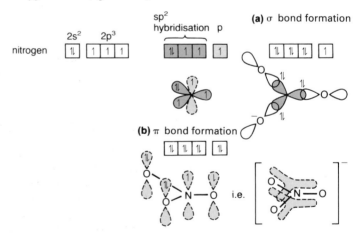

Figure 7.2 *π electron delocalisation in the NO_3 ion*

The electrons in this π orbital correspond to the double bond in each of the 'dot and cross' diagrams. A, B and C above, but are not restricted to a single pair of atoms. They are delocalised over the system as a whole, in effect giving each of the three bonds some 'double bond' character.

There are many such cases in which electrons are delocalised over π orbitals extending over three or more atoms. *They are generally easy to recognise since their structures may be represented by two or more equivalent 'dot and cross' diagrams.*

The carbonate ion, $CO_3{}^{2-}$, has exactly the same arrangement of electrons as the nitrate ion and possesses an identical structure. In the case of nitric acid, HNO_3, the oxygen atom linked to the hydrogen is unable to take part in π bonding and delocalisation is restricted to the nitrogen and the remaining two oxygen atoms.

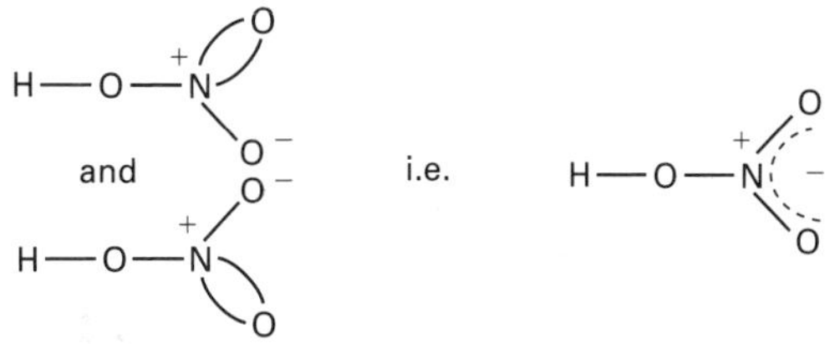

Similar delocalisation occurs in the nitrite ion, $NO_2{}^-$.

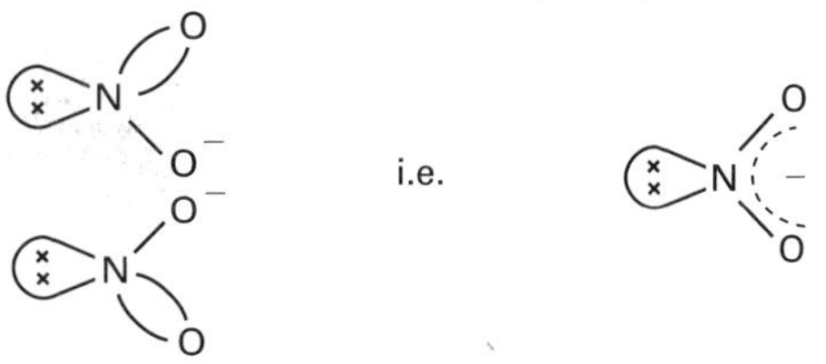

Although carboxylic acids, e.g. ethanoic acid, CH_3COOH, do not exhibit electron delocalisation, their anions, e.g. ethanoate, CH_3COO^-, do.

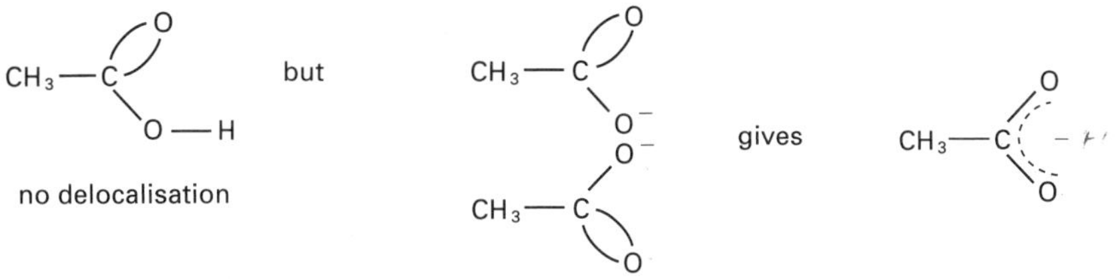

It should be noted that whilst electron delocalisation may affect relative bond lengths and angles, it will not change the basic shape of the structure determined using the electron repulsion theory described in section 7.1. This latter approach is perfectly adequate for predicting the basic shape of most non-transition metal species.

7.3 Shapes of 'd' block metal complexes

Care must be taken when predicting the shapes of complexes in which the central atom has a partially filled set of d orbitals. A detailed treatment of such species is beyond the scope of this book but the following generalisations may help.

▶ All 2-coordinate complexes are linear, e.g. $[Cu(NH_3)_2]^+$.
▶ All 6-coordinate complexes are octahedral, e.g. $[Ni(H_2O)_6]^{2+}$.
▶ Most 4-coordinate complexes are tetrahedral, e.g. $[CoCl_4]^{2-}$, but some are square planar, e.g. $[Ni(CN)_4]^{2-}$.

For more detail see section 30.3.

7.4 Comments on the activities

Activity 7.2

The key to all these observations is the *greater repulsive effect of lone pairs.*

1   Lone pairs in the triangular plane have only *two sets* of electrons at 90° to them. If they were placed in the other positions they would experience repulsion by *three sets* of electrons at right angles.

Figure 7.3   *Shapes of molecules and ions in activity 7.3*

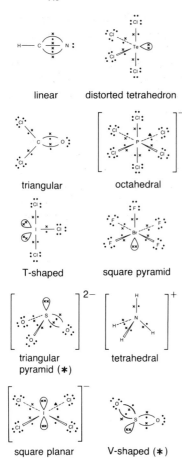

2   The bonding pairs are squeezed by the presence of the lone pairs, reducing the bond angle to less than 90°. The effect is similar to that described earlier for the series, methane, ammonia and water.

3   The five sets of electrons round the central iodine atom must consist of single bonds to each of the two chlorine atoms and three non-bonding lone pairs. Since, according to the arguments given in (1) above, the lone pairs will occupy all the positions in the triangular plane, the following **linear** shape results.

Activity 7.3

If you have difficulty in getting the answers shown in figure 7.3 then refer to the following procedure in which the shape of the tetrahydridoborate ion, BH_4^-, is deduced.

1   Use the Periodic Table to find the group in which each of the elements occurs. This gives the number of *outer* electrons on each kind of atom. Represent these by 'dots and crosses'.

B   and   4H •

2   If the species is **ionic** then add or subtract the number of electrons corresponding to the **charge**. Strictly speaking, we should add electrons to the more electronegative atom, or remove them from the less electronegative atom. In this case, therefore, we add an electron to one of the hydrogen atoms. (Don't worry if you pick the wrong kind of atom, since you should still get the right shape.)

B   3H •   and   H •

3   Construct a 'dot and cross' electron diagram showing the covalent bonds and any non-bonding lone pairs. Dative bonds may be represented as covalent bonds. At this stage do not worry about the shape of the species.

4   Count up the number of *different sets* of electrons round the central atom, *not forgetting to include any lone pairs*. Redraw the 'dot and cross' diagram, clearly showing the shape, if necessary referring to table 7.1.

7.5 Summary and Revision Plan

1   *Molecular shape is determined by mutual repulsion of different 'sets' of electrons in the valency shell of the central atom.* The basic shape of a species may be deduced from a 'dot and cross' diagram of its outer electron structure.

2   Although the presence of non-bonding **lone pairs** of electrons must be taken into account, they are not included in the 'description' of molecular shape. Thus, methane, ammonia and water all have four sets of electrons around their central atoms, but their shapes are respectively described as tetrahedral, pyramidal and angular.

3   *Lone pairs of electrons (and multiple bonds) repel more strongly than single bond pairs* and this will cause small distortions from regular shapes and bond angles.

4   Multiple bonds are usually shorter and stronger than single bonds. Bonds which are intermediate in type result from π **electron delocalisation**.

5   Simple electron repulsion theory does not always correctly predict the shape of 'd' block complexes, e.g. both tetrahedral and square planar 4-coordinate nickel complexes are known.

8

Gases and Liquids

Contents

Figure 8.1 *The relationship between the three main states of matter*

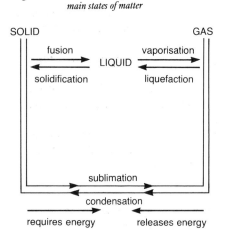

Matter can exist in three important states: solid, liquid and gas. Table 8.1 gives some characteristic properties of each state. Substances may undergo various changes of state; these are summarised in figure 8.1. This chapter and the next examine these properties and interpret them using the **Kinetic Theory of Matter**. Basically, this theory states that *all matter is made up of very small particles which are in constant motion.*

Table 8.1 *Comparing some properties of solids, liquids and gases*

	volume	shape	density	compressibility
solids	fixed	fixed	high	negligible
liquids	fixed	takes the shape of the container but may not fill it completely		very slight
gases	molecules will spread evenly throughout any container; thus volume is indefinite and shape is that of the container		low	very easily compressed

8.1 The ideal gas equation

Every year, massive amounts of gases are manufactured. These are used in thousands of different ways in various industries and in our homes. Of course, we often choose a gas because of its chemical properties. For example, hydrogen and helium are both lighter than air and could be used to fill balloons and airships. However, helium would be used because it is chemically inert whereas hydrogen may explode when mixed with air. To use a gas safely, we must also know about its physical properties. Most important is the way its volume varies with temperature and pressure. Let us consider two simple examples.

To make a sponge, air bubbles are forced into the cake mixture by whisking it. On cooking, these bubbles of air expand and the sponge 'rises'. So, when a gas is heated at constant pressure, its volume increases.

Suppose that a tyre is pumped up on a cold winter day at $0\,°C$. If no air is lost, then on a hot summer day at $27\,°C$, the inflation pressure would have increased by about 10%. So, when a constant volume of gas is heated, the pressure increases.

Accurate experiments with various gases show that the pressure (p), volume (V) and the absolute temperature (T) of a gas are related by the **ideal gas equation**,

$$pV = nRT$$

where n is number of moles of gas and R is called the **gas constant**. (The value of R depends on the units used, see table 8.2; at $X\,°C$, absolute temperature = X +

When using gases it is important to consider both their chemical and physical properties. Although hydrogen is the lightest gas, its use in the airship 'Hindenburg' in May 1937 proved disastrous because of its ability to form explosive mixtures with air. Helium, though much more expensive, is lighter than air and chemically inert making it very suitable for filling children's balloons. The volume of a fixed mass of gas changes with temperature and pressure. For example, the air bubbles in a sponge-cake mixture expand on heating and the sponge rises. Similarly, the inflation pressure of a car tyre will vary with the external temperature

273 K (Kelvin)). Since they vary with pressure and temperature, gas volumes are often compared under standard conditions. Thus, **standard temperature and pressure (s.t.p.)** is taken as 273 K (i.e. 0°C) and 101 325 Pa (i.e. 1 atm).

In fact, there are no ideal gases! However, under certain conditions, real gases can approximate to ideal behaviour, as we shall see in the next section.

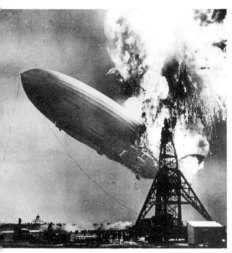

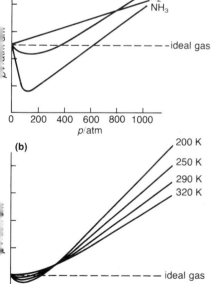

Figure 8.2 *Graphs of pV plotted against p for (a) the same number of moles of O₂(g), H₂(g), NH₃(g) and an ideal gas at constant temperature, and (b) 1 mole of nitrogen at different temperatures*

8.2 Real gases

Activity 8.1 will help you to identify the conditions under which a real gas will behave like an ideal gas.

Activity 8.1

1 Figure 8.2(a) shows how pV varies with p for an ideal gas and the real gases, ammonia, hydrogen and oxygen (at constant temperature, equal numbers of moles of each gas).
   Do the real gases behave ideally (i) at very low pressures and (ii) as the pressure is gradually increased?
2 Figure 8.2(b) shows the variation of pV with p for one mole of nitrogen at different temperatures. Does nitrogen resemble an ideal gas more closely at lower or higher absolute temperature?
3 Figures 8.2(a) and (b) are typical of the pV against p plots obtained with other real gases. Can you draw any conclusions, then, about the conditions under which real gases are most likely to behave ideally?

From this activity, we conclude that *real gases behave like ideal gases at*
▶ *low pressure*, e.g. 1 atmosphere (1 atm) = 101 325 Pa
▶ *high absolute temperature*, e.g. 293 K (i.e. 20 °C).

You may be wondering whether the ideal gas concept is much use! Well, most people experience gases at high absolute temperature and low pressure (e.g. 293 K and 1 atm). Since the ideal gas equation holds true under these conditions, it is often useful (for example, in calculating relative molecular masses, section 8.3).

· Deviations from ideal gas behaviour are considered further in section 8.9. In the meantime, we shall assume that our real gas samples are behaving ideally.

8.3 Using the ideal gas equation to work out the relative molecular masses of gases and volatile liquids

Although relative molecular masses may be very accurately measured using a **mass spectrometer** (section 2.3), these instruments are expensive and not always available. Simple, yet fairly accurate, methods for measuring the **relative molecular masses (M_r)** of gases and volatile liquids are based on the use of the ideal gas equation, $pV = nRT$. Now,

$$\text{number of moles of gas, } n = \frac{\text{mass of gas, } m}{\text{relative molecular mass, } M_r}$$

Substituting in the ideal gas equation, we get

$$pV = \frac{mRT}{M_r}$$

and, rearranging,

$$M_r = \frac{mRT}{pV}.$$

To find the relative molecular mass, M_r, therefore, we measure the mass m of a known volume V of gas at known absolute temperature T and pressure p. Finally, we substitute these values into the above equation, remembering to keep a consistent set of units (see table 8.2).

Figure 8.3 *Apparatus for determining the relative molecular mass of a gas*

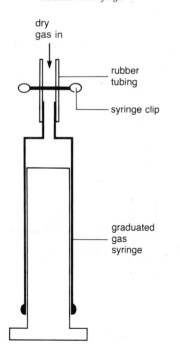

dry
gas in

rubber
tubing

syringe clip

graduated
gas
syringe

Table 8.2 *When using $pV = nRT$, use either box A or box B units but don't mix them. (If a pressure is given in mm Hg, convert it to atm or Pa; thus 1 mm Hg = 1.32×10^{-3} atm = 133.3 Pa)*

	box A	OR	box B
p = pressure in	atm		Pa
V = volume in	dm³		m³
R = gas constant	0.082 atm dm³ K⁻¹ mol⁻¹		8.31 J K⁻¹ mol⁻¹

n = number of gas moles
T = absolute temperature (K)

Full experimental details may be found in practical chemistry textbooks. However, two methods for finding the relative molecular mass of a gas and a volatile liquid are outlined below. Both methods involve the use of a glass gas syringe of capacity 100 cm³.

(a) Finding the relative molecular mass of gas X

1 A gas syringe, containing 10 cm³ of air, is fitted with a small piece of rubber tubing and a clip (figure 8.3).
2 The whole apparatus is weighed.
3 Then about 80 cm³ of dry X(g) is allowed into the syringe.
4 The apparatus containing the air/X(g) mixture is re-weighed.
5 Finally, the temperature and pressure are noted.

Specimen results
Step 1: volume of air $= \quad 10\,cm^3$
Step 2: mass of syringe, tubing, clip and air $= 200.00\,g$
Step 3: volume of air + X(g) $= \quad 90\,cm^3$
Step 4: mass of syringe, tubing, clip, air and X(g) $= 200.15\,g$
Step 5: **temperature = 21 °C (i.e. 294 K);**   **pressure** $=$ **750 mm Hg**

Calculation

1   volume of air + X(g) $= \quad 90\,cm^3$
       volume of air $= -10\,cm^3$

       volume of X(g), V $= \quad 80\,cm^3$
Now, $1\,cm^3 = 0.001\,dm^3$
       $V = 80\,cm^3 = 0.001 \times 80 = 0.08\,dm^3$

2   mass of syringe + cap + air + X(g) $= 200.15\,g$
       mass of syringe + cap + air $= 200.00\,g$

       mass of X(g), m $= \quad$ **0.15 g**

3   Convert mm Hg into atm:
       $760\,mm\,Hg = 1\,atm$
       $p = 750\,mm\,Hg = 1 \times 750/760 = 0.987\,atm$
       pressure, $p = 0.987\,atm$

4   For units of atm and dm^3, $R = 0.082\,atm\,dm^3\,K^{-1}\,mol^{-1}$.

5   Using the equation

$$M_r = \frac{mRT}{pV}$$

and substituting values,

$$M_r = \frac{0.15 \times 0.082 \times 294}{0.987 \times 0.08}$$

which gives $M_r\,(X(g)) = 46$.

These results were obtained for carbon dioxide, $M_r = 44$. Obviously, this method cannot be relied on to give very accurate relative molecular masses. However, the values obtained are sufficiently accurate to allow molecular formulae to be worked out from empirical formulae (section 6.2).

(b) Finding the relative molecular mass of a volatile liquid

This method can be used for liquids which boil below 80 °C.

1   A glass syringe (containing a little air) is placed into a steam jacket (figure 8.4). The air expands and its final volume is noted.

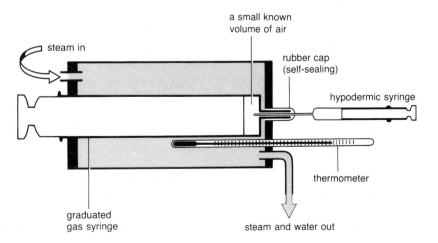

Figure 8.4 *Apparatus used to determine the relative molecular mass of a volatile liquid*

2 Next, a known mass of the volatile liquid is injected into the gas syringe. As the liquid vaporises, the syringe plunger is pushed out further and the final volume of vapour plus air is noted.

3 Finally, the temperature in the steam jacket and the atmospheric pressure are noted.

Calculation

The relative molecular mass is calculated using the same method as in (a) above.

Activity 8.2

Using the methods outlined above, a student obtained the following results:

1 For a gas

Step 1: volume of air	$= 10\,cm^3$
Step 2: mass of syringe, cap and air	$= 206.35\,g$
Step 3: volume of air + gas	$= 86\,cm^3$
Step 4: mass of syringe, cap, air and gas	$= 206.56\,g$
Step 5: temperature = 23 °C; pressure	$= 756\,mm\,Hg$

2 For a volatile liquid

Step 1: volume of air	$= 12\,cm^3$
Step 2: mass of volatile liquid	$= 0.24\,g$
volume of vapour + air	$= 95\,cm^3$
Step 3: temperature = 100 °C; pressure	$= 100\,680\,Pa$

In each case, calculate the relative molecular mass of the sample. (Remember, don't mix your units (see table 8.2).

8.4 The gas laws of Gay–Lussac and Avogadro

Towards the end of the eighteenth century, a lot of research was focused on the chemical reactions of gases. In 1809, Gay-Lussac published his **Law of Combining Volumes**: *the volumes of reacting gases and the volumes of any gas products are in a simple whole number ratio, providing temperature and pressure remain constant.* In 1811, Avogadro explained this law by supposing that *equal volumes of gases, at fixed temperature and pressure, contain the same number of molecules.* For example, in the reaction,

hydrogen + chlorine → hydrogen chloride

the volume ratio is . . .	1	:	1	:	2

Applying Avogadro's idea,

the ratio of molecules is also . . .	1	:	1	:	2

and the chemical equation must be . . . $H_2(g) + Cl_2(g) \rightarrow 2HCl(g)$.

At the time, Avogadro's idea was ignored, mainly because Dalton's Atomic Theory (1807) did not allow for 'X_2' type molecules. In fact, nearly fifty years passed before Avogadro's theory was accepted! Nowadays, it is often called **Avogadro's Law**.

Since we count molecules in mole quantities, it follows from Avogadro's Law that *equal volumes of all gases at constant temperature and pressure will contain the same number of moles of gas.* For example,

if **10** dm^3 of methane, $CH_4(g)$, contain **1** mole of gas
then **20** dm^3 of nitrogen, $N_2(g)$, will contain **2** moles of gas
and **40** dm^3 of helium, $He(g)$, will contain **4** moles of gas,

providing that temperature and pressure remain constant.

Avogadro's Law can be used to work out the volume change during a gas reaction, as shown below.

Example 1

Calculate the change in volume when $20\,cm^3$ of propane, C_3H_8, is burnt in $200\,cm^3$ of oxygen, assuming all products are gases (p and T constant).

Solution

The equation is

$$C_3H_8(g) + 5O_2(g) \rightarrow 3CO_2(g) + 4H_2O(g)$$

mole ratio	1	:	5	:	3	:	4
vol. ratio	1	:	5	:	3	:	4

Now, $20\,cm^3$ propane needs only $5 \times 20 = 100\,cm^3$ of oxygen
∴ $100\,cm^3$ are left over.
     Also, $3 \times 20 = 60\,cm^3$ of $CO_2(g)$ and $4 \times 20 = 80\,cm^3$ of $H_2O(g)$ are formed.
Thus,

$$\begin{array}{rr} \text{volume formed} = 60 + 80 = & 140 \\ + \text{ volume unused} = & + 100 \\ \hline \text{TOTAL} \quad = & 240 \end{array}$$

Subtracting the starting volume of $220\,cm^3$ gives a volume change $= +20\,cm^3$.

     This type of calculation can be used to determine the molecular formula of a hydrocarbon from the volume change during combustion (see activity 34.2).

8.5 Comparing the molar volumes of gas

The *volume of one mole of gas* is called its **molar volume, V_m**. It follows from Avogadro's Law that all ideal gases will have the same molar volume at constant temperature and pressure. For one mole of an ideal gas at s.t.p.,

$$pV_m = nRT$$

where $p = 101\ 325\,Pa$, $T = 273.15\,K$, $R = 8.31\,J\,K^{-1}\,mol^{-1}$ and $n = 1$. Substituting these values gives $V_m = 0.0224\,m^3$ or $22.4\,dm^3$. At s.t.p., then, the molar volume of an ideal gas is found to be $22.4\,dm^3$. Activity 8.3 considers the molar volumes of some real gases.

Activity 8.3

Table 8.3 lists the molar volumes of some gases at s.t.p., together with the temperatures at which they liquefy (at 1 atm).

Table 8.3 *Molar volumes at s.t.p. for some gases and their liquefaction temperatures (at 1 atm pressure)*

Gas	molar volume/dm^3	liquefaction temperature/K
helium	22.44	4.21
hydrogen	22.41	20.4
carbon dioxide	22.26	162
ethene, C_2H_4	22.25	169
ethyne, C_2H_2	22.16	189
ammonia	22.08	240

1   Which gases behave ideally at s.t.p.? Which do not?
2   Which gas least resembles an ideal gas under these conditions?
3   On lowering the temperature, which gases would liquefy first, the most or the least ideal?

Two points arise from this activity:

▶ *At s.t.p., many real gases behave ideally; others show slight deviations.* However, since the errors involved are so small (maximum about 1.5% for ammonia), *we assume that one mole of any real gas occupies a volume of 22.4 dm³ at s.t.p.*

▶ Not surprisingly, the gases which are least ideal tend to be the most easily liquefied.

8.6 Diffusion and effusion of gases: Graham's Law

Consider the two simple experiments described below.

Experiment I

When a few drops of bromine are placed in a gas jar, some of the bromine vaporises and spreads throughout the air in the jar. Eventually, the whole jar is filled with the red-brown bromine/air mixture. Although it is denser than air, the bromine moves upwards and mixes with the air. This *slow mixing of gases within a given volume* is known as **gaseous diffusion**.

Experiment II

The next question is, 'Do gases diffuse at the same speeds?' In this experiment, gas syringes containing ammonia and hydrogen chloride are connected to the ends of a long glass tube. On removing the clips, the gases are free to diffuse along the tube. After a few minutes, a white deposit of ammonium chloride forms on the side of the tube but nearer to the syringe which contained the hydrogen chloride. Thus, *ammonia must diffuse faster than hydrogen chloride.*

Experiment II suggests that gases diffuse at different rates. Graham measured the rates of diffusion of gases through a porous material and, in 1832, he published his **Law of Gaseous Diffusion**. This states that *the rate of diffusion of a gas, r_d, at constant temperature and pressure, is inversely proportional to the square root of its density, d.* Thus, $r_d \propto 1/\sqrt{d}$. If we apply this law to the diffusion rates of two gases, X and Y, we find that

$$\frac{r_d(X)}{r_d(Y)} = \sqrt{\frac{d(Y)}{d(X)}}$$

Now,

$$\text{density, } d = \frac{\text{mass of one mole of gas, } M_r}{\text{molar volume, } V_m}$$

Thus,

$$\frac{r_d(X)}{r_d(Y)} = \sqrt{\frac{d(Y)}{d(X)}} = \sqrt{\frac{M_r(Y)V_m(X)}{M_r(X)V_m(Y)}}$$

But, from Avogadro's Law, all ideal gases have the same molar volume at constant temperature and pressure. Thus, $V_m(X) = V_m(Y)$ and they cancel out, to give:

$$\frac{r_d(X)}{r_d(Y)} = \sqrt{\frac{M_r(Y)}{M_r(X)}}$$

The equation shows that *lighter gases diffuse faster than heavier gases* (e.g. ammonia ($M_r = 17$) diffused faster than hydrogen chloride ($M_r = 36.5$) in experiment II).

Figure 8.5 *Apparatus used to measure the rate of effusion of a gas. As the plunger moves downwards under gravity, the gas is forced through the pin-hole. We measure the time it takes for a known volume of gas to effuse*

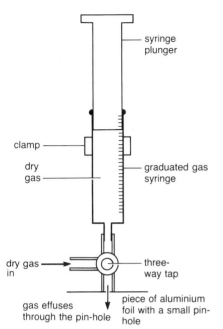

The relative molecular mass of a gas can be obtained from its rate of effusion. The *diffusion of a pressurised gas through a very small hole* is known as **effusion**. In practice, rates of effusion, r_e, are easier to measure than diffusion rates (figure 8.5), Also, we find that

$$\frac{r_e(X)}{r_e(Y)} = \sqrt{\frac{M_r(Y)}{M_r(X)}}$$

Consequently, we can measure the molecular mass of a gas by comparing its rate of effusion with that of a gas of known molecular mass. A typical calculation is shown below.

Example 2

When pressurised, $60\,cm^3$ of sulphur dioxide effuses through a very small hole in 176 s. Under the same conditions, $45\,cm^3$ of gas X effuses in 150 s. Calculate the relative molecular mass of gas X. $(A_r(S) = 32, A_r(O) = 16)$

Solution

1 Calculate the rates of effusion, r_e:

$$r_e(SO_2) = \frac{\text{volume effused}}{\text{time taken}} = \frac{60\,cm^3}{176\,s} = 0.34\,cm^3\,s^{-1}$$

$$r_e(X) = \frac{\text{volume effused}}{\text{time taken}} = \frac{45\,cm^3}{150\,s} = 0.30\,cm^3\,s^{-1}$$

2 Work out the molecular mass of the known gas; (here it is sulphur dioxide). Thus, $M_r(SO_2) = 32 + 2(16) = 64$

3 From Graham's Law:

$$\frac{r_e(SO_2)}{r_e(X)} = \sqrt{\frac{M_r(X)}{M_r(SO_2)}}$$

Substituting values,

$$\frac{0.34\,cm^3\,s^{-1}}{0.30\,cm^3\,s^{-1}} = \sqrt{\frac{M_r(X)}{M_r(SO_2)}}$$

$$1.13 = \sqrt{\frac{M_r(X)}{64}}$$

Square both sides and rearrange to get

$$1.28 \times 64 = M_r(X)$$
$$81.92 = M_r(X)$$

The relative molecular mass of X(g) is 82.

Activity 8.4

$360\,cm^3$ of oxygen diffuse through a porous material in 15 minutes. Under the same conditions, $600\,cm^3$ of unknown gas, X, diffuse in 30 minutes. Calculate the relative molecular mass of gas X. $(A_r(O) = 16)$

8.7 Dalton's Law of Partial Pressures

After studying the pressures of various gas mixtures, Dalton proposed the **Law of Partial Pressures** (1801). This states that *the total pressure of a gas mixture is equal to* the sum of the individual pressures that each gas would exert if it alone occupied the container. The individual pressure of each gas in the mixture is called its **partial pressure, p.** So, for a mixture of gases A, B, and C,

total pressure of the gas mixture = sum of the partial pressures

or $\qquad p_{total} \qquad = \qquad p_A + p_B + p_C$

The question is, 'How to calculate the partial pressure of each gas in the mixture?'

According to the Kinetic Theory (section 8.8), gas molecules exert a pressure by colliding with the retaining surface. Thus, the partial pressure of each gas in a mixture will be proportional to its mole fraction in the mixture, i.e.

$$p_X = \frac{\text{moles of X(g)}}{\text{total number of gas moles}} \times p_{total}$$

or $p_x = f_x \times p_{total}$ where f_x is the mole fraction of X(g) in the mixture.

Two calculations involving Dalton's Law are given below. Notice the use of Avogadro's Law in example 4.

Example 3

At 430 °C, a mixture of 1.48 moles A(g), 0.38 moles B(g) and 0.14 moles C(g) has a total pressure of 40 530 Pa. Calculate the partial pressure of each gas.

Solution

$$
\begin{aligned}
\text{Total number of gas moles} &= \text{moles A + moles B + moles C} \\
&= \quad 1.48 \quad + \quad 0.38 \quad + \quad 0.14 \\
&= 2.00 \text{ moles}
\end{aligned}
$$

From Dalton's Law,

$$p_A = f_A \times p_{total} = \frac{1.48}{2.00} \times 40\,530 = 29\,992 \text{ Pa}$$

$$p_B = f_B \times p_{total} = \frac{0.38}{2.00} \times 40\,530 = \quad 7701 \text{ Pa}$$

$$p_C = f_C = p_{total} = \frac{0.14}{2.00} \times 40\,530 = \quad 2837 \text{ Pa}$$

(Check your answer by adding the partial pressures: 29 992 + 7701 + 2837 = 40 530 Pa, as given.)

Example 4

At 450°C, a gas mixture has the volume composition 69% H_2(g), 23% N_2(g), 8% NH_3(g) and a total pressure of 45 atm. Calculate the partial pressure of each gas.

Solution

Equal gas volumes contain the same number of gas moles at constant T and p (Avogadro's Law). Thus:

If the volume ratio is $69\,H_2$(g): $23\,N_2$(g): $8\,NH_3$(g)
then the mole ratio is also $69\,H_2$(g) : $23\,N_2$(g) : $8\,NH_3$(g).
So, the percentage composition gives the mole fraction of each gas.

$$p_{H_2} = f_{H_2} \times p_{total} = \frac{69}{100} \times 45 = 31.05 \text{ atm}$$

$$p_{N_2} = f_{N_2} \times p_{total} = \frac{23}{100} \times 45 = 10.35 \text{ atm}$$

$$p_{NH_3} = f_{NH_3} \times p_{total} = \frac{8}{100} \times 45 = \quad 3.60 \text{ atm}$$

(Check: total pressure = 31.05 + 10.35 + 3.60 = 45.00 atm, as given.)

Activity 8.5

1   200 cm³ of hydrogen, 500 cm³ of nitrogen and 300 cm³ of helium, each at 20°C and 1 atm, were placed in a container of 500 cm³ capacity.
    (a) What will be the pressure of the gas mixture (assuming that the temperature remains constant)?
    (b) Calculate the partial pressures of each gas in the mixture. (Hint: see example 3).

2   Dinitrogen tetroxide dissociates according to the equation:

$$N_2O_4(g) \rightleftharpoons 2NO_2(g)$$

At 293 K and 4 atm pressure, the reaction mixture contains 94% N_2O_4 molecules. Calculate the partial pressure of each gas in the mixture.

8.8 The Kinetic Theory of Gases

All the gas laws mentioned so far are only *completely* accurate for ideal gases. In section 8.2, we saw that real gases deviate from ideal behaviour at low temperature and high pressure. Over the years, many scientists have put forward theories which account for the behaviour of ideal and real gases. One of these, the **Kinetic Theory of Gases**, was proposed by **Maxwell and Boltzmann** in 1859. This theory explains ideal gas behaviour by making five main assumptions:

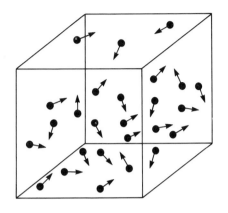

Figure 8.6 *Gas particles move rapidly in random directions*

1   *Gas molecules are always moving rapidly in random directions*, colliding with each other and the walls of the container. In this way, the gas molecules exert a pressure on the container's walls (figure 8.6). Between collisions, the molecules travel in straight lines.
2   Collisions are said to be **perfectly elastic**; this means that *there is no overall loss of kinetic energy on collision.*
3   *The distance between collisions, known as the **mean free path**, is massive compared to the molecules' size.* From this it follows that the volume of the molecules is negligible compared to that of the container.
4   Since the molecules are so far apart, *the attractive forces between them are negligible.*
5   *When a gas is warmed, the molecules convert all the heat energy into kinetic energy.* In fact, the average kinetic energy of the molecules is proportional to the absolute temperature.

Using this model of an ideal gas, **Clausius** derived the **kinetic theory equation** for a gas:

$$pV = \frac{1}{3} mn \sqrt{\overline{c^2}}$$

where p = pressure, V = volume, m = mass of the molecule, and n = number of molecules. $\sqrt{\overline{c^2}}$ is known as the **root mean square velocity**, and this may be thought of as the *average velocity during the molecule's 3-dimensional movement*. Since it is possible to derive all the gas laws from the kinetic theory equation, the five assumptions in the ideal gas model are justified. (A full mathematical treatment can be found in most advanced physical chemistry textbooks.)

8.9 Real gases and van der Waals' equation

Real gases only show ideal behaviour at low pressure and high temperature. To explain real gas behaviour at all pressures and temperatures, the ideal gas model must be modified. One such theory, due to van der Waals, is outlined below.

As pressure increases and temperature decreases, the gas molecules are forced closer together and this causes the mean free path to get smaller. Eventually, the mean free path is no longer massive compared to the molecule's size. When this happens:

▶ *the total volume of the molecules themselves, b, will not be negligible compared to the volume, V, of the container* (figure 8.7). Thus, the actual volume available for the gas molecules to move in will be (V−b).

Figure 8.7 *At high pressure and low temperature, the volume of gas molecules is not negligible compared to the volume of the container*

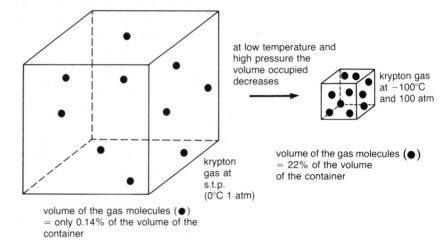

at low temperature and high pressure the volume occupied decreases

krypton gas at −100°C and 100 atm

volume of the gas molecules (●) = 22% of the volume of the container

krypton gas at s.t.p. (0°C 1 atm)

volume of the gas molecules (●) = only 0.14% of the volume of the container

▶ *the attractive forces between the molecules get stronger.* For a molecule in the middle of the gas volume, these forces cancel out (figure 8.8a). However, a molecule near the container wall experiences an overall inward force of attraction (figure 8.8b). Van der Waals proved that

$$\text{inward force} = \frac{a}{V^2}$$

where V is the volume and a is a constant for a given gas. Due to this inward force, *a real gas exerts less pressure on the retaining walls than does the same volume of an ideal gas.* Thus, under the same conditions,

pressure of an = pressure of a real gas + inward force
ideal gas

i.e.
$$p_{\text{ideal}} = p_{\text{real}} + \frac{a}{V^2}$$

Van der Waals took the ideal gas equation

$$p_{\text{ideal}} V_{\text{ideal}} = nRT$$

and substituted his modified volume and pressure terms:

$$\left(p_{\text{real}} + \frac{a}{V^2}\right)(V-b) = nRT$$

Figure 8.8 *Attractive forces between gas molecules in (a) the middle of the container and (b) near the wall of the container*

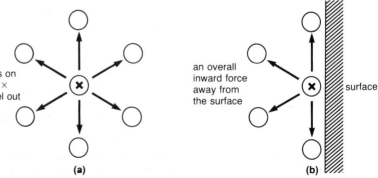

forces on atom × cancel out

an overall inward force away from the surface

surface

(a)

(b)

This is known as **van der Waals' equation**. Let us see how it explains real gas behaviour.

Real gases behave ideally at low pressure and high temperature. Under these conditions, *the volume (V) will be large*. Consequently, a/V^2 becomes very small and p_{real} approximates to p_{ideal}. Also, the volume occupied by the gas, V, will be much larger than the actual volume of the gas molecules, b. Thus, $(V-b) \simeq V_{ideal}$. As expected, this causes van der Waals' equation to simplify to the ideal gas equation.

Real gases show the greatest deviation from ideal behaviour at low temperature and high pressure. Under these conditions, the volume will not be large enough for the a/V^2 and b terms to be ignored. In fact, real gases having high values for a and b show the greatest deviation from the ideal gas model.

Experimental results show that the van der Waals' equation predicts, quite accurately, how the volume of a real gas varies with the temperature and pressure. In recognition of his work, the attractive forces between gas molecules were called **van der Waals' forces**. Lowering the temperature and raising the pressure causes an increase in the strength of the van der Waals' forces; eventually, the gas liquefies. (van der Waals' forces are discussed further in section 8.12).

8.10 The distribution of molecular speeds in gases

When gas molecules are warmed, they absorb heat energy and convert it into kinetic energy. Most of this energy is associated with translational motion, that is, the movement of the molecules through space (figure 8.9). *Due to their random motion*

Figure 8.9 *(a) Translational, (b) vibrational and (c) rotational motion in polyatomic gas molecules, (e.g. SO_2, H_2O, H_2S)*

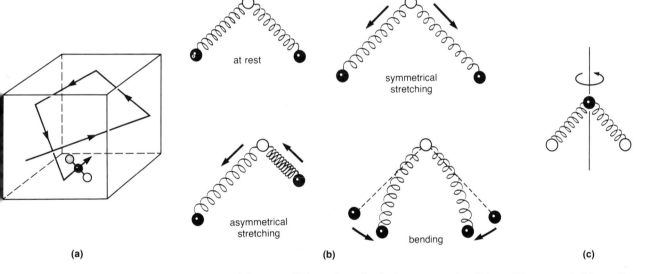

(a) (b) (c)

and frequent collisions, the molecules in a gas sample will have different speeds. Maxwell and Boltzmann calculated the **distribution of molecular speeds** in a gas at various temperatures (figure 8.10). You should note the following features of these curves:

▶ Very few molecules are slow moving and none are stationary.
▶ As the temperature is raised:
  (i) there is an increase in the average speed (and average translational kinetic energy);
  (ii) the shape of the curve alters, with more molecules having high speeds and fewer molecules having low speeds.
▶ The total number of molecules is proportional to the area under the curve. For the same gas sample, this area remains constant whatever the temperature.

Figure 8.10 *Distribution of molecular speeds in a gas sample at two different temperatures, T_1 and T_2*

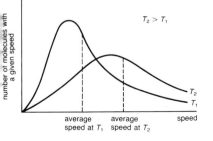

In section 12.3, we shall use these distribution curves to explain the effect of temperature on the rate of a reaction.

Figure 8.11 *(a) Intermolecular dipole–dipole attractions between propanone molecules; (b) hydrogen bonding between methanoic acid molecules*

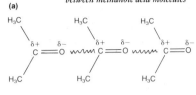

(a)

(b)

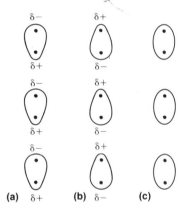

ʌʌʌ = dipole–dipole attraction

Figure 8.12 *(a) and (b) Unequal sharing of the molecular electron cloud at two instants in time. (c) Overall, though, the cloud is evenly distributed, that is, there is no permanent dipole*

Figure 8.13 *Branched alkanes have lower boiling points than straight chain isomers*

2,2-dimethylpropane
b.p. 10 °C

2- methylbutane
b.p. 28 °C

pentane
b.p. 36 °C

8.11 Applying Kinetic Theory to the liquid state

The Kinetic Theory proposes that, compared with gas molecules, those in a liquid
▶ *move less rapidly*, though still in random directions;
▶ *are much closer together and have appreciable attraction for each other.* These attractive forces enable the molecules of the liquid to form small groups, or **clusters**. These move through the bulk of the liquid which exists as single molecules.

8.12 Intermolecular forces

In section 8.9, we saw that *intermolecular forces get stronger as a gas is cooled and pressurised.* There are two main types of intermolecular force: dipole–dipole attractions and van der Waals' forces.

(a) Dipole–dipole attractions

These exist between unsymmetrical molecules which contain permanent dipoles, e.g. propanone (figure 8.11a),

Hydrogen bonds are an important type of dipole–dipole attraction. In these, *at least one of the interacting dipoles contains a hydrogen atom bonded directly to a nitrogen, oxygen or fluorine atom*, e.g. methanoic acid (figure 8.11b).

Dipole–dipole interactions and hydrogen bonding are also discussed in section 5.9.

(b) Van der Waals' forces

These are weak attractive forces which exist between closely positioned non-polar molecules (e.g. between bromine molecules).

A molecule's electron cloud is in a state of continual motion. At a given moment in time, the electron cloud may not be evenly spread over the molecule. The resulting temporary dipole induces dipoles in neighbouring molecules, and these then attract each other (figure 8.12a). In the next instant, the direction of polarity changes, but the intermolecular attraction remains (figure 8.12b). *Van der Waals' forces result from these induced dipole–induced dipole attractions.* Remember, however, that on average, the electron density remains evenly distributed within each molecule; thus, *the molecules do not have a permanent dipole.*

Van der Waals' forces will be stronger if:
▶ *the molecules have large electron clouds*, e.g.

	F_2	Cl_2	Br_2	I_2	
electron cloud	⟶				gets larger
van der Waals' forces	⟶				get stronger
boiling points/°C	−188	−34	58	183	increase

▶ *the molecules get closer to one another*, e.g. branched alkanes have lower boiling points than the straight chain isomers:

branching	⟶	decreases
electron cloud	⟶	gets less spherical
molecules	⟶	can get closer together
van der Waals' forces	⟶	get stronger
boiling points/°C	⟶	increase

Compared to chemical bond strengths, van der Waals' forces are extremely weak. However, as molecular size increases, there will be many points of contact between neighbouring molecules. In these cases, van der Waals' forces can make a significant contribution to the strength of the material, e.g. in non-polar polymers such as polythene (section 35.8).

8.13 Comments on the activities

Activity 8.1

1 (i) Yes, the curves for the real and ideal gases tend towards the same point at low pressure (e.g. 1 atm); (ii) generally speaking, as the pressure increases the gases show greater deviations from ideal behaviour.

2 Nitrogen, like other real gases, more closely resembles an ideal gas as the absolute temperature is raised.

3 *Real gases tend towards ideal behaviour at low pressure and high absolute temperature.*

Activity 8.2

Question 1

(Use box A units, table 8.2.)

1   volume of air + gas   = $86 \, cm^3$

           volume of air   = $10 \, cm^3$

      $\therefore$ volume of gas, V = $76 \, cm^3$

      Now, $1 \, cm^3 = 0.001 \, dm^3$

           $\therefore V = 76 \, cm^3 = 0.001 \times 76 = 0.076 \, dm^3$

2   mass of syringe + cap + air + gas   = $206.56 \, g$

           mass of syringe + cap + air   = $206.35 \, g$

      $\therefore$ mass of gas, m = $0.21 \, g$

3       $760 \, mm \, Hg = 1 \, atm$

      $p = 756 \, mm \, Hg = 756 \times 1/760 = 0.995 \, atm$

      $\therefore$ pressure, $p = 0.995 \, atm$

4   For units of atm and dm^3, $R = 0.082 \, atm \, dm^3 \, K^{-1} \, mol^{-1}$.

5   Using the equation

$$M_r = \frac{mRT}{pV}$$

and substituting,

$$M_r = \frac{0.21 \times 0.082 \times 296}{0.995 \times 0.076}$$

gives $M_r = 67.4$.

These results were obtained for sulphur dioxide, accurate $M_r = 64$.

Question 2

(Use box B units, table 8.2.)

1   volume of air + vapour   = $95 \, cm^3$

           volume of air   = $12 \, cm^3$

      $\therefore$ volume of gas, V = $83 \, cm^3$

      Now, $1 \, cm^3 = 10^{-6} \, m^3$

           $\therefore V = 83 \, cm^3 = 83 \times 10^{-6} \, m^3$

2   mass of volatile liquid, $m = 0.24 \, g$

3   For units of Pa and m^3, $R = 8.31 \, J \, K^{-1} \, mol^{-1}$.

4   Using the equation

$$M_r = \frac{mRT}{pV}$$

and substituting,

$$M_r = \frac{0.24 \times 8.31 \times 373}{100 \, 680 \times 83 \times 10^{-6}}$$

gives $M_r = 89.0$

These results were obtained for hexane, C_6H_{14}, accurate $M_r = 86$.

Activity 8.3

1 Helium and hydrogen; these have a molar volume which is almost identical to that of an ideal gas. As we descend table 8.3, the gases show greater deviations from ideal behaviour.
2 Ammonia.
3 The first gases to liquefy would be those which behave least like an ideal gas at s.t.p., e.g. ammonia and ethyne.

Activity 8.4

1 Calculate the rates of diffusion, r_d:

$$r_d(O_2) \quad = \frac{\text{volume diffused}}{\text{time taken}} = \frac{360\,\text{cm}^3}{15\,\text{min}} = 24\,\text{cm}^3\,\text{min}^{-1}$$

$$r_d(X) \quad = \frac{\text{volume diffused}}{\text{time taken}} = \frac{600\,\text{cm}^3}{30\,\text{min}} = 20\,\text{cm}^3\,\text{min}^{-1}$$

2 Work out the molecular mass of the known gas: here it is oxygen. Thus, $M_r(O_2) = 2(16) = 32$.
3 From Graham's Law:

$$\frac{r_d(O_2)}{r_d(X)} = \sqrt{\frac{M_r(X)}{M_r(O_2)}}$$

Substituting values,

$$\frac{24\,\text{cm}^3\,\text{min}^{-1}}{20\,\text{cm}^3\,\text{min}^{-1}} = \sqrt{\frac{M_r(X)}{M_r(O_2)}}$$

$$1.2 \quad = \sqrt{\frac{M_r(X)}{32}}$$

Square both sides and rearrange to get

$$1.44 \times 32 = M_r(X)$$
$$46.1 \quad = M_r(X)$$

The relative molecular mass of gas X is 46.

Activity 8.5

1 (a) Original total gas volume, $V_1 = 200 + 500 + 300 = 1000\,\text{cm}^3$ at $p_1 = 1\,\text{atm}$. Final volume, $V_2 = 500\,\text{cm}^3$ at $p_2 = ?\,\text{atm}$.
Since T remains constant, $p_1V_1 \quad = p_2V_2$
$$1 \times 1000 = p_2 \times 500$$
from which $p_2 = 1000/500 = 2\,\text{atm}$.

(b) Although the pressure changes, the number of gas moles remains constant. Thus, from Avogadro's Law:
if the volume ratio is $200\,H_2(g) : 500\,N_2(g) : 300\,He(g)$,
then the mole ratio is also $200\,H_2(g) : 500\,N_2(g) : 300\,He(g)$.
From Dalton's Law,

$$p_A \quad = f_A \quad \times p_{total}$$

$$p_{H_2} = f_{H_2} \quad \times p_{total} = \frac{200}{1000} \times 2 = 0.4\,\text{atm}$$

$$p_{N_2} = f_{N_2} \quad \times p_{total} = \frac{500}{1000} \times 2 = 1.0\,\text{atm}$$

$$p_{He} = f_{He} \times p_{total} = \frac{300}{1000} \times 2 = 0.6 \, atm$$

(Check: total pressure = 0.4 + 1.0 + 0.6 = 2 atm, as given.)

2 Equal gas volumes contain the same number of gas moles at constant T and p (Avogadro's Law). Thus,

if the volume ratio is $94 N_2O_4(g) : 6 NO_2(g)$,

then the mole ratio is also $94 N_2O_4(g) : 6 NO_2(g)$.

So, the percentage composition gives the mole fraction of each gas.

$$p_{N_2O_4} = f_{N_2O_4} \times p_{total} = \frac{94}{100} \times 4 = 3.76 \, atm$$

$$p_{NO_2} = f_{NO_2} \times p_{total} = \frac{6}{100} \times 4 = 0.24 \, atm$$

(Check: total pressure = 3.76 + 0.24 = 4 atm, as given.)

8.14 Summary and revision plan

1 The **absolute zero** of temperature, 0 Kelvin (K), is taken as $-273\,°C$. Thus,

$$X°C = (273 + X) K$$

2 **Ideal gases** obey the equation

$$pV = nRT$$

at all temperatures and pressures (where n = number of gas moles and R = the gas constant. Real gases behave like ideal gases at high absolute temperatures and low pressures (e.g. at 293 K and 1 atm (101 325 Pa).

3 When using the ideal gas equation, don't mix your units (see table 8.2).

4 The equation

$$\frac{p_1 V_1}{T_1} = \frac{p_2 V_2}{T_2}$$

is used to compare the volumes of a fixed mass of gas at different absolute temperatures and pressures.

5 Methods based on the ideal gas equation can be used to determine the relative molecular mass of (i) a gas and (ii) a volatile liquid, (section 8.3).

6 **Avogadro's Law** states that equal volumes of all gases contain the same number of molecules (i.e. the same number of moles of gas).

7 At s.t.p., the **molar volume** of an ideal gas is $22.4 \, dm^3$ (s.t.p. = 273 K and 1 atm (101 325 Pa)). Only small errors result if we use this value for real gases.

8 Since gas molecules move in random directions, they will spread themselves evenly throughout any volume they occupy. This process is known as **diffusion**.

9 **Graham's Law of Diffusion** states that the rate of diffusion of a gas, r_d, at constant temperature and pressure, is inversely proportional to the square root of its density. From this law, we derive the useful expression

$$\frac{r_d(X)}{r_d(Y)} = \sqrt{\frac{M_r(Y)}{M_r(X)}}$$

If r_d values are measured, and $M_r(Y)$ is known, then $M_r(X)$ can be determined. Rates of effusion (r_e), that is, the escape of a pressurised gas through a small hole, can also be used in the above equation instead of r_d.

10 **Dalton's Law of Partial Pressures** states that for a mixture of gases

$$p_{total} = p_A + p_B + p_C + \ldots$$

where $p_A, p_B, p_C, \ldots$ are the partial pressures of the individual gases, A, B, C, and so on. The partial pressure of a gas is the pressure that it would exert if it alone occupied the container.

11
$$\text{partial pressure of A(g)} = \frac{\text{moles of gas A}}{\text{total number of gas moles}} \times \text{total pressure of the gas mixture}$$

12 **The Kinetic Theory of Gases** states that ideal gas molecules
   (1) move rapidly in random directions,
   (2) undergo elastic collisions,
   (3) have a mean free path $\rangle\rangle$ the molecule's size,
   (4) do not attract each other,
   (5) have an average kinetic energy proportional to the absolute temperature.

13 Except at low temperatures and high pressures (when assumptions (3) and (4) above become untrue), real gases do fit in with the ideal gas model.

14 Real gas behaviour at all temperatures and pressures may be explained using **van der Waals' equation**,

$$\left(p_{\text{real gas}} + \frac{a}{V^2}\right)(V - b) = RT$$

where a/V^2 is the overall inward force of attraction on gas molecules near the container walls and b is the volume of the actual gas molecules.

15 The molecules in a gas have a range of speeds, as described by the **Maxwell–Boltzmann distribution** (figure 8.10).

16 Compared to gas molecules, those of liquids
   (1) move slower, but still randomly,
   (2) experience much stronger intermolecular forces,
   (3) move minute distances between collisions,
   (4) exist in small groups and as individual molecules.

17 Compared to chemical bond strengths, intermolecular forces are weak.

18 There are two types of intermolecular forces:
   ▶ **permanent dipole–dipole** intermolecular attractions (e.g. **hydrogen bonding**), exist between polar molecules;
   ▶ van der Waals' forces, which result from the interaction of **temporary dipoles**; these are the only attractive forces which exist between non-polar molecules.

9

Solids

Contents

Table 9.1 *The four main types of solid structure*

Name of structure	particles present
metallic	metal atoms
macromolecular	non-metal atoms
simple molecular	molecules
ionic	ions

Figure 9.1 *An electron density map of aluminium (contours in electrons per cubic Ångstrom, where $1Å = 10^{-10}$ m). The average electron density between ions is 0.21 electrons per cubic Ångstrom*

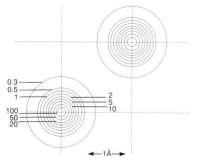

Two very large solid structures. The Forth Rail Bridge in Scotland, under construction in the late 1880s, and the Selangor Mosque in Malaysia

Kinetic Theory proposes that the particles in solids are held rigidly in a 3-dimensional arrangement called a **lattice**. However, the particles are *not* at rest: *they are vibrating around their average position*. On heating, these vibrations become more vigorous until, finally, the attractive forces between the particles are overcome and the solid melts.

Table 9.1 summarises the four main types of solid structure. Each is constructed from a particular kind of particle (atoms, ions or molecules). In this chapter, we shall

▶ look at examples of each structure;
▶ investigate the relationship between a solid's structure and its physical properties; and
▶ discuss the factors which govern the solubility of solids in liquids.

9.1 Metallic bonding

When subjected to X-ray diffraction, all metals produce similar electron density maps, e.g. aluminium (figure 9.1). These show that the atoms in the metallic lattice release some, or all, of their valence electrons, thereby forming positive ions (cations). These electrons are **delocalised** (i.e. move freely) throughout the lattice, as opposed to remaining in the vicinity of any one cation. Thus, a mobile electron cloud is produced. Since neighbouring cations are mutually attracted to this electron cloud, they will also be attracted to each other. These attractive forces exactly balance the repulsion between the like-charged cations. The overall result, therefore, is *a rigid 3-dimensional lattice of metal cations, embedded in a mobile electron cloud.*

What factors affect the strength of the metallic bonds? Have a look at figure 9.2.

Figure 9.2 *Metals with small highly charged ions form stronger metallic bonds. Here, metallic bond strength increases A < B < C*

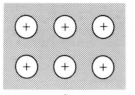

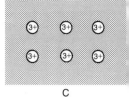

A	B	C

As we go from A→B→C, there is an increase in:
▶ the charge density (i.e. charge/size) of the cations; and
▶ the density of the mobile electron cloud, because the metal atoms are losing their valence electrons more readily.

The strongest metallic bonds will be formed between the cations and electron cloud which have the highest charge densities. Thus, metallic bond strength increases in the order: A < B < C.

If the metallic bonds are strong, the metal will be hard and have a high melting point. For example, let us compare sodium and aluminium:

	sodium	**aluminium**
electron configuration	$[Ne]3s^1$	$[Ne]\,3s^2\,3p^1$
cation charge	1+	3+
cation size (section 19.3)	larger	smaller
cation charge density	much smaller	much larger
density of delocalised electron cloud	low	high
∴ metallic bonds are	weaker	stronger

As expected, sodium is much softer and has a much lower melting point than aluminium. (Melting points: sodium 98°C; aluminium 659°C.)

Although it is over-simplified, this model of metallic bonding does account for the physical properties of metals (see table 9.2).

Table 9.2 *Physical properties of metals*

Physical property Metals are . . .	**explanation using our model**
good electrical conductors	when applied to the metal, an electromotive force (e.m.f.) can push the mobile electron cloud through the metallic lattice
good thermal conductors	when an area of the metal is heated, the kinetic energy of the electrons in that region increases; this causes them to flow quickly into the cooler parts of the metallic lattice
readily soluble in each other, when molten; on cooling alloys are formed	the mobile electron cloud can hold a variety of metal cations together, e.g. an alloy containing 1+ and 2+ cations

○ 1+ cations
● 2+cations
▨ electron cloud

| **malleable** (i.e. can be hammered into shape when red-hot, e.g. as a horseshoe) and **ductile** (i.e. can be drawn out into long wires) | the mobility of the electron cloud enables it to readily accomodate any distortion in the lattice e.g. |

cations   delocalised electron cloud

stress   gives

Activity 9.1

Using this simple model of metallic bonding, and atomic electron configurations, predict the trends in the melting points of:
    (a) potassium, calcium, scandium;
    (b) the Group 1 metals; and
    (c) the Group 2 metals.
(Note: The data in section 19.3 may help you.)

Figure 9.3 *Two single layers of spheres viewed from above. Those in (a) are close-packed*

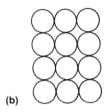

(a)

(b)

9.2 Types of metallic lattice

X-ray studies show that there are three common types of metallic lattice: **hexagonal close-packed (HCP)**, **cubic close-packed (CCP)** and **body centred cubic (BCC)**.

In close-packed structures, the spherical cations are positioned so as to fill as much space as possible (figure 9.3). Models made from polystyrene spheres can help us to see the structural difference between hexagonal and cubic close-packing. Each sphere represents a metal cation. A layer(A) of close-packed spheres is fixed on a white board and viewed from above. As you can see, this gives a hexagonal

arrangement with each sphere touching six neighbours. A second layer (B) is then placed into the depressions between spheres in layer (A). Now, looking from above, *we can see two sorts of gaps between the spheres in layer B*. Some gaps, marked ×, are almost hexagonal and reveal the white card. Others, marked ●, have a ▼ shape and are directly above spheres in layer A. This means, then, that *there will be two ways of placing a third layer of spheres, either above the ×'s or above the ●'s*.

Hexagonal close-packing

If the third layer is placed in the gaps marked ●, then we obtain the **hexagonal close-packed structure** (figure 9.4a). An exploded view (figure 9.4b) shows that

Figure 9.4 *Hexagonal close-packing of spheres*

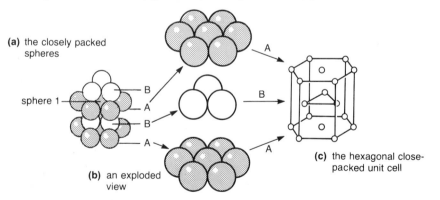

(a) the closely packed spheres

sphere 1

(b) an exploded view

(c) the hexagonal close-packed unit cell

▶ *alternate layers of spheres are positioned above each other.* Therefore, hexagonal close-packing is said to have an 'ABABAB' structure;

▶ *any given sphere* (e.g. sphere 1), *makes contact with twelve neighbours.* Thus, we say that each sphere has a **coordination number** of 12 (six in its own layer, three in the layer above and three in the layer below).

Close-packed structures are more clearly illustrated using unit cell diagrams (e.g. figure 9.4c). A **unit cell** *is the smallest part of the lattice which retains the structural properties of the solid*. Unit cells are the 'building blocks' of all solid structures, being repeated millions of times throughout the lattice. (Note: unit cell diagrams only gives the positions of the centres of the particles present.)

Zinc, magnesium and titanium are examples of metals whose atoms adopt a hexagonal close-packed structure.

Cubic close-packing

Look again at the photograph. By placing a third layer of spheres in the gaps marked ×, we will obtain the **cubic close-packed structure** (figure 9.5a). The exploded view (figure 9.5b) shows that:

Figure 9.5　*Cubic close-packing of spheres*

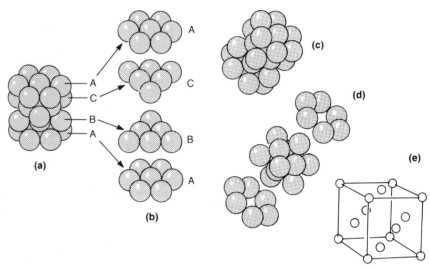

▶ *each sphere has a coordination number of 12* (six spheres in its own layer, three in the layer below and three in the layer above);
▶ *every third layer of spheres is located above each other.* So, we say that cubic close-packing has an 'ABCABC' structure.

At first glance, it may be difficult to see why this structure is classified as 'cubic'. However, imagine that figure 9.5a is rotated to give figure 9.5c. Now, by removing two hexagonal rings of spheres (figure 9.5d), we get a cubic close-packed unit cell, as shown in figure 9.5e. Since this cube has a sphere at each corner and one in each face, this unit cell is also known as a **face-centred cube.**

Calcium, aluminium and iron are examples of metals whose atoms adopt a cubic close-packed structure.

Body-centred cubic packing

The third common metal structure is not close-packed. As the name implies, the **body-centred cubic unit cell** has eight spheres at the corners of a cube with one sphere in the middle (figure 9.6). Each sphere has eight nearest neighbours; thus, the *coordination number is 8* (four in the layer above and four in the layer below).

Metals with a body-centred cubic structure include iron, tungsten and the alkali metals.

Figure 9.6　*Body-centred cubic packing of spheres*

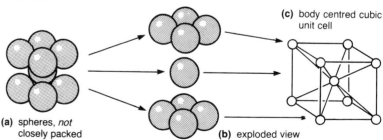

Go back over the examples of each metal structure. Do you notice anything interesting? Well, iron has *two* possible structures. It exists as a body-centred cubic lattice up to 960 °C. From 960 to 1401 °C, it is cubic close-packed. Above 1401 °C, it reverts to body-centred cubic. *The ability of a solid to exist in different crystalline structures* is known as **polymorphism**. Some other polymorphic substances are listed in table 9.3. The *polymorphic forms of an element* are known as **allotropes** (e.g. red and white phosphorus).

Table 9.3 *Some examples of polymorphic substances*

Substance	names of the polymorphs
sulphur	rhombic and monoclinic (ref: section 26.1)
phosphorus	white, red and black (ref: section 25.1)
calcium carbonate	aragonite and, the more common, calcite, e.g. as limestone and marble (made of large interlocking crystals) and chalk (a microcrystalline solid)

9.3 Macromolecular structures

A **macromolecular** *solid structure may be thought of as an enormous molecule made up of covalently bonded atoms.* Well-known examples of macromolecular solids are the carbon allotropes, diamond and graphite (figure 9.7). Diamond is an extremely hard solid because it has a very rigid tetrahedral arrangement of carbon atoms. On the other hand, graphite has sheets of carbon atoms bonded in a hexagonal pattern. Since adjacent sheets are only weakly held together by van der Waals' forces, they can slide over each other. Thus, graphite is a fairly soft solid and it can be used as a lubricant.

Figure 9.7 *Diamond and graphite, two allotropes of carbon*

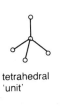

tetrahedral 'unit'

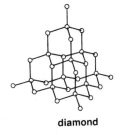

diamond

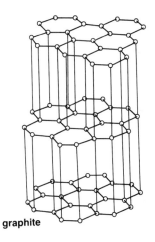

graphite

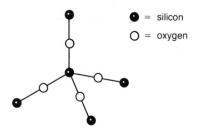

= silicon

◯ = oxygen

Figure 9.8 *In β-cristobalite, silicon atoms occupy the 'carbon' positions in the diamond structure. An oxygen atom is bonded between each pair of silicon atoms*

Boron and silicon are other examples of elements with macromolecular structures. However, the atoms in macromolecular solids *need not be identical*, for example in silica, SiO_2. In fact, silica adopts no less than six different macromolecular structures; thus, we have another example of polymorphism. One of the silica polymorphs, β-cristobalite, has a similar structure to that of diamond (figure 9.8). Do you think β-cristobalite will have a high or low melting point?

Activity 9.2 will help you to draw some conclusions about the physical properties of macromolecular solids.

Activity 9.2

We shall use table 9.4 to identify some patterns in the physical properties of macromolecular solids.

Note: $\Delta H^{\ominus}_{fus}$ = standard molar enthalpy of fusion and $\Delta H^{\ominus}_{vap}$ = standard molar enthalpy of vaporisation (see section 19.10)

Table 9.4 *Physical properties of some macromolecular solids*

	boron	silica (cristobalite)	diamond	graphite
physical state (25 °C, 1 atm)	solid	solid	solid	solid
hardness	hard	hard	hard	fairly soft
melting point/°C	?	1723	?	?
boiling point/°C	?	2230	?	?
$\Delta H^{\ominus}_{fus}$/kJ mol^{-1}	?	very high	?	?
$\Delta H^{\ominus}_{vap}$/kJ mol^{-1}	?	very high	?	?
electrical conductivity	←————— non-conductors —————→			good
solubility	insoluble in polar and non-polar solvents			

1 Copy the table and, by referring to chapter 19, fill in the missing values.
2 Now compare these values with the values of these properties for other elements and draw some general conclusions.
3 Account for the hardness, poor electrical conductivity and low solubility of macromolecular solids.
4 Why does graphite have some anomalous properties (Also, see section 24.1).

9.4 Simple molecular structures

In **simple molecular** structures, a *lattice of covalently bonded molecules is held together by weak intermolecular forces* (section 8.12). These solids may be broadly divided into two groups:

▶ Those made of **non-polar** molecules held together by **van der Waals' forces**, e.g. argon and iodine (figure 9.9).

Figure 9.9 *Simple molecular solid structures for (a) argon and (b) iodine. Both have a face-centred cubic unit cell*

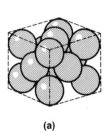

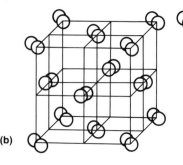

 show the centres of the iodine molecules

(a)   (b)

Figure 9.10 *Sulphur dioxide has an angular molecule in which the centres of positive and negative charge do not coincide, i.e. there is a permanent dipole*

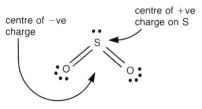

centre of −ve charge

centre of +ve charge on S

electronegativities S = 2.5, O = 3.5

Figure 9.11 *In ice, a lattice of water molecules is held together by hydrogen bonds. Each oxygen atom is surrounded tetrahedrally by four hydrogen atoms (two covalently bonded and two hydrogen bonded). Compared with the molecules in liquid water, those in ice are much less closely packed together*

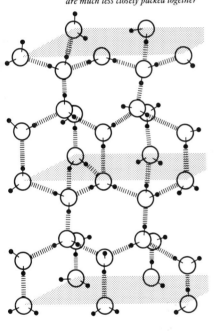

Icebergs float because ice, having a much less compact structure than water, is less dense. However, the 3-dimensional hydrogen-bonded structure of ice is very rigid. In 1912, the luxury passenger liner 'Titanic', on her maiden voyage, struck a massive iceberg and sank with the loss of 1500 lives

▶ Those made of **polar** molecules held together by **dipole–dipole attractions**, e.g. sulphur dioxide (figure 9.10). **Hydrogen bonding** is common in simple molecular solids, e.g. in ice (figure 9.11).

In practice, many simple molecular solids are held together by a *combination* of van der Waals' and dipole–dipole attractions. For example, phenol consists of a non-polar benzene ring joined to the polar —OH group:

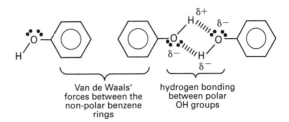

Van de Waals' forces between the non-polar benzene rings

hydrogen bonding between polar OH groups

Activity 9.3 will help you to deduce some properties of solids with simple molecular structures.

Activity 9.3

We shall use table 9.5 to identify any patterns in the physical properties of simple molecular solids.

1 Copy the table and, by referring to chapter 19, fill in the missing values.
2 Now compare these values with the values of these properties for metallic and macromolecular solids. Draw some general conclusions.
3 Does our model of a simple molecular solid account for these patterns in physical properties?

Table 9.5 *Physical properties of some substances with simple molecular solid structures*

	nitrogen	ice	sulphur	phosphorus (white)	iodine
molecular formula	N_2	H_2O	S_8	P_4	I_2
physical state (25 °C, 1 atm)	gas	liquid	solid	solid	solid
hardness	soft, in comparison to other types of solid				
melting point/°C	?	?	?	?	?
boiling point/°C	?	?	?	?	?
$\Delta H^{\ominus}_{fus}$/kJ mol^{-1}	?	6.0	?	?	?
$\Delta H^{\ominus}_{vap}$/kJ mol^{-1}	?	40.7	?	?	?
electrical conductivity	non-conductors				
solubility in polar and non-polar solvents	very slightly	only in polar	←——— only in non-polar ———→		

9.5 Ionic structures

When ions come together to form an ionic lattice, the electrostatic attraction between oppositely charged ions is exactly balanced by the repulsion between the electron clouds of the ions. Thus, a rigid 3-dimensional structure is build up.

Each type of ionic structure is described by the **coordination numbers** of ions present. *The coordination number tells us how many oppositely charged ions surround a particular ion.* In a **6 : 6 lattice** each ion is surrounded by six oppositely charged ions, for example, sodium chloride, NaCl (figure 9.12a). Similarly, when each ion has eight nearest neighbours, it is called an **8 : 8 lattice**, for example, caesium chloride, CsCl (figure 9.12b). If the cation and anion do not combine in a 1 : 1 ratio, the coordination numbers around each ion will not be equal. In calcium fluoride, CaF_2, for example, the Ca^{2+} ion is surrounded by a cube of eight F^- ions but each F^- ion has only four near Ca^{2+} neighbours held in a tetrahedral arrangement. So, calcium fluoride is said to adopt an **8 : 4** ionic structure.

Figure 9.12 *Crystal structures of (a) sodium chloride and (b) caesium chloride*

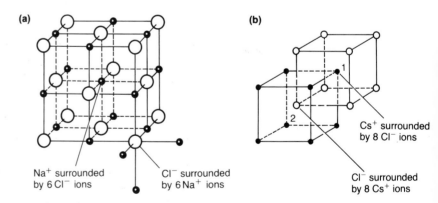

(a)

Na$^+$ surrounded by 6 Cl$^-$ ions   Cl$^-$ surrounded by 6 Na$^+$ ions

(b)

Cs$^+$ surrounded by 8 Cl$^-$ ions

Cl$^-$ surrounded by 8 Cs$^+$ ions

9.6 Ionic radii and radius ratio

Although sodium and caesium are in the same periodic group, their chlorides have different structures. Clearly, the '3-dimensional' structure adopted by the ions will depend on their size or, to be more exact, their **ionic radius**. But how do we define ionic radius?

Figure 9.13 *Electron density maps for (a) calcium fluoride and (b) sodium chloride (contours in electrons per cubic Ångstrom (10^{-10} m))*

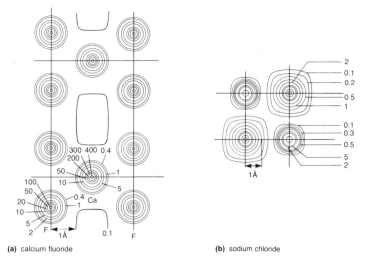

(a) calcium fluoride   (b) sodium chloride

Electron density maps of ionic structures show that the ions are *sometimes* spherical (e.g. in calcium fluoride, figure 9.13a). In many cases, though, the ions are *distorted* spheres (e.g. in sodium chloride, figure 9.13b). This distortion arises from the unequal repulsion of the ions' outermost electron clouds. In defining ionic radius, therefore, *we must assume that: (i) the ions are spherical and (ii) they touch each other.* Then the ionic radius can be depicted using a simple diagram (figure 9.14). X-ray diffraction can provide accurate values for the distance between the layers of ions, *d*. If the anion radius, r_A is known, the cation radius, r_C can be obtained by difference:

$$r_A + r_C = d$$
$$r_C = d - r_A$$

Figure 9.14 *We define ionic radius by assuming that ions are touching spheres, (r_C = cation radius, r_A = anion radius)*

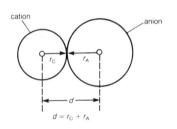

cation   anion

r_C r_A

d

$d = r_C + r_A$

Trends in ionic radii are discussed in section 19.3.

Ionic radii can also be measured for hydrated ions (section 9.9), by measuring the speed at which ions migrate towards an electrode during electrolysis.

We can use ionic radii to predict the type of ionic lattice which will be adopted by a given pair of ions. To do this, we calculate the **radius ratio** of the ions involved, where

$$\text{radius ratio} = \frac{\text{radius of the cation, } r_C}{\text{radius of the anion, } r_A}$$

Table 9.6 *Radius ratio and the structure of an ionic lattice*

Radius ratio	type of lattice formed	example
0.225–0.414	4:4	zinc sulphide, ZnS
0.414–0.732	6:6	potassium iodide, KI
0.732 and above	8:8	caesium bromide, CsBr

Table 9.6 shows the general relationship that exists between radius ratio and the type of ionic lattice.

Unfortunately, radius ratios do *not* always predict the correct structure. Lithium iodide, for example, has a radius ratio of 0.28. What structure would this suggest? From table 9.6, it should be a 4:4 lattice. However, X-ray diffraction shows it to be a 6:6 lattice, like sodium chloride. One reason for this discrepancy is that in lithium iodide there is a considerable degree of covalent character. As expected from Fajan's rules (section 5.10), the small lithium cation polarises the much larger iodide anion, with the resulting partial overlap of electron clouds. It is found, therefore, that the *radius ratio method usually works best for totally ionic solids.*

Figure 9.15 *Unit cells of the polymorphs zinc blende (a) and wurtzite (b)*

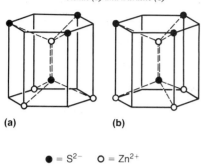

(a)   (b)

● = S²⁻   ○ = Zn²⁺

Polarisation of ions is a common feature of many ionic structures. A good example is zinc sulphide. This adopts a 4:4 ionic lattice and exists in two polymorphic forms, zinc blende and wurtzite (figure 9.15). Notice that zinc blende has the same structure as diamond, a macromolecular solid. Zinc sulphide is typical of the many thousands of compounds which cannot simply be described as having an ionic or macromolecular structure. Other examples of this include (i) silica, macromolecular yet partially ionic (figure 9.8), and (ii) cadmium iodide, which is ionic with appreciable macromolecular character.

9.7 Physical properties of ionic structures

Activity 9.4 will help you to make some general predictions about the physical properties of ionic solids.

Activity 9.4

Table 9.7 *Physical properties of some solids with ionic structures*

	sodium chloride	lead bromide	aluminium oxide	silver chloride
physical state (25 °C, 1 atm)	◀——————— solids ———————▶			
hardness	hard and brittle; they will **cleave** (split cleanly when hit by a sharp chisel)			
melting point/°C	808	370	2040	558
boiling point/°C	1465	914	2980	1504
ΔH_{fus}/kJ mol⁻¹ ΔH_{vap}/kJ mol⁻¹	high; comparable with those of metallic solids			
electrical conductivity	all conduct when molten or in aqueous solution			
solubility in polar solvents	good	very slightly	insoluble	insoluble
solubility in non-polar solvents	◀——————— insoluble ———————▶			

Table 9.7 lists some physical properties of a typical quartet of ionic solids. Use it to answer the following questions.

1   How do these physical properties compare with those of other types of solid structure? (Look back over previous activities, if necessary.)

2   Does our model of an ionic structure account for these patterns in physical properties?

9.8 The solubility of solids in liquids

Table 9.8 describes the general patterns in solubility of solids in polar and non-polar solvents. Let us consider the enthalpy changes (section 4.2) which occur when a solid dissolves in a liquid.

In a solution, the particles from the solid mix freely with those from the liquid. This process may be thought of as a combination of three enthalpy changes:

1   *The solid's lattice, made of atoms, molecules or ions, must be broken up.* This process will be *endothermic*, that is, enthalpy is absorbed (ΔH_1 is +ve).

2   Similarly, *the dipole–dipole and/or van der Waals' attractions in the liquid will be disrupted* to some extent. Once again, bonds are being broken and *enthalpy will be absorbed (ΔH_2 is +ve)*. However, ΔH_2 is usually much less than ΔH_1.

3   Now, if ΔH_1 and ΔH_2 were the only enthalpy changes involved, dissolution would *always* be an endothermic process. This is not the case; for example, try

Table 9.8 *Solid structures and their general pattern of solubility*

Structure	solvent	
	polar	non-polar
metallic		insoluble
macromolecular		insoluble
simple molecular	mostly insoluble	mostly soluble
ionic	mostly soluble	insoluble

measuring the temperature increase when one pellet of sodium hydroxide is dissolved in $1\,cm^3$ of water. Thus, *a release of enthalpy, ΔH_3, must accompany the formation of new bonds between the particles from the solid and liquid.*

Overall, then,

$$\begin{array}{llll} \text{enthalpy change, } \Delta H & = & \Delta H_1 & + & \Delta H_2 & + & \Delta H_3 \\ \text{on dissolving} & & \text{endothermic } (\Delta H = +\text{ve}) & & & & \text{exothermic } (\Delta H = -\text{ve}) \end{array}$$

Dissolving a solid in a liquid may be an endothermic or exothermic process, therefore, depending on the relative sizes of ΔH_1, ΔH_2 and ΔH_3.

Generally speaking, we find that a solid is more likely to dissolve in a liquid if the overall enthalpy change is exothermic. Putting it another way, *high solubility is more likely* if

strength of the attractions between solid and > *combined strengths of the attractions*
liquid particles in the solution   *between particles in the pure solid and pure liquid*

This simple 'rule of thumb' often helps us to explain the trends in solubility. For example, why is iodine soluble in hexane but not in water?

Well, iodine, I_2 and hexane, C_6H_{14}, are both *non-polar* substances. When mixed together a solution is formed because

the strength of I_2/hexane attractions in > combined strength of the attractions in
the solution (van der Waals' forces)   the solid (I_2/I_2; van der Waals' forces)
         and liquid (hexane/hexane; van der Waals' forces)

Now, water is a *polar* solvent, with its molecules engaged in extensive hydrogen bonding. When mixed with the non-polar iodine molecules, the resulting iodine/water attractions are extremely weak in comparison to the combined strengths of the hydrogen bonding in water and the van der Waals' forces in iodine. Consequently, iodine is virtually insoluble in water.

9.9 What happens when an ionic solid dissolves in water?

When an ionic solid dissolves in water, the water molecules penetrate the lattice and attach themselves to the ions (figure 9.16). This process is known as **hydration** and the ions are said to be **hydrated**.

Since new **ion–dipole attractions** are being formed, *hydration is an exothermic process.* Moreover, the energy released is large enough to enable the hydrated ions to move away from their oppositely charged neighbours (figure 9.16). Eventually, the lattice is completely destroyed, and all the ions become hydrated.

A simplified example of a hydrated ion is shown in figure 9.17. In reality, the sodium ion is surrounded by more than one layer of water molecules. *The number of water molecules in the innermost layer is given a familiar name, the* **coordination number.** For hydrated sodium ions, then, the coordination number is 4. The

Figure 9.16 *An ionic solid dissolving in water*

Figure 9.17 *A hydrated sodium ion. Four water molecules are attached via ion–dipole bonds, whilst the fifth H_2O is coordinated via hydrogen bonds. The hydration number is 5*

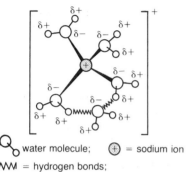

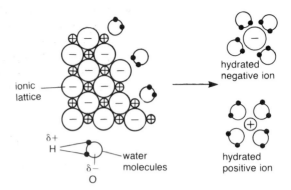

hydration number is the *total number of water molecules which are attached, however loosely, to an ion*. Hydration numbers are estimated from the speed at which the ions move during electrolysis. Some typical values are given in table 9.9. These show that *small, highly charged ions (i.e. those with the greatest charge density) are the most heavily hydrated*.

Finally, let us consider further the nature of the attractive forces between an ion and the water molecules. There are two kinds of attraction:

▶ **ion–dipole bonds:** These are physical attractions which exist between an ion and the oppositely charged part of a water molecule (figure 9.17).

▶ **dative covalent bonds:** If a metal ion possesses suitable empty orbitals at low enough energy it can form dative covalent bonds with the water molecules. As a result, **complex ions** are formed, e.g. the hexaaquaaluminium(III) ion (figure 9.18). Some common complex 'aqua-ions' are discussed in section 30.4.

(Note: The discussion above can also be applied to the solvation of ions by other polar solvents, such as methanol and propanone. When lithium chloride is dissolved in methanol, for example, each lithium ion is surrounded by about seven methanol molecules.)

Table 9.9 *Some approximate hydration numbers*

Ion	hydration number (± 1 unless stated)
Li^+	5
Na^+	5
K^+	4
Cl^-	1
Br^-	1
I^-	1
Mg^{2+}	15 ± 2
Ca^{2+}	13 ± 2
Al^{3+}	26 ± 3

9.10 Enthalpy changes on dissolving an ionic solid in water

An enthalpy change usually occurs when an ionic solid dissolves in water, and this can be described by an **enthalpy cycle** (figure 9.19). Each step has its own enthalpy term, as follows:

▶ $\Delta H_s^{\ominus}$ = **standard enthalpy change on solution**. This is the *enthalpy change when one mole of solute dissolves in so much solvent that further dilution produces a negligible enthalpy change, at 298 K and 1 atm*. (In this context, the solute is an ionic solid and the solvent is water.)

▶ $-\Delta H_1^{\ominus}$ = **the reverse of the lattice energy**. This will be *enthalpy needed to convert one mole of ionic lattice into gaseous ions*, e.g.

$$NaF(s) \rightarrow Na^+(g) + F^-(g) \qquad -\Delta H_1^{\ominus}[NaF(s)] = 918 \text{ kJ mol}^{-1}$$
$$\text{and } CaCl_2(s) \rightarrow Ca^{2+}(g) + 2Cl^-(g) \qquad -\Delta H_1^{\ominus}[CaCl_2(s)] = 2258 \text{ kJ mol}^{-1}$$

Figure 9.18 *Hexaaquaaluminium(III) ion, an example of a complex aqua-ion. It has an octahedral shape with aluminium having a coordination number of 6*

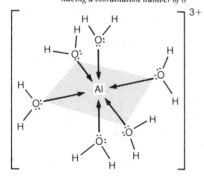

Figure 9.19 *An enthalpy cycle for the dissolution of M^+X^- (s) in water*

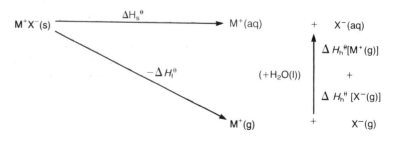

▶ $\Delta H_h^{\ominus}$ = **the standard enthalpy of hydration** of each ion, $M^+(g)$ and $X^-(g)$. It is defined as the *enthalpy change when one mole of gas ions are dissolved in so much water that more dilution produces no further enthalpy change, at 298 K and 1 atm pressure.*

Now, **Hess's Law** states that the enthalpy change during a reaction is independent of the route followed (section 4.11). Applying this to figure 9.19, we get

$$\Delta H_s^{\ominus}[M^+X^-(s)] \quad = \quad \underset{\text{endothermic (+ve)}}{-\Delta H_l^{\ominus}[M^+X^-(s)]} \quad + \quad \underset{\text{exothermic (−ve)}}{\Delta H_h^{\ominus}[M^+(g)] + \Delta H_h^{\ominus}[X^-(g)]}$$

From this equation, we see that:

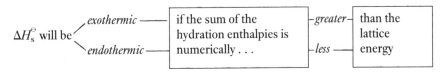

A worked example based on this enthalpy cycle is shown below.

Example

Use the following data to calculate the enthalpy of solution for magnesium chloride:

$$\Delta H_l^{\ominus}[MgCl_2(s)] \quad = \quad -2489\,kJ\,mol^{-1}$$
$$\Delta H_h^{\ominus}[Mg^{2+}(g)] \quad = \quad -1891\,kJ\,mol^{-1}$$
$$\Delta H_h^{\ominus}[Cl^-(g)] \quad = \quad -384\,kJ\,mol^{-1}$$

From figure 9.19 and Hess's Law,

$$\Delta H_s^{\ominus}[MgCl_2(s)] \quad = \quad -\Delta H_l^{\ominus}[MgCl_2(s)] \; + \; \Delta H_h^{\ominus}[Mg^{2+}(g)] \; + \; 2\{\Delta H_h^{\ominus}[Cl^-(g)]\}$$

$$\Delta H_s^{\ominus}[MgCl_2(s)] \quad = \quad -(-2489) \quad + \quad (-1891) \quad + 2(-384)$$

$$= \quad +2489 \quad - \quad 1891 \quad - 768$$

$$= \quad -170\,kJ\,mol^{-1}$$

(Note: Since 2 moles of $Cl^-(g)$ ions are hydrated, we must take $2 \times \Delta H_h^{\ominus}[Cl^-(g)]$.)

In these calculations, *beware the common error of failing to use multiples of the hydration enthalpies* (where necessary). For example, when 1 mole of iron(III) sulphate, $Fe_2(SO_4)_3$ is dissolved in water, you must take $2 \times \Delta H_h^{\ominus}[Fe^{3+}(g)]$ and $3 \times \Delta H_h^{\ominus}[SO_4^{2-}(g)]$.

Finally, we want to investigate whether there is a link between the water solubility of a salt and its enthalpy of solution. Can you draw any general conclusions from the data in table 9.10?

This data suggests that *a salt's solubility cannot be predicted solely on energetic grounds*, that is, by comparing $\Delta H_s^{\ominus}$ data. For example, although $\Delta H_s^{\ominus}[LiBr(s)]$ and $\Delta H_s^{\ominus}[LiCl(s)]$ are both exothermic, with similar values, the chloride is a hundred times more soluble in water. In fact, the energy changes on dissolving a solid are much more complex than those in our simple enthalpy cycle of figure 9.19. A full explanation is based on the concept of 'free energy', and this can be found in advanced physical chemistry texts. However, we can generalise by saying that an *ionic solid is more likely to be soluble in water if (i) it has a low lattice enthalpy and (ii) the constituent ions have high hydration enthalpies.*

Table 9.10 *Enthalpies of solution (ΔH_s) of some ionic solids and their solubilities in water (at 25°C)*

Name of solid	ΔH_s/kJ mol^{-1}	solubility/10^{-3} mol per 100 g water
Lithium bromide	-47	20
Barium iodide	-44	560
Lithium chloride	-35	2000
Sodium chloride	$+7$	650
Lead iodide	$+10$	0.2
Silver fluoride	$+21$	1420
Silver chloride	$+40$	0.001
Silver iodide	$+97$	0.00001

Is there a pattern here?

9.11 Comparing the physical properties of solids

The following activity will help you to compare the physical properties of metallic, macromolecular, simple molecular and ionic solid structures. This activity is a useful revision exercise.

Activity 9.5

Draw up a table which compares the physical properties of the four main types of solid. You should consider the following: hardness, melting points, boiling points, ΔH_{fus}, ΔH_{vap}, electrical conductivity and solubility in polar and non-polar solvents.

9.12 Comments on the activities

Activity 9.1

(a) Follow through this analysis:

	potassium	calcium	scandium
electron configuration	[Ar]4s^1	[Ar]4s^2	[Ar]3d^{1}4s^2
maximum number of electrons released per atom	1	2	3

∴ charge on the cation ——— increases ———→
size of cation ——— decreases ———→
∴ charge density on cation ——— increases ———→
density of electron cloud ——— increases ———→

Since the charge densities of both the electron cloud and the cations increase from sodium to scandium, there will be a corresponding increase in metallic bond strength. Thus, melting points should also increase and this is the case. (Melting points: K 64°C, Ca 850°C, Sc 1540°C.)

(b) Once again, follow through this analysis. Each Group 1 metal has an electron configuration of [noble gas] ns^1.

	Li	Na	K	Rb	Cs
maximum number of electrons released per atom	1	1	1	1	1

∴ charge on the cation   remains constant
size of cation   ———increases———→
∴ charge density on cation   ———decreases———→
density of electron cloud   ———decreases———→

Since the charge densities of both the electron cloud and the cations decrease from lithium to caesium, there will be a corresponding decrease in metallic bond strength. Thus, melting points should also decrease and this is the case. (Melting points: Li 180 °C, Na 98 °C, K 64 °C, Rb 39 °C, Cs 29 °C.)

(c) An argument similar to that in (b) predicts that the melting points of the Group 2 metals should also decrease down Group 2. In fact, the values are (°C):

beryllium	magnesium	calcium	strontium	barium
1280	650	850	768	714

We do not get the predicted steady decrease. This is because these metals, unlike the Group 1 elements, do not have the same '3-dimensional' arrangement of cations, and this is considered further in section 9.2.

Activity 9.2

2 You should have concluded that *macromolecular solids have very high melting points, boiling points and molar enthalpies of fusion and vaporisation.* These properties result from the strong covalent bonding between atoms in the lattice.

3 For the same reason, these solids are also *hard* and *virtually insoluble* (since too much energy is needed to break up the lattice).

4 Unlike other macromolecular solids, *graphite is fairly soft and conducts electricity*; this is explained in section 24.1.

Activity 9.3

2 You should have concluded that *simple molecular solids have very low melting points, boiling points and molar enthalpies of fusion and vaporisation.*

3 Yes, it does. The simple molecular lattice is only held together by weak intermolecular forces (i.e. van der Waals' forces and/or dipole–dipole attractions). Thus, a lattice of simple molecules will be broken up by a relatively small input of energy.

Simple molecular solids are *electrical non-conductors* because they contain neither a delocalised electron cloud nor mobile ions. The solubility of these solids is discussed in section 9.8.

Activity 9.4

Figure 9.20 *Cleavage in ionic solids: a layer of ions (a) before and (b) after cleavage*

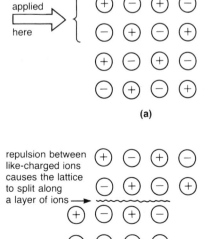

force applied here

repulsion between like-charged ions causes the lattice to split along a layer of ions ⟶

1 You should have concluded that, generally speaking, there is a pattern in the values of melting and boiling points and molar enthalpies of fusion and vaporisation, namely:

| *simple molecular* *all very low* | ≪ | *ionic & metals* *a few quite low, most high* | ≪ | *macromolecular* *all very high* |

2 In most cases, our structural model accounts very well for the physical properties of ionic solids. The large number of electrostatic interactions causes the lattice to be *strong* (with small, highly charged ions forming the strongest structures). Thus, we would expect not only the behaviour in (1) above, but also the hard, brittle nature.

Cleavage of the ionic crystal results from the mutual repulsion between neighbouring layers of ions which occurs when one is displaced, figure 9.20. Solid ionic salts are electrical non-conductors. However, *when heated or dissolved in water, the ionic lattice breaks up, the ions move freely and electricity is conducted.*

Surprisingly, perhaps, there is a *wide variation in solubilities* of ionic salts in water, and this is discussed in section 9.10.

Activity 9.5

See table 9.11 in section 9.13.

9.13 Summary and revision plan

1. **Kinetic Theory** proposes that, in solids, vibrating particles are held rigidly in a 3-dimensional lattice. These particles may be atoms, ions or molecules.
2. **X-ray diffraction** (section 6.4) is used to determine the arrangement of particles in the lattice.
3. There are four main types of solid structure: **metallic, macromolecular, simple molecular** and **ionic**. Their bonding, structure and physical properties are summarised in table 9.11.

Table 9.11 *Comparing the natures and properties of solid structures*

	metallic	macromolecular	simple molecular	ionic
examples	Na, Al, Fe	graphite, diamond, SiO_2	I_2, CH_4, CO_2, HF, H_2O	Na^+I^-, $Mg^{2+}O^{2-}$, $Ca^{2+}(2F^-)$
made up of	metal **atoms**	non-metal **atoms**	**molecules**	**ions**
bonding	**cations** mutually attracted to a mobile sea of electrons	atoms held together by strong **covalent** bonds	covalently bonded molecules held together by weak intermolecular forces: **van der Waals' forces** or **dipole–dipole attractions**	strong **electrostatic** attraction between oppositely charged ions
Properties physical state at 25 °C	solid, except Hg	solid	gas, liquid or solid	solid
hardness	variable: Na soft, Fe hard **malleable** and **ductile**	generally hard	soft	hard and brittle; undergoes **cleavage**
melting point	variable: Na 98 °C Fe 1500 °C	very high, SiO_2 2230 °C	very low H_2O 0 °C	high NaCl 808 °C
boiling point	variable: Na 890 °C Fe 2887 °C	very high diamond 5100 °C	very low H_2O 100 °C	high AgCl 1504 °C
$\Delta H^{\ominus}_{fus}$, $\Delta H^{\ominus}_{vap}$	some low, some high	very high	very low	high
electrical conductivity	good, whether solid or liquid	non-conductors (except graphite)	non-conductors	solids are non-conductors but will conduct when molten or in aqueous solution
solubility	nil, but dissolve in other metals → alloys	insoluble	usually soluble in a polar or non-polar solvent.	*usually* soluble in polar solvents; insoluble in non-polar solvents

4. The **coordination number** of an atom, ion or molecule tells us how many neighbouring particles are nearest to it.
5. A **unit cell** is the smallest part of the lattice which retains the structural properties of the solid.
6. Metals exist in three common crystalline structures (coordination numbers in brackets): **hexagonal close-packed (12), cubic close-packed (12) and body-centred cubic (8)** (section 9.2).
7. **Polymorphism** is the ability of a solid to exist in different crystalline structures. The polymorphic forms of an element are termed **allotropes**.
8. Ionic structures are often described by the coordination numbers of the ions present, e.g. NaCl, 6:6; CsCl, 8:8; ZnS, 4:4.
9. To define **ionic radius**, we assume that an ionic lattice consists of spherical ions which touch each other (section 9.6).
10. **Radius ratio** = radius of the cation/radius of the anion. For totally ionic solids, there is a link between the type of ionic lattice and the radius ratio of the ions.
11. Many solids have intermediate ionic/covalent bonds. As a result, they possess intermediate ionic/macromolecular structures.

12 Generally speaking, a solid is more likely to dissolve in a liquid if

strength of the attractions between solid and liquid particles in the solution	>	combined strengths of the attractions between particles in the pure solid and pure liquid

13 **Solvation** is the process in which solvent molecules penetrate a solid lattice and attach themselves to the particles present. If the solvent is water, the process is called **hydration**.

14 The **hydration number** of an ion is the number of water molecules which are attached, however loosely, to that ion. Small, highly charged ions have high hydration numbers, and vice versa.

15 Solvent molecules can be attached to the solute by (i) **van der Waals' forces** (I_2 in hexane), (ii) **dipole–dipole attractions** (phenol in water), (iii) **ion–dipole attractions** (Na^+ or Cl^- ions in water) or (iv) **dative covalent bonds** (Fe^{2+} ions in water).

16 The **standard enthalpy change on solution, $\Delta H_s^{\ominus}$**, is the enthalpy change when one mole of solute dissolves in so much solvent that further dilution produces a neglible enthalpy change, at 298 K and 1 atm pressure.

17 The **standard enthalpy of hydration, $\Delta H_h^{\ominus}$** is the enthalpy change when one mole of gas ions are dissolved in so much water that more dilution produces no further enthalpy change, at 298 K and 1 atm pressure.

18 Generally speaking, an ionic solid is more likely to be soluble in water if its lattice enthalpy is low and the hydration enthalpies of its ions are high.

□ C H A P T E R □

10

Isomerism

Contents

Molecular models of ethylmethanoate and propanoic acid, a pair of structural isomers both having the molecular formula C₃H₆O₂

Propanoic acid and ethyl methanoate have the same molecular formula, $C_3H_6O_2$. However, their structures and properties are different:

ethylmethanoate		propanoic acid
53	boiling point °C	141
very low	solubility in water	high

These molecules are **isomers**, that is, *they have the same molecular formula but their atoms are arranged in a different way.*

10.1 Types of isomerism

There are very many examples of isomerism in chemistry and these may be divided into two main classes:

STRUCTURAL ISOMERISM		STEREOISOMERISM
Isomers whose molecules have their atoms linked together in different bonding arrangements	and	Isomers whose molecules have their atoms linked together in the same bonding arrangement
Types of structural isomerism: ▶ chain isomerism ▶ positional isomerism ▶ functional group isomerism ▶ metamerism		Types of stereoisomerism: ▶ geometrical isomerism ▶ optical isomerism

As we describe each kind of isomerism, bear in mind two important points:
  ▶ how we tell the difference between isomers;
  ▶ isomerism is a property of both organic and inorganic compounds.

10.2 Structural Isomerism

There are four main types.

Chain isomerism

These isomers have different hydrocarbon chains. For example, C_5H_{12} is the molecular formula of the alkanes, pentane, 2-methylbutane and 2,2-dimethylpropane.

Chain isomers have similar chemical properties but different physical properties, e.g. melting and boiling points and densities (table 10.1). Thus, we can distinguish between chain isomers by measuring their melting or boiling points.

Before carrying on, a brief word about drawing structural formulae. *In many molecules, groups of atoms are able to rotate around σ bonds.* For example, look at the molecular model of propane, C_3H_8.

Due to the continual rotation around the C^1—C^2 bond, the hydrogen atoms and the —CH_3 group on C^2 are in equivalent positions. Hence, the three structural formulae in figure 10.1 are also equivalent. (Now would be a good time to try activity 34.1, question 1.)

Figure 10.1 *Due to the rotation about σ bonds, these structural formulae are all equivalent – they are not isomers*

Property	pentane	2-methylbutane	2,2-dimethylpropane
structural formula	H H H H H | | | | | H–C–C–C–C–C–H | | | | | H H H H H	H | H–C–H H H | H | | | | H–C–C–C–C–H | | | | H H H H	H | H–C–H H | H | | | H–C–C–C–H | | | H–C–H | H
melting point/°C	−130	−160	−16
boiling point/°C	36	28	10
density/g cm⁻³	0.63	0.62	0.59(liquid)

Table 10.1 *Physical properties of the isomers of molecular formula C_5H_{12}. Why do the boiling points decrease in the order shown?*

Positional isomerism

These isomers have a particular atom, or bond, or group of atoms, in different molecular positions. For example, there are two positional isomers of molecular formula C_3H_7Br.

2–bromopropane
(b.p. 60 °C)

1–bromopropane
(b.p. 71 °C)

Molecular models of the positional isomers, 2-bromopropane and 1-bromopropane

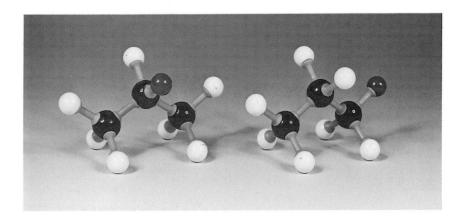

Positional isomers have different physical properties. They take part in similar chemical reactions, but often at different rates. For example, 2-bromopropane reacts faster with water than does 1-bromopropane (section 37.5.1). Thus, we can identify positional isomers by physical, and sometimes chemical, methods.

Other important examples of positional isomerism are found in: alkenes and alkynes (section 35.1), benzene derivatives (section 36.1) and alcohols (section 38.1).

Positional isomerism is fairly common in transition metal complex ions. A well-known example is the complex ion containing cobalt and the positional isomers of diaminopropane (figure 10.2).

Figure 10.2   *Cobalt complex ions containing the ligands 1,2-diaminopropane and 1,3-diaminopropane are positional isomers. (Note: the hydrogens have been omitted in the top diagrams for clarity)*

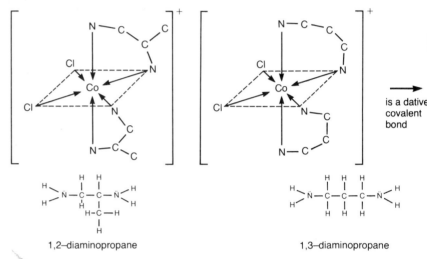

1,2–diaminopropane   1,3–diaminopropane

Activity 10.1

Draw structural formulae for
- (a)   four isomers of formula $C_3H_6Cl_2$;
- (b)   five isomers of formula C_4H_8;
- (c)   four isomers of C_4H_9Br;
- (d)   six isomers in which one methyl $(-CH_3)$ and two nitro $(-NO_2)$ groups are positioned around a benzene ring.

Functional group isomerism

Functional group isomers contain different organic functional groups (section 33.4). Alcohols and ethers are examples of functional group isomers, e.g.

ethanol   methoxymethane

Functional group isomers often display very different physical and chemical properties; see for example, table 10.2. Consequently, functional group isomers are easily distinguished by (i) measuring melting or boiling points or (ii) performing simple chemical tests (e.g. the different effects of sodium on ethanol and methoxymethane).

Functional group isomerism is found in alcohols and ethers (section 38.12), and carboxylic acids and their esters (sections 40.1, 40.8).

Table 10.2 *Comparing the physical and chemical properties of ethanol and methoxymethane, both of which have the same molecular formula, C_2H_6O. Why do the boiling points decrease in the order shown?*

Property	Ethanol	Methoxymethane
physical state at 25 °C	liquid	gas
boiling point/°C	78	−25
$\Delta H_f^{\ominus}/\text{kJ mol}^{-1}$	−277	−184
type of solvent	polar	almost non-polar
reaction with sodium metal (ref: section 38.5.1)	moderate, giving $H_2(g)$ and $C_2H_5O^- Na^+(s)$	no reaction
reaction with PCl_5 (ref: section 38.6.2)	vigorous giving $C_2H_5Cl(l)$	no reaction

Activity 10.2

Several compounds have the molecular formula $C_2H_4O_2$.
1   Three of these are functional group isomers containing a carbonyl group, $>C=O$. Give their structure.
2   Three other isomers contain a $C=C$ bond. Draw their structural formulae. How are these isomers related to those in part (1)?

Metamerism

These isomers contain different hydrocarbon skeletons linked by a common functional group, e.g. carboxylic acid esters:

methyl propanoate (b.p. = 80 °C)   ethyl ethanoate (b.p. = 77 °C)

Generally speaking, *metamers have different physical properties but similar chemical properties.*

Activity 10.3

Give structural formulae for the metamers of molecular formula:
(a) $C_4H_{10}O$ (ethers);   (b) $C_3H_6O_2$ (esters);   (c) $C_5H_{10}O$ (ketones).

10.3 Stereoisomerism I: geometrical isomerism

Stereoisomers are molecules which have different properties even though the same atoms are linked together in an identical bonding arrangement.
      Consider the molecular models of 1,2-dichloroethene shown in the photograph.

cis –1, 2–dichloroethene   *trans* –1, 2–dichloroethene

Each molecule has the same bonding arrangement. However, their '3-dimensional' structures differ because *the π electron cloud prevents rotation about the double bond.* Thus, *geometrical isomers have identical atoms, or groups, arranged either 'on the same side of' (**cis-**) or 'across' (**trans-**) a rigid section of the molecule's structure,* e.g. a C═C bond.

Geometrical isomers can be identified by their different physical properties, e.g. *cis-* and *trans*-but-2-ene:

cis–but–2– ene		*trans*–but–2–ene
–139	melting point / °C	–105
4	boiling point / °C	1
0.621	density /g cm⁻³	0.604

Although geometrical isomers have similar chemical properties, *their reactions often proceed at different rates,* e.g.

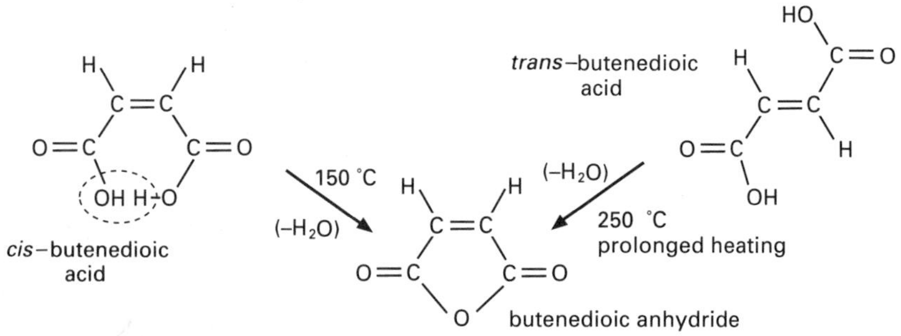

The *cis*-isomer loses water more readily because its —OH groups are closer together. Dehydration of the *trans*-isomer does occur, but a lot of energy is needed to rotate the C═C bond and bring the —OH groups close enough for a water molecule to be lost.

Geometrical isomerism is common in the chemistry of the *transition metal complex compounds and ions,* e.g. the square planar complexes

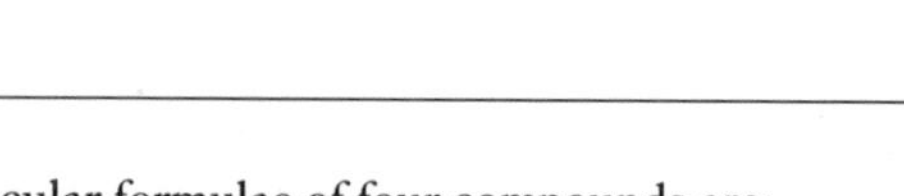

cis–dichlorodiammine   *trans*–dichlorodiammine
palladium (II)   palladium (II)

As expected, these isomers have different physical properties. Whilst they take part in similar reactions, these tend to occur at different rates. Other examples of geometrical isomerism in transition metal chemistry may be found in section 30.3.

Activity 10.4

1   The molecular formulae of four compounds are:
     (a) $C_2H_4Br_2$;   (b) C_2H_3Cl;   (c) $C_4H_6O_2$ (a carboxylic acid);
     (d) C_4H_7Br.
     Each contains a C═C bond. Draw out the possible structural formulae and classify the isomers (if any) as structural or geometrical.
2   The octahedral complex ion dichlorotetraaquachromium (III) has the molecular formula $[Cr(H_2O)_4Cl_2]^+$. Draw the *cis-* and *trans-* forms of this ion.

10.4 Stereoisomerism II: optical isomerism

Like geometrical isomers, optical isomers have their atoms linked together in the same bonding arrangement. They have identical physical and chemical properties *except in their behaviour towards plane polarised light.*

What is plane polarised light?

Have a look at figure 10.3.

Figure 10.3 *The production of plane polarised light. Light will not pass through two polaroid sheets whose polarising axes are at right angles to each other*

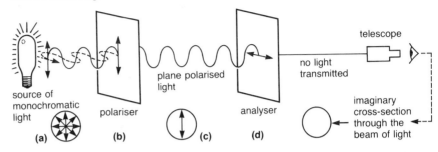

(a) A beam of light consists of an infinite number of waves vibrating in *all planes* at right angles to the direction of the beam's movement.

(b) Certain materials will let through light which vibrates in only one plane, called **plane polarised light**. One well-known **polariser** is the **polaroid sheet** used in sun-glasses.

(c) When it emerges from the polariser, the beam of light has vibrations in *only one plane*. It is plane polarised.

(d) To check for plane polarisation, the light is directed onto another polaroid sheet, known as the **analyser**. When the polarising axes of the polariser and analyser are at right angles, no light will be transmitted.

What happens when plane polarised light passes through chemical compounds?

These effects can be studied using a **polarimeter**. Its main components resemble figure 10.3, except that a polarimeter tube is placed between the polariser and analyser. First, the apparatus is adjusted so that no light is transmitted. Then the tube is filled with a solution of the sample and replaced in the polarimeter. If light can now be seen through the telescope, the sample must have rotated the plane of polarisation of the light. Thus, the compound is said to be **optically active.** To find the **angle of rotation,** α, and its direction, the analyser is rotated once again until no light is transmitted.

An isomer is said to be **dextrorotatory (+)** or **laevorotatory (−)**, depending on whether it rotates the plane of polarisation to the right or left, respectively. Under the same conditions, dextrorotatory and laevorotatory isomers produce the same angle of rotation. Some angles of rotation are given in table 10.3.

Table 10.3 *Specific rotations caused by some enantiomers. (The specific rotation is measured at a wavelength of 590 nm, temperature 20°C, polarimeter tube length 10 cm for a solution containing 1 g of enantiomer per cm³)*

Enantiomer	specific rotation [α]
(+)-tartaric acid	+12.0
(−)-tartaric acid	−12.0
alanine (2-aminopropanoic acid)	+2.7
(−)-lactic acid (2-hydroxypropanoic acid)	−3.3
natural glucose	+52.5
natural sucrose	−92.0

Which isomer rotates the plane of plane polarised light: (a) furthest to the right, (b) very slightly to the left?
What would be the angle of rotation if we made up equimolar mixtures of (a) (+) and (−)-tartaric acids, (b) glucose and sucrose?

Figure 10.4 *Your hands form non-superimposable mirror images*

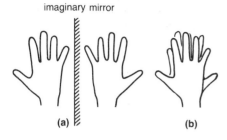

(a) **(b)**

Do optical isomers have a common structural feature?

If you hold up your hands, palms facing, they will form *mirror images* of each other (figure 10.4a). However, if you place one hand on top of the other, palms down, the fingers and thumbs do not line up (figure 10.4b). They are *non-superimposable*. Our hands are examples of structures which form **non-superimposable mirror images**. Research has shown that the molecules of optical isomers can exist as non-superimposable mirror images, and we call these **enantiomers**.

Consider, for example, the 'mirror-image' molecular models having four different groups arranged around a central carbon atom.

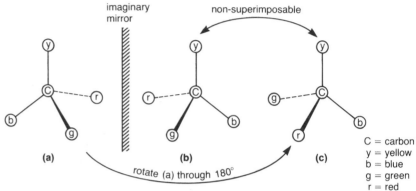

C = carbon
y = yellow
b = blue
g = green
r = red

(a) **(b)** **(c)**

rotate (a) through 180°

Figure 10.5 *When (a) is rotated through 180°, it cannot be superimposed on (b); thus, (a) and (b) are non-superimposable mirror-images*

Figure 10.5 shows these 'mirror-image' structures, (a) and (b). Now, if (a) is rotated through 180°, giving (c), it cannot be superimposed on (b). Thus, structures (a) and (b) would represent a pair of enantiomers. Two examples of this type of optical isomer are:

isomers of 2–aminopropanoic acid

is an imaginary mirror

isomers of 2–bromobutane

In fact, *any organic compound possessing one* **asymmetric carbon atom**, *that is, one bonded to four different atoms, or groups, must exist as optical isomers.*

Optical isomerism is particularly common in naturally occurring organic compounds such as amino acids, proteins, enzymes and sugars. An example is glucose, a sugar:

Optical isomerism is also found in inorganic chemistry, e.g. the complex ion, dichlorobis (1,2-diaminoethane) chromium (III):

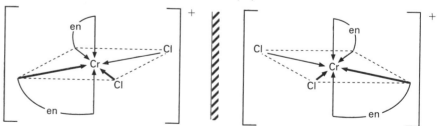

where en = 1,2-diaminoethane, $NH_2CH_2CH_2NH_2$, and $\rightarrow$ is a **dative covalent bond**. (Also, see figure 30.4b).

Racemic mixtures

2-hydroxypropanoic acid (lactic acid) and 2-aminopropanoic acid (alanine) each contain one asymmetric carbon. Each molecule can form enantiomers, with the (+) isomers occurring naturally in muscle and proteins, respectively.

$$\begin{array}{cc}
\text{COOH} & \text{COOH} \\
| & | \\
\text{H—C—OH} & \text{H—C—NH}_3 \\
| & | \\
\text{CH}_3 & \text{CH}_3
\end{array}$$

2–hydroxypropanoic   2–aminopropanoic
acid   acid

When the compounds are prepared in the laboratory, however, the products are found to be optically *inactive*. In fact, each sample contains an *equimolar mixture of the (+) and (−) isomer*. Both isomers rotate the plane of polarisation to the same extent but in *opposite* directions. Consequently, their individual effects on the plane of polarisation cancel out. *Any equimolar mixture of optical isomers is termed a* **racemic (±) mixture**. *It will be optically inactive.*

Although optical isomers are common in plant and animal life, they are seldom found as a racemic mixture. For example, all naturally occurring 2-amino acids are laevorotatory (−). However, *in any laboratory synthesis, the optical isomers will always form in equal amounts* (i.e. to give a racemic mixture).

Separating the isomers from a racemic mixture

Optical properties apart, enantiomers show exactly the same physical and chemical behaviour. Thus, we cannot separate them using physical methods, such as distillation, crystallisation and chromatography (described in chapter 32).

A few racemic mixtures may be separated by **hand-picking** the differently shaped crystals, e.g. the (+) and (−) forms of sodium ammonium tartrate (figure 10.6). Devised over 120 years ago, this method is very tedious and seldom used nowadays. Other techniques use (i) a **bacterium** to feed on one enantiomer or (ii) an **enzyme** to catalyse the reaction of just one enantiomer. In each case, this leaves the other enantiomer free for extraction by physical means.

However, by far the most common method of separating racemic mixtures involves the preparation of **diastereoisomers**. *These are the products formed when a racemic(±) mixture reacts with a pure optical isomer, (+) or (−).* For example:

$$\begin{array}{ccccc}
(+)\text{X} & & (+)\text{Y} & \rightarrow & (+)\text{X, }(+)\text{Y product} \\
(-)\text{X} & & & & (-)\text{X, }(+)\text{Y product} \\
\text{racemic mixture} & + & \text{optical isomer} & & \text{diastereoisomers}
\end{array}$$

Now, unlike optical isomers, *diastereoisomers have different physical properties*. Thus, they can be separated by the physical methods mentioned earlier. So,

$$\begin{array}{ccc}
(+)\text{X, }(+)\text{Y product} & \xrightarrow{\text{physical}} & (+)\text{X, }(+)\text{Y and }(-)\text{X, }(+)\text{Y} \\
(-)\text{X, }(+)\text{Y product} & \text{separation} & \text{product} \qquad \text{product} \\
\text{a mixture of} & & \text{separated} \\
\text{diastereoisomers} & & \text{diastereoisomers}
\end{array}$$

Finally, a chemical reaction is needed to recover the isomers, (+)X and (−)X, from the isolated diastereoisomers.

Figure 10.6 *The enantiomeric crystals of sodium ammonium tartrate can be separated by hand picking, but it's a very tedious process*

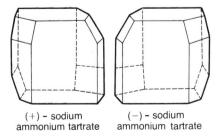

(+) – sodium   (−) – sodium
ammonium tartrate   ammonium tartrate

Activity 10.5

Draw 'mirror-image' structures for the optical isomers of formula
(a) $C_3H_6O_3$,   (b) $C_4H_{10}O$,   (c) C_3H_5NO and (d) C_4H_9Cl.
These structures have a common feature. What is it?

10.5 Comments on the activities

Activity 10.1

(a) There are *four* positional isomers:

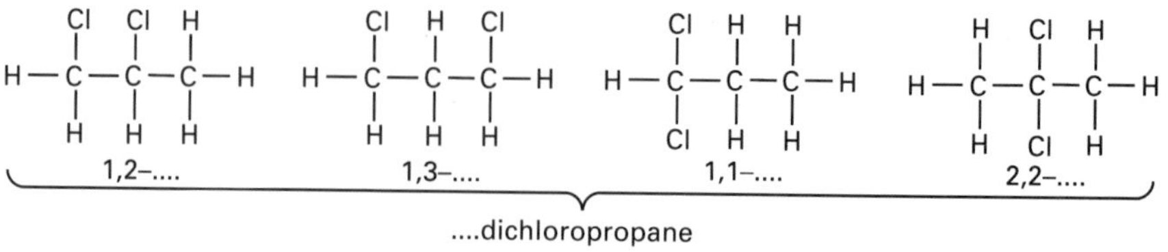

....dichloropropane

Once again, remember that rotation around the single bonds means that structural formulae such as

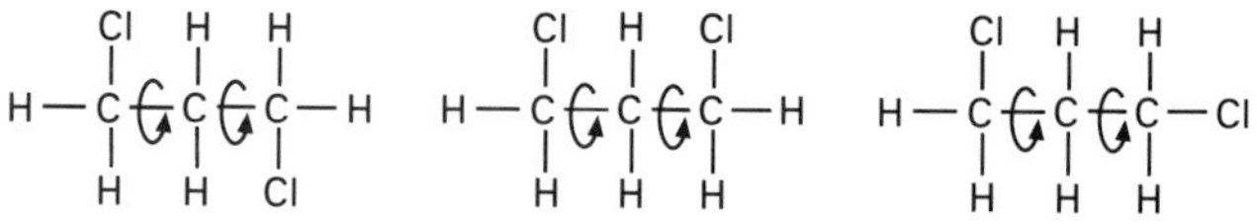

are all equivalent. They are not positional isomers.

(b) There are *five* chain isomers, *two* of which are also positional isomers:

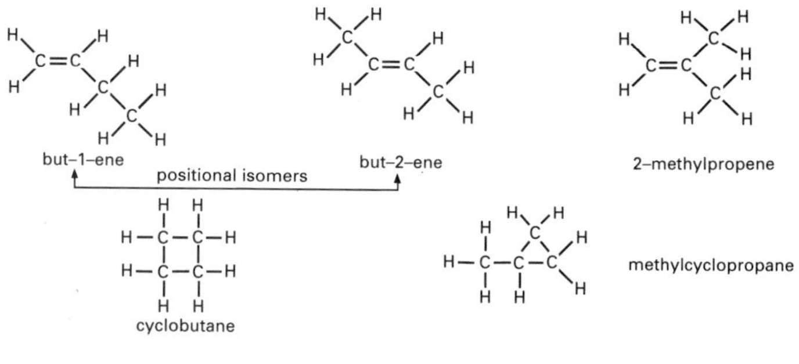

but–1–ene   but–2–ene   2–methylpropene

positional isomers

cyclobutane   methylcyclopropane

(c) There are *two pairs* of positional isomers:

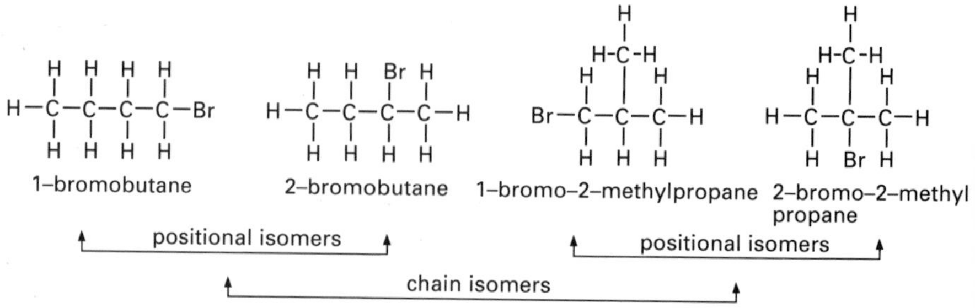

1–bromobutane   2–bromobutane   1–bromo–2–methylpropane   2–bromo–2–methyl propane

positional isomers   positional isomers

chain isomers

As you can see, each pair are chain isomers of the other pair.

(d) *Six* positional isomers are possible:

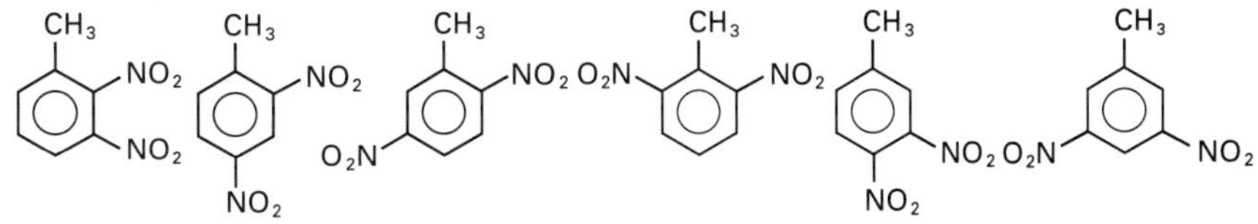

2,3–....   2,4–....   2,5–....   2,6–....   3,4–....   3,5–....

....dinitromethylbenzene

Activity 10.2

1

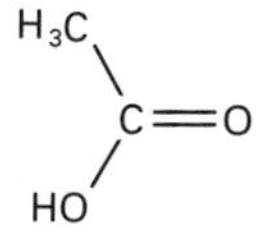

ethanoic acid
(a carboxylic acid)

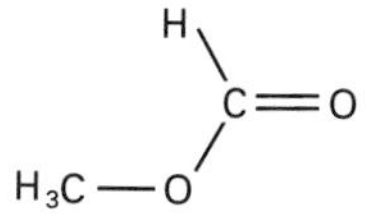

methyl methanoate
(an ester)

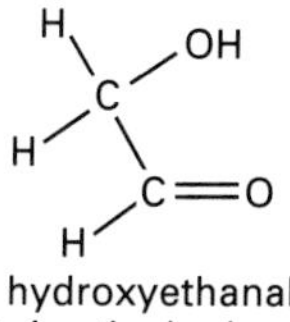

hydroxyethanal
(contains the hydroxy OH
and carbonyl C=O
functional groups)

2

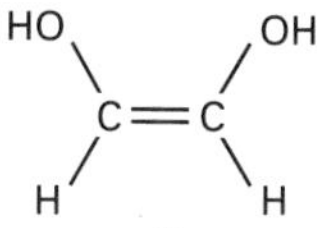

(i) 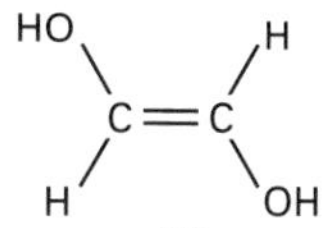   (ii) 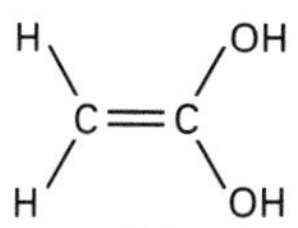   (iii)

These compounds are functional group isomers of those in 1. Finally, (i) and (ii) are examples of **geometrical isomerism**, as we shall see in section 10.3.

Activity 10.3

(a)

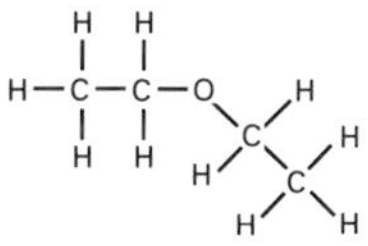

ethoxyethane 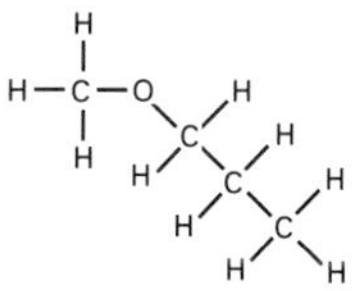   1–methoxypropane 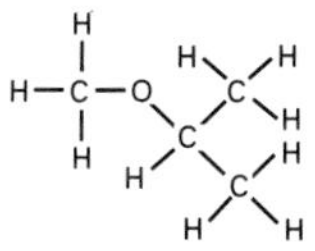   2–methoxypropane

(b)

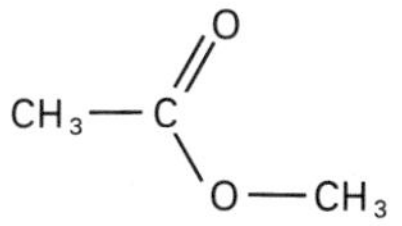

methyl ethanoate 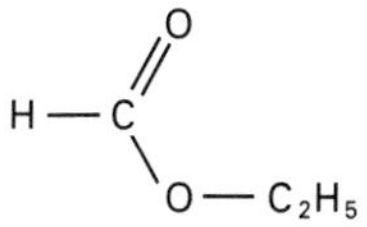   ethyl methanoate

(c)

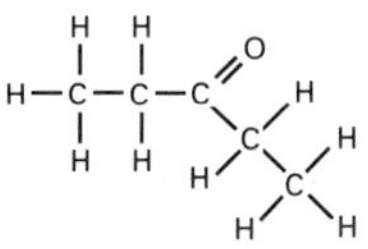

pentan–3–one 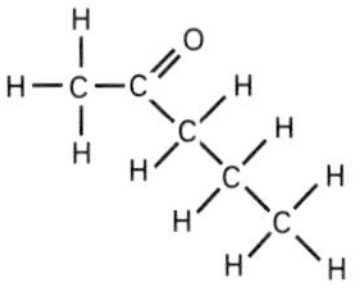   pentan–2–one 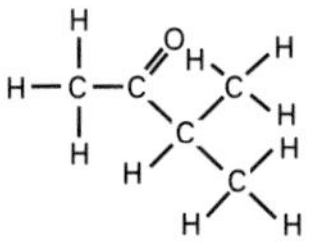   3–methylbutanone

Activity 10.4

1 (a)

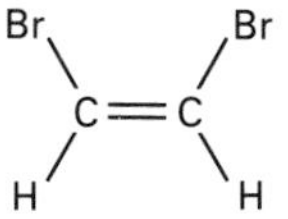

cis–.... 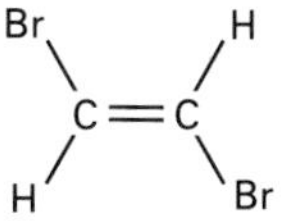   trans–....

1,2–dibromoethene (geometrical isomers)

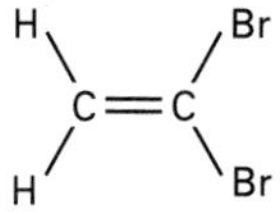

1,1–dibromoethene
structural isomer

(b)

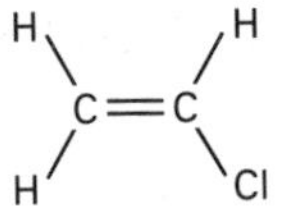

chloroethene, no isomers

(c)

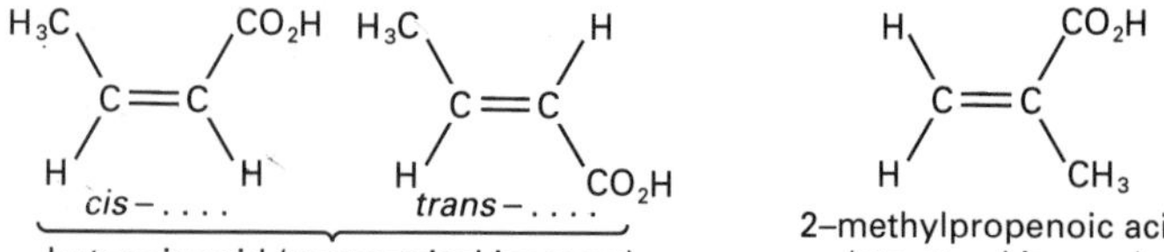

cis−....   trans−....

....butenoic acid (geometrical isomers)

2−methylpropenoic acid
(structural isomer)

(d)

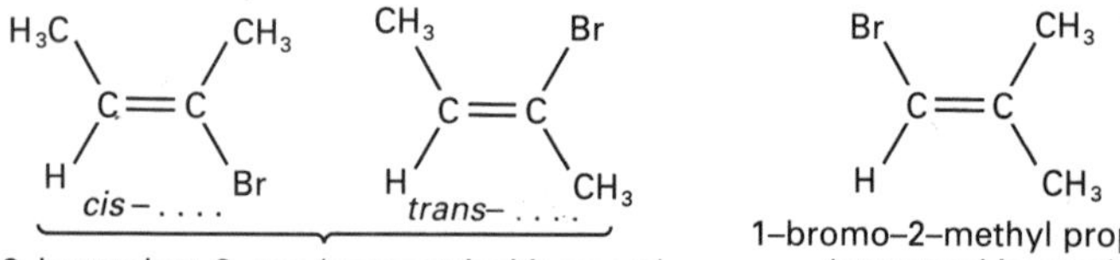

cis−....   trans−....

....2−bromobut−2−ene (geometrical isomers)

1−bromo−2−methyl propen
(structural isomer)

2

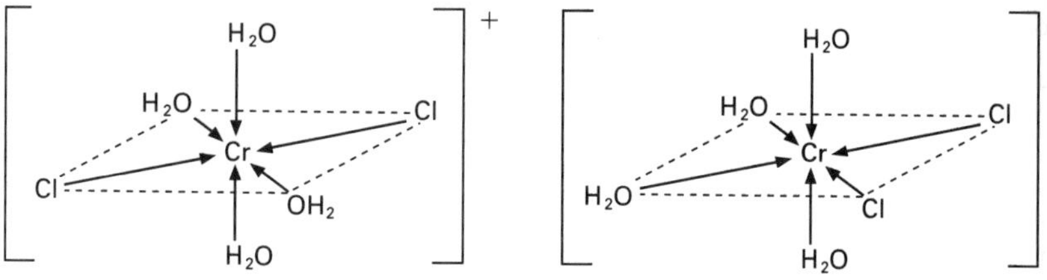

trans−....   cis−....

....dichlorotetraaquachromium (III)

Note that other equivalent drawings of these are possible, e.g.

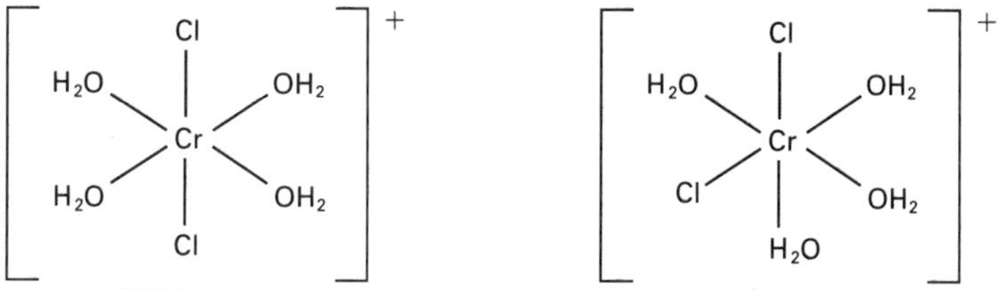

trans−....   cis−....

Activity 10.5

(a)   (b)

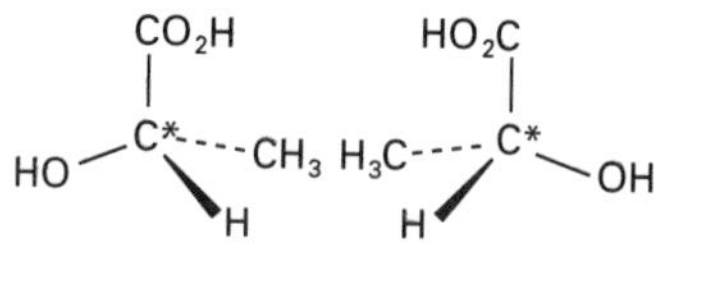

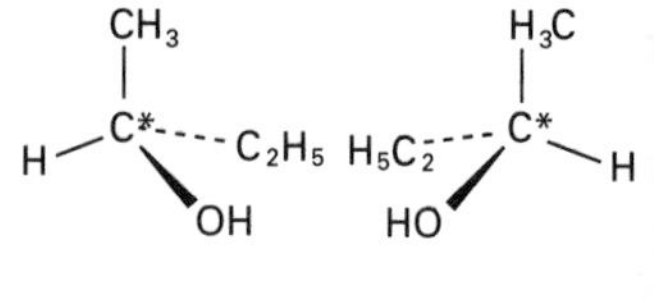

(c) 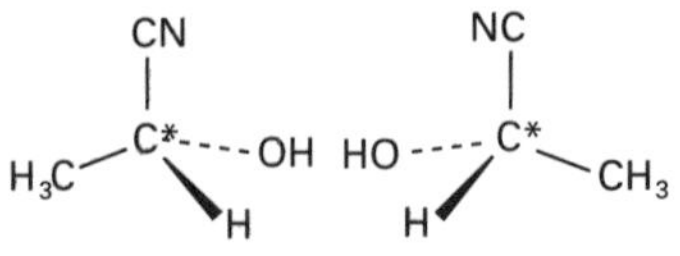   (d)

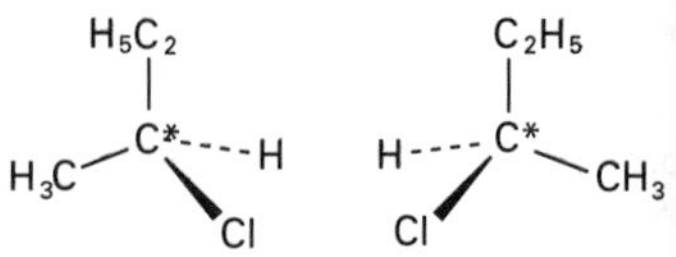

They are all enantiomers because they possess an **asymmetric carbon atom**,
marked ⋆.

10.6 Summary and revision plan

1   **Isomers** are compounds with the same molecular formula but different physical or chemical properties. Isomerism is a property of organic and inorganic compounds.
2   Isomers may be divided into two main classes: **structural isomers** and **stereoisomers**.
3   Molecules of structural isomers have the same atoms joined together in *different* bonding arrangements.
4   Molecules of stereoisomers have the same atoms joined together in *identical* bonding arrangements but they still have different '3-dimensional' structures.
5   The different types of isomer and their properties are summarised in table 10.4.

Table 10.4   *Types of isomer and their properties*

(a) STRUCTURAL ISOMERISM

Type of isomerism	isomeric molecules contain . . .	physical properties	chemical reactions	examples
chain isomerism	different hydrocarbon chains	different	same	$CH_3CH_2CH_2CH_3$ butane and 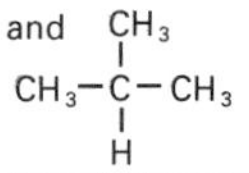 2-methylpropane
positional isomerism	a particular atom, bond or group of atoms in different positions on the same molecular skeleton	different	similar; often different rates	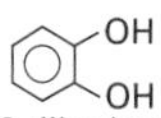 1,2-dihydroxybenzene and 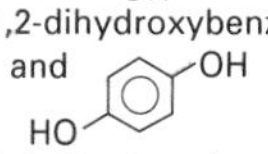 1,4-dihydroxybenzene
functional group isomerism	different organic functional groups	different	different	$CH_3CH_2CH_2CH_2OH$ butan-1-ol and $CH_3CH_2OCH_2CH_3$ ethoxyethane
metamerism	different hydrocarbon chains linked by a common organic functional group	different	same	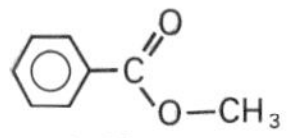 methyl benzoate and 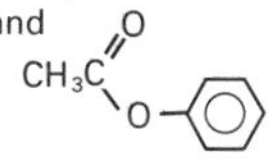 phenylethanoate

(b) STEREOISOMERISM

Type of isomerism	isomeric molecules . . .	physical properties	chemical reactions	examples
geometrical isomerism	have a rigid structure which prevents certain bonds from rotating	different	similar: often different rates	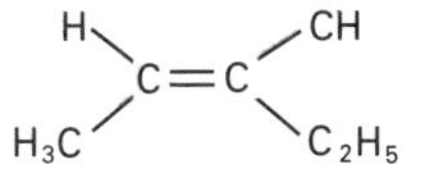 cis-.... 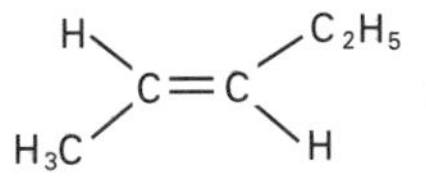 / trans-.... ....pent-2-ene
optical isomerism	exist as non-superimposable mirror images (enantiomers)	identical except towards plane polarised light		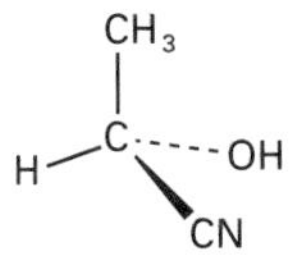 2-hydroxypropanonitrile

6   **Optical isomers** have identical properties except in their behaviour towards plane polarised light.

7   **Plane polarised light** is light which vibrates in only one plane. It is produced by passing monochromatic light through a polariser, such as polaroid sheet.

8   A **polarimeter** (figure 10.3), is used to study the effect of passing plane polarised light through chemical compounds.

9   An optical isomer is said to be **dextrorotatory** or **laevorotatory**, depending on whether it rotates the plane of polarisation to the right or left, respectively.

10   Dextrorotatory isomers are denoted by a ($+$) sign, laevorotatory isomers by a ($-$) sign.

11   The **angle of rotation**, α, depends on (i) the molecular structure of the isomer, (ii) the wavelength of light used, (iii) the temperature, (iv) the length of the polarimeter tube and (v) the concentration of the solution.

12   Under constant conditions, dextrorotatory and laevorotatory isomers produce the same angle of rotation.

13   All optical isomers have a common structural feature: their existence as non-superimposable mirror images, termed **enantiomers**.

14   A compound will always exist as optical isomers if it contains one **asymmetric carbon atom**, that is, one bonded to four different groups or atoms.

15   A **racemic mixture** contains ($+$) and ($-$) enantiomers in equimolar quantities. It will be optically inactive and is represented by a ($\pm$) sign. The laboratory synthesis of an optical isomer always leads to a racemic mixture.

16   The separation of enantiomers from a racemic mixture, termed **resolution**, is usually achieved by:

   (i)   preparing **diastereoisomers** by reacting the racemic($\pm$) mixture with a pure optical isomer, ($+$) or ($-$);

   (ii) separating the diastereoisomers using physical methods such as fractional distillation, crystallisation, chromatography and solvent extraction; and

   (iii) regenerating each isomer from the isolated diastereoisomers.

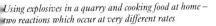

CHAPTER 11

Reaction Rates and their Measurement

Contents

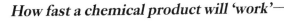

Using explosives in a quarry and cooking food at home – two reactions which occur at very different rates

Chemical reactions occur at different rates. Some are slow, e.g. on exposure to the atmosphere, copper statues or roofs slowly become coated with a green copper carbonate/hydroxide layer. Other reactions are very fast, e.g. the combustion of methane.

Every day our lives are influenced by the rates of chemical reactions. Boiling eggs, the hardening of resin-based glues and home-brewing are all examples of chemical reactions proceeding at different rates. Also, certain factors will affect the rate of reaction, e.g. glue will harden faster in warmer weather. *The study of reaction rates, and the factors which affect them, is known as* **reaction kinetics**.

11.1 Why measure reaction rates?

Kinetics studies play an important role in the chemical industry. They provide three main types of information.

How quickly, and economically, a product can be made

However good a chemical product may seem at the research and development stage, it will not be a commerical success if demand exceeds the supply. The consumer may then buy an inferior, yet more readily available, competing product. Consequently, many chemical processes are speeded up by increasing the temperature and/or pressure; in addition, a catalyst (section 12.5) may be added. For example, although ethene and water do not react together at room temperature, the reaction

$$\begin{array}{c} H \\ \diagdown \\ H \end{array} C = C \begin{array}{c} H \\ \diagup \\ \diagdown H\,(g) \end{array} \quad + \ H_2O(g) \quad \xrightarrow[\text{300 °C, 70 atm}]{\text{catalyst: conc. } H_3PO_4\,(l)} \quad C_2H_5OH(g)$$

is used to manufacture ethanol, C_2H_5OH (l). By studying the reaction kinetics, the industrial chemist can select a set of reaction conditions which give the most economical yield of ethanol.

How fast a chemical product will 'work'

This information enables the manufacturer to:
▶ adjust the properties of the product, e.g. the setting time for a glue;
▶ provide recommended instructions for the safe use of the product, e.g. finding the time that must elapse between spraying a pesticide and eating a vegetable crop.

The way in which a reaction occurs

Chemical reactions result from the redistribution of electron clouds. Bonds in the reactants break; at the same time, bonds in the products are being formed. This

Instructions for the use of a systemic insecticide indicate how long after spraying a food crop may be eaten. To work this out, the manufacturers will have studied the reaction kinetics for the breakdown of the insecticide within the plant

Molecular modelling of a drug's structure using a computer graphics system

Figure 11.1 *Reaction rates can be measured by drawing tangents to the '[   ] against time' graph. Also, the average rate over the time Δt_c is given by $\Delta[P]_c/\Delta t_c$*

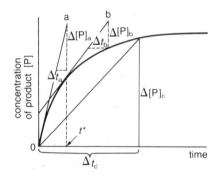

Figure 11.2 *Graphs of concentration of Reactant (——) or Product (– – – –) against time for the reaction $2R \rightarrow P$*

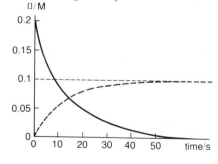

process, called the **reaction mechanism**, may occur in one step or in a sequence of steps.

A knowledge of the reaction mechanism helps the industrial chemist to modify a product, thereby increasing its effectiveness. For example, by slightly altering the molecular structure of a drug, its effects may be made more rapid and longer lasting.

In this chapter, we shall describe how reaction rates may be measured. Then we show how the results are analysed, thereby providing information about the reaction mechanism.

11.2 What is meant by the rate of a chemical reaction?

When we go on a journey, speed is defined as the distance travelled in a given time. Car speed, for example, is usually quoted in miles per hour. In a chemical reaction, as time passes, reactants are converted into products. Thus,

$$\text{rate of reaction} = \frac{\text{increase in [product]}}{\text{time taken}} \text{ or } \frac{\text{decrease in [reactant]}}{\text{time taken}}$$

where [ ] means concentration.

Figure 11.1 shows how the [product] increases during a typical reaction. There are three ways of obtaining a rate value from this graph.

▶ *The **rate at a given time** is obtained by measuring the gradient of the tangent drawn to the curve at that time.* For example, at t^*, rate $= \Delta[P]_b/t_b$. As time passes, the gradients become less steep, e.g. gradient b < gradient a. Hence, *the rate decreases as the reaction proceeds.*

▶ *Since the graph is almost linear at $t = 0$,* the **initial rate** can be measured quite accurately. Here, initial rate $= \Delta[P]_a/t_a$).

▶ An **average rate** can be measured over a given time (e.g. $\Delta[P]_c/t_c$).

Later on, we shall use each method in a kinetics study.

It is important to remember that *the rate of product formation need not equal the rate of reactant loss.* However, these rates will be related via the mole quantities in the chemical equation. For example, from the concentration changes during the reaction $2R \rightarrow P$ (figure 11.2) we find that

$$\text{rate} = \frac{\text{decrease in [R]}}{\text{time}} = 2 \times \frac{\text{increase in [P]}}{\text{time}}$$

(You might like to check this by estimating the initial rates in figure 11.2.) Thus, *rate values depend on which concentration is measured or* **'followed'**. A good example is the reaction of manganate(VII) (permanganate) ions with ethanedioate (oxalate) ions in acid solutions:

$$2MnO_4^-(aq) + 16H^+(aq) + 5C_2O_4^{2-}(aq) \rightarrow 2Mn^{2+}(aq) + 10CO_2(g) + 8H_2O(l)$$
$$2 \quad : \quad 16 \quad : \quad 5 \quad\quad\quad 2 \quad : \quad 10 \quad : \quad 8$$

The relative rates of reactant loss and product formation are shown in italics. When reporting rate values, then, you must state which concentration is being followed.

11.3 Methods of 'following' a concentration change

In the example above, we can choose to 'follow' the concentration of any one of the substances involved, i.e. $MnO_4^-(aq)$, $H^+(aq)$, $C_2O_4^{2-}(aq)$, $Mn^{2+}(aq)$, $CO_2(g)$ or $H_2O(l)$. Our choice will be based on which substance can be easily, yet accurately, analysed. Generally speaking, reaction kinetics are investigated in two ways: by sampling or continuous measurement.

Students using a sampling technique to study the kinetics of the acid catalysed reaction between aqueous manganate(VII) and ethanedioate ions

Sampling

The photograph shows how a typical sampling technique can be used to follow the $MnO_4^-(aq)/C_2O_4^{2-}(aq)$ reaction.

1 Starting the reaction: the reactants are mixed and a clock started.
2 Samples are withdrawn from the reaction mixture at regular intervals.
3 Noting the time, the reaction is halted by rapid cooling or by removing one of the reactants. In this case, we neutralise the hydrogen ions by running the sample into excess sodium hydrogen carbonate solution.
4 The concentration of a reactant or product is then estimated by titration. Here the remaining, unreacted, manganate(VII) ions are titrated with acidified iron(II) (aq):

$$MnO_4^-(aq) + 5Fe^{2+}(aq) + 8H^+(aq) \rightarrow Mn^{2+}(aq) + 5Fe^{3+}(aq) + 4H_2O(l)$$

Bearing in mind that each kinetic run may require many samples, this method can prove to be rather tedious. Also remember that the *titration volumes must be converted to give the concentration of the species we are following.*

Continuous measurement

In these experiments, we 'follow' the change in physical property of the reaction mixture, and then convert this into a concentration change. Some examples are:

Change in colour
Coloured chemicals give characteristic absorption spectra in the visible region (i.e. wavelength about 320 to 800 nm). These spectra can be recorded using an **ultraviolet/visible absorption spectrophotometer** (section 6.3).

A **simple colorimeter** is used to measure the absorbance of a solution at a fixed wavelength (figure 11.3). Monochromatic light is passed through the reaction mixture and the transmitted light is detected by the photoelectric cell.

Figure 11.3   *The main components of a colorimeter*

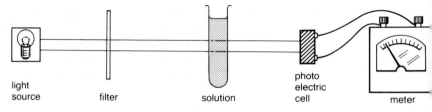

To follow a concentration change using colorimetry we need to:

1   test each filter so as to find a wavelength (x nm) which is absorbed strongly by only one of the reactant or product molecules, X, involved in the reaction;
2   measure the absorbance at x nm produced by solutions of known concentration in X. These results are used to plot a *calibration curve* of absorbance of X against [X] (figure 11.4);

Figure 11.4   *A colorimeter calibration curve for compound X absorbing visible radiation of wavelength x nm*

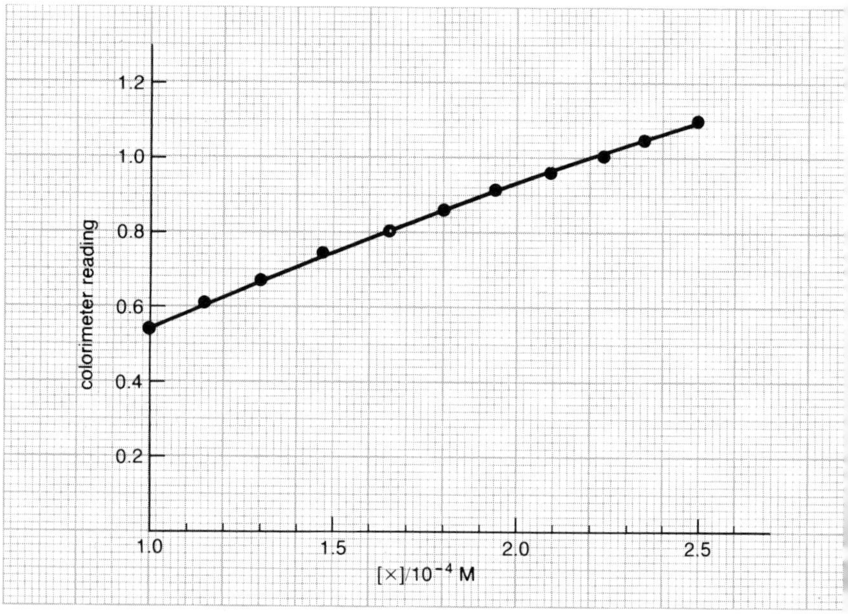

3   perform the reaction and measure the absorption at x nm at regular time intervals;
4   use the calibration curve to convert absorbance into [X];
5   plot a graph of [X] against time.

Activity 11.1

1   Use the calibration curve in figure 11.4 to complete the following table:

Time/min	0	1	2	3	4	5	6	7	8	9
Meter reading	1.1	1.05	1.00	0.95	0.92	0.88	0.85	0.81	0.78	0.75
[X]/M	?	?	?	?	?	?	?	?	?	?

2   Plot the graph of [X] (vertical axis) against time (horizontal axis).
3   Use your graph to determine the initial rate of reaction.

Figure 11.5 *Apparatus for measuring the volume of a gas evolved during a reaction*

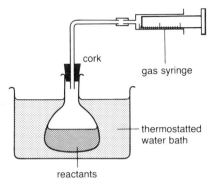

cork

gas syringe

thermostatted water bath

reactants

Change in the volume of a gas evolved

The kinetics of reactions which produce gases can be studied by measuring the volume of the gas produced at regular intervals. A suitable apparatus is given in figure 11.5.

When using this method, *the increase in gas volume must be converted to [reactant] or [product]* (since rate is a concentration change with time). For example, suppose that a known volume of 0.1 M aqueous hydrogen peroxide completely decomposes to $60 \, cm^3$ of oxygen. This means that each time $1 \, cm^3$ of oxygen is formed the concentration of hydrogen peroxide will drop by $1/60 \times 0.1 = 1.67 \times 10^{-3} \, M$.

Change in gas pressure

In some gas reactions, there is a change in the number of gas molecules present, e.g.

$$C_2H_4(g) + H_2(g) \rightarrow C_2H_6(g)$$
$$\text{2 moles} \qquad \text{1 mole}$$

From the **ideal gas equation, $pv = nRT$,** any decrease in the number of moles (n), at constant temperature (T) and volume (V), will lead to a corresponding decrease in pressure (p). On the other hand, if there is an increase in the number of gas moles present, the pressure will rise, e.g.

$$2N_2O_5(g) \rightarrow 4NO_2(g) + O_2(g)$$
$$\text{2 moles} \qquad \text{5 moles}$$

Such gas reactions can be studied, therefore, by performing the reaction in a closed metal container fitted with a pressure gauge.

Change in electrical conductivity

During some reactions, there is a change in the number of ions in solution and this will affect the electrical conductivity of the solution. For example, during the following reaction,

$$BrO_3^-(aq) + 5Br^-(aq) + 6H^+(aq) \rightarrow 3Br_2(aq) + 3H_2O(l)$$

there is a sharp decrease in the number of ions present. Consequently, the electrical conductivity of the solution also falls, and this can be observed using a **conductivity cell** (figure 11.6). Since ionic concentrations can be calculated from electrical conductivities, this gives us another way of following a reaction.

Figure 11.6 *A conductivity cell*

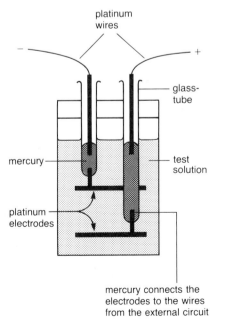

platinum wires

glass-tube

mercury

test solution

platinum electrodes

mercury connects the electrodes to the wires from the external circuit

Change in the optical rotation of the solution

When sucrose is hydrolysed in aqueous acid solution, there is a change in the optical rotation of the solution (see section 10.4). Thus,

$$C_{12}H_{22}O_{11}(aq) + H_2O(l) \rightarrow C_6H_{12}O_6(aq) + C_6H_{12}O_6(aq)$$

sucrose   (+)-glucose   (−)-fructose

dextrotatory, $[\alpha] = +66°$ overall laevorotatory, $[\alpha] = -20°$

A **polarimeter** (section 10.4) is used to measure the overall direction and angle of rotation. From this information, we can calculate the relative concentrations of the isomers and use these in our kinetics study.

Sometimes more than one method can be used for a particular reaction. For example, the reaction between permanganate and oxalate ions in acid solution,

$$2MnO_4^-(aq) + 16H^+(aq) + 5C_2O_4^{2-}(aq) \rightarrow 2Mn^{2+}(aq) + 8H_2O(l) + 10CO_2(g)$$

could be followed using three of the above 'continuous' methods. Which are they? Sampling is also a possibility. Quite often, our choice of technique may well depend on the apparatus which is available!

Activity 11.2

Which of the above methods could be used to investigate the kinetics of the following reactions?

1    $CH_3CHO(g) \xrightarrow{500\,°C} CH_4(g) + CO(g)$
ethanal   methane   carbon monoxide

2    $Br_2(aq) + HCOOH(aq) \xrightarrow{H^+, \text{catalyst}} 2Br^-(aq) + 2H^+(aq) + CO_2(g)$
methanoic acid

3

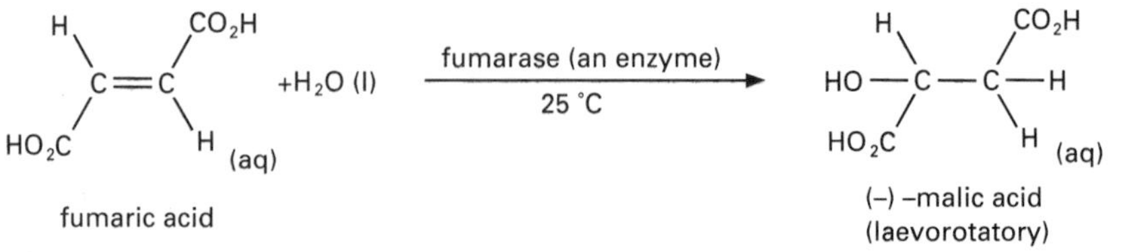

fumaric acid

(−) –malic acid
(laevorotatory)

4    $CH_3CO_2C_2H_5 (aq) + NaOH (aq) \rightarrow CH_3CO_2Na (aq) + C_2H_5OH (aq)$
ethyl ethanoate   sodium ethanoate   ethanol

11.4 Orders of reaction and rate equations

Once again, consider the reaction between bromate and bromide ions in acid solution:

$$BrO_3^-(aq) + 5Br^-(aq) + 6H^+(aq) \rightarrow 3Br_2(aq) + 3H_2O(l)$$
colourless solution   orange solution

The reaction kinetics can be studied by 'following' the formation of bromine using a colorimeter. Some results from this study, table 11.1, are analysed below.

Table 11.1   *Results from a kinetics study of the reaction between bromate and bromide ions in acid solution*

Mixture	$[BrO_3^- (aq)]/M$	$[Br^- (aq)]/M$	$[H^+ (aq)]/M$	relative rate
A	0.05	0.25	0.3	1
B	0.10	0.25	0.3	2
C	0.10	0.50	0.3	4
D	0.10	0.50	0.6	16

Comparing results from mixtures A and B:
Doubling the $[BrO_3^-]$ *doubles* the rate. Therefore, **rate** $\propto$ **$[BrO_3^-]$**.

Comparing results from mixtures B and C:
Doubling the $[Br^-]$ *doubles* the rate. Therefore, **rate** $\propto$ **$[Br^-]$**.

Comparing results from mixtures C and D:
Doubling the $[H^+]$ *quadruples* the rate. Therefore, **rate** $\propto$ **$[H^+]^2$**.

Combining these expressions,

$$\text{rate} \propto [BrO_3^-][Br^-][H^+]^2$$
$$\text{rate} = k\,[BrO_3^-][Br^-][H^+]^2$$

This is known as the **rate equation** for the reaction. Rate equations have the general form:

$$\text{rate} = k\,[A]^x\,[B]^y\,[C]^z \ldots$$

where k = the **rate constant** (or **rate coefficient**) and $x, y, z \ldots$ are the orders of reaction with respect to A, B, C . . .

The **order of reaction** *with respect to a given reactant is the power to which its concentration is raised in the rate equation. The overall order is the sum of the individual orders.* In our example, the reaction is said to be first order in BrO_3^- ions, first order

order in Br^- ions and second order in H^+ ions. Overall the reaction is fourth order. *Orders can be whole numbers or fractions, positive or negative.* We shall limit our discussion to reactions with rate equations containing zero, first or second order concentration terms.

Sometimes the individual orders or reaction are the same as the mole quantities in the balanced chemical equation; this is just a coincidence. *Orders must be found experimentally,* that is, by investigating how the rate varies with different reactant concentrations. Orders of reaction can help us to work out the reaction mechanism, as we shall see in the following case studies.

11.5 Studying kinetics I: by measuring initial rates

In section 11.1, we saw that the initial rate is obtained by measuring the gradient at time = 0 of a concentration against time graph (figure 11.1). A kinetics study based on initial rates is carried out in five stages. Let us work through each stage using, as an example, the acid catalysed iodination of propanone:

$$CH_3COCH_3(aq) + I_2(aq) \rightarrow CH_2ICOCH_3(aq) + HI(aq)$$

STAGE 1: (a) Choose a concentration to follow and (b) decide how you will follow it, by sampling or continuous measurement.

As this reaction proceeds, the reddish-brown colour of the iodine disappears. Thus, a colorimeter can be used to 'follow' the decrease in iodine concentration.

STAGE 2: Determine the initial rates for various initial concentrations of each reactant, whilst keeping the others constant.

First the colorimeter is calibrated (section 11.2). Then, the change in $[I_2(aq)]$ is followed for various reaction mixtures (table 11.2). (Note: [propanone] varies in A, B, C; $[H^+(aq)]$ varies in A, D, E; and $[I_2(aq)]$ varies in A, F, G; while the other concentrations remain constant.)

Table 11.2 *Results from a kinetics study of the reaction between propanone and iodine in acid solution at 25°C*

Expt.	CH$_3$COCH$_3$	H$^+$	I$_2/10^{-3}$	60 s	120 s	180 s	240 s	300 s
A	1.00	0.1	6.00	5.82	5.68	5.50	5.30	5.15
B	2.00	0.1	6.00	5.65	5.32	4.96	4.65	4.28
C	3.00	0.1	6.00	5.52	5.00	4.52	4.05	3.52
D	1.00	0.2	6.00	5.67	5.35	5.04	4.66	4.35
E	1.00	0.3	6.00	5.48	4.98	4.45	3.97	3.44
F	1.00	0.1	3.00	2.81	2.65	2.47	2.30	2.13
G	1.00	0.1	1.50	1.34	1.14	0.99	0.80	0.65

Column headers: starting concentrations/M (CH$_3$COCH$_3$, H$^+$, I$_2/10^{-3}$); $[I_2]/10^{-3}$ M remaining unreacted after (60 s, 120 s, 180 s, 240 s, 300 s)

STAGE 3: For each experiment, draw graphs of ['followed' reactant or product] plotted against time. Work out the initial rate from each graph.

Figure 11.7 shows the graphs of $[I_2(aq)]$ plotted against time (using the data in table 11.2). The initial rates, obtained by measuring the gradients of these lines, are listed in table 11.3.

STAGE 4: For each reactant, plot graphs of initial rate against starting concentration. Usually, these graphs will resemble one of those in figure 11.8. At this stage, you will have determined each order of reaction and can now write down the complete rate equation.

Table 11.3 *Initial rates obtained for the reaction of iodine with propanone in acid solution (see table 11.2 and figure 11.7)*

Expt.	initial rate/10^{-6} M s^{-1}
A	2.83
B	5.73
C	8.27
D	5.50
E	8.53
F	2.88
G	2.80

Figure 11.9 shows the 'initial rate against [reactant]' graphs obtained from the data in table 11.3. Comparing these graphs with those in figure 11.8, we can see that the reaction is first order in propanone, first order in hydrogen ions but zero order in iodine. Thus, we can write the rate equation:

Figure 11.7   *The data in table 11.2 for the iodination of propanone at 25°C plotted as graphs of concentration against time*

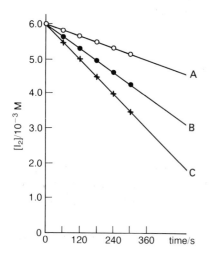

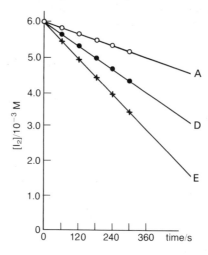

$$\text{rate} = k\,[CH_3COCH_3]\,[H^+]\,[I_2]^0$$
$$\therefore \text{rate} = k\,[CH_3COCH_3]\,[H^+]$$

(Note: any term to the power of zero = 1; thus $[I_2]^0 = 1$.)

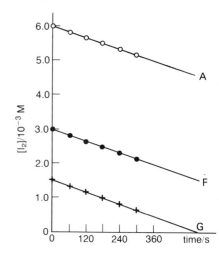

Figure 11.8   *Possible graphs of initial rate plotted against [A], whilst [B] and [C] remain constant, for the reaction $A + B + C \rightarrow$ products*

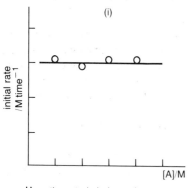

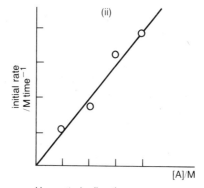

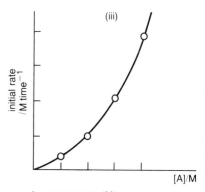

Here the rate is independent of [A]
∴ the reaction is zero order in A and
Rate ∝ $[A]^0$

Here rate is directly proportional to [A]
∴ Rate ∝ $[A]^1$
and the reaction is first order in A

In many cases, this type of graph will be due to a second order dependence i.e.
Rate ∝ $[A]^2$

Figure 11.9   *Graphs showing how the initial rates of the iodination of propanone (from figure 11.7) depend on the starting concentration of each reactant*

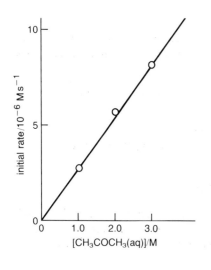

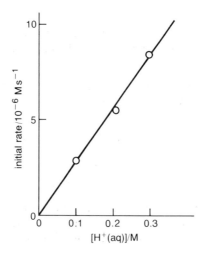

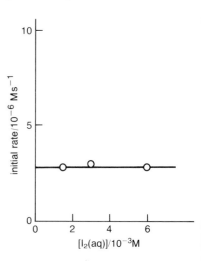

STAGE 5: Substitute each set of concentrations into the rate equation. This gives a series of values for the rate constant, k. If you have analysed the results correctly, these k values will agree within experimental error.

Take, for example, experiment A which has a rate =
$2.83 \times 10^{-6} \, M \, s^{-1}$ at $[CH_3COCH_3] = 1.00$ M and $[H^+] = 0.1$ M.
From the rate equation,

$$k = \frac{rate}{[CH_3COCH_3] \, [H^+]}$$

Substituting,

$$k = \frac{2.83 \times 10^{-6} \, M \, s^{-1}}{1.0 \times 0.1 \, M^2}$$

$$\boldsymbol{k = 2.83 \times 10^{-5} \, M^{-1} s^{-1}}$$

Similar calculations for experiments B to G give the following values for the rate constant 2.86, 2.76, 2.75, 2.84, 2.88, 2.80 (all $\times 10^{-5} \, M^{-1} \, s^{-1}$). These values show good agreement within experimental error and *confirm that the reaction is first order in both propanone and hydrogen ions.*

Orders of reaction provide information about the reaction's mechanism, as we shall now see.

11.6 Rate equations and reaction mechanisms

The following story should help with this section.

Al Chemist is desperate to get to college on time today; he has a chemistry test! Unfortunately, Al gets up late and can only catch his train by running to the station. After a superhuman effort, he reaches the station with three minutes to spare only to find that his train is running twenty minutes late! Even if Al ran faster, his overall rate of travel would still be totally dependent on the time he has to wait for the train.

Like Al's journey, *many chemical reactions:*

▶ *proceed via a sequence of distinct stages.* This sequence is known as the **reaction mechanism;**

▶ *possess an overall rate equal to that of the slowest step*, known as the **rate-determining step.** For example, the conversion of A + C → D may have the mechanism:

$$A \longrightarrow B \quad \text{slow, rate-determining step}$$
$$B + C \longrightarrow D \quad \text{very fast}$$

Here, *the rate at which D is formed depends on how quickly A gives B, not how quickly B reacts with C.* The rate equation would be

$$rate = k \, [A]^x$$

where *x* is the order of reaction. Note that [C] does not appear in the rate equation because C is not involved in the rate-determining step but only in the following fast step.

Now, let us see how our conclusions from section 11.5 fit in with the proposed mechanism of the reaction

$$CH_3COCH_3 + I_2 \xrightarrow{\quad H^+(aq) \text{ catalyst} \quad} CH_2ICOCH_3 + HI$$

To recap, this reaction has the rate equation:

$$rate = k[CH_3COCH_3] \, [H^+]$$

Since the reaction is zero order in iodine (i.e. $[I_2]$ does not affect the rate), the iodine molecule must be involved in a fast step. So, *the rate-determining step must involve only propanone and hydrogen ions.* The following mechanism has been suggested:

$$H_3C-\overset{\overset{\displaystyle H^+}{|}}{\underset{\|}{C}}-CH_3 \quad\xrightarrow{\text{slow}}\quad H_3C-\overset{\overset{\displaystyle O-H}{|}}{\underset{+}{C}}-CH_3 \qquad \text{the rate-determining step: formation of a carbonium ion}$$

$$H_3C-\overset{\overset{\displaystyle O-H}{|}}{\underset{+}{C}}-CH_3 \quad\xrightarrow{\text{fast}}\quad H^+ \ + \ H_2C=\overset{\overset{\displaystyle O-H}{|}}{C}-CH_3 \qquad \text{formation of an enol group} \qquad \overset{\diagdown}{}C=C\overset{OH}{\underset{\diagdown}{\diagup}}$$

$$H_2C=\overset{\overset{\displaystyle O-H}{|}}{C}-CH_3 \quad\xrightarrow{\text{fast}}\quad H-\overset{|}{\underset{|}{C}}-\overset{\overset{\displaystyle H\ O-H}{|}}{\underset{|}{C}}-CH_3 \qquad \text{addition of } I_2 \text{ to the C=C bond}$$

$$\underset{I-I}{}$$

$$H-\overset{\overset{\displaystyle H\ O-H}{|}}{\underset{|}{C}}-\overset{|}{\underset{|}{C}}-CH_3 \quad\xrightarrow{\text{fast}}\quad H-\overset{\overset{\displaystyle H\ O}{|}}{\underset{|}{C}}-\overset{\|}{C}-CH_3 \ + \ HI \qquad \text{elimination of HI}$$

Another aspect of each step in the mechanism is its **molecularity**. *This is the number of reacting species which take part in that step.* In the example above, the rate determining step involves one molecule and one ion. So, the molecularity is two and it is said to be *bimolecular*.

As we have seen, orders of reaction give us some idea of what happens in the rate-determining step. To work out the full reaction mechanism, though, we often need to use other techniques (e.g. isotopic labelling, section 40.5.3).

Activity 11.3

The decomposition of hydrogen peroxide in aqueous solution,

$$2H_2O_2(aq) \rightarrow 2H_2O(l) + O_2(g),$$

is catalysed by manganese dioxide, $MnO_2(s)$. Kinetics experiments can be carried out by following the rate of production of oxygen. Some experimental results are given in table 11.4.

Table 11.4 *Kinetics results for the manganese (IV) oxide catalysed decomposition of hydrogen peroxide. Initial concentrations of H_2O_2 are shown below as $[H_2O_2]_0$; volume of solution used $50\,cm^3$; mass of MnO_2 catalyst $50\,mg$; temperature $25°C$*

Experiment A $[H_2O_2]_0 = 0.05\,M$		Experiment B $[H_2O_2]_0 = 0.10\,M$		Experiment C $[H_2O_2]_0 = 0.20\,M$	
time/s	vol. of O_2/cm^3	time/s	vol. of O_2/cm^3	time/s	vol. of O_2/cm^3
12	0.16	12	0.38	12	0.67
24	0.33	24	0.72	24	1.31
36	0.50	36	1.05	36	2.02
48	0.65	48	1.33	48	2.67
60	0.82	60	1.65	60	3.30
72	0.96	72	1.96	72	3.97
84	1.13	84	2.25	84	4.50
96	1.28	96	2.53	96	5.05
108	1.42	108	2.83	108	5.56
120	1.58	120	3.14	120	6.08
final volume	30	final volume	60	final volume	120

1 Using the same axes plot graphs of volume of $O_2(g)$ (vertical axis) against time (horizontal axis), for the first 120s of each reaction.

2 Determine the initial gradients and note their units. Are these gradients actually the initial rates? (Remember, rate = [ ]/time.)

3 For these reaction conditions, what molarity of H_2O_2 solution would liberate $1 \, cm^3$ of oxygen?
4 Now convert your 'gradient' values into initial rates of loss of H_2O_2 (aq).
5 What is the effect on the initial rate of doubling $[H_2O_2]_0$? What is the order of reaction with respect to hydrogen peroxide?
6 Write down the rate equation and work out the rate constant.

11.7 Studying kinetics II: using a 'clock' reaction

In this method, we measure the average rate of forming a fixed concentration of product (figure 11.10). Thus,

$$\text{average rate} = \frac{\text{increase in [product]}}{\text{time taken for this increase}}$$

Our case study is the reaction between hydrogen peroxide and iodide ions in aqueous acid solution:

$$H_2O_2(aq) + 2H^+(aq) + 2I^-(aq) \rightarrow 2H_2O(l) + I_2(aq) \tag{I}$$

Iodine can be detected by the blue colour it gives in starch solution. However, if a small amount of aqueous sodium thiosulphate is added to the starch solution, the following rapid reaction takes place:

$$2Na_2S_2O_3(aq) + I_2(aq) \rightarrow Na_2S_4O_6(aq) + 2NaI(aq) \tag{II}$$

This prevents the iodine from reacting with the starch. Consequently, a blue colour will not be seen until all the sodium thiosulphate has been used up. Also, if each of the reaction mixtures has the same starting concentration of thiosulphate, they will turn blue only when each has produced the same concentration of iodine (i.e. that needed to react with all the thiosulphate ions).

Let us analyse the results from such a kinetics experiment (table 11.5).

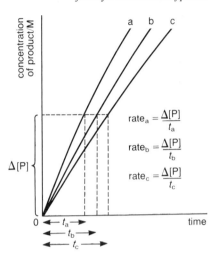

Figure 11.10 *Average rates are inversely proportional to the time it takes to form a fixed concentration of product*

Table 11.5 *Kinetics results for the reaction between hydrogen peroxide and iodide ions in aqueous acid solution. All concentrations have units = M; each reaction mixture contains starch indicator and a sodium thiosulphate concentration of $9.00 \times 10^{-5} M$*

Expt.	[KI(aq)]	[H^+(aq)]	[H_2O_2(aq)]	time taken, t/s	average rate/$10^{-6} M s^{-1}$
A	0.03	0.03	0.03	9.5	4.74
B	0.02	0.03	0.03	15.0	3.00
C	0.01	0.03	0.03	28.5	1.58
D	0.01	0.02	0.03	29.5	1.52
E	0.01	0.01	0.03	30.5	1.47
F	0.03	0.03	0.02	14.0	3.21
G	0.03	0.03	0.01	30.0	1.50
H	0.01	0.023	0.03	31.5	1.43
I	0.01	0.016	0.03	32.0	1.41

From the mole ratio in equation (II), we can see that the blue colour will appear when the iodine concentration reaches $\frac{1}{2}(9.00 \times 10^{-5})M = 4.50 \times 10^{-5} M$. Thus, for each mixture

$$\text{average rate} = \frac{4.50 \times 10^{-5} M s^{-1}}{\text{time taken}}$$

Values for the average rate are also given in table 11.5. From now on, the method resembles that in section 11.5, stages 4 and 5.

The **orders of reaction** *are obtained by plotting the average rates against the varying initial concentrations of each reactant* (figure 11.11). These graphs suggest that the reaction is first order in hydrogen peroxide, first order in iodide ions and probably zero order in hydrogen ions. Hence, the rate equation for this reaction is

$$\text{rate} = k \, [H_2O_2(aq)] \, [I^-(aq)]$$

Now we can determine the **rate constant** *from each experiment by substituting values into the rate equation.* For example, for experiment A we have:

$$k = \frac{\text{rate}}{[\text{H}_2\text{O}_2\,(\text{aq})]\,[\text{I}^-\,(\text{aq})]}$$

$$= \frac{4.74 \times 10^{-6}\,\text{M}\,\text{s}^{-1}}{0.03 \times 0.03\,\text{M}^2}$$

$$= 0.0053\,\text{M}^{-1}\,\text{s}^{-1}.$$

Figure 11.11 *Graphs of average rate plotted against the starting concentration of each reactant for the reaction:*

$$H_2O_2(aq) + 2I^-(aq) + 2H^+(aq) \rightarrow 2H_2O(l) + I_2(aq)$$

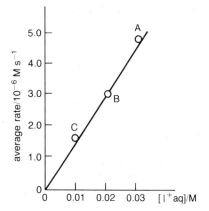

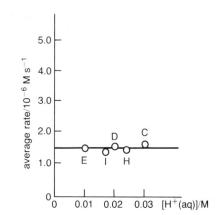

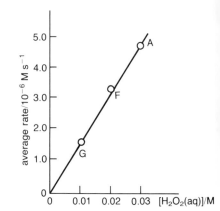

This calculation can be repeated using data from experiments B–I, giving the following values for k: 0.0050, 0.0053, 0.0051, 0.0049, 0.0053, 0.0050, 0.0048 and 0.0047, respectively. Also, the average value for the rate constant is found to be $0.005\,\text{M}^{-1}\,\text{s}^{-1}$. Within experimental error, the 'k' values show reasonable agreement and this suggests that our orders of reaction are probably correct. We can now see how the orders of reaction fit in with the proposed reaction mechanism.

Since the rate is independent of the concentration of hydrogen ions, these cannot be involved in the rate-determining step. The accepted mechanism is:

Step 1 $H_2O_2(aq) + I^-(aq) \rightarrow H_2O(l) + OI^-(aq)$ slow, rate-determining

Step 2 $H^+(aq) + OI^-(aq) \rightarrow HOI(aq)$ fast

Step 3 $HOI(aq) + H^+(aq) + I^-(aq) \rightarrow H_2O(l) + I_2(aq)$ fast

By adding the steps together, we get the overall chemical equation, given earlier. Notice that one molecule and one ion are reacting in the rate determining step; thus, it is *bimolecular*.

Activity 11.4

Iodide ions are oxidised in aqueous solution by peroxodisulphate (persulphate) ions. The equation is:

$$2I^-(aq) + S_2O_8^{2-}(aq) \rightarrow I_2(aq) + 2SO_4^{2-}(aq)$$

This reaction can be investigated by using the 'clock' technique. A set of results is shown in table 11.6.

Table 11.6 *Kinetics results for the oxidation of iodide ions by peroxosdisulphate ions in aqueous solution*

	volumes used/cm³						
Expt.	0.5 M $S_2O_8^{2-}$ (aq)	0.5 M I^- (aq)	0.01 M $Na_2S_2O_3$(aq)	0.2% w/w starch (aq)	water	total	time taken/s
A	2	60	20	5	13	100	6
B	2	40	20	5	33	100	10
C	2	20	20	5	53	100	19

1   Draw up a table which lists the concentrations of peroxodisulphate ions, iodide ions and sodium thiosulphate, in each experiment.
2   In these experiments, what concentration of iodine will be produced before the solution changes colour? (Notes: (i) the thiosulphate is diluted when the reaction mixture is made up; (ii) use equation (II), previous section.)
3   Calculate the average rate of reaction for each experiment.
4   What is the order of reaction with respect to I^- ions?
5   Other experiments indicate that the reaction is first order with respect to peroxodisulphate ions. Use this information to (a) write down the rate equation and (b) calculate the rate constant.

11.8 Studying kinetics III: by measuring half-lives

The **half-life, $t_{\frac{1}{2}}$,** of a reaction is defined as *the time it takes for a reactant concentration to fall to half of its original value.* Let us measure some half-lives for the manganese (IV) oxide catalysed decomposition of hydrogen peroxide.

$$2H_2O_2(l) \rightarrow 2H_2O(l) + O_2(g),$$

this being a first order reaction (see activity 11.3). Figure 11.12 shows a typical graph of $[H_2O_2]$ plotted against time. How long does it take for the hydrogen peroxide concentration to fall (i) from $0.1\,M$ to $0.05\,M$, (ii) from $0.05\,M$ to $0.025\,M$ and (iii) from $0.025\,M$ to $0.0125\,M$? What is interesting about your answers?

Figure 11.12 *A graph of concentration of hydrogen peroxide against time for its decomposition in aqueous solution, catalysed by manganese(IV) oxide at $25°C$*

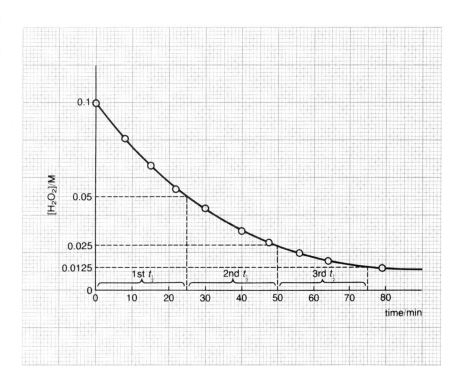

Well, within experimental error, the answers are the same, 25 minutes. We have measured the first, second and third half-lives for this first order reaction, and found them to be equal. In fact, it can be proved mathematically that *a first order reaction must have constant successive half-lives.* Because of this, we can identify any first order reaction from a single kinetics experiment. It is also possible to express a first order rate constant, k, in terms of its half-life:

$$k = \frac{0.693}{t_{\frac{1}{2}}}$$

In section 2.10, we saw that *radioactive isotopes have constant half-lives* (e.g. 1590 years for radium-226). Hence, *radioactive decay must be a first order reaction,* having the rate equation:

$$\text{rate} = \lambda \, [\text{isotope}]$$

Here, λ is a rate constant known as the **decay constant**. For radium-226,

$$\lambda = \frac{0.693}{1590} = 4.36 \times 10^{-4} \, \text{year}^{-1}$$

Activity 11.5

2-bromo-2-methylpropane (2-b-2-mp) is hydrolysed according to the equation:

1 How would you follow the kinetics of this reaction?
2 A student obtained the following results (at 25 °C):

time/h^{-1}	0	5	10	15	20	25	30	35	40	45
[2-b-2-mp]/M	0.210	0.164	0.128	0.097	0.076	0.058	0.044	0.034	0.027	0.023

(a) Plot the graph of [2-bromo-2-methylpropane] against time.
(b) By measuring half-lives, prove that the reaction is first order with respect to 2-bromo-2-methylpropane.
(c) Calculate the rate constant.
(d) Write down the rate equation.
(e) Give the molecularity of this reaction. Which molecule will be involved in the rate-determining step?
(f) By considering the bond polarities in the molecules, can you propose a reaction mechanism?

11.9 Units of rate constants

It is important that rate constants are quoted with the correct units. These can be worked out from the units of the individual terms in the rate equation, as follows.

Zero order reactions: have a rate equation, rate = k. Since rate has the units of concentration/time, it follows that the rate constant for a zero order reaction has units, M time^{-1}.

First order reactions have a rate equation, rate = k [ ]. Thus,

$$k = \frac{\text{rate}}{[\ ]} \xrightarrow{\text{substituting units}} \frac{\text{M time}^{-1}}{\text{M}} = \text{time}^{-1}$$

For first order reactions, then, the rate constant always has the unit time^{-1}.

Second order reactions have a rate equation, rate = k[ ]^2. Thus,

$$k = \frac{\text{rate}}{[\ ]^2} \xrightarrow{\text{substituting units}} \frac{\text{M time}^{-1}}{\text{M}^2} = \text{M}^{-1}\text{time}^{-1}$$

For second order reactions, then, the rate constant always has the unit $\text{M}^{-1}\text{time}^{-1}$.

Third order reactions have a rate equation, rate = k[ ]^3. Thus,

$$k = \frac{\text{rate}}{[\ ]^3} \xrightarrow{\text{substituting units}} \frac{\text{M time}^{-1}}{\text{M}^3} = \text{M}^{-2}\text{time}^{-1}$$

For third order reactions, then, the rate constant always has the unit $\text{M}^{-2}\text{time}^{-1}$.

11.10 Comments on the activities

Note: Your numerical answers may differ slightly from those in this section. This is to be expected because the drawing of graphs and tangents is a matter of personal judgement.

Activity 11.1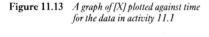

1   The completed table is:

Time/min	0	1	2	3	4	5	6	7	8	9
Meter reading	1.1	1.05	1.00	0.95	0.92	0.88	0.85	0.81	0.78	0.75
[X]/M	2.50	2.35	2.20	2.07	1.97	1.85	1.77	1.65	1.60	1.53

2   These results give the graph in figure 11.13.

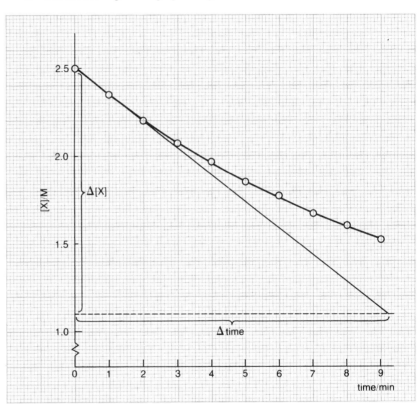

Figure 11.13 *A graph of [X] plotted against time for the data in activity 11.1*

3   The initial rate is obtained from the gradient of the tangent drawn at time = 0. Thus,

$$\text{initial rate (of removing X)} = \frac{\Delta[X]}{\Delta \text{ time}} = \frac{1.40\,M}{9.2\,\text{min}} = 0.15\,M\,\text{min}^{-1}$$

Activity 11.2

1   (i) Change in pressure; there is an increase in the number of gas moles, therefore pressure will increase as the reaction proceeds; (ii) increase in gas volume.

2   As the reaction proceeds there will be (i) a change in colour – the orange colour due to the bromine will disappear; (ii) an increase in the conductivity of the solution – more ions in the products; (iii) sampling: run the sample

into excess aqueous potassium iodide, titrating the iodine liberated against standard aqueous sodium thiosulphate. Following the increase in volume of CO_2 will not work because the gas is quite soluble in water.

3   As the reaction proceeds, there will be a change in the optical rotation of the solution.

4   Sampling; running the sample into ice-cold water (stops the reaction) then titrating the unreacted sodium hydroxide against a standard acid.

Activity 11.3

1   The graphs are shown in figure 11.14.

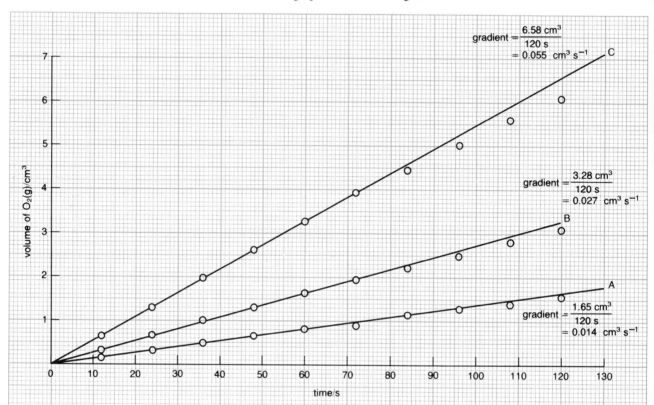

Figure 11.14   *Graphs of volume of oxygen produced plotted against time during the decomposition of aqueous hydrogen peroxide, catalysed by manganese(IV) oxide at 25°C*

2   The initial gradients are 0.014, 0.027 and 0.055 cm^3 s^{-1} for experiments A, B and C, respectively. These are not initial rates since *rate is a concentration change with time*. Thus, we must convert volume of oxygen into concentration of hydrogen peroxide.

3   Since the volume of peroxide solution is constant (50 cm^3), the final volume of O_2 gas will depend on the $[H_2O_2]_0$. Under these conditions using 50 cm^3 of 0.05, 0.10 or 0.20 M H_2O_2 solution produces 30, 60 or 120 cm^3 of oxygen, respectively. Hence,

1 cm^3 of oxygen is produced by 0.05/30 or 0.10/60 or 0.20/120
$$= 1.67 \times 10^{-3} \, M \, H_2O_2.$$

4   *Expt. A*, initial rate = 0.014 cm^3 s^{-1} × 1.67 × 10^{-3} M cm^{-3}
$$= 2.34 \times 10^{-5} \, M \, s^{-1}.$$

Expt. B, initial rate = 0.027 cm^3 s^{-1} × 1.67 × 10^{-3}
$$= 4.51 \times 10^{-5} \, M \, s^{-1}.$$

Expt. C, initial rate = 0.055 cm^3 s^{-1} × 1.67 × 10^{-3} M cm^{-3}
$$= 9.18 \times 10^{-5} \, M \, s^{-1}.$$

5   Doubling $[H_2O_2]_0$, doubles the rate. Thus, the reaction is first order in hydrogen peroxide.

6 The rate equation is rate $= k\,[H_2O_2]$.

Thus, $\quad k = \dfrac{\text{rate}}{[H_2O_2]}$

For experiment A, then,

$$k = \frac{2.34 \times 10^{-5}\,\text{M s}^{-1}}{0.05\,\text{M}} = 4.68 \times 10^{-4}\,\text{s}^{-1}.$$

Similarly, the results from experiments B and C give $k = 4.51 \times 10^{-4}$ and $4.59 \times 10^{-4}\,\text{s}^{-1}$, respectively. These values show good agreement within experimental error. The average value for k is $4.59 \times 10^{-4}\,\text{s}^{-1}$.

Activity 11.4

1 The concentrations are:

Expt.	$[S_2O_8{}^{2-}\,(aq)]$/M	$[I^-(aq)]$/M	$[Na_2S_2O_3\,(aq)]$/M	Average rate/10^{-4}M s^{-1}
A	0.01	0.3	0.002	1.67
B	0.01	0.2	0.002	1.00
C	0.01	0.1	0.002	0.53

2 Iodine and sodium thiosulphate react according to the equation:

$$2S_2O_3{}^{2-}(aq) + I_2(aq) \rightarrow S_4O_6{}^{2-}(aq) + 2I^-(aq)$$

Since 2 moles of $S_2O_3{}^{2-}$ ions give only 1 mole of I_2, the iodine concentration when the 'blue' appears will be $\frac{1}{2} \times 0.002 = 0.001$ M.

3 $\qquad\qquad$ Average rate $= \dfrac{\text{change in concentration}}{\text{time taken}}$

e.g. for experiment A,

$$\text{average rate} = \frac{0.001\,\text{M}}{6\,\text{s}} = 1.67 \times 10^{-4}\,\text{M s}^{-1}$$

4 The average rates are directly proportional to $[I^-]$. Thus, the reaction is first order in I^- ions.

5 (i) rate $= k\,[S_2O_8{}^{2-}(aq)]\,[I^-(aq)]$
$\quad$ (ii) Rearranging,

$$k = \frac{\text{rate}}{[S_2O_8{}^{2-}(aq)]\,[I^-(aq)]}$$

Substituting values for the average rates and concentrations we get values for $k = 0.056$, 0.050 and 0.053 M^{-1} s^{-1}, for experiments A, B and C, respectively. Once again, the answers show good agreement within experimental error, with an average $k = 0.053\,\text{M}^{-1}\text{s}^{-1}$.

Activity 11.5

1 The reaction may be followed by:
$\quad$ (i) sampling at regular intervals, cooling (to halt the reaction), and titrating the unreacted alkali against a standard acid; or
$\quad$ (ii) measuring the rate of decrease in pH (section 18.5).
In each case, the results obtained *must* be converted into the concentration of a reactant or product.

2 (a) See figure 11.15.
$\quad$ (b) Successive half-lives are constant, with an average value of 13.5 h. Thus, the reaction is *first order* in 2-bromo-2-methyl-propane, (2-b-2-mp).

(c) $k = \dfrac{0.693}{t_{\frac{1}{2}}} = \dfrac{0.693}{13.5\,\text{h}} = 0.05\,\text{h}^{-1}$

(d) Rate = k [2-b-2-mp]

(e) Only one molecule, 2-bromo-2-methylpropane, is involved in the rate-determining step; so, it is *unimolecular*.

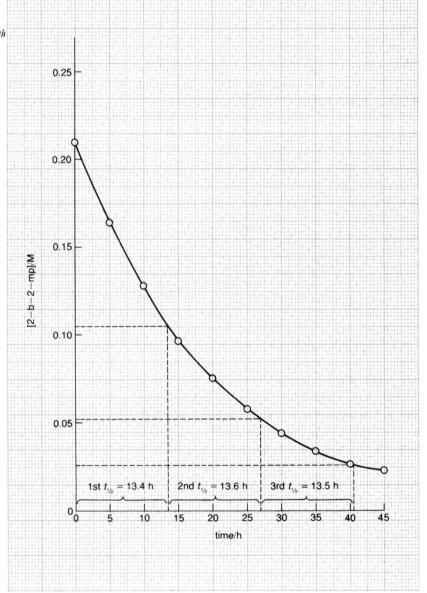

Step ①   H$_3$C—C(Br)(CH$_3$)—CH$_3$ $\xrightarrow{\text{slow}}$ H$_3$C—C$^+$(CH$_3$)—CH$_3$ + Br$^-$ unimolecular rate-determining step: ionisation of 2–b–2–mp

Step ②   H$_3$C—C$^+$(CH$_3$)—CH$_3$ + OH$^-$ $\xrightarrow{\text{fast}}$ H$_3$C—C(OH)(CH$_3$)—CH$_3$ nucleophilic attack by OH$^-$ (section **33.3**)

Figure 11.15 *A graph of the concentration of 2-bromo-2-methylpropane plotted against time, during its reaction with aqueous hydroxide ions*

1st $t_{1/2}$ = 13.4 h   2nd $t_{1/2}$ = 13.6 h   3rd $t_{1/2}$ = 13.5 h

[2–b–2–mp]/M

time/h

11.11 Summary and revision plan

1 **Rate of reaction** $= \dfrac{\text{increase in [product]}}{\text{time taken}}$ or $\dfrac{\text{decrease in [reactant]}}{\text{time taken}}$

2 Rate values, at a given time, can be obtained from the graph of [reactant], or [product], plotted against time (figure 11.1). The **initial rate** is the gradient of this curve at $t = 0$.

3 An **average rate** over a period of time $(\Delta t) = \Delta \text{[reactant]}/\Delta t$ or $\Delta \text{[product]}/\Delta t$.

4 Rate of product formation need not equal the rate of reactant loss.

5 The [reactant] or [product] is 'followed' by **sampling** or **continuous measurement** of a change in: **colour, gas volume, gas pressure, electrical conductivity** or **optical rotation**.

6 Rate equations have the general formula:

$$\text{rate} = k\,[\text{A}]^x[\text{B}]^y[\text{C}]^z \ldots$$

where $k =$ the **rate constant** and x, y and z are the **orders of reaction** with respect to A, B and C. The overall order is the sum of the individual orders. Orders need not be whole numbers and *must* be found experimentally; they help us to work out the **reaction mechanism** (section 11.6).

7 Orders of reaction and rate constants can be obtained by measuring **initial rates** (section 11.5), using a **'clock' reaction** (section 11.7) or measuring **successive half-lives** (section 11.8).

8 The slowest step in a reaction mechanism is known as the **rate-determining step**.

9 The number of reacting species involved in a reaction step is termed the **molecularity** of that step.

10 The **half-life, $t_{\frac{1}{2}}$,** of a reaction is the time it takes for the concentration of a reactant to fall to half of its original value. For a first order reaction, successive half-lives are constant and $k_{first\ order} = 0.693/t_{\frac{1}{2}}$.

11 The units of zero, first, second and third order rate constants are M time^{-1}, time^{-1}, $\text{M}^{-1}\text{time}^{-1}$ and $\text{M}^{-2}\text{time}^{-1}$.

□ CHAPTER □
CHAPTER
CHAPTER

12

CHAPTER
CHAPTER
□ CHAPTER □

Theories of Reaction Rates

Contents

During coal mining, the fine particles of coal dust produced by drilling are sprayed with water to prevent the dust igniting spontaneously

In chapter 11 we saw that changing a reactant's concentration often alters the rate of a reaction. Four other 'factors' may affect the rate of a reaction:

▶ **the size of the particles in a reacting solid**
   Rates get faster if solid reactants are ground up.

▶ **temperature**
   Reactions go faster at higher temperature.

▶ **light**
   Ultra violet light speeds up certain chemical reactions.

▶ **catalysts**
   Catalysts increase the rate of a reaction.

In this chapter, we shall see how a simple theory of reaction rates explains these effects.

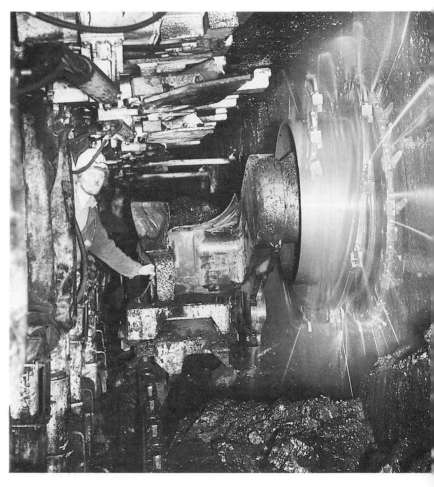

Fresh food can be kept longer in this frozen food store because bacteria breed much more slowly at low temperatures. Chickens, for example, can be stored for up to nine months in a freezer at $-15°C$

Magnesium was first used as a method of lighting in photography during the late nineteenth century

Fitting a catalytic converter to a car exhaust. The converter increases the rate of oxidation of the oxides of carbon, nitrogen and sulphur produced when petrol is burnt. Less harmful higher oxides are formed

The 'coconut shy' is a traditional fairground amusement. To win the coconut, it must be struck with enough force and at the correct angle

Figure 12.1 *In (a), the ball has enough kinetic energy to dislodge the coconut. In (b), although the ball has the same energy, it strikes the coconut at the wrong point (i.e. too near the top). Thus, the coconut remains in its holder*

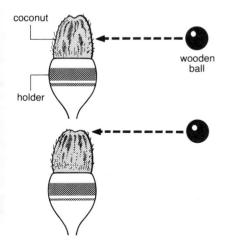

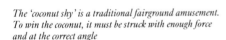

12.1 Collision Theory

In many ways the Collision Theory of Reaction Kinetics resembles a traditional fairground amusement, the 'coconut shy'. The idea is to throw a wooden ball at the coconut and knock it out of its holder. Then you can keep the coconut! Your success will depend on three factors:

▶ Does the ball hit the coconut, i.e. is there a *collision*?
▶ On collision, does the ball have *enough energy* to dislodge the coconut?
▶ Even if enough energy is present, does the ball strike the coconut at *a suitable point* (figure 12.1)?

Collision Theory suggests that products are formed only if the reactant molecules collide with:

▶ a certain minimum energy, known as the **activation energy, E_a**.
▶ the correct **collision geometry** (figure 12.2).

Figure 12.2 *Reactant molecules must collide with the correct collision geometry (b) if products are to be formed*

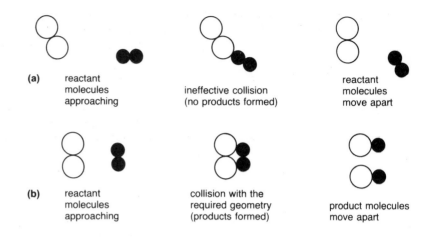

(a) reactant molecules approaching   ineffective collision (no products formed)   reactant molecules move apart

(b) reactant molecules approaching   collision with the required geometry (products formed)   product molecules move apart

Such collisions are said to be **activated**. Thus,

reaction rate = collision frequency × activated fraction

In fact, studies show that only a minute fraction of the total collisions are activated.

Figure 12.3 *Flasks with the same volumes but containing different numbers of moles of reactants*

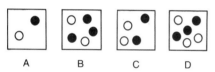

A   B   C   D

Figure 12.4 *When the same number of gas moles are subjected to an increase in pressure (at constant temperature), the volume decreases*

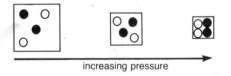

increasing pressure

These two flasks contain equal amounts of dilute hydrochloric acid and calcium carbonate. The reaction in the left-hand flask is much faster because we used powdered calcium carbonate, rather than large lumps

12.2 The effects of concentration and particle size on reaction rates?

Concentration

Increasing a reactant's concentration increases the collision frequency (figure 12.3). According to Collision Theory, this would lead to a faster rate of reaction (as is found for most reactions).

A similar effect is observed when we change the pressure of a gas reaction (figure 12.4).

Solid particle size

When a solid reacts, only the particles on its surface are available for reaction (figure 12.5). If the solid is ground up, its surface area gets larger and more particles will be available for collision. Thus, the frequency of collision increases and so does the rate of reaction.

To summarise, then, *changing a reactant's concentration, pressure (if gaseous) or surface area affects the collision frequency*. Since
reaction rate = collision frequency × activated fraction,
the reaction rate will also be affected by these changes.

12.3 The effects of temperature and light on reaction rates

Temperature

For *many* reactions, the rate roughly doubles every time the temperature is raised by 10°C. Collision Theory supposes that

reaction rate = collision frequency × activated fraction

fraction having correct geometry × fraction having the activation energy

Figure 12.5 *As the particles get smaller, their total surface area gets larger. Thus, more molecules are available for collision and the reaction rate increases*

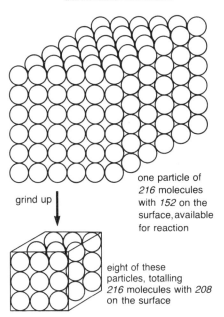

grind up ↓

one particle of *216 molecules* with *152* on the surface, available for reaction

eight of these particles, totalling *216 molecules* with *208* on the surface

Figure 12.6 *Distribution curves for the kinetic energies of gas molecules at different temperatures, where* $T_2 > T_1$

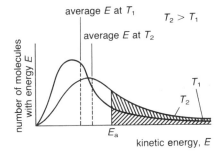

Now, if the reaction rate doubles, then so must the terms on the right hand side of this equation. Raising the temperature by 10 °C does indeed increase the collision frequency but only by a factor of about 1.016. Also, increasing the temperature does not alter the range of collision geometries. Therefore, *the effect of temperature on the reaction rate must result from more collisions having the activation energy.*

In 1859, Maxwell and Boltzmann calculated how the kinetic energy of gas molecules varies with temperature (figure 12.6.). At higher temperatures, the average kinetic energy of the molecules increases and there is a wider distribution of energies. For a reaction having an activation energy E_a, the number of molecules with E_a will be:

///// at the lower temperature T_1;

but //// + \\\\ at the higher temperature T_2.

A reaction will always be much faster at a higher temperature because many more molecules possess the activation energy on collision.

For any reaction, we find that the rate constant, k, and activation energy, E_a, are related by the equation:

$$k = A \times e^{-E_a/RT}$$

where A = the frequency of collisions with the correct geometry per unit volume;
   e = exponential constant (just a number = 2.718);
   R = gas constant = 8.31 J K^{-1} mol^{-1}. This tells us the increase in the kinetic energy of a gas which is produced by a certain temperature rise;
   T = the absolute temperature in K (i.e. °C + 273).

This equation was first suggested by Arrhenius in 1889 and it is known as the **Arrhenius equation**. It may be rewritten as

$$k = \frac{A}{e^{E_a/RT}}$$

This form makes it easier to see that:

▶ *raising T* makes E_a/RT (and e$^{E_a/RT}$) smaller ∴ k will increase and the reaction is *faster;* but
▶ *lowering T* makes E_a/RT (and e$^{E_a/RT}$) larger ∴ k will decrease and the reaction is *slower.*

By similar reasoning,

▶ if E_a *is low,* E_a/RT (and e$^{E_a/RT}$) will be small ∴ k will be large and the reaction will be *fast;* but
▶ if E_a *is high,* E_a/RT (and e$^{E_a/RT}$) will be large ∴ k will be small and the reaction will be *slow.*

Figure 12.7 shows how the activation energy contributes to the **enthalpy profile** for the reaction.

Figure 12.7 *Enthalpy profiles for endothermic (**a**) and exothermic (**b**, **c**) reactions*

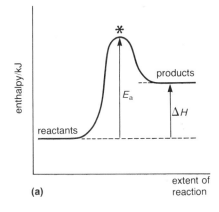

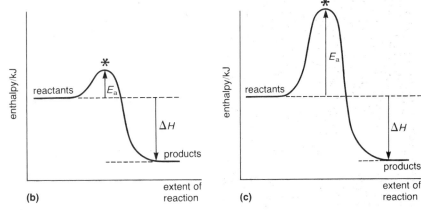

Activation energy must always be supplied to the reaction (i.e. it is endothermic (+ve)), whether or not the overall reaction is endothermic ($\Delta H = $ +ve, figure 12.7a) or exothermic ($\Delta H = $ −ve, figure 12.7b). The maximum energy state (marked *) is termed the **activated complex**. This may be thought of as *the instant in time when bonds in the reactants are broken as those in the product are formed.*

If you compare figures 12.7b and c, you will notice that ΔH is constant. In both reactions, the products are *energetically* more stable than the reactants. But which profile represents the faster reaction? You may remember that the *kinetic* stability of the reactants, relative to the products, decreases as the activation energy is lowered (section 4.13). Thus, the reactants in figure 12.7b are kinetically less stable than those in figure 12.7c, and we would expect figure 12.7b to represent the enthalpy profile of the faster reaction.

Light

Some reactions are faster in the presence of light. For example, the reaction

$$H_2(g) + Cl_2(g) \rightarrow 2HCl(g)$$

is explosive in sunlight but slow in the dark.

Light, like heat, is a form of energy. In photochemical reactions, the reactant molecules absorb the light, thereby increasing the fraction of collisions which possess the activation energy. Hence, the reaction rate increases. The most important photochemical reaction is **photosynthesis**. Plant leaves contain chlorophyll, a green pigment. In the presence of sunlight, chlorophyll catalyses the conversion of water and carbon dioxide into glucose:

$$6CO_2(g) + 6H_2O(l) \xrightarrow[\text{chlorophyll}]{\text{sunlight}} \underset{\text{glucose}}{C_6H_{12}O_6(aq)} + 6O_2(g) \quad \Delta H = +2826\,kJ$$

Due to photosynthesis, energy from the sun is converted into the chemical energy which is stored in our food and in fossil fuels (i.e. decayed plant or animal matter).

12.4 What are catalysts?

Catalysts *are substances which alter the rate of reaction whilst remaining chemically unchanged at the end of the reaction.* Their physical appearance, though, may change, e.g. a finely ground powder may end up as larger solid lumps. Since it is chemically unchanged, a small amount of catalyst may cause catalysis of a vast excess of reactants (figure 12.8).

Figure 12.8 *Catalytic action often continues until all the reactants have been converted into products*

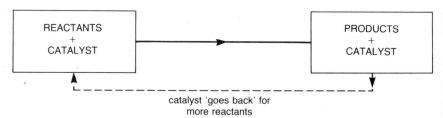

A catalyst which slows down the reaction is said to be a 'negative' catalyst or **inhibitor**. Anti-oxidants, for example, prevent fats from becoming rancid by slowing down their oxidation by atmospheric oxygen.

Now, from section 11.4, we know that

$$\text{rate of reaction} = k[A]^x[B]^y \ldots$$

Since its presence cannot change the reactant concentrations, *the catalyst must cause the rate constant to increase.* It can do this by:

▶ *bringing the reactant molecules closer together*, thereby increasing the collision frequency;

Figure 12.9 *This enthalpy profile shows how catalysts speed up reactions by providing an alternative route which has a lower activation energy*

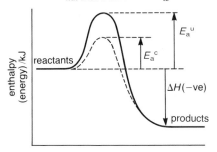

E_a^u activation energy for uncatalysed reaction
E_a^c activation energy for the catalysed reaction
$E_a^c < E_a^u$

▶ *orientating reactant molecules so that they achieve the correct collision geometry*; and

▶ *providing an alternative reaction route which requires a lower activation energy* (figure 12.9 and table 12.1). Thus, more molecules will possess this lower activation energy and a greater proportion of the collisions will be activated (figure 12.10).

In many cases, a catalyst speeds up the reaction by a combination of these three effects.

Table 12.1 *Activation energies for uncatalysed and catalysed reactions*

Reaction	Conditions	Activation energy/ $kJ\,mol^{-1}$
$2N_2O(g) \rightarrow 2N_2(g) + O_2(g)$	uncatalysed	245
	platinum catalysed	136
	gold catalysed	121
$2NH_3(g) \rightarrow N_2(g) + 3H_2(g)$	uncatalysed	335
	tungsten catalysed	162

What effect does adding a catalyst have on the activation energy of a reaction?

Finally, look again at figure 12.9. It is important to note that although a catalyst lowers the activation energy, *it does not alter the enthalpy change, ΔH, for the reaction.*

12.5 Types of catalyst

There are two main types of catalyst: heterogeneous and homogeneous.

Heterogeneous catalysts

A **heterogeneous catalyst** *is in a different physical state from the reactants.* By far the most common heterogeneous catalysts are finely divided solids.

Sometimes the reactants are liquids, e.g. in the preparation of oxygen from aqueous hydrogen peroxide:

$$2H_2O_2(aq) \xrightarrow[\text{manganese dioxide(s)}]{\text{catalyst}} 2H_2O(l) + O_2(g)$$

In most cases, though, the reactants are gases. Many important industrial processes use finely divided solids to catalyse gaseous reactions. For example, the Ostwald Process for the manufacture of nitric acid uses a platinum/rhodium mixture as catalyst:

$$4NH_3(g) + 5O_2(g) \xrightarrow{900°C, \ Pt/Rh_{(s)}} 4NO(g) + 6H_2O(g)$$

Figure 12.10 *Lowering the activation energy causes many more reactant molecules to take part in activated collisions, i.e. those giving products*

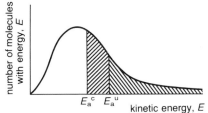

E_a^c = activation energy, catalysed reaction
E_a^u = activation energy, uncatalysed reaction
BUT
number of molecules with E_a^u = \\\\\\
number of molecules with E_a^c = \\\\\\ + /////

Table 12.2 *Some examples of heterogeneous catalysts*

Process/reaction	catalyst	reference section
Haber process: manufacture of ammonia $N_2(g) + 3H_2(g) \rightarrow 2NH_3(g)$	iron filings	25.7
Contact process: manufacture of sulphuric acid $2SO_2(g) + O_2(g) \rightarrow SO_3(g)$	vanadium pentoxide	26.7
hydrogenation reactions: e.g. manufacture of margarine	nickel powder	35.6.4

This man is holding up a large circular gauze woven from rhodium-platinum wire. It acts as a catalyst in the production of nitric acid by the oxidation of ammonia

Some other industrially important examples of heterogeneous catalysis are listed in table 12.2.

The behaviour of heterogeneous catalysts is explained by **Adsorption Theory**, as follows.

(a) Reactant molecules diffuse towards the catalyst surface . . .

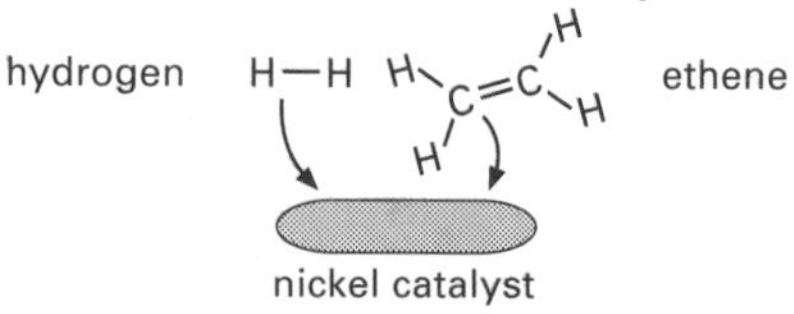

hydrogen   H—H   ethene

nickel catalyst

(b) . . . and are adsorbed on neighbouring **active sites**. Since the molecules are now closer together, *they have a higher collision frequency*. Also, the 'active sites' position the reactant molecules so that they will have the *correct collision geometry*. The overall process is termed **chemisorption**.

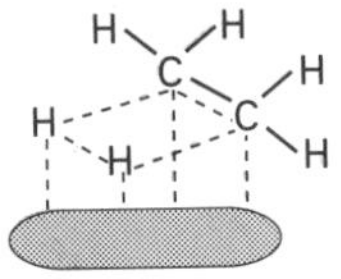

(c) Unlike simple physical adsorption (e.g. air bubbles on the side of a glass of water left overnight), chemisorption weakens the bonds in the adsorbed molecules (i.e. the reactants). As a result, *the reaction's activation energy is lowered and a greater proportion of the collisions will be activated* (figure 12.10).

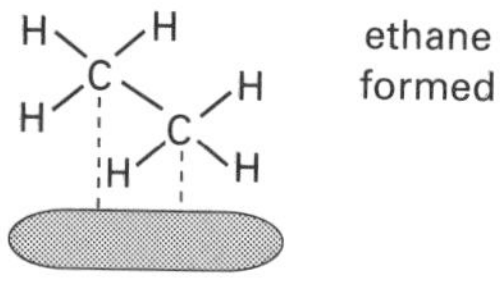

ethane formed

(e) Compared with the uncatalysed reaction, the products form more rapidly. However, the products are still chemisorbed. If they remain so, no more reactant molecules can get to the catalyst and the surface will become inactive. It is then said to be **poisoned**.

(f) To avoid this, the products are **desorbed**, that is, leave the catalyst surface. More reactants are chemisorbed and the whole process is repeated over and over again.

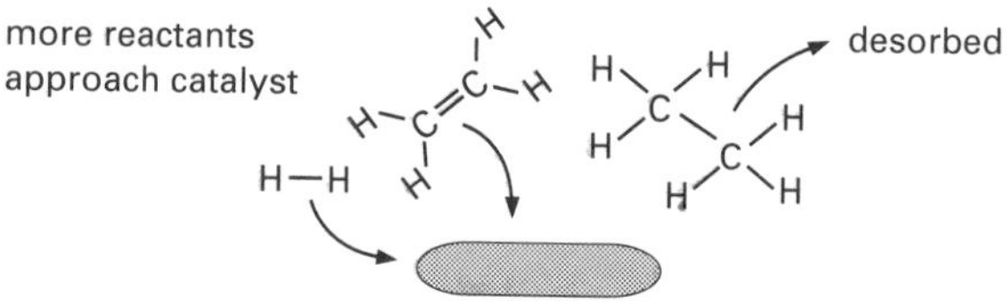

more reactants approach catalyst   desorbed

The action of a heterogeneous catalyst is very specific. Thus, even with the same reactants, different catalysts may give different products, e.g.

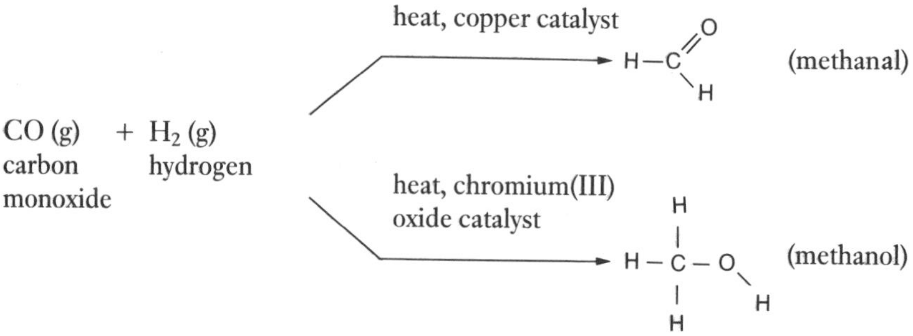

$$CO\,(g) + H_2\,(g)$$
carbon   hydrogen
monoxide

heat, copper catalyst → H—C=O, H   (methanal)

heat, chromium(III) oxide catalyst → H—C—O, H   (methanol)

Homogeneous catalysts

A **homogeneous catalyst** *is in the same physical state as the reactants.* Many of these reactions occur in solution. For example, the atmospheric oxidation of iron (II) ions in aqueous solution is catalysed by copper (II) ions:

$$2Fe^{2+}(aq) + \tfrac{1}{2}O_2(g) + 2H^+(aq) \xrightarrow{\text{catalyst: } Cu^{2+}(aq)} 2Fe^{3+}(aq) + H_2O(l)$$

Some reactions occur in the gas phase, e.g. the decomposition of ethanal is catalysed by iodine:

$$CH_3CHO(g) \xrightarrow{\text{catalyst: } I_2(g)} CH_4(g) + CO(g)$$

The main function of a homogeneous catalyst is to provide *an alternative reaction route which has an activation energy lower than that of the uncatalysed reaction.* In doing this, the catalyst forms an **intermediate compound** which decomposes at a later stage. Thus, for the reaction $A + B \rightarrow$ products:

$$\textbf{catalyst} \xrightarrow{+\textbf{A}} \begin{array}{c} \textbf{intermediate compound} \\ + \\ \textbf{product (sometimes)} \end{array} \xrightarrow{+\textbf{B}} \begin{array}{c} \textbf{catalyst} \\ + \\ \textbf{product} \end{array}$$

The above reactions illustrate this general mechanism:

$$I_2(g) \xrightarrow{+ CH_3CHO(g)} \begin{array}{c} CH_3I(g) \\ \\ \end{array} + HI(g) \xrightarrow{} \begin{array}{c} I_2(g) \\ + \\ CH_4(g) \end{array}$$
$$CO(g)$$

Catalyst $= I_2(g)$; intermediate compounds are $CH_3I(g)$ and $HI(g)$.

Also,

$$Cu^{2+}(aq) \xrightarrow{+ Fe^{2+}(aq)} \begin{array}{c} Cu^+(aq) \\ + \\ Fe^{3+}(aq) \end{array} \xrightarrow{+ \tfrac{1}{2}O_2(g) + 2H^+(aq)} \begin{array}{c} Cu^{2+}(aq) \\ + \\ H_2O(l) \end{array}$$

Catalyst $= Cu^{2+}(aq)$; intermediate $= Cu^+(aq)$.

During this redox reaction, the oxidation state of the copper ion changes from $+2 \rightarrow +1 \rightarrow +2$. Since most transition metals have variable oxidation states, their ions often prove to be useful homogeneous catalysts in redox reactions (section 29.3).

Some further examples of homogeneous catalysis are listed in table 12.3.

Table 12.3 *Some examples of homogeneous catalysts*

Reaction/process	catalyst	reference section
oxidation of iodide ions by peroxodisulphate ions: $2I^-(aq) + S_2O_8^{2-}(aq) \rightarrow I_2(aq) + 2SO_4^{2-}(aq)$	$Fe^{2+}(aq)$, $Fe^{3+}(aq)$ and $Cu^{2+}(aq)$ ions	29.3
ester formation: e.g. $HCO_2H(l) + CH_3OH(l) \rightarrow HCO_2CH_3(l) + H_2O(l)$ methyl methanoate	concentrated sulphuric acid	40.5.3
Friedel–Crafts reaction: helps substitution in the benzene ring e.g. $C_6H_6(l) + Cl_2(g) \rightarrow C_6H_5Cl(l) + HCl(g)$	aluminium chloride	36.5.3

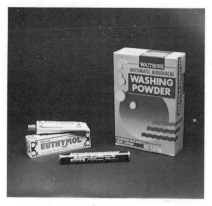

Enzymes are used in the production of many consumer products, including washing powder, toothpaste and soft-centred chocolates

12.6 Enzymes

Enzymes *are complex proteins which catalyse biochemical reactions in a highly specific way* (section 41.11). Molecules which react as a result of enzyme action are called **substrates**. Many biochemical processes are 'multi-step' and each substrate may require its own, specific, enzyme. Thus,

$$\text{SUBSTRATE 1} \xrightarrow{\text{enzyme 1}} \text{SUBSTRATE 2} \xrightarrow{\text{enzyme 2}} \text{SUBSTRATE 3} \xrightarrow{\text{enzyme 3}} \text{products}$$

For a reaction to occur, the enzyme and the substrate molecules must fit together like a '3-dimensional jigsaw puzzle'; hence the resulting highly specific action of a particular enzyme. Often the attractive forces between the substrate and the enzyme are due to hydrogen bonding.

Clearly, enzymes play an important role in living organisms. Some poisons destroy life by disrupting enzyme action. Moreover, enzymes will only work within certain pH and temperature ranges. Among their many applications, enzymes are used: to tenderise meat, to prevent hazes forming in chilled beers, and in the manufacture of toothpaste, cheese, washing powder and baby foods.

12.7 Autocatalysis

Autocatalysis *occurs when a reaction product catalyses the reaction.* A well-known example is the reaction between manganate(VII) ions and ethanedioate ions in acid solution:

$$2MnO_4^-(aq) + 5C_2O_4^{2-}(aq) + 16H^+(aq) \rightarrow 2Mn^{2+}(aq) + 10CO_2(g) + 8H_2O(l)$$

The reaction is catalysed by the manganese(II) ions, $Mn^{2+}(aq)$. Figure 12.11 describes how the manganate(VII) ion concentration changes with time.

Figure 12.11 *A typical graph of [reactant] plotted against time for an autocatalysed reaction, e.g.*

$$2MnO_4^-(aq) + 5C_2O_4^{2-}(aq) + 16H^+(aq) \rightarrow 2Mn^{2+}(aq) + 10CO_2(g) + 8H_2O(l)$$

Can you sketch the graph of $[Mn^{2+}(aq)]$ plotted against time?

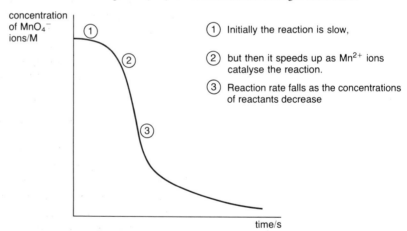

concentration of MnO_4^- ions/M

① Initially the reaction is slow,

② but then it speeds up as Mn^{2+} ions catalyse the reaction.

③ Reaction rate falls as the concentrations of reactants decrease

time/s

12.8 How good is Collision Theory?

A calculated value for any rate constant, k_{calc} can be obtained by substituting values into the Arrhenius equation (section 12.3). Kinetics studies can also provide an experimental value, k_{exp}, at the same temperature. If Collision Theory is completely accurate, k_{exp} *and* k_{calc} *should agree within experimental error*. In fact, this only really happens for the simplest of reactions.

A better explanation of reaction kinetics is given by **Transition State Theory**. This suggests that reacting molecules with enough activation energy will come together to form a **transition state**. Then the transition state decomposes to form either the products or the reactants. Thus,

$$\text{REACTANTS} \rightleftharpoons \text{TRANSITION STATE} \rightarrow \text{PRODUCTS}$$

The overall process is not reversible, even though the reactants and the transition state are in equilibrium (section 13.1). Eventually all of the reactants will be converted into products.

The main difference between the Collision and Transition State Theories is nicely illustrated by the decomposition of hydrogen iodide (figure 12.12).

Figure 12.12 *Comparing Collision and Transition State Theories*

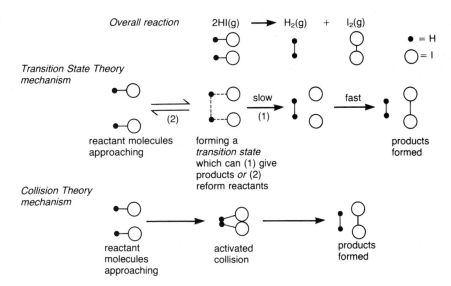

12.9 Summary and revision plan

1   The rate of a chemical reaction is affected by: (a) changing the reactant **concentrations** or their **particle size**, (b) varying the **pressure** (gas reactions) or **temperature** and (c) adding a **catalyst**.

2   **Collision Theory** proposes that products are formed when reactant molecules collide with: (a) a certain minimum energy, known as the **activation energy** and (b) the correct **collision geometry**. The fraction of the total collisions having these properties is known as the **activated fraction**. So,

rate of reaction = collision frequency × activated fraction

3   It follows from Collision Theory that increasing (a) the reactant concentrations, (b) the pressure in a gas reaction and (c) the surface area of the reactants (by decreasing their particle size) increases the collision frequency and, hence, the rate of reaction.

4   Raising the temperature: (a) only very slightly increases the collision frequency but (b) causes many more molecules to possess the activation energy. Thus, the activated fraction and, hence, the rate of reaction also increase. Lowering the temperature slows down the reaction rate.

5   The **Arrhenius equation** quantifies the temperature 'effect':

$$k = A \times e^{-E_a/RT}$$

where k = rate constant, A = the frequency of collisions with the correct collision geometry per unit volume, E_a is the activation energy and T = absolute temperature.

6   **Enthalpy profiles** describe the enthalpy changes during the reaction (figure 12.7).

7   **Catalysts** are substances which speed up the rate of reaction whilst remaining chemically unchanged at the end of the reaction.

8   Catalysts increase k (and hence the rate) by: (a) bringing the reactant molecules closer together, with the correct collision geometry; (b) providing a route which requires less activation energy than the uncatalysed reaction (figure 12.9).

9   A **heterogeneous** catalyst is in a different physical state from the reactants. Its action is explained by **Adsorption Theory**: (a) the reactants are **chemisorbed** on the catalyst surface, (b) they collide more frequently and with favourable geometry, (c) product molecules form and are desorbed. Then the whole process is repeated.

10 A **homogeneous** catalyst is in the same physical state as the reactants. Its action is explained by **Intermediate Compound Theory**, e.g. for the reaction $A + B \rightarrow$ product,

$$catalyst \xrightarrow{\quad +A \quad} \text{intermediate compound} \xrightarrow{\quad +B \quad} catalyst$$
$$+ \qquad\qquad\qquad\qquad\qquad +$$
$$\text{product (sometimes)} \qquad\qquad \text{product}$$

11 **Enzymes** are complex proteins which catalyse biochemical reactions in a highly specific way.

12 **Autocatalysis** occurs when a reaction product catalyses the reaction, e.g.

$$2MnO_4^-(aq) + 5C_2O_4^{2-}(aq) + 16H^+(aq)$$
$$\downarrow$$
$$Mn^{2+}(aq) + 10CO_2(g) + 8H_2O(l)$$

where $Mn^{2+}(aq)$ is the autocatalyst.

13 Collision theory is only really accurate for simple gas reactions. **Transition State Theory** gives a better, but more complex, explanation:

REACTANTS $\rightleftharpoons$ TRANSITION STATE $\rightarrow$ PRODUCTS (e.g. figure 12.12).

The Equilibrium State

Contents

A dramatic example of static equilibrium

Figure 13.1 *Different types of equilibrium: (a) static equilibrium, (b) dynamic equilibrium*

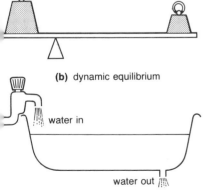

(a) static equilibrium

(b) dynamic equilibrium

water in

water out

In the dictionary, **equilibrium** is defined as *a state of balance*. We are all familiar with the example of loads balanced on a pivoted beam, e.g. the see-saw in figure 13.1a. In this case, in the balance position, no movement of any kind is taking place and the system is therefore said to be in **static** equilibrium.

The equilibria encountered in chemistry are somewhat different. At the balance point changes are taking place at the molecular level but in such a way that no overall change is observed. Since **movement** is involved, such equilibria are termed **dynamic**. We may make a simple analogy to the bath shown in figure 13.1b, which is *simultaneously* being *filled* with water from the tap and *drained*. The rate at which water enters the bath is controlled by the tap. The rate at which it drains away will increase as the level in the bath rises, since the water pressure will rise. Eventually, although water is still entering and leaving the bath, the observed water level will remain constant. The position of the equilibrium, i.e. in this case the depth of water in the bath, may be altered by changing the rate at which water either enters or leaves the bath.

Some of the characteristics of a dynamic equilibrium may be investigated in the experiment described in activity 13.1.

Activity 13.1

This simple experiment gives you considerable insight into the nature of a dynamic equilibrium and the theory of reversible reactions. We shall simulate the reaction,

$$A \rightleftharpoons B$$

by transferring water backwards and forwards between two troughs labelled A and B. The *depth* of water in each trough will be taken as a measure of the *amount* of each substance present.

You will need two glass troughs, labelled A and B, two beakers of equal size and one much smaller beaker.

   (a) Fill trough A with water so that one of the large beakers, lying on its side, is just submerged. If you wish, a little dye may be added to make it easier to see the level.
   (b) At the start of the experiment trough B is empty because no 'product' has been formed.
   (c) Now we may start the 'reaction'. Using the large beaker, scoop out as much liquid as you can from trough A and transfer it to trough B. You have now begun to form some 'product', B.
   (d) Since you now have some B, it will start to change back into A and so both reactions, $A \rightarrow B$ and $A \leftarrow B$, will occur simultaneously. To simulate this use the large beakers to scoop out liquid from each trough and transfer it to the other (do not tilt the troughs when doing this).

1 What happens to the relative liquid levels in A and B? Explain why this happens.

(e) Repeat step (d) several times.

2 What eventually happens to the liquid levels in A and B? How do you account for this?

Now repeat the experiment as above but use the smaller beaker to transfer liquid from trough B to trough A.

3 What differences do you notice and how do you explain them?

Simulating the setting up of a dynamic equilibrium (activity 13.1)

13.1 Reversibility of chemical reactions

Theoretically at least, all chemical reactions may be regarded as reversible. For any general reaction.

$$A \rightarrow B$$

We may construct an energy level diagram of the type shown in figure 13.2. If *one* of the activation energies (section 12.1) is *very high*, then this constitutes a *barrier* to the reaction which will therefore, for all practical purposes, take place in *one* direction only.

Figure 13.2 *Energy changes in a chemical reaction*

ΔH is the enthalpy change
$-$ve $A \rightarrow B$ or $+$ve $A \leftarrow B$

E_A is the activation energy for $A \rightarrow B$

E_B is the activation energy for $A \leftarrow B$

i.e. $\quad A \rightarrow B \quad$ or $\quad A \leftarrow B$
forward reaction $\quad$ reverse reaction
$E_B \gg E_A \quad\quad E_A \gg E_B$

Providing that conditions are such that both A and B molecules can attain their respective activation energies, then both the forward and reverse reactions will occur.

$$A \rightleftharpoons B$$

When the rates of both the forward and reverse reaction are equal, no further overall change will be observed and the system will be in **dynamic equilibrium**. Since the *rate* of any reaction depends upon the *concentration* of the reacting species, it follows that the **equilibrium position**, i.e. *the relative amounts of each substance in the system*, will be *constant* under any specified conditions.

Many industrially important reactions are reversible and it is therefore vital to be able to manipulate the equilibrium position so as to achieve the most *economical* yield of the desired product. Examples include the Haber process (section 25.7) and the Contact process (section 26.7).

13.2 Types of dynamic equilibrium

Chapters 14–18 are devoted to the theory of various reversible systems. Although the basic approach is similar throughout, it is convenient to classify equilibria into different types.

Homogeneous and heterogeneous equilibria

A **phase** is any *physically distinct* part of a system which itself is *homogeneous*, i.e. has a *uniform composition*. For instance, when sand is shaken with water it does not dissolve and the system is composed of two phases, solid sand and liquid water. Similarly, a mixture of oil and water will separate into two distinct liquid phases. However, if a little salt is shaken with water it will dissolve to give a single phase of salt solution.

Likewise, *miscible* liquids such as ethanol and water produce a single phase.

Any reversible system which involves only a *single phase* is said to be **homogeneous**. If there are *two or more phases* present, then the equilibrium is said to be **heterogeneous**.

Homogeneous chemical equilibria include all reactions which involve:

▶ only gases, e.g. $N_2(g) + 3H_2(g) \rightleftharpoons 2NH_3(g)$
▶ those which take place entirely in solution,
   e.g. $CH_3COOH(aq) \rightleftharpoons CH_3COO^-(aq) + H^+(aq)$
          $Fe^{2+}(aq) \rightleftharpoons Fe^{3+}(aq) + e^-$

Heterogeneous chemical equilibria include reactions between:

▶ solids and gases, e.g. $CaCO_3(s) \rightleftharpoons CaO(s) + CO_2(g)$
▶ solids and liquids, e.g. $AgCl(s) \rightleftharpoons Ag^+(aq) + Cl^-(aq)$
          $Zn(s) \rightleftharpoons Zn^{2+}(aq) + 2e^-$
▶ immiscible liquids,
   e.g. $CH_3COOC_2H_5(l) + H_2O(l) \rightleftharpoons CH_3COOH(l) + C_2H_5OH(l)$

Many *physical* processes involve heterogeneous equilibria. For example, changes in physical state:

$$H_2O(s) \rightleftharpoons H_2O(l)$$
$$H_2O(l) \rightleftharpoons H_2O(g)$$
$$C \text{ (diamond)} \rightleftharpoons C \text{ (graphite)}$$

Since a change of phase is involved, such physical equilibria are also referred to as **phase equilibria**. They are dealt with in chapter 16.

In the next two chapters, we shall examine the basic theory underlying simple homogeneous and heterogeneous equilibria and then consider some particular examples in more detail.

13.3 Comments on the activity

Activity 13.1

1 The level in A falls whilst the level in B *rises*. The *rate* at which liquid is transferred from a trough depends upon the *depth* of liquid in it. Since initially there is *more* water in trough A, the rate of transfer from A to B will be *greater* than from B to A.

   i.e. forward rate >backward rate

2 As the 'reaction' proceeds the level of water in A, and hence the rate of transfer to B, *falls*, whereas since the level in B is *rising*, the rate of transfer to A *increases*. Eventually the two rates become equal.

   i.e. forward rate = backward rate

An **equilibrium** has been established where both forward and backward 'reactions' are occurring at the *same* rate. No matter how long the process is continued, the water levels in each trough will remain *steady*, even though 'reactions' are still taking place. The equilibrium is, therefore, **dynamic**. Since the beakers used are of the same size, in this case we should expect the equilibrium levels in each trough to be identical.

3   When a *smaller* beaker is used to transfer water from B to A, a dynamic equilibrium is still reached, but here the final level of liquid in trough B is *higher* than that in A. The rate of transfer of water from B to A will be *lower* than before and the level of water in A will have to *fall* in order to make the rates of the forward and backward 'reactions' *equal* at equilibrium. This illustrates an important point in reversible reactions, that *though the forward and backward reaction rates must be equal at equilibrium, the concentrations of reactants and products need not be the same, and in fact very rarely are.*

13.4 Summary and revision plan

1   Theoretically, all chemical reactions are **reversible**, but, if the **activation energy** of the reverse reaction is too high, then effectively only the forward reaction occurs.

2   Reversible systems may eventually establish a **dynamic equilibrium** in which forward and backward reactions are still going on, but at equal rates.

3   **Homogeneous** systems involve only a single **phase**, i.e. gas reactions, miscible liquids.

4   Systems which contain two or more phases, e.g. solid/liquid, solid/gas, liquid/gas, immiscible liquids, are **heterogeneous**.

5   Reversible physical changes which involve a change of state, e.g. melting, evaporating, subliming, are known as **phase equilibria**.

□ C H A P T E R □

14

□ C H A P T E R □

Homogeneous Equilibria

Contents

14.1 The Equilibrium Law and equilibrium constants

Consider the general reaction,

$$aA + bB \rightleftharpoons cC + dD$$

Where the small letters represent the number of moles of each substance in the balanced chemical equation.

Suppose that we start with a mixture of A and B only. If the reaction mechanism involves only a single step, then the rate of the forward reaction, i.e. forming C and D, may be written,

$$\text{forward rate} = k_f [A]^a [B]^b$$

where k_f is the rate constant of the forward reaction.

As the forward reaction proceeds, its rate will *decrease* since A and B are being used up and their concentrations will fall. Once some C and D have been formed, the reverse reaction will start. Its rate may be written,

$$\text{reverse rate} = k_r [C]^c [D]^d$$

where k_r is the rate constant of the reverse reaction.

As the forward reaction proceeds, the concentrations of C and D will rise and thus the rate of the reverse reaction will *increase*. We therefore have the situation shown in figure 14.1. Since the rate of the forward reaction is decreasing, whilst the rate of the reverse reaction is increasing, eventually the two rates will become equal. At this point the rate at which any of the substances is being used up exactly equals the rate at which it is being formed. The concentrations of each substance will therefore remain *constant* and the system will have reached a **dynamic equilibrium**. Unless the reaction conditions are altered in some way, no further observable change will occur.

At equilibrium

$$\text{forward rate} = \text{reverse rate}$$
$$k_f [A]^a [B]^b = k_r [C]^c [D]^d$$

Thus,

$$K_c = \frac{k_f}{k_r} = \frac{[C]^c [D]^d}{[A]^a [B]^b}$$

Strictly speaking, this derivation applies only to simple one-step reactions. However, the **Equilibrium Law** above applies equally to multi-stage reactions.

K_c is known as the **equilibrium constant** for the reaction in terms of **molar concentrations**. Its value is fixed for any system at any given temperature and is of particular use for homogeneous reactions in solution.

Whilst K_c may be calculated for any homogeneous system, it is often more

Figure 14.1 *Change in the forward and back reactions in the reversible system $A + B \rightleftharpoons C + D$, starting with A and B only*

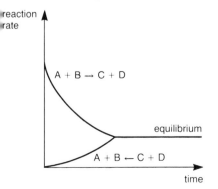

reaction rate

A + B → C + D

equilibrium

A + B ← C + D

time

convenient to define the equilibrium constant for a *gas* reaction in terms of the **partial pressures** of the components (section 8.7). In a mixture of gases the partial pressure of each component is proportional to its mole fraction and so may be used as an alternative to molar concentration in the equilibrium equation (figure 14.2).

Figure 14.2 *The partial pressure of each gas in a mixture of gases is proportional to its mole fraction*

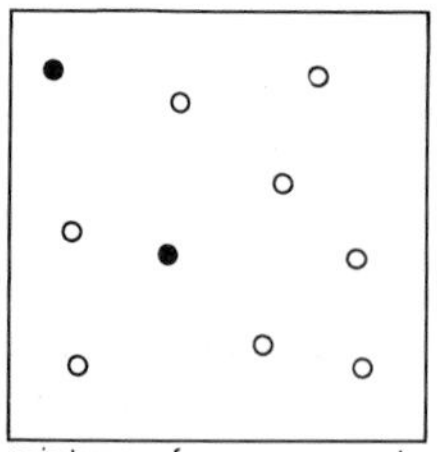

mixture of gases o and ●
in volume V
at total pressure
p atmospheres
Total number of moles = n

	o	●	total
number of moles	$0.8n$	$0.2n$	n
mole fraction	0.8	0.2	1
partial pressure	$0.8p$	$0.2p$	p
molar concentration	$\dfrac{0.8n}{V}$	$\dfrac{0.2n}{V}$	$\dfrac{n}{V}$

Thus,

$$K_p = \frac{p_C{}^c p_D{}^d}{p_A{}^a p_B{}^b}$$

where K_p is the **equilibrium constant** for the system in terms of the **partial pressures** of the components, p_A, p_B, p_C amd p_D. Alternatively, we may write,

$$K_p = \frac{(f_C P)^c (f_D P)^d}{(f_A P)^a (f_B P)^b}$$

where f_A, f_B, f_C and f_D are the **mole fractions** of each of the gases at equilibrium and P is the **total pressure** of the system.

The term 'equilibrium position' is sometimes used to indicate the relative amounts of reactants and products at equilibrium. In fact, the only precise measure of equilibrium position is given by the equilibrium constant. Clearly, *high* values of either K_c or K_p will mean that the equilibrium lies well to the *right*, i.e. the 'products' of the forward reaction will predominate, and vice versa. The 'position' of an equilibrium does not change unless the equilibrium constant changes.

14.2 Determination and use of equilibrium constants

The equilibrium constant for a reaction may be calculated if the equation for the reaction and the equilibrium concentrations or partial pressures of all the components are known.

Example 1

Ethanoic acid and ethanol react together to give ethyl ethanoate and water.

$$CH_3COOH(l) + C_2H_5OH(l) \rightleftharpoons CH_3COOC_2H_5(l) + H_2O(l)$$

In a series of experiments, various amounts of ethanoic acid, ethanol and water were allowed to react at a fixed temperature. The equilibrium amounts of each component were as follows (table 14.1).

Table 14.1

	moles present at equilibrium			
Experiment	CH_3COOH	C_2H_5OH	$CH_3COOC_2H_5$	H_2O
1	1.00	1.00	2.00	2.00
2	0.50	2.00	1.00	4.00
3	3.00	0.10	1.20	1.00
4	0.25	4.00	10.00	0.40

(a) Show that these figures are in agreement with the Equilibrium Law and calculate the value of the equilibrium constant for the reaction under these conditions.

(b) If one mole of ethanoic acid and two moles of ethanol are mixed under the same conditions, what will be the amount of each substance present at equilibrium?

Solution

(a) According to the Equilibrium Law,

$$K_c = \frac{[CH_3COOC_2H_{5(l)}]\,[H_2O_{(l)}]}{[CH_3COOH_{(l)}]\,[C_2H_5OH_{(l)}]}$$

We must show that when the equilibrium concentrations for each experiment are substituted into this expression, a constant result is obtained. In order to convert the *numbers of moles* in the table into *molar concentrations*, we must divide by the *volume in dm³* of the mixture at equilibrium.

Let the volume of the equilibrium mixture $= V\,dm^3$.

Expt. 1.

$$\frac{(2.00/V)\,(2.00/V)}{(1.00/V)\,(1.00/V)} = \frac{4.00 V^2\,M^2}{1.00 V^2\,M^2} = 4.00$$

Since the V^2 terms cancel here, the equilibrium is *independent* of total volume. Thus we may use the number of moles of each substance directly in the equation to calculate K_c.

Expt. 2.
$$\frac{(1)\,(4)}{(0.5)\,(2)} = \frac{4.00}{1.00} = 4.00$$

Expt. 3.
$$\frac{(1.2)\,(1)}{(3.0)\,(0.1)} = \frac{1.20}{0.30} = 4.00$$

Expt. 4.
$$\frac{(10.0)\,(0.4)}{(0.25)\,(4)} = \frac{4.00}{1.00} = 4.00$$

We have shown that the results obey the Equilibrium Law and that the equilibrium constant for the reaction is 4.00.

(b) We can now use this value of K_c to calculate equilibrium concentrations.

1 First write the balanced equation for the reaction:

$$CH_3COOH(l) + C_2H_5OH(l) \rightleftharpoons CH_3COOC_2H_5(l) + H_2O(l)$$

2 Under each component write the number of moles at the start of the reaction:

moles at START   1   2   0   0

3 Now write an expression for the number of moles of each substance **at equilibrium**. In this case let us suppose that x moles of ethanoic acid are *used up*. From the equation we can see that x moles of ethanol are also used up and that x moles of both ethyl ethanoate and water will be *formed*.

moles at $(1-x)$ $(2-x)$ x x
EQUILIBRIUM

4   Now we must remember that the expression for K_c is in terms of molar concentrations, so, as before, we must divide the molar amounts by the volume of the mixture *in dm³*.

molarities at $(1-x)/V$ $(2-x)/V$ x/V x/V
EQUILIBRIUM

5   Now write the expression for K_c and substitute the above molar concentrations.

$$K_c = \frac{[CH_3COOC_2H_{5(l)}][H_2O_{(l)}]}{[CH_3COOH_{(l)}][C_2H_5OH_{(l)}]}$$

$$4.00 = \frac{(x/V)^2}{\{(1-x)/V\}\{(2-x)/V\}} = \frac{x^2}{(1-x)(2-x)} \cdot \frac{V^2}{V^2}$$

$$4.00 = \frac{x^2}{x^2 - 3x + 2}$$

Rearranging,

$$4x^2 - 12x + 8 = x^2, \text{ i.e. } 3x^2 - 12x + 8 = 0$$

6   We must now solve this equation for x, the number of moles of ethanoic acid which are used up in the reaction. We may solve such a 'quadratic' equation of general type.

$$ax^2 + bx + c = 0$$

using the standard expression.

$$x = \frac{-b \pm \sqrt{b^2 - 4ac}}{2a}$$

where, a and b are the coefficients of x^2 and x respectively, and c is the constant. In this calculation, $a = 3$, $b = -12$ and $c = 8$

$$\therefore \quad x = \frac{12 \pm \sqrt{144 - 96}}{6}$$

$$= \frac{12 \pm \sqrt{48}}{6}$$

$$= \frac{12 \pm 6.93}{6}$$

$$\therefore \quad x = \frac{18.93}{6} \text{ or } \frac{5.07}{6}$$

i.e. $x = \quad 3.155$ or 0.845

7   Only one of these values can be correct! Clearly, since we only started with one mole of ethanoic acid, we cannot have used more than this so the right answer must be 0.845 moles of ethanoic acid used up.
    Now we find the equilibrium amounts of each component using the equation.

moles of ethanoic acid	$= 1-x$	$= 0.155$ moles
moles of ethanol	$= 2-x$	$= 1.155$ moles
moles of ethyl ethanoate	$= x$	$= 0.845$ moles
moles of water	$= x$	$= 0.845$ moles

8   Now, although the question does not ask us to do it, we can check that our answers are correct by recalculating K_c using these figures.

$$K_c = \frac{0.845^2}{(0.155)(1.155)} = 3.99$$

This is in good agreement with our original figure of 4.00 and confirms that our calculation is correct.

Activity 14.1

1   Use the equilibrium constant calculated in example 1(a) to determine the equilibrium amounts of each substance which would result from the reaction of one mole of ethyl ethanoate with two moles of water under the same conditions. You may use the method given in example 1(b).

2   Ethyl ethanoate is also formed by the reaction of ethene with ethanoic acid in an inert solvent:

$$C_2H_4 + CH_3COOH \rightleftharpoons CH_3COOC_2H_5$$

(a)   If you start with one mole of ethene and one mole of ethanoic acid and x moles of ethyl ethanoate are formed at equilibrium, write an expression for the equilibrium constant, K_c, in terms of the volume, V, of the mixture. Will the amount of ethyl ethanoate present at equilibrium depend on the volume of the inert solvent used?

(b)   In an experiment 0.050 moles of ethene was allowed to react with 0.020 moles of ethanoic acid at 10°C, the total volume being made up to 500 cm^3 with an inert solvent. When equilibrium had been established the mixture was found to contain 0.018 moles of ethyl ethanoate. Calculate:

(i)   the number of moles of ethene and ethanoic acid present at equilibrium;

(ii)   the molar concentration of each substance present at equilibrium;

(iii)   the value of K_c for the reaction under these conditions.

Example 2

Hydrogen iodide decomposes reversibly on heating

$$H_2(g) + I_2(g) \rightleftharpoons 2HI(g)$$

After heating at 448°C for some time, a mixture of hydrogen, iodine and hydrogen iodide was found to contain 7.83 moles of hydrogen, 1.68 moles of iodine and 25.54 moles of hydrogen iodide.

(a)   Calculate the equilibrium constant for the reaction in terms of partial pressures.

(b)   If 20 moles of hydrogen iodide are heated at the same temperature, what amounts of each of the three gases will be present at equilibrium?

The methods used are very similar to those used in example 1, but here we are dealing with the partial pressures of the components rather than molar concentrations.

Solution

(a)   The expression for the equilibrium constant is

$$K_p = \frac{p_{HI}^2}{p_{H_2} p_{I_2}}$$

1   Since we are not given the partial pressures, we must first calculate them from mole fractions.

	$H_2(g)$	$+$ $I_2(g)$	$\rightleftharpoons$ 2HI(g)	total
moles at EQUILIBRIUM	7.83	1.68	25.54	35.05
mole fraction	$\dfrac{7.83}{35.05}$	$\dfrac{1.68}{35.05}$	$\dfrac{25.54}{35.05}$	
i.e.	0.2234	0.0479	0.7287	

Let P be the total pressure at equilibrium. Then from Dalton's Law (section 8.7), partial pressures are: $0.2234P$ $0.0479P$ $0.7287P$

$$\therefore \quad K_p = \frac{(0.7287P)^2}{(0.2234P)(0.0479P)} = \frac{0.5310P^2}{0.0107P^2} = 49.63$$

2 Since here the P^2 terms cancel, K_p is independent of the total pressure. We may now use this value to calculate the equilibrium amounts of each component in part (b).

(b)

	$H_2(g) + I_2(g) \rightleftharpoons 2HI(g)$	total
moles at START	0 0 20	20 moles

1 Let x moles of hydrogen iodide decompose at equilibrium. From the equation we can see that half as many moles of both hydrogen and iodine are formed. We may then write the partial pressures of each component at equilibrium in terms of x and the total pressure P.

moles at EQUILIBRIUM	$x/2$	$x/2$	$20-x$	total 20 moles
mole fraction at EQUILIBRIUM	$\dfrac{x/2}{20}$	$\dfrac{x/2}{20}$	$\dfrac{20-x}{20}$	
partial pressure	$\dfrac{xP}{40}$	$\dfrac{xP}{40}$	$\dfrac{(20-x)P}{20}$	

2 Knowing the value of K_p we may now find x.

$$K_p = \frac{p_{HI}}{p_{H_2}p_{I_2}} = \frac{\{(20-x)/20\}^2}{(x/40)(x/40)} \cdot \frac{P^2}{P^2}$$

$$49.63 = \frac{4(20-x)^2}{x^2}$$

$$49.63x^2 = 1600 - 160x + 4x^2$$

$$45.63x^2 + 160x - 1600 = 0$$

3 We may now solve this quadratic equation as in example 1(b).

$$x = 4.41 \text{ (or } -7.93, \text{ clearly impossible)}$$

Thus from the equation, the number of moles of each substance at equilibrium will be

hydrogen	$= x/2$	$= 2.205$ moles
iodine	$= x/2$	$= 2.205$ moles
hydrogen iodide	$= 20-x$	$= 15.59$ moles

4 You might like to recalculate Kp, as described in example 1, in order to confirm these figures.

Activity 14.2

The molar concentration of a gas may be defined as the number of moles of that gas contained in $1\,dm^3$ of the mixture.

Use the equilibrium numbers of moles calculated in example 2 to determine the equilibrium constant in terms of molar concentration, K_c, for the decomposition of hydrogen iodide at 448 °C. You may take the total volume of the mixture to be $V\,dm^3$. How does your result compare with the value of K_p for this reaction?

14.3 Units of equilibrium constants

Let us return to our general equation for a reversible reaction,

$$aA + bB \rightleftharpoons cC + dD$$

and the corresponding expressions for the equilibrium constants.

$$K_c = \frac{[C]^c\,[D]^d}{[A]^a\,[B]^b} \quad \text{or} \quad K_p = \frac{p_C^c p_D^d}{p_A^a p_B^b}$$

The **units** of equilibrium constant will depend upon the *number of molecules on each side of the equation*.

$$K_c = \text{concentration}^{(c+d-a-b)} \quad \text{or} \quad K_p = \text{pressure}^{(c+d-a-b)}$$

Molar concentration has units of M, i.e. mole dm^{-3}. Pressure may be measured in atmospheres or Pa.

As we discovered in activity 14.2, K_c and K_p have no units and have the same value *only* if the number of molecules on each side of the equation are *equal*. Let us now consider an example of a reversible reaction in which there is a *change* in the total number of molecules.

Example 3

Dinitrogen tetroxide dissociates into nitrogen dioxide on heating:

$$N_2O_4(g) \rightleftharpoons 2NO_2(g)$$

At equilibrium under 2 atmospheres total pressure, dinitrogen tetroxide is 35% dissociated into nitrogen dioxide.
(a) calculate the value of K_p under these conditions.
(b) what will be the percentage dissociation of dinitrogen tetroxide at the same temperature but under a total pressure of one atmosphere?

Solution

(a) $\qquad\qquad\qquad\qquad\qquad N_2O_4(g) \quad \rightleftharpoons \quad 2NO_2(g)$

1   Let us suppose that we start with x moles of dinitrogen tetroxide.

			total
moles at START	x	0	x
moles at EQUILIBRIUM	$(1.00-0.35)x$	$2(0.35x)$	$1.35x$

Note that each mole of N_2O_4 which dissociates gives *two* moles of NO_2.

2   Note that in this reaction the total number of moles present at equilibrium depends upon the degree of dissociation. We may now calculate K_p as in example 2(a).

mole fraction at EQUILIBRIUM	$\dfrac{0.65x}{1.35x}$	$\dfrac{0.70x}{1.35x}$
i.e.	0.481	0.519

Since the total pressure at equilibrium is 2 atmospheres.

partial pressures	0.481×2	0.519×2
i.e.	0.962 atm	1.038 atm

but,

$$K_p = \frac{p_{NO_2}^2}{p_{N_2O_4}} = \frac{1.038^2\,\text{atm}^2}{0.962\,\text{atm}}$$

$$= \frac{1.077}{0.962}\,\text{atm}$$

$$= 1.12\,\text{atm}$$

(b) Since we are operating at the same temperature, the value of K_p will be unchanged. The **degree of dissociation**, i.e. *the fraction of dinitrogen tetroxide which decomposes at equilibrium* may be found directly if we assume that one mole of dinitrogen tetroxide is present at the start.

$$N_2O_4(g) \rightleftharpoons 2NO_2(g) \quad \text{total}$$

| moles at START | 1 | 0 | 1 |

Let the fraction of dinitrogen tetroxide which dissociates be x

| moles at EQUILIBRIUM | $1-x$ | $2x$ | $1+x$ |

| mole fraction at EQUILIBRIUM | $\dfrac{1-x}{1+x}$ | $\dfrac{2x}{1+x}$ | |

Since the total pressure at equilibrium is now 1 atmosphere,

| partial pressures | $\dfrac{1-x}{1+x}$ atm | $\dfrac{2x}{1+x}$ atm | |

But,

$$K_p = \frac{p_{NO_2}^2}{p_{N_2O_4}} = \frac{(2x)^2}{(1+x)^2} \cdot \frac{(1+x)}{(1-x)} = \frac{4x^2}{(1+x)(1-x)} \text{ atm}$$

So,

$$1.12 = \frac{4x^2}{1-x^2}$$

$$1.12\,(1-x^2) = 4x^2$$

$$1.12 - 1.12x^2 = 4x^2$$

$$1.12 = 5.12x^2$$

Therefore, $x^2 = 1.12/5.12 = 0.219$

and, $x = \sqrt{0.219} = 0.468$

Thus the fraction of dinitrogen tetroxide which dissociates at a total pressure of 1 atmosphere is 0.468, i.e. it is 46.8% dissociated.

In such a gaseous system as this, where the total number of molecules on each side of the equation differs, the number of moles of gas present will change as equilibrium is established. If the reaction is carried out in a closed vessel at *constant volume*, there will be a consequent *change in pressure* which may be used to follow the process.

14.4 Effect upon an equilibrium of changing the concentration or partial pressure of a component

Again let us start from the viewpoint of our general reversible reaction,

$$aA + bB \rightleftharpoons cC + dD$$

and the expressions for the equilibrium constants,

$$K_c = \frac{[C]^c\,[D]^d}{[A]^a\,[B]^b} \qquad K_p = \frac{p_C{}^c p_D{}^d}{p_A{}^a p_B{}^b}$$

If we change any of the concentrations or partial pressures, then the system will have to move in order to re-establish equilibrium, i.e. to keep K_c or K_p constant.

Suppose that we remove some product C, i.e. [C] falls. In order that K_c shall remain constant, more A and B must combine to produce C and D, i.e. the reaction moves to the right in an attempt to replace the C which has been removed. You may satisfy yourself from the above equations that *a change in concentration of any of the components will result in the system moving in such a direction as to attempt to reverse the imposed change. Exactly the same conclusion results if we consider partial pressures instead of concentrations.*

14.5 Effect upon equilibrium of changing total pressure

Liquids are virtually non-compressible, i.e. their volume hardly changes when the external pressure is altered. Molar concentration in the liquid phase, and therefore K_c, is *independent* of pressure. Any change in pressure will not affect a homogeneous liquid equilibrium.

In the case of a *gaseous* system, change in total pressure may or may not disturb the equilibrium. There are two possibilities to consider.

▸ If there are *equal* numbers of gas molecules on each side of the equation,

e.g. $H_2(g) + I_2(g) \rightleftharpoons 2HI(g)$ total pressure P

Here,

$$K_p = \frac{p_{HI}^2}{p_{H_2}p_{I_2}} = \frac{(f_{HI}P)^2}{(f_{H_2}P)(f_{I_2}P)}$$

$$= \frac{f_{HI}^2 P^2}{f_{H_2}f_{I_2}P^2}$$

$$= \frac{f_{HI}^2}{f_{H_2}f_{I_2}}$$

where f stands for the mole fraction of a component.

The total pressure does *not* affect the value of K_p and any such system at equilibrium is *not* disturbed by changing the overall pressure.

▸ If the number of gas molecules on each side of the equation are *different,*

e.g. $N_2O_4(g) \rightleftharpoons 2NO_2(g)$

Here,

$$K_p = \frac{p_{NO_2}^2}{p_{N_2O_4}} = \frac{(f_{NO_2}P)^2}{f_{N_2O_4}P}$$

$$= \frac{f_{NO_2}^2 P^2}{f_{N_2O_4}P}$$

$$= \frac{f_{NO_2}^2 P}{f_{N_2O_4}}$$

Here if the total pressure, P, is changed, then the mole fractions of the components must also change in order to keep K_p constant. In this case if P is increased, then f_{NO_2} must fall, i.e. the reaction moves to the left. Decreasing P will cause the system to move to the right, i.e. produce more nitrogen dioxide.

$$N_2O_4(g) \underset{\text{raise pressure}}{\overset{\text{reduce pressure}}{\rightleftharpoons}} 2NO_2(g)$$

1 mole   2 moles

This example illustrates an important general point. *If the total number of gas molecules on each side of the equation differs, then any increase in the total pressure*

Table 14.2 *Variation of K_p with temperature for the reaction of hydrogen and iodine*

Temperature/K	K_p
300	790
500	160
700	54

Figure 14.3 *Energy profile for the reversible reaction, $H_2(g) + I_2(g) \rightleftharpoons 2HI(g)$*

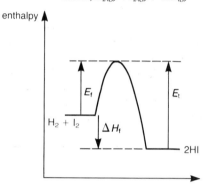

will cause the system to move towards the side which has fewer molecules. Similarly any decrease in pressure will result in the system moving towards the side containing more molecules in order to keep K_p constant.

14.6 Effect upon an equilibrium of changing temperature

Any change in temperature will alter the value of the equilibrium constant for a reaction, i.e. it will affect the concentrations of each component at equilibrium. For the formation of hydrogen iodide from its elements,

$$H_2(g) + I_2(g) \rightleftharpoons 2HI(g) \quad \Delta H = -10 \, kJ$$

K_p falls as the temperature is increased (table 14.2).

This means that increasing the temperature moves the system to the left, producing more hydrogen and iodine. As you can see from the above equation, the enthalpy change, ΔH, in this direction is positive, i.e. it is an endothermic process (heat is absorbed). It is interesting to note that increasing the temperature of the system moves it in such a way as to produce a 'cooling' effect. In any reversible system:

▸ *an increase in temperature favours the endothermic reaction;*
▸ *a decrease in temperature favours the exothermic reaction;*
▸ *the effect of both of the above is to counteract the change in temperature imposed on the system. In other words, a reversible system seems to 'resist' any change in temperature.*

We can explain these observations in terms of the energy changes involved. The energy 'profile' for the above reaction is shown in figure 14.3. The **activation energy** for the formation of hydrogen iodide, E_f, is *lower* than that for its decomposition, E_r. The distribution of molecular energies at low and high temperature is shown in figure 14.4. The *fraction* of molecules able to react upon collision is given by the area under the curve above the activation energy. Increasing the temperature increases the fraction of molecules able to undergo both the forward and reverse reactions, but the *percentage* increase is much greater for the endothermic change (*higher* activation energy) and so the reaction moves in this direction.

Rapid cooling may effectively 'freeze' the position of the equilibrium by slowing down both forward and backward reactions to a negligible rate. Quantitative analysis of the mixture will then give the molar concentrations of the components necessary to determine the equilibrium constant for the reaction at any particular temperature.

Figure 14.4 *Effect of activation energy on the number of molecules able to react at different temperatures*

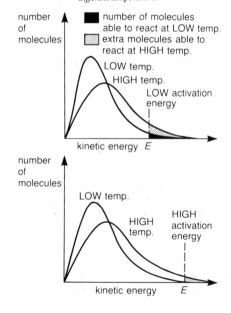

14.7 Use of catalysts in reversible reactions

A catalyst does *not* affect the *equilibrium constant* but enables the equilibrium state to be reached *more quickly*. Simply speaking, a catalyst provides an **alternative reaction pathway** with a *lower* activation energy. Figure 14.5 shows that the activation energies of both the forward and backward reactions are reduced by the *same* amount.

As a result both reactions are speeded up by the same factor and so the equilibrium constant does not change.

14.8 Summary of factors which may disturb an equilibrium: Le Chatelier's Principle

You may have notice a common factor running through sections 14.4 to 14.6. Let us first summarise the effect on any system at equilibrium of various changes in conditions (table 14.3).

Figure 14.5 *Effect of a catalyst on the energy changes in a reversible reaction*

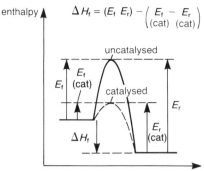

$$\Delta H_f = (E_f \; E_r) - \left(\begin{array}{cc} E_f & - & E_r \\ (cat) & & (cat) \end{array}\right)$$

Table 14.3

Change in conditions	direction in which the system moves
increasing the concentration or partial pressure of a component	to use up some of that component
increasing total pressure	if possible, shifts to reduce the total number of gas molecules and so reduce pressure
increasing temperature	to produce an endothermic change, so absorbing heat and cooling the system
adding a catalyst	no change

In every case the system proceeds to re-establish equilibrium. Wherever possible, the system moves in the direction which will oppose the change in conditions. This simple rule is known as **Le Chatelier's Principle** and is extremely useful in predicting which way a system will move if a certain change is made.

We shall use Le Chatelier's Principle to deduce qualitatively the conditions of temperature and pressure which, theoretically, will give the highest equilibrium yield of product from some commercially important reversible reactions. As we shall see, these are *not* necessarily the conditions which are used in practice.

The Haber process

Nitrogen and hydrogen are combined to give ammonia:

$$N_2(g) + 3H_2(g) \rightleftharpoons 2NH_3(g) \qquad \Delta H = -92\,kJ$$
$$\text{4 gas molecules} \qquad \text{2 gas molecules}$$

To get the maximum *theoretical* yield of ammonia we need:
> ▶ a *high* pressure, since the formation of ammonia is accompanied by a reduction in the total number of gas molecules. In practice, pressures of up to *1000 atmospheres* are used.
> ▶ a *low* temperature, since heat is evolved when ammonia is formed. In practice the process is carried out at about *450°C*, since below this temperature equilibrium is established too *slowly* to be economically viable. An *iron catalyst* is employed to further reduce the time taken to reach equilibrium.

Cooling the reaction mixture condenses the ammonia as a liquid and the unreacted nitrogen and hydrogen are recycled through the catalyst chamber. (The Haber process is discussed further in section 25.7.)

The Contact process

Sulphur dioxide and oxygen combine to give sulphur trioxide which is used to make sulphuric acid:

$$2SO_2(g) + O_2(g) \rightleftharpoons 2SO_3(g) \qquad \Delta H = -197\,kJ$$
$$\text{3 gas molecules} \qquad \text{2 gas molecules}$$

Again, since the production of sulphur trioxide is an exothermic process which involves a reduction in total volume, the *theoretical* conditions needed for the *best* yield are a *low* temperature and a *high* pressure.

As in the case of the Haber process, a moderately high temperature, about *450°C*, is chosen which, in conjunction with a *vanadium(V) oxide* catalyst, gives the most *economical compromise between reaction rate and equilibrium yield* of product.

In order to reduce costs, air is used rather than pure oxygen. An *excess* of air is employed to push the equilibrium in favour of the product. The process is operated at a *pressure only slightly above atmospheric*. Such conditions give over 99% conversion of sulphur dioxide and the extra expense involved in operating at high pressure would not be justified by the slight extra yield obtained. (The Contact process is discussed further in section 26.7.)

Activity 14.3

In the Birkeland–Eyde process, nitrogen and oxygen combine to give nitrogen monoxide (nitric oxide):

$$N_2(g) + O_2(g) \rightleftharpoons 2NO(g)$$

The formation of nitrogen monoxide is accompanied by the absorption of heat.

What are the *theoretical* optimum conditions of temperature and pressure required to give the *maximum* yield of nitrogen monoxide?

Activity 14.4

A major objective of any commercial organisation must be to make a profit. Clearly, this will be the difference between the production cost and the selling price. One of the functions of 'process development' is to investigate ways of reducing the production costs to a minimum.

We shall take an imaginary case of a chemical company manufacturing ammonia by the Haber process and consider a possible line of process development.

In section 14.8 we have outlined the optimum conditions for the most economical yield of ammonia, but there are other factors which should be taken into account, including:

▶ **Capital costs:** The cost of building the plant or modifying it to make it suitable or safe if the reaction conditions are changed. Ammonia plants are quite expensive, since the reaction vessel must withstand the high pressures used.

▶ **Energy:** Since the reaction is exothermic, the energy demand for heating is quite small. Electricity, however, is used to drive the gas compressors.

▶ **Catalyst:** The catalyst does not last forever. It slowly becomes 'poisoned' and loses its effectiveness and must be replaced periodically.

Normally the process is run continuously apart from breakdown, routine maintenance and safety inspections. Since the plant takes some time to get back into full operation after a shutdown, the catalyst is replaced during such operations, avoiding further loss of valuable production.

Your process presently uses a catalyst developed by a rival concern. Since they have 'patented' it, your company has to pay an annual licensing fee in order to use it. This, of course, increases the production costs. Your laboratory research department have discovered another material which catalyses the reaction on a small scale. As manager of a small 'pilot' production unit, you have been asked to evaluate the new catalyst under factory conditions.

Plan your evaluation program in the light of the above information, listing the factors you would choose to investigate and explaining your decisions on economic grounds.

14.9   Comments on the activities

Activity 14.1

1

$$CH_3COOH(l) + C_2H_5OH(l) \rightleftharpoons CH_3COOC_2H_5(l) + H_2O(l)$$

moles at START	0	0	1	2

Let x moles of ethyl ethanoate react at equilibrium,

moles at EQUILIBRIUM	x	x	$1-x$	$2-x$

Let the volume of the mixture at equilibrium be $V\,dm^3$.

molar concentration at EQUILIBRIUM	x/V	x/V	$(1-x)/V$	$(2-x)/V$

$$K_c = \frac{[CH_3COOC_2H_5(l)][H_2O(l)]}{[CH_3COOH(l)][C_2H_5OH(l)]} = \frac{(1-x)(2-x)}{x^2} \cdot \frac{V^2}{V^2}$$

$$4 = \frac{2 - 3x + x^2}{x^2}$$

So, $4x^2 = 2 - 3x + x^2$ or $3x^2 + 3x - 2 = 0$
Solving this quadratic equation for x,

$$x = \frac{-3 \pm \sqrt{9 + 24}}{6}$$

$$= \frac{-3 \pm 5.745}{6}$$

$$= \frac{2.745}{6} \quad \text{or} \quad \frac{-8.745}{6}$$

$$\therefore x = 0.458 \ (-1.458 \text{ is clearly impossible})$$

Thus, from the equation, the amounts of each component at equilibrium are:

ethanoic acid $= x$ $= 0.458$ moles
ethanol $= x$ $= 0.458$ moles
ethyl ethanoate $= 1-x$ $= 0.542$ moles
water $= 2-x$ $= 1.542$ moles

Again as a check we may use these figures to recalculate the value of K_c:

$$K_c = \frac{0.542 \times 1.542}{0.458^2} = 3.98 \text{ (agrees well with actual value of 4)}$$

2 (a)

	C_2H_4 +	CH_3COOH $\rightleftharpoons$	$CH_3COOC_2H_5$
moles at START	1	1	0
moles at EQUILIBRIUM	$1-x$	$1-x$	x

If the volume of the mixture is $V\,dm^3$.

molarity at EQUILIBRIUM	$\dfrac{1-x}{V}$	$\dfrac{1-x}{V}$	$\dfrac{x}{V}$

Then,

$$K_c = \frac{[CH_3COOC_2H_5]}{[C_2H_4][CH_3COOH]} = \frac{x/V}{((1-x)/V)^2} = \frac{xV}{(1-x)^2} \quad M^{-1}$$

As you can see, if the volume of inert solvent, V, is changed then the amount of ethyl ethanoate, x, produced at equilibrium must also change to keep K_c constant. Does a larger volume produce more or less ethyl ethanoate?

(b)

	C_2H_4 +	CH_3COOH $\rightleftharpoons$	$CH_3COOC_2H_5$
moles at START	0.050	0.02	0

(i) From the equation, the number of moles of ethyl ethanoate formed requires the reaction of an equal number of moles of both ethene and ethanoic acid.

moles at EQUILIBRIUM	(0.050−0.018)	(0.020−0.018)	0.018
i.e.	0.032	0.002	0.018

(ii) To find the molar concentration of each substance, we must divide by the volume of the solution *in dm³*, i.e. $500/1000 = 0.50$ dm³.

molarity at EQUILIBRIUM	0.032/0.5	0.002/0.5	0.018/0.5
i.e.	0.064 M	0.004 M	0.036 M

(iii)

$$K_c = \frac{[CH_3COOC_2H_5]}{[C_2H_4][CH_3COOH]}$$

Substituting our equilibrium concentrations calculated above,

$$K_c = \frac{0.036\,M}{0.064\,M \times 0.004\,M} = 141\,M^{-1}$$

Activity 14.2

Using the equilibrium numbers of moles given in example 2(a),

	H₂(g)	+	I₂(g)	⇌	2HI(g)
moles at EQUILIBRIUM	7.83		1.68		25.54

Since the total volume is V dm³.

molar concentration at EQUILIBRIUM	7.83/V	1.68/V	25.54/V

Now,

$$K_c = \frac{[HI(g)]^2}{[H_2(g)][I_2(g)]} = \frac{25.54^2}{7.83 \times 1.68} \cdot \frac{V^2}{V^2} = \frac{652.3}{13.15} = 49.59$$

In this reaction K_c and K_p are *identical*. This is not generally the case, but in any reaction which has the *same number of molecules* on each side of the equation, the *total volume* or *pressure* terms in the equilibrium expression cancel out and the equilibrium constant is a pure number, i.e. *without units*.

Reactions which have *different* numbers of molecules on each side of the equation are considered in section 14.3.

Activity 14.3

By Le Chatelier's Principle, since the formation of nitrogen monoxide is endothermic (absorbs heat), its equilibrium concentration will be *raised* by using a *high* temperature. In this case there is no conflict between rate of reaction and equilibrium position; a *high* temperature will give *more* product *more quickly*.

Since there is *no change* in the total number of gas molecules on forming nitrogen monoxide, any change in total pressure will *not* affect the position of the equilibrium. There is no advantage in operating the process either above or below atmospheric pressure.

Activity 14.4

There are many ways of tackling such an 'open-ended' problem, but we would suggest that you should consider the following points.

▶ Try the new catalyst under the reaction conditions which you use at present.

▶ If the new catalyst does not give an acceptable yield of ammonia, then try changing the temperature or pressure. If you decide to increase the pressure, then you must first test the 'pilot plant' reaction vessels to make sure it is safe! You should then estimate the cost of modifying the large-scale production plant to use the new conditions.

> ▸ Run the 'pilot plant' continously with the new catalyst to check that its 'life' is long enough to last between planned maintenance 'shutdowns'.
> ▸ If all is well so far, then you should make sure that the catalyst can be purchased or manufactured in sufficient quantities and at a price which makes it competitive with the present process.

14.10 Summary and revision plan

1 For any general reversible reaction,

$$aA + bB + \ldots \rightleftharpoons cC + dD + \ldots$$

The **Equilibrium Law** states that the **equilibrium constant** in terms of **molar concentrations, K_c**, is fixed at any given temperature:

$$K_c \; = \; \frac{[C]^c[D]^d \ldots}{[A]^a[B]^b \ldots}$$

In a gaseous system, the equilibrium constant may also be expressed in terms of the **partial pressures** of the components:

$$K_p \; = \; \frac{p_C{}^c p_D{}^d \ldots}{p_A{}^a p_B{}^b \ldots}$$

(Note that the partial pressure of a gas is obtained by multiplying its mole fraction by the total pressure.)

2 K_c and K_p are only identical if there are equal numbers of molecules on each side of the equation, and only in this case will the equilibrium constants have no units.

3 **Le Chatelier's Principle** states that, 'If any change is imposed on a system at equilibrium, then, if possible, it will move in such a direction as to try and remove the imposed change.'
This may be used to predict the effect (if any) on any particular equilibrium of changing concentration, temperature or pressure.

4 Addition of a **catalyst** does not affect the position of an equilibrium, but enables it to be reached more quickly by providing an alternative reaction pathway with a lower activation energy.

5 In industry, e.g. the Haber and Contact processes, conditions are chosen so as to give the most economical yield of product.

Heterogeneous Chemical Equilibria

15.1 Solid/liquid equilibria

The reaction between copper and aqueous silver ions may be represented:

$$Cu(s) + 2Ag^+(aq) \rightleftharpoons 2Ag(s) + Cu^{2+}(aq)$$

Applying the Equilibrium Law strictly to this system, we may define the equilibrium constant in terms of the molar concentrations of the components:

$$\text{constant} = \frac{[Ag(s)]^2\,[Cu^{2+}(aq)]}{[Cu(s)]\,[Ag^+(aq)]^2}$$

But, the *concentration of a pure solid is effectively constant*, it does *not* depend upon the *amount* of solid present. Hence the expression above may be reduced to

$$\text{constant} = \text{constant}' \times \frac{[Cu^{2+}(aq)]}{[Ag^+(aq)]^2}$$

$$\frac{\text{constant}}{\text{constant}'} = \frac{[Cu^{2+}(aq)]}{[Ag^+(aq)]^2}$$

In this case we define K_c as

$$K_c = \frac{[Cu^{2+}(aq)]}{[Ag^+(aq)]^2}$$

Activity 15.1

When excess copper metal is added to 2 M silver nitrate solution at 25 °C, the concentration of aqueous silver ions falls to 1.8×10^{-8} M at equilibrium,

$$Cu(s) + 2Ag^+(aq) \rightleftharpoons Cu^{2+}(aq) + 2Ag(s)$$

1   What is the reduction in concentration of aqueous silver ions?
2   What concentration of aqueous copper ions are formed? (*Hint:* look carefully at the above equation.)
3   Calculate the equilibrium constant, K_c, for the above reaction.
4   What would you observe when a copper rod is left in a solution of silver nitrate?

15.2 Solubility equilibria

Addition of solute to a fixed amount of solvent will eventually result in a **dynamic equilibrium** when *undissolved solid* is in contact with a *saturated solution*. The rate at which the solute *dissolves* will equal the rate at which it is *crystallising* out of the solution. For example

$$\text{sugar(s)} \rightleftharpoons \text{sugar(aq)}$$

The **solubility** *of the solid is defined as the maximum amount which will dissolve in a specified amount of solvent at a given temperature.* It may be expressed as a *molar concentration or as a mass of solute per specified volume of solvent.*

For an ionic solid such as silver chloride, the ions *separate* in solution:

$$AgCl(s) \rightleftharpoons Ag^+(aq) + Cl^-(aq)$$

Applying the Equilibrium Law.

$$constant = \frac{[Ag^+(aq)]\ [Cl^-(aq)]}{[AgCl(s)]}$$

Since we may assume the concentration of a pure solid to be constant,

$$constant = \frac{[Ag^+(aq)]\ [Cl^-(aq)]}{constant'}$$

or

$$K_s = [Ag^+(aq)]\ [Cl^-(aq)]$$

K_s is known as the **solubility product** *of silver chloride. It is the* **maximum product** *of the silver and chloride ion concentrations which can exist in aqueous solution at a given temperature. It should not be confused with solubility* (see above).

For the general case of a sparingly soluble ionic solid,

$$A_xB_y(s) \rightleftharpoons xA^{y+}(aq) + yB^{x-}(aq); K_s = [A^{y+}(aq)]^x\ [B^{x-}(aq)]^y$$

Note: This equation only holds strictly for *sparingly soluble ionic solids*, where the *ionic* concentration is *low*. In more concentrated solutions the ions may not act independently but associate because of electrostatic attraction.

Activity 15.2

1 To which of the following solids may the idea of 'solubility product' be correctly applied?
   (a) sodium chloride, (b) lead(II) chloride, (c) glucose, $C_6H_{12}O_6$, (d) benzoic acid, C_6H_5COOH.

2 For each of the following sparingly soluble ionic solids:
   (i) write an equation showing what happens when it dissolves in water;
   (ii) write the expression for the solubility product and give appropriate units.

   (a) $PbCl_2$ (b) Ag_2CrO_4 (c) $Fe(OH)_3$ (d) Ag_3PO_4 (e) Bi_2S_3

Example

The solubility of lead(II) chloride at $0\,°C$ is $0.70\,g$ per $100\,cm^3$ of water. Calculate (a) the solubility product of lead(II) chloride at this temperature, and (b) the approximate solubility of lead(II) chloride in $0.1\,M$ lead(II) nitrate solution. (Relative atomic masses: Pb = 207, Cl = 35.5)

Solution

(a)

1 First we must calculate the **molar concentration** of lead(II) chloride in saturated solution.

$$0.70\,g\ of\ PbCl_2\ per\ 100\,cm^3\ of\ water$$
$$\therefore\ 7.00\,g\ of\ PbCl_2\ per\ 1000\,cm^3\ of\ water$$

therefore, $\dfrac{7.00}{207 + 2(35.5)}$ moles of $PbCl_2$ per $1000\,cm^3$ of water

i.e. concentration of the saturated solution is $0.0252\,M\ PbCl_2$.

2   Now we find the molar concentrations of *each of the ions* present. *Do not assume that the ionic concentrations will be equal.* In this case the concentration of $Cl^-(aq)$ is double that of $Pb^{2+}(aq)$.

$$PbCl_2(aq) \rightleftharpoons Pb^{2+}(aq) \ + 2Cl^-(aq)$$
$$0.0252\,M \quad 0.0504\,M$$

3   Use these ionic concentrations to calculate the solubility product. *Do not forget to raise the concentration to the power of the number of ions in the equation,* i.e. in this case $[Cl^-(aq)]^2$.

$$K_s = [Pb^{2+}(aq)]\,[Cl^-(aq)]^2 = 0.0252 \times 0.0504^2 = 0.000\,064 \text{ M}^3$$

(b)

4   The first step here is to find the concentration of $Pb^{2+}(aq)$ resulting *from the lead(II) nitrate.*

For 0.1 M lead(II) nitrate solution,

$$Pb(NO_3)_2(s) \ \rightarrow \ Pb^{2+}(aq) \ + 2NO_3{}^-(aq)$$
$$0.1\,M \qquad\quad 0.1\,M$$

5   The concentration of lead ions in aqueous solution is *hardly changed* by the addition of *sparingly soluble* lead(II) chloride. Therefore, we may assume that $[Pb^{2+}(aq)]$ is *approximately* 0.1 M. Now we can use the value of K_s to calculate $[Cl^-(aq)]$.

$$K_s = [Pb^{2+}(aq)]\,[Cl^-(aq)]^2$$
$$0.000\,064 = 0.1 \times [Cl^-(aq)]^2$$
thus, $\qquad\qquad [Cl^-(aq)]^2 = 0.000\,64$
$$[Cl^-(aq)] = \sqrt{0.000\,64} = 0.0253\,M$$

6   Now, *all* the chloride ions in solution originate from the *lead(II) chloride*, so we may calculate its molar concentration.

$$Pb^{2+}(aq) \ + 2Cl^-(aq) \ \rightarrow PbCl_2(aq)$$
$$0.0253\,M \quad 0.0127\,M$$

7   The only step which remains is to convert the molar concentration of lead(II) chloride into solubility expressed in $g\,dm^{-3}$.

0.0127 moles of $PbCl_2$ has a mass of $0.0127 \times 278 = 3.53\,g$.

Thus, the approximate solubility of lead(III) chloride in 0.1 M lead(II) nitrate solution is $3.53\,g$ per $1000\,cm^3$ of solution.

The solubility of the lead(II) chloride has been *suppressed* by the presence of the lead(II) nitrate, or more specifically by the lead ions in this solution. This phenomenon is known as the **common ion effect** and may be predicted qualitatively using **Le Chatelier's Principle** (section 14.8).

$$PbCl_2(aq) \rightleftharpoons Pb^{2+}(aq) + 2Cl^-(aq)$$
$$\leftarrow \text{addition of more of either of these ions}$$

This treatment assumes that the chemical nature of the ions in solution does not change. In the above example, the solubility of lead(II) chloride actually *increases* at *high* chloride concentrations, owing to the formation of a *soluble* complex ion, $[PbCl_4]^{2-}$:

$$PbCl_2(s) + 2Cl^-(aq) \rightleftharpoons [PbCl_4]^{2-}(aq)$$

Activity 15.3

We have just seen that increasing the concentration of a 'common' ion in a saturated solution causes the solute to precipitate out. According to Le Chatelier's Principle we might expect addition of excess solid solute to the system to cause more to dissolve, thus increasing the solubility. Why does this not in fact happen?

15.3 Determination of solubility product

Since the solids concerned are only *sparingly* soluble, it is rarely possible to determine solubility *directly*, e.g. by evaporating a known volume of saturated solution and then weighing the residual solid.

Indirect methods which have been used include:

▶ **conductivity** – the conductivity of a solution is a measure of the concentration of the particular ions present;

▶ **electrode potential** – the potential developed on a metal in contact with a solution of its aqueous ions depends upon the molar concentration of the ions (the theory behind this technique is developed further in chapter 17);

▶ **radioactive tracer** – the concentration of a radioactive isotope in a saturated solution may be estimated by comparing the count rate with that of the solid sample.

15.4 Applications of solubility products

Several commercially important solids are isolated by precipitation reactions at the end of the manufacturing process. Clearly, conditions must be chosen so as to precipitate as much of the solid as possible and use may be made of the common ion effect. For example, soaps are the sodium salts of long chain organic acids. These are quite soluble in water but may be precipitated almost completely by addition of concentrated sodium chloride solution.

$$Na^+X^-(aq) \rightleftharpoons Na^+(aq) + X^-(aq)$$

Addition of concentrated salt solution increases the concentration of *sodium ions* to the point where the solubility product of the soap is exceeded. This process is known as **salting out**.

Precipitation reactions are also important in analytical chemistry. Qualitative analysis for some aqueous *metal ions* involves formation of their *sparingly soluble hydroxides*. Some typical solubility products are listed in table 15.1.

All of these hydroxides are precipitated on addition of aqueous ammonia. This is a weak base which ionises partially to give hydroxide ions:

$$NH_3(aq) + H_2O(l) \rightleftharpoons NH_4^+(aq) + OH^-(aq)$$

The concentration of hydroxide ions in solution is usually sufficient to ensure that the solubility product of all the above metal hydroxides is exceeded and precipitates are formed. If, however, ammonium chloride is added to the mixture this *suppresses* ionisation of the ammonia solution, via the common ion effect. The consequent *reduction* in hydroxide ion concentration ensures that only those metal hydroxides with a *very low* solubility product will now be precipitated. This forms the basis for part of the classical separation of metal ions in qualitative analysis.

Precipitation reactions may also be used in quantitative analysis. Chloride ions in aqueous solution may be estimated using silver nitrate solution. In this reaction, sparingly soluble *silver chloride* is precipitated:

$$Ag^+(aq) + Cl^-(aq) \rightleftharpoons AgCl(s)$$

One way of finding out the amount of chloride is to filter off, dry and weigh the silver chloride. Obviously, for accuracy the precipitation must be virtually *complete*. An *excess* of silver nitrate is used in the determination since the presence of the 'common' silver ion in solution will reduce the solubility of the silver chloride.

The same reaction may be used to determine chloride ion *volumetrically*. The solution under test is titrated with standard silver nitrate solution. The problem is in detecting when the precipitation of the silver chloride is *complete*. *Potassium chromate solution* may be used as an *indicator*, the *end point* being shown by the *first tinge of a red coloration* in the white precipitate of silver chloride. Only when virtually *all* the

Table 15.1 *Solubility products of some hydroxides*

very low solubility products/M^4	
$Fe(OH)_3$	2×10^{-39}
$Al(OH)_3$	1×10^{-33}

low solubility products/M^3	
$Mg(OH)_2$	1×10^{-11}
$Fe(OH)_2$	8×10^{-16}

chloride ions have been removed from solution will *silver chromate* be formed as a *red* precipitate.

$$2Ag^+(aq) + CrO_4{}^{2-}(aq) \rightleftharpoons Ag_2CrO_4(s)$$

The theory behind this technique is explored more fully in activity 15.4.

Activity 15.4

In an experiment, a solution which is 0.1 M with respect to chloride ions and 0.001 M with respect to chromate ions is titrated with silver nitrate solution. Answer the following questions using solubility product expressions for silver chloride and silver chromate.

1   What concentration of aqueous silver ions is required to precipitate (a) silver chloride, (b) silver chromate?
2   What concentration must the aqueous chloride ions fall to before silver chromate starts to precipitate?
(Solubility products: silver chloride $1.8 \times 10^{-10} \, M^2$; silver chromate $1.3 \times 10^{-12} \, M^3$.)

15.5 Solid/gas equilibria

Whereas in solid/liquid systems we use K_c, here we shall use K_p, the equilibrium constant in terms of the partial pressures of the components.

Calcium carbonate decomposes reversibly on heating as follows:

$$CaCO_3(s) \rightleftharpoons CaO(s) + CO_2(g)$$

Applying the Equilibrium Law,

$$\text{constant} = \frac{p_{CaO} \, p_{CO_2}}{p_{CaCO_3}}$$

Now the **vapour pressure** of any solid is constant at any particular temperature and it is usual to express the equilibrium constant in the simplest possible terms:

$$\text{constant} = \frac{\text{constant}' \times p_{CO_2}}{\text{constant}''}$$

i.e. $$K_p = p_{CO_2}$$

Thus, as in the case of solid/liquid systems, the position of this equilibrium is *independent* of the amounts of any *solids* present. At any given temperature, the partial pressure of carbon dioxide is *constant* and is known as the **dissociation pressure**. If calcium carbonate is heated in an open vessel the reaction will proceed to completion since the carbon dioxide will escape into the atmosphere and never reach its equilibrium partial pressure.

The reaction between iron and steam may be treated similarly:

$$3Fe(s) + 4H_2O(g) \rightleftharpoons Fe_3O_4(s) + 4H_2(g)$$

$$\text{constant} = \frac{p_{Fe_3O_4} \, p_{H_2}^4}{p_{Fe}^3 \, p_{H_2O}^4}$$

Since the partial pressures of the solids are constant,

$$\text{constant} = \frac{p_{H_2}^4}{p_{H_2O}^4}$$

$$K_p = \frac{p_{H_2}}{p_{H_2O}}$$

Thus at equilibrium, the partial pressures of hydrogen and steam are in a *constant ratio*. Altering the amounts of either solid has no effect on the equilibrium, but removal of hydrogen pushes the reaction to the right. This process has been used for the industrial manufacture of hydrogen.

Activity 15.5

A mixture of iron and steam is heated at constant temperature in a closed vessel until equilibrium is established. What effect, if any, would each of the following changes have upon the position of the equilibrium?
(a) Increasing the total pressure.
(b) More steam is introduced but the total volume is kept constant.
(c) More steam is added but the total volume is increased so that its partial pressure remains unchanged.
(d) Adding more iron.

15.6 Comments on the activities

Activity 15.1

1 The decrease in $[Ag^+(aq)]$ is $2 - 1.8 \times 10^{-8}$ M, i.e. about 2 M.
2 Looking at the equation for the reaction, half as many moles of Cu^{2+} are formed, therefore at equilibrium $[Cu^{2+}(aq)] = 1$ M.
3

$$Cu(s) + 2Ag^+(aq) \rightleftharpoons Cu^{2+}(aq) + 2Ag(s)$$

at EQUILIBRIUM $\qquad\qquad 1.8 \times 10^{-8}$ M $\qquad$ 1 M

$$K_c = \frac{[Cu^{2+}(aq)]}{[Ag^+(aq)]^2} = \frac{1}{(1.8 \times 10^{-8})^2} = 3.09 \times 10^{15} \ M^{-1}$$

4 Silver metal would deposit on the surface of the copper and the solution would turn blue owing to the presence of $Cu^{2+}(aq)$ ions.

Activity 15.2

1 Remember solubility product may only strictly be applied to sparingly soluble ionic solids.
(a) No – sodium chloride is ionic but quite soluble in water.
(b) Yes – lead(II) chloride is a sparingly soluble ionic solid.
(c) No – glucose is a water soluble covalent compound.
(d) No – although benzoic acid is only slightly soluble in cold water, it is a weak acid and hardly ionises in solution.

2 (a) $K_s = [Pb^{2+}(aq)] [Cl^-(aq)]^2 \qquad M^3$
(b) $K_s = [Ag^+(aq)]^2 [CrO_4^{2-}(aq)] \qquad M^3$
(c) $K_s = [Fe^{3+}(aq)] [OH^-(aq)]^3 \qquad M^4$
(d) $K_s = [Ag^+(aq)]^3 [PO_4^{3-}(aq)] \qquad M^4$
(e) $K_s = [Bi^{3+}(aq)]^2 [S^{2-}(aq)]^3 \qquad M^5$

Activity 15.3

The key factor is *not the amount* of substance in the system at equilibrium but its *concentration*. The concentration of any pure *solid* may be taken to be *constant* and thus addition of further excess will not increase the solubility.

Activity 15.4

1 For silver chloride:
$K_s = [Ag^+(aq)] [Cl^-(aq)]$
$1.8 \times 10^{-10} = [Ag^+(aq)] \times 0.1$
$[Ag^+(aq)] = 1.8 \times 10^{-9}$ M

For silver chromate:
$K_s = [Ag^+(aq)]^2 [CrO_4^{2-}(aq)]$
$1.3 \times 10^{-12} = [Ag^+(aq)]^2 \times 0.001$
$[Ag^+(aq)]^2 = 1.3 \times 10^{-9}$ M^2
$[Ag^+(aq)] = 3.6 \times 10^{-5}$ M

Thus, even though it has a *higher* solubility product than silver chromate, silver chloride will precipitate *first*.

2 Silver chromate will only start to precipitate when the concentration of the silver ions in solution reaches 3.6×10^{-5} M. We may use the solubility product of silver chloride to calculate the aqueous chloride ion concentration under these conditions.

$$K_s = [Ag^+(aq)]\,[Cl^-(aq)]$$
$$1.8 \times 10^{-10} = 3.6 \times 10^{-5}\,[Cl^-(aq)]$$
$$[Cl^-(aq)] = 5.0 \times 10^{-6}\,M$$

Since the original chloride ion concentration was 0.1 M, *virtually all* the aqueous chloride is precipitated *before* any silver chromate is produced. The first appearance of the red colour of the silver chromate in the mixture therefore indicates complete reaction of the chloride ions.

Activity 15.5

(a) No effect on equilibrium position. The partial pressures of both the steam and hydrogen would be increased by the same factor so K_p remains unchanged.

(b) The partial pressure of steam is increased whilst that of hydrogen remains the same. The system moves to the right, i.e. producing more hydrogen and using up steam.

(c) The effect is the same as that described in (2) above. The partial pressure of steam remains constant but because of the increase in volume, the partial pressure of hydrogen falls.

(d) No effect on equilibrium position. As explained in section 15.5, the equilibrium is independent of the amounts of any *solids* involved.

15.7 Summary and revision plan

1 The concentration or partial pressure of any solid (or pure liquid) is constant at any given temperature and does not appear in the expression for the equilibrium constant. Values of K_c and K_p 'incorporate' any such constant terms.

Changing the 'amount' of any solid (or pure liquid) in a heterogeneous system at equilibrium therefore has no effect.

2 **Solubility** is defined as the maximum amount (mass or moles) of solute which will dissolve in a fixed amount (usually $1\,dm^3$) of a particular solvent at a given temperature.

The effect on solubility of changing the temperature may be predicted, qualitatively, using **Le Chatelier's Principle** if the enthalpy change for dissolving the solid is known.

3 **Solubility product**, K_s, is defined as the product of the aqueous ionic concentrations, each raised to the power of the number of moles shown in the balanced equation, in a saturated solution of a sparingly soluble ionic solid. Like solubility, the value of K_s depends upon temperature.

4 The **common ion effect** refers to the lowering of the solubility of an ionic solid in any solution which contains an ion 'common' to the solute. This effect is due to that fact that 'solubility product' remains constant regardless of the common ion concentration.

5 The precipitation of sparingly soluble solids from solution has important applications in chemical analysis.

Physical or Phase Equilibria

Contents

Why does salt melt the ice and snow on roads in winter?
How can you separate pure 'alcohol' from beer or wine?
Why does oil mix with petrol but not with water?

The answers to these and many other questions involve a study of equilibria concerned with physical changes. Most of these involve a change of state, i.e. melting, subliming, evaporating or dissolving (figure 16.1).

Figure 16.1 *Changes of state*

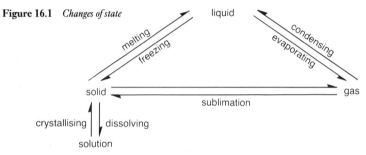

Since these processes involve a change of phase (section 13.2) the term **phase equilibria** is also used.

Our study will concentrate on the behaviour of mixtures rather than pure substances. We shall discover how the addition of an impurity can change the properties of a pure substance and how different types of mixture can be separated.

16.1 Miscible liquids: ideal behaviour and fractional distillation

At any given temperature, a pure liquid in a closed container will establish an equilibrium with its vapour

$$\text{liquid} \rightleftharpoons \text{vapour}$$

The equilibrium vapour pressure above the liquid will depend upon the temperature. Let us now consider mixing two liquids in different proportions. **Raoult's Law** *states that for an ideal mixture at a fixed temperature, the vapour pressure of each component is proportional to its mole fraction*, i.e. a graph of the vapour pressure of each component against its mole fraction will be a straight line passing through the origin (figure 16.2).

Here we shall consider the case of two volatile liquids, each of which contributes to the total vapour pressure. By Dalton's Law of partial pressures, the total vapour pressure of the mixture is the sum of that of the components and this will also give a straight line when plotted against molar composition as shown in figure 16.3.

For most purposes it is more convenient to plot the boiling point of the mixture

Figure 16.2 *The relationship between vapour pressure and mole fraction for a component in an ideal mixture*

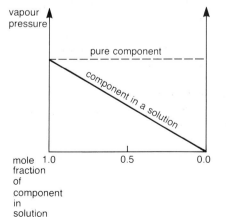

Figure 16.3 *The relationship between mole fractions and partial and total vapour pressures for an ideal mixture of two liquids*

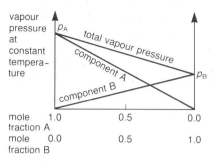

where, P_A is the vapour pressure of pure A
P_B is the vapour pressure of pure B

Figure 16.4 *Boiling point-composition diagram for the ideal liquid mixture represented in figure 16.3*

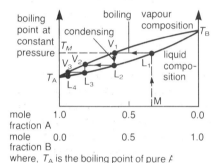

where, T_A is the boiling point of pure A
T_B is the boiling point of pure B

Figure 16.5 *Fractional distillation apparatus*

The fractionating column at Rastarura oil refinery, Saudi Arabia

against molar composition. The boiling point of a liquid is *the temperature at which its vapour pressure reaches the external atmospheric pressure.* Since the less volatile component will have the highest boiling point, the vapour pressure curves in figure 16.3 lead to the boiling point–composition graph shown in figure 16.4. Two curves are drawn on this diagram, since the liquid mixture and the vapour in equilibrium with it will *not* have the same composition. The vapour will always contain a higher proportion of the more volatile (lower boiling point) component. If we consider heating a liquid of composition M in figure 16.4, then it will boil at a temperature T_M. The vapour in equilibrium with the liquid, L_1, at this temperature has the composition V_1, and is considerably richer in component A (more volatile).

This difference in composition between the liquid and vapour phases in equilibrium enables such a liquid mixture to be separated by **distillation**. If the vapour V_1 in figure 16.4 is cooled, it condenses to a liquid of the same composition, L_2. Boiling this will produce vapour V_2 and if this process of condensing and reboiling is continued, the *final vapour will be pure A*. Meanwhile, the residual liquid has become less rich in the more volatile component A, and *its composition will follow the liquid composition curve until it contains only pure B.*

Thus, to separate a liquid mixture which obeys Raoult's Law we must repeatedly distil, i.e. boil the liquid and condense the vapour. This is known as **fractional distillation**, but rather than carry out each stage separately, it is convenient to use a **fractionating column** designed to allow many such steps to occur simultaneously. The fractionating column shown in figure 16.5 consists of a long tube filled with glass beads. The purpose of this packing is to provide a *large surface area* for condensation. The vapour rising from the flask warms up the bottom of the column and condenses back into liquid. As it falls it meets fresh hot vapour rising up the column. This process is repeated continually and each time the vapour rises further up the column and becomes richer in the more volatile component. If the column is long enough, the vapour which escapes at the top is the pure, more volatile component and this may be confirmed by checking its boiling point on the thermometer.

Each distillation step is known as a **theoretical plate** and clearly the greater the number of theoretical plates in the fractionating column, the more efficient it will be in separating the liquid mixture.

Fractional distillation is widely used in industrial chemistry for separating mixtures of miscible liquids which boil at different temperatures. For example:

▶ pure oxygen, nitrogen and the noble gases may be obtained from liquid air;
▶ the hydrocarbons in crude oil can be separated into useful 'fractions'.

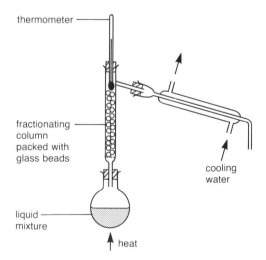

Figure 16.6 *Negative deviations from Raoult's Law*

(a) small deviation

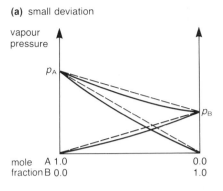

(b) large deviation

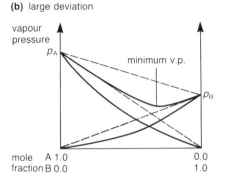

16.2 Deviations from ideal behaviour

Liquid mixtures which obey Raoult's Law exactly are quite rare. Usually in such cases the two components are chemically very similar, e.g. the alkanes, hexane, C_6H_{14}, and heptane, C_7H_{16}. This is because in an **ideal mixture** the *intermolecular attraction between different molecules must be the same as that between identical molecules.*

Often when liquids are mixed, heat is released and the total volume is less than that of the individual components. This suggests that the molecules of the two liquids *attract each other very strongly*. One such case is propanone, CH_3COCH_3, and trichloromethane, $CHCl_3$.

$$H_3C \diagdown$$
$$C = O \quad \overset{\delta-}{ } \quad \overset{\delta+}{ } \quad H - CCl_3$$
$$H_3C \diagup$$

Since the different molecules attract each other more strongly, they *cannot escape so readily* from the liquid and so the vapour pressure of each component is *less* than would be expected in the ideal case. This is known as **negative deviation** from Raoult's Law and leads to the kind of vapour pressure–composition curve shown in figure 16.6a. *Very large negative deviations* lead to a *minimum* in the vapour pressure curve as shown in figure 16.6b.

In contrast, other liquid pairs expand on mixing and absorb heat, e.g. water and ethanol. Here, strong intermolecular attraction within one or both of the components must be disrupted by mixing, i.e. the forces of attraction between *different* molecules are *weaker* than those between molecules of the *same* type. In the case of ethanol and water, the ethanol interferes with the strong hydrogen bonding between water molecules. Since the intermolecular attraction is reduced, each of the components vaporises *more easily* and this results in **positive deviation** from Raoult's Law, figure 16.7a. In figure 16.7b, the positive deviation is large enough to produce a *maximum* in the vapour pressure curve.

Figure 16.7 *Positive deviations from Raoult's Law*

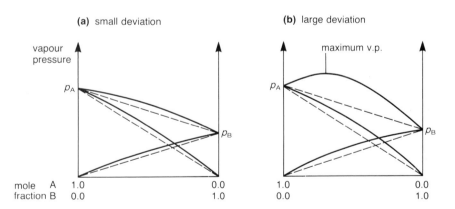

If the deviation from ideal behaviour is *small*, i.e. does not give rise to a minimum or maximum in the vapour pressure curve, then the boiling point–composition diagram is of the same form as that previously given for an ideal mixture in figure 16.4. As with an ideal mixture, fractional distillation will give a *complete separation* of the two components.

The situation is not so straightforward if the vapour pressure curve of the mixture contains a maximum or minimum and a complete separation cannot be achieved by fractional distillation.

16.3 Immiscible liquid mixtures – steam distillation

As the attraction between dissimilar molecules in a liquid mixture falls, positive deviation from Raoult's Law increases as shown in figure 16.8, and eventually the liquids become completely immiscible. Now the two liquids act *completely independently*. Since two layers are present, it is normally only the less dense component which is in contact with the vapour above the liquid. If, however, the system is constantly agitated both liquids will reach the surface and exert their full vapour pressure. Then the total vapour pressure of the system is the sum of the vapour pressures of the pure components and will be constant at any given temperature. Use is made of this behaviour in the purification of certain organic liquids by steam distillation.

Phenylamine, $C_6H_5NH_2$ (section 41.5), is a liquid that boils at about 184 °C at atmospheric pressure, but since it decomposes somewhat at this temperature it is difficult to purify by simple distillation. If, however, it is mixed with water, with which it is immiscible, then from figure 16.8 we can see that the total vapour pressure of the system is equal to the sum of the vapour pressures of each of the pure liquids. The mixture will therefore distil at a temperature *below* the boiling points of either of the individual components, actually at about 98 °C, and little decomposition of the phenylamine will occur at this lower temperature.

Figure 16.8 *Vapour pressure curves for miscible, partially miscible and immiscible liquid mixtures*

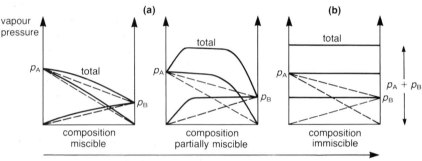

The apparatus for steam distillation is shown in figure 16.9. The mixture of the impure phenylamine and water is heated by steam, which also helps to agitate the system. In order to increase the temperature of the mixture more quickly and maintain it at the boiling point, gentle direct heat may be applied to the flask. A mixture of steam and phenylamine vapour distils out of the flask and the condensate is collected. On standing, the two layers may be separated using a tap funnel.

Figure 16.9 *Steam distillation apparatus*

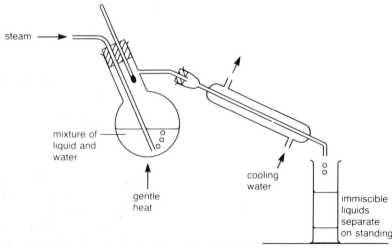

Steam distillation may be used with any liquid which is immiscible with water and which exerts a reasonable vapour pressure when boiled with water.

16.4 Solutions of solids in liquids – colligative properties

Many properties of solutions are **colligative**, i.e. *depend only upon the concentration of solute particles and not upon their chemical nature*. Such properties, including **elevation of boiling point** and **depression of freezing point**, may be of great value in the determination of the relative molecular mass of solutes. Care must, however, be taken where the solute ionises or associates in solution, since this will obviously affect the overall concentration of solute particles present.

Activity 16.1

Aluminium sulphate, $Al_2(SO_4)_3$, ionises completely in aqueous solution.
1   Write an equation for this process.
2   In a 0.1M aqueous solution of aluminium sulphate what is the molar concentration of:
(a) aluminium ions   (b) sulphate ions   (c) solute particles?

   For dilute solutions, the elevation of boiling point, ΔT, is directly proportional to the concentration of solute particles, n. Thus,

$$\Delta T = \mathbf{B}n$$

where B is known as the **boiling point elevation constant**, or **ebullioscopic constant**, of the solvent. It is the theoretical increase in the boiling point that would be produced by one mole of any solute particles in a specified mass, usually 100 g or 1000 g, of a particular solvent. It is *not* the *actual* increase in boiling point produced by one mole of solute, since such a solution would be *too concentrated* to be treated as above. The value of B is normally calculated by simple ratio from boiling point measurements in dilute solutions. Values of the boiling point elevation constant for some solvents are given in table 16.1.

   If the ebullioscopic constant of the solvent is known, boiling point elevation results may be used to find the relative molecular mass of solutes, as in the following examples.

Example 1

0.280 g of camphor dissolved in 16.0 g of ethanol increases the boiling point by 0.139 °C. If the boiling point elevation constant of ethanol is 1.15 °C per 1000 g of solvent, calculate the relative molecular mass of camphor.

Solution

   0.280 g camphor raises the b.p. of 16.0 g ethanol by 0.139 °C
   ∴ 0.280 g camphor raised the b.p. of 1 g ethanol by 0.139×16 °C

Mistakes are common in this type of simple ratio calculation, e.g. dividing by 16.0 above instead of multiplying. Always bear in mind that increasing the concentration of solute (in this case by reducing the amount of solvent) will increase the boiling point elevation.

   0.280 g camphor raises the b.p. of 1000 g ethanol by $\dfrac{0.139 \times 16 \,°C}{1000}$

   = 0.002 22 °C

Let the number of moles of camphor used be x,
                  x moles of camphor raises b.p. by 0.00 222 °C
         but, 1 mole of camphor raises b.p by 1.15 °C
         Thus, $x = 0.002\ 22/1.15 = 0.001\ 93$ moles of camphor.
         Now, 0.001 93 moles of camphor weigh 0.280 g
         so, 1 mole of camphor weighs $0.280/0.001\ 93 = 145$ g
         Hence, the relative molecular mass of camphor is 145.

Salt spreading on icy/snowy roads

You may know from experience that addition of a solute to a liquid depresses its melting point – for example, salt will cause the ice on a road to melt!

In *dilute* solution, as with elevation of boiling point, the depression of freezing point is proportional to the number of moles of solute particles, n:

i.e. $\Delta T = Fn$ for a fixed mass of solvent.

Here, F is the freezing point depression which would be produced by one mole of solute particles dissolved in a specified mass of the solvent, usually $100\,g$ or $1000\,g$, if the solution behaved as if it were very dilute. It is known as the **freezing point depression constant** or **cryoscopic constant**. Values for some common solvents are given in table 16.1.

Table 16.1 *Boiling point elevation constants and freezing point depression constants for some common solvents*

All constants in this table are given in °C for 1000 g of solvent. To find the constant for any other mass of solvent, g, multiply by 1000/g.

Solvent	boiling point elevation constant	freezing point depression constant
water	0.52	1.86
benzene	2.63	5.12
ethanoic acid	3.14	3.90
propanone	1.72	
methanol	0.83	
ethanol	1.20	
naphthalene		7.0
camphor		40.0

Activity 16.2

The following results were obtained in an experiment to find the relative molecular mass of ethanoic acid in benzene solution by measuring freezing point depression.

mass of benzene $= 50.67\,g$
mass of ethanoic acid $= 3.80\,g$

Beckmann thermometer readings:
freezing pt. of benzene $= 5.830\,°C$
freezing pt. of solution $= 2.630\,°C$

1 Use the freezing point depression constant for benzene given in table 16.1 to calculate the relative molecular mass of ethanoic acid in benzene solution.
(You may find it helpful to refer to the example above in which the M_r of camphor is calculated from boiling point measurements.)

2 How do you account for this figure in view of the fact that the formula of the acid is generally written as CH_3COOH?
(Relative atomic masses: H = 1, C = 12, O = 16)

16.5 Distribution of a solute between immiscible liquids

If a solute is shaken with a pair of immiscible solvents, then it will **distribute** itself between them in a dynamic equilibrium according to the **Partition Law**. This states that *the ratio of the concentrations of the solute in each of the solvents will be constant at a given temperature*, providing that the solubility in neither of the solvents is exceeded,

i.e.
$$K_d = \frac{\text{concentration of solute in solvent A}}{\text{concentration of solute in solvent B}}$$

where the constant, K_d, is known as the **partition coefficient** or **distribution coefficient** for the system.

Example 2

When various amounts of butanedioic acid were shaken with a mixture of water and ether the following concentrations were obtained.

concentration of acid in ether/$g\,dm^{-3}$	0.50	1.10	1.85
concentration of acid in water/$g\,dm^{-3}$	2.60	5.72	9.62

What is the distribution coefficient of butanedioic acid between water and ether?

Solution

Since the distribution coefficient was specified with water first we put this term on the top of the equation.

$$K_d = \frac{\text{concentration of acid in water}}{\text{concentration of acid in ether}}$$

=	2.60/0.50	5.72/1.10	9.62/1.85
=	5.20	5.20	5.20

The distribution coefficient of the acid between water and ether is 5.20. Organic solutes are generally more soluble in covalent solvents such as ether or trichloromethane. Since the latter are immiscible with water, they may be used to extract the organic compound from aqueous solution, leaving behind any ionic impurities. The organic solvent may then be distilled off, leaving the pure solid. More details of this technique, known as **solvent extraction** are given in section 32.3, but, as the following example shows, the extraction is more efficient if the solvent is used in successive small portions rather than all at once.

Example 3

The partition coefficient of an organic solid A between ether and water is 2. Calculate the mass of A extracted from $100\,cm^3$ of an aqueous solution which contains 6.00 g of the solute by
- (a) a single portion of $100\,cm^3$ of ether, and
- (b) two successive $50\,cm^3$ portions of ether.

Solution

- (a) Let x be the mass of A extracted by a single $100\,cm^3$ portion of ether.

$$\frac{\text{concentration in ether}}{\text{concentration in water}} = \frac{x/100}{(6-x)/100} = \frac{x}{6-x} = 2$$

  Hence, $x = 12 - 2x$, so $3x = 12$, i.e. $x = 4$.

  Mass of A extracted by one $100\,cm^3$ portion of ether = 4 g.
- (b) Let y be the mass of A extracted by the first $50\,cm^3$ portion of ether.

$$\frac{\text{concentration in ether}}{\text{concentration in water}} = \frac{y/50}{(6-y)/100} = \frac{2y}{6-y} = 2$$

  Hence, $2y = 12 - 2y$, so $4y = 12$, i.e. $y = 3$.

  Mass of A extracted by first portion of ether = 3 g, thus the mass solute remaining in the aqueous layer = $6 - 3 = 3$ g.

  Let z be the mass of A extracted by the second $50\,cm^3$ portion of ether.

$$\frac{\text{concentration in ether}}{\text{concentration in water}} = \frac{z/50}{(3-z)/100} = \frac{2z}{3-z} = 2$$

  Hence, $2z = 6 - 2z$, so $4z = 6$, i.e. $z = 1.5$.

Mass of A extracted by second portion of ether = 1.5 g; thus the total mass of A extracted by both ether portions is $3 + 1.5 = 4.5$ g, i.e. 0.5 g more than using the same volume of ether in a single extraction.

16.6 Comments on the activities

Activity 16.1

1    $Al_2(SO_4)_3(s)$ $2Al^{3+}(aq) + 3SO_4^{2-}(aq)$
2   0.1 moles   0.2 moles   0.3 moles
        i.e. a total of 0.5 moles of aqueous ions

(a) $[Al^{3+}(aq)] = 0.2M$.
(b) $[SO_4^{2-}(aq)] = 0.3M$.
(c) total concentration of ions = 0.5M.

Activity 16.2

1   Freezing point depression = $5.830 - 2.630 = 3.200°C$
3.80 g of ethanoic acid depresses f.p. of 50.67 g benzene by 3.20°C
3.80 g of ethanoic acid depresses f.p. of 1000 g benzene by $\dfrac{50.67 \times 3.2°C}{100}$

   $= 0.162°C$

But 1 mole of solute depresses f.p. of 1000 g benzene by 5.12°C.
Thus 0.162/5.12 moles of ethanoic acid must be present in solution.
i.e.   0.0316   moles of ethanoic acids weighs 3.80 g
        ∴ 1 mole of ethanoic acid weighs 3.80/0.0316 = 120 g
The relative molecular mass of ethanoic acid in benzene is 120.
2   The relative mass of the CH_3COOH molecule is,
            carbon $2 \times 12 = 24$
            hydrogen $4 \times 1 = 4$
            oxygen $2 \times 16 = 32$
                    total   60

The acid must associate into dimers in benzene solution under the conditions of the experiment,

$$2CH_3COOH \rightarrow (CH_3COOH)_2$$

(The mechanism for this process involves intermolecular hydrogen bonding, see section 5.9.)

16.7 Summary and revision plan

1   Phase equilibria involve reversible physical changes in which there is a change of state.

Miscible liquids
2   **Raoult's Law** states that, in an ideal mixture of miscible liquids, the vapour pressure of each component is directly proportional to its mole fraction.
3   **Positive** and **negative deviations** from ideal behaviour arise from differences in the strength of intermolecular attraction. Large deviations give rise to a **minimum** or **maximum** in the boiling point–composition curve and such mixtures cannot be completely separated by fractional distillation.

Immiscible liquids

4 In such mixtures, the attraction between dissimilar molecules is much lower than that between identical molecules and this leads to very large positive deviations from Raoult's Law.

5 In an agitated mixture of immiscible liquids, each component exerts its full vapour pressure and the boiling point will be lower than either of the pure components. This is made use of in the **steam distillation** of liquids which are immiscible with water.

Solutions of non-volatile solids

6 Many properties of solutions of non-volatile solids are **colligative**, i.e. they depend upon the mole fraction of the solute particles added and not upon their nature. Such properties include:
   (a) **elevation of boiling point**;
   (b) **depression of freezing point**;
   Care must be taken if the solute ionises or associates in solution, since this will affect the number of solute 'particles' present in the solution.

7 The relative molecular mass of a solute may be determined by measuring the above properties.

8 On shaking, a solute will **distribute** itself between two immiscible solvents in accordance with the **Partition Law**. This states that, provided that the solute is in the same molecular state in both solvents,

$$\text{partition coefficient of solute between solvent A and solvent B} = \frac{\text{concentration of solute in solvent A}}{\text{concentration of solute in solvent B}}$$

This is made use of in the purification of solids by **solvent extraction**.

□ CHAPTER □

17

CHAPTER
CHAPTER
CHAPTER
CHAPTER

□ CHAPTER □

Equilibria at Electrodes

Contents

17.1 Oxidation and reduction: redox reactions

The most useful definition of oxidation and reduction is given in terms of electron transfer.

▶ *A species is said to be* **oxidised** *if electrons are withdrawn from it.* The species which withdraws the electrons is said to be an **oxidising agent**.

Conversely,

▶ *A species is said to be* **reduced** *if it gains electrons.* The species which supplies the electrons is known as a **reducing agent**.

You should see from the above that when a substance acts as an oxidising agent, it is itself reduced and likewise a reducing agent is itself oxidised. Any reaction which involves both **red**uction and **ox**idation is referred to as a **redox** reaction.

Although most reactions involve the rearrangement of valency electrons, and therefore may properly be considered to be redox reactions, probably the easiest type to understand involves the formation of an ionic compound from its elements. Consider the following examples

magnesium sulphide, MgS:

$$Mg + S \rightarrow Mg^{2+} \quad S^{2-}$$
$$2.8.2 \quad 2.8.6 \qquad 2.8 \quad 2.8.8$$

Two electrons are transferred from a magnesium to a sulphur atom, i.e, magnesium is *oxidised* by sulphur. We may split the overall equation into two **half-equations**, one involving *oxidation* and one *reduction*.

$$Mg \rightarrow Mg^{2+} + 2e^- \quad \text{oxidation}$$
$$S + 2e^- \rightarrow S^{2-} \qquad \text{reduction}$$

Likewise, sodium chloride, NaCl:

$$2Na + Cl_2 \rightarrow 2Na^+ \, 2Cl^-$$

i.e.
$$2Na \rightarrow 2Na^+ + 2e^- \quad \text{oxidation}$$
$$Cl_2 + 2e^- \rightarrow 2Cl^- \qquad \text{reduction}$$

Activity 17.1

For the formation of each of the following ionic compounds from their elements:

    1 calcium oxide   2 potassium sulphide   3 aluminium fluoride
    4 aluminium oxide   5 magnesium nitride

(a) write an overall equation showing the formation of the ions;

(b) write half-equations showing the oxidation and reduction processes separately;

(c) state which element is acting as the reducing agent and which as the oxidising agent.

    At first sight the formation of a covalent compound such as hydrogen chloride, HCl, from its elements might not seem to be a redox reaction.

$$H_2 + Cl_2 \rightarrow 2HCl$$

However, if we look more closely at the electronic rearrangement which takes place, we can see that the bonding pair of electrons is *not equally shared* in the hydrogen chloride molecule.

equal sharing of electrons

chlorine has a greater share of the bonding electrons

Chlorine has a *higher* **electronegativity** than hydrogen and attracts the bonding electrons *more strongly*. It may be considered to have *partially gained* an electron, whilst the hydrogen atom has *partially lost* an electron. The hydrogen has thus been *oxidised* by the chlorine. In any covalent bond the more electronegative atom will develop a partial negative charge, $\delta-$, whilst the other atom will become slightly positive, $\delta+$. Knowing from chapter 5.9 that electronegativity generally increases on passing across a period but decreases on passing down any group in the Periodic Table, we may predict the partial charges present in any covalent molecule as shown in figure 17.1. Any atom which develops a positive charge may be considered to have partially lost electrons, whilst a negative charge indicates a partial gain of electrons.

The idea of **oxidation number** or **oxidation state** helps us to develop an understanding of redox reactions in the case of both ionic and covalent systems. *Oxidation number may be described as the number of electrons which the atom loses, or tends to lose, when it forms the substance in question. If the atom gains, or tends to gain electrons, then the oxidation number is negative.*

In the case of a simple ion the oxidation number of the element is obviously equal to the ionic charge, for example:

sodium chloride	Na^+	Cl^-
oxidation numbers	$+1$	-1
magnesium oxide	Mg^{2+}	O^{2-}
oxidation numbers	$+2$	-2
lithium nitride	$3Li^+$	N^{3-}
oxidation numbers	$3(+1)$	-3

For covalent compounds, the oxidation number may be regarded as the charge which the atom *would* develop if the electronegativity differences made the compound *fully ionic*: for example:

hydrogen chloride	H	Cl	(H^+ Cl^-)
oxidation numbers	$+1$	-1	
phosphorus trichloride	P	Cl_3	(P^{3+} $3Cl^-$)
oxidation states	$+3$	$3(-1)$	
sulphur trioxide	S	O_3	(S^{6+} $3O^{2-}$)
oxidation states	$+6$	$3(-2)$	

There are a number of simple rules which may help to determine the oxidation state of an element in any compound.
- *The oxidation number of an element in its free state is always zero.*
- *The sum of the oxidation numbers in a neutral molecule is always zero. In an ion, this sum equals the ionic charge.*

e.g. PCl_5 oxidation numbers   P $+5$ $= +5$
                             5Cl -1 each $= -5$
                                          ———
                                          0 total

Figure 17.1 *Examples of polar covalent molecules*

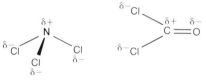

(note the size of the charge produced differs)

$$CO_3^{2-} \quad \text{oxidation numbers} \qquad \begin{array}{ll} C +4 & = +4 \\ 3O -2 \text{ each} & = -6 \\ \hline & -2 \text{ total} \end{array}$$

▶ *Some elements exhibit more or less fixed oxidation numbers in their compounds, e.g.*
Group I metals *always* show an oxidation number of $+1$.
Group II metals *always* show an oxidation number of $+2$.
Fluorine *always* shows an oxidation number of -1.
Oxygen *almost always* shows an oxidation number of -2 (except in oxygen difluoride, OF_2, and in peroxides and superoxides, e.g. Na_2O_2 and KO_2).
Hydrogen *usually* shows an oxidation number of $+1$ (except in the hydrides of more electropositive elements, e.g. NaH).

We may often use these rules to deduce the oxidation numbers of other elements in their compounds, e.g. manganese in $KMnO_4$:

$$\text{oxidation numbers} \quad \begin{array}{ccc} K & Mn & O_4 \\ +1 & +? & +4(-2) = 0 \end{array}$$

Since the compound as a whole is neutral, the oxidation number of the manganese must be $+7$. This is reflected in the systematic name of the compound, potassium manganate(VII), where the roman numerals indicate the oxidation state of the manganese.

Where there is more than one atom of a particular element present in a molecule or ion, this method will give use the *average* oxidation state, which may *not* be a whole number, e.g. sulphur in the tetrathionate ion, $S_4O_6^{2-}$

$$\begin{array}{cc} S_4 + & O_6 \\ \text{oxidation numbers} \quad 4(?) & 6(-2) = -2 \end{array}$$

The total of the oxidation numbers of the four sulphur atoms must be $+10$, so the average oxidation number of the sulphur is $+10/4 = +2.5$. This nicely illustrates the point that, whilst oxidation numbers provide a useful 'book-keeping' system for redox reactions, they must not be interpreted too literally.

If, during a reaction, the oxidation state of any atom becomes more positive then it has been oxidised. If the oxidation state becomes less positive then reduction has occurred.
Consider the reaction of manganate(VII) with iron(II) in aqueous acid solution:

$$\begin{array}{lccccc} & MnO_4^- + & 5Fe^{2+} + 8H^+ & \rightarrow Mn^{2+} & + 5Fe^{3+} & + 4H_2O \\ \text{oxidation numbers} & +7 & 5(+2) & +2 & 5(+3) & \\ \text{total} & & +17 & +17 & & \end{array}$$

The manganate(VII) has been *reduced* by the iron(II) and the iron(II) has been *oxidised* by the manganate(VII). *Note that the sum of the oxidation numbers on each side of any redox equation must be the same, since the number of electrons gained by the oxidising agent equals the number lost by the reducing agent.*

In section 17.8 we shall show how to derive the full equation for any redox reaction from a knowledge of the changes in oxidation number which take place.
Look at the following equation:

$$3ClO^-(aq) \rightarrow ClO_3^-(aq) + 2Cl^-(aq)$$
$$\text{oxidation state} \quad 3(+1) \qquad +5 \qquad 2(-1)$$

Chlorate(I), ClO^-, has been both oxidised to chlorate(V), ClO_3^-, and reduced to chloride, Cl^-. The chlorate(I) has acted simultaneously as an oxidising and a reducing agent. This **self oxidation and reduction** type of reaction is known as **disproportionation** and we shall meet several examples in our study of chemistry.

Activity 17.2

1   What is the oxidation number of each of the atoms in italics in the following molecules and ions?

(a) $CaCl_2$ (b) SiO_2 (c) KO_2 (d) NH_4^+ (e) $CuCl_4^{2-}$
(f) Na_3AlF_6

2 In each of the following equations,

$$Cl_2(aq) + 2KBr(aq) \rightarrow 2KCl(aq) + Br_2(aq)$$
$$2CrO_4^{2-}(aq) + 2H^+(aq) \rightarrow Cr_2O_7^{2-}(aq) + H_2O(l)$$
$$I_2(aq) + 2S_2O_3^{2-}(aq) \rightarrow 2I^-(aq) + S_4O_6^{2-}(aq)$$
$$3MnO_4^{2-}(aq) + 4H^+(aq) \rightarrow 2MnO_4^-(aq) + MnO_2(s) + 2H_2O(l)$$

(a) What are the oxidation numbers of the atoms in italics?
(b) Is the species concerned being oxidised? If so, what is the oxidising agent?
(c) Do any of the reactions involve disproportionation?

3 Oxidation and reduction were originally defined in terms of addition or removal of oxygen or hydrogen.
Oxidation is the addition of oxygen or the removal of hydrogen.
Reduction is the removal of oxygen or the addition of hydrogen.
On this basis, any element which combines with hydrogen to form a hydride is considered to have been reduced, e.g.

$$N_2(g) + 3H_2(g) \rightleftharpoons 2NH_3(g)$$
$$2Na(l) + H_2(g) \rightarrow 2NaH(s)$$

(a) Are both nitrogen and sodium 'reduced' in terms of gain of electrons?
(b) Under what circumstances may hydrogen act as an *oxidising* agent?
(c) What is the only element you might expect to be able to *oxidise* oxygen?

17.2 Metal/metal ion electrodes and electrode potential

When a metal is in contact with a solution containing its own ions, metal atoms tend to *lose* electrons and pass into the solution as aqueous ions and, conversely, aqueous ions may *gain* electrons and reform the metal.

$$M^{x+}(aq) + xe^- \rightleftharpoons M(s)$$

This is a **redox equilibrium**. Loss of electrons from the metal is an oxidation process, whereas the reverse is reduction.

The *ease* with which a metal tends to lose electrons is related to its reactivity. Fairly reactive metals, such as magnesium, lose electrons *readily* and so the above equilibrium will lie well to the *left*.

$$Mg^{2+}(aq) + 2e^- \rightleftharpoons Mg(s)$$

As a result, many electrons are released. These collect on the metal which therefore acquires a considerable *negative* charge. The solution in contact with the magnesium will become *positively* charged, since extra metal ions have been released into it.

Figure 17.2 *A metal in contact with a solution containing its own ions*

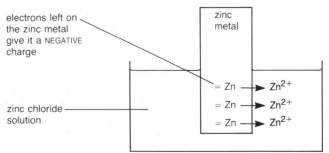

A less reactive metal, such as silver, will show much less tendency to ionise and the equilibrium will lie much further to the right.

$$Ag^+(aq) + e^- \rightleftharpoons Ag(s)$$

Figure 17.3 *A gas/ion electrode*

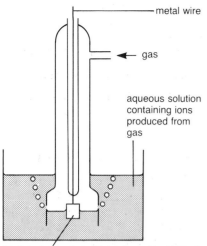

metal wire

gas

aqueous solution containing ions produced from gas

Platinim foil coated with 'platinum black' (finely divided platinum). The large surface area helps to establish equilibrium quickly.

Figure 17.4 *An electrochemical cell formed from a zinc electrode and a copper electrode*

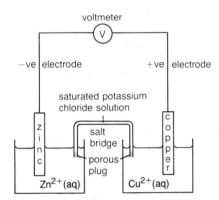

voltmeter

V

−ve | electrode   +ve | electrode

saturated potassium chloride solution

salt bridge

porous plug

zinc

copper

Zn^{2+}(aq) Cu^{2+}(aq)

As a result, *fewer* electrons will collect on the metal and the charge developed will be much *less negative*. In fact, if aqueous ions take electrons from the metal it will develop a *positive* charge.

Thus, whenever a metal is place in contact with a solution containing its own ions, an electric charge or potential will develop on the metal. The sign and size of this electrode potential will depend upon the relative *reactivity* of the metal.

The *absolute* potential of a single electrode cannot be measured in isolation. The determination of the potential of an electrode, relative to an arbitrary standard will be considered in section 17.7, following a discussion of electrochemical cells. The system of a metal in contact with a solution of its ions is often called a **half-cell**.

17.3 Other types of electrode

Any redox system, i.e. reversible reaction in which reactants and products are related by transfer of electrons, may be used to form an electrode. For example, any non-metal which forms aqueous ions:

$$H^+(aq) + e^- \rightleftharpoons \tfrac{1}{2}H_2(g)$$
or
$$\tfrac{1}{2}Cl_2(g) + e^- \rightleftharpoons Cl^-(aq)$$

In such cases the gas must be bubbled through a solution containing its ions. If the potential of such a system is to be measured, then it must be in contact with an **inert conductor**, such as platinum, which will accept or donate electrons as required and therefore acquire a charge. In such an electrode it is the potential of the inert conductor which is measured. The construction of a typical gas electrode is shown in figure 17.3.

Non-metals, such as chlorine, typically *gain* electrons to form negative ions. The electrons are taken from the inert conductor which therefore develops a *positive* charge. The size of this positive potential will be related to the ease with which the non-metal captures electrons, i.e. its oxidising power.

Another common type of electrode system consists of a mixture of aqueous ions of an element in *two different oxidation states* in the presence of an inert conductor, e.g.

$$Fe^{3+}(aq) \qquad\qquad + e^- \rightleftharpoons Fe^{2+}(aq)$$

$$MnO_4^-(aq) + 8H^+(aq) + 5e^- \rightleftharpoons Mn^{2+}(aq) + 4H_2O(l)$$

Again, any system which tends to *accept* electrons will develop a *positive* electrode potential, whereas *donation* of electrons will lead to a *negative* charge on the electrode.

17.4 Electrochemical cells

An **electrochemical cell** is formed by connecting two electrodes with *different* potentials, e.g. zinc and copper, as shown in figure 17.4. The two solutions must be connected by a **salt bridge**. This may be a glass tube containing saturated aqueous potassium chloride, sealed with a porous plug at each end, or simply a piece of filter paper soaked in this soltuion.

Zinc is more reactive than copper and will develop a more negative charge. When an electrical connection is made between the two metals, electrons will flow *from the zinc to the copper*. An electrical cell is set up with the zinc as the **negative** pole and copper as the **positive** pole, and the voltmeter will measure the **voltage** of the cell. The salt bridge completes the circuit by allowing the **transfer of ions** between the two solutions.

When a current is taken from the cell, the equilibrium at each electrode is disturbed. Electrons are *withdrawn* from the zinc and *added* to the copper. By Le Chatelier's Principle, the position of each equilibrium will move as follows:

$$Zn^{2+}(aq) + 2e^- \leftarrow Zn(s)$$
electrons
withdrawn

$$Cu^{2+}(aq) + 2e^- \rightarrow Cu(s)$$
electrons
added

OXIDATION occurs at NEGATIVE pole   REDUCTION occurs at POSITIVE pole

These processes may be represented using the following **cell diagram**.

[NEGATIVE electrode process]   [POSITIVE electrode process]
$$Zn(s) \,|\, Zn^{2+}(aq) \qquad\qquad \| \qquad\qquad Cu^{2+}(aq) \,|\, Cu(s)$$

By convention, the voltage of the cell is always given by

cell voltage = E (right hand electrode) − E (left hand electrode)

If we choose always to write the negative electrode process on the left, then the voltage of any working cell will always be *positive* and this represents the *flow of electrons from left to right in the cell*. Note that if the cell diagram were written the other way round, we would get a *negative* cell voltage indicating that energy must be *supplied* in order to drive electrons from the left hand side to the right (see electrolysis reactions, section 17.9).

In our cell diagram above, | separates different phases present in each electrode, and ‖ (or ⋮) indicates the salt bridge connecting the two solutions. Different species in the same phase, e.g. in aqueous solution, are separated by a comma (,). The presence of an inert conductor may also be shown, e.g. for platinum in a hydrogen electrode:

as the NEGATIVE pole $(Pt) \,|\, \tfrac{1}{2}H_2(g) \,|\, H^+(aq)$
as the POSITIVE pole $H^+(aq) \,|\, \tfrac{1}{2}H_2(g) \,|\, (Pt)$

Activity 17.3 gives you the opportunity to examine a range of other electrochemical cells in a similar manner.

Activity 17.3

The following list of electrodes is given in order of their potentials, from the most negative to the most positive:

(a) zinc in contact with aqueous zinc ions;
(b) tin in contact with aqueous tin(II) ions;
(c) hydrogen and aqueous hydrogen ions in contact with platinum;
(d) copper in contact with aqueous copper(II) ions;
(e) aqueous iron(II) and iron(III) ions in contact with platinum;
(f) chlorine and aqueous chloride ions in contact with platinum.

Write cell diagrams for the following combinations of electrodes so that electrons move from left to right in each case. Remember, reaction at the negative pole is written first as an oxidation process, followed by the reaction at the positive pole as a reduction process.

1 Electrodes (a) and (f).
2 Electrodes (c) and (d).
3 Electrodes (c) and (b).
4 Electrodes (a) and (e).
5 Electrodes (e) and (f).

17.5 Measurement of cell e.m.f.

The voltage supplied by any cell is not constant but depends upon the **current** being drawn from it, i.e. *the rate at which electrons are flowing from the negative to the positive electrode*. When a current flows, neither electrode is at equilibrium. In figure 17.4, for example, the zinc rod has fewer electrons and its potential is *less negative*, whilst the copper rod possesses more electrons, making its potential *less positive*.

If the current taken is progressively *reduced* by increasing the value of a variable resistance wired between the voltmeter and one of the electrodes in the apparatus shown in figure 17.4, then the cell voltage *rises*. The **electromotive force** *or* **e.m.f.**, E_{cell}, *is the voltage measured when no current is being taken from the cell, i.e. when each electrode is at equilibrium. This may be determined by using a high resistance voltmeter.*

The e.m.f. of any cell is given by the difference between the two electrode potentials involved. Using the convention mentioned in section 17.4, *the e.m.f. of a working cell will always be positive.* Thus,

$$E_{cell} = \quad E\ (\text{right hand}) \quad - \quad E\ (\text{left hand})$$

<table>
<tr><td>potential of
the POSITIVE electrode
REDuction</td><td>potential of
the NEGATIVE electrode
OXidation</td></tr>
</table>

Note that the e.m.f. of the cell tells us the difference between the two electrode potentials but gives no information regarding their individual values.

17.6 Standard electrode potentials

Since the reaction at any electrode is *reversible*, the position of the equilibrium, and hence the electrode potential, will depend upon the *experimental conditions* chosen. Take, for example, the zinc electrode.

$$Zn^{2+}(aq) + 2e^- \rightleftharpoons Zn(s)$$

By Le Chatelier's Principle increasing the concentration of the zinc ions will push the system to the *right*, removing electrons from the metal and making its potential *less negative*. On the other hand, raising the temperature favours the ionisation process, releasing more electrons to the metal and making its potential *more negative*. Changing the external pressure will hardly affect the potential of the zinc electrode but is important where a gas is involved. Thus for the hydrogen electrode,

$$H^+(aq) + e^- \rightleftharpoons \tfrac{1}{2}H_2(g)$$

Here an increase in the pressure of the hydrogen gas will push the system to the *left*, liberating more electrons and making the electrode potential *more negative*.

To make meaningful comparisons between the potentials of different electrode systems we must define a set of *standard* experimental conditions. *The* **standard potential of an electrode**, $E^\ominus$, *refers to a temperature of 25 °C and a pressure of one atmosphere with all aqueous concentrations of 1 M.* These values are also referred to as **standard redox potentials**.

17.7 Measuring standard electrode potentials

As we pointed out in section 17.5, the cell e.m.f. gives us the *difference* between the potentials of the two electrodes but does not tell us the *absolute* value of each. In fact all electrode potentials are measured *relative* to a **standard hydrogen electrode** which is assumed to have a potential of **zero**. In order to determine the potential of any other electrode, we must measure the e.m.f. of the cell illustrated in figure 17.5.

$$E_{cell} = E\ (\text{positive electrode}) \quad - E\ (\text{negative electrode})$$

If the hydrogen electrode forms the *negative* electrode in the cell, then

$$
\begin{aligned}
E_{cell} &= E\ (\text{positive electrode}) \quad - E^\ominus\ (\text{hydrogen}) \\
&= E\ (\text{positive electrode}) \quad - 0.00
\end{aligned}
$$

i.e. the potential of the test electrode equals the e.m.f. of the cell.

If the hydrogen electrode is the *positive* pole, then

$$
\begin{aligned}
E_{cell} &= E^\ominus(\text{hydrogen}) \quad\quad - E\ (\text{negative electrode}) \\
&= 0.00 \quad\quad\quad\quad\quad - E\ (\text{negative electrode}) \\
-E_{cell} &= E\ (\text{negative electrode})
\end{aligned}
$$

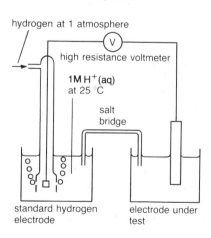

Figure 17.5 *Experimental determination of electrode potential*

hydrogen at 1 atmosphere

high resistance voltmeter

1M H⁺(aq) at 25 °C

salt bridge

standard hydrogen electrode

electrode under test

i.e. the potential of the test electrode is again numerically equal to the e.m.f. of the cell but has a *negative* value.

If standard conditions are chosen for the experiment, then such measurements will give the standard potential of the electrode under test.

Once the standard potential of any electrode has been found in this manner, it may be used as a **secondary reference electrode** to establish other electrode potentials. This is very useful, since in practice the hydrogen electrode is difficult to set up and maintain. The **calomel electrode** is a convenient secondary standard. It consists of a platinum wire dipping into mercury in contact with solid mercury(I) chloride and a saturated solution of mercury(I) chloride in 0.1 M potassium chloride.

You can see from the list of standard potentials in table 17.1 that, by convention, the electrode process is always written with the **Re**duced species on the **R**ight. Thus the hydrogen electrode is written:

$$H^+(aq) + e^- \rightleftharpoons \tfrac{1}{2}H_2(g)$$

Remember, however, if the electrode forms the negative pole in any cell it must be written the other way round, since it will be supplying electrons, e.g.

$$\tfrac{1}{2}H_2(g) \rightleftharpoons H^+(aq) + e^-$$

Example

A cell formed from the following standard electrodes,

$$Cu^{2+}(aq) + 2e^- \rightleftharpoons Cu(s) \text{ and } (Pt) H^+(aq) + e^- \rightleftharpoons \tfrac{1}{2}H_2(g)$$

has an e.m.f. of 0.34 volts. Hydrogen is the negative pole.

1 Write the cell diagram and calculate the standard potential of the copper electrode.

When the copper electrode is combined with a standard zinc electrode, the e.m.f. of the cell is +1.10 volts and zinc is the negative pole.

2 Draw the cell diagram and deduce the standard potential of the zinc electrode.

3 If the solution of zinc ions in the electrode is diluted, what would you expect to happen to the e.m.f. of the second cell?

Solution

1 The negative electrode process is written as an oxidation reaction on the left, followed by the positive electrode reduction process, connected by a salt bridge.

$$(Pt) \mid \tfrac{1}{2}H_2(g) \mid H^+(aq) \parallel Cu^{2+}(aq) \mid Cu(s)$$

$$E_{cell} = E \text{ (positive electrode)} - E \text{ (negative electrode)}$$
$$+0.34 = \quad E^\ominus \text{ (copper)} \quad -0.00$$

The standard potential of the copper electrode is +0.34 volts.

2 $$Zn(s) \mid Zn^{2+}(aq) \parallel Cu^{2+}(aq) \mid Cu(s)$$

$$E_{cell} = E \text{ (positive electrode)} - E \text{ (negative electrode)}$$
$$+1.10 = \quad +0.34 \quad -E^\ominus \text{ (zinc)}$$
$$E^\ominus \text{ (zinc)} = \quad +0.34 \quad -1.10 = -0.76 \text{ V}$$

The standard potential of the zinc electrode is −0.76 volts.

3 The equilibrium at the zinc electrode may be written,

$$Zn^{2+}(aq) + 2e^- \rightleftharpoons Zn(s)$$

According to Le Chatelier's Principle (section 14.8) reducing the concentration of aqueous zinc ions will push the system to the left, releasing more electrons. This will make the electrode more negative and hence increase the e.m.f. of the cell with the standard copper electrode.

Table 17.1   *Standard electrode potentials – an electrochemical series*

Note: *All potentials are quoted at 25°C, 1 atm pressure, with all aqueous concentrations being 1M. Electrode reactions are written as reduction processes, i.e. with electrons added on the left hand side*

Electrode process	$E^{\ominus}$/V
$Li^+(aq) + e^- \rightleftharpoons Li(s)$	−3.03
$Rb^+(aq) + e^- \rightleftharpoons Rb(s)$	−2.93
$K^+(aq) + e^- \rightleftharpoons K(s)$	−2.92
$Sr^{2+}(aq) + 2e^- \rightleftharpoons Sr(s)$	−2.89
$Ca^{2+}(aq) + 2e^- \rightleftharpoons Ca(s)$	−2.87
$Na^+(aq) + e^- \rightleftharpoons Na(s)$	−2.71
$Mg^{2+}(aq) + 2e^- \rightleftharpoons Mg(s)$	−2.37
$Be^{2+}(aq) + 2e^- \rightleftharpoons Be(s)$	−1.85
$Al^{3+}(aq) + 3e^- \rightleftharpoons Al(s)$	−1.66
$Mn^{2+}(aq) + 2e^- \rightleftharpoons Mn(s)$	−1.19
$Zn^{2+}(aq) + 2e^- \rightleftharpoons Zn(s)$	−0.76
$Cr^{3+}(aq) + 3e^- \rightleftharpoons Cr(s)$	−0.74
$2CO_2(g) + 2H^+(aq) + 2e^- \rightleftharpoons H_2C_2O_4(aq)$	−0.49
$Fe^{2+}(aq) + 2e^- \rightleftharpoons Fe(s)$	−0.44
$Cr^{3+}(aq) + e^- \rightleftharpoons Cr^{2+}(aq)$	−0.41
$Ti^{3+}(aq) + e^- \rightleftharpoons Ti^{2+}(aq)$	−0.37
$Ni^{2+}(aq) + 2e^- \rightleftharpoons Ni(s)$	−0.25
$Sn^{2+}(aq) + 2e^- \rightleftharpoons Sn(s)$	−0.14
$Pb^{2+}(aq) + 2e^- \rightleftharpoons Pb(s)$	−0.13
$H^+(aq) + e^- \rightleftharpoons \frac{1}{2}H_2(g)$	0.00
$Sn^{4+}(aq) + 2e^- \rightleftharpoons Sn^{2+}(aq)$	+0.15
$Cu^{2+}(aq) + e^- \rightleftharpoons Cu^+(aq)$	+0.15
$Cu^{2+}(aq) + 2e^- \rightleftharpoons Cu(s)$	+0.34
$\frac{1}{2}O_2(g) + H_2O(l) + 2e^- \rightleftharpoons 2OH^-(aq)$	+0.40
$Cu^+(aq) + e^- \rightleftharpoons Cu(s)$	+0.52
$\frac{1}{2}I_2(aq) + e^- \rightleftharpoons I^-(aq)$	+0.54
$MnO_4^-(aq) + e^- \rightleftharpoons MnO_4^{2-}(aq)$	+0.56
$Fe^{3+}(aq) + e^- \rightleftharpoons Fe^{2+}(aq)$	+0.77
$Ag^+(aq) + e^- \rightleftharpoons Ag(s)$	+0.80
$NO_3^-(aq) + 4H^+(aq) + 3e^- \rightleftharpoons NO(g) + 2H_2O(l)$	+0.96
$\frac{1}{2}Br_2(aq) + e^- \rightleftharpoons Br^-(aq)$	+1.09
$IO_3^-(aq) + 6H^+(aq) + 5e^- \rightleftharpoons \frac{1}{2}I_2(aq) + 3H_2O(l)$	+1.19
$MnO_2(s) + 4H^+(aq) + 2e^- \rightleftharpoons Mn^{2+}(aq) + 2H_2O(l)$	+1.23
$\frac{1}{2}Cr_2O_7^{2-}(aq) + 7H^+(aq) + 3e^- \rightleftharpoons Cr^{3+}(aq) + \frac{7}{2}H_2O(l)$	+1.33
$\frac{1}{2}Cl_2(aq) + e^- \rightleftharpoons Cl^-(aq)$	+1.36
$Mn^{3+}(aq) + e^- \rightleftharpoons Mn^{2+}(aq)$	+1.51
$MnO_4^-(aq) + 8H^+(aq) + 5e^- \rightleftharpoons Mn^{2+}(aq) + 4H_2O(l)$	+1.51
$Pb^{4+}(aq) + 2e^- \rightleftharpoons Pb^{2+}(aq)$	+1.69
$Co^{3+}(aq) + e^- \rightleftharpoons Co^{2+}(aq)$	+1.81
$S_2O_8^{2-}(aq) + 2e^- \rightleftharpoons 2SO_4^{2-}(aq)$	+2.01
$\frac{1}{2}F_2(g) + e^- \rightleftharpoons F^-(aq)$	+2.87

Are the species on the left hand side of these equations oxidising agents or reducing agents?

Activity 17.4

Here are some standard electrode potentials;

(a) $\frac{1}{2}Cl_2(g) \quad + e^- \quad \rightleftharpoons Cl^-(aq) \qquad E^{\ominus} +1.36$ volts

(b) $Cr^{3+}(aq) \quad + e^- \quad \rightleftharpoons Cr^{2+}(aq) \qquad E^{\ominus} -0.41$ volts

(c) $Zn^{2+}(aq) \quad + 2e^- \rightleftharpoons Zn(s) \qquad E^{\ominus} -0.76$ volts

    1   Write cell diagrams and deduce the cell e.m.f.s for the following combinations of electrodes:

        (i) (a) with a standard hydrogen electrode;

        (ii) (a) with (b);

        (iii) (b) with (c).

    2   A calomel electrode forms the positive pole in a cell with electrode (b). If the e.m.f. of the cell is +0.74 volts, what is the potential of the calomel electrode?

If you consult other textbooks you will probably find their approach to electrochemistry is quite different from that found in this chapter. Most treatments require you to learn (arbitrary) conventions which involve changing the sign of an electrode if its reaction is reversed. Here we use a more fundamental method in which the experimentally determined electrode potential is related to the oxidising or reducing power of a reversible system. **Do not use a mixture of both methods – use either one or the other**.

17.8 Predicting the direction of redox reactions

Table 17.1 lists a number of common electrodes in order of their standard redox potentials from the most *negative* through to the most *positive*. Such a list is known as the **electrochemical series** and as well as providing $E^\ominus$ values for calculating cell e.m.f.s, it gives much general information on redox systems.

You will probably have noticed that the *most reactive metals* are at the *top* of the series, whilst the *most reactive non-metallic elements* are at the *bottom*. This is to be expected, since metals always react by *losing* electrons and those elements which lose electrons most readily will have large *negative* electrode potentials. Non-metals, on the other hand, generally form negative ions by *gaining* electrons.

The value of the standard electrode potential indicates the oxidising or reducing power of the system. Negative values of $E^\ominus$ show that the electrode process releases electrons and hence acts a *reducing* agent. The greater the negative value of $E^\ominus$, the greater is the reducing power. On the other hand, *positive* standard electrode potentials indicate a capacity to accept electrons, i.e. *oxidising* power. *Any electrode system should reduce those below it in the electrochemical series, or put another way, any electrode system should oxidise those above it in the series.* We have already demonstrated this in the example in section 17.7. Oxidation always occurs at the negative electrode in a cell, whereas reduction always occurs at the positive electrode, e.g. for the zinc/copper cell,

NEGATIVE electrode (oxidation)   POSITIVE electrode (reduction)
$$Zn(s) \rightarrow Zn^{2+}(aq) + 2e^-$$ $$Cu^{2+}(aq) + 2e^- \rightarrow Cu(s)$$

The overall process is obtained by adding the half-equations for each electrode:

$$Zn(s) + Cu^{2+}(aq) \rightarrow Zn^{2+}(aq) + Cu(s)$$

Metallic zinc will reduce aqueous copper(II) ions even if an electrochemical cell is not set up. The electrons are simply transferred *directly* instead of via a connecting wire. If you add zinc metal to copper sulphate solution, you will see that the zinc becomes coated with a brown layer of copper and the blue colour of the solution fades.

We may thus investigate the feasibility of any redox reaction using the electrochemical series.

Example

Here are some standard electrode potentials obtained from table 17.1.

$$Mg^{2+}(aq) + 2e^- \rightleftharpoons Mg(s) \qquad -2.37V$$
$$Cu^{2+}(aq) + 2e^- \rightleftharpoons Cu(s) \qquad +0.34V$$
$$\tfrac{1}{2}Cl_2(g) \ + e^- \ \rightleftharpoons Cl^-(aq) \qquad +1.36V$$
$$H^+(aq) \ + e^- \ \rightleftharpoons \tfrac{1}{2}H_2(g) \qquad 0.00V$$
$$MnO_4^-(aq) + 8H^+(aq) + 5e^- \rightleftharpoons Mn^{2+}(aq) + 4H_2O(l) \ + 1.51V$$

Use these values to predict the reaction, if any, which occurs when each of the following is added separately to hydrochloric acid:

1 magnesium   2 copper   3 potassium manganate(VII).

We shall use the same basic procedure to tackle all these problems,

1   First, write down all the species present and decide which might possibly act as oxidising agents and which as reducing agents. Next to each system, write its standard electrode potential from the list.

oxidising agents: $H^+(aq) + e^- \rightarrow \frac{1}{2}H_2(g)$ $E^\ominus = 0.00\,V$

reducing agents: $Mg(s) \rightarrow Mg^{2+}(ag) + 2e^-$ $E^\ominus = -2.38\,V$

$Cl^-(aq) \rightarrow \frac{1}{2}Cl_2(g) + e^-$ $E^\ominus = +1.36\,V$

Look for the *best oxidising agent*, i.e. that with the *most positive* standard potential. Here, the only possible oxidising agent is $H^+(aq)$.

$$H^+(aq) + e^- \rightarrow \tfrac{1}{2}H_2(g) \quad \text{i.e. reduction reaction}$$

This system can only *oxidise* those systems with *more negative $E^\ominus$* values, i.e. in this case, only magnesium.

$$Mg(s) \rightarrow Mg^{2+}(aq) + 2e^- \quad \text{i.e. oxidation reaction}$$

Now we must combine the half-equations for reduction and oxidation to give the overall redox equation. Since the overall process involves electron transfer, we must ensure that the number of electrons supplied by the reducing agent exactly equals the number taken by the oxidising agent. *Note that we do NOT double the value of the electrode potential! This is independent of the number of moles in the overall redox equation.*

$$
\begin{array}{lll}
& Mg(s) & \rightarrow \quad Mg^{2+}(aq) + 2e^- \quad \text{oxidation} \\
2\{ & H^+(aq) + e^- & \rightarrow \quad \frac{1}{2}H_2(g) \qquad\qquad\; \} \quad \text{reduction} \\
\hline
& Mg(s) + 2H^+(aq) & \rightarrow \quad Mg^{2+}(aq) + H_2(g) \quad \text{overall redox}
\end{array}
$$

or $Mg(s) + 2HCl(aq) \rightarrow MgCl_2(aq) + H_2(g)$

Strictly speaking, we should check that none of the products might undergo further oxidation or reduction in one of the other electrode systems in the list. In this case no such reactions are possible.

2   Species present:

oxidising agents: $H^+(aq) + e^- \rightarrow \frac{1}{2}H_2(g)$ $E^\ominus = 0.00\,V$

reducing agents: $Cu(s) \rightarrow Cu^{2+}(aq) + 2e^-$ $E^\ominus = +0.34\,V$

$Cl^-(aq) \rightarrow \frac{1}{2}Cl_2(g) + e^-$ $E^\ominus = +1.36\,V$

Since there is no system present with a more negative $E^\ominus$ value than the only oxidising agent, $H^+(aq)$, no redox reaction is possible in this case.

3   Species present:

oxidising agents:

$MnO_4^-(aq) + 8H^+(aq) + 5e^- \rightarrow Mn^{2+}(aq) + 4H_2O(l)$ $E^\ominus = +1.52\,V$

$H^+(aq) + e^- \rightarrow \frac{1}{2}H_2(g)$ $E^\ominus = 0.00\,V$

reducing agents:

$Cl^-(aq) \rightarrow \frac{1}{2}Cl_2(g) + e^-$ $E^\ominus = +1.36\,V$

best oxidising agent:

$MnO_4^-(aq) + 8H^+(aq) + 5e^- \rightarrow Mn^{2+}(aq) + 4H_2O(l)$ (reduction)

only possible reducing agent:

$Cl^-(aq) \rightarrow \frac{1}{2}Cl_2(g) + e^-$ (oxidation)

Combining our two-half equations,

$$
\begin{array}{lll}
5\{Cl^-(aq) & \rightarrow \frac{1}{2}Cl_2(g) + e^- \quad \} & \text{(oxidation)} \\
MnO_4^-(aq) + 8H^+(aq) + 5e^- & \rightarrow Mn^{2+}(aq) + 4H_2O(l) & \text{(reduction)} \\
\hline
MnO_4^-(aq) + 8H^+(aq) + 5Cl^-(aq) \rightarrow & & \text{(redox)} \\
\quad Mn^{2+}(aq) + 4H_2O(l) + \frac{5}{2}Cl_2(g) & &
\end{array}
$$

or $2KMnO_4(aq) + 16HCl(aq) \rightarrow$
$\qquad 2KCl(aq) + 2MnCl_2(aq) + 8H_2O(l) + 5Cl_2(g)$

These predictions only refer to the *standard* conditions of electrochemistry, i.e. 25 °C, 1 atm pressure and molar concentration. However, providing that there is a *reasonably large difference* between the standard potentials of the oxidising and reducing systems, the reactions will probably occur over quite a *wide range* of conditions. Other factors may, however, be important in deciding whether the reaction will occur. For example a very high activation energy for one of the processes might prevent the reaction occurring at a measurable rate.

Activity 17.5

Use the standard potentials in table 17.1 to predict any redox reaction in each of the following mixtures.
  1 Fe^{3+}(aq) and I^-(aq)
  2 Ag(s) and Cu^{2+}(aq)
  3 Cl_2(g) and Br^-(aq)
  4 IO_3^-(aq) and I^-(aq) in acid solution
  5 Fe^{2+}(aq) and $Cr_2O_7^{2-}$(aq) in acid solution.

17.9 Electrolysis reactions

Electrical energy is *obtained* from a chemical cell when a *spontaneous* redox reaction is allowed to occur. In **electrolysis**, chemical changes are *forced* to take place by applying an **external voltage**. An electrolysis cell may be considered to be a chemical cell which is being *driven in the reverse direction*.

If we take a cell constructed from standard copper and silver electrodes, when we connect the two metals, electrons flow from the copper to the silver and the following spontaneous reactions occur,

Spontaneous redox reactions are the source of the voltage supplied by all of these batteries. Only certain types of battery, such as the nickel-cadmium ones in the bottom photo, can be recharged by applying an external voltage

electron flow

negative electrode	positive electrode
Cu(s) → Cu^{2+}(aq) + 2e$^-$	2Ag$^+$(aq) + 2e$^-$ → 2Ag(s)
OXIDATION	REDUCTION
$E^{\ominus}$ +0.34 V	$E^{\ominus}$ +0.80 V

$$E_{cell} = +0.80 - (+0.34) = +0.46\,V$$

The cell will not continue to supply electrical energy indefinitely, since eventually all the copper metal or silver ions will be used up. In simple terms, the 'battery' will go 'flat'. However, if we now connect an external electricity supply to the cell, such that the copper is connected to the negative pole and the silver to the positive pole, then if the external voltage is greater than 0.46 V, the cell is driven in reverse.

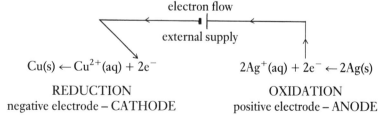

electron flow

external supply

Cu(s) ← Cu^{2+}(aq) + 2e$^-$	2Ag$^+$(aq) + 2e$^-$ ← 2Ag(s)
REDUCTION	OXIDATION
negative electrode – CATHODE	positive electrode – ANODE

Note that this reforms the copper metal and silver ions needed for the cell to supply electricity again. The cell has been **'recharged'** by electrolysis. Although 'rechargeable batteries' are available, we shall see in activity 17.6 that not all chemical cells may be renewed in this way.

We may extend this principle to the electrolysis of molten salts, e.g. sodium chloride.

▶ *Positive ions* (cations) are *reduced* at the *negative* electrode or **cathode**:

$$Na^+(l) + e^- \rightarrow Na(l)\ reduction$$

▶ *Negative ions* (anions) are *oxidised* at the *positive* electrode or **anode**:

$$Cl^-(l) \rightarrow \tfrac{1}{2}Cl_2(g) + e^- \quad \text{oxidation}$$

Overall $\qquad\qquad NaCl(l) \rightarrow Na(l) + \tfrac{1}{2}Cl_2(g) \quad \text{redox}$

If more than one reaction is possible, then the *most easily reduced* species is generally discharged at the *cathode* whilst the *most readily oxidised* species takes precedence at the *anode*. In the electrolysis of aqueous solutions, we must always take into account the possibility of the discharge of $H^+(aq)$ and $OH^-(aq)$ ions from the water.

$$H^+(aq) + e^- \rightarrow \tfrac{1}{2}H_2(g) \qquad\qquad \text{possible cathode process}$$
$$2OH^-(aq) \rightarrow H_2O(l) + \tfrac{1}{2}O_2(g) + 2e^- \quad \text{possible anode process}$$

Example

Predict the products of the electrolysis of aqueous sodium chloride, using inert platinum electrodes.

Solution

Ions present in solution, from sodium chloride $\quad Na^+(aq)$ and $Cl^-(aq)$
$\qquad\qquad\qquad\qquad\qquad$ from water $\qquad\quad H^+(aq)$ and $OH^-(aq)$

Possible reactions at cathode:

$$Na^+(aq) + e^- \rightarrow Na(s) \qquad E^\ominus = -2.71\,V$$
$$H^+(aq) \;\; + e^- \rightarrow \tfrac{1}{2}H_2(g) \qquad E^\ominus = \;\;\; 0.00\,V$$

Since $H^+(aq)$ has the more positive electrode potential, it is the more powerful oxidising agent and is therefore itself reduced more easily than $Na^+(aq)$. *Hydrogen gas* will be produced at the *cathode*.

Possible reactions at the anode:

$$Cl^-(aq) \qquad \rightarrow \tfrac{1}{2}Cl_2(g) + e^- \qquad\quad E^\ominus = +1.36\,V$$
$$2OH^-(aq) \rightarrow H_2O(l) + \tfrac{1}{2}O_2(g) + 2e^- \quad E^\ominus = +0.40\,V$$

Since $OH^-(aq)$ has the more negative electrode potential, it is the more powerful reducing agent and is therefore itself oxidised more easily than $Cl^-(aq)$. *Oxygen gas* is therefore *expected* at the *anode*.

We may get the overall reaction by combining the two half-equations:

$$2\{H^+(aq) + e^- \rightarrow \tfrac{1}{2}H_2(g)\} \qquad\qquad \text{reduction}$$
$$2OH^-(aq) \rightarrow H_2O(l) + \tfrac{1}{2}O_2(g) + 2e^- \qquad \text{oxidation}$$

$$2H^+(aq) + 2OH^-(aq) \rightarrow H_2(g) + \tfrac{1}{2}O_2(g) + H_2O(l) \qquad \text{redox}$$

Again it must be stressed that this prediction is strictly valid only under *standard* conditions. If the concentration of chloride ions is high enough then *chlorine gas* is produced at the anode. Chlorine is, in fact, manufactured by the electrolysis of *concentrated* salt solution.

Activity 17.6

1   Using the standard potentials in table 17.1 where necessary, predict the product at each electrode in the electrolysis of the following:
    (a) molten lead(II) bromide;
    (b) dilute hydrochloric acid;
    (c) silver sulphate solution.

2   The diagram of the Daniell cell is

$$Zn(s) \mid Zn^{2+}(aq) \parallel Cu^{2+}(aq) \mid Cu(s)$$

(a) What reactions would occur at each electrode on electrolysis? (Hint: you should consider all possible reactions.)

(b) Would it be possible to 'recharge' a 'flat' Daniell cell by this method?

17.10 Extraction of metals by reduction reactions

Metals have many unique and valuable properties. They are generally tough, flexible and of course readily conduct both heat and electricity. Apart from a few rather scarce unreactive metals, such as gold, they are not found as the free elements but as chemical compounds. There are several stages involved in extracting a pure metal from its naturally occurring ores:

▶ mining the crude ore;
▶ purifying the ore, i.e. removing non metal-bearing rock and waste;
▶ extracting the metal from the purified ore;
▶ if necessary, depending on the end use, refining or purifying the metal.

In this section we shall deal mainly with the extraction of the metal from a purified ore.

In their chemical compounds, most metals exist as *positive ions*. Extraction therefore involves a *reduction* process, i.e. addition of electrons,

$$M^{x+} + xe^- \rightarrow M$$

The reduction method chosen must give a product of acceptable quality as economically as possible. We are, in fact, reversing the natural tendency of most metals to form positive ions, thereby releasing electrons. The ease with which a metal ionises in aqueous solution is given by its standard electrode potential, $E^\ominus$. The very reactive metals at the top of the electrochemical series, i.e. with large negative $E^\ominus$ values, are more difficult to obtain by reduction than the less reactive metals towards the bottom of the series.

Electrolysis of molten compounds

This method is used for aluminium and all the metals *above it* in the electrochemical series. In the case of aluminium, the molten oxide is used as the electrolyte.

aluminium oxide Al_2O_3, ions present $2Al^{3+}$ and $3O^{2-}$

at the cathode $2Al^{3+}(l) + 6e^- \rightarrow 2Al(l)$

at the anode $3O^{2-}(l) \rightarrow \frac{3}{2}O_2(g) + 6e^-$

overall $Al_2O_3(l) \rightarrow 2Al(l) + \frac{3}{2}O_2(g)$

This is a very expensive process in energy terms, since the melting point of aluminium oxide is around 2000 °C. In such cases it is common practice to add an impurity which takes no part in the electrolysis process but which reduces the melting point of the electrolyte. In the extraction of aluminium, **cryolite** or **sodium aluminium fluoride**, Na_3AlF_6, is used as an inert 'solvent' for the molten aluminium oxide at a much reduced temperature.

Chemical reducing agents

Less reactive metals may generally be obtained more cheaply by chemical reduction. This generally involves heating the metal oxide with either **carbon** or **carbon monoxide**:

$$ZnO(s) + C(s) \rightarrow Zn(g) + CO(g)$$
$$Fe_2O_3(s) + 3CO(g) \rightarrow 2Fe(l) + 3CO_2(g)$$

If a very high purity product is required, then a **more reactive metal** may be used as the reducing agent. For example, titanium(IV) chloride may be reduced by heating with sodium or magnesium:

$$TiCl_4(g) + 2Mg(l) \rightarrow Ti(s) + 2MgCl_2(l)$$

Table 17.2   *Methods used for the extraction of some metals from their purified ores*

Metal	from	extraction method
lithium	LiCl	
sodium	NaCl	
potassium	KCl	
beryllium	BeF_2	electrolysis of fused* compounds
magnesium	$MgCl_2$	
calcium	$CaCl_2$	
strontium	$SrCl_2$	
barium	$BaCl_2$	
aluminium	Al_2O_3	
manganese	MnO_2	
zinc	ZnO	reduction with carbon
tin	SnO_2	
lead	PbO	
iron	Fe_2O_3	reduction with carbon monoxide
nickel	NiO	
titanium	$TiCl_4$	
chromium	Cr_2O_3	reduction with a more reactive metal
cobalt	Co_3O_4	
copper	Cu_2S	roasting the sulphide in air
mercury	HgS	

*Why can't these metals be extracted by electrolysis of aqueous solutions of their salts? (Hint: see section 17.9.)

Thermal decomposition

The compounds of *relatively unreactive* metals often decompose on heating. Mercury may be obtained simply by heating the purified sulphide ore in air:

$$HgS(s) + O_2(g) \rightarrow Hg(l) + SO_2(g)$$

Table 17.2 summarises some of the extraction methods used for a range of metals.

Activity 17.7

Using the information in table 17.2, write equations showing how each of the following metals may be extracted from their compounds:
1 sodium   2 chromium (using aluminium)
3 manganese   4 copper.

17.11 Comments on the activities

Activity 17.1

1   $2Ca + O_2 \rightarrow 2Ca^{2+} + 2O^{2-}$
    $2Ca \rightarrow 2Ca^{2+} + 4e^-$ oxidation
    $O_2 + 4e^- \rightarrow 2O^{2-}$ reduction
    Oxygen is the oxidising agent and calcium is the reducing agent.

2   $2K + S \rightarrow 2K^+ + S^{2-}$
    $2K \rightarrow 2K^+ + 2e^-$ oxidation
    $S + 2e^- \rightarrow S^{2-}$ reduction
    Potassium is the reducing agent and sulphur is the oxidising agent.

3   $2Al$ $+$ $3F_2 \rightarrow$ $2Al^{3+}$ $+$ $6F^-$

   $2Al$ $\rightarrow$ $2Al^{3+}$ $+$ $6e^-$ oxidation

   $3F_2$ $+$ $6e^- \rightarrow$ $6F^-$ reduction

Aluminium is the reducing agent and fluorine is the oxidising agent.

4   $4Al$ $+$ $3O_2 \rightarrow$ $4Al^{3+}$ $+$ $6O^2$

   $4Al$ $\rightarrow$ $4Al^{3+}$ $+$ $12e^-$ oxidation

   $3O_2$ $+$ $12e \rightarrow$ $6O^{2-}$ reduction

Aluminium is the reducing agent and oxygen is the oxidising agent.

5   $3Mg$ $+$ $N_2 \rightarrow$ $3Mg^{2+}$ $+$ $2N^3$

   $3Mg$ $\rightarrow$ $3Mg^{2+}$ $+$ $6e^-$ oxidation

   N_2 $+$ $6e^- \rightarrow$ $2N^{3-}$ reduction

Magnesium is the reducing agent and nitrogen is the oxidising agent.

Activity 17.2

1   Using the 'rules' given in section 17.1,

   (a) Ca Cl$_2$ (b) Si O$_2$ (c) K O$_2$ (d) N H$_4{}^+$

      +2 2(−1)   +4 2(−2)   +1 2(−0.5)   −3 4(+1)

   (e) Cu Cl$_4{}^{2-}$ (f) Na$_3$ Al F$_6$

      +2 4(−1)   3(+1) +3 6(−1)

2           $Cl_2(aq) + 2KBr(aq) \rightarrow 2KCl(aq) + Br_2(aq)$

                2(−1)   2(0)

Bromide has been oxidised by chlorine.

$$2CrO_4{}^{2-}(aq) + 2H^+(aq) \rightarrow Cr_2O_7{}^{2-}(aq) + H_2O(l)$$
  2(+6)   2(+6)

No oxidation has occurred.

$$I_2(aq) + 2S_2O_3{}^{2-}(aq) \rightarrow 2I^-(aq) + S_4O_6{}^{2-}(aq)$$
        4(+2)   4(+2.5)

The thiosulphate, $S_2O_3{}^{2-}$, has been oxidised by the iodine.

$$3MnO_4{}^{2-}(aq) + 4H^+(aq) \rightarrow 2MnO_4{}^-(aq) + MnO_2(s) + 2H_2O(l)$$
 3(+6)   2(+7)   +4

The manganate(VI), MnO_4^{2-}, has been oxidised by itself to manganate(VII). This is a *disproportionation* reaction.

3   (a) Nitrogen is *more electronegative* than hydrogen and so tends to *gain* electrons during the formation of ammonia. In terms of change in oxidation number, we can see that the nitrogen is reduced.

$$N_2(g) + 3H_2(g) \rightleftharpoons 2N \quad H_3(g)$$
  2(0)   6(0)   2(−3) 6(+1)

Sodium, however, is *less electronegative* than hydrogen. Group I metals only show an oxidation number of +1 in their compounds.

$$2Na(l) + H_2(g) \rightarrow 2Na \quad H(s)$$
  2(0)   2(0)   2(+1) 2(−1)

In this case the addition of hydrogen has *oxidised* the sodium.

(b) Hydrogen will only act as an oxidising agent if it gains or tends to gain an electron. It will only do this when combining with an element of *lower electronegativity*.

(c) In order to act as a reducing agent oxygen must lose or tend to lose electrons. Since it has a *very high electronegativity* this will be very rare. In fact only fluorine has a greater electronegativity than oxygen. Oxygen does in fact show an oxidation state of +2 in oxygen difluoride, OF_2, but this compound cannot be made by direct combination of the elements.

Activity 17.3

1   $Zn(s) \mid Zn^{2+}(aq) \parallel \frac{1}{2}Cl_2(g) \mid Cl^-(aq) \mid (Pt)$

2   $(Pt) \mid \frac{1}{2}H_2(g) \mid H^+(aq) \parallel Cu^{2+}(aq) \mid Cu(s)$

3   $Sn(s) \mid Sn^{2+}(aq) \parallel H^+(aq) \mid \frac{1}{2}H_2(g) \mid (Pt)$

4   $Zn(s) \mid Zn^{2+}(aq) \parallel Fe^{3+}(aq), Fe^{2+}(aq) \mid (Pt)$

5   $(Pt) \mid Fe^{2+}(aq), Fe^{3+}(aq) \parallel \frac{1}{2}Cl_2(g) \mid Cl^-(aq) \mid (Pt)$

Activity 17.4

1
$$(Pt) \mid \frac{1}{2}H_2(g) \mid H^+(aq) \qquad \parallel \qquad \frac{1}{2}Cl_2(g) \mid Cl^-(aq) \mid (Pt)$$
$$0.00\,V \qquad\qquad\qquad\qquad +1.36\,V$$
$$\text{e.m.f. } 1.36\,V$$

$$(Pt) \mid Cr^{2+}(aq), Cr^{3+}(aq) \qquad \parallel \qquad \frac{1}{2}Cl_2(g) \mid Cl^-(aq) \mid (Pt)$$
$$-0.41\,V \qquad\qquad\qquad\qquad +1.36\,V$$
$$\text{e.m.f. } 1.77\,V$$

$$Zn(s) \mid Zn^{2+}(aq), \qquad \parallel \quad Cr^{3+}(aq), Cr^{2+}(aq) \mid (Pt)$$
$$-0.76\,V \qquad\qquad\qquad\qquad -0.41\,V$$
$$\text{e.m.f. } 0.35\,V$$

2
$$(Pt) \mid Cr^{2+}(aq), Cr^{3+}(aq) \qquad \parallel \qquad \text{calomel electrode}$$
$$\text{e.m.f. } 0.74\,V$$
$$-0.41\,V \qquad\qquad\qquad\qquad\qquad +0.33\,V$$

i.e. the calomel electrode potential is $+0.33\,V$.

Activity 17.5

If you do not obtain the following answers, look carefully through the examples in section 17.8.

1   $\frac{1}{2}I_2(aq)/I^-(aq) +0.54V;$ $\qquad$ $I^-(aq) \rightarrow \frac{1}{2}I_2(aq) + e^-$ $\qquad$ oxidation

$Fe^{3+}(aq)/Fe^{2+}(aq) +0.77V;$ $\;$ $Fe^{3+}(aq) + e^- \rightarrow Fe^{2+}(aq)$ $\qquad$ reduction

$$\overline{Fe^{3+}(aq) + I^-(aq) \rightarrow Fe^{2+}(aq) + \tfrac{1}{2}I_2(aq)} \qquad \text{redox}$$

2   No reaction, $Cu(s)$ is a better reducing agent than $Ag(s)$.

3   $\frac{1}{2}Br_2(aq)/Br^-(aq) +1.09V;$ $\;$ $Br^-(aq) \rightarrow \frac{1}{2}Br_2(aq) + e^-$ $\qquad$ oxidation

$\frac{1}{2}Cl_2(g)/Cl^-(aq) + 1.36V;$ $\quad$ $\frac{1}{2}Cl_2(g) + e^- \rightarrow Cl^-(aq)$ $\qquad$ reduction

$$\overline{\tfrac{1}{2}Cl_2(g) + Br^-(aq) \rightarrow Cl^-(aq) + \tfrac{1}{2}Br_2(aq)} \qquad \text{redox}$$

4   $\frac{1}{2}I_2(aq)/I^-(aq) +0.54V;$ $\qquad$ $I^-(aq) \rightarrow \frac{1}{2}I_2(aq) + e^-$ $\qquad$ oxidation

$IO_3^-(aq)/\frac{1}{2}I_2(aq) + 1.19V;$

$IO_3^-(aq) +6H^+(aq) + 5e^- \rightarrow \frac{1}{2}I_2(aq) +3H_2O(l)$ $\qquad$ reduction

$$5\{I^-(aq) \qquad\qquad\qquad\qquad \rightarrow \tfrac{1}{2}I_2(aq) + e^-\}$$
$$IO_3^-(aq) + 6H^+(aq) + 5e^- \rightarrow \tfrac{1}{2}I_2(aq) + 3H_2O(l)$$

$$\overline{IO_3^-(aq) + 5I^-(aq) + 6H^+(aq) \rightarrow 3I_2(aq) + 3H_2O(l)} \qquad \text{redox}$$

5   $Fe^{3+}(aq)/Fe^{2+}(aq) -0.77V; Fe^{2+}(aq) \rightarrow Fe^{3+}(aq) + e^-$ $\qquad$ oxidation

$\frac{1}{2}Cr_2O_7^{2-}(aq)/Cr^{3+}(aq) + 1.33V;$

$\frac{1}{2}Cr_2O_7^{2-}(aq) + 7H^+(aq) + 3e^- \rightarrow Cr^{3+}(aq) + \frac{7}{2}H_2O(l)$ $\qquad$ reduction

$$3\{ Fe^{2+}(aq) \qquad\qquad \rightarrow \qquad Fe^{3+}(aq) + e^-\}$$
$$\tfrac{1}{2}Cr_2O_7^{2-}(aq) + 7H^+(aq) + 3e^- \rightarrow \qquad Cr^{3+}(aq) + \tfrac{7}{2}H_2O(l)$$

$$\overline{\tfrac{1}{2}Cr_2O_7^{2-}(aq) + 7H^+(aq) + 3Fe^{2+}(aq) \rightarrow}$$
$$Cr^{3+}(aq) + \tfrac{7}{2}H_2O(l) + 3Fe^{3+}(aq) \quad \text{redox}$$

Activity 17.6

1 (a) Ions present: Pb^{2+}(l) and Br^-(l)

        At cathode Pb^{2+}(l) $+ 2e^- \rightarrow Pb$(l)
        At anode Br^-(l) $\rightarrow \frac{1}{2}Br_2$(g) $+ e^-$

$$Pb^{2+}(l) + 2e^- \rightarrow Pb(l)$$
$$\underline{2\{\,Br(l) \rightarrow \tfrac{1}{2}Br_2(g) + e^-\,\}}$$
$$Pb^{2+}(l) + 2Br^-(l) \rightarrow Pb(l) + Br_2(g)$$

(b) Ions present, from hydrochloric acid: H^+(aq) and Cl^-(aq)
               from water: H^+(aq) and OH^-(aq)
At cathode: H^+(aq) $+ e^- \rightarrow \frac{1}{2}H_2$(g)

Possible anode reactions:

      Cl^-(aq) $\rightarrow \frac{1}{2}Cl_2$(g) $+ e^-$ $E^\ominus$ +1.36V
      $2OH^-$(aq)$\rightarrow H_2O$(l) $+ \frac{1}{2}O_2$(g) $+ 2e^-$ $E^\ominus$ +0.40V

Under standard conditons, oxygen gas is formed at the anode

$$2\{\,H^+(aq) + e^- \rightarrow \tfrac{1}{2}H_2(g)\,\}$$
$$\underline{2OH^-(aq) \rightarrow H_2O(l) + \tfrac{1}{2}O_2(g) + 2e^-}$$
$$2H^+(aq) + 2OH^-(aq) \rightarrow H_2(g) + \tfrac{1}{2}O_2(g) + H_2O(l)$$

(c) Ions present, from silver sulphate: Ag^+(aq) and $SO_4{}^{2-}$(aq)
                from water: H^+(aq) and OH^-(aq)

Possible cathode reactions:

      H^+(aq) $+ e^- \rightarrow \frac{1}{2}H_2$(g) $E^\ominus$ 0.00V
      Ag^+(aq) $+ e^- \rightarrow Ag$(s) $E^\ominus$ +0.80V

Under standard conditions, silver metal plates onto the cathode.

Possible anode reactions:

$2OH^-$(aq) $\rightarrow H_2O$(l) $+ \frac{1}{2}O_2$(g) $+ 2e^-$ $E^\ominus$ + 0.40V
$2SO_4{}^{2-}$(aq) $\rightarrow S_2O_6{}^{2-}$(aq) $+ 2e^-$ $E^\ominus$ + 2.01V

Hydroxide ions are discharged, producing oxygen gas at the anode

$$2\,\{\,Ag^+(aq) + e^- \rightarrow Ag(s)\,\}$$
$$\underline{2OH^-(aq) \rightarrow H_2O(l) + \tfrac{1}{2}O_2(g) + 2e^-}$$
$$2Ag^+(aq) + 2OH^-(aq) \rightarrow 2Ag(s) + H_2O(l) + \tfrac{1}{2}O_2(g)$$

2 (a) Species capable of being reduced at the cathode: Zn^{2+}(aq), H^+(aq)
Possible cathode reactions:

      Zn^{2+}(aq) $+ 2e^- \rightarrow Zn$(s) $E^\ominus$ -0.76V
      H^+(aq) $+ e^- \rightarrow \frac{1}{2}H_2$(g) $E^\ominus$ 0.00V

Under standard conditions hydrogen gas is formed at the cathode.
     Species capable of being oxidised at the anode: Cu(s), OH^-(aq)
Possible anode reactions:

      Cu(s) $\rightarrow Cu^{2+}$(aq) $+ 2e^-$ $E^\ominus$ $- 0.34$V
      $2OH^-$(aq) $\rightarrow H_2O$(l) $+ \frac{1}{2}O_2$(g) $+ 2e^-$ $E^\ominus$ $+ 0.40$V

Under standard conditions copper dissolves from the anode.

(b) It is not possible to recharge this cell by electrolysis. Although Cu^{2+} (aq) ions are replaced, hydrogen gas rather than the required zinc metal is formed at the other electrode.

Activity 17.7

1 Sodium is obtained by the electrolysis of its molten chloride,

at cathode $Na^+(l) + e^- \rightarrow Na(l)$
at anode $Cl^-(l) \rightarrow \frac{1}{2}Cl_2(g) + e^-$
overall $NaCl(l) \rightarrow Na(l) + \frac{1}{2}Cl_2(g)$

2 Chromium may be obtained by reducing chromium(III) oxide with aluminium.

$$Cr_2O_3 + 2Al \rightarrow 2Cr + Al_2O_3$$

3 Manganese is produced when manganese(IV) oxide is heated with carbon.

$$MnO_2 + 2C \rightarrow Mn + 2CO$$

4 Heating copper(I) sulphide in a limited supply of air gives the metal.

$$Cu_2S + O_2 \rightarrow 2Cu + 2SO_2$$

17.12 Summary and revision plan

1 **Oxidation** involves removal of electrons and **reduction**, addition of electrons. Each process may be represented by a **half-equation**.
2 **Redox** reactions involve complete or partial transfer of electrons. The number of electrons lost in the oxidation step must equal the number of electrons gained in the reduction process.
3 **Oxidation number** may be defined as the number of electrons which an atom of an element loses (or tends to lose) in a particular reaction. Oxidation involves a positive change in oxidation number, whereas reduction causes a negative change.
4 In a **half-cell** or electrode, a metal develops a potential by supplying or donating electrons to a redox equilibrium. Such **electrode potentials** cannot be measured in isolation but the difference in the potentials of two electrodes may be found by measuring the e.m.f. of the cell formed by connecting them with a **salt bridge**. In such a cell, oxidation takes place at the negative electrode and reduction at the positive electrode.
5 Electrode potential may depend upon temperature, pressure and ionic concentration. **Standard electrode potentials, $E^\ominus$**, are measured at 25 °C, 1 atm pressure and with all aqueous concentrations of 1 M. All standard potentials are compared to the **standard hydrogen electrode** which is assigned a value of **0.0 volts**.
6 The **electrochemical series** lists redox systems in order of standard potentials, from the most negative (best reducing agents) to the most positive (best oxidising agents). The electrochemical series may be used to predict whether a particular redox reaction will occur spontaneously (under standard conditions).
7 **Electrolysis** involves driving a spontaneous redox reaction in the reverse direction by applying a greater external voltage in opposition to the cell e.m.f. Thus reduction now takes place at the negative electrode (cathode) and oxidation at the positive electrode (anode).
8 The extraction of a metal from its purified ore involves a **reduction** process. The method chosen will depend upon the ease of reduction of the metal cation. Electrolysis of a molten compound must be used for the most reactive metals, but cheaper methods are available for less reactive metals.

Acid–base Equilibria

Contents

Figure 18.1 *Some examples of Brønsted–Lowry acids and bases*

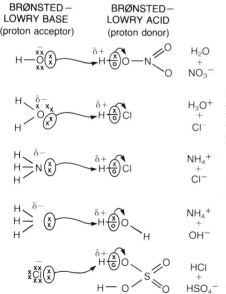

18.1 Definitions of acids and bases

Brønsted and **Lowry** (1923) defined an **acid** *as any species which donates a proton,* H^+, and a **base** as *a species which will accept a proton.* Figure 18.1 shows some reactions of Brønsted–Lowry acids and bases. Note that some substances, e.g. water, are **amphiprotic**, *capable of acting either as an acid or as a base depending upon conditions.*

In all cases when a Brønsted–Lowry acid reacts with a base, the base donates a lone pair of electrons to a positively charged hydrogen atom. **Lewis** (1938), extended the definition of acids to include any species which *accepts a lone pair of electrons.* Whilst all Brønsted–Lowry acids fall into this category, there are several Lewis acids which do not fit the Brønsted–Lowry description, e.g. boron trichloride. Although this cannot donate a proton, the boron atom, which has only six electrons in its valency shell, will readily accept a lone pair of electrons from a base such as ammonia:

For the purposes of this chapter we shall use the Brønsted–Lowry definition of acids and bases.

18.2 Acids and bases in aqueous solution

Strictly speaking, a substance can only function as an 'acid' in the presence of a proton acceptor, i.e. a 'base'. Water is an amphiprotic solvent since it may either accept or donate protons. An acid, HA, will ionise as follows in aqueous solution to give hydrated protons:

$$HA(aq) + H_2O(l) \rightleftharpoons H_3O^+(aq) + A^-(aq)$$
$$\text{acid} \qquad \text{base} \qquad \text{acid} \qquad \text{base}$$

Note that the reaction is reversible and leads to another acid and base. *An acid and base related by the loss of a proton, i.e. HA and A^- or H_3O^+ and H_2O, are referred to as a* **'conjugate pair'**. The **strength** *of an acid is a measure of its ability to donate a proton,* and is therefore related to the position of the above equilibrium. A **strong acid** will *ionise almost completely* which means that its conjugate base is weak, i.e. is reluctant to accept a proton. Conversely, a **weak acid** *ionises only slightly*, so its conjugate base will be strong, i.e. will accept a proton readily.

A base, B, in aqueous solution ionises to produce **hydroxide** ions,

$$B(aq) + H_2O(l) \rightleftharpoons BH^+(aq) + OH^-(aq)$$

$$\text{base} \qquad \text{acid} \qquad \text{acid} \qquad \text{base}$$

A **strong base** *ionises almost fully* in solution, whereas for a **weak base**, the above equilibrium will lie well to the *left*.

18.3 The ionic product of water

Although pure water is essentially covalent, it **self-ionises** to a slight extent through an acid–base reaction,

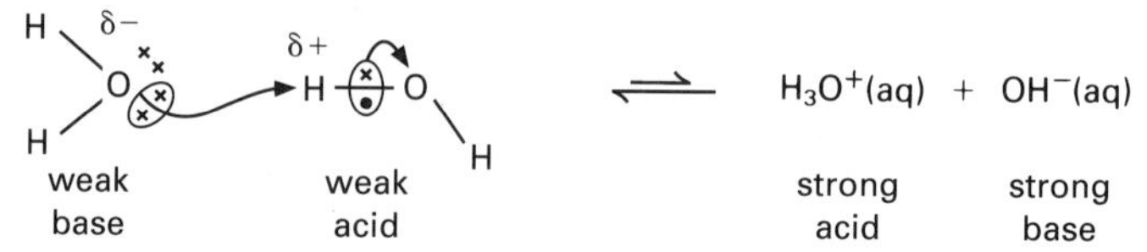

$H_3O^+(aq)$ is a strong acid and $OH^-(aq)$ is a strong base, so the equilibrium lies well to the left. The equilibrium constant, K_c, for the reaction is given by,

$$K_c = \frac{[H_3O^+(aq)] \, [OH^-(aq)]}{[H_2O(l)]^2}$$

Since the ionisation is very slight, the concentration of water is effectively constant and the **ionic product of water**, K_w, is given by,

$$K_w = [H_3O^+(aq)] \, [OH^-(aq)]$$

As for any equilibrium constant, the value of K_w is temperature dependent but at $25\,°C$ it is $10^{-14}\,M^2$. Since in pure water the concentrations of $H_3O^+(aq)$ and $OH^-(aq)$ must be equal, then under these conditons,

$$[H_3O^+(aq)] = [OH^-(aq)] = \sqrt{10^{-14}\,M^2} = 10^{-7}\,M$$

Any solution which has *equal* concentrations of $H_3O^+(aq)$ and $OH^-(aq)$ is **neutral**, i.e. neither acidic nor basic.

It is important to remember that the above equilibrium for water exists in *all* aqueous solutions. Addition of an acid will increase the concentration of $H_3O^+(aq)$ and, in order to maintain K_w constant, the concentration of $OH^-(aq)$ must fall. Similarly, an increase in $[OH^-(aq)]$ on adding a base will reduce the amount of $H_3O^+(aq)$ present. According to Le Chatelier's Principle, increase in the concentration of either $H_3O^+(aq)$ or $OH^-(aq)$ causes the above reaction to move to the left, i.e. removing ions from the solution to produce more water.

$$2H_2O(l) \rightleftharpoons H_3O^+(aq) + OH^-(aq)$$

$\leftarrow$ increase in the concentration of either ion

18.4 The pH scale of acidity and alkalinity

The **concentration of hydrogen ions** is a measure of the **acidity** or **alkalinity** of the solution. As we saw in section 18.3, if $[H_3O^+(aq)]$ exceeds $[OH^-(aq)]$ then the solution is *acidic*. Conversely, if $[H_3O^+(aq)]$ is less than $[OH^-(aq)]$ then the solution is *alkaline*. The ionic product of water is given by

$$K_w = [H_3O^+(aq)] \, [OH^-(aq)]$$

Taking logarithms to base 10,

$$\log_{10}K_w = \log_{10}[H_3O^+(aq)] + \log_{10}[OH^-(aq)]$$

or, $$-\log_{10}K_w = -\log_{10}[H_3O^+(aq)] - \log_{10}[OH^-(aq)]$$

Now, $-\log_{10}X$, *where X is any quantity, is known as pX*, so we may rewrite this equation as follows:

$$pK_w \quad = \quad pH \quad + \quad pOH$$

At 25 °C, K_w is $10^{-14}M^2$ and $[H_3O^+(aq)] = [OH^-(aq)] = 10^{-7}M$.

$$
\begin{array}{ccccc}
pK_w & = & pH & + & pOH \\
-\log_{10}10^{-14} & = & -\log_{10}10^{-7} & - & \log_{10}10^{-7} \\
14 & = & 7 & + & 7
\end{array}
$$

so

Thus the pH of a *neutral* solution at 25 °C is 7.

If acid is added, $[H_3O^+(aq)]$ increases, $\log_{10}[H_3O^+(aq)]$ also increases but pH, i.e. $-\log_{10}[H_3O^+(aq)]$ will decrease. Thus *acidic* solutions have pH values *below 7*. The lower the pH value, the more acidic is the solution.

Since addition of alkali will increase $[OH^-(aq)]$ and reduce $[H_3O^+(aq)]$, pH values *above 7* indicate increasingly *alkaline* solutions.

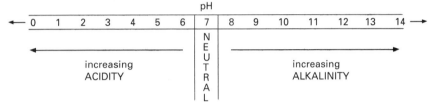

We often need to carry out simple calculations using the above quantities.

Examples

In all cases take K_w as $10^{-14}M^2$.

1. The concentration of hydroxide ions in an aqueous solution is $10^{-4}M$. Calculate the hydrogen ion concentration and hence the pH.

2. The pH of an aqueous solution is 2.5. What is the pOH of the solution and the molar concentrations of both hydrogen and hydroxide ions?

Solutions

1. $K_w = [H_3O^+(aq)] [OH^-(aq)]$
   $[H_3O^+(aq)] = K_w/[OH^-(aq)]$
   $\qquad\qquad = 10^{-14}/10^{-4}M$
   $\qquad\qquad = 10^{-10}M$
   $pH = -\log_{10}[H_3O^+(aq)]$
   $\qquad = -(-10)$
   $\qquad = 10$

2. $pK_w \ = pH + pOH$
   $14 \ = 2.5 + pOH$
   $pOH = 14 - 2.5 = 11.5$
   $pH \ = -\log_{10}[H_3O^+(aq)] = \ 2.5$
   $\qquad\quad \log_{10}[H_3O^+(aq)] = -2.5$

   Note: in calculating hydrogen ion concentration from pH, it is important to change the sign first BEFORE taking antilogs, otherwise we will get the wrong answer.

   Taking antilogs,
   $$[H_3O^+(aq)] = 3.16 \times 10^{-3}M$$

   $[OH^-(aq)] = K_w/[H_3O^+(aq)]$
   $\qquad\qquad = 10^{-14}/(3.16 \times 10^{-3})$
   $\qquad\qquad = 3.16 \times 10^{-12}M$

Activity 18.1

Complete the spaces in the following table. In all cases you may take the ionic product of water to be $10^{-14}M^2$.

[H$_3$O$^+$(aq)]/M	[OH$^-$(aq)]/M	pH	pOH
1.00			
	10^{-6}		
		1.8	
			9.0

18.5 Experimental determination of pH

There are two main methods available to determine the hydrogen ion concentration of a solution and hence its pH.

An approximate value may be obtained quickly by the use of **universal indicator** paper or solution. The indicator develops a colour dependent upon the pH of the solution. This may be compared with a colour chart prepared by adding the indicator to solutions of known pH. The theory of acid–base indicators is developed more fully in section 18.9.

Obviously the indicator method has its limitations. It is not suitable for highly coloured solutions, which would mask the indicator, and its accuracy depends on the skill and eyesight of the operator. A more accurate measure of pH may be found using a **pH meter**. This is an electrochemical cell which has one electrode whose

Using a pH meter to find the pH of yoghurt

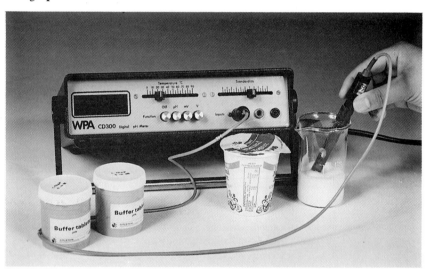

potential changes with the hydrogen ion concentration of the solution. The obvious choice is the hydrogen electrode, described in section 17.7,

$$H^+(aq) + e^- \rightleftharpoons \tfrac{1}{2}H_2(g)$$

At any given temperature, increasing the concentration of hydrogen ions will push the system to the right thus making the electrode potential more positive. When the hydrogen electrode is connected to another electrode of known potential, e.g. a calomel electrode, the e.m.f. of the cell gives a measure of the pH of the solution into which the hydrogen electrode dips. In practice, since the hydrogen electrode is difficult to set up and maintain, other pH-sensitive electrodes are preferred.

18.6 Acid and base strength: dissociation constants

A 0.1 M solution of hydrochloric acid has a pH of about 1, whereas the pH of 0.1 M ethanoic acid, CH$_3$COOH, is about 3. Although both acids are *monobasic* (contain only one donatable proton per molecule) and have the same molarity, the hydrochloric acid solution is more 'acidic', i.e. has a greater concentration of $H_3O^+(aq)$ ions. Hydrochloric acid must therefore ionise more fully in aqueous solution.

$$HCl(aq) \quad + H_2O(l) \rightleftharpoons H_3O^+(aq) + Cl^-(aq)$$

$$CH_3COOH(aq) + H_2O(l) \rightleftharpoons H_3O^+(aq) + CH_3COO^-(aq)$$

Hydrochloric acid is said to be a **stronger** acid than ethanoic acid because it ionises more fully. The equilibrium constant for the dissociation gives a numerical value of acid strength. For the general case of a monobasic acid, HA,

$$HA(aq) + H_2O(l) \rightleftharpoons H_3O^+(aq) + A^-(aq)$$

$$K_c = \frac{[H_3O^+(aq)] \ [A^-(aq)]}{[HA(aq)] \ [H_2O(l)]}$$

In dilute solutions, the concentration of water will be much higher than that of the other species and remain approximately constant regardless of the extent of ionisation. We may simplify the above to

$$HA(aq) \rightleftharpoons H^+(aq) + A^-(aq)$$

then,

$$K_a = \frac{[H^+(aq)] \ [A^-(aq)]}{[HA(aq)]}$$

where K_a is known as the **dissociation constant of the acid**. We may also define **pK_a** as follows,

$$pK_a = -\log_{10}K_a$$

Note that whereas weak acids will have a low value for K_a, the pK_a will be large.

For a weak monobasic acid of total concentration aM,

$$HA(aq) \rightleftharpoons H^+(aq) + A^-(aq)$$

molarity at START (before ionisation)	a	0	0
molarity at EQUILIBRIUM	$(a - x)$	x	x

where x is the molar concentration of acid which dissociates.
Then,

$$K_a = \frac{[H^+(aq)] \ [A^-(aq)]}{[HA(aq)]}$$

$$= \frac{x^2}{(a - x)}$$

Very strong acids, such as hydrochloric acid, ionise almost fully in aqueous solution, i.e. x is almost equal to a. This means that K_a for a strong acid is very high. In fact, we rarely quote dissociation constants for strong acids, but assume *complete* dissociation.

We need to be able to calculate the pH of any acid solution, given its molar concentration and dissociation constant.

Examples

1   What is the pH of (a) 0.01 M nitric acid, HNO_3 and (b) 0.01 M sulphuric acid, H_2SO_4, assuming both acids to be fully ionised under these conditions?

2   If the dissociation constant of ethanoic acid is 1.7×10^{-5} M at 25 °C, what is the pH of 0.1 M ethanoic acid at this temperature?

Solutions

1 (a)

$$HNO_3(aq) \rightarrow H^+(aq) + NO_3^-(aq)$$

	HNO_3(aq)	H^+(aq)	NO_3^-(aq)
molarity at START	0.01	0	0
molarity at EQUILIBRIUM	0	0.01	0.01 complete ionisation

$$\begin{aligned} pH &= -\log_{10} H^+(aq)] \\ &= -(-2) \\ &= 2 \end{aligned}$$

(b)

$$H_2SO_4(aq) \rightarrow 2H^+(aq) + SO_4^{2-}(aq)$$

	H_2SO_4(aq)	H^+(aq)	SO_4^{2-}(aq)
molarity at START	0.001	0	0
molarity at EQUILIBRIUM	0	0.02	0.01 complete ionisation

$$\begin{aligned} pH &= -\log_{10}[H^+(aq)] \\ &= -(-1.70) \\ &= 1.70 \end{aligned}$$

Note that sulphuric acid is *dibasic*, i.e. may donate *two* protons per molecule.

2

$$CH_3COOH(aq) \rightleftharpoons CH_3COO^-(aq) + H^+(aq)$$

	CH_3COOH(aq)	CH_3COO^-(aq)	H^+(aq)
molarity at START	0.1	0	0
molarity at EQUILIBRIUM	(0.1 − x)	x	x

Let x be the molarity of ethanoic acid which ionises,

Note that x is also the molarity of $H^+(aq)$ ions in the solution.

$$K_a = \frac{x^2}{(0.1 - x)}$$

Now since the acid is weak, very little of the acid ionises in solution and so $x \ll 0.1$. This means that the concentration of unionised acid $(0.1 - x)$ is almost equal to the total acid concentration, i.e. 0.1. Thus,

$$K_a = 1.7 \times 10^{-5} \simeq \frac{x^2}{0.1}$$

$$x = \sqrt{1.7 \times 10^{-6}} = [H^+(aq)]$$

$$= 1.30 \times 10^{-3} M$$

$$\begin{aligned} pH &= -\log_{10} [H^+(aq)] \\ &= -(-2.89) \\ &= 2.89 \end{aligned}$$

Activity 18.2

1 Complete the following table which lists values of K_a and pK_a for some organic acids.

Acid		K_a/M	pK_a
methanoic	HCOOH	1.78×10^{-4}	
ethanoic	CH_3COOH		4.76
propanoic	C_2H_5COOH		4.87
chloroethanoic	ClCH_2COOH	1.38×10^{-3}	

2 (a) Which of the above acids is the weakest?
(b) What is the approximate pH of a 1 M solution of methanoic acid?
(c) What would be the pH of a 1 M solution of a strong monobasic acid?

We may tackle the calculation of the pH of any alkaline solution in a similar way. Metal hydroxides ionise directly in aqueous solution, giving hydroxide ions, $OH^-(aq)$,

e.g.
$$NaOH(s) \xrightarrow{water} Na^+(aq) + OH^-(aq)$$

However, many bases produce hydroxide ions by reaction with water.

i.e.
$$B(aq) + H_2O(l) \rightleftharpoons BH^+(aq) + OH^-(aq)$$

The **strength** of the base is given by the **base dissociation constant, K_b,**

$$K_b = \frac{[BH^+(aq)]\,[OH^-(aq)]}{[B(aq)][H_2O(l)]}$$

Again, in *dilute* solution, the concentration of water may be taken as constant and we may write,

$$K_b = \frac{[BH^+(aq)][OH^-(aq)]}{[B(aq)]}$$

For a base of total concentration a M, where the molarity of base which ionises is x,

$$B(aq) \; + \; H_2O(l) \; \rightleftharpoons BH^+(aq) + OH^-(aq)$$

molarity at START (before dissociation)	a	constant	0	0
molarity at EQUILIBRIUM	$(a-x)$	constant	x	x

$$K_b \; = \frac{x^2}{(a-x)}$$

Again we may convert to pK_b:

$$\mathbf{pK_b = -\log_{10}K_b}$$

Note that *weak* bases will have a *small* value of K_b but consequently a *large pK_b*. When calculating the pH of an alkaline solution, we must first find the hydroxide ion concentration, $[OH^-(aq)]$, and then use the ionic product of water, K_w, to determine the hydrogen ion concentration, $[H^+(aq)]$.

Examples

The ionic product of water may be taken as $10^{-14}M^2$.
 1 Calculate the pH of a 0.1 M solution of the strong base sodium hydroxide.
 2 Ammonium hydroxide has a pK_b value of 4.75 at 25 °C. Calculate the approximate pH of a 2 M solution of ammonium hydroxide at this temperature.

Solutions

1
$$NaOH(aq) \rightarrow Na^+(aq) + OH^-(aq)$$

molarity at START	0.1	0	0
molarity at EQUILIBRIUM	0	0.1	0.1 complete ionisation

$$
\begin{aligned}
K_w &= [H^+(aq)][OH^-(aq)] = 10^{-14}M^2 \\
H^+(aq) &\times 0.1 = 10^{-14}M^2 \\
H^+(aq) &= 10^{-13}M \\
pH &= -\log_{10}[H^+(aq)] \\
&= -(-13) \\
&= 13
\end{aligned}
$$

2   First convert pK_b to K_b:

$$pK_b = -\log_{10}K_b = 4.75$$
$$-pK_b = \log_{10}K_b = -4.75$$
$$\text{antilog}_{10}(-pK_b) = K_b = 1.78 \times 10^{-5}\,\text{M}$$

$$NH_3(aq) + H_2O(l) \rightleftharpoons NH_4^+(aq) + OH^-(aq)$$

molarity at START   2   0   0

Let x be the molarity of ammonia solution which ionises.

molarity at EQUILIBRIUM $(2-x)$ x x

$$K_b = 1.78 \times 10^{-5} = \frac{x^2}{(2-x)}$$

Since from its very *low* dissociation constant, ammonia is a very *weak* base, little of it ionises and $x \ll 2$. So $(2-x) \simeq 2$.

$$1.78 \times 10^{-5} = \frac{x^2}{2}$$

$$\begin{aligned}
x = [OH^-(aq)] &= \sqrt{2 \times 1.78 \times 10^{-5}} \\
&= \sqrt{3.56 \times 10^{-5}} \\
&= 5.96 \times 10^{-3}\,\text{M}
\end{aligned}$$

But, $$\begin{aligned}
K_w = [H^+(aq)][OH^-(aq)] &= 10^{-14}\,\text{M}^2 \\
[H^+(aq)] &= 10^{-14}/(5.96 \times 10^{-3})\,\text{M} \\
&= 1.68 \times 10^{-12}\,\text{M} \\
pH = -\log_{10}[H^+(aq)] &= 11.78
\end{aligned}$$

Activity 18.3

Potassium hydroxide, KOH, is a strong base, whereas methylamine, CH_3NH_2, is a weak base with a dissociation constant of $4.37 \times 10^{-4}\,\text{M}$ at $25\,°C$.

1   What is the concentration of hydroxide ions in a $0.1\,\text{M}$ solution of each of these bases?
2   If the ionic product of water at $25\,°C$ is $10^{-14}\,\text{M}^2$, what is the pH of each of these solutions?

18.7   Experimental determination of dissociation constants

In section 18.6 we showed how to calculate the pH of a solution of a weak acid or base from its molar concentration and dissociation constant. If we know any two of these quantities we may calculate the third, so *to find the dissociation constant we need to determine the concentration and the pH of a solution*. We shall illustrate the method by considering the results of an experiment on a solution of the weak acid phenol, C_6H_5OH, which ionises as follows in water:

$$C_6H_5OH(aq) \rightleftharpoons C_6H_5O^-(aq) + H^+(aq)$$

The pH of an aqueous solution of phenol, measured on a pH meter at $25\,°C$ was found to be 5.35. We may use this value to determine the concentration of hydrogen ions in the solution.

$$\begin{aligned}
-\log_{10}[H^+(aq)] = \quad pH &= 5.35 \\
\log_{10}[H^+(aq)] = \quad -pH &= -5.35 \\
[H^+(aq)] = \text{antilog}_{10}(-pH) &= 4.47 \times 10^{-6}\,\text{M}
\end{aligned}$$

We now need to know the molar concentration of phenol in this solution. This may be determined by titrating with a standard solution of a strong alkali using a suitable acid–base indicator.

volume of phenol solution used in each titration $= 25.0\,cm^3$
titration volumes with 0.100 M sodium hydroxide (1) $50.1\,cm^3$
(2) $49.9\,cm^3$
(3) $50.0\,cm^3$
average titre $50.0\,cm^3$

The titration equation is $C_6H_5OH(aq) + NaOH(aq) \rightarrow C_6H_5ONa(aq) + H_2O(l)$

$\therefore$ moles of sodium hydroxide used in titration $= 0.100 \times 50.0/1000$
$= 0.0050$ moles

From the equation this also equals the number of moles of phenol used in the titration, therefore,

there are 0.0050 moles of phenol in $25.00\,cm^3$ of solution
there are $0.0050/25.0$ moles of phenol in $1.00\,cm^3$ of solution
there are $1000 \times 0.0050/25.0$ moles of phenol in $1000\,cm^3$ of solution
$= 0.200$ moles

Thus the total concentration of the phenol solution is 0.200 M.

Now we are in a position to calculate the acid dissociation constant of phenol.

$$C_6H_5OH(aq) \rightleftharpoons C_6H_5O^-(aq) + H^+(aq)$$

molarity at START   0.200   0   0
(no ionisation)

Since we know $[H^+(aq)]$ from the pH measurement,
molarity at EQUILIBRIUM $(0.200 - 4.47 \times 10^{-6})$ 4.47×10^{-6} 4.47×10^{-6}
$\simeq 0.200$

$$K_a = \frac{[C_6H_5O^-(aq)]\,[H^+(aq)]}{[C_6H_5OH(aq)]}$$

$$= \frac{(4.47 \times 10^{-6})^2}{0.200}$$

$$= 10^{-10}\,M$$

We shall leave a similar calculation to find the dissociation constant of a weak base to the next activity.

Activity 18.4

$25.0\,cm^3$ of a solution of ethylamine, $C_2H_5NH_2$, needed $37.5\,cm^3$ of 0.100 M hydrochloric acid solution for the following neutralisation,

$$C_2H_5NH_2(aq) + HCl(aq) \rightarrow C_2H_5NH_3^+(aq) + Cl^-(aq)$$

The pH of the ethylamine solution was found to be 11.95. Calculate:
1   the molar concentration of the ethylamine solution;
2   the concentration of hydrogen ions in the solution;
3   the concentration of hydroxide ions in the solution if the ionic product of water is $10^{-14}\,M^2$;
4   the value of the base dissociation constant for ethylamine which reacts as follows in water:

$$C_2H_5NH_2(aq) + H_2O(l) \rightarrow C_2H_5NH_3^+(aq) + OH^-(aq)$$

18.8 pH of salt solutions

Aqueous solutions of salts are not always neutral. The following table shows the approximate pH of 1 M solutions of a range of salts, together with data on the acids and bases from which they are derived.

Table 18.1

Salt	pH of solution	base	pK_b*	acid	pK_a*
sodium chloride NaCl	7.0	NaOH	s	HCl	s
sodium ethanoate CH_3COONa	9.4	NaOH	s	CH_3COOH	4.76
ammonium chloride NH_4Cl	4.6	NH_4OH	4.75	HCl	s
ammonium ethanoate CH_3COONH_4	7.0	NH_4OH	4.75	CH_3COOH	4.76

*s indicates a strong (fully ionised) acid or base

The following features should be apparent:

▶ A salt of a *strong acid* and a *strong base* is approximately *neutral* in aqueous solution (e.g. sodium chloride).

▶ The salt of a *strong base* with a *weak acid* is *alkaline* in solution (e.g. sodium ethanoate).

▶ A solution of a salt of a *weak base* with a *strong acid* is *acidic* (e.g. ammonium chloride).

▶ For the salt of a weak base with a weak acid the pH of the solution depends upon the relative strengths of the acid and base. In the case of ammonium ethanoate, ethanoic acid and aqueous ammonia are of similar strength, so the salt is approximately neutral in aqueous solution.

These values have important consequences when titrating acids and bases using indicators (see sections 18.9 and 18.10), and we must be able to account for the differences.

Let us consider the formation of a salt, M^+A^-, from an acid, HA, and a base. It will be easier to assume that all bases react as hydroxides, i.e. MOH. The neutralisation reaction may then be written

$$\underset{\text{base}}{MOH(aq)} + \underset{\text{acid}}{HA(aq)} \rightarrow \underset{\text{salt}}{M+(aq) + A^-(aq)} + \underset{\text{water}}{H_2O(l)}$$

This certainly does not suggest that the salt solution should be either acid or alkaline, but we must remember that the ions $M^+(aq)$ and $A^-(aq)$ are the conjugate partners of the starting materials and may also function as an acid or base respectively.

The cation, $M^+(aq)$, may react with water as follows:

$$M^+(aq) + H_2O(l) \rightleftharpoons \underset{\text{acidic}}{MOH(aq) + H^+(aq)}$$

i.e., hydrolysis of the *cation* to produce $H^+(aq)$ which will tend to make the solution *acidic*. If MOH is a strong base, its conjugate acid, M^+, will be very weak and any reaction with water will be slight. It is only when the base MOH is weak, that M^+ has appreciable acid strength and the effect will be noticeable.

The anion, $A^-(aq)$, may also react with water:

$$A^-(aq) + H_2O(l) \rightleftharpoons \underset{\text{alkaline}}{HA(aq) + OH^-(aq)}$$

i.e., in this case hydrolysis of the *anion* produces *hydroxide ions* which will tend to make the solution *alkaline*. Again, the effect is only noticeable if the acid HA is weak and its conjugate base A^- has appreciable strength.

The pH of any salt solution, therefore, depends upon the relative strengths of the acid and base used to prepare it. *As a 'rule of thumb', remember that if the acid is stronger than the base, the salt will be acidic in solution and vice versa.*

18.9 Acid–base indicators

An **acid-base** *indicator is any substance whose colour is dependent upon the pH of the solution.* Many natural dyes act as indicators, e.g. elderberry juice and 'red cabbage' extract. They are themselves weak acids or bases, in which the *ionised and unionised forms have different colours.* In the case of an indicator, HIn, which is a weak acid,

$$\text{HIn(aq)} \quad \rightleftharpoons \text{H}^+\text{(aq)} + \text{In}^-\text{(aq)}$$
colour 1   colour 2
(weak acid)   (strong base)

The acid dissociation constant, K_a, often referred to as the **indicator dissociation constant, K_{In}**, is given by

$$K_{In} = \frac{[\text{H}^+\text{(aq)}]\,[\text{In}^-\text{(aq)}]}{[\text{HIn(aq)}]}$$

rearranging,

$$[\text{H}^+\text{(aq)}] = K_{In} \frac{[\text{HIn(aq)}]}{[\text{In}^-\text{(aq)}]}$$

when $\quad [\text{H}^+\text{(aq)}] = K_{In}$, then $[\text{HIn(aq)}] = [\text{In}^-\text{(aq)}]$

Under these conditions, there will then be equal concentrations of both the unionised and ionised forms of the indicator and the overall colour will be a mixture of that of the two forms.

At lower pH, i.e. higher concentration of $\text{H}^+\text{(aq)}$, $[\text{HIn(aq)}] > [\text{In}^-\text{(aq)}]$, i.e. the colour of the *unionised* indicator, HIn, will predominate. In more alkaline conditions, $[\text{HIn(aq)}] < [\text{In}^-\text{(aq)}]$, i.e. the *ionised* form will predominate.

In practice, the colour of an indicator is observed to change gradually over about 2 or 3 pH units. Each indicator therefore has its own characteristic pH range, *dependent on the indicator constant,* over which it changes colour. Table 18.2 gives the pH ranges and colour changes of some common acid–base indicators.

We may use a range of indicators *separately* to find the approximate pH of any given solution, unless it is strongly coloured, but since indicators are themselves weakly acidic or alkaline we should use the *minimum* possible amounts. For instance, if a solution turns litmus blue but is colourless with phenolphthalein, we can see from table 18.2 that its pH must be about 8.

It is often more convenient to determine pH in a single experiment by using a **universal indicator** which is *mixture* of indicators that changes smoothly through a variety of colours over a wide pH range.

Table 18.2   *pH ranges over which some common acid-base indicators change colour*

Indicator	0	1	2	3	4	5	6	pH 7	8	9	10	11	12	13
bromophenol blue		YELLOW		*		*	BLUE							
methyl orange[†]				RED		*		*	YELLOW					
methyl red				RED		*		*	YELLOW					
litmus[†]					RED		*		*	BLUE				
bromothymol blue						YELLOW		*		*	BLUE			
phenolphthalein[†]							YELLOW(COLOURLESS)		*		*	RED		
thymolphthalein							COLOURLESS		*		*	BLUE		

[†]These indicators are amongst the commonest in general use.
What would be the approximate pH of a solution which gives a yellow colour with both methyl red and bromothymol blue?

18.10 Variation in pH during acid-base titrations: choice of indicator

First let us consider the titration of a **strong acid**, hydrochloric acid, with a **strong base**, sodium hydroxide. Both of these are *fully ionised* in solution.

$$HCl(aq) \rightarrow H^+(aq) + Cl^-(aq) \text{ and } NaOH(aq) \rightarrow Na^+(aq) + OH^-(aq)$$

The neutralisation reaction may therefore be written

$$H^+(aq) + OH^-(aq) \rightleftharpoons H_2O(l) \ (K_w = 10^{-14}M^2)$$

If we start with $25.0\,cm^3$ of $0.1\,M$ hydrochloric acid, i.e. 0.0025 moles HCl, and gradually add $0.1\,M$ sodium hydroxide, then we may calculate the pH whilst the acid is in excess as shown in table 18.3.

Table 18.3

cm³ base added	moles OH⁻ added	moles H⁺ left in solution	total volume of solution/cm³	[H⁺(aq)]/ M	pH
0	0	0.0025	25.0	0.1	1.0
5	0.0005	0.0020	30.0	0.067	– –
10	0.0010	0.0015	35.0	0.043	1.4
15	0.0015	0.0010	– – –	– – – –	– –
20	0.0020	0.0005	45.0	0.011	2.0
22	– – – – –	– – – – –	– – –	– – – –	– –
24	0.0024	0.0001	49.0	0.002	2.7

Can you fill in the blank spaces in this table?

When exactly $25\,cm^3$ of $0.1\,M$ sodium hydroxide has been added, the **equivalence point** will have been reached, i.e. exactly the right amount of base has been added to react with the acid present as shown in the balanced equation for the reaction. Since we are using a strong base and a strong acid, the salt, sodium chloride, will be *neutral* in aqueous solution and the pH will be 7.

Further addition of the sodium hydroxide solution will cause the pH to rise above 7 as shown by table 18.4.

Table 18.4

cm³ base added	moles OH⁻ added	moles OH⁻ left in solution	total volume of solution/cm³	[OH⁻(aq)]/M	pOH	pH
26	0.0026	0.0001	51.0	0.002	2.7	11.3
28	0.0028	0.0003	53.0	0.006	2.3	– – –
30	0.0030	0.0005	55.0	0.009	2.0	12.0
35	0.0035	0.0010	60.0	0.017	– –	– – –
40	0.0040	0.0015	65.0	0.023	1.6	12.4
45	0.0045	0.0020	– – –	– – – –	– –	– – –
50	0.0050	0.0025	75.0	0.033	1.5	12.5
60	– – – – –	– – – – –	– – –	– – – –	– –	– – –

Can you fill in the blank spaces in this table?

The variation in pH during the titration of the hydrochloric acid with the sodium hydroxide solution is shown graphically in figure 18.2a (You can check the missing pH values in the table above from this.) The important features are as follows.

(i) Initially the pH is low because the hydrochloric acid is strong.

(ii) Addition of sodium hydroxide has little effect on pH until the equivalence point is approached.

Figure 18.2 *pH changes during acid–base titrations*

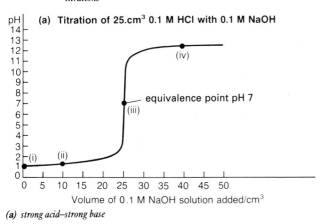

(a) *strong acid–strong base*

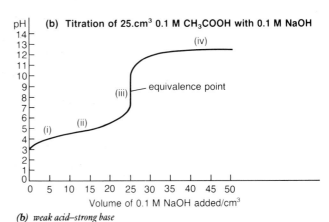

(b) *weak acid–strong base*

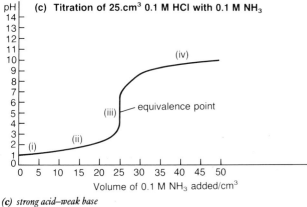

(c) *strong acid–weak base*

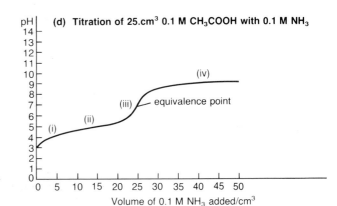

(d) *weak acid–weak base*

(iii) At the equivalence point there is a large, sudden increase in pH.

(iv) Soon after the equivalence point has been passed the pH curve flattens out at a high value, since sodium hydroxide is a strong base.

Since in an acid–base titration we need to find the *equivalence point*, we must choose an indicator which changes colour over the pH range of the *sharp vertical step* (iii) on the graph. For a strong acid–strong base titration this is very large, from about 3 to 11 in this example, and any indicator which changes colour over this pH range would be suitable. Any of the indicators listed in the table 18.2 would be satisfactory for determining the equivalence point in this titration.

If either the acid or the base used, or both, are *weak*, then we obtain somewhat different pH curves for the titration shown in figures 18.2b, 18.2c and 18.2d. Although we shall not attempt the detailed calculation of the pH change in such cases, we may explain the shapes of the graphs qualitatively and investigate the choice of indicator.

Weak acid–strong base, e.g. ethanoic acid and sodium hydroxide solution. The variation in pH is shown in figure 18.2b.

(i) At the start, since the acid is weak, the pH of the solution is *higher*.

(ii) Initially the pH rises rather faster than for a strong acid.

(iii) Again the pH rises quite sharply near the equivalence point but the *change in pH* in this region is *smaller*.

Remember that at the equivalence point we have the salt of a weak acid and a strong base in solution and *the pH will be greater than 7* (see section 18.8).

(iv) Beyond the equivalence point the pH curve flattens out at a high value since excess strong base is present.

Here we must be much more careful in our choice of indicator. In order to detect the sharp rise in pH at the equivalence point we need an indicator that changes over a pH range of about 7–12. From table 18.2 we can see that phenolphthalein or thymolphthalein could be used.

Strong acid–weak base, e.g. hydrochloric acid and aqueous ammonia. The pH curve for this titration is shown in figure 18.2c.
   (i) Since the acid is strong the starting pH is low.
  (ii) Addition of base causes only a small change in pH until the equivalence point is approached.
 (iii) The sharp increase in pH near the equivalence point is about the same size as that found in the weak acid–strong base titration but occurs at *lower pH*.

   At the equivalence point *the pH is less than 7*, since we have the salt of a strong acid and a weak base in solution (see section 18.8).
  (iv) After the equivalence point the pH curve flattens out at a *fairly low pH*, since the excess base present is weak.

We must choose an indicator for this titration which changes colour over the pH range of about 3–7. Bromothymol blue, methyl orange or methyl red from table 18.2 would be suitable.

Weak acid–weak base e.g. ethanoic acid and aqueous ammonia. Figure 18.2d shows the change in pH during this type of titration.
   (i) Since the acid is weak, *the starting pH is fairly high*.
  (ii) Addition of base causes the pH to rise steadily.
 (iii) Change in pH near the equivalence point is *much less sharp* than in any of the previous titrations.
  (iv) After the equivalence point, the pH flattens off at a *fairly low* value since the excess base present is weak.

Here the change in pH near the equivalence point does not occur sharply. *No indicator* will change colour *sharply* at the equivalence point but will do so gradually over quite a large volume of added alkali. *Such titrations cannot be followed accurately using indicators and a pH meter should be used to find the equivalence point.*

More complex pH curves occur if the acid is dibasic, i.e. can donate two protons per molecule, or if the base is diacidic, i.e. can accept two protons per molecule. The pH curve for the titration of a carbonate solution with a strong acid is shown in figure 18.3. It contains two equivalence points, A and B, which represent different reactions.

Figure 18.3 *pH curve for a carbonate–strong acid titration*

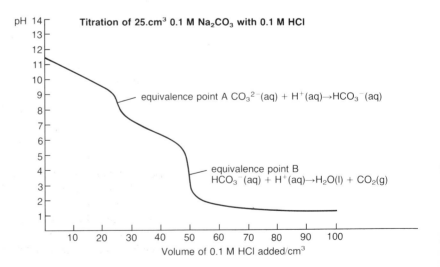

Titration of 25.cm³ 0.1 M Na₂CO₃ with 0.1 M HCl

equivalence point A $CO_3^{2-}(aq) + H^+(aq) \rightarrow HCO_3^-(aq)$

equivalence point B
$HCO_3^-(aq) + H^+(aq) \rightarrow H_2O(l) + CO_2(g)$

Volume of 0.1 M HCl added/cm³

Figure 18.4 *Data for activity 18.5*

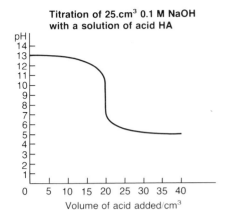

Titration of 25.cm³ 0.1 M NaOH
with a solution of acid HA

equivalence point A $CO_3^{2-}(aq) + H^+(aq) \rightarrow HCO_3^-(aq)$
                        carbonate   hydrogen carbonate

equivalence point B $HCO_3^-(aq) + H^+(aq) \rightarrow H_2O(l) + CO_2(g)$

The equivalence point that we detect will depend upon the pH range of the indicator which we choose for the titration.

Activity 18.5

1 Use the information contained in figure 18.3 and table 18.2 to answer the following question. In a carbonate–strong acid titration, choose an indicator which could be used to detect (a) the conversion of carbonate into hydrogen carbonate, (b) the conversion of carbonate into carbon dioxide and water.

2 Figure 18.4 shows the variation in pH on titrating 25.0 cm³ of 0.100 M sodium hydroxide solution with an aqueous solution of a monobasic acid HA.
   (a) Estimate the pH of the solution at the equivalence point and suggest a suitable indicator for this titration.
   (b) Is the acid strong or weak?
   (c) What volume of the acid solution is needed to use up all of the sodium hydroxide?
   (d) Write an equation for the reaction taking place in this titration and calculate the molarity of the acid.

3 If you have the facilities, confirm the shape of the pH curves given for all the titrations mentioned in section 18.10. A pH meter is not essential, since you may add universal indicator and estimate the pH from the colour of the solution at each stage.

18.11 Buffer solutions and their uses

A **buffer solution** *is one whose pH is resistant to change on the addition of moderate amounts of acid or alkali.* There are two main types:

▶ an aqueous solution of a **weak acid with its salt of a strong base** e.g. ethanoic acid, $CH_3COOH(aq)$ and sodium ethanoate, $CH_3COONa(aq)$. The weak acid, HA(aq), dissociates in aqueous solution as follows.

$$HA(aq) \rightleftharpoons H^+(aq) + A^-(aq)$$

$$K_a = \frac{[H^+(aq)]\,[A^-(aq)]}{[HA(aq)]}$$

Rearranging,

$$[H^+(aq)] = K_a \frac{[HA(aq)]}{[A^-(aq)]}$$

The pH of the solution is therefore determined by the ratio of unionised acid to the ionised form, i.e.

$$\frac{[HA(aq)]}{[A^-(aq)]}$$

Since the acid is weak, however, $[HA(aq)] >> [A^-(aq)]$.

Addition of acid, i.e. more $H^+(aq)$, will push the system to the left. The relative increase in [HA(aq)] is quite small but the 'relative' change in $[A^-(aq)]$ is considerable and the pH therefore decreases appreciably (i.e. $[H^+(aq)]$ increases).

Similarly, addition of an alkali will reduce $[H^+(aq)]$ and push the system to the right. Again there is a marked 'relative' change in the concentration of the ionised form, $A^-(aq)$, and the pH will rise (i.e. $[H^+(aq)]$ decreases).

Testing the acidity of soils in the laboratory. Much simpler soil-testing kits are available to amateur gardeners

When the sodium or potassium salt of the acid is added, it dissociates completely in solution:

$$NaA(aq) \rightarrow Na^+(aq) + A^-(aq)$$

This increases $[A^-(aq)]$ in the solution. The ratio $[HA(aq)]/[A^-(aq)]$ is no longer so sensitive to the position of the above equilibrium. Appreciable amounts of acid or alkali may now be added without drastically changing the pH of the solution. Such a mixture gives an **acidic buffer**, whose pH is determined by the *molar ratio of acid to salt* in the mixture and by the *acid dissociation constant*.

▶ an aqueous solution of a **weak base with its salt of a strong acid**, e.g. aqueous ammonia, $NH_3(aq)$, and ammonium chloride, $NH_4Cl(aq)$. This will give us a buffer solution with a pH *above 7*.

Buffer solutions have a wide range of uses. They may be used to calibrate pH meters and determine the pH ranges of indicator colour changes. Slight accidental contamination of such solutions will not affect the results. Many reactions, especially in biological systems, will only function correctly within quite narrow pH ranges and should be carried out in suitably buffered solutions. Blood, for example should have a pH of about 7.4. For this reason, injections are usually buffered by a mixture of carbonate and hydrogen carbonate ions. Certain plants also grow better when the soil is slightly alkaline or slightly acidic. Cabbages and sprouts, for example, favour alkaline conditions. The pH of soil may be tested using an indicator 'kit' and any excess acidity removed by applying calcium hydroxide ('slaked lime').

Activity 18.6

The dissociation constant of ethanoic acid, CH_3COOH, at 25 °C is 1.7×10^{-5} M. What is the pH of a buffer solution which contains 0.1 mol of ethanoic acid and 0.1 mol of sodium ethanoate in 1 dm³?

18.12 Comments on the activities

Activity 18.1

$[H_3O^+(aq)]/M$	$[OH^-(aq)]/M$	pH	pOH
1.00	10^{-14}	0	14
10^{-8}	10^{-6}	8	6
1.58×10^{-2}	6.31×10^{-13}	1.8	12.2
10^{-5}	10^{-9}	5.0	9.0

Activity 18.2

1

Acid		K_a/M	pK_a
methanoic	HCOOH	1.78×10^{-4}	3.75
ethanoic	CH_3COOH	1.74×10^{-5}	4.76
propanoic	C_2H_5COOH	1.35×10^{-5}	4.87
chloroethanoic	$ClCH_2COOH$	1.38×10^{-3}	2.86

2   (a) Propanoic acid is the weakest acid in the list. It has the lowest value of K_a and hence the highest pK_a.

(b) Using exactly the same method as in example 2 in section 18.6, you should find that the pH of 1 M methanoic acid is approximately 1.87.

(c) Using the method shown in example 1(a) in section 18.6, the pH of a 1 M solution of a strong (fully ionised) monobasic acid should be 0.

Activity 18.3

1
	$KOH(aq) \rightarrow K^+(aq)$ +		$OH^-(aq)$
molarity at START	0.1	0	0
molarity at EQUILIBRIUM	0	0.1	0.1 complete ionisation

Thus $[OH^-(aq)] = 0.1 M$

	$CH_3NH_2(aq) + H_2O(l) \rightarrow CH_3NH_3^+(aq)$ +	$OH^-(aq)$
molarity at START	0.1	0	0
molarity at EQUILIBRIUM	$(0.1 - x)$	x	x

where x is the molarity of the base which ionises.

$$K_b = \frac{[CH_3NH_3^+(aq)]\,[OH^-(aq)]}{[CH_3NH_2(aq)]}$$

$$= \frac{x^2}{(0.1 - x)}$$

But since methylamine is a very weak base, $x << 0.1$, so $(0.1 - x) \simeq 0.1$.

$$x^2 \simeq 0.1K_b \quad = 4.37 \times 10^{-5}$$

$$x = [OH^-(aq)] = \sqrt{4.37 \times 10^{-5}}\,M$$

$$= 6.61 \times 10^{-3}\,M$$

2   In order to calculate the pH of these solutions, we must first find the hydrogen ion concentration from the relation.

$$K_w = [H^+(aq)]\,[OH^-(aq)] \quad \text{i.e.} \quad [H^+(aq)] = K_w/[OH^-(aq)]$$
$$\therefore \text{ for } 0.1\,M \text{ KOH solution,} \quad [H^+(aq)] = 10^{-14}/0.1\,M$$
$$= 10^{-13}\,M$$

$$pH = -\log_{10}[H^+(aq)] = -(-13) = 13$$

For 0.1 M CH_3NH_2 solution, $\quad [H^+(aq)] = 10^{-14}/(6.61 \times 10^{-3})\,M$
$$= 1.51 \times 10^{-12}\,M$$
$$pH = -\log_{10}[H^+(aq)] = -(-11.82) \quad = 11.82$$

Activity 18.4

1   $C_2H_5NH_2(aq) + HCl(aq) \rightarrow C_2H_5NH_3^+(aq) + Cl^-(aq)$

Moles of hydrochloric acid used in titration $= 0.100 \times 37.5/1000$
$$= 0.00375 \text{ moles}$$

From the equation this also equals the number of moles of ethylamine.
There are 0.00375 moles of ethylamine in 25.0 cm³ of solution.
There are 0.00375/25.0 moles of ethylamine in 1 cm³ of solution.
There are $1000 \times 0.00375/25.0$ moles of ethylamine in 1000 cm³ of solution $= 0.150$ moles.
Thus the concentration of the ethylamine solution is 0.150 M.

2    $-\log_{10}[H^+(aq)] = pH$ = 11.95

$\log_{10}[H^+(aq)] = -pH$ = -11.95
$[H^+(aq)] = \text{antilog}_{10}(-pH) = 1.12 \times 10^{-12} M$

3        $[H^+(aq)][OH^-(aq)] = K_w = 10^{-14}$
$[OH^-(aq)] = 10^{-14}/(1.12 \times 10^{-12}) M$
$= 8.93 \times 10^{-3} M$

4                    $C_2H_5NH_3(aq)$ $+ H_2O(l) \rightarrow C_2H_5NH_3{}^+(aq) + OH^-(aq)$

molarity at   0.15   0   0
START

molarity at $(0.15 - 8.93 \times 10^{-3})$ 8.93×10^{-3} 8.93×10^{-3}
EQUILIBRIUM $\simeq 0.141$

$$K_b = \frac{[C_2H_5NH_3{}^+(aq)][OH^-(aq)]}{[C_2H_5NH_2(aq)]}$$

$$= \frac{(8.93 \times 10^{-3})^2}{0.141}$$

$$= 5.66 \times 10^{-4} M$$

Activity 18.5

1 (a) The first equivalence point occurs over a pH range of about 9.5–7. The best indicator in table 18.2 is phenolphthalein.
   (b) The second equivalence point ranges from about pH 5 to pH 2. Methyl orange or bromophenol blue would detect this.
2 (a) The equivalence point occurs at the sharpest change in pH. From figure 18.4 this occurs at a pH of about 9. Phenolphthalein and thymolphthalein change colour in this region and either would be a suitable indicator for this titration.
   (b) Since the pH of the solution at the equivalence point is above 7, the acid, HA, must be weak.
   (c) From figure 18.4, we can see that $20.0\,cm^3$ of acid must be added to reach the equivalence point, i.e. to react with all the sodium hydroxide present.
   (d) $HA(aq) + NaOH(aq) \rightarrow NaA(aq) + H_2O(l)$

$25.0\,cm^3$ of $0.100\,M$ NaOH contains $0.100 \times 25.0/1000$ moles
$= 0.0025$ moles NaOH

From the equation above, this reacts with an equal number of moles of acid. Thus,

$20.0\,cm^3$ of HA(aq) contains 0.0025 moles of HA
$1\ \ cm^3$ of HA(aq) contains 0.0025/20 moles of HA
$1000\,cm^3$ of HA(aq) contains $1000 \times 0.0025/20$ moles of HA

i.e. the concentration of the acid, HA, is $0.125\,M$.

Activity 18.6

$$CH_3COOH(aq) \rightleftharpoons CH_3COO^-(aq) + H^+(aq)$$
$$CH_3COONa(aq) \rightarrow CH_3COO^-(aq) + Na^+(aq)$$

$$[H^+(aq)] = \frac{K_a[CH_3COOH(aq)]}{[CH_3COO^-(aq)]}$$

Since ethanoic acid is weak, i.e. ionises only slightly,
[CH$_3$COOH(aq)] equals the concentration of acid added, i.e. $0.1\,M$,

and $[CH_3COO^-(aq)]$ equals the concentration of salt added, i.e. 0.1 M.

$$[H^+(aq)] = 1.7 \times 10^{-5} \times \frac{0.1}{0.1} = 1.7 \times 10^{-5} M$$

$$pH = -\log_{10}[H^+(aq)] = 4.77$$

18.13 Summary and revision plan

1   Acids and bases may be defined in two ways;
    (a) in terms of the **proton, H^+ (Brønsted and Lowry)**; an acid is a proton donor and a base is a proton acceptor.
    (b) in terms of a **lone pair of electrons (Lewis)**; an acid accepts a lone pair of electrons from a base.
    In this chapter we use the Brønsted–Lowry definition of acids and bases.

2   Acids ionise in aqueous solution to give the hydrated proton, $H^+(aq)$, whereas soluble bases (alkalis) give hydroxide ions, $OH^-(aq)$.

3   The acidity/alkalinity of an aqueous solution depends on the concentration of hydrogen ions and is usually quoted on the **pH scale**.

$$pH = -\log_{10}[H^+(aq)]$$

The lower the pH, the more acidic is the solution.

4   pH may be determined using **indicators** or a **pH meter**.

5   Water **self-ionises** slightly,

$$H_2O(l) \rightleftharpoons H^+(aq) + OH^-(aq)$$

The **ionic product** of water is given by

$$K_w = [H^+(aq)] \, [OH^-(aq)]$$
and so, $$pK_w = pH + pOH$$

6   The **strength** of an acid or base shows how far it ionises in solution and is measured by the **acid (or base) dissociation constant K_a (K_b)**. Weak acids (and bases) have very small dissociation constants and consequently high pK values.

7   The pH of any salt solution will depend upon the relative strengths of its parent acid and base. If the acid is stronger than the base, then the salt solution will be acidic, and vice versa.

8   Acid–base **indicators** are themselves weak acids or bases, where the unionised and ionised forms have different colours. The pH range over which an indicator changes colour depends upon the value of the **indicator constant K_{In}**.

9   An indicator for any acid–base titration must be chosen so that it changes colour over the sharp change in pH which occurs at the **equivalence point**. There is no suitable indicator in a titration where both the acid and base are weak.

10 A **buffer solution** resists change in its pH on addition of small amounts of acid or alkali. Acidic buffers contain a mixture of a weak acid with its salt of a strong base, whereas a mixture of a weak base with its salt of a strong acid gives an alkaline buffer.

Periodicity: Properties of the Elements

At first glance, the chemical elements seem to show a bewildering variety of properties. For example, if we arrange the elements in order of atomic number, then we find the totally inert gas neon 'sandwiched' between two of the most reactive elements, fluorine and sodium.

The Periodic Table which we use today resulted from the work of Mendeleev and others during the second half of the nineteenth century. They tried to classify the known elements on the basis of their physical and chemical properties. When the elements are arranged in order of atomic number many of their properties show a regular variation which repeats itself 'periodically'. We shall explain the form and construction of the modern Periodic Table and the properties of the individual elements in terms of atomic structure, which was unknown to the pioneers in this field.

Without doubt, the periodic classification of the elements is one of the greatest achievements in chemistry. A working knowledge of the material in chapters 19 and 20 gives us a theoretical framework within which to build up the detailed chemistry of the elements. From the well-defined trends, which we shall point out, it is also possible to predict, with a fair degree of confidence, the properties of any unfamiliar element from its position in the table.

Time spent in studying periodicity will certainly help to make inorganic chemistry seem clearer, more logical and therefore much simpler to understand and remember. You will find this part of the book easier to follow if you are familiar with the arrangement of electrons in atoms, covered in chapter 3.

19.1 The Periodic Table: atomic number and electron configuration

The elements are laid out in the Periodic Table, shown in figure 19.1, in the following way.

▶   They are in order of increasing atomic number.
▶   A new row is started when electrons start to enter a new principal energy level.
▶   Elements whose atoms have a similar electron configuration are placed in vertical columns.

We may subdivide the elements in the table in a number of ways, illustrated in figure 19.1:

▶   into to 's', 'p', 'd' and 'f' **blocks**. Within any block the final electron to be added to an atom enters a sub-level of the type shown by the block letter.
▶   into vertical columns, referred to as **groups**. *Elements in any particular group have similar outer electron configurations.* Subdivision into groups is particularly useful in the 's' and 'p' blocks.
▶   into horizontal rows, known as **periods**. *In any period, all the atoms have their 'outer' electrons in the same principal energy level.*

Figure 19.1 *Sub-divisions of the Periodic Table*

's' block — 'd' block — 'p' block

Group / Period	I	II											III	IV	V	VI	VII	0
1	1 H Hydrogen 1.0																	2 He Helium 4.0
2	3 Li Lithium 6.9	4 Be Beryllium 9.0											5 B Boron 10.8	6 C Carbon 12.0	7 N Nitrogen 14.0	8 O Oxygen 16.0	9 F Fluorine 19.0	10 Ne Neon 20.2
3	11 Na Sodium 23.0	12 Mg Magnesium 24.3											13 Al Aluminium 27.0	14 Si Silicon 28.1	15 P Phosphorus 31.0	16 S Sulphur 32.1	17 Cl Chlorine 35.5	18 Ar Argon 39.9
4	19 K Potassium 39.1	20 Ca Calcium 40.1	21 Sc Scandium 45.0	22 Ti Titanium 47.9	23 V Vanadium 50.9	24 Cr Chromium 52.0	25 Mn Manganese 54.9	26 Fe Iron 55.9	27 Co Cobalt 58.9	28 Ni Nickel 58.7	29 Cu Copper 63.5	30 Zn Zinc 65.4	31 Ga Gallium 69.7	32 Ge Germanium 72.6	33 As Arsenic 74.9	34 Se Selenium 79.0	35 Br Bromine 79.9	36 Kr Krypton 83.8
5	37 Rb Rubidium 85.5	38 Sr Strontium 87.6	39 Y Yttrium 88.9	40 Zr Zirconium 91.2	41 Nb Niobium 92.9	42 Mo Molybdenum 95.9	43 Tc Technetium (99)	44 Ru Ruthenium 101.1	45 Rh Rhodium 02.9	46 Pd Palladium 106.4	47 Ag Silver 107.9	48 Cd Cadmium 112.4	49 In Indium 114.8	50 Sn Tin 118.7	51 Sb Antimony 121.8	52 Te Tellurium 127.6	53 I Iodine 126.9	54 Xe Xenon 131.3
6	55 Cs Caesium 132.9	56 Ba Barium 137.3	57 La Lanthanum 138.9	72 Hf Hafnium 178.5	73 Ta Tantalum 178.5	74 W Tungsten 183.9	75 Re Rhenium 186.2	76 Os Osmium 190.2	77 Ir Iridium 192.2	78 Pt Platinum 195.1	79 Au Gold 197.0	80 Hg Mercury 200.6	81 Ti Thallium 204.4	82 Pb Lead 207.2	83 Bi Bismuth 209.0	84 Po Polonium (210)	85 At Astatine (210)	86 Rn Radon (223)
7	87 Fr Francium (223)	88 Ra Radium (226)	Ac Actinium (226)	104 Unq Unnil-quadium (261)	105 Unp Unnil-pentium (262)	106 Unh Unnil-hexium (263)												

'f' block

58–71 lanthanum series	58 Ce Cerium 140.1	59 Pr Praseo-dymium 140.9	60 Nd Neodymium (144.2)	61 Pm Promethium (147)	62 Sm Samarium 150.4	63 Eu Europium 152.0	64 Gd Gadolinium 157.3	65 Tb Terbium 158.9	66 Dy Dysprosium 162.5	67 Ho Holmium 164.9	68 Er Erbium 167.3	69 Tm Thulium 168.9	70 Yb Ytterbium 173.0	71 Lu Lutetium 175.0
90–103 actinium series	90 Th Thorium 232.0	91 Pa Protoactinium (231)	92 U Uranium 238.1	93 Np Neptunium (237)	94 Pu Plutonium (242)	95 Am Americium (243)	96 Cm Curium (247)	97 Bk Berkelium (251)	98 Cf Californium (251)	99 Es Einsteinium (254)	100 Fm Fermium (253)	101 Md Mendelevium (256)	102 No Nobelium (254)	103 Lr Lawrencium (257)

Key

atomic number
symbol
name
relative atomic mass

19.2 Atomic properties and bulk properties

In sections 19.3 to 19.8, we shall deal with properties of the elements which depend only upon the *structure of their atoms*. The variation in these **atomic properties** may be explained purely in terms of single isolated atoms.

Many of the most commonly measured physical properties, e.g. density, melting point and boiling point, do not depend only upon the characteristics of the separate atoms but also upon how they are linked or combined together into the *structure of the element*. These properties, which we shall refer to as **bulk properties,** are discussed in sections 19.9 and 19.10.

19.3 Atomic size: covalent, metallic, ionic and van der Waals' radii

We must first decide exactly what we mean by the 'size' of an atom, since this is not so straightforward as we might at first think. In chapter 3, we pointed out that the electrons within an atom occupy regions of space known as **orbitals**. We can never be absolutely certain where a given electron will be, so we generally limit the 'size' of an orbital to a region of space within which there is a certain probability of finding an electron in a particular energy level. But what 'probability' is acceptable? Shall we insist on 99% or will 95% or 90% do? (Figure 19.2.)

Clearly the 'size' of the atom, in these terms, will depend upon how we choose to describe the orbitals and would be very difficult to determine experimentally. A more practical approach is to determine the space which an atom *appears* to occupy in any structure.

Using the X-ray or electron diffraction techniques described in section 6.4, it is possible to determine the **internuclear distances** in any substance quite precisely. Assuming atoms to be spherical, we may 'interpret' the results as shown in the examples in figure 19.3. **Atomic radius** *is then defined as half the shortest internuclear distance found in the structure of the element.* Even then we must be a little more precise, since the observed 'radius' of the atom depends upon how it bonds or interacts with its neighbours. In a simple covalent structure such as iodine, shown in figure 19.3a, pairs of atoms are linked by a single covalent bond. The **covalent radius** of the iodine atom is defined as half the internuclear distance between iodine atoms which are bonded together. Note, however, that we might also define 'size' in terms of atoms which are not bonded to each other. The **van der Waals' radius** is defined as *half the shortest internuclear distance found between similar non-bonded atoms.* In a metal structure, such as that shown in figure 19.3b, the **metallic radius** is defined as *half the shortest internuclear distance.*

The question now arises, which of these three measures of atomic size do we use? Metallic radius is obviously restricted to those elements which form metallic lattices. Covalent radius may be measured for most elements, since even metals in the vapour phase often exist as diatomic molecules. Van der Waals' radius is most easily determined for non-metals, and is particularly useful for the lighter noble gases which do not form chemical bonds. As you can see from table 19.1, the three atomic radii have *different* values for the same element. In general the covalent radius is the smallest and the van der Waals' radius by far the largest. In comparing the 'size' of different atoms, therefore, we should always consider the *same type* of measurement.

Whichever measure of atomic radius we choose, the graph shown in figure 19.4 reveals the following definite trends within the Periodic Table.

▶ *On crossing a period, atomic radius generally decreases.*
This contraction is caused by the steadily increasing nuclear charge exerting a greater attraction on the outer electrons which occupy the same principal energy level. This trend is less marked in the 'd' block and, in fact, there is a slight rise towards the end of a transition series.

Figure 19.2 *How big is an atom?*

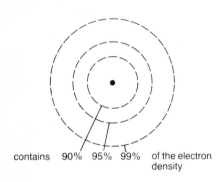

contains 90% 95% 99% of the electron density

Figure 19.3 *Interpretation of internuclear distances, found by X-ray diffraction results, in terms of atomic radii*

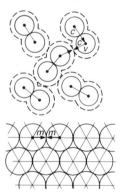

c = covalent radius half the internuclear distance between similar atoms joined by a covalent bond

v = van der Waals padius half the internuclear distance between non-bonded similar atoms at their closest approach

m = metallic radius hald the shortest internuclear distance in a metallic crystal lattice

	H	He
(i)	–	–
(ii)	0.037	–
	(0.12)	

	Li	Be		B	C	N	O	F	Ne
(i)	0.152	0.112		–	–	–	–	–	–
(ii)	0.123	0.089		0.080	0.077	0.074	0.074	0.072	–
						(0.15)	(0.140)	(0.135)	(0.160)

	Na	Mg		Al	Si	P	S	Cl	Ar
(i)	0.186	0.160		0.143					
(ii)	0.157	0.136		0.125	0.117	0.110	0.104	0.099	–
						(0.19)	(0.185)	(0.180)	(0.192)

	K	Ca	Sc	Ti	V	Cr	Mn	Fe	Co	Ni	Cu	Zn	Ga	Ge	As	Se	Br	Kr
(i)	0.231	0.197	0.160	0.146	0.131	0.125	0.129	0.126	0.125	0.124	0.128	0.133	0.141	–	–	–	–	–
(ii)	0.203	0.174	0.144	0.132	0.122	0.117	0.117	0.116	0.116	0.115	0.117	0.125	0.125	0.122	0.121	0.117	0.114	–
															(0.20)	(0.200)	(0.195)	(0.197)

	Rb	Sr	Y	Zr	Nb	Mo	Te	Ru	Rh	Pd	Ag	Cd	In	Sn	Sb	Te	I	Xe
(i)	0.244	0.215	0.180	0.157	0.141	0.136	0.135	0.133	0.134	0.138	0.144	0.149	0.166	0.162	–	–	–	–
(ii)	0.216	0.191	0.162	0.145	0.134	0.129	–	0.124	0.125	0.128	0.134	0.141	0.150	0.140	0.141	0.137	0.133	–
															(0.22)	(0.22)	(0.215)	(0.217)

	Cs	Ba	La	Hf	Ta	W	Re	Os	Ir	Pt	Au	Hg	Tl	Pb	Bi	Po	At	Rn
(i)	0.262	0.217	0.188	0.157	0.143	0.137	0.137	0.134	0.135	0.138	0.144	0.152	0.171	0.175	0.170	0.14	–	–
(ii)	0.235	0.198	0.169	0.144	0.134	0.130	0.128	0.126	0.126	0.129	0.134	0.144	0.155	0.154	0.152	–	0.140	–

	Fr	Ra	Ac
(i)	0.27	0.220	0.20
(ii)	–	–	–

Table 19.1 *Metallic, covalent and van der Waals' radii*

(i) metallic radius/nm
(ii) single bond covalent radius/nm
The figure in parentheses is the van der Waals' radius/nm

Figure 19.4 *Periodicity in atomic radius*

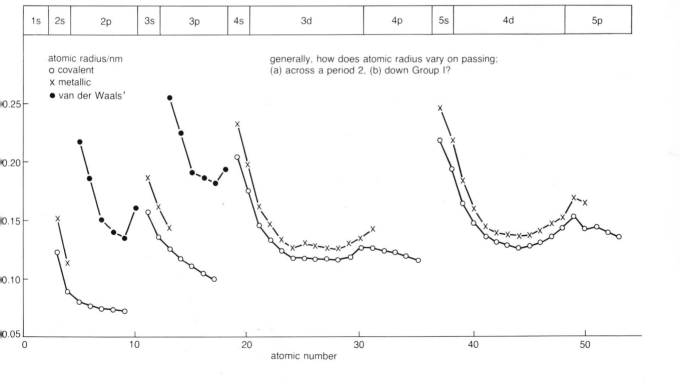

▷ *On descending a group, atomic size increases.*
Although nuclear charge increases on passing down a group, the outer electrons are entering a new principal quantum level. There are also more inner electrons to 'screen' the outer electrons from the attraction of the nucleus.

In the fourth period, K–Kr, there are an extra ten elements of the first transition series between group II and group III. Since atomic size generally decreases on passing across the 'd' block, this means that there is less difference in size than might be expected between the second and third elements in 'p' block groups. This effect is known as the **'d' block contraction** and is shown by the covalent radii in figure 19.5.

Figure 19.5 *The 'd' block contraction*

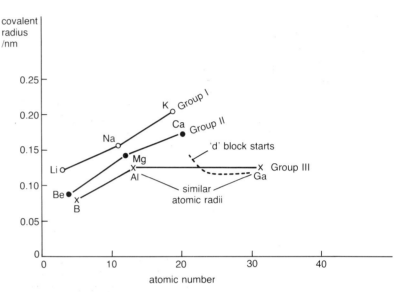

Figure 19.6 *Internuclear distance = cation radius (r_C) + anion radius (r_A)*

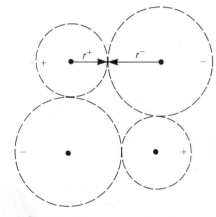

Before leaving this subject, it is worth considering what happens to the size of an atom when it forms an ion. The internuclear distances found from X-ray diffraction studies give us the *sum* of the radii of the cation and anion (figure 19.6). By comparing the internuclear distances for a whole range of compounds we may establish the radii of the individual ions. Figure 19.7 shows the covalent radii of the elements in the third period, Na–Ar, together with the radii of their ions. You should note that:

▷ *positive ions are always smaller than their parent atoms;*
▷ *negative ions are always larger than their parent atoms;*
▷ *the relative difference in size between an atom and its ion increases with the charge on the ion.*

We can explain this in terms of the attraction of the nucleus for the outer electrons of the ion. A cation has fewer electrons than the atom, so the nucleus attracts them more strongly causing a reduction in size. An anion has more electrons than the atom, so the attraction of the nucleus for each electron is reduced, resulting in expansion.

A knowledge of the way in which atomic and ionic size changes within the Periodic Table is important in explaining many other properties.

19.4   Ionisation energies: metallic character

We have already touched on the periodicity in first ionisation energy in section 3.7 as evidence for the existence of electronic energy sub-levels in atoms. If you remember, the first ionisation energy of an element, $\Delta H_i(1)$, is defined as the enthalpy change on converting one mole of gaseous atoms into one mole of gaseous unipositive ions,

$$M(g) \rightarrow M^+(g) + e^-   \Delta H_i(1)$$

Figure 19.7 *Comparison of covalent and ionic radii in period 3*

Ar, Cl⁻, S²⁻, K⁻ and Ca²⁺ have the same arrangement of electrons. Place these particles in order of increasing size.

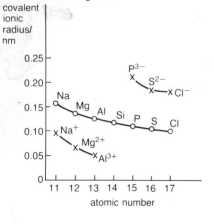

A graph of the first ionisation energy of the first 54 elements against atomic number is shown in figure 19.8. The main points to note are:

▶ *ionisation energy generally increases on passing from left to right across a period;*
▶ *ionisation energy generally decreases on passing down a group.*

Figure 19.8   *Variation in first ionisation energy for the first 54 elements*

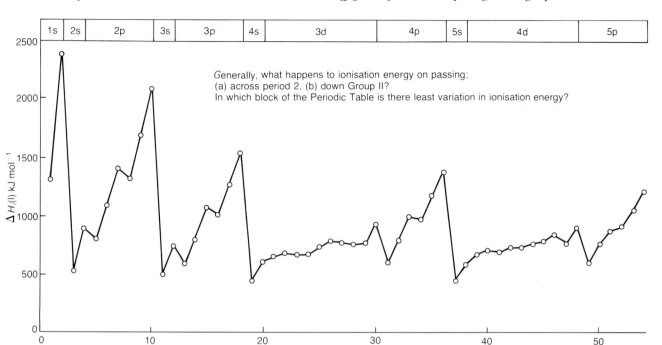

Generally, what happens to ionisation energy on passing:
(a) across period 2, (b) down Group II?
In which block of the Periodic Table is there least variation in ionisation energy?

We may explain these trends in terms of the changes in nuclear charge, atomic radius and the number of inner electrons in the atom, summarised in figure 19.9. First ionisation energy is clearly directly related to the attraction of the nucleus for the most loosely bound electron. On passing across a period, the nuclear charge steadily *increases* and the atomic radius *falls*. Both of these changes *increase* the nuclear attraction, resulting in an *increase* in ionisation energy.

You will notice that *ionisation energy does not, however, increase smoothly on passing across a period*. The three 'breaks' in the ionisation energy graph on passing across the second period, Li (atomic number 3) to fluorine (atomic number 10), are due to the existence of '*s*' and '*p*' *sub-levels* (figure 19.10). Boron has a lower *first* ionisation energy than beryllium because its outer electron is in the 2p sub-level which is less tightly held than a 2s electron. The drop in $\Delta H_i(l)$ at oxygen is due to electrons starting to '*pair up*' in 2p orbitals. Mutual repulsion will make a paired electron rather easier to remove.

Although on passing down a group the nuclear charge *increases*, the outer

Figure 19.9   *Variation in first ionisation energy on passing across a period and down a group*

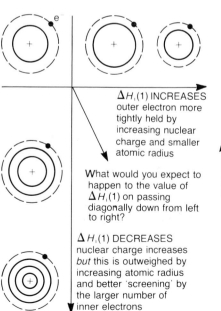

$\Delta H_i(1)$ INCREASES
outer electron more tightly held by increasing nuclear charge and smaller atomic radius

What would you expect to happen to the value of $\Delta H_i(1)$ on passing diagonally down from left to right?

$\Delta H_i(1)$ DECREASES
nuclear charge increases *but* this is outweighed by increasing atomic radius and better 'screening' by the larger number of inner electrons

Figure 19.10   *Ionisation energy does not increase smoothly across a period*

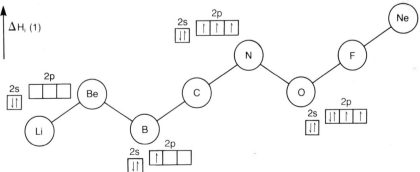

NON-METALS

METALS

SEMI-METALS

1	2	3	4	5	6	7	8	9	10	11	12	13	14	15	16	17	18
1 H 10																	2 He 4.0
3 Li 69	4 Be 90											5 B 10.8	6 C 12.0	7 N 14.0	8 O 16.0	9 F 19.0	10 Ne 20.2
11 Na 23.0	12 Mg 24.3											13 Al 27.0	14 Si 28.1	15 P 31.0	16 S 32.1	17 Cl 35.5	18 Ar 39.9
19 K 39.1	20 Ca 40.1	21 Sc 45.0	22 Ti 47.9	23 V 50.9	24 Cr 52.0	25 Mn 54.9	26 Fe 55.9	27 Co 58.9	28 Ni 56.7	29 Cu 63.5	30 Zn 65.4	31 Ga 69.7	32 Ge 72.6	33 As 74.9	34 Se 79.0	35 Br 79.9	36 Kr 83.8
37 Rb 85.5	38 Sr 87.6	39 Y 88.9	40 Zr 91.2	41 Nb 92.9	42 Mo 95.9	43 Tc (99)	44 Ru 101.1	45 Rh 102.9	46 Pd 106.4	47 Ag 107.9	48 Cd 112.4	49 In 114.8	50 Sn 118.7	51 Sb 121.8	52 Te 127.6	53 I 126.9	54 Xe 131.3
55 Cs 132.9	56 Ba 137.3	57 La 136.9	72 Hf 178.5	73 Ta 178.5	74 W 183.9	75 Re 186.2	76 Os 190.2	77 Ir 192.2	78 Pt 195.1	79 Au 197.0	80 Hg 200.6	81 Ti 204.4	82 Pb 207.2	83 Bi 209.0	84 Po (210)	85 At (210)	86 Rn (223)
87 Fr (223)	88 Ra (226)	Ac (226)	104 Unq (261)	105 Unp (262)	106 Unh (263)												

58–71 lanthanum series

58 Ce 140.1	59 Pr 140.9	60 Nd (144.2)	61 Pm (147)	62 Sm 150.4	63 Eu 152.0	64 Gd 157.3	65 Tb 158.9	66 Dy 162.5	67 Ho 164.9	68 Er 167.3	69 Tm 168.9	70 Yb 173.0	71 Lu 175.0

90–103 actinium series

90 Th 232.0	91 Pa (231)	92 U 236.1	93 Np (237)	94 Pu (242)	95 Am (243)	96 Cm (247)	97 Bk (251)	98 Cf (251)	99 Es (254)	100 Fm (253)	101 Md (256)	102 No (254)	103 Lr (257)

Figure 19.11 *Metallic character in the Periodic Table*

electrons are *further away* from the nucleus and are better **screened** from its attraction by the increased number of inner electrons. Hence the ionisation energy *falls*.

The above effects are much less marked in the 'd' block. Their *fairly constant* ionisation energies result from the following factors.

▶ Atomic size decreases only slightly on passing across a transition series.
▶ Electrons are filling into an inner 'd' sub-level which helps to screen the most loosely bound outer 's' electrons from the increased attraction of the nucleus.

Now, in section 5.8, we described the structure of metals as consisting of positive ions held together by free valency electrons. Clearly, the *more loosely bound* the outer electrons are, i.e. the *lower* the ionisation energy, the easier it will be for the element to adopt a **metallic lattice** structure. As expected, metallic 'character' *decreases* on passing from left to right across the Periodic Table, but *increases* on passing down any group, as shown by figure 19.11. This has important consequences for the properties of compounds which will be dealt with in the next chapter.

19.5 Electron affinity

The first electron affinity of an element is defined as *the enthalpy change on converting one mole of gaseous atoms into gaseous uninegative ions*:

$$X(g) + e^- \rightarrow X^-(g) \quad \Delta H_e(1) \text{ (electron affinity)}$$

Electron affinity is difficult to measure, but from values below we can see that:

▶ on passing across a period from left to right, atoms attract an extra electron more easily (electron affinity tends to become more exothermic);
▶ the ability to attract an electron decreases on passing down a group.

First electron affinities of some elements (kJ mol^{-1})

N −3	O −142	F −348
		Cl −364
		Br −342
		I −314

As we might have expected, these trends are exactly opposite to those found for first ionisation energies. The ability to attract an extra electron will increase as nuclear charge increases and atomic radius falls (i.e. across a period), but will decrease as the number of inner 'screening' electrons rises (i.e. down a group).

You may have noticed that *the electron affinity of fluorine is less exothermic than expected.* Since it has a small atom, its electrons are densely packed and will strongly repel an incoming electron before it feels the attraction from the nucleus. Considerable energy must be supplied to force the extra electron close enough to be captured by the nucleus and so the overall energy released is lower.

Further addition of electrons to gaseous anions gives rise to successive electron affinities for elements. The *second* electron affinity of oxygen is the enthalpy change for the process:

$$O^-(g) + e^- \rightarrow O^{2-}(g) \quad \Delta H_e(2) = +790 \text{kJ mol}^{-1}$$

The second electron affinities of all elements are endothermic since energy must be supplied to overcome the repulsion between the negative ion and the incoming electron.

19.6 Electronegativity

We used the idea of electronegativity in section 5.9 to explain bond polarity. Whereas electron affinity is related to the ease with which an atom completely captures an extra electron to form a negative ion, **electronegativity** *measures the attraction of the nucleus of an atom for the electrons in a covalent bond.*

Figure 19.12 shows a graph of electronegativity plotted against atomic number. As you can see, electronegativity generally *increases* on passing from left to right *across a period* but *decreases* on passing *down any group*. Again we may explain these trends by considering how nuclear charge, atomic size and the screening effect of inner electrons vary with position in the Periodic Table.

On passing across a period, the nuclear charge steadily increases and atomic radius falls. Both of these effects result in increased attraction of the nucleus for bonding electrons, i.e. an increase in electronegativity. Although, on passing down a group, nuclear charge increases, this effect is outweighed by the increase in both atomic radius and the number of inner electrons 'screening' the bonding electrons from the attraction of the nucleus, causing the electronegativity to decrease.

Figure 19.12   *Electronegativities of the first 54 elements*

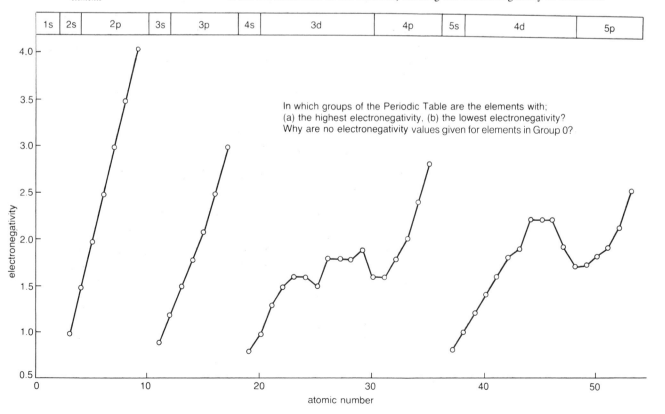

In which groups of the Periodic Table are the elements with;
(a) the highest electronegativity, (b) the lowest electronegativity?
Why are no electronegativity values given for elements in Group 0?

19.7 Oxidation states

We defined **oxidation state** or **number** in section 17.1 as *the number of electrons which an atom loses, or tends to lose, when it forms a particular compound.* Negative values indicate a tendency to gain electrons. Some of the common oxidation states of the first 54 elements are shown in figure 19.13. Of course, all elements show an oxidation state of zero when uncombined.

Figure 19.13 *Common oxidation numbers shown by the first 54 elements*

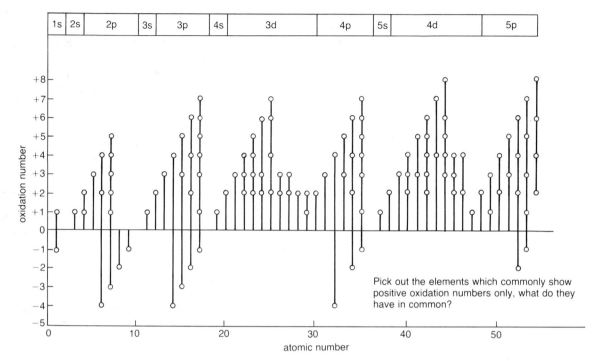

Pick out the elements which commonly show positive oxidation numbers only, what do they have in common?

Oxidation number will clearly be related to the number of valency electrons in an atom, and as we might expect, the oxidation numbers exhibited by elements in the same group tend to be similar. On passing across a period from Group I to Group VII, the elements tend to show a greater variety in oxidation state, and negative values become more common. We shall consider the differences between metals and non-metals in each of the 's', 'p' and 'd' blocks of the Periodic Table.

Metals

Referring to figure 19.13, we can see that metals commonly show *positive* oxidation states only, i.e. their atoms lose, or tend to lose, electrons, on forming compounds. This is to be expected since the ionisation energies and electronegativities of metals are *low*.

The metals in the 's' block, i.e. in Groups I and II only, show an oxidation number equal to the group number. The atoms form positive ions by losing their outer 's' electrons, e.g.

$$\text{sodium chloride NaCl,} \quad \text{magnesium oxide MgO}$$
$$+1 \qquad\qquad\qquad +2$$

In the 'p' block again, metals generally show a *maximum* oxidation state equal to the group number, i.e. they may lose, or tend to lose, all of their valency electrons, e.g.

$$TlF_3, \quad SnF_4 \quad \text{and} \quad BiF_5$$
$$+3 \qquad +4 \qquad\qquad +5$$

The degree of covalency in the bonding increases with oxidation number (see Fajan's Rules, section 5.10).

On passing across the 'p' block, however, there is an increasing tendency for the elements near the bottom of the Periodic Table to show an oxidation state of *two less* than the group number. This is the so called **inert pair effect** *where the outer 's' electrons of the atom are reluctant to take part in chemical bonding*, e.g.

$$TlCl, \quad SnCl_2, \quad and \quad BiCl_3$$
$$+1 \qquad +2 \qquad\qquad +3$$

The 'inert pair' effect will be considered more fully with the detailed chemistry of Group IV in section 24.3.

The 'd' block metals show the greatest variation in oxidation number. They may use electrons from the inner d sub-level as well as the outer s orbital in forming compounds. Generally, the widest range of oxidation number is found near the middle of the 'd' block. Manganese, for example, commonly shows oxidation states between +2 (only 4s electrons used) and +7 (all 3d electrons used as well as 4s), e.g.

$$MnCl_2 \qquad MnO_2, \qquad K_2MnO_4 \qquad KMnO_4$$
$$+2 \qquad\quad +4 \qquad\quad\;\; +6 \qquad\qquad +7$$

Non-metals

The only non-metal in the 's' block which forms chemical compounds is hydrogen. It shows an oxidation number of +1 or −1 depending upon the electronegativity of the element with which it combines, e.g.

$$HCl, \quad NaH$$
$$+1 \qquad -1$$

When non-metals in the 'p' block combine with *more electronegative* elements, they may use *all* their outer electrons in bond formation and show a *positive* oxidation state equal to the group number, e.g.

$$SiO_2, \quad P_2O_5 \quad SO_3, \quad Cl_2O_7$$
$$+4 \qquad +5 \qquad +6 \qquad +7$$

Lower positive oxidation states may also occur, when the atom retains some of its valency electrons as non-bonding lone pairs, e.g.

$$P_2O_3, \qquad SO_2, \; HClO_3$$
$$+3 \qquad\quad +4 \qquad +5$$

$$SCl_2, \; HClO_2$$
$$+2 \qquad +3$$

$$HClO$$
$$+1$$

When a non-metal combines with a *less electronegative* element it will show a *negative* oxidation state. Since it will generally gain, or attempt to gain, electrons to achieve a noble gas configuration, these negative oxidation states are generally equal to (8 − group number), e.g.

$$CH_4, \quad NH_3, \; H_2O, \quad HF$$
$$-4 \qquad -3 \qquad -2 \qquad -1$$

Fluorine is a somewhat special case. Since it is the *most electronegative* element, it can *only* show an oxidation state of −1. Similarly, oxygen, which is also very electronegative *generally* shows an oxidation state of −2. This difference between the first member of a 'p' block group and the rest of the elements will be studied more closely in chapter 20.

Figure 19.14 *Origin of the diagonal relationship in the Periodic Table*

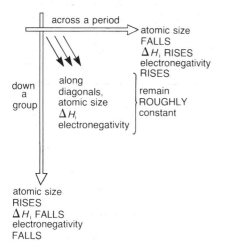

across a period → atomic size FALLS ΔH_i RISES electronegativity RISES

along diagonals, atomic size ΔH_i electronegativity remain ROUGHLY constant

down a group

atomic size RISES ΔH_i FALLS electronegativity FALLS

19.8 The diagonal relationship

We have seen that the trend in any atomic property on passing from left to right across the Periodic Table is generally *counterbalanced* by an opposite trend on passing from top to bottom. It follows, therefore, that along any diagonal line running from top left to bottom right in the Periodic Table the elements will have *similar* atomic sizes, ionisation energies and electronegativities, as shown in figure 19.14. We have already seen some evidence for such 'diagonal' relationships in figure 19.11, which shows the dividing line between metals and non-metals in the Periodic Table. The relationship is particularly marked towards the *top left* of the Periodic Table, i.e. before the appearance of the 'd' block elements. More detailed reference to the similarities between the following pairs of elements,

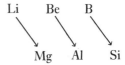

Li Be B

Mg Al Si

will be made in chapter 20 and in the sections dealing with the detailed chemistry of the main groups.

19.9 Atomic volume and density

The *actual* 'volume' of an *isolated* atom is clearly related to its radius. As such it will *decrease* steadily on passing across a period and *rise* on passing down a group. *The term* **atomic volume,** *however, does not refer to individual atoms, but is defined as the volume occupied by one mole of atoms of the element in the liquid or solid state.* It might be better called 'molar' volume, but this term is reserved for gases. Since it is a 'bulk' property, atomic volume depends largely upon *how closely packed* the atoms are in the structure of the element. Thus small atoms which are widely spaced will have a *larger* atomic volume than bigger atoms which are closely packed together (figure 19.15).

The solid line in figure 19.16 shows the variation in atomic volume of the first 54 elements. By and large, for the 's' and 'd' block elements, the trends follow the

Figure 19.15 *How structure influences 'atomic volume'*

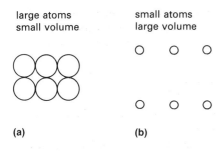

large atoms small volume

small atoms large volume

(a)   (b)

Figure 19.16 *Periodicity in atomic volume*

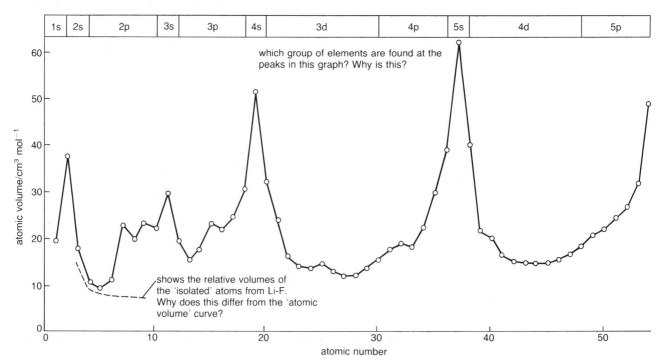

which group of elements are found at the peaks in this graph? Why is this?

shows the relative volumes of the 'isolated' atoms from Li–F. Why does this differ from the 'atomic volume' curve?

atomic volume/cm³ mol⁻¹

atomic number

variation in the calculated volumes of the *individual* atoms, i.e. *increase* on passing down a group and *decrease* on passing across a period. All of these elements have a *metallic structure* in which the atoms are *packed closely together* and the dominant feature is the variation in *atomic radius*. In the 'p' block, apart from macromolecular structures such as carbon, the elements consist of *separate small covalent molecules* which are *widely spaced* and thus their atomic volumes are quite *high*.

Let us consider the elements of the second period, lithium to neon (table 19.2).

Table 19.2 *Relating atomic volume to an element's structure*

	Li	Be	B	C*	N	O	F	Ne
atomic volume/ cm³ mol⁻¹	13.1	4.87	4.61	3.42	17.3	13.9	17.1	16.8
covalent radius/ nm	0.123	0.89	0.080	0.077	0.074	0.074	0.072	–
type of structure	<metallic>		<macromolecule>		N₂ <simple	O₂ small	F₂ molecules>	Ne
space between particles	←————small————→				←————large————→			

atomic volume/ cm^3 mol^{-1} — N_2 O_2 F_2 Ne — <simple small molecules>

*diamond

The *sharp rise* in atomic volume between carbon and nitrogen can be seen to be due to a change from a close-packed structure to widely spaced separate molecules.

The density of an element in the solid or liquid state is *inversely* related to atomic volume:

$$\text{density} = \frac{\text{mass of one mole}}{\text{atomic volume}}$$

As shown in figure 19.17, the variation in density with position in the Periodic Table is thus exactly opposite to that of atomic volume;

▶ *those elements which have the highest atomic volumes, e.g. the alkali metals and simple covalent structures, have the lowest densities;* whereas,

▶ *the elements with small atomic volumes, e.g. the transition metals, are among the densest.* In fact the element with the highest density of all, 22.5 g cm⁻³, is osmium in the 'd' block.

Figure 19.17 *Densities of the first 54 elements (liquid or solid state as appropriate)*

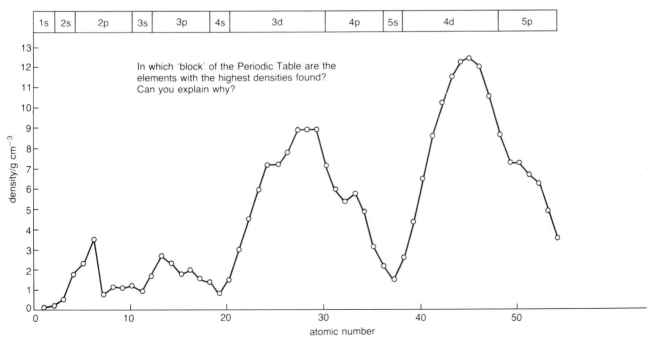

In which 'block' of the Periodic Table are the elements with the highest densities found? Can you explain why?

19.10 Melting point, boiling point, enthalpies of fusion and vaporisation

All of these quantities are concerned with changes of physical state, i.e. between solid, liquid and gas. If enough heat energy is supplied to a solid, then the regular lattice arrangement will break down and, when the particles are able to slide past each other, melting occurs. The temperature at which this occurs is the **melting point** and *the amount of energy which must be supplied to convert one mole of the solid at its melting point into liquid at the same temperature is the* **molar enthalpy of fusion**. Clearly, both these quantities are dependent upon the strength of the attractive forces between the particles making up the structure. Figure 19.18 shows the variation in both melting point and the molar enthalpy of fusion for the first 54 elements.

Figure 19.18 *Variation in melting point and enthalpy of fusion for the first 54 elements*

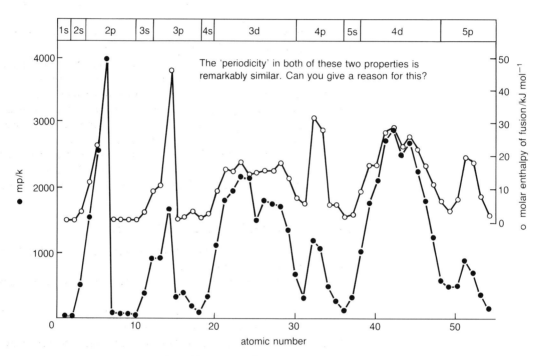

It is interesting to note that the form of both of these graphs compares quite closely with that for density in figure 19.17 and we may use structural arguments similar to those developed in the last section to account for this. Again taking the period from lithium to neon:

▶ Lithium and beryllium both have a metallic structure in which positive ions are held together by mobile valency electrons. Beryllium has a *higher* melting point than lithium since it has *more* outer electrons which can be used in binding.

▶ Boron and carbon have macromolecular covalent structures, where each atom is *strongly bonded* to *all* its neighbours. Considerable energy is required to break these bonds, so again the melting points of these elements are *very high*.

▶ The remaining elements in the period, i.e. nitrogen to neon, have very *low* melting points. Their structures contain simple, small covalent molecules held together only by weak van der Waals' attractive forces. *It is very important to realise that when such elements are melted, covalent bonds are not broken and that the molecules remain intact.*

Boiling point and **molar enthalpy of vaporisation,** *i.e. the enthalpy change on converting one mole of liquid to one mole of vapour at the boiling point*, again depend upon the forces of attraction between the particles in the structure. The periodic variation in these properties, shown in figure 19.19, is similar to that described above.

Figure 19.19 *Variation boiling point and enthalpy of fusion for the first 54 elements*

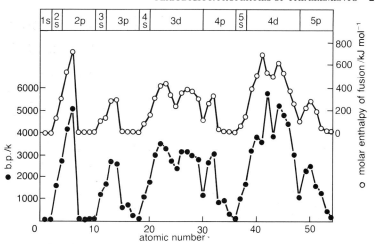

To summarise, *these properties indicate the strength of attraction between the particles in the structure.* We may identify three types of attraction in elements,

▶ **Metallic bonding.** This increases in strength as the atoms become smaller and the number of electrons available for bonding increases. As a result, transition metals tend to have high melting and boiling points.

▶ **Covalent bonding.** This is only important in macromolecular structures. Covalent bond strength generally increases as atomic size decreases and as the number of bonds formed by the atom decreases.

▶ **Van der Waals' forces.** These are weak forces of attraction between separate small covalent molecules (section 8.12). As a rule, such intermolecular attraction will increase with relative molecular mass.

19.11 Summary and revision plan

1 An understanding of **periodicity** helps us to explain and predict the properties of elements and their compounds.

2 The **Periodic Table** consists of the elements arranged in atomic number order and in:

(a) **groups** – vertical columns of generally similar elements where each atom has the same number of outer electrons;

(b) **periods** – horizontal rows where the 'outer' electrons are in the same principal quantum level;

(c) **blocks** – according to the type of sub-level into which the last electron is added in each atom, i.e. 's', 'p', 'd' (and 'f').

3 Some properties (**atomic properties**) of an element depend largely, on the nature of individual atoms. Others, such as melting point and density, are **bulk properties** since they also depend on how the atoms are linked together into a 'structure', e.g. simple molecular, macromolecular or metallic.

The general trends in some 'key' properties on passing across a period and down a group are shown in table 19.3.

Table 19.3 *Trends in some key properties of elements*

Property	across a period	down a group
atomic radius	decreases	increases
ionisation energy	increases	decreases
electronegativity	increases	decreases
metallic character	decreases	increases
maximum oxidation state	increases	similar

4 There are some similarities between certain **diagonally related** elements in the Periodic Table, e.g., lithium and magnesium, beryllium and aluminium.

CHAPTER 20

Periodicity: Properties of Compounds

In this chapter we shall largely restrict ourselves to the compounds of the elements from lithium to argon. We shall be most concerned with the trends on passing across those two periods and with the similarities of the compounds of diagonally related elements. More detailed comparisons of the compounds of the elements within any particular group can be found in chapters 21 to 28.

20.1 Physical properties of the oxides, chlorides and hydrides

Tables 20.1, 20.2 and 20.3 list some of the important physical properties for a range of the oxides, chlorides and hydrides of the elements from lithium to argon.

As we cross both periods, the melting points of the compounds and their electrical conductivity in the liquid state generally *fall*. Both of these trends suggest that *the bonding type is changing from essentially ionic to predominantly covalent*. The unusually high melting points of compounds such as beryllium oxide and silicon oxide indicate a *macromolecular* rather than a simple covalent structure.

Within any particular group, the compounds of the lower elements tend to be somewhat more ionic in character, as shown by the data for the oxides and chlorides of beryllium and magnesium. This trend is quite predictable. The ease with which the elements form simple positive ions is inversely related to their ionisation energies, which decrease on passing down a group.

20.2 Thermal stability of the oxides, chlorides and hydrides

Tables 20.1, 20.2 and 20.3 also show the **standard enthalpies of formation** (section 4.7) for the oxides, chlorides and hydrides respectively. *Negative* values indicate that the compound is *energetically more stable* than its elements, whereas *positive* values show it to be *less stable*.

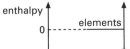

enthalpy

0 ---- elements

Increasingly POSITIVE ΔH_f values: Compounds becoming progressively LESS stable

Increasingly NEGATIVE ΔH_f values: Compounds becoming progressively MORE stable

If we compare the enthalpies of formation *per mole of oxygen or chlorine*, we can see that *the oxides and chlorides tend to become less stable with respect to the elements as we pass from left to right across a period*. Since oxygen and chlorine are both very electronegative elements, they will bond most strongly to the less electronegative elements on the left of the Periodic Table. Compounds with a large positive enthalpy of formation are energetically unstable and will often spontaneously decompose, sometimes explosively, e.g. nitrogen chloride.

$$2NCl_3(l) \rightarrow N_2(g) + 3Cl_2(g)$$

Table 20.1 *Some of the oxides of the elements lithium to argon, showing their enthalpies of formation, melting and boiling points, electrical conductivity in the liquid state and structure*

Element	oxide	$\Delta H_f^{\ominus}$/kJ mol^{-1}	$\Delta H_f^{\ominus}$ per mol of O /kJ	m.p./°C	b.p./°C	electrical conductivity (molten)	structure
lithium	Li_2O	−596	−596	>1000 sublimes	—	yes	ionic
beryllium	BeO	−611	−611	2250	4120	no	macromolecular
boron	B_2O_3	−1264	−421	460	1860	no	macromolecular
carbon	CO	−111	−111	−210	−191	—	simple covalent molecules
	CO_2	−394	−197	−78 sublimes	—	—	
nitrogen	N_2O	+82	+82	−91	−88	no	
	NO	+90	+90	−163	−152	no	
	NO_2	+34	+17	−11	−21	no	
fluorine	F_2O	+23	+23	−224	−145	no	
sodium	Na_2O	−416	−416	920	1275	yes	ionic
	Na_2O_2	−505	−253	460 decomposes	—	yes	
magnesium	MgO	−602	−602	2900	3600	yes	
aluminium	Al_2O_3	−1669	−556	2040	2980	yes	
silicon	SiO_2	−858	−429	1610	2230	no	macromolecular
phosphorus	P_2O_3	−820	−273	24	175	no	simple covalent molecules
	P_2O_5	−1506	−301	300 sublimes	—	no	
sulphur	SO_2	−297	−149	−75	−10	no	
	SO_3	−395	−132	17	45	no	
chlorine	Cl_2O	+76	+76	−20	2	no	
	Cl_2O_7	+265	+38	−59	10	no	

Note: '—' means 'not applicable' in this table and in tables 20.2 and 20.3; '?' means that the value is difficult to determine experimentally.

How is $\Delta H_f^{\ominus}$ related to energetic stability?
What happens to the stability of the oxides on passing across each period?
How and why do the structures of the oxides vary on passing across each period?

Table 20.2 *Some of the chlorides of the elements from lithium to argon showing enthalpy of formation, melting and boiling points, electrical conductivity in the liquid state and structure*

Element	chloride	$\Delta H_f^{\ominus}$/kJ mol^{-1}	$\Delta H_f^{\ominus}$ per mol of Cl /kJ	m.p./°C	b.p./°C	electrical conductivity (molten)	structure
lithium	LiCl	−409	−409	614	1382	yes	ionic
beryllium	$BeCl_2$	−512	−256	410	547	no	macromolecular
boron	BCl_3	−418	−139	−107	13	no	simple covalent molecules
carbon	CCl_4	−139	−35	−23	77	no	
nitrogen	NCl_3	+233	+78	−37	71	no	
oxygen	Cl_2O	+76	+38	−20	2	no	
	Cl_2O_7	+265	+133	−59	10	no	
fluorine	ClF	−56	−56	−154	−101	no	

Table 20.2 *(Continued)*

Element	chloride	$\Delta H_f^\ominus$/kJ mol^{-1}	$\Delta H_f^\ominus$ per mol of Cl /kJ	m.p./°C	b.p./°C	electrical conductivity (molten)	structure
sodium	NaCl	−411	−411	808	1465	yes	ionic
magnesium	$MgCl_2$	−642	−321	714	1418	yes	ionic
aluminium	$AlCl_3$	−695	−232	178 sublimes	—	poor	simple covalent molecules
silicon	$SiCl_4$	−640	−160	−70	57	no	simple covalent molecules
phosphorus	PCl_3	−339	−113	−92	76	no	simple covalent molecules
	PCl_5	−463	−93	160 sublimes	—	no	simple covalent molecules
sulphur	S_2Cl_2	−60	−30	−80	136	no	simple covalent molecules
	SCl_2	?	?	−78	59	no	simple covalent molecules
	SCl_4	?	?	−31	decomposes	no	simple covalent molecules

One of the group V chlorides is explosively unstable. From the above enthalpies of formation which would you expect this to be?

Table 20.3 *Some hydrides of the elements from lithium to argon showing enthalpy of formation, melting and boiling points, electrical conductivity in the liquid state and structure*

Element	hydride	$\Delta H_f^\ominus$/kJ mol^{-1}	$\Delta H_f^\ominus$ per mol of H	m.p./°C	b.p./°C	electrical conductivity (molten)	structure
lithium	LiH	−91	−91	688 decomposes	—	yes	ionic
beryllium	BeH_2	?	?	260 decomposes	—	no	macromolecular?
boron	BH_3	+16	+5	−165	−92	no	simple covalent molecules
carbon	CH_4	−75	−19	−182	−161	no	simple covalent molecules
nitrogen	NH_3	−46	−15	−78	−33	no	simple covalent molecules
oxygen	H_2O	−242	−121	0	100	poor	simple covalent molecules
fluorine	HF	−269	−269	−83	20	poor	simple covalent molecules
sodium	NaH	−57	−57	800 decomposes	—	yes	ionic
magnesium	MgH_2	?	?	700 decomposes	—	?	?
aluminium	AlH_3	?	?	?	?	no	macromolecular?
silicon	SiH_4	−62	−16	−185	−112	no	simple covalent molecules
phosphorus	PH_3	+9	+3	−133	−90	no	simple covalent molecules
sulphur	H_2S	−20	−10	−85	−60	no	simple covalent molecules
chlorine	HCl	−92	−92	−114	−85	no	simple covalent molecules

Which are energetically more stable, the hydrides of period 2 or those of period 3? Check with tables 20.1 and 20.2. to see if the same relative stability is found for the oxides and chlorides.

In the case of the hydrides, the pattern of stability is somewhat different since hydrogen is much *less* electronegative than either oxygen or chlorine. As a result, although the ionic hydrides formed by lithium and sodium are energetically quite stable, *the most stable hydrides are formed by the very electronegative elements on the right of the Periodic Table.*

We must always remember that the enthalpy of formation only indicates the energetic stability of a compound *in comparison with its elements.* A large negative value does not *necessarily* mean that it will be generally unreactive, since it may combine exothermically with other substances. Thus, although the enthalpy of formation of silicon chloride is $-640 \, kJ \, mol^{-1}$, it reacts vigorously with water (see section 20.5).

20.3 Preparation of the oxides, chlorides and hydrides

As we might expect, if a binary compound has an appreciably *negative* enthalpy of formation, then it is usually (but not always) possible to prepare it by **direct combination** of the elements. We can see from the data in tables 20.1 and 20.2 that most of the elements will combine exothermically with both oxygen and chlorine. Even some compounds which are energetically less stable than the elements may be prepared by this method. For example, nitrogen and oxygen in the air will combine to give nitrogen monoxide using the energy from lightning during thunderstorms:

$$N_2(g) + O_2(g) \rightleftharpoons 2NO(g)$$

An electrical storm

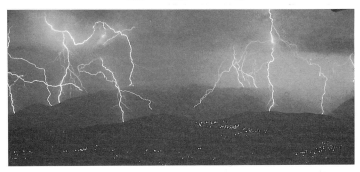

By and large, however, the less stable compounds must be made by **indirect** methods. Nitrogen chloride cannot be made by direct combination of the elements but is formed an explosive oil when chlorine is bubbled through ammonium chloride solution:

$$NH_4Cl(aq) + 3Cl_2(g) \rightarrow NCl_3(l) + 4HCl(aq)$$

Even when direct combination is possible, it may be more *convenient* to use an indirect method of preparation. Thus sodium chloride may be made by burning sodium in chlorine:

$$2Na(s) + Cl_2(g) \rightarrow 2NaCl(s)$$

but it is rather easier to neutralise sodium hydroxide solution with dilute hydrochloric acid and obtain pure sodium chloride by evaporating the water from the solution:

$$NaOH(aq) + HCl(aq) \rightarrow NaCl(aq) + H_2O(l)$$

Tables 20.4, 20.5 and 20.6 indicate which of the oxides, chlorides and hydrides may be made by direct combination. Where appropriate, examples of indirect methods are also outlined. Further details of the preparation of oxides, chlorides and hydrides are given in the chapters dealing with the chemistry of particular groups.

Table 20.4   *Methods of preparing the oxides of the elements from lithium to argon*

Oxide	direct combination?	indirect methods	
Li_2O	yes	$4LiNO_3 \xrightarrow{heat} 2Li_2O + 4NO_2 + O_2$	(a)
BeO	yes		
B_2O_3	yes	$2H_3BO_3 \xrightarrow[c.H_2SO_4]{heat} B_2O_3 + 3H_2O$	(b)
CO	yes (limited O_2)	$HCOOH \xrightarrow{c.H_2SO_4} CO + H_2O$	(b)
CO_2	yes	$CO_3^{2-} + 2H^+ \rightarrow CO_2 + H_2O$	(b)
N_2O	no	$NH_4NO_3 \xrightarrow{heat} N_2O + 2H_2O$	
NO	yes but difficult	$3Cu + 8HNO_3 \rightarrow 3Cu(NO_3)_2 + 2NO + 4H_2O$ (50%)	(c)
NO_2	no	$Cu + 4HNO_3 \rightarrow Cu(NO_3)_2 + 2NO_2 + 2H_2O$ conc.	(c)
OF_2	no	$2F_2 + 2OH^- \rightarrow OF_2 + 2F^- + H_2O$	
Na_2O	yes (limited O_2)		
Na_2O_2	yes (excess O_2)		
MgO	yes	$MgCO_3 \xrightarrow{heat} MgO + CO_2$	(a)
Al_2O_3	yes		
SiO_2	yes		
P_2O_3	yes (limited O_2)		
P_2O_5	yes (excess O_2)		
SO_2	yes	$Cu + 2H_2SO_4 \xrightarrow{heat} CuSO_4 + SO_2 + 2H_2O$ conc.	(c)
SO_3	no	$2SO_2 + O_2 \underset{catalyst}{\overset{heat}{\rightleftharpoons}} 2SO_3$	
Cl_2O	no	$2Cl_2 + 2HgO \rightarrow Cl_2O + HgO.HgCl_2$	
Cl_2O_7	no	$2HClO_4 \xrightarrow{P_2O_5} Cl_2O_7 + H_2O$	(b)

Note general methods for preparation of oxides;
   metal oxides: (a) thermal decomposition of carbonates or nitrates.
non–metal oxides: (b) dehydration of an acid
                  (c) reduction of an acid

Table 20.5   *Preparation of some chlorides of the elements lithium to argon*

Chloride	direct combination?	indirect methods	
$LiCl$	yes	$Li_2O + 2HCl \rightarrow 2LiCl + H_2O$	(a)
$BeCl_2$	yes		
BCl_3	yes		
CCl_4	no	$CS_2 + 3Cl_2 \xrightarrow{I_2} CCl_4 + S_2Cl_2$	(b)
NCl_3	no	$NH_4Cl + 3Cl_2 \rightarrow NCl_3 + 4HCl$	(b)
Cl_2O	no	$2Cl_2 + 2HgO \rightarrow HgCl_2.HgO + Cl_2O$	
Cl_2O_7	no	$2HClO_4(l) \xrightarrow{P_2O_5/distil} Cl_2O_7(l) + H_2O(l)$	
ClF	yes		

Table 20.5 *(continued)*

Chloride	direct combination?	indirect methods	
NaCl	yes	$NaOH + HCl \rightarrow NaCl + H_2O$	(a)
$MgCl_2$	yes	$MgCO_3 + 2HCl \rightarrow MgCl_2 + CO_2 + H_2O$	(a)
$AlCl_3$	yes	$2Al + 6HCl \rightarrow 2AlCl_3 + 3H_2$	(a)
$SiCl_4$	yes	$SiO_2 + 2C + 2Cl_2 \xrightarrow{heat} SiCl_4 + 2CO$	(b)
PCl_3	yes (limited Cl_2)		
PCl_5	yes (excess Cl_2)	$PCl_3 + Cl_2 \xrightarrow{heat} PCl_5$	(c)
S_2Cl_2	yes		
SCl_2	no	$S_2Cl_2 + Cl_2 \rightleftharpoons 2SCl_2$	(c)

Note general methods for the preparation of chlorides:
    metal chlorides: (a) action of hydrochloric acid on the metal, its oxide, hydroxide or carbonate
non-metal chloride: (b) substitution of chlorine atoms for oxygen, sulphur or hydrogen
                 (c) action of chlorine on a lower chloride of the element

Table 20.6 *Preparation of some hydrides of the elements from lithium to argon*

Hydride	direct combination?	indirect methods
LiH	yes	
BeH_2	no	
B_2H_6	no	
CH_4	yes but difficult	$Al_4C_3 + 12H_2O \rightarrow 4Al(OH)_3 + 3CH_4$
NH_3	yes	$Mg_3N_2 + 3H_2O \rightarrow 3MgO + 2NH_3$
H_2O	yes	
HF	yes	$NaF + H_2SO_4 \rightarrow HF + NaHSO_4$
NaH	yes	
MgH_2	yes	
AlH_3	yes	
SiH_4	no	$Mg_2Si + 4H_2O \xrightarrow{acid} 2Mg(OH)_2 + SiH_4$
PH_3	no	$Ca_3P_2 + 6H_2O \rightarrow 3Ca(OH)_2 + 2PH_3$
H_2S	yes	$FeS + 2HCl \rightarrow FeCl_2 + H_2S$
HCl	yes	$NaCl + H_2SO_4 \rightarrow NaHSO_4 + HCl$

Note general methods for preparing hydrides:
    metal hydrides: (a) direct combination
non-metal hydrides: (b) displacement of a metal in a binary compound with
                      hydrogen from water or an acid

20.4 Action of water on the oxides

Table 20.7 shows that *on passing across both of the periods, lithium to neon and sodium to argon, the oxides change in nature from alkaline or basic to acidic.* This trend may be explained in terms of the difference in bonding type in the oxides.

Table 20.7 *Action of water on the oxides of the elements from lithium to argon*

Oxide	solubility in water	reaction with water
Li_2O	soluble – alkaline	$Li_2O + H_2O \rightarrow 2LiOH$
BeO	insoluble (amphoteric)	
B_2O_3	soluble – weakly acidic	$B_2O_3 + 3H_2O \rightarrow 2H_3BO_3$
CO_2	soluble – weakly acidic	$CO_2 + H_2O \rightleftharpoons H_2CO_3$
NO_2	soluble – acidic	$2NO_2 + H_2O \rightarrow HNO_3 + HNO_2$
OF_2	reacts – acidic	$OF_2 + H_2O \rightarrow O_2 + 2HF$
Na_2O	soluble – very alkaline	$Na_2O + H_2O \rightarrow 2NaOH$
MgO	almost insoluble (basic)	
Al_2O_3	insoluble (amphoteric)	
SiO_2	insoluble (acidic)	
P_2O_5	soluble – acidic	$P_2O_5 + H_2O \rightarrow 2HPO_3$
SO_2	soluble – acidic	$SO_2 + H_2O \rightarrow H_2SO_3$
SO_3	soluble – strongly acidic	$SO_3 + H_2O \rightarrow H_2SO_4$
Cl_2O_7	soluble – strongly acidic	$Cl_2O_7 + H_2O \rightarrow 2HClO_4$

How and why does the acid–base nature of the oxides vary on passing across a period?

The oxides of **electropositive metals** are *ionic*, e.g. sodium monoxide, $[Na^+]_2\, O^{2-}$. If the oxide is soluble in water then the O^{2-} ion will react to give hydroxide ions, OH^-, making the solution *alkaline,*

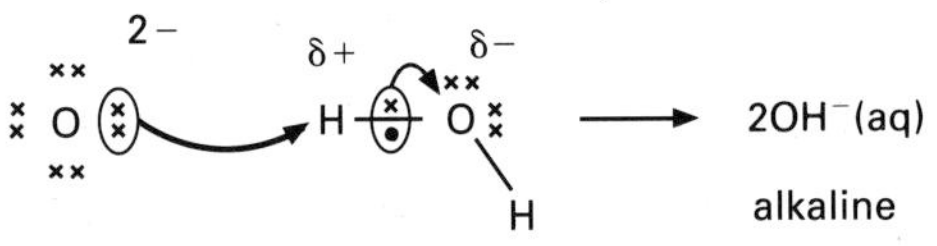

Insoluble metal oxides also act as *bases*, e.g. magnesium oxide will accept protons from acids, forming water.

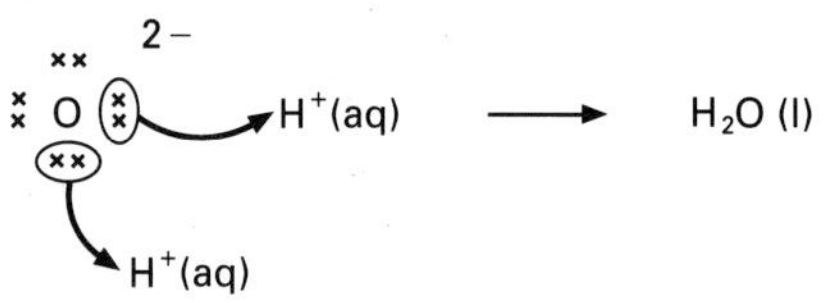

If the metal ion is small and highly charged, it may also react with water molecules, releasing protons, i.e. acting as a **Brønsted–Lowry acid** (section 18.1).

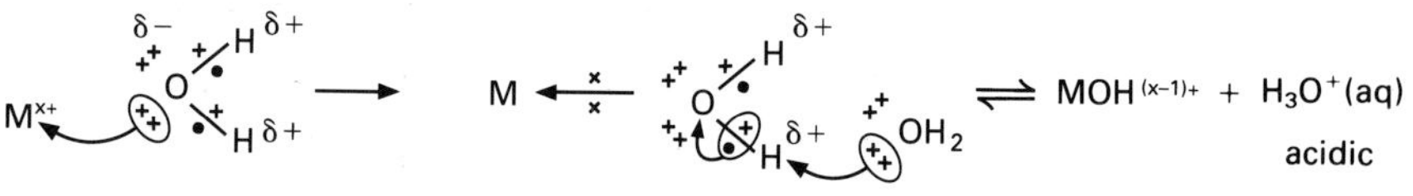

Thus beryllium and aluminium oxides are **amphoteric** and may act as *either bases or acids*, e.g.

$$Al_2O_3(s) + 6HCl(aq) \rightarrow 2AlCl_3(aq) + 3H_2O(l)$$
$$Al_2O_3(s) + 2NaOH(aq) + 3H_2O(l) \rightarrow 2Na[Al(OH)_4](aq)$$

Non–metal oxides are *covalent* in character and since the oxygen atom only carries a slight negative charge it cannot easily act as a proton acceptor. If soluble in water, non–metal oxides hydrate to produce *acids*, e.g. sulphur dioxide, SO_2, may be regarded as the **anhydride** of sulphurous acid, H_2SO_3.

$$H_2O + SO_2 \rightleftharpoons \quad O = S \quad \rightleftharpoons \quad H^+(aq) + HSO_3^-(aq)$$

Macromolecular non-metal oxides such as silicon dioxide, SiO_2, are insoluble in water but will form salts when fused with alkalis,

e.g. $$Na_2O(l) + SiO_2(l) \rightarrow Na_2SiO_3(l)$$

The acidic nature of non-metal oxides is more pronounced in *high* oxidation states. Since the central atom carries a greater partial positive charge it accepts a lone pair of electrons from a water molecule very readily. For example, carbon dioxide, CO_2, behaves as a weak acid, whereas carbon monoxide is insoluble in water and is generally regarded as neutral. Even so, it will form sodium methanoate on heating with concentrated sodium hydroxide solution.

$$NaOH(aq) + CO(g) \xrightarrow{heat} HCOONa(aq)$$

20.5 Action of water on the chlorides

Table 20.8 shows that *the chlorides become increasingly acidic on passing across the Periodic Table.* The chlorides of Group I are essentially ionic and dissolve in water giving virtually *neutral* solutions containing hydrated ions, e.g. sodium chloride,

$$NaCl(s) \rightarrow Na^+(aq) + Cl^-(aq)$$

Table 20.8 *Action of water on some chlorides of the elements from lithium to argon*

Chloride	solubility in water	reaction with water
LiCl	soluble – weakly acidic	
$BeCl_2$	soluble – acidic	
BCl_3	soluble – acidic	$BCl_3 + 3H_2O \rightarrow B(OH)_3 + 3HCl$
CCl_4	insoluble	
NCl_3	soluble – acidic	$NCl_3 + 3H_2O \rightarrow NH_3 + 3HOCl$
Cl_2O_7	soluble – very acidic	$Cl_2O_7 + H_2O \rightarrow 2HClO_4$
ClF	soluble – acidic	
NaCl	soluble – neutral	
$MgCl_2$	soluble – weakly acidic	
$AlCl_3$	soluble – very acidic	see section 23.4
$SiCl_4$	soluble – very acidic	$SiCl_4 + 4H_2O \rightarrow Si(OH)_4 + 4HCl$
PCl_5	soluble – very acidic	$PCl_5 + H_2O \rightarrow POCl_3 + 2HCl$
S_2Cl_2	soluble – acidic	$S_2Cl_2 + 2H_2O \rightarrow 2HCl + SO_2 + H_2S$

How and why does the acidity of the chlorides vary on passing down a group in the 's' block?

Figure 20.1 *Mechanism of the hydrolysis of silicon tetrachloride, SiCl₄*

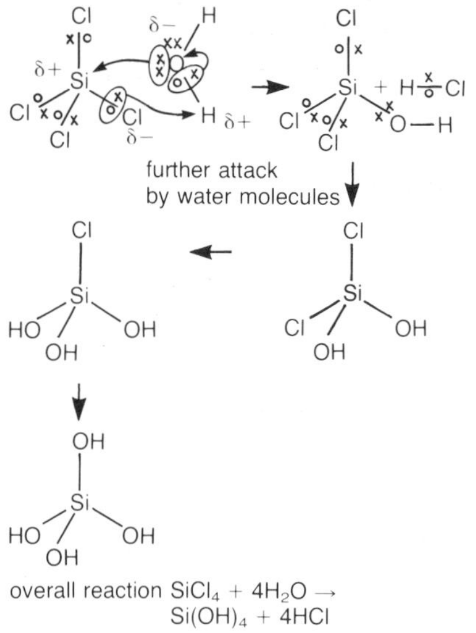

further attack
by water molecules

overall reaction $SiCl_4 + 4H_2O \rightarrow$
$Si(OH)_4 + 4HCl$

As the charge on the cation rises and its size decreases, the solutions become increasingly acidic. The metal ion attracts the electrons on the water molecule more strongly, making the release of hydrogen ions more likely, as outlined in section 20.4.

Non-metal chlorides are essentially *covalent* but the bonds may have some *polarity* depending upon the difference in electronegativity between chlorine and the element concerned. *It is largely this bond polarity which makes non-metal chlorides liable to attack by water.* As an example we shall look at silicon chloride, $SiCl_4$, which dissolves exothermically in water giving a *strongly acidic* solution. The silicon atom carries a slight positive charge and can accept a lone pair of electrons from the oxygen atom on a water molecule into an empty 'd' orbital in its valency shell. This brings a positive hydrogen atom close to a negative chlorine atom, and hydrogen chloride is eliminated. This mechanism is repeated until all the chlorine atoms have been replaced by hydroxide groups as shown in figure 20.1.

It is interesting to note that not all non-metal chlorides react readily with water in this way. Tetrachloromethane, CCl_4, might be expected to resemble silicon tetrachloride but the carbon atom, although slightly positively charged, has *no empty orbitals in its valency shell which can accept a lone pair of electrons from the water molecule.* Such differences in the chemistry of the first elements in the 'p block' groups will be covered in more detail in chapters 23 to 27 but another such example is considered in activity 20.1.

Activity 20.1

Nitrogen chloride, NCl_3, is only slowly attacked by water as follows:

$$NCl_3(l) + 3H_2O(l) \rightarrow NH_3(aq) + 3HOCl(aq)$$

Phosphorus trichloride, PCl_3, is immediately and vigorously attacked by water according to the following equation:

$$PCl_3(l) + 3H_2O(l) \rightarrow H_3PO_3(aq) + 3HCl(aq)$$

1 How do you explain the fact that NCl_3 reacts much more slowly than PCl_3 with water?
2 The products of the two reactions are quite different. Suggest a mechanism in each case.
3 Why cannot NCl_3 react with water in the same way as PCl_3?

To summarise, *soluble ionic chlorides always dissociate into ions in aqueous solution.* If the cation has a high charge density then the hydrated cation will release protons, making the solution *acidic*. Soluble covalent chlorides always hydrolyse to give acidic aqueous solutions.

Since most chlorides dissolve in or react with water to produce chloride ions, their empirical formula may be determined by estimating the amount of chloride ion produced from a known mass of sample. The chloride may either be precipitated as silver chloride and estimated by accurate weighing or be titrated with standard silver nitrate in neutral solution using potassium chromate as indicator as discussed in section 15.4. Activity 20.2 gives some experimental data for a chloride of phosphorus from which you may find its empirical formula.

Activity 20.2

$0.500\,g$ of a phosphorus chloride was dissolved in an excess of water. On addition of silver nitrate solution and nitric acid, $1.722\,g$ of silver chloride was precipitated

$$AgNO_3(aq) + Cl^-(aq) \rightarrow AgCl(s) + NO_3^-(aq)$$

(Relative atomic masses: $P = 31$, $Cl = 35.5$, $Ag = 108$)

1 How many moles of silver chloride were precipitated in the experiment?

2 How many moles of chlorine atoms were in the original phosphorus chloride sample?

3 What mass of chlorine was in the sample of phosphorus chloride?

4 What mass of phosphorus did the original sample contain?

5 How many moles of phosphorus atoms did the original sample contain?

6 What is the empirical formula of the phosphorus chloride?

20.6 Action of water on the hydrides

Table 20.9 shows the reaction of the hydrides with water. The ionic hydrides all react to give an *alkaline* solution and liberate *hydrogen* gas. This results from the presence of the **hydride ion** H^-:

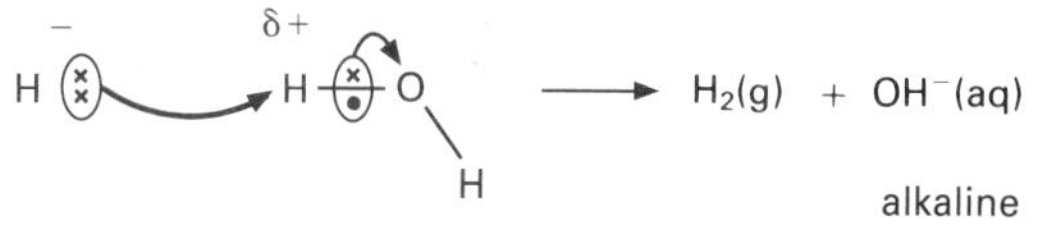

alkaline

Table 20.9 *Action of water on some hydrides of the elements lithium to argon*

Hydride	solubility in water	reaction
LiH	soluble – alkaline	$LiH + H_2O \rightarrow LiOH + H_2$
BeH$_2$		
B$_2$H$_6$	complex behaviour	
CH$_4$	insoluble	
NH$_3$	soluble – weakly alkaline	$NH_3 + H_2O \leftrightharpoons NH_4^+ + OH^-$
H$_2$O	neutral	$2H_2O \rightleftharpoons H_3O^+ + OH^-$
HF	soluble – weakly acidic	$HF + H_2O \rightleftharpoons H_3O^+ + F^-$
NaH	soluble – very alkaline	$NaH + H_2O \rightarrow NaOH + H_2$
MgH$_2$		
AlH$_3$	complex behaviour	
SiH$_4$	reacts – neutral	$SiH_4 + 4H_2O \rightarrow Si(OH)_4 + 4H_2$
PH$_3$	insoluble	
H$_2$S	soluble – weakly acidic	$H_2S + H_2O \rightleftharpoons H_3O^+ + HS^-$
HCl	soluble – very acidic	$HCl + H_2O \rightarrow H_3O^+ + Cl^-$

What ion do all 'alkaline' hydrides contain and how does this ion react with water?

Silicon hydride also gives hydrogen with water, the mechanism for the hydrolysis being similar to that shown for the chloride in figure 20.1.

$$SiH_4(g) + 4H_2O(l) \rightarrow Si(OH)_4(s) + 4H_2(g)$$

The other non–metals hydrides, if soluble in water, tend to become progressively *more acidic* on passing across a period. If we take the hydrides of carbon, nitrogen, oxygen and fluorine as an example. Methane does *not* react with water, since it may neither accept nor donate a lone pair of electrons. Ammonia, NH_3, is readily soluble in water, giving a *weakly alkaline* solution. The nitrogen atom donates a lone pair of electrons to the hydrogen of a water molecule, i.e. it acts as a *Lewis base*.

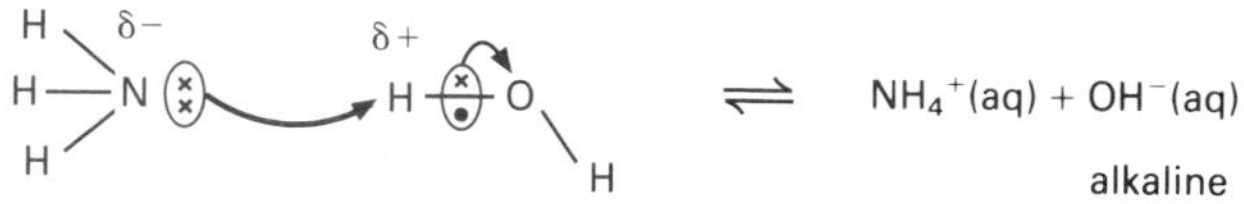

alkaline

Water self-ionises to a small extent, since it may act *both* as a Lewis acid and as a Lewis base. Since equal amounts of $H^+(aq)$ and $OH^-(aq)$ are produced, water is *neutral*:

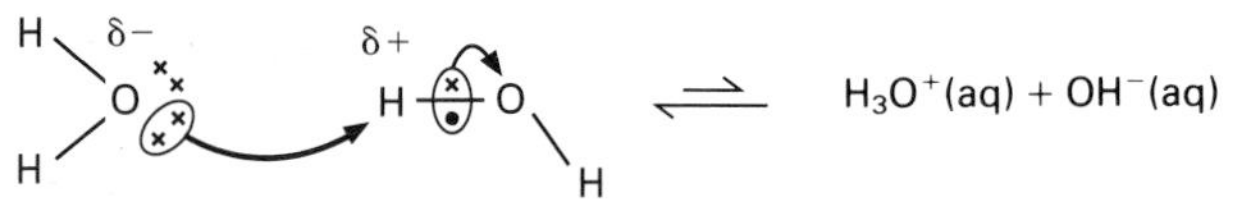

$$\rightleftharpoons \quad H_3O^+(aq) + OH^-(aq)$$

In hydrogen fluoride, the very high electronegativity of the fluorine atom causes the hydrogen atom to develop an appreciable positive charge. This can *accept* a lone pair of electrons from the oxygen atom of a water molecule forming H_3O^+ which makes the solution *acidic*:

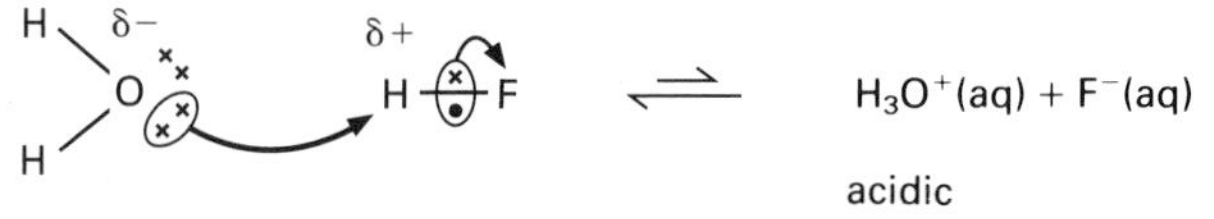

$$\rightleftharpoons \quad H_3O^+(aq) + F^-(aq)$$

acidic

20.7 Diagonal relationships

We have explained the variation in the properties of compounds on passing across a period largely in terms of the gradual change in such atomic properties as ionisation energy, electronegativity and atomic size. Although, by and large, the chemistry of the compounds within a particular group is similar, *the first element often shows marked differences from the rest*. In chapter 19 we noted that the atomic properties of the diagonally related elements lithium and magnesium were quite similar. This is reflected in the properties of some of their compounds. Table 20.10 lists some of the main ways in which the compounds of lithium differ from those of the rest of the metals in Group I and resemble those of magnesium.

Table 20.10 *The diagonal relationship – how lithium compounds differ from those of the rest of the Group I metals and resemble those of magnesium*

Compound	Group I, except lithium	lithium and magnesium
oxides	form peroxides and superoxides, e.g. Na_2O_2 and KO_2	form a monoxide only Li_2O and MgO
carbonates	soluble in water thermally stable	sparingly soluble decompose on heating to give the metal oxide $Li_2CO_3 \rightarrow Li_2O + CO_2$ $MgCO_3 \rightarrow MgO + CO_2$
hydrogen carbonates	stable in the solid state	known only in solution
nitrates	decompose on heating to give nitrites, e.g. $2NaNO_3 \rightarrow 2NaNO_2 + O_2$	decompose to the metal oxide on heating $4LiNO_3 \rightarrow 2Li_2O + 4NO_2 + O_2$ $2Mg(NO_3)_2 \rightarrow 2MgO + 4NO_2 + O_2$
hydroxides	thermally stable	lose water on heating to give the metal oxide $2LiOH \rightarrow Li_2O + H_2O$ $Mg(OH)_2 \rightarrow MgO + H_2O$
nitrides	not formed by direct combination	both formed by direct combination with nitrogen $6Li + N_2 \xrightarrow{cold} 3Li_3N$ $3Mg + N_2 \xrightarrow{burn} Mg_3N_2$

20.8 Comments on the activities

Activity 20.1

1   The hydrolysis of a non-metal chloride depends largely upon the polarity of the covalent bonds. Since nitrogen and chlorine have approximately the same electronegativity, the bonds in NCl_3 are virtually non-polar and neither of the atoms will attract a polar water molecule. Phosphorus has a lower electronegativity than chlorine and hence the $P^{\delta+}$—$Cl^{\delta-}$ bonds are more polar and susceptible to hydrolysis.

2   We can explain the different products by assuming that NCl_3 acts as an electron pair donor, whilst PCl_3 accepts a lone pair of electrons from the water molecule.

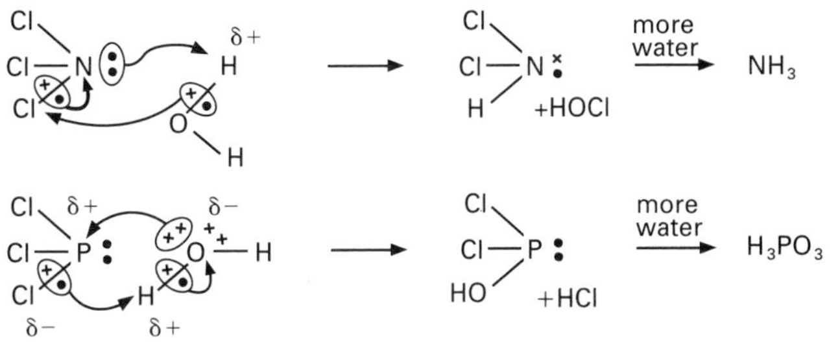

3   NCl_3 *cannot* act as a Lewis acid, i.e. an electron pair acceptor, since the nitrogen atom *cannot* accommodate any more electrons in its valency shell. It may *only* react by *donating* the lone pair on the nitrogen atom.

Activity 20.2

1   Mass of one mole of silver chloride $= 108 + 35.5 = 143.5\,g$
    $1.722\,g$ of silver chloride $= 1.722/143.5 = 0.012\,mol$.

2   $0.012\,mol$ AgCl contains $0.012\,mol$ of Cl, therefore the phosphorus chloride sample contained $0.012\,mol$ of chlorine atoms.

3   $0.012\,mol$ of chlorine atoms weigh $0.012 \times 35.5 = 0.426\,g$.

4   Since $0.500\,g$ of the chloride contains $0.426\,g$ of chlorine, the mass of phosphorus present must be $0.500 - 0.426 = 0.074\,g$.

5   $0.074\,g$ phosphorus $= 0.074/31 = 0.0024\,mol$ of phosphorus atoms.

6   The molar ratio of phosphorus atoms to chlorine atoms is
    $0.0024\,P : 0.012\,Cl$ *or*
    $1\,P : 5\,Cl$
    Thus the empirical formula of the chloride is PCl_5.

20.9 Summary and revision plan

The trends in structure and bonding, thermal stability, and a range of physical and chemical properties, for some common compounds of the elements in periods 2 and 3 (lithium to argon) are summarised in tables 20.1 to 20.10. The numerical data are meant for reference only and you should concentrate on understanding the overall 'trends' in properties on passing across a period, down a group, and diagonally in the Periodic Table.

CHAPTER 21

Hydrogen

Contents

Potentially, hydrogen is an excellent fuel. Since on combustion only water is produced, it poses much less of a pollution problem than conventional hydrocarbon fuels.

$$2H_2(g) + O_2(g) \rightarrow 2H_2O(g) \quad \Delta H = -483\,kJ$$

However, although liquid hydrogen has been used as rocket fuel, this can be hazardous and it is currently quite expensive to produce. Research is being carried out into cheap methods of obtaining hydrogen by catalytic decomposition of its most plentiful source, sea-water.

In the oxy-hydrogen welding torch, heat is produced by burning hydrogen in oxygen. Alternatively, in atomic hydrogen welding, hydrogen molecules are dissociated into atoms by an electric arc. The large amount of energy which is released when these recombine to form molecules is sufficient to melt many metals.

$$2H(g) \rightarrow H_2(g) \quad \Delta H = -436\,kJ$$

The hydrogen atmosphere helps to prevent oxidation, and the technique is particularly suitable for metals such as aluminium which do not readily combine with hydrogen.

Hydrogen is also important in the food industry. Ammonia formed by the combination of hydrogen and nitrogen in the Haber process (section 25.7) is converted into nitrogen fertilisers such as ammonium salts and nitrates.

Margarine and other fats are made by passing hydrogen through a heated vegetable oil in the presence of a catalyst. Under these conditions, hydrogen adds on

Some of the wide range of uses of hydrogen

across some, or all, of the double bonds in the oil, thereby increasing its melting point (section 35.6.4).

$$-CH = CH - \ + \ H_2 \qquad \xrightarrow[\text{200\,°C}]{\text{finely divided nickel}} \qquad -CH_2{-}CH_2-$$
'unsaturated' oil   'saturated' fat

The manufacture of many important inorganic and organic chemicals requires hydrogen. Methanol, for example, may be made from hydrogen and carbon monoxide.

$$CO(g) + 2H_2(g) \xrightarrow[\text{400\,°C, high pressure}]{Cr_2O_3/ZnO \text{ catalyst}} CH_3OH(g)$$

21.1 The element

The hydrogen atom is the simplest known. It has one proton in the nucleus and, in its ground state, one electron in the 1s orbital. There are three isotopes of hydrogen.

^1_1H	^2_1H (or D)	^3_1H (or T)
hydrogen	deuterium	tritium

Tritium is radioactive but all three isotopes have very similar chemical properties.

Hydrogen exists as diatomic H_2 molecules. It is a colourless, odourless gas of very low density and almost insoluble in water. In the laboratory it is conveniently prepared by the action of dilute sulphuric or hydrochloric acid on a moderately reactive metal such as zinc, e.g.

$$Zn(s) + 2HCl(aq) \rightarrow ZnCl_2(aq) + H_2(g)$$

Industrially, hydrogen may be manufactured from hydrocarbons by cracking (section 34.6) or by reaction with steam, e.g. methane from natural gas:

$$CH_4(g) + 2H_2O(g) \xrightarrow[\text{750\,°C}]{\text{nickel catalyst}} CO_2(g) + 4H_2(g)$$

This process is considered in more detail in section 25.7 which deals with the manufacture of ammonia.

Although a very abundant element, almost all of the earth's hydrogen is chemically combined. It will, in fact, form binary compounds called **hydrides** with most other elements except the noble gases. Some of the principal reactions of hydrogen are shown in figure 21.1 and chemistry of the hydrides is considered more fully in sections 21.2. and 21.3.

Figure 21.1 *Some reactions of hydrogen*

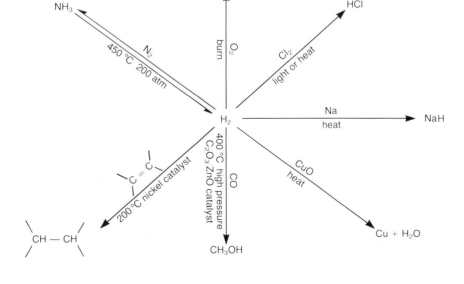

21.2 Binary compounds of hydrogen: a brief survey of the hydrides

Most elements, except the noble gases, will form some sort of compound with hydrogen. These 'hydrides' may be divided up into three main types, ionic, covalent and interstitial, as shown in table 21.1.

Table 21.1 *Classification of hydrides*

LiH	$(BeH_2)_x$			$(BH_3)_2$*	CH_4*	NH_3	OH_2	FH
NaH	$(MgH_2)_x$			$(AlH_3)_x$	SiH_4	PH_3	SH_2	ClH
KH	CaH_2	Sc → Zn		GaH_3	GeH_4	AsH_3	SeH_2	BrH
RbH	SrH_2	Y →	In	SnH_4	SbH_3	TeH_2	IH
ionic hydrides		intersitial hydrides				covalent hydrides		

*These elements form a wide range of hydrides

Ionic hydrides, formed by the very electropositive Group I metals and all except beryllium and magnesium in Group II, contain the hydride ion, H^-. They are high melting point crystalline solids which in the molten state undergo electrolysis giving hydrogen gas at the anode:

$$H^- \rightarrow \tfrac{1}{2}H_2 + e^-$$

They are very powerful reducing agents and react vigorously with water, giving hydrogen and an alkaline solution of the metal hydroxide:

$$H^- + H_2O \rightarrow H_2 + OH^-$$

Most of the 'p' block elements form well-characterised **covalent hydrides** which are mainly gases or liquids of low boiling point. Carbon forms a very extensive range of hydrocarbons, largely owing to its ability to **catenate**, *i.e. form chains and rings of carbon atoms, and form stable multiple bonds* which gives rise to the alkenes and alkynes. Boron also forms several hydrides, but not the simple BH_3 molecule which would be 'electron deficient' with only six electrons in the valency shell of the boron atom. The simplest hydride of boron is B_2H_6 in which the boron atoms are linked by two 'bridging' hydrogen atoms. Here three atoms, both of the borons and a bridging hydrogen, are bonded by a single pair of electrons.

The hydrides of beryllium, magnesium and aluminium are covalent macromolecules which contain similar 'bridging' hydrogen atoms. Boron and aluminium also form complex tetrahydrido ions in which the central atom is tetrahedrally linked to four hydrogen atoms. **Lithium tetrahydridoaluminate**, $LiAlH_4$, a very useful reducing agent in organic chemistry, may be prepared from lithium hydride and aluminium chloride:

$$4LiH + AlCl_3 \xrightarrow[\text{solution}]{\text{ethoxyethane}} Li^+[AlH_4]^- + 3LiCl$$

A comparison of the properties of some of the hydrides of the elements in the periods Li–Ne and Na–Ar may be found in chapter 20.

Elements of the 'd' block also often absorb appreciable amounts of hydrogen on heating. Such materials are frequently **non-stoichiometric**, *i.e. do not have a simple fixed chemical formula*, and have properties similar to the parent metal. The bonding is uncertain but the hydrogen atoms appear to occupy 'holes' in the metallic lattice. These compounds are often referred to as **interstitial hydrides**.

Table 21.2

$X_2(g)$	atomisation energy/kJ i.e. $\frac{1}{2}X_2(g) \rightarrow X(g)$
H_2	$+218$
F_2	$+79$
Cl_2	$+121$

21.3 Energetics of hydride formation

Before hydrogen can react to form a compound, its molecules must be dissociated into atoms. The atomisation energy of hydrogen is *very high* compared with similar singly bonded diatomic molecules. Unlike the other molecules, there are *no* non-bonding electrons on the hydrogen atoms which could repel each other and thus weaken the bond.

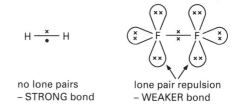

no lone pairs – STRONG bond lone pair repulsion – WEAKER bond

This relative stability of the hydrogen molecule explains why the gas is regarded as being only moderately reactive.

From our study of bonding in chapter 5, we might expect that the hydrogen atom could achieve a stable electronic structure in three different ways:

▶ by **gaining** an electron to form the hydride ion, H^-;
▶ by **losing** an electron leaving a bare proton, H^+;
▶ by **sharing** an electron with another atom to form a single covalent bond.

We shall examine each of these possibilities in more detail.

Table 21.3

$X(g)$	electron affinity/kJ i.e. $X(g) + e^- \rightarrow X^-(g)$
H	-72
F	-348
Cl	-364
Br	-342
I	-314

Formation of the hydride ion, H^-

Here, the hydrogen atom must gain an electron from an electropositive element such as sodium.

The electron affinity values in Table 21.3 show that the hydrogen atom does not form a negative ion as readily as the halogens.

Figure 21.2 compares the energy changes in forming sodium hydride and sodium chloride. Although energetically more stable than its elements, the hydride is not as stable as the chloride. The much less exothermic value for the enthalpy of formation of the hydride is due largely to the higher atomisation energy of hydrogen and its lower electron affinity. *Stable ionic hydrides are likely to be formed only by those metals whose ionisation energies are sufficiently low to result in a negative enthalpy of formation.* In practice, this is restricted to the Group I metals and calcium, strontium and barium in Group II.

Formation of the proton, H^+

Although we might expect the hydrogen atom to lose an electron to very electronegative elements, *the free proton does not exist in chemical compounds.*

Since the hydrogen atom is small and possesses no inner electrons to screen the nuclear charge, its electron is very tightly held. At $+1310\,\text{kJ mol}^{-1}$, the ionisation energy of hydrogen is the highest of all the 's' block elements, except helium, and is greater even than the first ionisation energy of the noble gas xenon. Even in combination with the most electronegative element fluorine, the lattice energy released would be insufficient to produce a stable ionic hydride.

We may also explain the non-existence of the free H^+ ion in terms of its very small size. According to **Fajan's rules**, discussed in section 5.10, a cation with a high charge density will attract electrons from the anion, leading to covalent character in the bonding. The following data show that the proton is by far the most polarising cation because of its extremely small radius and consequent immense charge/size ratio.

Although the proton is not found in the free state in chemical compounds, it may be produced in a high voltage discharge tube where sufficient energy is available to atomise and ionise the hydrogen gas. In the next section we shall examine the existence of the hydrogen ion in association with electron pair donors such as water.

Figure 21.2 *Enthalpy cycles for the formation of sodium hydride and sodium chloride*

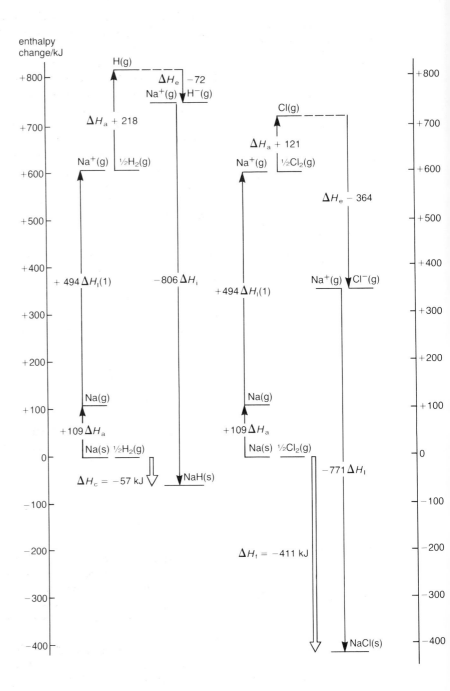

Table 21.4 *Approximate radii and charge/radius ratios of some cations*

Cation	approx. radius/nm	approx. charge/radius ratio
H^+	0.000002	500000
Li^+	0.060	17
Na^+	0.095	11
Mg^{2+}	0.065	31
Al^{3+}	0.050	60

Table 21.5 *Polarity of some 'covalent' hydrides*

This table shows the difference in electronegativity values between hydrogen and each element and the sign of the partial charge on the hydrogen atoms in the corresponding hydride

CH_4	NH_3	OH_2	FH
0.4 +	0.9 +	1.4 +	1.9 +
SiH_4	PH_3	SH_2	ClH
0.3 −	0.0	0.4 +	0.9 +
GeH_4	AsH_3	SeH_2	BrH
0.3 −	0.1 −	0.3 +	0.7 +
SnH_4	SbH_4	TeH_2	IH
0.3 −	0.2 −	0.0	0.4 +

Why is ammonia, NH_3, much more soluble in water than the hydrides of the other Group V elements?

Table 21.6 *Average bond energy terms for the hydrides of 'p' block elements (kJ mol^{-1})*

C—H	N—H	O—H	F—H
416	391	464	567
Si—H	P—H	S—H	Cl—H
323	321	367	431
Ge—H	As—H	Se—H	Br—H
289	297	316	366
Sn—H	Sb—H	Te—H	I—H
253	254	266	298

How and why does the bond energy vary on passing (a) across a period, (b) down a group?

Covalent bonding

Most of the elements in the 'p' block form covalent hydrides but in most cases the bonding will be polar to some extent. As explained in section 5.9, the atoms of the more electronegative element will develop a partial negative charge. Table 21.5 compares the electronegativity of the elements in Groups IV–VII with hydrogen and indicates the sign of the charge on the hydrogen atoms.

The thermal stabilities of these compounds, with respect to dissociation into the elements, depend largely on the strength of the covalent bonds present. Table 21.6 shows that, in general, the strength of covalent bonds involving hydrogen generally *increases* on passing across the 'p' block but *decreases* on passing down a particular group. Both of these trends may be explained if we assume that it is largely the atomic size of the 'p' block element which determines the strength of the covalent bond. *In general, larger atoms form weaker covalent bonds. Since the shared pair of electrons is further away from the nucleus and screened by more inner electrons, it is attracted less strongly.*

21.4 The hydrogen ion

Several covalent hydrides dissolve exothermically in water to produce solutions which readily conduct electricity. In each case a positive ion is produced which contains a proton associated with a **Lewis base**, i.e. an electron pair donor. If the solution is *alkaline*, e.g. ammonia, the *water* acts as a **Lewis acid,** accepting a lone pair of electrons via one of its positively charged hydrogen atoms.

$$\rightleftharpoons \quad NH_4^+(aq) + OH^-(aq)$$

alkaline

In *acidic* solutions, e.g. hydrogen chloride, the *water* acts as a Lewis base by donating a lone pair of electrons to the positive hydrogen atom on the hydride, forming a hydrated proton or **hydroxonium ion, H_3O^+**.

$$\longrightarrow \quad H_3O^+(aq) + Cl^-(aq)$$

acidic

The reason for the ready formation of the hydroxonium ion in aqueous solution becomes clear if we consider the energy changes involved. The energy cycle for dissolving hydrogen chloride in water is shown in figure 21.3. As you can see, *the energy released on hydrating the gaseous ions, especially the proton, more than compensates for the energy required to dissociate the hydrogen chloride molecule and ionise the hydrogen atom.*

The first step in the formation of the hydroxonium ion involves donation of a lone pair of electrons from the water molecule, so we might expect acid nature to increase with the degree of positive charge on the hydrogen atom, i.e. with increasing electronegativity of the other element. Although this trend is observed on passing across a period, acidity rather unexpectedly increases on passing down a group. Again the explanation lies in the energetics of the process. Hydroxonium ions can only be formed if the covalent bond in the hydride is broken. Since bond strength *falls* on passing down a group, as shown in table 21.6, the hydrides *ionise more readily* and their acid strength *increases*.

Activity 21.1

1   Use the information in figure 21.3 and table 21.6 together with the following electron affinities and hydration energies (all expressed in

Figure 21.3 *Enthalpy cycle for dissolving hydrogen chloride in water*

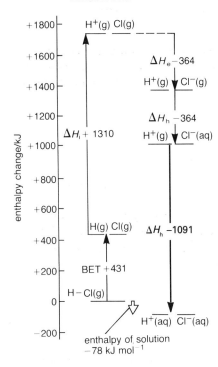

kJ mol^{-1}) to estimate the enthalpy change on dissolving each of the hydrogen halides in water.

electron affinities ΔH_e, i.e. $X(g) + e^- \rightarrow X^-(g)$
F -348, Br -342, I -314

hydration energies ΔH_h, i.e. $X^-(g) \rightarrow X^-(aq)$
F$^-$ -506, Br$^-$ -335, I$^-$ -293

2 How do these values correspond with the increase in the acid strength of the hydrides in aqueous solution on passing down Group VII?

21.5 The hydrogen bond

Figure 21.4 shows that the boiling points of the covalent hydrides of any particular group generally increase quite smoothly with relative molecular mass. This is to be expected since normally the main intermolecular attraction is in the form of van der Waals' forces. These are weak forces whose strength increases with the size of the electron cloud in the molecule. You should notice, however, that the boiling points

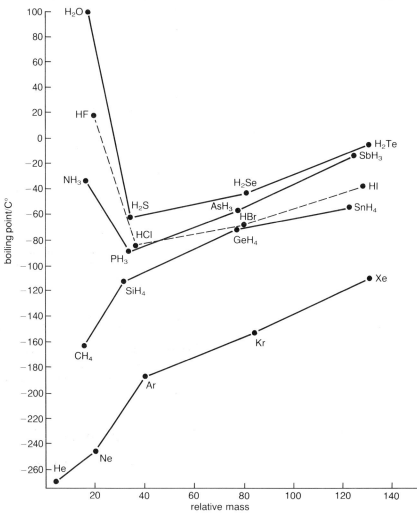

Figure 21.4 *Variation in the boiling point of some 'p' block hydrides - why are the boiling points of H₂O, NH₃ and HF so high?*

of ammonia, water and hydrogen fluoride do not fit this pattern, being *abnormally high*. Clearly, there must be stronger *intermolecular attraction* in these compounds, i.e. where hydrogen is bonded directly to either nitrogen, oxygen or fluorine. Each of these elements is very electronegative, and the bonding in their hydrides will be correspondingly quite polar.

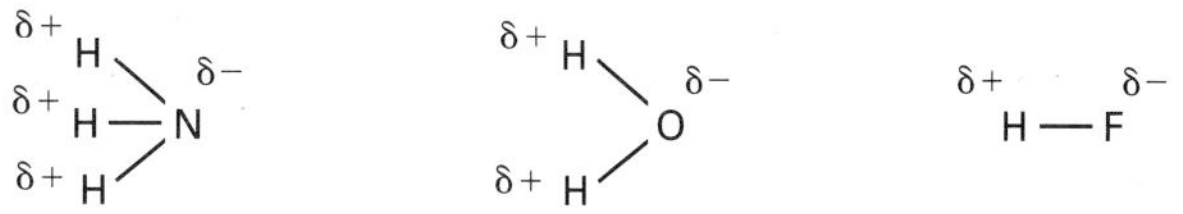

As a result, there is quite a strong electrostatic attraction between the positive hydrogen atoms on one molecule and the negative nitrogen, oxygen or fluorine on other molecules. In the case of hydrogen fluoride, this **hydrogen bonding** results in the formation of zig-zag molecular chains.

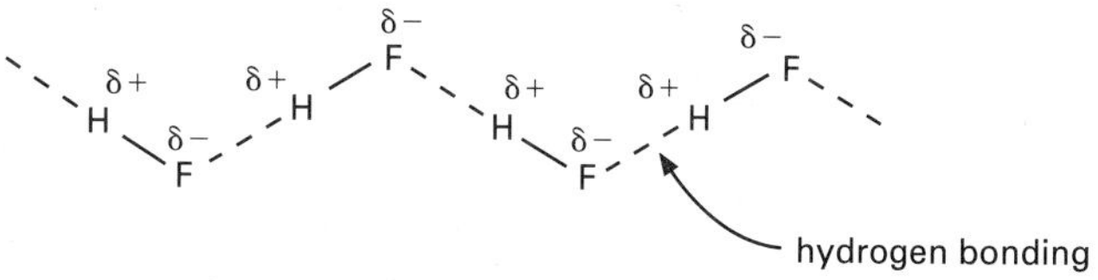

It is important to remember that *appreciable hydrogen bonding can only occur in molecules where a hydrogen atom is directly bonded to either a nitrogen, oxygen or fluorine atom.* Thus, whilst the hydrogenfluoride ion, HF_2^-, is well known, there is no evidence for the hydrogenchloride ion, HCl_2^-.

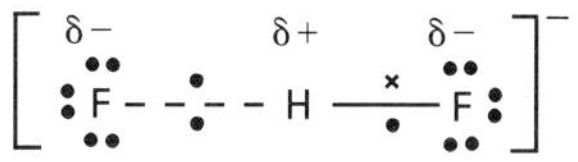

Other instances of hydrogen bonding include:
  ▶ the dimerisation of carboxylic acids in non–polar solvents such as benzene,

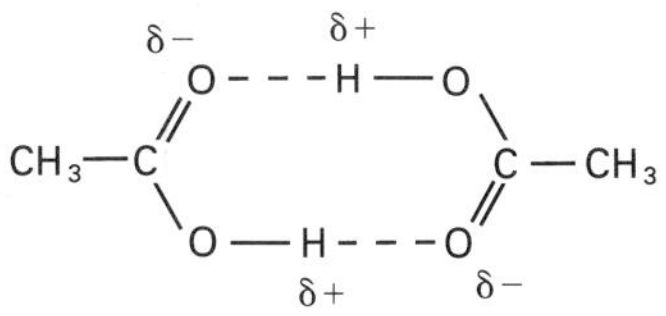

  ▶ the structure of some biologically important molecules. Hydrogen bonding is, for instance, essential in the double helix structure of deoxyribonucleic acid (DNA) which carries the 'genetic code' necessary for reproduction of living cells.

21.6 The position of hydrogen in the periodic table

Although quite unique in many of its properties, it is possible to make out a case for placing hydrogen together with either the alkali metals or the halogens. Table 21.7 summarises the similarities and differences between hydrogen and each of these groups.

21.7 Comments on the activity 21.1

1 Estimated enthalpies of solution: HF -68
   (kJ mol^{-1})   HCl -78
                       HBr -92
                       HI -90

2 The figures above show that the ionisation process,

$$HX(g) \rightleftharpoons H^+(aq) + X^-(aq),$$

becomes energetically *more* favourable as the size of the halogen atom increases, i.e. more hydroxonium ions will be formed, making the solution

Table 21.7   *A comparison of the properties of hydrogen with the alkali metals and the halogens*

Property	Group I elements (Li–Cs)		Hydrogen	Group VII elements (F–I)
electron configuration	ns^1 one electron in outer shell		$1s^1$ BOTH one electron in outer shell, AND one electron less than a noble gas	$ns^2 np^5$ one electron LESS than a noble gas
structure	metallic		covalent, diatomic molecules, H_2	covalent diatomic molecules
first ionisation energy, $\Delta H_i(1)$	low		high	high
electronegativity	<1.0		2.1	4.0–2.5
redox action	reducing agents		generally reducing but oxidises Group I metals	oxidising agents
standard electrode potential $E^\ominus$ (volts)	$\simeq -3$		0.00	+2.9 to +0.5
bonding types				
+ve ions	yes, e.g. Na^+		yes but only as complex ions, e.g. H_3O^+	uncommon
−ve ions	no		yes, H^-, in hydrides of electropositive metals	yes, e.g. Cl^- in metallic halides
covalent bonds	no		yes, in non-metallic hydrides	yes in halides of non-metals

Look carefully at the table above. In what ways does hydrogen closely resemble: (a) Group I elements, (b) Group VII elements? Which properties of hydrogen resemble neither of these groups?

more acidic. Hydrogen fluoride is a *weak* acid since it is only *slightly* ionised in aqueous solution, whereas the other hydrogen halides are almost *fully* dissociated i.e. *strong* acids.

21.8   Summary and revision plan

1   In the laboratory hydrogen is made by the reaction of a moderately reactive metal, e.g. zinc, with dilute sulphuric or hydrochloric acid. Industrial manufacturing methods include hydrocarbon **'cracking'** and the high temperature reaction of methane with steam.

2   Hydrogen is used on a large scale in welding and in the manufacture of ammonia and margarine.

3   Hydrides of very electropositive metals are ionic and contain the H^- ion. Most other hydrides are essentially covalent in character.

4   The hydrogen ion, H^+, exists only in chemical compounds in association with electron pair donors, e.g. as H_3O^+ and NH_4^+. The high **hydration energy** of H^+ is the driving force when polar covalent hydrides of the type $^{\delta+}H—X^{\delta-}$ dissolve in water to give acidic solutions.

5   The very polar covalent bond formed between hydrogen and nitrogen, oxygen or fluorine leads to strong intermolecular attraction known as **hydrogen bonding**. This is responsible for the abnormally high boiling points of ammonia, water and hydrogen fluoride.

6   Hydrogen is normally placed in a separate block with helium at the top of the Periodic Table. In terms of electron configuration and properties it shows some similarities to both Group I and Group VII.

Groups I and II, the Alkali and Alkaline Earth Metals

Contents

Despite their high reactivity, the metals themselves have several commercially important uses. Sodium and magnesium are the most widely used and are produced in bulk, but small quantities of the other metals are needed for special applications.

Over 100 000 tonnes of sodium are used annually, alloyed with lead, in the manufacture of tetraethyl lead, an 'anti-knock' additive for petrol (section 34.5).

$$Pb/4Na + 4C_2H_5Cl \rightarrow Pb(C_2H_5)_4 + 4NaCl$$

Their excellent thermal conductivity and relatively low melting points make the alkali metals very efficient coolants. Some nuclear reactors use circulating molten sodium to absorb the heat produced in their cores.

Sodium is also employed as a laboratory reducing agent and has been used commercially in the extraction of titanium from its chloride.

$$TiCl_4 + 4Na \rightarrow Ti + 4NaCl$$

Magnesium is widely used in alloys with aluminium. These have a low density but are much tougher and stronger than pure aluminium and find use in the aircraft and aerospace industries. Since on ignition magnesium burns with an intense white flame, it has also been used in fireworks, flares and photographic flashbulbs.

Some familiar uses of the Group I and II metals

Strontium, barium and all the alkali metals give characteristic flame colours (table 22.1).

Table 22.1

Element	flame coloration	Element	flame coloration
lithium	red		
sodium	golden yellow		
potassium	lilac	calcium	'brick' red
rubidium	red	strontium	red
caesium	blue	barium	green

The yellow-orange colour of the sodium emission spectrum is used in modern street lighting.

It is now a legal requirement that all pre-packaged food is labelled with its ingredients. You will often see 'E' numbers quoted on food and drink labels. These are additives, such as colours, flavourings and preservatives, which are approved as 'safe' by the European Economic Community. Figure 22.1 shows some of the many

Figure 22.1 *Many compounds of the metals of Groups I and II are used as food additives*

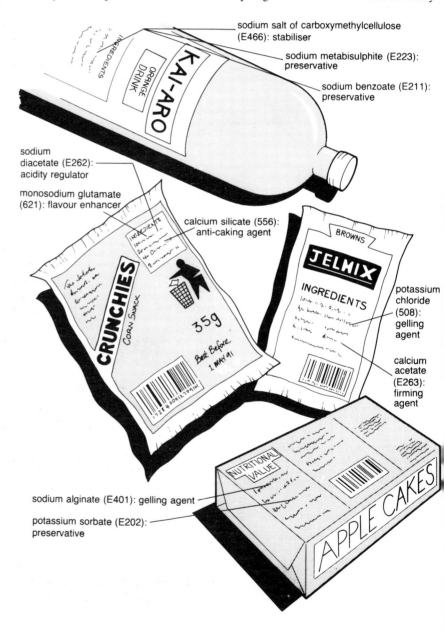

compounds of sodium, potassium and calcium which are used as food additives. The metal ion is usually not the 'active' constituent, but since sodium and potassium salts are generally water soluble, they are easily blended into various foods.

Other important uses of compounds of the alkali and alkaline earth metals are summarised in table 22.2.

Table 22.2 *Some uses of the compounds of the alkali and alkaline earth metals*

Type of compound	metal		main uses
oxide	magnesium	MgO	'basic' furnace lining (very high melting point)
	calcium	CaO	to remove acidic oxides as 'slag' in the extraction of iron
hydroxide	sodium	NaOH	very strong alkali used in many manufacturing processes, e.g. soap and paper making
	calcium	$Ca(OH)_2$	'slaked lime' – a soil conditioner used to remove excess acidity (oxide and carbonate also used for this purpose)
	magnesium	$Mg(OH)_2$	in suspension as 'milk of magnesia', a mild stomach antacid
carbonate	sodium	Na_2CO_3	water softener – 'washing soda' also used in glassmaking and the textiles industry
	calcium	$CaCO_3$	used in cement making
sulphate	calcium	$CaSO_4$	the 'hemihydrate', $CaSO_4.\frac{1}{2}H_2O$ is plaster of Paris
	barium	$BaSO_4$	'barium meal' – insoluble and opaque to X-rays, used to diagnose stomach disorders such as ulcers
nitrate	potassium	KNO_3	an ingredient of 'gunpowder'
hydride	lithium	$LiAlH_4$	reducing agents, especially useful in organic chemistry
	sodium	$NaBH_4$	

22.1 The elements: their atomic and physical properties

Although there are very close similarities in the chemistry of all the elements within a particular group, there are well-defined trends which may be explained largely in terms of atomic and ionic size. In particular, the small ionic radius of the first element in each group leads to some unusual properties. As explained in section 20.7, there are some similarities in the chemistry of the 'diagonally related' elements, lithium and magnesium.

We shall first examine, and account for, the trends in the properties of the elements which are listed in table 22.3.

Atomic and ionic size

Within any period the atomic and ionic radii of the Group II element are *smaller* than those of the Group I metal. The nuclear charge of the Group II atom is *greater* and thus pulls the electrons closer to it.

On passing down either of the groups, atomic and ionic size *increase*. The greater number of inner electrons progressively 'screen' the outer electrons more effectively from the bigger nuclear charge.

These variations in atomic and ionic size are very important in explaining the trends in many of the properties outlined below.

Density

Since their atoms are somewhat smaller, the densities of Group II metals are *higher* than those of the corresponding elements in Group I. On passing down Group I density *rises* quite smoothly, because atomic mass is increasing rather more rapidly

Table 22.3 *Data sheet for the elements of Groups I and II*

Element	atomic number	electron configuration	atomic radius /nm	ionic radius /nm	ionisation energies /kJ mol⁻¹ 1st 2nd 3rd			electro- negativity	$E^{\ominus}$ /volts	density /g cm⁻³	m.p. /°C
Group I											
lithium Li	3	[He] $2s^1$	0.152	0.060	519	7300	11800	1.0	−3.04	0.53	180
sodium Na	11	[Ne] $3s^1$	0.186	0.095	494	4560	6940	0.9	−2.71	0.97	98
potassium K	19	[Ar] $4s^1$	0.231	0.133	418	3070	4600	0.8	−2.92	0.86	64
rubidium Rb	37	[Kr] $5s^1$	0.244	0.148	402	2650	3850	0.8	−2.92	1.53	39
caesium Cs	55	[Xe] $6s^1$	0.262	0.169	376	2420	3300	0.7	−2.92	1.90	29
francium Fr	87	[Rn] $7s^1$	0.270	0.176	381	?	?	0.7	?	?	(27)
Group II											
beryllium Be	4	[He] $2s^2$	0.112	(0.031)	900	1760	14800	1.5	−1.85	1.85	1280
magnesium Mg	12	[Ne] $3s^2$	0.160	0.065	736	1450	7740	1.2	−2.38	1.74	650
calcium Ca	20	[Ar] $4s^2$	0.197	0.099	590	1150	4940	1.0	−2.87	1.54	850
strontium Sr	38	[Kr] $5s^2$	0.215	0.113	548	1060	4120	1.0	−2.89	2.62	768
barium Ba	56	[Xe] $6s^2$	0.217	0.135	502	966	3390	0.9	−2.90	3.51	714
radium Ra	88	[Rn] $7s^2$	0.220	0.140	510	979	?	0.9	−2.92	5.0	700

What is the general trend in the value of standard electrode potential, $E^{\ominus}$, on passing (a) down a group, (b) from group I to group II? The standard electrode potential of lithium does not fit this pattern. Can you explain why?

than atomic size. In general, the same is true in Group II but the trend is not perfect as there are differences in the way in which the atoms pack together in the crystal lattice.

Melting point

This may be taken as a measure of the 'strength' of the metallic bonding in the crystal lattice. In simple terms, cations are held together by the attraction of mobile valency electrons. Since Group II elements have two valency electrons per atom, as against only one for the alkali metals, we should expect their melting points to be *higher*. This is confirmed by the data in table 22.3 and we can also see that melting point tends to fall on passing down each group. The 'binding power' of the valency electrons decreases as the cations become larger, i.e. as their charge density falls.

Again, the irregularity in the melting points of the Group II metals may be explained in terms of differences in crystal structure.

Electronegativity

Remember that this measures the attraction of the atom for the electrons in a covalent bond. Since it is the nucleus of the atom which attracts electrons, electronegativity should *decrease* as both atomic radius and the number of inner 'screening' electrons *increase*. As expected, table 22.3 reveals that the electronegativity *increases* on passing from Group I to Group II but *falls* on descending the Periodic Table.

Ionisation energies

Figure 22.2 *Increase in successive ionisation energies*

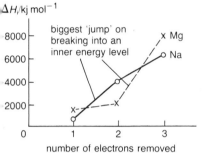

These measure the ease with which electrons are progressively stripped from the gaseous atoms. Again, atomic size is very important. Decrease in atomic radius will mean progressively stronger nuclear attraction and ionisation energies will increase. As a result, the first ionisation energy of a Group II element is *higher* than that of the corresponding element in Group I. On passing down each group ionisation energies will *fall*, owing to the increase in both atomic radius and the number of inner 'screening' electrons.

It is interesting to compare the relative values of the first three ionisation energies of the elements in each group. Although the first ionisation energy of a Group I element is less than that of its Group II neighbour, its second ionisation energy is very much *higher*. This is because, in the case of Group I, the second electron is taken from an inner energy level which is closer to the nucleus, whilst for Group II the second electron is withdrawn from the outer 's' sub-level. The third ionisation energy of all the elements is high, since in both groups the electron is removed from an inner energy level. *The large 'jump' in ionisation energy on breaking into an inner energy level has important consequences for the chemistry of the alkali and alkaline earth metals* (figure 22.2).

Standard electrode potential

This property refers to the tendency of an element to form cations in aqueous solution:

$$M^{x+}(aq) + xe^- \rightleftharpoons M(s)$$

As we described in section 17.2, the *more readily* the atom ionises, the *more negative* will be its standard electrode potential, $E^\ominus$. Although electrode potential involves the formation of ions *in solution*, whilst ionisation energy refers to the *gaseous* state, we might expect some correspondence between these properties, as both require the atoms to *lose* electrons. Bearing in mind the above trends in ionisation energies, we might therefore expect electrode potential to become steadily more negative on passing from Group II to Group I and on descending the Periodic Table. Whilst the data in table 22.3 generally support this, the electrode potentials of lithium and the alkaline earth metals are rather more negative than expected. The higher *charge density* of their ions means that they can attract water molecules more strongly, making the hydration process energetically more favourable (table 22.4).

Table 22.4 *Relative charge densities and standard enthalpies of hydration of Group I and II cations.*

Ion	relative charge density (ionic charge/ionic radius)	$\Delta H^\ominus_h$, hydration enthalpy of gaseous cation/kJ mol^{-1}
Li^+	16.7	-519
Na^+	10.5	-406
K^+	7.5	-322
Rb^+	6.8	-301
Cs^+	5.9	-276
Be^{2+}	64.5	-2150
Mg^{2+}	30.8	-1920
Ca^{2+}	20.2	-1650
Sr^{2+}	17.7	-1480
Ba^{2+}	14.8	-1360

22.2 Chemical properties and bonding type

All the metals are quite *reactive*, especially towards electronegative non-metals such as the halogens and oxygen. Table 22.5 shows some of their principal reactions. Their compounds, except those of beryllium and to some extent lithium, are predominantly ionic. The *alkali metals show an oxidation state of +1* and the *alkaline earth metals +2*, i.e. the atoms lose their outer electrons on forming compounds. Reactivity *increases* on passing down both groups, and the elements of Group I are generally *more reactive* than those of Group II. The alkali metals are so reactive that they are usually stored under oil in order to prevent atmospheric attack.

We shall try to account for these trends by a closer examination of the reaction of the elements with chlorine, oxygen and water.

Table 22.5 *Some chemical reactions of the elements of Groups I and II*

Reaction	GROUP I					GROUP II				
	Li	Na	K	Rb	Cs	Be	Mg	Ca	Sr	Ba
heat in excess oxygen	normal oxide Li_2O	peroxide Na_2O_2	← superoxides →		MO_2	← normal oxides → MO			peroxides MO_2	
heat in chlorine	← chlorides → MCl					← chlorides → MCl_2				
heat in nitrogen	nitride Li_3N	← no action →				← nitrides → M_3N_2				
heat in hydrogen	← hydrides → MH					no action	← hydrides → MH_2			
cold water	← hydroxides → MOH					←no action→	← hydroxides → $M(OH)_2$			
heat in steam	oxide Li_2O	← hydroxide → (very vigorous reaction)				no action	← oxides → MO			
dilute acids	← $M^+(aq)$ → explosively vigorous reaction					← $M^{2+}(aq)$ → vigour of reaction increases →				

In which of the above reactions does lithium resemble magnesium more than the other Group I metals? By what name is this relationship known?

Reaction with chlorine

It is often stated that the atoms of Group I and Group II lose their outer electrons to form a 'stable' noble gas configuration. The energy changes involved in forming sodium and magnesium chlorides from their elements have been discussed in section 5.2. *A stable product is only likely to be formed if the lattice energy released on forming the crystal lattice is greater than the energy required to form the separate gaseous ions from the elements.* Even though the lattice energy of $NaCl_2$ is much *greater* than that of NaCl, the latter is energetically much more stable. The main reason for this is the relatively high *second* ionisation energy of sodium which involves removal of an electron from an 'inner' energy level. Group I metals can easily lose only a single electron, whereas Group II metals can lose both outer electrons, before the 'big jump' in further ionisation energy makes ionic bonding unfavourable.

That accounts for the oxidation states shown by the elements of Group I and Group II, but how do we explain the fact that the elements react *more vigorously* on passing from Group II to Group I and going down the Periodic Table? The most important factor in deciding how vigorous the reaction will be is not the amount of energy released but how *quickly* it is released, i.e. *the vigour of the reaction depends largely upon its rate*. The activation energy for reaction of the Group I elements is *less* than that for those of Group II, largely because much less energy is needed to ionise the metal atom. If, using the data in table 22.3, you compare the energy needed to form an M^{2+} ion with that needed to form an M^+ ion, then you will readily appreciate why the alkaline earth metals tend to react rather more slowly and less vigorously than the alkali metals.

Reaction with oxygen

All the elements burn on heating in oxygen and, apart from beryllium and magnesium, are oxidised by air at room temperature. Although, as always, the oxidation states of the Group I and Group II metals are $+1$ and $+2$ respectively, there are differences in the type of compound formed, owing to the ability of oxygen to form different anions. Table 22.5 shows that *lithium, beryllium, magnesium and calcium form only the normal oxide, containing the O^{2-} ion. With excess oxygen, sodium, strontium and barium form peroxides, containing the O_2^{2-} ion, and the lower Group I metals form superoxides, containing the O_2^- ion.*

the oxide ion	the peroxide ion	the superoxide ion
O^{2-}	O_2^{2-}	O_2^-

We may account for these differences in behaviour in terms of the *charge densities* of the metal cations. The greater the charge/size ratio, or charge density, of the positive ion, the more powerfully it will attract the electrons on the anion. In the case of peroxide and superoxide ions, this may break the bond between the two oxygen atoms, forming the simple oxide.

electrons attracted
to cation

Reaction with water

Apart from beryllium and magnesium, all the elements react with cold water to give hydrogen and a solution of the metal hydroxide.

Group I $M(s) + H_2O(l) \rightarrow M^+(aq) + OH^-(aq) + \frac{1}{2}H_2(g)$

Group II $M(s) + 2H_2O(l) \rightarrow M^{2+}(aq) + 2OH^-(aq) + H_2(g)$

As with the formation of a solid ionic compound, we may construct an enthalpy cycle for the reaction. In the case of an alkali metal such as sodium,

overall	$Na(s) + H_2O(l)$	$\rightarrow Na^+(aq) + OH^-(aq) + \frac{1}{2}H_2(g)$	
step 1.	$Na(s)$	$\rightarrow Na(g)$	ΔH_a
2.	$Na(g)$	$\rightarrow Na^+(g) + e$	$\Delta H_i(1)$
3.	$Na^+(g)$	$\rightarrow Na^+(aq)$	ΔH_h
4.	$H_2O(l)$	$\rightarrow H^+(aq) + OH^-(aq)$	$-\Delta H_n$
5.	$H^+(aq)$	$\rightarrow H^+(g)$	$-\Delta H_h$
6.	$H^+(g)$	$\rightarrow H(g)$	$-\Delta H_i(1)$
7.	$H(g)$	$\rightarrow \frac{1}{2}H_2(g)$	$-\Delta H_a$

From figure 22.3, which shows the complete enthalpy cycle approximately to scale, we can see that the main exothermic term which favours the reaction is the reverse of the ionisation energy of hydrogen, i.e. step 6 above.

Figure 22.3   *Enthalpy cycle for the reaction of sodium with water (approximately to scale)*

ΔH_n *is the enthalpy of neutralisation, i.e. for the reaction*

$$H^+(aq) + OH^-(aq) \rightarrow H_2O(l)$$

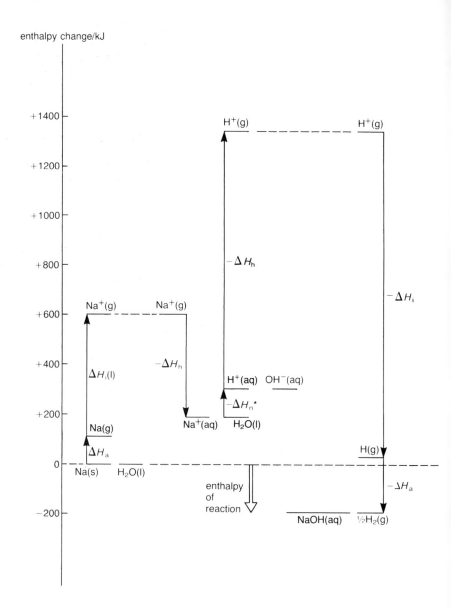

Activity 22.1

1   Sketch an enthalpy level diagram, similar to that in figure 22.3, but for the reaction of a Group II metal with water.

2   The theoretical enthalpy of reaction for each of the metals with water, calculated from such enthalpy cycles, is given below.

Group I	$\Delta H/kJ\ mol^{-1}$	Group II	$\Delta H/kJ\ mol^{-1}$
Li	−224	Be	+61
Na	−188	Mg	−354
K	−199	Ca	−487
Rb	−198	Sr	−478
Cs	−200	Ba	−486

(a)   Which of the metals would be energetically least likely to react with water?

(b) How do you account for the following?

    (i) Magnesium does not react noticeably with cold water but will react on heating in steam.

    (ii) Lithium has the most exothermic enthalpy of reaction of all the alkali metals, yet reacts least vigorously with water.

22.3 Properties of the compounds

Here we shall survey the physical properties, water solubility and thermal stability of some compounds of the alkali and alkaline earth metals.

Physical properties

Since the bonding in their simple compounds is almost invariably ionic, most are white crystalline solids with relatively high melting point. Also, when in solution or in the molten state, they will conduct electricity readily. However, beryllium chloride and lithium chloride are somewhat soluble in organic solvents such as ethanol, indicating considerable covalent character in the bonding.

Water solubility

A full treatment of the tendency of ionic solids to dissolve in water relies upon the concept of 'free energy' change which can be found in more advanced textbooks. Here we shall discuss solubility in terms of the simple enthalpy cycle shown in figure 22.4. *Energy must be supplied by hydration of the ions in order to overcome the attractive forces holding them together in the crystal.*

Figure 22.4 *Energy cycle for dissolving M^+X^- (s) in water*

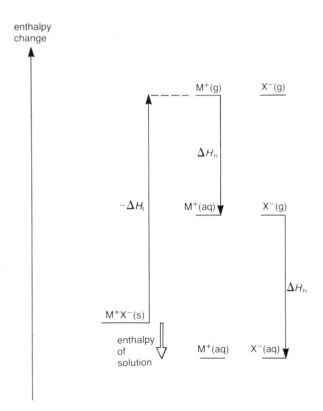

Let us assume that the activation energy for the dissolving process depends upon the attractive forces holding the ions together in the crystal. Compounds with a *high lattice energy* will then tend to be *less* soluble in water. Ions with high charge/size ratio will attract oppositely charged ions more strongly, so we should expect, on the whole, that the solubility of Group II compounds should be somewhat *lower* than the corresponding compounds of the alkali metals (figure 22.5).

Figure 22.5   *Lattice energy and solubility*

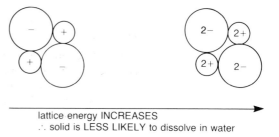

lattice energy INCREASES
∴ solid is LESS LIKELY to dissolve in water

You can see from table 22.6 that this is generally true for the hydroxides and carbonates. In the case of large, singly charged anions, such as nitrate and hydrogencarbonate, which have a low charge/size ratio, the relatively low lattice energy leads to all the compounds being appreciably soluble in water.

Table 22.6   *Thermal stability and water solubility of some compounds of the elements of Groups I and II*

Compounds	Group I					Group II				
	Li	Na	K	Rb	Cs	Be	Mg	Ca	Sr	Ba
hydroxides	←——————— MOH ———————→					←——————— M(OH)$_2$ ———————→				
heat	oxide ←—————— stable ——→					←—————— oxides ———————→				
water solubility	←——— very soluble ———→					slight ←——soluble——→				
carbonates	←——————— M$_2$CO$_3$ ———————→					←——————— MCO$_3$ ———————→				
heat	oxide ←——— stable ———→					←——————— oxides ———————→				
water solubility	slight ←———— soluble————→					←——————— insoluble ———————→				
hydrogen-carbonates*	←——————— MHCO$_3$ ———————→					←——————— M(HCO$_3$)$_2$ ———————→				
heat	←————— carbonates ————→					←————— carbonates ————→				
water solubility	←————— soluble ————→					←————— soluble ————→				
nitrates	←——————— MNO$_3$ ———————→					←——————— M(NO$_3$)$_2$ ———————→				
heat	oxide ←————nitrite————→					←——————— oxides ———————→				
water solubility	←————— soluble ————→					←——————— soluble ———————→				

*The hydrogencarbonates of lithium and all the Group II metals are stable only in aqueous solution.

Potassium nitrate and calcium nitrate are both white solids. How could you distinguish between them experimentally?

The action of water on the oxides presents an interesting case. The oxide ion has quite a high charge/size ratio but the oxides of all the elements except beryllium and magnesium dissolve readily. In fact they *react* to form the metal hydroxide:

$$O^{2-}(s) + H_2O(l) \rightarrow 2OH^-(aq)$$

The peroxides and superoxides also react with water, giving *strongly alkaline* solutions containing *hydroxide* ions:

$$O_2^{2-}(s) + 2H_2O(l) \rightarrow H_2O_2(aq) + 2OH^-(aq)$$
$$2O_2^-(s) + 2H_2O(l) \rightarrow H_2O_2(aq) + 2OH^-(aq) + O_2(g)$$

The oxide and hydroxide of beryllium are unique in the 's' block in showing **amphoteric nature**, e.g. they will dissolve readily in concentrated alkali, forming a solution containing the beryllate ion $[Be(OH)_4]^{2-}$.

Thermal stability

There are some similarities in the action of heat on the corresponding compounds of Group I and Group II, e.g. the hydrogencarbonates break down into carbonates on heating,

$$\text{i.e.} \quad 2HCO_3^- \rightarrow CO_3^{2-} + H_2O + CO_2$$

However, table 22.6 shows that, apart from lithium, the compounds of the Group I elements tend to be thermally more stable than the corresponding compounds of the alkaline earth metals. For example,

▶ Group I **carbonates** generally do not decompose on heating, but those of lithium and Group II break down to give the metal oxide and carbon dioxide,

e.g.
$$Li_2CO_3(s) \rightarrow Li_2O(s) + CO_2(g)$$
$$CaCO_3(s) \rightarrow CaO(s) + CO_2(g)$$

▶ Group I **nitrates** normally give the metal nitrite and oxygen on heating, whereas those of lithium and Group II break down further to give the metal oxide and nitrogen dioxide in addition to oxygen,

e.g.
$$2NaNO_3(s) \rightarrow 2NaNO_2(s) + O_2(g)$$
but
$$4LiNO_3(s) \rightarrow 2Li_2O(s) + 4NO_2(g) + O_2(g)$$
$$2Mg(NO_3)_2(s) \rightarrow 2MgO(s) + 4NO_2(g) + O_2(g)$$

▶ The **hydroxides** of Group I are generally thermally stable, whereas those of lithium and Group II are dehydrated on heating to give the oxide,

e.g.
$$2LiOH(s) \rightarrow Li_2O(s) + H_2O(g)$$
$$Ba(OH)_2(s) \rightarrow BaO(s) + H_2O(g)$$

As with so much of the chemistry of these elements, the explanation for these differences in behaviour involves the *charge/size ratio* of the *metal cations*. Ions with a high charge density will attract electrons powerfully and this will weaken any covalent bonds in the anion as shown in figure 22.6. Thermal stability of the hydroxides, hydrogencarbonates, carbonates and nitrates therefore is *greater* in Group I than Group II and *increases* on passing down the Periodic Table.

Figure 22.6 *Thermal dissociation as a result of anion polarisation - which of the Group I metal nitrates gives nitrogen dioxide on heating? Why is this?*

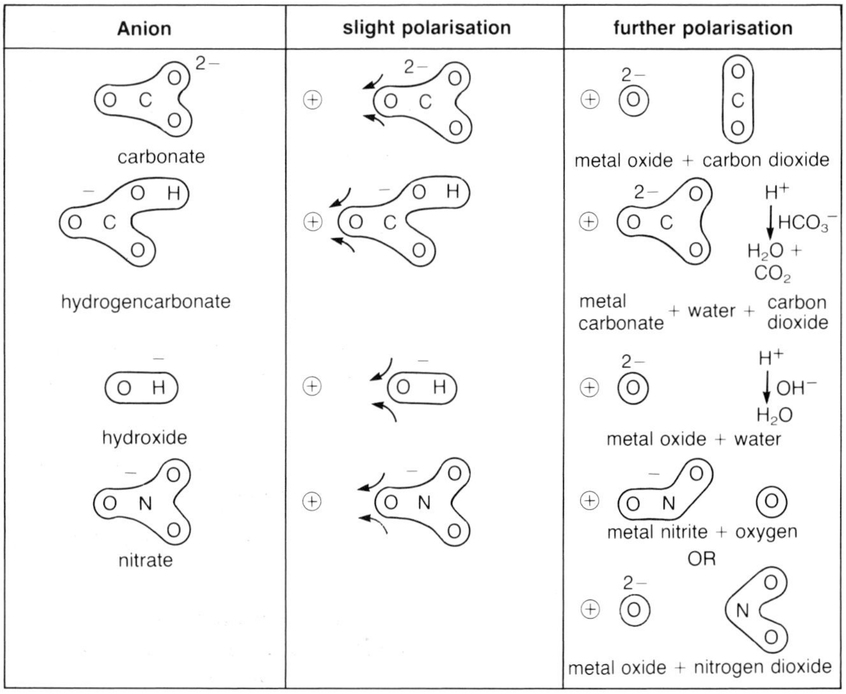

Figure 22.7 *Relative abundance by mass of the alkali and alkaline earth metals*

% by
mass

4.0
3.5
3.0
2.5
2.0
1.5
1.0
0.5

Ca | Na | K | Mg | others

22.4 Occurrence and extraction of the elements

All the metals are too reactive to be found in the free state. Figure 22.7 indicates the relative abundance of the metals in nature and table 22.7 gives a reference list of some of their more important minerals.

Since they are so reactive, the metals may only be extracted by **electrolysis of their molten compounds**. Sodium for example may be extracted from its chloride, obtained from sea-water, using the Down's cell.

at the cathode $\quad Na^+(l) \quad + e^- \rightarrow Na(l) \qquad$ reduction
at the anode $\quad\;\; Cl^-(l) \qquad\quad \rightarrow \frac{1}{2}Cl_2(g) + e^- \quad$ oxidation

A little calcium chloride is added to reduce the melting point of the sodium chloride.

	Group I			Group II	
lithium	$LiAl(SiO_3)_2$	spodumene	**beryllium**	$BeAl_2(SiO_3)_6$	beryl (emerald)
sodium	$NaCl$	rocksalt	**magnesium**	$MgCO_3$	magnesite
	$NaNO_3$	'Chile' saltpetre		$MgSO_4.H_2O$	kieserite
potassium	KNO_3	saltpetre	**calcium**	$CaCO_3$	chalk/limestone/marble
	$KCl. MgCl_2. 6H_2O$	carnallite		$CaSO_4.2H_2O$	gypsum
rubidium	as chlorides usually found with sodium and		**strontium**	as carbonates or sulphates usually found with	
caesium	potassium compounds		**barium**	magnesium and calcium compounds	

Table 22.7 *Some naturally occurring compounds containing the alkali and alkaline earth metals*

22.5 Comments on the activity

Activity 22.1

1 See figure 22.8.

Figure 22.8 *Enthalpy cycle for the reaction of a Group II metal with water
Why are these standard enthalpy changes multipled by 2?

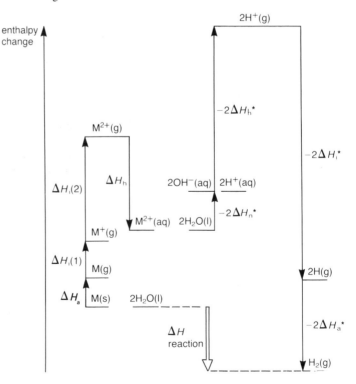

2   (a) Beryllium would be least likely to react with water, since the enthalpy change for the reaction is positive. Beryllium will not, in fact, even react with steam at red heat.

    (b) (i) This is an example of a reaction which is 'energetically' favourable but 'kinetically' unfavourable, i.e. very slow (section 4.13). The relatively high ionisation energies of magnesium make the activation energy of the reaction too high for it to occur at a reasonable rate at room temperature. Magnesium will, however, react on heating with steam to produce hydrogen and the metal oxide.

        (ii) As we pointed out for the action of chlorine on the elements, it is largely the rate of release of energy which determines how vigorous the reaction will be. The rate of reaction will be lower for lithium, since its relatively high ionisation energy is likely to result in a high activation energy.

22.6 Summary and revision plan

1   All these elements are reactive **electropositive** metals. Group I metals are more reactive than those of Group II and reactivity increases on passing down each group.

2   Almost invariably the alkali metals exist as M^+ ions in their compounds and the alkaline earth metals form M^{2+} ions.

3   The **charge density** of the cations is higher for Group II and decreases on passing down each group as ionic radius increases. This variation in cation charge density often explains trends in the properties of the compounds of 's' block elements. For example:

    (a) Many compounds of beryllium (and to a lesser extent lithium) are appreciably covalent owing to the polarising power of the small cation.

    (b) The compounds of Group I metals are generally more soluble than the corresponding compounds of Group II since their **lattice energies** are smaller.

    (c) Except for lithium, the nitrates and carbonates of Group I are thermally more stable than those of Group II, since their cations are less polarising.

    (d) Lithium, beryllium, magnesium and calcium form only **normal oxides,** whereas the other metals form **peroxides** and sometimes **superoxides**.

    (e) The similarity in the charge densities of the cations of the **diagonally related** elements lithium and magnesium lead to considerable similarity in their chemistry.

4   Owing to their high reactivity, the metals are extracted by **electrolysis** of their molten chlorides.

5   Magnesium is used extensively as a constituent of low density alloys, e.g. with aluminium, and sodium is used in the manufacture of the petrol additive, tetraethyl lead.

Boron and Aluminium in Group III

Contents

Aluminium has a very wide range of uses, from cooking foil to aircraft and engine construction. Its low density and very good electrical conductivity, together with its corrosion-resistant oxide layer, makes it very useful for overhead electricity power cables. For many purposes, however, aluminium is alloyed with other metals to improve its strength. Over a hundred different aluminium alloys are available but two of the commonest are

duralumin   95% Al; 4% Cu; 0.5% Mg; 0.5% Mn
magnalium   95% Al; 5% Mg

Food-packing foil, electric power cables and pans: some of the common uses of aluminium and its alloys

Different forms of corundum (aluminium oxide) in their natural and processed states

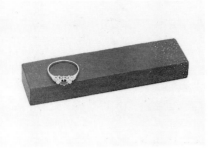

The surface oxide layer on aluminium may be thickened by **anodising**. Here, aluminium is made the anode in the electrolysis of dilute sulphuric acid. At the anode:

$$2OH^-(aq) \rightarrow H_2O(l) + \tfrac{1}{2}O_2(g) + 2e^-$$

The oxygen released at the surface of the metal reacts to form more of the oxide. 'Anodised' aluminium may be readily coloured, since the oxide layer readily takes up dyes. Aluminium sulphate solution may be used in a similar way as a 'mordant' to fix dyes onto fabrics. Treatment with an alkali precipitates aluminium hydroxide in the pores of the cloth.

Corundum is a very hard natural form of aluminium oxide. It is used as an abrasive and as gemstones, e.g. emerald, amethyst and ruby. The colours of these minerals are due to traces of 'd' block compounds.

Boron occurs naturally as borax, $Na_2B_2O_7.10H_2O$. This is used in pottery glazing and the manufacture of 'borosilicate' glass.

23.1 The elements: their atomic and physical properties

Boron is the only non-metal in the group. It has a **macromolecular** covalent structure. As table 23.1 shows, the outer electronic structure of all the atoms is $\mathbf{ns^2np^1}$. The elements all show an oxidation state of $+3$, but gallium, indium and thallium show a progressive tendency to exhibit an oxidation state of $+1$, somewhat resembling the Group I metals.

Data for the properties outlined below may be found in table 23.1. You should particularly note the large differences between boron and the rest of the elements in the group.

Atomic and ionic size

For the same reasons as those already explained in the 's' block, both *atomic and ionic radii tend to increase on passing down the group*. There is, however, little difference in atomic size between aluminium and gallium as a result of the 'd' block contraction, discussed in section 19.3.

Table 23.1 *Data sheet for the elements of Group III*

Element	atomic number	electron configuration	atomic radius* /nm	ionic radius† /nm	ionisation energies/ kJ mol^{-1}				electro- negativity	$E^\ominus$ /V‡	density /g cm^{-3}	m.p. /°C
					1st	2nd	3rd	4th				
boron B	5	[He]$2s^2 2p^1$	0.080	(0.020)	799	2420	3660	25000	2.0		2.34	2300
aluminium Al	13	[Ne]$3s^2 3p^1$	0.125	0.050	577	1820	2740	11600	1.5	−1.66	2.70	660
gallium Ga	31	[Ar]$3d^{10} 4s^2 4p^1$	0.125	0.062	577	1980	2960	6190	1.6	−0.53	5.91	30
indium In	49	[Kr]$4d^{10} 5s^2 5p^1$	0.150	0.081	556	1820	2700	5230	1.7	−0.34	7.30	157
thallium Tl	81	[Xe]$4f^{14} 5d^{10}$ $6s^2 6p^1$	0.155	0.095	590	1970	2870	4900	1.8	+0.72	11.8	304

*values are 'covalent' radii
†for the 3 + ions – the value for B^{3+} is theoretical only, since the ion does not exist. Why?
‡for the process $M^{3+}(aq) + 3e^- \rightleftharpoons M(s)$

Why are the atomic radii of aluminium and gallium similar?
Which is the better oxidising agent $Al^{3+}(aq)$ or $Tl^{3+}(aq)$?

Density

Although boron is a non-metal, its structure is similar to the other members of the group in that its atoms are packed quite closely together. Since, on passing down the Periodic Table, atomic mass increases more rapidly than atomic size, *the density of the elements rises.*

Melting point

This effectively measures the strength of the attraction between the particles in the structure. Since in the boron macromolecule the atoms are interconnected by strong covalent bonds, its melting point is very high. The metals in the group melt at much lower temperatures but there is no well-defined trend on passing from aluminium to thallium.

Electronegativity

As we might expect, *boron, the only non-metal in Group III, has the highest electronegativity,* i.e. its atoms show the greatest tendency to attract the electrons in covalent bonds. Unlike the 's' block elements, the electronegativities of the metals increase slightly on passing down the group.

Ionisation energies

The fourth ionisation energy of all the elements is much larger than the first three, since then the outer valency electrons have been removed and an 'inner' shell is being disturbed. As explained in section 19.4, ionisation energies tend to *fall* on passing down the Periodic Table, although there is relatively little difference in the corresponding ionisation energies of the metallic elements in this group.

23.2 Chemical properties and bonding types

Table 23.2 shows some of the principal reactions of boron and aluminium.

Aluminium is somewhat *less reactive* than might be expected from its quite *negative* electrode potential. It will not, for example, react with water or steam, since

Table 23.2 *A comparison of the reactions of boron and aluminium*

Reaction with	boron	aluminium
oxygen	burns on heating to give boron(III) oxide $4B + 3O_2 \rightarrow 2B_2O_3$	burns on heating to give aluminium(III) oxide $4Al + 3O_2 \rightarrow 2Al_2O_3$
nitrogen	burns on heating to give the nitride $2B + N_2 \rightarrow 2BN$	burns on heating to give the nitride $2Al + N_2 \rightarrow 2AlN$
chlorine	burns on heating to give the trichloride $2B + 3Cl_2 \rightarrow 2BCl_3$	burns on heating to give the trichloride $2Al + 3Cl_2 \rightarrow Al_2Cl_6$
sulphur	burns on heating to give the sulphide $2B + 3S \rightarrow B_2S_3$	violent reaction on heating gives the sulphide $2Al + 3S \rightarrow Al_2S_3$
water	reduces steam at red heat $2B + 3H_2O \rightarrow B_2O_3 + 3H_2$	no action even on heating in steam
acids	no reaction with dilute hydrochloric or sulphuric acid. Oxidised by dilute nitric acid to boric acid: $2B + 6HNO_3 \rightarrow 2H_3BO_3 + 6NO_2$ Oxidised to boric acid by conc. nitric or sulphuric acid (see above)	little or no reaction with dilute sulphuric or nitric acids owing to protection by the oxide layer. Oxide layer dissolves in dil. hydrochloric acid, metal reacts to give the chloride: $2Al + 6HCl \rightarrow 2AlCl_3 + 3H_2$ Unaffected by conc. nitric acid. Conc. hydrochloric and sulphuric acid give the chloride and sulphate respectively
alkalis	reacts with molten alkalis to give a metal borate and hydrogen e.g. $2B + 2NaOH + 2H_2O \rightarrow 2NaBO_2 + 3H_2$	reacts with aqueous alkali to give a metal aluminate and hydrogen $2Al + 2NaOH + 10H_2O \rightarrow 2Na[Al(OH)_4(H_2O)_2] + 3H_2$

it is normally protected by a very thin but impervious *oxide layer*. If this is removed chemically, e.g. by rubbing with mercury(II) chloride solution, the metal reacts rapidly and exothermically with atmospheric moisture to give aluminium hydroxide.

The central area of this sheet of aluminium foil has reacted with moisture in the surrounding air following the removal of its oxide layer

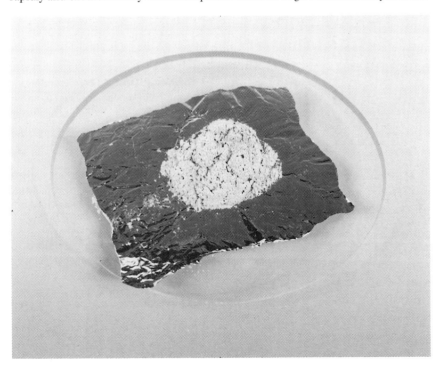

Table 23.3 *A comparison of the properties of some compounds of boron and aluminium*

Compound	boron	aluminium
OXIDE		
empirical formula	B_2O_3	Al_2O_3
structure	covalent polymer	ionic lattice
m.p./°C	450	2017
water	dissolves to give a solution of boric acid $B_2O_3 + 3H_2O \rightarrow 2H_3BO_3$	insoluble
acids	generally no reaction	reacts to give a salt and water $Al_2O_3 + 6H^+ \rightarrow 2Al^{3+} + 3H_2O$
alkalis	reacts to give a borate and water $B_2O_3 + 2OH^- \rightarrow 2BO_2^- + H_2O$	reacts to give an aluminate $Al_2O_3 + 2OH^- + 7H_2O \rightarrow 2[Al(OH)_4(H_2O)_2]^-$
HYDROXIDE		
empirical formula	$B(OH)_3$ or H_3BO_3	$Al(OH)_3$
water	dissolves giving a weakly acidic solution	insoluble
acids	generally no reaction	gives aluminium salts and water e.g. $Al_2O_3 + 3H_2SO_4 \rightarrow Al_2(SO_4)_3 + 3H_2O$
alkalis	reacts to give a borate e.g. $H_3BO_3 + NaOH \rightarrow NaH_2BO_3 + H_2O$	reacts to give an aluminate $Al(OH)_3 + NaOH + 2H_2O \rightarrow Na[Al(OH)_4(H_2O)_2]$
CHLORIDE		
empirical formula	BCl_3	$AlCl_3$
structure	covalent monomer	covalent dimer, Al_2Cl_6 (monomeric at very high temperatures)
m.p./°C	−107	192
water	hydrolyses violently $BCl_3 + 3H_2O \rightarrow H_3BO_3 + 3HCl$	hydrolyses vigorously e.g. $AlCl_3 + 6H_2O \rightleftharpoons [AlOH(H_2O)_5]Cl_2 + HCl$
HYDRIDE		
empirical formula	simplest is BH_3	AlH_3
structure	covalent dimer, B_2H_6	covalent polymer, $(AlH_3)_n$
m.p./°C	−166	decomposes at 100
lithium hydride	gives lithium tetrahydridoborate $2LiH + B_2H_6 \rightarrow 2LiBH_4$	gives lithium tetrahydridoaluminate $LiH + AlH_3 \rightarrow LiAlH_4$

In which of the above reactions do boron and aluminium compounds react in a similar way?

The oxidising nature of concentrated nitric acid stabilises the oxide layer on aluminium and the metal is said to be **passified**.

Although all the elements form compounds in which they show the group oxidation state of +3, considerable energy is required to remove the three electrons in the valency shell of each atom. Indeed boron shows no tendency to form simple ions in its compounds. The fluoride and oxide of aluminium conduct electricity when molten (see the extraction of aluminium in section 23.7) and may be considered to contain simple Al^{3+} ions, but most other binary compounds of aluminium are essentially polar covalent in nature. *The tendency to form positive ions increases on passing down the group*, especially in the +1 oxidation state shown by the lower members. This is explained more fully in section 24.3, which deals with the 'inert pair' effect. Thallium(I) hydroxide, TlOH, is a strong base and closely resembles sodium hydroxide in its properties.

Boron and aluminium form mainly covalent compounds in which their atoms form three covalent bonds. This gives a total of six electrons in the outer energy level, i.e. two electrons short of a noble gas configuration. As a result these molecules tend to act as electron pair acceptors, i.e. Lewis acids, and this is an important feature of their chemistry.

In sections 23.3 to 23.5 we shall compare the properties of some of the compounds of boron and aluminium, shown in table 23.3.

23.3 Oxides and hydroxides

Aluminium oxide has a very much higher melting point than boron oxide, since it is essentially ionic in character. Boron oxide is a covalent polymer which dissolves in water to give an *acidic* solution,

$$B_2O_3(s) + 3H_2O(l) \rightarrow 2H_3BO_3(aq)$$
$$\text{boric acid}$$

Boric acid is very weak, and therefore has a high pK_a value:

$$H_3BO_3(aq) \rightleftharpoons H^+(aq) + H_2BO_3^-(aq) \quad pK_a = 9.2$$

On heating, boric acid is progressively dehydrated to metaboric acid, HBO_2, and finally to boron oxide:

$$H_3BO_3(s) \rightarrow HBO_2(s) + H_2O(g)$$
$$2HBO_2(s) \rightarrow B_2O_3(s) + H_2O(g)$$

Both H_3BO_3 and HBO_2 form **borates** on reaction with alkalis, e.g.

$$HBO_2(aq) + OH^-(aq) \rightarrow BO_2^-(aq) + H_2O(l)$$

Aluminium oxide and aluminium hydroxide are almost insoluble in water but resemble the boron compounds in showing acid character. Thus they will dissolve in alkalis to give **aluminates**, e.g.

$$[Al(OH)_3(H_2O)_3](s) + OH^-(aq) \rightleftharpoons [Al(OH)_4(H_2O)_2]^-(aq) + H_2O(l)$$

Unlike the corresponding boron compounds, aluminium oxide and hydroxide are *amphoteric* and will act as *bases,* dissolving in acids to give aluminium salts, e.g.

$$[Al(OH)_3(H_2O)_3](s) + 3H^+(aq) \rightleftharpoons [Al(H_2O)_6]^{3+}(aq)$$

23.4 Halides

Boron and aluminium react directly with fluorine, chlorine, bromine and iodine to give trihalides. An apparatus suitable for the preparation and collection of anhydrous aluminium chloride is shown in figure 23.1. At room temperature BF_3 and BCl_3 are gaseous, BBr_3 is liquid and BI_3 is a low melting point solid. The aluminium halides, especially the fluoride, are much less volatile.

Figure 23.1 *Laboratory preparation of anhydrous aluminium chloride*

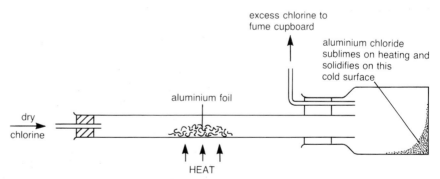

All of the boron halides exist as *plane triangular covalent molecules*, in which the central boron atom has only six electrons in its valency shell:

Since the boron atom is two electrons short of a 'noble gas' configuration, these compounds are excellent Lewis acids. The molecules readily accept a lone pair of electrons, e.g. from ammonia:

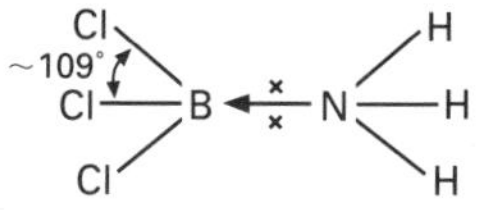

why has the Cl–B–Cl bond angle changed from its value in BCl_3?

Similar reactions occur with water, but only the fluoride forms a stable 'hydrate':

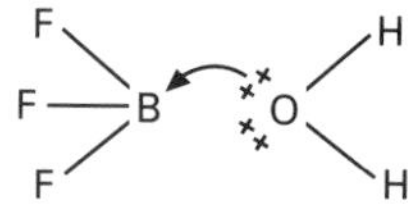

The other boron halides **hydrolyse** in water, giving a mixture of boric and the hydrohalic acids:

$Cl_2BOH + HCl$

excess water

$H_3BO_3 + 3HCl$

Aluminium fluoride is *ionic* in nature, but the other aluminium halides exist as **polar covalent dimers**, in which two halogen atoms 'bridge' the aluminium atoms, completing their 'noble gas' electron configuration. At high temperatures in the vapour phase, the dimers dissociate to give triangular molecules similar in structure to the boron halides:

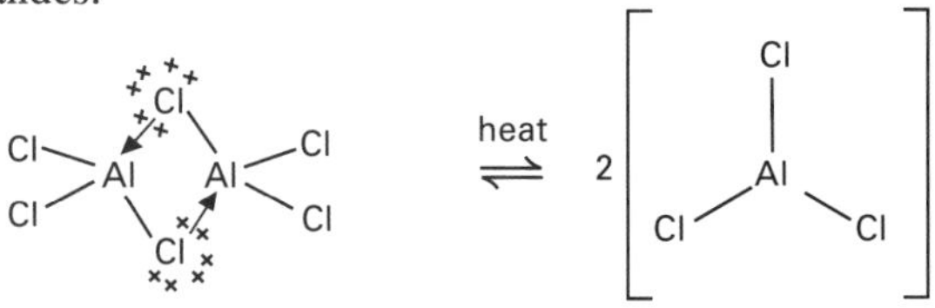

At first glance we might not expect the dimeric aluminium halides to act as Lewis acids, since the outer electronic octet of the aluminium atoms has been completed by the bridging halogen atoms. However the compounds will dissolve in Lewis bases such as ether to give monomeric species:

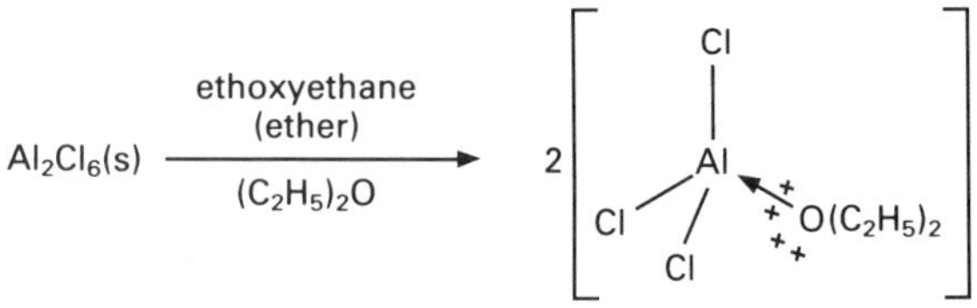

Aluminium fluoride is insoluble in water but the other halides dissolve, giving out considerable heat. The solutions formed readily conduct electricity, showing that the bonding must have changed from covalent to ionic:

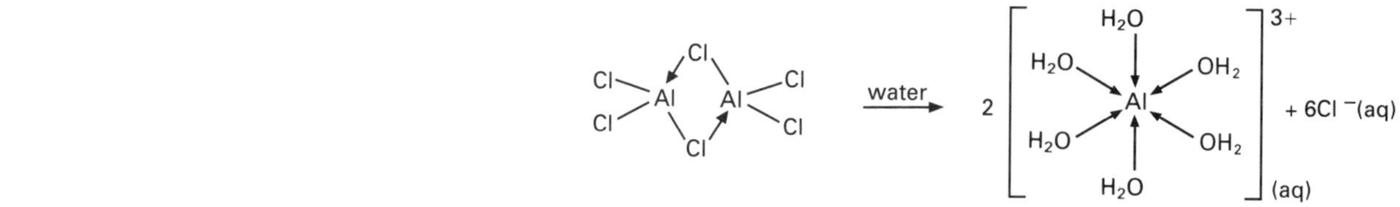

Activity 23.1

1   Using the following enthalpy changes construct an enthalpy cycle for the
    reaction,

$$\tfrac{1}{2}Al_2Cl_6(s) \xrightarrow{\text{water}} Al^{3+}(aq) + 3Cl^-(aq)$$

enthalpy of formation $\Delta H_f[\tfrac{1}{2}Al_2Cl_6]$		=	$-697\,kJ$
atomisation enthalpies ΔHa	[Al]	=	$314\,kJ$
	[Cl]	=	$121\,kJ$
ionisation energies ΔH_i 1st	[Al]	=	$578\,kJ$
ΔH_i 2nd	[Al]	=	$1816\,kJ$
ΔH_i 3rd	[Al]	=	$2744\,kJ$
electron affinity ΔH_e	[Cl]	=	$-364\,kJ$
hydration energies ΔH_h	$[Al^{3+}]$	=	$-4690\,kJ$
	$[Cl^-]$	=	$-364\,kJ$

2   Calculate the theoretical enthalpy change for the above reaction.

3   Which of the above standard enthalpy changes is largely responsible for the
    exothermic reaction on dissolving aluminium chloride in water?

In addition, these solutions are *strongly acidic*, the $[Al(H_2O)_6]^{3+}$ ion readily losing
protons, as outlined in section 23.3.

$$[Al(H_2O)_6]^{3+}(aq) \xrightarrow{-H^+} [AlOH(H_2O)_5]^{2+}(aq) \xrightarrow{-H^+} [Al(OH)_2(H_2O)_4]^+(aq) \quad \text{etc.}$$

Addition of a base causes further ionisation and results in the precipitation of
hydrated aluminium hydroxide:

$$[Al(OH)_2(H_2O)_4]^+(aq) \xrightleftharpoons{-H^+} [Al(OH)_3(H_2O)_3](s)$$

If the base is weak, e.g. aqueous ammonia, the reaction stops at this stage, but as
described in section 23.3, aluminium hydroxide is amphoteric and will dissolve in
excess *strong base*, such as sodium hydroxide, to give an *aluminate*:

$$[Al(OH)_3(H_2O)_3](s) \xrightarrow{-H^+} [Al(OH)_4(H_2O)_2]^-(aq)$$

Activity 23.2

When sodium carbonate solution is added to aqueous aluminium chloride, a white
precipitate is formed and bubbles of a colourless gas are evolved.

1   What is the colourless gas?
2   What is the white precipitate? (It is NOT aluminium carbonate.)
3   Complete the following ionic equation for the reaction

$$[Al(H_2O)_6]^{3+}(aq) + CO_3^{2-}(aq) \rightarrow$$

The Lewis acid nature of the boron and aluminium halides makes them useful
catalysts for some organic reactions. The use of aluminium chloride in the
Friedel–Crafts reaction is outlined in section 36.5.3.

23.5 Hydrides

Aluminium forms only a single hydride, prepared by adding lithium hydride to a
solution of aluminium chloride in ether. It is a polymeric white solid of uncertain
structure which is stable up to $100\,°C$:

$$3LiH + AlCl_3 \rightarrow 3LiCl + AlH_3$$

If *excess* lithium hydride is used, the ether-soluble compound **lithium
tetrahydridoaluminate** is formed:

$$4LiH + AlCl_3 \rightarrow 3LiCl + LiAlH_4$$

This contains the tetrahedral tetrahydridoaluminate complex ion, AlH_4^-, and is a very useful reducing agent in organic chemistry. Its use in reducing carbonyl compounds to alcohols is described in section 39.8.2. In contrast to aluminium, boron forms a wide range of hydrides called **boranes**. These fall into two groups having the general formulae B_nH_{n+4} and B_nH_{n+6}, where n is a whole number between 2 and 10. The simplest boron hydride is diborane, B_2H_6, whose structure was mentioned in section 21.2. It may be made by the action of lithium hydride on boron trifluoride:

$$6LiH + 2BF_3 \rightarrow 6LiF + B_2H_6$$

A mixture of the higher boranes may be obtained by passing diborane through a heated tube. Most are rather unstable gases which are readily hydrolysed by water and oxidised by air.

If diborane is passed into a solution of lithium hydride in ether, **lithium tetrahydridoborate** is formed:

$$2LiH + B_2H_6 \rightarrow 2LiBH_4$$

Like lithium tetrahydridoaluminate, this is a very useful reducing agent in organic chemistry.

23.6 Complex ions

Throughout this chapter we have stressed the tendency of both boron and aluminium compounds to act as *Lewis acids* by accepting a lone pair of electrons to complete the 'noble gas' electron configuration of the central atom. Such compounds, therefore, readily combine with a range of electron pair donors to form complexes. Amongst the examples we have already considered in this chapter are the hydride complexes, BH_4^- and AlH_4^-. Boron forms a similar *tetrahedral* complex, BF_4^- with fluoride ions, but the aluminium fluoro complex, AlF_6^{3-}, is *six-coordinate octahedral*.

In common with all the elements in the second period, a boron atom can only accommodate eight electrons in its valency shell and is therefore restricted to a a maximum covalency of four. Although aluminium resembles boron in forming several 4-coordinate tetrahedral complexes, the presence of empty 'd' orbitals in its valency shell means that the atom may hold more than eight electrons in its outer shell by accepting more than one lone pair of electrons. This behaviour is particularly common with oxygen donors and all water/hydroxo complexes of Al^{3+} are octahedral, e.g. $[Al(H_2O)_6]^{3+}$, $[Al(OH)_3(H_2O)_3]$ and $[Al(OH)_4(H_2O)_2]^-$.

Some common complex ions of boron and aluminium are compared in table 23.4.

Table 23.4 *A comparison of some complex ions containing boron and aluminium*

	hydride	fluoride	chloride	bromide	water/hydroxide
boron	BH_4^-	BF_4^-	–	–	–
aluminium	AlH_4^-	AlF_6^{3-}	$AlCl_4^-$	$AlBr_4^-$	$[Al(H_2O)_6]^{3+}$ through to $[Al(OH)_4(H_2O)_2]^-$

Why can aluminium, but not boron, form 6-coordinate complexes?

What will be the shapes of BF_4^- and AlF_6^{3-}?

23.7 Extraction of aluminium

Aluminium, which comprises about 7.5% of the earth's crust, is the *most abundant metal*. Although widely distributed in clay and many rocks, it is often present in low concentration and the only *commercially important* source is bauxite which contains about 50% of aluminium oxide together with iron oxide and other impurities. The production of aluminium involves purification of the bauxite followed by electrolytic reduction of the alumina or aluminium oxide.

Separation of the aluminium oxide from the iron oxide and other impurities in bauxite depends upon its amphoteric nature. The bauxite is treated with sodium hydroxide solution which dissolves the alumina as sodium aluminate:

$$Al_2O_3(s) + 2NaOH(aq) + 7H_2O(l) \rightarrow 2Na[Al(OH)_4(H_2O)_2](aq)$$

Insoluble impurities, including iron(III) oxide, are filtered off and hydrated aluminium oxide, $Al_2O_3.3H_2O$, is precipitated by introducing a 'seed' of the pure solid. The water of crystallisation is driven off by heating, which leaves pure anhydrous aluminium oxide:

$$Al_2O_3.3H_2O(s) \xrightarrow{\text{ignite}} Al_2O_3(s) + 3H_2O(g)$$

Electrolysis of fused aluminium oxide gives **molten aluminium** at the cathode and **oxygen** at the anode.

cathode reaction: $\quad Al^{3+} + 3e^- \rightarrow Al \qquad$ reduction
anode reaction: $\quad O^{2-} - 2e^- \rightarrow O \rightarrow \frac{1}{2}O_2$ oxidation

In practice, since the melting point of alumina exceeds 2000°C, it is dissolved in molten sodium aluminium fluoride (cryolite), Na_3AlF_6, when the electrolysis may be carried out at about 1000°C. The concentration of alumina in the mixture is maintained at about 5% and under these conditions the cryolite remains unchanged. Molten aluminium is siphoned off from the base of the electrolysis cell shown in figure 23.2. The carbon anodes must be replaced periodically since they are slowly oxidised to carbon dioxide by the oxygen produced at such high temperatures.

Two carbon anodes for use in an electrolysis cell producing aluminium. The first was photographed before use and the second after use. Why does the appearance of the anode change during the electrolysis?

Figure 23.2 *Production of aluminium by electrolysis of molten alumina*

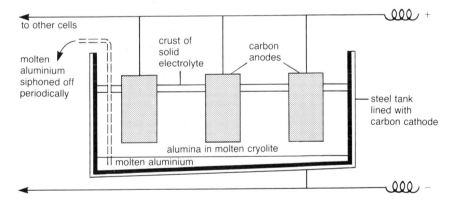

23.8 Comments on the activities

Activity 23.1

1 See figure 23.3.
2 The theoretical enthalpy change for the reaction is −362 kJ.
3 The driving force for the reaction is the highly exothermic hydration energy of the Al^{3+} ion, which more than offsets the energy required to form the Al^{3+} ion. The high charge density on the Al^{3+} ion makes it extremely attractive to the polar water molecules.

Figure 23.3 *Enthalpy level diagram for dissolving anhydrous aluminium chloride in water*

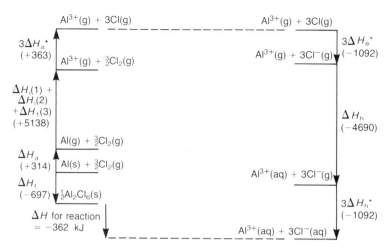

Activity 23.2

1 The gas is carbon dioxide.
2 The white precipitate is hydrated aluminium hydroxide, $[Al(OH)_3(H_2O)_3]$.
3 $[Al(H_2O)_6]^{3+}(aq)$ readily loses protons. Since it is acidic, it will liberate carbon dioxide from carbonates. Sodium carbonate is a fairly weak base and will not form aluminate solutions with hydrated aluminium hydroxide.

$$[Al(H_2O)_6]^{3+}(aq) \rightarrow [Al(OH)_3(H_2O)_3](s) + 3H^+(aq) \times 2$$
$$CO_3{}^{2-}(aq) + 2H^+(aq) \rightarrow (H_2CO_3) \rightarrow H_2O(l) + CO_2(g) \times 3$$

$$2[Al(H_2O)_6]^{3+}(aq) + 3CO_3{}^{2-}(aq) \rightarrow 2[Al(OH)_3(H_2O)_3](s) + 3H_2O(l) + 3CO_2(g)$$

No carbonates of M^{3+} ions exist, since they are all sufficiently acidic in aqueous solution to liberate carbon dioxide from $CO_3{}^{2-}$.

23.9 Summary and revision plan

1 Metallic character in the 'p' block increases on passing down the group. Boron is the only non-metal in Group III.
2 Boron always, and aluminium usually, bond covalently in their compounds. The **maximum covalency** of boron is **4**, whereas that of aluminium is **6**.
3 The oxide and hydroxide of boron are acidic whereas the corresponding aluminium compounds are **amphoteric**, i.e. act as either acids or bases.
4 Anhydrous aluminium chloride is prepared by direct combination of the elements. It exists as the **dimer**, Al_2Cl_6, in the solid state but $AlCl_3$ molecules are formed in the vapour. The solid dissolves exothermically in water to give an ionic, acidic solution. The driving force for the reaction is the high hydration enthalpy of the small, highly charged Al^{3+} ion.

   Anhydrous aluminium chloride is used as a catalyst in Friedel-Crafts reactions in organic chemistry (section 36.5.3).
5 Boron forms an extensive range of hydrides called **boranes**, most of which contain '3-centre' covalent bonds.

   Tetrahydrido complexes of boron and aluminium, $BH_4{}^-$ and $AlH_4{}^-$, are used as powerful reducing agents, e.g. in the reduction of ketones to secondary alcohols (section 39.8.2).
6 Aluminium is manufactured by the electrolysis of molten aluminium oxide. Its low density, good electrical conductivity and corrosion resistant **oxide layer** make it ideal for use in overhead power cables.

   Aluminium may be **anodised** by making it the anode in the electrolysis of dilute sulphuric acid. This thickens the surface oxide layer, increasing corrosion resistance and allowing the metal to be readily 'dyed'.

CHAPTER
24
Group IV

Contents

Can you say which Group IV elements or their compounds are illustrated in these photographs?

These elements show, perhaps, the widest variation in properties of any group in the Periodic Table. Carbon and silicon are non-metals, germanium is a semi-metal, but both tin and lead are typical metals. As might be expected from their diagonal relationship in the Periodic Table, silicon and boron are quite similar in many of their properties.

All the elements have important uses. **Carbon** in the form of diamond is used in cutting tools as well as in jewellery, whereas graphite has lubricant properties and forms the 'lead' in pencils.

Silicon and **germanium** become semiconductors when 'doped' with certain impurities. Such materials have led to the miniaturisation of electronic circuits by the development, first of the transistor, and, more recently, of large scale integrated circuits. Modern microchips may contain the equivalent of hundreds of thousands of individual components. Glass also contains silicon, as do the silicones, polymers used as waterproofing agents and lubricants.

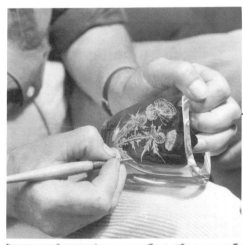

Industrial diamonds

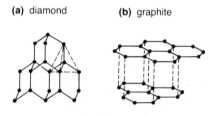

(a) diamond   **(b)** graphite

Figure 24.1 *The structure of the allotropes of carbon*

Sand is mainly silicon oxide

Tin is used in alloys such as type metal, solder, bronze and pewter. Its major use is in plating steel food and drink cans to prevent rusting.

Most of the world's **lead** production is converted into tetraethyl lead, $Pb(C_2H_5)_4$, an anti-knock additive for petrol. Every year it is estimated that almost 10 000 tonnes of lead compounds are released into the air from engine exhaust fumes. This is a severe environmental problem, since lead is a dangerous cumulative poison. Lead metal, itself, is used as a roofing material, in car batteries, and in alloys such as solder.

24.1 The elements: structure, atomic and physical properties

Whilst the trends in properties on passing down the group from silicon to lead are fairly smooth, and in general quite predictable, carbon is often significantly different. *Although the first members of many groups are often untypical, the differences between carbon and the rest of the group IV are quite dramatic.*

Carbon exists in two allotropic forms, **diamond** and **graphite**, both of which are **macromolecular**. In diamond each carbon atom is linked by single covalent bonds to four others in a tetrahedral shape as shown in figure 24.1a. This very rigid arrangement accounts for the extreme *hardness* of diamond. The graphite structure is unique to carbon and results from its ability to form stable multiple bonds. It consists of flat macromolecular sheets in which each carbon atom is bonded to three others in a hexagonal arrangement. In this structure, shown in figure 24.1b, each carbon atom uses only three of its valency electrons to form σ bonds, leaving one electron in a 2p orbital perpendicular to the plane of the sheet. These overlap to form a π molecular orbital which extends over all the atoms in each sheet. Since the 2p electrons are delocalised, graphite readily *conducts electricity* in the plane of the 'sheets' but not perpendicular to them. Adjacent sheets are only weakly held together by van der Waals' forces and may readily slide over each other, thus accounting for the excellent *lubricating* properties of graphite. Under normal conditions graphite is energetically slightly more stable than diamond.

$$C_{(diamond)} \rightarrow C_{(graphite)} \quad \Delta H = -2 \, kJ$$

At high temperature and pressure, however, the relative stabilities are reversed and under such conditions graphite may be converted into 'industrial' diamond. Since the activation energy for the process is high, the rate of conversion is slow even in the presence of a catalyst.

Silicon and germanium exist *only* in the 'diamond' type structure. At low temperatures tin also adopts this structure but normally it exists as an allotrope with a metallic lattice. Lead does *not* exhibit allotropy, and always adopts a metallic structure.

Activity 24.1

High temperature reduction of silicon oxide, SiO_2, with carbon gives carbon monoxide and silicon carbide, SiC. The latter is a high melting, extremely hard substance and under its common name, carborundum, is used as an abrasive.

1. Write an equation for the formation of silicon carbide by the above reaction.
2. Bearing in mind its hardness, what kind of structure would you expect silicon carbide to possess?
3. Why should silicon carbide adopt this structure?

Some of the main atomic and physical properties of the elements are summarised in table 24.1.

Table 24.1 *Data sheet for the elements of group IV*

Element	atomic number	electron configuration	atomic radius /nm*	ionic radius /nm†	ionisation energies/kJ mol⁻¹					electro-negativity	density /g cm⁻³	m.p. /°C
					1st	2nd	3rd	4th	5th			
carbon C	6	[He]$2s^2 2p^2$	0.077	–	1090	2350	4610	6220	37800	2.5	$2.25^{(1)}$ $3.51^{(2)}$	3730 (sub)
silicon Si	14	[Ne]$3s^2 3p^2$	0.117	–	786	1580	3230	4360	16000	1.8	2.33	1410
germanium Ge	32	[Ar]$3d^{10}4s^2 4p^2$	0.122	0.093	762	1540	3300	4390	8950	1.8	5.35	937
tin Sn	50	[Kr]$4d^{10}5s^2 5p^2$	0.140	0.112	707	1410	2940	3930	7780	1.8	7.28	232
lead Pb	82	[Xe]$4f^{14}5d^{10}6s^2 6p^2$	0.154	0.120	716	1450	3080	4080	6700	1.8	11.3	327

*values are 'covalent' radii
†for the 2+ ions
(1) graphite; (2) diamond

Why is diamond denser than graphite?

Why is there a 'big jump' between the values of the 4th and 5th ionisation energies for all these elements?

Atomic and ionic size

As with all groups, *atomic radius increases on passing down the Periodic Table.* Although the nuclear charge increases, new electron principal energy levels are started and more inner 'screening' electrons are present. You should note that, unlike Group III, there is a small increase on passing from period 3, silicon, to period 4, germanium, despite the 'contraction' caused by the first row of the 'd' block.

Carbon and silicon form *no* simple cations, and apart from tin(IV) fluoride and lead(IV) fluoride, it is doubtful whether any compounds contain true 4+ ions. Tin, lead, and possibly germanium, do form 2+ ions and, as expected, the size of these increases on passing down the group.

Density

All the elements have a quite close-packed structure, carbon, silicon and germanium being macromolecular and tin and lead having a metallic lattice. Since atomic mass increases more rapidly than atomic volume, this leads to a *general increase in density on passing down the group.* The one exception to this is diamond, which has a greater density than silicon. This is caused by the quite large increase in atomic radius on passing from carbon to silicon.

Melting point

Diamond and graphite do not melt under atmospheric pressure but sublime at over 3700 °C. This indicates the great strength of carbon–carbon bonds within these macromolecules. Silicon and germanium, with structures similar to diamond, melt at fairly high temperatures but the data in table 24.1 indicate that the bonding here is not quite so strong as in carbon. Tin and lead have much lower melting points which suggest *comparatively weak* metallic bonding in their lattices. This may be due in part to the **inert pair effect** (section 24.3), *i.e. the reluctance of their atoms to use the outer pair of 's' electrons in bonding.* Solder, an important low melting alloy, is composed largely of tin and lead.

Electronegativity

This is fairly constant within the group except for carbon which is considerably more electronegative, i.e. it has the greatest tendency to attract the electrons in a covalent bond. This has important consequences for the chemistry of the hydrides which is discussed in section 24.5.

24.2 Chemical properties and bonding types

Some of the main reactions of the Group IV elements are summarised in table 24.2.

Table 24.2   *A comparison of the reactions of the elements of Group IV*

Reaction with	carbon	silicon	germanium	tin	lead
excess oxygen	burns on heating $C + O_2 \rightarrow CO_2$	burns on heating $Si + O_2 \rightarrow SiO_2$	burns on heating $Ge + O_2 \rightarrow GeO_2$	burns on heating $Sn + O_2 \rightarrow SnO_2$	oxidises progressively on heating to PbO and Pb_3O_4
sulphur	heat $C + 2S \rightarrow CS_2$	heat $Si + 2S \rightarrow SiS_2$	heat $Ge + 2S \rightarrow GeS_2$	heat $Sn + S \rightarrow SnS$	heat $Pb + S \rightarrow PbS$
halogens	combines directly only with fluorine heat $C + 2F_2 \rightarrow CF_4$	combines directly with all halogens heat $Si + 2X_2 \rightarrow SiX_4$	combines directly with all halogens heat $Ge + 2X_2 \rightarrow GeX_4$	combines directly with all halogens heat $Sn + 2X_2 \rightarrow SnX_4$	PbI_2, $PbBr_2$ $PbCl_4$ (unstable) and PbF_4 on direct combination
water	decomposes steam at red heat $C + H_2O \rightarrow CO + H_2$	reacts on heating in steam $Si + 2H_2O \rightarrow SiO_2 + 2H_2$	reacts on heating in steam $Ge + 2H_2O \rightarrow GeO_2 + 2H_2$	reacts on heating in steam $Sn + 2H_2O \rightarrow SnO_2 + 2H_2$	no reaction
acids	unaffected by dilute acids oxidised to CO_2 by c.HNO_3 or c.H_2SO_4 $C + 4HNO_3 \rightarrow CO_2 + 2H_2O + 4NO_2$	unaffected by dilute acids unaffected by concentrated acids	little reaction with dilute acids oxidised to hydrated GeO_2 by c.HNO_3 or c.H_2SO_4	slowly gives Sn^{2+}(aq) with dilute acids reacts to give Sn^{2+}(aq) with c.HCl gives hydrated SnO_2 with c.HNO_3, and Sn^{4+} with c.H_2SO_4	little reaction with dilute acids reacts to give Pb^{2+}(aq) with HNO_3 and hot c.HCl
alkalis	no reaction	reacts to give solutions of silicates $Si + 2OH^- + H_2O \rightarrow SiO_3{}^{2-} + 2H_2$	reacts to give solutions of germanates $Ge + 2OH^- + H_2O \rightarrow GeO_3{}^{2-} + 2H_2$	reacts to give solutions of stannate(IV) $Sn + 2OH^- + H_2O \rightarrow SnO_3{}^{2-} + 2H_2$	reacts to give solutions of plumbate(II) $Pb + 2OH^- \rightarrow PbO_2{}^{2-} + H_2$

Compare the reaction of tin and lead with the halogens. PbI_4 and $PbBr_4$ do not exist. Can you explain why?

Covalent Bonding

All the elements react with non-metals such as fluorine and oxygen to form largely covalent compounds in which they show a valency of **four**. The ease with which these compounds are formed seems to depend largely on the electronegativity difference between the two elements. Thus, unlike the rest of the group, the more electronegative carbon will not combine directly with chlorine.

The four outer electrons of a Group IV atom are arranged:

ns^2 np^2

In order to form four covalent bonds, one of the outer 's' electrons must be **promoted** to the vacant 'p' orbital to give four unpaired electrons:

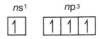

In theory, the atom may then complete its 'noble gas' electron configuration in one of the three ways illustrated in figure 24.2, i.e. by forming either

▶ four single bonds;
▶ two single and one double bond;
▶ either two double bonds, or one single and one triple bond.

Figure 24.2 *Covalent bonding in the compounds of Group IV elements*

(a) four single bonds

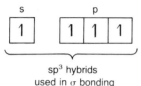

sp³ hybrids used in σ bonding

e.g.

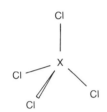

(b) one double and two single bonds

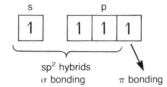

sp² hybrids σ bonding   π bonding

e.g.

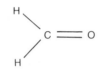

(c) two double bonds, or one triple and one single bond

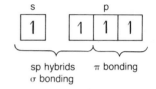

sp hybrids σ bonding   π bonding

e.g.

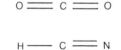

and

As we shall see in later sections, *carbon shows a much greater tendency to form stable multiple bonds than any of the other elements in the group.* This readiness of carbon to form multiple bonds also accounts for the fact that it alone in the group forms a stable covalent monoxide. Its structure will be considered in section 24.4.

Although many of the divalent halides of tin and lead are predominantly ionic in aqueous solution, in the vapour phase they exist as V-shaped covalent molecules. Here only the outer 'p' electrons are used in bond formation, the 's' electrons remaining as a lone pair:

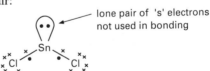

lone pair of 's' electrons not used in bonding

Ionic Bonding

The ionisation energies given in table 24.1 may be used to show that the energy required to produce the 4+ ion *decreases* on passing down the group. *Lead(IV) fluoride and tin(IV) fluoride are the only tetravalent compounds to show ionic properties.*

On passing down the group, however, from germanium there is an increasing tendency for the atoms to form 2+ ions. Here only the outer 'p' electrons are lost and the atom retains its outer 's' electron pair.

$$X \xrightarrow{} X^{2+} + 2e^-$$
$$/ns^2np^2 \qquad /ns^2$$

This tendency, shown also by the lower elements in other 'p' block groups, is known as the **inert pair effect** and will be discussed in greater detail in the next section.

Although carbon does not form simple cations, it combines on heating with several electropositive metals to form ionic compounds. Most of these **carbides** are thought to contain the C_2^{2-} ion, since on hydrolysis they give ethyne, e.g.

$$Na_2C_2 + 2H_2O \rightarrow 2NaOH + C_2H_2$$
$$(C_2^{2-} + 2H^+ \rightarrow C_2H_2)$$

Aluminium and beryllium carbides, however, give methane on hydrolysis, e.g.

$$Al_4C_3 + 12H_2O \rightarrow 4Al(OH)_3 + 3CH_4$$

24.3 The inert pair effect

This may be stated as follows:

'On passing down Group IV there is an increasing tendency for the outer pair of 's' electrons to remain inert, i.e. not to take part in bonding, resulting in greater stability of the divalent compounds.'

Let us examine a piece of evidence in support of this claim.

▶ The standard enthalpies of formation, *quoted per mole of oxygen atoms* in table 24.3, show that the energetic stability of the monoxide relative to the dioxide *increases* on passing down the group.

Lead(IV) oxide, as might be expected from these figures, is an excellent **oxidising agent** and decomposes on gentle heating to give the monoxide and oxygen. This instability of lead(IV) with respect to lead(II) is also found in aqueous solution, $Pb^{4+}(aq)$ being much more readily reduced than $Sn^{4+}(aq)$:

$$Sn^{4+}(aq) + 2e^- \rightleftharpoons Sn^{2+}(aq); \quad E^{\ominus} +0.15 \text{ volts (mild oxidant)}$$
$$Pb^{4+}(aq) + 2e^- \rightleftharpoons Pb^{2+}(aq); \quad E^{\ominus} +1.69 \text{ volts (powerful oxidant)}$$

Table 24.3 *Standard enthalpies of formation for the Group IV oxides*

$\Delta H_f^{\ominus}(XO)/$ kJ mol^{-1}		$\Delta H_f^{\ominus}(XO_2)/$ kJ mol^{-1} of oxygen atoms	
CO	−111	CO_2	−197
SiO	*	SiO_2	−429
GeO	*	GeO_2	−269
SnO	−286	SnO_2	−291
PbO	−218	PbO_2	−139

*no stable monoxide formed

Which monoxide is energetically more stable than its dioxide? Why should we compare the enthalpies of formation per mole of oxygen atoms?

24.4 Oxides

Preparation

Carbon forms three well defined *gaseous* oxides. All three may be prepared by dehydration of the corresponding acid. Carbon dioxide, CO_2, is normally prepared by the action of a dilute acid on a carbonate. This may be considered to liberate the weak 'carbonic acid', H_2CO_3, which immediately decomposes to give carbon dioxide and water:

$$CO_3^{2-} + 2H^+(aq) \rightarrow [H_2CO_3(aq)] \rightarrow H_2O(l) + CO_2(g)$$
$$\text{(unstable)}$$

Carbon monoxide is formed when methanoic acid is dehydrated by concentrated sulphuric acid:

$$HCOOH(l) \xrightarrow[\text{(−H}_2\text{O)}]{\text{c.H}_2\text{SO}_4 \text{ warm}} CO(g)$$

Carbon suboxide is the *anhydride* of propanedioic acid:

$$HOOC.CH_2.COOH(s) \xrightarrow[\text{(−2H}_2\text{O)}]{\text{P}_2\text{O}_5 \text{ heat}} C_3O_2(g)$$

Both carbon monoxide and carbon suboxide form carbon dioxide on burning in excess air or oxygen.

Silicon forms the dioxide only, SiO_2, which exists naturally in several forms, including quartz. As with the dioxides of germanium and tin, it may be prepared by igniting the element in air or oxygen:

$$Si(s) + O_2(g) \xrightarrow{\text{ignite}} SiO_2(s)$$

Heating **lead** in air does *not* give the dioxide but first the monoxide, PbO, which is converted into triplumbic tetroxide, Pb_3O_4, at about 450°C:

$$2Pb(s) + O_2(g) \xrightarrow{\text{heat}} 2PbO(s)$$
$$\text{yellow}$$

$$6PbO(s) + O_2(g) \xrightarrow{450°C} 2Pb_3O_4(s)$$
$$\text{orange}$$

Lead(IV) oxide may be prepared by oxidising a solution of lead(II) nitrate with sodium chlorate(I):

$$Pb(NO_3)_2(aq) + H_2O(l) + NaOCl(aq) \rightarrow PbO_2(s) + NaCl(aq) + 2HNO_3(aq)$$
$$\text{brown}$$

It is a powerful oxidising agent and decomposes on heating into lead(II) oxide and oxygen.

Thermal decomposition of tin(II) ethanedioate gives **tin(II) oxide**:

$$Sn(COO)_2(s) \xrightarrow{\text{heat}} SnO(s) + CO_2(g) + CO(g)$$
$$\text{black}$$

It is rather easily oxidised to tin(IV) oxide but the reducing atmosphere created by the carbon monoxide helps to prevent this.

We shall now consider some of the important properties of the oxides of Group IV, summarised in table 24.4.

Structure

All the oxides of the group are solid, except for those of carbon which are gaseous at room temperature and pressure. The latter are composed of **simple small covalent molecules**, *whose structures demonstrate the ability of carbon atoms to form stable multiple bonds.*

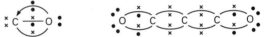

The high melting point of silicon dioxide results from a **macromolecular** covalent structure, in which each silicon atom is linked by *single* covalent bonds to four oxygen atoms in a tetrahedral arrangement.

repeated to give a macromolecular structure of empirical formula SiO_2

The relatively high melting points of the other dioxides in the group also suggest a macromolecular structure, whilst tin(II) oxide and lead(II) oxide are more ionic in character.

The structure of triplumbic tetroxide, Pb_3O_4, is of interest since it behaves as a molecular mixture of lead(IV) oxide and lead(II) oxide. X-ray studies show that each layer of PbO_2 is 'sandwiched' between two layers of PbO.

Acid/base nature

All the oxides show acidic character to some extent. Carbon suboxide dissolves in water to give propanedioic acid, and carbon dioxide is somewhat soluble giving the unstable weak carbonic acid:

$$C_3O_2(g) + 2H_2O(l) \rightarrow HOOCCH_2COOH(aq)$$
$$CO_2(g) + H_2O(l) \rightleftharpoons H_2CO_3(aq)$$

Table 24.4 *A comparison of the properties of some compounds of Group IV elements*

Compound	carbon	silicon	germanium	tin	lead
(IV) oxides m.p./(°C)	CO_2 -56	SiO_2 1710	GeO_2 1120	SnO_2 1800 (sublimes)	PbO_2 300 (decomp.)
water	dissolves to give a weak acid $H_2O + CO_2 \rightleftharpoons H_2CO_3$	insoluble	insoluble	insoluble	insoluble
sodium hydroxide	gives a carbonate or hydrogencarbonate $CO_2 + 2OH^- \rightarrow CO_3^{2-} + H_2O$ $CO_2 + OH^- \rightarrow HCO_3$	gives a silicate $SiO_2 + 2OH^- \rightarrow SiO_3^{2-} + H_2O$	gives a germanate $GeO_2 + 2OH^- \rightarrow GeO_3^{2-} + H_2O$	gives a stannate(IV) $SnO_2 + 2OH^- \rightarrow SnO_3^{2-} + H_2O$	gives a plumbate(IV) $PbO_2 + 2OH^- \rightarrow PbO_3^{2-} + H_2O$
(II) oxides m.p./(°C)	CO -199	–	(GeO unstable)	SnO 1077 (decomp.)	PbO 888
oxygen	burns on heating $2CO + O_2 \rightarrow 2CO_2$		readily oxidised $2GeO + O_2 \rightarrow 2GeO_2$	oxidised on warming $2SnO + O_2 \rightarrow 2SnO_2$	oxidised to Pb_3O_4 at 400°C
water	insoluble			insoluble	insoluble
sodium hydroxide	gives a methanoate $CO + OH^- \rightarrow HCOO^-$			gives a stannate(II) $SnO + 2OH^- \rightarrow SnO_2^{2-} + H_2O$	gives a plumbate(II) $PbO + 2OH^- \rightarrow PbO_2^{2-} + H_2O$
other oxides	C_3O_2				Pb_3O_4
hydrides b.p./(°C)	CH_4 (+ many others) -161	SiH_4* -112	GeH_4* -90	SnH_4 (unstable) ?	PbH_4 (very unstable) ?
oxygen	burn on ignition	burns spontaneously	rapidly oxidised	?	?
water	insoluble	rapid hydrolysis $SiH_4 + 4H_2O \rightarrow Si(OH)_4 + 4H_2$	no reaction	no reaction	?
sodium hydroxide	no reaction	vigorous hydrolysis $SiH_4 + 2OH^- + H_2O \rightarrow SiO_3^{2-} + 4H_2$	no reaction	no reaction	?
(IV) chlorides b.p./(°C)	CCl_4 (+ many others) 77	$SiCl_4$ 58	$GeCl_4$ 83	$SnCl_4$ 114	$PbCl_4$ 105 (decomp.)
water	no reaction	rapidly hydrolysed $SiCl_4 + 4H_2O \rightarrow Si(OH)_4 + 4HCl$	hydrolysed $GeCl_4 + 4H_2O \rightarrow Ge(OH)_4 + 4HCl$	hydrolysed $SnCl_4 + 4H_2O \rightarrow Sn(OH)_4 + 4HCl$	hydrolysed $PbCl_4 + 4H_2O \rightarrow Pb(OH)_4 + 4HCl$
conc. HCl	no reaction	no reaction (except hydrolysis)	no reaction (except hydrolysis)	forms chlorostannate(IV) $SnCl_4 + 2Cl^- \rightarrow SnCl_6^{2-}$	forms chloroplumbate(IV) $PbCl_4 + 2Cl^- \rightarrow PbCl_6^{2-}$
(II) chlorides m.p./(°C)	–			$SnCl_2$ 247	$PbCl_2$ 500
water				soluble in cold water (hydrolyses in dil. soln.) $SnCl_2 + H_2O \rightleftharpoons Sn(OH)Cl + HCl$	soluble only in hot water
sodium hydroxide				precipitate of hydroxide, soluble in excess giving stannate $Sn(OH)_2 \rightarrow SnO_2^{2-}$	precipitate of hydroxide, soluble in excess giving plumbate $Pb(OH)_2 \rightarrow PbO_2^{2-}$
conc. HCl				gives chlorostannate(II) $SnCl_2 + 2Cl^- \rightarrow SnCl_4^{2-}$	gives chloroplumbate(II) $PbCl_2 + 2Cl^- \rightarrow PbCl_4^{2-}$

*There are a few other hydrides of these elements corresponding to the higher alkanes

How does the stability of the +2 oxidation state vary on passing down the group?

All the other oxides are insoluble in water, but they will react with *alkalis* to give *anions*. Carbon monoxide dissolves in hot concentrated sodium hydroxide solution to give sodium methanoate:

$$CO(g) + OH^-(aq) \rightarrow HCOO^-(aq)$$

The oxides of the other elements react with alkali to give silicates, germanates, stannates and plumbates. In simple terms, the reactions may be represented:

$$XO_2(s) + 2OH^-(aq) \rightarrow XO_3^{2-}(aq) + H_2O(l)$$
$$XO(s) + 2OH^-(aq) \rightarrow XO_2^{2-}(aq) + H_2O(l)$$

The oxides of carbon and silicon show no basic nature, but those of the other elements, especially in the lower oxidation state, become more amphoteric on passing down the group and give salts with strong acids:

$$XO(s) + 2H^+(aq) \rightarrow X^{2+}(aq) + H_2O(l)$$

24.5 Hydrides

All the elements form a simple hydride, **XH$_4$**: CH$_4$ methane, SiH$_4$ silane, GeH$_4$ germane, SnH$_4$ stannane, PbH$_4$ plumbane. These are all *tetrahedral* in shape, the central atom forming covalent single bonds with each hydrogen atom.

Carbon forms an *almost infinite* series of alkanes which contain chains and/or rings of carbon atoms. This ability to **catenate**, that is link together, decreases markedly on passing down the group. Hydrides containing chains of up to six silicon atoms and eight germanium atoms are known, but there are no corresponding compounds of tin and lead. The explanation for this lies in *the marked decrease in the strength of the X—X covalent bond on passing down the group.*

	C—C	Si—Si	Ge—Ge	Sn—Sn	Pb—Pb
Bond energies/kJ mol^{-1}	331	196	163	152	145

The ability of carbon to form stable multiple bonds leads to the existence of the alkenes, alkynes and the aromatic hydrocarbons, but compounds of this type are unknown for the other elements.

The hydrocarbons are much more stable than the other hydrides of the group. Methane, for example, decomposes into its elements at about 800°C, whereas plumbane is unstable even at 0°C. This may be attributed to the *weakening of the X—H bond on passing down the group.*

	C—H	Si—H	Ge—H	Sn—H	Pb—H
Bond energies/kJ mol^{-1}	416	323	289	253	209?

All the elements form stronger bonds with oxygen than with hydrogen *and their hydrides* consequently burn in excess air or oxygen, generally giving the dioxide and water:

$$XH_4 + 2O_2 \rightarrow XO_2 + 2H_2O$$

The silicon hydrides are *least* stable in this respect and are spontaneously inflammable in air at room temperature.

Although stable in pure water, the addition of a very small trace of alkali is sufficient to *hydrolyse* silane rapidly to hydrated silicon dioxide Si(OH)$_4$ and hydrogen:

$$SiH_4(g) + 4H_2O(l) \rightarrow Si(OH)_4(s) + 4H_2(g)$$

Nucleophilic attack on the slightly positive silicon atom, which can accept a lone pair of electrons into an empty 3d orbital, is the first step in the reaction:

Methane does not react with water. The carbon atom is showing its maximum covalency of four and, since it has no empty atomic orbitals in its valency shell, it cannot function as an electron pair acceptor. Some of the main properties of the hydrides are summarised in table 24.4.

24.6 Halides

Tetrahalides

Carbon, unlike the rest of the elements, forms an extensive range of halides, owing to *its ability to catenate and form stable multiple bonds.* The only halogen which will react directly with carbon is fluorine, giving the tetrafluoride:

$$C(s) + 2F_2(g) \xrightarrow{\text{heat}} CF_4(g)$$

The other carbon tetrahalides must be prepared by indirect methods, e.g.

$$CS_2(l) + 3Cl_2(g) \xrightarrow{\text{I}_2 \text{ catalyst}} CCl_4(l) + S_2Cl_2(l)$$

CBr_4 is made by a similar reaction, but the iodide is formed by a halogen exchange reaction:

$$CCl_4(l) + 4C_2H_5I(l) \xrightarrow{\text{AlCl}_3} CI_4(s) + 4C_2H_5Cl(g)$$

Silicon, germanium and tin all form the tetrahalides by direct combination, *but lead(IV) bromide and lead(IV) iodide do not exist.* As a result of the 'inert pair effect', Pb(IV) will *oxidise* bromide and iodide ions to give the free halogen and the more stable Pb(II), e.g.

$$Pb^{4+} + 2I^- \rightarrow Pb^{2+} + I_2$$

Apart from SnF_4 and PbF_4, which are appreciably ionic, all the tetrahalides are essentially covalent, existing as simple tetrahedral molecules. With increasing relative molecular mass, their melting and boiling points generally *increase*, but they *decompose more readily* on heating. This is largely due to a decrease in bond strength as the atoms get bigger.

Except for carbon, all the tetrahalides are attacked by water to some degree. The first step involves donation of a lone pair of electrons from a water molecule to the central Group IV atom:

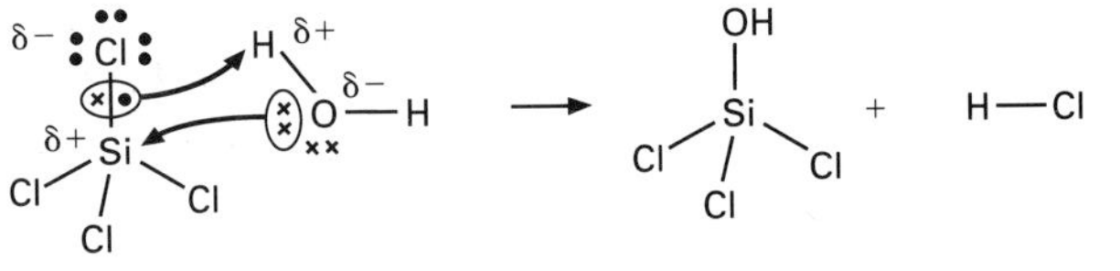

Apart from the fluoride, the silicon halides give hydrated silicon oxide, $Si(OH)_4$, as the final product, e.g.

$$SiCl_4(l) + 4H_2O(l) \rightarrow Si(OH)_4(s) + 4HCl(aq)$$

In the case of SiF_4, the hydrofluoric acid produced reacts further with some of the $Si(OH)_4$ to give the complex **hexafluorosilicate ion, SiF_6^{2-}**:

$$Si(OH)_4(s) + 6HF(aq) \rightarrow H_2SiF_6(aq) + 4H_2O(l)$$

Similar reactions occur on hydrolysis of the tetrahalides of tin and lead. The tetrachlorides readily dissolve in concentrated hydrochloric acid to give hexachloro species, e.g.

$$SnCl_4(l) + 2HCl(aq) \rightarrow 2H^+(aq) + SnCl_6^{2-}(aq)$$

The resistance of the carbon halides to hydrolysis and the absence of hexachloro-carbon species results from the *inability of the carbon atom to act as an electron pair acceptor* (see section 24.5).

Dihalides

Only tin and lead form reasonably stable dihalides. Anhydrous tin(II) chloride may be made by passing dry hydrogen chloride over the heated metal:

$$Sn(s) + 2HCl(g) \xrightarrow{\text{heat}} SnCl_2(s) + H_2(g)$$

Since all the lead(II) halides are sparingly soluble in water they are conveniently prepared by precipitation reactions, e.g.

$$Pb(NO_3)_2(aq) + 2HCl(aq) \rightarrow PbCl_2(s) + 2HNO_3(aq)$$

All the dihalides are solid and are *much more ionic* in character than the corresponding tetrahalides. They are much less susceptible to hydrolysis and readily form tetrahalo complex anions, e.g.

$$PbI_2(s) + 2I^-(aq) \rightarrow PbI_4{}^{2-}(aq)$$

Some of the important properties of the Group IV chlorides are summarised in table 24.4.

24.7 Atypical properties of carbon

Activity 24.2

Throughout this chapter we have stressed the differences between carbon and its compounds and the rest of the group. The main reasons for the unique properties of carbon include:

▶ the strength of carbon–carbon bonds which results in catenation, i.e. the formation of chains and rings of carbon atoms;
▶ the ability of carbon atoms to form stable multiple bonds;
▶ the maximum covalency of four shown by carbon.

Tabulate all the differences between carbon and the rest of the elements of the group that you can find in this chapter and select the reason(s) above which account for each. You should include:

(a) the structure and physical properties of the elements;
(b) the structure and properties of the oxides;
(c) the variety and stability of the hydrides;
(d) the action of water on the halides.

24.8 Comments on the activities

Activity 24.1

1 $SiO_2(s) + 3C(s) \rightarrow SiC(s) + 2CO(g)$
2 From its high melting point silicon carbide must be macromolecular. Its hardness indicates that it has the 'diamond' type structure shown in figure 24.1a, containing alternate carbon and silicon atoms.
3 Although carbon also forms the 'graphite' structure, the presence of silicon atoms forces the compound to adopt the 'diamond' type lattice. Silicon forms only *single* covalent bonds and is unable to use its 'p' electrons in π bonding.

Activity 24.2

Compare your answers with table 24.5.

Table 24.5 *Some properties of carbon and its compounds which are not typical of Group IV as a whole*

	difference from the rest of the group	main reason
(a) the element	▶ the structure of the graphite allotrope	stable multiple bonding (π electron delocalisation)
(b) its oxides	▶ gaseous, simple covalent molecules ▶ covalent monoxide	stable multiple bonding
(c) its hydrides	▶ extensive series of alkanes	ability to catenate – strong C—C bonds
	▶ existence of unsaturated hydrocarbons	stable multiple bonding
	▶ resistance to hydrolysis	full valency shell – maximum covalency 4
(d) its halides	▶ resistance to hydrolysis ▶ absence of halo complex anions	full valency shell – maximum covalency 4

24.9 Summary and revision plan

1 Metallic character increases on passing down the group. Carbon and silicon are non-metals, germanium is a semi-metal, but tin and lead are metals.

2 All the elements show an oxidation state of $+4$ but the $+2$ oxidation state becomes relatively more stable on passing down the group (**inert pair effect**).

Compounds in which the elements show an oxidation state of $+4$ are generally covalent but, except for carbon, the $+2$ oxidation state is essentially ionic.

3 The $+4$ oxides are more acidic in nature than the $+2$ oxides and the acidity of each type of oxide decreases on passing down the group.

4 Carbon has several properties unique in the group. There are two main reasons for this:

(a) A carbon atom can only hold a maximum of eight electrons in its valency shell.

▶ Carbon shows a maximum covalency of **4** compared to **6** for the other elements.

▶ The hydrides and halides of carbon are much more resistant to hydrolysis than the halides of the other elements.

(b) Carbon atoms **catenate** (link together) readily and form stable **multiple bonds.**

▶ Carbon is the only element in the group to exist in a 'graphite' type of structure.

▶ Carbon forms an extensive range of hydrides.

▶ The common oxides of carbon are simple small covalent molecules and are gaseous at room temperature.

5 Silicon and germanium are used to make microchips for the electronics industry. The main use of tin is in plating food and drink cans and most lead is used in the manufacture of petrol additives.

Nitrogen and Phosphorus in Group V

Contents

Figure 25.1 *World population growth and ammonia production in the 20th century - estimate the likely world population in the year 2000*

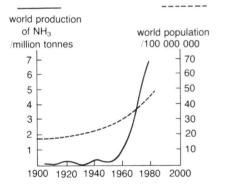

Nitrogen gas is used to provide an unreactive atmosphere in many processes. To avoid the risk of explosion, nitrogen may be used to flush the air out of oil pipelines before welding repairs are carried out. **Phosphorus**, on the other hand, is a much more reactive element and burns readily in air. It is a consitituent of match heads and has been used to make incendiary (fire) bombs.

Compounds of nitrogen and phosphorus are also manufactured in large quantities. World production of ammonia now exceeds sixty million tonnes a year and is still increasing. With the problems of feeding the earth's population, which is expected to double in the last quarter of this century, it is not surprising that most of this ammonia is used in the manufacture of **nitrogenous fertilisers**. The major growth area is likely to be in the underdeveloped countries. Other important products dependent on ammonia include polyurethane plastics, polyamide synthetic fibres, dyestuffs and explosives.

Phosphoric acid is used as an additive in food and drink, and phosphates are used in detergents and water softeners.

Incendiary bombs, fertilisers, matches and water softeners: just a few of the applications of phosphorus and nitrogen

25.1 The elements: structure, atomic and physical Properties

Nitrogen gas exists as simple diatomic molecules, N_2, containing a triple covalent bond:

The other elements in the group do not show the same tendency to π bond and their structures contain single bonds only.

Phosphorus exists in three main **allotropic** forms, referred to by their colours. White phosphorus consists of separate tetrahedral P_4 molecules, each atom being linked to three others by single covalent bonds:

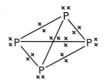

The red and black allotropes of phosphorus are both macromolecular.

Arsenic and antimony are semi-metals which also exhibit allotropy. The 'yellow' form of each has a structure similar to 'white' phosphorus. Bismuth is the most metallic element in the group but has an essentially macromolecular structure.

Some of the main atomic and physical properties of the Group V elements are summarised in table 25.1.

Table 25.1 *Data sheet for the elements of Group V*

Element	atomic number	electron configuration	atomic radius /nm*	ionisation energies/kJ mol⁻¹						electro-negativity	density /g cm⁻³	m.p. /°C
				1st	2nd	3rd	4th	5th	6th			
nitrogen N	7	$[He]2s^2 2p^3$	0.074	1400	2860	4590	7480	9440	53200	3.0	0.81[1]	−210
phosphorus P	15	$[Ne]3s^2 3p^3$	0.110	1060	1900	2920	4960	6280	21200	2.1	1.82[2] 2.34[3]	44[2] 590[3]
arsenic As	33	$[Ar]3d^{10}4s^2 4p^3$	0.121	966	1950	2730	4850	6020	12300	2.0	5.72	613 (sublimes)
antimony Sb	51	$[Kr]4d^{10}5s^2 5p^3$	0.141	833	1590	2440	4270	5360	10400	1.9	6.62	630
bismuth Bi	83	$[Xe]4f^{14}5d^{10}6s^2 6p^3$	0.152	703	1610	2460	4350	5400	8500	1.9	9.80	271

*Values are 'covalent' radii (1) measured for the liquid at its boiling point (−196 °C); (2) for 'white' phosphorus; (3) for 'red' phosphorus

How does electronegativity vary on passing down the group?
Can you explain this trend?

What do the comparative densities and melting points suggest about the structures of 'white' and 'red' phosphorus?

Atomic size and ionisation energies

Activity 25.1

How do you account for the following trends on passing down Group V?
(a) The increase in atomic radius
(b) The general decrease in ionisation energies.

Melting point

Very little energy is needed to overcome the weak **van der Waals' attractive forces** between N_2 molecules and consequently the melting point and boiling point of nitrogen are very low. If we consider the allotropes of phosphorus, arsenic and antimony which consist of separate X_4 molecules, then, as expected, *melting and boiling points rise with relative molecular mass.* The comparatively low melting point of bismuth indicates fairly weak metallic bonding.

Density

Since atomic mass increases rather more rapidly than the volume of the atom on passing down the group, we would expect a steady increase in density. We must also take into account, however, structural differences which affect how closely the atoms are packed together. Thus liquid nitrogen, consisting of separate N_2 molecules, has a low density and white phosphorus is less dense than its macromolecular allotropes.

Electronegativity

This measures the attraction of the atom for the electrons in a covalent bond and *decreases down the group.* Nitrogen has by far the highest electronegativity in Group V, since it has the smallest atomic radius and the fewest number of inner electrons to 'screen' the attraction of the nucleus. As we shall see in section 25.6, this has important consequences for the properties of ammonia.

25.2 Chemical properties and bonding types

Table 25.2 *A comparison of the reactions of nitrogen and phosphorus*

We can see from table 25.2 that *nitrogen is generally much less reactive than phosphorus.* Its only reaction at room temperature is to slowly form a nitride with lithium.

Reaction with	nitrogen	phosphorus
oxygen	combination takes place in an electric arc: $$N_2 + O_2 \rightarrow 2NO$$ further oxidation then occurs: $$2NO + O_2 \rightarrow 2NO_2$$	all allotropes burn in air on heating and white phosphorus smoulders spontaneously at room temperature. Phosphorus(III) oxide is formed in a limited supply of oxygen but phosphorus(V) oxide results in excess oxygen: $$4P + 3O_2 \rightarrow P_4O_6 \xrightarrow{2O_2} P_4O_{10}$$
hydrogen	reversible reaction under high pressure at $450\,°C$ using an iron catalyst (see section 25.7): $$N_2 + 3H_2 \rightleftharpoons 2NH_3$$	no reaction
chlorine	no reaction	white phosphorus burns spontaneously. Normally the trichloride is formed but this gives the pentachloride with excess chlorine: $$2P + 3Cl_2 \rightarrow 2PCl_3 \xrightarrow{[2Cl_2\ (0\,°C)]} 2PCl_5$$
metals	ionic nitrides formed by lithium and Group II metals on heating, e.g. $3Mg + N_2 \rightarrow Mg_3N_2$	complex phosphides formed by many electropositive metals
acids	unaffected by any acids	oxidised by concentrated nitric acid: $$4P + 10HNO_3 + H_2O \rightarrow 4H_3PO_4 + 5NO + 5NO_2$$
sodium hydroxide solution	no reaction	white phosphorus reacts on warming to give the hydride: $$4P + 3NaOH + 3H_2O \rightarrow PH_3 + 3NaH_2PO_2$$

Which is more reactive, nitrogen or phosphorus?   Can you explain why?

Reactivity depends partly upon the energy required to atomise the element. *The inert nature of nitrogen is due mainly to the great strength of the N≡N bond.*

$$N_2(g) \rightarrow 2N(g) \quad \Delta H = 946\,kJ$$

The white allotrope is the most reactive form of phosphorus, since the P_4 molecules are *highly strained*. The P—P—P bond angles are only 60°, whereas the most stable arrangement with minimum repulsion for four sets of electrons demands an angle of about 109°.

The atoms of Group V all have the outer electron configuration:

$$ns^2np^3 \quad \text{i.e.} \quad \boxed{\uparrow\downarrow} \quad \boxed{\uparrow \mid \uparrow \mid \uparrow}$$

We must now consider how these may achieve a stable configuration by compound formation.

Ionic bonding

The combined value of the first five ionisation energies is too high for any of the elements to form an X^{5+} ion. However, as in Group IV, the **inert pair effect** operates for the heavier elements. Bismuth, and to some extent antimony, react with electronegative elements to form compounds containing X^{3+} ions:

$$\text{e.g.} \quad \underset{/6s^2 6p^3}{\text{Bi}} \quad \xrightarrow{-3e^-} \quad \underset{/6s^2}{\text{Bi}^{3+}}$$

Only nitrogen, and to a lesser extent phosphorus, are sufficiently electronegative to gain a noble gas configuration by attracting electrons from metals, forming X^{3-} ions:

$$\text{e.g.} \quad \underset{/2s^2 2p^3}{\text{N}} \quad \xrightarrow{+3e^-} \quad \underset{/2s^2 2p^5}{\text{N}^{3-}}$$

Nitrogen atoms may also achieve a noble gas configuration by a combination of electron gain *and* covalent bond formation, e.g. in the NH_2^- and NH^{2-} ions:

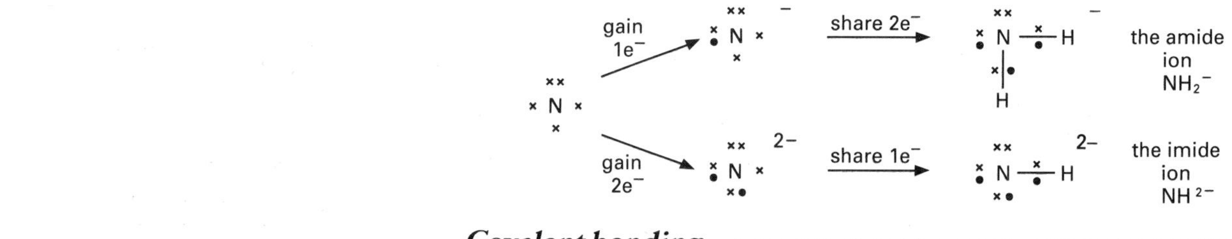

Covalent bonding

All the atoms may complete their outer 'octet' of electrons by forming pyramidal molecules containing three covalent bonds, e.g. NH_3:

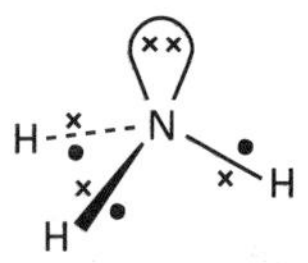

This leaves a **lone pair** of electrons on the central atom which may be donated, forming a **dative bond**, as in the tetrahedral ammonium ion NH_4^+. This tendency to act as a **Lewis base** decreases on passing down the group:

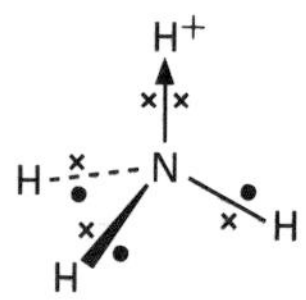

The maximum covalency of nitrogen is four, since its valency shell may only hold a maximum of eight electrons. The other elements may, however, promote an outer 's' electron into an empty 'd' orbital and form trigonal bipyramidal molecules with five covalent bonds, e.g. PF_5:

Phosphorus, in fact, shows a maximum covalency of six, in the complex ion $PF_6{}^-$. Here the phosphorus atom accepts a lone pair from an F^- ion into another of its 'd' orbitals:

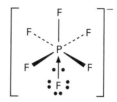

25.3 Oxides

The properties of the main oxides of nitrogen and phosphorus are compared in table 25.3.

The phosphorus oxides are prepared by direct combination of the elements, P_4O_6 being formed in a limited supply of oxygen and P_4O_{10} in excess. Nitrous

Table 25.3 *A comparison of the properties of some compounds of nitrogen and phosphorus*

Compound	nitrogen					phosphorus	
Oxides common name	N_2O nitrous oxide	NO nitrogen monoxide	NO_2 nitrogen dioxide	N_2O_4 dinitrogen tetroxide	N_2O_5 dinitrogen pentoxide	P_4O_6 phosphorus trioxide	P_4O_{10} phosphorus pentoxide
oxidation state	+1	+2	+4	+4	+5	+3	+5
physical state (room temp & pressure)	gas	gas	gas	gas	solid	solid	solid
$\Delta H_f^{\ominus}/\text{kJ mol}^{-1}$	+82	+90	+34	+10	−42	−1640	−3012
water	N_2O and NO do not react. The other oxides dissolve to give acidic solutions, e.g. $2NO_2 + H_2O \rightarrow HNO_3 + HNO_2$ $N_2O_5 + H_2O \rightarrow 2HNO_3$					dissolve to give acidic solutions $P_4O_6 + 6H_2O \rightarrow 4H_3PO_3$ $P_4O_{10} + 6H_2O \rightarrow 4H_3PO_4$	
Hydrides common name	NH_3 ammonia		N_2H_4 hydrazine			PH_3 phosphine	P_2H_4 diphosphine
b.p./°C	−33		114			−87	52?
$\Delta H_f^{\ominus}/\text{kJ mol}^{-1}$	−46		+50			+9	?
water	very soluble, giving an alkaline solution $NH_3 + H_2O \rightleftharpoons NH_4^+ + OH^-$		soluble, gives a stable hydrate $N_2H_4.H_2O$			sparingly soluble	insoluble
oxygen	ignites $4NH_3 + 3O_2 \rightarrow 2N_2 + 6H_2O$		spontaneously inflammable $N_2H_4 + O_2 \rightarrow N_2 + 2H_2O$			readily ignites $4PH_3 + 8O_2$ $\rightarrow P_4O_{10} + 6H_2O$	spontaneously inflammable $2P_2H_4 + 7O_2$ $\rightarrow P_4O_{10} + 4H_2O$

Compound	nitrogen	phosphorus	
Chlorides	NCl_3	PCl_3	PCl_5
b.p./°C	71 (explodes)	76	162 (sublimes)
$\Delta H_f^{\ominus}/kJ\ mol^{-1}$	+232	−339	−463
water	hydrolyses slowly	hydrolyse rapidly	
	$NCl_3 + 3H_2O \rightarrow NH_3 + 3HOCl$	$PCl_3 + 3H_2O$ $\rightarrow H_3PO_3 + 3HCl$	$PCl_5 + 4H_2O$ $\rightarrow H_3PO_4 + 5HCl$

Which are energetically more stable, the oxides of nitrogen or the oxides of phosphorus?
Why is ammonia much more soluble in water than phosphine?

oxide, N_2O, is made by gently heating ammonium nitrate:

$$NH_4NO_3 \xrightarrow{\text{heat}} N_2O + 2H_2O$$

Depending upon its concentration, nitric acid will give either nitrogen monoxide or nitrogen dioxide with copper:

$$Cu(s) + 4HNO_3(l)\ (conc) \rightarrow Cu(NO_3)_2(aq) + 2NO_2(g) + 2H_2O(l)$$
$$3Cu(s) + 8HNO_3\ (50\%\ aq) \rightarrow 3Cu(NO_3)_2(aq) + 2NO(g) + 4H_2O(l)$$

As we shall see in the next section, nitrogen dioxide may also be prepared by the thermal decomposition of many metal nitrates. Dinitrogen pentoxide results from the dehydration of concentrated nitric acid with phosphorus pentoxide:

$$2HNO_3(l) \quad \frac{P_2O_5,\ distil}{(-H_2O)} \quad N_2O_5(s)$$

Nitrogen, the first member of the group, forms more oxides than the other elements. Most of the nitrogen oxides exist as simple small molecules and are *gaseous* at room temperature and pressure. Figure 25.2 shows that, as with carbon in Group IV, this results from the greater tendency of nitrogen atoms to form multiple

Figure 25.2 *The molecular structure of the nitrogen oxides*

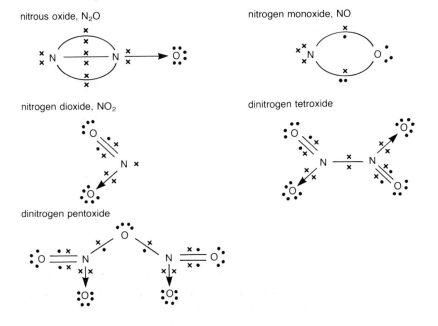

nitrous oxide, N_2O

nitrogen monoxide, NO

nitrogen dioxide, NO_2

dinitrogen tetroxide

dinitrogen pentoxide

Figure 25.3 *Molecular structure of the phosphorus oxides*

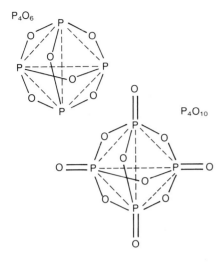

P_4O_6

P_4O_{10}

bonds. The structure of nitrogen dioxide is unusual in that the nitrogen atom has only *seven* outer electrons. The nitrogen atoms may complete their octet by **dimerising** to give dinitrogen tetroxide. These two oxides generally exist in equilibrium, the formation of nitrogen dioxide being favoured by high temperature and low pressure:

$$\underset{\text{pale yellow}}{N_2O_4(g)} \underset{\xrightarrow{\hspace{3cm}}}{\overset{\text{high temperature/low pressure}}{\rightleftharpoons}} \underset{\text{dark brown}}{2NO_2(g)}$$

The two main oxides of phosphorus are solid. Each consists of molecules containing four phosphorus atoms linked by bridging oxygen atoms as shown in figure 25.3.

In common with many nitrogen compounds, most of the oxides have endothermic enthalpies of formation (section 4.7). They often decompose into the elements on heating. Thus, even the heat from a glowing splint will produce oxygen from nitrous oxide, causing the splint to be rekindled.

$$2N_2O(g) \xrightarrow{\text{heat}} 2N_2(g) + O_2(g)$$

The driving force for this reaction is the great stability of the N_2 molecule.

Both of the phosphorus oxides dissolve vigorously in water, forming solutions containing phosphorus oxoacids:

$$P_4O_6(s) + 6H_2O(l) \rightarrow 4H_3PO_3(aq)$$
$$P_4O_{10}(s) + 6H_2O(l) \rightarrow 4H_3PO_4(aq)$$

Nitrous oxide and nitrogen monoxide are *neutral* but, both nitrogen dioxide and dinitrogen pentoxide give *acidic* aqueous solutions:

$$2NO_2(g) + H_2O(l) \rightarrow HNO_3(aq) + HNO_2(aq)$$
$$N_2O_5(s) + H_2O(l) \rightarrow 2HNO_3(aq)$$

25.4 Oxoacids

The properties of a range of nitrogen and phosphorus oxoacids are shown in table 25.4, and their structures are illustrated in figure 25.4.

Nitrous acid, HNO_2, used in the preparation of azo dyes (section 41.9), may be

Table 25.4 *Properties of some oxoacids of nitrogen and phosphorus*

Oxoacid	HNO_2	HNO_3	H_3PO_3	H_3PO_4*
common name systematic name	nitrous acid nitric(III) acid	nitric acid nitric(V) acid	phosphorous acid phosphoric(III) acid	orthophosphoric acid phosphoric(V) acid
oxidation state	+3	+5	+3	+5
physical state (room temp. & pressure)	stable only in aqueous solution	liquid b.p. 86°C	solid m.p. 74°C	solid m.p. 47°C
acid strength	weak	strong	moderate	moderate
basicity†	1	1	2	3
Redox behaviour	oxidising	oxidising	reducing	stable

* may be progressively dehydrated to pyrophosphoric acid, $H_4P_2O_7$, and metaphosphoric acid, HPO_3
† i.e. the number of acidic hydrogens per molecule which may be replaced by other cations.

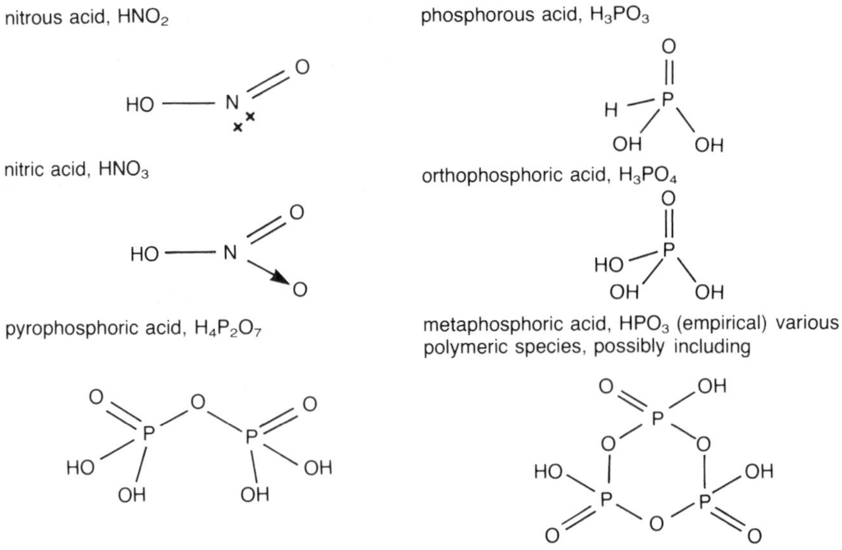

Figure 25.4 *Structures of some oxoacids of nitrogen and phosphorus*

nitrous acid, HNO_2

nitric acid, HNO_3

pyrophosphoric acid, $H_4P_2O_7$

phosphorous acid, H_3PO_3

orthophosphoric acid, H_3PO_4

metaphosphoric acid, HPO_3 (empirical) various polymeric species, possibly including

made by adding sodium nitrite to ice-cold, dilute hydrochloric acid:

$$NaNO_2(aq) + HCl(aq) \xrightarrow{<5\,^\circ C} NaCl(aq) + HNO_2(aq)$$

It is unstable and **disproportionates** on warming:

$$3HNO_2(aq) \rightarrow HNO_3(aq) + 2NO(g) + H_2O(l)$$
$$3(+3) \qquad\quad +5 \qquad\quad 2(+2)$$

Nitric acid, HNO_3, is manufactured by the catalytic oxidation of ammonia (section 25.7) but is prepared in the laboratory by distilling a mixture of sodium nitrate and concentrated sulphuric acid.

$$NaNO_3(s) + H_2SO_4(l) \rightarrow NaHSO_4(s) + HNO_3(l)$$

Pure nitric acid, although largely covalent, **self-ionises** slightly:

$$2HNO_3(l) \rightleftharpoons NO_3^-(l) + H_2NO_3^+(l)$$
$$H_2NO_3^+(l) \rightarrow H_2O(l) + NO_2^+(l) \quad \text{(nitryl cation)}$$

The **nitryl cation** is the species responsible for the nitration of aromatic hydrocarbons (section 36.5.1). *Nitric acid is a good oxidising agent, especially when hot and concentrated, when it is reduced to nitrogen dioxide.* It converts non-metallic elements and some less electropositive metals, such as tin, into their oxide. For example, sulphur:

	S	SO$_3$	
ox. state	0	+6	change +6 (oxidation)
	HNO$_3$	NO$_2$	
ox. state	+5	+4	change −1 (reduction)

therefore $S + 6HNO_3 \rightarrow SO_3 + 6NO_2 + 3H_2O$

Most other metals form **ionic nitrates**. For example, copper:

	Cu	Cu^{2+}	
ox. state	0	+2	change +2 (oxidation)
	HNO$_3$	NO$_2$	
ox. state	+5	+4	change −1 (reduction)

therefore $Cu + 2HNO_3 \rightarrow Cu^{2+} + 2NO_2 + 2OH^-$

But, *since OH^- ions react with further nitric acid to form water,* the overall reaction is

$$Cu(s) + 4HNO_3(aq) \rightarrow Cu(NO_3)_2(aq) + 2NO_2(g) + 2H_2O(l)$$

Aluminium, iron and chromium are, however, *unattacked* by the concentrated acid which *produces a stable oxide layer on the surface of these metals.*

Activity 25.2

Derive balanced equations for the following oxidising reactions of concentrated nitric acid, assuming that nitrogen dioxide is produced in each case:
(a) carbon to carbon dioxide;
(b) silver to silver nitrate.

The salts of nitric acid are **thermally unstable**. Most metal nitrates give the metal oxide and nitrogen dioxide on heating, e.g.

$$2Cu(NO_3)_2(g) \xrightarrow{\text{heat}} 2CuO(s) + 4NO_2(g) + O_2(g)$$

Apart from lithium nitrate, however, the nitrates of the **alkali metals** give the nitrite, e.g.

$$2NaNO_3(s) \xrightarrow{\text{heat}} 2NaNO_2(s) + O_2(g)$$

Phosphorous acid, H_3PO_3, is formed when phosphorus trioxide is dissolved in water. It functions as a *dibasic* acid, since one of the hydrogen atoms is bonded directly to the 5-valent phosphorus as shown in figure 25.3. It is a quite powerful reducing agent and decomposes on heating to give orthophosphoric acid and phosphine:

$$4H_3PO_3(l) \rightarrow 3H_3PO_4(l) + PH_3(g)$$

Orthophosphoric acid, H_3PO_4, is manufactured by heating calcium phosphate with sulphuric acid:

$$Ca_3(PO_4)_2(s) + 3H_2SO_4(aq) \rightarrow 3CaSO_4(s) + 2H_3PO_4(aq)$$

If the amount of sulphuric acid used is restricted, then calcium dihydrogenphosphate is formed:

$$Ca_3(PO_4)_2(s) + 2H_2SO_4(aq) \rightarrow 2CaSO_4(s) + Ca(H_2PO_4)_2(aq)$$

This mixture of calcium sulphate and calcium dihydrogenphosphate is sold under the name of **superphosphate** as a 'phosphorus' fertiliser.

Orthophosphoric acid is a moderately strong *tribasic* acid and will form *three* salts with sodium hydroxide:

$$H_3PO_4 \xrightarrow{\text{NaOH}} NaH_2PO_4 \xrightarrow{\text{NaOH}} Na_2HPO_4 \xrightarrow{\text{NaOH}} Na_3PO_4$$

The trisodium salt is widely used in detergents and water softeners.

The other phosphoric acids may be obtained by heating orthophosphoric acid, which progressively dehydrates:

$$2H_3PO_4 \xrightarrow{(-H_2O)} H_4P_2O_7 \xrightarrow{(-H_2O)} 2HPO_3$$

25.5 Halides

Table 25.3 includes a comparison of the chlorides of nitrogen and phosphorus.

As explained in section 25.2, *nitrogen only forms trihalides, since it can only hold eight electrons in its valency shell.* None of the nitrogen halides may be prepared by direct combination and only the gaseous trifluoride is energetically more stable than the elements. The trichloride is an unstable, explosive yellow oil formed by passing chlorine through a solution of ammonium chloride:

$$NH_4Cl(aq) + 3Cl_2(g) \rightarrow NCl_3(l) + 4HCl(aq)$$

The bromide and iodide are both solids which decompose explosively into the elements on impact or heating.

Nitrogen trichloride is hydrolysed by water to ammonia and chloric(I) acid:

$$NCl_3(l) + 3H_2O(l) \rightarrow NH_3(aq) + 3HOCl(aq)$$

The first step in this reaction is the donation of a lone pair of electrons from the nitrogen atom to the slightly positive hydrogen of the water molecule:

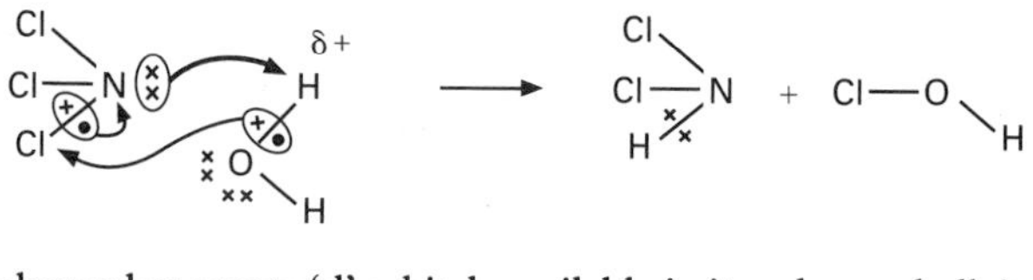

Since phosphorus has empty 'd' orbitals available in its valency shell, it may form pentahalides as well as trihalides. Presumably it is not possible to pack five large iodine atoms around one phosphorus atom, since PI_5 does not exist. Except for PF_3, all of the compounds may be prepared by direct combination. All the trihalides and phosphorus pentafluoride exist as simple covalent molecules but PCl_5 and PBr_5 are *ionic* in the solid state:

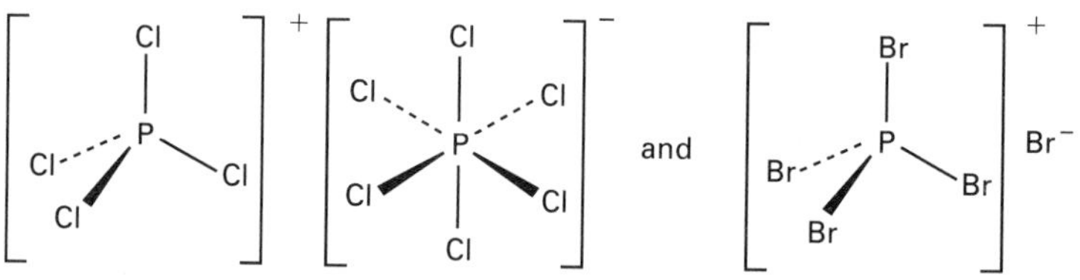

The non-existence of $[PBr_6]^-$ may be due to the large size of the bromine atoms. In the *vapour phase*, both PCl_5 and PBr_5 form trigonal bipyramidal covalent molecules. All the phosphorus halides react vigorously with water.

$$PCl_3(l) + 3H_2O(l) \rightarrow H_3PO_3(aq) + 3HCl(aq)$$

$$PCl_5(s) + 4H_2O(l) \rightarrow H_3PO_4(aq) + 5HCl(aq)$$

Note that PCl_3 does not hydrolyse in the same way as NCl_3. Since the phosphorus atom has empty 'd' orbitals available in its valency shell it acts as a Lewis acid by accepting a lone pair of electrons from the water molecule.

The remaining two chlorine atoms are then replaced in the same way. Both phosphorus chlorides are used in organic chemistry to replace the −OH group in alcohols or carboxylic acids by chlorine (section 37.3).

25.6 Hydrides

Nitrogen and phosphorus each form *two* hydrides, XH_3 and X_2H_4. Although their structures are similar, table 25.3 shows that their properties differ considerably:

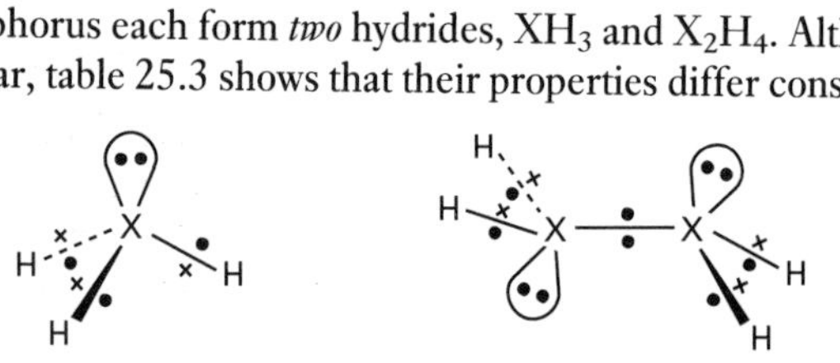

Only **ammonia**, energetically the most stable of the hydrides, may be made by direct combination of the elements. Oxidation of ammonia by sodium chlorate(I) gives **hydrazine**:

$$2NH_3(g) + NaOCl(aq) \rightarrow N_2H_4(l) + NaCl(aq) + H_2O(l)$$

Phosphine is prepared by warming white phosphorus in sodium hydroxide solution:

$$P_4(s) + 3OH^-(aq) + 3H_2O(l) \rightarrow PH_3(g) + 3H_2PO_2^-(aq)$$

The boiling points of ammonia and hydrazine are *much higher* than those of the corresponding phosphorus hydrides. *The polarity of the N—H bonds, caused by the high electronegativity of the nitrogen, leads to extensive intermolecular* **hydrogen bonding** *in the liquid state,* as explained in section 5.9.

Diphosphine is spontaneously inflammable in air. Hydrazine and phosphine burn in air when lit, but ammonia burns only in oxygen. The nitrogen hydrides give nitrogen on combustion, whereas the phosphorus hydrides give phosphorus pentoxide,

e.g. $4NH_3(g) + 3O_2(g) \rightarrow 2N_2(g)\ + 6H_2O(g)$
$4PH_3(g) + 8O_2(g) \rightarrow P_4O_{10}(g) + 6H_2O(g)$

Hydrazine is a powerful, if somewhat hazardous fuel, and has been used with liquid oxygen as the propellant system in some space rockets.

Unlike the phosphorus hydrides, both ammonia and hydrazine dissolve readily in water to give alkaline solutions. The more electronegative nitrogen atoms are able to function as **Lewis bases** by donating their lone pairs of electrons:

Both ammonia and phosphine form *salts* with strong acids, e.g. with hydrogen iodide:

$$NH_3(g) + HI(g) \xrightleftharpoons{200\,°C} NH_4^+I^-(s)\ \text{ammonium iodide}$$

$$PH_3(g) + HI(g) \xrightleftharpoons{60\,°C} PH_4^+I^-(s)\ \text{phosphonium iodide}$$

The hydrides may be reformed from these salts by displacement with a stronger base. Sodium hydroxide must be used to obtain ammonia but water alone will decompose phosphonium salts.

$$NH_4^+ + OH^- \rightarrow NH_3 + H_2O$$
$$PH_4^+ + H_2O \rightarrow PH_3 + H_3O^+$$

Activity 25.3

In the last chapter you were asked to list the differences between the first element, carbon, and the rest of Group IV. You will have noticed that the chemistry of the first element in Group V, nitrogen, also differs considerably from that of the next member, phosphorus. Tabulate these differences and account for them as far as possible in atomic terms.

25.7 Manufacture of ammonia

Ammonia is manufactured by the **Haber process** in which nitrogen and hydrogen are combined directly at *high pressure* in the presence of an *iron catalyst* at about *450°C.* The reasons for the choice of these conditions, both chemical and economic, have already been discussed in section 14.8.

$$N_2(g) + 3H_2(g) \xrightleftharpoons[\text{finely divided iron catalyst}]{450°C, \text{ up to } 1000 \text{ atmospheres}} 2NH_3(g) \quad \Delta H = -92\,kJ$$

Air is used as the source of nitrogen, and in Britain the hydrogen is usually obtained by high temperature reduction of steam with natural gas.

The technical details of the process are quite complex but the main stages, illustrated in the flow diagram in figure 25.5 are described below.

Figure 25.5 *Simplified flow diagram for the Haber process*

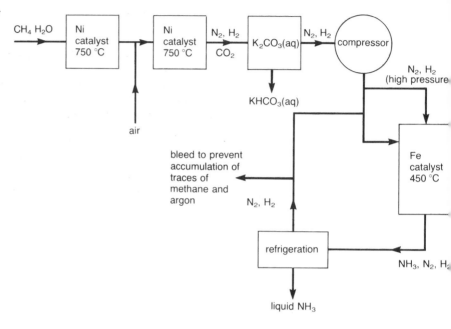

Formation of hydrogen

Purified methane is reacted with steam over a nickel catalyst at about 750°C which favours the endothermic reaction:

$$CH_4(g) + 2H_2O(g) \rightleftharpoons CO_2(g) + 4H_2(g) \quad \Delta H \text{ +ve}$$

Addition of air

This is added to give the required nitrogen: hydrogen ratio of 1:3. Some of the hydrogen burns in the oxygen from the air to give water but this is converted back to hydrogen by reaction with more methane as above.

Removal of carbon dioxide

At this stage the mixture contains approximately 18% of carbon dioxide, most of which is removed by **scrubbing** with potassium carbonate solution. The carbon dioxide dissolves to form potassium hydrogen carbonate:

$$K_2CO_3(aq) + H_2O(l) + CO_2(g) \rightarrow 2KHCO_3(aq)$$

Compression

The composition of the gas, by volume, at this stage is approximately
   74.3% N_2
   24.6% H_2
    0.8% CH_4
    0.3% Ar (from the air)
The mixture is progressively pressurised to at least 200 atmospheres and its temperature is adjusted to about 400°C.

A 1200 tonne/day ammonia plant at Billingham

Synthesis

Since the reaction is exothermic, the temperature of the gas is increased to its optimum value of about $450\,°C$ as it passes over the iron catalyst. The product leaving the catalyst chamber contains about 15% of ammonia together with unreacted gases. The catalyst has a 'life expectancy' of several years, which enables each plant to operate continuously, apart from periodic safety inspections and breakdowns.

Removal of ammonia

Since ammonia has a much higher boiling point than the other gases in the mixture it may be removed as a liquid by **refrigeration**. The unreacted gases are recycled to the catalyst chamber, but periodically some of the gas is **bled off** to prevent the build up of methane and argon which take no part in the reaction.

Britain has the capacity to produce almost three million tonnes of ammonia per year. The major plants are operated by ICI at Billingham on the River Tees. This is well placed to make use of the surplus electric power generated in the Durham coalfields and is also convenient for the supply of North Sea gas. Other factors which are important in the choice of site include a good supply of water and adequate transport facilities for distribution of the product.

Although ammonia may be used directly on the land, it is rather more convenient to transport and apply a solid fertiliser. One of the most widely used is **ammonium nitrate**, NH_4NO_3, made by neutralising ammonia with nitric acid:

$$NH_3(aq) + HNO_3(aq) \rightarrow NH_4NO_3(aq)$$

The nitric acid required is made by a process which involves the *oxidation* of ammonia. A mixture of ammonia and air is passed over a platinum catalyst. An electric spark starts the following reaction which then releases sufficient energy to maintain the catalyst at red heat:

$$4NH_3(g) + 5O_2(g) \rightarrow 4NO(g) + 6H_2O(g)$$

On cooling, the nitrogen monoxide is oxidised by more air to give nitrogen dioxide:

$$2NO(g) + O_2(g) \rightarrow 2NO_2(g)$$

This is dissolved in hot water, when further oxidation gives nitric acid:

$$4NO_2(g) + O_2(g) + 2H_2O(l) \rightarrow 4HNO_3(aq)$$

25.8 Comments on the activities

Activity 25.1

If necessary refer to chapter 19 and the relevant parts of section 24.1.

Activity 25.2

(a)

$$C \rightarrow CO_2$$

ox. state $\quad$ 0 $\quad$ +4 $\quad$ change +4

$$HNO_3 \rightarrow NO_2$$

ox. state $\quad$ +5 $\quad$ +4 $\quad$ change -1

therefore $C(s) + 4HNO_3(l) \longrightarrow CO_2(g) + 4NO_2(g) + 2H_2O(l)$

(b)

$$Ag \rightarrow Ag^+$$

ox. state $\quad$ 0 $\quad$ +1 $\quad$ change +1

$$HNO_3 \rightarrow NO_2 \quad \text{change} -1$$
$$+5 \quad\quad +4$$

therefore $Ag + HNO_3 \longrightarrow Ag^+ + NO_2 + OH^-$

OH^- then reacts with further acid to give water, so the overall reaction is

$$Ag(s) + 2HNO_3(l) \longrightarrow AgNO_3(aq) + NO_2(g) + H_2O(l)$$

Activity 25.3

Compare your answers with table 25.5.

Table 25.5   *Some differences in the properties of nitrogen and phosphorus*

	differences	reasons
the elements	Nitrogen exists as gaseous N_2 molecules Phosphorus is solid and exists as either P_4 molecules or macromolecules	Nitrogen atoms, unlike phosphorus, are able to form multiple bonds with each other by π overlap
	Phosphorus (especially white) is much more reactive than nitrogen	The triple bond in N_2 is very strong. The P_4 molecule is highly 'strained'
the oxides	Nitrogen forms a greater variety of oxides	Largely as a result of the greater tendency of nitrogen atoms to π bond
the hydrides	Ammonia is much less volatile than phosphine	Appreciable hydrogen bonding in ammonia, owing to the high electronegativity of nitrogen
	The nitrogen hydrides are much more basic than those of phosphorus	The nitrogen atom donates its lone pair of electrons more readily
the chlorides	The highest chloride of nitrogen is NCl_3 whereas that of phosphorus is PCl_5. NCl_3 can only act as an electron pair donor, whereas PCl_3 and PCl_5 generally act as electron pair acceptors	Unlike nitrogen, phosphorus has empty 'd' orbitals in its valency shell and hence may show covalencies greater than 4

25.9 Summary and revision plan

1   The difference in structure and reactivity of nitrogen and phosphorus is largely due to the ability of nitrogen to form strong **multiple bonds**.

2   Nitrogen can only hold a maximum of 8 electrons in its valency shell. Thus, although both elements show a **maximum oxidation state** of $+5$, the **maximum covalency** of nitrogen is **4**, whereas that of phosphorus is **6**.

3   The hydrides of nitrogen are much more basic in character than those of phosphorus. Their boiling points are also significantly higher owing to strong **intermolecular hydrogen bonding**.

4   The halides of nitrogen are much less thermally stable than those of phosphorus and decompose explosively.

5   Both elements form acidic oxides and a range of oxoacids.

6   **Ammonia** is one of the most important compounds of nitrogen and is extensively used in the production of **nitrogenous fertilisers**. It is manufactured from its elements by the **Haber process**.

Oxygen and Sulphur in Group VI

Contents

Figure 26.1 *Where does Britain's sulphuric acid go?*

Industrial and medical uses of oxygen: burning off impurities during steel-making and maintaining respiration during surgery

The role of **oxygen** in respiration and combustion is well known and in steelmaking the pure gas is used to burn off the carbon impurity from the molten 'pig' iron. **Sulphur** is used in gunpowder and in the 'vulcanisation' (hardening) of rubber. Although many sulphur compounds are commercially important, sulphuric acid is produced in the largest quantities with world production now exceeding 100 million tonnes per year.

It is no exaggeration to say that the manufacture of sulphuric acid is essential to modern industrial society. Indeed the level of sulphuric acid production is a good indicator of economic prosperity. Fertiliser manufacture takes the largest share of the UK annual production of over 3 million tonnes, but, as figure 26.1 shows, the acid is required in the processing of many other materials. In the UK almost all the sulphuric acid is manufactured from sulphur using the Contact process described in section 26.7.

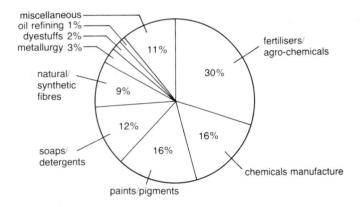

26.1 The elements: structure, atomic and physical properties

As in previous 'p' block groups, metallic character increases with relative atomic mass. Oxygen and sulphur are non-metals, selenium and tellurium are semi-metals, and polonium is a radioactive metal.

Both oxygen and sulphur exhibit **allotropy**. The most stable form of oxygen is the diatomic molecule O_2, but this is converted into ozone, O_3, by solar energy in the upper atmosphere:

$$3O_2(g) \rightleftharpoons 2O_3(g)$$

It is formed in the laboratory by passing a stream of dry oxygen through a silent electrical discharge. Atmospheric ozone plays an important role in absorbing much of the harmful ultraviolet radiation in sunlight. Certain chemicals, such as chlorofluorocarbons (CFCs) are now known to damage the ozone layer. Their use

Police drivers training on a skid-pan. Many parts of their cars rely on oxygen, sulphur and sulphuric acid. Oxygen is used in making the steel for the bodywork and chassis. Sulphur is used to vulcanise the tyre rubber. Sulphuric acid is used in the car battery and in the production of nylon for the upholstery and seatbelts, of white pigment for the paintwork and even of oil and petrol

as aerosol propellants and refrigerant liquids is now discouraged. You will probably have seen labels on deodourant products claiming to be 'ozone friendly'. The molecular structures of both oxygen and ozone indicate *the readiness of oxygen atoms to link using multiple bonds*. This behaviour is also shown by carbon and nitrogen, the preceding elements in the period.

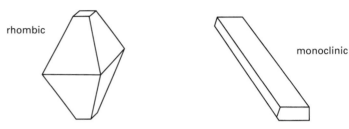

Crystallisation of sulphur from carbon disulphide solution at room temperature gives diamond shaped crystals of **rhombic** sulphur, whereas slow cooling of molten sulphur produces needle-shaped **monoclinic** crystals.

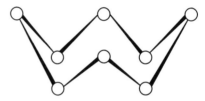

Above 95.5 °C, monoclinic sulphur is the more stable allotrope, but on cooling this slowly reverts to the rhombic form. Each contains separate 'crown-shaped' S_8 molecules, but packed together differently.

Table 26.1 *Data sheet for the elements of group VI*

The trends in the main atomic and physical properties of the elements, shown in table 26.1, are explained in chapter 19.

Element	atomic number	electron configuration	atomic radius /nm*	ionisation energies/kJ mol⁻¹							electro-negativity	density /g cm⁻³	m.p. /°C
				1st	2nd	3rd	4th	5th	6th	7th			
oxygen O	8	[He]2s²2p⁴	0.074	1310	3390	5320	7450	11 000	13 300	71 000	3.5	1.15†	−218
sulphur S	16	[Ne]3s²3p⁴	0.104	1000	2260	3390	4540	6990	8490	27 100	2.5	2.07 (rhombic)	113
selenium Se	34	[Ar]3d¹⁰4s²4p⁴	0.117	941	2080	3090	4140	7030	7870	16 000	2.4	4.81	217
tellurium Te	52	[Kr]4d¹⁰5s²5p⁴	0.137	870	1800	3010	3680	5860	7000	13 200	2.1	6.25	450
polonium Po	84	[Xe]4f¹⁴5d¹⁰6s²6p⁴	0.14	812							2.0	9.32	254

*values are 'covalent' radii

†measured for the liquid at its boiling point (−183 °C)

Why is the melting point of oxygen much lower than that of the other elements?

Why is there a 'big jump' between the values of the 6th and 7th ionisation energies for all these elements?

26.2 Chemical properties and bonding types

Some of the reactions of oxygen and sulphur are compared in table 26.2. Although oxygen is generally considered to be more reactive, it does *not* combine directly with more electronegative elements such as fluorine or chlorine.

Table 26.2 *A comparison of some reactions of oxygen and sulphur*

Reaction with	oxygen	sulphur
oxygen	–	Burns with a blue flame to give sulphur dioxide: $S + O_2 \rightarrow SO_2$ This combines reversibly on heating with more oxygen in the presence of a catalyst to give sulphur trioxide: $2SO_2 + O_2 \rightleftharpoons 2SO_3$
metals	All except the less reactive 'noble' metals form ionic oxides on heating, e.g. $2Mg + O_2 \rightarrow 2MgO$	Most metals combine on heating to give ionic sulphides: e.g. $Mg + S \rightarrow MgS$
hydrogen	Mixtures explode when ignited, $2H_2 + O_2 \rightarrow 2H_2O$	Reacts reversibly at its b.p.: $H_2 + S \rightleftharpoons H_2S$
chlorine	no reaction	Molten sulphur gives disulphur dichloride: $2S + Cl_2 \rightarrow S_2Cl_2$ Further chlorination takes place at low temperature, giving SCl_2 and SCl_4
acids	no reaction	Oxidised by hot concentrated nitric or sulphuric acid: e.g. $S + 2H_2SO_4 \rightarrow 3SO_2 + 2H_2O$
sodium hydroxide	no reaction	Dissolves in hot concentrated solutions: $3S + 6OH^- \rightarrow 2S^{2-} + SO_3^{2-} + 3H_2O$ Further reaction gives a mixture of polysulphides and thiosulphate

Which has a wider range of reactions, oxygen or sulphur?

All the atoms of Group VI have the outer electron configuration.

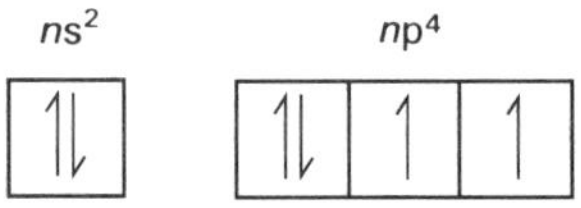

They may take part in chemical bonding in several ways.

Ionic bonding

Ionisation to give the X^{6+} ion is energetically impossible for all the elements. Polonium, and to a slight extent tellurium, show the **inert pair effect** (section 24.3) in forming X^{4+} ions.

The atoms may form X^{2-} ions by *gaining* electrons from electropositive metals:

$$X \xrightarrow[ns^2np^4]{\quad +2e^- \quad} X^{2-}_{ns^2np^6}$$

Since there are more inner electrons to 'screen' the nuclear attraction, the tendency to form simple negative ions decreases on passing down the group.

Both oxygen and sulphur atoms may achieve a noble gas configuration by a combination of electron gain *and* covalent bond formation, e.g. with hydrogen:

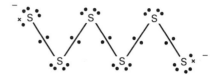

i.e. hydroxide, OH⁻
or hydrogensulphide, SH⁻

Anions containing two oxygen atoms, O_2^{2-} and O_2^-, have been mentioned in section 22.2, but sulphur shows a much greater tendency to catenate, forming a range of **polysulphide** ions, $(S_n)^{2-}$, e.g:

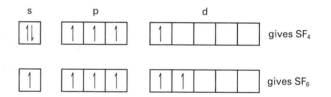

Covalent bonding

All the atoms may complete their outer 'octet' of electrons by forming two covalent bonds, e.g. in the hydrides:

The oxygen atom cannot hold more than eight electrons in its outer shell but may show a maximum covalency of **three** by donating one of its lone pairs of electrons, e.g. in the hydroxonium ion H_3O^+:

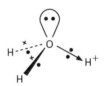

Sulphur atoms may also show covalencies of four and six by promoting electrons into empty 'd' orbitals in their valency shell, e.g. in the fluorides:

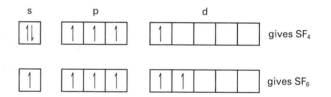

26.3 Halides

Some of the more stable fluorides and chlorides of oxygen and sulphur are shown in table 26.3.

Activity 26.1

Draw 'dot and cross' diagrams to show the bonding and molecular shapes of the fluorides of oxygen and sulphur described in table 26.3. If necessary, refer to the 'electron repulsion' theory covered in chapter 7.

Table 26.3 *A comparison of the properties of some compounds of oxygen and sulphur*

Compound	oxygen				sulphur		
Oxides					SO_2		SO_3
common name					sulphur dioxide		sulphur trioxide
systematic name					sulphur(IV) oxide		sulphur(VI) oxide
physical state (room temp. & pressure)					gas		solid (m.p. 18 °C)
$\Delta H_f^{\ominus}/\text{kJ mol}^{-1}$					-297		-395
water					soluble		vigorous reaction
					$H_2O + SO_2 \rightleftharpoons H_2SO_3$		$H_2O + SO_3 \rightarrow H_2SO_4$
Hydrides	H_2O		H_2O_2		H_2S		
b.p./°C	100		150 (decomp.)		-61		
$\Delta H_f^{\ominus}/\text{kJ mol}^{-1}$	-286		-188		-20		
redox behaviour	–		oxidising		reducing		
Fluorides	OF_2					SF_4	SF_6
b.p./°C	-145					-40	-51
$\Delta H^{\ominus}/\text{kJ mol}^{-1}$	23					?	-1100
Chlorides	Cl_2O	ClO_2	Cl_2O_6	Cl_2O_7	S_2Cl_2	SCl_2	SCl_4
b.p./°C	-2	11	decomp.	81	138	decomp.	decomp.
$\Delta H_f^{\ominus}/\text{kJ mol}^{-1}$	76	103	?	265	-60	?	?

Can you work out an equation for the reaction between hydrogen peroxide solution and hydrogen sulphide?

Oxygen does not combine directly with fluorine or chlorine and its compounds with these elements are generally energetically *less stable* than those of sulphur. The main reason for this seems to be the greater strength of the S—F bond.

$$\text{BET (kJ mol}^{-1}\text{)} \quad \text{O—F} \quad 214, \quad \text{S—F} \quad 327.$$

The most stable fluoride of oxygen is OF_2, which is made by passing fluorine through dilute sodium hydroxide solution:

$$2F_2(g) + 2OH^-(aq) \rightarrow F_2O(g) + H_2O(l) + 2F^-(aq)$$

It reacts slowly with water, but explosively with steam, to give oxygen:

$$F_2O(g) + H_2O(l) \rightarrow 2HF(aq) + O_2(g)$$

By contrast, sulphur hexafluoride, SF_6, made by direct combination of the elements, is extremely stable and is almost as unreactive as the noble gases. The tetrafluoride, SF_4, is much more reactive and is readily hydrolysed by water:

$$SF_4(g) + 2H_2O(l) \rightarrow 4HF(aq) + SO_2(g)$$

By looking at the hydrolysis of the halides of silicon and phosphorus (sections 24.6 and 25.5), you should be able to suggest a mechanism for this reaction.

All four chlorine oxides are dangerously explosive compounds which are energetically less stable than the elements. They may be regarded as **anhydrides** of the oxoacids of chlorine and form salts with alkalis:

$$Cl_2O(g) + 2OH^-(aq) \rightarrow 2ClO^-(aq) + H_2O(l)$$

$$2ClO_2(g) + 2OH^-(aq) \rightarrow ClO_2^-(aq) + ClO_3^-(aq) + H_2O(l)$$

$$Cl_2O_6(l) + 2OH^-(aq) \rightarrow ClO_3^-(aq) + ClO_4^-(aq) + H_2O(aq)$$

$$Cl_2O_7(l) + 2OH^-(aq) \rightarrow 2ClO_4^-(aq) + H_2O(l)$$

The most stable chloride of sulphur is disulphur dichloride, S_2Cl_2, made by passing chlorine through molten sulphur. Sulphur dichloride, SCl_2, and the tetrachloride, SCl_4, readily decompose to give S_2Cl_2 and chlorine.

Activity 26.2

Draw 'dot and cross' diagrams showing the bonding in, and the shapes of, the following chlorides of oxygen and sulphur:
(a) Cl_2O (b) ClO_2 (c) Cl_2O_7 (d) S_2Cl_2 (e) SCl_2 (f) SCl_4

Sulphur combines directly with bromine to give S_2Br_2, but there are *no* known iodides. The oxides of bromine are unstable but iodic acid dehydrates on heating to give iodine(V) oxide:

$$2HIO_3(s) \xrightarrow{\text{heat}} I_2O_5(s) + H_2O(l)$$

26.4 Hydrides

Oxygen forms two hydrides, water and hydrogen peroxide, H_2O_2:

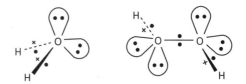

Sulphur forms similar compounds but hydrogen persulphide, H_2S_2, is very unstable.

Both water and hydrogen sulphide may be made by direct combination of the elements. The reaction with sulphur is, however, slow and reversible and hydrogen sulphide is usually prepared by the action of dilute acid on a metal sulphide.

$$S^{2-}(s) + 2H^+(aq) \rightarrow H_2S(g)$$

A solution of hydrogen peroxide can be prepared by adding dilute sulphuric acid to barium peroxide and filtering off the insoluble barium sulphate.

$$BaO_2(s) + H_2SO_4(aq) \rightarrow BaSO_4(s) + H_2O_2(aq)$$

We shall now compare the properties of water, hydrogen peroxide and hydrogen sulphide, summarised in table 26.3.

Boiling point

The boiling points of water and hydrogen peroxide are much higher than that of hydrogen sulphide, owing to extensive **intermolecular hydrogen bonding** *in the liquid state.* This results from appreciable bond polarity caused by the very electronegative nature of oxygen and has been described in section 5.9.

Thermal stability

As expected from its high negative enthalpy of formation, water is the most stable of the hydrides and decomposes only slightly into its elements at temperatures above 1000 °C. S—H bonds are considerably weaker than O—H bonds and hydrogen sulphide dissociates at red heat. Hydrogen peroxide is energetically unstable with respect to water and oxygen and its decomposition is catalysed by many metal compounds, e.g. in the laboratory preparation of oxygen:

$$2H_2O_2(aq) \xrightarrow{MnO_2(s)} 2H_2O(l) + O_2(g)$$

Acid–base behaviour

Water may act either as a **Lewis base** or a **Lewis acid** by respectively *donating* or *accepting* a lone pair of electrons:

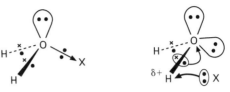

It self-ionises slightly in the liquid state.

$$2H_2O(l) \rightleftharpoons H_3O^+(aq) + OH^-(aq) \quad K_w = 10^{-14}M^2$$

Where K_w is the ionic product of water (section 18.3).

Hydrogen peroxide solution is slightly more acidic than water, owing to the presence of two highly electronegative oxygen atoms.

$$H_2O_2(aq) + H_2O(l) \rightleftharpoons H_3O^+(aq) + HO_2^-(aq) \quad K_a = 10^{-12}M$$

Hydrogen sulphide dissolves in water to give a weakly acidic solution.

$$H_2S(aq) + H_2O(l) \rightleftharpoons H_3O^+(aq) + SH^-(aq) \quad K_a = 10^{-7}M$$

The greater acidity of hydrogen sulphide is largely due to the relative weakness of the H—S bond, compared to the H—O bond in water. This means that it breaks more easily, releasing hydrogen ions.

Redox behaviour

In water, the oxygen atom is in its most stable oxidation state of -2 and it shows little tendency to act either as an oxidising or reducing agent. *Hydrogen peroxide contains oxygen in an oxidation state of -1 and acts mainly as an oxidising agent, forming water in acidic solution*, e.g. with iodide ions:

$$H_2O_2(aq) + 2H^+(aq) + 2e^- \rightarrow 2H_2O(l)$$

oxidation $2(-1)$ $2(-2)$ change -2
state   (reduction)

$$I^-(aq) \quad\quad \rightarrow \tfrac{1}{2}I_2(aq) + e^-$$

oxidation -1 0 change $+1$
state   (oxidation)

Therefore, $H_2O_2(aq) + 2H^+(aq) + 2I^-(aq) \rightarrow 2H_2O(l) + I_2(aq)$

It is, however, oxidised to oxygen gas by strong oxidising agents such as chlorine:

$$H_2O_2(aq) + Cl_2(g) \rightarrow 2HCl(aq) + O_2(g)$$
$$2(-1) \qquad\qquad\qquad\qquad\qquad 2(0)$$

Hydrogen sulphide acts as a reducing agent, since sulphur in its lowest oxidation state of -2 is easily oxidised. Thus hydrogen sulphide burns readily on igniting in excess air to give sulphur(IV) oxide:

$$2H_2S(g) + 3O_2(g) \rightarrow 2H_2O(l) + 2SO_2(g)$$
$$2(-2) \qquad\qquad\qquad\qquad\qquad 2(+4)$$

In aqueous solution, hydrogen sulphide generally forms free sulphur when it acts as a reducing agent, e.g. with bromine:

$$H_2S(aq) \rightarrow 2H^+(aq) + S(s) + 2e^-$$

oxidation -2 0 change $+2$
state   (oxidation)

$$\tfrac{1}{2}Br_2(aq) + e^- \rightarrow Br^-(aq)$$

oxidation 0 -1 change -1
state   (reduction)

Therefore, $H_2S(aq) + Br_2(aq) \rightarrow 2HBr(aq) + S(s)$

Solvent action

The solvent properties of water are discussed in section 9.9.

26.5 Oxides and oxoacids of sulphur

The only stable oxides of sulphur are the dioxide, SO_2, and the trioxide, SO_3. Sulphur burns with a blue flame on heating in air or oxygen to give the dioxide:

$$S(s) + O_2(g) \xrightarrow{\text{burn}} SO_2(g)$$

Although further oxidation to the trioxide is energetically favourable, the high activation energy means that in practice a catalyst must be used at a moderately high temperature:

$$2SO_2(g) + O_2(g) \underset{\text{platinum/450°C}}{\rightleftharpoons} 2SO_3(g) \quad \Delta H = -196\,kJ$$

The manufacture of sulphuric acid by the Contact process, described in section 26.7, is based upon this reaction.

The physical properties of SO_2 and SO_3 are compared in table 26.3. In the solid state the trioxide polymerises, but in the vapour phase both compounds exist as separate molecules:

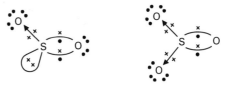

Each of the oxides dissolve in water to give an *acidic* solution:

$$H_2O(l) + SO_2(g) \rightleftharpoons H_2SO_3(aq) \quad \text{sulphuric(IV) (sulphurous) acid}$$

$$H_2O(l) + SO_3(g) \rightarrow H_2SO_4(l) \quad \text{sulphuric(VI) (sulphuric) acid}$$

We shall consider the nature of the acids separately.

Sulphurous acid

This is a *moderately strong dibasic acid* which exists only in aqueous solution.

$$H_2SO_3(aq) \rightleftharpoons HSO_3^-(aq) + H^+(aq) \quad K_a(1) = 1.2 \times 10^{-2}\,M$$

$$HSO_3^-(aq) \rightleftharpoons SO_3^{2-}(aq) + H^+(aq) \quad K_a(2) = 6.2 \times 10^{-8}\,M$$

It forms two series of salts with alkalis, e.g.

$$H_2SO_3(aq) \xrightarrow{\text{NaOH(aq)}} NaHSO_3(aq) \xrightarrow{\text{NaOH(aq)}} Na_2SO_3(aq)$$

sodium hydrogensulphite   sodium sulphite

The *reducing* nature of sulphurous acid and its salts will be considered in the next section.

Coal-burning power stations emit considerable quantities of sulphur dioxide into the atmosphere resulting from the combustion of sulphur impurities in the fuel. This is a serious atmospheric pollutant since it dissolves in rain, making it acidic. This **acid rain** is thought to be responsible for damaging forests and killing freshwater fish. Because of the prevailing south-west winds, most of the sulphur dioxide produced in Britain is 'exported' to Northern Europe. Plans to fit 'scrubbers' to power station chimneys to reduce sulphur dioxide emissions are being considered, but this will increase the cost of electricity.

Emissions from coal-fired power stations contain sulphur dioxide, a dangerous atmospheric pollutant that causes acid rain

Sulphuric acid

Pure sulphuric acid is a dense viscous liquid. It is essentially covalent in nature and its high boiling point (330 °C) indicates extensive hydrogen bonding between the H_2SO_4 molecules:

Concentrated sulphuric acid dissolves exothermically in water to give a highly acidic solution:

$$H_2SO_4(aq) \rightarrow H^+(aq) + HSO_4^-(aq) \quad \text{(in dilute solution)}$$
$$HSO_4^-(aq) \rightleftharpoons H^+(aq) + SO_4^{2-}(aq) \quad K_a(2) = 1.2 \times 10^{-2} M$$

Dilute sulphuric acid behaves as a typical strong dibasic acid, forming two series of salts, e.g. with sodium hydroxide:

$$H_2SO_4 \xrightarrow{\text{NaOH(aq)}} \underset{\substack{\text{sodium} \\ \text{hydrogensulphate}}}{NaHSO_4(aq)} \xrightarrow{\text{NaOH(aq)}} \underset{\substack{\text{sodium} \\ \text{sulphate}}}{Na_2SO_4(aq)}$$

We shall now consider some of the important chemical properties of concentrated sulphuric acid.

As a dehydrating agent
As its highly exothermic enthalpy of solution suggests, *concentrated sulphuric acid has a great affinity for water.* It is used as a drying agent for many gases and will remove the water of crystallisation from salts, e.g.

$$CuSO_4.5H_2O(s) \xrightarrow{\text{c.}H_2SO_4} CuSO_4(s)$$
$$\text{blue} \qquad (-5H_2O) \qquad \text{white}$$

The elements of water are also removed from many organic compounds. In the case of ethanol, C_2H_5OH, two dehydration products are possible,

$$C_2H_5OH(l) \xrightarrow[170°C\ (-H_2O)]{H_2SO_4(l)} C_2H_4(g) \text{ major product with excess } H_2SO_4$$
$$\text{ethene}$$

$$2C_2H_5OH(l) \xrightarrow[140°C\ (-H_2O)]{H_2SO_4(l)} (C_2H_5)_2O(g) \text{ major product with excess } C_2H_5OH$$
$$\text{ethoxyethane}$$

(See also section 38.6.1.)

In displacing volatile acids
Addition of concentrated sulphuric acid to the salt of another acid, e.g. sodium nitrate, will set up an equilibrium of the following type:

$$H_2SO_4(l) + NaNO_3(s) \rightleftharpoons NaHSO_4(s) + HNO_3(l)$$

Since the boiling point of sulphuric acid is high, heating will cause the more volatile nitric acid to distil off first, driving the reaction to the right.

Acids with very low boiling points, e.g. hydrogen chloride, may be displaced completely from their salts at room temperature:

$$H_2SO_4(l) + NaCl(s) \rightarrow NaHSO_4(s) + HCl(g)$$

Note that a hydrogensulphate, rather than a sulphate, is formed in the presence of excess concentrated sulphuric acid.

As an oxidising agent
Although not as powerful as nitric acid, hot concentrated sulphuric acid is a useful oxidising agent. Hydrogen sulphide or sulphur may be formed, but the usual reduction product of concentrated sulphuric acid is sulphur dioxide:

$$\begin{array}{ccc} & H_2SO_4 & SO_2 \\ \text{ox. state} & +6 & +4 \qquad \text{change} -2 \end{array}$$

Non-metallic elements generally give their oxides, e.g. carbon:

$$\begin{array}{ccc} & C \longrightarrow & CO_2 \\ \text{ox. state} & 0 & +4 \qquad \text{change} +4 \end{array}$$

Thus one mole of carbon reacts with two moles of sulphuric acid:

$$C(s) + 2H_2SO_4(l) \rightarrow CO_2(g) + 2SO_2(g) + 2H_2O(l)$$

Metals are oxidised to their positive ions, e.g. copper:

$$\begin{array}{ccc} & Cu \longrightarrow & Cu^{2+} \\ \text{ox. state} & 0 & +2 \qquad \text{change} +2 \end{array}$$

Thus one mole of copper reacts initially with one mole of sulphuric acid:

$$Cu(s) + H_2SO_4(l) \rightarrow Cu^{2+}(s) + SO_2(g) + 2OH^-$$

However, the hydroxide ions react with further sulphuric acid to give water and sulphate ions:

$$2OH^- + H_2SO_4(l) \rightarrow 2H_2O(l) + SO_4^{2-}(aq)$$

So the overall equation is

$$Cu(s) + 2H_2SO_4(l) \rightarrow Cu^{2+}SO_4^{2-}(s) + SO_2(g) + 2H_2O(l)$$

It is not possible to prepare hydrogen bromide or hydrogen iodide from their salts by displacement with sulphuric acid. In each case the oxidising action of the acid gives some free halogen:

$$3H_2SO_4(l) + 2NaBr(s) \rightarrow 2NaHSO_4(s) + 2H_2O(l) + SO_2(g) + Br_2(l)$$

As a sulphonating agent

Hot concentrated sulphuric acid reacts slowly with benzene to give benzenesulphonic acid:

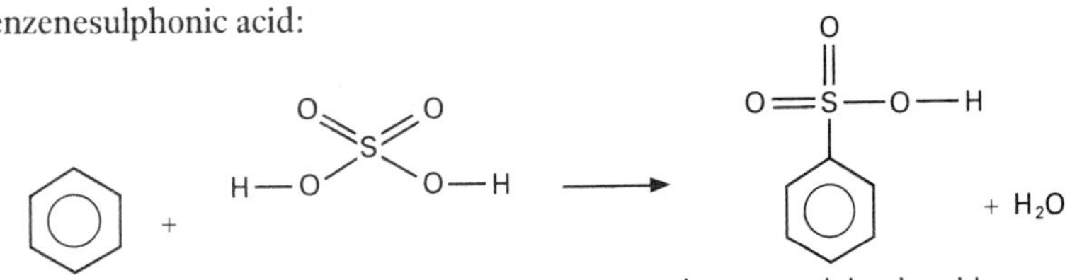

benzenesulphonic acid

The same reaction takes place more rapidly at lower temperatures if sulphur trioxide is dissolved in the sulphuric acid (section 36.5.2).

Concentrated sulphuric acid also aids the **nitration** of benzene by encouraging the formation of the nitryl cation, NO_2^+:

$$H_2SO_4(l) + HNO_3(l) \rightleftharpoons HSO_4^-(l) + H_2NO_3^+(l)$$
$$H_2NO_3^+(l) \rightarrow H_2O(l) + NO_2^+(l)$$

26.6 Oxoanions of sulphur

We have already mentioned sulphite, SO_3^{2-}, and sulphate, SO_4^{2-}, derived from sulphurous and sulphuric acid respectively. Figure 26.2 shows other oxoanions together with the oxidation states of the sulphur atoms. Most of these other species result from the ability of sulphur atoms to bond directly together, but **peroxodisulphate**, $S_2O_8^{2-}$, contains a **peroxo** linkage, O—O. These oxygen atoms are in an oxidation state of -1 whilst all the others are in their most stable oxidation state of -2.

The redox behaviour of the oxoanions is quite complex and depends considerably upon the pH of the solution. In general terms, however, *the most stable oxidation state of sulphur is +6, and most of the species will undergo redox reactions to give sulphate ions.*

Figure 26.2 *Structures of some oxoanions of sulphur, showing the oxidation states of the sulphur*

S—O bonds only

sulphite SO_3^{2-}

with S—S

thiosulphate $S_2O_3^{2-}$
(average o.n. = 2)

with O—O bonds

peroxodisulphate $S_2O_8^{2-}$

sulphate SO_4^{2-}

dithionate $S_2O_6^{2-}$

tetrathionate $S_4O_6^{2-}$
(average o.n. = 2.5)

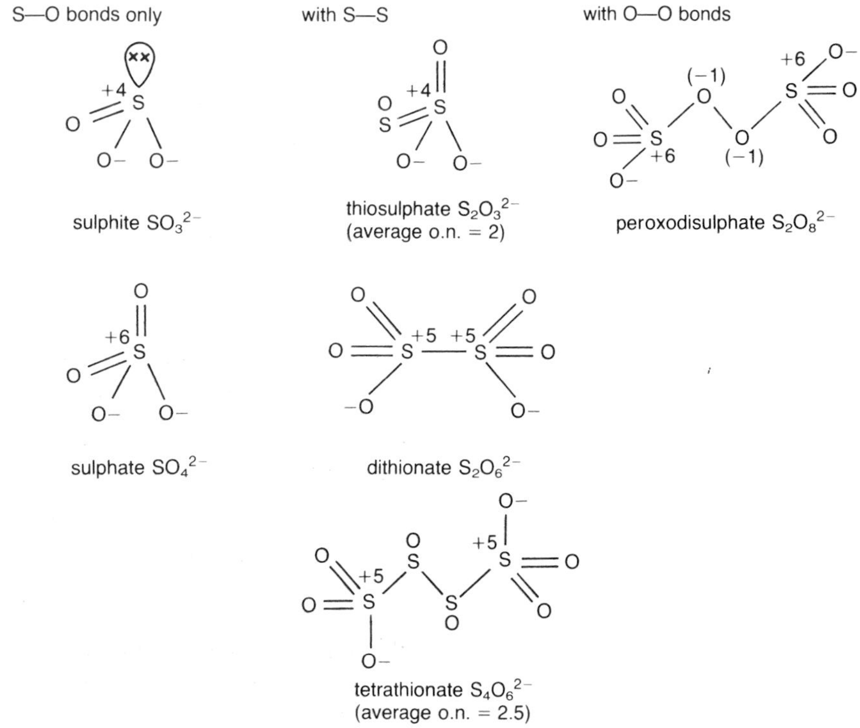

Activity 26.3

Bearing in mind that the most stable oxidation state of sulphur in its oxoanions is +6, and that the most stable oxidation state of oxygen is −2, which of the species illustrated in figure 26.2 would you expect to be oxidising agents, and which reducing agents?

Those ions which contain sulphur atoms not linked directly to oxygen atoms tend to **disproportionate**, e.g. thiosulphate in acid solution,

$$S_2O_3^{2-}(aq) + 2H^+(aq) \rightarrow SO_2(g) + H_2O(l) + S(s)$$
$$2(+2) \qquad\qquad\qquad\qquad +4 \qquad\qquad\qquad 0$$

Iodine may be estimated volumetrically by titration with thiosulphate but in this case tetrathionate rather than sulphate is produced,

$$2S_2O_3^{2-}(aq) + I_2(aq) \rightarrow S_4O_6^{2-}(aq) + 2I^-(aq)$$
$$4(+2) \qquad\qquad\qquad\quad 4(+2.5)$$

Sodium thiosulphate solution, under the name of 'hypo', is also used as a 'fixer' in photography. After developing the film, it is used to remove unreacted silver bromide as a soluble complex, so preventing further darkening on exposure to light.

26.7 Manufacture of sulphuric acid

The 'flow diagram' in figure 26.3 shows the main stages in the manufacture of sulphuric acid from sulphur.

Figure 26.3 *Flow diagram for the production of sulphuric acid by the Contact process*

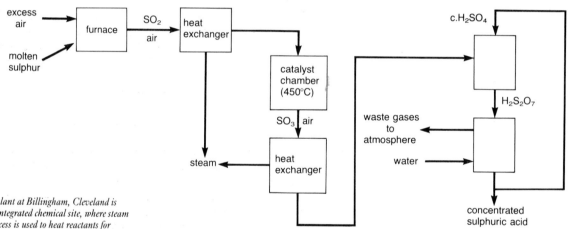

The sulphuric acid plant at Billingham, Cleveland is part of a very large integrated chemical site, where steam generated in one process is used to heat reactants for another

Sulphur burning

Molten sulphur is burned in excess air to give sulphur dioxide:

$$S(l) + O_2(g) \rightarrow SO_2(g) \quad \Delta H = -297kJ$$

The mixture of sulphur dioxide and air leaves the furnace at over 1000°C and must be cooled by passing it through a heat exchanger before the next stage. This produces *steam* which may be sold for electricity production, thereby helping to offset running costs.

Sulphur trioxide formation

Sulphur dioxide and oxygen combine in the presence of a **vanadium(V) oxide** catalyst at about **450°C** to give sulphur trioxide. The reasons for the choice of these conditions are explained in section 14.8.

$$2SO_2(g) + O_2(g) \rightleftharpoons 2SO_3(g) \quad \Delta H = -196kJ$$

In modern plants at least 99.5% of the sulphur dioxide is oxidised to sulphur trioxide. The hot gases, which contain about 10% of sulphur trioxide, are cooled, again producing valuable steam, before being passed to the next stage.

Oleum production

It is impractical to dissolve sulphur trioxide directly in water, since the very exothermic reaction produces a dangerous fine mist of sulphuric acid. To prevent this the sulphur trioxide is first dissolved in concentrated sulphuric acid to give 'fuming' sulphuric acid or **oleum**:

$$H_2SO_4(l) + SO_3(g) \rightarrow H_2S_2O_7(l)$$

Sulphuric acid production

Oleum may be safely diluted with water to give concentrated sulphuric acid:

$$H_2S_2O_7(l) + H_2O(l) \rightarrow 2H_2SO_4(l)$$

Part of the acid is **recirculated** to the oleum production stage. The waste gases from the process are vented from the top of the vessel. Current legislation demands that the sulphur dioxide content of these emissions does not exceed 0.05% and at this level the contribution to **acid rain** is negligible compared with that of a coal burning power station.

There are several factors which must be taken into account in siting a sulphur acid plant.

▶ Since sulphur has to be imported from the USA or Sicily, the plant should be close to a **port**.
▶ For large scale production, **transport** costs are important. Sulphuric acid is also a hazardous material and the plant should be as close as possible to its major customers and well served by adequate road and rail links.
▶ Proximity to a **power** station which will buy the surplus steam produced will reduce production costs.
▶ A good reliable **water** supply is required.

Activity 26.4

There are many factors which must be taken into account when deciding whether to build a chemical factory and where to site it. In this activity we shall consider a 'fertiliser' company which uses sulphuric acid in the manufacture of *ammonium sulphate*. At present it buys in all the sulphuric acid it uses, but as the price has recently risen, the company is considering building its own Contact process plant. As part of a 'feasibility study', you have been asked to report on the advantages and disadvantages of building a sulphuric acid plant at each of the three possible locations described below and illustrated on the map in figure 26.4.

Location A

This is where your ammonia plant is situated and where all your sulphuric acid is actually used. Although there is just enough room to build a sulphuric acid production plant, this would mean having to find alternative storage space for the ammonium sulphate fertiliser before delivery to customers. The factory is close to London with good links to the motorway system.

Location B

This is a disused factory in Sheffield. There are several other chemical firms in the area which also use sulphuric acid in their manufacturing processes. The site has been empty for some time and is for sale at a reasonable price. It is near to the Yorkshire coalfields and a power station.

Figure 26.4 *Map showing possible sites for the sulphuric acid plant in activity 26.4*

Location C

This is a completely undeveloped 'greenfield' site on the coast just north of Belfast in Northern Ireland. There is no traditional chemical industry in the region, but it has good port facilities and, because of very high unemployment in this area, government grants are available to developers. The proposed site is, however, close to an area of outstanding natural beauty and there is an active local conservation group.

You are not expected to make a definite choice in your report, but to argue possible advantages and disadvantages of each site with particular respect of each of the following factors.

1. The cost of building the plant and supplying the main services, i.e. water and electricity.
2. The availability of fuel for the sulphur burners.
3. Transport costs: both to deliver the raw material, sulphur, to the plant and, if necessary, transport the sulphuric acid after manufacture.
4. Possible extra sources of income: perhaps by selling surplus acid or other products of the process.
5. The ease of recruiting the skilled and semi-skilled labour to operate and maintain the plant.
6. Environmental factors associated with the disposal of waste products, or more seriously, with possible malfunction of the plant.

26.8 Comments on the activities

Activity 26.1

Compare your answers with figure 26.5.

Figure 26.5 *Molecular structure of the fluorides of oxygen and sulphur*

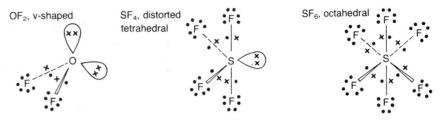

Activity 26.2

Compare your answers with figure 26.6. Note that double bonds may be used in place of dative bonds in these diagrams.

Figure 26.6 *Molecular structure of some chlorides of oxygen and sulphur*

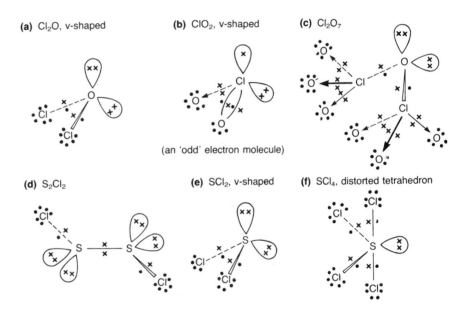

Activity 26.3

Peroxodisulphate contains two oxygen atoms in an oxidation state of -1 and should act as an *oxidising* agent by accepting electrons. This is in fact the case, peroxodisulphate is one of the strongest oxidising agents known,

$$S_2O_8^{2-}(aq) + 2e^- \rightarrow 2SO_4^{2-}(aq) \quad E^{\ominus} + 2.01 \text{ volts}$$

All the other ions in figure 26.2 contain sulphur in an average oxidation state below $+6$ and act as reducing agents under certain conditions by donating electrons, e.g.

$$SO_3^{2-}(aq) + H_2O(l) \rightarrow SO_4^{2-}(aq) + 2H^+(aq) + 2e^-$$

Activity 26.4

Building costs
The actual cost of building the sulphuric acid plant at site A should be the lowest, as you already own the land. Finding alternative storage space for the ammonium sulphate could be expensive, however, given the high cost of property near London.

Site C is likely to be more expensive to develop than site B, since it will need to be connected to mains water and electricity supplies. Government grants may, however, make this a financially attractive proposition.

Fuel supplies
Site B probably has a clear advantage here, as it is close to the South Yorkshire coalfields.

Transport
Since sulphur is imported, sites A and C have an advantage in being close to major ports. In terms of transport of the sulphuric acid, it is best to produce it where it is to be used, that is, at site A.

Extra income
Site B has two advantages here. There are potential customers for your surplus sulphuric acid nearby, and also a power station which might buy the steam made in the process to generate electricity.

Labour
Site A could use existing management but extra labour might be more expensive here than in the more depressed areas around the other two sites. Skilled labour is likely to be easier to find at site B than at site C which has no local chemical industry.

Environmental factors
Although modern Contact process plants are very safe and emit negligible quantities of sulphur dioxide, you are still likely to face stiff opposition from conservation groups if you decide to build near site C. If there were to be a serious accident, site C has the advantage that it is least populated and that the prevailing winds would probably blow any poisonous emissions out to sea.

26.9 Summary and revision plan

1 Both elements exhibit **allotropy**. The allotropes of oxygen are gaseous (and contain multiple bonds), whereas those of sulphur are solid at room temperature.

2 Both elements show an oxidation state of -2 in their simple anions, X^{2-}. Sulphur commonly also shows oxidation states of $+6$ and $+4$, but since oxygen is far more electronegative it does not generally show positive oxidation states.

3 The **maximum covalency** of sulphur is six, whereas that of oxygen is three.

4 The hydrides of oxygen, i.e. water and hydrogen peroxide, have higher boiling points than hydrogen sulphide owing to strong **intermolecular hydrogen bonding**.

    Hydrogen sulphide acts as a reducing agent and as a weak acid in aqueous solution.

5 Owing to its polar nature, water is an excellent solvent for ionic compounds.

6 Sulphur forms two oxides, SO_2 and SO_3, both of which dissolve in water to give acidic solutions.

    Sulphur dioxide is a serious air pollutant which largely arises from burning coal in power stations. It is a major cause of **acid rain** which is harmful to vegetation and fish and damages stonework.

7 Large quantities of sulphuric acid are manufactured by the **Contact process**. The acid is used in the production of a wide range of materials including fertilisers and detergents.

    The concentrated acid acts as a **dehydrating** agent, an **oxidising** agent and a **sulphonating** agent. When dilute, it behaves as a typical **strong dibasic acid**.

27

Group VII: The Halogens

Contents

During this century world production of chlorine has risen from about 0.1 million tonnes to over 29 million tonnes per year. Table 27.1 shows that the petrochemicals industry consumes well over half of the chlorine produced in Britain. In carefully controlled amounts, the poisonous nature of chlorine is useful in killing bacteria in drinking water. Many chlorine compounds are also toxic and, despite concern over environmental pollution, continue to be used as insecticides or weedkillers.

Fluorides are used in 'fluoride' toothpastes and organic fluorine compounds are found in non-stick coatings on pans, and in aerosol sprays. Silver bromide and iodide are light-sensitive compounds used in photographic films.

Swimming pools, non-stick pans, fluoride toothpaste and photographic film – all depend on halogen chemistry

Table 27.1   *Some major uses of chlorine in Britain*

Approx. % of total chlorine production	intermediate product(s)	end use(s)
Petrochemicals		
27	chloroethene (vinyl chloride) CH_2CHCl	poly(chloroethene), i.e. poly(vinyl chloride), PVC
17	chloromethanes $CHCl_3$, CCl_4 CH_3Cl	refrigerant liquids and aerosol 'propellants' petrol 'antiknock' additives
16	other chlorinated hydrocarbons, e.g. $CCl_2.CHCl$ $CCl_2.CCl_2$	metal 'degreasing' solvent 'dry-cleaning' solvent
6	propene oxide	car brake fluid polyurethane plastics many pharmaceutical products
Inorganics		
13		extraction of magnesium, titanium and bromine manufacture of hydrochloric acid
1	sodium chlorate(I), NaClO	paper and pulp bleach
Miscellaneous		
20		sterilisation of water manufacture of disinfectants, anaesthetics, insecticides and dyestuffs, etc.

Table 27.2   *Data sheet for the elements of Group VII*

Element	atomic number	electron configuration	atomic radius /nm*	ionisation energies /kJ mol^{-1}								electron affinity /kJ mol^{-1}	electro-negativity	standard electrode potential $E^{\ominus}$/V†	density /g cm^{-3}	m.p. /°C
				1st	2nd	3rd	4th	5th	6th	7th	8th					
fluorine F	9	[He]$2s^2 2p^5$	0.072	1680	3370	6040	8410	11000	15100	17900	91600	−348	4.0	+2.87	1.11‡	−220
chlorine Cl	17	[Ne]$3s^2 3p^5$	0.099	1260	2300	3850	5150	6540	9330	11000	33600	−364	3.0	+1.36	1.56‡	−101
bromine Br	35	[Ar]$3d^{10} 4s^2 4p^5$	0.114	1140	2030	3460	4850	5770	8370	10000	20300	−342	2.8	+1.07	3.12	−7
iodine I	53	[Kr]$4d^{10} 5s^2 5p^5$	0.133	1010	1840	3000	4030	5000	7400	8700	16400	−314	2.5	+0.54	4.93	114
astatine At	85	[Xe]$4f^{14} 5d^{10} 6s^2 6p^5$	0.140	920								?	2.2	?	?	302

*values are 'covalent' radii

†$E^{\ominus}$ is the standard electrode potential for the reaction $\frac{1}{2}X_2 + e \rightleftharpoons X^-$ in aqueous solution

‡measured for the liquid at its boiling point

Are you surprised by the trend in the values of electron affinity?

What do the above $E^{\ominus}$ values show about the relative oxidising power of the halogens in aqueous solution?

27.1 The elements: structure, atomic and physical properties

The elements of Group VII, known collectively as the **halogens**, are similar in many ways. They are all non-metals and exist as diatomic molecules, X_2:

$$:\overset{..}{\underset{..}{X}} \overset{}{\underset{}{\text{———}}} \overset{..}{\underset{..}{X}}:$$

In common with the previous 'p' block groups, the chemistry of the first element, fluorine, shows several unique features. It is the most electronegative element and by far the most reactive non-metal. Throughout this chapter we shall contrast the chemistry of fluorine with the quite smooth variation in properties on passing from chlorine to iodine.

All isotopes of the heaviest halogen, astatine, are intensely radioactive with short half-lives. Other than showing how this element fits in with the main group trends, we shall not consider its chemistry further.

Table 27.2 gives value for some of the main atomic and physical properties of the halogens. Since there are no complications caused by differences in molecular structure, the main trends are quite predictable and are explained fully in chapter 19.

27.2 Bonding types

All the atoms of Group VII have the outer electron configuration

ns^2ns^5 i.e.

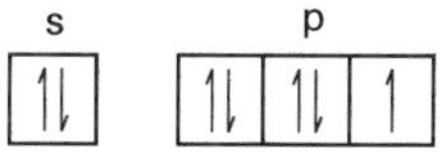

s	p
↑↓	↑↓ ↑↓ ↑

They may achieve a stable noble gas electron configuration in *two* ways.

Ionic bonding

All the elements form **ionic halides** with electropositive metals. The halogen atom, X, achieves a noble gas configuration by gaining one electron to form a halide ion, X^-:

$$\underset{/ns^2np^5}{X} \quad + \quad e^- \rightarrow \quad \underset{/ns^2np^6}{X^-}$$

Polyhalide ions are also known which contain one or more halogen molecules attached to a halide ion. One of the commonest is triiodide, I_3^-, formed on dissolving iodine in aqueous iodide solution:

$$I_2(aq) + I^-(aq) \rightleftharpoons I_3^-(aq)$$

Iodine has the lowest first ionisation energy in the group and can also form cations. The I^+ ion is stabilised by electron pair donors such as pyridine, C_5H_5N, e.g. in the complex:

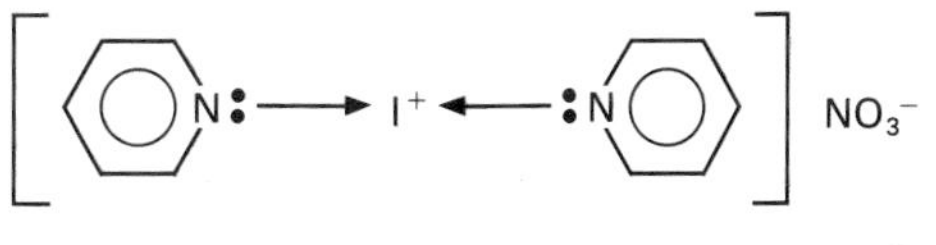

$$\left[\langle\bigcirc\rangle N: \longrightarrow I^+ \longleftarrow :N \langle\bigcirc\rangle \right] NO_3^-$$

Covalent bonding

All the halogen atoms may achieve a noble gas electron configuration by forming a single covalent bond, e.g. in the hydrogen halides, HX:

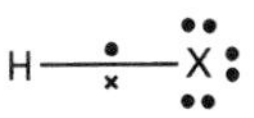

$$H \overset{}{\underset{\times}{\text{———}}} \overset{..}{\underset{..}{X}}:$$

Except for fluorine, the halogens can also show covalencies of 3, 5 and 7, by promoting electrons from 'p' orbitals into empty 'd' orbitals in the valency shell. Iodine, for example, shows covalencies of 1, 3, 5 and 7 in **interhalogens**, i.e. compounds of two halogens:

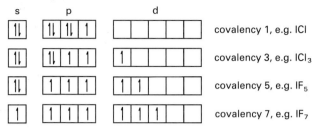

Activity 27.1

1 Why can fluorine atoms form only a single covalent bond whereas all the other halogens have maximum covalencies greater than one? (If in doubt, look at sections 25.2 and 26.2.)
2 Draw 'dot and cross' diagrams clearly showing the bonding in, and the shape of, the following interhalogen molecules:
   (a) ICl (b) ICl_3 (c) IF_5 (d) IF_7
   (Hint: don't forget any lone pairs of electrons on the central atom.)

Hydrogen bonding is also possible in compounds containing hydrogen and fluorine atoms linked directly together. This will be considered in more detail in the chemisty of the hydrogen halides in section 27.5.

27.3 Chemical properties and reactivity

The halogens react with a wide range of metallic and non-metallic elements. Some of their principal reactions are shown in figure 27.1. As you can see, the chemistry of chlorine and bromine is virtually identical but fluorine and to some extent iodine, show differences.

Reactivity *decreases* markedly on passing down the group. Fluorine, for instance, is the only halogen to react directly with carbon. All the elements form hydrogen halides on combination with hydrogen but the conditions needed vary considerably.

$$H_2(g) + F_2(g) \xrightarrow{\text{explosive under all conditions}} 2HF(g)$$

$$H_2(g) + Cl_2(g) \xrightarrow{\text{explodes in direct sunlight}} 2HCl(g)$$

$$H_2(g) + Br_2(g) \xrightarrow{300\,°C, \text{ platinum catalyst}} 2HBr(g)$$

$$H_2(g) + I_2(g) \xrightleftharpoons{300\,°C, \text{ platinum catalyst}} 2HI(g)$$

We can explain this trend in reactivity by considering the *enthalpy cycle* and data shown in figure 27.2. The standard enthalpies of formation show that the hydrogen halides become relatively less stable with respect to the elements on passing down the group. *The high reactivity of fluorine results from its comparatively low atomisation energy and the great strength of the H—X bond.* At first glance it might seem strange that fluorine should form strong covalent bonds with other atoms, whilst the F—F bond itself is rather weak. In fact, the strength of a fluorine covalent bond decreases with the number of lone pairs in the valency shell of the other atom:

Figure 27.1 *Some reactions of the halogens*

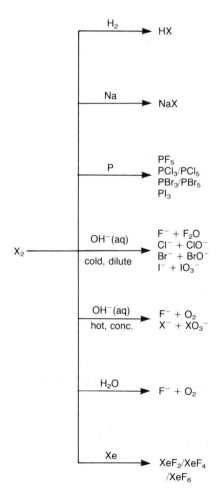

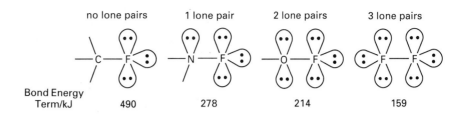

	no lone pairs	1 lone pair	2 lone pairs	3 lone pairs

| Bond Energy Term/kJ | 490 | 278 | 214 | 159 |

Increased repulsion between the lone pairs is responsible for the weakening of these short covalent bonds.

The strength of the covalent bonds which fluorine forms with other elements also helps to explain why it brings out their *maximum* covalency. Sulphur, for example forms a hexafluoride, SF_6, while its highest chloride is only SCl_4. It is also rather easier to pack the small fluorine atoms around the central sulphur atom.

Figure 27.2 *Enthalpy cycle for the formation of a hydrogen halide, HX*

enthalpy

	ΔH_a /kJ mol^{-1}
fluorine	79
chlorine	121
bromine	112
iodine	107
hydrogen	218

	bond energy /kJ mol^{-1}	ΔH_f /kJ mol^{-1}
H—F	567	−269
H—Cl	431	−92
H—Br	366	−36
H—I	298	+27

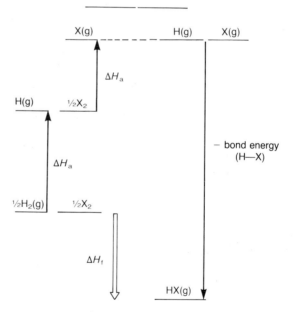

27.4 Oxidising power

Oxidation involves the total or partial removal of electrons from species. All the halogens act as oxidising agents when they react with more electropositive elements. They will totally remove electrons from reactive metals, being themselves reduced to halide ions, e.g.

$$2Na \rightarrow 2Na^+ + 2e^- \quad \text{oxidation}$$
oxidation states   2(0)   2(+1)

$$X_2 + 2e^- \rightarrow 2X^- \quad \text{reduction}$$
oxidation states   2(0)   2(−1)

Less electronegative non-metals are also oxidised, although here the halogen atom only partially withdraws electrons, forming a polar covalent bond, e.g.

$$H \overset{\times}{-} H \; + \; :\overset{..}{X} \overset{..}{-} \overset{..}{X}: \longrightarrow \; 2 \; H \overset{\delta+ \quad \delta-}{\overset{..}{-}\overset{..}{X}:}$$

oxidation
states   2 (0)   2 (0)   2 (+1)   2 (−1)

We should be able to judge the relative oxidising 'power' of the halogens by comparing their electron affinities, electronegativities and standard electrode potentials given in table 27.2.

Both electronegativity values and standard electrode potentials indicate that oxidising strength should *decrease* on descending the group. Except in the case of fluorine, this is confirmed by the electron affinity data. *Despite having a less exothermic electron affinity, however, fluorine is a more powerful oxidising agent than chlorine.* We must remember that we are concerned with the oxidising power of the X_2 molecules and that these must be *atomised* before halide ions, X^-, can be formed.

$$\tfrac{1}{2}X_2 \xrightarrow[\text{atomisation energy}]{\Delta H_a} X(g) \xrightarrow[\text{electron affinity}]{\Delta H_e} X^-(g)$$

If we add atomisation energy and electron affinity (below), then the figures confirm that fluorine is the most powerful oxidising agent in Group VII.

	F_2	Cl_2	Br_2	I_2
atomisation energy/kJ mol^{-1}	79	121	112	107
electron affinity/kJ mol^{-1}	−348	−364	−342	−314
atomisation energy + electron affinity/kJ mol^{-1}	−269	−243	−230	−207

Further experimental confirmation of the decrease in oxidising power on passing down the group is given by the **displacement** reactions. *Any halogen will oxidise a halide ion below it in the group,* e.g.

$$Cl_2(aq) \; + 2Br^-(aq) \rightarrow 2Cl^-(aq) \; + Br_2(aq)$$
2(0)   2(−1)   2(−1)   2(0)

but $I_2(aq) \; + 2Br^-(aq)$ no reaction

We may explain this very simply in terms of the relative sizes of the halogen atoms. In a *large* halide ion, the outer electrons are *more easily removed*, being further from the nucleus and *'screened'* from its attraction by a greater number of inner electrons. *Small* halide ions hold onto their outer electrons *more strongly*. Conversely, small halogen atoms are able to attract electrons more powerfully than larger ones.

Chlorine and bromine are very similar in their oxidising reactions but fluorine and iodine sometimes behave differently. Fluorine, for example, is the only halogen powerful enough to oxidise water directly:

$$2F_2(g) \; + 2H_2O(l) \rightarrow 4HF(aq) + O_2(g)$$
4(0)   2(−2)   4(−1)   2(0)

Astatine apart, iodine is the weakest oxidising agent in the group. Hence it converts thiosulphate, $S_2O_3{}^{2-}$, into tetrathionate, $S_4O_6{}^{2-}$.

$$I_2(aq) \; + 2S_2O_3{}^{2-}(aq) \rightarrow 2I^-(aq) \; + S_4O_6{}^{2-}(aq)$$
2(0)   4(+2)   2(−1)   4(+2$\tfrac{1}{2}$)

but, Cl_2 can oxidise thiosulphate to sulphate ions

$$4Cl_2(aq) + \; S_2O_3{}^{2-}(aq) \; + 5H_2O(l) \rightarrow 8Cl^-(aq) \; + \; 2SO_4{}^{2-}(aq) \; + 10H^+(aq)$$
8(0)   2(+2)   8(−1)   2(+6)

Activity 27.2

1 Complete each of the following equations, stating clearly if there is no reaction:
   (a) $Cl_2(aq) + 2NaF(aq) \rightarrow$
   (b) $Br_2(aq) + 2KAt(aq) \rightarrow$
   (c) $At_2(aq) + 2NaI(aq) \rightarrow$
   (d) $I_2(aq) + 2KCl(aq) \rightarrow$
   (e) $F_2(g) + 2NaI(aq) \rightarrow$

2 Use the change in oxidation states of the atoms in italics below to balance the following redox equations involving iodine.
   (a) $Ce^{4+}(aq) + I^-(aq) \rightarrow Ce^{3+}(aq) + I_2(aq)$
   (b) $Cu^{2+}(aq) + I^-(aq) \rightarrow CuI(s) + I_2(aq)$
   (c) $IO_4^-(aq) + I^-(aq) + H^+(aq) \rightarrow I_2(aq) + H_2O(l)$

27.5 Hydrogen halides

Hydrogen fluoride and hydrogen chloride are prepared in the laboratory by the action of concentrated sulphuric acid on an appropriate metal halide, e.g.

$$CaF_2(s) + 2H_2SO_4(l) \xrightarrow{\text{warm}} Ca(HSO_4)_2(s) + 2HF(g)$$

$$NaCl(s) + H_2SO_4(l) \xrightarrow{\text{room temp.}} NaHSO_4(s) + HCl(g)$$

Since concentrated sulphuric acid oxidises both Br^- and I^- to the free halogen, *a different method must be used to prepare hydrogen bromide and hydrogen iodide.* The halogen is added to phosphorus to give the phosphorus trihalide which is then decomposed by a little water, e.g.

$$2P + 3Br_2 \rightarrow 2PBr_3$$
$$\text{then}\quad PBr_3 + 3H_2O \rightarrow 3HBr + H_3PO_3$$

Some of the main properties of the hydrogen halides are compared in table 27.3.

Table 27.3 *Properties of the hydrogen halides*

Hydrogen halide	boiling point /°C	$\Delta H_f^{\ominus}$ /kJ mol^{-1}	bond enthalpy, H—X /kJ mol^{-1}	acid dissociation constant, K_a, in aqueous solution /M
hydrogen fluoride, HF	20	-269	567	7×10^{-4}
hydrogen chloride, HCl	-85	-92	431	10^7
hydrogen bromide, HBr	-69	-36	366	$>10^7$
hydrogen iodide, HI	-35	$+26$	298	$>10^7$

How and why do (i) the boiling points and (ii) the strength of the H—X covalent bond vary on passing down the group?

You will notice that, in general, boiling point rises with relative molecular mass indicating an increase in intermolecular attraction. *Hydrogen fluoride, however, has by far the highest boiling point. In the liquid state its molecules are linked into long chains by quite strong hydrogen bonding, as described in section 5.9:*

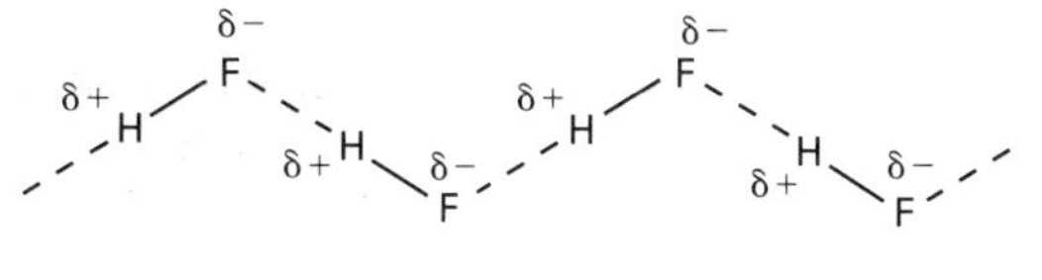

As we might expect from the decrease in the strength of the H—X bond and the trend in enthalpies of formation shown in table 27.2, *the thermal stability of the hydrogen halides falls on passing down the group*. This is especially noticeable with hydrogen iodide, which readily dissociates into its element on heating:

$$2HI(g) \underset{\text{at } 1000\,°C}{\overset{\text{about 30\% dissociation}}{\rightleftharpoons}} H_2(g) + I_2(g)$$

As we might expect, the polar covalent hydrogen halides are appreciably soluble *without dissociation* in organic solvents such as benzene. They are also highly soluble in water, but here *ionisation* occurs giving solutions containing the corresponding **hydrohalic acids**:

$$HX(g) + H_2O(l) \rightleftharpoons H_3O^+(aq) + X^-(aq)$$

The dissociation constants given in table 27.2 show that *the strength of the hydrohalic acids increases on passing down the group*. The comparative weakness of hydrofluoric acid has been explained in section 21.3, largely in terms of the great strength of the H—F bond. The increase in acid strength mirrors the decrease in H—X bond strength.

Figure 27.3 *Detection of halide ions in aqueous solution using silver nitrate*

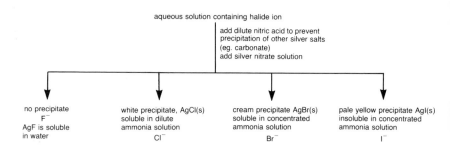

Since halides are so common it is important that we should be able to identify the presence of each ion. The analysis scheme shown in figure 27.3 is based on differences in solubility between the silver halides. Silver nitrate solution may also be used for quantitative determination of chloride, either by weighing the precipitated silver chloride or by titration, as described in section 15.4.

27.6 Oxides and oxoacids

The oxides and oxoacids in which the halogens show their common oxidation of 1, 3, 5 and 7 are shown in table 27.4. The oxides, which may be regarded as the anhydrides of the oxoacids, have been described in section 26.3. All the halogens, *except fluorine*, form some halic acids of the following types.

Table 27.4 *Main oxides and oxoacids of the halogens*

Halogen	oxidation state of the halogen							
	+1		+3		+5		+7	
fluorine	F_2O^*							
chlorine	Cl_2O	HClO		$HClO_2$		$HClO_3$	Cl_2O_7	$HClO_4$
bromine	Br_2O	HBrO				$HBrO_3$		
iodine		HIO			I_2O_5	HIO_3		HIO_4

*Since fluorine is more electronegative than oxygen its oxidation state is -1

Why are there no oxoacids of fluorine?

Halic(I) acids, HXO

Halic(III) acids, HXO₂

The only definite compound of this type is chloric(III) acid.

Halic(V) acids, HXO₃

Halic(VII) acids, HXO₄

These acids may be prepared by displacing them from their salts with sulphuric acid. In general, *as the oxidation state of the halogen increases, so acid strength and thermal stability increase but oxidising power decreases.*

Activity 27.3

Explain the following:
1 Chlorine, bromine and iodine all form halic(V) acids, whereas fluorine cannot.
2 The strengths of the chloric acids increase as the number of oxygen atoms in the molecule increases.

27.7 Oxoanions

Most, but not all, of the halogen oxoacids react with alkali to form stable salts containing halogen oxoanions.

Halate(I), XO⁻

Sodium chlorate(I) is formed when chlorine is bubbled through *dilute* sodium hydroxide solution *at or below room temperature:*

$$2NaOH(aq) + Cl_2(g) \xrightarrow{\text{room temperature}} NaCl(aq) + NaClO(aq) + H_2O(l)$$
$$\qquad\qquad\quad 2(0) \qquad\qquad\qquad\qquad\quad -1 \qquad\quad +1$$

Bromate(I) may be made by a similar reaction but only at temperatures below $0\,^\circ$C. Iodate(I) does not exist, iodate(V) being formed immediately upon dissolving iodine in alkali.

Chlorate(III)

Sodium chlorate(III) is formed when chlorine dioxide is dissolved in sodium hydroxide solution.

$$2NaOH(aq) + 2ClO_2(l) \rightarrow NaClO_2(aq) + NaClO_3(aq) + H_2O(l)$$
$$2(+4) \qquad\qquad -3 \qquad\qquad +5$$

Halate(V), XO_3^-

All may be prepared by adding the appropriate halogen to *hot concentrated* alkali, e.g.

$$6NaOH(aq) + 3Cl_2(aq) \xrightarrow{\text{heat}} NaClO_3(aq) + 5NaCl(aq) + 3H_2O(l)$$
$$6(0) \qquad\qquad +5 \qquad\quad 5(-1)$$

Halate(VII), XO_4^-

Potassium chlorate(V) **disproportionates** on controlled heating to give potassium chlorate(VII).

$$4KClO_3(s) \xrightarrow{480\,^\circ C} 3KClO_4(s) + KCl(s)$$
$$4(+5) \qquad\qquad 3(+7) \qquad -1$$

Iodate(VII) may be made by bubbling chlorine through a boiling solution of iodine in sodium hydroxide solution. This effectively oxidises I(V) to I(VII).

The oxo-salts of each particular halogen are interlinked by the series of disproportionation reactions shown in figure 27.4, for chlorine.

Figure 27.4 *Disproportionation reactions involving oxoanions of chlorine*

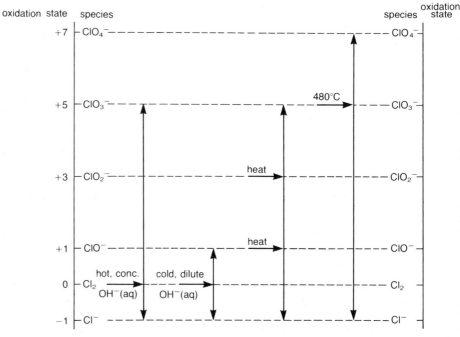

Activity 27.4

1   Draw 'dot and cross' diagrams clearly showing the electronic structure and shape of the following ions:
(a) ClO_2^- (b) ClO_3^- (c) ClO_4^-

2 Deduce balanced ionic equations for the following disproportionation reactions:
(a) chlorate(I) into chloride and chlorate(V);
(b) chlorate(III) into chloride and chlorate(V).
(See section 17.8 if you are unsure how to do this.)

Like their parent acids, the oxo-salts of the halogens are usually good oxidising agents. Potassium iodate(V) may be used to standardise sodium thiosulphate solution, since it liberates iodine from slightly acidic iodine solutions.

$$IO_3^-(aq) + 5I^-(aq) + 6H^+(aq) \rightarrow 3I_2(aq) + 3H_2O(l)$$
$$+5 \qquad 5(-1) \qquad\qquad\qquad 6(0)$$

Potassium iodate(VII) is sufficiently powerful to oxidise $Mn^{2+}(aq)$ to $MnO_4^-(aq)$ in the presence of nitric acid.

Several oxo-salts of chlorine are commercially important as a result of their oxidising nature. Chlorate(I), either as the sodium salt in solution or as the solid calcium salt, is an excellent domestic disinfectant and bleach. Sodium chlorate(III) is an industrial textile bleach and sodium chlorate(V) is a powerful weedkiller.

27.8 Manufacture of chlorine

Chlorine is manufactured by the electrolysis of concentrated sodium chloride solution or 'brine'. The overall process also gives sodium hydroxide and hydrogen.

$$2NaCl(aq) + H_2O(l) \xrightarrow{\text{electrolysis}} Cl_2(g) + H_2(g) + 2NaOH(aq)$$
$$2(-1) \quad 2(+1) \qquad\qquad\qquad 2(0) \quad 2(0)$$

In fact, sodium hydroxide is almost as valuable a chemical as chlorine, and the above reaction forms the basis of the **'chlor-alkali' industry**. We shall describe the construction and operation of the **diaphragm cell** illustrated in figure 27.5.

The titanium anodes and steel cathodes are separated by a porous asbestos 'diaphragm'. This is needed to separate the sodium hydroxide and chlorine which would react as follows on mixing:

$$2NaOH(aq) + Cl_2(g) \rightarrow NaCl(aq) + NaClO(aq) + H_2O(l)$$

Saturated brine is continually fed into the anode compartment. This contains Na^+ and Cl^- ions, together with H^+ and OH^- from the water. Approximately half of the chloride ions are converted into chlorine gas which is piped from the cell:

anode reaction: $2Cl^-(aq) \rightarrow Cl_2(g) + 2e^-$

The liquid seeps through the diaphragm and hydrogen gas is formed at the cathode:

cathode reaction: $2H^+(aq) + 2e^- \rightarrow H_2(g)$

Workers charging the rock-face with explosives and detonators in a salt mine in Austria, and strange natural formations at the Dead Sea salt works

An alternative method of electrolysing brine to produce chlorine is to use a battery of mercury cells. This one is at a chemical plant in Cheshire

The solution leaving the cathode compartment is rich in Na^+ and OH^- ions which do not take part in the electrolysis reactions but a considerable concentration of Cl^- ions remains. On partial evaporation, the less soluble sodium chloride crystallises out leaving a concentrated solution of sodium hydroxide. The recovered sodium chloride is, of course, recycled to the electrolysis cell.

Electrical energy is one of the major costs of a chlor-alkali plant, since a typical factory consumes the total output of a large modern power station. The ICI installation at Runcorn on Merseyside is close to the energy resource of the Lancashire coalfields and obtains its brine from the nearby Cheshire salt beds. Good road and rail links are also important for transport of the chlorine and sodium hydroxide to customers. Both of these are hazardous materials, usually transported as liquids in special tankers.

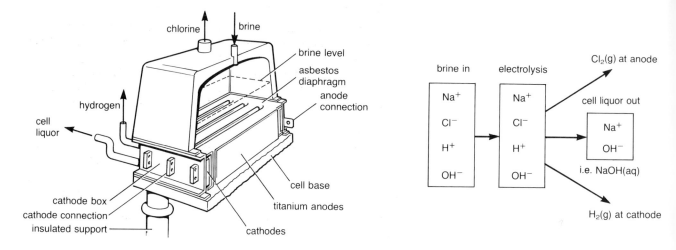

Figure 27.5 *Construction and operation of the 'diaphragm' cell*

27.9 Comments on the activities

Activity 27.1

1 *The valency shell of the fluorine atom can contain a maximum of eight electrons only. It has no accessible 'd' orbitals into which it may promote its 2p electrons. In this respect fluorine resembles the earlier 'p' block elements in this period, i.e. carbon, nitrogen and oxygen.*

Fluorine atoms show little tendency to donate lone pairs to electron deficient species and hence show a maximum covalency of one.

Figure 27.6 *Electronic structure and shapes of some interhalogen molecules*

(a) ICl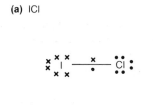

(b) ICl_3 T-shaped

(c) IF_5 square pyramid

(d) IF_7 pentagonal bipyramid

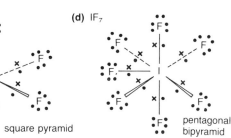

2 The bonding and shape of the iodine interhalogen molecules is shown in figure 27.6.

Activity 27.2

1 Remember that a halogen will only oxidise a halide ion below it in the group, so:

(a) $Cl_2(aq) + 2NaF(aq) \rightarrow$ no reaction

(b) $Br_2(aq) + 2KAt(aq) \rightarrow 2KBr(aq) + At_2(aq)$

(c) $At_2(aq) + 2NaI(aq) \rightarrow$ no reaction

(d) $I_2(aq) + 2KCl(aq) \rightarrow$ no reaction

(e) $F_2(g) + 2NaI(aq) \rightarrow 2NaF(aq) + I_2(aq)$

2 (a) $2Ce^{4+}(aq) + 2I^-(aq) \rightarrow 2Ce^{3+}(aq) + I_2(aq)$
     2(+4)   2(−1)   2(+3)   2(0)

(b) $2Cu^{2+}(aq) + 4I^-(aq) \rightarrow 2CuI(s) + I_2(aq)$
     2(+2)   4(−1)   2(+1)(−1)   2(0)

(c) $IO_4^-(aq) + 7I^-(aq) + 8H^+(aq) \rightarrow 4I_2(aq) + 4H_2O(l)$
     + 7   7(−1)   8(0)

Activity 27.3

1 Unlike the heavier halogens, fluorine can accommodate a maximum of only eight electrons in its valency shell. Accordingly it has a maximum covalency of one and is unable to form HFO_3.

2 The very electronegative oxygen atoms attached to the chlorine atom withdraw electron density from the O—H bond. This *weakens* the bond, favouring release of hydrogen ions and therefore *increasing* acid strength.

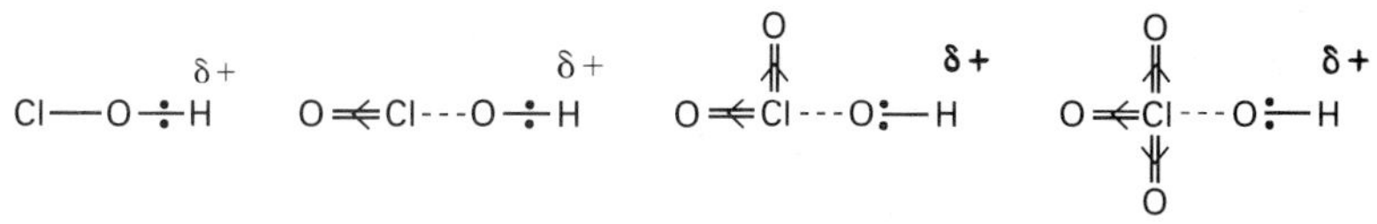

Activity 27.4

1 The electronic structures and shapes of the oxoanions of chlorine are shown in figure 27.7.

Figure 27.7 *Shapes of some oxoanions of chlorine*

v-shaped or angular   triangular pyramid   tetrahedral

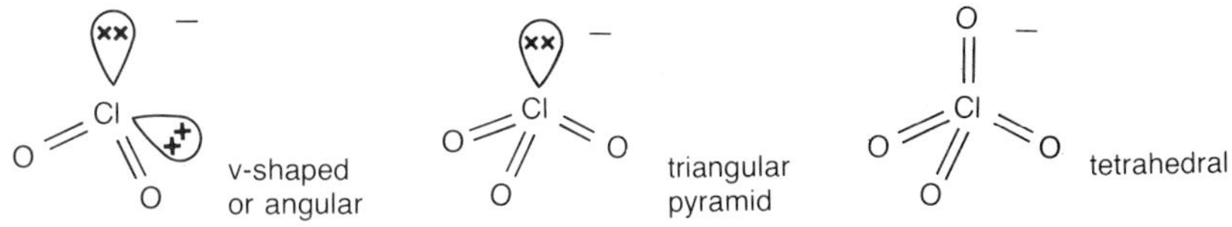

2 (a) $3ClO^-(aq) \rightarrow ClO_3^-(aq) + 2Cl^-(aq)$
       $3(+1)$ $+5$ $2(-1)$

   (b) $3ClO_2^-(aq) \rightarrow 2ClO_3^-(aq) + Cl^-(aq)$
       $3(+3)$ $2(+5)$ -1

27.10 Summary and revision plan

1 All the halogens exist as diatomic covalent molecules. Melting point and boiling point increase with relative molecular mass as van der Waals' forces of attraction between the molecules get stronger.

2 All halogen atoms can achieve a 'noble gas' electron configuration, either by, gaining one electron to form a halide ion, X^-, or by forming a single covalent bond. In such reactions they act as oxidising agents. The oxidising 'power' of the halogens decreases on passing down the group and they become less reactive.

3 As the first member of the group, fluorine has several unique properties for the following reasons:

(a) Fluorine is the most electronegative of all elements.
   ▶ Whereas all the other halogens show positive oxidation states, fluorine only shows an oxidation state of -1 in its compounds.
   ▶ Hydrogen fluoride has the highest boiling point of the hydrogen halides, owing to strong intermolecular hydrogen bonding.

(b) The fluorine atom can hold a maximum of 8 electrons only in its valency shell.
   ▶ Fluorine atoms generally form only one covalent bond, whereas the maximum covalency of the other halogens is higher (up to 7 for iodine).
   ▶ Fluorine is the only halogen not to form oxoacids.

4 On passing down the group the hydrides become thermally less stable and stronger acids in aqueous solution, owing to the decreasing strength of the H—X covalent bond.

5 Halide ions may be detected in aqueous solution using silver nitrate solution. Chloride ions may also be determined, gravimetrically or volumetrically, by precipitation of silver chloride.

6 Chlorine may be manufactured by the electrolysis of concentrated sodium chloride solution in the **diaphragm cell**. It is used in water treatment and in the manufacture of a range of chemicals including plastics, disinfectants and insecticides.

□ CHAPTER □
28
CHAPTER

Group 0: The Noble Gases

Everyone who has seen pink fluorescent advertising lights in shop windows is familiar with at least one use of the noble gas neon. Table 28.1 lists some other uses of these elements, many of which rely upon their generally unreactive nature.

Table 28.1 *Some uses of the noble gases*

helium	Very low density and non-inflammable, has replaced hydrogen as the gas used in airships and metereological balloons
	Less soluble in blood than nitrogen under pressure. An oxygen/helium mixture is breathed by deep-sea divers to avoid the 'bends', i.e. decompression sickness
	Provides an inert atmosphere for certain welding operations
neon	Characteristic atomic emission spectrum. Gives a pinkish glow in electric discharge tubes used for advertising signs and street lighting
argon	The most abundant and the cheapest of the noble gases
	Provides an inert atmosphere in 'argon-arc' welding
krypton	Used in electric gas dicharge tubes for lighting
xenon	Quite rare and comparatively expensive
	No large scale uses
radon	Because of its radioactivity, this has been used in the treatment of cancers

Neon lights and a helium-filled airship: two familiar uses of noble gases

Table 28.2	*Percentage by volume of the noble gases in air*

Element	% by volume in air
helium	0.00052
neon	0.00182
argon	0.934
krypton	0.00114
xenon	0.0000087
radon	negligible
Total (approx)	0.938

The first five members may be isolated by methods which involve the fractional distillation of liquid air (table 28.2). The earth's gravity is not strong enough to prevent the escape of the least dense gas, helium, but its atmospheric concentration remains roughly constant since it is formed by natural radioactive decay processes. Radon is not generally found in appreciable quantities in the atmosphere as all of its isotopes are radioactive with short half-lives.

Activity 28.1

Some samples of granite are mildly radioactive and produce radon and helium gases. Here is part of a decay series involving an isotope of radon:

$$^{226}Ra \longrightarrow \underset{\text{and X}}{^{222}Rn} \longrightarrow \underset{\text{and X}}{^{218}Po} \longrightarrow \underset{\text{and Y}}{^{218}At}$$

1   Use the Periodic Table to find the atomic numbers of these elements.
2   What are the particles X and Y?
3   How do you explain the formation of helium gas?
(If you have difficulty with this activity, revise the work in sections 2.5 to 2.8.)

Most of the early work on the noble gases was carried out on the most abundant member, argon. This, together with helium and neon, has so far proved to be totally unreactive and for this reason the elements of Group 0 were referred to as the 'inert' gases. For many years it was believed that their electron configuration was so stable that none of the gases would undergo any chemical reactions. However, in 1962 Bartlett found that platinum(VI) fluoride, would *oxidise* the oxygen molecule:

$$O_2(g) + PtF_6(g) \longrightarrow O_2{}^+[PtF_6]^-(s)$$
$$\text{dioxygenyl hexafluoroplatinate(V)}$$

Since the first ionisation energy of xenon, $1170\,kJ\,mol^{-1}$, is slightly *less* than the energy required to remove an electron from the oxygen molecule, $1183\,kJ\,mol^{-1}$, he reasoned that this should form a similar compound. In fact the following reaction occurred simply on mixing the gases, and **xenon hexafluoroplatinate(V)** was the first *true* compound of a Group 0 element to be prepared:

$$Xe(g) + PtF_6(g) \rightarrow Xe^+[PtF_6]^-(s)$$
$$\text{orange-yellow}$$

This observation sparked off considerable interest amongst chemists and since then several other xenon compounds containing fluorine and oxygen have been prepared. The chemistry of xenon will be considered in more detail in section 28.2.

Since at least one of the elements forms a limited range of chemical compounds, the term 'inert' gases does not strictly apply. The elements of Group 0 are now generally referred to as the **noble gases**, presumably because they are 'reluctant' to combine with most of the 'common' elements.

28.1 Atomic and physical properties

Table 28.3 shows that the trends in atomic radius and ionisation energies on passing down the group follow, almost perfectly, those predicted in chapter 19.

With the exception of helium which has a full first shell only, $1s^2$, all the atoms have an outer electron configuration of ns^2np^6. Note that only helium and neon may be correctly described as having 'full' outer energy levels, since from argon onwards, each atom has empty 'd' orbitals in its valency shell.

All the elements exist as separate simple atoms. Their melting and boiling points are very low, but, as expected, increase with relative molecular mass as the

Table 28.3 *Data sheet for the elements of Group 0*

Element	atomic number	electron configuration	atomic radius* /nm	ionisation energies /kJ mol^{-1}								density /g cm^{-3} †	b.p. /°C	m.p. /°C
				1st	2nd	3rd	4th	5th	6th	7th	8th			
helium He	2	$1s^2$	0.12	2370	5250	–	–	–	–	–	–	0.147	−269	−270
neon Ne	10	$[He]2s^22p^6$	0.16	2080	3950	6150	9290	12100	15200	20000	23000	0.20	−246	−249
argon Ar	18	$[Ne]3s^23p^6$	0.192	1520	2660	3950	5770	7240	8790	12000	13800	1.40	−186	−189
krypton Kr	36	$[Ar]3d^{10}4s^24p^6$	0.197	1350	2370	3560	5020	6370	7570	10700	12200	2.16	−152	−157
xenon Xe	54	$[Kr]4d^{10}5s^25p^6$	0.217	1170	2050	3100	4300	5800	8000	9800	12200	3.52	−108	−112
radon Rn	86	$[Xe]4f^{14}5d^{10}6s^26p^6$?	?	1040	1930	2890	4250	5310	?	?	?	4.4	−62	−71

*values are van der Waals' radii
†measured for the liquid at its boiling point

How and why do the boiling points of these elements vary on passing down the group?

van der Waals' forces of attraction become stronger. The behaviour of helium on cooling is rather unusual. It forms a normal liquid at about 4 K but below 2 K a dramatic change occurs. Its viscosity falls to a point where it will readily 'flow' uphill and it becomes an excellent conductor of heat. Helium can only be solidified under high pressure.

The water solubility of the gases increases with relative molecular mass. Their atoms become physically 'trapped' in 'cages' formed by hydrogen bonding between the water molecules. Similar **clathrates** are formed by argon, krypton and xenon with benzene-1, 4-diol. These are quite stable solids but the noble gas is released on melting or dissolving the crystals.

28.2 Chemical compounds of xenon

Fluorine is the only element which has so far been found to combine directly with xenon. Xenon hexafluoride reacts with water to give a range of oxofluorides, oxides and oxoacids. These reactions are summarised in figure 28.1.

Figure 28.1 *Fluorine and oxygen compounds of xenon - what is meant by 'disproportionation'?*

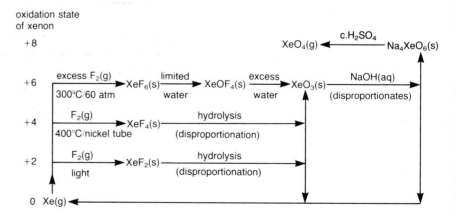

The xenon fluorides are energetically more stable than the elements but the oxides are unstable endothermic compounds. Xenon(VI) oxide decomposes explosively and, since it is formed from the fluorides by traces of moisture, presents a considerable hazard in xenon chemistry.

The simple binary compounds are *covalent* in nature. In its fluorides, the xenon atom must promote one or more of its outer 'p' electrons into empty 'd' orbitals:

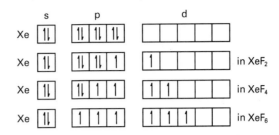

Similar promotion could lead to double bonding with oxygen, although here dative bonding is also possible.

The molecular *shapes* of some covalent xenon compounds are illustrated in figure 28.2. They are as predicted by the 'electron repulsion' theory described in chapter 7.

Fluorides of krypton have also been reported but these are much less stable than the xenon compounds.

Figure 28.2 *Molecular shapes of some xenon compounds*

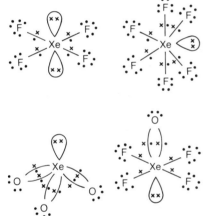

Activity 28.2

1 Draw diagrams illustrating the bonding and shaping of the following xenon species: (a) XeF_2 (b) XeO_4 (c) XeO_6^{4-}
2 No compounds of helium or neon have yet been prepared and many chemists have claimed that this would be 'impossible'. How far do you think that this view is justified in terms of:
   (a) the values of their first ionisation energies;
   (b) their outer electronic structures?

28.4 Comments on the activities

Activity 28.1

1 $$\underset{88}{\overset{226}{Ra}} \underset{\text{and X}}{\longrightarrow} \underset{86}{\overset{222}{Rn}} \underset{\text{and X}}{\longrightarrow} \underset{84}{\overset{218}{Po}} \underset{\text{and Y}}{\longrightarrow} \underset{85}{\overset{218}{At}}$$

2 In order for the mass numbers and atomic numbers to balance in each step, X must be $_2^4\alpha$ particles and Y must be a $_{-1}^0\beta$ particle.

3 $_2^4\alpha$ particles are helium ions, i.e. He^{2+}. A helium atom is formed when an α particle captures two $_{-1}^0\beta$ particles (electrons).

$$\alpha \text{ (i.e. } He^{2+}) + 2\beta \text{ (i.e. } 2e^-) \rightarrow He$$

Activity 28.2

1   Compare your answers with figure 28.3.

Figure 28.3 *Molecular/ionic shapes for activity 28.2*

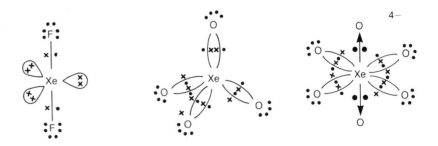

2   (a) From table 28.3 we can see that the first ionisation energies of helium and neon are the *highest* in the group. These atoms are, therefore, unlikely to form positive ions of the type found in xenon hexafluoroplatinate(V), described earlier.

    (b) To form covalent compounds, noble gas atoms must 'promote' one or more of their 'paired' valency electrons. Unlike the heavier atoms, helium and neon have *no* empty 'd' orbitals in their valency shell. Promotion of electrons into a new principal energy level is the only possibility but this would require much more energy than that released on forming covalent bonds. So, helium and neon are unlikely to form covalent compounds.

28.4 Summary and revision plan

1   Group 0 contains the least reactive elements in the Periodic Table. They all exist as **simple monatomic gases** at room temperature.

2   The unreactive nature of the elements results from the stable outer electron configurations of their atoms, i.e. full outer 's' and (except for helium) 'p' sub-levels.

3   Xenon reacts directly with fluorine to form true chemical compounds. It does this by promoting electrons into its empty outer 'd' orbitals. Although it might be possible for krypton or argon to react in a similar way, it seems unlikely that true chemical compounds of helium or neon will ever be prepared, since their atoms have no empty orbitals available in the valency shell.

The 'd' Block Elements: An Introduction

Contents

Metals from the 'd' block of the Periodic Table have played an important part in our history. **Copper** and **iron** were amongst the first metals to be used for weapons and tools, whilst coins were minted from **gold** and **silver**. Although no longer generally used in coinage, reserves of these precious metals are still an important measure of a nation's wealth.

In more recent times, some of the metals and their compounds have been found to act as catalysts in the manufacture of important chemicals. Many of the metals also have more specialised applications which depend upon their individual properties. Some of these uses, together with more general information, are summarised in table 29.1.

Some of the ways in which 'd' block metals have been used from Roman times to the present day. Can you identify the metal in each case?

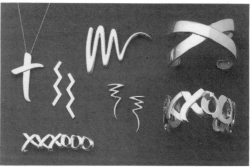

Table 29.1 *Occurrence, extraction and uses of some 'd' block metals*

Metal	abundance in earth's crust/%	principal ores	method of extraction	use of metal, other than in steels or as catalysts	useful compounds
titanium	0.6	ilmenite $FeTiO_3$ rutile TiO_2	reduction of $TiCl_4$ with Mg or Na	high strength to weight ratio, used in aircraft construction	TiO_2 as a white pigment in paint
chromium	0.02	chromite $FeCr_2O_4$	reduction of oxide by Al	electroplating onto steel	chromium(VI) compounds are good oxidising agents
manganese	0.09	pyrolusite MnO_2	reduction of oxide by Al	forms many useful alloys	manganate(VII) is a powerful oxidant and a 'germicide'
iron	4.5	haematite Fe_2O_3 magnetite Fe_3O_4	reduction of oxide by CO	metal castings electromagnets	pigments: Fe_2O_3 red, $KFe[Fe(CN)_6]$ blue; weedkiller, $FeSO_4$
cobalt	0.004	cobaltite CoAsS	reduction of oxide by C or Al	alloys	$CoCl_2$ as a test for water
nickel	0.01	pentlandite NiS (with FeS)	reduction of oxide with CO/H_2	alloys e.g. in coinage electroplating	
copper	0.01	malachite $Cu_2(OH)_2CO_3$ some free metal	heat mixture of Cu_2O/Cu_2S	electrical wiring, alloys, e.g. brass, bronze and coinage metal; boilers	$CuSO_4, 5H_2O$ as a fungicide
zinc	0.02	zinc blende ZnS	reduction of oxide with C	'galvanising' iron, alloys, e.g. brass	ZnO in cosmetics and medicinal creams
silver	0.00002	some free metal		jewellery, etc.	silver halides in photographic films

In the next three chapters we shall examine the chemistry of the 'd' block in general, and that of the first row elements and silver in particular. Many distinctive properties, e.g. catalytic activity and the formation of coloured compounds, are due to the presence of a partially full 'd' sub-level in the atom or ion of the element concerned.

The term **transition** element is generally reserved for *an element which has an atom, or forms an ion, which contains an incomplete inner electronic sub-level*. We shall consider the implications of this definition later but it is interesting to note that **zinc**, although a member of the 'd' block, is *not* regarded as a transition element.

29.1 Atomic and physical properties

All the 'd' block elements are typical metals and are characterised by their *electron configuration*, shown in figure 29.1. The last electron fills into an inner principal energy level. In the first row, scandium to zinc, the outer 4s sub-level is full and electrons enter the 3d sub-level; in the second and third rows, they fill the 4d and 5d orbitals respectively. The appearance of the 'f' block series after lanthanum, shown in figure 29.1, arises because the 4f orbitals are filled after a single electron has entered the 5d sub-level. A similar situation occurs with the 'actinides' in the third row.

Table 29.2 lists some atomic and physical properties of the first row 'd' block elements and silver. Data on calcium and gallium, the elements preceding and following the 1st row of the 'd' block, are included for comparison.

Table 29.2 *Data sheet for the elements of the first row of the 'd' block and silver*

Element	atomic number	atomic radius /nm	ionisation energies /kJ mol⁻¹						maximum oxidation state	electro-negativity	$E^\ominus$ /volts	density /g cm⁻³	m.p. /°C
			1st	2nd	3rd	4th	5th	6th					
GROUP II calcium Ca	20	0.197	590	1150	4940	6480	8120	10700	+2	1.0	−2.87	1.54	850
scandium Sc	21	0.160	632	1240	2390	7110	8870	10700	+3	1.3		2.99	1540
titanium Ti	22	0.146	661	1310	2720	4170	9620	11600	+4	1.5	−1.63	4.54	1675
vanadium V	23	0.131	648	1370	2870	4600	6280	12400	+5	1.6	−1.2	5.96	1900
chromium Cr	24	0.125	653	1590	2990	4770	7070	8700	+6	1.6	−0.91	7.19	1890
manganese Mn	25	0.129	716	1510	3250	5190	7360	9750	+7	1.5	−1.18	7.20	1240
iron Fe	26	0.126	762	1560	2960	5400	7620	10100	+3 commonly	1.8	−0.44	7.86	1535
cobalt Co	27	0.125	757	1640	3230	5100	7910	10500	+3	1.8	−0.28	8.90	1492
nickel Ni	28	0.124	736	1750	3390	5400	7620	10900	+2	1.8	−0.25	8.90	1453
copper Cu	29	0.128	745	1960	3550	5690	7990	10500	+2	1.9	+0.34	8.92	1083
zinc Zn	30	0.133	908	1730	3828	5980	8280	11000	+2	1.6	−0.76	7.14	420
GROUP III gallium Ga	31	0.141	577	1980	2960	6190	8700	11400	+3	1.6		5.91	30
silver Ag	47	0.144	732	2070	3360	5000	6700	8400	+1	1.9	+0.80	10.5	961

Underlined figures show the LARGEST single jump between successive ionisation energies. What causes these?

Which of the above metals would you not expect to give hydrogen with dilute sulphuric acid and why? (Section 17.8)

Figure 29.1 *The electron configuration of the 'd' block elements - why aren't the electron configurations of Cr and Cu 3d⁴4s² and 3d⁹4s² respectively?*

1st row [Ar]
Sc 3d¹,4s² Ti 3d²,4s² V 3d³,4s² Cr 3d⁵,4s¹ Mn 3d⁵,4s² Fe 3d⁶,4s² Co 3d⁷,4s² Ni 3d⁸,4s¹ Cu 3d¹⁰,4s² Zn 3d¹⁰,4s²

2nd row [Kr]
Y 4d²,5s² Zr 4d¹,5s² Nb 4d⁴,5s¹ Mo 4d⁵,5s¹ Tc 4d⁶,5s¹ Ru 4d⁷,5s¹ RH 4d⁸,5s¹ Pd 4d¹⁰,5s⁰ Ag 4d¹⁰,5s¹ Cd 4d¹⁰,5s²

3rd row [Xe]
La* 5d¹,6s² Hf 5d²,6s¹ Ta 5d³,6s² V 5d⁴,6s² Re 5d⁵,6s² Os 5d⁶,6s² Ir 5d⁹,6s⁰ Pt 5d⁹,6s¹ Au 5d¹⁰,6s¹ Hg 5d¹⁰6s²

4th row [Rn]
Ac** 6d¹,7s²

'f' block elements * the lanthanides Ce – Lu (electrons enter 4f sub-level)
** the actinides Th – Lr (electrons enter 5f sub-level)

Atomic radius

The general decrease in size on passing across the block, known as the **'d' block contraction**, is caused by the increase in nuclear charge. Towards the end of the row the increased 'screening' effect of the added 3d electrons outweighs the greater nuclear charge, and atomic radius increases slightly (figure 29.2).

Figure 29.2 *The 'd' block contraction*

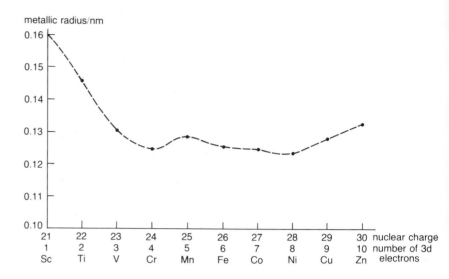

Density

All the 'd' block elements are quite *dense*. In fact the densest element of all is osmium in the third row ($22.5\,\text{g cm}^{-3}$ compared to $11.3\,\text{g cm}^{-3}$ for lead). The small atomic size obviously partly accounts for this, but also the atoms are packed very tightly together in the metallic lattice. This is because, in addition to the outer 's' electrons, the inner 'd' electrons may also contribute to the pool of delocalised electrons used in metallic bonding (section 5.8).

Melting point

As we might expect from the use of 'd' electrons in metallic bonding, the attractive forces between the atoms in the lattice are usually *very strong*. Melting points are consequently *generally high* e.g. tungsten ($3410\,°\text{C}$) has the highest melting point of all the metals. However there are exceptions, notably mercury, which is the only metallic element to exist as a *liquid* at room temperature.

Electronegativity

The electronegativity of the 'd' block elements is rather higher than that of the metals of Groups I and II. Because of their smaller atomic size, bonding electrons are more strongly attracted by the nucleus. There is *litte variation in electronegativity on passing across the row*, since the rise in nuclear charge is largely 'screened' by the addition of electrons to the inner 'd' sub-level.

Ionisation energies

As we might predict, since atomic radius falls slightly whilst the nuclear charge rises, *first ionisation energy generally increases on passing across the first row*. The figures for the 'd' block elements are appreciably *higher* than those for the corresponding 's' block metals.

It is important to remember that, although the last electron to be added to a 'd' block atom enters the inner 'd' sub-level, the outer 4s electrons are the first to be removed. This happens because the energy of the 4s sub-level rises on adding electrons to the 3d orbitals. In simple terms, electrons in the 3d sub-level penetrate closer to the nucleus, effectively, 'screening' the 4s electrons and making them relatively easier to remove (figure 29.3).

Figure 29.3

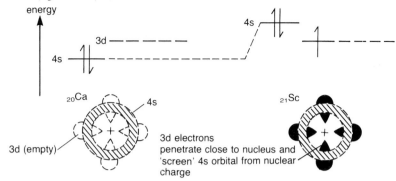

In the case of 's' and 'p' block elements there is a dramatic 'jump' in ionisation energy when an inner principal level is broken. Since the energies of the 4s and 3d sub-levels in a 'd' block atom are quite similar, there is a *steady rise in successive ionisation energies until the 'noble gas core' is broken,* i.e. an inner 'p' sub-level is disturbed, (figure 29.4). The consequences of this for bonding within the compounds of 'd' block elements are discussed in section 29.2.

Figure 29.4   *Successive ionisation energies for titanium and calcium*

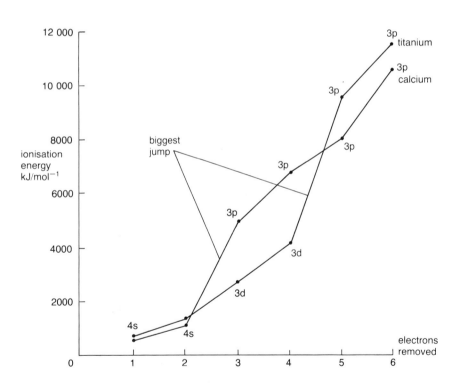

Standard electrode potential

A comparison of table 29.2 with table 22.3 shows that *the standard electrode potentials of the 'd' block elements are much less negative than those of the 's' block metals,* i.e. they are more reluctant to form positive ions in aqueous solution. Positive $E^\ominus$ values for silver and copper indicate that these metals are so unreactive that they will *not liberate hydrogen from dilute acid.*

Again we may explain the lower reactivity of the 'd' block elements compared to the 's' block metals largely in terms of greater nuclear attraction for the most loosely bound electrons.

29.2 Oxidation states and chemical bonding

'd' block atoms *always* lose their outer 4s electrons on forming compounds. Since the 3d electrons are also relatively loosely held, some or all of these may also be involved in bond formation. As a result, many of the elements show a *variety* of oxidation states, some of the commonest being shown in table 29.3. This table also indicates that most of the compounds which contain a *partially full* 3d sub-level are *coloured*.

Table 29.3 *Common oxidation states of the first row 'd' block elements and silver, showing the characteristic colours in aqueous solution, and stability towards redox reactions*

| Metal | common oxidation states | | | | | | |
	+1	+2	+3	+4	+5	+6	+7
scandium	–	–	colourless*	–	–	–	–
titanium	–	unstable in water	violet	colourless*	–	–	–
vanadium	–	violet	green	blue*	pale yellow	–	–
chromium	–	blue	green*	–	–	yellow or orange	–
manganese	–	very pale pink*	–	generally insoluble	–	dark green	intens purpl
iron	–	pale green	yellow brown*	–	–	–	–
cobalt	–	pink*	orange yellow	–	–	–	–
nickel	–	green*	–	–	–	–	–
copper	colourless	blue*	–	–	–	–	–
zinc	–	colourless*	–	–	–	–	–
silver	colourless*	–	–	–	–	–	–

*Indicates the most stable state of the element with respect to redox reactions. However this may vary with conditions as discussed in chapter 31
In terms of their electron configuration, what do all the 'colourless' oxidation states above have in common?

Some anhydrous compounds of the 'd' block elements, particularly in low oxidation states with very electronegative elements such as fluorine and oxygen, possess simple ionic lattice structures. However, in higher oxidation states and especially in aqueous solution, the chemistry of these elements generally involves the formation of **coordination compounds** or **complexes**. Because of their relatively small size, 'd' block ions possess a considerable positive charge density and will attract electron pair donors, such as water molecules, quite strongly. For example, cobalt(II) in aqueous solution exists in association with six water molecules:

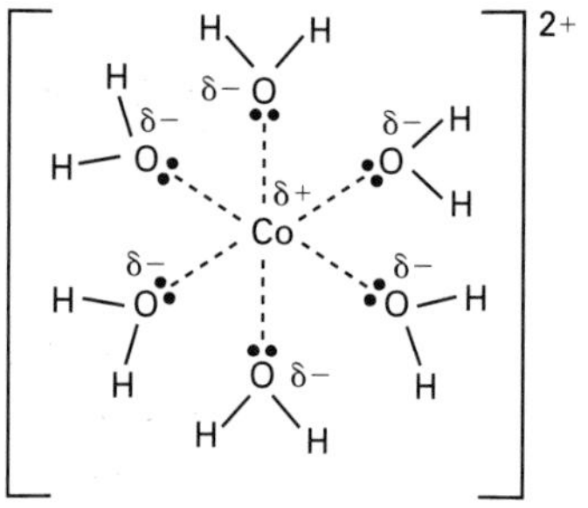

The species $[Co(H_2O)_6]^{2+}$ is known as a **complex ion**, and the electron pair donors, i.e. water in this case, are called **ligands**. The number of ligands associated with the central metal ion is known as the **coordination number**. If the charge on the central metal ion is low, then the 'bonding' with the ligands may be regarded largely as simple electrostatic attraction. For high oxidation states, though, the electron pair on each ligand will be attracted so strongly towards the metal species that it effectively produces a **dative** (or **coordinate**) **covalent bond**, e.g. in the manganate(VII) ion, MnO_4^-. In most cases it is convenient to treat all bonding within complexes as *dative covalent*:

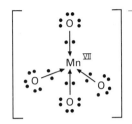

The shape, colour, magnetic properties and characteristic reactions of complex ions will be covered in some detail in chapter 30.

Trace amounts of some 'd' block elements are essential to life, since many enzymes and other biologically active substances contain complexed transition metal ions. For example, figure 29.5 shows **haemoglobin**, the oxygen carrier in red blood cells, which contains an **iron(II) complex** attached to a large protein molecule.

Figure 29.5 *Schematic structure of haemoglobin and its function as an 'oxygen carrier' in the blood*

oxygen molecule weakly attached to iron – easily removed when required by the body

The 'haem' group. Fe^{2+} complexed by nitrogen atoms in a 'porphyrin' ring ligand

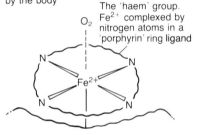

large protein molecule which contains four 'haem' groups

Activity 29.1

Answer the following questions, using table 29.3 and the electron configurations in figure 29.1.

1   Which is the only element in the first row of the 'd' block:
   (a) not to show an oxidation state of $+2$;
   (b) to show an oxidation state of $+1$?
2   The electron configuration of Ti(II) may be written [Ar] $3d^24s^0$. Write the electron configurations of all the common oxidation states shown in table 29.3 in a similar way.
   How does the ability of an atom to use its 3d electrons in bonding vary with its position in the first row of the 'd' block?

29.3 Redox behaviour and catalytic properties

The oxidation states of the first row 'd' block elements generally accepted as being most stable are shown in table 29.3. If the element can exist in different oxidation states its compounds will undergo *oxidation* and/or *reduction*.

The most stable state of chromium is $+3$. Cr(II) will donate an electron to achieve this stable state, thereby acting as a **reducing agent**, and being *itself oxidised*:

$$Cr^{2+}(aq) \rightarrow Cr^{3+}(aq) + e^-$$
$$+2 \qquad\qquad +3$$

On the other hand, Cr(VI) will act as an **oxidising agent** by *accepting* electrons, e.g. dichromate(VI) in acid solution:

$$\tfrac{1}{2}Cr_2O_7^{2-}(aq) + 7H^+(aq) + 3e^- \rightarrow Cr^{3+}(aq) + \tfrac{7}{2}H_2O(l)$$
$$+6 \qquad\qquad\qquad\qquad\qquad +3$$

The **standard electrode potentials**, $E^\ominus$ in table 17.1, give a guide as to the reducing or oxidising *power* of a particular 'd' block species. The *more negative* the electrode potential, the *more powerfully reducing* is the system and vice versa.

Activity 29.2

1   Using the standard electrode potentials in table 17.1, list the systems,

$$M^{3+}(aq) + e^- \rightarrow M^{2+}(aq)$$

in order from the strongest reducing agent to the strongest oxidising agent, where M may be any of the metals from titanium to cobalt.

2   How, in general, does the stability towards oxidation of the +2 oxidation state vary on passing across the first row of the 'd' block?

The ability of many 'd' block ions to accept and donate electrons whilst changing their oxidation state often makes them very useful **catalysts** for **redox** reactions. Theories of catalysis were discussed in section 12.5, but here we shall look at one particular example from the 'd' block.

Peroxodisulphate ion, $S_2O_8^{2-}$, will oxidise iodide ions, I^-, to iodine in aqueous solution, being itself reduced to sulphate:

$$\tfrac{1}{2}S_2O_8^{2-}(aq) + I^-(aq) \rightarrow \quad SO_4^{2-}(aq) + \tfrac{1}{2}I_2(aq)$$

The standard electrode potentials for the two half-equations involved are

$$\tfrac{1}{2}S_2O_8^{2-}(aq) + e^- \rightarrow SO_4^{2-}(aq) \qquad E^\ominus = +2.01\,V$$
$$\tfrac{1}{2}I_2(aq) \qquad\quad + e^- \rightarrow I^-(aq) \qquad E^\ominus = +0.54V$$

This reaction is catalysed by $Fe^{3+}(aq)$ or $Fe^{2+}(aq)$ and the standard electrode potential of this system is

$$Fe^{3+}(aq) + e^- \rightarrow Fe^{2+}(aq) \qquad E^\ominus = +0.77V$$

It seems likely that the iron ions catalyse the reaction by acting as *intermediates* for the exchange of electrons between the peroxodisulphate and iodide ions. This is possible because, as the above electrode potentials show, peroxodisulphate will oxidise $Fe^{2+}(aq)$:

$$\tfrac{1}{2}S_2O_8^{2-} + Fe^{2+}(aq) \rightarrow SO_4^{2-}(aq) + Fe^{3+}(aq)$$

and iodide will reduce $Fe^{3+}(aq)$:

$$Fe^{3+}(aq) + I^-(aq) \quad \rightarrow Fe^{2+}(aq) \quad + \tfrac{1}{2}I_2(aq)$$

This provides an alternative reaction route with a *lower activation energy* than that involved in the direct transfer of electrons from iodide to peroxodisulphate. *Any redox system with a standard potential which is between that of the half-equations in the desired reaction may possibly act as a catalyst.*

Activity 29.3

Which of the following redox systems might catalyse the oxidation of iodide ions by peroxodisulphate in aqueous solution?

1   $Cr_2O_7^{2-}(aq) + 14H^+(aq) + 6e^- \rightarrow 2Cr^{3+}(aq) + 7H_2O(l)$ $E^\ominus +1.33\,V$
2   $MnO_4^-(aq) + 8H^+(aq) + 5e^- \rightarrow Mn^{2+}(aq) + 4H_2O(l)$ $E^\ominus +1.52\,V$
3   $Sn^{4+}(aq) \qquad\qquad\qquad\quad + 2e^- \rightarrow Sn^{2+}(aq)$ $E^\ominus +0.15\,V$

Examples of industrially important redox reactions which are catalysed by transition metals or their compounds include the following:

The Contact process (section 26.7)

In the manufacture of sulphuric acid, sulphur dioxide is oxidised by air at 450 °C in the presence of a **vanadium(V) oxide, V_2O_5,** catalyst:

$$2SO_2(g) + O_2(g) \rightleftharpoons 2SO_3(g)$$

The Haber process (section 25.7)

Nitrogen and hydrogen combine under pressure at about 450 °C in the presence of a finely divided **iron** catalyst:

$$N_2(g) + 3H_2(g) \rightleftharpoons 2NH_3(g)$$

Oxidation of ammonia (section 25.7)

Ammonia may be oxidised to nitrogen monoxide, prior to conversion into nitric acid. The reaction is carried out at high temperature using a catalyst which contains **platinum**:

$$4NH_3(g) + 5O_2(g) \rightarrow 4NO(g) + 6H_2O(g)$$

Hydrogenation of alkenes (section 35.6.4)

Unsaturated vegetable oils may be 'hardened' by treatment with hydrogen at 200 °C using a **nickel** catalyst. Hydrogen is added on across some or all of the double bonds, converting the liquid oil into margarine, a solid fat.

29.4 Occurrence and extraction

Although some of the less reactive metals, e.g. copper, silver and gold, are found in the free state, most of the 'd' block elements exist as compounds in nature. Iron is by far the most abundant of these elements and, at about 4.5% of the earth's crust, is second only to aluminium amongst the metals. World production of iron exceeds two hundred million tonnes per annum, most of which is used in steel manufacture.

The general principles involved in the extraction of metals from their purified ores have been covered in section 17.10. Generally, the 'd' block metals are only moderately reactive and may be obtained by reducing their oxides with *carbon* or *carbon monoxide*. However, if carbon impurities have an adverse effect upon the strength of the metal, e.g. titanium, than a more reactive metal such as sodium, magnesium or aluminium may be used to reduce the chloride.

Table 29.4 *The composition, properties and uses of some common steels*

Type of steel	composition excluding iron	properties and uses
mild	0.1 – 0.2% C	soft but very malleable, readily shaped into sheet and rods
high carbon	0.7 – 1.5% C	very hard, used for tools such as hammers and punches
stainless	18% Cr, 8% Ni, some C	very corrosion resistant, used in cutlery
manganese	13% Mn, some C	very tough, used for drilling through rock
tungsten	5% W, some C	very hard, used in high speed cutting tools
permalloy	78% Ni, some C	strongly magnetised in an electric field but loses magnetism when current is switched off, used in electromagnets

Since the atomic radii of the first row metals are similar, they readily form *alloys* with each other. The most important of these are the various *steels* in which carbon and various 'd' block metals are incorporated into the crystal structure of iron. The composition, properties and uses of some common steels are listed in table 29.4.

29.5 Comments on the activities

Activity 29.1

1 (a) Scandium does *not* show an oxidation state of $+2$. Whenever it forms compounds it loses its single 3d electron as well as the outer 4s electrons to form an ion with a 'noble gas' configuration. As such it behaves as a typical *Group III metal* and its chemistry closely resembles that of *aluminium*.

  (b) Copper is unique in the first row in forming reasonably stable compounds in an oxidation state of $+1$. One reason for this is that the Cu^+ ion, formed on losing the single 4s electron, has *extra stability* because it retains a *completely full 3d sub-level*.

2 Sc(III) [Ar] $3d^0\ 4s^0$

Ti(III) [Ar] $3d^1\ 4s^0$ Ti(IV) [Ar] $3d^0\ 4s^0$

V(II) [Ar] $3d^3\ 4s^0$ V(III) [Ar] $3d^2\ 4s^0$ V(IV) [Ar] $3d^1\ 4s^0$ V(V) [Ar] $3d^0\ 4s^0$

Cr(II) [Ar] $3d^4\ 4s^0$ Cr(III) [Ar] $3d^3\ 4s^0$ Cr(VI) [Ar] $3d^0\ 4s^0$

Mn(II) [Ar] $3d^5\ 4s^0$ Mn(IV) [Ar] $3d^3\ 4s^0$ Mn(VI) [Ar] $3d^1\ 4s^0$

Mn(VII) [Ar] $3d^0\ 4s^0$

Fe(II) [Ar] $3d^6\ 4s^0$ Fe(III) [Ar] $3d^5\ 4s^0$

Co(II) [Ar] $3d^7\ 4s^0$ Co(III) [Ar] $3d^6\ 4s^0$

Ni(II) [Ar] $3d^8\ 4s^0$

Cu(I) [Ar] $3d^{10}\ 4s^0$ Cu(II) [Ar] $3d^9\ 4s^0$

Zn(II) [Ar] $3d^{10}\ 4s^0$
(Remember, the atom will *always* lose its 4s electrons.)

Up to and including manganese (i.e. a half full 3d sub-level), the atoms may use *all* their 3d electrons in bonding, i.e. the maximum oxidation state increases steadily from $+3$ at scandium to $+7$ at manganese. After this, however, the tendency to use the 3d electrons in bonding *decreases*. Both iron and cobalt generally lose only one 3d electron to form the $+3$ oxidation state. Nickel and zinc are reluctant to lose any of their 3d electrons and copper may use one in forming Cu^{2+}.

Activity 29.2

1 The systems with the most negative $E^\ominus$ values will be the best reducing agents, so

M	$E^{\ominus}$ M^{3+}, M^{2+} (aq)/V	
Cr	-0.41	
Ti	-0.37	reducing power of M^{2+} decreases
V	-0.26	
Fe	$+0.77$	oxidising power of M^{3+} increases
Mn	$+1.51$	
Co	$+1.81$	

2   We can see from the above figures that generally it becomes *more difficult* to oxidise M^{2+}(aq) as we pass across the first row of the 'd' block. There are no M^{3+}/M^{2+} $E^{\ominus}$ values for the last three elements, i.e. nickel, copper and zinc, since their M^{2+} ions are extremely resistant to oxidation.

Activity 29.3

System 3 would not be expected to act as a catalyst for the peroxodisulphate/iodide reaction. Although Sn^{2+} will reduce peroxodisulphate ions, Sn^{4+} cannot oxidise iodide.

Both of the other systems might be expected to catalyse the reaction. In fact, although manganese compounds *do* act as catalysts, chromium species *do not*. It is important to realise that a study of $E^{\ominus}$ values will only indicate if an alternative to the direct reaction is *possible*. The reaction will only be speeded up if this alternative pathway has a *lower activation energy*.

29.6   Summary and revision plan

1   In the 'd' block, the last electron to be added to an atom enters an inner 'd' sub-level.
      The term **transition metal** is usually reserved for those elements which have a common oxidation state containing a partly filled inner 'd' sub-level.
2   All the 'd' block elements are metals and generally have small atomic radii, high densities and high melting points.
3   Apart from scandium, all the elements may react by losing their outer 4s electrons only. Most also exhibit higher oxidation states by using some, or all, of their inner 3d electrons in bonding.
4   In their compounds, especially in solution, most of the 'd' block elements are found as **complexes**, i.e. a metal cation associated with electron pairs donors known as **ligands**. The number of ligands attached to a metal ion is known as the **coordination number**.
5   The elements are only moderately reactive and are generally extracted from their oxides by reduction with carbon, carbon monoxide or a more reactive metal.
6   The elements and their compounds are frequently excellent catalysts, especially for redox reactions.

'd' Block Complexes

30.1 Types of ligand

Complex formation involves the 'donation' of a pair of electrons from the ligand to a cation. The metal ion is, therefore, acting as a Lewis acid, or *electrophile*, whilst the ligand is a Lewis base, or *nucleophile* (*section 33.3*).

$$M^{x+} \longleftarrow \text{(:)} \quad \text{ligand}$$

Clearly, *a species can only act as a ligand if it has a pair of electrons, usually a non-bonded 'lone' pair, capable of being donated.* It may be a negative ion, e.g. chloride or oxide, or a neutral molecule such as water or ammonia:

It should be noted that the tendency of a particular species to complex a metal cation will depend to large extent on its basic 'strength', i.e. the ease with which it can donate its electron pair. Thus although 'noble gas' atoms possess four lone pairs of electrons in the outer energy level, these are strongly attracted by the nucleus and cannot be donated to a metal ion.

All the ligands that we have considered so far are **monodentate** (literally, 'one-toothed'), *i.e. they can only donate one pair of electrons to a particular metal ion.* Some ligands which contain more than one atom capable of electron pair donation are shown in figure 30.1a. These may form complexes of the type illustrated in figure 30.1b, called **chelates**, in which the metal and ligand form *ring* structures.

Figure 30.1 **(a)** *Examples of ligands which contain more than one electron pair donor atoms;*

BIDENTATE ligands
(2 electron pair donors)

POLYDENTATE ligands
(several electron pair donors)

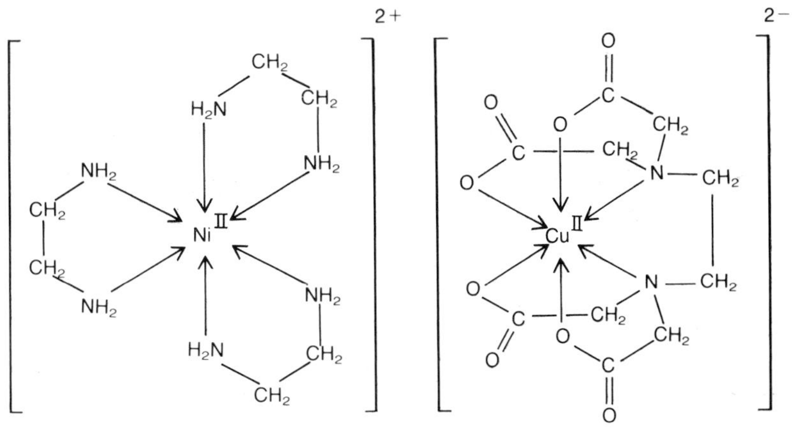

Figure 30.1 *(b) Examples of 'chelate' (ring-containing) complexes of bi- and poly-dentate ligands*

Activity 30.1

1 By considering their electronic structure, suggest which of the following molecules and ions might act as ligands. Which, if any, of these might act as bidentate ligands?

(a) CH_4 (b) CN^- (c) CO (d) NH_4^+
(e) BCl_3 (f) SO_4^{2-} (g) OH^- (h) Br^-
(i) $CH_3-CH_2-O-CH_2-CH_3$ (j) $CH_3-\underset{\substack{\| \\ O}}{C}-CH_2-\underset{\substack{\| \\ O}}{C}-CH_3$

2 Ammonia, NH_3, is a better ligand than nitrogen trichloride, NCl_3, but not so good as trimethylamine, $N(CH_3)_3$. Account for this in terms of the effect of the rest of the molecule upon the ease of donation of the lone pair of electrons on the nitrogen atoms of each of the species.

30.2 Naming of complexes

Before we can work out the systematic name of a complex, we must first decide:

▶ the overall charge, if any, on the complex, and
▶ the oxidation state of the central metal species.

By convention, the formula of a complex is enclosed in square brackets. Let us consider some examples.

1. *[Fe(H₂O)₆]Cl₂*

Applying the oxidation state calculation methods developed in section 17.1, this is made up of,

▶ the complex cation $[Fe(H_2O)_6]^{2+}$
▶ the simple anions $2Cl^-$

Since, overall, the water molecules are electrically neutral, the oxidation state of the iron must equal the charge on the complex, i.e. $+2$. Thus,

$$[Fe(H_2O)_6]^{2+}$$
$$+2 \quad 6(0) \qquad = +2$$

2. *[Cr(OH)₃(H₂O)₃]*

No simple ions are present, so this complex must be electrically neutral. Since each hydroxide ion has a charge of -1, the chromium must be in an oxidation state of $+3$.

$$[Cr\ (OH)_3\ (H_2O)_3]$$
$$+3 \quad 3(-1) \quad 3(0) \quad = 0$$

3. $K_2[CoCl_4]$

The compound consists of the simple cations $2K^+$ and the complex anion $[CoCl_4]^{2-}$. The cobalt must be in an oxidation state of $+2$, since the charge on each chloride is -1.

$$[CoCl_4]^{2-}$$
$$+2 \quad 4(-1) \quad = \quad -2$$

Now for the actual rules applied in naming such compounds.

1 (a) Electrically **neutral** complexes, e.g. $[Cr(OH)_3(H_2O)_3]$, have *single word* names.
   (b) In ionic compounds, e.g. $[Fe(H_2O)_6]Cl_2$ and $K_2[CoCl_4]$, the cation is always named *before* the anion.
2 In any complex the ligands are named *before* the central metal;
   (a) Negative ligands, e.g. Cl^- and OH^-, are named before electrically neutral ligands, e.g. H_2O, each set being given in alphabetical order.
   (b) The names of **negative** ligands end in 'o', e.g. Cl^- chloro, OH^- hydroxo, NO_2^- nitrito, CN^- cyano, SO_4^{2-} sulphato.
   (c) Neutral ligands usually keep their normal names, except for H_2O aqua, NH_3 ammine, CO carbonyl, NO nitrosyl.
   (d) The number of each type of ligand present is indicated by the following prefixes to their names:
      1 mono-, 2 di-, 3 tri-, 4 tetra-, 5 penta-, 6 hexa-.
4 (a) If the complex is **negatively** charged, e.g. $[CoCl_4]^{2-}$, then **'ate'** is added *after* the metal name.
      Some metals take their Latin name in anionic complexes, e.g.
      iron becomes ferrate
      copper becomes cuprate
      silver becomes argentate.
   (b) The **oxidation state** of the central metal, *in Roman numerals*, is given in brackets *after* its name.

Let us now apply these rules to the examples we introduced earlier.

1. $[Fe(H_2O)_6]^{2+} 2Cl^-$

We name the complex cation first – since we have six water molecules as ligands and iron in an oxidation state of II, this will be

hexaaquairon(II)

The name of the simple anion is then added, i.e. chloride. Note that we do not need to say dichloride, since the number of chloride ions needed to balance the charge on the cation is fixed.

The full systematic name of the compound is, therefore, **hexaaquairon(II) chloride**.

2. $[Cr(OH)_3(H_2O)_3]$

The complex is electrically neutral and will be named in a single word. We give the negative OH^- ligands before the neutral H_2O, so the name becomes **trihydroxotriaquachromium(III)**.

3. $2K^+ [CoCl_4]^{2-}$

Again we name the cation first, in this case it is simply potassium. The complex anion is tetrachlorocobaltate(II) – note the ending 'ate' to indicate its overall negative charge. So the full name of the compound is, **potassium tetrachlorocobaltate(II)**. Again the number of potassium ions is fixed by the overall charge on the anion and need not be specified.

Of course, it is equally possible to use the rules to work out the structure of a coordination compound from its systematic name, e.g. **dichlorotetraamminecobalt(III) chloride**. This compound is made up of a complex cation, dichlorotetraamminecobalt(III) and simple chloride ions. The complex contains two Cl^- ions and four NH_3 molecules as ligands and cobalt(III), i.e.

$$[Co \quad Cl_2 \quad (NH_3)_4]^+$$

charges $\quad +3 \quad 2(-1) \quad 4(0) \quad = +1$

For electrical neutrality, the compound must contain only one simple Cl^- ion, so the complete formula is **$[CoCl_2(NH_3)_4]Cl$**. *Note the way in which the endings 'o' and 'ide' distinguish between chlorine acting as a ligand and as a simple ion.*

Activity 30.2 provides more practice in naming complexes from their formulae and vice versa.

Activity 30.2

Using the methods described in section 30.2, answer these questions

1 Name the following compounds:
   (a) $[Ni(H_2O)_6]SO_4$ (b) $[CoCl_3(NH_3)_3]$
   (c) $[Co(NH_3)_6]Cl_3$ (d) $K_3[Fe(CN)_6]$
   (e) $K_4[Fe(CN)_6]$ (f) $[Cu(NH_3)_4(H_2O)_2](NO_3)_2$

2 Write the formulae of the following compounds:
   (a) ammonium hexachlorotitanate(IV);
   (b) triamminetriaquachromium(III) hydroxide;
   (c) dihydroxotetraaquairon(II);
   (d) sodium hexanitritocobaltate(III);
   (e) potassium tetrachlorocuprate(II);
   (f) chloropentaamminecobalt(III) chloride.

30.3 The shapes of complexes and isomerism

By and large, we may use the electron repulsion theory described in chapter 7 to predict the shapes of most complexes. In the first row of the 'd' block, the only exceptions are the square planar 4-coordinate complexes of nickel(II) which are discussed in more detail in section 31.5.

The common **coordination numbers** with their corresponding shapes, are summarised in figure 30.2, together with some examples.

Isomerism in general has been considered in chapter 10, but here we shall look briefly at some specific examples involving 'd' block complexes.

Structural isomers (section 10.2)

The simplest case occurs in complex cations, where different anions may act as ligands. Thus, for example, the following two compounds have the same 'molecular' formula but different structures, i.e. *a different arrangement of ligands.*

$[Co(NH_3)_4Cl_2]NO_2$ and $[Co(NH_3)_4ClNO_2]Cl$
containing NO_2^- as a simple   containing NO_2^- as a ligand
anion

We may distinguish between the above two isomers since free chloride ions will give an *immediate* precipitate with aqueous silver nitrate, whereas chloro ligands will not.

$[Co(NH_3)_4Cl_2]NO_2(aq) + Ag^+(aq) \rightarrow$ no immediate reaction
$[Co(NH_3)_4ClNO_2]Cl(aq) + Ag^+(aq) \rightarrow [Co(NH_3)_4ClNO_2]^+(aq) + AgCl(s)$

Figure 30.2 *Coordination numbers and shapes of 'd' block complexes*

Coordination number	shape of complex		representative examples
6	octahedral 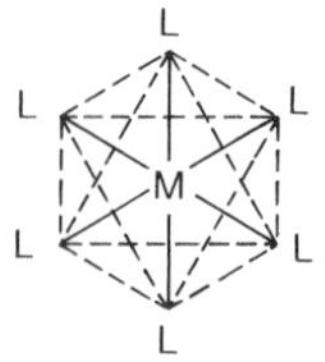		The most common shape All M^{2+} and M^{3+} aqua complexes, except $[Zn(H_2O)_4]^{2+}$ Most ammines of M^{2+} and M^{3+} ions, e.g. $[Co_4(NH_3)_6]^{3+}$ and mixed ammine-aqua complexes, e.g. $[Cu(NH_3)_4(H_2O)_2]^{2+}$
4	tetrahedral 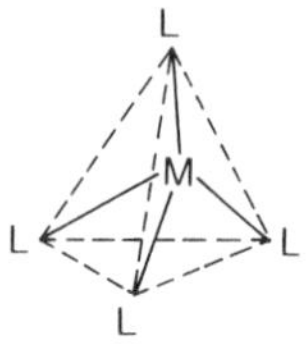		Quite common, in fact the most common shape for Zn(II) complexes, e.g. $[Zn(H_2O)_4]^{2+}$ All 4-coordinate halo complexes, e.g. $[CoCl_4]^{2-}$
	square planar 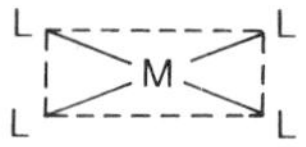		In the 1st row of the 'd' block only some Ni(II) complexes have this shape, e.g. $[Ni(CN)_4]^{2-}$
2	linear	L——M——L	Amongst the metals in the 1st row of the 'd' block this shape is only found in Cu(I) complexes e.g. $[Cu(NH_3)_2]^+$ Ag(I) also forms linear complexes, e.g. $[AgCl_2]^-$

Geometrical isomers (section 10.3)

These are possible when octahedral and square planar complexes contain at least two different types of ligand. If we draw the octahedral complex cation, dichlorotetraamminecobalt(III), we may place the two chloride ions either *adjacent* to each other, figure 30.3a, or *opposite* as shown in figure 30.3b. Similarly, two geometrical isomers of the square planar dichlorodiammineplatinum(II) are illustrated in figure 30.3c.

Figure 30.3 *Examples of geometrical isomerism in complexes*

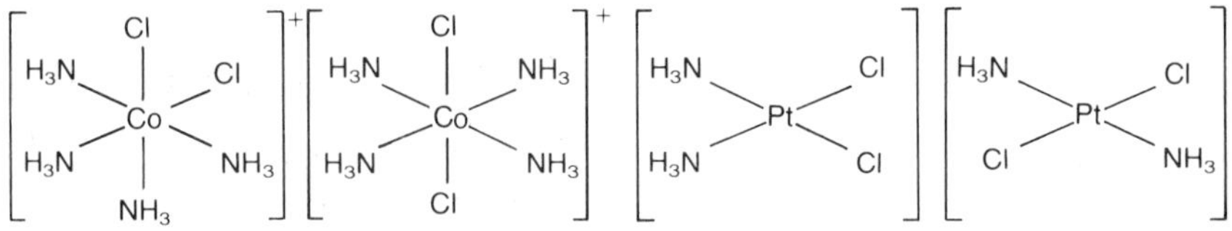

'cis' isomer   'trans' isomer   'cis' isomer   'trans' isomer

Optical isomers (section 10.4)

None of the isomers we have looked at so far in this section is optically active. If you compare the complexes with their 'mirror images' you will find that they are *superimposable*, i.e. identical, as shown for dichlorotetraamminecobalt(III) in figure

Figure 30.4 *Optical activity in octahedral complexes*

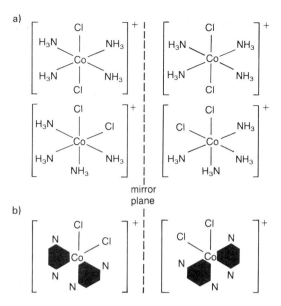

30.4a. If however, the two mirror image forms *cannot* be superimposed, they will be **enantiomers**, *i.e. they will rotate the plane of polarised light equally but in opposite directions*. An example of an optically active octahedral complex which contains bidentate ligands is illustrated in figure 30.4b. You may find it helpful to construct 'ball and stick' models of the mirror image forms to convince yourself that they are indeed different.

Activity 30.3

1   Consulting figure 30.2 if necessary, deduce the shapes of the following complexes:
    (a) $[Ag(NH_3)_2]^+$ (b) $[CuCl_4]^{2-}$ (c) $[Cu(NH_3)_4(H_2O)_2]^{2+}$
2   Could the 'trans' isomer of the complex illustrated in figure 30.4b show optical activity? Explain your answer.
3   (a) A chromium compound X has the formula $CrCl_3(H_2O)_6$. If the coordination number of the chromium is six, give the four possible structural isomers of the chromium species.
    (b) When excess silver nitrate solution is added to 0.01 mole of X, 0.01 moles of silver chloride are precipitated. Which of the above species is present in X?
    (c) Draw the geometrical isomers of the chromium complex. Could either of these isomers show optical activity?

30.4 Acid–base reactions of aqua ions

In common with many metal ions, *'d' block cations in aqueous solution are acidic to some extent.* As the approximate pH values in table 30.1 show, $M^{3+}(aq)$ ions are appreciably *more* acidic than $M^{2+}(aq)$ species.

In section 23.4 we pointed out, with reference to $Al^{3+}(aq)$, that a cation will attract electrons from associated water molecules, favouring the release of $H^+(aq)$ ions into solution. $M^{3+}(aq)$ is more acidic than $M^{2+}(aq)$ since the central metal ion has a higher charge density and will be more attractive to electrons:

Table 30.1 *The acidity of some 'd' block cations in aqueous solution*

Metal ion	approximate pH in dilute aqueous solution	pK_1†
$Sc^{3+}(aq)$	3	4.9
$Ti^{3+}(aq)$	2	2.6
$V^{3+}(aq)$	2	2.6
$Cr^{3+}(aq)$	3	3.9
$Mn^{2+}(aq)$	5	10.9
$Fe^{2+}(aq)$	5	9.5
$Fe^{3+}(aq)$	2	2.2
$Co^{2+}(aq)$	4	7.0
$Ni^{2+}(aq)$	5	8.9
$Cu^{2+}(aq)$	5	8.0
$Zn^{2+}(aq)$	5	9.0

† See section 18.6

Which is more acidic $M^{2+}(aq)$ or $M^{3+}(aq)$? How do you explain this?

Theoretically, hexaaqua ions may act as polybasic acids, i.e. the complex may release *several* hydrated protons, e.g.

1 $[M(H_2O)_6]^{3+}(aq) \rightleftharpoons [MOH(H_2O)_5]^{2+}(aq) + H^+(aq)$
2 $[MOH(H_2O)_5]^{2+}(aq) \rightleftharpoons [M(OH)_2(H_2O)_4]^+(aq) + H^+(aq)$
3 $[M(OH)_2(H_2O)_4]^+(aq) \rightleftharpoons [M(OH)_3(H_2O)_3](s) + H^+(aq)$

Usually however, in the absence of added base, only reaction 1 is important. The pK_a values shown for this process in table 30.1 show the relative acid strengths of various 'd' block aqua ions.

If a base such as $OH^-(aq)$ is added to the solution, $H^+(aq)$ ions are removed, pushing the above systems to the right and precipitating the electrically neutral *hydroxoaqua* complex. In some cases, e.g. $Cr^{3+}(aq)$ and $Zn^{2+}(aq)$, *this precipitate will dissolve in excess alkali*, losing further $H^+(aq)$ ions to give complex *anions*, i.e.

4 $[M(OH)_3(H_2O)_3](s) \rightleftharpoons [M(OH)_4(H_2O)_2]^-(aq) + H^+(aq)$ .... etc.

Such precipitates which dissolve in excess alkali are known as **amphoteric** hydroxides, since they may both accept and donate $H^+(aq)$, i.e. act as both a base and an acid.

Because of the considerable difference in acidity, *$M^{2+}(aq)$ and $M^{3+}(aq)$ solutions generally react quite differently with $CO_3{}^{2-}(aq)$*. $M^{2+}(aq)$ gives a precipitate of the insoluble metal carbonate, e.g.

$$[Fe(H_2O)_6]^{2+}(aq) + CO_3{}^{2-}(aq) \rightarrow FeCO_3(s) + 6H_2O(l)$$

However, *no carbonates containing M^{3+} ions exist*. Since $Fe^{3+}(aq)$ is a stronger acid than $H_2CO_3(aq)$, it will displace this from solution, giving bubbles of carbon dioxide gas and a precipitate of the electrically neutral hydroxoaqua iron complex:

$$[Fe(H_2O)_6]^{3+}(aq) \rightleftharpoons [Fe(OH)_3(H_2O)_3](s) + 3H^+(aq)$$
and $\quad CO_3{}^{2-}(aq) + 2H^+(aq) \rightarrow H_2CO_3(aq) \rightarrow H_2O(l) + CO_2(g)$

The overall reaction may be written:

$$2[Fe(H_2O)_6]^{3+}(aq) + 3CO_3{}^{2-}(aq) \rightarrow$$
$$2[Fe(OH)_3(H_2O)_3)](s) + 3H_2O(l) + 3CO_2(g)$$

Activity 30.4

Iron(III) chloride solution reacts with magnesium ribbon to give a brown precipitate and hydrogen gas. Write a balanced equation for this reaction and explain why a solution of iron(II) chloride does not react in a similar way.

30.5 Stability of complexes and ligand substitution reactions

If another ligand is added to a solution of an aqua complex, then it will *compete* with the water molecules to complex the metal ion. For example, additon of aqueous ammonia to the *green* $[Ni(H_2O)_6]^{2+}(aq)$ gives a *violet* solution containing **ammine** complexes. In many cases the **substitution** of one ligand for another may be regarded as a *stepwise* reaction, e.g.

$[Ni(H_2O)_6]^{2+}(aq) + NH_3(aq) \rightleftharpoons [Ni(H_2O)_5NH_3]^{2+}(aq) + H_2O(l) \; K_1$

$[Ni(H_2O)_5NH_3]^{2+}(aq) + NH_3(aq) \rightleftharpoons [Ni(H_2O)_4(NH_3)_2]^{2+}(aq) + H_2O(l) \; K_2$

$[Ni(H_2O)_4(NH_3)_2]^{2+}(aq) + NH_3(aq) \rightleftharpoons [Ni(H_2O)_3(NH_3)_3]^{2+}(aq) + H_2O(l) \; K_3$

$[Ni(H_2O)_3(NH_3)_3]^{2+}(aq) + NH_3(aq) \rightleftharpoons [Ni(H_2O)_2(NH_3)_4]^{2+}(aq) + H_2O(l) \; K_4$

$[Ni(H_2O)_2(NH_3)_4]^{2+}(aq) + NH_3(aq) \rightleftharpoons [NiH_2O(NH_3)_5]^{2+}(aq) + H_2O(l) \; K_5$

$[NiH_2O(NH_3)_5]^{2+}(aq) + NH_3(aq) \rightleftharpoons [Ni(NH_3)_6]^{2+}(aq) + H_2O(l) \; K_6$

The concentrations of each of these species in the solution will depend upon the *relative concentrations of the competing ligands* and the *individual equilibrium constants* of the above steps, K_1 to K_6. The **stability constant, K_{st}**, of a particular complex is defined as *the equilibrium constant for its formation from the metal aqua ion*. Thus for the hexaamminenickel(II) ion, the overall equation for its formation from hexaaquanickel(II) is

$$Ni(H_2O)_6^{2+}(aq) + 6NH_3(aq) \rightarrow Ni(NH_3)_6^{2+}(aq) + 6H_2O(l)$$

$$\text{and, } K_{st} = \frac{[Ni(NH_3)_6^{2+}(aq)]}{[Ni(H_2O)_6^{2+}(aq)] \, [NH_3(aq)]^6}$$

where the square brackets here indicate molar concentration.

You can easily show that K_{st} is the product of the equilibrium constants of all the separate stages. For example for the hexaamminenickel (II) ion above

$$K_{st} = K_1.K_2.K_3.K_4.K_5.K_6$$

In some cases, not all of the water molecules may be substituted. In aqueous solution, for example, only *four* water molecules in the hexaaquacopper(II) ion may be exchanged for ammonia, i.e. the process stops at $[Cu(H_2O)_4(NH_3)_2]^{2+}(aq)$.

$$[Cu(H_2O)_6]^{2+}(aq) + 4NH_3(aq) \rightarrow [Cu(H_2O)_2(NH_3)_4]^{2+}(aq) + 4H_2O(l)$$

The stability constant for this complex is given by

$$K_{st} = \frac{[Cu(H_2O)_2(NH_3)_4^{2+}(aq)]}{[Cu(H_2O)_6^{2+}(aq)] \, [NH_3(aq)]^4}$$

The higher the value of K_{st} for a complex, the more readily it can be formed in aqueous solution by addition of the appropriate ligand. The wide variation in stability constants can be seen from the examples in table 30.2.

Ligand substitution may also affect the relative stabilities of different oxidation states of the transition metal. For example, although $Co(H_2O)_6^{2+}(aq)$ is quite

Table 30.2 *Approximate stability constants of some 'd' block complexes*

Ligand	Cl^-	CN^-	NH_3	da, i.e. $H_2N\text{-}CH_2\text{-}CH_2\text{-}NH_2$
	$[FeCl_4]^-\ 10^{-2}$	$[Fe(CN)_6]^{4-}\ 10^{24}$		
		$[Fe(CN)_6]^{3-}\ 10^{31}$		
			$[Co(NH_3)_6]^{2+}$ $\quad10^6$	
			$[Co(NH_3)_6]^{3+}$ $\quad10^{33}$	
			$[Ni(NH_3)_6]^{2+}$ $\quad10^7$	$[Ni(da)_3]^{2+}\ 10^{18}$
	$[CuCl_4]^{2-}\ 10^5$		$[Cu(H_2O)_2(NH_3)_4]^{2+}\ 10^{13}$	$[Cu(da)_3]^{2+}\ 10^{20}$

Which of the above complexes is (a) most stable, (b) least stable, in aqueous solution?

stable, $Co(NH_3)_6^{2+}(aq)$ is *readily oxidised by air to* $Co(NH_3)_6^{3+}(aq)$. This, together with examples taken from iron chemistry, will be covered in more detail in chapter 31.

Activity 30.5

Hexaamminenickel(II) chloride may be obtained by adding aqueous ammonia to a solution of hexaaquanickel(II).

$$Ni(H_2O)_6^{2+}(aq) + 6NH_3(aq) \rightleftharpoons Ni(NH_3)_6^{2+}(aq) + 6H_2O(l)$$

The stability constant of $Ni(NH_3)_6^{2+}$ is 10^7. What is the ratio of the concentration of the hexaammine complex to the hexaaqua complex if the concentration of free ammonia is $0.1\,M$?
(You may find it helpful to refer to section 14.2.)

30.6 Colour and magnetic properties of complexes

The origin of colour in transition metal complexes and their behaviour in a magnetic field are most interesting topics and deserve a brief mention.

Colour

White light is a mixture of all the visible colours in a quite narrow frequency range in the electromagnetic spectrum. The colour of a substance exposed to white light will depend upon whether it absorbs none, all, or some of the radiation. The *observed* colour will be a mixture of all the frequencies which are *not* absorbed by the sample. If *no* visible light is absorbed then the substance will appear *white*, whereas if *all* frequencies are absorbed it will be *black*. Only if just a part of the visible light is absorbed will the sample be 'coloured', as shown in figure 30.5.

A species will absorb radiation of a particular 'colour' only if this corresponds *exactly* to the energy required to promote one of its electrons to a higher level. We have noted already that colour in transition metal compounds is largely associated with the presence of an *incomplete inner 'd' sub-level*. Since all *free* transition metal ions are colourless, colour must somehow be developed by the interaction of the *ligands* with the metal ion during complex formation. In the free metal ion, all five of the 3d orbitals have the *same* energy, but the approach of ligands during complex formation *disturbs* the energy levels of the 'd' orbitals. Without giving a detailed explanation, figure 30.6 shows that for 6-coordinate octahedral complexes, the 3d orbitals are *split into two sets*, separated by an energy difference known as the **crystal field splitting energy**, Δ. If an electron in the lower state can be **promoted** to the higher level by absorbing a particular wavelength of visible radiation, then the substance will be coloured. If the crystal field splitting energy is too high or too low,

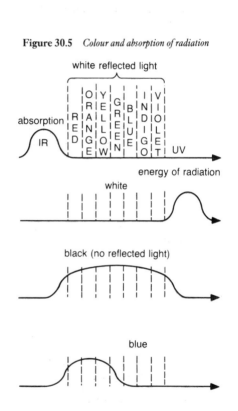

Figure 30.5 *Colour and absorption of radiation*

Figure 30.6 *The effect of octahedral complex formation on the energies of electrons in the 'd' orbitals of a metal ion*

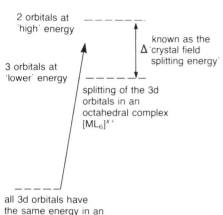

2 orbitals at 'high' energy

known as the Δ 'crystal field splitting energy'

3 orbitals at 'lower' energy

splitting of the 3d orbitals in an octahedral complex $[ML_6]^{x+}$

all 3d orbitals have the same energy in an isolated gaseous transition metal ion, M^{x+}

then the sample will be white, since it will absorb **ultra violet** or **infrared** radiation respectively.

Clearly, if the 3d orbitals are completely empty or completely full, then no such movement of electrons is possible and the substance should be *white*. Whilst this is true for $3d^{10}$ configurations, complexes containing no 3d electrons are often intensely coloured, especially when the metal is in a high oxidation state, e.g. MnO_4^- is deep purple. Colour here is caused by **charge transfer**, i.e. exchange of electrons between the ligands and the metal.

Magnetism

Electrons may be regarded as 'spinning' charged particles, and act as tiny magnets. They may 'react' to an external magnetic field in two ways. A sample which contains *paired* electrons only will be **diamagnetic**, i.e. it is *repelled* very weakly by an external field. The presence of *unpaired* electrons, however, will cause the sample to be *attracted* towards a magnetic field. The strength of this **paramagnetic** attraction will depend upon the *number* of unpaired electrons present. Here we shall only consider the case of 6-coordinate octahedral complexes where the 'd' orbitals are split as shown in figure 30.6.

Clearly, metal ions which contain an empty 'd' sub-level, e.g. in scandium(III) and titanium(IV) complexes, and those which have a full 'd' sub-level, e.g. in copper(I) and zinc(II) complexes, must be diamagnetic:

$$d^0 \qquad\qquad\qquad d^{10}$$

Metal ions with a partly filled 'd' sub-level may, however, be paramagnetic. For example, nickel(II) complexes have two unpaired electrons, since the eight electrons in the 3d orbitals are arranged as follows:

$$d^8$$

Magnetic measurements can give much information about the electronic structure of a complex.

30.7 Comments on the activities

Activity 30.1

1   'Dot and cross' electron diagrams reveal that the following possess atoms with 'lone' pairs of electrons and could, therefore, act as ligands:

(b)   :C≡N:⁻   (c)   :C≡O: (f)   [O₂S O₂]²⁻   (g)   ⁻:O—H

(h)   Br:⁻   (i)   CH₃—CH₂—Ö—CH₂—CH₃   (j)   CH₃—C—CH₂—C—CH₃ with :O and O:

(For clarity, any extra lone pairs on particular donor atoms have been omitted.) The remaining species cannot function as ligands as they possess no 'lone' pairs of electrons.

Since (b), (c), (f) and (j) above contain more than one atom with an available lone pair, we might expect them to behave as bi- (or in the case of

SO_4^{2-} poly-) dentate ligands. In practice only species (j) donates more than one pair of electrons to a particular metal ion, since only this molecule possesses the 'flexibility' required to bend itself into the necessary shape.

2   The key to complexing ability is the ease with which a pair of electrons is donated. In nitrogen trichloride the very electronegative chlorine atoms attract electron density away from the nitrogen atoms, making it more *reluctant* to donate its lone pair. Methyl groups are, however, electron repelling, and in trimethylamine, *improve* the donating power of the nitrogen atom by *increasing* the electron density around it.

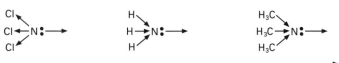

increasing electron density on the nitrogen atom improves complexing ability

Activity 30.2

1   (a)   hexaaquanickel(II) sulphate
    (b)   trichlorotriamminecobalt(III)
    (c)   hexaamminecobalt(III) chloride
    (d)   potassium hexacyanoferrate(III)
    (e)   potassium hexacyanoferrate(II)
    (f)   tetraamminediaquacopper(II) nitrate

2   (a) $(NH_4)_2[TiCl_6]$
    (b) $[Cr(NH_3)_3(H_2O)_3](OH)_3$
    (c) $[Fe(OH)_2(H_2O)_4]$
    (d) $Na_3[Co(NO_2)_6]$
    (e) $K_2[CuCl_4]$
    (f) $[CoCl(NH_3)_5]Cl_2$

Activity 30.3

1   (a) linear (b) tetrahedral (c) octahedral.

2   No. The two 'mirror image' forms are identical (superimposable):

3   (a)   We must have six ligands, which must be combinations of Cl^- and H_2O:

$[Cr(H_2O)_6]^{3+}$ $3Cl^-$ $[CrCl(H_2O)_5]^{2+}2Cl^-$
$[CrCl_2(H_2O)_4]^+Cl^-$ $[CrCl_3(H_2O)_3]$

   (b)   Since 0.01 moles of X gives 0.01 moles of AgCl, the sample must have contained 0.01 moles of simple chloride ions. Each mole of X must therefore contain *one mole* of chloride ions. The chromium species present in X must therefore be dichlorotetraaquachromium(III), $[CrCl_2(H_2O)_4]^+$.

   (c)   *Cis* and *trans* isomers are possible but neither of these will be optically active:

cis   trans

Activity 30.4

$$[Fe(H_2O)_6]^{3+}(aq) \rightleftharpoons [Fe(OH)_3(H_2O)_3](s) + 3H^+(aq)$$

and

$$Mg(s) + 2H^+(aq) \rightarrow Mg^{2+}(aq) + H_2(g)$$

Overall the equation may be written,

$$2[Fe(H_2O)_6]^{3+}(aq) + 3Mg(s) \rightarrow 2[Fe(OH)_3(H_2O)_3](s) + 3Mg^{2+}(aq) + 3H_2(g)$$

Iron(II) chloride does not give a similar reaction because the $[Fe(H_2O)_6]^{2+}(aq)$ is a weaker acid than H_2CO_3. Because of its lower charge density, the Fe^{2+} ion does not polarise co-ordinated water molecules to the same extent as Fe^{3+}.

Activity 30.5

$$K_{st} = \frac{[Ni(NH_3)_6{}^{2+}(aq)]}{[Ni(H_2O)_6{}^{2+}(aq)]\,[NH_3(aq)]^6}$$

Substituting the figures given in the question,

$$10^7 = \frac{[Ni(NH_3)_6{}^{2+}(aq)]}{[Ni(H_2O)_6{}^{2+}(aq)].(0.1)^6}$$

$$10 = \frac{[Ni(NH_3)_6{}^{2+}(aq)]}{[Ni(H_2O)_6{}^{2+}(aq)]}$$

i.e. $[Ni(NH_3)_6{}^{2+}(aq)] = 10\,[Ni(H_2O)_6{}^{2+}(aq)]$

Thus the concentration of the hexaammine complex will be ten times that of the hexaaqua ion in this solution.

30.8 Summary and revision plan

1 **Ligands** may be classified as follows:
   ▶ either **neutral** molecules or **anions**;
   ▶ in terms of the number of lone pairs of electrons which they may donate to a metal ion.

2 There is a systematic method for deriving the name of a complex from its structure, or vice versa.

3 The number of ligands attached to a particular metal is known as the **coordination number**. Common values in 'd' block complexes are **6, 4** and **2**.

4 The shape of a 'd' block complex is largely determined by its coordination number:
   ▶ 6-coordinate complexes are **octahedral** (most common);
   ▶ 4-coordinate complexes are normally **tetrahedral**, but some complexes of nickel are **square planar**;
   ▶ 2-coordinate complexes are **linear** (copper(I) and silver(I)).

5 **Geometrical** and/or **optical isomerism** is possible in some complexes.

6 The acidity of aqua-complexes in solution increases with the charge density on the central metal ion. Addition of alkali generally precipitates a neutral hydroxo-aqua complex which, if **amphoteric**, dissolves in excess alkali to give an anionic complex.

7 Ligand substitution reactions result from competition between different ligands to complex a metal ion. The **stability constant, K_{st},** of a complex is the overall equilibrium constant for its formation from an aqua ion in solution. The higher the value of K_{st}, the more readily the complex will be formed.

8 Change in ligand type can sometimes reverse the redox stabilities of different oxidation states of a given metal.

9 The presence of ligands in a complex causes the metal 'd' orbitals to split into groups at different energies. A complex in which the central metal ion has a partly filled inner 'd' sub-level is often coloured since electrons may be 'promoted' by absorbing visible radiation.

10 **Paramagnetism** is the attraction of a species towards an applied magnetic field and results from the presence of unpaired electrons.

□ CHAPTER □

31

Further Aspects of the Chemistry of 'd' Block Elements

Contents

For each of the following metals we shall survey the preparation, properties and reactions of typical species which illustrate the chemistry of the main oxidation states. Brief summaries of important reaction sequences are given in the figures accompanying each section.

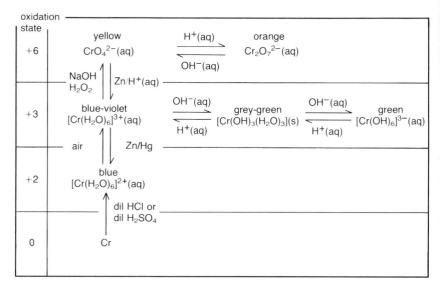

Figure 31.1 *Outline chemistry of chromium*

31.1 Chromium

Common oxidation states: $+2$, $+3$ and $+6$.

2+

Dilute hydrochloric and sulphuric acids react slowly with the metal, liberating hydrogen and producing solutions containing the sky blue hexaaquachromium(II) ion:

$$Cr(s) + 2H^+(aq) + 6H_2O(l) \rightarrow [Cr(H_2O)_6]^{2+}(aq) + H_2(g)$$
$$\text{blue}$$

Cr(II) is a powerful **reducing agent** and in solution is rapidly oxidised by air to Cr(III); $(Cr^{3+}(aq)/Cr^{2+}(aq), E^{\ominus} = -0.41\,V)$.

3+

Generally the *most stable* oxidation state of chromium, being neither powerfully oxidising nor reducing in nature. Although the hexaaqua complex itself is blue-violet, $Cr^{3+}(aq)$ solutions are often green in colour, owing to ligand exchange. With strong alkali, the trihydroxotriaqua complex is first precipitated. This is *amphoteric*, dissolving in excess alkali to give solutions containing hexahydroxochromate(III):

$$[Cr(H_2O)_6]^{3+}(aq) \underset{H^+(aq)}{\overset{OH^-(aq)}{\rightleftharpoons}} [Cr(OH)_3(H_2O)_3](s) \underset{H^+(aq)}{\overset{OH^-(aq)}{\rightleftharpoons}} [Cr(OH)_6]^{3-}(aq)$$
blue-violet $\qquad$ grey-green $\qquad$ green

Addition of ammonia to solutions of chromium(III) can give a wide range of **ammine** complexes including hexaamminechromium(III):

$$[Cr(H_2O)_6]^{3+}(aq) + 6NH_3(aq) \rightarrow [Cr(NH_3)_6]^{3+}(aq) + 6H_2O(l)$$
violet

Reduction of Cr(III)(aq) with a zinc mercury amalgam gives Cr(II)(aq):

$$2[Cr(H_2O)_6]^{3+}(aq) + Zn(Hg) \rightarrow 2[Cr(H_2O)_6]^{2+}(aq) + Zn^{2+}(aq)$$

6+

The yellow chromate(VI) ion is formed by the oxidation of Cr(II)(aq) by hydrogen peroxide in alkaline solution. We may derive the overall equation by combining the following two half-equations:

$$Cr^{3+}(aq) + 8OH^-(aq) \qquad \rightarrow CrO_4^{2-}(aq) + 4H_2O(l) + 3e^- \qquad (\times 2)$$

$$H_2O_2(aq) + 2e^- \qquad \rightarrow 2OH^-(aq) \qquad (\times 3)$$

$$2Cr^{3+}(aq) + 16OH^-(aq) + 3H_2O_2(aq) \rightarrow 2CrO_4^{2-}(aq) + 8H_2O(l) + 6OH^-(aq)$$

Cancelling the $OH^-(aq)$ on each side of the equation, this gives

$$2Cr^{3+}(aq) + 10OH^-(aq) + 3H_2O_2(aq) \rightarrow 2CrO_4^{2-}(aq) + 8H_2O(l)$$
green $\qquad\qquad\qquad\qquad\qquad\qquad\qquad\qquad$ yellow

In solution, chromate(VI) exists in equilibrium with dichromate(VI). The position of the equilibrium is dependent upon pH, with acid conditions favouring the formation of dichromate(VI).

$$2CrO_4^{2-}(aq) + 2H^+(aq) \underset{alkali}{\overset{acid}{\rightleftharpoons}} Cr_2O_7^{2-}(aq) + H_2O(l)$$
yellow $\qquad\qquad\qquad\qquad\qquad$ orange

Chromium(VI) is a good **oxidising agent** and since potassium dichromate(VI) may be obtained in high purity and is quite stable in aqueous solution it is used as a **primary standard*** in volumetric oxidation. When it acts as an oxidising agent in acid solution, it is converted into Cr(III)(aq), according to the following half-equation:

$$Cr_2O_7^{2-}(aq) + 14H^+(aq) + 6e^- \rightarrow 2Cr^{3+}(aq) + 7H_2O(l) \quad (E^\ominus = +1.33\,V)$$

Unlike manganate(VII), dichromate(VI) solutions may be used to carry out volumetric oxidations in the presence of hydrochloric acid, since it is not powerful enough to convert chloride ions into chlorine. One disadvantage of dichromate(VI) in volumetric analysis is the difficulty in determining the end point, since the green Cr(III)(aq) produced obscures the first appearance of the excess orange dichromate(VI) solution. Special indicators have been developed, however, for use in titrating iron(II) with dichromate(VI).

---

*This means that it is possible to prepare a solution of known molarity directly by dissolving a weighed sample in a known volume of solution. It is not necessary to standardise this solution against a reducing agent of known molarity.

This is not true of all volumetric solutions; see, for example, the comments on potassium manganate(VII) in section 31.2.

Activity 31.1

Potassium dichromate(VI) will oxidise iron(II) in acid solution as follows:

$$Fe^{2+}(aq) \rightarrow Fe^{3+}(aq) + e^-$$

1 Complete the following equation for the reaction between dichromate(VI) and iron(II) under these conditions.

$$Cr_2O_7^{2-}(aq) + H^+(aq) + Fe^{2+}(aq) \rightarrow$$

2 Iron dissolves in dilute hydrochloric acid as follows:

$$Fe(s) + 2H^+(aq) \rightarrow Fe^{2+}(aq) + H_2(g)$$

1.400 g of a sample of steel was dissolved in hydrochloric acid and diluted to exactly 250 cm³ with water in a graduated flask. 25 cm³ portions of this solution required 20.5 cm³ of 0.02 M potassium dichromate(VI) solution for complete oxidation. Calculate
   (a) the number of moles of dichromate(VI) used in the titration;
   (b) the number of moles of iron present in the original steel sample;
   (c) the % by mass of iron in the steel.

(Relative Atomic Mass: Fe = 56)

31.2 Manganese

Common oxidation states: +2, +4, +6 and +7.

Figure 31.2 *Outline chemistry of manganese*

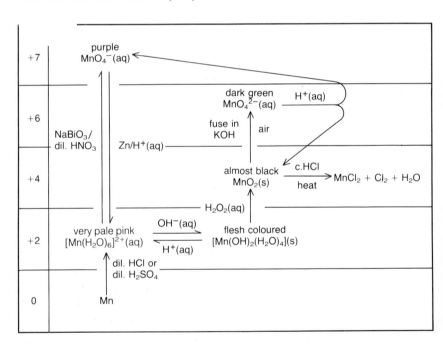

2+

Generally the *most stable* oxidation state of manganese, especially in aqueous solution. This is possibly due to the presence of a half-full 3d sub-level in Mn(II). The metal will react with dilute hydrochloric or sulphuric acids, liberating hydrogen and giving a very pale pink, almost colourless, solution containing the hexaaqua complex:

$$Mn(s) + 2H^+(aq) + 6H_2O(l) \rightarrow [Mn(H_2O)_6]^{2+}(aq) + H_2(g)$$
$$\text{very pale pink}$$

Addition of alkali to this solution gives a flesh coloured precipitate of the dihydroxotetraaqua complex:

$$[Mn(H_2O)_6]^{2+}(aq) + 2OH^-(aq) \rightarrow [Mn(OH)_2(H_2O)_4](s) + 2H_2O(l)$$

very pale pink   flesh coloured

This precipitate is insoluble in excess alkali but darkens, owing to oxidation, on exposure to air. Addition of hydrogen peroxide solution produces the very dark brown (almost black) manganese(IV) oxide:

$$[Mn(OH)_2(H_2O)_4](s) + H_2O_2(aq) \rightarrow MnO_2(s) + 6H_2O(l)$$

flesh coloured   dark brown

4+

The only important compound of manganese(IV) is the almost black oxide, MnO_2. Its stability results from its *insolubility*, since *manganese(IV) is a powerful oxidising agent in solution*. It will dissolve in concentrated hydrochloric acid on warming to give chlorine and manganese(II) chloride:

$$MnO_2(s) + 4HCl(aq) \rightarrow MnCl_2(aq) + 2H_2O(l) + Cl_2(g)$$

6+

The dark green manganate(VI) ion, MnO_4^{2-}, is prepared by fusing manganese(IV) oxide with potassium hydroxide pellets. Air acts as the oxidising agent, but a little potassium nitrate may be added if desired:

$$\overset{\text{fuse}}{2MnO_2(s) + O_2(g) + 4OH^-(l) \rightarrow 2MnO_4^{2-}(l) + 2H_2O(g)}$$

almost black   dark green

Manganese(VI) is stable only under very alkaline conditions. In neutral or acid solution it **disproportionates**, *i.e. undergoes self oxidation and reduction, into purple manganate(VII) solution and solid manganate(IV) oxide.*

oxidation: $MnO_4^{2-}(aq)$ $\rightarrow MnO_4^-(aq) + e^-$
            +6   +7

reduction: $MnO_4^{2-}(aq) + 4H^+(aq) + 2e^-$ $\rightarrow MnO_2(s) + 2H_2O(l)$
            +6   +4

overall: $3MnO_4^{2-}(aq) + 4H^+(aq)$ $\rightarrow 2MnO_4^-(aq)$ + $MnO_2(s) + 2H_2O(l)$
            3(+6)   2(+7)   +4
            dark green   purple   almost black

7+

The most important species is the intense purple manganate(VII). It may be prepared by the disproportionation of manganate(VI) in neutral or acid solution as described above, or by the action of a very powerful oxidising agent such as sodium bismuthate(V) on manganese(II) solutions in dilute nitric acid.

$2Mn^{2+}(aq)$ + $5BiO_3^-(aq) + 14H^+(aq) \rightarrow$ $2MnO_4^-(aq)$ + $5Bi^{3+}(aq) + 7H_2O(l)$
2(+2)   5(+5)   2(+7)   5(+3)
very pale pink   purple

The distinctive colour of the manganate(VII) solutions makes this a useful chemical test for the presence of Mn(II).

Potassium manganate(VII) is a powerful and widely used **oxidising agent**. In alkaline solution it is first reduced to manganate(VI) and finally to manganese(IV) oxide. In volumetric analysis it is almost always used in *acid* solution, when it is reduced directly to Mn(II):

$$MnO_4^-(aq) + 8H^+(aq) + 5e^- \rightarrow Mn^{2+}(aq) + 4H_2O(l) \quad (E^\ominus = +1.52V)$$

Under such conditions, manganate(VII) is a more powerful oxidant than dichromate(VI) and will convert chloride ions into chlorine. *It should therefore never be used in the analysis of solutions which contain chloride.* Since it is rather unstable in solution, potassium manganate(VII) is not used as a primary standard. Solutions should be standardised, e.g. with an iron(II) solution, immediately before use. No indicator is needed in these titrations, since the first excess of manganate(VII) is revealed by its purple colouration.

Activity 31.2

Ethanedioic acid is oxidised to carbon dioxide by manganate(VII):

$$H_2C_2O_4(aq) \rightarrow 2H^+(aq) + 2CO_2(g) + 2e^-$$

1   Complete the following balanced equation for the oxidation of ethanedioic acid by manganate(VII).

$$MnO_4^-(aq) + H^+(aq) + H_2C_2O_4(aq) \rightarrow$$

2   In an experiment to standardise an approximately 0.02 M solution of potassium manganate(VII), 0.630 g of hydrated ethanedioic acid, $H_2C_2O_4.2H_2O$, was dissolved in water and the volume of the solution made up to exactly $100\,cm^3$ in a graduated flask. $25\,cm^3$ portions of this solution needed $27.9\,cm^3$ of the potassium manganate(VII) solution for complete oxidation.

    (a) How many moles of hydrated ethanedioic acid were present in the original sample?

    (b) How many moles of the acid were present in the titration?

    (c) How many moles of manganate(VII) were used in the titration?

    (d) What is the molarity of the potassium manganate(VII) solution?

(Relative Atomic Masses: H = 1, C = 12, O = 16)

31.3 Iron

Common oxidation states: +2 and +3.

Figure 31.3 *Outline chemistry of iron*

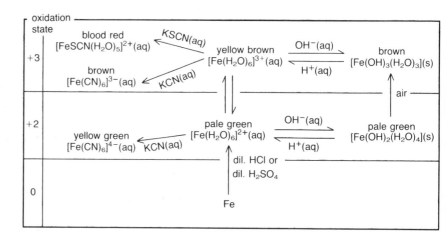

2+

The pale green hexaaquairon(II) ion is formed when iron reacts with dilute hydrochloric or sulphuric acids.

$$Fe(s) + 2H^+(aq) + 6H_2O(l) \rightarrow [Fe(H_2O)_6]^{2+}(aq) + H_2(g)$$
$$\text{pale green}$$

It is also formed by the reduction of aqueous iron(III) by zinc in the presence of dilute acid:

$$2Fe^{3+}(aq) + Zn(s) + 12H_2O(l) \rightarrow 2[Fe(H_2O)_6]^{2+}(aq) + Zn^{2+}(aq)$$

yellow-brown   pale green

In *acid* solution, hexaaquairon(II) is *slowly* oxidised by air to brown iron(III). Addition of sodium hydroxide solution precipitates the pale green dihydroxotetraaquairon(II) complex which is insoluble in a moderate excess of alkali:

$$[Fe(H_2O)_6]^{2+}(aq) + 2OH^-(aq) \underset{H^+(aq)}{\overset{OH^-(aq)}{\rightleftharpoons}} [Fe(OH)_2(H_2O)_4](s) + 2H_2O(l)$$

pale green   pale green

Since iron is not readily complexed by ammonia, exactly the same precipitate is obtained if ammonia solution is used as the alkali. Under *alkaline* conditions the atmospheric oxidation of iron(II) to iron(III) is *speeded up*, and on exposure to air the green dihydroxotetraaquairon(II) precipitate darkens rapidly, eventually giving brown trihydroxotriaquairon(III):

$$4[Fe(OH)_2(H_2O)_4](s) + O_2(g) \rightarrow 4[Fe(OH)_3(H_2O)_3](s) + 2H_2O(l)$$

pale green   brown

Hexaaquairon(II) undergoes several ligand substitution reactions. For example, addition of a concentrated chloride solution gives the tetrahedral tetrachloroferrate(II), $[FeCl_4]^{2-}(aq)$. Except for hexacyanoferrate(II), *most iron(II) complexes are readily oxidised to iron(III) compounds.*

3+

Oxidation of aqueous hexaaquairon(II) gives a yellow-brown solution containing hydroxoaqua species, e.g. $[FeOH(H_2O)_5]^{2+}(aq)$. The purple hexaaquairon(III) is formed only in very strongly acidic conditions:

$$[Fe(H_2O)_6]^{3+}(aq) \rightleftharpoons [FeOH(H_2O)_5]^{2+}(aq) + H^+(aq)$$

purple   yellow-brown

Addition of alkali produces a brown precipitate of trihydroxotriaquairon(III) which is insoluble in moderate excess of alkali:

$$[FeOH(H_2O)_5]^{2+}(aq) + 2OH^-(aq) \underset{H^+(aq)}{\overset{OH^-(aq)}{\rightleftharpoons}} [Fe(OH)_3(H_2O)_3](s) + 2H_2O(l)$$

yellow-brown   brown

As with iron (II), iron (III) hydroxoaqua complexes undergo a variety of **ligand exchange reactions.** With potassium thiocyanate solution, KSCN(aq), a deep blood red thiocyanatoaqua complex is formed:

$$[FeOH(H_2O)_5]^{2+}(aq) + SCN^-(aq) \rightarrow [FeSCN(H_2O)_5]^{2+}(aq) + OH^-(aq)$$

yellow brown   intense blood red

This reaction is used as a very sensitive test for the presence of iron(III) in solution.

Although, generally, iron(III) is the most stable oxidation state, replacement of hydroxo and water ligands by cyanide ions gives hexacyanoferrate(III) which is *readily reduced* to hexacyanoferrate(II):

$$[FeOH(H_2O)_5]^{2+}(aq) + 6CN^-(aq) \rightarrow [Fe(CN)_6]^{3-}(aq) + OH^-(aq) + 5H_2O(l)$$

yellow-brown   brown
not readily reduced   easily reduced

Thus changing the type of ligand from OH⁻ and H₂O to CN⁻ has reversed the relative stabilities of iron(II) and iron(III).

31.4 Cobalt

Common oxidation states: +2 and +3.

Figure 31.4 *Outline chemistry of cobalt*

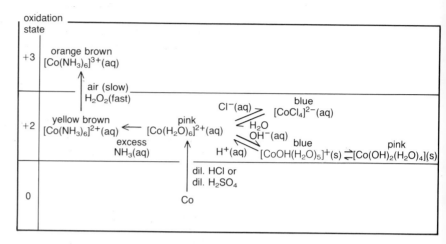

2+

The pink hexaaquacobalt(II) ion is obtained in solution when cobalt reacts with dilute hydrochloric or sulphuric acid.

$$Co(s) + 2H^+(aq) + 6H_2O(l) \rightarrow [Co(H_2O)_6]^{2+}(aq) + H_2(g)$$
$$\text{pink}$$

Cobalt(II) is generally the most stable oxidation state and this solution is very resistant to oxidation. The hexaaqua ion undergoes several ligand displacement reactions. Addition of aqueous sodium hydroxide first gives a blue precipitate containing the hydroxopentaaqua ion, but on standing in excess alkali pink dihydroxotetraaquacobalt(II) is formed.

$$[Co(H_2O)_6]^{2+}(aq) \underset{H^+(aq)}{\overset{OH^-(aq)}{\rightleftharpoons}} [CoOH(H_2O)_5]^+(s) \underset{H^+(aq)}{\overset{OH^-(aq)}{\rightleftharpoons}} [Co(OH)_2(H_2O)_4](s)$$
$$\text{pink} \qquad\qquad \text{blue} \qquad\qquad \text{pink}$$

High concentrations of chloride ions give the blue tetrachlorocobaltate(II) complex.

$$[Co(H_2O)_6]^{2+}(aq) + 4Cl^-(aq) \rightleftharpoons [CoCl_4]^{2-}(aq) + 6H_2O(l)$$
$$\text{pink} \qquad\qquad\qquad \text{blue}$$

The *ratio* of tetrachloro to hexaaqua complex in the solution depends upon the relative concentrations of the two ligands, i.e. H_2O and Cl^-. This reaction forms the basis for the well-known 'cobalt chloride' paper test for the presence of water. If a filter paper soaked in cobalt chloride solution is heated the water is driven off, leaving the blue tetrachloro complex. Exposure to water, even moist air, causes the colour to change to pink, owing to the formation of $[Co(H_2O)_6]^{2+}$.

Dropwise addition of ammonia solution to $[Co(H_2O)_6]^{2+}(aq)$ first gives a precipitate containing the blue hydroxopentaaqua ion,

$$[Co(H_2O)_6]^{2+}(aq) + OH^-(aq) \rightarrow [CoOH(H_2O)_5]^+(s) + H_2O$$

but this dissolves in excess ammonia to give yellow-brown hexaamminecobalt(II) ions:

$$[CoOH(H_2O)_5]^+(s) + 6NH_3(aq) \rightarrow [Co(NH_3)_6]^{2+}(aq) + OH^-(aq) + 5H_2O(l)$$
$$\text{blue} \qquad\qquad\qquad\qquad \text{yellow-brown}$$

With ammonia ligands, however, cobalt(II) is not the most stable oxidation state and it is readily oxidised to orange-brown hexaamminecobalt(III) by air, or more rapidly by hydrogen peroxide solution.

$$2[Co(NH_3)_6]^{2+}(aq) + H_2O_2(aq) \rightarrow 2[Co(NH_3)_6]^{3+}(aq) + 2OH^-(aq)$$
yellow-brown   orange-brown

3+

As we noted above, the ammine is the only common cobalt complex stable in this oxidation state. If the ammonia ligands are driven off by boiling with sodium hydroxide solution, a black precipitate of trihydroxotriaquacobalt(III) is produced.

$$[Co(NH_3)_6]^{2+}(aq) + 3OH^-(aq) + 3H_2O(l) \longrightarrow [Co(OH)_3(H_2O)_3](s) + 6NH_3(aq)$$
orange-brown   black

Unlike the stable hexaammine, the hydroxoaqua cobalt complex is readily reduced to cobalt(II) and acts as a powerful **oxidising agent**. It will, for example, produce iodine from an acidic solution of iodide ions:

$$Co^{3+}(aq) + I^-(aq) \rightarrow Co^{2+}(aq) + \tfrac{1}{2}I_2(aq)$$

31.5 Nickel

Common oxidation states: +2 only.

Figure 31.5 *Outline chemistry of nickel*

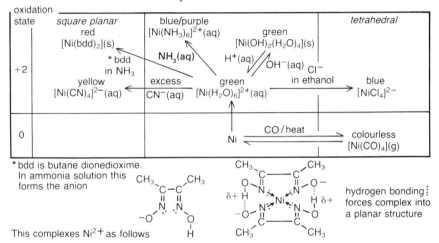

* bdd is butane dionedioxime.
In ammonia solution this forms the anion

This complexes Ni^{2+} as follows

hydrogen bonding forces complex into a planar structure

Nickel dissolves in dilute hydrochloric or sulphuric acid to give the green hexaaqua complex.

$$Ni(s) + 2H^+(aq) + 6H_2O(l) \rightarrow [Ni(H_2O)_6]^{2+}(aq) + H_2(g)$$
green

Addition of aqueous sodium hydroxide to this solution precipitates pale green dihydroxotetraaquanickel(II) which is insoluble in moderate excess of alkali:

$$[Ni(H_2O)_6]^{2+}(aq) + 2OH^-(aq) \underset{H^+(aq)}{\overset{OH^-(aq)}{\rightleftharpoons}} [Ni(OH)_2(H_2O)_4](s) + 2H_2O(l)$$
green   pale green

Ammonia solution first gives the dihydroxotetraaqua complex but this dissolves in excess of the reagent to give a purple solution containing hexaamminenickel(II):

$$[Ni(H_2O)_6]^{2+}(aq) + 6NH_3(aq) \rightarrow [Ni(NH_3)_6]^{2+}(aq) + 6H_2O(l)$$
green   purple

Nickel(II) also forms several 4-coordinate complexes. The blue tetrachloro complex formed in non-aqueous solution is **tetrahedral**,

$$[Ni(H_2O)_6]^{2+} + 4Cl^- \rightleftharpoons [NiCl_4]^{2-} + 6H_2O$$

but *nickel(II) also forms many square planar complexes which are generally yellow or red.* Addition of aqueous cyanide to a solution of hexaaquanickel(II) first gives a pale green precipitate of nickel(II) cyanide, but this dissolves in excess to give the **square planar** yellow tetracyanonickelate(II) ion.

$$[Ni(H_2O)_6]^{2+}(aq) + 2CN^-(aq) \rightarrow Ni(CN)_2(s) + 6H_2O(l)$$
green   pale green

$$Ni(CN)_2(s) + 2CN^-(aq) \rightarrow [Ni(CN)_4]^{2-}(aq)$$
pale green   yellow

The red square planar complex formed by nickel(II) with butanedione dioxime in ammonia solution, illustrated in figure 31.5, is used as a test for the presence of nickel(II). The metal may also be estimated *quantitatively* by filtering off, drying and then weighing the precipitate.

Activity 31.3

0.119 g of a nickel(II) compound was dissolved in water. Addition of ammonia and a slight excess of butanedione dioxime solution, $C_4H_8N_2O_2$, quantitatively precipitated the complex $[Ni(C_4H_7N_2O_2)_2]$. When this was filtered off and dried its mass was found to be 0.145 g.

1. What mass of nickel(II) is contained in the precipitate?
2. What is the % by mass of nickel in the original sample?

(Relative Atomic Masses: Ni = 59, O = 16, C = 12, N = 14, H = 1)

Finely divided nickel reacts with carbon monoxide on gentle warming to give the gaseous tetracarbonylnickel(0). Since the ligand is a neutral molecule the oxidation state of the metal in this complex is zero:

$$Ni(s) + 4CO(g) \underset{\text{heat strongly}}{\overset{\text{warm gently}}{\rightleftharpoons}} [Ni(CO)_4](g)$$
tetracarbonylnickel(0)

This reaction has been used in the 'Mond' process for the purification of nickel. The gaseous complex is separated from any solid impurity and the pure metal recovered by raising the temperature.

31.6 Copper

Common oxidation states: +1 and +2.

Figure 31.6   *Outline chemistry of copper*

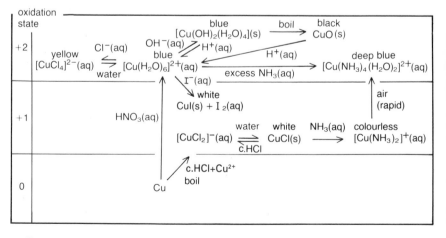

+2

We shall deal with this oxidation state first since it is generally more stable, especially in aqueous solution. Copper does *not* react with dilute hydrochloric or sulphuric acids but gives a blue solution containing hexaaquacopper(II) ions with nitric acid. Hydrogen is not produced but oxides of nitrogen are given off, nitrogen dioxide from concentrated acid but mainly nitrogen monoxide from more dilute solution:

$$Cu(s) + 4HNO_3(aq) + 4H_2O(l) \rightarrow [Cu(H_2O)_6]^{2+}(aq) + 2NO_2(aq) + 2NO_3^-(aq)$$
conc.   blue

$$3Cu(s) + 8HNO_3(aq) + 14H_2O(l) \rightarrow 3[Cu(H_2O)_6]^{2+}(aq) + 2NO(g) + 6NO_3^-(aq)$$
dil.

Addition of sodium hydroxide solution gives a blue precipitate of dihydroxotetraaquacopper(II) which is insoluble in moderate access of the alkali:

$$[Cu(H_2O)_6]^{2+}(aq) + 2OH^-(aq) \rightleftharpoons [Cu(OH)_2(H_2O)_4](s) + 2H_2O(l)$$
blue

If the mixture is boiled the precipitate turns black, since loss of water occurs to give copper(II) oxide:

$$[Cu(OH)_2(H_2O)_4](s) \xrightarrow{\text{heat}} CuO(s) + 5H_2O(l)$$
blue   black

If ammonia solution is used instead of sodium hydroxide, the hydroxoaqua complex is precipitated first but this dissolves in excess ammonia to give a deep blue solution containing tetraamminediaquacopper(II) ions. This characteristic colour change is used as a test for the presence of Cu^{2+} in aqueous solution:

$$[Cu(H_2O)_6]^{2+}(aq) + 4NH_3(aq) \rightarrow [Cu(NH_3)_4(H_2O)_2]^{2+}(aq) + 4H_2O(l)$$
blue   (excess)   deep blue

Addition of concentrated hydrochloric acid to the blue hexaaqua ion gives the tetrahedral yellow tetrachlorocuprate(II) ion. The reaction is reversed by diluting with water:

$$[Cu(H_2O)_6]^{2+}(aq) + 4Cl^-(aq) \underset{H_2O(l)}{\overset{Cl^-(aq)}{\rightleftharpoons}} [CuCl_4]^{2-}(aq) + 6H_2O(l)$$
blue   yellow

+1 ───

Copper(I) is normally made by *reducing* copper(II) in aqueous solution. Copper(I) chloride, for example, may be made by reducing boiling tetrachlorocuprate(II) with copper in concentrated hydrochloric acid. This forms the linear dichlorocuprate(I) ion:

$$[CuCl_4]^{2-}(aq) + Cu(s) \xrightarrow{\text{boil}} 2[CuCl_2]^-(aq)$$
yellow

Copper(I) chloride separates as a white precipitate when this solution is poured into excess water.

$$[CuCl_2]^-(aq) \underset{\text{c. HCl(aq)}}{\overset{H_2O(l)}{\rightleftharpoons}} CuCl(s) + Cl^-(aq)$$
white

A red precipitate of copper(I) oxide is formed by reduction of a copper(II) complex in alkaline solution. This forms the basis of **Fehling's test** for aldehydes in organic chemistry, e.g.

$$2Cu^{2+}(aq) + CH_3CHO(aq) + OH^-(aq) + H_2O(l)$$
$$\text{blue} \qquad \text{(aldehyde)}$$

$$\rightarrow Cu_2O(s) + CH_3COO^-(aq) + 4H^+(aq)$$
$$\text{red} \qquad \text{(acid salt)}$$

Iodide ions immediately reduce $Cu^{2+}(aq)$, giving an off-white precipitate of copper(I) iodide:

$$Cu^{2+}(aq) + 2I^-(aq) \rightarrow CuI(s) + \tfrac{1}{2}I_2(aq)$$
$$\text{blue} \qquad\qquad \text{off-white} \quad \text{brown}$$

The iodine liberated in this reaction may be titrated with standard sodium thiosulphate solution, giving a measure of the $Cu^{2+}(aq)$ originally present in the solution.

Activity 31.4

The following experiment was carried out on a sample of hydrated copper(II) chloride in order to find the number of molecules of water of crystallisation, x, in the formula $CuCl_2.xH_2O$.

4.668 g of the solid was dissolved in water and the volume of the solution made up to exactly 250 cm³ in a graduated flask. Excess aqueous potassium iodide was added to 25 cm³ portions of this solution. In a titration, 27.3 cm³ of 0.1 M sodium thiosulphate were needed to react with the liberated iodine, according to the equation:

$$I_2(aq) + 2S_2O_3^{2-}(aq) \rightarrow 2I^-(aq) + S_4O_6^{2-}(aq)$$

1 How many moles of sodium thiosulphate were used in the titration?
2 How many moles of iodine were produced from 25 cm³ of the copper chloride solution?
3 How many moles of $Cu^{2+}(aq)$ were present in 25 cm³ of solution?
4 How many moles of anhydrous copper chloride, $CuCl_2$, were present in the original sample?
5 What was the mass of $CuCl_2$ in the original sample?
6 What mass of water did the original sample contain?
7 How many moles of water did the sample contain?
8 How many molecules of water of crystallisation are associated with one mole of copper chloride?

(Relative Atomic Masses: Cu = 64, Cl = 35.5, H = 1, O = 16)

You may have noticed that, with the exception of the dichlorocuprate(I) complex ion, most of the copper(I) species we have mentioned so far are *insoluble* solids. This is because *in aqueous solution simple $Cu^+(aq)$ ions are unstable. They undergo self oxidation–reduction, i.e.* **disproportionation**, *to give copper and $Cu^{2+}(aq)$.* For example, copper(I) oxide reacts with dilute acid as follows:

$$Cu_2O(s) \xrightarrow{H^+(aq)} 2Cu^+(aq) \xrightarrow[\text{reaction}]{\text{immediate}} Cu(s) + Cu^{2+}(aq)$$
$$2(+1) \qquad\qquad 2(+1) \qquad\qquad (0) \qquad (+2)$$
$$\text{red} \qquad\qquad \text{colourless} \qquad\qquad \text{brown} \quad \text{blue}$$

Most other copper(I) complex ions, although not subject to disproportionation are quite readily *oxidised* to copper(II). Thus copper(I) chloride will dissolve in ammonia to give a colourless solution containing the linear diamminecopper(I) ion. On exposure to air, however, this is rapidly converted into deep blue tetraamminediaquacopper(II).

$$CuCl(s) + 2NH_3(aq) \rightarrow [Cu(NH_3)_2]^+(aq) \xrightarrow{\text{air}} [Cu(NH_3)_4(H_2O)_2]^{2+}(aq)$$
$$\text{white} \qquad\qquad\qquad \text{colourless} \qquad\qquad \text{deep blue}$$

31.7 Zinc

Common oxidation state: +2 only.

Figure 31.7 *Outline chemistry of zinc*

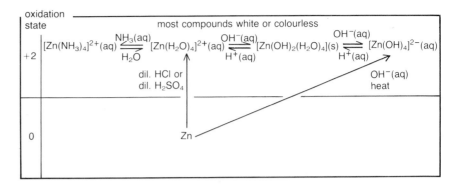

Figure 31.7 *Outline chemistry of zinc*

As the last member of the 'd' block row, both zinc and zinc(II) have a *completely full* 3d electronic sub-level. As a result, neither the element nor its compounds exhibit the properties characteristic of transition metals and *it more closely resembles Group II in its chemistry*. Most zinc complexes are, for example, colourless or white.

Zinc forms a **tetraaqua complex** on dissolving in dilute acid.

$$Zn(s) + 2H^+(aq) + 4H_2O(l) \rightarrow [Zn(H_2O)_4]^{2+}(aq) + H_2(g)$$

Addition of sodium hydroxide first gives a precipitate of dihydroxodiaquazinc(II) which dissolves in excess of the alkali to give tetrahydroxozincate(II). Similar observations are made if ammonia solution is used in place of sodium hydroxide, but the final solution contains the tetraammine complex:

$$[Zn(H_2O)_4]^{2+}(aq) \underset{H^+(aq)}{\overset{OH^-(aq)}{\rightleftharpoons}} [Zn(OH)_2(H_2O)_2](s) \underset{H^+(aq)}{\overset{OH^-(aq)}{\rightleftharpoons}} [Zn(OH)_4]^{2-}(aq)$$

$$\text{NH}_3(aq) \, \Big\Updownarrow \, H_2O(l)$$

$$[Zn(NH_3)_4]^{2+}(aq)$$

Zinc metal itself will dissolve *directly* in hot concentrated sodium hydroxide solution to give a solution of tetrahydroxozincate(II), this reflecting the amphoteric nature of zinc metal.

31.8 Silver

Common oxidation state: +1 only.

Figure 31.8 *Outline chemistry of silver*

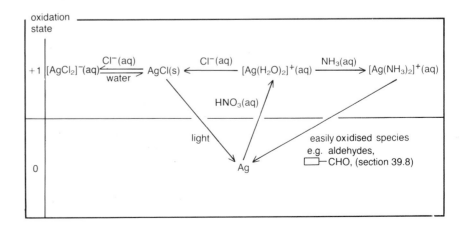

Figure 31.8 *Outline chemistry of silver*

As we might expect, the chemistry of silver shows some similarity to that of copper. The main difference is the greater stability of silver(I), which unlike copper(I), is resistant to disproportionation and oxidation.

Like copper, silver is not sufficiently electronegative to displace hydrogen from dilute acids, but it will dissolve in nitric acid to give oxides of nitrogen and a solution containing diaquasilver(I) ions, e.g.

$$3Ag(s) + 4HNO_3(aq) + 4H_2O(l) \rightarrow 3[Ag(H_2O)]^+(aq) + 3NO_3^-(aq) + NO(g)$$
(dilute)   colourless

Addition of sodium hydroxide to diaquasilver(I) first gives a precipitate of the unstable hydroxide which decomposes to leave brown silver(I) oxide:

$$2[Ag(H_2O)_2]^+(aq) \xrightarrow{\text{OH}^-(aq)} 2AgOH(s) \longrightarrow Ag_2O(s)$$
colourless   brown

If ammonia is used in place of the sodium hydroxide solution, the silver(I) oxide dissolves in excess to give a colourless solution containing diamminesilver(I), $[Ag(NH_3)_2]^+$. This liquid, known as **Tollen's reagent**, is used in organic analysis as a test for aliphatic aldehydes (section 39.8.1). The aldehyde reduces diamminesilver(I) to a silver 'mirror', being itself oxidised to a carboxylic acid:

$$2[Ag(NH_3)_2]^+(aq) + 2OH^-(aq) + CH_3CHO(aq) \rightarrow$$
$$2Ag(s) + H_2O(l) + CH_3COONH_4(aq) + 3NH_3(aq)$$

Except for fluoride, addition of halide ions to $[Ag(H_2O)_2]^+(aq)$ first gives a precipitate of the insoluble silver(I) halide. Silver(I) chloride dissolves in concentrated chloride solutions to give dichloroargentate(I):

$$[Ag(H_2O)_2]^+(aq) \xrightarrow{\text{Cl}^-(aq)} AgCl(s) \xrightarrow{\text{Cl}^-(aq)} [AgCl_2]^-(aq)$$
colourless   (dilute)   white   (conc.)   colourless

Silver(I) chloride also dissolves in *dilute* ammonia solution, giving the diammine. Silver bromide undergoes a similar reaction with *concentrated* ammonia solution, but the iodide is *insoluble*. In common with many silver(I) compounds, the halides are light sensitive, undergoing **photochemical decomposition** into the elements:

$$\text{e.g.} \quad 2AgCl(s) \xrightarrow{\text{light}} 2Ag(s) + Cl_2(g)$$
white   black

Photographic film depends upon this type of 'photochemical' reaction.

31.9 Comments on the activities

Activity 31.1

1   Combining the two half-equations,

$$Cr_2O_7^{2-}(aq) + 14H^+(aq) + 6e^- \rightarrow 2Cr^{3+}(aq) + 7H_2O(l)$$
$$Fe^{2+}(aq) \rightarrow Fe^{3+}(aq) + e^- \qquad (\times 6)$$

$$Cr_2O_7^{2-}(aq) + 14H^+(aq) + 6Fe^{2+}(aq) \rightarrow 2Cr^{3+}(aq) + 7H_2O(l) + 6Fe^{3+}(aq)$$

2   (a) $1000\,cm^3$ of $0.02\,M\ K_2Cr_2O_7$ contains $0.02\,mol\ Cr_2O_7^{2-}$

        $20.5\,cm^3$ of $0.02\,M\,K_2Cr_2O_7$ contains $\dfrac{0.02 \times 20.5}{1000} = 0.00041\,mol$

(b) Moles of iron in titration $= 6 \times 0.00041 = 0.00246$. *But only a tenth of the total solution was used in the titration,* so moles of iron in original sample $= 0.0246$.

(c) Mass of iron in steel sample $= 0.0246 \times 56 = 1.3776\,g$

$\therefore$ % by mass of iron in the steel $= \dfrac{1.3776}{1.400} \times 100 = 98.4\%$.

Activity 31.2

1   Combining the two half-equations,

$$MnO_4^-(aq) + 8H^+(aq) + 5e^- \rightarrow Mn^{2+}(aq) + 4H_2O(l) \qquad (\times 2)$$
$$H_2C_2O_4(aq) \rightarrow 2H^+(aq) + 2CO_2(aq) + 2e^- \; (\times 5)$$

$$2MnO_4^-(aq) + 16H^+(aq) + 5H_2C_2O_4(aq) \rightarrow$$
$$2Mn^{2+}(aq) + 8H_2O(l) + 10H^+(aq) + 10CO_2(g)$$

Cancelling $H^+(aq)$ ions on each side of the equation, this becomes

$$2MnO_4^-(aq) + 6H^+(aq) + 5H_2C_2O_4 \rightarrow$$
$$2Mn^{2+}(aq) + 8H_2O(l) + 10CO_2(g)$$

2   (a) M_r of $H_2C_2O_4.2H_2O = 126$. Thus,

moles of acid $= 0.630/126 = 0.005$ moles

(b) Moles of acid used in the titration $= 0.005 \times 25/100$
$= 0.00125$ moles

(c) Moles of manganate(VII) used in titration $= 0.00125 \times 2/5$
$= 0.0005$ moles

(d) There are 0.0005 moles of MnO_4^- in $27.9\,cm^3$ of solution.

Therefore, $\dfrac{0.0005 \times 1000}{27.9} = 0.0179$ moles per dm^3.

Concentration of $KMnO_4$ solution $= 0.0179\,M$.

Activity 31.3

1   $Ni^{2+}(aq) \rightarrow [Ni(C_4H_7N_2O_2)_2]$
     1 mole   1 mole
     59 g   289 g

i.e. each gram of complex contains $59/289 = 0.204\,g$ of nickel. Precipitate contains $0.204 \times 0.145 = 0.0296\,g$ of nickel.

2   % of nickel in original sample $= \dfrac{\text{mass of nickel}}{\text{mass of sample}} \times 100$

$= \dfrac{0.0296}{0.119} \times 100$

$= 24.9\%$ of nickel

Activity 31.4

1   $1000\,cm^3$ of $0.1\,M$ $Na_2S_2O_3$ contains 0.1 moles.
$27.3\,cm^3$ of $0.1\,M$ $Na_2S_2O_3$ contains $0.1 \times 27.3/1000 = 0.00273$ moles.

2   From the equation given, 2 moles of $Na_2S_2O_3$ are needed for each mole of I_2.
Therefore $0.00273/2 = 0.001\,365$ moles of I_2 are liberated by $25\,cm^3$ of the copper chloride solution.

3   From the equation in section 31.6, 2 moles of Cu^{2+} (aq) are needed to liberate each mole of I_2.
    Therefore $0.001365 \times 2 = 0.00273$ moles of Cu^{2+}(aq) are present in $25 \, cm^3$ of solution.

4   *Since only 25 cm³ out of a total 250 cm³ of solution were used in the titration,* there must have been $0.00273 \times 10 = 0.0273$ moles of $CuCl_2$ in the original sample.

5   Mass of 1 mole of $CuCl_2 = 64 + 2(35.5) = 135 \, g$,
    Thus mass of $CuCl_2$ in original sample $= 0.0273 \times 135 = 3.686 \, g$.

6   Since $4.668 \, g$ of original sample contains $3.686 \, g$ of $CuCl_2$, it must contain $4.668 - 3.686 = 0.982 \, g$ water of crystallisation.

7   1 mole of water weighs $18 \, g$,
    therefore $0.982 \, g$ water $= 0.982/18 = 0.546$ moles.

8   The sample contains $0.0273 \, mol \, CuCl_2$ and $0.0546 \, mol \, H_2O$. Molecules of water associated with each $CuCl_2 = 0.0546/0.0273 = 2$.
    Thus, formula of the hydrated copper(II) chloride is $CuCl_2.2H_2O$.

31.10   Summary and revision plan

Figures 31.1 to 31.8 summarise the chemistry of some important 'd' block complexes. Use these, together with your examination syllabus, to devise a revision scheme.

Organic Chemistry – an Overview

In 1807, the famous Swedish chemist Berzelius proposed that chemicals should be divided into two distinct categories, organic and inorganic. Substances which existed in, or were created by, plants or animals were termed **organic**. It was thought that these materials could only be formed in living organisms via some kind of mystical **'vital force'**. **Inorganic** compounds, on the other hand, were far less mysterious since they could easily be obtained from mineral sources. This division largely resulted from chemists' lack of knowledge of naturally occurring compounds. At that time, it was very difficult to extract organic chemicals in a pure enough form for analysis.

Up to 1828, only a handful of organic chemicals had been identified. It was in that year, though, that the German chemist Wohler made a remarkable discovery. He prepared one of these organic compounds, urea, from an inorganic starting material, ammonium cyanate:

$$NH_4CNO(aq) \xrightarrow{\text{evaporation}} \begin{array}{c} H_2N \\ \diagdown \\ C=O \\ \diagup \\ H_2N \end{array}$$

ammonium cyanate   urea

At first, Wohler's research made little impact on the supporters of the 'vital force' theory. Indeed, it was not until the 1850s that the idea of a vital force was finally discredited. By that time, many more organic compounds had been prepared and successfully analysed. Consequently, with a few exceptions (e.g. CO, CO_2 and carbonates), organic chemistry was re-defined as *the chemistry of carbon compounds*.

During the last 140 years, our knowledge of organic compounds, and their uses, has increased many times over. Indeed, a recent estimate suggested that there are upwards of 2.5 million known organic compounds.

In the late nineteenth century, the main source of organic chemicals was coal tar, a by-product of the coal industry. This was used as starting material in the manufacture of a variety of household and industrial products, such as dyes, paints, disinfectants and solvents. Nowadays, about 80% of organic substances are made, directly or indirectly, from one of the components of crude oil or **petroleum** (section 34.4). Petroleum, then, is the world's major organic chemical feedstock.

A large number of organic products are now a common, and often irreplaceable, feature of everyday life. Some are prepared in vast amounts (e.g. plastics, detergents and solvents); others are manufactured in small quantities for more specialist uses (e.g. drugs and pesticides).

Although many organic compounds occur naturally, most commercial products are synthetic; this process is called **synthesis**. Some synthetic pathways are short and straightforward, e.g. the manufacture of ethanol by the hydration of ethene:

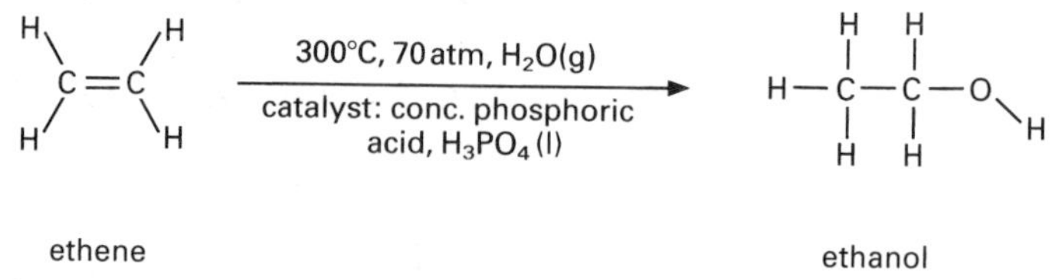

ethene ethanol

More complex organic substances often need longer synthetic routes, e.g. aspirin:

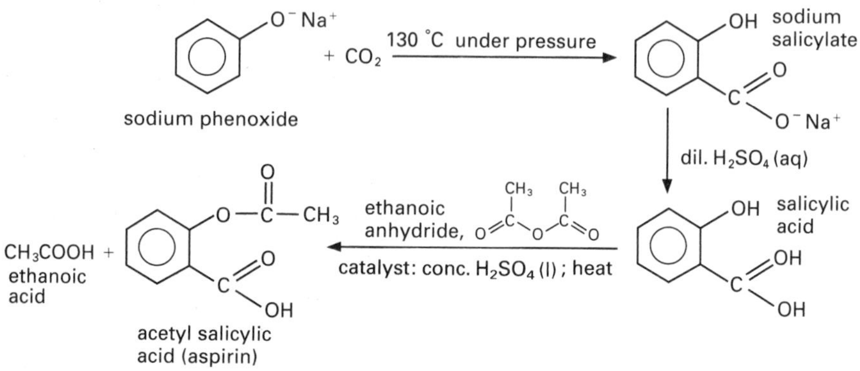

Aspirin, one of the first synthetic drugs, was developed in 1899. Since then, thousands of drugs have been prepared and, in many cases, these are sold under a variety of trade names.

As you can imagine, the business of selling drugs and other organic chemicals is highly profitable, especially when petroleum prices are low. Very often, though, these profits are needed to finance the enormous capital investment associated with the research, development, testing and production of a new chemical product. A new drug, for example, will seldom go from planning to production in less than 15 years.

The purpose of our study is to give you an insight into the world of the organic chemist. Whether in the school or industrial laboratory, organic chemistry is based on common principles and techniques. Admittedly, you will only have access to situations involving relatively simple organic materials. However, the way problems are tackled requires an approach almost identical to that used by industrial organic chemists.

When working through each of the following chapters, you will find it useful to keep in mind three general points.

1 Organic synthesis

Organic synthesis changes a starting material into the required product via one, or more, stages. Usually, each stage will involve a chemical reaction between the **starting material** (or an intermediate product), and a **chemical reagent**.

$$\text{STARTING MATERIAL} \xrightarrow{\text{Reagent 1}} \text{INTERMEDIATE PRODUCT} \xrightarrow{\text{Reagent 2}} \text{FINAL PRODUCT}$$

For example, in the manufacture of ethanol, given earlier, the reagent is steam in the presence of concentrated phosphoric acid as catalyst. This reagent does a certain 'job', namely, it adds water to a $C{=}C$ bond; consequently, $H_2O(g)$/conc. $H_3PO_4(l)$ is called a **hydrating agent**.

The aim of any synthesis is to cause a desired alteration to a molecule's structure. To do this, we must use a suitable reagent, often under *carefully controlled conditions*. You would not use, for example, a toothbrush to paint a door in the pouring rain!

One **key aspect** of our work, then, is the planning of synthetic pathways. When you have to do this:

▶ *remember that reagents do specific 'jobs'*. Thus, get to know these reagents and, perhaps, compile a list as you work through the text.

▶ *always state the temperature, pressure and, where relevant, physical states of the reactants, reaction times and any special reaction techniques.*

We shall expand on this in chapter 32.

2   *The systematic nature of organic chemistry*

There are over 2.5 million organic chemicals. It would be a very large book or computer file which could store the chemical properties of all these compounds. Yet, after studying chapters 32 to 41, you will be able to comment on the probable chemical reactions of almost any organic substance just by looking at its molecular structure.

For the purpose of ordering the study, the following chapters are arranged under functional group headings. A **functional group** *is an atom, or group of atoms, which impart characteristic chemical properties to any organic compound in which they appear.* It is very important that you do not view each chapter as an isolated mass of information. Look out for the links between functional groups which are stressed in the text and the activities. In this way, you will develop the systematic approach which leads to a better understanding of organic chemistry.

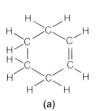

(a)

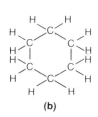

(b)

3   *Identification of organic compounds*

To determine the molecular structure of an organic compound, we need to use the modern instrumental techniques described in chapter 6. However, where these are not available, *we can still identify the presence of a particular functional group by studying simple chemical reactions of the compound.* Suppose, for example, that you were asked to distinguish between the liquids cyclohexene (a) and cyclohexane (b). From their structural formulae, we can see that both molecules possess C—H and C—C bonds but only the cyclohexene has a C=C bond. Hence, we test each liquid with a reagent which reacts with a C=C bond but not with a C—H or C—C bond, e.g. by shaking with bromine water.

cyclohexane + bromine water → no reaction
BUT cyclohexene + bromine water → reaction (orange bromine
colour disappears)

Thus, the colour change, or lack of it, distinguishes the compounds.

The identification of functional groups using simple laboratory tests is another **key aspect** *of this study.*

□ CHAPTER □
CHAPTER · CHAPTER

32

CHAPTER · CHAPTER
□ CHAPTER □

Organic Synthesis

Contents

Converting an organic starting material into the final pure product may require a number of synthetic steps. Each step involves:

▶ planning and performing the chemical reaction;
▶ separating the crude product and purifying it;
▶ analysing the product to ensure that it is the desired compound.

This chapter looks at some of the ways you might carry out these tasks.

32.1 Planning and performing the experiment

If the reaction has been performed before, you will be able to find the procedure in a reference text. Some modifications may be needed; for example, if double the quantity of product is required, then the amounts of reactants will also need to be doubled. However, if you are the first person to try the synthesis, it may be necessary to repeat the reaction under varied experimental conditions (e.g. reactant concentrations, temperature and pressure, ways of mixing the reactants and so on). Eventually, you can work out which set of conditions gives the most economical yield of product (section 32.9).

Organic chemicals are usually volatile and inflammable; many are also toxic. These hazards must be borne in mind when planning the experimental procedure and designing the apparatus. Nowadays, small-scale organic syntheses are performed in

Smoke billows from a chemical plant at Flixborough, near Scunthorpe, after a massive explosion ripped through it on 6th January 1974. Buildings were levelled to the ground and dozens of people were injured or killed. Like the accident at Chernobyl, this one was attributed to human error rather than poor plant design

hard glassware which fits closely together via ground glass joints. Before use, these joints are lightly smeared with high melting point grease. This improves the seal and allows the glassware to be easily dismantled after use. In industry, large-scale preparations are usually carried out in stainless steel vessels.

Whether it is performed in school or industry, there are three important aspects of any organic synthesis, and these are described below.

Heating and cooling the reaction mixture

When heating is necessary, a **reflux apparatus** is used (figure 32.1). As the reaction mixture boils, vapour passes into the condenser where it is liquefied and falls back into the flask. No vapour is able to escape into the atmosphere.

Another consideration is the source of heat. Obviously, using a Bunsen burner could present a danger of fire or explosion. Thus, we use (i) a bath containing water (up to 100°C) or liquid paraffin (up to 220°C) or (ii) an electric heater (up to 300°C).

For highly exothermic reactions, cooling may be necessary. To do this, the reaction flask is placed in one of the following: (i) cold water (room temperature), (ii) an ice/salt/water mixture (−10°C) or (iii) a mixture of solid carbon dioxide and ethanol (−40°C). The temperatures of these cooling mixtures are shown in brackets.

Mixing the reactants together

Often, it is necessary to mix the reactants together in small portions whilst the reaction is proceeding. This is achieved by using a double (or triple) necked flask fitted with a dropping funnel.

One interesting example of the value of gradually mixing reactants is the preparation of ethanal by using acidified potassium dichromate(VI)(aq) to oxidise ethanol. If the reactants are mixed before heating, any ethanal which forms is further oxidised to ethanoic acid:

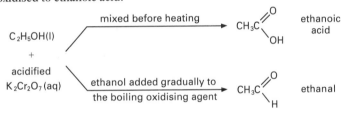

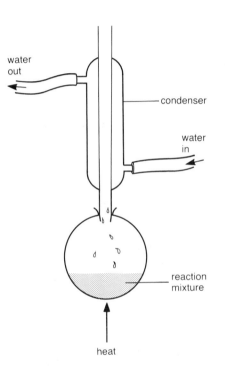

Figure 32.1 *A reflux apparatus allows us to boil reaction mixtures containing volatile substances*

However, if the ethanol is added *gradually* to the hot oxidising agent, ethanal can be distilled off as it is formed. Ethanal has a much lower boiling point (20°C) than ethanol (78°C), since the latter contains fairly strong hydrogen bonds. So, by adding the ethanol dropwise to the oxidising agent (at 70°C), the ethanal distils off and further oxidation is minimised. Using this method, only a small amount of ethanoic acid (b.p. = 118°C) is formed and this remains in the reaction flask.

Stirring the reaction mixture

Stirring is used to help the reactants mix together and to distribute heat evenly throughout the reaction mixture. Two types of stirrer are available: (i) a mechanical overhead stirrer or (ii) a magnetic stirring bead which spins round in time with a larger magnet rotating below the reaction flask.

We can also make reaction mixtures boil more 'evenly' by adding a few small bits of porcelain called **'anti-bumping' granules**.

Finally, we must stress the need for stringent **safety precautions** when preparing organic compounds. Where possible, reactions should be performed in a fume cupboard, away from any naked flames. Of course, safety clothing and goggles should be worn. It is also important to know the location of fire-fighting equipment and how to use it.

A triple-necked flask fitted with a dropping funnel and an overhead mechanical stirrer being refluxed on an electric heating mantle. The student is adding one of the reactants in portions from the dropping funnel

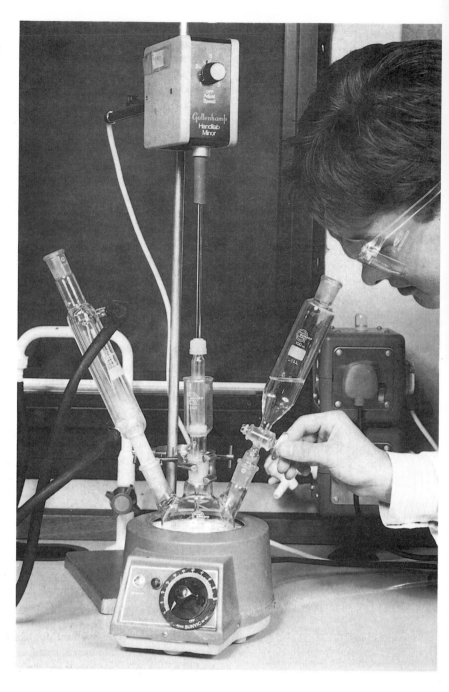

32.2 Separating the crude product and purifying it

When the reaction has finished, the desired product is described as being in a **crude** state. Often, it is heavily contaminated, perhaps by unused reactants, a catalyst, solvent or a reaction by-product. Thus, the synthetic chemist's next job is to separate the product from these impurities.

Some of the most commonly used separation techniques are listed in table 32.1. As you can see, the choice of technique is governed by the physical states of the product and its impurities.

We shall now look briefly at each method.

Table 32.1 *Some common separation techniques and their uses*

Technique	used to separate
solvent extraction	a solid or liquid from its solution
distillation	a liquid from a dissolved non-volatile solid or liquids with very different boiling points
fractional distillation	liquids which have similar boiling points
steam distillation	a high boiling point liquid from a non-volatile solid
recrystallisation	a solid from other solid impurities
filtration	an insoluble solid from a liquid
chromatography (various techniques)	mixtures of solids, volatile liquids or gases

Which technique(s) could be used to separate the following mixtures:
(a) propan–l–ol, b.p. 97 °C and 1-iodopropane, b.p. 103 °C;
(b) phenylamine, b.p. 184 °C and tin(II) chloride;
(c) pentane, b.p. 36 °C, hexane, b.p. 69 °C and heptane, b.p. 99 °C;
(d) benzoic acid(s) contaminated by charcoal dust?

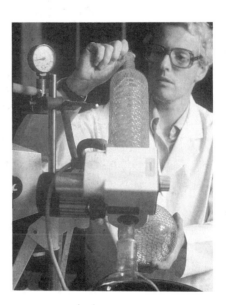

A rotary evaporator in use

32.3 Distillation and fractional distillation

Have a quick look at the description of these techniques in section 16.1.

Distillation is used to separate a liquid from either a dissolved non-volatile solid or another liquid. In the latter case, the two liquids must have *very different* boiling points, e.g. the separation of phenylamine (b.p. = 184 °C) from its solution in ethoxyethane (b.p. = 25 °C). Mixtures of miscible liquids with *similar* boiling points can often be separated by using **fractional distillation**. This technique is widely used in the chemical industry, e.g. to separate the hydrocarbon components in petroleum (section 34.4).

Distillation and fractional distillation can be performed at reduced pressure, e.g. by using a **rotary evaporator**. A liquid boils when its vapour pressure equals the external pressure. Therefore, by lowering the external pressure, the liquid will boil at a lower temperature. Hence, distillation at reduced pressure is used to purify liquids which decompose below their boiling points.

32.4 Steam distillation

An organic liquid which has a *high boiling point and very low solubility in water* can be removed from a mixture by **steam distillation**. Steam is passed through the hot mixture and the distillate is collected (see figure 16.9). On standing, the distillate forms two layers; one is the organic product, the other is aqueous. These are separated and any product in the aqueous layer is removed by **solvent extraction**. The theory of steam distillation was discussed in section 16.3.

32.5 Solvent extraction

In this technique, the 'crude' product is shaken up with a small quantity of a volatile solvent in which only the product is soluble. After filtering off any solid impurities (if necessary), the mixture is transferred to a separating funnel. On standing, the mixture divides into two distinct layers, which can be run off separately. We keep the layer containing the product; this is called an **extract**. Since small amounts of product still remain in other layer, the shaking and separation procedure is repeated twice, each time using fresh solvent. All the product extracts are combined.

Solvent extraction is often used to separate an organic product which is contaminated by an aqueous solution. Such extracts will always contain a small amount of water and this is removed by 'drying' it with an *anhydrous* ionic salt, e.g. magnesium sulphate. Usually, drying takes a few hours, after which time the ionic salt (which is now partially hydrated) is filtered off.

Finally, we must remove the volatile solvent from the dried extracts. This is easily achieved using a rotary evaporator. The resulting product is then further purified by fractional distillation (for liquids), or recrystallisation (for solids).

The theory of solvent extraction is discussed in section 16.5.

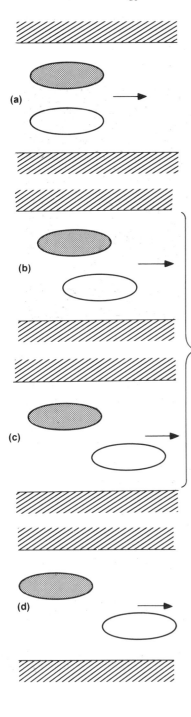

Figure 32.2 *Chromatographic separation of two substances ○ and ◉, as time passes from (a) → (d). Since ○ is less strongly attracted to the stationary phase, it moves along more readily with the moving phase.*

(a)

(b)

(c)

direction of moving phase

(d)

32.6 Recrystallisation

Recrystallisation is used to separate a solid product from other solid impurities. In this technique, we choose a solvent in which:

▶ the product readily dissolves when hot but hardly does so when cold;
▶ the impurities must either not dissolve or remain dissolved at low temperatures.

Often, the selection of this solvent is simply a case of 'trial and error'.
A solid product can be purified by recrystallisation from water. The impure solid is dissolved in the minimum quantity of hot water. Impurities which are insoluble in water can be removed by quickly filtering through a fluted filter paper held in a hot funnel. What would happen if the funnel was cold?

As the filtrate cools, any soluble impurities remain in solution while the pure product crystallises out. The crystals are filtered off using a **vacuum filtration** apparatus. Apart from giving a rapid filtration, vacuum filtration has the added advantage that the flow of air past the crystals helps them to dry out.

The final drying of an organic solid is carried out in either a desiccator at low pressure or an oven. The method chosen will depend on the properties of the solvent and the solid, e.g. the latter might decompose in an oven.

32.7 Chromatography

Chromatography is a particularly valuable technique since it enables us to separate very complex mixtures, even where the components are present in small amounts.

In chromatography, *the components can be separated because of their different strengths of attraction for a stationary phase and a moving phase* (figure 32.2). As a result, the moving phase carries the components through the stationary phase at different rates and a separation is achieved.

There are various chromatographic methods and you can find full experimental details in a practical chemistry textbook. We shall just outline two procedures commonly used by organic chemists: thin-layer chromatography and gas–liquid chromatography.

Thin-layer chromatography

This is used to separate a mixture of solids. As the name implies, the stationary phase is a thin layer of solid, supported on a glass plate. The moving phase is a liquid.

The photograph describes the use of thin-layer chromatography (TLC) to separate the coloured components in black ink. Here the stationary phase is alumina (Al_2O_3) and the moving phase is a mixture of butan-1-ol, ethanol and ammonia. Why choose this mixture? Simply, because it gives a good separation! Very often the choice of stationary and moving phases is based on 'trial and error' experiments.

Thin layer chromatography. A drop of black ink is applied to a thin layer plate using a fine capillary tube. The thin layer plate is allowed to dip into the solvent (a mixture of butan-1-ol, ethanol and aqueous ammonia) contained in a gas jar. After a while the different components in the ink form separate 'spots' as the solvent front rises up the plate

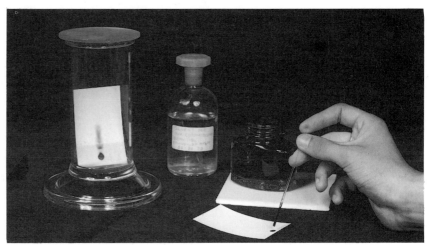

When a mixture of colourless solids is used, we locate their positions (or spots) on the **chromatogram** by:

▶ detecting the glowing 'spots' under an ultraviolet lamp; or

▶ exposing the chromatogram to a substance which reacts with the 'spots' and causes them to darken. For example, ninhydrin makes amino acid spots turn purple.

Gas–liquid chromatography

Gas–liquid chromatography (GLC) is used to separate mixtures of gases and volatile liquids. A typical gas–liquid chromatograph is shown in figure 32.3.

Figure 32.3 *The main features of a gas–liquid chromatograph and a typical recorder trace for a mixture of four volatile liquids A, B, C and D*

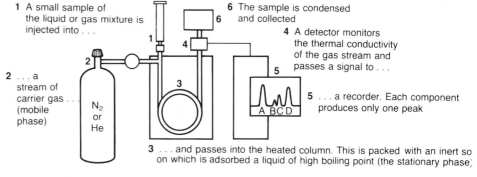

1 A small sample of the liquid or gas mixture is injected into . . .

2 . . . a stream of carrier gas . . . (mobile phase)

3 . . . and passes into the heated column. This is packed with an inert so on which is adsorbed a liquid of high boiling point (the stationary phase)

4 A detector monitors the thermal conductivity of the gas stream and passes a signal to . . .

5 . . . a recorder. Each component produces only one peak

6 The sample is condensed and collected

The time it takes for each substance to pass through the column is called its **retention time**. For a given set of conditions (i.e. length of column, speed of carrier gas and type of stationary phase), a substance will have a *constant* retention time. Thus, each peak on the recorder trace can be assigned to a given compound. Also, *the area under each peak corresponds to the amount of that compound in the mixture.*

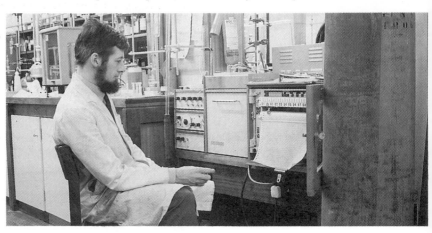

A gas–liquid chromatograph (GLC) is used to purify and identify gases and volatile liquids

To conclude, then, gas–liquid chromatography (GLC) is mainly used as a rapid means of separating, identifying and determining the purity of gases and volatile liquids. GLC is used, for example, to measure accurately the alcohol content of a motorist's blood.

32.8 Testing the purity of a synthetic product

Once the synthetic product has been obtained in its purified form, it is necessary to test its purity. Sometimes small amounts of impurities may be tolerated, e.g. if the product is to be used in another synthesis. However, other products must be absolutely pure, e.g. if they are to be used as drugs or food additives.

In industry, gas–liquid chromatography provides an easy, yet accurate, way of testing a sample's purity. As we have seen, a pure compound will give a chromatogram consisting of only one peak and this will have a characteristic retention time. **Infrared absorption, nuclear magnetic resonance** and **mass spectra** are also used because each pure compound gives its own unique **fingerprint** spectrum (see chapter 6).

Where these instrumental techniques are not available, the purity of a sample can be tested by measuring its **melting point** or **boiling point**. These values can then be checked against those in a data book.

A commercial apparatus for determining melting point

32.9 Calculating the percentage yield of product

Whenever we write a chemical equation, it is understood that the reactants will form the theoretical quantities of products, that is, there is a 100% yield.

In real life this is never the case, and in organic chemistry in particular, the actual yield of purified product is often well below the theoretical yield. Thus, we say that

$$\% \text{ yield} = \frac{\text{actual yield of purified product}}{\text{theoretical yield}} \times 100$$

A worked example is shown below.

Example

When 15 g of butan-1-ol(A) and 10 g of ethanoic acid(B) were refluxed together in the presence of concentrated sulphuric acid, 17.8 g of 1-butylethanoate(C) were formed.

$$C_4H_9OH + H_3C-C\overset{O}{\underset{OH}{\diagup}} \longrightarrow H_3C-C\overset{O}{\underset{OC_4H_9}{\diagup}} + H_2O$$

    (A)   (B)   (C)

Calculate the percentage yield of C.

Solution

First of all, we must work out which reactant is present in excess because this will not affect the yield of product. Thus, we use the expression,

$$\text{number of moles used} = \frac{\text{mass used}}{\text{relative molecular mass } (M_r)}$$

Now, $M_r(A) = 74$ and $M_r(B) = 60$ and the equation is:

$$C_4H_9OH + H_3C-C\overset{O}{\underset{OH}{\diagup}} \longrightarrow H_3C-C\overset{O}{\underset{OC_4H_9}{\diagup}} + H_2O$$

number of moles used: $\dfrac{15}{74}$ $\dfrac{10}{60}$

i.e.   0.203   0.167

Hence, the amount of ethanoic acid will determine the product yield: butan-1-ol is in excess.

Now, 1 mole of ethanoic acid forms 1 mole of 1-butylethanoate

∴ 0.167 moles of ethanoic acid forms 0.167 moles of 1-butylethanoate

Thus,

$$\text{theoretical mass of 1-butylethanoate} = 0.167 \times M_r = 0.167 \times 116 = 19.37\,\text{g}$$

Finally,

$$\% \text{ yield} = \frac{\text{actual yield of purified product}}{\text{theoretical yield}} \times 100$$

$$= \frac{17.8}{19.37} \times 100$$

giving % yield of C = 92%

In reality, yields do not closely approach 100%. Indeed, a 90% yield would often be thought of as being most satisfactory. There are three main reasons for a lowering of the percentage yield:

▶ *the reactants may not be completely pure,* e.g. some moisture may be present;
▶ *loss of product during purification,* e.g. small quantities of solid left on the filter paper or funnel during recrystallisation;
▶ *side reactions which give rise to by-products.*

Often, product yields can be improved by carrying out the synthesis using an excess of one (or more) reactant.

Sometimes, we have to accept a low yield. For example, there may be no other method of making the compound. Also, a low yield does not necessarily mean that a reaction is uneconomical, since a popular product can still be sold at a profit.

Activity 32.1

1   A chemist prepared 5.9 g of aspirin by warming 5.0 g of 2-hydroxybenzoic acid with 7.5 g of ethanoic anhydride at 60 °C. The equation is:

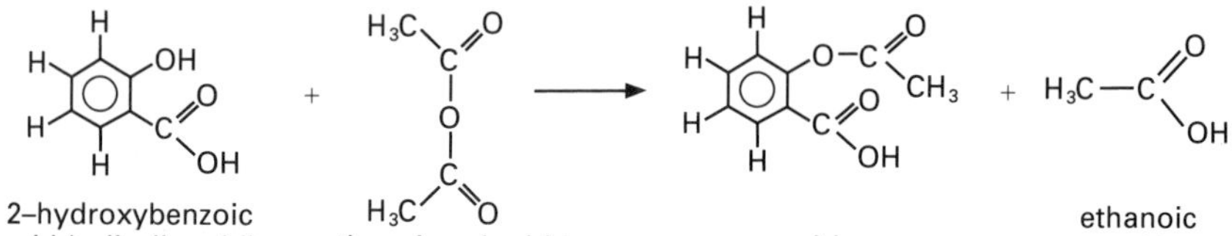

| 2–hydroxybenzoic acid (salicylic acid) | ethanoic anhydride | aspirin | ethanoic acid |

Calculate the percentage yield of aspirin.

2   When 6.2 g of anhydrous 2-methylpropan-2-ol(A) are treated with *excess* concentrated hydrochloric acid at room temperature, 6.2 g of 2-chloro-2-methylpropane(B) are formed:

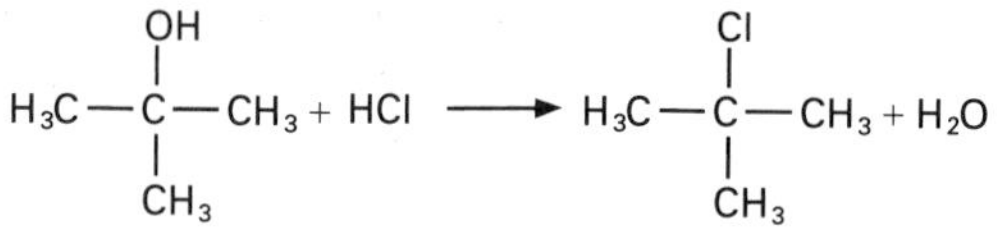

Calculate the percentage yield of B.

32.10 Comments on the activity

1

$$\text{2-hydroxybenzoic acid (salicylic acid)} + \text{ethanoic anhydride} \rightarrow \text{aspirin} + \text{ethanoic acid}$$

moles used: $\dfrac{5.0}{138}$ $\dfrac{7.5}{102}$
              $= 0.036$ $= 0.074$

Hence, the amount of salicylic acid will determine the product yield; ethanoic anhydride is in excess.

Now, 1 mole of salicylic acid forms 1 mole of aspirin
∴ 0.036 moles of salicyclic acid forms 0.036 moles of aspirin.
So the theoretical yield of aspirin $= 0.036 \times M_r = 0.036 \times 180 = 6.48 \text{ g}$
Finally,

$$\% \text{ yield} = \frac{\text{actual yield of purified product}}{\text{theoretical yield}} \times 100$$

$$= \frac{5.9}{6.48} \times 100$$

$$\% \text{ yield} = 91\%$$

2 The equation is:

$$
\underset{\text{(A)}}{H_3C-\underset{\underset{CH_3}{|}}{\overset{\overset{OH}{|}}{C}}-CH_3} + HCl \longrightarrow \underset{\text{(B)}}{H_3C-\underset{\underset{CH_3}{|}}{\overset{\overset{Cl}{|}}{C}}-CH_3} + H_2O
$$

In theory,

$$74\,\text{g will form } 92.5\,\text{g}$$

$$\therefore \quad 1\,\text{g will form } \frac{92.5\,\text{g}}{74}$$

and

$$6.2\,\text{g will form } \frac{92.5}{74} \times 6.2 = 7.75\,\text{g}$$

So, theoretical yield of product = 7.75 g and the actual yield = 6.2 g. Thus,

$$\% \text{ yield } = \frac{\text{actual yield of purified product}}{\text{theoretical yield}} \times 100$$

$$= \frac{6.2}{7.75} \times 100$$

$$\therefore \quad \% \text{ yield of B } = 80\%$$

32.11 Summary and revision plan

1 Organic synthesis involves three main tasks: (i) planning and performing the chemical reaction; (ii) separating the crude product and purifying it; (iii) checking the purity of the final product.

2 Any organic preparation that you devise should give information about: the concentrations of the reactants and the way they are mixed, the use of any catalyst, temperature and pressure. In industry, these conditions would be chosen so as to give the most economical yield of product.

3 Organic chemicals are often volatile, flammable and toxic. Hence, organic reaction mixtures are heated under **reflux** (figure 32.1).

4 Crude organic products can be purified by: **distillation techniques, solvent extraction, recrystallisation** and **chromatography** (table 32.1).

5 In chromatography, the components in the mixture are separated because of their different strengths of attraction for a stationary phase and a moving phase. Two important techniques are: **thin-layer chromatography (TLC)** and **gas–liquid chromatography (GLC)**.

6 GLC is mainly used as a rapid means of separating, identifying and determining the purity of gases and volatile liquids.

7 The time it takes for each component to pass through the GLC column is called its **retention time**. Under fixed conditions, retention times are constant and can be used to identify components in the mixture.

8 Spectra of pure organic compounds are like 'fingerprints'. Hence, **infrared, ultraviolet, nuclear magnetic resonance** and **mass spectra** are used to identify a compound and to estimate its purity.

9 Pure organic compounds also have characteristic **melting** and **boiling points**.

10 $$\frac{\textbf{\% yield}}{\textbf{of pure product}} = \frac{\textbf{actual yield of pure product}}{\textbf{theoretical yield}} \times \textbf{100}$$

The reactant present in excess will not govern the yield of product (see the worked example).

11 Percentage yields are always *less* than 100%. The reasons for this might be impure reactants, loss of product during purification or the formation of reaction by-products.

□ C H A P T E R □

33

The Reactivity of Organic Compounds

When ethene is bubbled through bromine dissolved in tetrachloromethane, at room temperature, the orange colour of the bromine quickly disappears. However, if the experiment is repeated, this time using ethane instead of ethene, *no* reaction is observed.

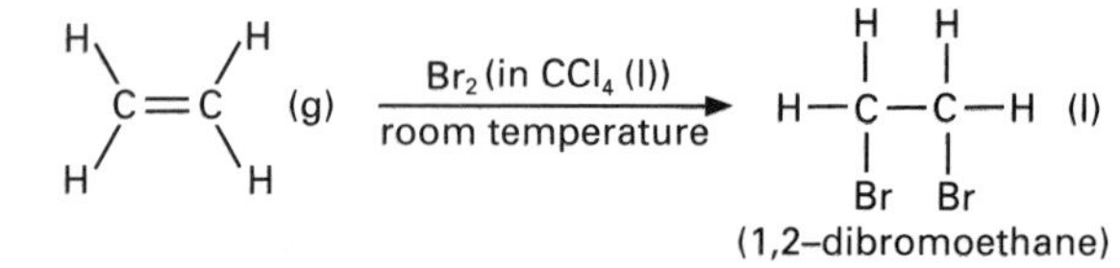

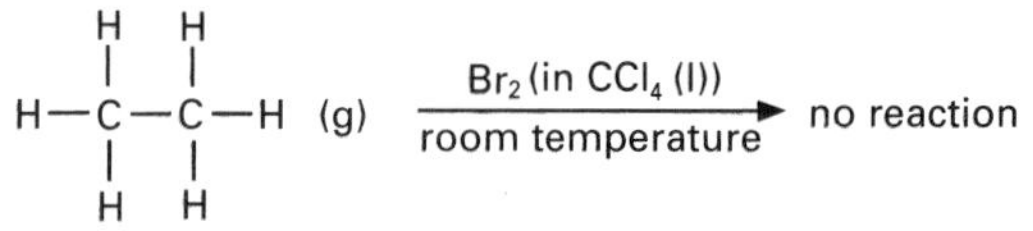

$$\underset{H}{\overset{H}{>}}C=C\underset{H}{\overset{H}{<}} \text{ (g)} \xrightarrow[\text{room temperature}]{Br_2\,(\text{in } CCl_4\,(l))} H-\underset{\underset{Br}{|}}{\overset{\overset{H}{|}}{C}}-\underset{\underset{Br}{|}}{\overset{\overset{H}{|}}{C}}-H \text{ (l)}$$
(1,2–dibromoethane)

$$H-\underset{\underset{H}{|}}{\overset{\overset{H}{|}}{C}}-\underset{\underset{H}{|}}{\overset{\overset{H}{|}}{C}}-H \text{ (g)} \xrightarrow[\text{room temperature}]{Br_2\,(\text{in } CCl_4\,(l))} \text{no reaction}$$

Since each molecule contains C—H bonds, the reaction must be characteristic of the C=C bond present in ethene, but not in ethane. This is an example of an **addition** reaction. In fact, we find that *bromine can be added to any molecule containing a C=C bond.* Thus, we say that the C=C bond is a **reactive centre** in the molecule.

Although ethane will not react with bromine in tetrachloromethane, a gas phase reaction will occur in the presence of ultra violet light:

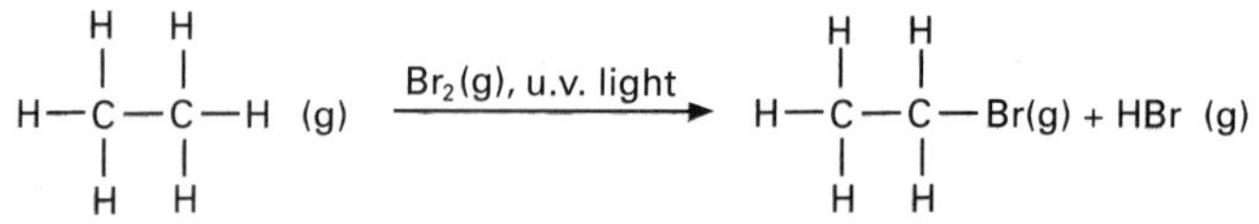

$$H-\underset{\underset{H}{|}}{\overset{\overset{H}{|}}{C}}-\underset{\underset{H}{|}}{\overset{\overset{H}{|}}{C}}-H \text{ (g)} \xrightarrow{Br_2(g),\, u.v.\, light} H-\underset{\underset{H}{|}}{\overset{\overset{H}{|}}{C}}-\underset{\underset{H}{|}}{\overset{\overset{H}{|}}{C}}-Br(g) + HBr \text{ (g)}$$

In this case, a bromine atom has **substituted** for a hydrogen atom and the reactive centre in the alkane is the C—H bond. As expected, *other compounds containing C—H bonds will react with bromine in the same way,* under these conditions.

In the examples above, bromine's behaviour depends on the experimental conditions. The reason for this is that the bromine molecule can split up in two ways and these give rise to the different mechanisms for the addition and substitution reactions. **Reaction mechanisms** *explain how the electron clouds move around during a chemical reaction.* An understanding of why and how these clouds shift will help you to predict the outcome of mixing organic chemicals together.

The purpose of this chapter is to lay the foundations upon which our study of organic reactions is based. To do this, we shall:

▶ review the concept of **electronegativity** and use this to identify the reactive centres in a variety of molecules;

▶ discuss **bond fission** (i.e. the ways in which covalent bonds can be broken); and

▶ survey some common types of organic reaction mechanism.

After working through this chapter, you will be better able to detect and analyse the many patterns of behaviour that run through chapters 34 to 41.

33.1 Electronegativity and bond polarity

Electronegativity may be defined as the *power of an atom in a covalent bond to attract the bonding electron cloud to itself.* The values suggested by Pauling are listed in table 5.2, to which you should now refer. If the atom has a *high* electronegativity, it will attract the bonding electron cloud *very strongly*, and vice versa. When two atoms of unequal electronegativity are bonded together, a **permanent dipole** will result, e.g.

	$\delta+$ $\delta-$	$\delta+$ $\delta-$	$\delta-$ $\delta+$
	C—F	C=O	N—H
electronegativities	2.5 4.0	2.5 3.5	3.0 2.1

Electronegativity values, therefore, allow us to work out the polarity of the bonds in an organic molecule.

Activity 33.1

Look again at table 5.2, and then answer these questions.

1   Use $\delta+$ and $\delta-$ signs to show the polarity of the following bonds:

   C—Br   O—H   N—H   S—O   C=O   C≡N
   C—Cl   C—F

2   The greater the difference in the electronegativities of the bonded atoms, the more polarised the bond will be. Hence, place the bonds above in order of *increasing* polarity.

33.2 Breaking covalent bonds

When a molecule absorbs energy, the bonded atoms vibrate more vigorously around their mean positions. If enough energy is supplied **bond fission** will occur. This can happen in two ways, known as homolytic and heterolytic bond fission.

Homolytic bond fission

As the bond breaks, both atoms take an equal share of the bonding electron cloud:

$$A{\overset{\times}{\bullet}}B \rightarrow A^{\times} + {\bullet}B$$

At the instant of their formation, $A^{\times}$ and ${\bullet}B$ are *very excited atoms, or groups of atoms, possessing an unpaired electron*; these are known as **free radicals**. Free radicals are highly energetic because the previously bonded electrons have not yet returned to their lower energy ground states. Needless to say, *free radicals are very reactive particles*.

   Two examples of free radical formation are given below:

$$Cl \overset{\times}{\bullet} Cl \rightarrow \quad Cl^{\times} + {\bullet}Cl \quad \Delta H = +242\,kJ$$
$$H_3C \overset{\times}{\bullet} H \rightarrow H_3C^{\times} + {\bullet}H \quad \Delta H = +435\,kJ$$

Generally speaking, homolytic fission occurs in non-polar, or only slightly polar, molecules.

Heterolytic bond fission

In this very common process, *one atom takes both bonding electrons* and ions are formed:

$$A{\overset{\times}{\bullet}}B \rightarrow [A]^{+} + [{\overset{\times}{\bullet}}B]^{-}$$

Before fission, atoms A and B may each be thought of as effectively 'owning' one electron in the shared pair. When the bond breaks:

▶   atom A loses its 'owned' electron ($^{\times}$). By losing a negative charge, atom A becomes a **positive ion**;

▶   atom B withdraws its own electron (${\bullet}$) but also gains an electron ($^{\times}$).

Thus, atom B becomes a **negative ion**.

Clearly, this approach is simplistic since we know that chemical bonds are formed by the redistribution of electron clouds, not particles. Also, by using this idea of 'owned' electrons, we have ignored polarity in the chemical bonds. However, as long as you realise its limitations, *this idea of an atom 'owning' a shared electron will prove very useful when we discuss reaction mechanisms.*

Heterolytic bond fission occurs when the bonded atoms have very different electronegativities. After fission, the more electronegative atom will form the negative ion, e.g.

Here chlorine is more electronegative than carbon.

33.3 Reagents in organic chemistry

From a knowledge of bond polarities, we can also predict which types of reagent might attack the organic molecule. **Chemical reagents** *are substances which bring about a desired structural change in another molecule.* For example, phosphorus pentachloride, $PCl_5(s)$, is a reagent used to substitute a $-Cl$ atom for the $-OH$ group in alcohols or carboxylic acids, e.g.

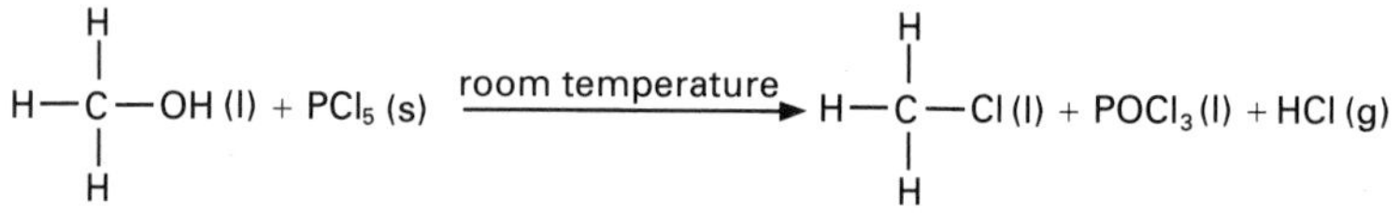

There are three main classes of reagent: free radicals, electrophiles and nucleophiles.

Free radicals

As mentioned earlier, free radicals are highly reactive atoms or groups of atoms. They are usually formed by the homolytic fission of non-polar bonds.

Electrophiles

These are *electron-poor species which will attack an electron rich, ($\delta-$) centre in the organic molecule.* Electrophiles may be either molecules with an incomplete outer shell of electrons (e.g. sulphur trioxide, SO_3) or positive ions (e.g. H^+, NO_2^+, Cl^+, Br^+, CH_3^+). 'Dot and cross' diagrams show why these molecules and ions can act as electron acceptors (figure 33.1).

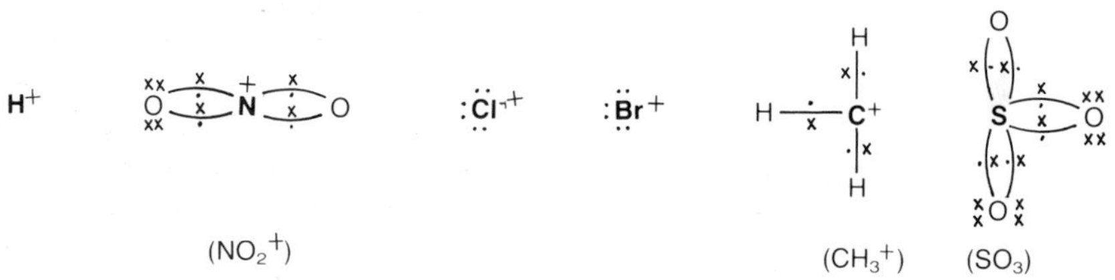

Figure 33.1 *'Dot and cross' diagrams of some common electrophiles. These are electron acceptors because they contain an atom (in bold print) which has an incomplete outer electron shell*

Nucleophiles

Nucleophiles are *electron-rich species which will attack electron-poor ($\delta+$) centres in an organic molecule.* Nucleophiles may be either negative ions (e.g. OH^-, CN^-, Cl^-,

CH_3O^-) or molecules (e.g. NH_3, H_2O, CH_3OH). An essential property of a nucleophile is the presence of at least one lone pair of electrons (figure 33.2).

Figure 33.2 *'Dot and cross' diagrams of some common nucleophiles. These are electron donors because they contain an atom (in bold print) which has at least one lone pair of electrons. (▲ is the electron left behind following the loss of a positive ion)*

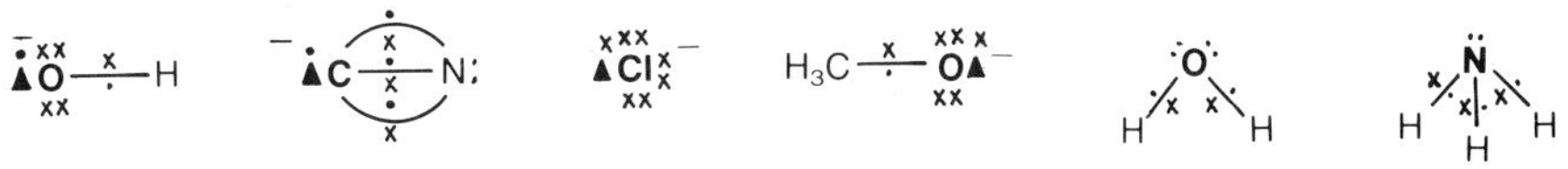

Activity 33.2 gives you some practice in predicting the type of reagent which will attack a given organic molecule.

Activity 33.2

Use δ+ and δ− signs to show the bond polarities in the following structural units:

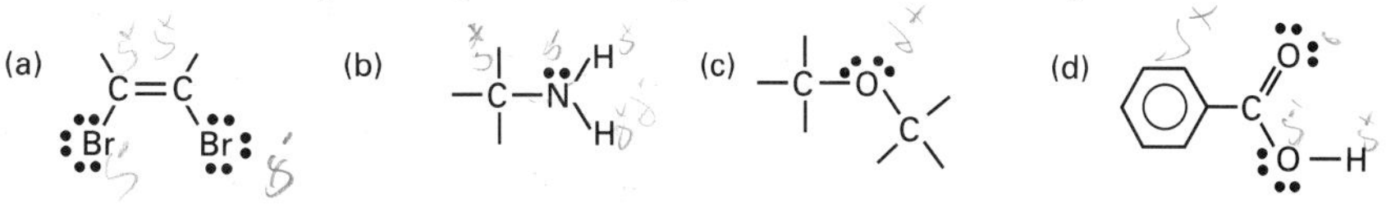

(a)   (b)   (c)   (d)

(Note: ignore the reactivity of the C—H bonds in the benzene ring.)

At what positions might these structures be attacked by (i) electrophiles and (ii) nucleophiles?

33.4 Types of reactive centre

Generally speaking, an organic molecule may be pictured as having two types of reactive centre:

▶ a **hydrocarbon framework** or **skeleton**, that is, one made of carbon and hydrogen atoms;

▶ one, or more, **functional groups**, which are attached to the hydrocarbon skeleton, figure 33.3. Functional groups are single atoms, or groups of atoms, which give characteristic chemical properties to any organic molecule in which they are found.

Let us survey the main types of hydrocarbon skeleton and functional groups.

Figure 33.3 *Organic compounds may be thought of as a hydrocarbon skeleton which may be attached to one, or more, functional groups FG*

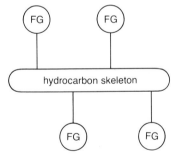

The hydrocarbon skeleton

In section 24.5, we saw that the high bond energy term for the C—C bond enables carbon to form **catenated** compounds. These compounds consist of chains or rings of carbon atoms linked together via single or multiple bonds, (e.g. C=C and C≡C). Each catenated carbon atom displays a valency of four by also bonding to hydrogen atoms or functional groups.

The most common structural features of the hydrocarbon skeleton are C—H, C—C, C=C, C≡C bonds and the C—C bonds in the benzene ring (section 5.8). More than one of these structural features may be present. If so, each will impart its own unique chemical properties to the skeleton. For example, consider the phenylethene skeleton (figure 33.4). This gives reactions typical of:

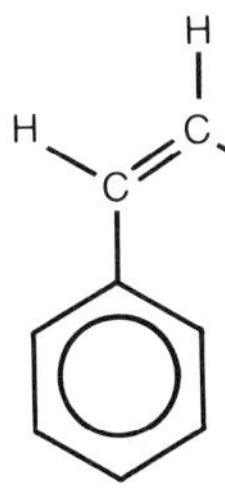

▶ the C=C bond, e.g. by adding hydrogen bromide at room temperature section 35.6.2:

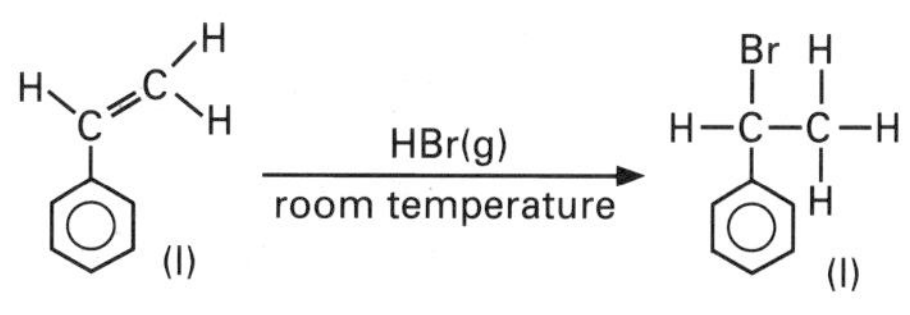

Figure 33.4 *The phenylethene molecule*

- the C—H bond in benzene, e.g. by reacting with iodomethane (section 36.5.3):

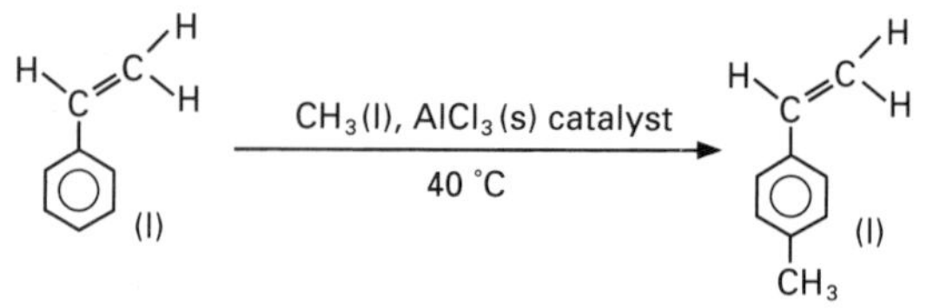

To conclude, then, *each reactive centre in the hydrocarbon skeleton will cause the compound to have certain predictable chemical properties.*

Functional groups

Functional groups *are atoms, or groups of atoms, which have been subsituted for a hydrogen in the hydrocarbon skeleton.* Table 33.1 lists the main types of functional group and some compounds in which they are found.

Table 33.1 *The main types of functional group (The way we name these compounds is discussed in chapters 34–41; □– is a hydrocarbon skeleton)*

Functional group	... is found in ...	aliphatic example		aromatic example	
–halogen	organic halogen compounds	CH_3-CH_2-Br	bromoethane	C_6H_5-I	iodobenzene
–OH	alcohols	$CH_3-CH_2-CH_2-OH$	propan–1–ol	$C_6H_5-CH_2-OH$	phenylmethanol
	phenols (if the –OH is joined directly to a benzene ring)			C_6H_5-OH	phenol
–O–□	ethers	$H_3C-O-CH_3$	methoxymethane	$C_6H_5-O-CH_3$	methoxybenzene
–C(=O)H	aldehydes	$H_3C-C(=O)H$	ethanal	$C_6H_5-C(=O)H$	benzaldehyde
–C(=O)–□	ketones	$H_3C-C(=O)CH_3$	propanone	$C_6H_5-C(=O)CH_3$	phenylethanone
–C(=O)OH	carboxylic acids	$H_3C-C(=O)OH$	ethanoic acid	$C_6H_5-C(=O)OH$	benzoic acid
–C(=O)Cl	acid chlorides	$H_3C-C(=O)Cl$	ethanoyl chloride	$C_6H_5-C(=O)Cl$	benzoyl chloride
–C(=O)NH2	acid amides	$H_3C-C(=O)NH_2$	ethanamide	$C_6H_5-C(=O)NH_2$	benzamide
–C(=O)O–□	acid esters	$H_3C-C(=O)O-CH_3$	methyl ethanoate	$C_6H_5-C(=O)O-CH_3$	methyl benzoate
$-NO_2$	nitro compounds	H_3C-NO_2	nitromethane	$C_6H_5-NO_2$	nitrobenzene
$-NH_2$	amines	H_3C-NH_2	methylamine	$C_6H_5-NH_2$	phenylamine
–C≡N	nitriles	H_3C-CN	ethanonitrile	C_6H_5-CN	benzonitrile

When predicting the chemical properties of a molecule, we must consider each functional group in the context of the whole molecule. For example, the reactivity of a hydrocarbon skeleton is often modified by the presence of functional groups:

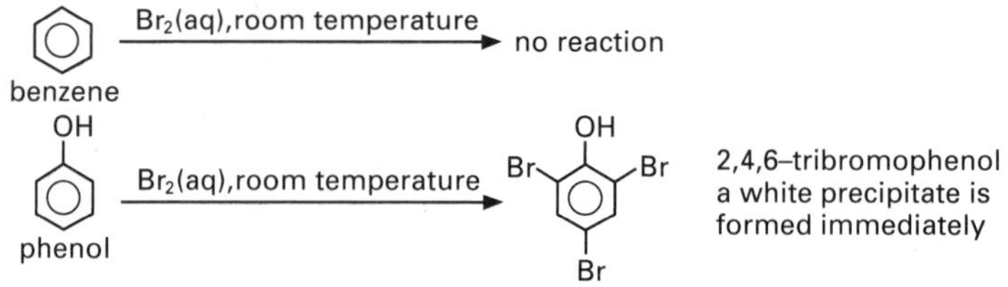

Here the –OH functional group activates the benzene ring and makes reaction possible.

Likewise, the type of hydrocarbon skeleton can affect the reactivity of a functional group. Compare, for example, the relative rates of hydrolysis of chloromethane and chlorobenzene:

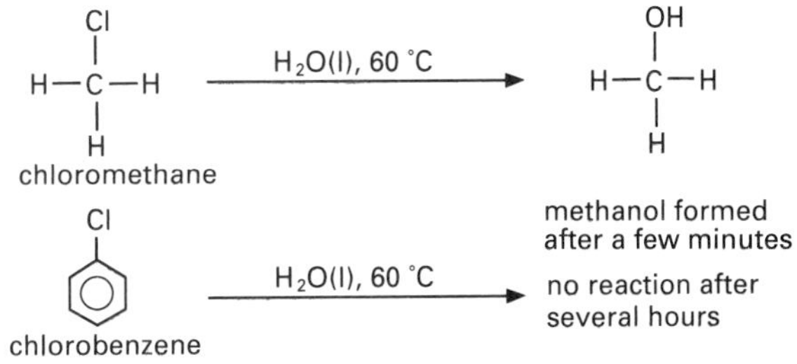

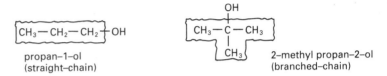

These reactions are discussed further in section 37.5.1.

As you read through the text, you will see that *the reactivity of a given functional group is often heavily dependent on its molecular environment,* and this is a **key aspect** of our study. In particular, we shall compare the reactivities of a given functional group, X, in:

▶ **aliphatic** and **aromatic** molecules.
   Aliphatic compounds contain **straight-** or **branched-chain** hydrocarbon skeletons, e.g.

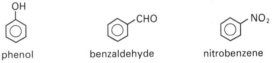

propan–1–ol (straight–chain)	2–methyl propan–2–ol (branched–chain)

Aromatic compounds are derived from benzene, e.g.

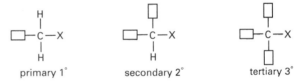

phenol   benzaldehyde   nitrobenzene

▶ **primary, secondary** and **tertiary** compounds.
   These have the general form

primary 1°   secondary 2°   tertiary 3°

where ☐ *means a hydrocarbon skeleton, whether aliphatic or aromatic.* (This notation is used throughout the book.)

They are known as............................**primary, secondary** and **tertiary** compounds because they have ....**one,   two   ** and **three** hydrocarbon skeletons bonded to the carbon which is attached to the functional group, X.

33.5 Predicting the reactivity of a functional group

In section 33.1, we saw that electronegativities can be used to work out bond polarities. From these, we can predict which type of reagent, electrophilic or nucleophilic, *might* attack a given bond. We can also do this for a functional group (and its neighbouring carbon atom), as shown below:

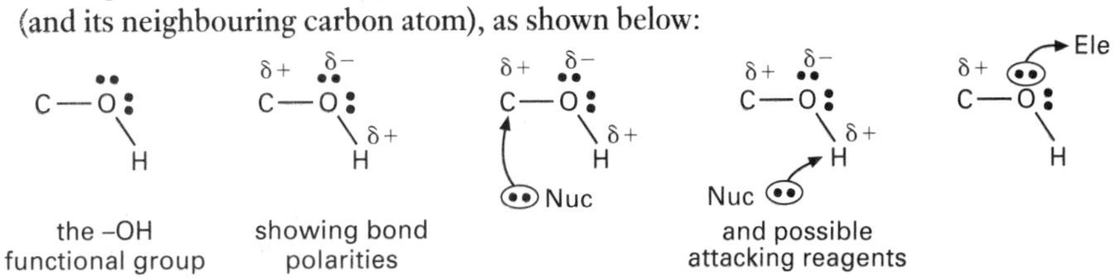

the –OH functional group	showing bond polarities		and possible attacking reagents	

There are three possible reactive centres $C^{\delta+}$, $H^{\delta+}$ and $O^{\delta-}$. The $\delta+$ and $\delta-$ centres will be targets for nucleophilic (Nuc) and electrophilic (Ele) attacks, respectively. Note the use of **'curly' arrows** *to show the direction of movement of the electron cloud due to two electrons.*

To conclude, then, you should note the importance of identifying a molecule's reactive centres. These help us to predict chemical properties of the molecule.

33.6 Mechanisms of organic reactions

Reaction mechanisms *describe the way in which electron clouds shift during the reaction.* Although there are millions of organic reactions, many have one of a small group of well-known mechanisms and these are outlined below.

Organic reaction mechanisms are usually classified according to:

▶ the nature of the reagent molecule, or ion, which *first* attacks the organic compound. Reagents may be **free radical, electrophilic** or **nucleophilic** (section 33.3);

▶ the type of structural change that the organic compound undergoes. Frequently, this involves

(i) **addition** to a C=C, C≡C or C=O bond, e.g.

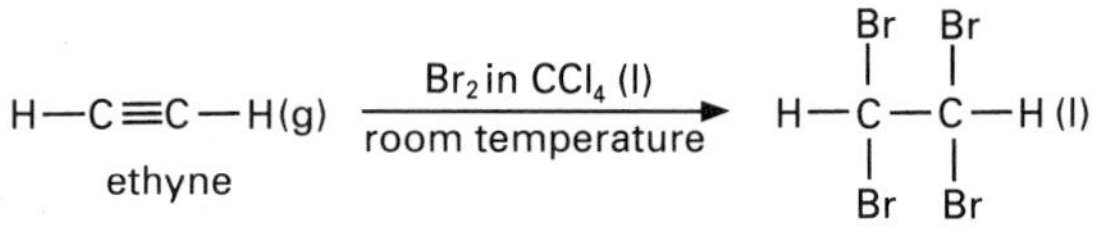

$$H-C \equiv C-H(g) \xrightarrow[\text{room temperature}]{Br_2 \text{ in } CCl_4 \text{ (l)}} \begin{array}{c} Br\ \ Br \\ |\ \ \ | \\ H-C-C-H \text{ (l)} \\ |\ \ \ | \\ Br\ \ Br \end{array}$$

ethyne

(ii) **substitution** of one functional group for another, e.g.

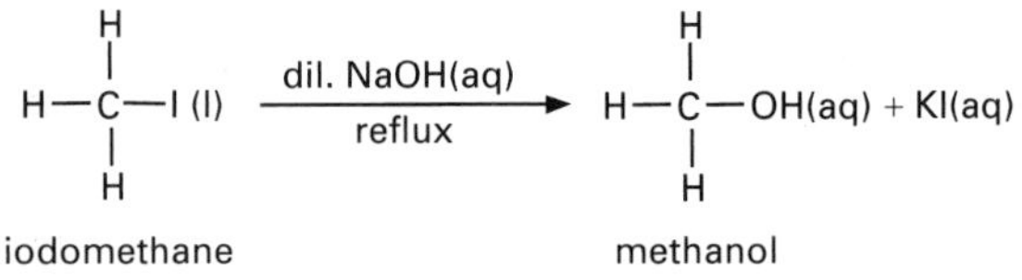

$$\begin{array}{c} H \\ | \\ H-C-I \text{ (l)} \\ | \\ H \end{array} \xrightarrow[\text{reflux}]{\text{dil. NaOH(aq)}} \begin{array}{c} H \\ | \\ H-C-OH(aq) + KI(aq) \\ | \\ H \end{array}$$

iodomethane   methanol

(iii) **elimination** of a small molecule e.g.,

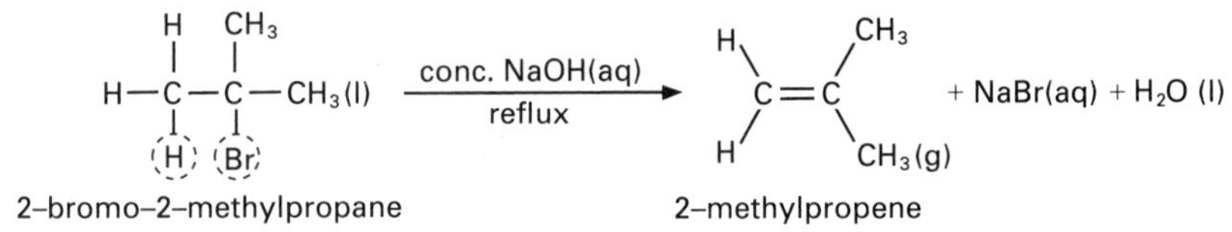

$$\begin{array}{c} H\ \ CH_3 \\ |\ \ \ | \\ H-C-C-CH_3 \text{ (l)} \\ |\ \ \ | \\ (H)\ (Br) \end{array} \xrightarrow[\text{reflux}]{\text{conc. NaOH(aq)}} \begin{array}{c} H \\ \diagdown \\ \diagup \\ H \end{array} C=C \begin{array}{c} CH_3 \\ \diagup \\ \diagdown \\ CH_3 \text{ (g)} \end{array} + NaBr(aq) + H_2O \text{ (l)}$$

2–bromo–2–methylpropane   2–methylpropene

Finally, you should note that organic compounds take part in many important **redox** reactions, e.g.

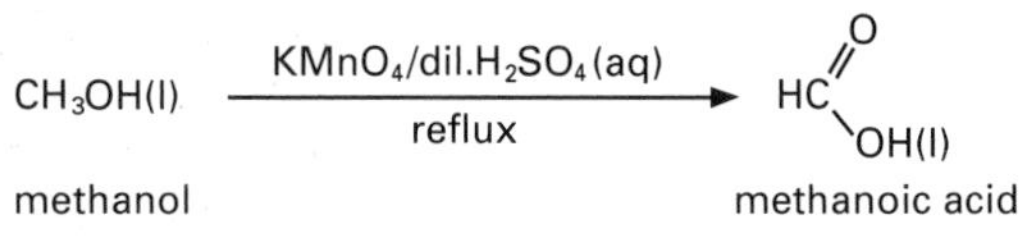

$$CH_3OH(l) \xrightarrow[\text{reflux}]{KMnO_4/\text{dil.}H_2SO_4 \text{(aq)}} HC\overset{\displaystyle O}{\underset{OH(l)}{\diagup}}$$

methanol   methanoic acid

The mechanisms of redox reactions are rather complex, and go beyond this study.

33.7 Comments on the activities

Activity 33.1

1 $\overset{\delta+\ \delta-}{\text{C-Br}}$ $\overset{\delta-\ \delta+}{\text{O-H}}$ $\overset{\delta-\ \delta+}{\text{N-H}}$ $\overset{\delta+\ \delta-}{\text{S-O}}$ $\overset{\delta+\ \delta-}{\text{C=O}}$ $\overset{\delta+\ \delta-}{\text{C≡N}}$ $\overset{\delta+\ \delta-}{\text{C-Cl}}$ $\overset{\delta+\ \delta-}{\text{C-F}}$

2 Increasing polarity:	$\delta+\ \delta-$	$\delta+\ \delta-$	$\delta+\ \delta-$	$\delta-\ \delta+$	$\delta+\ \delta-$
electronegativity	C—Br	C—Cl	C—N	N—H	C=O
difference	0.3	0.5	0.5	0.9	1.0

	$\delta+\ \delta-$	$\delta-\ \delta+$	$\delta+\ \delta-$
electronegativity	S—O	O—H	C—F
difference	1.0	1.4	1.5

Activity 33.2

The reactive centres and possible types of attacking reagents are shown below:

Electron-rich centres ($\delta-$) are likely to be attacked by electrophiles; these will also attack the ring of delocalised electrons in benzene (section 5.8). Nucleophiles will attack the electron-poor ($\delta+$) centres.

33.8 Summary and revision plan

1 **Electronegativity** is the power of an atom in a covalent bond to attract the bonding electron cloud to itself (see table 5.2).

2 Electronegativities can be used to deduce the polarity of covalent bonds and, hence, to identify the **reactive centres** in an organic molecule.

3 An organic molecule may have two main types of reactive centre: its **hydrocarbon skeleton** and **functional groups** (section 33.4). Each reactive centre will cause the compound to display certain predictable chemical properties.

4 **Functional groups** are atoms, or groups of atoms, which have been substituted for a hydrogen in the hydrocarbon skeleton. Functional groups can be identified by their characteristic chemical properties.

5 A **key aspect** of our study is the comparison of a functional group's behaviour in different molecular locations, such as in (i) **aliphatic** and **aromatic** molecules and (ii) **primary, secondary** and **tertiary** compounds (section 33.4).

6 The nature of the hydrocarbon skeleton can modify the reactivity of a functional group, and vice versa.

7 By attacking its reactive centre(s), chemical reagents bring about a desired structural change in the organic molecule.

8 There are three main classes of reagent: free radicals, electrophiles and nucleophiles (section 33.3).

9 **Free radicals** are highly excited atoms, or groups of atoms, which have an unpaired electron. They are very reactive.

10 An **electrophile** is an electron-poor species which will attack an electron-rich ($\delta-$) reactive centre in the organic molecule.

11 A **nucleophile** is a species which possesses at least one lone pair of electrons. It is electron-rich and will attack an electron-poor ($\delta+$) reactive centre in the organic molecule.

12 **Reaction mechanisms** explain how the electron clouds move around during a chemical reaction (section 33.6). **'Curly' arrows** show the shift of cloud due to two electrons.

13 **Homolytic bond fission:** both atoms take an equal share of the bonding electron clouds, and free radicals are formed.

14 **Heterolytic bond fission:** one atom takes both bonding electrons, and ions are formed.

Alkanes

Contents

In the early days of coal-mining, many lives were lost because of explosions caused by combustible gases in the coal seam. One of these gases is **methane, CH_4,** the simplest alkane. Alkanes are hydrocarbons in which each carbon is bonded to four other atoms. *They contain only single bonds and are said to be saturated compounds.*

The miner's safety lamp (left) was invented by Humphry Davy in 1815. It dramatically reduced the number of deaths caused by methane explosions in coal mines. At the Houghton Main Colliery near Barnsley (right), methane is now harnessed as a resource. All of the surface buildings are heated by burning the methane gas released from the coal seams

Methane is also found in stagnant ponds, swamps and marshes where it is formed by the bacterial decay of plants and animals. In some countries, the controlled decay of sewage material is used to produce small quantities of methane, and this can be used by the local community as cheap fuel (e.g. for heating, cooking or gas-powered cars).

A more plentiful source of methane is **natural gas**. Typically, this contains

A tanker being filled with methane obtained from the treatment of sewage at a processing plant in Essex

about 75% methane, 21% other gaseous alkanes and 4% of other gases, such as hydrogen sulphide. Often, natural gas is found together with **crude oil**. This is a complex mixture of many thousands of different hydrocarbons, most of which are alkanes. The actual composition of crude oil varies with its place of origin (e.g. USA, Middle East, USSR, etc.). At present, the UK is self-sufficient in natural gas and crude oil as a result of their discovery about two miles below the bed of the North Sea (figure 34.1).

Figure 34.1   *The location of the UK oil wells and pipelines*

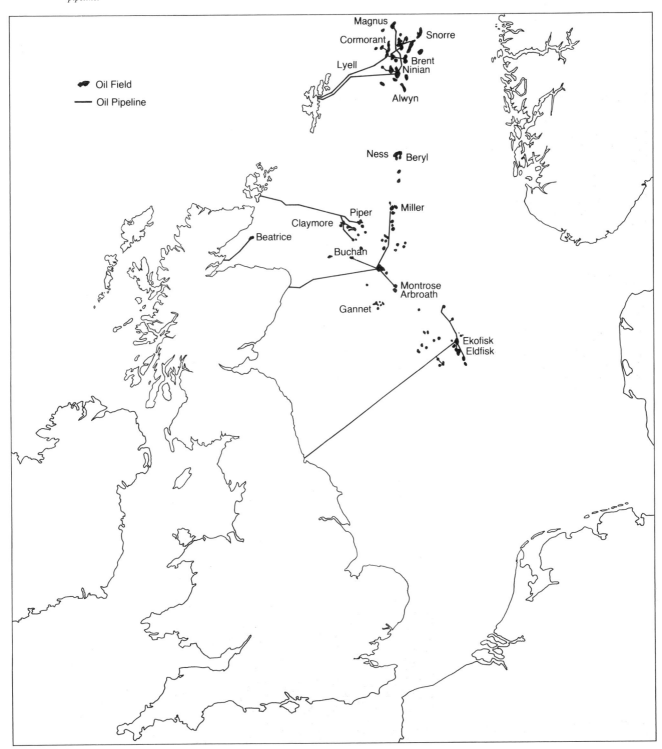

Environmentally safe alternatives to fossil fuels: a wind-powered electrical generator and a tidal power scheme. Although 'safe', they are not without environmental implications

Natural gas and crude oil are thought to have been formed from the decay of animals and plants which inhabited shallow seas many millions of years ago. As these died, they sank to the sea-bed where they were gradually covered with layers of sand, mud and weathered rocks. This 'burial' caused the plant and animal remains to decompose under pressure and at high temperature. Natural gas and crude oil, the decay products, were then absorbed by porous rocks, such as limestone. Thus, crude oil is more accurately known as **petroleum** which comes from the Greek words for rock (*petra*) and oil (*oleum*). The refining of petroleum is described in section 34.4.

Because they take such a long time to form, natural gas and petroleum are **finite resources** i.e. *they cannot be replaced.* At present, about 65% of the world's energy comes from oil. Yet, it is generally agreed that natural gas and oil supplies will only last about another 50 years. What do you think could, or should, replace it as a source of energy?

34.1 The structure of alkanes

A molecular model of methane is shown in photograph A. It consists of four hydrogen atoms arranged tetrahedrally around an 'sp^3 hybridised' carbon atom (section 5.6). The electron clouds in the C—H bonds are mutually repulsive and this results in bond angles of **109.5°**, *not* 90° as might be suggested by the structural formula.

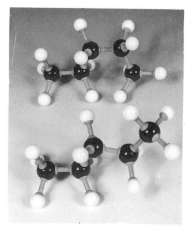

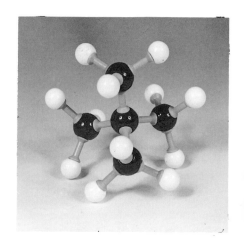

A)

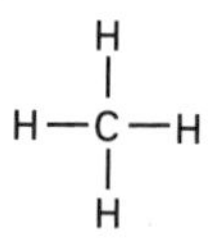

$$H-\underset{\underset{H}{|}}{\overset{\overset{H}{|}}{C}}-H$$

B)

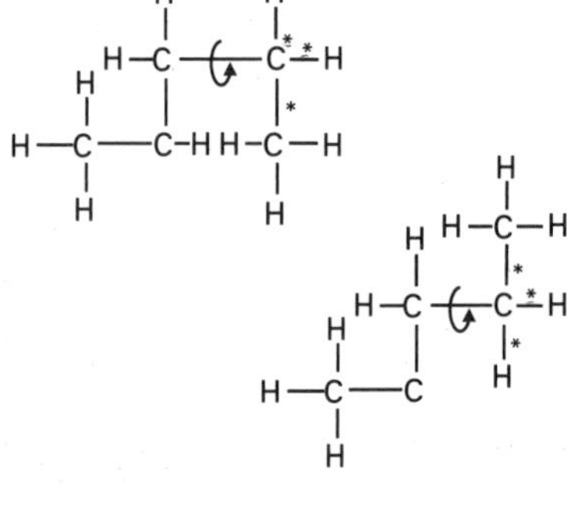

C)

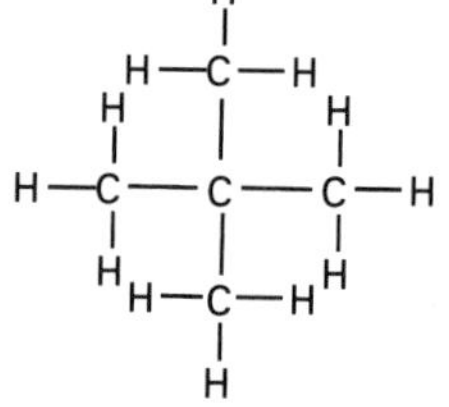

Table 34.1 *Names and molecular formulae of the first eight straight-chain alkanes*

Name	molecular formula
methane	CH_4
ethane	C_2H_6
propane	C_3H_8
butane	C_4H_{10}
pentane	C_5H_{12}
hexane	C_6H_{14}
heptane	C_7H_{16}
octane	C_8H_{18}

Can you work out a link between the number of carbon and hydrogen atoms in each molecule?

Table 34.2 *Names of some alkyl groups used, for example, to name branched alkanes*

Name of group	molecular formula
methyl	$-CH_3$
ethyl	$-C_2H_5$
propyl	$-C_3H_7$
butyl	$-C_4H_9$

When naming alkanes, and other organic compounds, remember that a structural formula represents the molecule's *'3-dimensional'* shape. For example, consider the molecular models of pentane, C_5H_{12}, a **straight-chain** alkane, shown in photograph B. Both models, and their structural formulae, are equivalent and correct. They are not structural isomers (section 10.2), because the bonds marked * are equivalent due to the continuous rotation around single bonds. However, photograph C shows the molecular model of 2,2-dimethylpropane. This is one of the two **branched-chain** alkanes which are structural isomers of pentane. Can you write down the structural formula of the other isomer?

34.2 Naming alkanes

To name an alkane, we follow a set of five rules.

1   Identify and name the longest straight chain. The name consists of two parts:

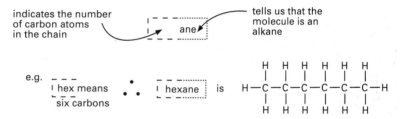

Table 34.1 lists the name of the first eight straight-chain alkanes.

2   For branched-chain alkanes, name each 'branch' and state its point of attachment to the longest straight chain. These 'branches' are known as **alkyl** groups (table 34.2). Some examples:

2–methylbutane   3–methylpentane   3–ethylpentane

Where the point of attachment could be described by two numbers, we choose the smaller, e.g.

2–methylpentane
(not 4–methylpentane)

3–ethylheptane
(not 5–ethylheptane)

3   If the same 'branch' appears more than once, we must
   (i)   prefix the alkyl group name with *di-, tri-, tetra-, penta-* etc.; and
   (ii) give the positions of each alkyl group on the longest straight chain, *keeping the numbers as small as possible.*

Some examples are:

2,2–dimethylpropane

2,3,5–trimethylhexane
(not 2,4,5–trimethylhexane)

2,2,4–trimethylpentane
(not 2,4,4–trimethylpentane)

4 If a branched-chain alkane contains more than one type of alkyl group, we give them in alphabetical order, e.g.

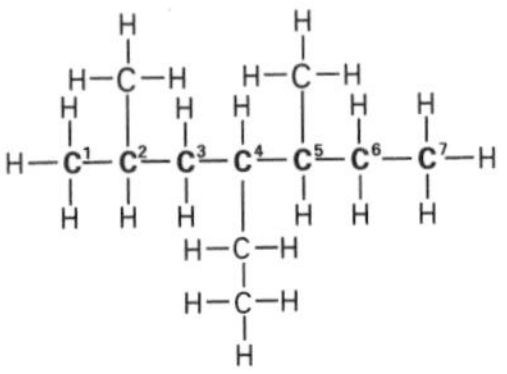

4–ethyl–2,5–dimethylheptane

5 Finally, when naming cycloalkanes we use the prefix *cyclo-* and the rules above, e.g.

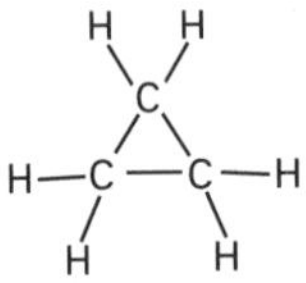

cyclopropane

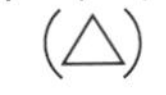

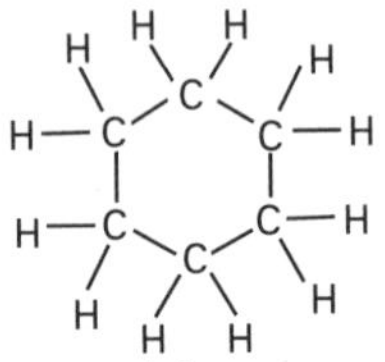

cyclohexane

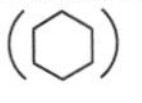

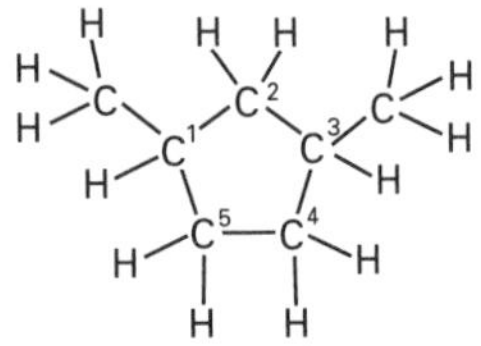

1,3–dimethylcyclopentane

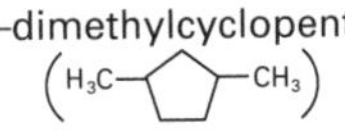

In the shorthand versions of these molecules (shown in brackets), the presence of the 'ring' carbon and hydrogen atoms is understood.

Activity 34.1

1 From the structural formulae shown below, select those which are (a) equivalent and (b) structural isomers.

(i)

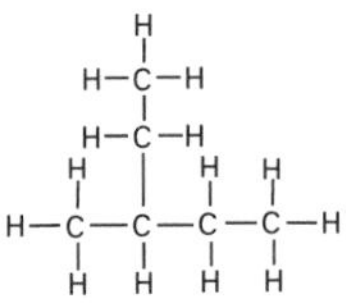

(ii)

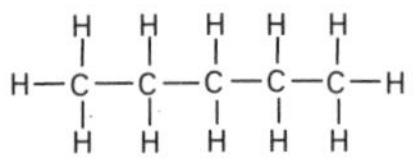

(iii)

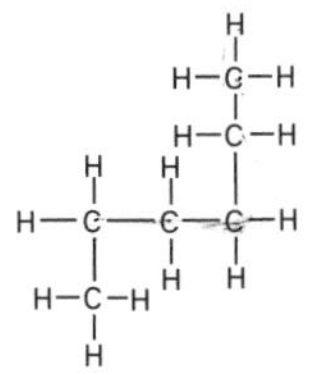

(iv)

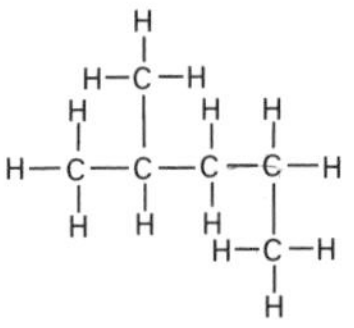

(v)

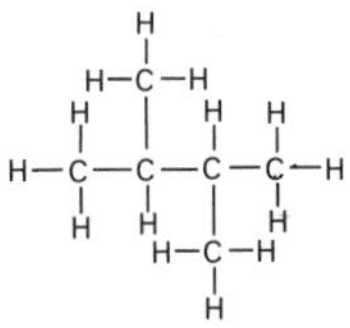

(vi)

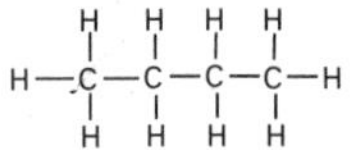

(vii)

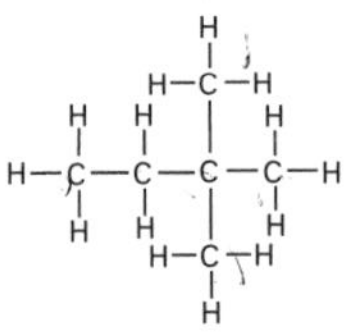

(viii)

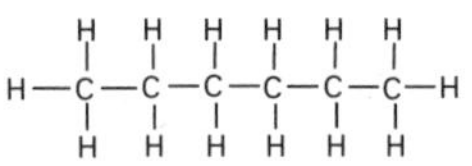

(ix)

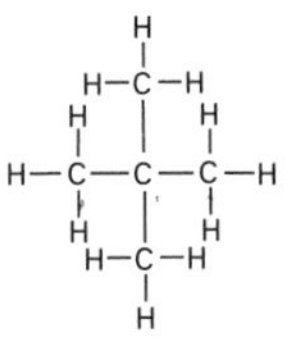

(x)

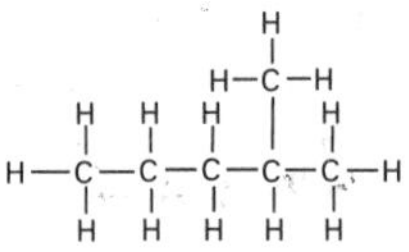

(xi)

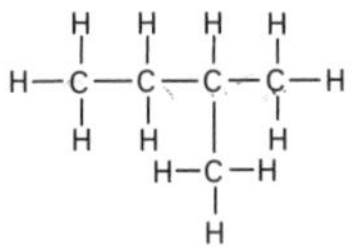

(xii)

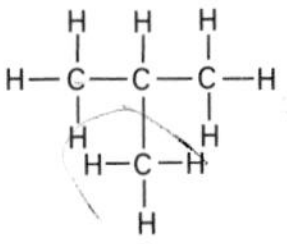

2 Now name all the alkanes drawn in question 1.

3 Name the following branched-chain alkanes. (Hint: first, draw the structural formula; bracketed groups are attached to the previous carbon atom.)
   (a) $CH_3C(CH_3)_2CH_2CH_3$
   (b) $CH_3CH(CH_3)CH_2CH_3$
   (c) $CH_3CH_2C(C_2H_5)_2CH_2CH_2CH_3$
   (d) $CH_3CH(CH_3)CH_2CH(CH_3)CH_3$
   (e) $CH_3CH_2CH(CH_3)CH(C_2H_5)CH_2C(CH_3)_2CH_3$

4 Draw structural formulae for the following alkanes:
   (a) 2-methylpropane (b) 3-methylheptane (c) 2,3-dimethylbutane
   (d) 2,2,6-trimethyloctane (e) 4-ethyl-2,3-dimethylheptane
   (f) 1,3-diethylcyclobutane

5 There are nine structural isomers which have the molecular formula C_7H_{16}. Draw their structural formulae and name them.

34.3 Physical properties of the alkanes

Some properties of alkanes are given in table 34.3. Notice that the molecular formulae of successive members of the alkane family *differ by a* $-CH_2-$ *unit*. Such compounds are said to form a **homologous series**. Moreover, they have a general formula, namely C_nH_{2n+2}, (and C_nH_{2n} for cycloalkanes).

Table 34.3 *Physical properties of some straight-chain alkanes*

Name	formula	state (at 298 K)	melting point/°C	boiling point/°C	density /g cm^{-3}	$\Delta H_c^{\ominus}$ /kJ mol^{-1}
methane	CH_4	gas	−183	−162	0.424(L)	−890
ethane	C_2H_6	gas	−172	− 89	0.546(L)	−1560
propane	C_3H_8	gas	−188	− 42	0.582(L)	−2220
butane	C_4H_{10}	gas	−135	0	0.579(L)	−2877
pentane	C_5H_{12}	liquid	−130	36	0.626	−3509
hexane	C_6H_{14}	liquid	− 95	−169	0.659	−4195
heptane	C_7H_{16}	liquid	− 91	98	0.684	−4853
octane	C_8H_{18}	liquid	− 57	126	0.703	−5512
nonane	C_9H_{20}	liquid	− 54	151	0.718	−6124
decane	$C_{10}H_{22}$	liquid	− 30	174	0.730	−6778

(L) means density in the liquid state

Is there any pattern in the boiling points, densities and standard enthalpies of combustion of these alkanes?

As you work throught the text, you will see that the *members of a homologous series* have:

▶ *similar chemical properties;*
▶ *gradually changing physical properties.*

The alkanes provide an excellent example of this behaviour.

Alkanes are non-polar substances. As such, their molecules are attracted to each other by **van der Waals' forces** (section 8.12). These intermolecular forces result from the mutual attraction between molecules which contain *induced* dipoles. Larger molecular electron clouds are more easily polarised and give rise to stronger van der Waals' forces. As the alkane gets larger, therefore, more energy is needed to separate neighbouring molecules and *the boiling points of the straight-chain alkanes*

Figure 34.2   *Graph of the boiling points of straight-chain alkanes plotted against the number of carbon atoms in the molecule*

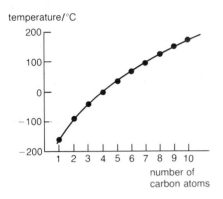

Figure 34.3   *Graph of the standard enthalpies of combustion, $\Delta H_c^{\ominus}$, of the straight-chain alkanes plotted against the number of carbon atoms in the molecule*

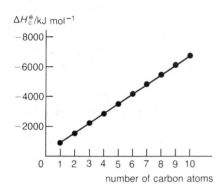

Figure 34.4   *A 'pie chart' showing the use of the world's energy resources (1990) How might this pie chart differ from that for our use of energy in the year 2100?*

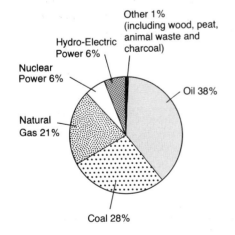

show a steady increase. Indeed, plotting their boiling points against molecular mass gives a smooth curve (figure 34.2).

Similar reasoning explains why *branched-chain alkanes have lower boiling points and densities than their straight-chain isomers* (table 34.4). Branching prevents the close contact of neighbouring molecules, thereby producing a more open structure. Consequently, the density is lowered and the strength of the van der Waals' forces is reduced.

Table 34.4   *Physical properties of some isomeric alkanes*

Name	structure (H atoms omitted)		state (at 298 K)	boiling point/°C	density /gcm^{-3}
butane	C—C—C—C		gas	0	0.579 (L)
		isomers of C_4H_{10}			

2-methylpropane	C—C—C
	    |
	    C
			gas	−12	0.557 (L)

pentane	C—C—C—C—C		liquid	36	0.626

2-methylbutane	C—C—C—C
	      |
	      C
			liquid	28	0.620

		isomers of C_5H_{12}			
2,2-dimethylpropane	C | C—C—C | C		gas	10	0.591 (L)

What happens to (i) the boiling point and (ii) the density of the isomers as their molecules become more branched?

Another feature of a homologous series is that the **enthalpies of combustion** *of successive members increase fairly steadily* by about 600–650 kJ mol^{-1} (see figure 34.3). This is to be expected since we are burning an extra $-CH_2-$ unit each time.

34.4   Refining petroleum

In its crude state, petroleum is a virtually useless material. However, when refined, the hydrocarbons it contains:

▶ supply almost half of the world's current energy needs (figure 34.4); and
▶ are the starting materials from which about 90% of the world's organic chemicals are made.

Refined petroleum, then, is highly valued as a source of fuel and a chemical feedstock.

In the UK, underwater pipelines or tankers carry the crude oil to the refinery. After the removal of water and any insoluble impurities, the petroleum is heated to about 400°C and then fractionally distilled. The fractionating column is about 60 metres high and contains layers of trays fitted with **bubble caps** (figure 34.5). Six main fractions are taken off the column during the primary distillation.

At the bottom of the column, the temperature is high enough to vaporise all but the highest boiling point hydrocarbons, that is, those with boiling points greater than about 350°C. These hydrocarbons, known as the **residue**, remain as liquids at the bottom of the column and can be run off. Petroleum also contains very volatile alkanes, having boiling points less than 20°C. These are removed as **refinery gases** at the top of column. The four other fractions, termed **gasoline, naptha, kerosene** and **gas oil**, are removed at intervals along the column.

Figure 34.5 *The primary fractionation of petroleum. A fractionating column contains many layers of 'bubble caps'. (% = approximate % by weight of that fraction in petroleum; length = number of carbon atoms in the molecules of the alkanes found in that fraction)*

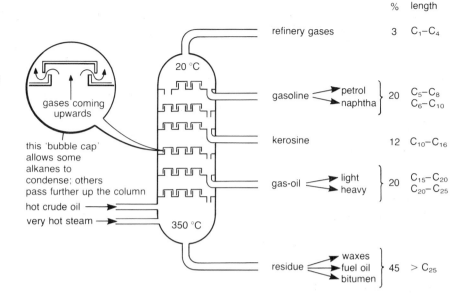

	%	length
refinery gases	3	C_1–C_4
gasoline → petrol, naphtha	20	C_5–C_8, C_6–C_{10}
kerosine	12	C_{10}–C_{16}
gas-oil → light, heavy	20	C_{15}–C_{20}, C_{20}–C_{25}
residue → waxes, fuel oil, bitumen	45	> C_{25}

gases coming upwards

this 'bubble cap' allows some alkanes to condense; others pass further up the column

hot crude oil →
very hot steam →

20 °C
350 °C

The effect of 'acid rain' on the stonework figures at York Minster and on trees in a Czechoslovakian forest

Before the fractions can be used, sulphur compounds (e.g. hydrogen sulphide) must be removed, and this is done by washing them with aqueous sodium hydroxide solution. Since massive amounts of petroleum, and natural gas, are purified in this way, we can extract appreciable amounts of sulphur and *it is a valuable by-product.*

Unfortunately, even after purification, petroleum fuels still contain small amounts of sulphur compounds. On combustion, these form sulphur dioxide which passes into the atmosphere and dissolves in rain. Wherever **acid rain** falls, it damages the stonework of buildings, kills trees and makes rivers and lakes uninhabitable. Such is the concern over acid rain pollution that many western countries have imposed laws controlling the levels of sulphur, and nitrogen oxides which are emitted by power stations and industrial consumers.

The further treatment and uses of the petroleum fractions are described in the next two sections.

34.5 Combustion of alkanes and their use as fuels

Alkanes burn readily in air to form carbon dioxide and water, e.g.

$$C_4H_{10}(g) + \tfrac{13}{2}O_2(g) \rightarrow 4CO_2(g) + 5H_2O(l) \ \Delta H = -2877\,\text{kJ mol}^{-1}$$
butane

Although the combustion of an alkane is a highly exothermic process, no reaction will occur unless the activation energy is supplied (figure 34.6). Thus, with respect to the reaction products, *an alkane/air mixture is energetically unstable, but kinetically stable* (section 4.13). As a result, alkanes can safely be used as fuels.

Figure 34.6 *Enthalpy profile for the combustion of an alkane. Compared to the combustion products, the alkane and oxygen are energetically unstable (i.e. ΔH is large and exothermic), but kinetically stable (i.e. E_a is large)*

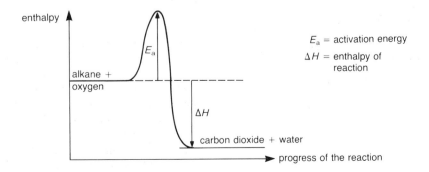

enthalpy

E_a

alkane + oxygen

ΔH

carbon dioxide + water

progress of the reaction

E_a = activation energy

ΔH = enthalpy of reaction

A 1200 litre tank provides butane gas for a whole house – central heating, cooking and a living-flame fire – and is particularly useful where there is no mains gas supply

Figure 34.7 *A piston and cylinder from an internal combustion engine. (a) The piston compresses the mixture of petrol vapour and air. (b) Maximum compression of the petrol/air mixture coincides with ignition by an electrical spark. (c) Spontaneous combustion occurs before maximum compression is obtained; this is termed 'knocking'*

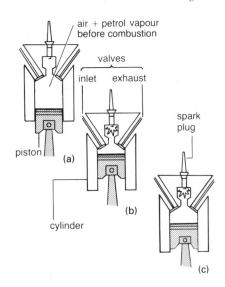

Figure 34.8 *2,2,4-trimethylpentane, an alkane with a very high resistance to knocking*

The **refinery gases** are valuable fuels. In some cases, the mixture is used directly at the refinery, e.g. to heat the incoming crude petroleum. Alternatively, the refinery gases can be liquefied and then fractionally distilled to produce the individual gases (methane, ethane, propane and butane). Since propane and butane are easily condensed, they are stored, and sold, as a liquid fuel, such as 'Calor' gas.

Further fractionation of **gasoline** yields **petrol** (C_5–C_8 alkanes). In the internal combustion engine, a mixture of air and petrol vapour is compressed by a piston (figure 34.7a). At the point of maximum compression, the petrol/air mixture is ignited by an electrical spark and an explosion occurs (figure 34.7b). A typical reaction would be the combustion of octane:

$$C_8H_{18}(g) + \tfrac{25}{2} O_2(g) \rightarrow 8CO_2(g) + 9H_2O(g) \quad \Delta H = -5470 \text{kJ mol}^{-1}$$

The hot gaseous products expand against the piston and force it downwards. This mechanical energy is transmitted to the drive wheels of the car, thus enabling it to move.

Petrol also contains various additives such as lubricants, rust inhibitors and **anti-knock** agents. Some hydrocarbons have a tendency to ignite spontaneously before maximum compression is achieved (figure 34.7c). This premature explosion, known as **knocking**, still forces the piston downwards and powers the vehicle. However, the chemical energy in the petrol is less efficiently converted into mechanical energy. As a result, *the vehicle will do fewer miles per gallon. Moreover, 'knocking' causes a rough ride and excessive engine wear.*

Nowadays, the anti-knock properties of petrol must conform to an international standard known as the **octane** scale. Branched-chain alkanes have been found to be much more resistant to knocking than their straight-chain isomers. In particular, **2,2,4-trimethyl pentane** (figure 34.8), has been identified as having an exceptionally *high* resistance to knocking. Thus, we say that pure 2,2,4-trimethylpentane has an octane number of 100. On the other hand, pure heptane is given an octane number of 0, because it is the straight-chain alkane with the *lowest* resistance to knocking. By comparing the anti-knock performance of 2,2,4-trimethylpentane/heptane mixtures with that of the petrol, we can give the latter an octane number (table 34.5).

Table 34.5 *Octane numbers of some petrol samples. Which sample would you use?*

Sample . . .	behaves like a mixture of		its octane
	. . % 2,2,4-tmp	+ . . % heptane	number is
A	55	45	55
B	95	5	95

(2,2,4-tmp = 2,2,4-trimethylpentane)

To summarise then, by using petrol with a high octane number (i.e. very resistant to knocking), we can increase the engine's efficiency and prolong its life. There are two important ways of increasing the petrol's octane number:

▶ *By adding about 2% by mass of* **tetraethyl lead**, *$(C_2H_5)_4Pb$, an anti-knock agent.* This breaks up during the combustion to form tiny lead(IV) oxide particles which ensure even combustion of the fuel at a moderate rate. To prevent a build-up of lead(IV) oxide in the cylinder, a small amount of 1,2-dibromoethane ($BrCH_2CH_2Br$) is added to the petrol. This reacts with the residual lead oxide to produce lead bromide, a fairly volatile compound. Consequently, it passes with the other exhaust gases into the atmosphere.

Unfortunately, *lead compounds are known to be very toxic.* In recent years, much attention has been focused on the dangers of the atmospheric lead

Kerosene, a mixture of C₁₀–C₁₆ alkanes, is used as aviation fuel

All petrol-driven cars being manufactured in the UK today must be able to run on unleaded petrol

pollution which arises from the use of tetraethyl lead. Inhalation of lead-polluted air causes a build-up of lead in the blood, and this is thought to impair the brain's activity. In acute cases, lead-poisoning can cause permanent brain damage.

Such is the concern over the effects of lead pollution that many countries are phasing out the use of tetraethyl lead. In Britain, for example, all new petrol-driven vehicles built since 1990 have to run on unleaded petrol.

▸ Prohibiting the use of tetraethyl lead will certainly clean up the atmosphere, especially in inner city areas. However, we will still be faced with the problem of petrol wastage and engine wear caused by 'knocking'. Apart from modifying the engine's design, *'knocking' can be prevented by increasing the proportion of branched alkanes, cycloalkanes and aromatic hydrocarbons in the petrol*. Now, although these compounds have excellent 'anti-knock' properties, only relatively small amounts occur naturally in crude oil. Thus, the refinery makes them from the other crude oil fractions using **cracking** and **reforming** processes (section 34.6).

The other petroleum fractions are also used as fuels. **Kerosene** is used as fuel in jet engines and, domestically, as 'paraffin' for lamps and heaters. **Light gas-oil** is used in oil-fired central heating systems. **Heavy gas-oil** finds widespread use as **diesel** fuel. In the diesel engine, compression of the air/fuel vapour mixture causes it to ignite spontaneously. Thus, no sparking plugs are needed and the common problems associated with an electrical ignition are avoided. Unfortunately, unlike petrol, diesel will freeze in very cold weather! Most of the thick oily **residue** from the primary fractionation can be used as fuel oil to power ships or electrical generators.

Whenever alkanes are burnt in a *limited* supply of oxygen (e.g. in a petrol engine), **incomplete combustion** will occur. Apart from carbon, another product of incomplete combustion is **carbon monoxide**. This is a very poisonous gas because it can block the uptake of oxygen by the haemoglobin in blood (figure 29.5). Car exhaust fumes always contain up to about 10% by volume of carbon monoxide, together with other pollutants (e.g. nitrogen oxides and unburnt hydrocarbons). In some countries, car exhausts must be fitted with **catalytic converters** which convert these pollutants into harmless substances. Unfortunately, since the catalyst is poisoned by lead, these devices can only be used if the engine runs on unleaded petrol.

Activity 34.2

The molecular formula of any gaseous hydrocarbon can be calculated from the volume change on combustion. An example is given below.

A known volume of an alkane is completely burnt in an excess of oxygen and the volume of residual gases ($CO_2(g)$ + unreacted $O_2(g)$) is measured. These are then shaken with aqueous sodium hydroxide solution so that the carbon dioxide is absorbed. Once again, the volume of gas (only unreacted $O_2(g)$) is measured. (Note: all gases are measured at room temperature and pressure; thus, the water formed is a liquid not a gas volume.) Some typical results might be:

volume of alkane	=	$30\,cm^3$
volume of O_2 added	=	$340\,cm^3$
volume of O_2 (left) + CO_2	=	$250\,cm^3$
volume of O_2 (left)	=	$100\,cm^3$

Use the general equation for the combustion of a hydrocarbon,

$$C_xH_y(g) + (x + y/4)\,O_2(g) \rightarrow x\,CO_2(g) + y/2\,H_2O(l)$$

An oil refinery in the Netherlands, where a great number of heavy chemical plants have been sited to take advantage of North Sea oil and gas and the excellent port facilities

and Avogadro's Law to calculate the relative molecular mass of the alkane. (Hint: see section 8.4.)

Write down the possible structures of this alkane.

34.6 Cracking and reforming the petroleum fractions

Although 90% of petroleum is used as fuel, fractionating petroleum is only part of the refinery's work. Many other process plants will be based on site (see photograph, left). Two important types of process are **cracking** and **reforming**.

Cracking

Only about a fifth of crude oil is gasoline and this does not produce enough petrol to satisfy world demands. However, there is a surplus of kerosene and light gas oil. Thus, chemists have developed a process called cracking, which *converts large alkane molecules into smaller molecules (alkanes, alkenes or hydrogen)*.

Since strong C—C and C—H bonds must be broken, cracking is carried out at high temperature, often using a catalyst. For example, kerosene can be cracked at 500 °C in the presence of powdered silicon and aluminium oxides, e.g.

$$C_{12}H_{26}(g) \xrightarrow[\substack{SiO_2/Al_2O_3 \\ \text{(catalyst)}}]{500\,°C} C_9H_{20}(g) + CH_3CH{=}CH_2(g)$$

$$\text{dodecane} \qquad\qquad\qquad \text{nonane} \qquad \text{propene}$$

An added benefit of cracking is that the products are often rich in *branched* alkanes. As we have seen, these are valued for their high resistance to 'knocking'. Cracking nearly always gives a mixture of organic products. These are then passed to a fractionating column for separation.

Apart from supplementing petrol supplies, cracking also produces alkenes. Because they contain C=C bonds, *alkenes are more reactive then alkanes*. Hence, they are a convenient starting point from which to make other organic chemicals. In particular, the manufacture of plastics and organic solvents requires vast amounts of ethene and propene. These can be made by cracking the ethane and propane obtained from refinery and natural gas:

$$H_3C{-}CH_3(g) \xrightarrow{700\,°C} H_2C{=}CH_2(g) + H_2(g)$$

$$H_3C{-}CH_2{-}CH_3(g) \xrightarrow[\substack{\text{catalyst:} \\ Cr_2O_3/Al_2O_3}]{500\,°C} H_3C{=}CH{-}CH_2(g) + H_2(g)$$

Note here that (i) no alkanes are produced, and (ii) the hydrogen gas is a valuable by-product, e.g. for making ammonia in the Haber process.

Reforming

In these processes, alkane molecules are either restructured or combined to form larger molecules.

Isomerisation and alkylation When heated in the presence of an aluminium chloride catalyst, *straight-chain alkanes can be converted into their branched-chain isomers*. This process is called **isomerisation**. For example, butane from refinery or natural gas yields the rather more useful, branched isomer, 2-methylpropane:

butane → 2-methylpropane (500 °C, catalyst: AlCl₃)

Branched-chain alkanes are valuable because they can be added to petrol, thereby increasing its octane number. Alternatively, they can be reacted with alkenes (e.g. from cracking) to form longer chain branched alkanes. This process, known as **alkylation**, occurs at low temperatures and is catalysed by concentrated sulphuric acid, e.g.

2-methylpropene + 2-methylpropane → 2,2,4-trimethylpentane (25 °C, catalyst: conc. H₂SO₄(l))

As we have seen, 2,2,4-trimethylpentane has excellent 'anti-knock' properties.

Cyclisation and aromatisation In these processes, cycloalkanes and aromatic hydrocarbons are made from the straight-chain 'C₆–C₁₀' alkanes in naptha. The naphtha vapour is heated to 500 °C and then passed, at high pressure, over a catalyst of platinum metal absorbed on aluminium oxide. A typical reaction would be:

hexane → cyclohexane (500 °C, 20 atm, catalyst: Pt/Al₂O₃(s), cyclisation) → benzene (same conditions, aromatisation)

Cycloalkanes can be added to petrol to increase its octane number. Benzene is used as a solvent and as starting material in the manufacture of many important aromatic compounds.

34.7 Some other uses of the alkanes in petroleum

Large quantities of the **methane** in refinery and natural gases are reacted with steam at 450 °C, using a nickel catalyst:

$$CH_4(g) + H_2O(g) \rightarrow CO(g) + 3H_2(g)$$

After separation, the hydrogen is used in the manufacture of ammonia (refer to the Haber process, section 25.7).

Some of the **residue** is redistilled under reduced pressure (section 32.3). This yields a variety of **lubricating oils**, each containing dissolved **paraffin wax** which is removed by solvent extraction. After purification, paraffin wax is used to waterproof paper cartons and in the manufacture of candles and petroleum jelly (Vaseline).

Like naphtha, paraffin wax can be cracked by mixing it with steam at 500 °C. The products are valuable alkenes containing 5 to 18 carbon atoms and a terminal double bond, e.g. $CH_3(CH_2)_{14}CH{=}CH_2$. After fractional distillation, the smaller alkenes are passed to the alkylation plant. The longer chain alkenes are used in the manufacture of **detergents** (section 40.11).

After vacuum distillation of the original residue, we are left with a thick tarry solid. Even this substance, called **bitumen**, is not discarded but is used to surface roads and in the manufacture of roofing felt and damp-proof coursing.

(The key aspects of petroleum refining are summarised in section 34.10.)

34.8 Free radical substitution reactions in alkanes

Due to the overall non-polarity of an alkane molecule, the C—H bonds will undergo **homolytic fission**:

$$C \overset{\times}{\underset{\bullet}{-}} H \rightarrow C_\bullet + {}^\times H$$

Free radicals are formed (section 33.2). Generally speaking, alkanes react with non-polar reagents whose bonds can also break up homolytically. Thus, alkanes do not react with $H^+(aq)$ or $OH^-(aq)$ ions. They do take part, though, in the following **free radical substitution reactions**.

34.8.1 With halogens

Alkanes react with the halogens to form halogenoalkanes. In these compounds, one or more halogen atoms substitute for hydrogen atoms in the hydrocarbon skeleton, e.g.

$$C_2H_6(g) + Cl_2(g) \xrightarrow{\text{dull sunlight}} C_2H_5Cl(g) + HCl(g)$$
$$\text{ethane} \qquad\qquad\qquad\qquad \text{chloroethane}$$

Table 34.6 summarises the effects of mixing each halogen with an excess of methane. The results show that:

▶ the reactivity of the halogens with alkanes increases in the order: $I_2 < Br_2 < Cl_2 < F_2$;
▶ the reactions involving chlorine and bromine obtain their activation energies by absorbing ultraviolet light. Thus, they are termed **photochemical** reactions.

Table 34.6 *Observations on mixing a halogen with an alkane*

Halogen used	conditions: at 30 °C and . . .	
	. . . in the dark	. . . exposed to ultra violet light
fluorine	explosion	explosion
chlorine	no reaction	green colour of $Cl_2(g)$ quickly disappears
bromine	no reaction	brown colour of $Br_2(g)$ slowly disappears
iodine	no reaction	no reaction

Do these results show a trend in the reactivity of the halogens with alkanes?

Mechanism

The chlorination of methane has been well researched; it is thought to have a 'three step' mechanism.

Step 1: Initiation
Chlorine molecules absorb the ultra violet light. Some homolytic bond fission takes place, and Cl free radicals are produced:

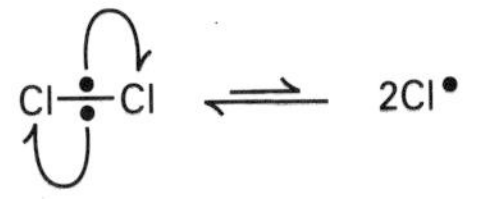

$$Cl \overset{\curvearrowright}{\underset{\curvearrowright}{-}} Cl \rightleftharpoons 2Cl^\bullet$$

($\curvearrowright$ represents the movement of the charge cloud due to one electron.)

Step 2: Propagation
The $Cl^\bullet$ free radical is a highly reactive atom and this pulls an H atom off the methane molecule. Hydrogen chloride and a methyl radical are formed.
    The methyl radical then reacts with an undissociated chlorine molecule, thereby forming chloromethane and providing a $Cl^\bullet$ to take part in another

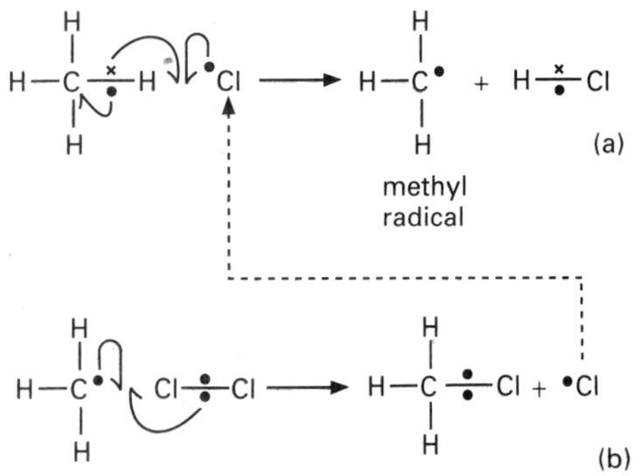

(a)

methyl
radical

(b)

reaction (a). This leads to a rapid repetition of the propagating reactions ((a) . . (b) . . (a) . . (b) . . and so on); this is termed a free radical **chain** reaction.

Step 3: Termination

When one of the reactants has been used up, the chain reaction is terminated by the combination

with
excess
halogen:

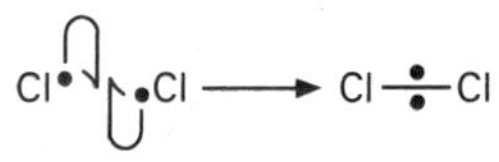

with
excess
methane:

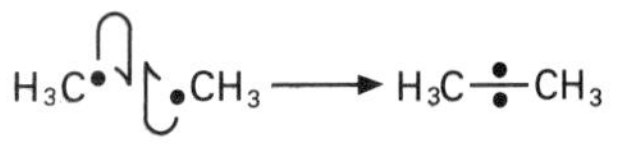

If the chlorine is in excess, further free radical substitution will occur:

$$CH_3Cl(g) + Cl_2(g) \rightarrow CH_2Cl_2(g) + HCl(g)$$
$$CH_2Cl_2(g) + Cl_2(g) \rightarrow CHCl_3(g) + HCl(g)$$
$$CHCl_3(g) + Cl_2(g) \rightarrow CCl_4(g) + HCl(g)$$

The halogenation of larger alkanes proceeds through an identical mechanism to give a mixture of products, e.g.

$$CH_3CH_2CH_3(g) \xrightarrow[\text{u.v. light}]{Br_2(g)} CH_3CH_2CH_2Br(g) + CH_3CHBrCH_3(g)$$

propane   1-bromopropane   2-bromopropane
(in excess)

Of course, a 'multi-product' reaction may have limited synthetic value because of the cost of separating the products. However, the chloro-compounds of methane and ethane are made this way. These are valuable solvents, e.g. 1,1,1-trichloroethane is used in 'Tipp-Ex' correction fluid.

34.8.2 With nitric acid vapour

Although alkanes do not react with concentrated nitric acid at room temperature, a vapour phase substitution reaction can occur:

$$CH_4(g) + HNO_3(g) \xrightarrow[\text{10 atm}]{400°C} CH_3NO_2(g) + H_2O(g)$$

A nitroalkane is formed. Nitroalkanes are used as fuels, solvents and in the synthesis of amines (section 41.2).

Activity 34.3

1   Give the name and structural formula of the organic product formed in each of the following reactions.

(a)   ethane $\xrightarrow[\text{u.v. light}]{\text{excess } Cl_2(g)}$

(b)   cyclohexane $\xrightarrow[\text{u.v. light}]{\text{equimolar } Br_2(g); \text{ heat}}$

(c) $C_2H_6 \xrightarrow[\text{10 atm}]{\text{equimolar } HNO_3(g), 400°C}$

2   (a) Write balanced equations for the complete combustion of the following alkanes: (i) ethane, (ii) 3-methylpentane and (iii) cyclobutane.
    (b) What other products would be formed if these alkanes were burnt in a poor supply of oxygen?

3   Give the reagent and the reaction conditions needed for the following conversions:

(a) C_7H_{16} (heptane) $\longrightarrow$ ⬡—CH_3 (methylbenzene)

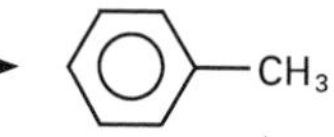

(b) $CH_3COOH \longrightarrow CH_2ClCOOH$

(c)  ⬡ $\longrightarrow$ ⬡—NO_2

4   Write down the mechanism for the following reaction:

$$CHBr_3(g) + Br_2(g) \rightarrow CBr_4(g) + HBr(g)$$

34.9 Comments on the activities

Activity 34.1

1   (a) Equivalent structures: (iii) and (viii), both hexane
                                (iv) and (x), both 2-methylpentane.
    (b) Isomeric structures: (i), (iii) or (viii), (iv) or (x), (v) and (vii) are all C_6H_{14};
                              (ii), (ix) and (xi) are all C_5H_{12};
                              (vi) and (xii) are both C_4H_{10}.

2   (i) 3-methylpentane; (ii) pentane; (iii) and (viii) hexane;
    (iv) and (x) 2-methylpentane; (v) 2,3-dimethylbutane
    (vi) butane; (vii) 2,2-dimethylbutane;
    (ix) 2,2-dimethylpropane; (xi) 2-methylbutane
    (xii) 2-methylpropane.

3

(a) 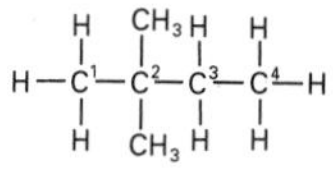   2,2-dimethylbutane

(b) 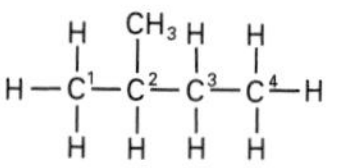   2-methylbutane

(c) 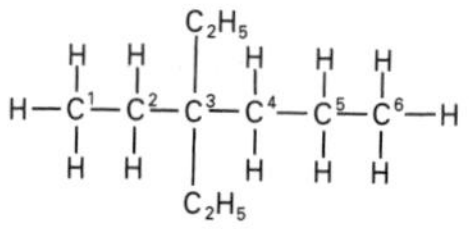   3,3-diethylhexane

(d) 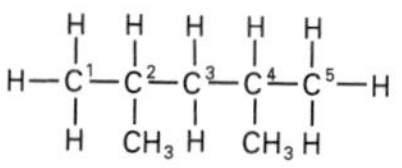   2,4-dimethylpentane

(e) 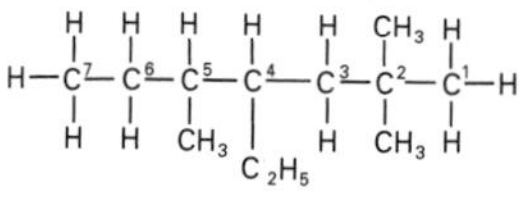   4-ethyl-2,2,5-trimethylheptane

4

(a)

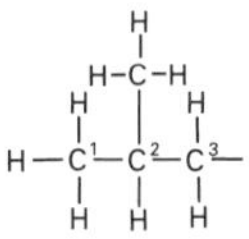

(b)

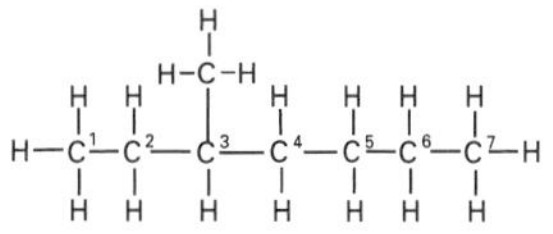

(c)

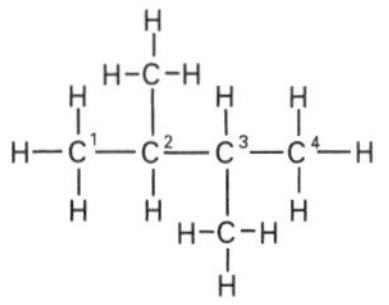

(d)

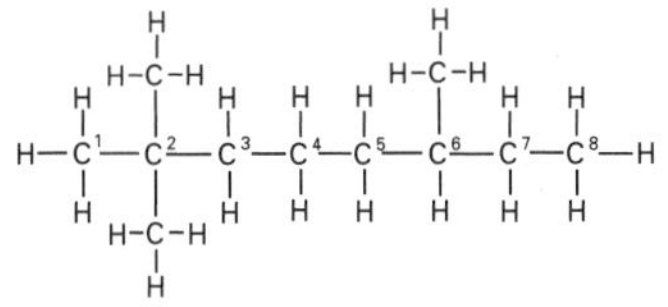

(e)

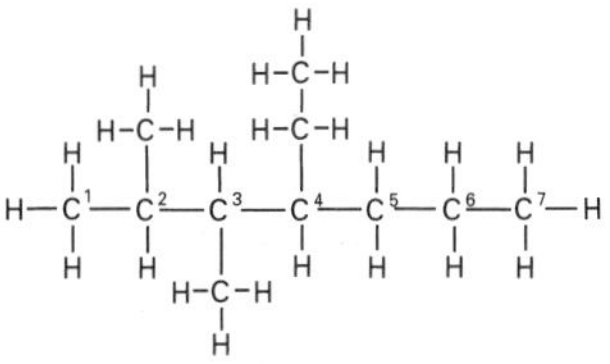

(f)

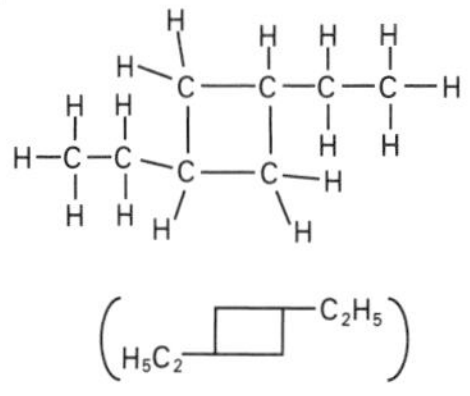

$$\left(H_5C_2 \boxed{\quad}^{C_2H_5} \right)$$

5

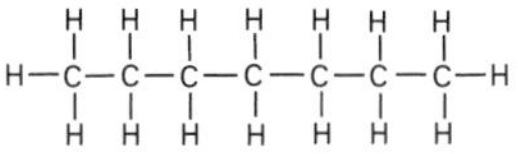

heptane

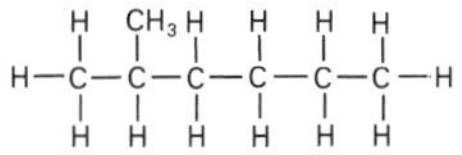

2–methylhexane

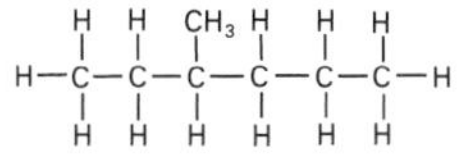

3–methylhexane

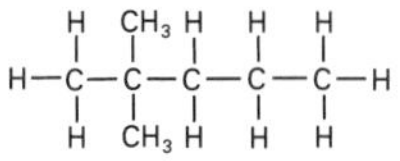

2,2–dimethylpentane

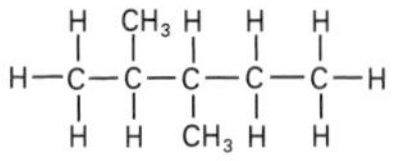

2,3–dimethylpentane

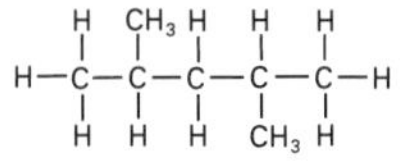

2,4–dimethylpentane

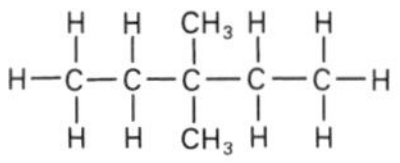

3,3–dimethylpentane

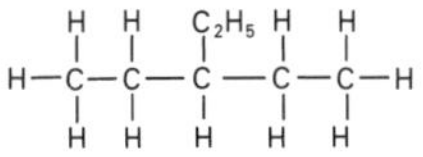

3–ethylpentane

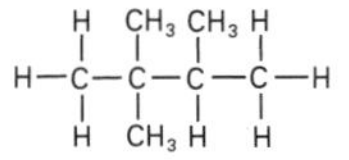

2,2,3–trimethylbutane

Activity 34.2

(a) These results show that
   (i) the volume of $CO_2(g)$ formed $= 250 - 100 = 150\,cm^3$
   (ii) the volume of $O_2(g)$ used $= 340 - 100 = 240\,cm^3$
   The general equation for the combustion of alkanes is:

$$C_xH_y \ + (x + y/4)O_2 \ \longrightarrow x CO_2 \ + y/2 H_2O$$
$$\text{1 mole} \quad (x + y/4)\text{ moles} \quad x\text{ moles} \ + y/2 \text{ moles}$$

From Avogadro's Law:
$$\begin{array}{llll} 1\text{ vol} & (x + y/4)\text{ vols} & \longrightarrow x\text{ vols} & + \text{ liquid} \\ 30 & 240 & 150 & - \qquad (cm^3) \end{array}$$

where vol = a certain volume of gas.
Now, since $30\,cm^3 = 1\,vol$, $150\,cm^3 = 5\,vols$; thus, $x = 5$.
Similarly, $240\,cm^3 = 8\,vols$
and $x + y/4 \ = 8$, but $x = 5$
$\therefore$ $5 + y/4 \ = 8$
            $y/4 \ = 8 - 5 = 3$
from which $y = 12$.
Thus, the formula of the alkane is C_5H_{12}.

(b) There are three isomeric alkanes:

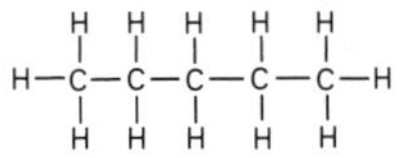

pentane

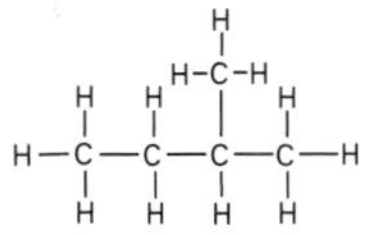

2–methylbutane

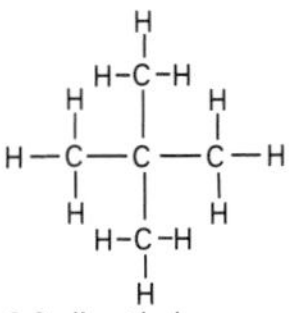

2,2–dimethylpropane

Activity 34.3

1 (a) hexachloroethane

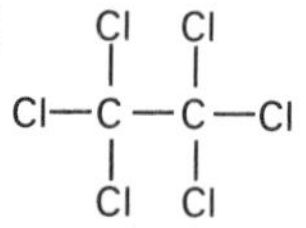

(b) bromocyclohexane

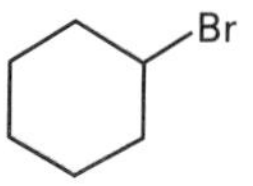

(c) nitroethane

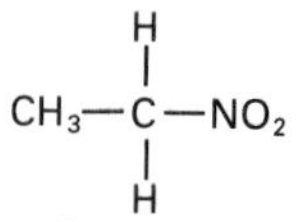

2 (a) (i) $C_2H_6(g) + \frac{7}{2}O_2(g) \rightarrow 2CO_2(g) + 3H_2O(l)$
        (ii) $CH_3CH_2CH(CH_3)CH_2CH_3(l) + \frac{19}{2}O_2(g) \rightarrow 6CO_2(g) + 7H_2O(l)$
        (iii) $C_4H_8(g) + 6O_2(g) \rightarrow 4CO_2(g) + 4H_2O(l)$

3 (a) 500°C, 20 atm, catalyst: $Pt/Al_2O_3(s)$
    (b) equimolar $Cl_2(g)$, u.v. light
    (c) equimolar $HNO_3(g)$, 400°C, 10 atm

4

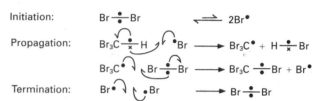

Initiation:

Propagation:

Termination:

34.10 Summary and revision plan

1 Alkanes are **saturated** hydrocarbons, that is, they contain only single bonds. Each carbon is tetrahedrally surrounded by four other atoms, thereby giving bond angles of 109.5°.

2 Alkanes are named by using the set of five rules given in section 34.2. Structural (**chain**) isomers are a common feature.

3 Alkanes form an **homologous series** of general formula C_nH_{2n+2}. They have identical chemical properties and their physical properties change gradually with increasing molecular mass. Alkanes have non-polar molecules, which are weakly attracted to each other via van der Waals' forces.

4 Alkanes occur naturally in **natural gas** and **petroleum**. These were formed by the bacterial decay of marine plants and animals which lived millions of years ago. Alkanes are used as fuels and as a feedstock for the chemical industry. Figure 34.9 summarises the main aspects of the refining of petroleum and the uses of the products.

5 Alkanes take part in three main types of reaction: (i) **free radical substitution** of the hydrogen atoms, (ii) **combustion** and (iii) **cracking**. These are summarised in figure 34.10.

6 Substitution in alkanes occurs via a free radical chain reaction. The mechanism involves **initiation, propagation** and **termination**. Remember there are **two** propagating steps.

7 Alkanes are good fuels because they readily burn in air to form mainly carbon dioxide and water. A small amount of incomplete combustion, giving C(s) and CO(g), may occur, especially where the oxygen supply is restricted.

8 The quantitative combustion of a hydrocarbon can be used to determine its molecular formula (see activity 34.3).

9 The conversion of a longer chain alkane into a shorter chain alkane and/or an alkene is known as **cracking**. This is carried out at high temperature, often in the presence of a catalyst.

10 The new reagents used in this chapter are shown in table 34.7.

Table 34.7 *New reagents used in chapter 34*

Reagent	conditions	what it does to an alkane
$Cl_2(g)$ or $Br_2(g)$	presence of u.v. light	converts C—H into C—Hal
$HNO_3(g)$	400°C, 10 atm	converts C—H into C—NO$_2$

Figure 34.9 *The key aspects of the petroleum and petrochemicals industries*

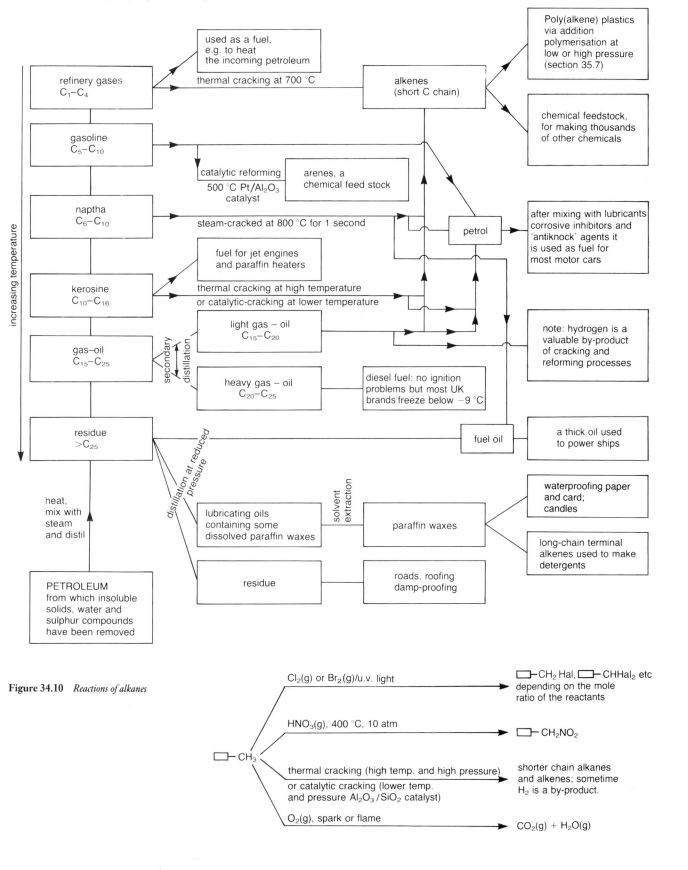

Figure 34.10 *Reactions of alkanes*

Alkenes and Alkynes

Contents

Carrier bags, records, antifreeze, 'throwaway' cups and washing powder all have something in common – they contain materials made from **alkenes**. Alkenes are hydrocarbons which contain at least one C═C bond, e.g. ethene, $H_2C═CH_2$. Because they contain a multiple bond, alkenes are said to be **unsaturated** compounds.

Alkynes are another type of unsaturated hydrocarbon; they contain at least one C≡C bond. The simplest alkyne, ethyne, HC≡CH, is the fuel for the oxy-acetylene torch used to weld and cut metals.

In this chapter, we shall compare the properties of alkenes and alkynes and discuss further their many uses.

35.1 Naming alkenes and alkynes

Like alkanes, the names of unsaturated hydrocarbons consist of two parts:

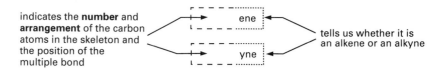

indicates the **number** and **arrangement** of the carbon atoms in the skeleton and the position of the multiple bond

ene

yne

tells us whether it is an alkene or an alkyne

For example,

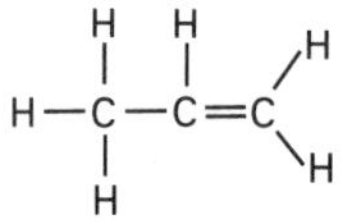

propene C_3H_6 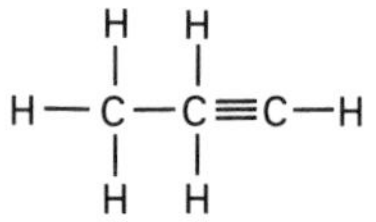   propyne C_3H_4

For unsaturated hydrocarbons with four, or more, carbon atoms, there is the possibility of **positional isomerism**:

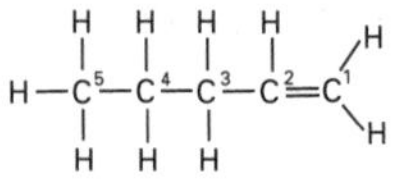

pent–1–ene   and 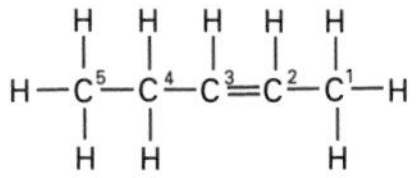   pent–2–ene

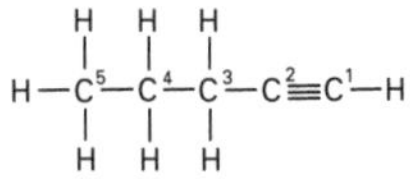

pent–1–yne   and 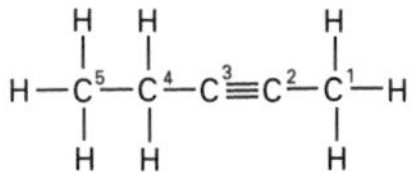   pent–2–yne

The numbers refer to the position of the *first* unsaturated carbon. Where two numbers are possible, the *smaller* must be used, e.g.

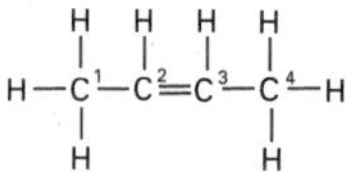

is   but–2–ene   and not but–3–ene.

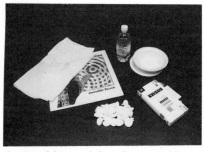

A variety of objects made from alkenes: carrier bags (polythene), records (PVC), bottles and videotapes (polyester) and plates and packing material (polystyrene)

Both alkenes and alkynes can display **chain isomerism**, e.g.

A welder using an oxy-acetylene torch. The flame has a temperature of about 2000°C

3–methylbut–1–ene   3–methylbutyne

are   chain isomers of the pentenes or pentynes shown earlier

Alkenes, but not alkynes, can form **geometrical isomers** (section 10.3), e.g.

cis–pent–2–ene   *trans*–pent–2–ene

Does pent–1–ene exhibit geometrical isomerism?

If a molecule contains more than one C=C, or C≡C bond, then the position of each must be stated, e.g.

penta–1,3–diene   penta–1,4–diene

In complex molecules, we often use a 'common' name, e.g. vitamin A (figure 35.1). Notice that the molecules of vitamin A and penta-1,3-diene both contain *alternating single and double bonds*; thus, they are termed **conjugated** alkenes. Synthetic rubber can be made from buta-1,3-diene, the simplest conjugated alkene (section 35.9).

Figure 35.1 *Vitamin A, a conjugated alkene*

Activity 35.1

1 Name the unsaturated hydrocarbons whose formulae are shown below:

(a) $CH_3CH_2CH_2CH=CHCH_3$ (b) $CH_3CH(CH_3)CH=CHCH_3$

(c) $CH_3C≡C-CH(CH_3)_2$

(d)

(e)

(f) $CH_3CH(CH_3)C≡CCH_2CH_3$

(You may find it helpful to draw out the structural formulae, where necessary.)

2 Draw structural formulae for the following alkenes and alkynes:
(a) 2,3-dimethylbut-2-ene; (b) 4-methylhex-1-yne;
(c) 3,4-diethylhex-2-ene; (d) *cis*-hex-3-ene; (e) phenylethene;
(f) 4-ethylcyclohex-1-ene; (g) 2-methylbuta-1,3-diene.

3 Which of the following compounds exhibit geometrical isomerism?
(a) hex-2-ene; (b) but-1-ene (c) 1-phenylpropene
(d) 2-methylpropene (e) penta-1,3-diene
(Hint: in each case, first draw out the structural formulae.)

35.2 Physical properties of unsaturated hydrocarbons

Some properties of unsaturated hydrocarbons are listed in table 35.1.

Table 35.1 *Some properties of unsaturated hydrocarbons*

Name	formula	state at 298 K	melting point/°C	boiling point/°C	density /g cm^{-3}	$\Delta H_c^{\ominus}$ /kJ mol^{-1}
ethene	C_2H_4	gas	−169	−102	0.610 (L)	−1411
propene	C_3H_6	gas	−185	−48	0.514 (L)	−2058
but-1-ene	C_4H_8	gas	−185	−6	0.595 (L)	−2717
but-2-ene	C_4H_8	gas	−139	3	0.621 (L)	−2710
hex-1-ene	C_6H_{12}	liquid	−139	64	0.673	−4004
cyclohexene	C_6H_{10}	liquid	−104	83	0.811	−4128
ethyne	C_2H_2	gas	−80	−83	0.618 (L)	−1300
propyne	C_3H_4	gas	−103	−23	0.671 (L)	−1938

(L) means density in the liquid state

What effect does increasing chain length have on the boiling points, densities and standard enthalpies of combustion of the straight-chain alkenes?

What value would you predict for the standard enthalpy of combustion of pent-1-ene?

Figure 35.2 *Graphs of (a) the boiling points of straight-chain alkenes (•) and alkynes (×), and (b) the standard enthalpies of combustion of straight-chain alkenes, $\Delta H_c^{\ominus}$, each plotted against the number of carbon atoms in the molecule*

(a) boiling point /°C

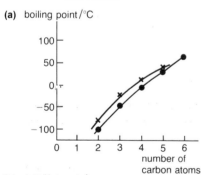

(b) $\Delta H_c^{\ominus}$/kJ mol^{-1}

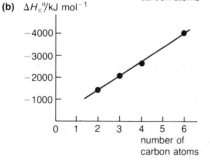

Alkenes and alkynes both form **homologous series**. As such, the members of each series have:

▶ a general formula, namely, C_nH_{2n} and C_nH_{2n-2} for aliphatic alkenes and alkynes, respectively;
▶ gradually increasing boiling points (figure 35.2a) and enthalpies of combustion (figure 35.2b);
▶ similar chemical properties.

As expected, the lower members of each series are gases. With increasing molecular size, the hydrocarbons are found as liquids and, eventually, as solids. Can you explain why?

Since alkenes and alkynes are non-polar substances, they are insoluble in water. However, they are readily soluble in many organic solvents.

35.3 Making unsaturated hydrocarbons

Manufacture

Unlike alkanes, simple unsaturated hydrocarbons occur naturally in only minute quantities. Although alkanes are excellent fuels, they do not take part in a wide range of reactions and this limits their use as a chemical feedstock. The greater reactivity of alkenes and alkynes makes them convenient starting materials in the synthesis of other chemicals (table 35.2).

Ethene and propene are made by cracking (i) the naphtha or gas-oil fractions of petroleum or (ii) the ethane and propane from natural gas (section 34.6).

Ethyne is made by heating methane (from natural gas), at 1500 °C for about 0.01 seconds:

$$2CH_4(g) \xrightarrow[0.01 \text{ seconds}]{1500\,°C} HC≡CH(g) + 3H_2(g)$$

Unless the heating time is very short, the ethyne will decompose into carbon and hydrogen.

Table 35.2 *Some examples of the use of alkenes as a chemical feedstock*

Starting material	commercial product	use
ethene	plastics (35.8)	construction, packaging etc.
	ethanol (38.3)	solvent, cosmetics
	epoxyethane (35.7.1)	manufacture of antifreeze (35.7.1) polyester (40.11) and detergents (40.11)
propene	propanone, as a by-product of the manufacture of phenol (38.3)	solvent, plastics
buta-1,3-diene	synthetic rubber (35.9)	tyres, electrical insulation

Laboratory preparation

Alkenes may be prepared from:

▶ an alcohol, by refluxing it with excess concentrated sulphuric acid, e.g.

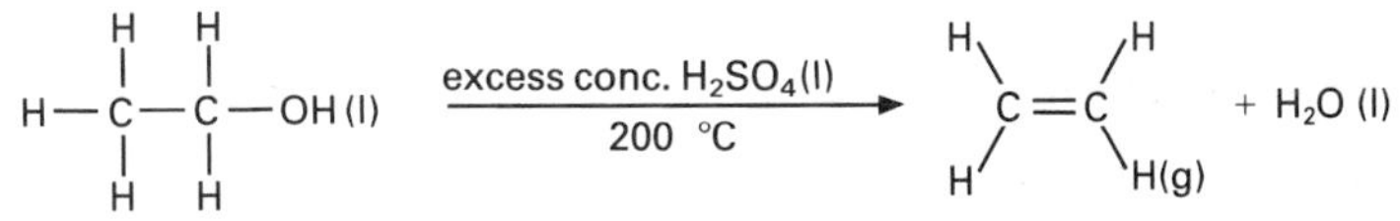

$$H-\underset{\underset{H}{|}}{\overset{\overset{H}{|}}{C}}-\underset{\underset{H}{|}}{\overset{\overset{H}{|}}{C}}-OH(l) \xrightarrow[200\ °C]{\text{excess conc. } H_2SO_4(l)} \underset{H}{\overset{H}{>}}C=C\underset{H(g)}{\overset{H}{<}} + H_2O\ (l)$$

Since *water is eliminated from the alcohol*, this is termed a **dehydration** reaction. Concentrated sulphuric acid is acting as a **dehydrating agent**.

▶ a halogenoalkane, by refluxing it with potassium hydroxide dissolved in ethanol, e.g.

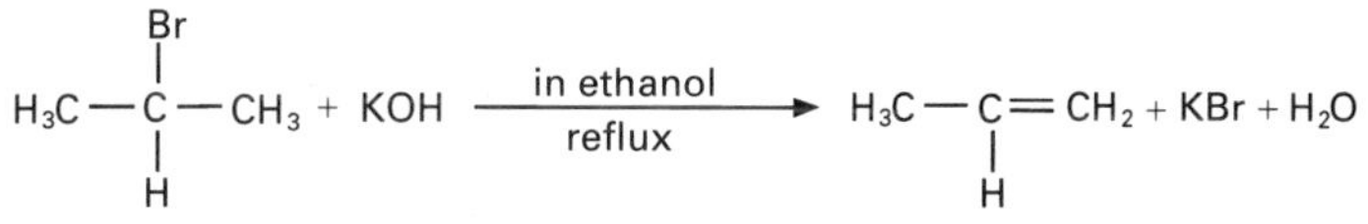

$$H_3C-\underset{\underset{H}{|}}{\overset{\overset{Br}{|}}{C}}-CH_3 + KOH \xrightarrow[\text{reflux}]{\text{in ethanol}} H_3C-\underset{\underset{H}{|}}{C}=CH_2 + KBr + H_2O$$

2–bromopropane   propene

Here the hydrogen halide is eliminated.

The method above can also be used to prepare an alkyne. In this case, *two molecules of hydrogen halide must be removed across the same C—C bond*, e.g.

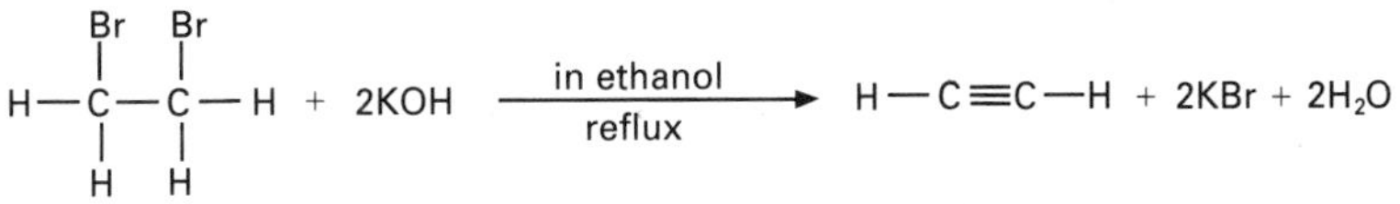

$$H-\underset{\underset{H}{|}}{\overset{\overset{Br}{|}}{C}}-\underset{\underset{H}{|}}{\overset{\overset{Br}{|}}{C}}-H + 2KOH \xrightarrow[\text{reflux}]{\text{in ethanol}} H-C≡C-H + 2KBr + 2H_2O$$

1,2–dibromoethane   ethyne

Although ethyne can be made this way, a cheaper method is the dropwise addition of water to calcium carbide:

$$CaC_2(s) + 2H_2O(l) → HC≡CH(g) + Ca(OH)_2(s)$$

Here *a weaker acid, ethyne, is displaced from its salt by a stronger acid, water*. Until recently, most industrial ethyne was produced in this way.

35.4 Electronic structures of alkenes and alkynes

The **bond energy term (BET)** for a carbon–carbon single bond is $348\,kJ\,mol^{-1}$. What values might you expect, then, for the BETs of C=C and C≡C bonds? Well, if the multiple bonds are made up of identical single bonds, we would expect BETs for C=C and C≡C to be about 692 and $1038\,kJ\,mol^{-1}$, respectively. Actually, the values are

C—C	C=C	C≡C	$kJ\,mol^{-1}$
348	611	837	

These values suggest that different types of bond contribute to the multiple covalent bond. Let us briefly consider the structure of these bonds.

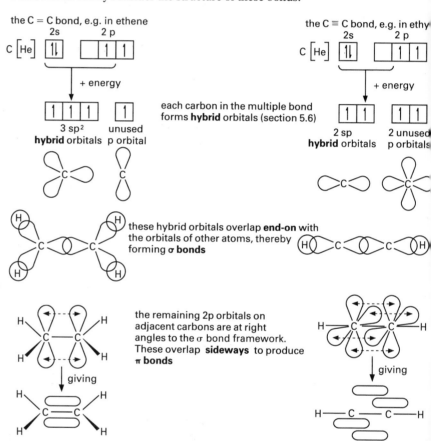

Since the electron cloud of the σ bond is concentrated between the bonding nuclei, it holds them firmly together. However, the π bond electron cloud is spread out *further* from the nuclei. Hence, π bonds make a somewhat *smaller* contribution to the multiple bond strength, and this accounts for the BET values given above.

35.5 Predicting the reactivity of alkenes and alkynes

The presence of the π bonds causes alkenes and alkynes to have very similar chemical properties. Thus, the multiple bonds are:
▶   *centres of high electron density*, which will be attacked by
    (i) electrophiles, e.g. Br^+, H^+; and
    (ii) oxidising agents, e.g. alkaline potassium manganate(VII).
▶   *under strain*. Four covalent bonds around carbon would be energetically more stable if they were arranged tetrahedrally, as in alkanes (table 35.3). Consequently, alkenes and alkynes readily add molecules across their multiple bonds, e.g.

Table 35.3 *Standard enthalpies of formation, $\Delta H_f^\ominus$, of some hydrocarbons. The more exothermic (−ve) the value, the greater the* **energetic stability** *of the hydrocarbon (see section 4.13)*

Compound	$\Delta H_f^\ominus/kJ\,mol^{-1}$
ethane	− 84.6
ethene	+ 52.3
ethyne	+226.8
propane	−103.8
propene	+ 20.4
propyne	+185.4

Is there a link between energetic stability and the number of π bonds?

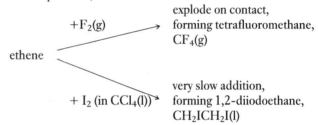

Unsaturated hydrocarbons, then, are much more reactive than the corresponding alkanes, and undergo (i) addition, (ii) oxidation and (iii) polymerisation reactions. We shall now consider each in turn.

35.6 Addition reactions of alkenes and alkynes

35.6.1 With halogens

When unsaturated hydrocarbons react with halogens, the order of increasing reactivity is $I_2 < Br_2 < Cl_2 < F_2$.
Thus, at room temperature,

ethene
$+F_2(g)$ → explode on contact, forming tetrafluoromethane, $CF_4(g)$
$+ I_2$ (in $CCl_4(l)$) → very slow addition, forming 1,2-diiodoethane, $CH_2ICH_2I(l)$

Alkynes are more reactive than alkenes. For example, at room temperature,

chlorine
$+$ ethene → rapid addition, forming 1,2-dichloroethane, $CH_2ClCH_2Cl(g)$
$+$ ethyne → explosion, forming $C(s) + 2HCl(g)$

Addition of chlorine to ethyne can be achieved, though, by mixing the gases in an inert solvent such as tetrachloromethane.

We can use these addition reactions as a **test for unsaturation**. Usually the unknown hydrocarbon is shaken vigorously with a solution of bromine dissolved in tetrachloromethene and the mixture is placed in a dark cupboard. If the sample is unsaturated, the orange colour of the bromine will disappear in a matter of minutes. Why wouldn't an alkane react under these conditions? (See section 34.8.)

Mechanism

Useful information about the reaction mechanism comes from the reaction of ethene with bromine water. *Two* products are formed:

Since ethene does not react directly with OH^-(aq) ions, the reaction's first step must involve only ethene and bromine. However, if this were a simple sideways attack

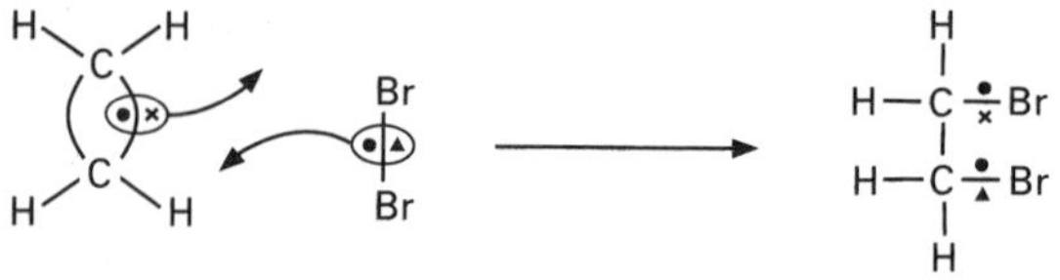

only *one* product, 1,2-dibromoethane, would be formed. In fact, our results support the following step-wise mechanism:

(i) Reactant molecules approach and **polarise** each other. The induced dipoles hold the molecules loosely together.

(ii) Electron cloud from the π bond moves into the space between the $\delta-$ carbon and the positively charged bromine atom. A **dative covalent bond** is formed; at the same time, **heterolytic fission** of the Br—Br bond occurs.

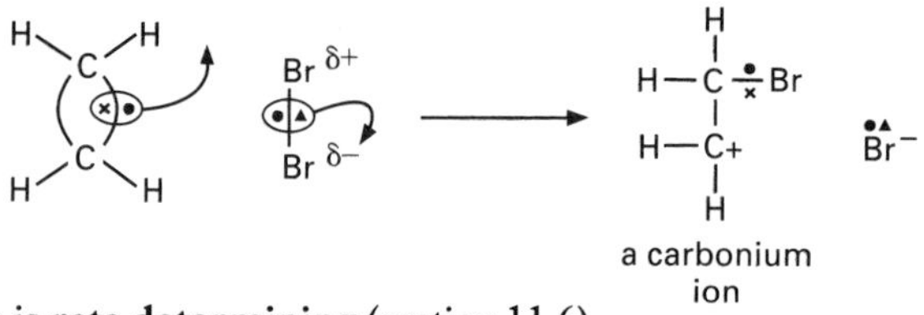

a carbonium ion

This step is **rate determining** (section 11.6).

Now, counting up the electrons, we can see that we have formed a Br^- ion and a **carbonium ion** (that is, a species with a positively charged carbon). The carbon has a positive charge because it has lost an electron, ✗.

(iii) Finally, the carbonium ion is rapidly attacked by a nucleophile (Br^- or H_2O):

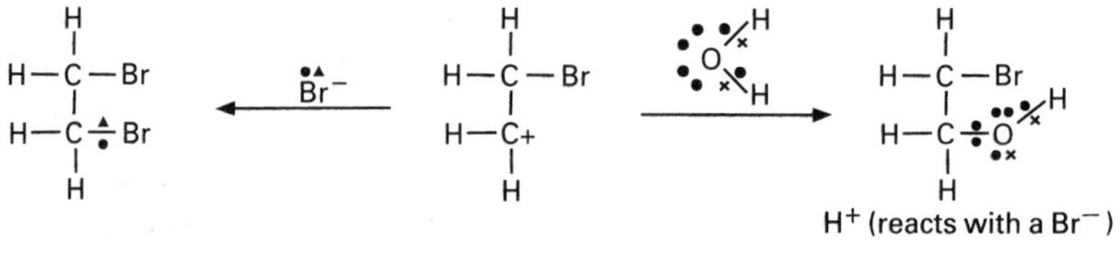

H^+ (reacts with a Br^-)

Since an *addition* reaction has occurred, via the *initial attack of the electrophile*, the entire mechanism is known as **electrophilic addition**. Alkynes are halogenated via a similar mechanism. Of course, two molecules of halogen may be added to the triple bond, and these are added one at a time.

35.6.2 With hydrogen halides

Unsaturated hydrocarbons are attacked by hydrogen halides, either as gases or dissolved in a non-polar solvent, e.g.

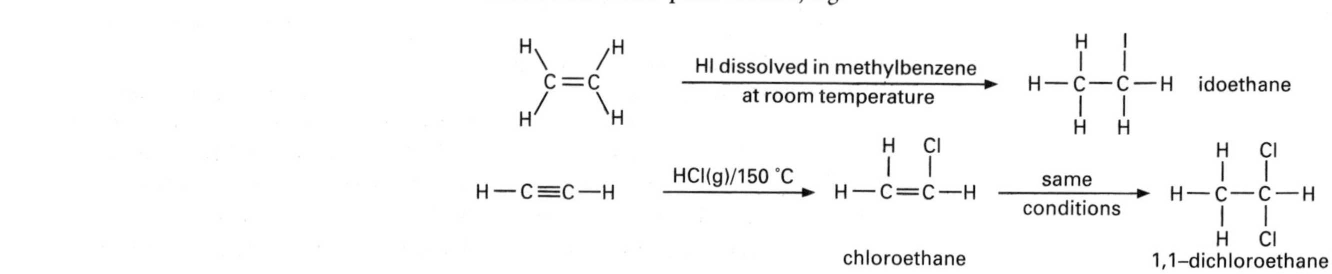

chloroethane   1,1–dichloroethane

There are two points to note here:

▶ reactivity *increases* in the order HCl < HBr < HI.
This is explained by the corresponding ease with which the H—Hal bond is broken:

	HCl	HBr	HI
bond energy terms/kJ mol^{-1}	431	366	299

▶ with alkynes, two moles of H—Hal can be added. *Notice, though, that both halogen atoms add to the same carbon.* We will see why later on.

Hydrohalogenation of propene produces interesting results. For example, with hydrogen bromide we obtain two products:

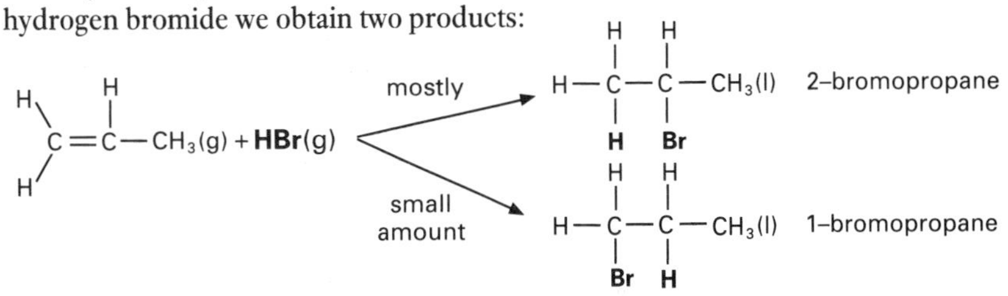

$$C=C-CH_3(g) + \mathbf{HBr}(g) \xrightarrow{mostly} H-C-C-CH_3(l) \quad \text{2-bromopropane}$$

$$\xrightarrow[\text{amount}]{small} H-C-C-CH_3(l) \quad \text{1-bromopropane}$$

Once again, the mechanism is electrophilic addition (see above). However, in this case, step (ii) of the mechanism can give *two different* carbonium ions via shift of electron cloud from the π bond to a or b:

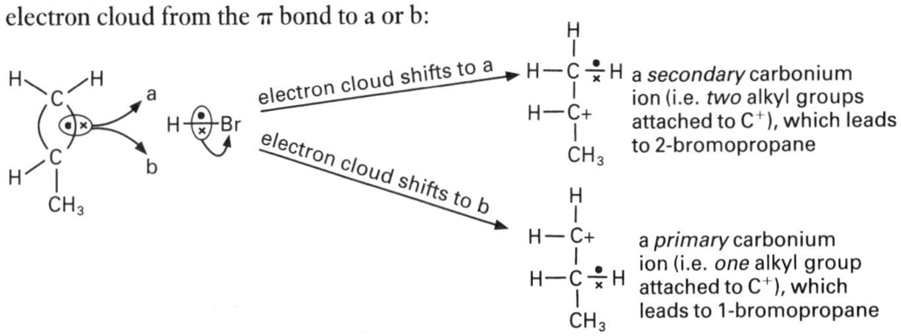

electron cloud shifts to a → a *secondary* carbonium ion (i.e. *two* alkyl groups attached to C$^+$), which leads to 2-bromopropane

electron cloud shifts to b → a *primary* carbonium ion (i.e. *one* alkyl group attached to C$^+$), which leads to 1-bromopropane

Since 2-bromobutane is the main product, the secondary carbonium ion must be formed in preference. Thus, it is the more stable. But why?

Well, *alkyl groups are said to have a* **positive inductive effect**. This means that *they tend to push electron cloud away from themselves*. In so doing, the carbon's positive charge can be **delocalised** (i.e. spread out) over the whole molecule:

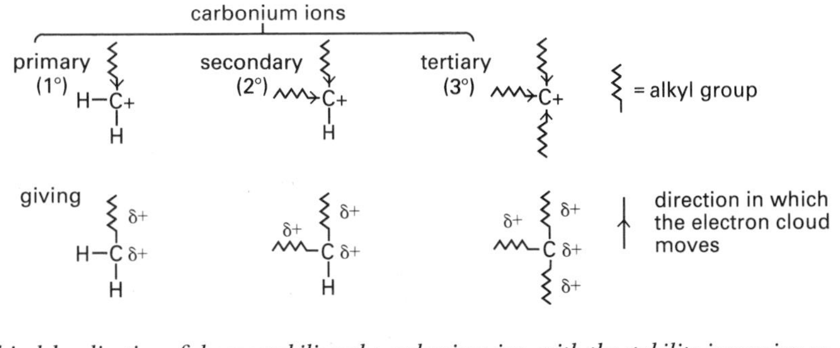

carbonium ions

primary (1°)   secondary (2°)   tertiary (3°)   ∫ = alkyl group

giving   H-C δ+   ...   ...   direction in which the electron cloud moves

This delocalisation of charge stabilises the carbonium ion, with the stability increasing as more alkyl groups are attached to the C$^+$, i.e. 1° < 2° < 3°.

Markovnikov found that other asymmetric alkenes and alkynes behaved in this way, and he produced a useful rule:

'When an HX molecule adds to an asymmetric alkene or alkyne, the hydrogen atom is more likely to add to the unsaturated carbon which already has the most hydrogen atoms.'

Typically H—X can be H—Cl, H—Br, H—I, H—OH (H_2O) and H—OSO$_3$H (H_2SO_4). (It is important to note that it is the relative stabilities of the carbonium ions, *not* Markovnikov's rule, which explains the experimental results.)

We saw earlier that when two H—Hal molecules add to ethyne, both halogen atoms add to the same carbon. Markovnikov's Rule predicts that this should be the case:

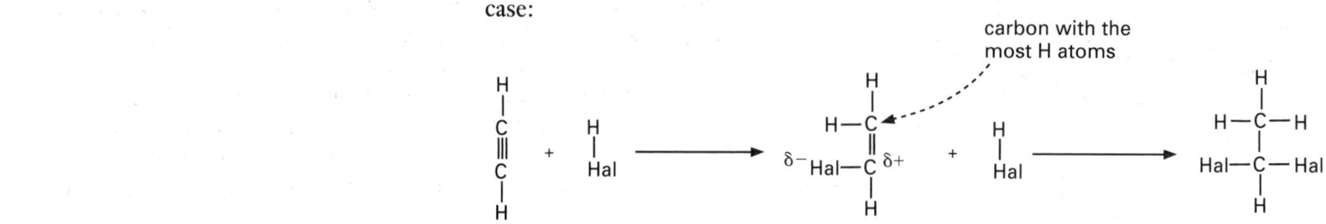

Due to the addition of the first H—Hal molecule, a polarised C—Hal bond is formed. Since this $C^{\delta+}$ is less attractive to the incoming H^+ electrophile, the latter adds to the other unsaturated carbon atom.

35.6.3 With sulphuric acid

Alkenes slowly add concentrated sulphuric acid at room temperature, e.g.

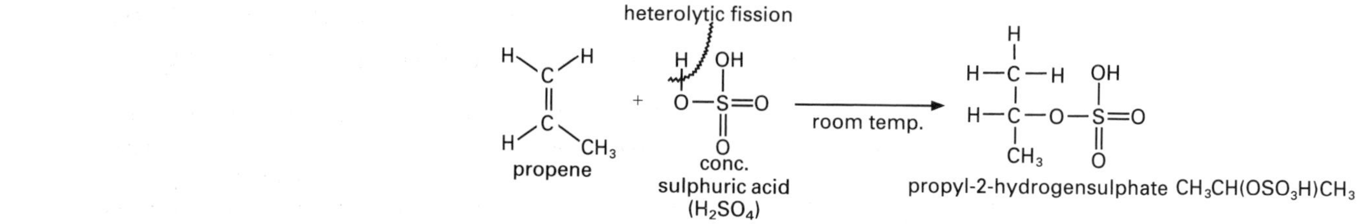

Once again, the mechanism is electrophilic addition (section 35.6.1). Also, notice that *Markovnikov's Rule is followed.* Alkyl hydrogensulphates are useful products because they can be readily hydrolysed to alcohols:

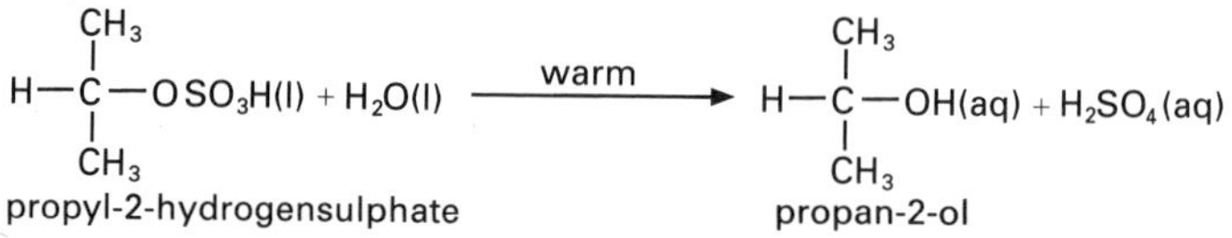

The net result here is **hydration**, that is *the addition of water across the C=C bond.*

Alkynes are readily hydrated by dilute sulphuric acid containing dissolved mercury(II) sulphate as catalyst:

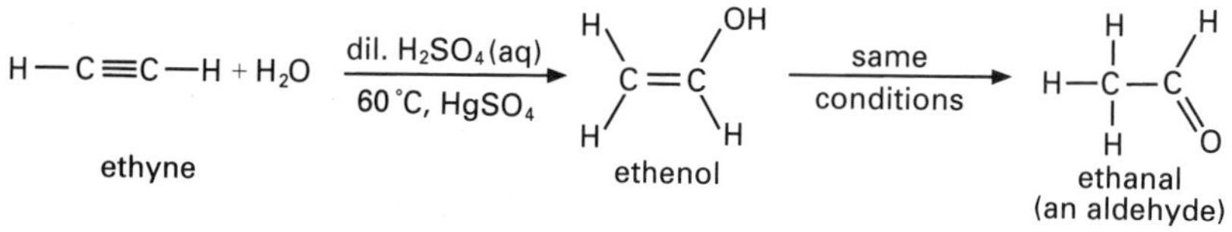

Ethenol is unstable and rearranges to form ethanal.

35.6.4 With hydrogen

Both alkenes and alkynes are reduced by hydrogen at 200°C in the presence of a finely divided nickel catalyst. e.g.

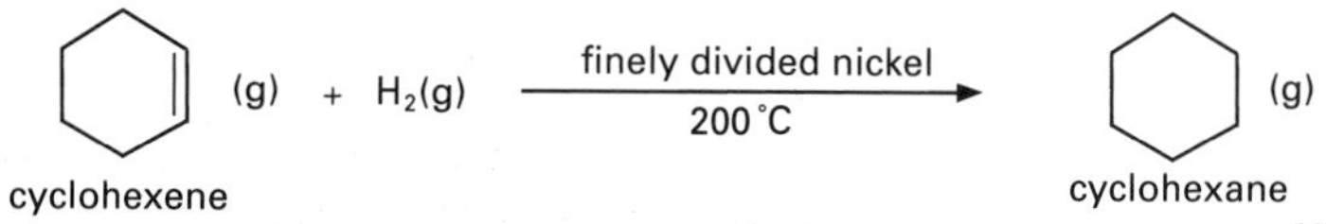

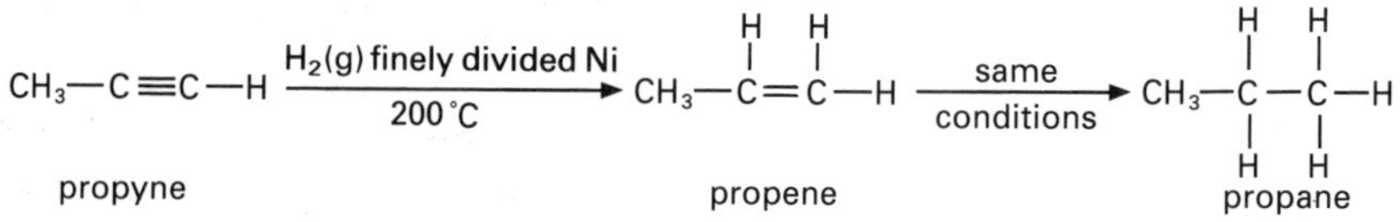

Nowadays, a major use of catalytic hydrogenation is in the **margarine industry**. In the middle of the last century, there was a world shortage of butter and

In the manufacture of sunflower margarine, oil is extracted from the sunflower seeds and then transferred to this hydrogenator where it is reacted with hydrogen in the presence of a nickel catalyst

animal fats. Thus, scientists investigated ways of converting oils into solid fats. Commercially, the first real success came in 1910 when it was found that vegetable oils could be hydrogenated at 200 °C in the presence of finely divided nickel. Vegetable oils, such as those from sunflower seeds, soya beans and ground nuts, have molecules which contain a number of C=C bonds. Hydrogenation of these *unsaturated* oils produces *saturated* oils which form soft solid fats on cooling. These fats are separated, purified and then shaken up with milk. Vitamins A and D, food colouring and various other additives are mixed in before the margarine finds its way to the customer.

35.7 Oxidation of alkenes and alkynes

35.7.1 Reaction with oxygen

All unsaturated hydrocarbons burn readily in air or oxygen. Ethene and ethyne, for example, can react explosively, e.g.

$$C_2H_4(g) + 3O_2(s) \rightarrow 2CO_2(g) + 2H_2O(g) \quad \Delta H_c^{\ominus} = -1411 \text{ kJ mol}^{-1}$$

$$C_2H_2(g) + \tfrac{5}{2}O_2(g) \rightarrow 2CO_2(g) + H_2O(g) \quad \Delta H_c^{\ominus} = -1297 \text{ kJ mol}^{-1}$$

As you can see, the reactions are highly exothermic. Indeed, by controlling the combustion of ethyne in oxygen, an **oxy-acetylene torch** can produce a flame temperature in excess of 2000 °C. These torches can be used for welding and cutting metals. Generally speaking, though, alkenes and alkynes are *not* useful fuels because:

▶ they are more valuable as a **chemical feedstock**;
▶ some **incomplete combustion** occurs as a result of their high carbon content (e.g. ethyne contains 92% carbon by mass). Compared to alkanes, then, unsaturated hydrocarbons burn in air with a more luminous, sooty flame.

In industry, the addition of oxygen to ethene is catalysed by finely divided silver at 200 °C:

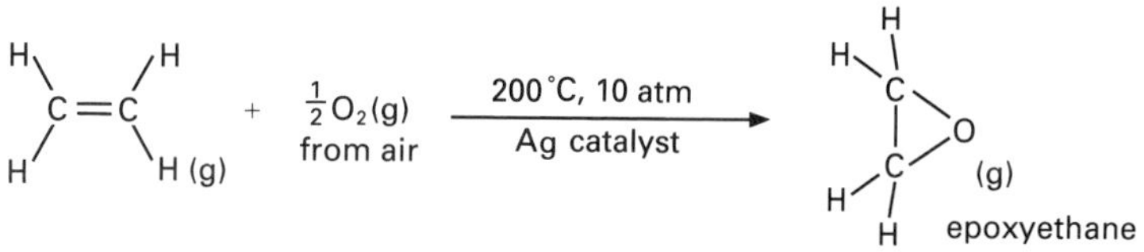

$$\begin{array}{c}
\text{H}_2\text{C}=\text{CH}_2 \\
\end{array} + \tfrac{1}{2}\text{O}_2(g) \xrightarrow[\text{from air}]{\substack{200\,°\text{C, 10 atm} \\ \text{Ag catalyst}}} \text{epoxyethane (g)}$$

Epoxyethane is an unstable molecule which is involved in a variety of important organic syntheses. For example, it can easily be hydrolysed to form ethane-1,2-diol:

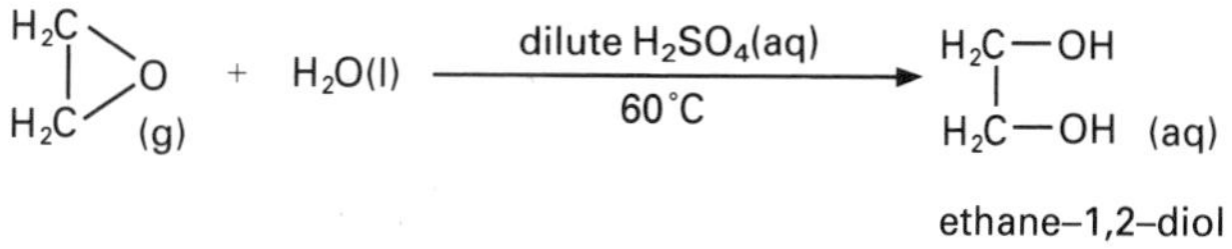

$$\text{epoxyethane (g)} + \text{H}_2\text{O(l)} \xrightarrow[\text{60 °C}]{\text{dilute H}_2\text{SO}_4\text{(aq)}} \begin{array}{c} \text{H}_2\text{C}-\text{OH} \\ | \\ \text{H}_2\text{C}-\text{OH} \end{array} \text{(aq)}$$

ethane-1,2-diol

Ethane-1,2-diol is used as antifreeze and in the manufacture of polyesters (section 40.11).

35.7.2 Reaction with aqueous potassium manganate(VII)

Unsaturated hydrocarbons are oxidised by acidified potassium manganate(VII) (potassium permanganate). With an alkene, the product is a alkanediol, e.g.

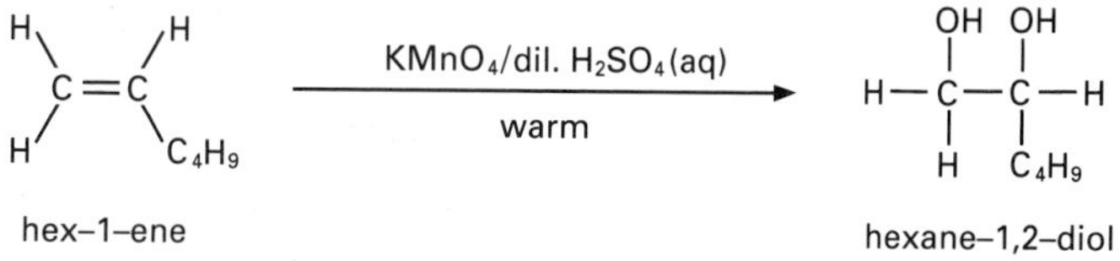

$$\begin{array}{c}
\text{H} \quad \quad \text{H} \\
\text{C}=\text{C} \\
\text{H} \quad \quad \text{C}_4\text{H}_9
\end{array} \xrightarrow[\text{warm}]{\text{KMnO}_4/\text{dil. H}_2\text{SO}_4\text{(aq)}} \begin{array}{c} \text{OH} \quad \text{OH} \\ | \quad \quad | \\ \text{H}-\text{C}-\text{C}-\text{H} \\ | \quad \quad | \\ \text{H} \quad \quad \text{C}_4\text{H}_9 \end{array}$$

hex-1-ene   hexane-1,2-diol

Many everyday products are made completely, or in part, from plastics. In Western Europe, over half of the plastics produced are used in packaging and building materials

Figure 35.3 *Uses of petroleum products in Western Europe*

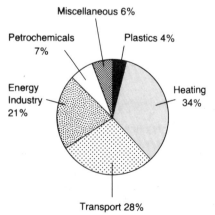

Miscellaneous 6%
Petrochemicals 7%
Plastics 4%
Energy Industry 21%
Heating 34%
Transport 28%

Ethyne is converted into ethanedioic (oxalic) acid:

$$H-C\equiv C-H \xrightarrow[\text{warm}]{\text{KMnO}_4/\text{dil. H}_2\text{SO}_4\text{(aq)}}$$

ethyne   ethanedioic acid

During these reactions, a *colour change* is observed:

$$\underset{\text{purple}}{\text{MnO}_4^-\text{(aq)}} \rightarrow \underset{\text{brown}}{\text{MnO}_2\text{(s)}} \rightarrow \underset{\text{colourless}}{\text{Mn}^{2+}\text{(aq)}}$$

Since alkanes do not react in this way, *acidified potassium manganate(VII) can be used to distinguish alkenes from alkanes.*

Activity 35.2

1 You have been given three unlabelled bottles containing the liquids hexane, hex-1-ene and hex-1-yne. What chemical tests could you use to distinguish them?

2 Describe the reagents and reaction conditions that you would use to convert pent-1-ene into:
   (a) 1,2-dibromopentane; (b) 2-bromopentane; (c) pentan-2-ol;
   (d) pentane; (e) pentane-1,2-diol.

3 Give the name and structural formula of the organic product(s) formed by the following reactions:

   (a) but-1-ene $\xrightarrow[\text{room temp.}]{\text{Cl}_2\text{(g)}}$?

   (b) propyne $\xrightarrow[\text{room temp.}]{\text{I}_2 \text{ in CCl}_4\text{(l)}}$?

   (c) *cis*-pent-2-ene $\xrightarrow[\text{room temp.}]{\text{HI(g)}}$?

   (d) *trans*-but-2-ene $\xrightarrow[\text{warm}]{\text{KMnO}_4/\text{dil.H}_2\text{SO}_4\text{(aq)}}$?

   (e) but-1-ene $\xrightarrow[\text{room temp.}]{\text{conc. H}_2\text{SO}_4\text{(l)}}$? $\xrightarrow{\text{H}_2\text{O(l), reflux}}$?

   (f) but-1-yne $\xrightarrow[\text{divided Ni(s), 200°C}]{\text{H}_2\text{(g), finely}}$?

35.8 Polymerisation of unsaturated hydrocarbons

Without a doubt, 'modern' living is strongly influenced by the pace of chemical research and development. Over the last fifty years, one particular range of synthetic materials has made a dramatic contribution to our lifestyle. What are these materials? **Plastics**. No matter where you look nowadays, plastic objects appear everywhere. (Although in fact, the manufacture of plastics accounts for only about 4% of the petroleum products consumed in Western Europe figure 35.3.)

Plastics are made up of massive molecules, called **polymers**, *which have been formed by joining together many small molecules, called* **monomers**. This process, known as **polymerisation**, can occur in two ways.

In **condensation** polymerisation, a small molecule (e.g. H_2O) is liberated each time a monomer—monomer linkage is formed. Thus,

monomer molecules → a polymer molecule + small molecules

The manufacture of **polyester** (section 40.11) and **nylon** (section 40.11) are examples of condensation polymerisation.

For the moment, though, we are interested in **addition polymerisation**. In this case, *the polymer is the only product,* i.e.

$$\text{monomer molecules} \rightarrow \text{a polymer molecule}$$

Also, we find that the molecules of monomer and polymer have the same empirical formula.

Alkenes, and substituted alkenes, undergo addition polymerisation to form a wide variety of plastics. The general reaction is:

Table 35.4 *Addition polymers of some alkenes and their derivatives (n is usually between 500 and 5000)*

where n is a large number (typically between 500 and 5000). Obviously, *the properties and uses of the plastic will depend on (i) the value of n, (ii) the nature of the $-X$ group and (iii) the reaction conditions.*

Monomer	ethene	phenylethene	chloroethene (vinyl chloride)	propenonitrile
Polymer	poly(ethene)	poly(phenylethene)	poly(chloroethene)	poly(propenonitrile)
Common name	polythene	polystyrene	PVC (polyvinyl chloride)	Acrilan
Formula				
Manufacture	(I) 200 °C, 1000 atm, free radical initiator; or use (II)	(II) 50–100 °C, 5–20 atm, Ziegler catalyst (a mixture of titanium(IV) chloride and an organo-aluminium compound)		
Properties	(I) produces low density polyethene which easily softens at 105 °C. It is a **thermoplastic**, i.e. *one which melts on gentle heating and can then be reshaped* (II) gives high density polyethene. It is fairly rigid with a higher melting point of 135 °C	Thermoplastic which is rigid but fractures easily. Polystyrene can be made into a foam by dissolving it and then distilling off the solvent	Thermoplastic whose properties can be adjusted by mixing in various additives. More rigid than polyethene, yet still a flexible product	Thermoplastic of great strength; thus it is used to make fibres
		All plastics will burn, often giving off a poisonous vapour		
Uses	I – plastic bags II – bottles, cups, buckets	cups, wall insulation, packaging foam, egg boxes	shoes and clothing (imitation leather), electrical insulation, records	clothes, carpets

Some common addition polymers are described in table 35.4. Although they are made from fairly similar monomers, the polymers show a wide variation in physical properties. These properties can be related to the polymer's '3-dimensional' structure (table 35.5).

Table 35.5 *Comparing polymer structures*

Polymer made up of . . .	branched chains	unbranched chains	unbranched chains with cross-linking bonds
∴ the chains will be . . .	further apart ←	→	closer together
Consequently, density will be . . .	LOW	HIGH	VERY HIGH
Also, van der Waals' forces will be . . .	WEAK	STRONG	VERY STRONG
∴ melting points will be . . .	LOW	HIGH	VERY HIGH
and the polymers will be . . .	SOFT and FLEXIBLE	HARDER	VERY HARD and RIGID
Example	low density polythene	high density polythene	perspex
Uses	'plastic' bags	bottles, cups, bowls	replacement for glass in windows, 'see-through' roof tiles

Figure 35.4 *The energy needed to produce 100 cm³ of various materials*

- ☐ as energy
- ▨ as proportion of oil

- poly(propene)
- poly(ethene), low density
- poly(ethene), high density
- PVC, poly(chloroethene)
- poly(phenylethene)
- steel
- copper
- alluminium

relative energy consumption
0   5   10   15

Nowadays, plastics have taken the place of many natural materials, e.g. in the construction and clothing industries. Generally speaking, plastics are *more versatile, last longer* and are *cheaper* than alternative natural materials (figure 35.4). However, the widespread use of plastics does pose one problem, that of disposal. Plastics are **non-biodegradable**, that is, *they are not broken down by bacteria*, such as those in the soil. Unlike metals, glass and paper, the recycling of these synthetic polymers is usually an uneconomical process but research continues. At present most waste plastic is either buried or burnt.

A plastic recycling operation in Japan. The material is compressed into discs of uniform size before being processed

Activity 33.3

Write down the structures of the polymers formed from
   (a) tetrafluoroethene, $F_2C{=}CF_2$
   (b) but-1-ene
   (c) 2-methylpropene
   (d) 2,3-dimethylbut-2-ene.

35.9 Conjugated alkenes: their properties and uses

Conjugated alkenes are *molecules which have alternating C—C and C=C bonds along their chain length.* Some conjugated alkenes are large molecules, e.g. β-carotene, the orange pigment found in carrots:

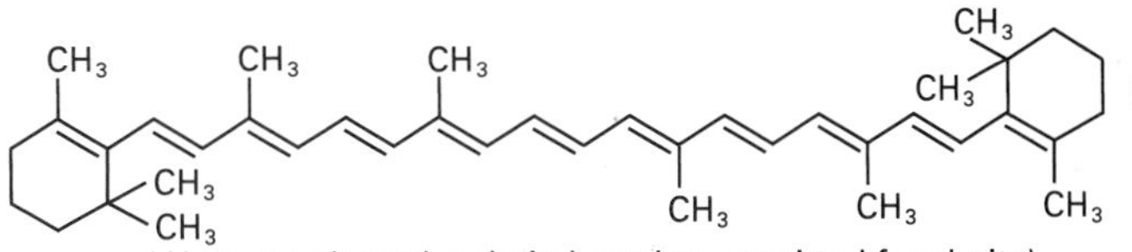

(H atoms along the chain have been omitted for clarity)

The smallest conjugated alkene is buta-1,3-diene:

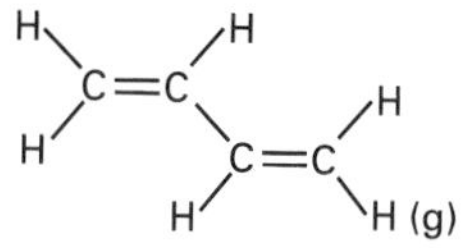

Like benzene, buta-1,3-diene is a molecule which contains **delocalised** electrons. Where this occurs, *the negative charge cloud is spread out, thereby stabilising the molecule* (figure 35.5). Because of this delocalisation, buta-1,3-diene and other conjugated

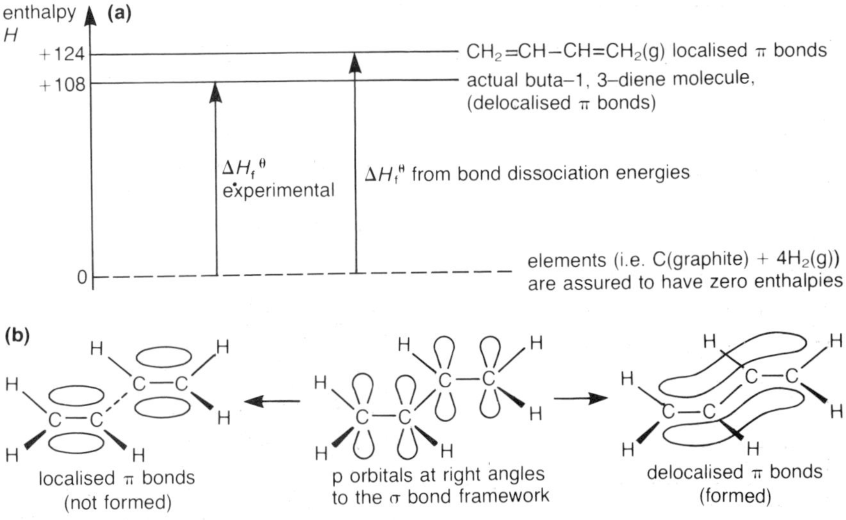

Figure 35.5 *(a) The actual buta-1,3-diene molecule is about $16\,kJ\,mol^{-1}$ more energetically stable than the localised π bond structure.* **(b)** *This suggests that buta-1,3-diene contains delocalised π bonds*

alkenes have some interesting properties. Many of them are highly coloured, e.g. β-carotene. Also, they give some *unexpected* addition reactions. For example, when buta-1,3-diene reacts with bromine in equimolar quantities, we get 1,2 *and* 1,4 addition:

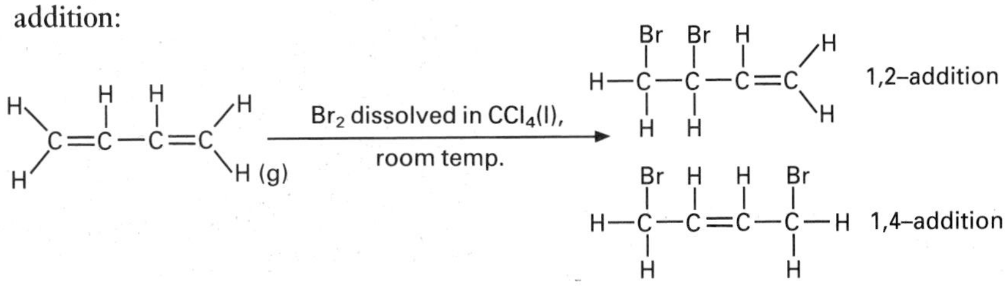

Sap being drained from a rubber tree in Malaysia. It is easy to see why synthetic rubber had to be developed

Buta-1,3-diene's most important reaction is its polymerisation to form synthetic rubber.

For nearly two hundred years, people have extracted natural rubber from a tropical tree called *Hevea brasiliensis*. At first, rubber had limited usefulness because it was rather soft and became sticky in hot weather. However, in 1839, Goodyear solved this problem by heating the natural rubber with a small amount of sulphur. During this process, known as **vulcanisation**, the sulphur atoms form cross-linkages between neighbouring rubber molecules. This produces a stronger and more elastic product.

The tread-cutting process in the manufacture of tyres

By the start of this century, demand for rubber (e.g. for tyres) began to exceed the natural supply. Consequently, chemists turned their attention to the synthesis of rubber substitutes. One of the first synthetic rubbers, called **Buna rubber**, was obtained from the sodium catalysed polymerisation of buta-1,3-diene:

$$n \ H_2C{=}C(H){-}C(H){=}CH_2(g) \xrightarrow{\text{Na(g) catalyst}} {\left(CH_2{-}C(H){=}C(H){-}CH_2\right)}_n$$

Buna rubber

Here n may be up to 2000. Nowadays, the most popular synthetic rubber is a co-polymer of 80% buta-1,3-diene and 20% phenylethene.

35.10 Comments on the activities

Activity 35.1

1 (a) hex-2-ene*;   (b) 4-methylpent-2-ene*;
   (c) 4-methylpent-2-yne;   (d) *cis*-hept-3-ene;
   (e) *trans*-3-methylpent-2-ene;   (f) 2-methylhex-3-yne.
   (*may be *cis* or *trans*– isomers).

2 Remember always to draw the longest unbranched chain first of all.

(a) 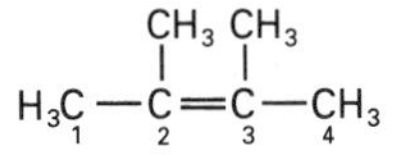 $H_3C-\overset{CH_3}{\underset{2}{C}}=\overset{CH_3}{\underset{3}{C}}-\underset{4}{CH_3}$ (b) $H-\overset{1}{C}\equiv\overset{2}{C}-\overset{CH_3}{\underset{H}{C}}-\overset{H}{\underset{H}{C}}-\overset{H}{\underset{H}{C}}-\overset{H}{\underset{H}{C}}-H$

(c) $H-\overset{H}{\underset{H}{C}}-\overset{H}{\underset{2}{C}}=\overset{C_2H_5}{\underset{3}{C}}-\overset{H}{\underset{C_2H_5}{C}}-\overset{H}{\underset{H}{C}}-\overset{H}{\underset{H}{C}}-H$ (d) 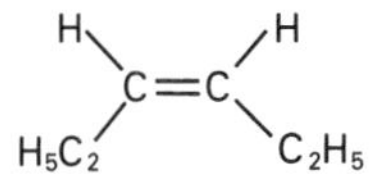 $\underset{H_5C_2}{\overset{H}{\diagdown}}C=C\underset{\diagup C_2H_5}{\overset{H}{}}$

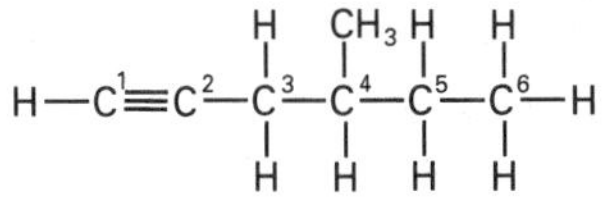

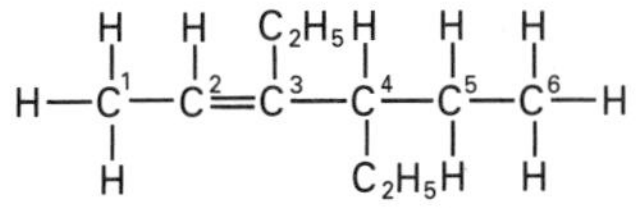

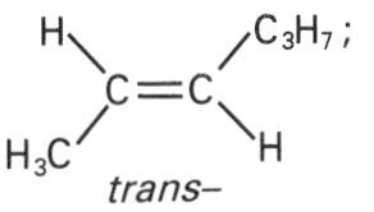

(e) 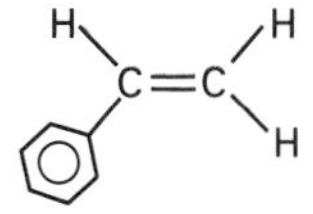 phenyl $C=C$ with H, H groups

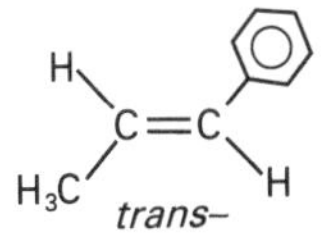

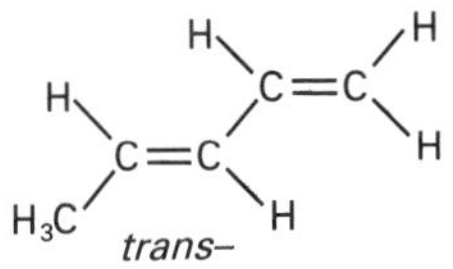

(f) 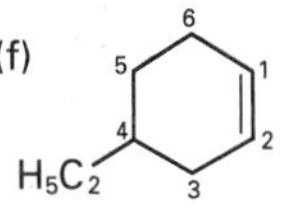 ring structure, H_5C_2

(g) 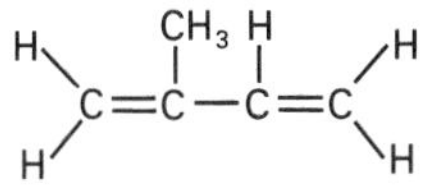 $\overset{H}{\underset{H}{\diagdown}}C=\overset{CH_3}{\underset{H}{C}}-\overset{H}{\underset{H}{C}}=C\overset{H}{\underset{H}{}}$

3

(a) Yes, 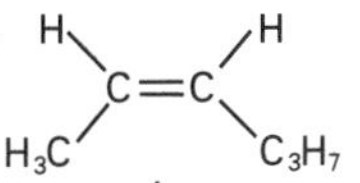 *cis-* form (H_3C, C_3H_7) ; *trans–* form (H_3C, C_3H_7)

(b) No ;   (c) Yes, 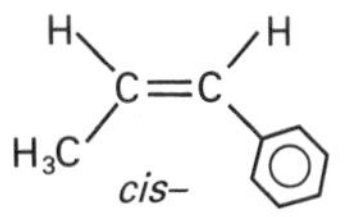   *cis–* form ; *trans–* form

(d) No ;   (e) Yes, 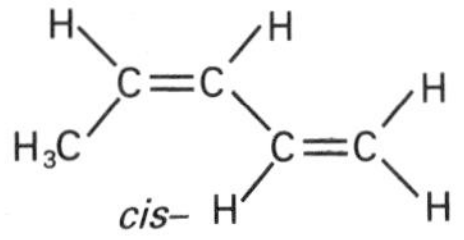   *cis–* form ; *trans–* form

Activity 35.2

1 You could use any reaction which gives a different observation with saturated hydrocarbons, e.g. see table 35.6:

Table 35.6   *Tests to distinguish saturated and unsaturated hydrocarbons*

Hydrocarbon	Reagent	
	Br_2 dissolved in CCl_4 room temp. in the dark	$KMnO_4$/dil. H_2SO_4(aq) reflux
Hexane	no reaction	no reaction
Hex-1-ene or Hex-1-yne	bromine (orange) decolorised	colour changes from purple through brown to colourless

Hex-1-ene and hex-1-yne can be distinguished by determining the number of moles of Br_2 which add to the multiple bond: alkenes add 1 mole, alkynes add 2 moles.

2 (a) Br_2 dissolved in $CCl_4(l)$, at room temperature;
  (b) HBr (in $CCl_4(l)$) or HBr(g), warm;
  (c) Two steps: firstly, conc. $H_2SO_4(l)$ at room temperature;
      then, $H_2O(l)$ warm;
  (d) $H_2(g)$, finely divided nickel, 200 °C;
  (e) $KMnO_4$/dil. $H_2SO_4(aq)$, reflux.

3

(a)

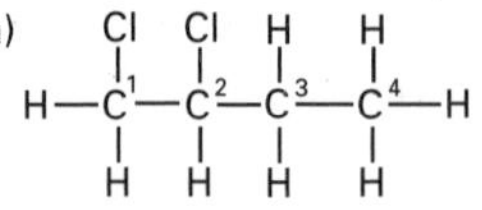

1,2–dichlorobutane

(b)

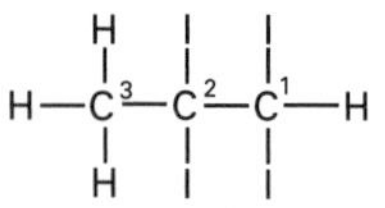

1,1,2,2–tetraiodopropane

(c)

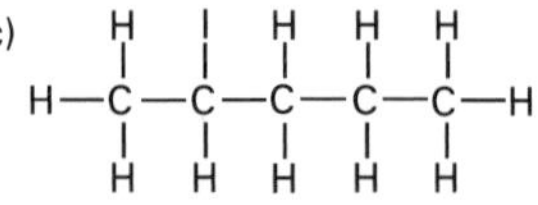

2–iodopentane

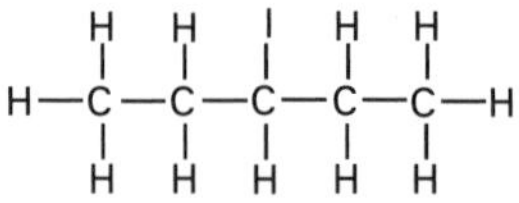

3–iodopentane

(d)

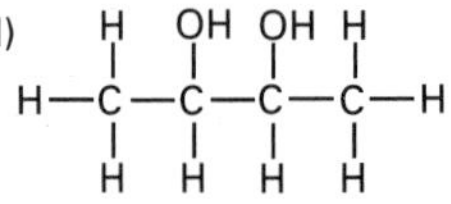

butane–2,3–diol

(e)

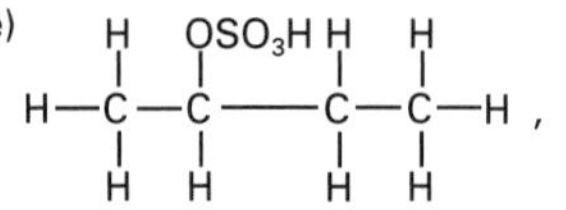

butyl–2–hydrogensulphate

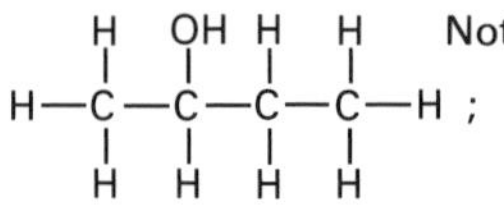

butan–2–ol

Note: **Markovnikov's Rule** is followed. Only a very small amount of butyl-1-hydrogen sulphate and butan-1-ol will be formed.

(f)

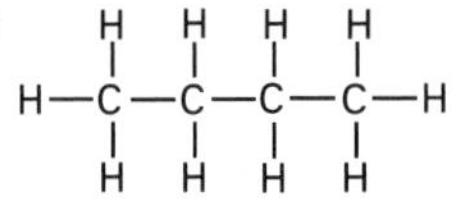

butane

Activity 35.3

(a)

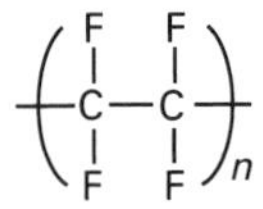

(b)

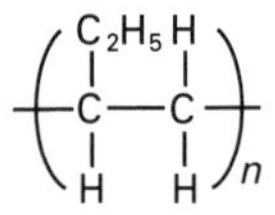

(c)

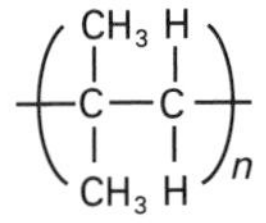

(d)

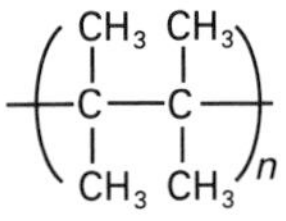

Note: When drawing structures derived from the monomer, remember that each repeating unit contributes only two carbon atoms to the chain.

35.11 Summary and revision plan

1 Alkenes and alkynes are **unsaturated** hydrocarbons, that is, they contain at least one C=C or C≡C bond, respectively.
2 When naming alkenes and alkynes, you must state the position of the multiple carbon–carbon bond(s).
3 The presence of the C=C bond enables some alkenes to exist as **geometrical isomers** (section 10.3).
4 Alkenes and alkynes both form **homologous series**, with the general formulae C_nH_{2n} and C_nH_{2n-2}, respectively.
5 Alkenes are manufactured by cracking the naphtha or gas-oil fractions from petroleum. Ethene and propene are extremely valuable starting materials in industrial organic synthesis.

6 A C=C bond is made up of a σ bond and a π bond. A C≡C bond consists of a σ bond and two π bonds at right angles to each other (section 35.4).

7 Since C=C and C≡C bonds are electron-rich reactive centres, they will add on **electrophiles** and react with oxidising agents. They can also 'link' together to form **addition polymers**.

8 Some important reactions of alkenes and alkynes are shown in figure 35.6.

9 **Markovnikov's Rule** says that 'when an H—X molecule adds to an alkene or alkyne, the hydrogen atom is more likely to add to the unsaturated carbon which already has the most hydrogen atoms'. The relative stabilities of **carbonium ions** (i.e. 3° > 2° > 1°) explain this behaviour (section 35.6.2.).

Figure 35.6 *Some important reactions of alkenes and alkynes. Notes: (1) decolorisation of Br₂ is a test for an alkene or alkyne; (2) Markovnikov's Rule is followed; (3) the basis of the margarine industry; (4) ozonolysis and identification of the products enables us to work out the position of an alkene's C=C bond. (□- is a hydrocarbon skeleton)*

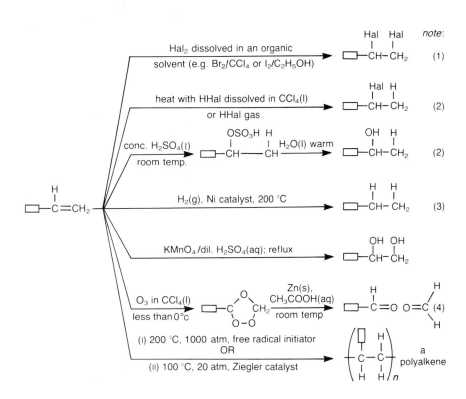

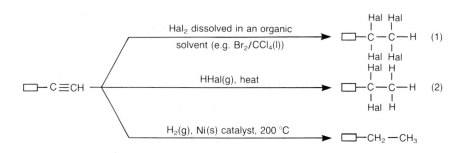

Table 35.7 *Important reagents used in this chapter. Try to learn them*

Reagent	conditions	what it does	notes
Excess conc. H_2SO_4(l)	reflux	**a dehydrating agent** (i.e. removes H_2O); converts  $-\overset{H}{\underset{\vert}{C}}-\overset{OH}{\underset{\vert}{C}}- \longrightarrow\ \ \rangle C{=}C\langle\ +H_2O$	
KOH in ethanol	reflux	removes H—Hal, converts  $H-\overset{\vert}{\underset{\vert}{C}}-\overset{\vert}{\underset{\vert}{C}}-Hal \longrightarrow\ \rangle C{=}C\langle\ +HHal$ or $H-\overset{Hal}{\underset{\vert}{C}}-\overset{Hal}{\underset{\vert}{C}}-H \longrightarrow\ -C{\equiv}C-\ +2HHal$ 	
Cl_2(g), Br_2 in CCl_4(l) or I_2 in CCl_4(l)	room temp, in the dark	converts  $\rangle C{=}C\langle\ \longrightarrow\ Hal-\overset{\vert}{\underset{\vert}{C}}-\overset{\vert}{\underset{\vert}{C}}-Hal$ or $-C{\equiv}C-\ \longrightarrow\ Hal-\overset{\vert}{\underset{Hal}{C}}-\overset{\vert}{\underset{Hal}{C}}-Hal$ 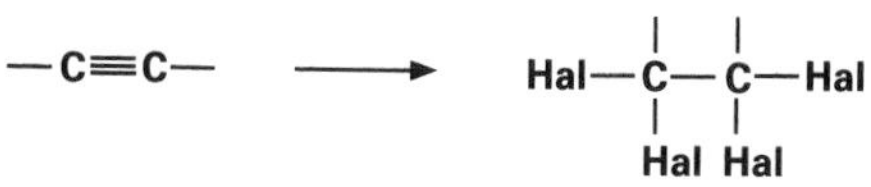	Test for unsaturation
H Hal(g) or H Hal (in non-polar solvent)	room temp. (alkenes) or heat (alkynes)	converts 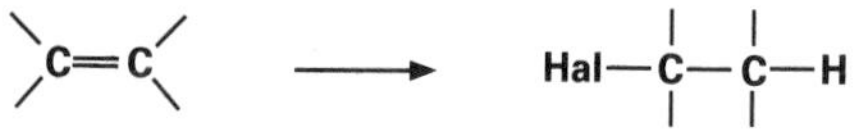 $\rangle C{=}C\langle\ \longrightarrow\ Hal-\overset{\vert}{\underset{\vert}{C}}-\overset{\vert}{\underset{\vert}{C}}-H$ or $-C{\equiv}C-\ \longrightarrow\ Hal-\overset{\vert}{\underset{Hal}{C}}-\overset{\vert}{\underset{H}{C}}-H$ 	Markovnikov's Rule applies here
(I) conc. H_2SO_4(l), (II) H_2O(l)	(I) room temperature (II) reflux	hydration of C=C bond i.e.  $\rangle C{=}C\langle\ \longrightarrow\ -\overset{H}{\underset{\vert}{C}}-\overset{OH}{\underset{\vert}{C}}-$	As above
H_2(g), Ni(s) catalyst	200°C	**reduce** C=C and C≡C bonds to give the corresponding alkane	Important in the margarine industry
$KMnO_4$/dil. H_2SO_4(aq)	reflux	oxidises alkenes → diols i.e.  $\rangle C{=}C\langle\ \longrightarrow\ -\overset{\vert}{\underset{OH}{C}}-\overset{\vert}{\underset{OH}{C}}-$	Test for unsaturation

10 **Polymers** are formed by the joining together of many small molecules, called **monomers**. This process is called **polymerisation**.

11 Molecules which have alternating C—C and C=C bonds along their chain length are known as **conjugated** alkenes and contain a delocalised π electron cloud. Synthetic rubber is a co-polymer of a buta-1,3-diene, the simplest conjugated alkene.

12 The new reagents used in this chapter are shown in table 35.7. Try to learn them.

CHAPTER

36

Aromatic Hydrocarbons

Contents

Figure 36.1 *Kekulé's structure for benzene*

Figure 36.2 *The delocalised π bond system in benzene results from the sideways overlap of the p orbitals on the carbon atoms*

So far, we have looked at two types of hydrocarbon, saturated and unsaturated. **Saturated** hydrocarbons contain only σ bonds and undergo substitution reactions. **Unsaturated** hydrocarbons contain σ and π bonds, and take part in substitution and addition reactions.

During the early years of organic research, chemists were puzzled by the structures of some hydrocarbons which were unsaturated, *yet resisted addition reactions*. Originally, these compounds were termed **aromatic** because of their rather pleasant smell. In 1834, the molecular formula of the simplest aromatic hydrocarbon, **benzene**, was found to be C_6H_6. Following this discovery, various 'alkene-like' structures were suggested, e.g.

$$CH_2{=}C{=}CH{-}CH{=}C{=}CH_2$$

However, such structures posed two problems:

▶ unlike alkenes, benzene is almost unreactive at room temperature (whereas the above compound would be highly reactive);

▶ benzene only gives *one* mono-substitution product, suggesting that the molecular positions of the six hydrogen atoms are equivalent.

In fact, benzene's structure remained unclear for many years until, in 1865, Kekulé suggested that it was a cyclic triene (figure 36.1). Kekulé's model puts the hydrogen atoms in equivalent positions but it still does not explain benzene's reluctance to give addition reactions. Even so, it found favour and was accepted for a long time. X-ray studies and thermochemical data now suggest that benzene contains **delocalised π bonds** located above and below the σ bond framework (figure 36.2). (The structure of benzene was discussed fully in section 5.8.)

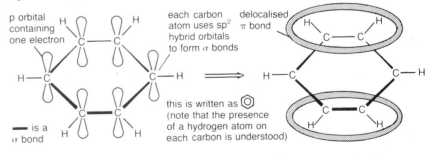

Nowadays, thousands of organic compounds are known to contain a benzene ring. Many are foul-smelling and toxic. Even so, they are still described by the traditional term 'aromatic'. Some examples are:

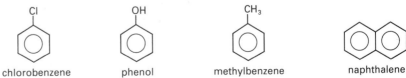

chlorobenzene   phenol   methylbenzene   naphthalene

Aromatic hydrocarbons, such as methylbenzene and naphthalene, are often called **arenes**.

36.1 Naming aromatic compounds

Aromatic compounds can be named in *three* ways:

▶ by identifying the functional groups and/or hydrocarbon chains which are attached to the benzene ring, e.g.

ethylbenzene   iodobenzene   nitrobenzene

▶ by using the name **phenyl** to identify each ⬡ group in the molecule,

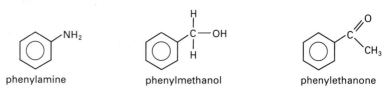

phenylamine   phenylmethanol   phenylethanone

▶ sometimes a molecule will also be known by a historical (trivial) name e.g.

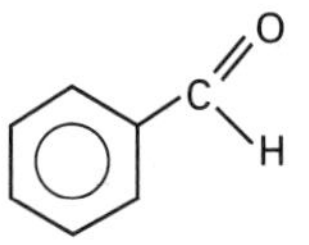

benzaldehyde
(benzenecarbaldehyde)

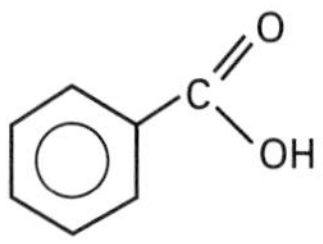

benzoic acid
(benzenecarboxylic acid)

In section 10.2, we saw that **positional isomerism** can occur in substituted benzenes. When naming these compounds, we must number the relative positions of the substituent groups, e.g.

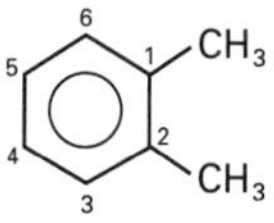

1,2–dimethylbenzene 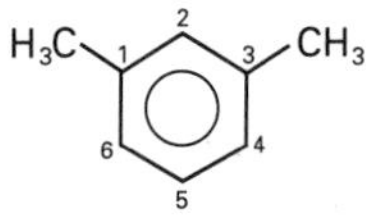   1,3–dimethylbenzene 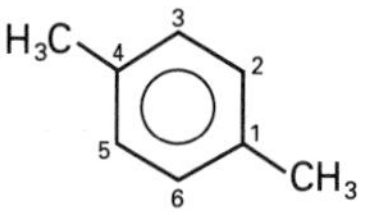   1,4–dimethylbenzene

There are two points to note here:

▶ 1,5- and 1,6-dimethylbenzene are non-existent because they are identical to the 1,3- and 1,2- isomers, respectively;

▶ avoid thinking of the benzene ring solely in terms of clockwise numbering with position 1 at the top.

Often a substituted benzene has a name based on a common 'parent' molecule e.g.

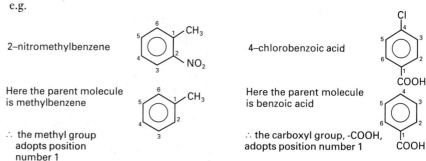

2–nitromethylbenzene

Here the parent molecule is methylbenzene

∴ the methyl group adopts position number 1

4–chlorobenzoic acid

Here the parent molecule is benzoic acid

∴ the carboxyl group, -COOH, adopts position number 1

Activity 36.1

1 Name the aromatic compounds whose structural formulae are shown below:

(a) [benzene ring with C_2H_5 and C_2H_5]

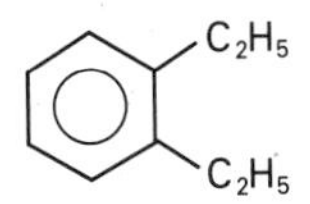

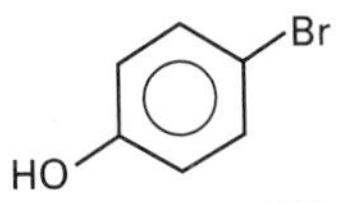

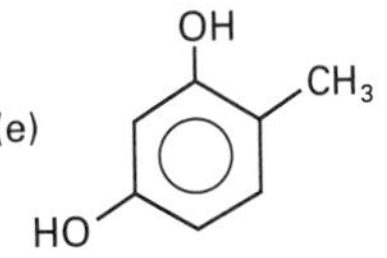

(b) [benzene ring with Br and HO]

(c) [benzene ring with COOH and NO_2]

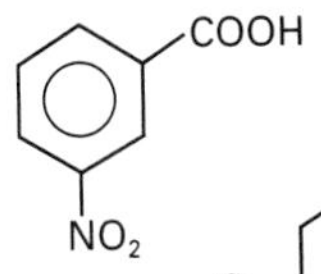

(d) [benzene ring with NH_2, Br, Br, Br]

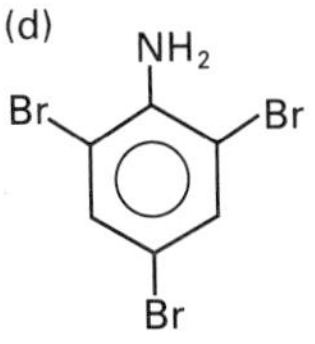

(e) [benzene ring with OH, CH_3, HO]
(–OH is an hydroxy group)

(f) [benzene ring with CH_2Cl]

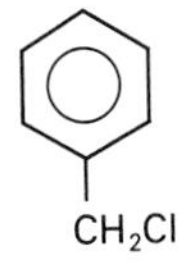

(g) [benzene ring with CH_3 and Cl]

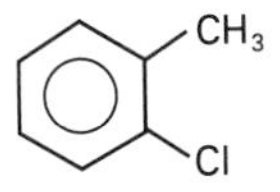

(h) [benzene ring with Br and $C=O$, CH_3]

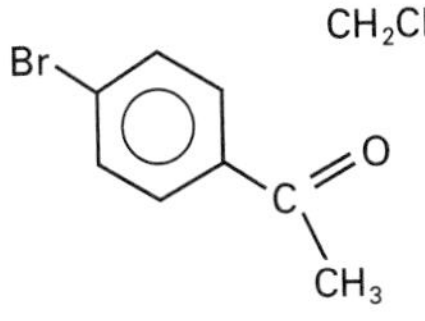

2 Draw structural formulae for the following compounds.
(a) 2-phenylpropane (b) 1,2-dihydroxybenzene
(c) 4-nitrophenol (d) phenylethanone (e) 3-chlorobenzaldehyde;
(f) 3-chlorobenzoic acid (g) 2,4,6-tribromophenol.

36.2 Uses and manufacture of benzene and methylbenzene

Although benzene and methylbenzene are poisonous, they are both widely used as (i) non-polar solvents and (ii) starting materials in the manufacture of many commerically important aromatic compounds, e.g. polystyrene and trinitrotoluene (TNT).

Arenes are not found naturally in large amounts. There are two main methods of producing benzene and methylbenzene: (i) by **cracking** and **reforming** the naphtha fraction from petroleum (section 34.6) and (ii) by heating **coal** in the absence of air.

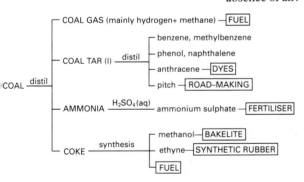

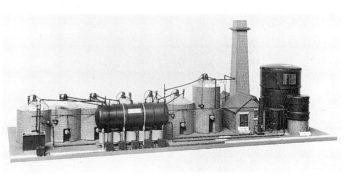

A model of a nineteenth century plant for the continuous distillation of coal-tar, which yielded (among other products) benzene and methylbenzene

36.3 Physical properties of benzene and methylbenzene

Benzene and methylbenzene are colourless liquids with boiling points of 80 and 111 °C and densities of 0.88 and 0.87 g cm^{-3}, respectively. Both liquids are almost insoluble in water. They are good solvents for non-polar compounds, the one drawback being that benzene is very poisonous.

36.4 The reactivity of benzene

Like alkenes and alkynes, benzene has an **electron rich reactive centre**, namely, its delocalised ring of π electrons. Consequently, benzene will also be a target for

electrophilic attack, for example by Cl^+ and Br^+. Also, since benzene is an unsaturated molecule, we would expect it to undergo addition reactions. In fact, benzene resists most of the addition reactions shown by alkenes and alkynes, e.g.

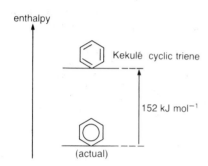

Benzene has a delocalised π bond system, rather than three separate double bonds. As we saw with buta-1,3-diene (section 35.9), delocalisation of the π electron cloud stabilises the molecule, and benzene is said to have a delocalisation energy of about $150 \, kJ \, mol^{-1}$. This means that *the 'delocalised' structure is said about $150 \, kJ \, mol^{-1}$ more stable than the 'Kekulé' cyclic triene* (figure 36.3). To undergo an electrophilic addition reaction, therefore, a benzene molecule would need to absorb enough energy to localise the double bonds, i.e. about $150 \, kJ \, mol^{-1}$. Such reactions would have very high activation energies, and this prevents them from occurring. Electrophilic addition to the localised π bond in an alkene requires much less activation energy; thus, the reaction occurs quite readily.

It is important to remember, then, that *benzene, though unsaturated, normally takes part in electrophilic substitution reactions*. A few addition reactions do take place but these occur via a free radical mechanism (section 36.6).

Figure 36.3 *The relative energetic stabilities of benzene and Kekulé's cyclic triene*

enthalpy

Kekulé cyclic triene

152 kJ mol⁻¹

(actual)

36.5 Substitution reactions

In these reactions, a C—H bond is converted into a C—X unit, where X may be $-NO_2$, $-SO_3H$, $-CH_3$ or another alkyl group, $-COCH_3$, Cl or Br.

36.5.1 Nitration

The structural change $C—H \rightarrow C—NO_2$ is termed **nitration**.

Benzene is nitrated by refluxing it with a **nitrating mixture** of concentrated nitric acid and concentrated sulphuric acid. At 50°C, nitrobenzene is formed:

$$\text{(l)} + HNO_3(aq) \text{ conc.} \xrightarrow[50°C]{\text{conc. } H_2SO_4(l)} \text{nitrobenzene (l)} \quad NO_2 \quad + H_2O \text{ (l)}$$

On diluting the reaction mixture with water, an oily layer of nitrobenzene appears and this can be separated by solvent extraction. After drying with anhydrous calcium chloride, the pure nitrobenzene (b.p. = 210°C) is obtained by distillation. In the manufacture of certain dyes, nitrobenzene is made this way and then reduced to give phenylamine (section 41.5).

When benzene and the nitrating mixture are refluxed at 100°C, the chief product is 1,3-dinitrobenzene, a yellow solid:

$$\text{(l)} + 2HNO_3(aq) \text{ conc.} \xrightarrow[100°C]{\text{conc. } H_2SO_4(l)} \text{(s)} \quad NO_2 \quad NO_2 \quad + 2H_2O$$

Mechanism of the nitration of benzene

Individually, concentrated nitric or sulphuric acids do *not* react with benzene at 50°C. On mixing, though, they form the **nitryl cation, NO_2^+**. Evidence for this

Figure 36.4 *Infrared spectra of (a) 'nitrating' mixture and (b) aqueous nitronium chlorate(VII), $NO_2^+ ClO_4^-$ (aq). In both, the peak at 7.1 μm is due to the nitryl cation, NO_2^+*

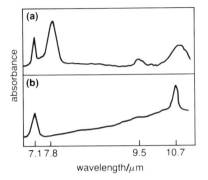

comes from the similar infrared absorption spectra of 'nitrating mixture' and nitronium chlorate(VII), $NO_2^+ ClO_4^-$ (s) (figure 36.4). Furthermore, like 'nitrating mixture', nitronium chlorate(VII) will nitrate benzene. Thus, we conclude that *the nitryl cation is responsible for the nitration of benzene*, according to the following mechanism.

Nitryl cation formation   Sulphuric acid is so strong that it can **protonate** a nitric acid molecule, forming an $H_2NO_3^+$ ion. This breaks up to give a nitryl cation, NO_2^+:

$$HNO_3 + 2H_2SO_4 \rightarrow NO_2^+ + H_3O^+ + 2HSO_4^-$$

Attack of the NO_2^+ electrophile on the benzene ring   The nitryl cation is attracted to the benzene's delocalised π electron cloud, and it bonds with one of the carbon atoms. Notice that this removes the stability of the π electron cloud. However, the reaction is feasible because the intermediate cation is *also* stabilised, to some extent, by the delocalisation of the remaining four π electrons over the other five carbon atoms (figure 36.5).

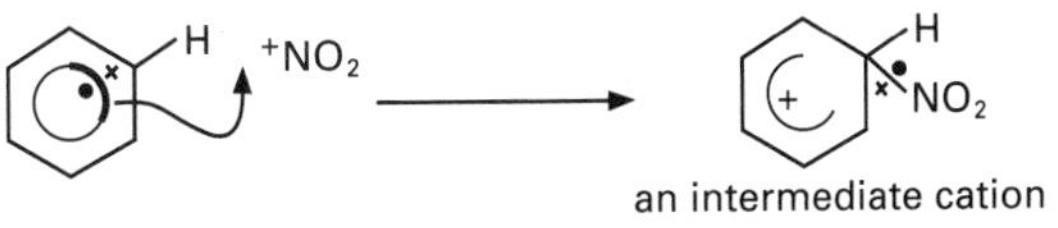

Figure 36.5 *Energy profile for the reaction between benzene and the nitryl cation*

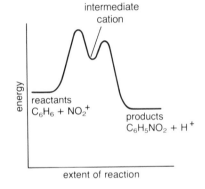

(here the '+' means that the positive charge from the $^+NO_2$ is now spread over carbon atoms 2–6)

an intermediate cation

Proton loss   The intermediate cation rapidly ejects a proton, H^+, thereby reforming the ring of delocalised π electrons and stabilising the product:

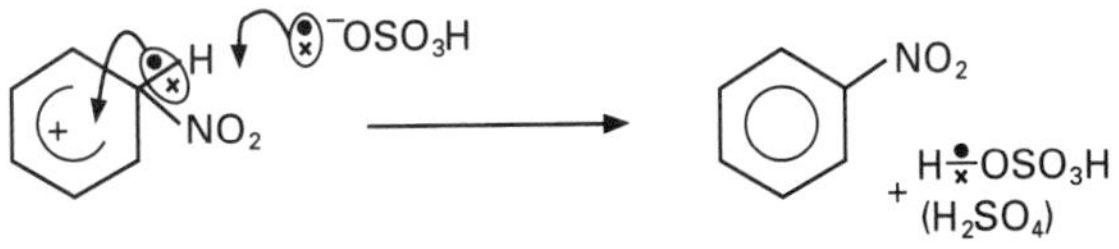

Notice here that sulphuric acid is acting as a **homogeneous catalyst**.

36.5.2 Sulphonation

The structural change $C—H \rightarrow C—SO_3H$ is called **sulphonation**.

Benzene is sulphonated by refluxing it with concentrated sulphuric acid for several hours:

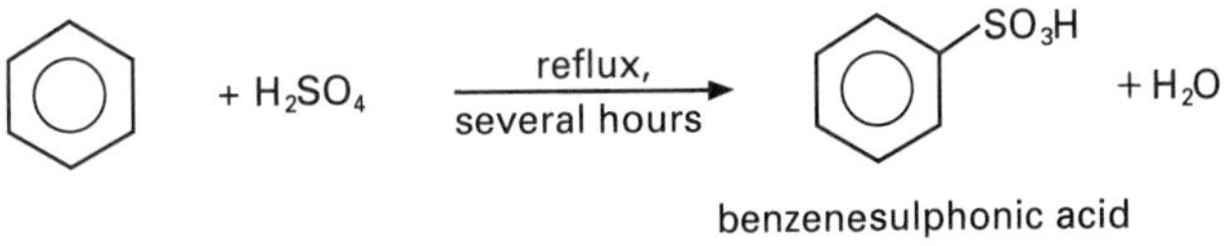

benzenesulphonic acid

Benzenesulphonic acid, a **strong** acid, is a crystalline solid which is very soluble in water. Thus, *by sulphonating an aromatic compound we can make it water soluble*. For this reason, a sulphonation reaction is often used in the manufacture of water soluble dyes and detergents (section 40.11). Benzenesulphonic acid is also an intermediate compound in the laboratory synthesis of phenol:

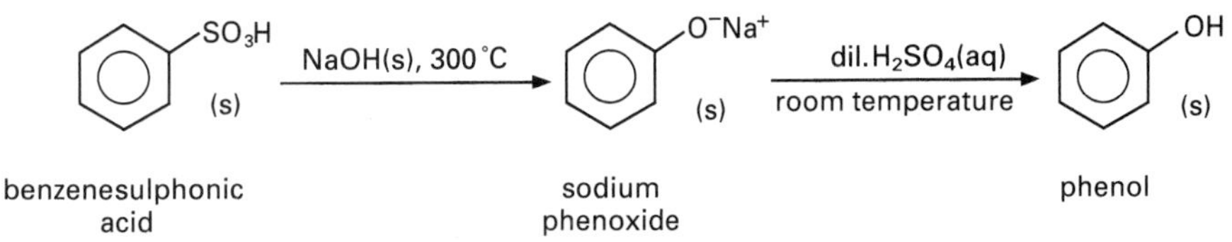

benzenesulphonic acid   sodium phenoxide   phenol

Figure 36.6 *Sulphur trioxide can act as an electrophile because the sulphur atom has an incomplete outer electron shell*

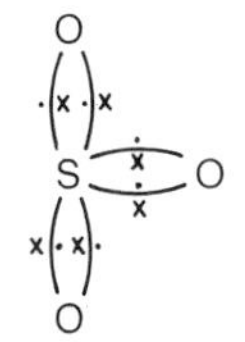

The mechanism of sulphonation resembles that for nitration except that, this time, the electrophile is **sulphur trioxide, SO_3**, a neutral molecule (figure 36.6).

36.5.3 Alkylation, acylation, and halogenation

These names are used here to describe the following structural changes:

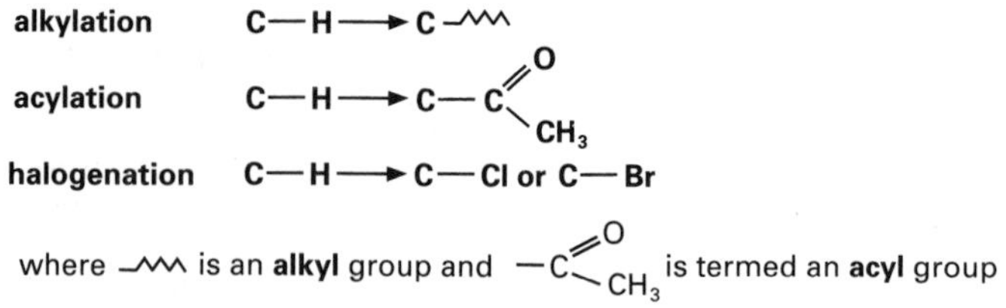

where $\wedge\!\wedge\!\wedge$ is an **alkyl** group and $-C{\diagup}^O_{\diagdown CH_3}$ is termed an **acyl** group

These reactions are grouped together because *they occur under similar conditions*, namely, in the presence of a **Friedel-Crafts catalyst**. Originally discovered by Friedel and Crafts in 1877, *these catalysts promote the formation of the electrophiles which can then attack the benzene ring*. Commonly used Friedel-Crafts catalysts include **aluminium chloride** and **iron(III) bromide**.

Alkylation

When benzene is warmed with a halogenoalkane and anhydrous aluminium chloride, an alkylbenzene is formed, e.g.

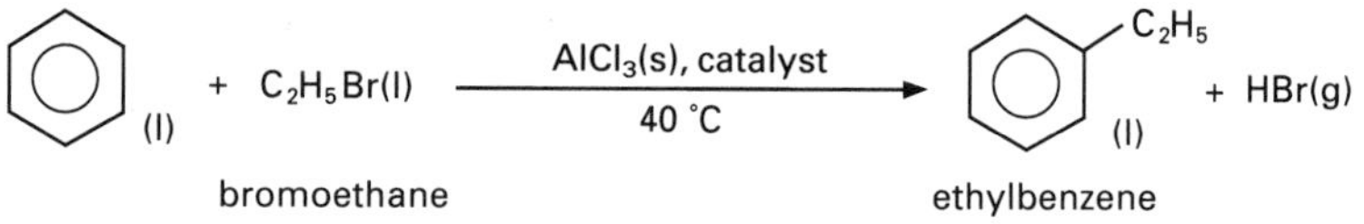

In industry, the alkylation of benzene is an important synthetic step in the manufacture of polystyrene, phenol (section 38.3) and detergents (section 40.11).

Acylation

When benzene is warmed with an acid chloride and a Friedel–Crafts catalyst, we get acylation. For example,

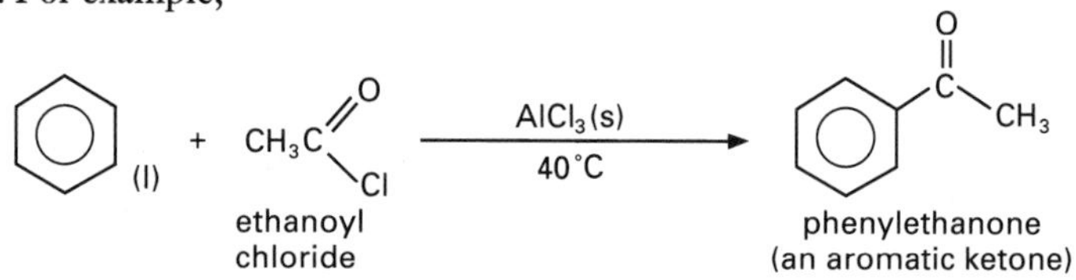

Halogenation

Although benzene is unsaturated, it does not react with halogens in the dark unless a Friedel–Crafts catalyst is present, e.g.

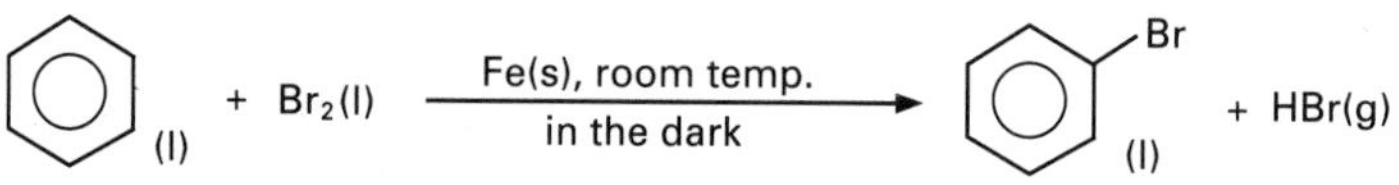

Here the $FeBr_3$ catalyst is made from the metal and halogen *in situ*, that is, *in the same flask we use for the main reaction*. There are two important points to note:

▶ *Iodine does not react in this way* because hydrogen iodide, being a powerful reducing agent, converts any iodobenzene back into benzene. (To prepare iodobenzene, see section 41.9.)

▶ In bright sunlight, chlorine and bromine will *add* to the benzene molecule, section 36.6.

Mechanism of alkylation, acylation and halogenation

Not surprisingly, these reactions have almost identical mechanisms. Of most interest is the role of the Friedel–Crafts catalyst (e.g. $AlCl_3(s)$). These catalysts are *electron-pair acceptors,* that is, *Lewis acids* (section 18.1). Thus, they attract the electron cloud in the C—Hal or Hal—Hal bond:

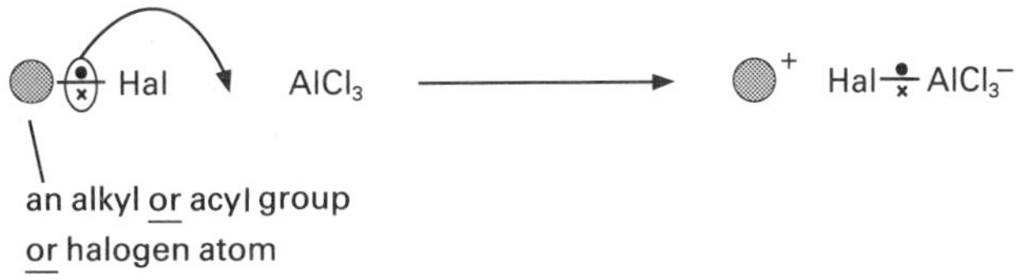

an alkyl or acyl group
or halogen atom

A complex ionic compound is formed. Since this possesses an electron-poor centre (i.e. the positive ion), it can act as an electrophile. As in the nitration of benzene, the electrophile attacks benzene's π electron ring (1) and, finally, a proton is lost (2):

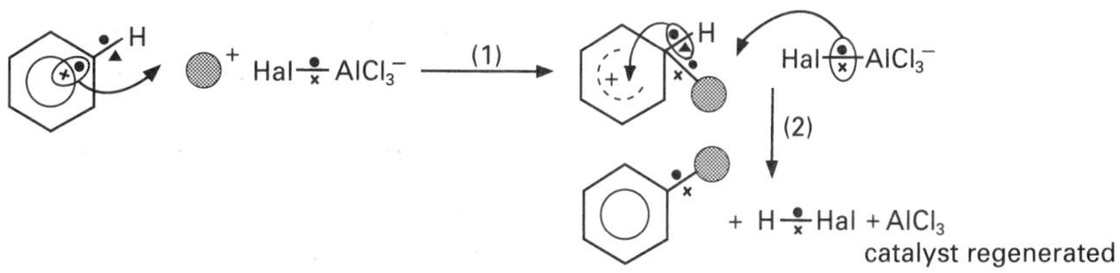

catalyst regenerated

36.6 Addition reactions of benzene

Unlike other unsaturated hydrocarbons, *benzene shows a reluctance to take part in addition reactions,* because these have extremely high activation energies. Even so, benzene does take part in some addition reactions, e.g.

▶ **hydrogenation**

When heated to 200 °C in the presence of finely divided nickel, benzene adds hydrogen to form cyclohexane:

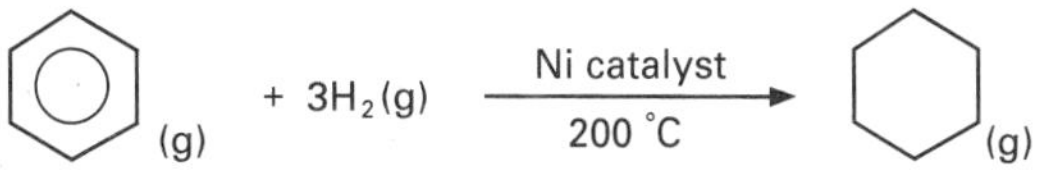

Studies of the energetics of this reaction provide evidence that benzene contains a delocalised π electron cloud (section 5.8);

▶ **halogenation in the presence of u.v. light**

When chlorine, or bromine, are bubbled through boiling benzene in the presence of u.v. light, or bright sunlight, addition occurs:

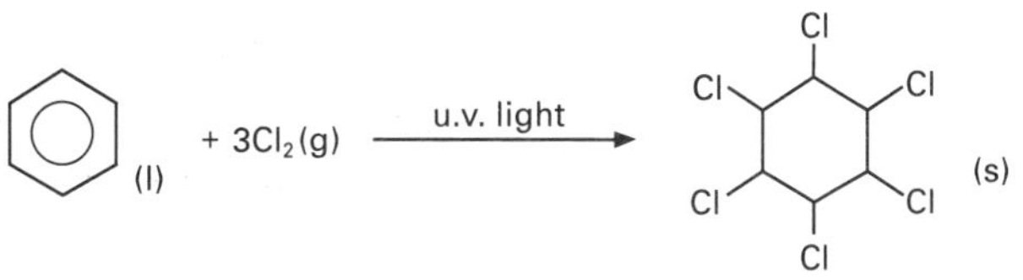

1,2,3,4,5,6-hexachlorocyclohexane can exist as eight geometrical isomers. One of these isomers, known as **Gammexane**, is used as an insecticide.

These addition reactions confirm that *benzene does have an unsaturated nature.* Interestingly, though, they proceed via a free radical, rather than an electrophilic, mechanism.

36.7 Oxidation reactions of benzene and methylbenzene

Benzene, and other aromatic hydrocarbons, burn readily when ignited. In theory, the combustion products are carbon dioxide and water, e.g.

$$C_6H_6(l) + \tfrac{15}{2}O_2(g) \rightarrow 6CO_2(g) + 3H_2O(l) \quad \Delta H = -3268 \text{ kJ mol}^{-1}$$

However, the very high carbon content in aromatic hydrocarbons (benzene, for example, is 92% C by mass), causes a lot of **incomplete combustion**. Thus, aromatic hydrocarbons burn with a bright orange, sooty flame and they are not used as fuels.

Unlike other unsaturated hydrocarbons, *the benzene ring is not attacked by common oxidising reagents*, such as acidified $KMnO_4(aq)$. However, one important synthetic reaction is the oxidation of the methyl side chain in methylbenzene:

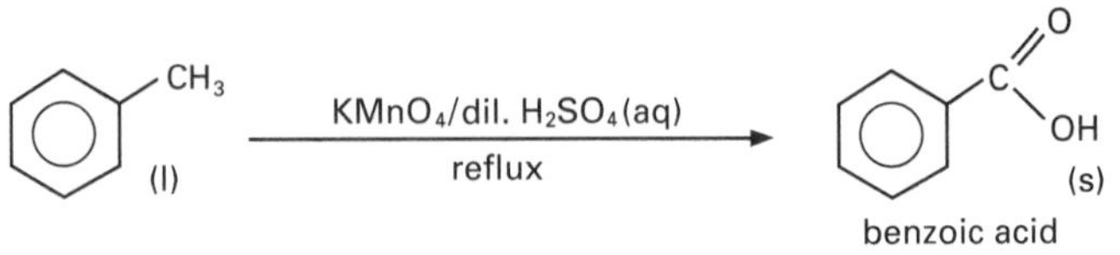

Under similar conditions, methane is totally unreactive. Thus, the benzene ring must **activate** the methyl side chain towards the oxidising agent.

Since this reaction also produces a colour change, purple $MnO_4^-(aq)$ to colourless $Mn^{2+}(aq)$, we can use it to tell the difference between methylbenzene and benzene.

Activity 36.2

1 Describe the reagents and reaction conditions that you would use to convert benzene into: (a) methylbenzene; (b) 1,3-dinitrobenzene; (c) bromobenzene; (d) phenol; (e) benzoic acid.
   (Hint: parts (d) and (e) need more than one step.)

2 Give the names and formulae of the products formed when benzene reacts with:
   (a) conc. HNO_3/H_2SO_4 at 50°C;   (b) conc. H_2SO_4 reflux for several hours;

   (c) CH_3I, $FeBr_3$ catalyst, 40°C;   (d) $CH_3C{\Large\diagdown}_{Cl}^{O}$, $AlCl_3$, 40°C;

   (e) Cl_2, Fe catalyst, room temp.;   (f) I_2, $AlCl_3$, 40°C;
   (g) H_2, Ni catalyst, 200°C;   (h) Br_2, u.v. light, reflux.

36.8 Comparing the reactions of hydrocarbons

In an examination, you may well be asked to compare the properties of an alkane, alkene, alkyne and benzene. Thus, it is a valuable revision exercise to make a table summarising these properties. Activity 36.3 suggests how you might do this.

Activity 36.3

Draw up a table which compares, and contrasts, the reactions of hexane, hex-1-ene, hex-1-yne and benzene with the following reagents:
1 $O_2(g)$;   2 Cl_2, Br_2;   3 HCl(g), HBr(g) and HI(g);
4 conc. $H_2SO_4(l)$;   5 $KMnO_4/dil$. $H_2SO_4(aq)$;   6 $H_2(g)/Ni(s)$;
7 conc.$HNO_3/conc$. $H_2SO_4(l)$;   8 Friedel–Crafts reagents.

36.9 Comments on the activities

Activity 36.1

1 (a) 1,2-diethylbenzene;   (b) 4-bromophenol;
   (c) 3-nitrobenzoic acid;   (d) 2,4,6-tribromophenylamine;
   (e) 2,4-dihydroxymethylbenzene;   (f) (chloromethyl) benzene – note the

use of the bracket to show that the chlorine is attached to the methyl carbon; (g) 2–chloromethylbenzene; (h) 4-bromophenylethanone.

2

(a) $CH_3-\overset{2}{CH}-CH_3$ (with numbering 1, 2, 3; phenyl group attached to central carbon)

(b) benzene ring with OH at position 1 and OH at position 2

(c) benzene ring with NO$_2$ at position 4, HO at position 1, position 2 marked, position 3 marked

(d) benzene ring with $C\!\!=\!\!O$ and CH_3 group

(e) benzene ring with $C\!\!=\!\!O$ and H, Cl at position 3, positions 1, 2 marked

(f) benzene ring with Cl at position 3, position 2 marked, COOH at position 1

(g) benzene ring with OH at position 1, Br at position 6, Br at position 2, Br at position 4, positions 5, 3 marked

Activity 36.2

1 (a) halogenomethane, AlCl$_3$ catalyst, 40°C;
   (b) conc.HNO$_3$/conc. H$_2$SO$_4$(l), 100°C;
   (c) Br$_2$, Fe or AlCl$_3$ catalyst, 40°C;

(d) benzene $\xrightarrow[\text{H}_2\text{SO}_4\text{(l), reflux}]{\text{conc.}}$ benzene-SO$_3$H $\xrightarrow[\text{NaOH(s)}]{\text{heat with}}$ benzene-O$^-$Na$^+$ $\xrightarrow[\text{room temp.}]{\text{dil. HCl(aq)}}$ benzene-OH

(e) benzene $\xrightarrow[\text{40°C}]{\text{CH}_3\text{Hal,AlCl}_3\text{(s)}}$ benzene-CH$_3$ $\xrightarrow[\text{reflux}]{\text{KMnO}_4/\text{dil. H}_2\text{SO}_4\text{(aq)}}$ benzene-COOH

2

(a) nitrobenzene, benzene–NO$_2$

(b) benzenesulphonic acid benzene–SO$_3$H

(c) methylbenzene, benzene–CH$_3$

(d) phenylethanone benzene–C$\!\!=\!\!$O, CH$_3$

(e) chlorobenzene, benzene–Cl

(f) no reaction (see section 36.5.3)

(g) cyclohexane, cyclohexane ring

(h) 1, 2, 3, 4, 5, 6-hexabromo– cyclohexane (cyclohexane ring with Br on each carbon)

Activity 36.3

Compare your answer with table 36.2.

36.10 Summary and revision plan

1 Aromatic compounds have a common structural feature, the benzene ring. Aromatic hydrocarbons are known as **arenes**.

2 Benzene's molecule contains a **delocalised π bond system** above and below the σ bond framework (covered in section 5.8).

3 **Positional isomerism** can occur in 'multi-substituted' benzene derivatives. Thus, you must always number the relative positions of the substituent groups in these compounds.

4 Benzene and methylbenzene are widely used in industry as (i) solvents and (ii) starting materials in the manufacture of other aromatic compounds. They are obtained from coal and by the catalytic reforming of naphtha.

5 *Benzene, though unsaturated, resists electrophilic addition reactions* (e.g. like those of alkenes and alkynes). Such reactions would have very high activation energies because delocalisation of the π electron cloud stabilises the benzene molecule. Some free radical addition reactions are known, and these demonstrate the unsaturated nature of benzene.

6 The reactions of benzene, and other arenes, fall into three main categories:
   (i) **electrophilic substitution** of hydrogen (ii) **addition** reactions

Figure 36.7　*Some important reactions of benzene*

Notes: *(1) $I_2(s)$ does not work in this reaction*
(2) ΔH_r value is evidence for electron delocalisation in benzene

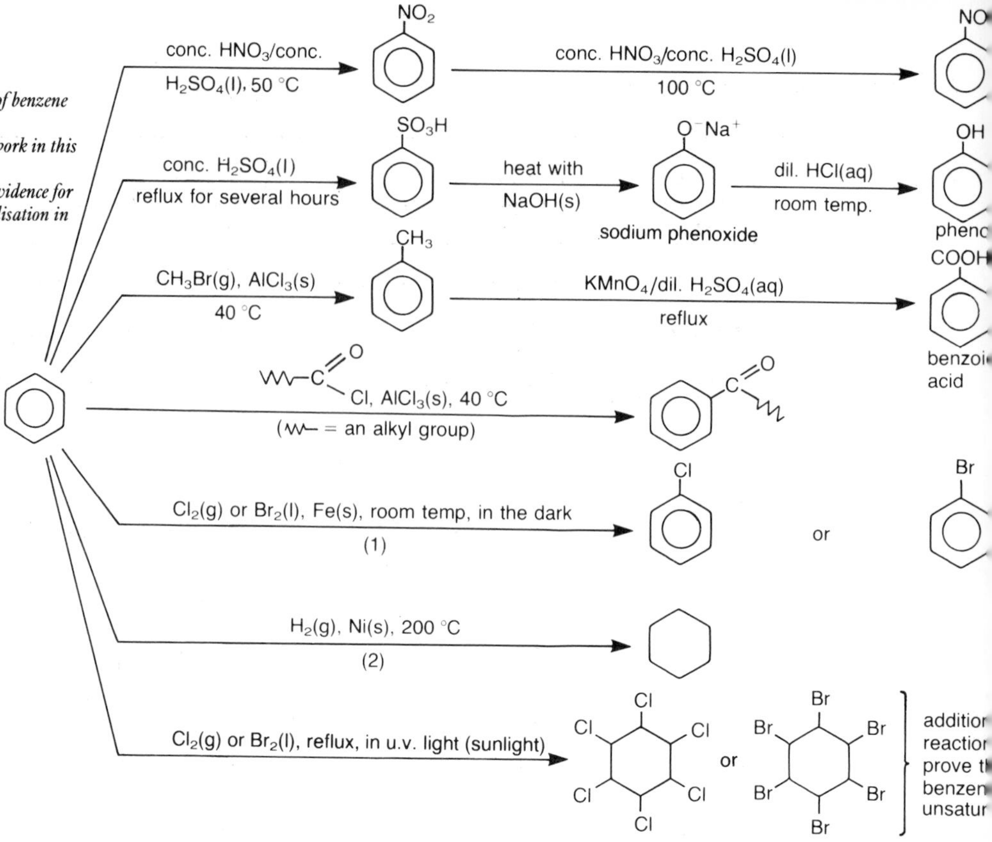

and　(iii) **oxidation** reactions. These reactions and some useful synthetic routes, are summarised in figure 36.7.

7　In the substitution reactions a C—H bond is converted into a C—X unit, where X may be $-NO_2$, $-SO_3H$, $-CH_3$ or another alkyl group, $-\overset{\displaystyle O}{\underset{}{C}}-CH_3$, $-Cl$ or $-Br$. These reactions have similar 'three-step' mechanisms.

Table 36.1　*Important reagents used in this chapter. Try to learn them*

Reagent	conditions	what it does
conc. HNO_3/conc. $H_2SO_4(l)$	50°C	**nitrates** benzene 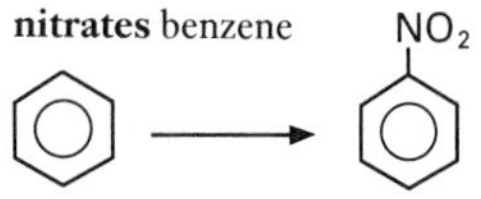
conc. $H_2SO_4(l)$	reflux, for several hours	**sulphonates** benzene 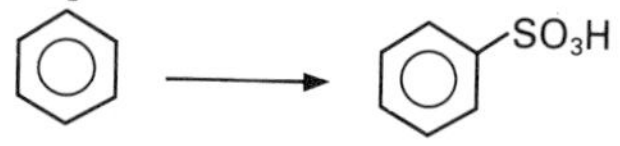
$AlCl_3$ catalyst, $\wedge\!\wedge$—Hal	40°C	**alkylates** benzene 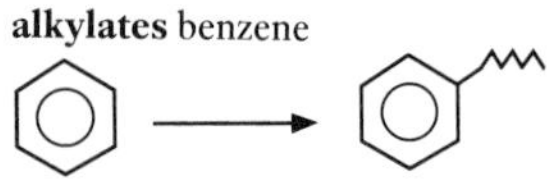
$AlCl_3$ catalyst, 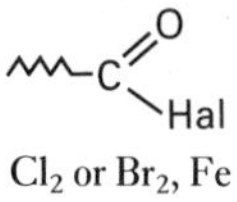 $\wedge\!\wedge$—C(=O)—Hal	40°C	**acylates** benzene 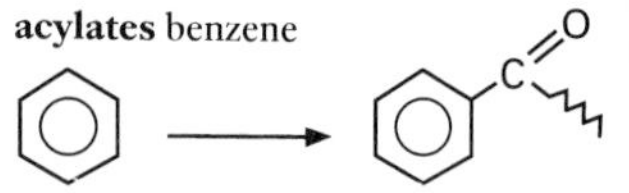
Cl_2 or Br_2, Fe catalyst	room temperature, in the dark	**halogenates** benzene 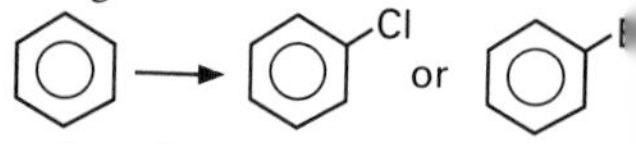
$H_2(g)$, Ni catalyst	200°C	**reduces** benzene 
$KMnO_4$/dil. $H_2SO_4(aq)$	reflux	**oxidises** methyl side-chain 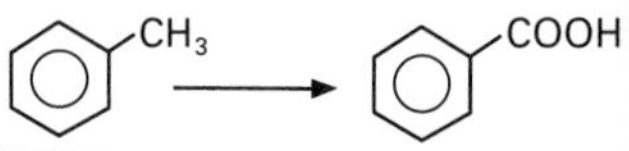

Table 36.2 *Comparing the reactions of hydrocarbons*

Reagent	alkanes, e.g. C_6H_{14} hexane	alkenes e.g. $C_4H_9-CH=CH_2$ hex-1-ene	alkynes e.g. $C_4H_9-C\equiv CH$ hex-1-yne	arenes e.g.  benzene
O_2(g), ignited	⟵ all burn; main products CO_2(g) and H_2O(l); more incomplete combustion as % of carbon increases ⟶			
Cl_2, Br_2	**substitution** in u.v. light→ a mixture of **halogenoalkanes** e.g. $C_6H_{13}Cl$	**addition** in the dark at room temp. → $C_4H_9-C(H)(Hal)-C(H)(Hal)-H$	**addition** in the dark at room temp. → $C_4H_9-C(Hal)(Hal)-C(H)(Hal)-H$	**substitution** in the dark at room temp., 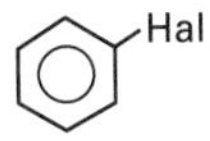 → (ring)–Hal **addition** in u.v. light → C_6Hal_6
		⟵ A test for localised π bonds ⟶		
HCl, HBr, HI gases	no reaction	**addition** at room temp. → $C_4H_9-C(H)(Hal)-C(H)(H)-H$	**addition** may need heating → $C_4H_9-C(H)(Hal)-C(H)(Hal)-H$	no reaction
		⟵ Markovnikov's Rule will apply ⟶		
conc. H_2SO_4(l)	no reaction	**addition** at room temp. Markovnikov's Rule will apply → $C_4H_9-C(H)(OSO_3H)-C(H)(H)-H$	dilute H_2SO_4(aq) → +$HgSO_4$ at 60°C $C_5H_{11}C(OH)=O$	**substitution** on refluxing 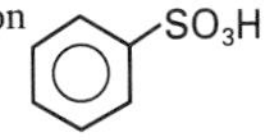 → (ring)–SO_3H
$KMnO_4$/dil. H_2SO_4(aq) reflux	no reaction	**oxidised** → diols	**oxidised** → carboxylic acids	no reaction (but see section 36.7)
H_2(g), Ni(s) at 200°C	no reaction	⟵ **reduction** → C_6H_{14}, hexane ⟶		**reduction**  → cyclohexane
conc. HNO_3/H_2SO_4(l)	no reaction	⟵ **oxidation** to give carboxylic acids ⟶		**nitration** at 55°C 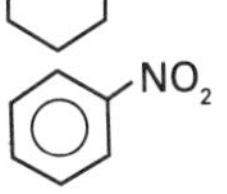 → (ring)–NO_2
Friedel–Crafts reactions (see section 36.5.3)	no reaction	⟵ no reaction ⟶		**alkylation**, e.g. 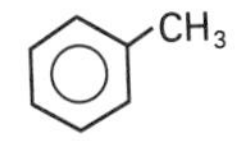 (ring)–CH_3 ; **acylation**, e.g. 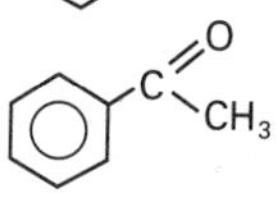 (ring)–C(=O)CH_3 ; **halogenation**, e.g. 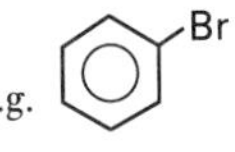 (ring)–Br

mechanisms: (i) formation of the electrophile, (ii) its attack on benzene's π electron ring and (iii) the rapid loss of a proton from the resulting cation.

8 Methylbenzene, but not benzene, will react with acidified $KMnO_4$(aq), (purple MnO_4^-(aq) giving colourless Mn^{2+}(aq)). Thus, we can use this reaction to tell the difference between these two arenes.

9 New reagents used in this chapter are given in table 36.1.

10 Table 36.2 compares the reactions of benzene with those of other hydrocarbons.

□ CHAPTER □
CHAPTER · CHAPTER
37

Organic Halogen Compounds

Contents

DDT was used during the Second World War to kill lice at home and mosquitoes at the battlefront

Figure 37.1 *The properties of an organic halogen compound depend on (i) the type of halogen atom and (ii) its molecular location*

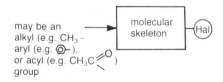

may be an
alkyl (e.g. CH₃–
aryl (e.g. ⬡–),
or acyl (e.g. CH₃C⟨O)
group

Figure 37.2 *The molecular structure of dichlorodiphenyltrichloroethane (DDT)*

An **organic halogen compound** has a halogen functional group attached to a hydrocarbon skeleton (figure 37.1). A most notorious example is the insecticide **DDT** (figure 37.2).

Although DDT was first prepared in 1874, it was not widely used until the Second World War. Due to the poor sanitation in wartime, soldiers and civilians were perfect hosts for parasites such as body lice. Apart from causing discomfort, these insects were a threat to life because they carried typhus, a deadly micro-organism. Fortunately, the lice could be killed by dusting with DDT powder.

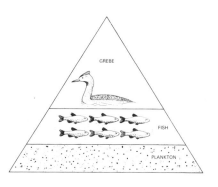

Figure 37.3 *DDT affected not only the insects that it was intended to kill, but also those organisms that fed on the insects. In this case the concentration of insecticide in the animals body gradually increases as it passes from the plankton to the fish and then to the grebes*

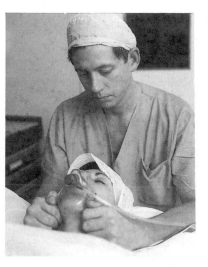

Halothane is widely used in hospitals as an anaesthetic. It is an organic halogen compound with the formula $CF_3CHBrCl$

Similarly, when the Allies liberated the Pacific islands, 'airborne' spraying of DDT was used to destroy the mosquitoes which spread malaria.

After the war, DDT was used by farmers to selectively kill insects while leaving animals unharmed. At first, the treatment appeared to be extremely successful and other organochlorine insecticides were developed. However, before long, certain insects were showing a resistance to DDT, and there was growing concern about the increased dosage that was being applied. Even more worrying was the discovery of appreciable amounts of DDT in dead birds found in regions where the insecticide had been used. This happened because the DDT molecule is extremely stable, and remains unchanged for a long time after spraying. It is also soluble in body fat and so builds up in the bodies of organisms that eat it. When it was used to kill midges over American lakes, the DDT was taken in by plankton in the water, which were then eaten by fish, which were then eaten by birds. As each fish ate millions of plankton and each bird ate many fish, the concentration of DDT in the bird's body was high enough to kill it (figure 37.3). By the mid-1960s, the concern over the use of DDT caused many countries, including the UK, to restrict its use.

DDT is just one of the many organic halogen compounds that have made an impact on everyday life. Nowadays, they have numerous uses, ranging from solvents to anaesthetics, from aerosol propellants to plastics. Organic halogen compounds also display a wide variety of chemical reactions, and this makes them useful in organic synthesis.

37.1 The different types of organic halogen compounds

There are three main types of organic halogen compound: halogenoalkanes, halogenoarenes and carboxylic acid halides.

Halogenoalkanes

Here one, or more, hydrogens in the alkane have been replaced by halogen atoms:

$$
\begin{array}{ccc}
\underset{\text{chloromethane}}{H-\overset{\displaystyle H}{\underset{\displaystyle H}{C}}-Cl} &
\underset{\text{dibromomethane}}{Br-\overset{\displaystyle H}{\underset{\displaystyle H}{C}}-Br} &
\underset{\text{iodoethane}}{H-\overset{\displaystyle H}{\underset{\displaystyle H}{C}}-\overset{\displaystyle H}{\underset{\displaystyle H}{C}}-I}
\end{array}
$$

If the halogenoalkane can exist as structural isomers, you must indicate the position(s) of the halogen atom(s) along the hydrocarbon chain:

1–chlorobutane, a primary...

2–chlorobutane, a secondary...

2–chloro–2–methylpropane a tertiary...

...halogenoalkane

Notice here the classification of halogenoalkanes as **primary, secondary** and **tertiary** compounds. Thus, we say that

▶ PRIMARY (1°) halogenoalkanes have the general formula:

▶ SECONDARY (2°) halogenoalkanes have the general formula:

▶ TERTIARY (3°) halogenoalkanes have the general formula:

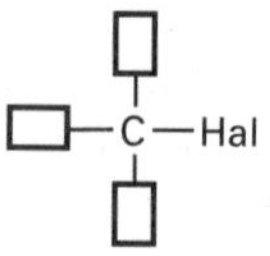

where ☐ is a hydrocarbon skeleton and Hal = F, Cl, Br or I.

The difference in the reactivity of 1°, 2° and 3° halogenoalkanes is a key aspect of our study.

Before we carry on, can you identify the type of isomerism shown by (i) 1,2-dibromoethene and (ii) 2-bromobutane? Draw the isomers. (For help, see sections 10.3 and 10.4, respectively.)

Halogenoarenes

Here, halogen atoms have been substituted for one, or more, of the hydrogens in benzene. For example,

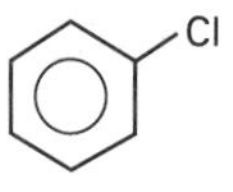

but not

chlorobenzene 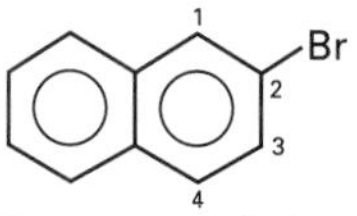   2–bromonaphthalene   (chloromethyl)benzene

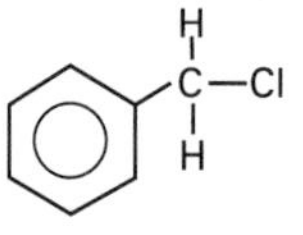

(Chloromethyl)benzene is *not* a halogenoarene because the halogen atom is *not directly attached* to the ring but is located in an alkyl side chain. Do you think that the chemical properties of (chloromethyl)benzene would resemble those of chlorobenzene or chloromethane?

Positional isomerism may occur in halogenoarenes, e.g.

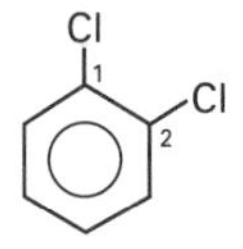

1,2–dichlorobenzene 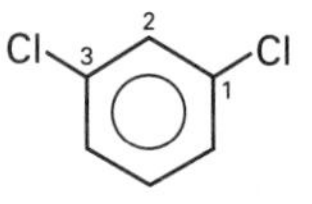   1,3–dichlorobenzene 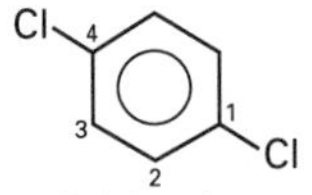   1,4–dichlorobenzene

Carboxylic acid halides

Here the −OH group in the carboxylic acid has been replaced by a halogen atom, e.g.

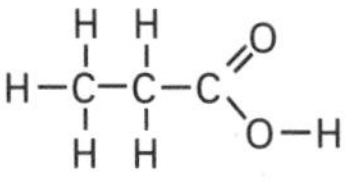

propanoic acid 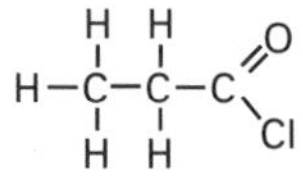   propanoyl chloride   benzoic acid 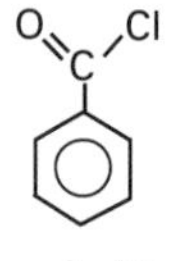   benzoyl chloride

Acid halides are named by replacing the '−oic' of the acid name by '−oyl halide'.

Activity 37.1

1   Name the following organic halogen compounds;

(a) CH_3CH_2Cl

(b) $CH_3-\overset{\overset{\displaystyle Br}{|}}{\underset{\underset{\displaystyle CH_3}{|}}{C}}-CH_3$

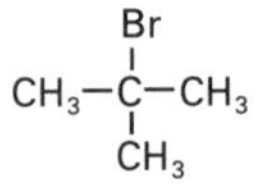

(c) $CH_3CH_2CHICH_3$

(d) Br

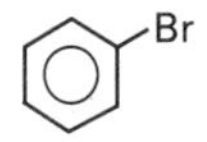

(e) CH_2Br

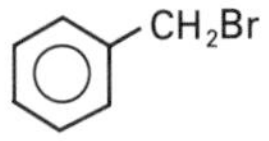

(f)

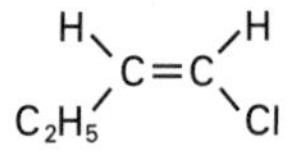

2   Write down structural formulae for the following compounds.
    (a) 2-iodo-2-methylpentane   (b) 1-chloro-1-phenylethane
    (c) 1-bromo-4-iodobenzene   (d) triiodomethane (iodoform)
    (e) 1-bromo-3-chloro-4-methylhexane
    (f) 1,2-dibromocyclohexane

3   Of the *saturated* compounds given in questions 1 and 2, which are (i) primary, (ii) secondary and (iii) tertiary?

4   A compound of molecular formula $C_3H_4Cl_2$ is known to have seven non-cyclic isomers. Draw their structural formulae and name them.

5   (a) Name these acid halides:

    (b) Draw structural formulae for (i) butanoyl iodide and (ii) 2-phenylethanoyl bromide.

37.2 Physical properties of organic halogen compounds

Some properties of organic halogen compounds are shown in table 37.1. Activity 37.2 will help you to analyse this data and explain any trends which are found.

Table 37.1 *Some properties of organic halogen compounds*

Name	formula	state (at 25°C)	melting point/°C	boiling point/°C	density /g cm^{-3}	$\Delta H_c^{\ominus}$ /kJ mol^{-1}
chloromethane	CH_3Cl	gas	− 98	−24	0.92 (L)	− 687
chloroethane	C_2H_5Cl	gas	−136	12	0.90 (L)	−1325
1-chloropropane	C_3H_7Cl	liquid	−123	47	0.89	−2001
2-chloropropane	$CH_3CHClCH_3$	liquid	−117	36	0.86	−2028
1-chlorobutane	$CH_3(CH_2)_3Cl$	liquid	−123	79	0.89	−2704
2-chlorobutane	$C_2H_5CHClCH_3$	liquid	−131	68	0.87	
2-chloro-2-methylpropane	$(CH_3)_2CClCH_3$	liquid	− 25	51	0.84	−2693
chlorobenzene	C_6H_5Cl	liquid	− 45	132	1.11	−3112
ethanoyl chloride	CH_3COCl	liquid	−112	51	1.10	
bromomethane	CH_3Br	gas	− 93	4	1.68 (L)	− 770
bromoethane	C_2H_5Br	liquid	−118	38	1.46	−1425
1-bromopropane	C_3H_7Br	liquid	−110	71	1.35	−2057
2-bromopropane	$CH_3CHBrCH_3$	liquid	− 89	60	1.31	−2052
1-bromobutane	$CH_3(CH_2)_3Br$	liquid	−112	102	1.28	
2-bromobutane	$C_2H_5CHBrCH_3$	liquid	−112	91	1.26	−2705
2-bromo-2-methylpropane	$(CH_3)_2CBrCH_3$	liquid	− 16	73	1.22	
bromobenzene	C_6H_5Br	liquid	− 32	156	1.49	
ethanoyl bromide	CH_3COBr	liquid	− 96	77	1.66	
iodomethane	CH_3I	liquid	− 66	33	2.28	− 815
iodoethane	C_2H_5I	liquid	−111	72	1.94	−1490
1-iodopropane	C_3H_7I	liquid	−101	103	1.75	−2152
2-iodopropane	CH_3CHICH_3	liquid	− 91	90	1.70	
1-iodobutane	$CH_3(CH_2)_3I$	liquid	−130	131	1.61	
2-iodobutane	$C_2H_5CHICH_3$	liquid	−104	120	1.59	
2-iodo-2-methylpropane	$(CH_3)_2CICH_3$	liquid	− 38	103	1.57	
iodobenzene	C_6H_5I	liquid	− 30	189	0.90	−3193
ethanoyl iodide	CH_3COI	liquid	0	108	1.98	

(L) means density in the liquid state

Can you predict the standard enthalpies of combustion of the following compounds (a) 1-chlorobutane (b) 1-iodobutane and (c) bromobenzene?

Activity 37.2

Briefly study table 37.1 and then work through the following questions.

1 Do the halogenoalkanes form a homologous series? If so, what is their general formula?

2 For the primary halogenoalkanes *only*, plot graphs of (a) boiling point and (b) standard enthalpy of combustion, $\Delta H_c^{\ominus}$ against the number of carbon atoms in the chain. Account for the shape of the graphs. (For help here, and in questions 3 and 4, see section 34.3.)

3 Compare (a) the boiling points and (b) the densities of primary, secondary and tertiary isomeric compounds containing the same halogen atom. Do you detect any trends in the values? If so, what explanation can you give for this behaviour?

4 Compare the boiling points of the halogenoalkanes which have different halogen atoms attached to the same hydrocarbon skeleton. Once again, can you detect, and explain, any trends in the values?

Solubility

Since they contain polar C—Hal bonds, halogenoalkanes and halogenoarenes usually dissolve in polar organic solvents, such as ethanol and propanone. However, they are almost insoluble in water. Can you explain why? (See section 9.8.)

Finally, let us consider **tetrachloromethane**, $CCl_4(l)$. Although it contains polarised bonds, the molecule is non-polar overall (section 5.9). Thus, tetrachloromethane can be used as a non-polar solvent.

37.3 Making organic halogen compounds

Halogenoalkanes

These can be made in two ways:

▶ **from alcohols;**
A halogenoalkane can be prepared by the action of a halogenating agent on an alcohol, e.g.

Some other halogenating agents which convert C—OH into C—Hal are given in table 37.2.

▶ **from alkenes and alkynes;**
A halogen, or hydrogen halide, reacts with an alkene or alkyne to form a halogenoalkane (or halogenoalkene), e.g.

Notice that the addition of hydrogen halide follows Markovnikov's Rule (section 35.6.2).

Table 37.2 *These common halogenating agents convert 1°, 2° amd 3° alcohols into the corresponding halogenoalkanes*

Reagent	reaction conditions
$PCl_5(s)$ $PCl_3(l)$	} room temperature
$P(red) + Br_2(l)$ $P(red) + I_2(s)$ (giving $PHal_3$ *in situ*) $SOCl_2(l)$ conc. $HCl(aq)$ $KBr(s)/$conc. $H_3PO_4(l)$ $KI(s)/$conc. $H_3PO_4(l)$ (giving conc. HHal *in situ*)	} reflux

Notes: (1) one mole of PCl_5 can only halogenate one mole of —OH bonds, whereas $PHal_3$ can halogenate three moles of —OH bonds;
(2) $SOCl_2$ is a useful reagent because the unwanted products, being gases (SO_2 and HCl), are easily removed;
(3) *in situ* means making one reactant in the presence of the other reactants or just before they are added

Acid halides

These are made by reacting a carboxylic acid with one of the halogenating agents in table 37.2, e.g. sulphur dichloride oxide:

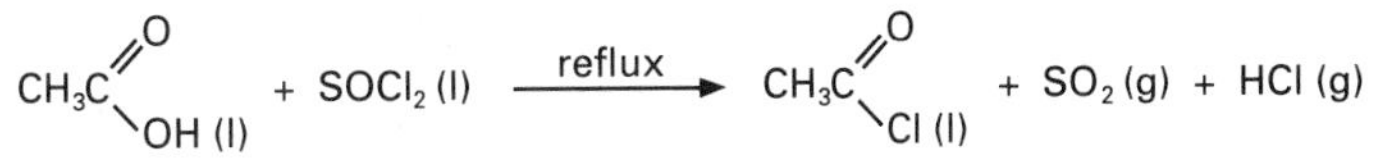

$$CH_3C\overset{O}{\underset{OH\ (l)}{\diagup}} + SOCl_2\ (l) \xrightarrow{\text{reflux}} CH_3C\overset{O}{\underset{Cl\ (l)}{\diagup}} + SO_2\ (g) + HCl\ (g)$$

Halogenoarenes

Chloro and bromoarenes are obtained by reacting the arene with the halogen in the presence of a Friedel–Crafts catalyst (section 36.5.3), e.g.

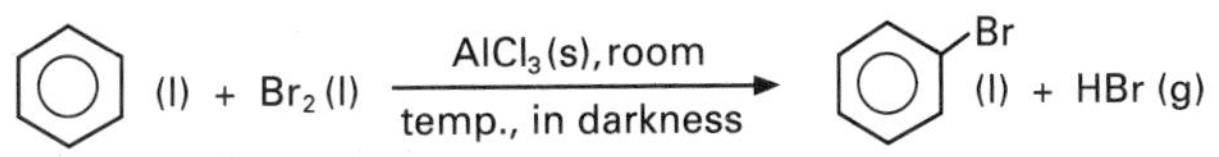

$$\bigcirc\!\!\!\!\!\bigcirc (l) + Br_2\ (l) \xrightarrow[\text{temp., in darkness}]{AlCl_3\ (s),\ room} \bigcirc\!\!\!\!\!\bigcirc\!\!^{Br} (l) + HBr\ (g)$$

Halogenoarenes can also be easily prepared from diazonium salts (section 41.9).

Activity 37.3

Using a different reagent each time, explain how you would perform the following conversions:

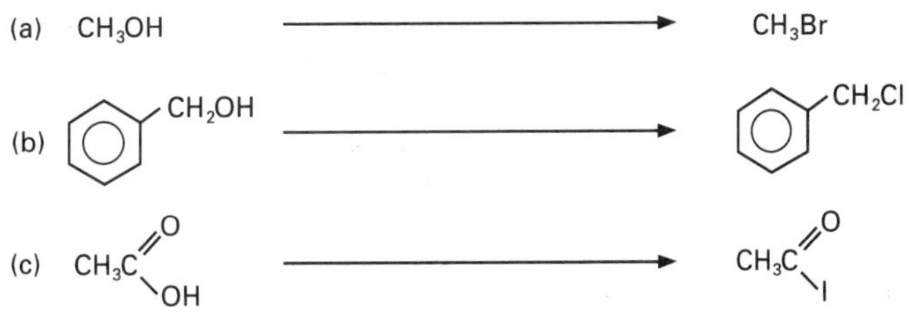

(a) CH_3OH ⟶ CH_3Br

(b)   ⟶

(c) $CH_3C\overset{O}{\underset{OH}{\diagup}}$ ⟶ $CH_3C\overset{O}{\underset{I}{\diagup}}$

(d) butan-2-ol → 2-chlorobutane
(e) benzene   → chlorobenzene
(f) but-2-ene → 2-iodobutane.

37.4 Predicting the reactivity of organic halogen compounds

The chemical properties of an organic halogen compound will depend on:

▶   *which halogen atom (F, Cl, Br or I), is present.*
    Looking at the bond energy terms in table 37.3, we can see that the C—F bond is very strong. It is not surprising, therefore, that organic fluorine compounds are found to be extremely unreactive. We shall concentrate, then, on the reactions of chloro, bromo and iodo compounds.
▶   *the location of the C—Hal bond within the molecule.*
    It will be interesting to see how the chemical reactivity of a given C—Hal bond, say C—Cl, depends on its structural position within the molecule.
Due to the C—Hal bond polarities, **nucleophiles** should attack the $C^{\delta+}$, thereby displacing a halogen ion, e.g.

$$\overset{\delta-}{Hal}—\overset{\delta+}{C} + \underset{\text{a nucleophile}}{Nuc^-} \longrightarrow Hal^- + C—Nuc$$

Apart from nucleophilic substitution, we would expect two other types of reaction:

▶   **elimination** of hydrogen halide from a halogenoalkane or halogenoalkene, to form an alkene or alkyne, respectively:

Tape made from PTFE is used by plumbers for sealing and by electricians for insulation

Table 37.3   *Some bond energy terms*

Bond	bond energy term (BET)/ $kJ\ mol^{-1}$
C—F	484
C—Cl	338
C—Br	276
C—I	238
C—H	412

Can you explain the trend in C—Hal bond strength?

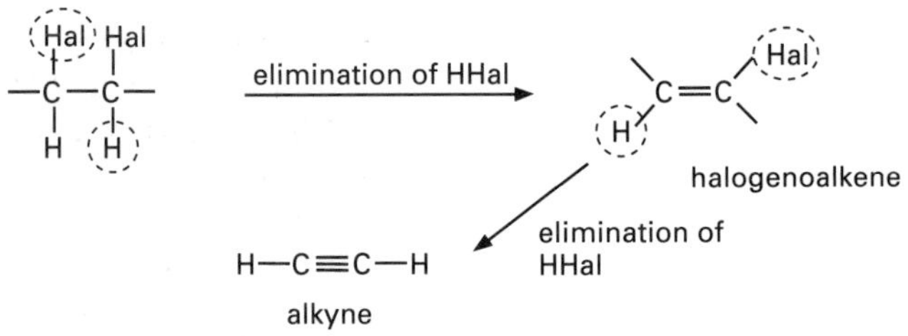

- **electrophilic substitution** of the 'ring' hydrogens in halogenoarenes (section 36.5). For example:

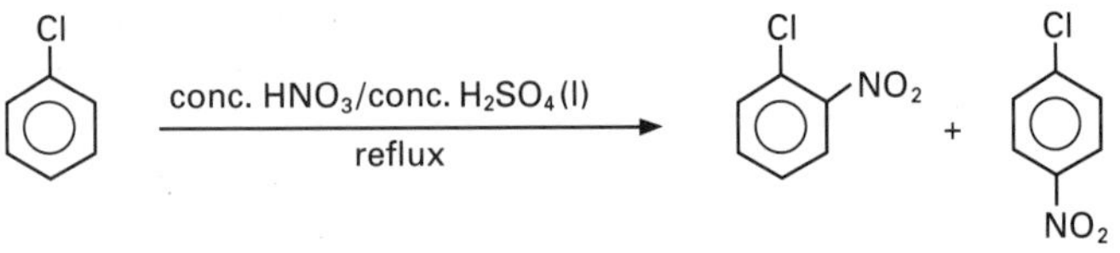

37.5 Nucleophilic substitution reactions

37.5.1 Substitution of —Hal by —OH

The reactivity of an organic halogen compound depends on (i) the type of halogen atom and (ii) its location within the molecule. These effects can be easily studied by measuring the relative rates of hydrolysis of various organic halogen compounds i.e.

$$C—Hal + H_2O \rightarrow C—OH + HHal$$

Experiment 1

To study the effect of different halogen atoms on the rate of hydrolysis

Method   Three test-tubes, each containing aqueous silver nitrate ($1\,cm^3$, $0.1\,M$) and ethanol ($2\,cm^3$) are placed in a water bath at $60\,°C$. After five minutes, we add 2 drops of 1-chlorobutane to the first tube, 2 drops of 1-bromobutane to the second and 2 drops of 1-iodobutane to the third. Each tube is shaken, loosely corked and observed at $60\,°C$ for ten minutes. (Note: (i) the nucleophile is $H_2O(l)$ from $AgNO_3(aq)$, not NO_3^- (aq); and (ii) the ethanol is not a reactant but acts as a solvent.)

Observations   A precipitate of silver halide appears in each tube. We find that:

AgCl(s)	AgBr(s)	AgI(s)
white	cream	yellow

precipitate forms more rapidly →

Explanation   As soon as the halide ion is displaced from the halogenoalkane, it reacts with the $Ag^+(aq)$ ion to give the precipitate of silver halide:

$$Ag^+(aq) + Hal^-(aq) \rightarrow AgHal(s)$$

Thus, the rates of hydrolysis are proportional to the amount of AgHal that is formed in a given time. Our results show that

1-chlorobutane	1-bromobutane	1-iodobutane

increasing rate of hydrolysis →

Similar trends are found when these halogen compounds react with other nucleophiles, such as NH_3^- and CN^-.

Two opposing factors govern the rate of nucleophilic substitution in halogenoalkanes:

▶ *the polarity of the C—Hal bond.* Electronegativity decreases in going from chlorine to iodine. This suggests that *1-chlorobutane should react fastest* with nucleophiles because it contains the most electron-poor ($\delta+$) carbon atom.

▶ *the C—Hal bond strength.* For substitution to occur, the C—Hal bond must be broken, and this will happen more readily if the bond is weak. The C—Hal bond energy terms in table 37.3 suggest that *1-iodobutane would react fastest* because it has the weakest C—Hal bond.

Since 1-iodobutane did hydrolyse most rapidly, *the effect of the bond strength seems to outweigh that of the bond polarity.* Hence, for the same hydrocarbon skeleton, we find that:

chloroalkanes	bromoalkanes	iodoalkanes

$\longrightarrow$

rates of nucleophilic substitution increase

Experiment 2

To study the effect of changing the molecular location of the halogen atom on the rate of hydrolysis

Method   We use the same method as in experiment 1, but this time compare the rates of hydrolysis of five types of chlorocompound:

$CH_3CH_2CH_2CH_2Cl$

1–chlorobutane
(primary, 1°)

$CH_3CH_2-\overset{\overset{\displaystyle H}{|}}{\underset{\underset{\displaystyle Cl}{|}}{C}}-CH_3$

2–chlorobutane
(secondary, 2°)

$CH_3-\overset{\overset{\displaystyle CH_3}{|}}{\underset{\underset{\displaystyle Cl}{|}}{C}}-CH_3$

2–chloro–2–methylpropane
(tertiary, 3°)

chlorobenzene
(aromatic)

$CH_3C\overset{\displaystyle O}{\underset{\displaystyle Cl}{\diagup}}$

ethanoyl chloride
(an acid chloride)

Observation   Figure 37.4 describes the appearance of the reactive mixtures after ten minutes. These results clearly show that *the rate of hydrolysis does depend on the molecular location of the halogen atom.* For a given halogen, we find that:

halogenoarenes $<<<$ 1° $<$ 2° $<$ 3° $<<$ acid halides

$\longrightarrow$

increasing rate of hydrolysis

Reactions with other nucleophiles confirm this trend in reactivity.

Figure 37.4   *Observations from experiment 2: the appearance of the reaction mixtures after ten minutes*

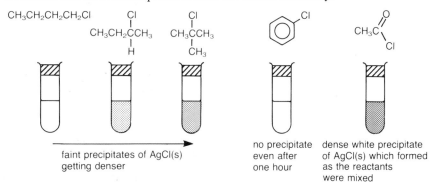

faint precipitates of AgCl(s) getting denser

no precipitate even after one hour

dense white precipitate of AgCl(s) which formed as the reactants were mixed

Explanation   The increase in rate of nucleophilic substitution as we go from 1° to 2° to 3° halogenoalkanes occurs because these reactions have *different mechanisms*, and these are described in section 37.6.

Figure 37.5 *The delocalised π bond system in halogenoarenes both strengthens the C—Hal bond and decreases its polarity*

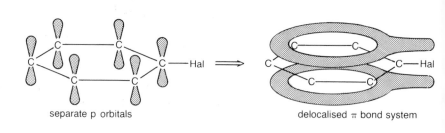

separate p orbitals

delocalised π bond system

Halogenoarenes do not give nucleophilic substitution reactions under normal laboratory conditions. The reason for this is that the p orbitals on the carbon and halogen atoms overlap sideways to form a **delocalised π bond system** (figure 37.5). This has two effects:

▶ *the C—Hal bond gains some π bond character,* making it stronger, and less reactive, than the same C—Hal bond in a halogenoalkane; and

▶ *the C—Hal bond polarity is decreased,* making the $C^{\delta+}$ atom much less susceptible to nucleophilic attack.

Compared to halogenoalkanes of similar mass, aliphatic **acid halides** are vigorously hydrolysed at room temperature, e.g.

$$CH_3CH_2C \overset{\delta-}{\underset{\delta-}{\overset{O}{\diagup}}}_{Br\ (l)}^{\delta+} + H_2O\ (l) \xrightarrow[\text{temp.}]{\text{room}} CH_3CH_2C \overset{O}{\underset{OH\ (aq)}{\diagup}} + HBr\ (aq)$$

propanoyl bromide   propanoic acid

Although aromatic acid halides are less reactive, they are still quickly hydrolysed by boiling water, e.g.

benzoyl chloride   benzoic acid

$$+ H_2O\ (l) \xrightarrow{100\,°C} + HCl\ (aq)$$

Figure 37.6 *In acid halides, both the O and Hal atoms can withdraw electron cloud from the neighbouring C atom, making it highly susceptible to nucleophilic attack*

In acid halides, the polarisation of the $\overset{\partial+}{C}=\overset{\partial-}{O}$ and the $\overset{\partial+}{C}-\overset{\partial-}{Hal}$ bonds produces a highly *electron-poor (δ+) carbon atom,* towards which nucleophiles are strongly attracted (figure 37.6). Consequently, we find that acid halides undergo nucleophilic substitution faster than the halogenoalkanes of similar mass. Also, we find that:

acid iodides	acid bromides	acid chlorides

increasing rate of nucleophilic substitution →

This trend is exactly the opposite of that found for halogenoalkanes (see experiment 1). For acid halides, then, the order of reactivity depends more on the strength of attraction between the nucleophile and $C^{\delta+}$, than on the C—Hal bond strength.

To summarise, then, the tendency of organic halogen compounds to undergo nucleophilic substitution is described by the following trends:

chloro-	bromo-	iodoalkanes or arenes

GET FASTER

BUT acid chlorides	bromides	iodides

GET SLOWER

primary	secondary	tertiary halogenoalkanes

GET FASTER

halogenoarenes	halogenalkanes	acid halides

GET MUCH FASTER

Primary alcohols may be prepared, in good yields, by the alkaline hydrolysis of a primary halogenoalkane, e.g.

$$CH_3CH_2CH_2I(l) \xrightarrow[\text{reflux}]{\text{dil. NaOH(aq)}} CH_3CH_2CH_2OH(aq) + NaI(aq)$$

Under the same conditions, secondary and tertiary halogenoalkanes do form the alcohols, *but the yields are poor*, e.g.

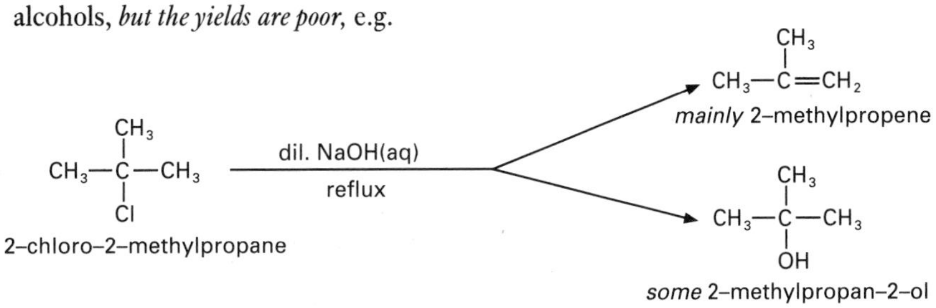

2-chloro-2-methylpropane

mainly 2-methylpropene

some 2-methylpropan-2-ol

Here the alkene is produced by an **elimination** reaction. Whenever halogenoalkanes react with hydroxide ions, *substitution and elimination reactions are in competition*. This topic is further discussed in section 37.7.

In fact, a secondary or tertiary alcohol is made by refluxing a halogenoalkane with water:

$$CH_3CHICH_3(l) \xrightarrow[\text{reflux}]{H_2O(l)} CH_3CH(OH)CH_3$$
2-iodopropane   propan-2-ol

37.5.2 Substitution of −Hal by −CN

When an ethanolic solution of a halogenoalkane and potassium cyanide is refluxed, a **nitrile** is formed, e.g.

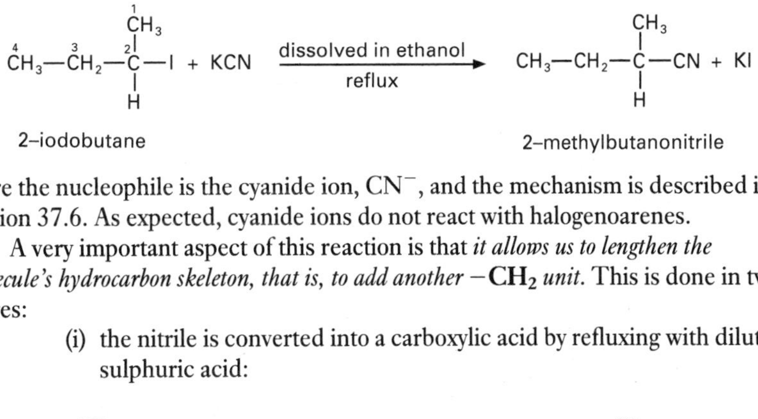

2-iodobutane

2-methylbutanonitrile

Here the nucleophile is the cyanide ion, CN^-, and the mechanism is described in section 37.6. As expected, cyanide ions do not react with halogenoarenes.

A very important aspect of this reaction is that *it allows us to lengthen the molecule's hydrocarbon skeleton, that is, to add another* −CH_2 *unit*. This is done in two stages:

    (i) the nitrile is converted into a carboxylic acid by refluxing with dilute sulphuric acid:

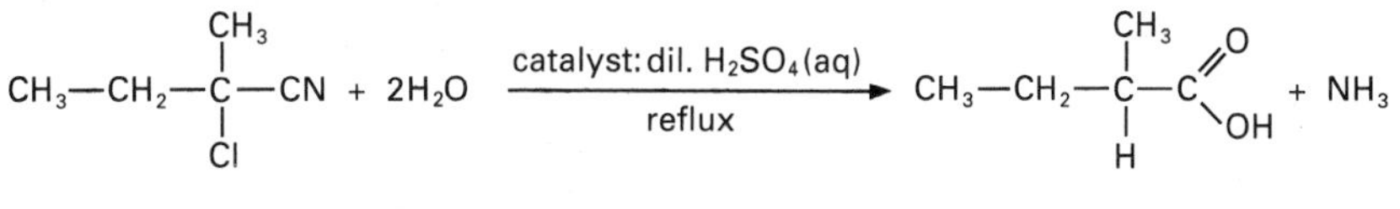

    (ii) the carboxylic acid is reduced by refluxing with lithium tetrahydridoaluminate $Li^+[AlH_4]^-$ dissolved in ethoxyethane, $C_2H_5OC_2H_5$:

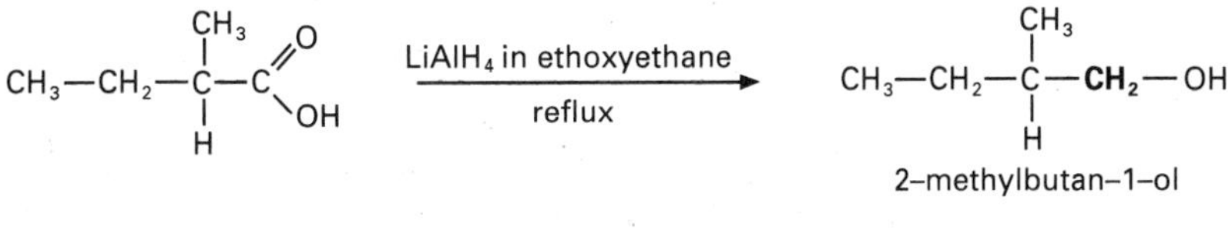

2-methylbutan-1-ol

37.5.3 Substitution of −Hal by −NH₂

When a halogenoalkane and ammonia dissolved in ethanol are heated in a sealed tube (to create a high pressure), an amine is formed, e.g.

$$\text{C}_2\text{H}_5\text{I} + \text{NH}_3 \xrightarrow[\text{high pressure}]{\text{ethanol solvent; heat;}} \text{C}_2\text{H}_5\text{NH}_2$$

iodoethane   ethylamine

Since it has one hydrocarbon skeleton attached to the nitrogen atom, ethylamine is termed a primary (1°) amine.

Like ammonia, amines have a lone pair of electrons on the nitrogen atom, and they can behave as nucleophiles (section 41.8). Thus, if the reaction above is carried out with the halogenoalkane in excess, we obtain a mixture of secondary(2°) and tertiary(3°) amines, and a quaternary ammonium salt, e.g.

$$\overset{\bullet\bullet}{\text{C}_2\text{H}_5\text{NH}_2} \xrightarrow{\text{C}_2\text{H}_5\text{I}} (\text{C}_2\text{H}_5)_2\overset{\bullet\bullet}{\text{NH}} \xrightarrow{\text{C}_2\text{H}_5\text{I}} (\text{C}_2\text{H}_5)_3\overset{\bullet\bullet}{\text{N}} \xrightarrow{\text{C}_2\text{H}_5\text{I}} (\text{C}_2\text{H}_5)_4\text{N}^+\text{I}^-$$

ethylamine   diethylamine   triethylamine   tetraethylammonium
(1°)   (2°)   (3°)   iodide

Since such mixtures are hard to separate, secondary and tertiary amines are not made this way (see section 41.5). *Secondary* and *tertiary* amines have *two* and *three* hydrocarbon skeletons respectively, attached to the nitrogen atom.

Halogenoarenes do not react with ammonia, or amines, under similar conditions. However, acid halides react violently with ammonia at room temperature and pressure to form **acid amides**, e.g.

$$\text{CH}_3\text{C}\underset{\text{Cl (l)}}{\overset{\text{O}}{{\Big\backslash}}} + 2\text{NH}_3\,(\text{aq}) \xrightarrow{\text{room temp.}} \text{CH}_3\text{C}\underset{\text{NH}_2\,(\text{aq})}{\overset{\text{O}}{{\Big\backslash}}} + \text{NH}_4\text{Cl}\,(\text{aq})$$

conc.   ethanamide

37.5.4 Substitution of —Hal by —O—□, where —□ is a hydrocarbon skeleton

An **ether** can be prepared by refluxing a primary halogenoalkane with an alcoholic solution of a **sodium alkoxide**, e.g.

$$\text{CH}_3\text{CH}_2\text{O}^-\text{Na}^+(\text{s}) + \text{ICH}_3(\text{l}) \xrightarrow[\text{reflux}]{\text{in an alcohol}} \text{CH}_3\text{CH}_2\text{OCH}_3(\text{l}) + \text{NaI}(\text{s})$$

sodium ethoxide   methoxyethane
                                                              (an ether)

The sodium alkoxide is prepared by the action of sodium on excess alcohol, e.g.

$$\text{CH}_3\text{CH}_2\text{OH}(\text{l}) + \text{Na}(\text{s}) \xrightarrow[\text{temp.}]{\text{room}} \text{CH}_3\text{CH}_2\text{O}^-\text{Na}^+(\text{s}) + \tfrac{1}{2}\text{H}_2(\text{g})$$

sodium ethoxide

Sodium phenoxide reacts with primary halogenoalkanes in the same way, e.g.

phenol   sodium phenoxide   phenoxyethane
                                                                        (an aromatic ether)

Similar reactions with secondary or tertiary halogenoalkanes produce only very small amounts of ethers. Instead, the major product is an alkene, e.g.

$$\text{CH}_3\overset{\overset{\displaystyle |}{|}}{\underset{\underset{\displaystyle \text{H}}{|}}{\text{C}}}\text{CH}_3\,(\text{l}) + \text{CH}_3\text{O}^-\text{Na}^+\,(\text{s}) \xrightarrow{\text{reflux}} \text{CH}_3\text{—CH}\text{=}\text{CH}_2\,(\text{g}) + \text{CH}_3\text{OH}\,(\text{l}) + \text{NaI}\,(\text{s})$$

Elimination of a hydrogen halide has taken place, and this is discussed further in section 37.7.

As expected, we find that alkoxide ions, or phenoxide ions, (i) do not react with halogenoarenes and (ii) often react vigorously with acid halides, even at room temperature, to form **acid esters**, e.g.

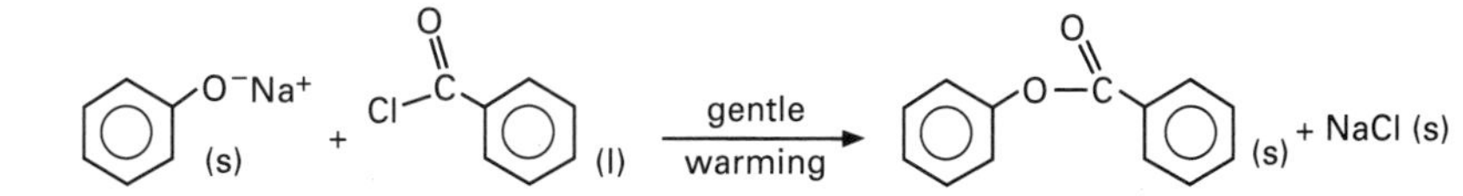

sodium phenoxide   benzoyl chloride   phenyl benzoate
                                                              (an aromatic ester)

37.5.5 Substitution of −Hal by −OC−□

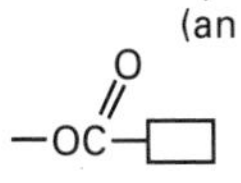

Acid esters are formed when the sodium salt of the carboxylic acid is refluxed with a halogenoalkane, e.g.

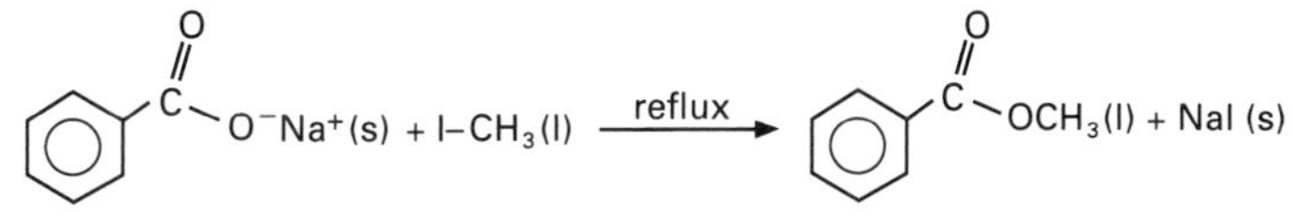

sodium benzoate   iodomethane   methyl benzoate

Of course, halogenoarenes will not react in this way because their delocalised π bond system strengthens the C—Hal bond and reduces its polarity (figure 37.5).

On heating an acid halide with the sodium salt of a carboxylic acid, an **acid anhydride** distils off. For example,

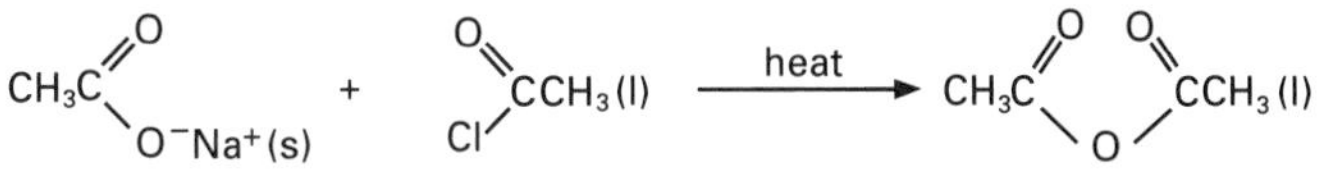

sodium   ethanoyl   ethanoic
ethanoate   chloride   anhydride

Activity 37.4

1   Draw the structural formulae of: propanoyl iodide, chlorobenzene, 2-bromo-2-methylpropane, 2-chloro-2-methylpropane, propanoyl chloride, 2-chlorobutane, 2-iodo-2-methylpropane, (chloromethyl) benzene.
    Number these structures in order of their *increasing* reactivity with water.

2   Give the name and structural formula of the organic product(s) formed in the following reactions:

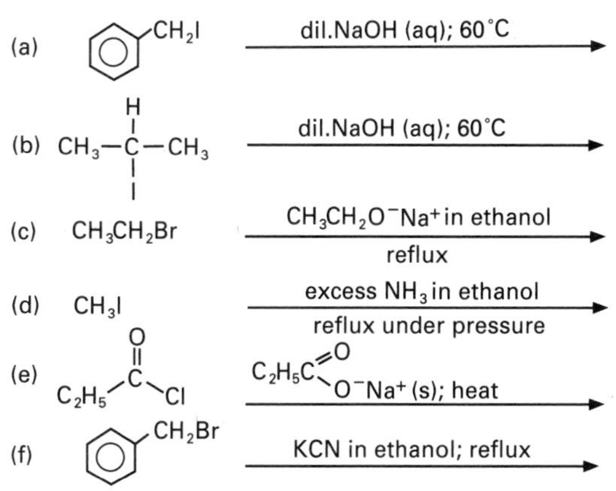

3   Give the reagents and reaction conditions needed for the following conversions:

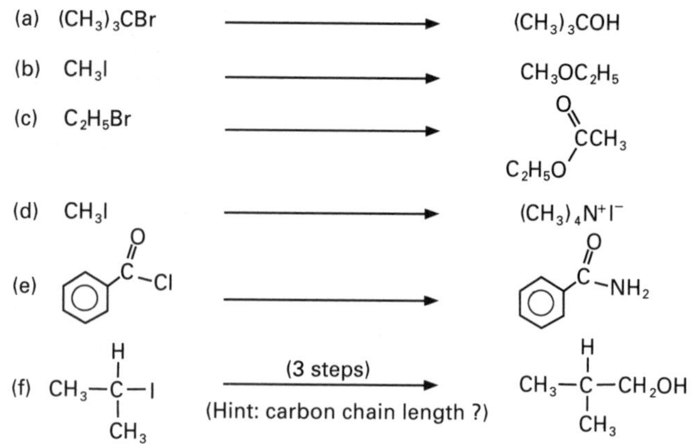

(a) $(CH_3)_3CBr$ $\longrightarrow$ $(CH_3)_3COH$

(b) CH_3I $\longrightarrow$ $CH_3OC_2H_5$

(c) C_2H_5Br $\longrightarrow$

(d) CH_3I $\longrightarrow$ $(CH_3)_4N^+I^-$

(e)

(f)

37.6 The mechanism of nucleophilic substitution in halogenoalkanes

In chapter 11, we saw that kinetics studies provide information about a reaction's mechanism. We are going to investigate the kinetics of the following reactions:

I $\quad CH_3-CH_2-CH_2-CH_2Br \xrightarrow[60°C]{\text{dil. NaOH(aq)}} CH_3-CH_2-CH_2-CH_2OH$

1-bromobutane   butan-1-ol
(a 1° halogenoalkane)

II

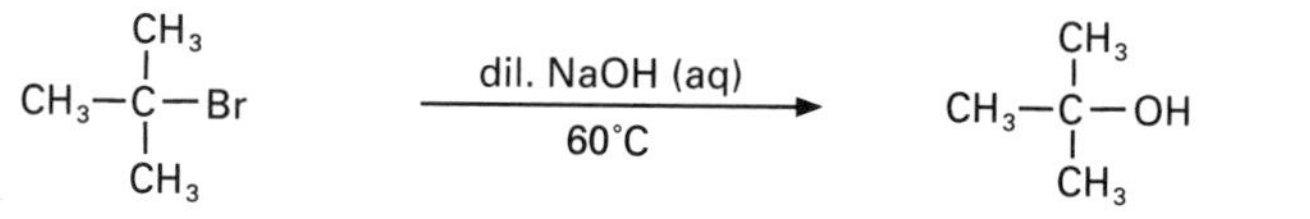

2–bromo–2–methylpropane   2,2–dimethylpropan–1–ol
(a 3° halogenoalkane)

Scan through sections 11.3, 11.4 and 11.6 and then try activity 37.5.

Activity 37.5

1   How might we follow the kinetics of reactions I and II?

2   A series of experiments gave the results shown below.
(2-b-2-mp = 2-bromo-2-methylpropane)

Reaction I

[1-bromobutane]/M	[OH⁻(aq)]/M	relative rate
0.01	0.3	1
0.02	0.3	2
0.03	0.3	3
0.03	0.6	6
0.03	1.2	12

Reaction II

[2-b-2mp]/M	[OH⁻(aq)]/M	relative rate
0.01	0.3	1
0.02	0.3	2
0.03	0.3	3
0.03	0.6	3
0.03	1.2	3

(a) How does the rate of reaction I vary with (i) [halogenoalkane] and (ii) $[OH^-(aq)]$?
(b) Hence, write down the individual, and overall, orders of reaction.
(c) Give the rate equation for the reaction.
(d) Which molecule(s) will be involved in the rate-determining step?
(e) Can you propose a possible reaction mechanism?

3 Repeat question 2, but using the results from reaction II.

The results from activity 37.5, and those with other nucleophiles, show that substitution in primary (1°) and tertiary (3°) halogenoalkanes proceeds via different mechanisms, and these are discussed below.

Nucleophilic substitution in primary halogenoalkanes

These are **second order** reactions with the rate equation:

$$\text{rate} = k\,[1° \text{ halogenoalkane}]\,[\text{Nuc}^-]$$

where k = the rate constant and Nuc^- = nucleophile.
Since the concentration of *each* reactant affects the reaction rate, *both* molecules must be involved in the **rate-determining step**.
The following mechanism fits in with these results.

Electron cloud from the nucleophile shifts towards $C^{\delta+}$, and a **dative covalent bond** starts to form. As this happens, the C—Hal bond is weakened; eventually, this breaks heterolytically:

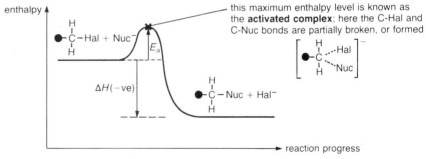

There is only one step, so it must be rate-determining. Since it involves *two* molecules, the reaction mechanism is termed **bimolecular nucleophilic substitution** and given the symbol S_N2. Figure 37.7 shows the **enthalpy profile** for a typical S_N2 reaction. The **activated complex** is the structure at the instant in time when the new C—Nuc bond forms just as the old C—Hal breaks.

Figure 37.7 *An enthalpy profile for an exothermic S_N2 reaction of a primary halogenoalkane. Can you draw the profile for an endothermic S_N2 reaction?*

enthalpy ▲

this maximum enthalpy level is known as the **activated complex**; here the C-Hal and C-Nuc bonds are partially broken, or formed

$$\left[\begin{array}{c} H \\ | \\ \bullet-C\cdots\text{Hal} \\ | \\ H \end{array}\cdots\text{Nuc}\right]^-$$

$$\begin{array}{c} H \\ | \\ \bullet-C-\text{Hal} + \text{Nuc}^- \\ | \\ H \end{array}$$

E_a

$\Delta H(-ve)$

$$\begin{array}{c} H \\ | \\ \bullet-C-\text{Nuc} + \text{Hal}^- \\ | \\ H \end{array}$$

reaction progress ➤

(E_a = activation energy; ΔH = enthalpy of reaction;
● = H or a hydrocarbon skeleton)

Nucleophilic substitution in tertiary halogenoalkenes

Our results in activity 37.5 suggest that nucleophilic substitution in tertiary halogenoalkanes is a **first order** reaction with the rate equation:

$$\text{rate} = k\,[3° \text{ halogenoalkane}]$$

where k = the rate constant. Only the 3° halogenoalkane is involved in the rate-determining step and this is explained by the following mechanism.

First, the C—Hal bond breaks heterolytically, giving a **tertiary carbonium ion** and a Hal$^-$ ion. This step is slow and rate determining:

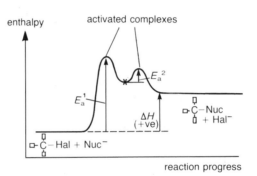

a 3° carbonium ion

The second step is very much faster since it involves the combination of a nucleophile (an electron-rich particle) with the positively charged (electron-poor) carbonium ion:

Since the rate-determining step involves only one reactant molecule, this mechanism is described as **unimolecular nucleophilic substitution**. It is given the symbol S_N1. Figure 37.8 shows the **enthalpy profile** for a typical S_N1 reaction.

Figure 37.8 *An enthalpy profile for an endothermic S_N1 reaction of a tertiary halogenoalkane. Can you draw the profile for an exothermic S_N1 reaction?*

enthalpy

activated complexes

E_a^2

E_a^1

ΔH (+ve)

$\square$—C—Hal + Nuc$^-$

$\square$—C—Nuc + Hal$^-$

reaction progress

✗ this point represents the enthalpy of the intermediate 3° carbonium ion plus the halide ion

$\square$—C$^+$+Hal$^-$

(E_a^1 and E_a^2 are the activation energies for the first (rate-determining) and second reaction steps, respectively; ΔH = the enthalpy of reaction; $\square$— = a hydrocarbon skeleton).

You may be wondering why nucleophilic substitution in 1° and 3° halogenoalkanes occurs via different mechanisms. Well, we saw in section 35.6.2 that the **inductive effect** of alkyl groups causes carbonium ion stability to increase in the order

primary   secondary   tertiary
→
carbonium ions increase in stability

Thus, primary halogenoalkanes do not react via the S_N1 route because the primary carbonium ion is highly unstable and will not form. Tertiary halogenoalkanes do not give an S_N2 reaction because the three bulky hydrocarbons skeletons hinder the approach of the nucleophile.

There are two other important points to note:
▶ experiments with isomeric halogenoalkanes show that *S_N1 reactions are faster than S_N2 reactions*;
▶ nucleophilic substitution in *secondary* halogenoalkanes proceeds via a *combination* of S_N1 and S_N2 mechanisms.

Thus, for isomeric halogenoalkanes, we find that

1°   2°   **3° halogenoalkanes**
→
increasing rate of nucleophilic substitution

37.7 Elimination reactions

When halogenoalkanes react with nucleophiles *which are also strong bases*, such as OH$^-$ and C$_2$H$_5$O$^-$ ions, there is *competition* between nucleophilic substitution and elimination reactions. A mixture of products is obtained:

alcohol, via nucleophilic substitution of Hal$^-$ by OH$^-$

ether, via nucleophilic substitution of Hal$^-$ by C$_2$H$_5$O$^-$

$\xleftarrow{\text{OH}^-\text{(aq)}}$ halogenoalkane $\xrightarrow{\text{C}_2\text{H}_5\text{O}^-\text{(ethanol)}}$

alkene, via the elimination of HHal

The alkenes result from the elimination of a molecule of hydrogen halide, e.g.

2–iodo–2–methylbutane $\xrightarrow[\text{reflux}]{\text{dil. KOH (aq)}}$ 2–methylbut–2–ene + HI (aq)

1–bromo–1–phenylethane $\xrightarrow[\text{(produces some C}_2\text{H}_5\text{O}^-\text{ ions),reflux}]{\text{conc. NaOH in ethanol}}$ phenylethene + HBr (ethanol)

Figure 37.9 *(Iodomethyl)benzene – can it give an elimination reaction?*

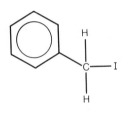

Table 37.4 *The effect of the reagent on the competing nucleophilic substitution and elimination reactions of halogenoalkanes (the main product is stated)*

Notice how the H and Hal atoms come off adjacent carbon atoms. So, could (iodomethyl)benzene eliminate an HI molecule (figure 37.9)?
2-iodo-2-methylbutane gives two elimination products; one is 2-methylbut-2-ene – what is the other?

When using these reactions in organic synthesis, we need to know which set of reactants and conditions favour elimination, and which favour substitution. This information is summarised in table 37.4.

Halogenoarenes and acid halides do not give simple elimination reactions. Can you explain why?

Type of halogenoalkane	Reagents (reflux in each case)		
	H$_2$O(l)	dil. NaOH(aq)	conc. NaOH dissolved in ethanol
primary	alcohol	alcohol	alcohol
secondary	alcohol	alcohol	alkene
tertiary	alcohol	alkene	alkene

substitution □   elimination ▨

Which type of halogenoalkane is most resistant to elimination reactions? And the least resistant?

Activity 37.6

1   By reference to table 37.4, arrange the following compounds in order of increasing tendency towards elimination reactions:

2-bromo-2-methylbutane, 1-bromopentane, 2-bromopentane.

2   Give the reagents and reaction conditions needed for the following conversions.
(a) 2-iodobutane $\longrightarrow$ butan-2-ol

These bath books are made from poly(chloroethene), commonly known as PVC

(b) 2-iodopropane   ⟶   propene

(c) bromoethane   ⟶   ethoxyethane ($H_5C_2OC_2H_5$)

(d) 2-iodo-2-methyl propane ⟶ 2-methyl propene

(e) 2-iodo-2-methylpropane ⟶ 2-methylpropan-2-ol

(f) 1,2-diiodoethane   ⟶   ethyne

3   When 1-iodopropane reacts with a hot concentrated solution of sodium hydroxide in ethanol, two organic products are obtained.

    (a) Give the name and structural formula of the major organic product and write a balanced equation for its formation.

    (b) Give the name and structural formula of the organic by-product and write a balanced equation for its formation.

    (c) Write down the mechanism for the reaction in part (a).

37.8 Uses of organic halogen compounds

Organic halogen compounds have a wide range of applications, some of which are outlined in table 37.5. They are also valuable intermediates in synthetic pathways, as shown in activity 37.7.

Table 37.5 *Some uses of organic halogen compounds*

Compound	use	notes
dichlorodifluoromethane, $CF_2Cl_2(l)$	aerosol propellant	It has a b.p. of $-30\,°C$. Thus, it is easily liquefied under pressure but it readily vaporises when the pressure is released (i.e. when the aerosol is used). However, the use of these chlorofluorocarbons (CFCs) in aerosols is becoming unpopular because they are thought to destroy the ozone layer which absorbs harmful UV radiation from the sun.
chloroalkenes e.g. 'trichlor', $CCl_2{=}CHCl(l)$	non-polar solvents	They dissolve a wide range of non-polar substances. Used, for example, by dry-cleaners to remove the layer of greases which holds dirt on clothes.
certain chloroarenes	insecticides (e.g. DDT) and herbicides	These selectively kill pests or unwanted plants (e.g. weeds in grass).
chloroethene	manufacture of poly(chloroethene)	This is a plastic used, for example, to make clothing and records (section 35.8).
1,2-dibromoethane	petrol additive	This additive converts the lead from tetraethyl lead (an 'anti-knock' agent) into lead bromide. At the engine's operating temperature, lead bromide is volatile and passes into the atmosphere via the vehicle's exhaust system (see section 34.5).
halothane, $CF_3{—}CHClBr$	anaesthetic	Developed over thirty years ago, this compound contains a C—Cl bond for its anaesthetic properties and C—F bonds for their inertness. The bromine atom increases its boiling point, thus making it easier to store.

Activity 37.7

Give the reagents and reaction conditions which are need to perform the following conversions.

(a) $CH_3CH{=}CH_2$ $\xrightarrow{\text{2 steps}}$ $CH_3{-}\underset{\underset{CH_3}{|}}{\overset{\overset{H}{|}}{C}}{-}NH_2$

(b) CH_3OH $\xrightarrow{\text{3 steps}}$ $CH_3C\overset{O}{\underset{OH}{\diagup}}$

(c) $CH_3CHBrCH_3$ $\xrightarrow{\text{2 steps}}$ $CH_3CHBrCH_2Br$

(d) $CH_3C\overset{O}{\underset{OH}{\diagup}}$ $\xrightarrow{\text{2 steps}}$ $CH_3C\overset{O}{\underset{NH_2}{\diagup}}$

(e) C_2H_6 $\xrightarrow{\text{3 steps}}$ $C_2H_5C\overset{O}{\underset{OH}{\diagup}}$

(f) ⬡—$CHICH_3$ $\xrightarrow{\text{2 steps}}$ ⬡—$CH(OH)CH_2OH$

(g) C_2H_6 $\xrightarrow{\text{2 steps}}$ $C_2H_5O{-}\overset{O}{\overset{\|}{C}}CH_3$

(h) ⬡ $\xrightarrow{\text{2 steps}}$ ⬡ with CH_3 and Cl substituents

(Note: conversions (e) to (h) need synthetic steps from earlier chapters.)

37.9 Comparing the reactions of organic halogen compounds

A common examination question asks you to compare the reactivities of the three main types of organic compound: halogenoalkanes, halogenoarenes and acid halides. Activity 37.8 suggests how this might be done in tabular form. It provides a useful revision exercise.

Activity 37.8

Prepare a summary table which compares the reactions of halogenoalkanes, halogenoarenes and acid halides. You should consider their reactions with the following reagents: 1. $H_2O(l)$ and dil.NaOH(aq), 2. hot conc.NaOH (in ethanol), 3. KCN (in ethanol), 4. NH_3 (in ethanol), 5. alkoxide ions (e.g. $C_2H_5O^-$), 6. carboxylic acid salts, 7. electrophiles such as NO_2^+, Cl^+, CH_3CO^+.

37.10 Comments on the activities

Activity 37.1

1. (a) chloroethane; (b) 2-bromo-2-methylpropane; (c) 2-iodobutane;
   (d) bromobenzene; (e) (bromomethyl) benzene;
   (f) *cis*-1-chlorobut-1-ene (both H's on the same side of the C=C bond).

2.

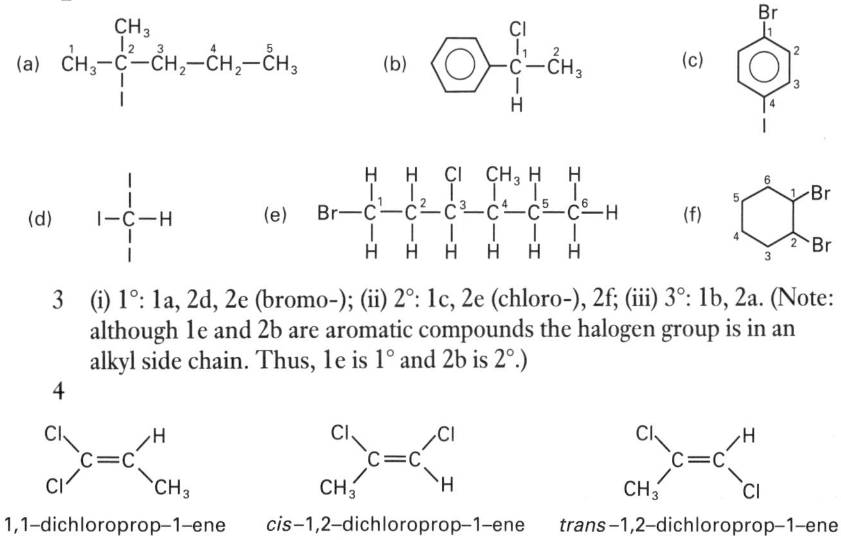

3. (i) 1°: 1a, 2d, 2e (bromo-); (ii) 2°: 1c, 2e (chloro-), 2f; (iii) 3°: 1b, 2a. (Note: although 1e and 2b are aromatic compounds the halogen group is in an alkyl side chain. Thus, 1e is 1° and 2b is 2°.)

4.

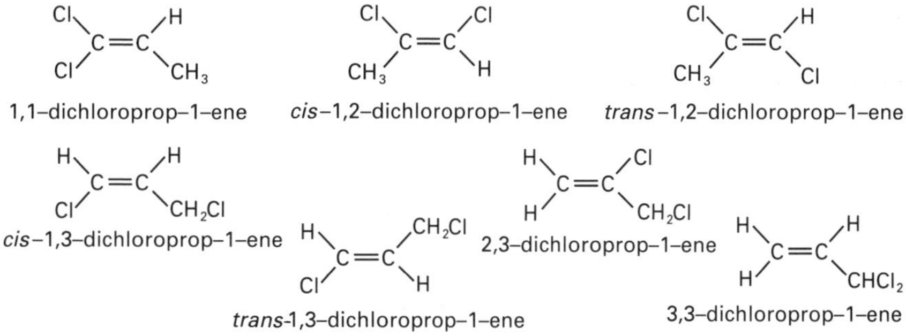

1,1–dichloroprop–1–ene   *cis*-1,2–dichloroprop–1–ene   *trans*-1,2–dichloroprop–1–ene

cis-1,3–dichloroprop–1–ene   *trans*-1,3–dichloroprop–1–ene   2,3–dichloroprop–1–ene   3,3–dichloroprop–1–ene

5. (a) (i) ethanoyl iodide   (ii) benzoyl bromide

   (b) (i) $CH_3-CH_2-CH_2-C$ (ii)

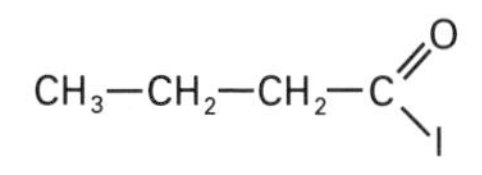

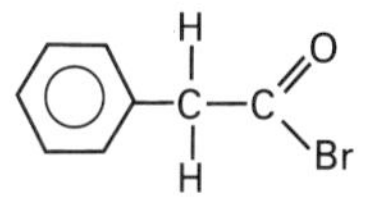

Activity 37.2

1. As expected, halogenoalkanes form a homologous series with the general formula $C_nH_{2n+1}Hal$.

Figure 37.10 *The relationship between the boiling points of some primary halogenoalkanes and the number of carbon atoms in the molecule*

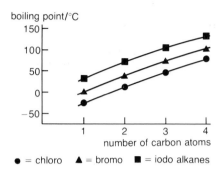

boiling point/°C

● = chloro   ▲ = bromo   ■ = iodo alkanes

Figure 37.11 *The relationship between the standard enthalpies of combustion, $\Delta H_c^\ominus$, of some primary halogenoalkanes and the number of carbon atoms in the molecule*

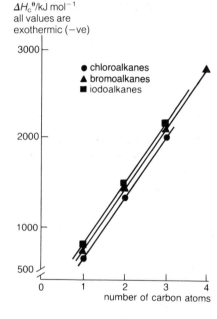

$\Delta H_c^\ominus$/kJ mol^{-1}
all values are
exothermic (−ve)

● chloroalkanes
▲ bromoalkanes
■ iodoalkanes

number of carbon atoms

2 (a) For the primary halogenoalkanes, graphs of boiling point against molecular mass are smooth curves (figure 37.10). As the hydrocarbon chain length is increased, the molecule's electron cloud gets larger and is more easily polarised by neighbouring molecules. Thus, the **van der Waals' forces** will be strongest, and boiling points will be highest, in halogenoalkanes with long straight chains.

   (b) The regular increase in $\Delta H_c^\ominus$ values is typical of compounds which form a homologous series (figure 37.11). Roughly speaking, the increase corresponds to the enthalpy of combustion of a CH_2 group.

3 For a given halogen atom, we find that *boiling points and densities decrease* in the order: *1° halogenoalkane > 2° halogenoalkane > 3° halogenoalkane*.

   On going from 1°→2°→3° halogenoalkanes, the molecules become less able to make such a close contact with their neighbours. A more open structure is produced and, hence, the densities decrease. Also, the van der Waals' forces become weaker, thereby causing the boiling points to decrease.

4 For organic halogen compounds with the same hydrocarbon skeleton, the *boiling points increase* in the order: *chloro- < bromo- < iodo-compound*

chlorobenzene   bromobenzene   iodobenzene
(b.p. 132 °C)   (b.p. 156 °C)   (b.p. 189 °C)

As molecular mass increases, so does the size of the molecular electron cloud, making it more easily polarised by neighbouring molecules. Thus, the van der Waals' forces will be strongest in the iodo compounds and these will have the highest boiling points.

Activity 37.3

(a) P(red) + Br$_2$(l)/reflux or NaBr(s) + conc. H$_3$PO$_4$(l)/reflux.
(b) and (d) PCl$_5$(s)/room temp., PCl$_3$(l)/room temp., SOCl$_2$(l)/reflux or conc. HCl(aq)/reflux.
(c) and (f) P(red) + I$_2$(s)/reflux or NaI(s) + conc. H$_3$PO$_4$(l)/reflux.
(e) Cl$_2$(g) + AlCl$_3$(s)/40 °C.

Activity 37.4

1 The structural formulae are:

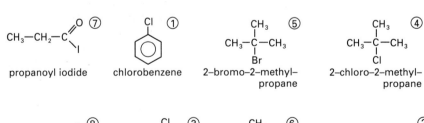

Increasing reactivity with water: ① → ⑧.

2

(a) 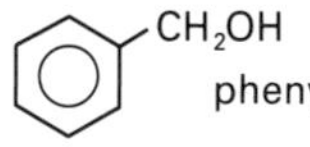 CH$_2$OH phenylmethanol (b) mainly CH$_3$CH=CH$_2$ propene; some CH$_3$–$\overset{\text{H}}{\underset{\text{OH}}{\text{C}}}$–CH$_3$ propan–2–ol

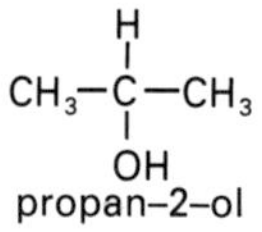

(c) CH$_3$CH$_2$OCH$_2$CH$_3$ ethoxyethane   (d) CH$_3$NH$_2$ methylamine

(e) 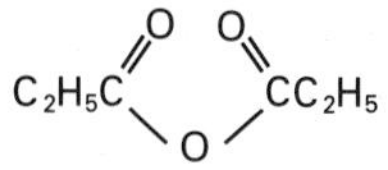 C$_2$H$_5$C$\diagdown$O$\diagup$CC$_2$H$_5$ propanoic anhydride   (f) 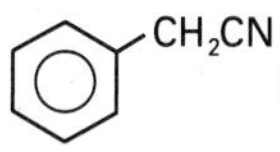 CH$_2$CN phenylethanonitrile

3 (a) H$_2$O(l), reflux.
   (b) C$_2$H$_5$O$^-$Na$^+$ in ethanol, reflux.
   (c) reflux,

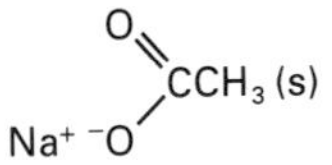

   $\overset{\text{O}}{\underset{\text{Na}^+\ ^-\text{O}}{\text{CCH}_3}}$ (s)

   (d) conc. NH$_3$ dissolved in ethanol; heat in a sealed tube; iodomethane in excess.
   (e) conc. NH$_3$(aq), room temperature.
   (f)

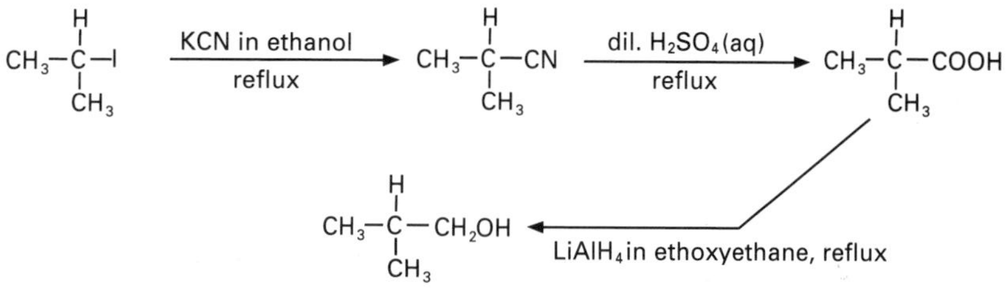

CH$_3$–$\overset{\text{H}}{\underset{\text{CH}_3}{\text{C}}}$–I $\xrightarrow[\text{reflux}]{\text{KCN in ethanol}}$ CH$_3$–$\overset{\text{H}}{\underset{\text{CH}_3}{\text{C}}}$–CN $\xrightarrow[\text{reflux}]{\text{dil. H}_2\text{SO}_4\text{(aq)}}$ CH$_3$–$\overset{\text{H}}{\underset{\text{CH}_3}{\text{C}}}$–COOH

CH$_3$–$\overset{\text{H}}{\underset{\text{CH}_3}{\text{C}}}$–CH$_2$OH $\xleftarrow{\text{LiAlH}_4\text{ in ethoxyethane, reflux}}$

Activity 37.5

1 *Sampling:* stopping the reaction, at fixed time intervals, by adding the sample to excess crushed ice. Then the concentration of unused OH$^-$ ions is obtained by titration against standard acid.
   Continuous method: following the decrease in pH.

2 (a) (i) As [1-bromobutane] doubles, so does the rate.
          (ii) As [OH$^-$(aq)] doubles, so does the rate.
      (b) First order in both 1-bromobutane and OH$^-$(aq) ions. Second order overall.
      (c) Rate = k [1-bromobutane] [OH$^-$(aq)].
      (d) 1-bromobutane and OH$^-$(aq) ions.
      (e) The mechanism follows this activity.

3 (a) (i) As [2-b-2-mp] doubles, so does the rate.
          (ii) As [OH$^-$(aq)] doubles, the rate remains constant.
      (b) First order in 2-b-2-mp and zero order in OH$^-$(aq) ions. First order overall.
      (c) Rate = k [2-b-2-mp].
      (d) 2-bromo-2-methylpropane only.
      (e) The mechanism follows this activity.

Activity 37.6

1

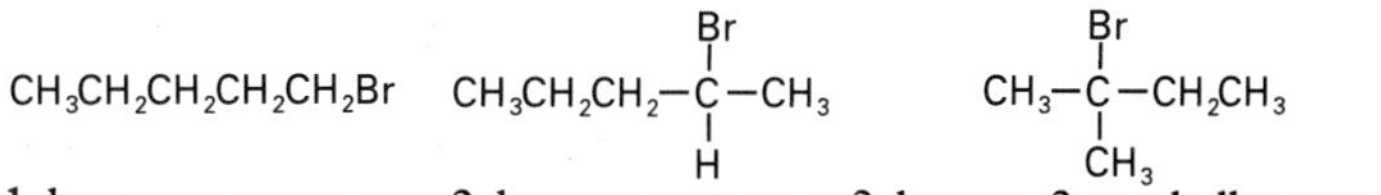

CH$_3$CH$_2$CH$_2$CH$_2$CH$_2$Br   CH$_3$CH$_2$CH$_2$–$\overset{\text{Br}}{\underset{\text{H}}{\text{C}}}$–CH$_3$ CH$_3$–$\overset{\text{Br}}{\underset{\text{CH}_3}{\text{C}}}$–CH$_2CH_3$

1-bromopentane << 2-bromopentane < 2-bromo-2-methylbutane
i.e.   1°   <<   2°   <   3°

2 (a) dilute $NaOH(aq)$ or $H_2O(l)$; reflux.
   (b) concentrated NaOH (ethanol); reflux.
   (c) reflux with $C_2H_5O^-Na^+(s)$ in ethanol (1° halogenoalkanes *resist* elimination reactions).
   (d) dilute NaOH(aq); reflux. (3° halogenoalkanes are *very susceptible* to elimination reactions, even under these conditions.)
   (e) $H_2O(l)$; reflux.
   (f) concentrated NaOH (ethanol); reflux.
   (Note: potassium salts can also be used in these reactions.)

3 (a) 1-ethoxypropane; the equation is:

$$CH_3CH_2CH_2I + Na^{+-}OC_2H_5 \rightarrow CH_3CH_2CH_2OCH_2CH_3 + NaI$$

formed from NaOH
and C_2H_5OH
1-ethoxypropane

   (b) propene; the equation is:

$$CH_3CH_2CH_2I + Na^{+-}OC_2H_5 \rightarrow CH_3CH=CH_2 + C_2H_5OH + NaI$$

propene

   (c) The mechanism in (a) is bimolecular nucleophilic substitution, S_N2:

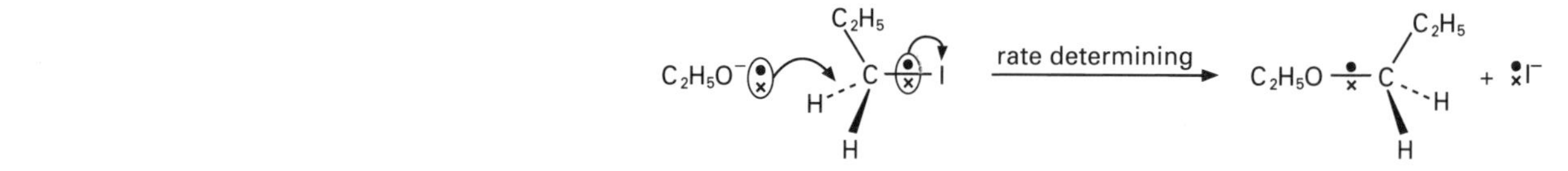

Activity 37.7

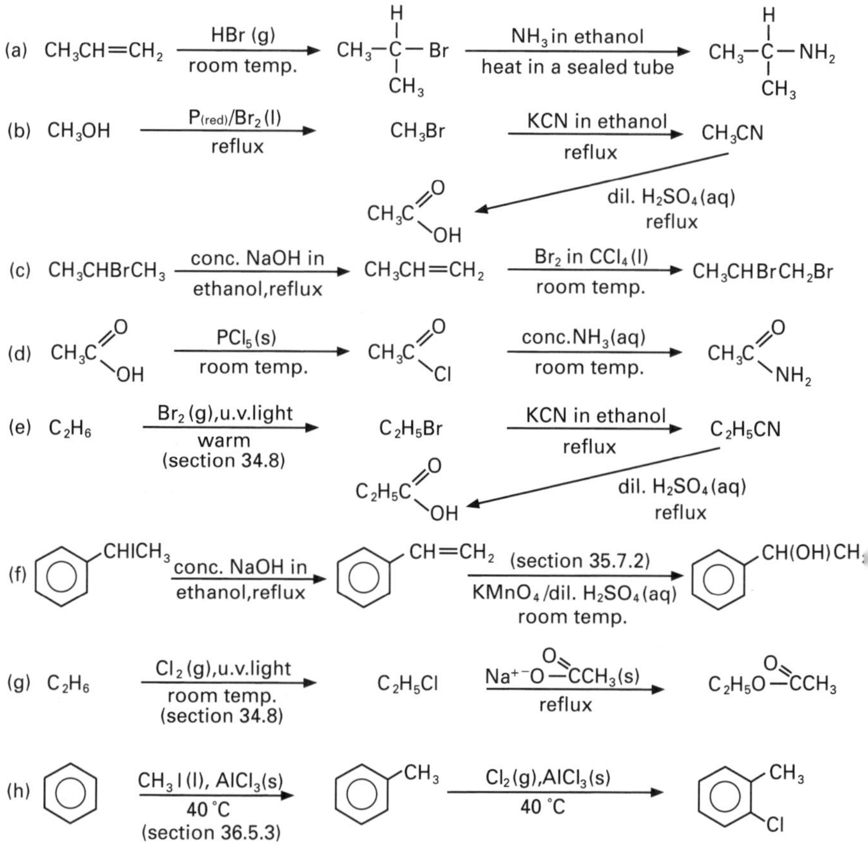

Activity 37.8

Compare your answer with table 37.6.

37.11 Summary and revision plan

1. There are three main types of halogen compound: **halogenoalkanes, halogenoarenes** and **acid halides**.

2. To name a halogenoalkane, put a prefix (i.e. fluoro-, chloro-, bromo- or iodo-) before the name of the parent hydrocarbon. If structural isomers are possible, you must state the numbered position(s) of the halogen atom(s) along the hydrocarbon skeleton.

3. Halogenoalkanes are described as being **primary (1°), secondary (2°)** or **tertiary (3°)**, depending on whether there are one, two or three alkyl groups attached to the carbon of the C—Hal bond.

4. Halogenoalkanes form **homologous series** of formulae, $C_nH_{2n+1}Hal$. Thus, their physical properties change gradually as the molecular mass is increased.

5. To name a halogenoarene, put the halogen prefix (e.g. iodo-) before the name of the arene. If **positional isomers** are possible, you must state the ring position of each halogen atom.

6. Acid halides are named by replacing the '−oic' of the carboxylic acid name by '−oyl halide'.

Table 37.6 *Comparing the chemical properties of halogenoalkanes, halogenoarenes and acid halides, with some examples*

Reagent	halogenoalkanes e.g. C_2H_5I	halogenoarenes e.g.	acid halides e.g. CH_3COCl
warm $H_2O(l)$ or dil. NaOH(aq)	**alcohols** formed C_2H_5OH	no reaction	**carboxylic acids** formed, CH_3COOH
hot. conc. NaOH (or KOH) in ethanol	1° mainly **alcohols** 2° mainly **alkenes** 3°	no reaction	a violent reaction giving esters
KCN (ethanol) reflux	**nitriles** formed C_2H_5CN	no reaction	mainly esters
reflux with NH_3 (ethanol) under pressure	1°, 2°, 3° **amines** or **quaternary ammonium salts**	no reaction	a mixture of amides and esters
conc. solution of sodium alkoxide in alcohol	mainly **ethers** formed $C_2H_5OC_2H_5$	no reaction	**esters** formed
carboxylic acid salts e.g.	**esters** formed	no reaction	**acid anhydrides** formed
electrophiles such as NO_2^+, Cl^+, CH_3^+	no reaction	slow ring substitution in the 2,4 positions	no reaction

7. The chemical properties of an organic halogen compound depend on (i) which halogen atom is present and (ii) its molecular location. Table 37.6 compares the chemical properties of these three types of organic halogen compound.

8. Some important synthetic steps are shown in figure 37.12 on page 493.

9. The relative rates of nucleophilic substitution in organic halogen compounds show a clear pattern:

(a) chloro-   bromo-   iodo-   alkanes or arenes
     GET FASTER →

(b)   acid chlorides   bromides   iodides
          GET SLOWER →

(c)   primary   secondary   tertiary halogenoalkanes

→

GET FASTER

(d)   halogenoarenes   halogenoalkanes   acid halides

→

GET MUCH FASTER

10   Brief explanations of the trends in 9:
    (a) is caused by the decrease in bond strength as we go from C—Cl to C—Br to C—I.
    (b) is due to the polarity of the $\overset{\delta+}{C}-\overset{\delta-}{Hal}$ bonds: C—I < C—Br < C—Cl.
    (c) occurs because the reactions have different mechanisms: primary is S_N2, tertiary is S_N1 and secondary is a combination of S_N1 and S_N2. For isomeric halogenoalkanes, the S_N1 route is faster than the S_N2 route.
    (d) Halogenoarenes resist nucleophilic substitution because **partial π bonding** (i) strengthens the C—Hal bond and (ii) decreases the C—Hal bond polarity (figure 37.5). In acid halides, polarisation of the C=O and the C—Hal bonds produces a highly electron-poor ($\delta+$) carbon atom, towards which nucleophiles are strongly attracted (figure 37.6). Thus, acid halides react readily with nucleophiles.

11   Lengthening the hydrocarbon chain in bromo or iodoalkanes is an important synthetic step (section 37.5.2).

12   When halogenoalkanes react with nucleophiles which are also strong bases (such as OH^- and $C_2H_5O^-$ ions), *nucleophilic substitution and elimination reactions will be in competition.* The tendency of a halogenoalkane to undergo elimination increases in the order: *primary << secondary < tertiary*

13   Halogenoalkanes can be prepared by reacting:
    (a) alcohols with halogenating agents (e.g. $PCl_5(s)$, P(red) + $Br_2(l)$ *in situ* or $KI/H_3PO_4(l)$ *in situ*);
    (b) alkenes or alkynes with the halogen or hydrogen halide. (Remember that Markovnikov's Rule will be followed.)

14   Halogenoarenes are prepared by using (i) a Friedel–Crafts reaction, (section 36.5.3) or (ii) a diazonium salt (section 41.9).

15   Important new reagents used in this chapter are listed in table 37.7.

Table 37.7 *Important reagents used in this chapter. Try to learn them (▭— is a hydrocarbon skeleton)*

Reagent	conditions	what it does to a halogenoalkane
dil. NaOH(aq) or $H_2O(l)$	reflux	converts **C—Hal → C—OH**, an alcohol (acid halides give similar reactions)
KCN in ethanol	reflux	converts **C—Hal → C—CN**, a nitrile (this is one step in the lengthening of the hydrocarbon skeleton).
excess NH_3 in ethanol	heated in a sealed tube	converts **C—Hal → C—NH₂**, a primary amine
sodium alkoxide or phenoxide in ethanol $Na^{+-}O—▭$	reflux	converts **C—Hal → C—O—▭** an ether
sodium salt of a carboxylic acid $Na^{+-}O—\overset{O}{\overset{\|\|}{C}}—▭$ (s)	reflux	converts **C—Hal → C—O—\overset{O}{\overset{||}{C}}—▭** an ester (also converts $\overset{O}{\overset{\|\|}{C}}—Hal$ → $\overset{O}{\overset{\|\|}{C}}—O—\overset{O}{\overset{\|\|}{C}}—▭$ an acid anhydride)
conc. NaOH (or KOH) in ethanol	reflux	converts: 2° or 3° **C—Hal** into one, or two, **alkenes**; 1° **C—Hal** give mainly **alcohols**

Figure 37.12 *Important reactions of halogenoalkanes and halogenoarenes (●- is a hydrogen atom or hydrocarbon skeleton)*

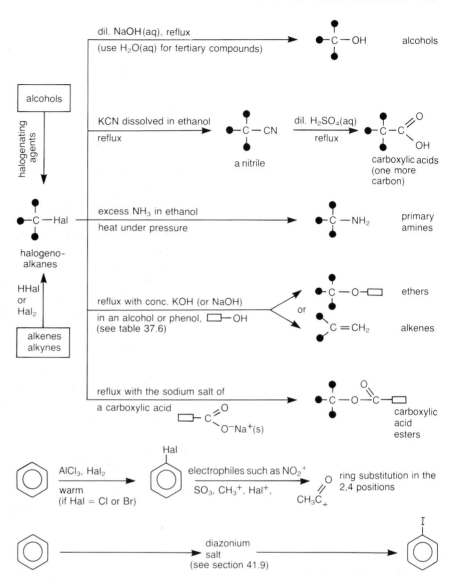

Alcohols, Phenols and Ethers

Contents

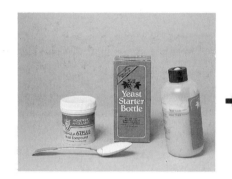

Making wine at home. Yeast is mixed with sugar and water in a starter bottle and kept warm until fermentation starts. The starter yeast mixture is then added to the fruit extract in a large jar fitted with a bubble trap. The trap allows carbon dioxide to escape but no air to get in. After about three weeks the fermentation is complete and the wine is filtered. After standing for a few more weeks, the filtered wine becomes clear and can be bottled

Over the last twenty years, making wine and beer at home has become a very popular hobby. Nowadays, you can buy kits which contain all the necessary ingredients and equipment and, providing the instructions are followed, these can give good results. Brewing and wine-making are chemical processes involving the **fermentation** of the **glucose** obtained from fruit, or grain:

$$C_6H_{12}O_6(aq) \longrightarrow 2C_2H_5OH(aq) + 2CO_2(g) \quad \Delta H = -\text{ve}$$
$$\text{glucose} \qquad\qquad \text{ethanol}$$

Table 38.1 *Typical percentages by volume of ethanol in various 'alcoholic' drinks*

Drink	beer	wine	sherry	brandy
% ethanol	4	11	15	40

A breathalyser contains orange crystals of potassium dichromate. These are reduced by any ethanol in the motorist's breath, and turn a green colour in the process. The greener the crystals, the greater the amount of alcohol that has been consumed

The reaction is catalysed by zymase, an enzyme present in **yeast**. Yeast is a living organism which obtains its energy from the heat released during the reaction.

All 'alcoholic' drinks are products of this reaction. They are, in effect, flavoured aqueous solutions containing different concentrations of **ethanol** (table 38.1). When the ethanol content of the brew reaches about 15%, it poisons the yeast and the fermentation stops. However, some people prefer stronger drinks such as whisky, gin and rum. These contain 40% ethanol and are known as 'spirits' because they are distilled off the fermented liquids.

Contrary to much common belief, alcoholic drinks are not stimulants. By drinking small quantities, people feel more relaxed and, of course, this is usually a good thing. However, over indulgence temporarily dulls the senses and increases reaction times; hence the need to prevent people from drinking and driving. It is also too easy to forget, perhaps, that ethanol is an addictive and toxic chemical. Long-term heavy 'drinking' can cause depression, liver disease and, ultimately, death.

Ethanol is a **hydroxy** compound, that is, *an organic molecule containing an –O—H functional group.* Two important types of hydroxy compound are alcohols and phenols. An **alcohol** has at least one hydroxy group attached to the *aliphatic part* of a hydrocarbon skeleton:

methanol cyclohexanol ethenol ethane-1,2-diol

Ethane-1,2-diol is a dihydric alcohol, that is, it contains more than one —OH group. **Phenols** are compounds which have an —OH group *directly* bound to a benzene ring:

phenol naphthalene-2-ol

In this chapter, we shall see how the properties of alcohols and phenols depend on the molecular location of their –OH group.

38.1 Naming alcohols and phenols

Alcohols

These are named by changing the final **e** of the hydrocarbon name to **ol**. Where structural isomers are possible, the *position* of the —OH group must be stated:

butan–1-ol
(primary,1°)

butan–2-ol
(secondary,2°)

2-methylpropan–2-ol
(tertiary,3°)

Like halogenoalkanes, alcohols are also classified as being **primary (1°), secondary (2°)** or **tertiary (3°)** compounds, depending on whether they have one, two or three hydrocarbon skeletons, respectively, attached to the carbon bonded to the —OH group.

It is important to remember that *an alcohol can be aromatic without being a phenol,* e.g. 2-phenylethanol (figure 38.1).

Figure 38.1 *2-phenylethanol is an aromatic alcohol because the –OH group is attached to the aliphatic part of the molecule*

Phenols

Substituted phenols can exist as positional isomers:

2–nitrophenol   4–nitrophenol   2–hydroxybenzoic acid   3–hydroxybenzoic acid

Activity 38.1

1   Name the following hydroxy compounds:

(a) $CH_3CH_2CH_2CH_2CH_2OH$

(b) $CH_3\overset{\quad OH}{\underset{\;\;\,H}{C}}CH_2CH_2OH$

(c)

(d) $CH_3\overset{H}{\underset{OH}{C}}-\overset{Br}{\underset{H}{C}}CH_3$

(e) $CH_3\overset{OH}{\underset{H}{C}}-\overset{OH}{\underset{H}{C}}-CH_3$

(f)

2   Write down structural formulae for the following compounds:
    (a) pentan-2-ol   (b) 3-methylhexan-1-ol
    (c) 2-phenylpropan-2-ol   (d) cyclohexane-1,3-diol
    (e) 4-chlorophenol   (f) 1,2-dihydroxybenzene

3   Of the *alcohols* in questions 1 and 2 which are
    (a) aliphatic,   (b) aromatic,   (c) primary,   (d) secondary and
    (e) tertiary?

4   Three diols have the same molecular formula, $C_2H_4O_2$. Draw their structural formulae and name them.

38.2 Physical properties of alcohols and phenols

Some properties of alcohols and phenols are listed in table 38.2. Activity 38.2 will help you to pick out certain trends in these values.

Table 38.2 *Some properties of alcohols and phenols*

Name	formula	State (at 25 °C)	melting point/°C	boiling point/°C	density /gcm^{-3}	$\Delta H_c^{\ominus}$ /kJ mol^{-1}
methanol	CH_3OH	liquid	−98	65	0.79	−726
ethanol	C_2H_5OH	liquid	−114	78	0.79	−1367
propan-1-ol	C_3H_7OH	liquid	−126	97	0.80	−2017
propan-2-ol	$CH_3CH(OH)CH_3$	liquid	−88	83	0.78	−1987
butan-1-ol	$CH_3(CH_2)_3OH$	liquid	−89	118	0.81	−2675
butan-2-ol	$C_2H_5CH(OH)CH_3$	liquid	−115	100	0.81	—
2-methylpropan-1-ol	$(CH_3)_2CHCH_2OH$	liquid	−108	108	0.80	—
2-methylpropan-2-ol	$(CH_3)_3COH$	liquid	25	82	0.79	−2644
pentan-1-ol	$CH_3(CH_2)_3CH_2OH$	liquid	−78	138	0.81	−3323
hexan-1-ol	$CH_3(CH_2)_4CH_2OH$	liquid	−44	157	0.82	−3976
heptan-1-ol	$CH_3(CH_2)_5CH_2OH$	liquid	−34	176	0.82	−4623
octan-1-ol	$CH_3(CH_2)_6CH_2OH$	liquid	−16	195	0.83	−5280
ethane-1,2-diol	CH_2OHCH_2OH	liquid	−13	197	1.11	−1179
propane-1,2,3-triol	$CH_2OHCH(OH)CH_2OH$	liquid	19	290	1.26	−1661
phenylmethanol	$C_6H_5CH_2OH$	liquid	−15	205	1.04	−3756
phenol	C_6H_5OH	solid	41	182	1.08	−3056

Are there any patterns in the boiling points, densities and standard enthalpies of combustion of the primary aliphatic alcohols?
What value would you predict for the standard enthalpy of combustion of butan-2-ol?

Figure 38.2 *Hydrogen bonding between molecules of ethanol*

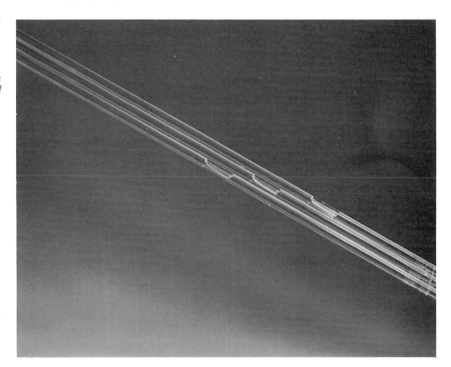

|||||| hydrogen bonds

Table 38.3 *Boiling points of propane and some related alcohols*

Compound	boiling point/°C
propane	−42
propan-1-ol	97
propane-1,2-diol	189
propane-1,2,3-triol	290

What happens to the boiling points as the number of —OH groups rises?

These three sealed tubes are filled with (from left to right) propan-1-ol (I), propane-1, 2-diol (II) and propane-1, 2, 3-triol (III), and a bubble of air is trapped at the top of each tube. When the apparatus is inverted, the air bubbles move upwards through the liquids at different speeds: I>II>III. This shows that the viscosity increases as the degree of hydrogen bonding increases: propan-1-ol (one –OH group) < propane-1, 2-diol (two –OH groups) < propane-1, 2, 3-triol (three –OH groups)

|||||| = hydrogen bonds

Figure 38.3 *Hydrogen bonding between molecules of ethanol and water*

Activity 38.2

Briefly study table 38.2 and then work through the following questions.

1. Do the alcohols form a homologous series? If so, what is their general formula?
2. For the *primary* monohydric alcohols (i.e. those with only one OH group), plot graphs of (a) boiling point and (b) $\Delta H_c^{\ominus}$ against the number of carbon atoms in the molecule (horizontal axis). Account for the shape of these graphs.
3. Look at the boiling points of the isomeric alcohols of molecular formula C_4H_9OH. Do you detect any trends in the values? If so, what explanation can you give for this behaviour?
4. Compare the boiling points of the alcohols with those of alkanes of similar mass (table 34.3). Once again, can you detect, and explain, any trends in the values?

This activity shows that alcohol molecules take part in strong **intermolecular hydrogen bonding** (figure 38.2).

Further evidence for the existence of these hydrogens bonds comes from the data in table 38.2. As the number of —OH groups is increased, there is a greater degree of hydrogen bonding. As a result, in going from propan-1-ol → propane-1,2-diol → propane-1,2,3-triol:

▶ the boiling points rise dramatically (table 38.3);
▶ the alcohols become much more viscous. You can prove this by timing how quickly a bubble of air moves through each liquid.

Since alcohols form hydrogen bonds, we might expect them to dissolve in water and other polar solvents. Certainly, this is true for the lower members of the series (see table 38.4). *Methanol, ethanol and propan-1-ol are completely miscible with water,* and 'new' hydrogen bonds are formed between alcohol and water molecules (figure 38.3). As the non-polar hydrocarbon chain gets longer, the water solubility of alcohols drops markedly. At the same time, though, the alcohols become better solvents for non-polar substances.

The lower alcohols are valuable solvents. Ethanol, for example, is often used to enable non-polar and polar chemical reactants to mix together:

$$\text{C}_2\text{H}_5\text{I} + \text{KCN} \xrightarrow{\text{in ethanol, reflux}} \text{C}_2\text{H}_5\text{CN} + \text{KI}$$

Table 38.4 *Solubilities of some alcohols in water*

Compound	formula	solubility (g in $100\,\text{cm}^3$ water at $20\,^\circ\text{C}$)
methanol	CH_3OH	∞
ethanol	$\text{C}_2\text{H}_5\text{OH}$	∞
butan-1-ol	$\text{C}_4\text{H}_9\text{OH}$	8.0
hexan-1-ol	$\text{C}_6\text{H}_{13}\text{OH}$	0.6
heptan-1-ol	$\text{C}_7\text{H}_{15}\text{OH}$	0.1
hexandecan-1-ol	$\text{C}_{16}\text{H}_{33}\text{OH}$	0.0

What happens to the solubility as the hydrocarbon chain gets longer?

As we have seen, polyhydric alcohols are able to form extensive hydrogen bonds. Thus, they are extremely soluble in water (table 38.5).

Table 38.5 *Solubility of hexane and its related alcohols*

Compound	hexane	hexan-1-ol	hexane-2,3-diol
Solubility in water (g/$100\,\text{cm}^3$ at $20\,^\circ\text{C}$)	0.01	0.60	$\propto$ (i.e. it is miscible)

An important polyhydric alcohol is the wood-working adhesive **poly(ethenol)**, commonly known as PVA.

Generally speaking, phenols are colourless, low-melting point, solids. Like alcohols, phenols have somewhat higher melting and boiling points than those of hydrocarbons of comparable molecular mass:

methylbenzene($M_r=92$)
m.p.–95°C; b.p.111°C

phenol($M_r=94$)
m.p.41°C ; b.p.182°C

Once again, this pattern emerges because the intermolecular forces in phenols are due to hydrogen bonds *as well as* van der Waals' forces.

Although they can form hydrogen bonds with water, phenols also contain the non-polar benzene nucleus. As a result, many phenols tend to be slightly soluble in cold water but very soluble in hot water (section 16.3).

38.3 Making alcohols and phenols

Alcohols

Many alcohols are manufactured from the 'cracked' petroleum fractions (section 34.6). The alkenes are catalytically hydrated by steam:

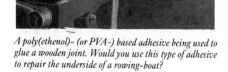

A poly(ethenol)- (or PVA-) based adhesive being used to glue a wooden joint. Would you use this type of adhesive to repair the underside of a rowing-boat?

propene $\; + \text{H}_2\text{O (g)} \xrightarrow[\text{conc. phosporic acid, H}_3\text{PO}_4\,\text{(l)}]{300°C, 70 \text{ atm; catalyst:}}$ propan–2-ol

Some industrial ethanol is produced by fermentation but the process is only economic where there is a plentiful supply of sugar cane or starch. Enzymes catalyse the conversion of starch into glucose, which is then fermented.

Alcohols are best prepared in the laboratory from alkenes, e.g.

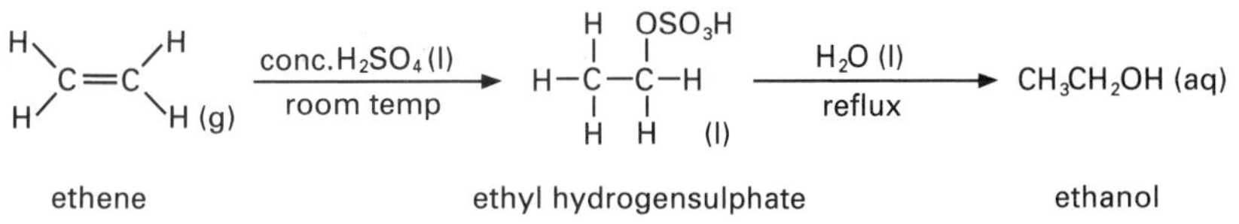

$$
\text{ethene} \xrightarrow[\text{room temp}]{\text{conc.} H_2SO_4 \text{(l)}} \text{ethyl hydrogensulphate} \xrightarrow[\text{reflux}]{H_2O \text{(l)}} CH_3CH_2OH \text{(aq)}
$$

ethene — ethyl hydrogensulphate — ethanol

or halogenoalkanes, e.g.

$$
CH_3CH_2I \text{(l)} \xrightarrow[\text{reflux}]{\text{dil. NaOH (aq)}} CH_3CH_2OH \text{(aq)}
$$

iodoethane — ethanol

Both of these processes yield ethanol in aqueous solution. Fractional distillation of this solution gives a distillate which contains about 96% ethanol and boils at 78.1 °C. Pure ethanol, commonly known as 'absolute' ethanol is obtained by refluxing the distillate for several hours with freshly prepared quicklime (calcium oxide). This drying agent absorbs the water so that further distillation gives 'absolute' ethanol (b.p. 78.5 °C).

Aqueous ethanol is here being produced in a computer-controlled plant by the fermentation of glucose, using the yeast Saccharomyces cerevisiae. Absolute ethanol can then be obtained by distillation

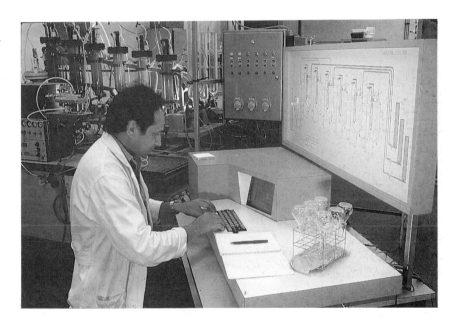

Phenol

Nowadays, most phenol is made from petroleum:

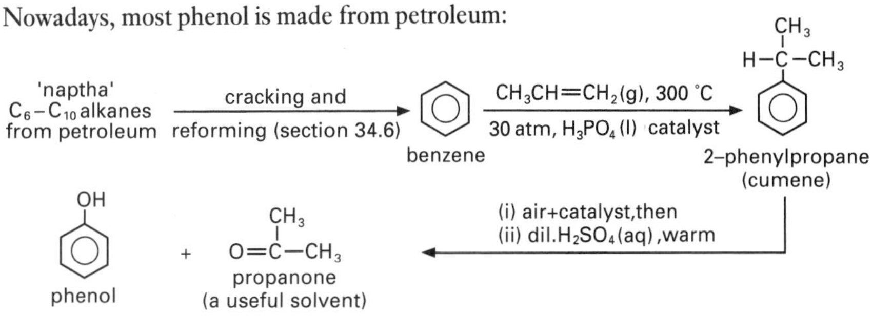

'naptha'
$C_6 - C_{10}$ alkanes from petroleum $\xrightarrow[\text{reforming (section 34.6)}]{\text{cracking and}}$ benzene $\xrightarrow[\text{30 atm, } H_3PO_4 \text{ (l) catalyst}]{CH_3CH=CH_2 \text{(g), 300 °C}}$ 2-phenylpropane (cumene)

phenol (OH) + propanone $O=C-CH_3$ (a useful solvent) $\xleftarrow[\text{(ii) dil.} H_2SO_4 \text{(aq) ,warm}]{\text{(i) air+catalyst,then}}$

Figure 38.4 *The polar nature of the C—O—H structure*

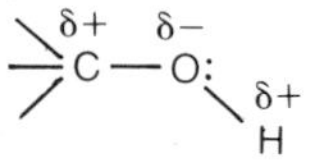

Small quantities of phenol are extracted from coal tar. Which of these methods might be favoured in, say, 100 years time?

Phenols can be prepared in the laboratory from sulphonic acids (section 36.5.2) or diazonium salts (section 41.9).

Activity 38.3

1. Give reagents and conditions for the preparation (a) butan-2-ol from but-2-ene, (b) propan-1-ol from 1-chloropropane and (c) propan-1-ol from ethanol. (Hint: for part (c), look at section 37.5.2.)
2. Give reagents and conditions for the laboratory synthesis of phenol from benzene.

38.4 Predicting the reactivity of alcohols and phenols

All alcohols and phenols contain the C—O—H structure. Electronegativities indicate that these will be polar bonds (figure 38.4). We would predict, then, that the reactions of this structure might involve:

▶ **fission of the O—H bond,** caused by the attack of a nucleophile, or base, at $H^{\delta+}$:

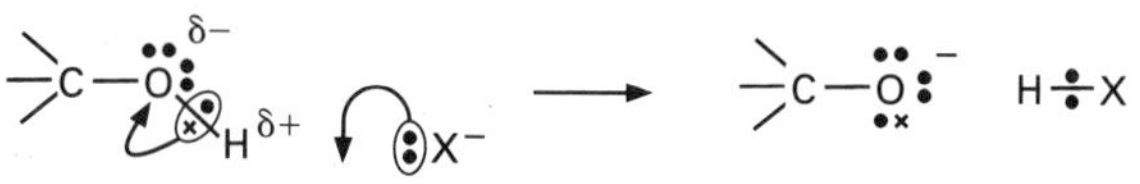

($\overset{\bullet\bullet}{\bullet}X^-$ is a base or a nucleophile)

▶ **fission of the C—O bond,** caused by the attack of a nucleophile at $C^{\delta+}$, e.g.

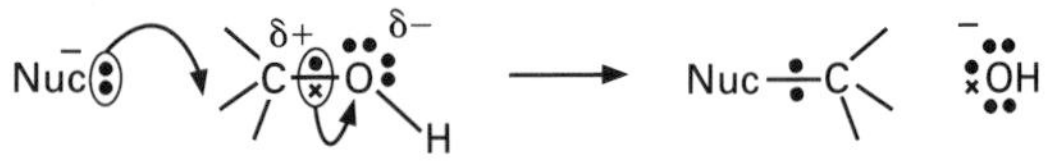

($Nuc^-\!\!\overset{\bullet\bullet}{}$ is a nucleophile)

We shall look at both types of reaction, together with:

▶ the **oxidation reactions** of alcohols and phenols; and
▶ the reactions of the **hydrocarbon skeleton**, e.g. electrophilic substitution in the benzene ring of a phenol.

As you work through sections 38.5 to 38.9, make a special note of any occasions where the reactivity of the —OH group is affected by its **molecular location**. This is a *key aspect* of our study.

38.5 Reactions involving fission of the O—H bond

38.5.1 Acidity

Table 38.6 describes how ethanol, water and phenol react with (i) sodium metal and (ii) aqueous sodium hydroxide.

Sodium metal and hydroxide ions are **bases**. Where a reaction occurs, therefore, ethanol, water and phenol must behave as **acids**. Moreover, the relative rates of reaction suggest that:

ethanol	water	phenol

increasing acid strength →

Table 38.6 *(i) Observations when ethanol, water and phenol react with a small pellet of sodium at room temperature*

Reactant	observations
Ethanol	Sodium sinks; steady evolution of hydrogen (tested with a lighted splint); an exothermic reaction.
Water	Sodium moves quickly around the surface of the water; vigorous evolution of hydrogen; an exothermic reaction
Phenol (solution in ethanol)	Sodium sinks; vigorous evolution of hydrogen; a very exothermic reaction

(ii) Observations when ethanol, water and phenol are treated with dilute NaOH(aq) at room temperature

Reactant	observations
Ethanol	No noticeable reaction
Water	No noticeable reaction
Phenol	Phenol is much more soluble in NaOH(aq) than it is in water; a slight temperature rise occurs.

Which of these hydroxy compounds seems to be the strongest acid?

Although it is the strongest of these three acids, phenol is still several hundred times weaker than a carboxylic acid, such as benzoic acid. Thus, we find that benzoic acid, *but not phenol*, will liberate carbon dioxide from a hydrogencarbonate:

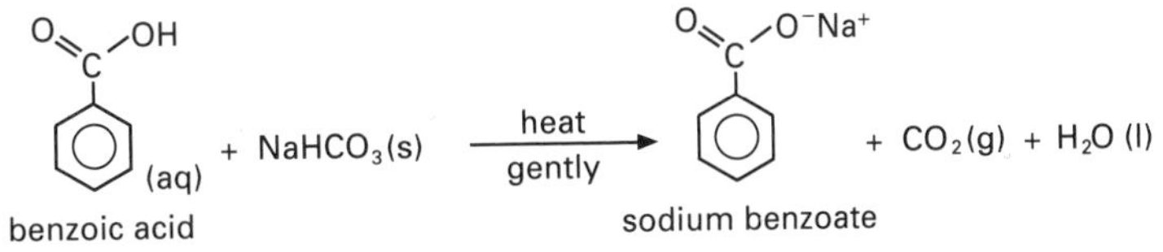

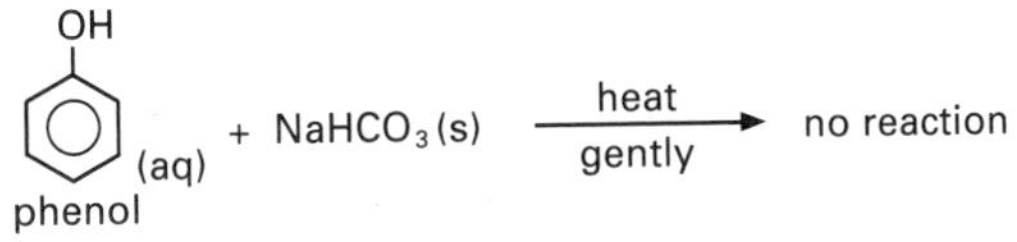

Note, then, how *the acidity of the hydroxy group varies with its molecular location* (i.e. in an alcohol, phenol or carboxylic acid).

Phenol and, to a much lesser extent, ethanol dissociate in aqueous solution:

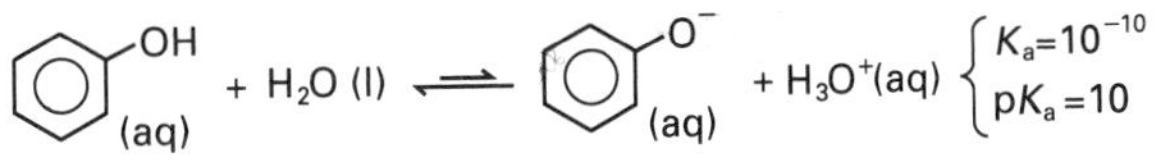

$$C_2H_5OH(aq) + H_2O(l) \rightleftharpoons C_2H_5O^-(aq) + H_3O^+(aq) \quad \begin{cases} K_a = 10^{-18} \\ pK_a = 18 \end{cases}$$

The meanings of K_a (the acid dissociation constant) and pK_a were given earlier (section 18.6). Just a reminder, then, that when comparing acid strengths, a *weaker* acid will have a *lower* K_a but a *higher* pK_a.

Values for K_a and pK_a show that both the above equilibria lie heavily to the left hand side. Phenol is a stronger acid than ethanol because it dissociates to a greater extent. But can this behaviour be related to the molecular structure?

Well, on dissolving a weak oxoacid, XO—H, in water, the following equilibrium is set up:

$$XO—H(aq) + H_2O(l) \rightleftharpoons XO^-(aq) + H_3O^+(aq)$$

The acid will be stronger, that is, more likely to dissociate:

▶ *if the O—H bond is weak and breaks easily;* and
▶ *if the negative charge on the oxygen in XO$^-$ is delocalised over the entire anion.* This will stabilise the anion by lowering its ability to attract a proton and reform an undissociated molecule.

Both these factors are influenced by the **inductive effect** of the X group, that is *its ability to attract or repel the electron cloud.*

In the ethanol molecule and the ethoxide ion, the ethyl group pushes electrons away from itself:

the electron cloud shift **strengthens** the O—H bond, making the loss of the H$^+$ **more difficult**

the electron cloud shift localises the negative charge on the O$^-$, making it **more easily protonated, i.e. less stable**

Overall, these effects *decrease* the degree of dissociation of ethanol. Consequently, *ethanol, and other alcohols, are very weak acids.*

Figure 38.5 *The delocalised π bond system in the phenoxide ion is formed by the sideways overlap of the p orbitals on the carbon and oxygen atoms. A similar π bond system is found in phenol itself*

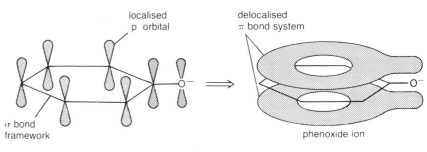

localised p orbital

delocalised π bond system

σ bond framework

phenoxide ion

However, in the phenol molecule and the phenoxide ion, *the lone pair in oxygen's p orbital overlaps sideways with benzene's π electron ring* (figure 38.5). As a result, electron cloud from the oxygen and the O—H bond is drawn towards the benzene ring:

the electron cloud shift **weakens** the O—H bond making it **easier to lose** the H$^+$

the electron cloud shift **delocalises** the negative charge on the O$^-$ making it **less** easily protonated, i.e. **more** stable

Due to these effects, *phenol is a stronger acid, that is, a better proton donor, than ethanol.*

The presence of electron *withdrawing* substituent groups, such as $-NO_2$ and $-COCH_3$, *increases* the acidity of a phenol. Such groups enhance the drift of electron cloud away from the oxygen atom and the O—H bond. For example, 2,4,6-trinitrophenol is a fairly strong acid:

Figure 38.6 *The electron releasing effects of the methyl and amino groups cause the electron cloud to move towards the benzene ring and then into the –OH group*

2,4,6-trinitrophenol
(K_a=0.1, pK_a=1)

$+ H_2O$ (l) ⇌ $+ H_3O^+$(aq)

Like the mineral acids, 2,4,6-trinitrophenol is able to displace carbon dioxide from carbonates. As expected, electron *donating* ring substituents, such as $-CH_3$ and $-NH_2$, *decrease* the acid strength of the phenol (figure 38.6).

Although phenol is a stronger acid than ethanol, remember that they are both weak acids. Thus, *they are both displaced from their salts by stronger acids:* e.g.

$$CH_3CH_2O^-Na^+(s) + H_2O(l) \rightarrow CH_3CH_2OH(l) + NaOH(aq)$$
$$\text{sodium ethoxide}$$

Water, the stronger acid, displaces ethanol, the weaker acid, from its salt. In section 40.5.2, we shall compare the acid strengths of alcohols and phenols with those of carboxylic and sulphonic acids.

38.5.2 Esterification

Due to bond polarisation and the presence of lone pairs, a dense electron cloud surrounds the oxygen atom in an alcohol or phenol. Hence, they act as **nucleophiles**, via this $O^{\delta-}$ atom, and attack electron-poor (δ^+) centres. An important example of this type of reaction is **esterification**.

A carboxylic acid ester is best prepared by reacting an alcohol with an *acid chloride*, e.g.

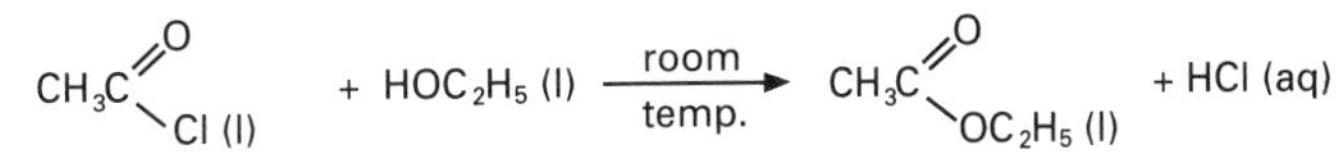

ethanoyl chloride   ethyl ethanoate

Due to the delocalisation of the oxygen's lone pair of electrons, *phenols are weaker nucleophiles than alcohols* (see figure 38.5). Compared to alcohols, then, phenols form esters much less readily. In fact, phenyl esters are best prepared by first converting phenol into the **phenoxide ion**. This is a much stronger nucleophile which readily reacts with acid chlorides:

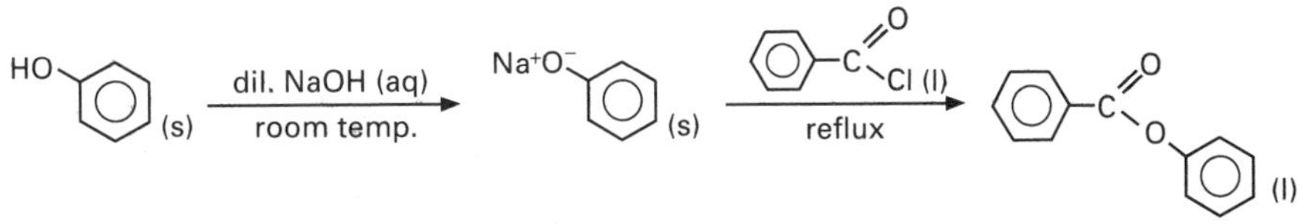

phenol   sodium phenoxide   phenyl benzoate

38.6 Reactions involving fission of the C—O bond

38.6.1 With concentrated sulphuric acid

When alcohols react with concentrated sulphuric acid, different products are formed according to the reaction conditions.

At **140 °C**, in the presence of **excess alcohol**, the main product is an **ether**:

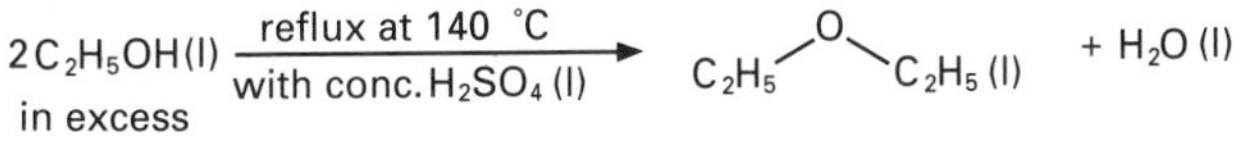

ethoxyethane

This is a **nucleophilic substitution** reaction (of OH^- by $C_2H_5O^-$). However, at **170 °C**, in the presence of **excess concentrated sulphuric acid**, a molecule of water is **eliminated** and the main product is an **alkene**:

$$CH_3CH_2CH_2OH(l) \xrightarrow[\text{excess conc. } H_2SO_4(l)]{\text{reflux at 170°C}} CH_3CH{=}CH_2(g) + H_2O(l)$$

There are two points to note here:

▶ concentrated sulphuric acid acts as a dehydrating agent in both reactions;
▶ like the halogenoalkanes, alcohols can become involved in *competing* nucleophilic substitution and elimination reactions.

When phenols react with concentrated sulphuric acid, the only reaction is electrophilic substitution in the benzene ring:

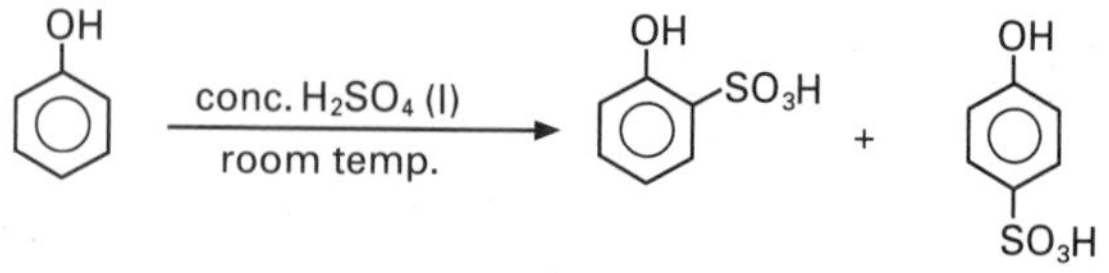

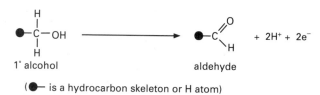

To sulphonate benzene, it must be *refluxed* with concentrated sulphuric acid. Why does the above reaction occur under such mild conditions?

38.6.2 With halogenating agents

As we saw in section 37.3, halogenoalkanes are prepared by treating an alcohol with a halogenating agent. Table 37.2 summarised these reactions.

Phenol does *not* give substitution reactions with halogenating agents because the C—O bond is strengthened, and its polarity decreased, by partial π bonding (figure 38.5). However, carboxylic acids (another type of hydroxy compound) react readily with halogenating agents (section 40.5.3):

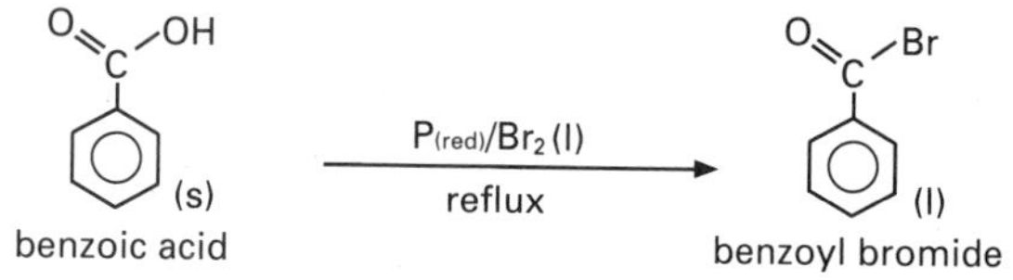

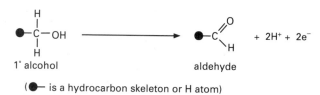

38.7 Oxidation reactions

Although alcohols burn in air with a clean flame, the cost of production limits their use as a 'bulk' fuel. However, ethanol is used in some countries as a petrol additive or substitute. Due to their high carbon/hydrogen ratio, phenols burn in air with a sooty flame.

The controlled oxidation of alcohols is used (i) in organic synthesis and (ii) to distinguish between primary, secondary and tertiary alcohols.

Primary and secondary alcohols are easily oxidised by refluxing them with a solution of potassium dichromate, $K_2Cr_2O_7$, in dilute sulphuric acid. *An acidified dichromate ion readily accepts electrons:*

$$Cr_2O_7^{2-}(aq) + 14H^+(aq) + 6e^- \longrightarrow 2Cr^{3+}(aq) + 7H_2O(l)$$

orange   green

and this makes it a powerful **oxidising agent** (see section 31.1). Also, the colour change indicates that a reaction is occurring.

On oxidation, a **primary alcohol** first forms an **aldehyde**:

(⬤— is a hydrocarbon skeleton or H atom)

Then the aldehyde is further oxidised to a **carboxylic acid**:

The ethanol in brandy burns with a clean blue flame

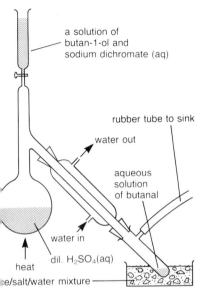

a solution of butan-1-ol and sodium dichromate (aq)

rubber tube to sink

water out

aqueous solution of butanal

water in

dil. H_2SO_4(aq)

heat

ice/salt/water mixture

For example,

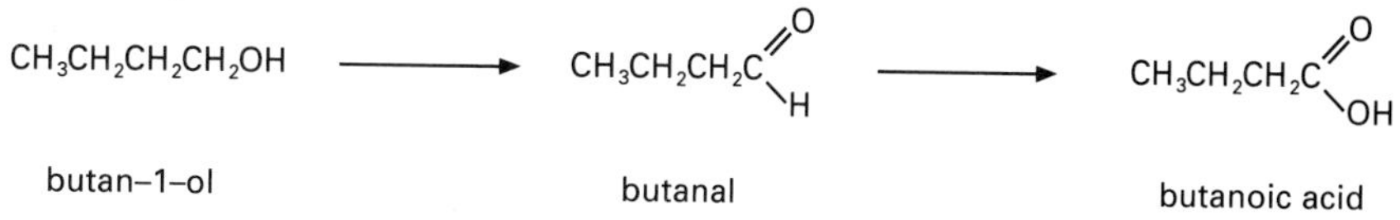

$CH_3CH_2CH_2CH_2OH \longrightarrow CH_3CH_2CH_2C\overset{O}{\underset{H}{}} \longrightarrow CH_3CH_2CH_2C\overset{O}{\underset{OH}{}}$

butan-1-ol   butanal   butanoic acid

If the aldehyde is the desired product, it must be distilled off as it is formed, as shown in figure 38.7.

Secondary alcohols are oxidised to **ketones**:

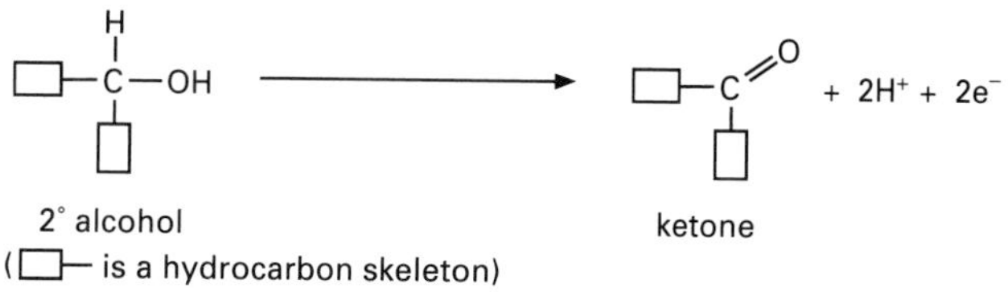

2° alcohol → ketone $+ 2H^+ + 2e^-$

($\square$— is a hydrocarbon skeleton)

For example,

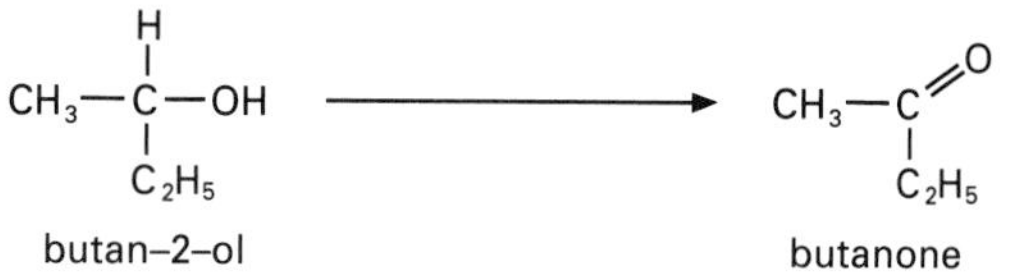

$CH_3-\overset{H}{\underset{C_2H_5}{C}}-OH \longrightarrow CH_3-C\overset{O}{\underset{C_2H_5}{}}$

butan-2-ol   butanone

Under these conditions, ketones resist further oxidation (but see section 39.8.1).

During the oxidation of primary and secondary alcohols, hydrogen atoms are removed from the carbon atom bearing the $-OH$ group. Since they have no such hydrogen atoms, **tertiary alcohols** *are not oxidised by hot acidified potassium dichromate.* However, prolonged treatment with a very strong oxidising agent, such as hot concentrated nitric acid, converts them into a mixture of ketones, carboxylic acids and carbon dioxide.

A variety of oxidising agents are used, both in the laboratory and industrially, to convert alcohols into aldehydes, ketones and carboxylic acids. Some examples are given in table 38.7.

Table 38.7 *Some reagents commonly used to oxidise alcohols*

Reagent	reaction conditions	notes
potassium dichromate(VI), $K_2Cr_2O_7$ in dilute H_2SO_4(aq)	reflux	colour change: *orange* Cr (VI) to *blue-green* Cr(III) confirms the reaction
potassium manganate(VII), $KMnO_4$ in dilute H_2SO_4(aq)	reflux	colour change: *purple* Mn(VII) to *colourless* Mn(II) confirms the reaction
air + silver oxide catalyst	600°C	manufacture of methanal from methanol
air + copper catalyst	500°C	manufacture of propanone from propan-2-ol

We can distinguish between primary, secondary and tertiary alcohols by analysing their oxidation products. Simple chemical tests are used to identify any aldehydes, ketones or carboxylic acids which are formed (see sections 39.6.4 and 41.8). Alternatively, the oxidation products might be separated, purified and then analysed using the instrumental methods given in chapter 6.

A simple way of distinguishing between certain alcohols is to use the **iodoform test**. *Alcohols which contain the structure below, react with iodine (dissolved in KI(aq)) and aqueous sodium hydroxide to give a yellow precipitate of triiodomethane, $CHI_3(s)$.* This compound is commonly known as iodoform.

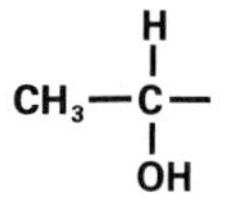

$CH_3-\overset{H}{\underset{OH}{C}}-$

Ethanol and propan-2-ol, for example, will form iodoform:

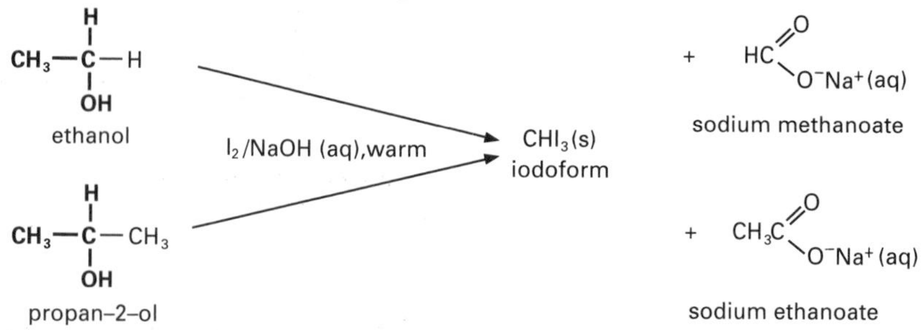

$$CH_3-\overset{\overset{\displaystyle H}{|}}{\underset{\underset{\displaystyle OH}{|}}{C}}-H$$

ethanol

$$CH_3-\overset{\overset{\displaystyle H}{|}}{\underset{\underset{\displaystyle OH}{|}}{C}}-CH_3$$

propan–2-ol

$\xrightarrow{I_2/NaOH \text{ (aq),warm}}$

$CHI_3(s)$
iodoform

$+ \quad HC\overset{\displaystyle O}{\underset{\displaystyle O^-Na^+ \text{(aq)}}{\diagdown}}$

sodium methanoate

$+ \quad CH_3C\overset{\displaystyle O}{\underset{\displaystyle O^-Na^+ \text{(aq)}}{\diagdown}}$

sodium ethanoate

However, propan-1-ol does *not* have the $-CH(OH)CH_3$ group; consequently, it gives a negative iodoform test. The iodoform reaction is further discussed in section 39.7.2.

Finally, you should note that the $-OH$ group in phenols and carboxylic acids does not give similar oxidation results.

38.8 Reactions of the hydrocarbon skeleton

When predicting the reactions of a particular alcohol, remember that the hydrocarbon skeleton also has some characteristic reactions. Thus, a C—H bond will undergo photocatalysed bromination:

$$CH_3OH(l) \xrightarrow[\text{light}]{Br_2(l) \text{ in u.v.}} CBr_3OH(l)$$

This is a free radical substitution reaction (section 34.8).

Often, the reactivity of the hydrocarbon skeleton is *modified* by the presence of the $-OH$ group. For example, due to the activating effect of the hydroxy group, the benzene ring in phenol is very susceptible to electrophilic attack. Even under mild conditions, substitution will readily occur in the 2-, 4- and 6- positions:

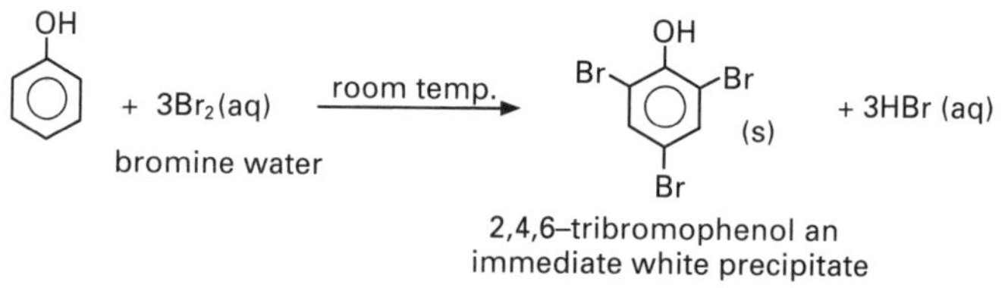

2,4,6–tribromophenol an immediate white precipitate

Would benzene react with bromine under these conditions?

Some other electrophilic substitution reactions of phenol are summarised in table 38.8.

Table 38.8 *Some electrophilic substitution reactions of phenol*

Reagent	conditions	product(s)
dil. HNO_3(aq)	room temperature	2- and 4-nitrophenols
Br_2(aq)	room temperature	2,4,6-tribromophenol (white ppt.)
conc. H_2SO_4(l)	room temperature	2- and 4-sulphonic acids of phenol
methanal, HCHO + conc. H_2SO_4 (catalyst)	gentle heating	Bakelite (a condensation polymer, section 39.10)

Can you remember if benzene will react with nitric or sulphuric acid under these conditions?

Finally, we must mention the industrial hydrogenation of phenol vapour:

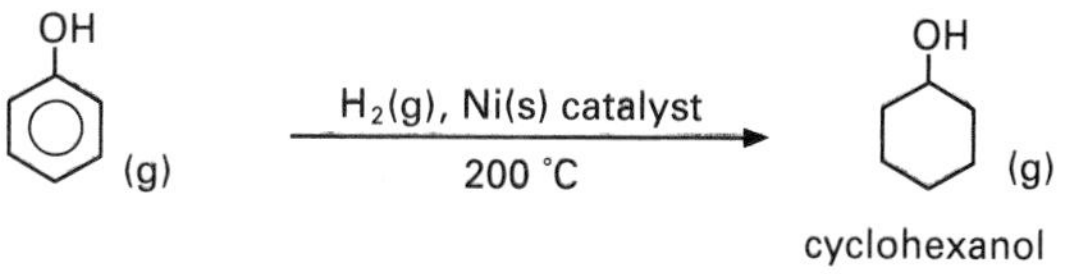

cyclohexanol

This is an important reaction because large quantities of cyclohexanol are used to make **nylon** (section 40.11).

38.9 A simple chemical test for phenol

Phenols react with a neutral solution of **iron(III) chloride** to give brightly coloured compounds. These substances are complex ions of iron(III) with ligands containing the enol group,

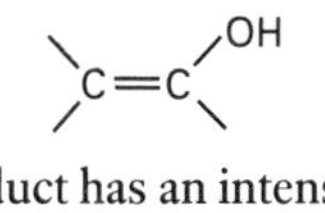

$$\begin{array}{c}\diagup\\ \diagup\end{array}C{=}C\begin{array}{c}{}^{OH}\\ \diagdown\end{array}$$

With phenol itself, the product has an intense violet colour.

Activity 38.4

1   Place the following weak acids in order of increasing acidity: F_2CHOH, $ClCH_2OH$, F_3COH, CH_3OH, $FCH_2(OH)$.

2   Give the name(s) and formula(e) of the organic product(s) formed by the following reactions:

(a) sodium methoxide $\xrightarrow[\text{temperature}]{\text{dil. }H_2SO_4\text{(aq), room}}$

(b) 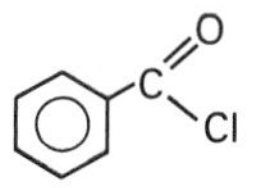 [structure] benzoyl chloride $\xrightarrow{CH_3OH\text{(l), warm}}$

(c) butan-2-ol $\xrightarrow[\text{reflux at }170\,°C]{\text{conc. }H_2SO_4\text{(l) in excess}}$

(d) methanol (excess) $\xrightarrow[\text{at }140\,°C]{\text{conc. }H_2SO_4\text{(l), reflux}}$

(e) 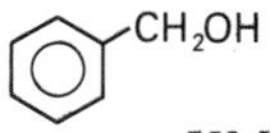 [structure with $-CH_2OH$] $\xrightarrow{P_{red},\ Br_2\text{(l) reflux}}$

(f) methanol $\xrightarrow[\text{reflux}]{KMnO_4/\text{dil. }H_2SO_4\text{(aq)}}$

(g) 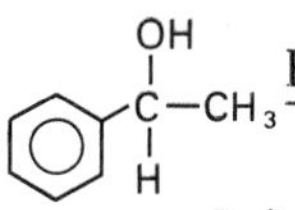 [structure with OH, $C{-}CH_3$, H] $\xrightarrow[\text{reflux}]{K_2Cr_2O_7/\text{dil. }H_2SO_4\text{(aq)}}$

(h) hexan-2-ol $\xrightarrow{I_2/NaOH\text{(aq), warm}}$

3   Give the reagents and reaction conditions needed for the eight following conversions:

(a) [phenol structure OH] $\longrightarrow$ [structure $O{-}\overset{\overset{O}{\|}}{C}{-}C_2H_5$] phenylpropanoate (a phenylester)

(b) methanol $\longrightarrow$ $CH_3{-}O{-}CH_3$

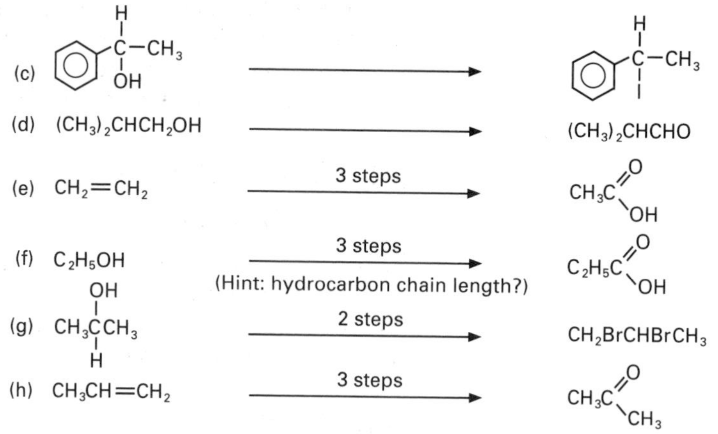

(c) [structure: phenyl-CH(CH₃)OH] ⟶ [structure: phenyl-CH(CH₃) with H]

(d) $(CH_3)_2CHCH_2OH$ ⟶ $(CH_3)_2CHCHO$

(e) $CH_2{=}CH_2$ —— 3 steps ⟶ $CH_3C{\lesssim}^O_{OH}$

(f) C_2H_5OH —— 3 steps (Hint: hydrocarbon chain length?) ⟶ $C_2H_5C{\lesssim}^O_{OH}$

(g) $CH_3\underset{H}{\overset{OH}{C}}CH_3$ —— 2 steps ⟶ $CH_2BrCHBrCH_3$

(h) $CH_3CH{=}CH_2$ —— 3 steps ⟶ $CH_3C{\lesssim}^O_{CH_3}$

4 Describe simple chemical test(s) by which you could distinguish between
(a) butan-1-ol, butan-2-ol and 2-methylpropan-2-ol;
(b) phenol and phenylmethanol

38.10 Use of alcohols and phenols

Large quantities of the lower alcohols are used as *solvents*, e.g. in the manufacture of drugs, cosmetics and varnishes. Alcohols are also used as a *chemical feedstock* in the synthesis of other organic compounds. Two of these are mentioned below.

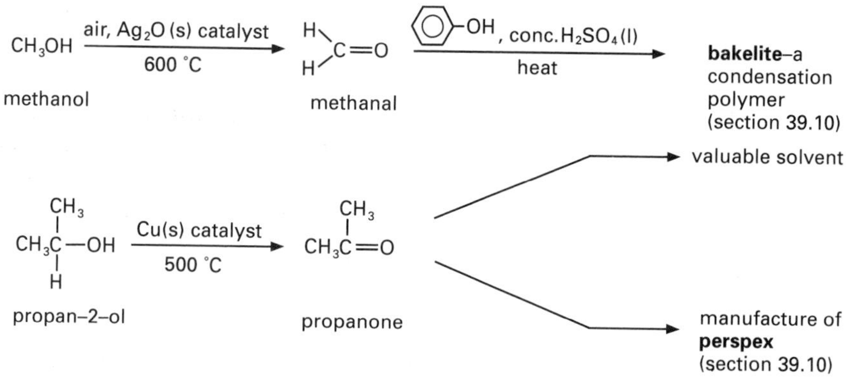

CH_3OH —— air, Ag₂O (s) catalyst / 600 °C ⟶ $\underset{H}{\overset{H}{>}}C{=}O$ —— phenol-OH, conc. H₂SO₄ (l) / heat ⟶ **bakelite**—a condensation polymer (section 39.10)

methanol   methanal

↗ valuable solvent

$CH_3\underset{H}{\overset{CH_3}{C}}{-}OH$ —— Cu(s) catalyst / 500 °C ⟶ $CH_3\overset{CH_3}{C}{=}O$

propan–2-ol   propanone

↘ manufacture of **perspex** (section 39.10)

Dihydric and polyhydric alcohols also have their uses. *Ethane-1,2-diol* is used as antifreeze and in the manufacture of *polyester* (section 40.11). Propane-1,2,3-triol is used to make nitroglycerine the explosive material in dynamite.

A dilute aqueous solution of phenol has powerful *antiseptic* properties. Known as 'carbolic acid', this solution was first used in 1867 by Lister, a famous surgeon. By spraying a fine mist of aqueous phenol near a wound, Lister was able to hinder the development of bacterial diseases during the operation or the patient's recovery period. Although the use of 'carbolic acid' increased the chances of the patient surviving surgery, it tended to burn the skin around the wound. In fact, we now know that phenol is poisonous by skin absorption. Nowadays, *derivatives* of phenol are used as antiseptics, e.g.

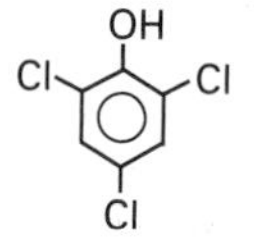

[structure: benzene ring with OH at top, Cl at positions 2, 4, 6]
2, 4, 6–trichlorophenol
('TCP')

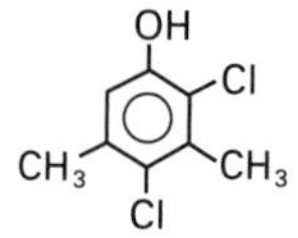

[structure: benzene ring with OH at top, Cl, CH₃ substituents]
2,4–dichloro-3,5–dimethylphenol
('Dettol')

Not only are these much more active anti-bacterial agents than phenol, but they are also much less toxic and do not irritate the skin.

As mentioned earlier, phenol is also used to make phenol–methanal plastics (e.g. Bakelite) and nylon (via cyclohexanol).

38.11 Comparing the reactions of alcohols and phenol

We are very interested in how the chemical reactivity of the hydroxy group depends on its molecular location. Activity 38.5 will help you to compare the behaviour of ethanol (1°), propan-2-ol (2°), 2-methylpropan-2-ol (3°) and phenol. This activity is a very useful revision exercise.

Activity 38.5

Prepare a summary table which compares the reactivity of ethanol, propan-2-ol, 2-methylpropan-2-ol and phenol. You should consider their reactions with the following reagents: 1. sodium metal;   2. $CH_3COCl(l)$;
3. conc. $H_2SO_4(l)$;   4. $PCl_5(s)$;   5. conc. HHal(aq);
6. $K_2Cr_2O_7$/dil. H_2SO_4(aq);   7. I_2/NaOH(aq);   8. Br_2(aq);
9. neutral $FeCl_3$(aq);   10. electrophiles such as NO_2^+, Cl^+, CH_3^+ and SO_3.

38.12 Ethers

Ethers have the general formula:

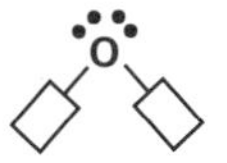

where ☐− is a hydrocarbon skeleton. A simple ether has identical ☐− groups whereas a mixed either has different ☐− groups.

Ethers are named as alkoxy- or phenoxy- derivatives of the longest hydrocarbon chain or benzene ring:

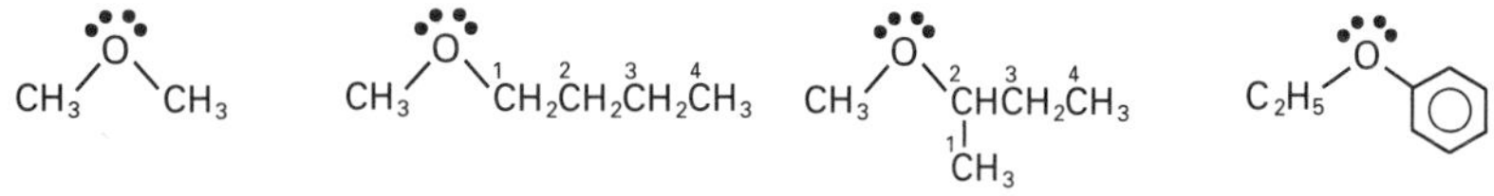

CH₃OCH₃   CH₃O¹CH₂²CH₂³CH₂⁴CH₃   CH₃O²CH³CH₂⁴CH₃   C₂H₅O⟨ring⟩
                                                                              |
                                                                             CH₃

methoxymethane   1–methoxybutane   2–methoxybutane   ethoxybenzene
                                                                            (or phenoxyethane)

metamers

Since structural isomerism can occur, we must number the carbon atom which bears the **oxy** group. In fact, the isomers above are examples of **metamers**. This means that *they have the same functional group, but different alkyl groups*.

Preparing ethers

Ethers may be prepared in two ways:
▶ by refluxing concentrated sulphuric acid with an excess of an alcohol at 140°C:

$$CH_3OH(l) \xrightarrow[\text{reflux}]{\text{conc. } H_2SO_4(l)} CH_3OCH_3(g)$$
excess

As we saw in section 38.6.1, the sulphuric acid acts as a dehydrating agent. This reaction, which always produces a simple aliphatic ether, is used to manufacture *ethoxyethane*, the most commonly used ether.
▶ by heating a sodium alkoxide, or sodium phenoxide with an iodoalkane, (section 37.5.4):

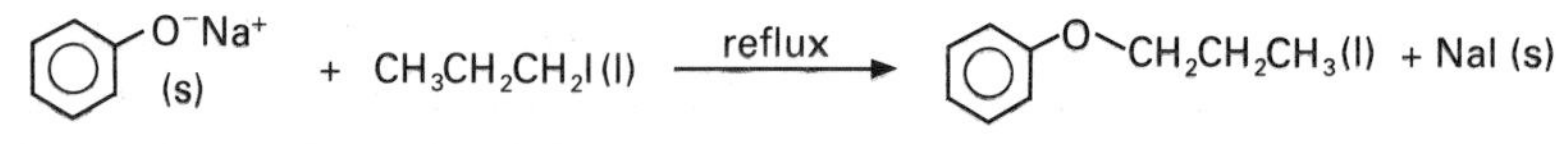

sodium phenoxide   1–iodopropane   1–phenoxypropane

Simple and mixed ethers can be prepared in this way.

Physical properties of ethers

Aliphatic ethers form a homologous series of general formula $C_nH_{2n+2}O$. Ethers and alcohols are functional group isomers (section 10.2), e.g.

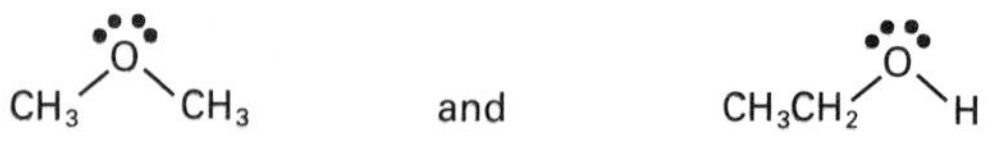

methoxymethane   and   ethanol

Since they are unable to form hydrogen bonds, ethers have much lower boiling points than the isomeric alcohols. Indeed, ethers are as volatile as alkanes of similar mass. This would suggest that the dipole–dipole attractions in ethers, via their polar C—O bonds, must be very weak. Ethers, then, are essentially non-polar compounds, whose molecules are held together by weak van der Waals' forces. Hence, ethers are only slightly water-soluble but they are good solvents for non-polar substances.

Chemical properties of ethers

Ethers burn readily in air, forming carbon dioxide and water:

$$C_2H_5OC_2H_5(l) + 6O_2(g) \rightarrow 4CO_2(g) + 5H_2O(l) \quad \Delta H = -2761\,kJ\,mol^{-1}$$

Ethoxyethane, for example, is a highly flammable liquid (b.p. = 35 °C), which forms an explosive mixture with air. Since it is denser than air, ethoxyethane vapour diffuses through the laboratory at bench level, creating a danger of a fire well away from the actual source of the 'ether'. Even so, ethoxyethane is very widely used as a non-polar solvent.

Combustion apart, *ethers are rather inert compounds*. Although the oxygen atom bears two lone pairs of electrons, *ethers are only weak bases* (i.e. proton acceptors). Thus, they dissolve in strong acids forming oxonium salts:

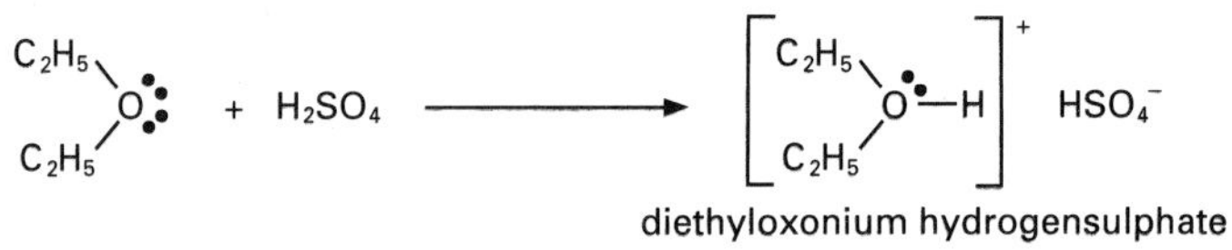

diethyloxonium hydrogensulphate

From the C—O bond polarity, *we might expect an ether to behave as a nucleophile at $O^{\delta-}$*. In fact, there is only one noteworthy example of this, namely, the reaction with concentrated hydriodic acid. An aliphatic ether yields two iodoalkanes, e.g.

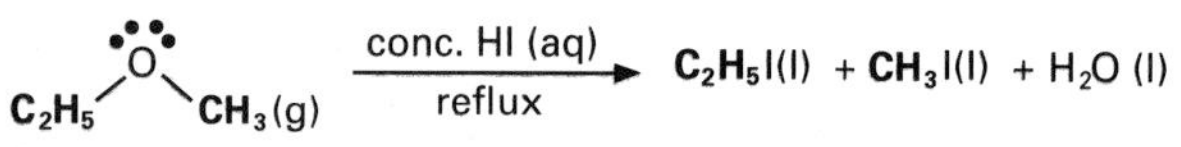

Hydriodic acid is a very strong acid; thus, it *protonates* the ether and makes it more reactive towards the I^- nucleophile. A similar reaction with an aromatic ether produces a phenol and an iodoalkane.

Uses of ethers

Due to their lack of chemical reactivity, ethers are *valuable solvents* for covalent compounds. In particular, large quantities of ethoxyethane are used in industrial organic chemistry. As well as helping reactants mix together, ethoxyethane is also frequently used to solvent extract crude products from aqueous reaction mixtures (see section 32.5).

Figure 38.8 *Epoxyethane, an industrially important ether. Would you expect it to be very reactive?*

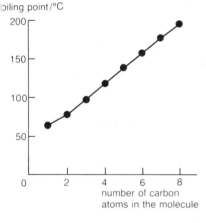

Figure 38.8 *Epoxyethane, an industrially important ether. Would you expect it to be very reactive?*

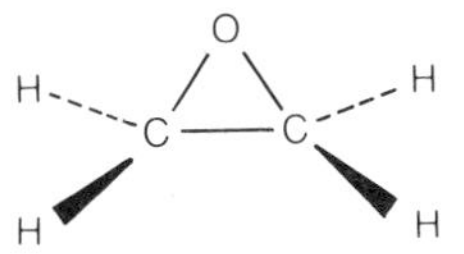

Another ether of industrial importance is *epoxyethane* (figure 38.8). Owing to the strain in its three-membered ring, epoxyethane is far more reactive than non-cyclic ethers. It is used, for example, in the manufacture of antifreeze (section 35.7.1).

Activity 38.6

1 Write down the names and structural formulae of the ethers of molecular formula, $C_4H_{10}O$.
2 Give the reactants and conditions you would use to prepare
   (a) ethoxyethane, (b) 1-ethoxypropane, (c) 2-methoxybutane and
   (d) phenoxyethane.
3 Describe one physical method and one chemical method of distinguishing between phenoxymethane and phenylmethanol.

38.13 Comments on the activities

Activity 38.1

1 (a) pentan-1-ol (b) 3-phenylbutan-1-ol (c) 1-methylcyclohexanol
   (d) 3-bromobutan-2-ol (e) butane-2,3-diol (f) 3-nitrophenol

2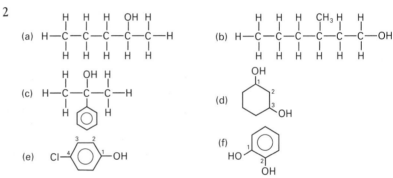

3 (a) aliphatic: 1a, 1c, 1d, 1e, 2a, 2b, 2d; (b) aromatic: 1b, 2c;
   (c) 1°: 1a, 1b, 2b; (d) 2°: 1d, 1e, 2a, 2d; (e) 3°: 1c, 2c.

4

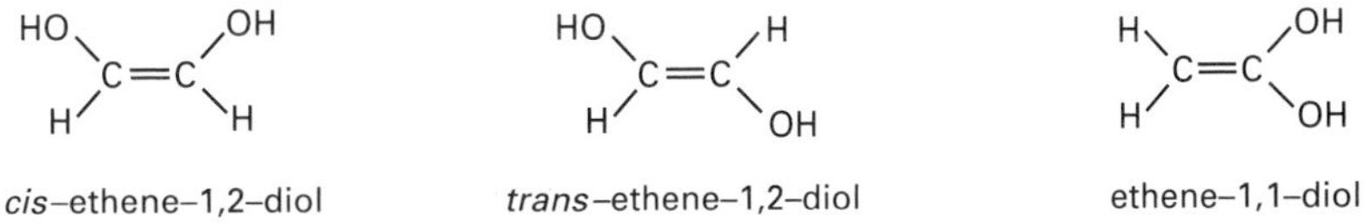

cis–ethene–1,2–diol   *trans*–ethene–1,2–diol   ethene–1,1–diol

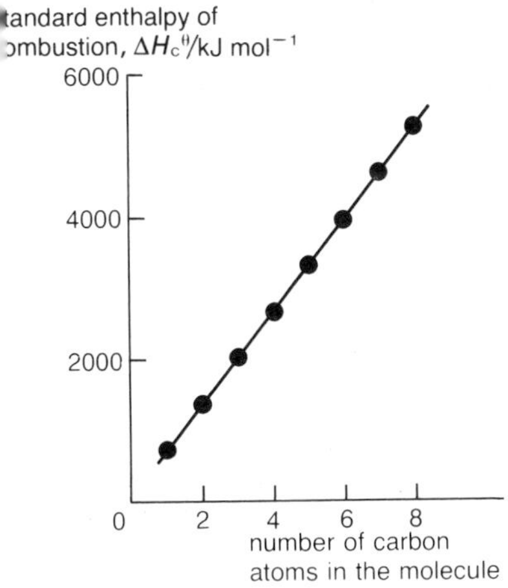

Activity 38.2

1 As expected, the alcohols form a **homologous series** with the general formula $C_nH_{2n+1}OH$.
2 (a) A graph of boiling point against the number of carbon atoms in the chain is a smooth curve (figure 38.9). As the hydrocarbon chain gets longer, the size of the molecular electron cloud also increases. Larger electron clouds are more easily polarised by neighbouring molecules. Thus, the van der Waals' forces will be strongest, and *boiling points will be highest, for alcohols with long hydrocarbon chains*.
   (b) The regular increase is $\Delta H_c^{\ominus}$ values is typical of compounds which form a homologous series (figure 38.10). As in other homologous series, the successive increase roughly corresponds to the enthalpy of combustion of a CH_2 unit.
3 Boiling points decrease in the order:

   butan-1-ol > 2-methylpropan-1-ol > butan-2-ol > 2-methylpropan-2-ol

Figure 38.9 *A graph of the boiling points of some straight-chain alcohols plotted against the number of carbon atoms in the molecule*

boiling point/°C

Figure 38.10 *A graph of the standard enthalpies of combustion, $\Delta H_c^{\ominus}$, of some straight-chain alcohols plotted against the number of carbon atoms in the molecule*

standard enthalpy of combustion, $\Delta H_c^{\ominus}$/kJ mol^{-1}

'This trend is typical of those already seen for alkanes, alkenes and halogenoalkanes, namely, *greater branching produces lower boiling points*. On going from $1° \rightarrow 2° \rightarrow 3°$ alcohols, the molecules become less able to make such a close contact with their neighbours. Thus, van der Waals' forces become weaker, thereby causing the boiling points to decrease.

4   Alcohols have much higher boiling points than the alkanes of similar mass, e.g. propane ($M_r = 44$), b.p. $= -42°C$; ethanol ($M_r = 46$), b.p. $= 78°C$. This effect results from the differing strengths of the intermolecular attractions. Whilst fairly weak van der Waals' forces operate in both alcohols and alkanes, *alcohol molecules are also mutually attracted via much stronger* **hydrogen bonds** (figure 38.2).

Activity 38.3

1   (a)   Two ways:

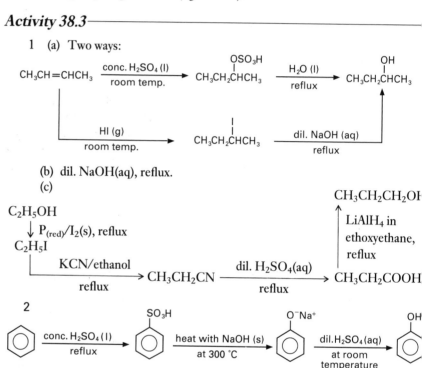

(b)   dil. NaOH(aq), reflux.

(c)

2

benzene · · · benzenesulphonic acid · · · sodium phenoxide · · · pheno

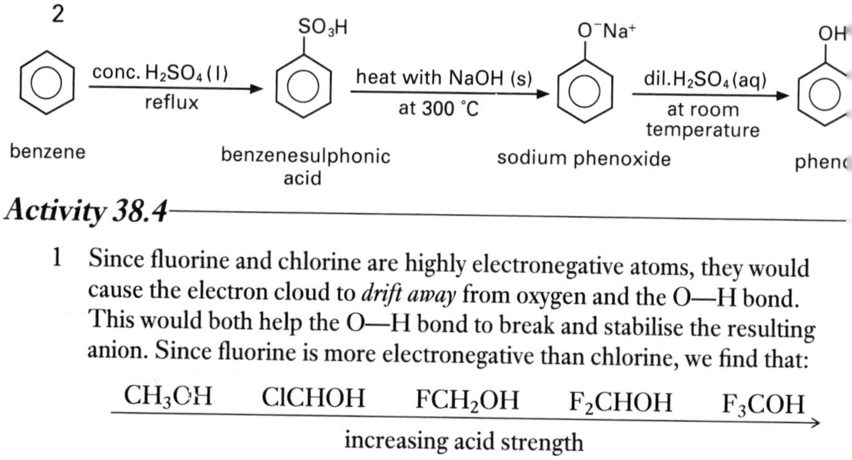

Activity 38.4

1   Since fluorine and chlorine are highly electronegative atoms, they would cause the electron cloud to *drift away* from oxygen and the O—H bond. This would both help the O—H bond to break and stabilise the resulting anion. Since fluorine is more electronegative than chlorine, we find that:

$$CH_3OH \quad ClCHOH \quad FCH_2OH \quad F_2CHOH \quad F_3COH$$

increasing acid strength

2   (a)   methanol, CH_3OH; this very weak acid is displaced from its salt by the strong acid, H_2SO_4(aq).

(b)   methyl benzoate

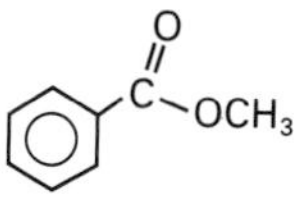

(c)   a *mixture* of but-1-ene, $CH_3CH_2CH=CH_2$ (via 1,2 elimination) and but-2-ene $CH_3CH=CHCH_3$ (via 2,3 elimination).

(d)   methoxymethane CH_3—O—CH_3

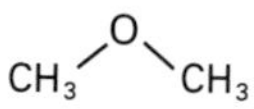

(e) (bromomethyl) benzene

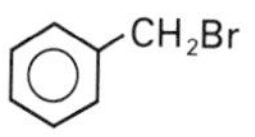

(f) methanal

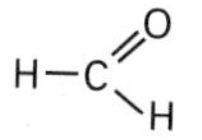

H—C(=O)H and then methanoic acid H—C(=O)OH

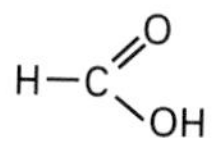

(g) phenylethanone

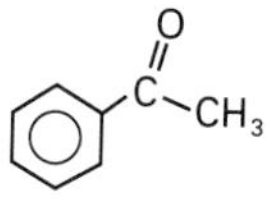

(h) triiodomethane (iodoform), CHI_3 and sodium pentanoate

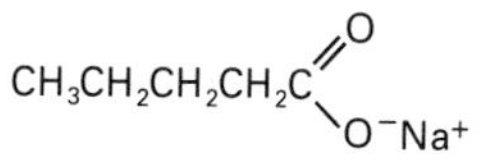

$CH_3CH_2CH_2CH_2C(=O)O^-Na^+$

3 (a) reflux with propanoyl chloride $C_2H_5C(=O)Cl$

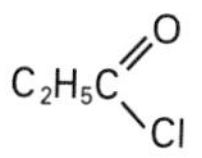

and dil.NaOH(aq) as a catalyst (section 38.5.2).
(b) reflux at 140 °C with conc. H_2SO_4(l); alcohol in excess.
(c) reflux with *either* (i) $P_{(red)}$ + I_2(s) *or* (ii) NaI, conc. H_3PO_4(l).
(d) boiling $K_2Cr_2O_7$/dil.H_2SO_4(aq) *or* $KMnO_4$/dil.H_2SO_4(aq); distil off the aldehyde as it forms (figure 38.7).
(e)

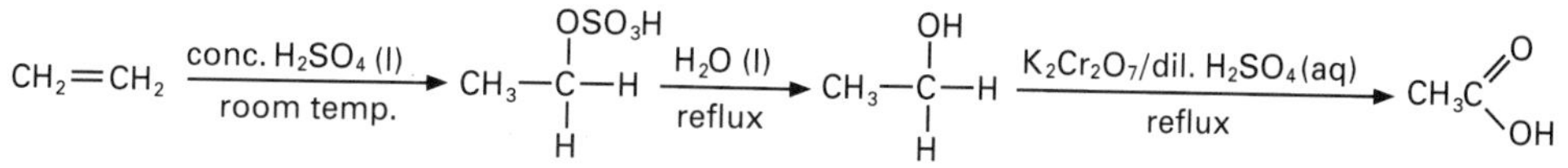

$CH_2=CH_2 \xrightarrow[\text{room temp.}]{\text{conc. }H_2SO_4 \text{ (l)}} CH_3-\underset{H}{\overset{OSO_3H}{C}}-H \xrightarrow[\text{reflux}]{H_2O \text{ (l)}} CH_3-\underset{H}{\overset{OH}{C}}-H \xrightarrow[\text{reflux}]{K_2Cr_2O_7/\text{dil. }H_2SO_4\text{(aq)}} CH_3C(=O)OH$

(f) $C_2H_5OH \xrightarrow[\text{or HI }in situ]{P_{(red)}/I_2 \text{ reflux}} C_2H_5I \xrightarrow[\text{reflux}]{KCN/\text{ethanol}} C_2H_5CN \xrightarrow[\text{reflux.}]{\text{dil.}H_2SO_4\text{(aq)}} C_2H_5COOH$

(g) 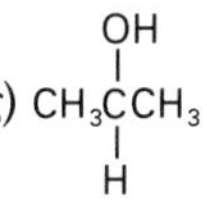 $CH_3\underset{H}{\overset{OH}{C}}CH_3 \xrightarrow[\text{reflux at 170 °C}]{\text{conc.}H_2SO_4 \text{ (l) in excess}} CH_2=CHCH_3 \xrightarrow[\text{room temp.}]{Br_2 \text{ in }CCl_4\text{(l)}} CH_2BrCHBrCH_3$

(h) $CH_3CH=CH_2 \xrightarrow{\text{HBr(g), warm}} CH_3CHBrCH_3$

dil.NaOH(aq) reflux

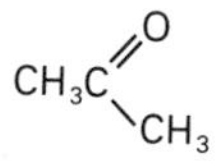

$CH_3C(=O)CH_3 \xleftarrow[\text{reflux}]{K_2Cr_2O_7/\text{dil.}H_2SO_4\text{(aq)}} CH_3CHOHCH_3$

4 (a) $CH_3CH_2CH_2CH_2OH$ (1°) $\xrightarrow[\text{test}]{\text{iodoform}}$ -ve $\xrightarrow[\text{reflux for five minutes}]{K_2Cr_2O_7/\text{dil.}H_2SO_4\text{(aq)}}$ butanoic acid formed colour change orange → green

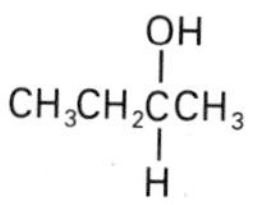

$CH_3CH_2\underset{H}{\overset{OH}{C}}CH_3$ (2°) $\xrightarrow[\text{test}]{\text{iodoform}}$ +ve ∴ identified

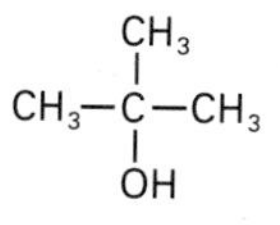

$CH_3-\underset{OH}{\overset{CH_3}{C}}-CH_3$ (3°) $\xrightarrow[\text{test}]{\text{iodoform}}$ -ve $\xrightarrow[\text{propan-1-ol}]{\text{as above for}}$ no reaction, no colour change

(b)

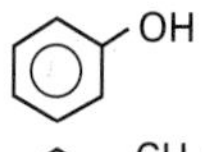

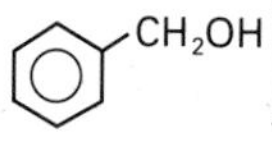

many possible test reactions (see table 38.9). For example neutral iron (III) chloride gives an intense violet colour with phenol, but not with phenylmethanol

Activity 38.5

Compare your answer with table 38.9.

Activity 38.6

1

| ethoxyethane | 1–methoxypropane | 2–methoxypropane |

2 (a) *either* C_2H_5OH(excess) + conc. H_2SO_4(l), reflux at $140\,°C$ *or* ethanolic $C_2H_5O^-Na^+$ + C_2H_5I(l), reflux

(b) ethanolic $C_2H_5O^-Na^+$ + $CH_3CH_2CH_2I$(l), reflux

(c) ethanolic $CH_3O^-Na^+$ + $CH_3CH_2\overset{|}{\underset{|}{C}}CH_3$ (l) reflux

(d) 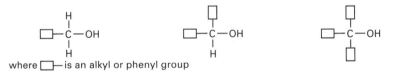 + C_2H_5I(l), reflux

3 **Physical test:** boiling point determination. Unlike phenylmethanol, phenoxymethane has no hydrogen bonds so it will distil at a lower temperature.
Chemical test: Since ethers are very unreactive, any characteristic reaction of an alcohol (e.g. with sodium) can be used.

38.14 Summary and revision plan

1 Alcohols may be thought of as alkanes, alkenes or alkynes in which at least one hydrogen atom has been replace by a hydroxy ($-OH$) group. To name them, change the final **e** of the hydrocarbon name to **ol**. Where structural isomers are possible, the position of each $-OH$ group must be stated.

2 Alcohols are described as being **primary (1°)**, **secondary (2°)** or **tertiary (3°)**:

where ☐— is an alkyl or phenyl group

3 Phenols are compounds which have at least one $-OH$ group *directly bound* to a benzene ring. (Remember that phenylmethanol, ⬡-CH₂OH, is not a phenol but an aromatic alcohol.)

4 Saturated alcohols form a **homologous series** of general formula $C_nH_{2n+1}OH$.

5 There is strong intermolecular **hydrogen bonding** in alcohols. Thus, (i) boiling points of the alcohols $>>$ boiling points of alkanes of comparable M_r and (ii) the lower alcohols are extremely soluble in water. The solubility in water decreases rapidly as the non-polar hydrocarbon chain gets longer. The lower alcohols are valuable solvents.

6 Most phenols are colourless, low melting point, solids. They are only slightly soluble in cold water.

7 Many alcohols are manufactured from petroleum. Some ethanol is obtained from the **fermentation** of glucose. In the laboratory, alcohols may be prepared from alkenes or halogenoalkanes, (section 38.3).

Table 38.9 *Important reactions of alcohol and phenols*

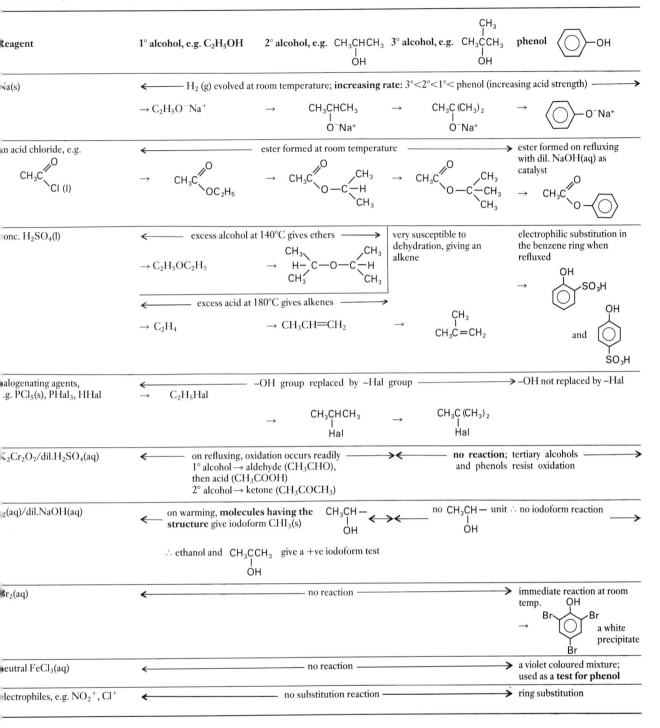

8 Most phenol is made from petroleum (section 38.3). Phenol can be prepared in the laboratory from sulphonic acids (section 36.5.2) or diazonium salts (section 41.9).

9 There are four main types of reactions of alcohols and phenols: (i) **as acids**, (ii) **as nucleophiles** (iii) **oxidation reactions** and (iv) reactions of the **hydrocarbon skeleton**. Some important reactions are summarised in table 38.9. This shows how the reactivity of the −OH group is affected by its molecular location in 1°, 2° and 3° alcohols and phenols.

10   Oxoacids dissociate in aqueous solution:

$$XO\text{—}H(aq) + H_2O(l) \rightleftharpoons H_3O^+(aq) + XO^-(aq)$$

The oxoacids become stronger, that is, dissociate to a greater extent, as the X group becomes more able to draw the electron cloud towards itself (section 38.5.1). Thus, we observe the pattern:

—**alcohols—water—phenols—carboxylic acids → increasing acid strength**

11   Phenols are weaker nucleophiles than alcohols (see figure 38.5).

12   Primary alcohols are readily oxidised to aldehydes and then to carboxylic acids. (Note: figure 38.7.) Secondary alcohols are oxidised to ketones. Tertiary alcohols will only be oxidised by very strong oxidising agents; a C—C bond is broken and a mixture of carboxylic acids is produced. We can distinguish between 1°, 2° and 3° alcohols by analysing their oxidation products.

13   All alcohols having the $-CH(OH)CH_3$ group will give a **positive iodoform test**.

14   The hydroxy group in a phenol makes the benzene ring more susceptible to electrophilic attack.

15   A simple chemical test for phenol: reaction with neutral $FeCl_3(aq)$ gives a violet coloured product.

16   **Ethers** have the general formula ▢–O–▢ where ▢– is a hydrocarbon chain benzene ring. They are named as alkoxy– or phenoxy– derivatives of the longest hydrocarbon chain or benzene ring.

17   Ethers may be prepared from (i) alcohols and (ii) iodoalkanes (section 38.12).

18   Although esters and alcohols are **functional group isomers**, only the alcohols display hydrogen bonding. Thus, the alcohol has a much higher boiling point than its isomeric ether.

19   Ethers are fairly unreactive compounds and they are useful solvents for non-polar substances.

20   Important new reagents used in this chapter are listed in table 38.10.

Table 38.10   *Important reagents used in this chapter.*

Reagent	conditions	what it does to a hydroxy compound
an acid chloride, ▢–C(=O)Cl	room temp., (alcohol); reflux with dil. NaOH(aq), (phenol)	converts alcohol or phenol into an **ester**
conc. $H_2SO_4(l)$ (a dehydrating agent)	(i) excess alcohol, 140°C (ii) excess acid, 180°C	(i) converts 1°, 2° alcohol → **ether** (ii) converts 1°, 2°, 3° alcohol → **alkene**
PCl_5 .... $P_{(red)} + Br_2$, $P_{(red)} + I_2$	room temp. reflux	converts alcohol → **halogen compound** i.e. $(-OH) \rightarrow (-Hal)$
$K_2Cr_2O_7/dil.H_2SO_4(aq)$ *or* $KMnO_4/dil.\ H_2SO_4(aq)$	reflux	oxidises 1° alcohol → **aldehyde** → **carboxylic acid** oxidises 2° alcohol → **ketone**
$I_2(aq)/dil.NaOH(aq)$ (iodoform test)	warm	**iodoform, CHI₃**, is formed if the alcohol has this group: CH_3-CH- with OH below
neutral $FeCl_3(aq)$	room temp.	a test for **phenol**: if present, the mixture turns a violet colour
lithium tetrahydridoaluminate $LiAlH_4$ in ethoxyethane	reflux	reduces: **carboxylic acids → 1° alcohols** **aldehydes → 1° alcohols** **ketones → 2° alcohols**

How can we ensure that a primary alcohol is oxidized to an aldehyde rather than on to the carboxylic acid?

Aldehydes and Ketones

Contents

Slug-bait and sweets are both made from compounds containing the carbonyl group, C=O

At first glance, slug-bait, squash courts and sweets don't seem to have much in common! However, they can all be made from compounds which contain the **carbonyl** functional group:

(electronegativities, C = 2.5, O = 3.5)

Since oxygen is much more electronegative than carbon, the carbonyl bond is strongly polarised and, as we shall see, this has a big effect on the properties of these compounds.

39.1 Types of carbonyl compound

Broadly speaking, there are two main types of carbonyl compound:

aldehydes and ketones

carboxylic acids and their derivatives, e.g.

aldehydes   ketones   carboxylic acids   acid amides   acid esters

(Here □— is a hydrocarbon skeleton and ●— is a hydrocarbon skeleton or hydrogen atom.)

In this chapter, and the next, we shall see how the chemical properties of the carbonyl group are affected by its different molecular locations.

39.2 Naming aldehydes and ketones

Aliphatic aldehydes and ketones are named as derivatives of the hydrocarbon with the same carbon 'skeleton'. Thus, the final e of an alkane name is replaced by **al** or **one** for an **al**dehyde or a ket**one**, respectively. For example:

ethanal
(acetaldehyde)   butanal   propanone
(acetone)   pentan–2–one   pentan–3–one

Whilst the carbonyl group in an aldehyde is always at the end of the chain, *ketones can exist as positional isomers*. So, when naming a ketone, you may need to number the 'carbonyl' carbon. (Note: some historical names are given in the brackets.)

In aromatic aldehydes and ketones, the carbonyl group is bonded to a benzene ring, e.g.

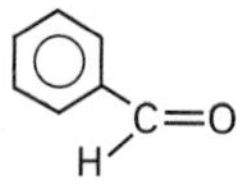

benzenecarbaldehyde
(benzaldehyde–often used)

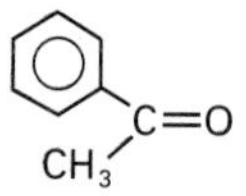

phenylethanone
(acetophenone)

Activity 39.1

1   Name the following carbonyl compounds:

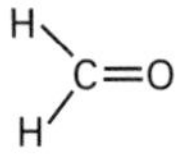

2   Write down the structural formulae for the following compounds:
   (a) cyclohexanone   (b) 3-methylbutanal
   (c) 2,2-dimethylpropanal   (d) 3-phenylbutan-2-one
   (e) phenylpropanone   (f) 4-phenylpentanal

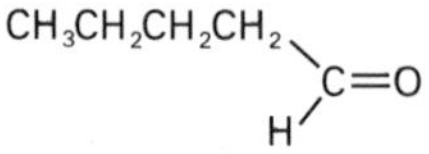

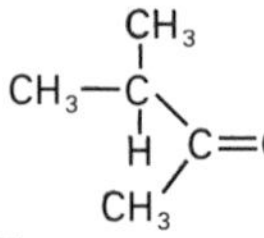

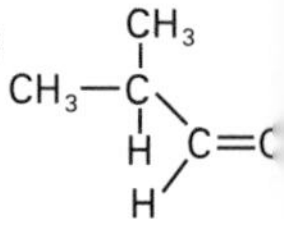

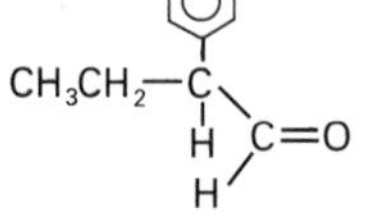

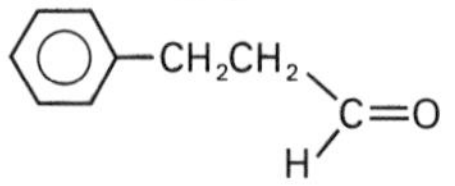

3   Of the compounds in 1 and 2, which are structural isomers?

39.3 Physical properties

Table 39.1 *Some properties of aldehydes and ketones*

Some properties of aldehydes and ketones are given in table 39.1.

Name	formula	state (at 25 °C)	melting point/°C	boiling point/°C	density /g cm^{-3}	$\Delta H_c^{\ominus}$ /kJ mol^{-1}
methanal	HCHO	gas	− 92	− 19	0.81 (L)	− 550
ethanal	CH$_3$CHO	gas	−123	21	0.78 (L)	−1167
propanal	CH$_3$CH$_2$CHO	liquid	− 80	48	0.80	−1817
butanal	CH$_3$CH$_2$CH$_2$CHO	liquid	− 96	72	0.80	−2497
2-methylpropanal	(CH$_3$)$_2$CHCHO	liquid	− 65	64	0.79	−2497
benzaldehyde	C$_6$H$_5$CHO	liquid	− 26	178	1.05	−3520
propanone	CH$_3$COCH$_3$	liquid	− 95	56	0.78	−1821
butanone	CH$_3$CH$_2$COCH$_3$	liquid	− 87	80	0.80	−2438
pentan-2-one	CH$_3$CH$_2$CH$_2$COCH$_3$	liquid	− 39	102	0.81	−3078
phenylethanone	C$_6$H$_5$COCH$_3$	liquid	− 80	198	1.03	−4137

(L) means density in the liquid state

Can you see any patterns in these values?

Both aldehydes and ketones form **homologous series** which have the same general formula $C_nH_{2n}O$. For example, C_4H_8O could be

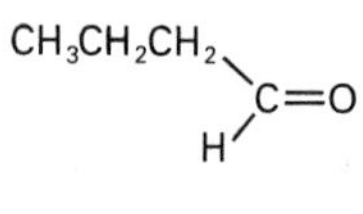

butanal 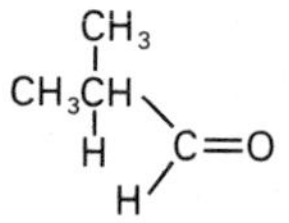   2–methylpropanal   or 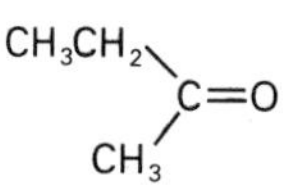   butanone

Once again, there is a steady rise in boiling points and $\Delta H_c^{\ominus}$ values with increasing carbon chain length (figure 39.1). These graphs are typical of those given by compounds which form a homologous series.

When comparing compounds of similar molecular mass, we find that:

alkanes   aldehydes/ketones   alcohols

boiling points increase →

Figure 39.1 *Steady increases in (a) the boiling points and (b) the $\Delta H_c^{\ominus}$ values of some straight-chain aldehydes (○) and ketones (×) as the hydrocarbon chain gets longer. What does this suggest?*

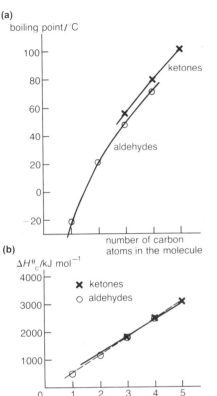

(a)

(b)

e.g. propane ($M_r = 44$)
b.p. $-42\,°C$
and pentane ($M_r = 72$)
b.p. $36\,°C$

ethanal ($M_r = 44$)
b.p. $20.5\,°C$
butan-2-one ($M_r = 72$)
b.p. $80\,°C$

ethanol ($M_r = 46$)
b.p. $78.5\,°C$
butan-1-ol ($M_r = 74$)
b.p. $118\,°C$

This pattern reflects the increasing strength of the intermolecular attractions:

strength of the intermolecular attractions increases →

ALKANES	ALDEHYDES or KETONES	ALCOHOLS
molecules experience only *van der Waals' forces* (i.e. weak intermolecular forces resulting from the attraction between temporary dipoles)	molecules experience *van der Waals' forces plus permanent dipole-dipole attractions, i.e.*	molecules experience *van der Waals' forces plus strong permanent dipole–dipole attractions i.e. hydrogen bonds*

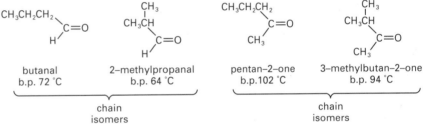

$\wedge\!\wedge\!\wedge$ = a dipole–dipole attraction

$\mid\mid\mid\mid\mid$ = hydrogen bonds

Since their molecules make closer contact, straight-chain aldehydes and ketones possess stronger intermolecular forces, and hence higher boiling points, than their branched-chain isomers, e.g.

butanal
b.p. 72 °C

2–methylpropanal
b.p. 64 °C

chain isomers

pentan–2–one
b.p.102 °C

3–methylbutan–2–one
b.p. 94 °C

chain isomers

Due to their polarity, aldehydes and ketones of low molecular mass are very soluble in water. They are also able to dissolve a wide range of polar and non-polar solutes. Indeed, *propanone is an important industrial solvent*. Of course, as the hydrocarbon skeleton gets larger, the polar C=O group has less effect on the physical properties of the compound. Thus, benzaldehyde, C_6H_5CHO is almost insoluble in water.

Aldehydes and ketones are strongly smelling compounds. The pungent smell of formalin (a 40% aqueous solution of methanal) for example, will be well known to students who work with preserved biological specimens. On the other hand, in small amounts benzaldehyde has a pleasant smell of almonds and these nuts actually contain a benzaldehyde derivative.

39.4 Making aldehydes and ketones

Manufacture

Generally speaking, aldehydes and ketones are manufactured by the **catalytic oxidation** of primary or secondary alcohols, respectively, e.g.

$$\text{methanol} + \tfrac{1}{2}O_2(g) \xrightarrow[500\,°C]{\text{catalyst: Ag(s)}} \text{methanal} + H_2O\,(l)$$

methanol

methanal

Formalin, a 40% aqueous solution of methanal, is used to preserve biological specimens. This is a lung

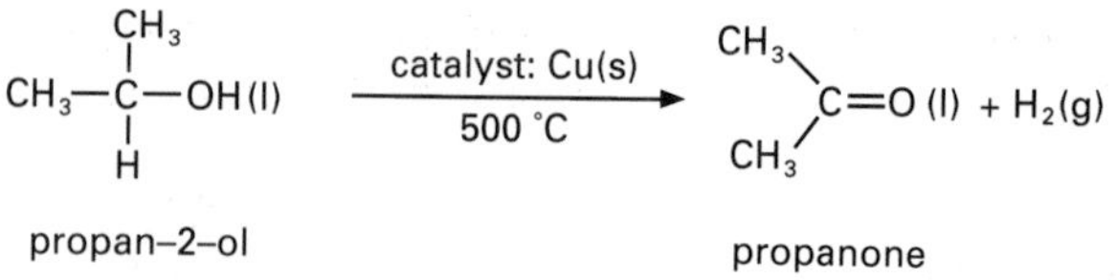

$$CH_3-\underset{\underset{H}{|}}{\overset{\overset{CH_3}{|}}{C}}-OH\,(l) \xrightarrow[500\ °C]{catalyst:\ Cu(s)} \underset{CH_3}{\overset{CH_3}{>}}C{=}O\,(l) + H_2(g)$$

propan–2–ol

propanone

Considerable amounts of propanone are obtained as a by-product from the manufacture of phenol (section 38.3).

Laboratory preparation

Aldehydes and ketones are usually prepared by the oxidation of alcohols. As we saw in section 38.7, *primary alcohols give aldehydes and secondary alcohols give ketones.* Usually, we use acidified sodium (or potassium) dichromate as oxidising agent, e.g.

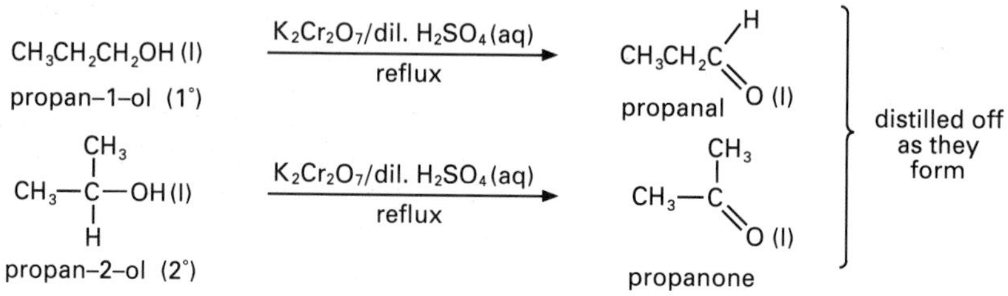

$$CH_3CH_2CH_2OH\,(l) \xrightarrow[reflux]{K_2Cr_2O_7/dil.\ H_2SO_4(aq)} CH_3CH_2C\overset{\overset{H}{\diagup}}{\underset{\diagdown}{O}}\,(l)$$

propan–1–ol (1°)   propanal

$$CH_3-\underset{\underset{H}{|}}{\overset{\overset{CH_3}{|}}{C}}-OH\,(l) \xrightarrow[reflux]{K_2Cr_2O_7/dil.\ H_2SO_4(aq)} CH_3-\underset{\diagdown O}{\overset{\overset{CH_3}{|}}{C}}\,(l)$$

propan–2–ol (2°)   propanone

} distilled off as they form

To avoid the problem of further oxidation, *an aldehyde must be distilled off as it forms,* using the apparatus shown in figure 38.7. Although ketones resist oxidation, it is often convenient to use the same apparatus for their preparation.

Benzaldehyde is made from methylbenzene:

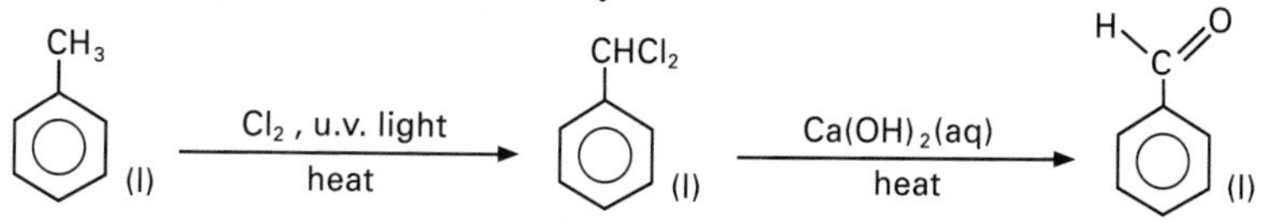

and aromatic ketones are obtained from Friedel–Crafts reactions, e.g.

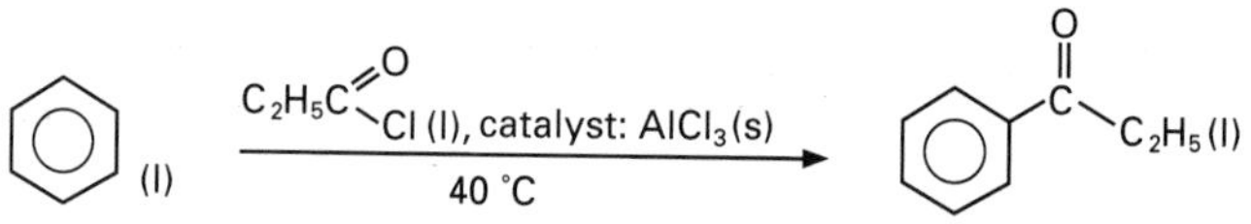

Activity 39.2

Give the names and formulae of the alcohols which can be oxidised to give the following carbonyl compounds:
(a) butanal   (b) 3-methylbutan-2-one   (c) 2-methylpropanal   (d) cyclohexanone
(e) 3-phenylbutanal   (f) benzaldehyde   (g) pentan-2-one   (h) phenylethanone

39.5 Predicting the reactivity of aldehydes and ketones

Firstly, let us look more closely at the electronic structure of the carbonyl group, taking methanal as an example.

The carbon atom forms three **sp² hybrid orbitals**:

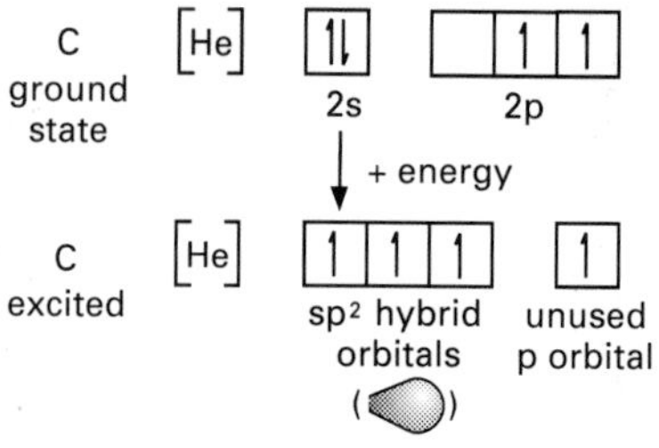

Figure 39.2 *Electronic structure of the C═C bond in ethene*

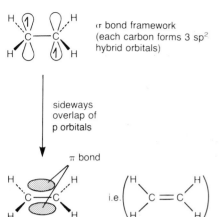

σ bond framework
(each carbon forms 3 sp² hybrid orbitals)

sideways overlap of p orbitals

π bond

i.e.

Two of these orbitals form **σ bonds** with the 1s orbitals of hydrogen. The third sp² hybrid orbital overlaps **end-on** with a 2p orbital on oxygen, giving another σ bond:

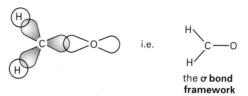

i.e.

the **σ bond framework**

The remaining 2p orbitals on carbon and oxygen overlap **sideways-on** to form a **π bond**:

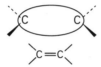

sideways overlap of p orbitals

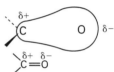

i.e.

π bond

Now, compare the electronic structure of the C═O bond with that of the C═C bond (figure 39.2). At first glance, these bonds appear to be closely related: *both are planar, each consisting of a σ and a π bond*. But does this similarity extend to their chemical properties?

Due to their unsaturated nature, *both C═C and C═O bonds undergo addition reactions*. Generally speaking, though, *they do not react with the same reagents* (table 39.2). This interesting behaviour is explained by the different distributions of the bonding electron clouds:

no permanent dipole, although the π bond is easily polarised, and attacked, by **electrophiles** (e.g. Br^+ or H^+)

a permanent dipole results from the different electonegativities of carbon and oxygen; addition occurs via an initial **nucleophilic** attack (e.g. by CN^- or NH_3)

Table 39.2 *Comparing the addition reactions of the C═O bond in aldehydes/ketones with the C═C bond in alkenes*

Reagent	aldehydes/ketones ($\overset{\delta+}{C}=\overset{\delta-}{O}$)	alkenes (C═C)
KCN/NaOH(aq)		
NaHSO₃(aq)	addition occurs	no addition
NH₃(aq)		
Cl₂, Br₂, I₂ HCl, HBr, HI } (g)	no addition	addition occurs
conc.H₂SO₄(l)		

In aldehydes and ketones, the carbonyl group creates two main centres of reactivity: (i) the *carbonyl bond* itself which will take part in nucleophilic addition reactions (section 39.6); (ii) the *α-hydrogen atoms*, that is, those on the carbon next to the carbonyl group (section 39.7). A third key aspect of this study is the *redox chemistry* of aldehydes and ketones (section 39.8).

39.6 Nucleophilic addition reactions

39.6.1 With hydrogen cyanide

Aliphatic aldehydes and all ketones will add hydrogen cyanide in cold, alkaline solution; the products are **hydroxynitriles,** e.g.

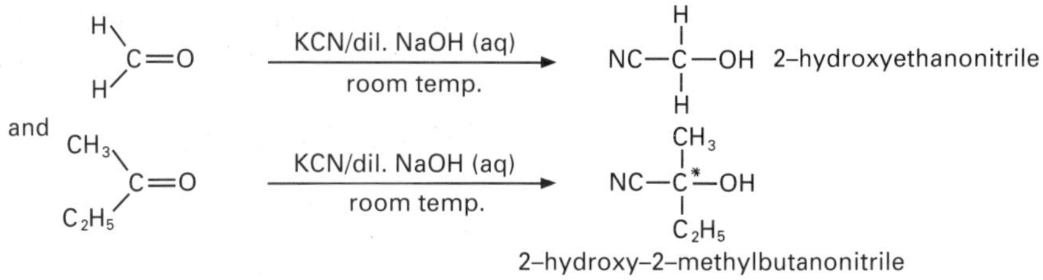

2-hydroxyethanonitrile

2-hydroxy-2-methylbutanonitrile

The reaction is a useful synthetic step because it increases the length of the carbon skeleton. Also, note that some hydroxynitriles will possess an asymmetric carbon atom, C*. When this occurs, the products will form a racemic mixture which, on separation, will give the two optical isomers (section 10.4).

In this reaction, the potassium cyanide hydrolyses, giving hydrogen cyanide:

$$K^+(aq) + CN^-(aq) + H_2O(l) \rightleftharpoons K^+(aq) + HCN(aq) + OH^-(aq)$$

Since hydrogen cyanide is a very weak acid, this equilibrium lies heavily to the *right* hand side. We work in alkaline solution because OH^- ions react with the HCN and the equilibrium is displaced to the *left* (see Le Chatelier's principle, section 14.8). Consequently, the concentration of free CN^- ions is increased and so is the rate of reaction.

Kinetics studies show that the reaction mechanism is quite straightforward.

In the *rate-determining step*, electron cloud from the cyanide ion is used to form a dative covalent bond with the 'carbonyl' carbon. At the same time, the π bond weakens and then breaks *heterolytically* with oxygen taking both bonding electrons:

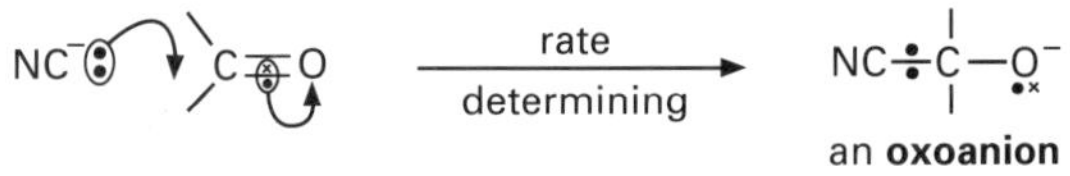

an **oxoanion**

This oxoanion rapidly accepts a proton from an H_3O^+ ion, thereby forming the hydroxynitrile:

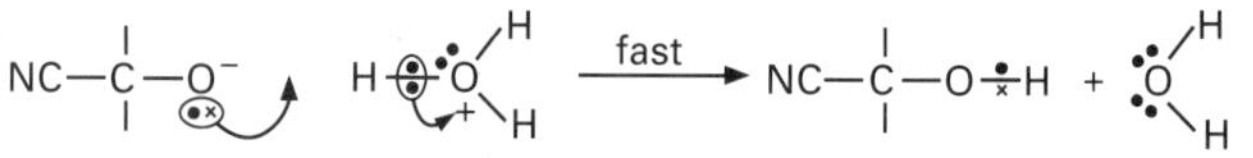

39.6.2 With sodium hydrogensulphite

Aldehydes and methylketones will slowly form addition compounds when shaken with a cold saturated solution of sodium hydrogensulphite, e.g.

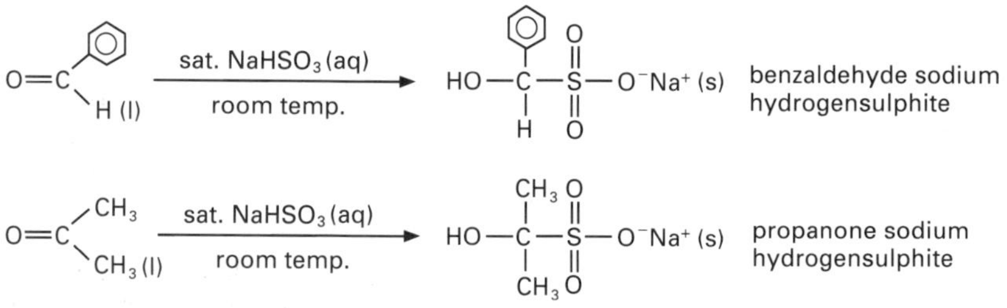

benzaldehyde sodium hydrogensulphite

propanone sodium hydrogensulphite

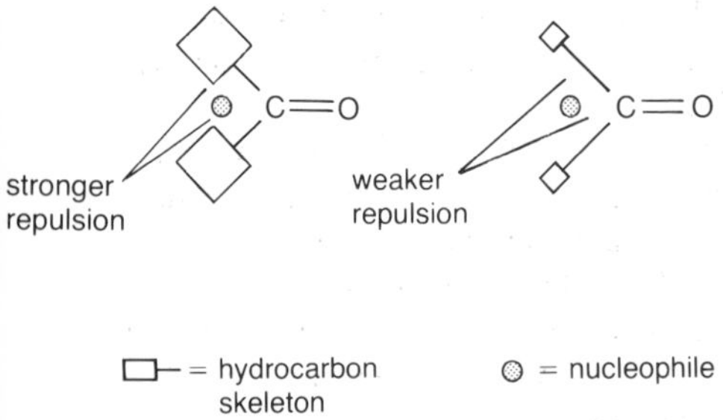

The mechanism resembles that in section 39.6.1, the reaction proceeding mainly via nucleophilic attack of SO_3^{2-} ions. Since SO_3^{2-} ions are bulky nucleophiles, the reaction takes place slowly. Not surprisingly, their movement towards the carbonyl carbon is *hindered* by the presence of large hydrocarbon skeletons (figure 39.3). Thus, *only aldehydes and methylketones react with sodium hydrogensulphite*.

The addition of sodium hydrogensulphite across a carbonyl bond may be used to introduce a water soluble group into the molecule. For example, by forming the hydrogensulphite, an aldehyde or methylketone can be separated from non-water

Figure 39.3 *Large hydrocarbon skeletons can hinder the nucleophile's attack on the C = O bond; this effect is an example of steric hindrance*

stronger repulsion

weaker repulsion

□— = hydrocarbon skeleton   ⊚ = nucleophile

soluble impurities. The free carbonyl compound is then recovered by treating the hydrogensulphite with dilute acid or alkali.

39.6.3 With water

In aqueous solution, the lower aldehydes and ketones exist to a very small extent as diols, e.g.

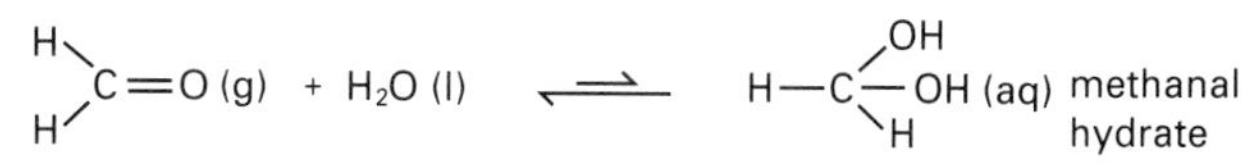

These diols are unstable and cannot be isolated from solution. However, **trichloroethanal (chloral)** and water form a stable solid addition compound:

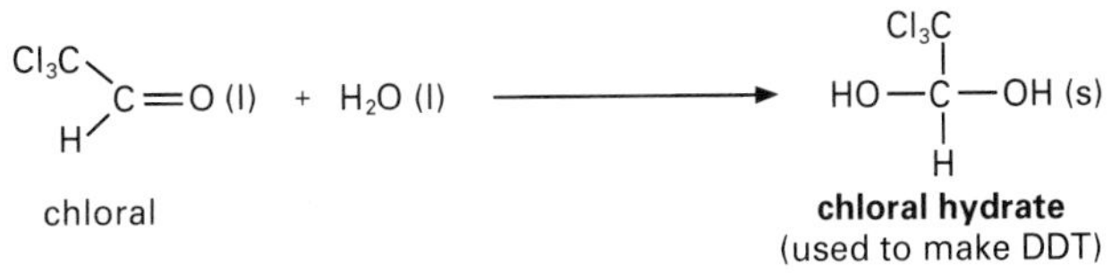

chloral   **chloral hydrate**
                                          (used to make DDT)

In both of the above reactions, an addition product is formed via the nucleophilic attack of H_2O on the electron-poor 'carbonyl' carbon. Since a C=C bond is not attacked by water, this reaction further illustrates *the different natures of the C=O and C=C bonds* (section 39.5).

39.6.4 Addition–elimination reactions

Although aliphatic aldehydes (except methanal) will add on ammonia,

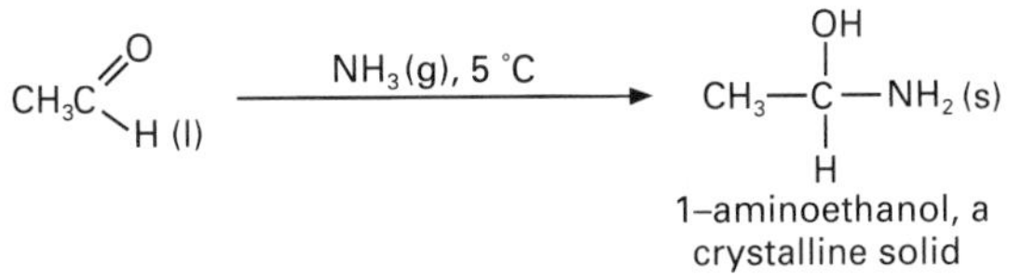

1-aminoethanol, a
crystalline solid

these compounds are readily decomposed (e.g. by water). Indeed 'ketone–ammonia' addition compounds are too unstable to exist. However, similar reactions using molecules of general formula : **NH₂X** produce rather different results.

Firstly, let us consider the reactions of aldehydes and ketones with **hydroxylamine, : NH₂OH**. These produce fairly stable crystalline solids, called **oximes**, e.g.

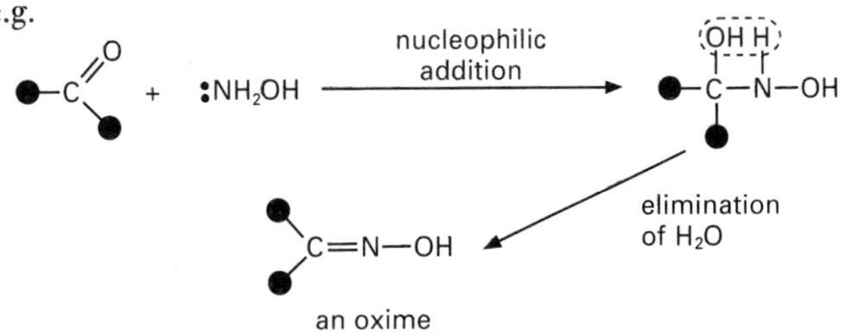

an oxime

In this type of reaction, a molecule of water is **eliminated** from the initial **addition** product. Hence, it is termed an **addition–elimination** or **condensation** reaction.

Some other ':NH₂X' molecules which give addition–elimination reactions with aldehydes and ketones are given in table 39.3.

Apart from the hydrazones, which are liquids, the other condensation products are *crystalline solids*. When purified, *these have sharp melting points which can be used to identify the parent carbonyl compound*. Suppose, for example, you were asked to distinguish between samples of pentanal (b.p. 104 °C) and pentan-2-one (b.p. 102 °C). Clearly, a boiling point determination would be inconclusive. Thus, a 2,4-dinitrophenylhydrazone is prepared from each sample, purified and its melting point taken (section 32.8). A firm identification is possible because:

Table 39.3 *Some reagents which give addition–elimination reactions with aldehydes and ketones (●— is H or a hydrocarbon skeleton)*

pentanal 2,4-dinitrophenylhydrazone melts at 98 °C but pentan-2-one 2,4-dinitrophenylhydrazone melts at 141 °C.

Reagent	product
hydroxylamine, :NH$_2$OH (+ conc.NaOH(aq) catalyst, warm gently)	an oxime 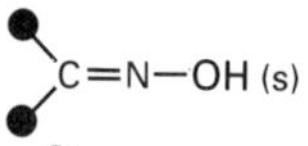 C=N—OH (s)
hydrazine, :NH$_2$NH$_2$ (+ conc.NaOH(aq) catalyst, warm gently)	a hydrazone 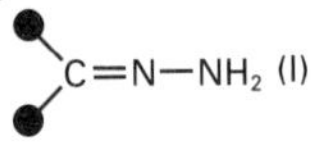 C=N—NH$_2$ (l)
2,4-dinitrophenylhydrazine 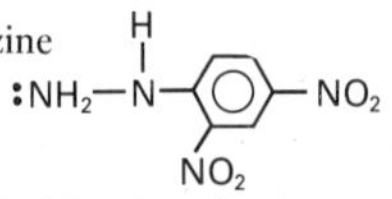 :NH$_2$—N(H)—⟨ring⟩—NO$_2$ / NO$_2$ (dissolved in dil.H$_2$SO$_4$(aq)/methanol, room temperature)	a 2,4-dinitrophenylhydrazone 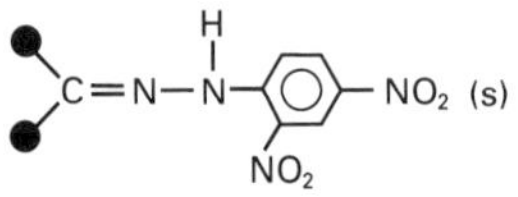 C=N—N(H)—⟨ring⟩—NO$_2$ (s) / NO$_2$

Activity 39.3

1 Give the name and structural formula of the organic product formed in each of the following reactions:
(a) ethanal + KCN/OH$^-$(aq)
(b) pentan-2-one + KCN/OH$^-$(aq)
(c) methanal + NaHSO$_3$(aq)
(d) ethanal + NH$_2$OH(l)
(e) phenylethanone + 2,4-dinitrophenylhydrazine.
Which reactions will yield a racemic mixture?

2 Give the reagents and reaction conditions needed for the following conversions:
(a) propanal → 2-hydroxybutanonitrile
(b) butan-2-one → butan-2-one sodium hydrogensulphite

(c) 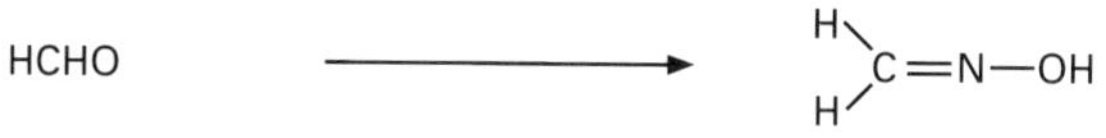   HCHO ⟶ $\begin{smallmatrix}H\\H\end{smallmatrix}$C=N—OH

(d)  ⟨ring⟩—CHCl$_2$ $\xrightarrow{\text{(2 steps)}}$ ⟨ring⟩—C(H)=N—NH—⟨ring⟩(NO$_2$)—NO$_2$

(e) 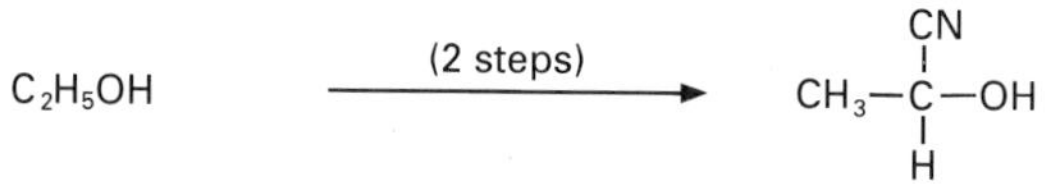   C$_2$H$_5$OH $\xrightarrow{\text{(2 steps)}}$ CH$_3$—C(CN)(OH)—H

(f) 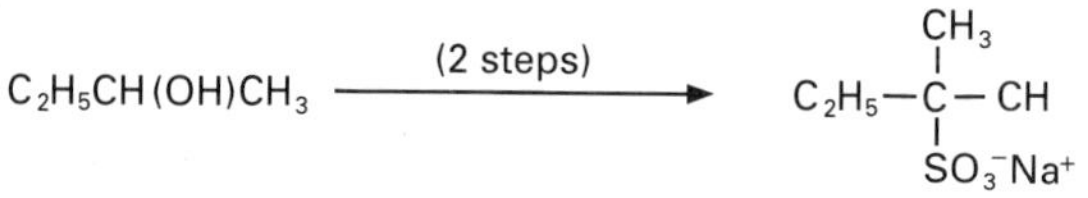   C$_2$H$_5$CH(OH)CH$_3$ $\xrightarrow{\text{(2 steps)}}$ C$_2$H$_5$—C(CH$_3$)—CH / SO$_3^-$Na$^+$

3 Of the following carbonyl compounds:
butanal, benzaldehyde, pentan-3-one, phenylethanone
benzophenone (⟨O⟩—C(=O)—⟨O⟩) , methanal,

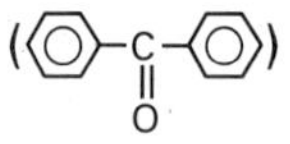

which will *not* react with NaHSO$_3$(aq)? Explain why.

4 Describe how you would distinguish chemically between butanal and 2-methylpropanal.

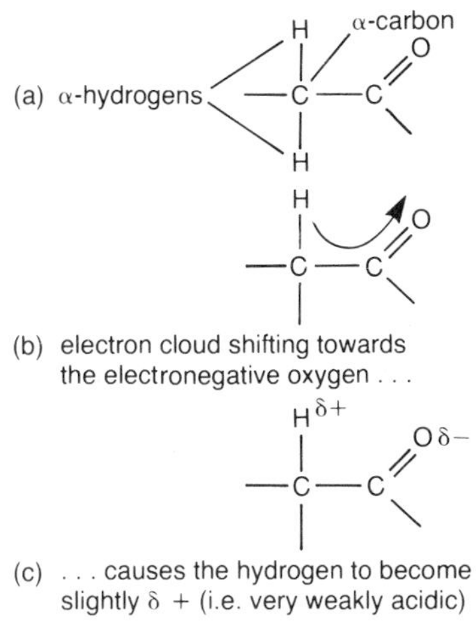

39.7 Reactions of the α-hydrogen

A carbon atom which is attached to the carbonyl group is termed an **α-carbon** (figure 39.4a). Each hydrogen atom on the α-carbon is termed an **α-hydrogen**. Since the carbonyl group is strongly polarised it can withdraw electron density from the α-carbon and its C—H bonds (figure 39.4b). Hence, each αC—H bond becomes slightly polarised (figure 39.5c). Overall, this weakens the αC—H bond, *making the electron-poor hydrogen more easily removed by a base.*

Two important types of reaction result from the presence of an α-hydrogen: (i) dimerisation/polymerisation and (ii) halogenation.

39.7.1 Dimerisation and polymerisation

Aldehydes which possess α-hydrogens readily form dimers and polymers. For example, ethanal will dimerise in *dilute* sodium hydroxide solution, forming 3-hydroxybutanal (an **aldol**):

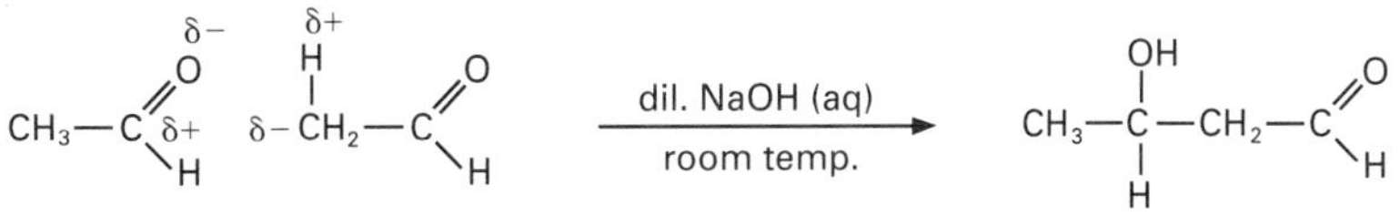

ethanal molecules → 3-hydroxybutanal

dil. NaOH (aq)
room temp.

Notice that the aldol reaction provides a useful method of creating a new C—C bond. When ethanal is heated with *concentrated* alkali, a brown resinous polymer is formed:

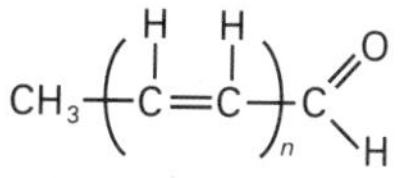

where *n* depends on the reaction conditions

Under similar conditions, ketones will dimerise, *but they will not form polymers,* e.g.

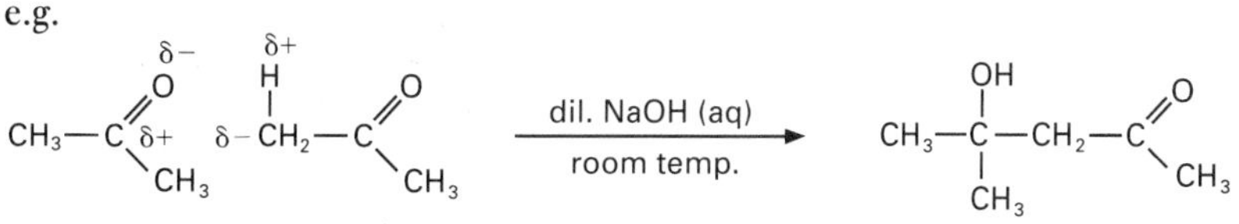

propanone molecules → 4-hydroxy-4-methylpentan-2-one

dil. NaOH (aq)
room temp.

Looking carefully at the products from the above reactions, you will notice that each results from the nucleophilic addition of the carbonyl compound to itself. The nucleophile is a **carbanion** which is formed when an OH⁻ ion removes the α-hydrogen, e.g.

a carbanion (i.e. an ion with negative charge on carbon)

Aldehydes can also form polymers in neutral and acidic solutions but these are not 'α-hydrogen' reactions (table 39.4).

39.7.2 Halogenation

In aldehydes and ketones, one or more α-hydrogen can be easily replaced by halogen atoms. Chlorine, for example, will react with ethanal at room temperature to form trichloroethanal (chloral):

$$CH_3CHO(l) \xrightarrow[\text{room temp.}]{Cl_2(g)} CCl_3CHO(l)$$
chloral

Chloral is used to make insecticides, such as DDT.

Figure 39.4 *Reactivity of the α-hydrogen(s) in aldehydes and ketones*

(a) α-hydrogens

(b) electron cloud shifting towards the electronegative oxygen . . .

(c) . . . causes the hydrogen to become slightly δ + (i.e. very weakly acidic)

Table 39.4 *Some polymers formed by ethanal in acidic solution*

Polymer	formed by	use
paraldehyde liquid, b.p. 128°C 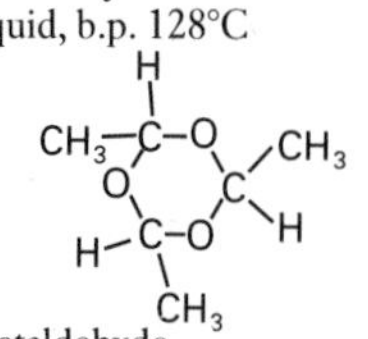	adding conc.H_2SO_4 to ethanal at room temp.	way of storing ethanal in the laboratory: paraldehyde $\downarrow$ dil.H_2SO_4(aq) ethanal (b.p. 21°C)
metaldehyde 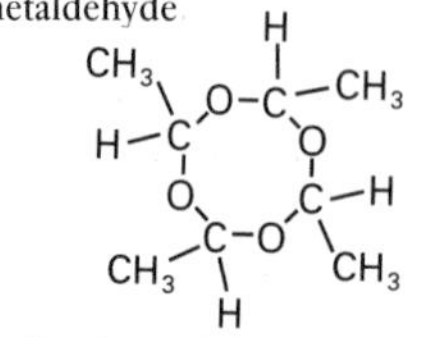 a colourless solid	adding conc.H_2SO_4 to ethanal at 0°C	fuel and as a slug-killer

Similar reactions with bromine and iodine are carried out in the presence of a dilute acid *or* base catalyst, e.g.

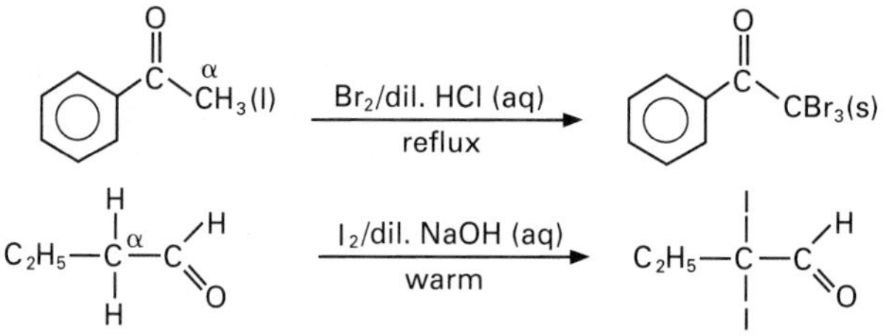

Of particular interest is the base catalysed halogenation of ethanal and methylketones. These compounds, all of which contain the $CH_3C{=}O$ structure, give trihalogenated products which are then decomposed by the excess base:

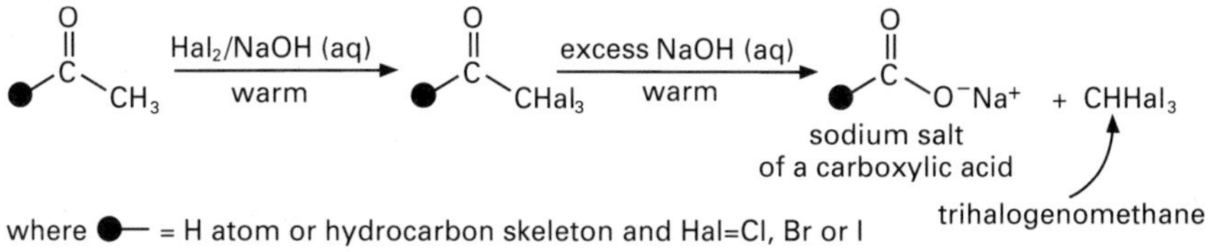

where ●— = H atom or hydrocarbon skeleton and Hal=Cl, Br or I

Since triiodomethane (iodoform) is a yellow solid which is insoluble in aqueous solution, it can easily be recognised as a reaction product. Thus, we often use the reagent I_2/dil.NaOH(aq) to test for a $CH_3{-}C{=}O$ group, and this is known as the **iodoform test**. Alcohols containing the $CH_3{-}CH(OH){-}$ group are oxidised to $CH_3{-}C{=}O$ by I_2/dil.NaOH(aq). Thus, they will also give a positive iodoform test.

Activity 39.4

1 Give the formulae of the organic products formed when (a) propanal and (b) propanone react with (i) dil.NaOH(aq), (ii) conc.NaOH(aq), (iii) equimolar I_2/dil.HCl(aq) and (iv) I_2/dil.NaOH(aq).

2 By drawing the structures of the following compounds, state which will give a positive iodoform test:
(a) benzaldehyde   (b) propanal   (c) ethanol   (d) butanone
(e) 2-methylpropan-2-ol   (f) phenylethanone   (g) propan-2-ol.

39.8 Redox chemistry of the aldehydes and ketones

39.8.1 Oxidation

Aldehydes are easily oxidised to carboxylic acids, even by mild oxidising agents, e.g.

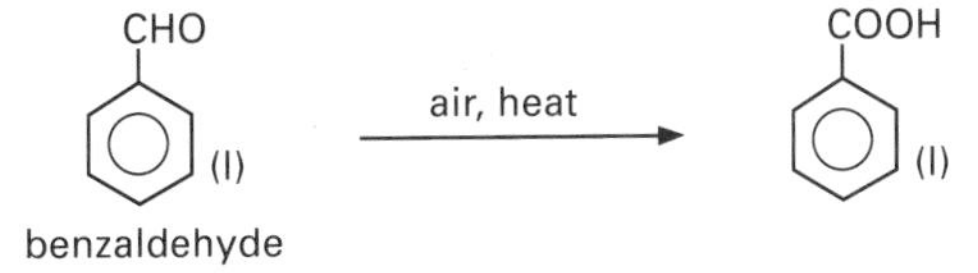

benzaldehyde

On the other hand, *ketones resist oxidation*, and will only react after prolonged treatment with a powerful oxidising agent. A mixture of carboxylic acids is usually formed, e.g.

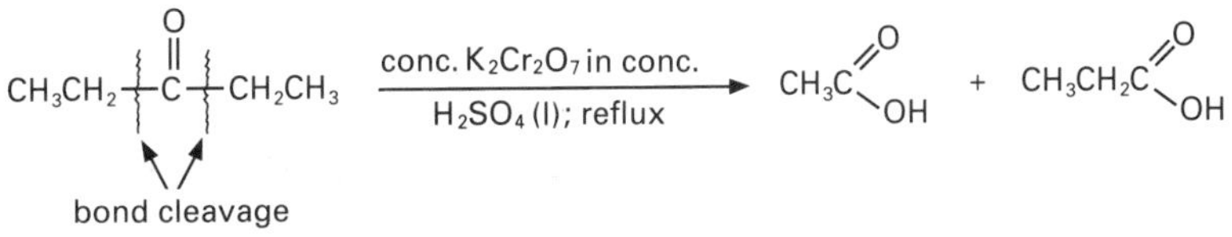

In this reaction, the C—C bond on each side of the carbonyl group is broken.

This difference in reactivity towards oxidising agents enables us to distinguish between an aldehyde and a ketone. *On testing each sample with a mild oxidising agent, the aldehyde, but not the ketone, will react.* Two mild oxidising agents are commonly used:

▶ **Tollen's reagent**
This is an aqueous solution of the complex **diamminesilver(I) ion, $Ag(NH_3)_2^+(aq)$**. It is made by dissolving silver nitrate in aqueous ammonia. On reacting with an aldehyde, the complex ion is reduced to silver metal and this often appears as a **silver 'mirror'** on the sides of the test-tube, e.g.

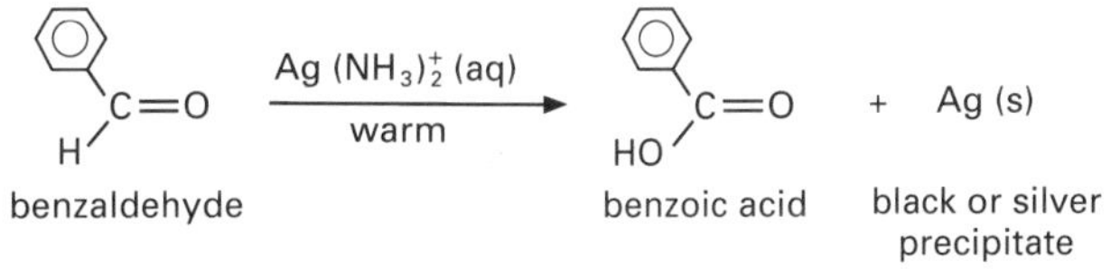

benzaldehyde   benzoic acid   black or silver precipitate

Of course, with ketones there will be *no* reaction.

▶ **Fehling's solution**
This is a clear blue solution which contains a **complex ion of copper(II)**. Most aldehydes reduce it to give a red-brown precipitate of **copper(I) oxide**, e.g.

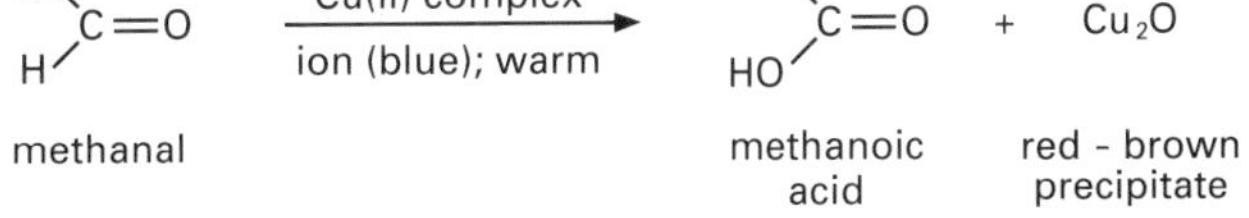

methanal   methanoic   red - brown
acid   precipitate

As expected, Fehling's solution is too mild an oxidising agent to react with ketones.

39.8.2 Reduction

Aldehydes and ketones are easily reduced to primary and secondary alcohols, respectively, e.g.

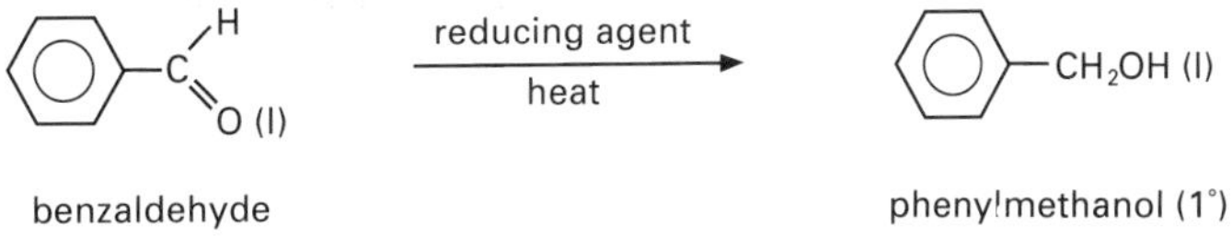

benzaldehyde   phenylmethanol (1°)

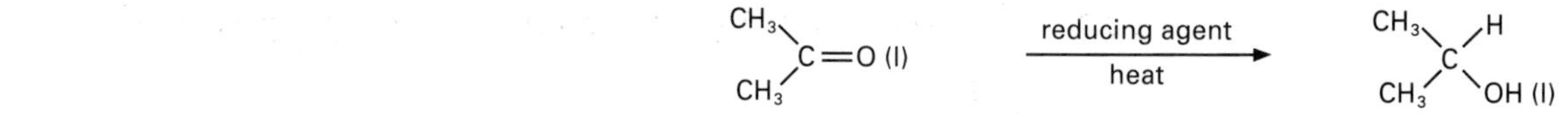

propanone   propan–2–ol (2°)

Various reducing agents can be used, such as lithium tetrahydridoaluminate (LiAlH₄) in ethoxyethane, sodium tetrahydridoborate (NaBH₄) in ethanol or zinc in dilute ethanoic acid.

It is worth noting here that *LiAlH₄ and NaBH₄ will reduce a C=O bond but not a C=C bond*. This is not really surprising because these reducing agents add H₂ to the C=O bond by acting as *nucleophiles* (via the AlH₄⁻ and BH₄⁻ ions). Since a C=C bond is not attacked by nucleophiles (section 39.5), it cannot be reduced by LiAlH₄ or NaBH₄. Once again, *we have observed a difference in the properties of the C=C and C=O bonds*.

39.8.3 The Cannizzaro reaction

When treated with hot concentrated alkali, aldehydes having α-hydrogen atoms form polymers (section 39.7.1). In fact, Cannizzaro found that an aldehyde without an α-hydrogen atom, such as methanal, will also react under these conditions. The products, though, are an alcohol and the salt of a carboxylic acid. Methanal, for example, forms methanol and sodium methanoate:

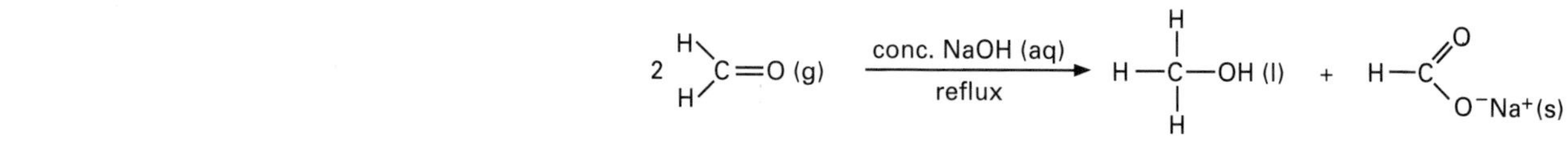

Benzaldehyde also gives a Cannizzaro reaction:

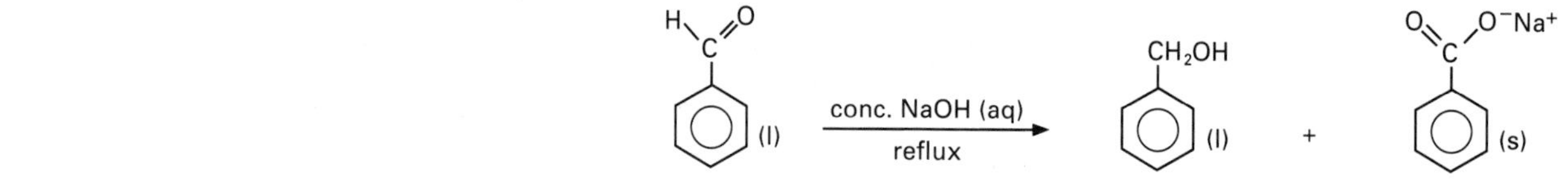

phenylmethanol   sodium benzoate

But are these redox reactions?

Well, half of the aldehyde molecules are reduced to an alcohol; the rest are oxidised to the carboxylic acid salt. So, a redox reaction *is* taking place. Since this is a **self reduction-oxidation** reaction, it is also known as **disproportionation**.

Activity 39.5

1   From the following compounds select those that will react with (a) Tollen's reagent and (b) Fehling's solution: ethanal, propanone, phenylethanone, propanal, methanal.

2   Give the name(s) and formula(e) of the organic product(s) formed in each of the following reactions.

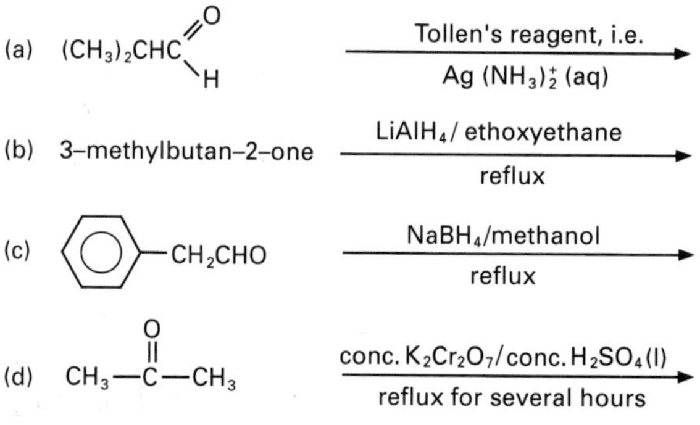

39.9 Comparing the reactivity of aldehydes and ketones

Looking back over the reactions of aldehydes and ketones, would you describe these compounds as having mainly similar or different properties? Well, activity 39.6 should help you to decide. It is also a useful revision exercise.

Activity 39.6

Prepare a summary table which compares the reactions of aldehydes and ketones. You should consider their reactions with the following reagents:
1. KCN/dil.NaOH(aq);   2. $NaHSO_3$(aq);   3. NH_2OH(l)/conc.NaOH(aq);
4. 2,4-dinitrophenylhydrazine;   5. $LiAlH_4$/ethoxyethane;
6. Tollen's reagent;   7. Fehling's solution;   8. conc.NaOH(aq);
9. $K_2Cr_2O_7$/dil.H_2SO_4(aq);   10. I_2/dil.NaOH(aq).

In your opinion, do aldehydes and ketones have similar, or different, chemical properties?

39.10 Uses of aldehydes and ketones

Aldehydes and ketones are widely used both as bulk and specialist chemicals.

Propanone is used in bulk as an *industrial solvent* and in the manufacture of **Perspex**:

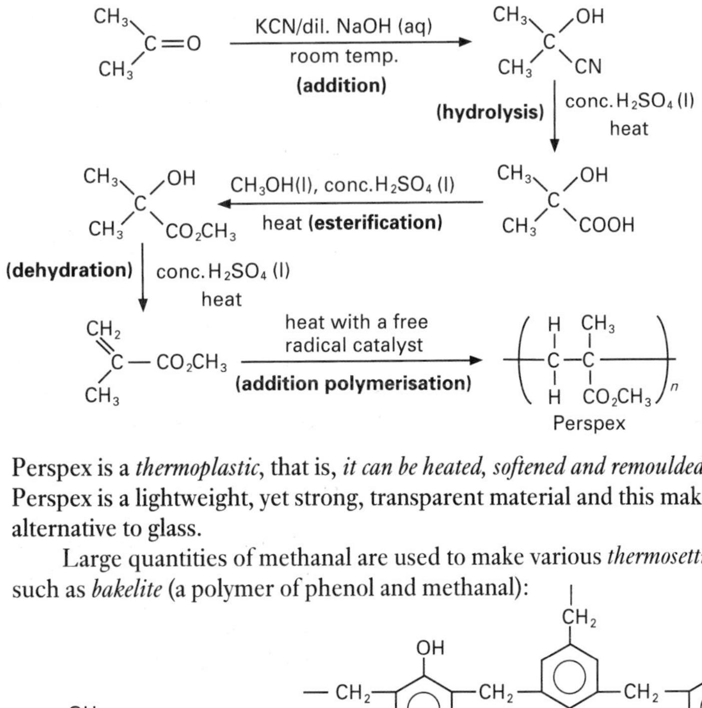

Perspex is a *thermoplastic*, that is, *it can be heated, softened and remoulded into shape.* Perspex is a lightweight, yet strong, transparent material and this makes it a valuable alternative to glass.

Large quantities of methanal are used to make various *thermosetting plastics*, such as *bakelite* (a polymer of phenol and methanal):

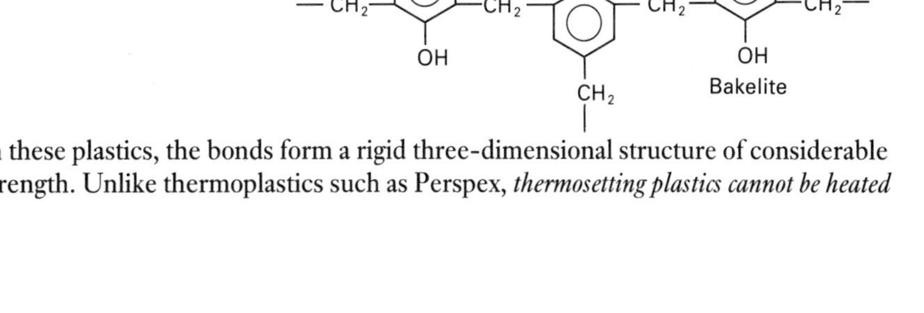

In these plastics, the bonds form a rigid three-dimensional structure of considerable strength. Unlike thermoplastics such as Perspex, *thermosetting plastics cannot be heated*

The characteristic 'almondy' smell of benzaldehyde and its derivatives is used in the formulation of perfumes

and remoulded. Thus, dyes and fillers are added to the monomers and they are polymerised within the mould of the desired article. *Thermosetting plastics have high decomposition temperatures and do not conduct electricity.* Hence, they are often used as electrical insulators in plugs and switches.

Formalin, a 40% aqueous solution of methanal, is used to preserve biological specimens. *Ethanal* is mainly used to make *ethanoic acid.* As we saw earlier, chlorination of ethanal produces *trichloroethanal (chloral)* and this is a starting material in the manufacture of certain insecticides. *Benzaldehyde* is used to make perfumes and artificial flavourings.

39.11 Carbohydrates

Carbohydrates are compounds with the general formula, $C_x(H_2O)_y$.

This formula might suggest that they are hydrates of carbon (hence the name), but nothing could be further from the truth.

There are three main types of carbohydrate: monosaccharides and disaccharides (both commonly known as **sugars**), and polysaccharides.

Monosaccharides

These are colourless crystalline solids of low molecular mass (e.g. glucose, $C_6H_{12}O_6$). They taste sweet and are very soluble in water. Most monosaccharide molecules are either **pentoses** or **hexoses**, that is, they contain **five** or **six** carbon atoms, respectively, e.g.

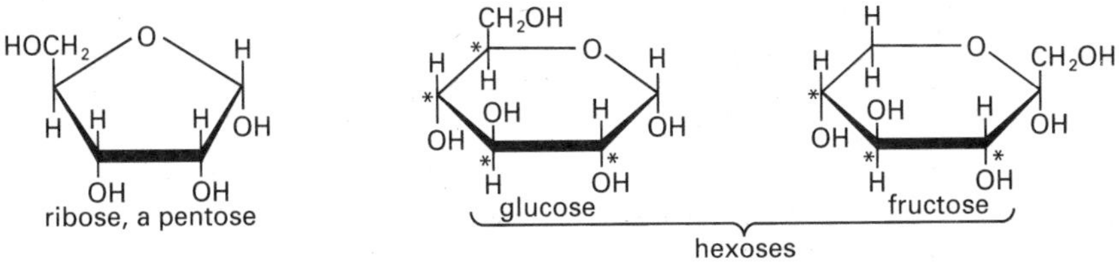

(structures: ribose, a pentose; glucose and fructose — hexoses)

Monosaccharides are the 'building bricks' from which other carbohydrates are made. Two important examples are the hexoses, **glucose** and **fructose**, shown above. Each molecule contains:

▶ five hydroxyl groups, enabling them to form extensive *hydrogen bonding.* This accounts for their high melting points and their good solubility in water.

▶ asymmetric carbon atoms (four in glucose, three in fructose, marked *). Thus, they form a number of *optical isomers,* and this is a general feature of mono- and di-saccharide chemistry.

Table 39.5 *Some reactions of glucose and fructose*

Reagent/conditions	product formed by glucose or fructose
$CH_3COOH(l) + conc.H_2SO_4(l)$; reflux	a pentaethanoate (i.e. five ester groups are present)
$LiAlH_4$ in ethoxyethane; reflux	reduction occurs, giving another $-OH$ group.
KCN/dil.NaOH(aq); room temp.	hydroxynitrile formed
2,4-dinitrophenylhydrazine solution; room temp.	addition–elimination to give a 2,4-dinitrophenylhydrazone
Tollen's reagent	silver 'mirror' formed
Fehling's solution	red-brown precipitate of $Cu_2O(s)$

Would you expect these reactions from the 'ring' structures of glucose and fructose?

On investigating the chemical reactions of glucose and fructose, we find some very interesting results (table 39.5). Although ester formation is to be expected (because of the five −OH groups), the other reactions suggest that glucose and fructose are *carbonyl* compounds! Looking at the structure above, you would not class glucose and fructose as aldehydes or ketones. However, one of the most interesting properties of sugars is *their ability to exist in an equilibrium between ring and open chain forms*, e.g.

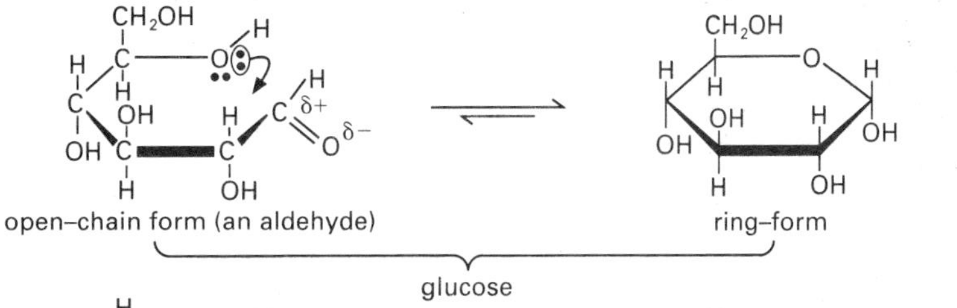

open–chain form (an aldehyde) ⇌ ring–form

glucose

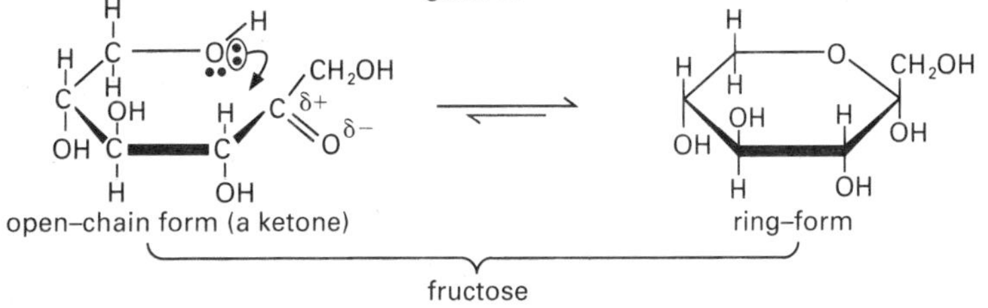

open–chain form (a ketone) ⇌ ring–form

fructose

The ring is reformed via the nucleophilic addition of an −OH group across the carbonyl bond. *Both equilibria almost completely favour the ring form.* Even so, glucose and fructose will give reactions typical of an aldehyde and ketone, respectively. Monosaccharides which form an open-chain aldehyde (e.g. glucose) are called **aldoses**; those giving an open-chain ketone (e.g. fructose) are termed **ketoses**.

Surprisingly, like aldehydes, fructose and other ketoses, will reduce Tollen's reagent and Fehling's solution. Hence, all monosaccharides are described as **reducing** sugars.

Disaccharides

Disaccharides are made up of two monosaccharides which have linked together via the loss of a water molecule. Like monosaccharides, they also have a sweet taste and are very soluble in water. Two important disaccharides are **sucrose** (or cane sugar) and **maltose**. Both compounds have the same molecular formula, $C_{12}H_{22}O_{11}$.

When hydrolysed by hot dilute hydrochloric acid, sucrose yields equimolar amounts of glucose and fructose and this indicates that *sucrose has a* glucose — fructose *structure*. However, unlike glucose and fructose, sucrose neither reduces Fehling's solution nor Tollen's reagent. This tells us that the monosaccharides are linked together via the aldehyde group of glucose and the ketone group of fructose. Thus, sucrose is termed a **non-reducing** sugar and it does not react like a typical aldehyde or ketone.

On the other hand, the enzyme-catalysed hydrolysis of maltose yields only one monosaccharide, glucose. Thus, *maltose must be made up of two glucose units*. Like glucose, maltose is a reducing sugar because it has an open-chain form which contains the aldehyde functional group.

Polysaccharides

Polysaccharides are tasteless powders of very high molecular mass. They are slightly soluble in water and organic solvents. As the name implies, these are polymers of monosaccharides. The most important polysaccharides are **starch** and **cellulose**.

When starch is hydrolysed in acid solution, the only product is glucose. This indicates that starch is a polymer of glucose. Plants store starch for use as an energy supply where photosynthesis is not possible, e.g. during the underground sprouting

These foods can supply all the carbohydrate that we need for a healthy diet. Digestible carbohydrates, such as sugar and starch, provide us with energy. Non-digestible carbohydrates, such as cellulose, provide no energy but act as dietary fibre. Fibre assists the passage of food through the body and helps prevent various diseases, such as bowel cancer and coronary heart disease. How many of these foods do you eat?

of a potato tuber or a daffodil bulb. Starch is the main carbohydrate in our diet, appearing in foods such as potatoes, corn, rice and vegetables. During digestion, starch is converted into glucose via two enzyme-catalysed processes:

$$2(C_6H_{10}O_5)_n + nH_2O \xrightarrow[\text{found in saliva}]{\text{enzyme: amylase}} nC_{12}H_{22}O_{11}$$

starch (*n* can be from about 60 to 600) — maltose

$$C_{12}H_{22}O_{11} + H_2O \xrightarrow{\text{enzyme: maltase}} 2C_6H_{12}O_6$$

maltose — glucose

Cellulose is the main material in the cell walls of plants and only certain herbivorous animals (e.g. cows) can digest it. An analysis of its hydrolysis products shows that cellulose, like starch, is also a polymer of glucose. However, these polysaccharides differ in the 3-dimensional orientation of the glucose units.

39.12 Comments on the activities

Activity 39.1

1 (a) pentanal (b) 3-methylbutan-2-one (c) 2-methylpropanal
   (d) 2-phenylbutanal (e) 3-phenylpropanal (f) methanal

2

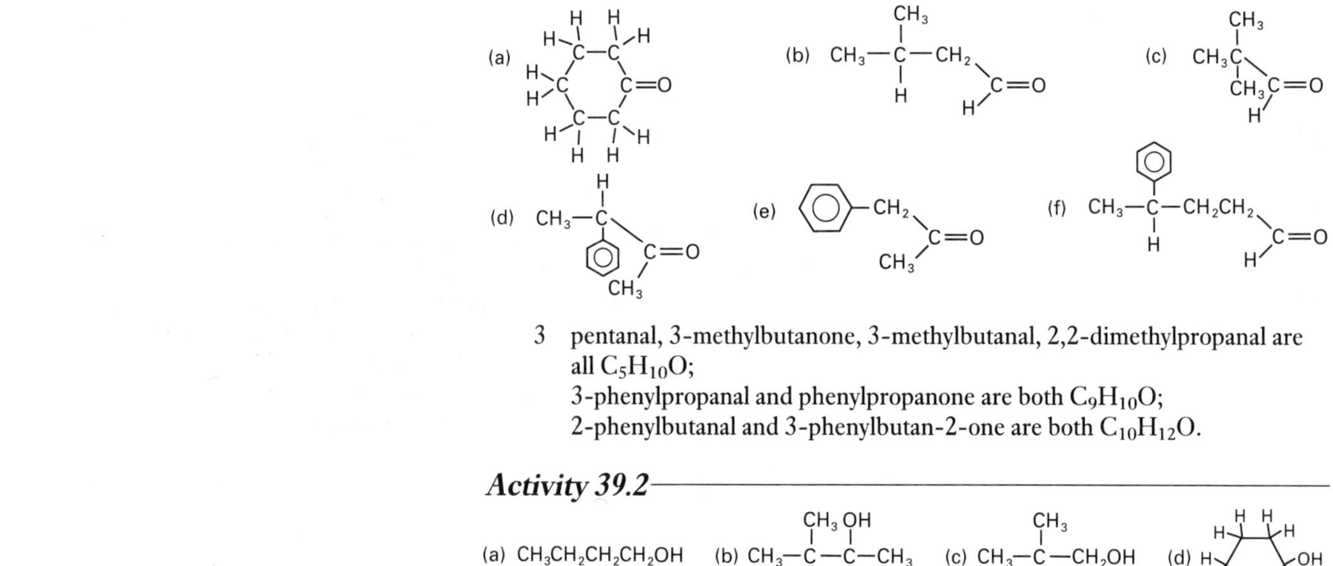

3 pentanal, 3-methylbutanone, 3-methylbutanal, 2,2-dimethylpropanal are all $C_5H_{10}O$;
   3-phenylpropanal and phenylpropanone are both $C_9H_{10}O$;
   2-phenylbutanal and 3-phenylbutan-2-one are both $C_{10}H_{12}O$.

Activity 39.2

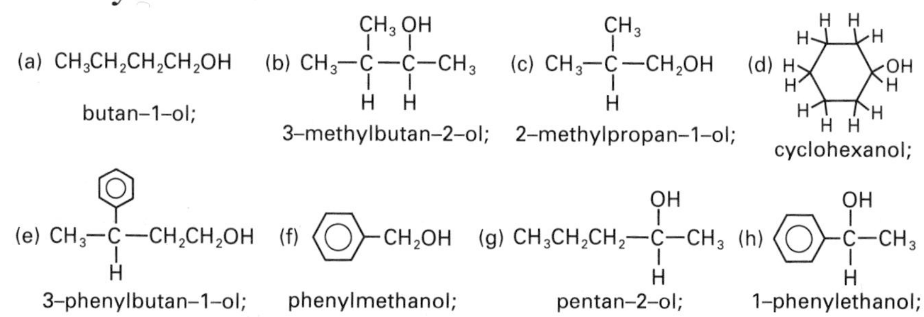

(a) $CH_3CH_2CH_2CH_2OH$
butan-1-ol;

(b) $CH_3-\overset{CH_3}{\underset{H}{C}}-\overset{OH}{\underset{H}{C}}-CH_3$
3-methylbutan-2-ol;

(c) $CH_3-\overset{CH_3}{\underset{H}{C}}-CH_2OH$
2-methylpropan-1-ol;

(d) cyclohexanol;

(e) $CH_3-\overset{}{\underset{H}{C}}-CH_2CH_2OH$ (with phenyl group)
3-phenylbutan-1-ol;

(f) phenyl–CH_2OH
phenylmethanol;

(g) $CH_3CH_2CH_2-\overset{OH}{\underset{H}{C}}-CH_3$
pentan-2-ol;

(h) phenyl–$\overset{OH}{\underset{H}{C}}-CH_3$
1-phenylethanol;

Activity 39.3

1

(a) 2-hydroxypropanonitrile $CH_3-\overset{OH}{\underset{H}{\overset{*}{C}}}-CN$

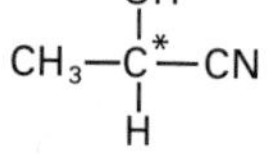

(b) 2-hydroxy-2-methylpentanonitrile $CH_3CH_2CH_2-\overset{OH}{\underset{CH_3}{\overset{*}{C}}}-CN$

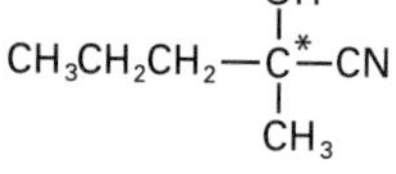

(c) methanal sodium hydrogensulphite

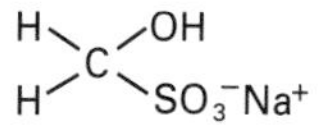

$$H-\overset{\displaystyle H}{\underset{\displaystyle SO_3^-Na^+}{C}}-OH$$

(d) ethanal oxime

$$\overset{\displaystyle CH_3}{\underset{\displaystyle H}{}}C=N-OH$$

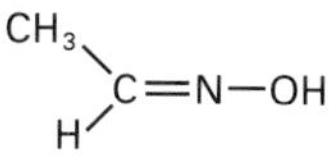

(e) phenylethanone–2,4–dinitrophenylhydrazone

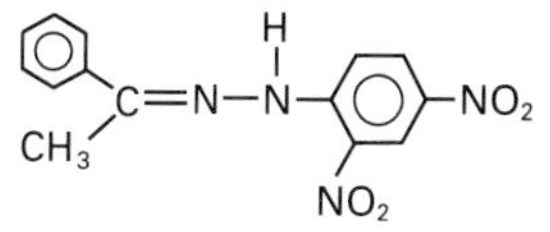

Optically active: (a) and (b); each molecule of product contains an asymmetric carbon atom, C*.

2 (a) KCN/dil. NaOH(aq), room temp.
   (b) Saturated NaHSO₃(aq), room temp.
   (c) NH₂OH/conc.NaOH(aq), warm.

(d)

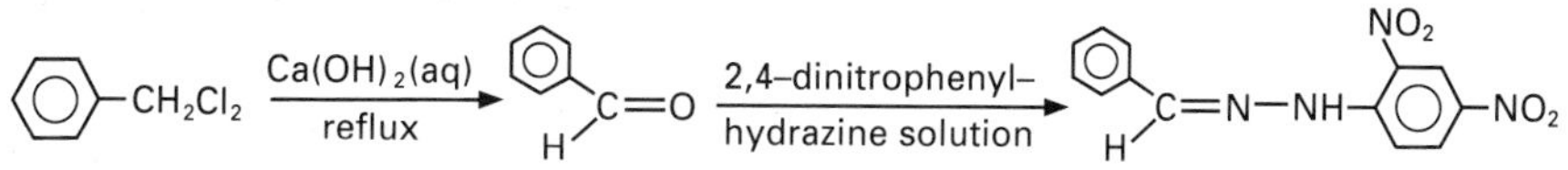

(e) 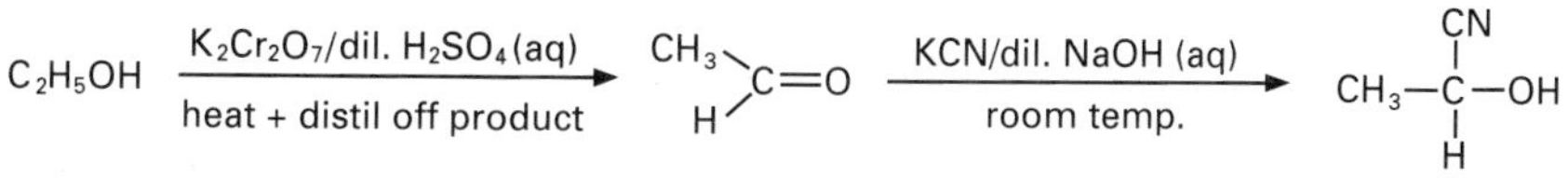 C_2H_5OH $\xrightarrow[\text{heat + distil off product}]{K_2Cr_2O_7/\text{dil. } H_2SO_4(aq)}$

(f) 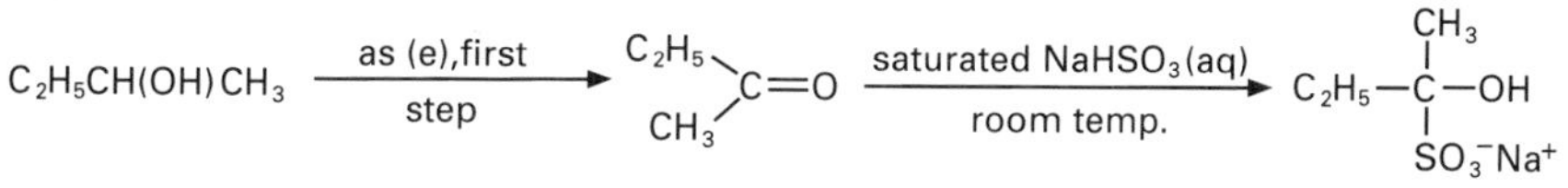 $C_2H_5CH(OH)CH_3$ $\xrightarrow[\text{step}]{\text{as (e),first}}$

3

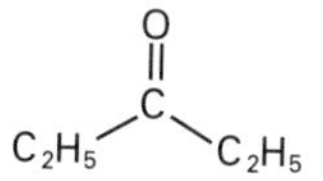

pentan–3–one 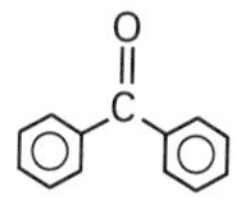   benzophenone

Reason: Since these are not aldehydes or methyl ketones, the approach of the bulky SO_3^{2-} nucleophile is hindered.

4 Prepare, purify and dry the 2,4-dinitrophenylhydrazones (or oximes) of each compound. Take the melting points and check these with a book of data, e.g. butanal-2,4-dinitrophenylhydrazone m.p. 123 °C
2-methylpropanal-2,4-dinitrophenylhydrazone m.p. 187 °C.
Thus, the compounds can be *characterised* (identified).

Activity 39.4

1

(a) (i) 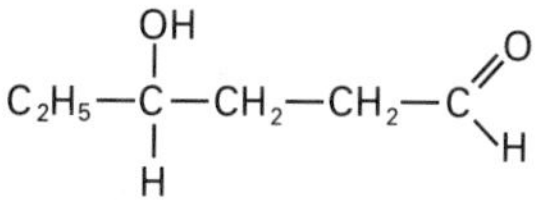 $C_2H_5-\overset{\displaystyle OH}{\underset{\displaystyle H}{C}}-CH_2-CH_2-C\overset{\displaystyle O}{\underset{\displaystyle H}{}}$ at room temp.

(b) (i) 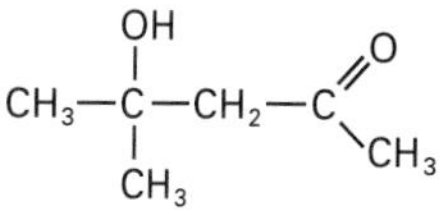 $CH_3-\overset{\displaystyle OH}{\underset{\displaystyle CH_3}{C}}-CH_2-C\overset{\displaystyle O}{\underset{\displaystyle CH_3}{}}$ at room temp.

(ii) 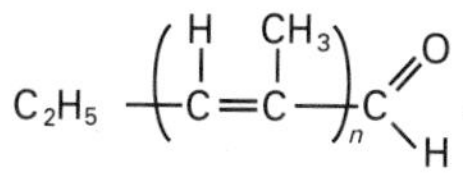 $C_2H_5\left(\overset{\displaystyle H \quad CH_3}{\underset{}{C=C}}\right)_n C\overset{\displaystyle O}{\underset{\displaystyle H}{}}$ on heating

(b) (ii) no polymerisation but product in (b) (i) is formed.

(iii) 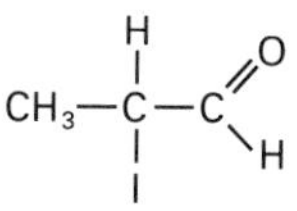 $CH_3-\overset{\displaystyle H}{\underset{\displaystyle I}{C}}-C\overset{\displaystyle O}{\underset{\displaystyle H}{}}$

(iii) 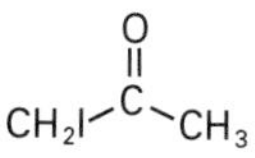 $CH_2I-\overset{\displaystyle O}{\overset{\|}{C}}-CH_3$

(iv) no iodoform formed but α–hydrogens are substituted to give:

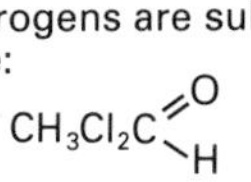

$$CH_3Cl_2C\overset{\displaystyle O}{\underset{\displaystyle H}{}}$$

(iv) CHI₃ formed (+ ve iodoform test) because propanone has the $CH_3-C=O$ group

2 positive iodoform test:

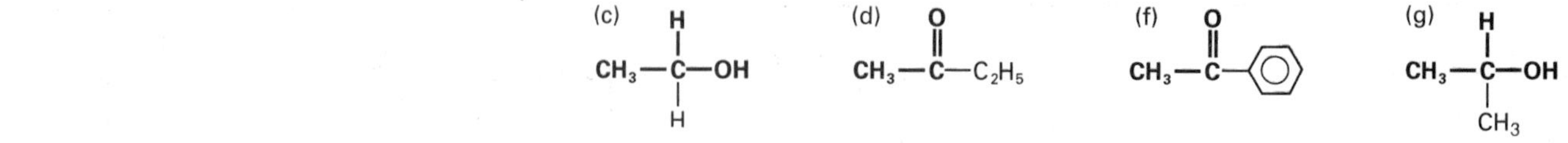

(c)

$$CH_3-\overset{\overset{\displaystyle H}{|}}{\underset{\underset{\displaystyle H}{|}}{C}}-OH$$

(d)

$$CH_3-\overset{\overset{\displaystyle O}{\|}}{C}-C_2H_5$$

(f)

$$CH_3-\overset{\overset{\displaystyle O}{\|}}{C}-\bigcirc$$

(g)

$$CH_3-\overset{\overset{\displaystyle H}{|}}{\underset{\underset{\displaystyle CH_3}{|}}{C}}-OH$$

because they contain the required structural units (shown in bold print).

Activity 39.5

1 (a) ethanal, propanal, methanal; (b) as (a).

2

(a) 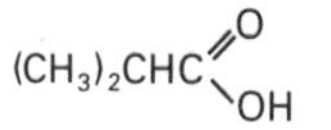 $(CH_3)_2CHC\overset{\nearrow O}{\underset{\searrow OH}{}}$ 2-methylpropanoic acid

(b) 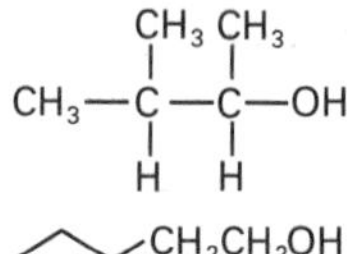 $CH_3-\overset{\overset{\displaystyle CH_3}{|}}{\underset{\underset{\displaystyle H}{|}}{C}}-\overset{\overset{\displaystyle CH_3}{|}}{\underset{\underset{\displaystyle H}{|}}{C}}-OH$ 3-methylbutan-2-ol

(c) 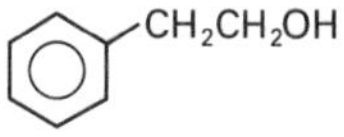 $\bigcirc\!\!-\!CH_2CH_2OH$ 2-phenylethanol

(d) methanoic acid, $H-C\overset{\nearrow O}{\underset{\searrow OH}{}}$ and ethanoic acid $\overset{O\diagdown}{\underset{HO\diagup}{}}C-CH_3$

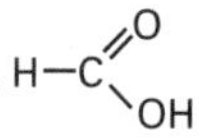

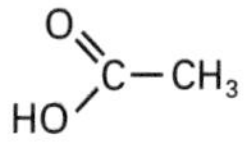

Activity 39.6

Compare your answer with table 39.6.

39.13 Summary and revision plan

1 Carbonyl compounds contain the **carbonyl bond, C=O**. There are two main classes of compound: (i) aldehydes and ketones and (ii) carboxylic acids and their derivatives.

2 To name an aldehyde or ketone, replace the final **e** of the parent hydrocarbon's name by **al** for an aldehyde or **one** for a ketone. If the ketone exists as isomers, number the 'carbonyl' carbon.

3 Aldehydes and ketones form **homologous series** which have the same general formula $C_nH_{2n}O$.

4 The carbonyl bond is strongly polarised, $\overset{\delta+}{C}=\overset{\delta-}{O}$, and this gives rise to *dipole–dipole attractions* between neighbouring molecules. As a result, aldehydes and ketones: (i) have higher boiling points than the alkanes of similar mass and (ii) are very soluble in water (unless the hydrocarbon skeleton is large).

5 Aldehydes and ketones are made by oxidising primary or secondary alcohols, respectively. In the laboratory, hot acidified sodium (or potassium) dichromate is used as oxidising agent. To prevent further oxidation (to a carboxylic acid), an aldehyde must be distilled off as it forms (see figure 38.7). Aromatic ketones can also be made via a Friedel–Crafts reaction.

6 Aldehydes and ketones take part in three main types of reaction:
 ▶ **nucleophilic addition** to the carbonyl bond (section 39.6);
 ▶ reactions involving the α-**hydrogen(s)** (section 39.7); and
 ▶ **redox** reactions (section 39.8).
 Some of these reactions are summarised in table 39.6. Also, remember that the hydrocarbon skeleton may display its own typical reactions.

7 Although, both the C=O bond and C=C bond are planar and consist of one σ and one π bond, they differ in their polarities:

Table 39.6   *Comparing some important reactions of aldehydes and ketones*

Reagent/conditions	aldehydes e.g. $\begin{smallmatrix}CH_3\\H\end{smallmatrix}C=O$	ketones e.g. $\begin{smallmatrix}CH_3\\CH_3\end{smallmatrix}C=O$	notes
KCN/dil.NaOH(aq), room temp.	**hydroxynitriles** are formed and the hydrocarbon chain is **lengthened** $\longrightarrow$ $CH_3-\overset{\overset{H}{\mid}}{\underset{\underset{CN}{\mid}}{C}}-OH$ or $CH_3-\overset{\overset{CH_3}{\mid}}{\underset{\underset{CN}{\mid}}{C}}-OH$		
sat.NaHSO$_3$(aq), room temp.	a crystalline **sodium hydrogensulphite** is formed $\longrightarrow$ $CH_3-\overset{\overset{H}{\mid}}{\underset{\underset{SO_3^-Na^+}{\mid}}{C}}-OH$ or $CH_3-\overset{\overset{CH_3}{\mid}}{\underset{\underset{SO_3^-Na^+}{\mid}}{C}}-OH$		(1)
:NH$_2$OH(l), conc.NaOH(aq), warm	addition–elimination reactions to give **oximes** $\longrightarrow$ $\begin{smallmatrix}CH_3\\H\end{smallmatrix}C=N-OH$ or $\begin{smallmatrix}CH_3\\CH_3\end{smallmatrix}C=N-OH$		(2)
:NH$_2$-N(H)-C$_6$H$_3$(NO$_2$)NO$_2$ solution, room temp.	addition–elimination reactions to give **2,4-dinitrophenylhydrazones** $\longrightarrow$ $\begin{smallmatrix}CH_3\\H\end{smallmatrix}C=N-\overset{H}{N}-C_6H_3(NO_2)-NO_2$ or $\begin{smallmatrix}CH_3\\CH_3\end{smallmatrix}C=N-\overset{H}{N}-C_6H_3(NO_2)-NO_2$		(2)
LiAlH$_4$/ethoxyethane, reflux	reduction to an **alcohol** (aldehyde $\rightarrow$1°, ketone $\rightarrow$ 2°) $\rightarrow CH_3CH_2OH$, $\rightarrow CH_3CH(OH)CH_3$		
Tollen's reagent, warm	**silver 'mirror'** and a carboxylic acid are formed $\rightarrow CH_3COOH + Ag(s)$	no reaction	(3)
Fehling's solution, warm	**red-brown Cu$_2$O(s)** and a carboxylic acid are formed $\rightarrow CH_3COOH + Cu_2O(s)$	no reaction	(3)
conc. NaOH(aq), heat	a resin is formed – **aldehydes polymerise** $CH_3\text{-}\left(\overset{\overset{H}{\mid}}{C}=\overset{\overset{H}{\mid}}{C}\right)_n\text{-}C\overset{O}{\underset{H}{}}$	no noticeable reaction	
K$_2$Cr$_2$O$_7$/dil.H$_2$SO$_4$(aq)	rapidly oxidised on warming to a **carboxylic acid** $\rightarrow CH_3COOH$	refluxing for *several hours* with concentrated oxidising agent gives a **mixture of carboxylic acids** $\rightarrow CH_3COOH + HCOOH$	
I$_2$(aq)/dil.NaOH(aq)	only ethanal and methyl ketones will react to form **iodoform**, CHI$_3$(s)		(4)

Notes: (1) Will all ketones form a sodium hydrogensulphite?

    (2) Why do we prepare these compounds?

    (3) Why do ketones resist oxidation?

    (4) What structural feature of the molecules is responsible for the reaction?

C=C is non-polar and undergoes **electrophilic** addition (e.g. of Hal_2, HHal, H_2SO_4) but $\overset{\delta+}{C}=\overset{\delta-}{O}$ is polarised and undergoes **nucleophilic** addition (e.g. of HCN, $NaHSO_3$, NH_2OH)

8   Addition of HCN to an aldehyde or ketone: (a) gives an hydroxynitrile which may be optically active and (b) is a step in lengthening the hydrocarbon chain (section 39.6.1).

9   An unknown aldehyde or ketone can be identified by preparing a pure sample of its **2,4-dinitrophenylhydrazone** and taking its melting point. This value is then compared with those in a data book.

10 Any carbon atom which is attached to the carbonyl group is termed an α-carbon. Each hydrogen atom on the α-carbon is termed an α-**hydrogen**. Two important reactions arise from the presence of an α-hydrogen: (i) **dimerisation/polymerisation** and (ii) **halogenation**.

11 A positive **iodoform test** proves that a molecule contains a $CH_3-\overset{|}{C}=O$ or $CH_3-CH(OH)-$ structural unit. The reagent for the iodoform test is **I_2/dil.NaOH(aq)**.

12 Aldehydes are easily oxidised to carboxylic acids, even by mild oxidising agents (such as **Tollen's reagent** and **Fehling's solution**); under the same conditions, ketones resist oxidation. These reagents can be used, therefore, to distinguish between an aldehyde and a ketone.

13 The chemical properties of aldehydes and ketones are compared in table 39.6.

14 Aldehydes and ketones are widely used as solvents and in the manufacture of plastics.

15 Carbohydrates are compounds with the general formula $C_x(H_2O)_y$.

16 There are three main types of carbohydrates: monosaccharides, disaccharides and polysaccharides.

17 **Monosaccharides** are colourless crystalline solids, most of which contain either five or six carbon atoms. They taste sweet and are very soluble in water. Their chemical properties resemble those of either an aldehyde (e.g. glucose) or a ketone (e.g. fructose).

18 A **disaccharide** is formed when two monosaccharides join together via the loss of an H_2O molecule. Disaccharides have a sweet taste and are very soluble in water. Two important disaccharides are sucrose (glucose–fructose structure) and maltose (glucose–glucose structure). **Optical isomerism** is a common feature of mono- and di-saccharide chemistry. The chemical properties of disaccharides depend on the way the monosaccharide 'units' have joined together.

19 **Polysaccharides** are tasteless powders of very high molecular mass. Some are soluble in water, others are not. They are polymers of monosaccharides, the most important being starch and cellulose. These are both polymers of glucose but differ in the 3-dimensional orientation of the glucose units.

20 Important reagents used in this chapter are listed in table 39.6.

Carboxylic Acids and their Derivatives

Every time you drink orange juice or milk, eat a pickled onion or annoy an ant, you will come into contact with a carboxylic acid! These organic acids contain the **carboxyl group**:

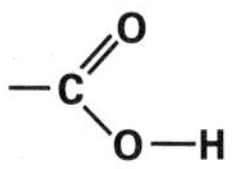

As you can see, this consists of a carbonyl group, $C=O$, joined to a hydroxyl group, $-OH$. Later on, we shall see whether these groups *behave in isolation* or *influence each other* during physical and chemical changes. Firstly, let us look at the way we name these compounds.

40.1   Naming carboxylic acids

Monocarboxylic acids contain *one* carboxyl group. To name them, work out the name of the hydrocarbon which has the same number of carbon atoms, and then replace the final 'e' by 'oic acid'. For example,

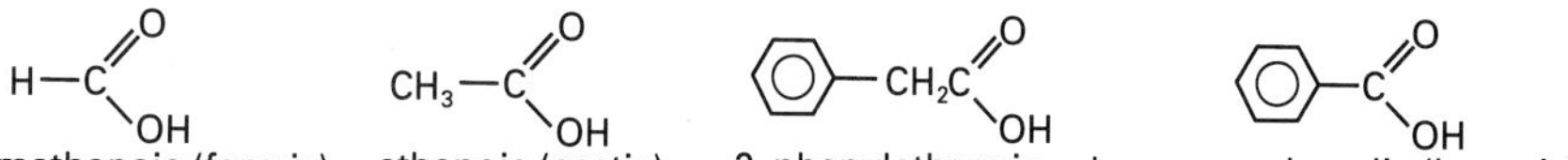

methanoic (formic)   ethanoic (acetic)   2–phenylethanoic   benzenecarboxylic (benzoic)
acid   acid   acid   acid

Of the common names shown in brackets, only benzoic acid will be used in this text.
    Dicarboxylic acids contain *two* carboxyl groups, e.g.

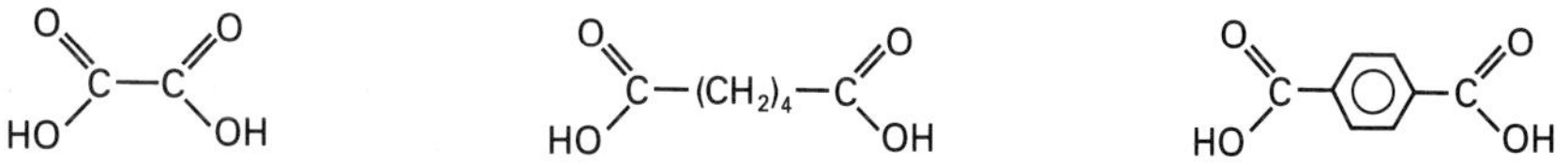

ethanedioic acid   hexanedioic acid   benzene–1, 4–dicarboxylic acid
(oxalic acid)   (used to make   (used to make 'Terylene',
                          nylon, section 40.10)   a polyester, section 40.10)

Activity 40.1

1   Name the following carboxylic acids:

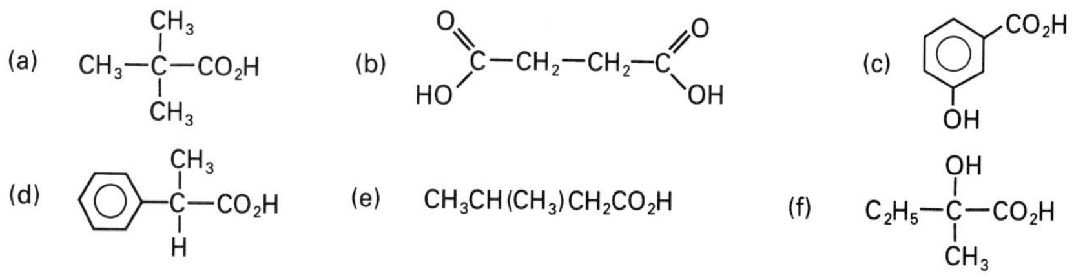

(a) $CH_3-\overset{\overset{\displaystyle CH_3}{|}}{\underset{\underset{\displaystyle CH_3}{|}}{C}}-CO_2H$ (b)   (c)

(d)   (e) $CH_3CH(CH_3)CH_2CO_2H$ (f) $C_2H_5-\overset{\overset{\displaystyle OH}{|}}{\underset{\underset{\displaystyle CH_3}{|}}{C}}-CO_2H$

2   Write down the structural formulae for the following compounds:
    (a) pentanoic acid (b) 3-phenylpropanoic acid (c) butenedioic acid
    (2 answers) (d) 2-hydroxybenzoic acid (e) chloroethanoic acid
    (f) 2-hydroxybutanoic acid.

3   Of the compounds in 1 and 2, which are: (a) structural isomers; (b) optically active?

40.2 Physical properties

Monocarboxylic acids of low molecular mass are pungent smelling, colourless liquids. As expected, the higher members are solids (e.g. benzoic acid). Some properties of carboxylic acids are given in table 40.1.

Table 40.1 *Properties of some carboxylic acids*

Name	formula	state (at 25 °C)	melting point/°C	boiling point/°C	density /g cm^{-3}	$\Delta H_c^{\ominus}$ /kJ mol^{-1}
methanoic acid	HCOOH	liquid	9	101	1.22	− 270
ethanoic acid	CH$_3$COOH	liquid	17	118	1.05	− 873
propanoic acid	CH$_3$CH$_2$COOH	liquid	− 21	141	0.99	−1574
butanoic acid	CH$_3$CH$_2$CH$_2$COOH	liquid	− 4	164	0.96	−2194
2-methylpropanoic acid	(CH$_3$)$_2$CHCOOH	liquid	− 47	154	0.95	−2344
ethanedioic acid	(CO$_2$H)$_2$	solid	157	189	1.65	− 246
benzoic acid	C$_6$H$_5$COOH	solid	122	249	1.32	−3228

Although they have very similar relative molecular masses butanoic acid is a liquid but ethanedioic acid is a solid (at 25 °C). Can you explain why?

Figure 40.1 *Bond polarisation in carboxylic acids and their ability to form hydrogen bonds*

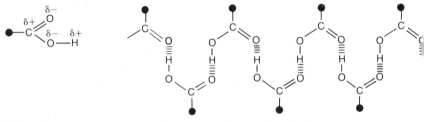

(a) bond polarities

(b) the strong hydrogen bonding in carboxylic acids ($\equiv$ are hydrogen bonds)

Figure 40.2 *Carboxylic acids form dimers in the vapour state and when dissolved in organic solvents*

Aliphatic monocarboxylic acids form a homologous series of general formula C$_n$H$_{2n+1}$COOH, and this is reflected by the steady increases in their boiling point and $\Delta H_c^{\ominus}$ values. Electronegativities show that *the bonds in the carboxyl group are polarised* (figure 40.1a). As a result, the acids form strong intermolecular hydrogen bonds (figure 40.1b). Hence, their melting and boiling points are much higher than those of the alkanes of comparable molecular mass (e.g. ethanoic acid, M_r = 60, b.p. 118 °C but butane M_r = 58, m.p. 0 °C). Indeed, their great ability to form hydrogen bonds enable the lower acids to:

▶   **dimerise** in the vapour state or when dissolved in an organic solvent (figure 40.2); and

▶   dissolve readily in water and other polar solvents. As expected, their water solubility *decreases* as the hydrocarbon skeleton gets *larger*. Benzoic acid, C$_6$H$_5$COOH, for example, is only slightly soluble in cold water.

Since dicarboxylic acids can form hydrogen bonds via both carboxyl groups, they exist as high melting point solids (e.g. ethanedioic acid melts at 157 °C).

40.3 Making carboxylic acids

Manufacture

Methanoic acid is made by heating carbon monoxide with concentrated aqueous sodium hydroxide under pressure:

$$\text{CO(g)} + \text{NaOH (aq)} \xrightarrow{150\,^{\circ}\text{C, 10 atm}} \text{H}-\text{C} \underset{\text{O}^-\text{Na}^+ \text{(aq)}}{\overset{\text{O}}{\diagup}}$$

The methanoic acid is then displaced from its salt by the addition of a strong acid:

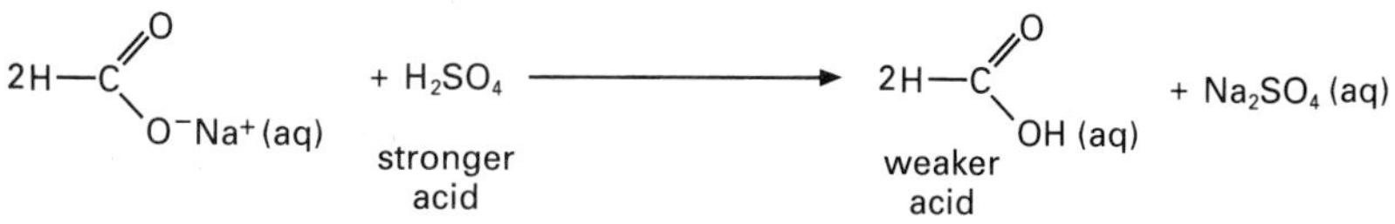

$$2H-C\overset{O}{\underset{O^-Na^+(aq)}{}} + H_2SO_4 \longrightarrow 2H-C\overset{O}{\underset{OH\ (aq)}{}} + Na_2SO_4\ (aq)$$

stronger acid   weaker acid

Methanoic acid is used in the dyeing of cotton and as a preservative.

Ethanoic acid is a petrochemical, being produced by the catalytic oxidation of a mixture of C_5–C_7 alkanes:

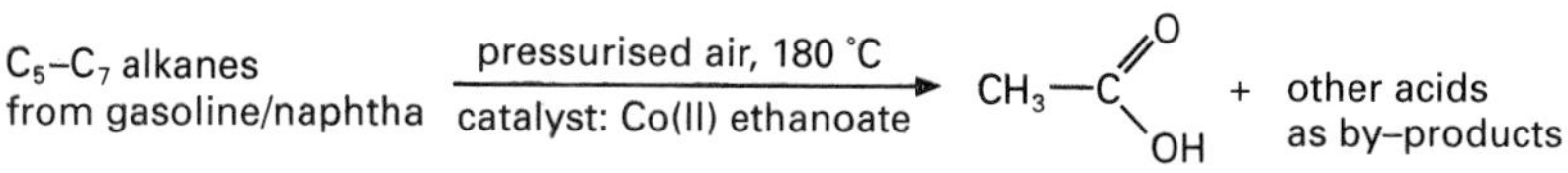

C₅–C₇ alkanes from gasoline/naphtha $\xrightarrow[\text{catalyst: Co(II) ethanoate}]{\text{pressurised air, 180 °C}}$ $CH_3-C\overset{O}{\underset{OH}{}}$ + other acids as by–products

Most ethanoic acid is converted into ethanoic anhydride for use in the manufacture of rayon, a semi-synthetic fibre derived from cellulose.

Benzoic acid is manufactured by a similar process:

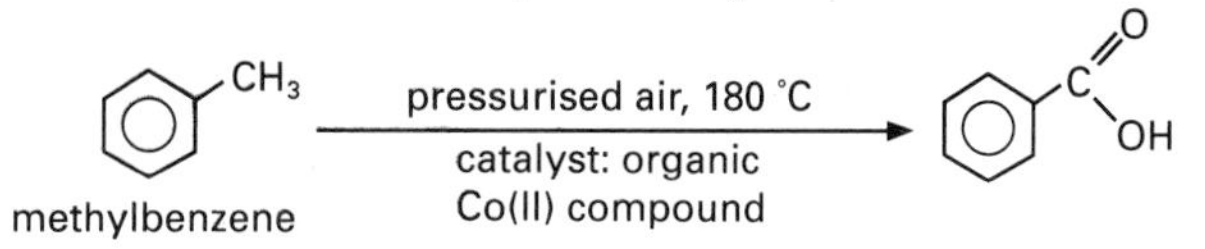

methylbenzene $\xrightarrow[\substack{\text{catalyst: organic}\\\text{Co(II) compound}}]{\text{pressurised air, 180 °C}}$

The methylbenzene is obtained from the catalytic reforming of naphtha (section 34.6). Benzoic acid is mainly used as a preservative in canned fruit and soft drinks.

Laboratory preparation

Many methods are available, three of which are given below.

▶ *Oxidation of a primary alcohol, or aldehyde,* by refluxing with acidified aqueous potassium dichromate or potassium manganate(VII), e.g.

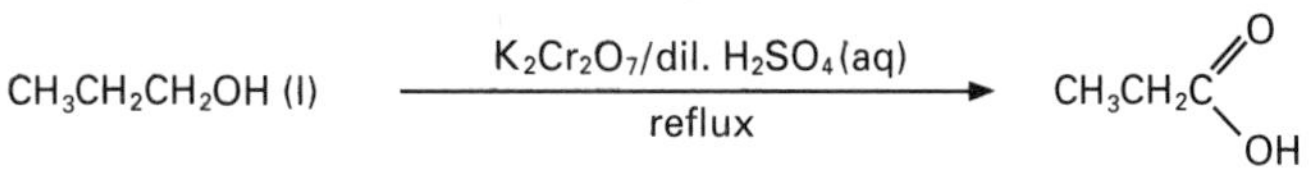

$$CH_3CH_2CH_2OH\ (l) \xrightarrow[\text{reflux}]{K_2Cr_2O_7/\text{dil. }H_2SO_4(aq)} CH_3CH_2C\overset{O}{\underset{OH}{}}$$

▶ *Hydrolysis of a nitrile, or an acid amide,* by refluxing with hot aqueous acid, e.g.

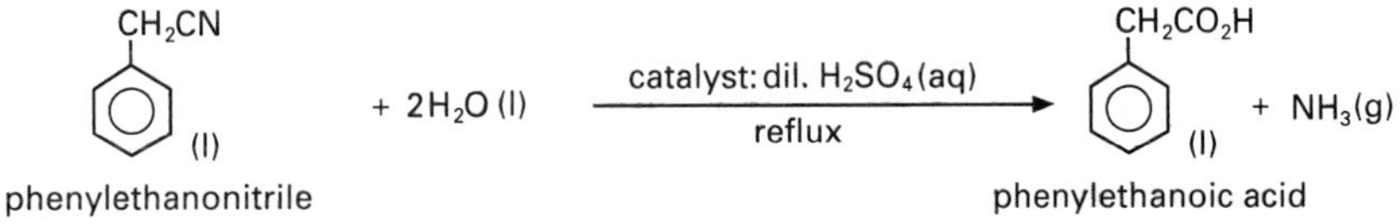

phenylethanonitrile (l) $+ 2H_2O\ (l)$ $\xrightarrow[\text{reflux}]{\text{catalyst: dil. }H_2SO_4(aq)}$ phenylethanoic acid (l) $+ NH_3(g)$

Nitriles are easily prepared from halogenoalkanes (section 37.5.2).

▶ *Benzoic acid can be made by oxidising methylbenzene* with hot acidified potassium manganate(VII):

(l) $\xrightarrow[\text{reflux}]{KMnO_4/\text{dil. }H_2SO_4(aq)}$ (s)

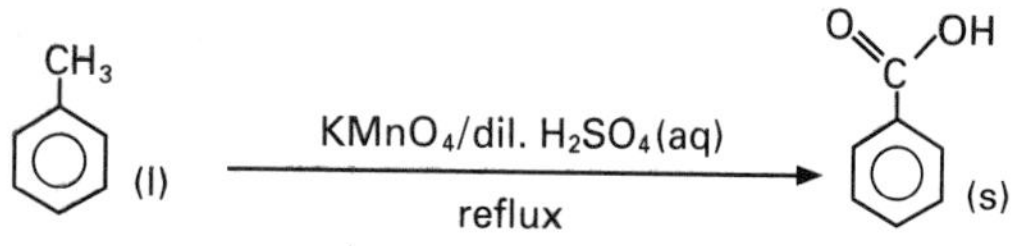

Activity 40.2

State the reagents and the reaction conditions which are used in the laboratory synthesis of propanoic acid from (a) propan-1-ol; (b) propanonitrile; (c) propanal; (d) propanamide, $CH_3CH_2CONH_2$; (e) bromoethane (two steps).

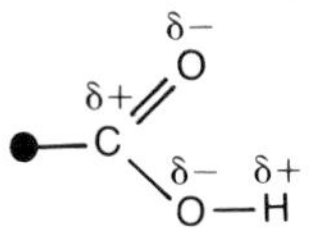

40.4 Predicting the reactivity of carboxylic acids

Looking at the general structure of a carboxylic acid in figure 40.3, we can identify three main reactive centres:

Figure 40.3 *General structure of a carboxylic acid*

▶ the **carbonyl bond** which, like that in aldehydes and ketones, may give **nucleophilic addition** reactions:

$$\underset{OH}{\overset{O}{\underset{\delta+}{\bullet-C}}}{\overset{\delta-}{\diagup}} + X-Y \longrightarrow \bullet-\underset{OH}{\overset{X}{\underset{|}{C}}}-OY$$

▶ the **O—H bond**, fission of which gives rise to the **acidic** character of the carboxyl group:

$$\bullet-C{\overset{O}{\underset{\underset{\delta-\;\;\delta+}{O-H}}{\diagup}}} + \textbf{:Base} \longrightarrow \bullet-C{\overset{O}{\underset{O^-}{\diagup}}} + [H \textbf{:Base}]^+$$

A similar process occurs in alcohols and phenols.

▶ the **C—O bond**, which may break heterolytically during the substitution of the −OH group:

$$\bullet-\underset{\delta+}{C}{\overset{O}{\underset{\underset{\delta-}{OH}}{\diagup}}} + X^- \longrightarrow \bullet-C{\overset{O}{\underset{X}{\diagup}}} + OH^-$$

Once again, alcohols take part in similar substitution reactions.

A **key aspect** of our study is a comparison of the chemistry of the carboxyl group with that of the C=O group in aldehydes/ketones and the O—H bond in alcohols. Try to keep this in mind as you work through sections 40.5 and 40.6.

40.5   Reactions of carboxylic acids

40.5.1 Nucleophilic addition to the C=O bond

In section 39.6, we saw that the carbonyl bond in aldehydes and ketones readily adds nucleophiles, such as HCN and $NaHSO_3$. However, when carboxylic acids are treated with these reagents there are *no* addition reactions. So, why does the C=O bond in acids resist addition reactions?

Figure 40.4a shows the σ bond framework of the carboxyl group, together with the p orbitals which are available for π bonding. Sideways overlap of these p orbitals produces a **delocalised π bond system** (figure 40.4b). A molecule, or ion, becomes more energetically stable if it contains delocalised electrons, e.g. benzene (section 5.8). *An addition reaction would remove the electron delocalisation in the carboxyl group, thereby destabilising the addition product.* Hence, carboxylic acids resist addition to their C=O bond. Aldehydes and ketones, on the other hand, contain a localised double bond and this readily adds other molecules.

Figure 40.4 *Electron delocalisation in carboxylic acids*

(a)
s orbital
containing two
electrons

p orbitals
containing one
electron

(b)

i.e. $\bullet-C{\overset{\overset{\delta+}{O-H}}{\underset{\underset{\delta-}{O}}{\diagdown}}}$

In fact, carboxylic acids will give *one* addition reaction: *reduction*. Hydrogen is added by refluxing the acid with lithium tetrahydridoaluminate in ethoxyethane, e.g.

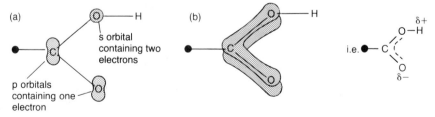

40.5.2 Fission of the O—H bond: behaviour as acids

Four main types of organic hydroxy compounds have an acidic nature:

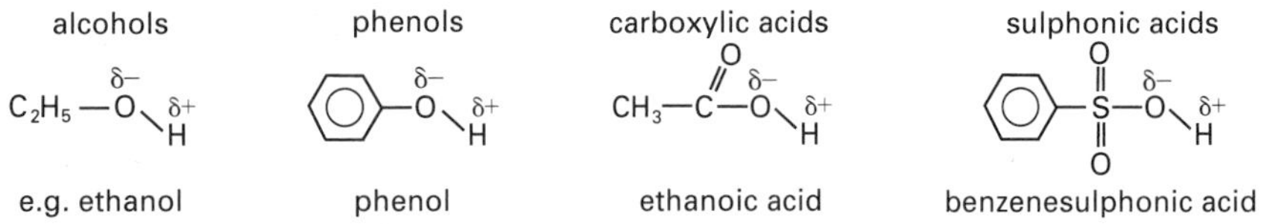

alcohols	phenols	carboxylic acids	sulphonic acids

e.g. ethanol	phenol	ethanoic acid	benzenesulphonic acid

They are all **oxoacids**, that is, *they lose a proton via the fission of an O—H bond*. By comparing their acid strength, therefore, we should be able to see how the acidic nature of the O—H group is affected by its molecular location. A similar comparison showed why phenols are stronger acids than alcohols (section 38.5.1). You will find it helpful to scan through that section before carrying on.

Carboxylic acids are weak acids, dissociating only slightly in aqueous solution:

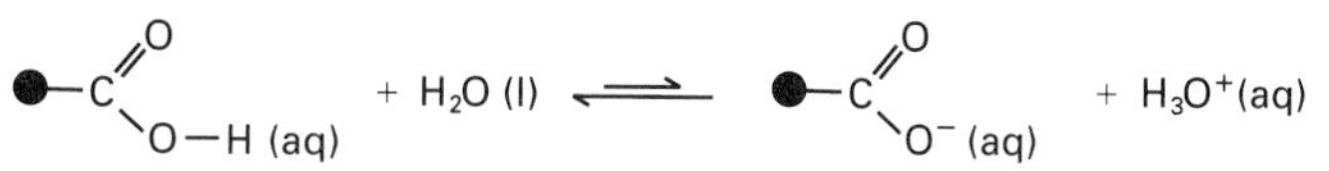

These equilibria lie heavily to the left hand side. For example, in 0.1 M ethanoic acid, only about 1.3% of acid molecules dissociate into ions.

Like phenols, carboxylic acids react with metals and alkalis, giving salts:

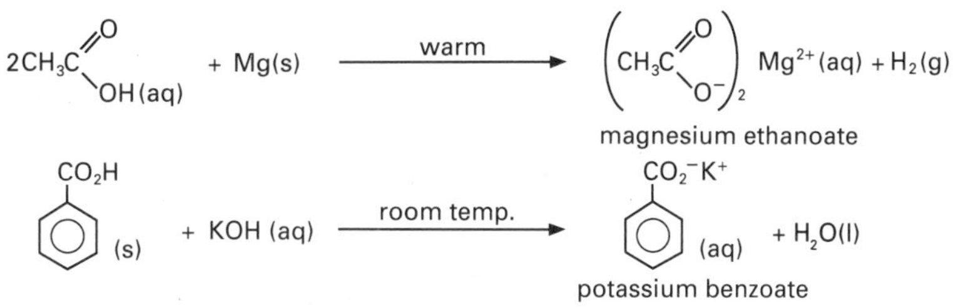

However, *carboxylic acids are much stronger acids than phenols*, and this is shown by their ability to:

▶ *liberate carbon dioxide from a hydrogencarbonate* (a weak base):

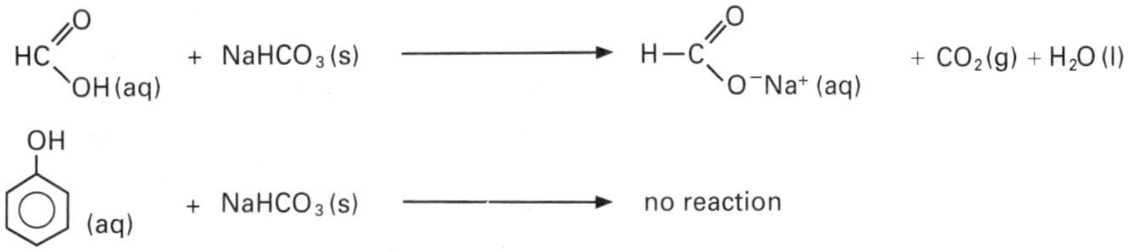

Indeed, this reaction may be used to distinguish carboxylic acids from phenols.

▶ *displace a phenol from its salt:*

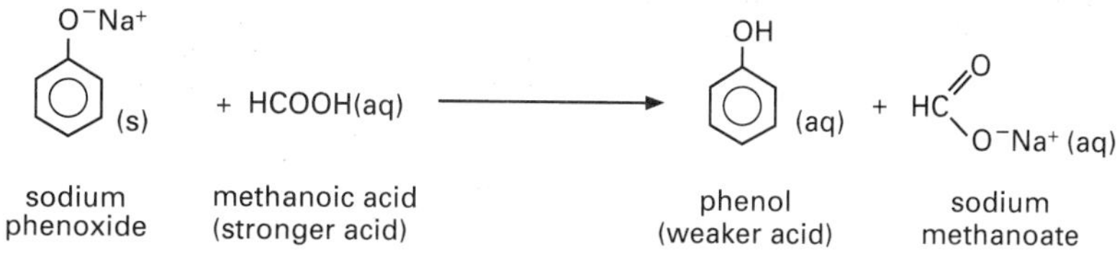

Similarly, a stronger acid (e.g. benzenesulphonic acid) will free a carboxylic acid from its salt:

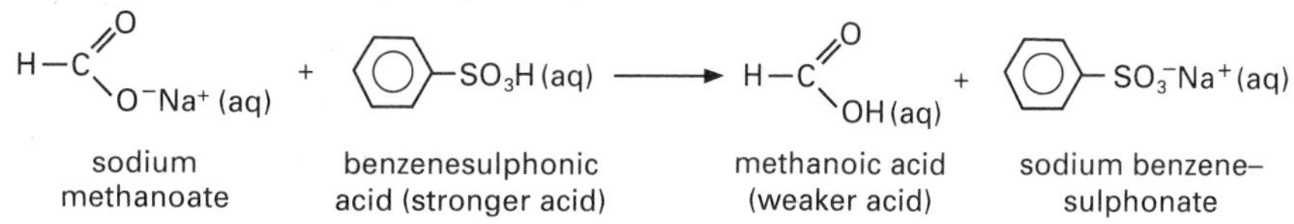

Table 40.2 *Dissociation constants, K_a, for some oxoacids. (Remember that a stronger acid has a larger K_a and a smaller pK_a.)*

Acid	formula	K_a at 25°C/M	pK_a
(a)			
methanoic	HCOOH	1.6×10^{-4}	3.8
ethanoic	CH₃COOH	1.7×10^{-5}	4.8
propanoic	CH₃CH₂COOH	1.3×10^{-5}	4.9
butanoic	CH₃CH₂CH₂COOH	1.5×10^{-5}	4.8
benzoic	C₆H₅COOH	6.3×10^{-5}	4.2
ethanol	C₂H₅OH	10^{-16}	16.0
phenol	C₆H₅OH	10^{-10}	10.0
benzenesulphonic acid (a strong acid)	C₆H₅SO₃H	very high	very low
(b)			
ethanoic	CH₃COOH	1.7×10^{-5}	4.8
iodoethanoic	ICH₂COOH	6.9×10^{-4}	3.2
bromoethanoic	BrCH₂COOH	1.3×10^{-3}	2.9
chloroethanoic	ClCH₂COOH	1.4×10^{-3}	2.85
dichloroethanoic	Cl₂CHCOOH	5.0×10^{-2}	1.3
trichloroethanoic	Cl₃CCOOH	2.3×10^{-1}	0.7
(c)			
ethanoic	CH₃COOH	1.7×10^{-5}	4.8
propanoic	CH₃CH₂COOH	1.3×10^{-5}	4.9
2,2-dimethylpropanoic	(CH₃)₃CCOOH	1.0×10^{-5}	5.0
(d)			
benzoic	C₆H₅COOH	6.3×10^{-5}	4.2
4-nitrobenzoic	NO₂C₆H₄COOH	4.0×10^{-4}	3.4
4-methylbenzoic	CH₃C₆H₄COOH	4.6×10^{-5}	4.3
4-hydroxybenzoic	HOC₆H₄COOH	3.0×10^{-5}	4.5

In this table, which is (i) the strongest acid and (ii) the weakest acid? Is benzoic acid stronger or weaker than propanoic acid?

This behaviour suggests that the strengths of organic acids increase in the order:

alcohols	**phenols**	**carboxylic acids**	**sulphonic acids**

increasing acid strength →

Confirmation of this trend comes from the K_a and pK_a values listed in table 40.2a. These can be related to the molecular structure of the oxoacid, as shown below.

An oxoacid, X—O—H, dissociates in aqueous solution:

$$X—O—H(aq) + H_2O(l) \rightleftharpoons X—O^-(aq) + H_3O^+(aq)$$

The *stronger* the acid, the *greater* the degree of dissociation (i.e. the more the equilibrium will lie to the right hand side). This is more likely to happen if

▶ *the O—H bond breaks easily;* and

▶ *the negative charge on the oxoanion is delocalised*, thereby making protonation more difficult and increasing the stability of the oxoanion.

In phenols, carboxylic acids and sulphonic acids, the X group has the ability to pull electron cloud towards itself:

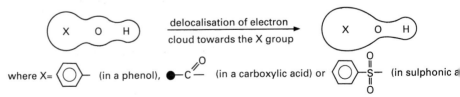

In each case, this electron delocalisation weakens the O—H bond and encourages the loss of a proton.

Of more importance, though, is the stability of the oxoanions, and this increases in the order:

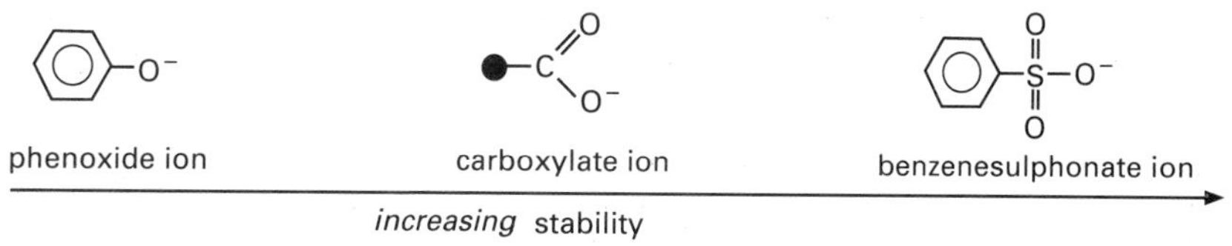

| phenoxide ion | carboxylate ion | benzenesulphonate ion |

increasing stability

Electron delocalisation occurs in each oxoanion, thereby spreading out its negative charge (figure 40.5). However, we find that *the greatest oxoanion stability (i.e. resistance to protonation) is achieved where there are most oxygen atoms to share the negative charge.* Thus, the trend in acid strength is directly related to stability of the oxoanion.

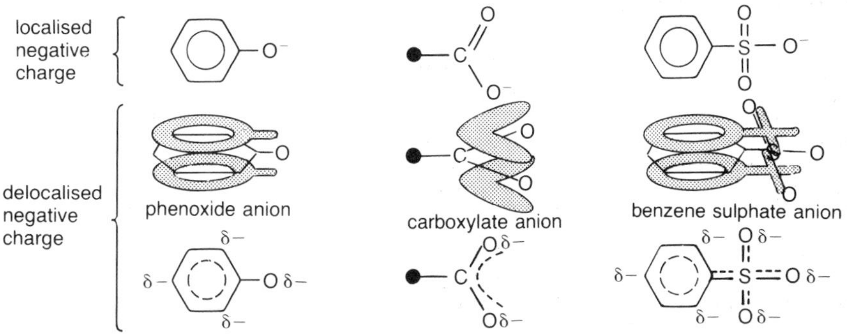

Figure 40.5 *Delocalisation of the negative charge on the oxygen stabilises an oxoanion*

Finally, we need to investigate how the strength of a carboxylic acid, Y—COOH, depends on the nature of the Y group. Look at the K_a and pK_a data in table 40.2 b–d. Can you detect any patterns in the values?

Well, *as the electron-attracting power of Y becomes greater, the acids get progressively stronger* (higher K_a, lower pK_a). For example, the strengths of the monohalogenated ethanoic acids increases with the electronegativity of the halogen atom:

H—CH₂CO₂H   I—CH₂CO₂H   Br—CH₂CO₂H   Cl—CH₂CO₂H

				increasing acid strength
pK_a 4.8	3.2	2.9	2.85	

Similarly, the electron-attracting power of the Y group increase as more halogen atoms are attached:

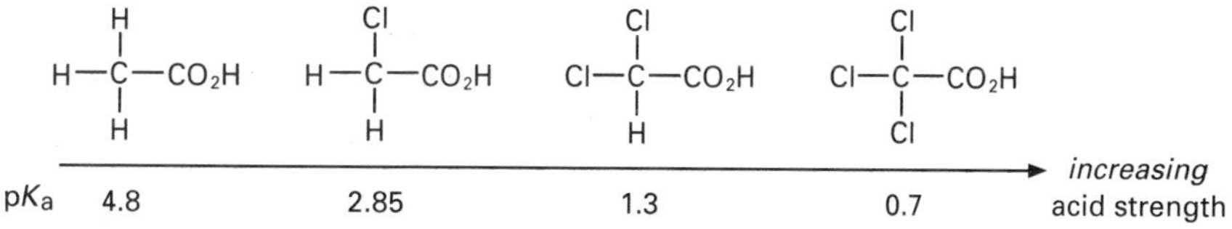

				increasing acid strength
pK_a 4.8	2.85	1.3	0.7	

Increasing the electron-attracting power of the Y group both assists proton loss and stabilises the resulting oxoanion. Hence the corresponding increase in acid strength.

Conversely, if the Y group has an *electron-releasing* effect, the O—H bond will be strengthened and the acid oxoanion will be encouraged to accept a proton. Thus, the acid will dissociate to a lesser extent, that is, *it will be weaker.* For example, the acid strength decreases as the alkyl chain is lengthened:

H—CO₂H   CH₃—CO₂H   CH₃CH₂—CO₂H

			decreasing acid strength
pK_a 3.8	4.8	4.9	

and with the number of alkyl groups:

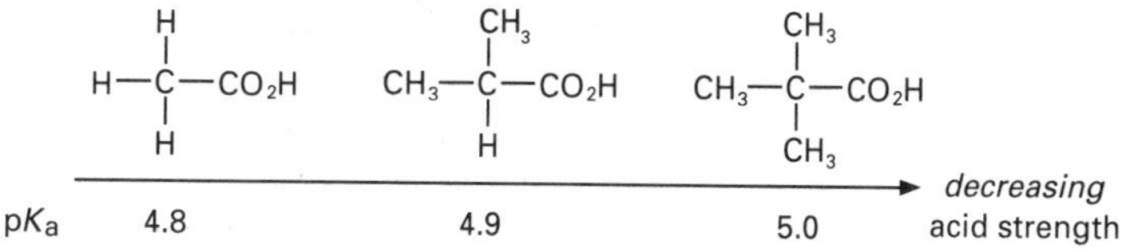

			decreasing acid strength
pK_a 4.8	4.9	5.0	

For similar reasons, an *electron-attracting* ring substituent (e.g. $-NO_2$) *increases* the strength of a benzoic acid. Conversely, an *electron-releasing ring* substituent (e.g. $-OH$) *decreases* the acid's strength:

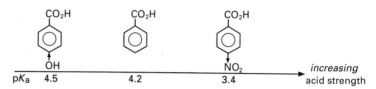

Activity 40.3 will help you to apply these ideas in some unfamiliar situations.

Activity 40.3

1 Name the products, if any, obtained from the following reactions:
   (a) chloroethanoic acid + sodium benzoate:
   (b) methanoic acid + sodium butanoate;
   (c) potassium methanoate + hydrochloric acid;
   (d) magnesium bromoethanoate + propanoic acid;
   (e) magnesium bromoethanoate + benzenesulphonic acid.
2 Arrange the following compounds in order of increasing acid strength:
   (a) $ClCH_2CH_2COOH$, $ClCH_2COOH$, $ClCH_2CH_2CH_2COOH$;
   (b) 2-iodopropanoic acid, 2-methylpropanoic acid, propanoic acid;
       2-bromopropanoic acid, 2-chloropropanoic acid, 3-iodopropanoic acid
   (c) 2,4-dichlorobenzoic acid, benzoic acid, 4-methylbenzoic acid;
       4-chlorobenzoic acid.

40.5.3 Fission of the C—O bond

Halogenation

Apart from their acidic nature, *the hydroxyl groups in a carboxylic acid and an alcohol have similar reactions with halogenating agents.* Thus, carboxylic acids react with phosphorus trihalides to give **acid halides**:

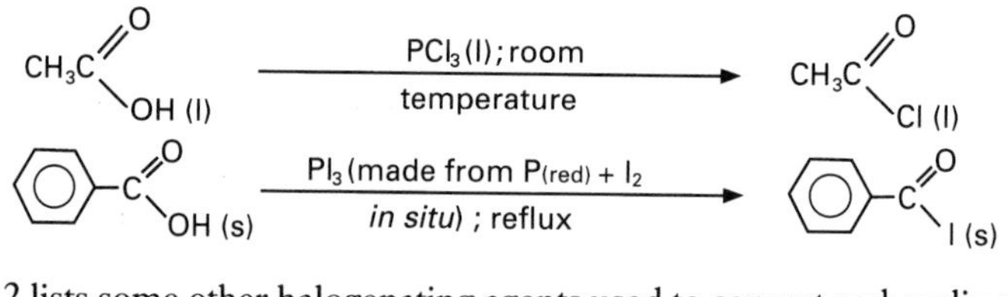

Table 37.2 lists some other halogenating agents used to convert carboxylic acids into their halides.

Esterification

When a carboxylic acid is refluxed with an alcohol for several days, an **acid ester** is formed in an equilibrium mixture, e.g.

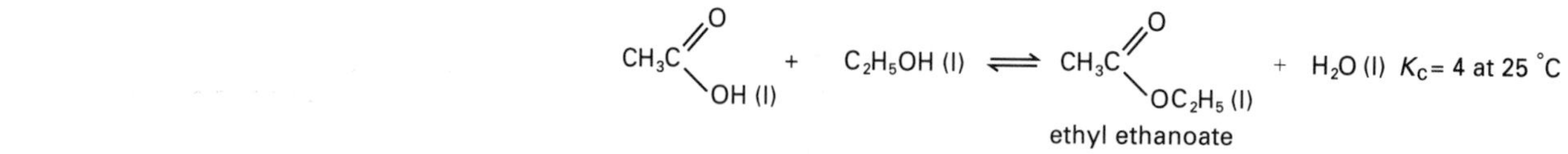

Fortunately, small amounts of concentrated sulphuric acid, or dry hydrogen chloride, catalyse the reaction, giving an equilibrium after a few hours. Also, if an excess of alcohol is used, the equilibrium shifts towards the ester, thereby increasing its yield. Even so, good yields are only obtained with primary alcohols.

The mechanism of esterification is interesting. At first glance, it may appear to be a simple **acid/base** reaction:

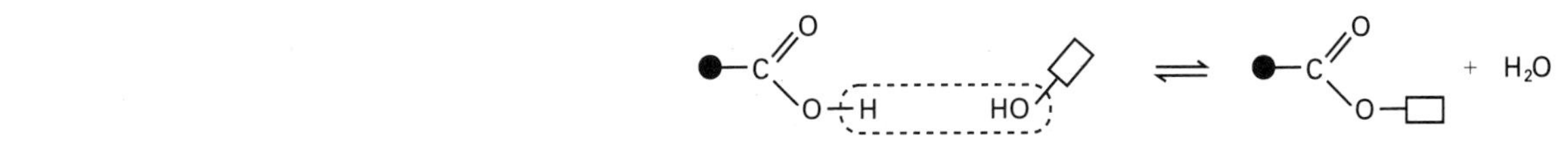

In theory, though, bond fission may occur in *two* ways:

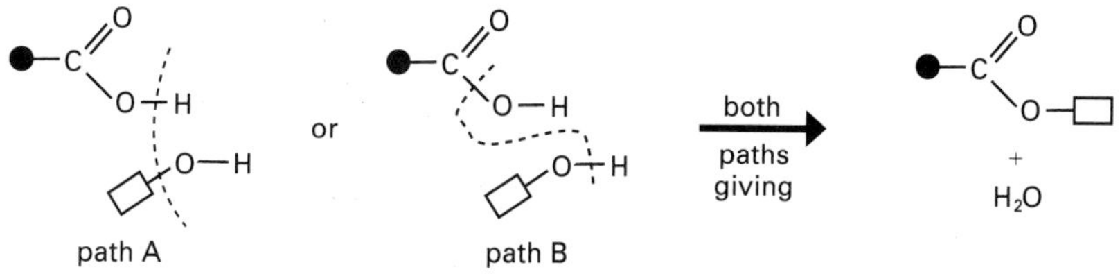

path A   path B

For the simple acid/base reaction, path A, the oxygen from the alcohol would end up in the water molecule. Alternatively, **nucleophilic attack** by the alcohol on the carbonyl carbon, path B, would leave the alcohol's oxygen in the ester. So which mechanism is correct?

This problem provides a good example of how **radioactive isotopes** are used to help work out a reaction mechanism. To follow the fate of a particular atom during a reaction, we 'label' it by using a radioactive isotope. After the reaction, we can analyse the products to find out which contains the labelled atom. In this case, we want to know what has happened to the alcohol's oxygen. Thus, we prepare an alcohol labelled with ^{18}O and use it in the esterificaton.

Consider, for example, the reaction of ethanoic acid with labelled ethanol, $C_2H_5{}^{18}OH$. Two esters are possible:

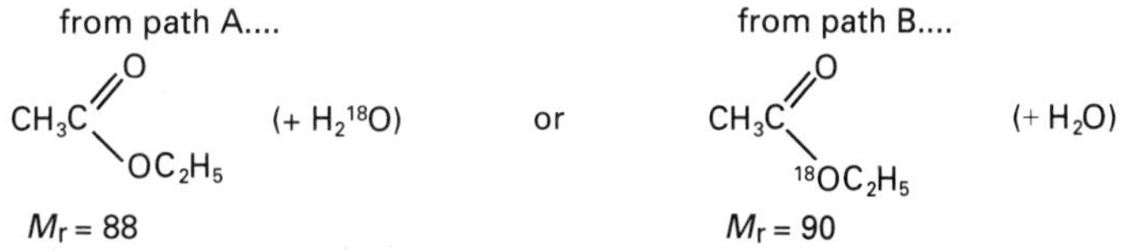

A **mass spectrum** of the purified ester gives a molecular ion of $M_r = 90$ (section 6.2). Hence, the alcohol's oxygen ends up in the ester and *the reaction must proceed via path B.*

Activity 40.4

1 Give the name and structural formula of the organic product formed in each of the following reactions.

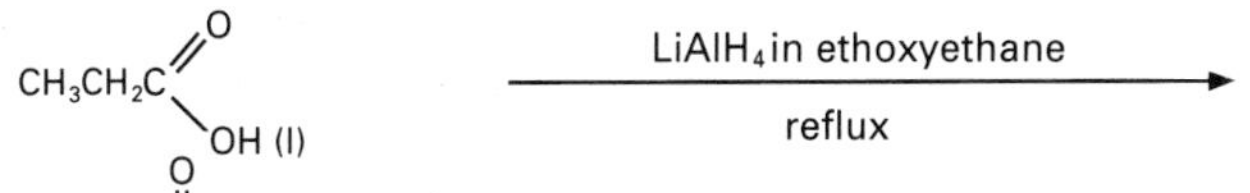

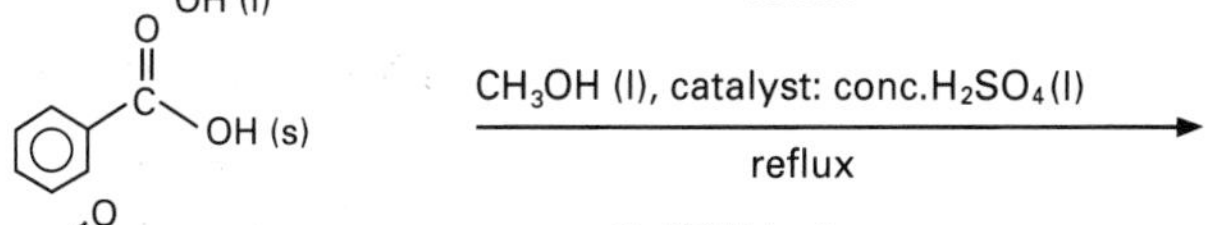

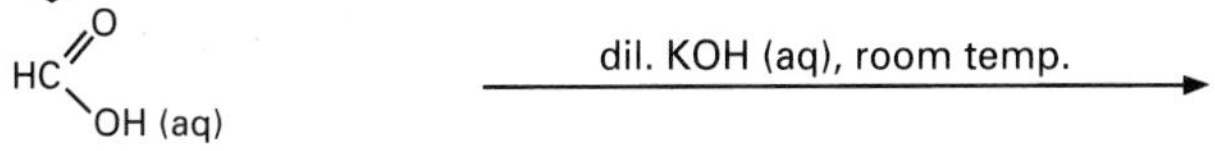

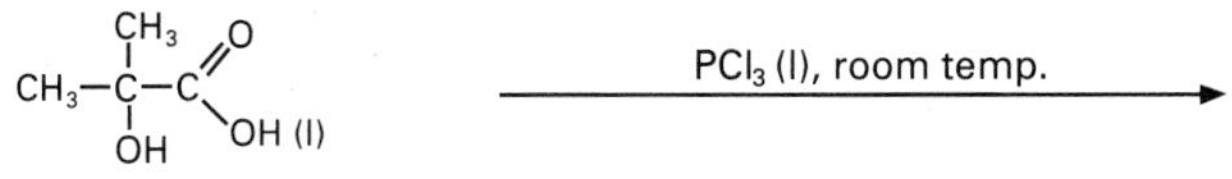

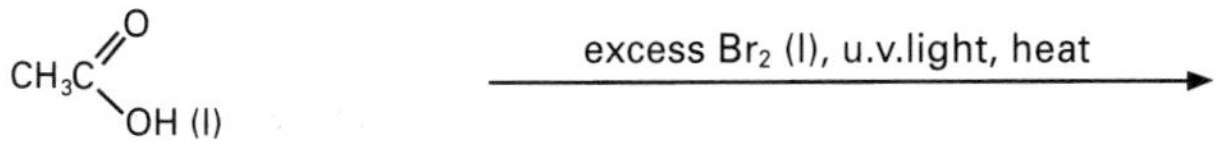

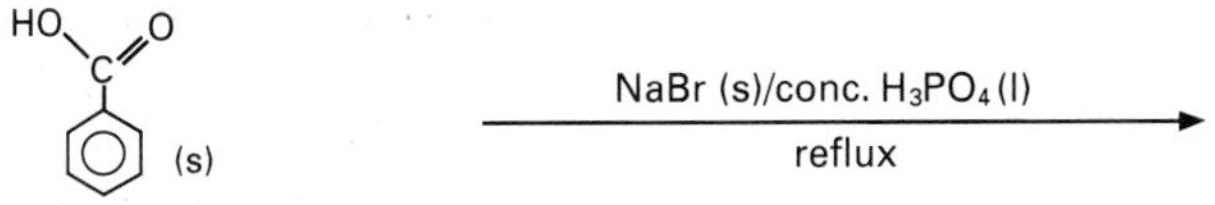

2 Give the reagents and reaction conditions needed for the following conversions:

(a) ethanol → ethylpropanoate;

(b) ethanoic acid → ethanoyl iodide.

(c)  (2 steps) →

(d) CH_3CH_2CN (2 steps) → $CH_3CH_2CH_2OH$

(e) 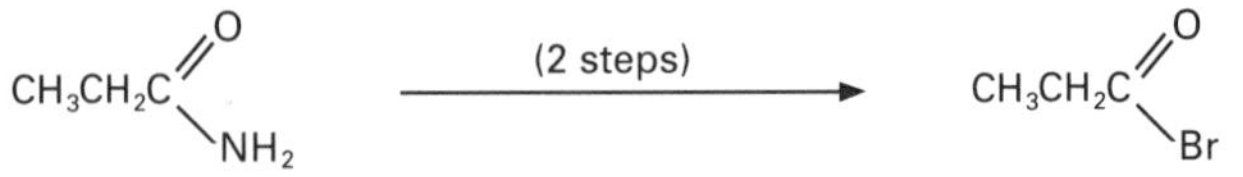 CH_3CH_2C (with $=O$ and NH_2) (2 steps) → CH_3CH_2C (with $=O$ and Br)

Parts (f) to (h) cover the material in sections 40.3, 40.5 and earlier chapters.

(f) $CH_3CH_2CO_2H$ $\xrightarrow{(3\ steps)}$ $CH_3CHBrCH_2Br$

(g) CH_3CH_2Cl $\xrightarrow{(3\ steps)}$ $ClCH_2CO_2H$

(h) $CH_3CH=CH_2$ $\xrightarrow{(3\ steps)}$ $\underset{CH_3CHCH_3}{\overset{COOH}{|}}$

40.6 Special chemical properties of methanoic and ethanedioic acids

These acids have the structural formulae

methanoic acid

ethanedioic acid

Generally speaking, they display the typical reactions of carboxylic acids, such as reduction, salt formation, esterification and halogenation (section 40.5). However, unlike most carboxylic acids, methanoic and ethanedioic acid are really oxidised and dehydrated, as shown in table 40.3.

Table 40.3 *Special reactions of methanoic and ethanedioic acids*

Reagent/conditions	what it does to methanoic and ethanedioic acids
potassium dichromate/ dil.H_2SO_4(aq), warming	both acids are readily **oxidised**: 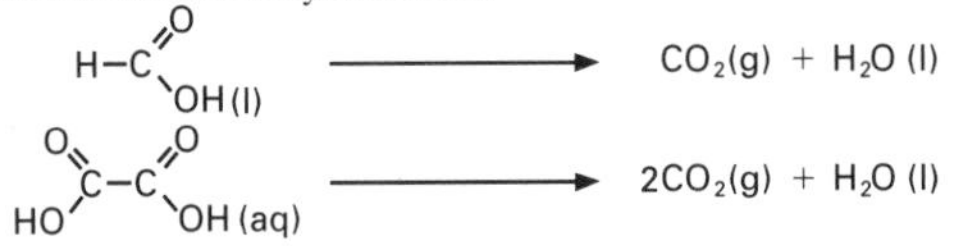 $H-C$ ($=O$, OH) (l) → $CO_2(g) + H_2O(l)$ $C-C$ (HO, OH) (aq) → $2CO_2(g) + H_2O(l)$
concentrated sulphuric acid, warming	both acids are **dehydrated**: 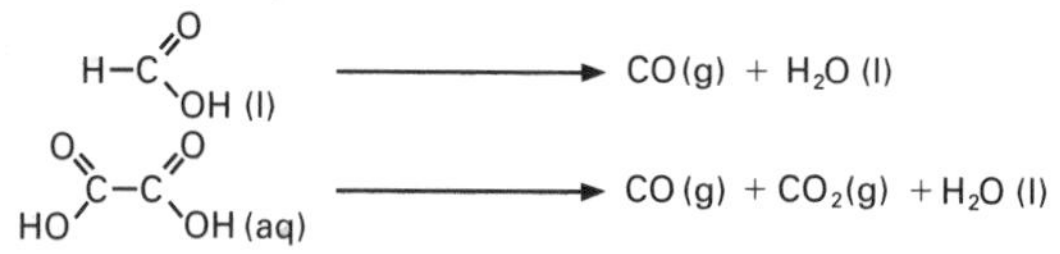 $H-C$ ($=O$, OH) (l) → $CO(g) + H_2O(l)$ $C-C$ (HO, OH) (aq) → $CO(g) + CO_2(g) + H_2O(l)$
Tollen's reagent, i.e. $[Ag(NH_3)_2]^+$(aq) (section 39.8.1)	methanoic acid is **oxidised** and silver is precipitated: 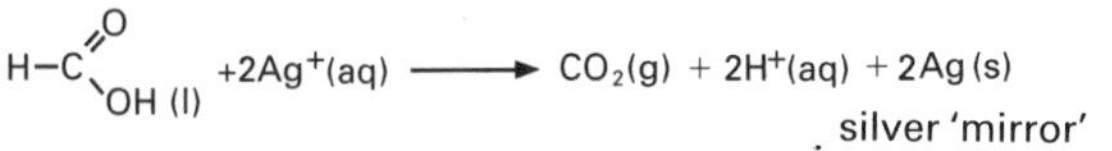 $H-C$ ($=O$, OH) (l) $+2Ag^+$(aq) → $CO_2(g) + 2H^+$(aq) $+ 2Ag(s)$ silver 'mirror' Like aldehydes, methanoic acid contains the **H—C=O** group; thus, it is oxidised by Tollen's reagent. Ethanedioic acid has no H—C=O group so it does not react

How would you distinguish between aqueous solutions of methanoic and ethanedioic acids?

40.7 Salts of the carboxylic acids

Salts of the carboxylic acids are prepared by reacting the acid with a moderately reactive metal, e.g.

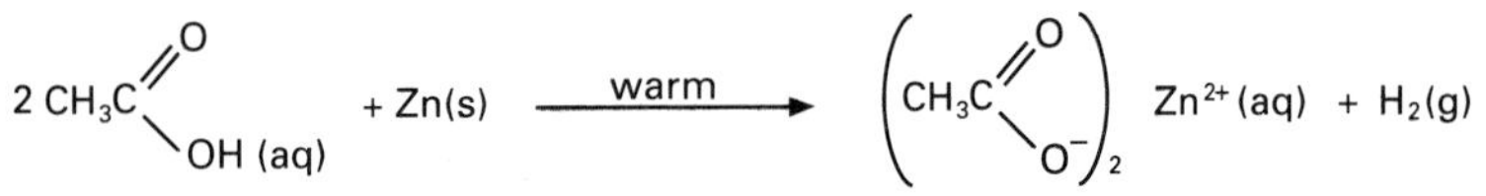

$$2\ CH_3C\!\!\diagup_{OH\ (aq)}^{O} + Zn(s) \xrightarrow{\text{warm}} \left(CH_3C\!\!\diagup_{O^-}^{O}\right)_{\!2} Zn^{2+}(aq)\ +\ H_2(g)$$

ethanoic acid   zinc ethanoate

or an alkali, e.g.

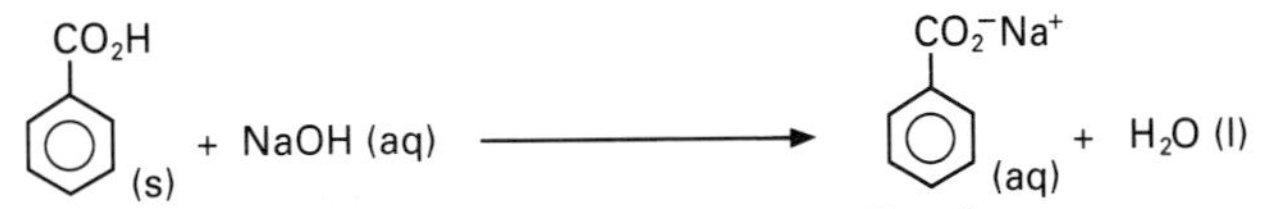

CO₂H (s) + NaOH (aq) ⟶ CO₂⁻Na⁺ (aq) + H₂O (l)
    sodium benzoate

The solid salts can be obtained by evaporating the aqueous solution. Notice how the **carboxylate ion** is named by changing the 'oic acid' to 'oate'.

Most widely used are the salts of sodium and potassium. These are white, crystalline solids. Due to their ionic nature, they have high melting points and are very soluble in water. Since they are the salts of a weak acid and a strong base, their aqueous solutions undergo **salt hydrolysis** (section 18.8), e.g.

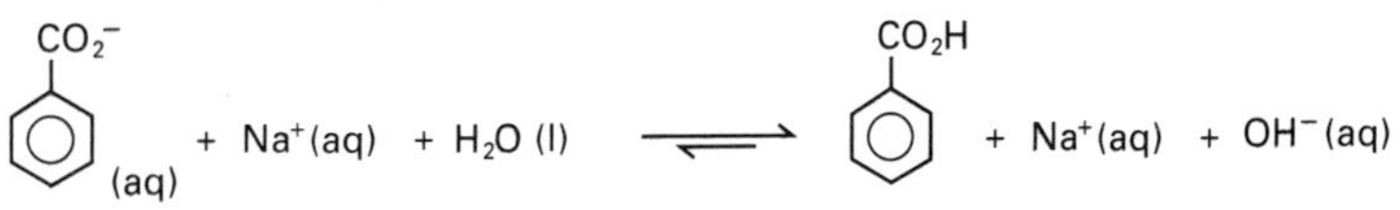

CO₂⁻ (aq) + Na⁺(aq) + H₂O (l) ⇌ CO₂H + Na⁺(aq) + OH⁻(aq)

Thus, their dilute aqueous solutions have a pH of about 9.

Some uses of carboxylic acid salts are given below.

▶ **Decarboxylation**

When heated with soda-lime (NaOH(s)/CaO(s)), the sodium or potassium salt of an aliphatic acid forms an alkane which contains *one less* carbon atom;

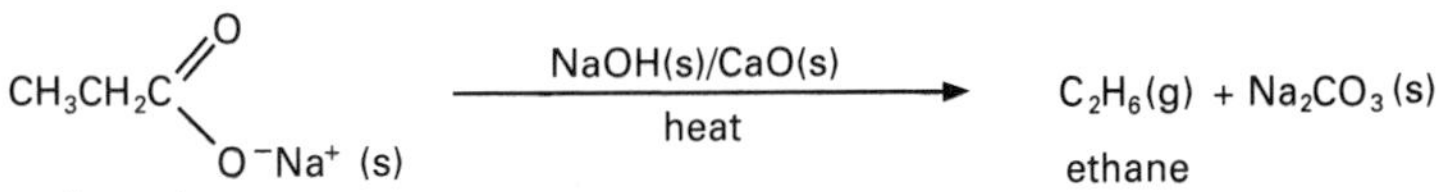

$$CH_3CH_2C\!\!\diagup_{O^-Na^+\ (s)}^{O} \xrightarrow[\text{heat}]{NaOH(s)/CaO(s)} C_2H_6(g)\ +\ Na_2CO_3\,(s)$$

sodium propanoate   ethane

With a benzoate, the product is benzene:

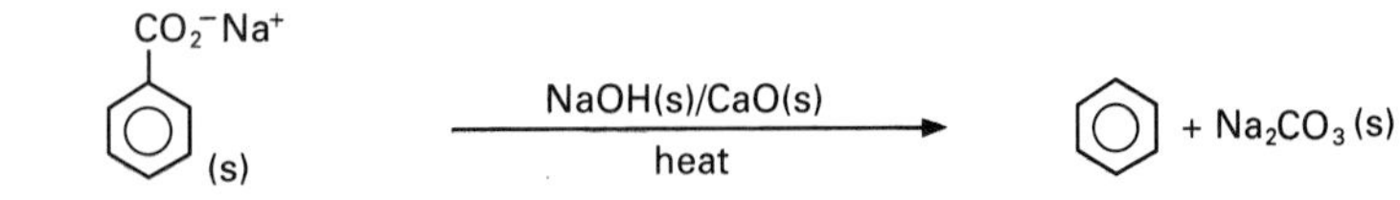

CO₂⁻Na⁺ (s) $\xrightarrow[\text{heat}]{NaOH(s)/CaO(s)}$ benzene + Na₂CO₃ (s)

sodium benzoate   benzene

Decarboxylation also occurs if the carboxylic acid is heated with soda-lime.

As you can see, decarboxylation can be used in organic synthesis to shorten a carbon chain.

▶ **The preparation of acid anhydrides**

When an anhydrous sodium salt is heated with an acid chloride, an acid anhydride is formed, e.g.

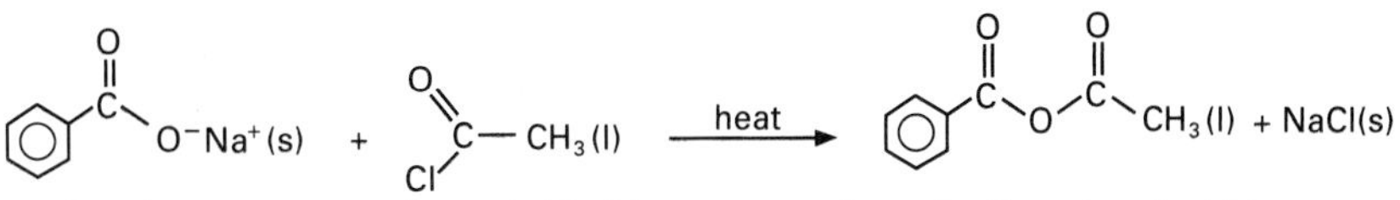

sodium benzoate + ethanoyl chloride $\xrightarrow{\text{heat}}$ benzoic ethanoic anhydride + NaCl(s)

▶ **The preparation of acid amides**

Carboxylic acids react readily with ammonium carbonate to give the ammonium salt:

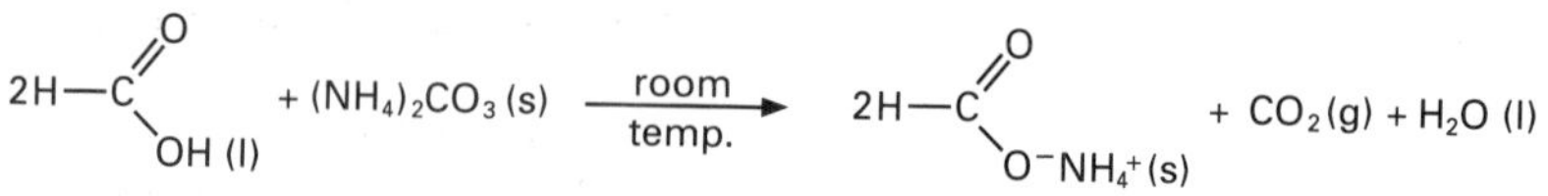

$$2H-C\underset{OH\ (l)}{\overset{O}{\Big\langle}} + (NH_4)_2CO_3\ (s) \xrightarrow[\text{temp.}]{\text{room}} 2H-C\underset{O^-NH_4^+\ (s)}{\overset{O}{\Big\langle}} + CO_2(g) + H_2O\ (l)$$

ammonium
methanoate

If *excess* acid is used, and the mixture is refluxed, the salt is dehydrated and an amide is formed:

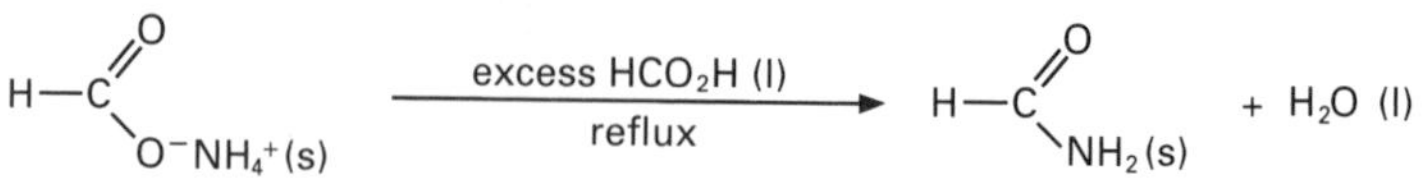

$$H-C\underset{O^-NH_4^+(s)}{\overset{O}{\Big\langle}} \xrightarrow[\text{reflux}]{\text{excess } HCO_2H\ (l)} H-C\underset{NH_2(s)}{\overset{O}{\Big\langle}} + H_2O\ (l)$$

methanamide

▶ **Soaps**

Soaps are the sodium, or potassium, salts of long-chain carboxylic acids. They are prepared by the alkaline hydrolysis of naturally occurring esters (section 40.11).

Finally, we must mention a valuable 'spot' test for the lower carboxylic acids and their salts. These react with a neutral solution of iron(III) chloride to give a red/brown solution of iron alkanoate, e.g.

$$3CH_3COO^-(aq) + Fe^{3+}(aq) \rightarrow (CH_3COO)_3Fe(aq)$$

iron(III) ethanoate,
a red solution

On boiling this solution, we get a brown precipitate of the basic iron(III) ethanoate e.g. $CH_3COOFe(OH)_2(s)$.

Benzoic acid will give similar reactions, but basic iron(III) benzoate is buff coloured.

Activity 40.5

Give the reagents and reaction conditions that you would use to convert propanoic acid into: (a) calcium propanoate, (b) ethane, (c) propanoic anhydride $(C_2H_5CO)_2O$ (2 steps) and (d) propanamide.

40.8 What are carboxylic acid derivatives?

Carboxylic acid derivatives may be thought of as a parent acid in which the hydroxy group has been replaced by another functional group, i.e.

$$\bullet-C\underset{O-H}{\overset{O}{\Big\langle}} \qquad\qquad \bullet-C\underset{X}{\overset{O}{\Big\langle}}$$

parent acid   acid derivative

Here ●— is an H atom or a hydrocarbon skeleton and X is one of *four* functional groups:—**Hal** in acid halides, $-O\overset{O}{\overset{\|}{-}}C-\square$ in acid anhydrides, $-O-\square$ in acid esters or $-NH_2$ in acid amides.

Naming acid derivatives

Acid halides

Name the parent acid and replace '**oic acid**' by '**oyl halide**', e.g.

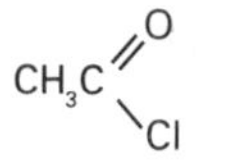

$$CH_3C\underset{Cl}{\overset{O}{\Big\langle}} \qquad CH_3-\underset{\underset{H}{|}}{\overset{\overset{CH_3}{|}}{C}}-C\underset{Br}{\overset{O}{\Big\langle}} \qquad \bigcirc\!\!\!\!\!\!-C\underset{I}{\overset{O}{\|}}$$

ethanoyl chloride 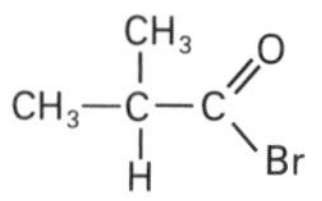   2–methylpropanoyl bromide 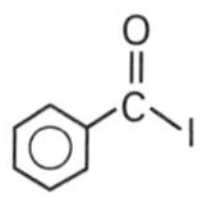   benzoyl iodide

Methanoyl chloride does not exist under normal laboratory conditions.

Acid anhydrides

Anhydrides consist of two carboxylic acid molecules which have been linked together with the loss of a water molecule. Thus, we just place the name(s) of the parent acid(s) in front of the word **anhydride**.

ethanoic anhydride   benzoic anhydride   benzoic propanoic anhydride

Note that methanoic anhydride does not exist.

Acid esters

Esters are named as though they are **alkyl** or **phenyl salts** of the parent acid, e.g.

methyl methanoate   phenyl ethanoate   ethyl benzoate

Acid amides

Name the parent acid and replace '**oic acid**' by '**amide**', e.g.

ethanamide   2–methylpropanamide   benzenecarbamide
(acetamide)   (benzamide)

Activity 40.6

1   Name the following carboxylic acid derivatives:

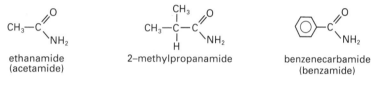

(a) CH_3-C ... (b) $CH_3CH_2CH_2C$ ... OCH_3 ... (c) $H-C$ ... NH_2

(d) ... (e) $C_2H_5CO_2C_2H_5$ ... (f) ...

2   Write down the structural formulae for the following compounds:
    (a) phenylethanoate (b) 2-phenylpropanamide (c) propanoic anhydride
    (d) 4-methylbenzoyl iodide (e) ethyl butanoate (f) methylbenzoate.

3   Which of the compounds in 1 and 2 are structural isomers?

40.9 The preparation and physical properties of acid derivatives

Preparation

Acid halides are easily prepared by treating the acid with a halogenating agent, e.g.

CH_3C ... OH (l) $+ SOCl_2$ (l) $\xrightarrow{\text{reflux}}$ CH_3C ... Cl (l) $+ SO_2$(g) $+ HCl$(g)

Some other halogenating agents are given in table 37.2.

Figure 40.6 *General structure of an acid derivative*

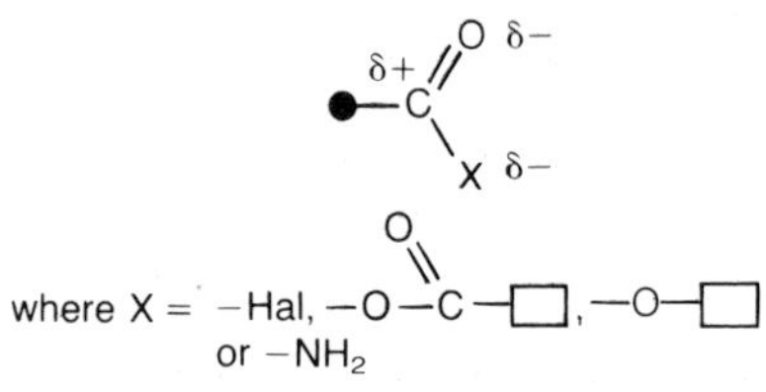

where X = −Hal, −O−C—□, −O—□
or −NH₂

Although various methods can be used, the other acid derivatives are conveniently prepared from acid chlorides (figure 40.7).

Physical properties

Whilst we need not discuss these in detail, certain trends are worth noting. The lower mass esters, halides and anhydrides are all fairly volatile liquids. They have strong odours, *the esters having well-known 'fruity' smells.*

For compounds of similar molecular mass, we find that:

esters/halides	anhydrides	acids	amides
	boiling points increase →		

This is explained by a corresponding increase in the strengths of the intermolecular forces.

Acid amides form extensive intermolecular *hydrogen bonds*:

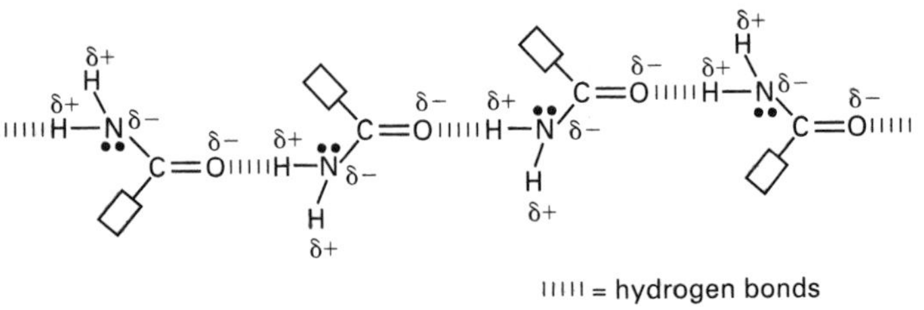

| | | | = hydrogen bonds

Consequently, apart from methanamide, which is a liquid, *the amides are white crystalline solids of fairly high melting point.* When purified, an amide can often be identified from its sharp melting point.

The *water solubility* of the aliphatic acid derivatives, of low molecular mass, increases in the order:

esters (insoluble)	anhydrides	acids	amides (very soluble)
	increasing solubility in water →		

Esters are insoluble because they are unable to hydrogen bond with water; amides do so readily, and this makes them very soluble in water.

40.10 Reactions of the acid derivatives

As well as reactions of the hydrocarbon skeleton, we might expect an acid derivative (figure 40.6) to give two types of reaction:

▶ *addition to the C=O bond* (as in aldehydes and ketones); and
▶ *substitution of the X-group*, via a nucleophilic attack at $C^{\delta+}$.

Since almost identical reactive centres are found in carboxylic acids, there should be some similarity between reactions of the acids and their derivatives. Bear this in mind as you work through this section. (For simplicity, the chloride is taken as an example of an acid halide; bromides and iodides have similar, yet slower, reactions.)

40.10.1 Addition reactions across the C=O bond

Like the carboxylic acids themselves, the derivatives do not give the typical addition reactions shown by aldehydes and ketones (e.g. with HCN or NaHSO₃). Once again, the only addition reaction is *reduction*, that is, the addition of hydrogen. When refluxed with lithium tetrahydridoaluminate in ethoxyethane, acid halides, esters and anhydrides give the corresponding alcohol(s), e.g.

Amides are reduced to amines, e.g.

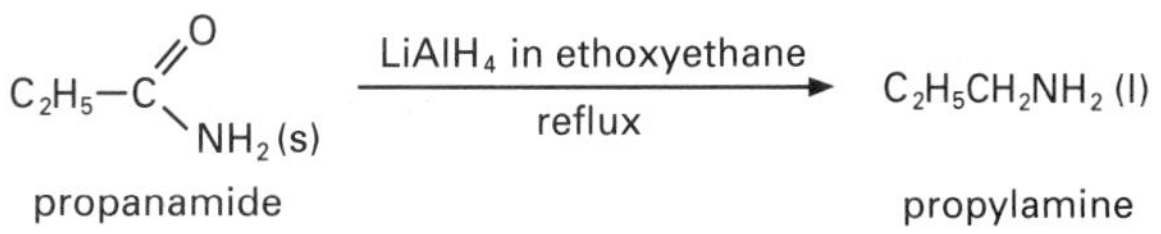

$$C_2H_5-C\overset{O}{\underset{NH_2(s)}{\Big\backslash}} \quad \xrightarrow[\text{reflux}]{\text{LiAlH}_4 \text{ in ethoxyethane}} \quad C_2H_5CH_2NH_2 \text{ (l)}$$

propanamide propylamine

40.10.2 Substitution of the −X group

Acid derivatives, like the parent acids, take part in a number of substitution reactions, and these are summarised in figure 40.7. These reactions occur at very

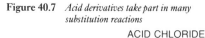

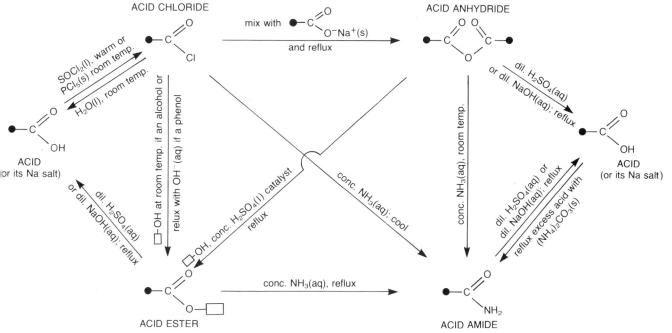

different rates. For example, ethanoyl chloride is vigorously hydrolysed by cold water:

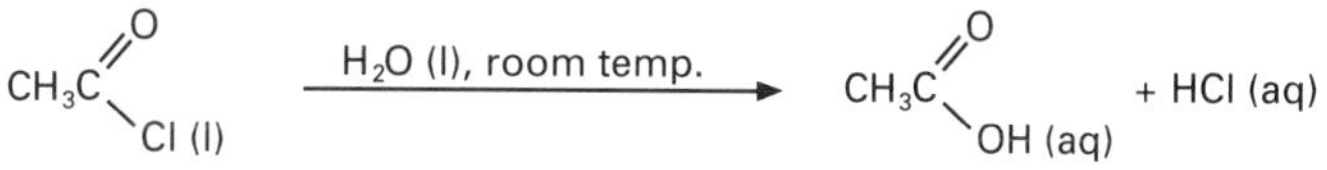

$$CH_3C\overset{O}{\underset{Cl\,(l)}{\Big\backslash}} \quad \xrightarrow{\text{H}_2\text{O (l), room temp.}} \quad CH_3C\overset{O}{\underset{OH\,(aq)}{\Big\backslash}} + HCl \text{ (aq)}$$

However, the hydrolysis of ethanamide by boiling water is slow unless an acid or base catalyst is added, e.g.

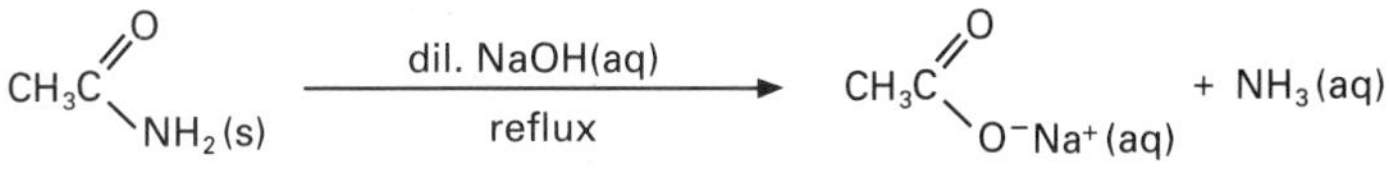

$$CH_3C\overset{O}{\underset{NH_2(s)}{\Big\backslash}} \quad \xrightarrow[\text{reflux}]{\text{dil. NaOH(aq)}} \quad CH_3C\overset{O}{\underset{O^-Na^+(aq)}{\Big\backslash}} + NH_3 \text{ (aq)}$$

In fact, for the same attacking nucleophile, the rates of substitution reactions increase in the order:

amides   esters   anhydrides   carboxylic acids   acid chlorides

→ rates get faster

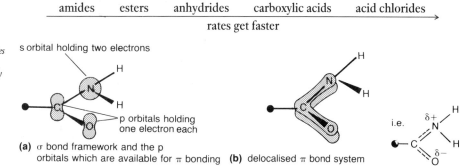

(a) σ bond framework and the p orbitals which are available for π bonding **(b)** delocalised π bond system

Amides are especially resistant to nucleophilic attack because of electron delocalisation (figure 40.8). This has two effects:

▶ it decreases the δ+ charge on the carbon, making it less attractive to the attacking nucleophile; and

▶ it gives some π bond character to the C—N bond, making it more difficult to break.

Another effect of this delocalisation is that amides are much weaker bases than amines (see section 41.7).

Nucleophilic substitution reactions of acid derivatives proceed via two main steps. First, the nucleophile attacks the carbonyl carbon:

Then, the carbonyl bond reforms and the leaving group departs:

Soaps are the salts of long-chain carboxylic acids. They are manufactured by the alkaline hydrolysis, or **saponification**, of naturally occurring esters (section 40.11). In fact, soap-making dates back to Roman times, and the name saponification comes from the Latin *sapons facio*: to make soap.

40.10.3 Some important reactions of acid amides

Although it is resistant to nucleophilic substitution, the $-NH_2$ group in an amide undergoes three important reactions.

▶ **Dehydration**
We can prepare a **nitrile** by heating a mixture of an amide and phosphorus(V) oxide (a strong dehydrating agent), e.g.

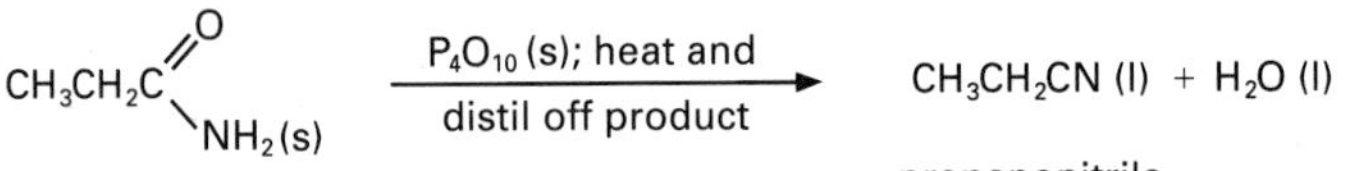

▶ **With nitrous acid**
Nitrous acid, which is prepared *in situ* from sodium nitrite and hydrochloric acid, converts an amide into its parent *acid*, e.g.:

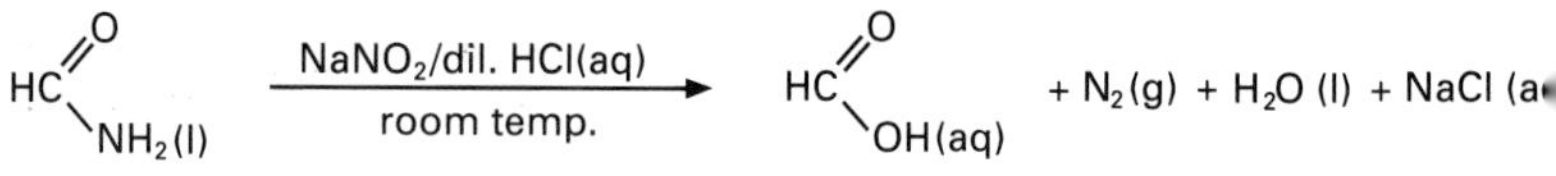

A similar reaction is used to identify the $-NH_2$ group in a primary aliphatic amine (section 41.8.3).

▶ **Hofmann's degradation**
When treated with bromine and concentrated potassium hydroxide, an amide yields an *amine containing one less carbon atom*:

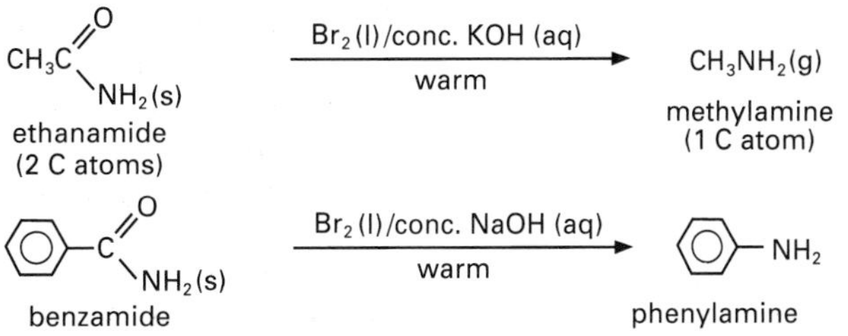

The reaction, known as the Hofmann degradation, is carried out by (i) mixing the amide with bromine; (ii) adding aqueous sodium or potassium hydroxide, with shaking, until the mixture turns yellow; (iii) adding potassium hydroxide pellets and warming at about 70 °C.

Hofmann's degradation is useful in synthesis because *it provides a way of shortening a hydrocarbon chain*. Also note that amides can be reduced to give amines containing the *same* number of carbon atoms, e.g.

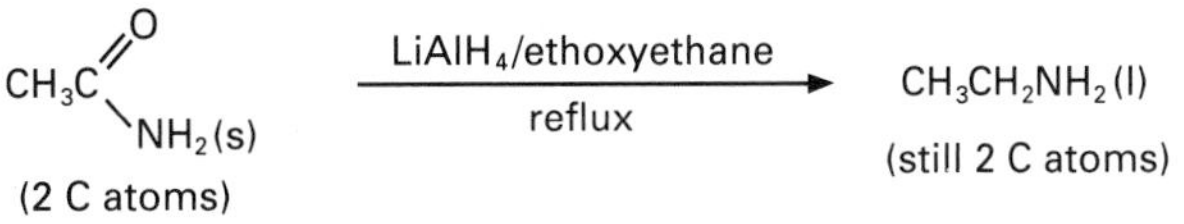

Activity 40.7

1   Give the name(s) and structural formula(e) of organic product(s) formed in the following reactions:

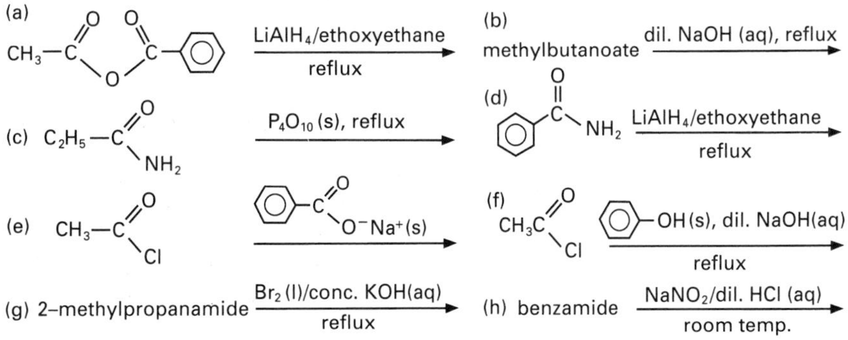

2   This question covers the material in sections 40.4 to 40.11. Give the reagents and reaction conditions needed for the following conversions:

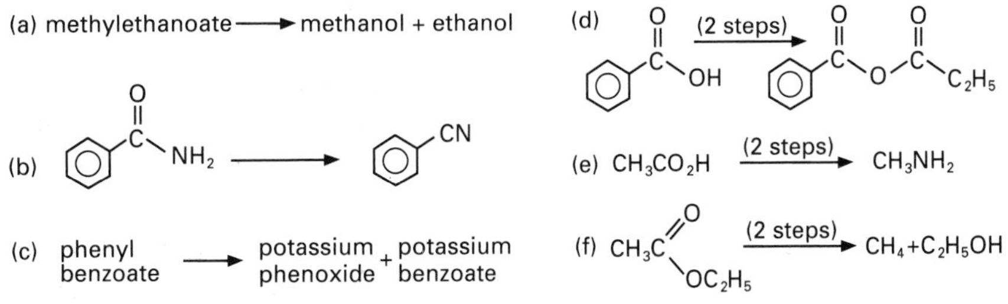

Parts (g) to (j) cover material from this chapter and earlier chapters:

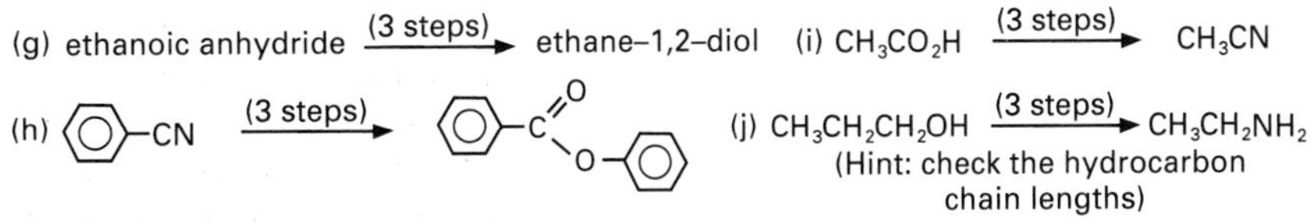

Nylon (a polyamide) and polyester fibres are used in enormous quantities in the manufacture of fabrics for clothing

Soaps are made by hydrolysing naturally-occurring carboxylic esters

3 Explain how conc. $NH_3(aq)$ can be used to identify an unknown acid chloride.

40.11 Important industrial applications of acid derivatives

Unless you are reading this book in the bath, there is a good chance that you are wearing a carboxylic acid derivative! Indeed, when you take a bath, or shower, you will probably use a substance which was made from an acid derivative. Puzzled? Have a look at the photograph.

Nowadays, a lot of clothing is made from fabric which contains a mixture of *natural* fibres (e.g. wool, silk and cotton) and *synthetic* fibres (e.g. polyester and nylon). Synthetic fabrics, though not as soft as the natural materials, are cheaper, harder wearing and wash well. Common examples of a **nylon (Nylon 66)** and a **polyester (Terylene)** are given below:

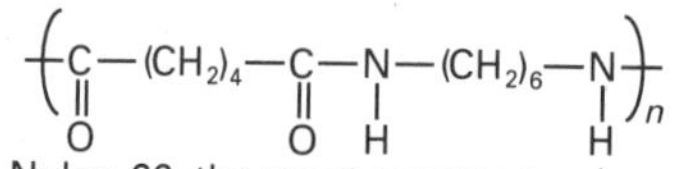

Nylon 66, the most common nylon, is a polyamide; $n \simeq 40-80$

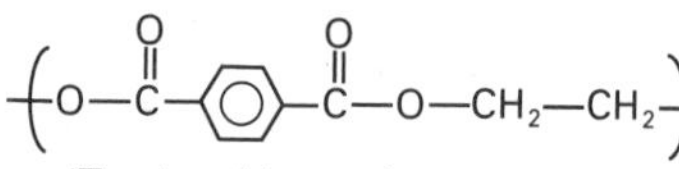

'Terylene' is a polyester; $n \simeq 80$

Soaps are the long-chain salts of carboxylic acids, such as **sodium stearate, $CH_3(CH_2)_{16}CO_2^- Na^+$**. They are made by the saponification of various naturally occurring esters.

In this section, we shall briefly describe the manufacture of Nylon 66, Terylene and soap.

Nylon 66

First marketed in 1940, Nylon 66 was the first completely synthetic fibre. It was developed at the same time in **N**ew **Y**ork and **Lon**don; hence the name. Nylon 66 is now prepared by the co-polymerisation of **hexanedioic acid** and **1,6-diaminohexane**:

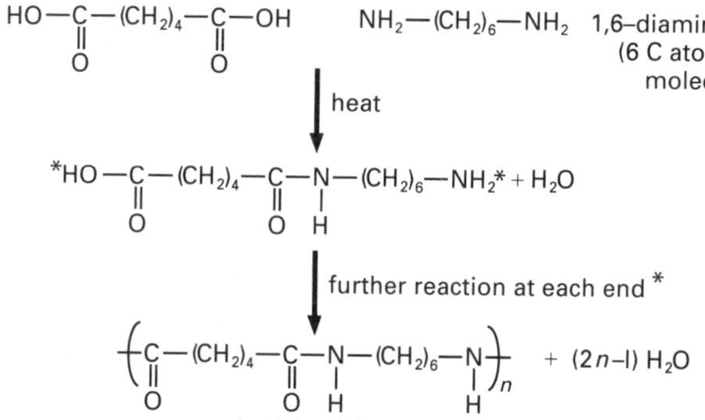

hexanedioic acid (6 C atoms per molecule)

$NH_2-(CH_2)_6-NH_2$ 1,6-diaminohexane (6 C atoms per molecule)

heat

further reaction at each end *

Nylon 66

The product is known as Nylon 66 because both of the monomers have molecules which contain **6** carbon atoms. Each monomer is attached to its neighbour by a **peptide link**, (section 41.11). Every time a peptide link is formed, a water molecule is released. Thus, this is an example of a **condensation** reaction (i.e. *one in which a small molecule, such as H_2O, is released*).

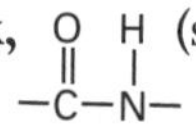

The monomers are made from benzene, as shown below:

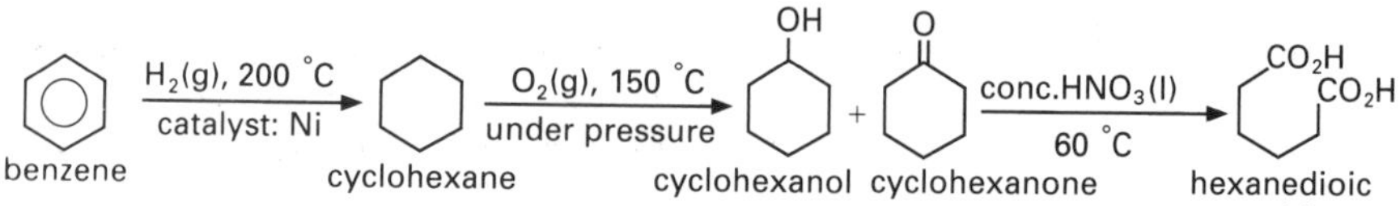

benzene $\xrightarrow[\text{catalyst: Ni}]{H_2(g), 200\,°C}$ cyclohexane $\xrightarrow[\text{under pressure}]{O_2(g), 150\,°C}$ cyclohexanol + cyclohexanone $\xrightarrow[60\,°C]{conc.HNO_3(l)}$ hexanedioic acid

What properties of nylon make it suitable for use in inflatable boats?

Figure 40.9 *The polymer chains of a nylon are (a) disordered after extrusion, (i.e. forcing through small holes). On 'cold drawing' (i.e. gentle stretching), the chains adopt the same orientation*

Some hexanedioic acid is converted into 1,6-diaminohexane:

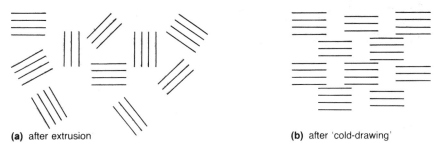

Since nylons melt without decomposition, the hot polymer can be **extruded**, that is, forced through small holes called **spinnerets**. As they emerge, the streams of liquid polymer are cooled and they solidify. In this state, the fibres have little strength because the long chain molecules of the polymer are disordered. However,

(a) after extrusion **(b)** after 'cold-drawing'

when the fibres are gently stretched, the molecular chains adopt the same orientation (figure 40.9). This enables the fibres to *cross-link* via *hydrogen bonding*:

Due to this treatment, the nylon fibres become much stronger and more elastic. These properties, and its ability to wash well, have made nylon a popular material in the clothing industry. Nylon is used in many other situations, e.g. carpet piles, brushes and fishing lines.

Figure 40.10 shows how easy it is to prepare Nylon 66 in the laboratory.

Figure 40.10 *The laboratory preparation of Nylon 66 is quite simple. A pair of tongs is used to pull out the nylon which forms at the interface between the solutions. The reaction is*

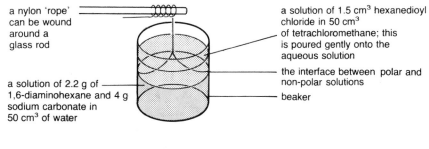

a nylon 'rope' can be wound around a glass rod

a solution of 2.2 g of 1,6-diaminohexane and 4 g sodium carbonate in 50 cm³ of water

a solution of 1.5 cm³ hexanedioyl chloride in 50 cm³ of tetrachloromethane; this is poured gently onto the aqueous solution

the interface between polar and non-polar solutions

beaker

Terylene

'Terylene', another condensation polymer, also made its commercial impact in the 1940s. It is a polyester formed by the condensation co-polymerisation of **benzene-1,4-dicarboxylic acid** and **ethane-1,2-diol**:

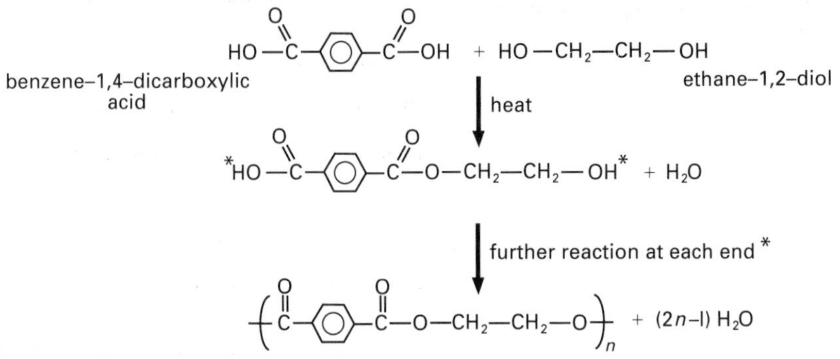

benzene–1,4–dicarboxylic acid   ethane–1,2–diol

where n is usually about 80. Both monomers are obtained from petroleum, as shown below:

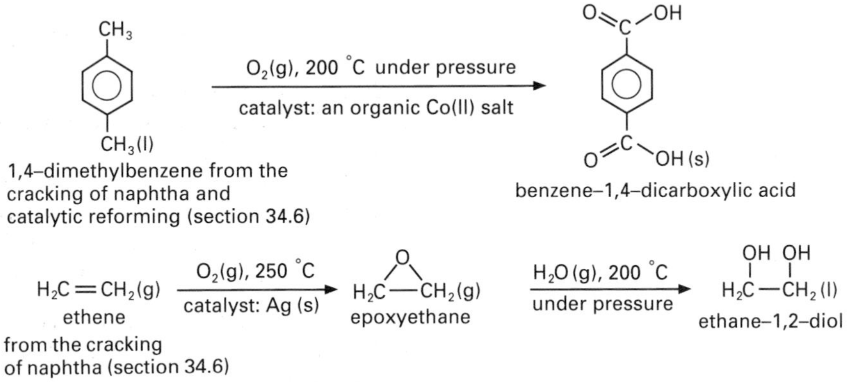

1,4–dimethylbenzene from the cracking of naphtha and catalytic reforming (section 34.6)

benzene–1,4–dicarboxylic acid

ethene
from the cracking of naphtha (section 34.6)

epoxyethane

ethane–1,2–diol

Like nylon, molten Terylene can be extruded and stretched. This allows cross-linking of chains to occur via *dipole–dipole bonding*:

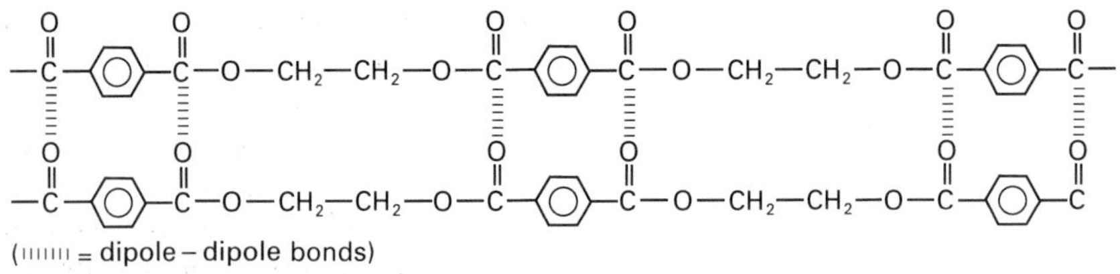

(⁞⁞⁞⁞⁞ = dipole – dipole bonds)

Once again, strong, highly elastic fibres are produced and these are mainly used to make clothing.

Soaps and detergents

Soaps are made by the saponification, that is, alkaline hydrolysis, of fats and oils. These are known as **glycerides** because they are the triesters of propane-1,2,3-triol (glycerol) and long-chain aliphatic carboxylic acids. The general reaction is

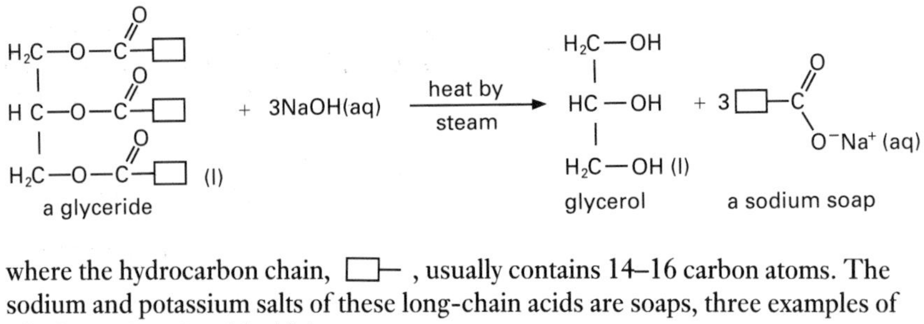

a glyceride   glycerol   a sodium soap

where the hydrocarbon chain, ☐─ , usually contains 14–16 carbon atoms. The sodium and potassium salts of these long-chain acids are soaps, three examples of which are given in table 40.4.

Table 40.4 *Some common soaps and the fats/oils from which they are made*

Source	soap	formula
animal fats	sodium stearate	$CH_3(CH_2)_{16}COO^-Na^+$
palm oil	sodium palmitate	$CH_3(CH_2)_{14}COO^-Na^+$
olive oil	potassium oleate	$CH_3(CH_2)_7CH{=}CH(CH_2)_7COO^-Na^+$

Although they have long hydrocarbon chains, soaps dissolve in water. Can you explain why?

In the manufacture of a sodium soap, steam is passed for several hours through a mixture of the molten fats, oils and aqueous sodium hydroxide. During saponification, some soap floats to the top of the reaction mixture where it is skimmed off. However, much of the soap is dissolved in the aqueous solution,

$$\boxed{}{-}CO_2^-Na^+(s) \rightleftharpoons \boxed{}{-}CO_2^-(aq) \quad + \quad Na^+(aq)$$

Adding sodium chloride causes the system to shift to the left, thereby precipitating the soap. This technique, known as **salting out**, is an example of the **common ion effect** (section 15.4).

After removing the soap, the glycerol is obtained from the aqueous solution by distillation. Since glycerol has many uses (e.g. medicines, manufacture of nitroglycerine), it is a marketable by-product. In a more modern method, soap is made by using superheated steam to hydrolyse the fats.

Identical methods can be used to make potassium soaps. These are *softer* and *more soluble* in water than sodium soaps. Most commerical products are a mixture of various soaps, disinfectants, perfumes and colouring agents.

Activity 40.8

Soaps work by helping water to remove the thin layer of grease which holds particles of 'dirt' on our bodies, clothes, plates, etc. To observe this effect, try the following simple experiment.

1 Place 10 drops of cooking oil in a test-tube and gently swirl it round. Add $2\,cm^3$ of distilled water. Cork the test-tube, shake vigorously and leave the test-tube to stand for a couple of minutes. What do you see?
2 Empty the test-tube and look at its walls. Are they clean?
3 Repeat 1 and 2, but using $2\,cm^3$ of aqueous soap solution instead of water. What do you see this time?

Soaps help grease, a *non-polar* substance, to mix with water, a *polar* solvent. Looking at the structure of a soap, we can see why this happens:

long hydrocarbon chain
(non–polar) will mix with
grease (also non–polar)

ionic part will mix
with water (polar)

Whilst the long hydrocarbon chain readily dissolves non-polar molecules, such as grease, the ionic $-COO^-$ group enables the soap to dissolve in water.

Soapless detergents have similar structures:

← - - - - - - non–polar part - - - - - - - - → ← polar →
(ionic)
part

They are made from **alkylbenzenes** produced in the petroleum industry, e.g.

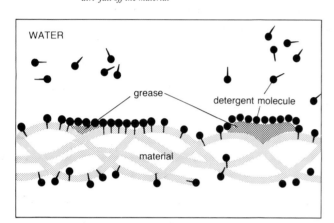

Figure 40.11 *Detergents enable grease and water to mix together. Once the thin layer of grease is removed, the particles of 'dirt' fall off the material*

a soapless detergent

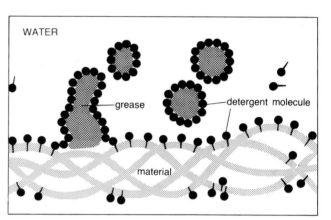

Figure 40.11 hows how soaps and detergents remove grease from clothing. Soaps have the disadvantage that they form a precipitate, or **scum** with the calcium and magnesium ions found in hard water, e.g.

Apart from its unpleasant appearance, the formation of a 'scum' wastes a lot of soap. Detergents, on the other hand, do not form 'scums' because their calcium and magnesium salts are soluble in water.

40.12 Comments on the activities

Activity 40.1

1 (a) 2,2-dimethylpropanoic acid. (b) butanedioic acid.
   (c) 3-hydroxybenzoic acid. (d) 2-phenylpropanoic acid.
   (e) 3-methylbutanoic acid. (f) 2-hydroxy-2-methylbutanoic acid.

2

(a) $CH_3CH_2CH_2CH_2C$ with $=O$ and OH (pentanoic acid structure)

(b) Phenyl ring $-\overset{3}{C}H_2\overset{2}{C}H_2\overset{1}{C}$ with $=O$ and OH

(c) $HO-C(=O)-CH=CH-C(=O)-OH$ with H atoms below

cis–butenedioic acid

$HO-C(=O)-C=C$ with H and $C(=O)OH$

trans–butenedioic acid

(d) $HO-C=O$ attached to benzene ring with OH

(e) $Cl-\overset{H}{\underset{H}{C}}-C$ with $=O$ and OH

(f) $CH_3CH_2-\overset{OH}{\underset{H}{C}}-C$ with $=O$ and OH

3 (a) pentanoic acid, 3-methylbutanoic acid and 2,2-dimethylpropanoic acid are all $C_5H_{10}O_2$;
3-hydroxybenzoic acid and 2-hydroxybenzoic acid, both $C_7H_6O_3$;
2-phenylpropanoic acid and 3-phenylpropanoic acid, both $C_9H_{10}O_2$.

(b) 2-phenylpropanoic acid, 2-hydroxy-2-methylbutanoic acid and 2-hydroxybutanoic acid; all have an *asymmetric* carbon atom.

Activity 40.2

(a) $K_2Cr_2O_7$/dil. H_2SO_4(aq), reflux; *or* $KMnO_4$/dil.H_2SO_4(aq), reflux.
(b) dil.H_2SO_4(aq), reflux.
(c) as (a).
(d) as (b).

(e) $C_2H_5Br \xrightarrow[\text{reflux}]{\text{KCN in ethanol}} C_2H_5CN \xrightarrow[\text{reflux}]{\text{dil. } H_2SO_4\text{(aq)}} C_2H_5CO_2H$

Activity 40.3

1 Apart from (d), each reaction involves *a stronger acid displacing a weaker acid from its salt*. Thus, the products will be: (a) sodium chloroethanoate and benzoic acid, (b) sodium methanoate and butanoic acid, (c) potassium chloride and methanoic acid (e) magnesium benzenesulphonate and bromoethanoic acid. In (d), there will be no reaction because bromoethanoic acid is a stronger acid than propanoic acid.

2 (a) $ClCH_2CH_2CH_2COOH$, $ClCH_2CH_2COOH$, $ClCH_2COOH$. Reason: increasing acidity as the halogen atom gets *closer* to the carboxyl group.

(b) 2-methylpropanoic acid, propanoic acid, 3-iodopropanoic acid, 2-iodopropanoic acid, 2-bromopropanoic acid, 2-chloropropanoic acid. Reason: increasing acidity as the Y group in $Y-CO_2H$ becomes better able to *attract* electron cloud to itself.

(c) 4-methylbenzoic acid, benzoic acid, 4-chlorobenzoic acid and 2,4-dichlorobenzoic acid. Reason: increasing ability of the substituent group(s) to *attract* electron cloud.

Activity 40.4

(a) $CH_3CH_2CH_2OH$
propan–1–ol

(b) Benzene ring $-C(=O)-OCH_3$
methyl benzoate

(c) HC with $=O$ and O^-K^+
potassium methanoate

(d) $CH_3-\overset{CH_3}{\underset{Cl}{C}}-C$ with $=O$ and Cl
2–chloro–2–methyl propanoyl chloride

(e) CBr_3C with $=O$ and OH
tribromoethanoic acid

(f) $Br-C=O$ attached to benzene ring
benzoyl bromide

2

(a) CH_3CH_2C (with =O and OH), catalyst: conc. H_2SO_4 (l), reflux.

(b) $P_{(red)} + I_2$ (s), reflux *or* $NaI(s)/conc. H_3PO_4$ (l), reflux.

(c)

$\xrightarrow[\text{reflux}]{K_2Cr_2O_7/\text{dil. } H_2SO_4 \text{(aq)}}$ ... $\xrightarrow[\text{conc. } H_2SO_4 \text{(l) reflux}]{CH_3OH(l),\text{catalyst:}}$

(d) CH_3CH_2CN $\xrightarrow[\text{reflux}]{\text{dil. } H_2SO_4 \text{(aq)}}$ $CH_3CH_2CO_2H$ $\xrightarrow[\text{reflux}]{LiAlH_4/\text{ethoxyethane}}$ $CH_3CH_2CH_2OH$

(e) CH_3CH_2C (with =O and NH_2) $\xrightarrow[\text{reflux}]{\text{dil. } H_2SO_4 \text{(aq)}}$ CH_3CH_2C (with =O and OH) $\xrightarrow[\text{reflux}]{P_{(red)}/Br_2(l)}$ CH_3CH_2C (with =O and Br)

(f) $CH_3CH_2CO_2H$ $\xrightarrow[\text{reflux}]{LiAlH_4/\text{ethoxyethane}}$ $CH_3CH_2CH_2OH$ $\xrightarrow[\text{180 °C}]{\text{conc. } H_2SO_4 \text{(l) excess}}$ $CH_3CH=CH_2$

$CH_3CHBrCH_2Br$ $\xleftarrow[\text{room temp.}]{Br_2 \text{ in } CCl_4 \text{(l)}}$

(g) CH_3CH_2Cl $\xrightarrow[\text{reflux}]{\text{dil. NaOH(aq)}}$ CH_3CH_2OH $\xrightarrow[\text{reflux}]{K_2Cr_2O_7/\text{dil. } H_2SO_4 \text{(aq)}}$ CH_3CO_2H

$ClCH_2CO_2H$ $\xleftarrow[\text{heat}]{Cl_2(g), \text{ u.v. light}}$

(h) $CH_3CH=CH_2$ $\xrightarrow[\substack{\text{temp.} \\ \text{(Markovnikov's Rule} \\ \text{obeyed)}}]{HI(g),\text{room}}$ CH_3CHICH_3 $\xrightarrow[\text{reflux}]{KCN/\text{ethanol}}$ CH_3CHCH_3 (with CN)

CH_3CHCH_3 (with COOH) $\xleftarrow[\text{reflux}]{\text{dil. } H_2SO_4 \text{(aq)}}$

Activity 40.5

(a) Ca(s) room temperature; you could also heat the acid with $Ca(OH)_2$(s) or $CaCO_3$(s).

(b) Soda-lime (NaOH(s)/CaO(s)), heat.

(c)

$CH_3CH_2CO_2H(l)$ $\xrightarrow[\text{room temp.}]{\text{dil. NaOH(aq)}}$ $CH_3CH_2CO_2^- Na^+$ (s) $\xrightarrow[\text{reflux}]{CH_3CH_2C(\text{=O})Cl(l)}$ $(CH_3CH_2C(\text{=O}))_2O$ (l)

propanoic acid — sodium propanoate

(d) $(NH_4)_2CO_3$(s) with excess $CH_3CH_2CO_2H$(l), reflux.

Activity 40.6

1 (a) ethanoyl iodide   (b) methylbutanoate
   (c) methanamide   (d) ethanoic butanoic anhydride
   (e) ethyl propanoate   (f) 3-phenylpropanoyl chloride

2

(a) CH_3-C (=O, O-phenyl)

(b) $CH_3-C(H)-C$ (=O, NH_2) with phenyl

(c) CH_3CH_2C (=O)-O-(=O)CCH_2CH_3

(d) CH_3-(phenyl labelled 4,3,2,1)-C(=O, I)

(e) $CH_3CH_2CH_2C$ (=O, OC_2H_5)

(f) phenyl-C (=O, OCH_3)

3 Methyl benzoate and phenyl ethanoate, both $C_8H_8O_2$; ethanoic butanoic anhydride and propanoic anhydride, both $C_6H_{10}O_3$.

Activity 40.7

1

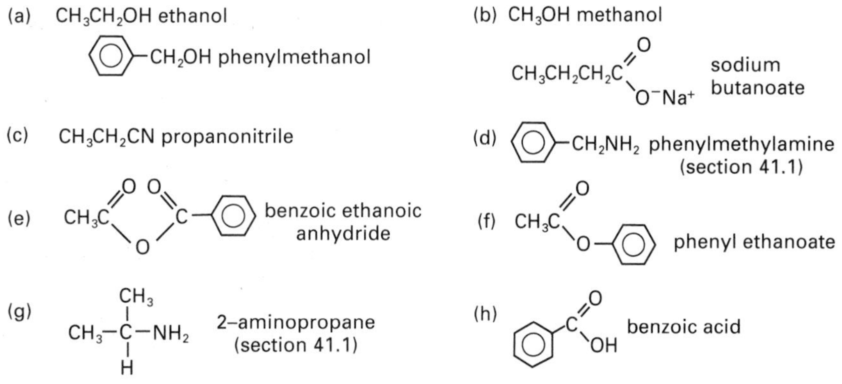

(a) CH$_3$CH$_2$OH ethanol

    ⬡—CH$_2$OH phenylmethanol

(b) CH$_3$OH methanol

    CH$_3$CH$_2$CH$_2$C(=O)O$^-$Na$^+$ sodium butanoate

(c) CH$_3$CH$_2$CN propanonitrile

(d) ⬡—CH$_2$NH$_2$ phenylmethylamine (section 41.1)

(e) CH$_3$C(=O)—O—C(=O)—⬡ benzoic ethanoic anhydride

(f) CH$_3$C(=O)—O—⬡ phenyl ethanoate

(g)
       CH$_3$
       |
  CH$_3$—C—NH$_2$ 2–aminopropane (section 41.1)
       |
       H

(h) ⬡—C(=O)OH   benzoic acid

2 (a) LiAlH$_4$/ethoxyethane, reflux.
   (b) P$_4$O$_{10}$(s), heat and distil off the product.
   (c) dil. KOH(aq), reflux.

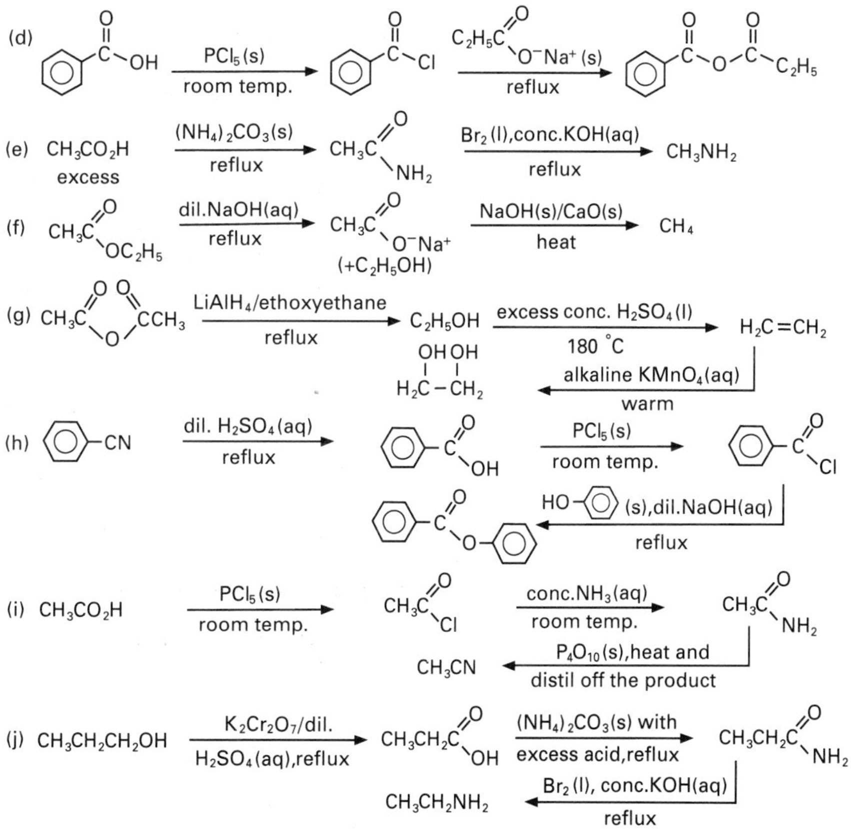

(d) ⬡—C(=O)OH →[PCl$_5$(s), room temp.] ⬡—C(=O)Cl →[C$_2$H$_5$C(=O)O$^-$Na$^+$(s), reflux] ⬡—C(=O)—O—C(=O)—C$_2$H$_5$

(e) CH$_3$CO$_2$H (excess) →[(NH$_4$)$_2$CO$_3$(s), reflux] CH$_3$C(=O)NH$_2$ →[Br$_2$(l), conc.KOH(aq), reflux] CH$_3$NH$_2$

(f) CH$_3$C(=O)OC$_2$H$_5$ →[dil.NaOH(aq), reflux] CH$_3$C(=O)O$^-$Na$^+$ (+C$_2$H$_5$OH) →[NaOH(s)/CaO(s), heat] CH$_4$

(g) CH$_3$C(=O)—O—C(=O)CH$_3$ →[LiAlH$_4$/ethoxyethane, reflux] C$_2$H$_5$OH →[excess conc. H$_2$SO$_4$(l), 180 °C] H$_2$C=CH$_2$ →[alkaline KMnO$_4$(aq), warm] OHOH | | H$_2$C–CH$_2$

(h) ⬡—CN →[dil. H$_2$SO$_4$(aq), reflux] ⬡—C(=O)OH →[PCl$_5$(s), room temp.] ⬡—C(=O)Cl →[HO—⬡ (s), dil.NaOH(aq), reflux] ⬡—C(=O)—O—⬡

(i) CH$_3$CO$_2$H →[PCl$_5$(s), room temp.] CH$_3$C(=O)Cl →[conc.NH$_3$(aq), room temp.] CH$_3$C(=O)NH$_2$ →[P$_4$O$_{10}$(s), heat and distil off the product] CH$_3$CN

(j) CH$_3$CH$_2$CH$_2$OH →[K$_2$Cr$_2$O$_7$/dil. H$_2$SO$_4$(aq), reflux] CH$_3$CH$_2$C(=O)OH →[(NH$_4$)$_2$CO$_3$(s) with excess acid, reflux] CH$_3$CH$_2$C(=O)NH$_2$ →[Br$_2$(l), conc.KOH(aq), reflux] CH$_3$CH$_2$NH$_2$

3 Prepare the amide,

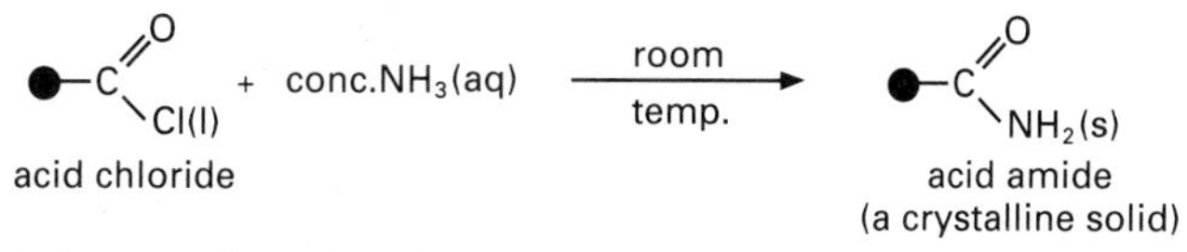

●—C(=O)Cl(l) + conc.NH$_3$(aq) →[room temp.] ●—C(=O)NH$_2$(s)

acid chloride   acid amide (a crystalline solid)

purify it and take its melting point. Look up the value in a book of data and identify the acid amide. Hence work out the acid chloride from which it was made.

Activity 40.8

You have probably made the following observations:

1 When the oil is shaken with distilled water, a cloudy emulsion is formed. On standing, this separates to give two layers: oil on top, water below.
2 Although we can now remove some of the oil by emptying the test-tube, oily drops still remain on its walls. It is still 'greasy'.
3 In the presence of soap, though, the oil and water give a cloudy mixture which does not form layers on standing. Moreover, on emptying the tube its walls are found to be clean, not 'greasy'.

40.13 Summary and revision plan

1 Carboxylic acids contain the **carboxyl group, $-COOH$**.
2 To name an aliphatic carboxylic acid, name the hydrocarbon with the same number of carbon atoms, and then replace the final 'e' by **'oic acid'**. The simplest aromatic carboxylic acid is benzoic acid, $C_6H_5COOH(s)$.
3 Aliphatic carboxylic acids form a **homologous series** of general formula $C_nH_{2n+1}COOH$. There is a steady rise in boiling points and $\Delta H_c^{\ominus}$ values as the hydrocarbon chain length increases.
4 Because of the polarisation in the COOH group (figure 40.3), the acids form strong intermolecular **hydrogen bonds**. Hence, (i) they dimerise when dissolved in an organic solvent and (ii) the lower acids are very soluble in water.
5 Aliphatic carboxylic acids are prepared by (i) oxidising a primary alcohol with hot $K_2Cr_2O_7/dil.H_2SO_4(aq)$ or (ii) hydrolysing a nitrile with hot $dil.H_2SO_4(aq)$.

  Benzoic acid is prepared by oxidising methylbenzene with hot acidified $KMnO_4(aq)$.
6 Carboxylic acids may take part in three main types of reaction:
  ▶ **nucleophilic addition** to the $C{=}O$ bond; this is uncommon (see section 40.5.1);
  ▶ as an **acid**, via heterolytic fission of the O—H bond (section 40.5.2); and
  ▶ **substitution** of the $-OH$ group by a nucleophile (section 40.5.3).
  Some important examples of these reactions are given in table 40.5. Also, remember that the hydrocarbon skeleton will display its own typical reactions.
7 The $C{=}O$ bond in a carboxylic acid resists addition reactions because these would remove the stability resulting from **delocalisation** of the π electron cloud over the O—C—O atoms (figure 40.4b). However, the localised $C{=}O$ bond in aldehydes and ketones readily undergoes nucleophilic addition (e.g. by HCN, H_2 and $NaHSO_3$).
8 Oxoacids dissociate in aqueous solution:

$$XO{-}H(aq) + H_2O(l) \rightleftharpoons H_3O^+(aq) + XO^-(aq)$$

The oxoacids become stronger, that is, they dissociate to a greater extent, as the X group becomes more able to draw electron cloud towards itself (section 40.5.2). Thus, we observe the pattern:

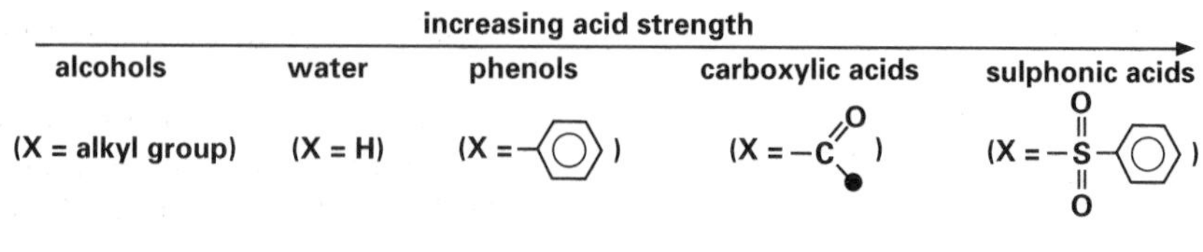

		increasing acid strength		
alcohols	water	phenols	carboxylic acids	sulphonic acids
(X = alkyl group)	(X = H)	(X = ⬡)	(X = $-C\underset{\diagdown}{\overset{\diagup O}{}}$)	(X = $-S$⬡)

Table 40.5 *Important reactions of carboxylic acids*

Reagent/conditions	products formed by a carboxylic acid	notes
LiAlH₄/ethoxyethane; reflux	Reduction to a **1° alcohol** (addition of H₂ to the C=O bond); e.g. CH₃COOH → C₂H₅OH	(1)
various bases, e.g. NaHCO₃(s)	Form **salts**, e.g. CH₃COOH + NaHCO₃ → CH₃COONa + CO₂ + H₂O	
PCl₃(l), P_red + Br₂(l), P_red + I₂(s), SO₂Cl₂(l), reflux; *or* PCl₅ room temp.	**Halogenation**, e.g.	(2)
alcohol, catalyst of conc. H₂SO₄(l) *or* dry HCl(g); reflux	**Esterification**, e.g.	(3)
(NH₄)₂CO₃(s); reflux with excess acid	Forms an **acid amide**, e.g.	
soda-lime (NaOH/CaO(s)); heat	**Decarboxylation**, i.e. removal of a CO₂ group, e.g.	

$$CH_3C\underset{OH}{\overset{O}{<}} \xrightarrow{\text{halogenating agent}} CH_3C\underset{Hal}{\overset{O}{<}} + HHal$$

$$CH_3C\underset{OH}{\overset{O}{<}} + C_2H_5OH \rightleftharpoons CH_3C\underset{OC_2H_5}{\overset{O}{<}} + H_2O$$

$$CH_3C\underset{OH}{\overset{O}{<}} \longrightarrow CH_3C\underset{NH_2}{\overset{O}{<}}$$

$$CH_3C\underset{OH}{\overset{O}{<}} \longrightarrow CH_4$$

(2 carbon atoms)   (1 carbon atom)

Notes: (1) Addition to the carboxyl C=O bond is uncommon.
(2) Methanoic acid does not form acid halides.
(3) Isotopic labelling is used to work out the mechanism.

The strength of the carboxylic acid Y—COOH also increases as the electron withdrawing power of Y is increased, e.g. as more halogen atoms are added.

A stronger acid will displace a weaker acid from its salt.

9 Esterication of a carboxylic acid can be studied by labelling the alcohol's oxygen with ^{18}O. The reaction proceeds via the nucleophilic attack of the alcohol's oxygen on the C$^{\delta+}$ of the carboxyl group.

10 Like aldehydes, methanoic acid contains the **H—C=O** group. Thus, it will react with oxidising agents (e.g. Tollen's reagent, Fehling's solution and KMnO₄/dil.H₂SO₄(aq)). Methanoic and ethanedioic acids are easily dehydrated. Other carboxylic acids do not give these reactions.

11 Carboxylic acids react with metals and alkalis to form salts, whose reactions are summarised in figure 40.12.

12 Carboxylic acid derivatives have the general formula:

$$\bullet - C\underset{X}{\overset{O}{<}} \quad \text{where X} = -Hal, -NH_2, -\square \text{ or } -O-C\overset{O}{<}$$

13 Acid halides are formed when a carboxylic acid reacts with a halogenating agent (table 37.2). Other acid derivatives are made from acid chlorides (figure 40.7).

14 Some important reactions of the acid derivatives are also summarised in figure 40.7. Reactivity increases in the order:

amides << esters < anhydrides < carboxylic acids < acid halides.

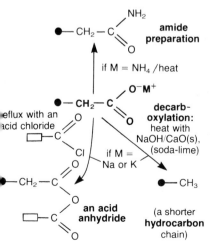

Figure 40.12 *Some reactions of carboxylic acid salts*

amide preparation

if M = NH₄ /heat

decarboxylation: heat with NaOH/CaO(s), (soda-lime)

reflux with an acid chloride

if M = Na or K

an acid anhydride

(a shorter hydrocarbon chain)

15 Acid derivatives play an important role in everyday life (section 40.11). Three examples: (i) **nylons** are polyamides, used to make clothing, carpet pile and ropes; (ii) **polyesters**, such as Terylene are also used as synthetic fibres in clothing; (iii) the triesters of glycerol and various long-chain carboxylic acids are used to make **soaps**. Soaps are the sodium or potassium salts of these acids (e.g. sodium stearate, $CH_3(CH_2)_{16}CO_2^- Na^+(s)$).

16 Important reagents used in this chapter are listed in table 40.6.

Table 40.6 *Important reagents used in this chapter*

Reagent/conditions	what it does
Each reagent in table 40.5	converts carboxylic acids into various products
$K_2Cr_2O_7/dil.H_2SO_4(aq)$; reflux	oxidises **1°alcohols** → **carboxylic acids** e.g. $C_2H_5OH \rightarrow CH_3COOH$
dil. $H_2SO_4(aq)$, reflux	hydrolysis of **nitrile** (CH_3CN) to **carboxylic acid** (CH_3COOH)
$KMnO_4/dil.H_2SO_4(aq)$ reflux	oxidises **methylbenzene** 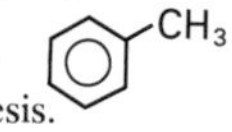 to **benzoic acid** 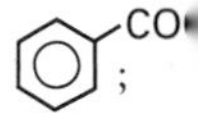 ; valuable in organic synthesis.
conc. $H_2SO_4(l)$, reflux	a dehydrating reagent, e.g. $HCOOH \rightarrow CO + H_2O$
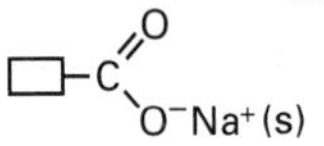 reflux ◻–C(=O)O⁻Na⁺(s)	converts **acid chloride** into **acid anhydride** 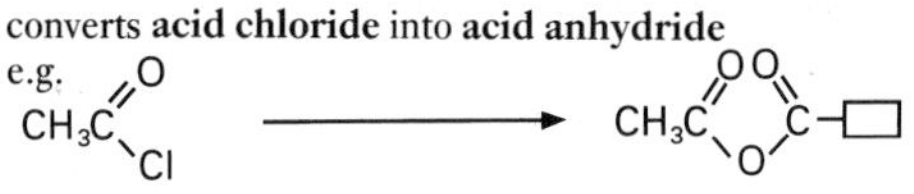
alcohol, room temp, *or* phenol, reflux with $OH^-(aq)$	converts **acid chloride** into **acid ester** 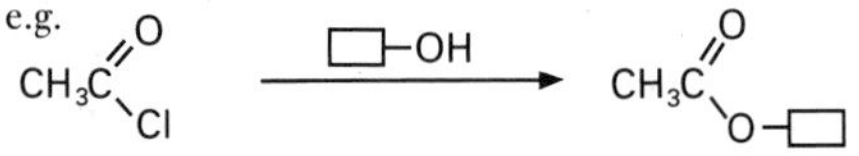
conc. $NH_3(aq)$, room temp.	converts (i) **acid** → **ammonium salt** (ii) **acid chloride** → **acid amide** 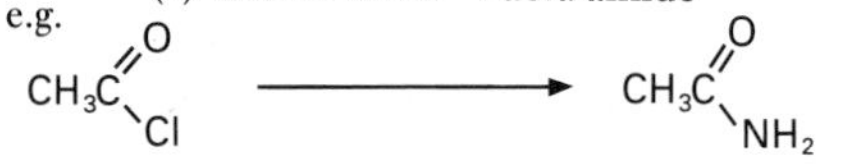
dil.NaOH(aq), reflux	hydrolyses acid derivative → sodium salt of the carboxylic acid 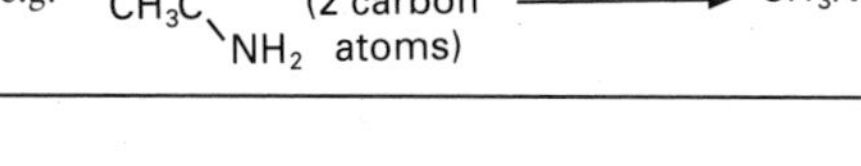
$P_4O_{10}(s)$, heat	a dehydrating reagent; converts **amide** → **nitrile** e.g. $CH_3C(=O)NH_2 \rightarrow CH_3CN + H_2O$
$Br_2(l)/conc. KOH(aq)$; reflux	Hofmann's degradation; converts **amide** → **amine** *with one less C atom* e.g. $CH_3C(=O)NH_2$ (2 carbon atoms) → CH_3NH_2 (1 carbon atom)

Organic Nitrogen Compounds

Contents

Figure 41.1 *The importance of proteins in the human body*

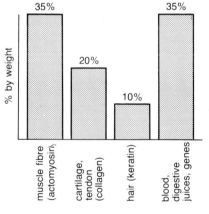

Figure 41.2 *General formula of a 2-amino acid (● is a hydrogen atom or hydrocarbon skeleton)*

Nitrogen atoms are found in a wide variety of organic molecules. Of most importance are **proteins**. These make up about a sixth of our bodyweight and are found, for example, in muscle, hair, skin and blood (figure 41.1). We need proteins for the growth and repair of body tissue, and the maintenance of our normal bodily functions.

All naturally occurring proteins are polymeric molecules containing a unique combination of **2-amino acids** (figure 41.2). A living organism can control the exact sequence in which these 2-amino acids join together to form the protein. This behaviour is almost incredible, especially when you bear in mind that over 3 million different sequences can be made from just 10 different amino acid residues.

We obtain our supply of 2-amino acids from the proteins in meat, fish and vegetables. Digestive enzymes in the stomach and intestines catalyse the hydrolysis of these proteins. After hydrolysis, the amino acids are carried by the bloodstream to the various organs and body tissues where they are converted into the necessary proteins.

In this chapter, we shall discuss the chemistry of amino acids and four other types of organic nitrogen compound: **nitro compounds, nitriles, amines** and **amides**.

41.1 Naming organic nitrogen compounds

Nitro compounds

These compounds contain the **nitro group, $-NO_2$**, having the general formula $\boxed{}-NO_2$. They are named by using the prefix **nitro-**, for example

CH_3NO_2 nitromethane

$CH_3-\underset{\underset{H}{|}}{\overset{\overset{CH_3}{|}}{C}}-NO_2$ 2–nitropropane

nitrobenzene

1,3,5–trinitrobenzene

Nitriles

These contain the **cyano group, $-C\equiv N$**, and have the general formula $\boxed{}-CN$. To name them, name the hydrocarbon with the same number of carbons and replace the final 'e' with 'onitrile' e.g.

CH_3CN ethanonitrile

propenonitrile

benzonitrile (not benzenonitrile)

Amines

Most of this chapter will be about the chemistry of amines. These are classified as **primary, secondary** or **tertiary** compounds:

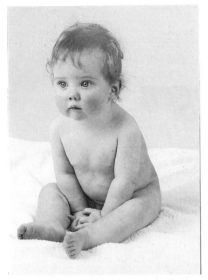

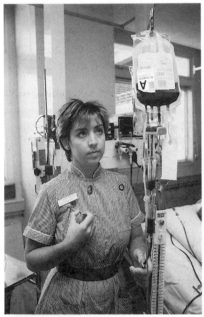

Growth, repair and maintenance – all depend on proteins

ammonia

primary (1°)
(1 ☐– group)

secondary (2°)
(2 ☐– groups)

tertiary (3°)
(3 ☐– groups)

Notice how these structures resemble that of ammonia. Perhaps this similarity will extend to their chemical properties?

Naming an amine is sometimes a bit tricky. Usually, we place the names of their alkyl, or phenyl, groups in front of the word '-amine', naming the shortest first, e.g.

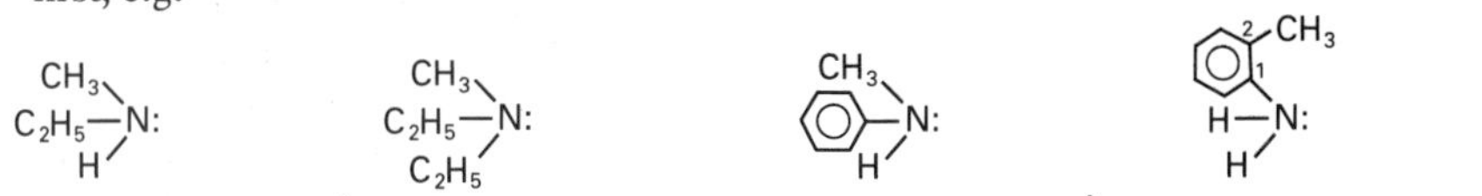

methylethylamine (2°)

methyldiethylamine (3°)

N–methylphenylamine (2°)

(2–methylphenyl) amine (1°)

The last two amines are isomers. To distinguish them, place 'N-' in front of each group which is attached to the nitrogen atom. Also, note the use of a bracket to clarify the name of a substituted ☐– group.

Sometimes 'amino-' is used to denote an $-NH_2$ group, e.g.

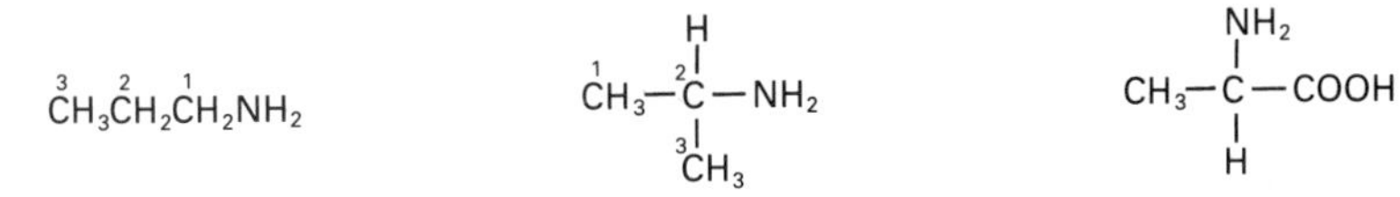

$\overset{3}{C}H_3\overset{2}{C}H_2\overset{1}{C}H_2NH_2$

1-aminopropane (1°)

$\overset{1}{C}H_3-\overset{2}{C}H-NH_2$ with $\overset{3}{C}H_3$

2-aminopropane (1°)

$CH_3-C-COOH$ with NH_2 and H

2-aminopropanoic acid (1°)

This is very useful where positional isomers exist or the molecule contains more than one functional group.

Amides

Amides are derivatives of carboxylic acids:

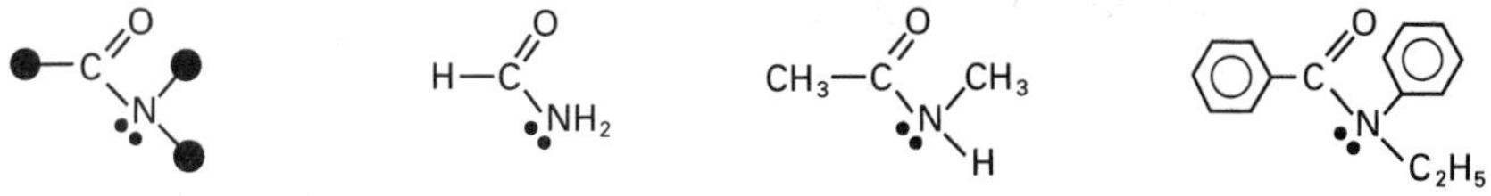

general formula

examples: methanamide

N–methyl-ethanamide

N–ethyl,N–phenyl benzamide

Their names and chemistry were discussed in sections 40.8–10. Like amines, amides have a lone pair of electrons on the nitrogen atom. Perhaps their chemical properties will also be similar?

Amino acids

Amino acids are compounds whose molecules contain both the **amino-, $-NH_2$,** and the **carboxylic acid, $-COOH$,** functional groups. They are named as 'amino-' substituted acids:

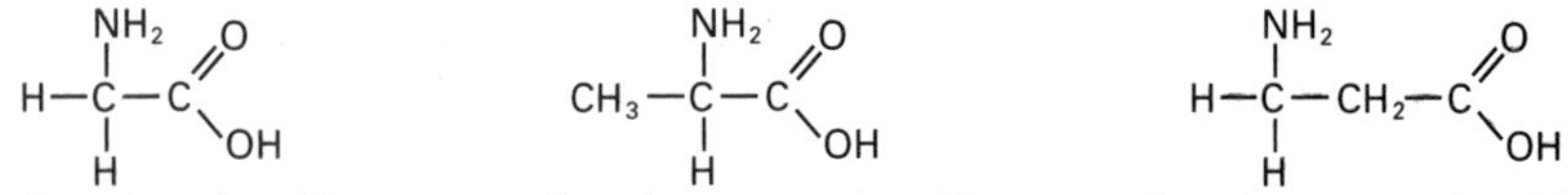

2-aminoethanoic acid (glycine)

2-aminopropanoic acid (alanine)

3-aminopropanoic acid

Later on, we shall see if the chemistry of the amino acids resembles that of amines and/or carboxylic acids.

Activity 41.1

1   Name the following organic nitrogen compounds.

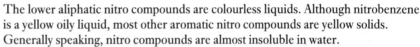

(a) $CH_3CH_2CH_2CH_2NO_2$ (b) CH_3CH_2CN (c) $(C_2H_5)_3N$

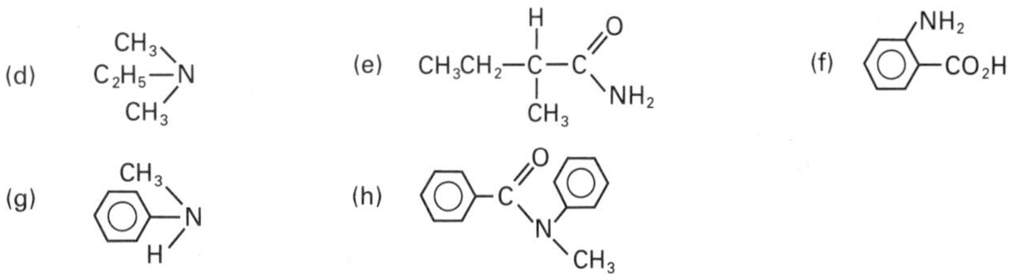

(d) 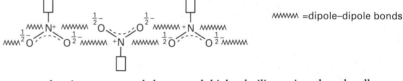   (e) (structure)   (f) (structure)

(g) (structure)   (h) (structure)

2   Write down the structural formulae for the following compounds:
   (a) 2-nitro-3-methylbutane   (b) 2-methylbutanonitrile;
   (c) 3-aminopentane   (d) phenylmethylamine;
   (e) N,N-dimethylphenylamine   (f) N-phenylpropanamide;
   (g) 2-amino-4-methylpentanoic acid (leucine).
3   Draw out the structures of the following amines and then classify them as
   1°, 2° or 3°: N-ethylphenylamine, propylamine, triphenylamine,
   phenylamine, N-methyl-N-ethylphenylamine, diethylamine,
   (4-methylphenyl) amine, 1,4-diaminobenzene.

41.2 Nitro compounds

Physical properties

The lower aliphatic nitro compounds are colourless liquids. Although nitrobenzene
is a yellow oily liquid, most other aromatic nitro compounds are yellow solids.
Generally speaking, nitro compounds are almost insoluble in water.
   Due to its polarity the nitro group forms strong dipole-dipole intermolecular
attractions:

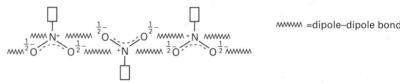

wwww =dipole–dipole bonds

Nitroalkanes are used as fuel in high speed dragster racing

Consequently, nitro compounds have much higher boiling points than the alkanes
of comparable molecular mass, e.g. nitromethane $M_r = 61$, b.p. 101 °C; butane M_r
= 58, b.p. 0 °C.
   Another interesting example of dipole–dipole attraction is provided by the
isomers of **nitrophenol**:

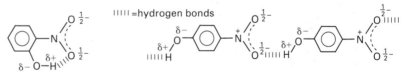

||||| =hydrogen bonds

2–nitrophenol (b.p. 216 °C)
intramolecular hydrogen bonds

4–nitrophenol (b.p. 279 °C)
intermolecular hydrogen bonds

Since the 4-isomer forms intermolecular hydrogen bonds, more energy will be
needed to separate neighbouring molecules. Thus, it has the *higher* boiling point.

Manufacture and uses

Nitroalkanes are made by heating the alkane with nitric acid vapour under pressure
(section 34.8). They are used as industrial solvents, in the preparation of aliphatic
amines and as fuels.

Nitrobenzene is made by refluxing benzene with a 'nitrating' mixture of concentrated nitric and sulphuric acids (section 36.5.1). Large quantities of aromatic nitro compounds are converted into amines, and most of these are used to make dyes (section 41.9).

Reactions

By far the most important reaction of nitro compounds is their reduction to amines. Nitroalkanes are reduced by hydrogen when the hot gases are passed over a nickel catalyst:

$$\underset{\text{2–nitropropane}}{CH_3-\underset{\underset{H}{|}}{\overset{\overset{NO_2}{|}}{C}}-CH_3\,(l)} \xrightarrow{H_2(g),\,Ni\;catalyst,\,150\;°C} \underset{\text{dimethylamine}}{CH_3-\underset{\underset{H}{|}}{\overset{\overset{NH_2}{|}}{C}}-CH_3}$$

In the laboratory, aromatic nitro compounds are reduced by refluxing with tin and concentrated hydrochloric acid:

$$C_6H_5-NO_2 \xrightarrow{Sn(s),\,conc.\;HCl\,(l)\,,reflux} C_6H_5-NH_2$$

phenylamine

The same method is used industrially except that iron, a cheaper metal, is used instead of tin.

As expected, the benzene ring of aromatic nitro compounds will undergo **electrophilic substitution** reactions (section 36.5).

41.3 Nitriles

Physical properties

The lower aliphatic nitriles are colourless, pleasantly smelling, liquids which are fairly soluble in water. Benzonitrile is a colourless oily liquid, insoluble in water. All nitriles dissolve readily in organic solvents. Although hydrogen cyanide, HCN, is extremely poisonous, nitriles are only mildly toxic.

Like the nitro group, the $-\overset{\delta+}{C}\equiv\overset{\delta-}{N}$ bond is polarised and this enables nitriles to form quite strong intermolecular dipole-dipole attractions. As a result, their boiling points are much higher than those of hydrocarbons of comparable molecular mass, e.g. ethanonitrile $M_r = 41$, b.p. $81\,°C$; propane $M_r = 44$, b.p. $-42\,°C$.

$$\underset{\text{ammonium ethanoate}}{CH_3C\overset{\overset{O}{\diagup}}{\underset{O^-NH_4^+\,(s)}{\diagdown}}} \xrightarrow{P_4O_{10}(s),\,reflux} CH_3C\overset{\overset{O}{\diagup}}{\underset{NH_2\,(s)}{\diagdown}} + H_2O\,(l)$$

$$\downarrow{P_4O_{10}(s),\,reflux}$$

$$CH_3CN\,(l) + H_2O\,(l)$$

Chemical reactions

Nitriles are valuable intermediates in organic synthesis. As we have seen, *the introduction of* the *cyano-group* into the molecule lengthens its hydrocarbon chain:

$$CH_2CH_2Br(l) \xrightarrow{KCN\;(ethanol),\,reflux} CH_3CH_2CN(l) \qquad \text{(section 37.5.2)}$$

$$CH_3C\overset{\overset{O}{\diagup}}{\underset{H(l)}{\diagdown}} \xrightarrow[\text{room temp.}]{KCN/dil.NaOH(aq)} CH_3-\underset{\underset{H}{|}}{\overset{\overset{OH}{|}}{C}}-CN(l) \qquad \text{(section 39.6.1)}$$

The nitrile can then be:

▶ *hydrolysed* by boiling with aqueous acid, e.g.

OH
|
CH_3-C-CN (l) $\xrightarrow{\text{dil. H}_2\text{SO}_4\text{(aq), reflux}}$ $CH_3-C-COOH$(l)
| |
H   H

OH
|

2–hydroxypropanoic acid

▶ *reduced* to an amine, by refluxing with lithium tetrahydridoaluminate in ethoxyethane, e.g.

$$CH_3CH_2CN(l) \xrightarrow[\text{reflux}]{\text{LiAlH}_4/\text{ethoxyethane}} CH_3CH_2CH_2NH_2(l)$$

Activity 41.2

1 State the reagents and the reaction conditions which are used to synthesise 2-methylbutanonitrile from (a) 2-bromobutane;
(b) 2-methylbutanoic acid (two steps needed).

2 Give the names and structural formulae of the organic product(s) formed in the following reactions:

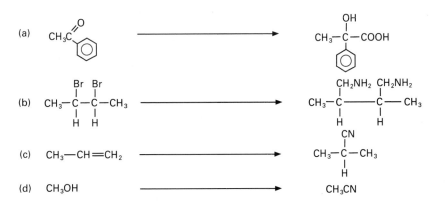

(a) $CH_3-\langle\bigcirc\rangle-NO_2$ $\xrightarrow[\text{reflux}]{\text{Sn(s)/conc.HCl(aq)}}$

(b) $CH_3-\overset{CH_3}{\underset{CH_3}{\overset{|}{\underset{|}{C}}}}-CN$ $\xrightarrow{\text{dil.H}_2\text{SO}_4\text{(aq), reflux}}$

(c) $\langle\bigcirc\rangle-CN$ $\xrightarrow{\text{H}_2\text{(g), Ni catalyst, 200 °C}}$

(d) $CH_3-C\overset{O}{\underset{CH_3}{\diagdown}}$ $\xrightarrow[\text{room temp}]{\text{KCN/dil.NaOH(aq)}}$? $\xrightarrow[\text{reflux}]{\text{dil. H}_2\text{SO}_4\text{(aq)}}$?

3 Give the reagents and reaction conditions needed for the following conversions, each of which involves *two* steps:

(a) $CH_3C\overset{O}{\diagdown}\langle\bigcirc\rangle$ ⟶ $CH_3-\overset{OH}{\underset{\langle\bigcirc\rangle}{\overset{|}{\underset{|}{C}}}}-COOH$

(b) $CH_3-\overset{Br}{\underset{H}{\overset{|}{\underset{|}{C}}}}-\overset{Br}{\underset{H}{\overset{|}{\underset{|}{C}}}}-CH_3$ ⟶ $CH_3-\overset{CH_2NH_2}{\underset{H}{\overset{|}{\underset{|}{C}}}}-\overset{CH_2NH_2}{\underset{H}{\overset{|}{\underset{|}{C}}}}-CH_3$

(c) $CH_3-CH=CH_2$ ⟶ $CH_3-\overset{CN}{\underset{H}{\overset{|}{\underset{|}{C}}}}-CH_3$

(d) CH_3OH ⟶ CH_3CN

(Note: parts (c) and (d) cover material from section 41.3 and earlier chapters.)

41.4 Amines: their physical properties

Some properties of common amines are listed in table 41.1.

The lower aliphatic amines are gases or volatile liquids which often have a fishy smell. Indeed, various amines are found in rotting fish. Each type of amine (1°, 2° and 3°) forms a *homologous series*; thus, we can observe the typical steady increase in boiling points and standard enthalpies of combustion, $\Delta H_c^\ominus$ (figure 41.3).

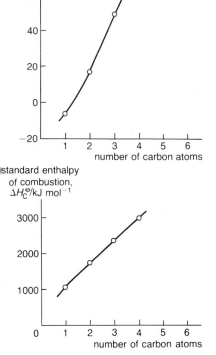

Figure 41.3 *Steady increases in (a) the boiling points and (b) the $\Delta H_c^\ominus$ values of some straight-chain primary aliphatic amines*

Table 41.1   *Some properties of amines*

Name	formula	state (at 25 °C)	melting point/°C	boiling point/°C	density /g cm^{-3}	$\Delta H_c^{\ominus}$ /kJ mol^{-1}
methylamine	CH_3NH_2	gas	−93	−6	0.66(L)	−1079
dimethylamine	$(CH_3)_2NH$	gas	−92	7	0.66(L)	−1760
trimethylamine	$(CH_3)_3N$	gas	−117	3	0.63(L)	−2419
ethylamine	$C_2H_5NH_2$	gas	−81	17	0.68(L)	−1739
1-aminopropane	$CH_3CH_2CH_2NH_2$	liquid	−83	49	0.72	−2336
2-aminopropane	$CH_3CHNH_2CH_3$	liquid	−95	33	0.69	−2354
1-aminobutane	$CH_3(CH_2)_3NH_2$	liquid	−49	78	0.73	−2973
2-aminobutane	$CH_3CHNH_2CH_2CH_3$	liquid	−84	68	0.73	−2986
phenylamine	$C_6H_5NH_2$	liquid	−6	184	1.02	−3396

(L) means density in the liquid state

Why do the secondary amines have lower boiling points than the isomeric primary amines?

Boiling points of primary and secondary amines are *higher* than those of similar molecular mass hydrocarbons, e.g.

	methylamine	ethane	dimethylamine	propane
M_r	31	30	45	44
b.p./°C	−6	−89	7	−42

The values point to the existence of strong intermolecular forces in these amines, and these result from *hydrogen bonding*, e.g.

molecules of a primary amine

☐ = hydrocarbon skeleton

IIIII = hydrogen bonds

However, since tertiary amines have no N—H bonds, they are unable to form hydrogen bonds. Consequently, their molecules experience only weak van der Waals' forces, and their boiling points do not differ greatly from branched alkanes of similar mass:

trimethylamine
(M_r=59, b.p. 3 °C)

2-methylpropane
(M_r=58, b.p. −15 °C)

Like ammonia, the lower aliphatic amines are readily soluble in water because they interact forming strong hydrogen bonds:

IIIII = hydrogen bonds

hydrogen bonding between
ammonia and water molecules

hydrogen bonding between dimethylamine (2°)
and water molecules

Because of their non-polar benzene rings, aromatic amines are virtually insoluble in water. They do dissolve, though, in organic solvents.

41.5 Preparation of amines and their uses

Primary aliphatic amines are prepared in the laboratory by:

▶ *the reduction of nitriles or amides:*

$$CH_3CN(l) \xrightarrow[\text{reflux}]{\text{LiAlH}_4/\text{ethoxyethane}} CH_3CH_2NH_2(l)$$

ethanonitrile   ethylamine

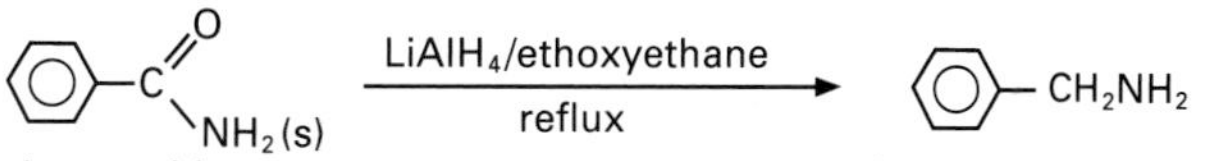

benzamide   phenyl methylamine

▶ *the Hofmann degradation of amides:*

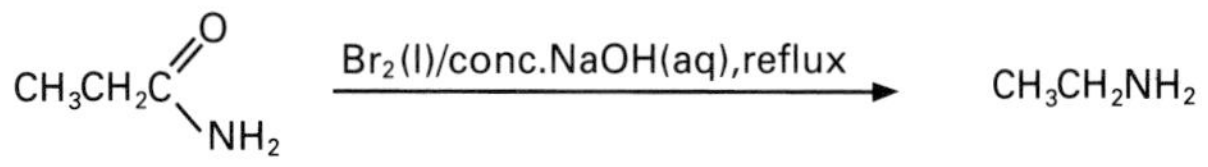

propanamide   ethylamine
(3 carbon atoms)   (2 carbon atoms)

Primary aromatic amines are formed by the *reduction of nitro compounds* with tin and concentrated hydrochloric acid:

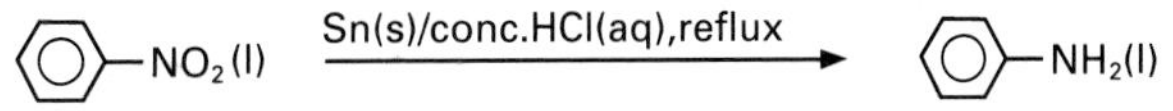

nitrobenzene   phenylamine

Secondary and tertiary amines are best prepared in the laboratory by reducing N-substituted amides:

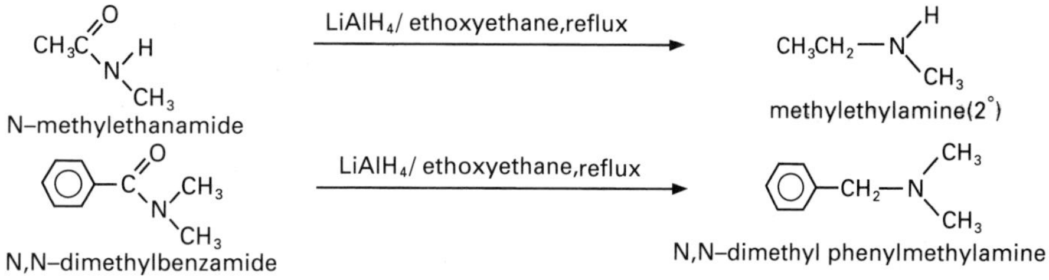

N–methylethanamide   methylethylamine(2°)

N,N–dimethylbenzamide   N,N–dimethyl phenylmethylamine

Industrially, amines are made by reducing a nitro compound (above), reacting a halogenoalkane with ammonia (section 37.5.3) or heating an alcohol with ammonia under pressure, e.g.

$$C_2H_5OH \xrightarrow[\text{400°C, pressure}]{\text{NH}_3(g), \text{Co salt as catalyst}} C_2H_5NH_2$$

By far, their most important uses are the manufacture of dyes from primary aromatic amines (section 41.9), and the production of nylon from 1,6-diaminohexane (section 40.11).

41.6 Predicting the reactivity of amines

Looking at their general formula,

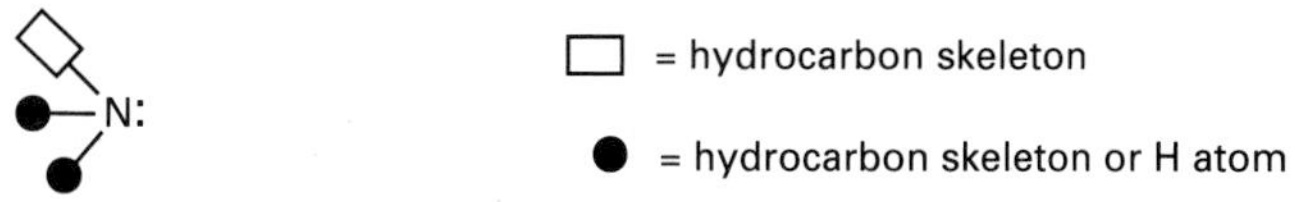

□ = hydrocarbon skeleton

● = hydrocarbon skeleton or H atom

we would expect the chemistry of amines to be dominated by the reactivity of nitrogen's lone pair of electrons. This is certainly the case, with amines reacting as **bases** and as **nucleophiles**. Of course, reactions can also occur in the hydrocarbon skeleton.

41.7 The basicity of amines

When tested with universal indicator, aqueous solutions of aliphatic amines, and ammonia, are found to be weak bases (table 41.2). Base dissociation constants, K_b, for the equilibria

$$\underset{/}{\overset{\diagdown}{-}}N\!:\ (aq)\ +\ H_2O\ (l)\ \rightleftharpoons\ \left[\underset{/}{\overset{\diagdown}{-}}N\!-\!H\right]^+ (aq)\ +\ OH^-(aq)$$

Table 41.2 *The pH of some aqueous amines and their base dissociation constants, K_b. (Remember that a stronger base has a larger K_b, and a smaller pK_b)*

Amine	formula		colour of solution + universal indicator	pH range	K_b at 25 °C/M	pK_b
ammonia	NH_3				1.8×10^{-5}	4.8
methylamine	CH_3NH_2	(1°)			4.4×10^{-4}	3.4
dimethylamine	$(CH_3)_2NH$	(2°)			5.9×10^{-4}	3.3
trimethylamine	$(CH_3)_3N$	(3°)	blue/purple	10–12	6.3×10^{-5}	4.2
ethylamine	$CH_3CH_2NH_2$	(1°)			5.4×10^{-4}	3.3
diethylamine	$(C_2H_5)_2NH$	(2°)			1.3×10^{-3}	2.9
triethylamine	$(C_2H_5)_3N$	(3°)			1.0×10^{-3}	3.0
phenylmethylamine	⬡–CH₂NH₂	(1°)			2.2×10^{-5}	4.7
phenylamine	⬡–NH₂	(1°)	green	about 7	4.2×10^{-10}	9.4

Which is the stronger base, trimethylamine or diethylamine?

fit in with these observations. Remember the higher K_b, and the lower pK_b, the stronger the base (section 18.6). Clearly, aliphatic amines and phenylmethylamine are bases of strength similar to ammonia. However, in phenylamine, the direct attachment of the $-NH_2$ group to the benzene ring considerably reduces its basic nature, that is, its ability to accept protons. Note that phenylmethylamine, though aromatic, is a slightly stronger base than ammonia. This is because its $-NH_2$ group is in an aliphatic side chain and not bonded directly to the benzene ring.

The values in table 41.2 are typical of a general pattern in basicity, namely,

phenylamine<<ammonia	tertiary aliphatic	primary aliphatic	secondary aliphatic

→

increasing base strength

But can we explain this pattern in terms of the molecular structures of these amines?

In phenylamine, the lone pair of electrons on nitrogen is held in a p orbital. This can overlap *sideways* with benzene's π electron ring (figure 41.4). Due to this

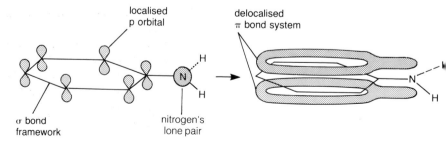

Figure 41.4 *In phenylamine, sideways overlap of p orbitals produces a delocalised electron cloud over the carbon and nitrogen atoms*

Figure 41.5 *The electron releasing ability of an alkyl chain both (a) localises electron cloud on the nitrogen atom of an amine and (b) delocalises the positive charge on the alkylammonium cation*

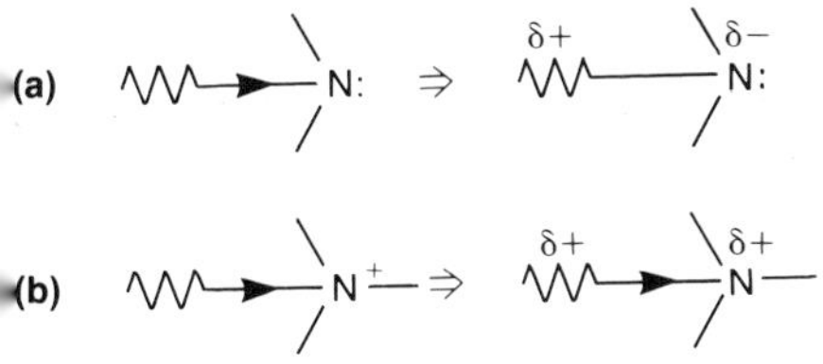

delocalisation, the lone pair is less available for dative covalent bonding with a proton. Thus, *phenylamine is a poor proton-acceptor, making it a very weak base.*

Exactly the opposite case can be made for aliphatic amines. As we have seen before, *alkyl groups are able to push electrons away from themselves,* and this has two effects. Firstly, an alkyl group can assist protonation by localising electron cloud on nitrogen (figure 41.5a). Secondly, an alkyl group will help stabilise the resulting cation by delocalising its positive charge (figure 41.5b). Both effects would aid proton-acceptance, making the base stronger. Thus, *in theory,* we would expect basicity of aliphatic amines to *increase* with the number of alkyl groups attached to nitrogen. In real life, though, this is not quite true; tertiary amines are weaker bases than primary amines! Clearly, another factor must be involved.

When an alkylammonium ion is hydrated, it is stabilised by *hydrogen bonding with water molecules:*

ᴡᴡ⁻ = alkyl group
‖‖‖‖ = hydrogen bonds

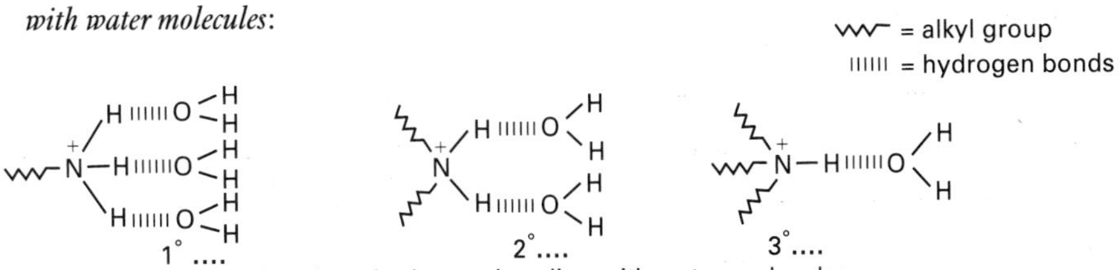

....alkylammonium ions hydrogen bonding with water molecules

As the number of N—H bonds decreases, the ion becomes less able to form hydrogen bonds. Hence, the *stabilities of aqueous alkylammonium ions decrease in the order $1° > 2° > 3°$.* Tertiary amines are surprisingly weak bases, therefore, because they have the *least* stable aqueous alkylammonium ions.

Amines react with strong acids to form salts, e.g.

$$2CH_3\overset{..}{N}H_2(g) + H_2SO_4(aq) \xrightarrow[\text{temp.}]{\text{room}} (CH_3\overset{+}{N}H_3)_2\,SO_4^{2-}(aq)$$
methylammonium sulphate

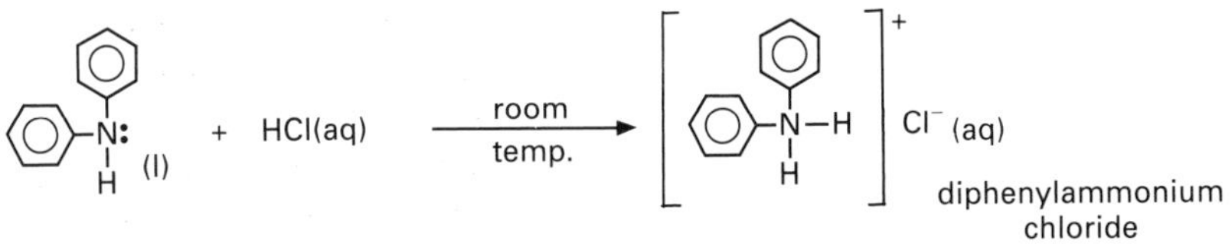

On evaporating their aqueous solutions, these salts are obtained as white crystalline solids. Generally speaking, they show the typical properties of ionic solids, e.g. fairly high melting points and good solubility in water.

Stronger bases displace the amines from their salts:

$$CH_3CH_2\overset{+}{N}H_3\,Cl^-(s) + KOH(aq) \xrightarrow{\text{warm}} CH_3CH_2NH_2 + KCl(aq) + H_2O(l)$$

ethylammonium chloride (strong base) ethylamine (weak base)

Activity 41.3

1 Arrange the following nitrogen compounds in order of increasing base strength:
   ethylamine, phenylamine, tetraethylammonium hydroxide, diethylamine, triethylamine, ammonia, triphenylamine.

2 Complete the following equations:
   (a) $2C_2H_5NH_2(l) + H_2SO_4(aq) \rightarrow$
   (b)

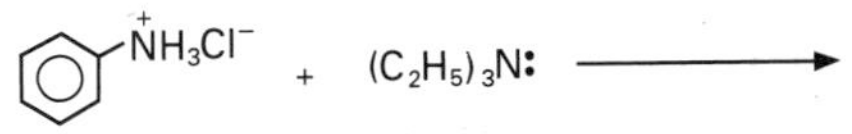

(c) $[(C_2H_5)_3NH]^+Cl^- + NaOH \rightarrow$

3 Scan through section 18.6. Now, calculate the pH of a 0.01 M aqueous solution of each of the following amines: methylamine, dimethylamine and trimethylamine. (You will need data from table 41.2.)

41.8 Reactions as nucleophiles

41.8.1 With acid chlorides and acid anhydrides

Amines react vigorously with acid chlorides to give N-substituted amides:

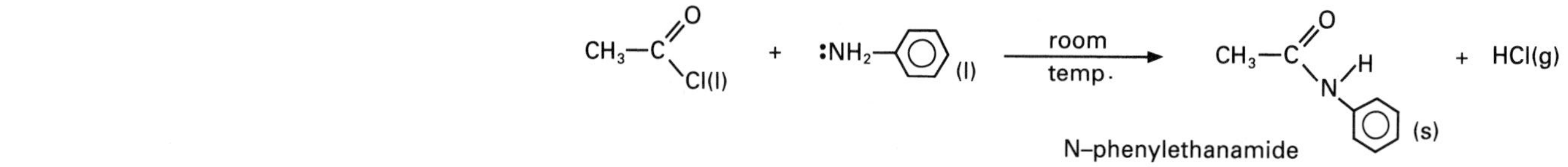

Acid anhydrides give similar reactions, though less readily:

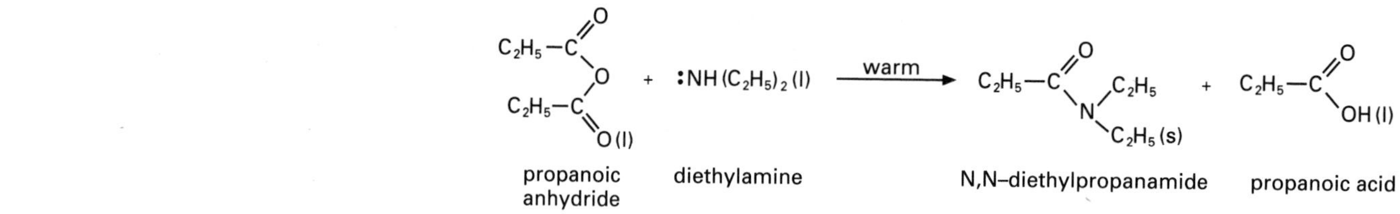

These reactions are examples of **acylation**, that is the introduction of an acyl group, $\square-C\!\!\!\diagup^{O}_{\diagdown}$, into the molecule. When $\square-$ is a phenyl group, $\bigcirc-$, the process is also known as **benzoylation**.

Amines are benzoylated by refluxing them with benzoyl chloride, using a strong base as catalyst:

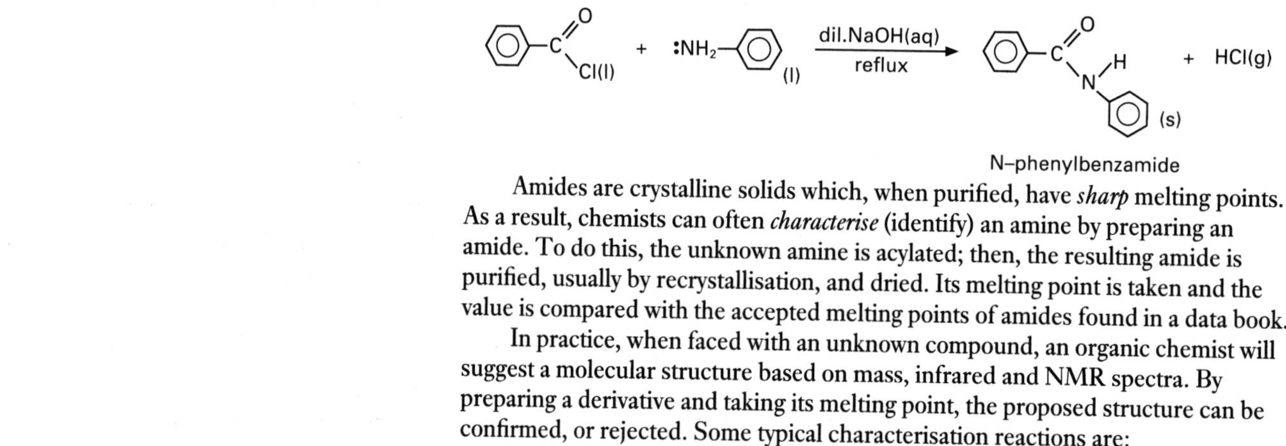

Amides are crystalline solids which, when purified, have *sharp* melting points. As a result, chemists can often *characterise* (identify) an amine by preparing an amide. To do this, the unknown amine is acylated; then, the resulting amide is purified, usually by recrystallisation, and dried. Its melting point is taken and the value is compared with the accepted melting points of amides found in a data book.

In practice, when faced with an unknown compound, an organic chemist will suggest a molecular structure based on mass, infrared and NMR spectra. By preparing a derivative and taking its melting point, the proposed structure can be confirmed, or rejected. Some typical characterisation reactions are:

▶ aldehyde or ketone → 2,4-dinitrophenylhydrazone (section 39.6.4);
▶ acid, acid derivative or amine → amide, using the above method.

41.8.2 With halogenoalkanes

When an ethanolic solution of an aliphatic amine and a halogenoalkane alkane is heated under pressure (in a sealed metal container), a mixture of secondary, tertiary and quaternary alkylammonium salts is formed (section 37.5.3). The composition of this mixture depends on the mole quantities of the reactants used, e.g.

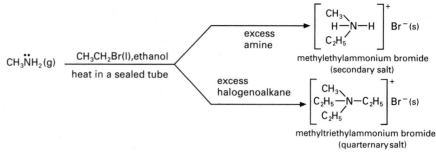

$CH_3\ddot{N}H_2(g)$ $\xrightarrow[\text{heat in a sealed tube}]{CH_3CH_2Br(l),ethanol}$

excess amine → methylethylammonium bromide (secondary salt)

excess halogenoalkane → methyltriethylammonium bromide (quarternary salt)

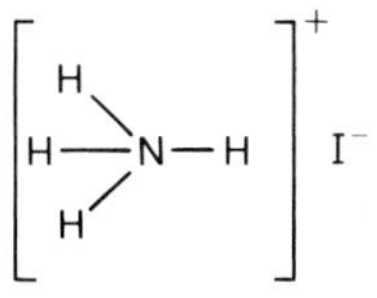

Notice the structural similarity between alkylammonium salts and simple ammonium salts, e.g. ammonium iodide (figure 41.6). Since the free amines are *weak* bases, they can be liberated from these salts by a *strong* base, e.g.

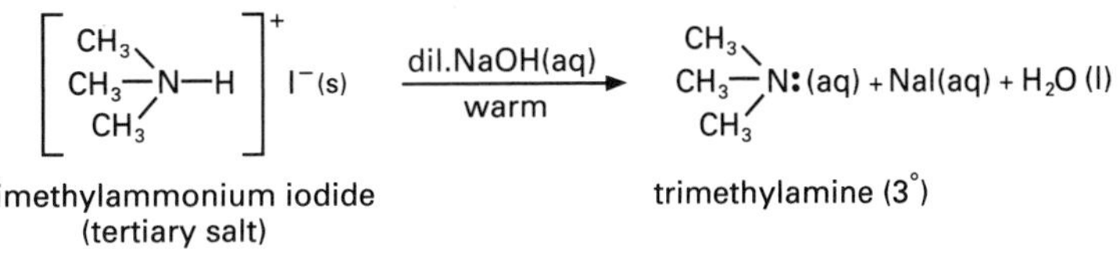

Figure 41.6 *Ammonium iodide, NH_4I*

trimethylammonium iodide (tertiary salt) $\xrightarrow[\text{warm}]{dil.NaOH(aq)}$ trimethylamine (3°)

$+ NaI(aq) + H_2O (l)$

This synthesis is of limited value because the mixture of amines produced is difficult to separate, so 2° and 3° amines are usually prepared by reducing acid amides.

41.8.3 With nitrous acid, HNO_2

Figure 41.7 *Nitrous acid, HNO_2 exists as an equilibrium mixture*

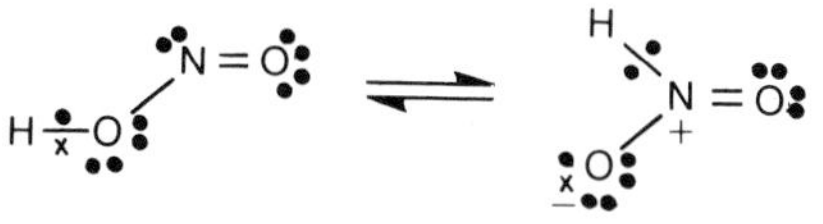

Nitrous acid is unstable and exists only in solution (figure 41.7). At room temperature, an aqueous solution decomposes fairly rapidly, eventually forming nitric acid and nitrogen monoxide. Hence, to test its reactions, we prepare small quantities of nitrous acid *in situ* from ice-cold solutions of sodium nitrite and dilute hydrochloric acid:

$$NaNO_2(aq) + HCl(aq) \xrightarrow{\text{at about } 5\,°C} HNO_2(aq) + NaCl(aq)$$

When formed, the nitrous acid solution is kept below 5 °C by cooling in an ice/water mixture. Table 41.3 describes the reactions of amines with nitrous acid at 5 °C.

Table 41.3 *Reactions of amines with nitrous acid at 5 °C. (The nitrous acid is made in situ from $NaNO_2(aq) + HCl(aq)$)*

Amine used	observation	product(s)
1° aromatic e.g. 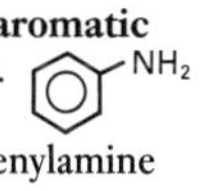 phenylamine	colourless solution, *no* gas bubbles	a **diazonium salt**, e.g. 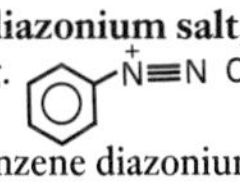 benzene diazonium choride
1° aliphatic e.g. CH_3NH_2 methylamine	colourless solution, gas bubbles slowly released	Firstly, a diazonium salt, $CH_3-\overset{+}{N}\equiv N\ Cl^-$, which rapidly decomposes giving $N_2(g)$, and an **alcohol** as the main organic product e.g. $CH_3OH + N_2(g)$ methanol
2° aliphatic or aromatic e.g. 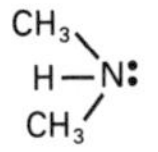 dimethylamine	a yellow oil slowly separates out	the oil is a **nitrosamine**, it will be extremely toxic e.g. 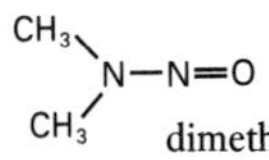 dimethyl nitrosamine
3° aromatic e.g. 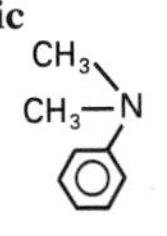	the solution turns green/yellow	a **nitroso salt**, 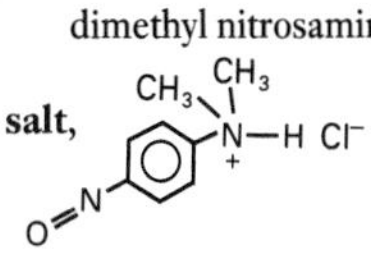 N,N-dimethyl-4-nitrosophenylammonium chloride
3° aliphatic e.g. 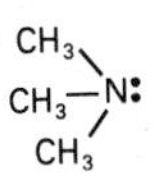	the solution remains colourless	a simple **nitrite salt**, trimethylammonium nitrite 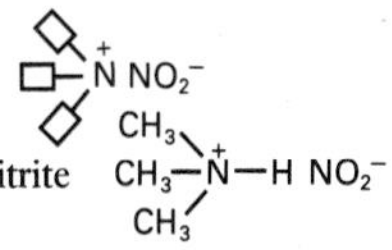 $CH_3-\overset{+}{N}-H\ NO_2^-$

Using these simple reactions, we can identify all amines *except* 1° aromatic and 3° aliphatic. Both of these give colourless solutions. However, on gentle warming the **aromatic diazonium salt** decomposes and we see a rapid release of nitrogen gas bubbles:

1° aromatic amine $\xrightarrow{\text{NaNO}_2/\text{dil. HCl(aq); 5°C}}$ diazonium salt colourless soln. $\xrightarrow{\text{gentle heat}}$ rapid release of $N_2(g)$ bubbles

3° aliphatic amine $\xrightarrow{\text{NaNO}_2/\text{dil. HCl(aq); 5°C}}$ nitrite colourless soln. $\xrightarrow{\text{gentle heat}}$ no immediate change

As we shall see in the next section, *aromatic diazonium salts are extremely valuable in organic synthesis.*

Activity 41.4

1 Give the name(s) and structural formula(e) of the organic products formed in the following reactions:

(a) $(C_2H_5)_2\overset{\bullet\bullet}{N}H$ $\xrightarrow[\text{room temp.}]{\text{dil. H}_2\text{SO}_4\text{(aq)}}$? $\xrightarrow[\text{warm}]{\text{dil. KOH(aq)}}$?

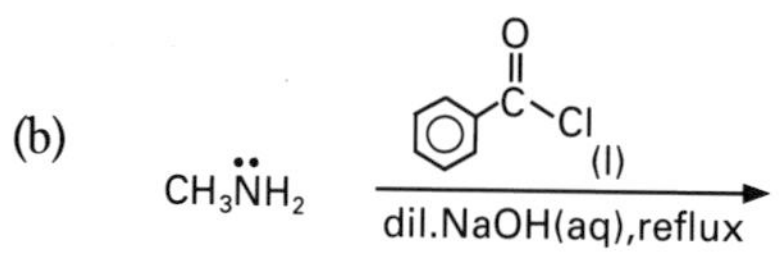

(b) $CH_3\overset{\bullet\bullet}{N}H_2$ + (benzoyl chloride) $\xrightarrow{\text{dil.NaOH(aq),reflux}}$

(c) $CH_3\overset{\bullet\bullet}{N}H_2$ $\xrightarrow[\text{heat in sealed tube}]{\text{excess CH}_3\text{I(l) in ethanol}}$

2 Give the reagents and reaction conditions which are needed for the following conversions:

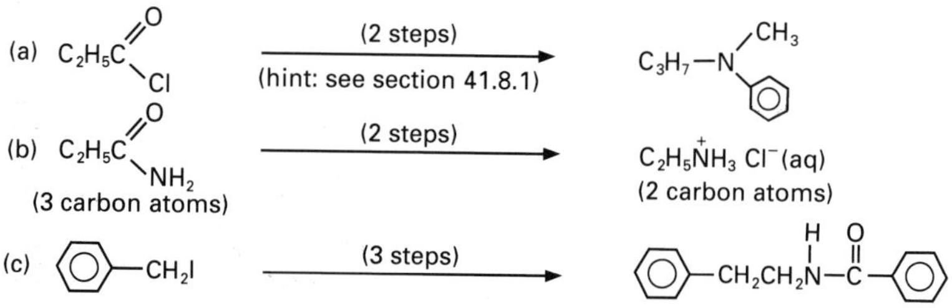

(a) $C_2H_5C\overset{\displaystyle O}{\underset{\displaystyle Cl}{\big\langle}}$ $\xrightarrow[\text{(hint: see section 41.8.1)}]{\text{(2 steps)}}$ $C_3H_7-N\overset{\displaystyle CH_3}{\underset{\displaystyle \langle O\rangle}{\big\langle}}$

(b) $C_2H_5C\overset{\displaystyle O}{\underset{\displaystyle NH_2}{\big\langle}}$ (3 carbon atoms) $\xrightarrow{\text{(2 steps)}}$ $C_2H_5\overset{+}{N}H_3\ Cl^-\text{(aq)}$ (2 carbon atoms)

(c) $\langle O\rangle -CH_2I$ $\xrightarrow{\text{(3 steps)}}$ $\langle O\rangle -CH_2CH_2\overset{H}{N}-\overset{O}{C}-\langle O\rangle$

3 Describe two chemical tests that can be used to distinguish between

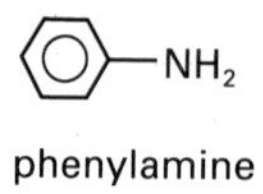

$\langle O\rangle -NH_2$ and $\langle O\rangle -CH_2NH_2$

phenylamine   phenylmethylamine

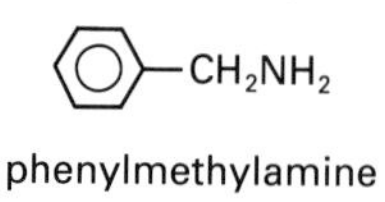

41.9 Diazonium salts

Diazonium salts are formed when primary amines react with nitrous acid at about 5°C:

$$\boxed{}-\ddot{N}H_2 \xrightarrow{\text{NaNO}_2/\text{HCl(aq), 5 °C}} \boxed{}-\overset{+}{N}\equiv N \;\; Cl^-$$

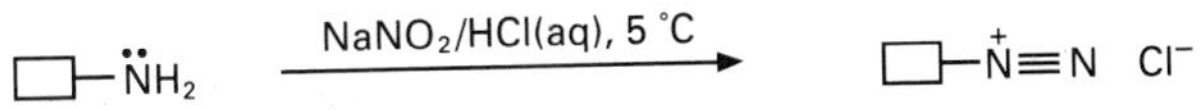

a diazonium chloride

Even at this low temperature, though, *aliphatic* diazonium ions decompose fairly quickly, giving nitrogen gas and a mixture of organic products, e.g.

$$C_2H_5-\overset{+}{N}\equiv N \; Cl^-\text{(aq)} \xrightarrow[\text{even at low temp.}]{\text{decomposes rapidly}}$$

ethyl diazonium
chloride

$C_2H_5OH\text{(aq)}$ ethanol

$C_2H_4\text{(g)}$ ethene $+ N_2\text{(g)}$

$C_2H_6\text{(g)}$ ethane

However, *aromatic diazonium salts are more stable and can exist in aqueous solution, providing that the temperature does not rise above 5°C.* Although solid diazonium salts have been isolated, they are very unstable and most are explosive.

Aromatic diazonium salts take part in *two* types of reaction: (i) those in which $N_2\text{(g)}$ is evolved and (ii) those in which the nitrogen atoms are retained.

Reactions in which N₂(g) is evolved

Loss of N_2 from the benzenediazonium ion gives a phenyl cation,

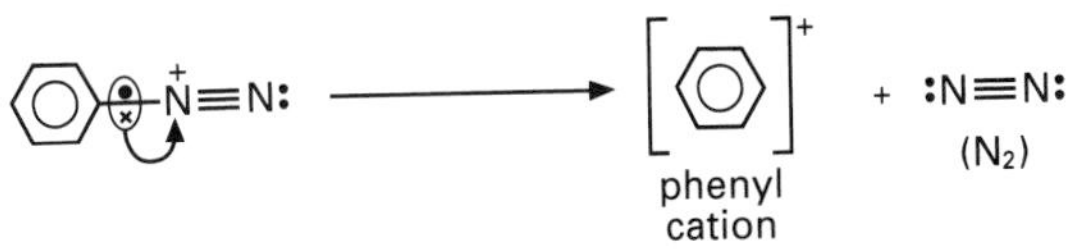

This girl has diabetes. She needs regular injections of insulin to prevent the concentration of sugar in her blood from reaching dangerous levels

which readily reacts with a nucleophile. *The overall effect is the attachment of a nucleophilic group to the benzene ring.* Since the benzene ring normally reacts with electrophiles (section 36.5), this is an extremely useful synthetic step. Some important examples are given below:

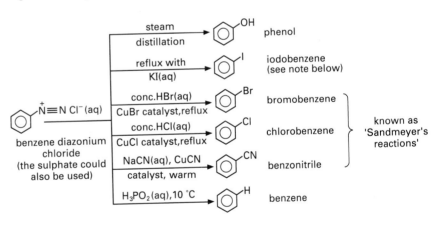

There are two particularly satisfying features of these syntheses:
- ▶ *the ease with which we can make iodobenzene,* a preparation which is difficult by any other route (e.g. refluxing benzene with iodine and concentrated nitric acid!); and
- ▶ the crude organic products are easily obtained from the reaction mixture (e.g. by solvent extraction).

Reactions in which the nitrogen atoms are retained

Aromatic diazonium salts react with cold alkaline solutions of aromatic amines and phenols to give coloured **azo-compounds**, e.g.

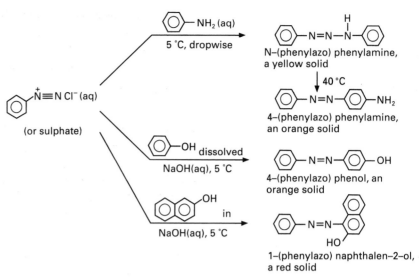

Figure 41.8 *Delocalisation of the electron cloud from the N≡N bond towards benzene's π electron ring produces a δ+ charge on the end nitrogen atom. This enables it to act as an electrophile in coupling reactions*

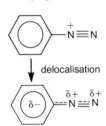

Because they give such clear results, *these* **azo-coupling** *reactions can be used to detect primary aromatic amines* (as their diazonium salts). Azo-coupling reactions have three common features:

▶ the diazonium ion acts as an *electrophile* (see figure 41.8);
▶ the $-NH_2$ and $-OH$ groups *activate* the benzene ring, making it slightly nucleophilic at the 2- and 4- positions:

the NH_2 and OH groups release the electron cloud from their lone pair(s) towards the benzene ring

As a result, the coupling reaction occurs rapidly even at low temperature.

▶ each product contains *two* benzene rings linked by an **azo-group**, $-N=N-$ and it is this structural grouping which causes the molecules to be coloured.

Azo-coupling reactions are used industrially to make **azo-dyes**. For example, an azo-dye known commercially as **Acid Orange 7**, is manufactured by the following coupling reaction:

41.10 Amides

Amides are carboxylic acid derivatives and, as such, their chemistry was discussed in sections 40.8–10. One final point to stress is the difference in behaviour of the $-NH_2$ group in amines and amides.

Because of their -NH_2 group, *amines react as weak bases and nucleophiles*. In amides, however, the lone pair of electrons on nitrogen is delocalised over the N—C—O σ bond framework (figure 40.8). Consequently, the lone pair on the amide's nitrogen is less available for donation to electron-poor species, such as the H^+ ion. Consequently, *amides are extremely weak bases*, e.g.

$$CH_3C\overset{O}{\underset{NH_2(aq)}{}} + H_2O\,(l) \rightleftharpoons CH_3C\overset{O}{\underset{\overset{+}{N}H_3(aq)}{}} + OH^-(aq) \qquad K_b = 7.9 \times 10^{-16}\,M$$
$$pK_b = 15.1 \text{ at } 25\,°C$$

Also, *they react as nucleophiles only in one important reaction*, namely, with nitrous acid:

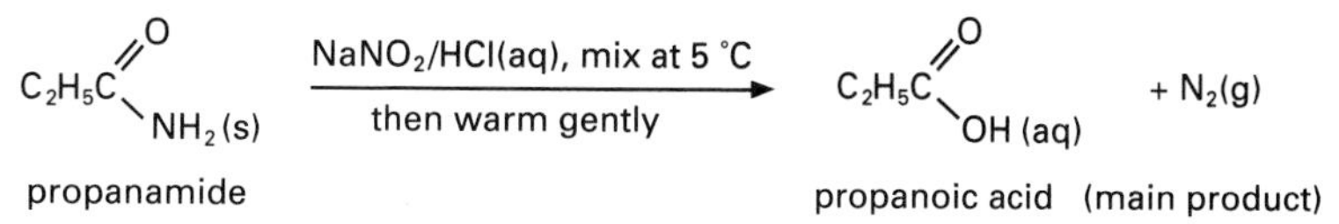

$$C_2H_5C \overset{O}{\underset{NH_2 (s)}{\big\langle}} \xrightarrow[\text{then warm gently}]{NaNO_2/HCl(aq), \text{ mix at 5 °C}} C_2H_5C \overset{O}{\underset{OH (aq)}{\big\langle}} + N_2(g)$$

propanamide   propanoic acid (main product)

41.11 Amino acids and proteins

As mentioned earlier, amino acids have molecules which contain both the amino, $-NH_2$, and carboxylic, $-COOH$, functional groups. Although a variety of amino acids can be prepared, we shall limit our discussion to just a few of the *naturally* occurring compounds. These are all **2-amino acids** because they have both functional groups attached to the same carbon:

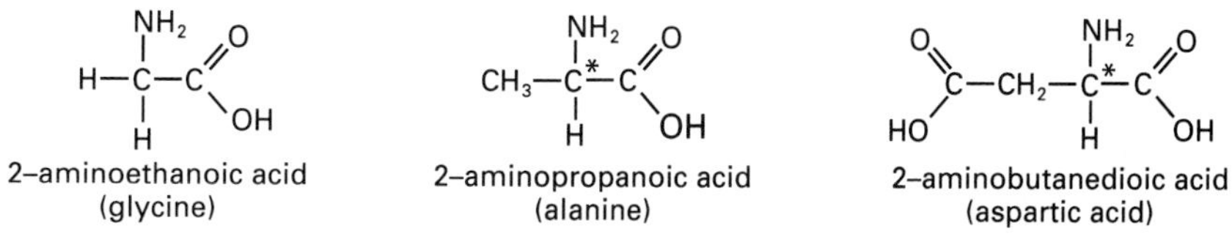

2–aminoethanoic acid (glycine)   2–aminopropanoic acid (alanine)   2–aminobutanedioic acid (aspartic acid)

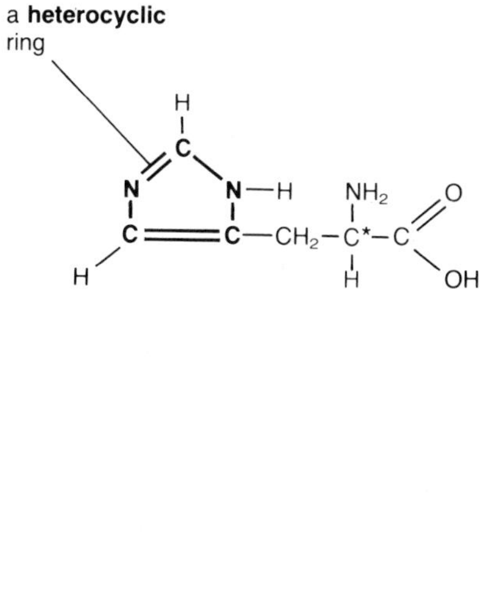

Common names are often used, especially where the amino acid has a complex structure, e.g. histidine (figure 41.9). Can you predict what physical property will result from the presence of the C* atom in these molecules? (Hint: see section 10.4.)

Figure 41.9 *Histidine, one of the more complex amino acid structures. Heterocyclic rings are common in naturally occurring organic compounds*

a **heterocyclic** ring

Preparation

Synthesis of the more complex amino acids, such as histidine, can be a lengthy process. However, simpler 2-amino acids can be prepared from carboxylic acids, using the following route:

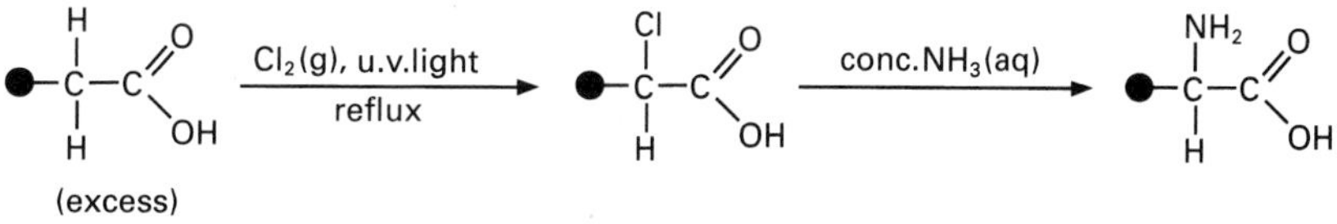

(excess)

Physical and chemical properties

Amino acids are high melting point solids (e.g. glycine melts at 235 °C). Generally speaking, they are very soluble in water, but only dissolve slightly in organic solvents. These physical properties are typical of those shown by an *ionic* solid, such as sodium chloride. In fact, in the solid state and in solution, *amino acids exist as internal ionic salts, called* **zwitterions**:

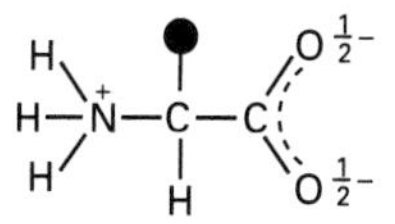

(*Zwitter* is the German word for 'between'). Here a proton has shifted from the carboxyl group to the amino group, the salt having both an anion and cation in the same molecule.

Further evidence for zwitterion formation comes from their migration in an electric field, as shown in figure 41.10. This experiment, known as **electrophoresis**, shows that:

▶ when it is dissolved in strong *acid*, the zwitterion is *protonated*,

$$H_3\overset{+}{N}-\underset{\underset{H}{|}}{\overset{\bullet}{C}}-CO_2^- \quad \xrightarrow{\text{dil. H}^+\text{(aq)}} \quad H_3\overset{+}{N}-\underset{\underset{H}{|}}{\overset{\bullet}{C}}-CO_2H, \text{ a positive ion}$$

and moves towards the cathode.

▶ when it is dissolved in strong *base*, the zwitterion *loses a proton*

$$H_3\overset{+}{N}-\underset{\underset{H}{|}}{\overset{\bullet}{C}}-CO_2^- \quad \xrightarrow{\text{dil. OH}^-\text{(aq)}} \quad H_2O + H_2\overset{\bullet\bullet}{N}-\underset{\underset{H}{|}}{\overset{\bullet}{C}}-CO_2^-, \text{ a negative ion}$$

and moves towards the anode.

Figure 41.10 *(a) Electrophoresis is a variation on paper chromatography. (b) The positions of the amino acids may be found by spraying the filter paper with ninhydrin, when purple dots will be seen*

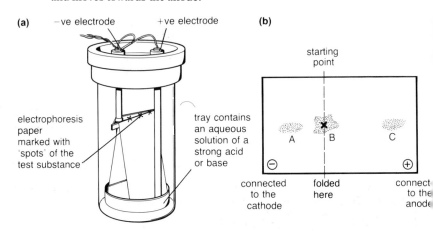

(a) −ve electrode   +ve electrode

electrophoresis paper marked with 'spots' of the test substance

tray contains an aqueous solution of a strong acid or base

(b)

starting point

A B C

⊖ ⊕

connected to the cathode   folded here   connected to the anode

By carefully controlling the pH of the solution, we can prevent the zwitterion from moving at all. *This pH, known as the* **isoelectric point,** *is characteristic of the amino acid used.* For example, glycine and aspartic acid have isoelectric points of 6.0 and 2.8, respectively. Hence, electrophoresis is sometimes used to help separate and identify a mixture of amino acids.

With the exception of glycine, the 2-amino acids contain an asymmetric carbon atom; thus, they can exist as **optical isomers.** Interestingly, all of the naturally occurring amino acids exist as the (−)-isomer (i.e. they are **laevorotatory** (section 10.4).

As we have seen, amino acids can behave as weak acids (via the -COOH group) or weak bases (via -NH$_2$ group):

$$CH_3-\underset{\underset{H}{|}}{\overset{\overset{\overset{\bullet\bullet}{NH_2}}{|}}{C}}-C\overset{\displaystyle O}{\underset{\displaystyle OH\text{(s)}}{}} \quad \xrightarrow[\text{room temp.}]{\text{dil.NaOH(aq),}} \quad CH_3-\underset{\underset{H}{|}}{\overset{\overset{\overset{\bullet\bullet}{NH_2}}{|}}{C}}-C\overset{\displaystyle O}{\underset{\displaystyle O^-Na^+\text{(aq)}}{}} \quad + H_2O \text{ (l)}$$

$$CH_3-\underset{\underset{H}{|}}{\overset{\overset{\overset{\bullet\bullet}{NH_2}}{|}}{C}}-C\overset{\displaystyle O}{\underset{\displaystyle OH\text{(s)}}{}} \quad \xrightarrow[\text{room temp.}]{\text{dil.HCl(aq),}} \quad CH_3-\underset{\underset{H}{|}}{\overset{\overset{\overset{\overset{+}{NH_3}Cl^-}{}}{|}}{C}}-C\overset{\displaystyle O}{\underset{\displaystyle OH\text{ (aq)}}{}}$$

Amino acids also give other reactions which are typical of carboxylic acids and amines, and these are summarised below:

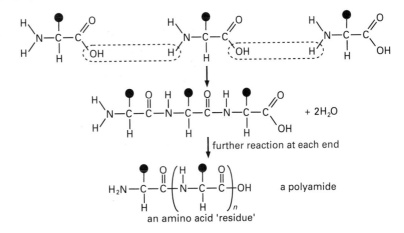

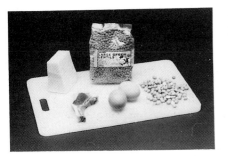

All of these foods are rich in protein. Digestive enzymes catalyse the hydrolysis of the proteins, forming polypeptides and individual amino acids

Polypeptides and proteins

Amino acids undergo **condensation polymerisation** to form long-chain **polyamide** molecules:

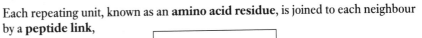

Each repeating unit, known as an **amino acid residue**, is joined to each neighbour by a **peptide link**,

These **'peptisation'** reactions occur readily in living organisms because they are **enzyme-catalysed**. If $n <$ about 50, the product is termed a **polypeptide**; if $n >$ about 50 the product is a **protein**. Proteins fall into two categories: fibrous and globular. Body tissue, such as muscle, hair and skin, is made of **fibrous** (or structural) proteins. These have long straight-chain molecules which are insoluble in water. Fibrous proteins derive their strength from the well-organised close packing of the long molecular chains. These chains are *cross-linked*, often via *hydrogen bonds*, to their neighbours. Two examples of fibrous proteins are **fibroin** (found in silk) and **keratin** (found in hair), and their structures are described in figure 41.11.

Figure 41.11 *Fibroin (a) and keratin (b), two examples of fibrous proteins. Due to hydrogen bonding, the keratin molecule adopts a helical structure. (Dotted lines represent hydrogen bonds)*

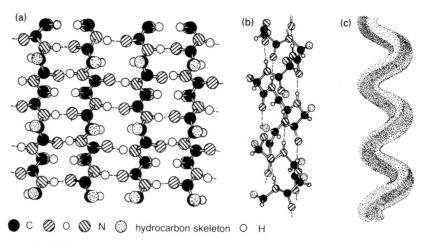

● C   ⊘ O   ⦼ N   ⊙ hydrocarbon skeleton   ○ H

As their name implies, **globular** proteins tend to have a more spherical shape, e.g. myoglobin (figure 41.12). Indeed, globular proteins have complex 3-dimensional molecular structures which govern the way they function, for example, as enzymes and hormones.

Figure 41.12 *Myoglobin, a globular protein, has a complex 3-dimensional structure. Straight sections of helical structure are joined together via non-helical linkages. A haem group is held in position between the chains*

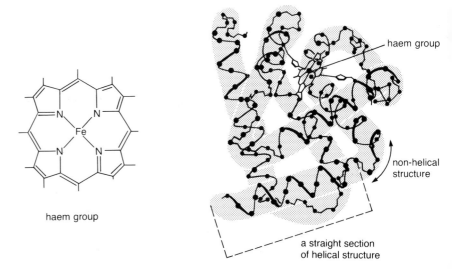

haem group

haem group

non-helical structure

a straight section of helical structure

Figure 41.13 *The 'lock and key' theory of enzyme action. (a) The enzyme and protein molecules approach each other. (b) They fit together like a 'key' in a 'lock'. This creates an unstable energy system, which leads to chemical reaction. In (c) the protein molecule is split into two. (d) The reaction products (peptide fragments) and enzyme molecule separate*

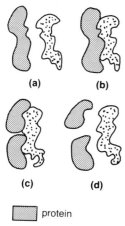

(a)   (b)

(c)   (d)

▓ protein

░ enzyme

An **enzyme** is an organic catalyst which brings about a specific reaction of a biochemical compound, termed the **substrate**. Each enzyme has its substrate. For example, α-amylase, an enzyme which is found in saliva, breaks down starch, its substrate, to give maltose, a sugar. Enzyme action may be simply explained by using the **'lock and key'** theory (figure 41.13). A rise in temperature or a change in pH can alter the 3-dimensional structure of the enzyme molecule and, as a result, its catalytic ability may be removed. In this case, the enzyme is said to be **denatured**.

Hormones control the growth rate and regulate metabolic reactions. For example, sugar metabolism is governed by the hormone **insulin**. This is a globular protein which is made up of fifty-one amino acid residues. In 1954, insulin became the first protein to have its amino acid sequence worked out. This followed ten years of painstaking research by Sanger, who was later awarded the Nobel Prize for Chemistry. First of all, Sanger broke down the insulin in various ways (e.g. acid catalysed hydrolysis) to produce smaller molecular fragments. These were separated and identified using **paper chromatography** (figure 41.14). Eventually, Sanger was able to fit these fragments to give the complete amino acid sequence. Nowadays, the complex 3-dimensional structures of proteins are investigated using X-ray diffraction and electron microscopy.

Figure 41.14 *The 17 amino acids of insulin can be separated using paper chromatography. A mixture of the free acids is obtained by hydrolysing the insulin. A 'spot' of this mixture is placed on the + mark. The amino acids are partially separated using a butan-1-ol/ethanoic acid solvent. The separation is completed by turning the paper through 90° and using aqueous phenol as solvent. The positions of the amino acids are obtained by spraying the chromatogram with ninhydrin spray, when purple dots will appear*

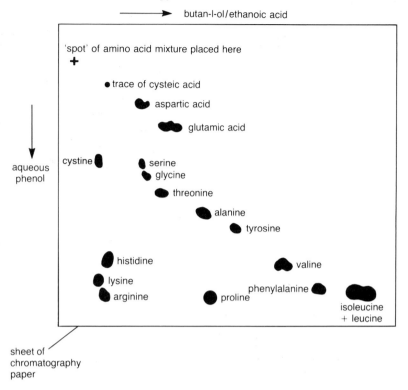

butan-1-ol / ethanoic acid

'spot' of amino acid mixture placed here

trace of cysteic acid
aspartic acid
glutamic acid
cystine
serine
glycine
threonine
alanine
tyrosine
histidine
valine
lysine
phenylalanine
arginine
proline
isoleucine + leucine

aqueous phenol

sheet of chromatography paper

41.12 Comments on the activities

Activity 41.1

1   (a) 1-nitrobutane (b) propanonitrile (c) triethylamine
     (d) dimethylethylamine (e) 2-methylbutanamide (f) 2-aminobenzoic acid
     (g) N-methylphenylamine (h) N-methyl-N-phenylbenzamide.

2

(a) $CH_3-\overset{\overset{\displaystyle NO_2H}{|}}{\underset{\underset{\displaystyle H}{|}}{C}}-\overset{\overset{\displaystyle}{}}{\underset{\underset{\displaystyle CH_3}{|}}{C}}-CH_3$

(b) $CH_3-CH_2-\overset{\overset{\displaystyle CH_3}{|}}{\underset{\underset{\displaystyle H}{|}}{C}}-CN$

(c) $CH_3CH_2-\overset{\overset{\displaystyle NH_2}{|}}{\underset{\underset{\displaystyle H}{|}}{C}}-CH_2CH_3$

(d) $\langle\bigcirc\rangle-CH_2NH_2$

(e) $CH_3-\overset{\overset{\displaystyle CH_3}{|}}{N}$ (ring)

(f) $CH_3CH_2C\overset{\displaystyle O}{\underset{\displaystyle N-H}{\big\backslash}}$ (ring)

(g) $^5CH_3-\overset{\overset{\displaystyle CH_3}{|}}{\underset{\underset{\displaystyle H}{|}}{\overset{4}{C}}}-\overset{3}{CH_2}-\overset{\overset{\displaystyle NH_2}{|}}{\underset{\underset{\displaystyle H}{|}}{\overset{2}{C}}}-\overset{1}{C}\overset{\displaystyle O}{\underset{\displaystyle OH}{\big\backslash}}$

3

1°: $CH_3CH_2CH_2NH_2$ $\langle\bigcirc\rangle-NH_2$ $CH_3-\langle\bigcirc\rangle-NH_2$ $H_2N-\langle\bigcirc\rangle-NH_2$
       propylamine   phenylamine   (4-methylphenyl)amine   1,4-diaminobenzene

2°: $\overset{\displaystyle C_2H_5}{\underset{\displaystyle H}{\diagdown}}N$ (ring) $\overset{\displaystyle C_2H_5}{\underset{\displaystyle C_2H_5}{\big\backslash}}N$ with H

       N-ethylphenylamine   diethylamine

3°:

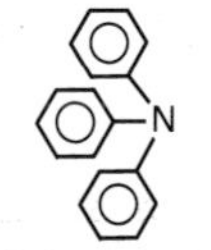

triphenylamine 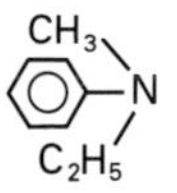   N–methyl–N–ethylphenylamine

Activity 41.2

1 (a) KCN (ethanol), reflux.

(b)
$$CH_3CH(C_2H_5)-COOH \xrightarrow[\text{room temp.}]{\text{conc.NH}_3\,(aq)} CH_3CH(C_2H_5)-COO^-NH_4^+ \xrightarrow[\text{reflux}]{P_4O_{10}\,(s)} CH_3CH(C_2H_5)-CN$$

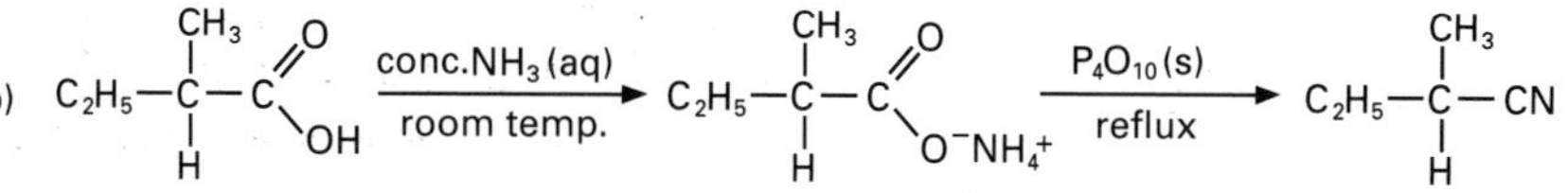

2

(a) (4–methylphenyl)amine $CH_3-\!\!\bigcirc\!\!-NH_2$

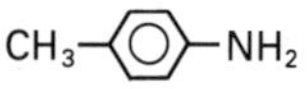

(b) 2,2–dimethyl–propanoic acid $CH_3-C(CH_3)_2-COOH$

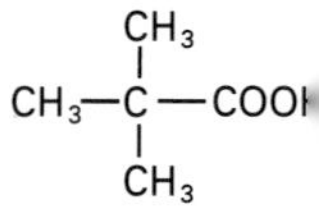

(c) phenylmethylamine $\bigcirc\!\!-CH_2NH_2$

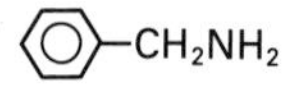

(d) 1st step: 2–hydroxy–propanonitrile $CH_3-CH(OH)-CN$

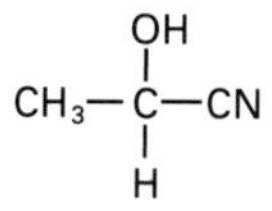

2nd step: 2–hydroxypropanoic acid $CH_3-CH(OH)-COOH$

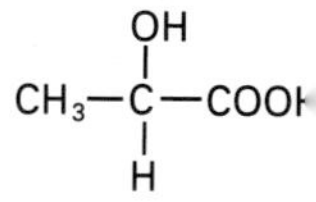

3.

(a) $CH_3-C(=O)-\bigcirc \xrightarrow[\text{room temp}]{\text{KCN, dil.NaOH(aq)}} CH_3-C^*(OH)(\bigcirc)-CN \xrightarrow[\text{reflux}]{\text{dil. H}_2SO_4\,(aq)} CH_3-C^*(OH)(\bigcirc)-COOH$

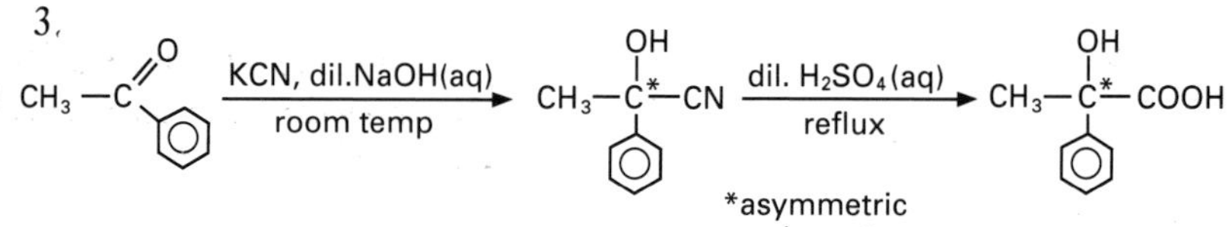

*asymmetric carbon atom

(b) $CH_3-CBr_2-CH_3 \xrightarrow[\text{reflux}]{\text{KCN (ethanol)}} CH_3-C(CN)_2-CH_3 \xrightarrow[\substack{\text{ethoxyethane}\\ \text{reflux}}]{\text{LiAlH}_4 \text{ in}} CH_3-C(CH_2NH_2)_2-CH_3$

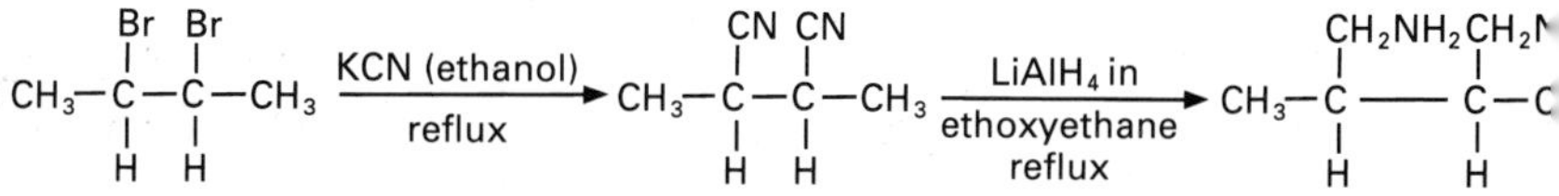

(c) $CH_3CH=CH_2 \xrightarrow[\text{room temp.}]{\text{HBr(g)}} CH_3-CBr(H)-CH_3 \xrightarrow[\text{reflux}]{\text{KCN (ethanol)}} CH_3-C(CN)(H)-CH_3$

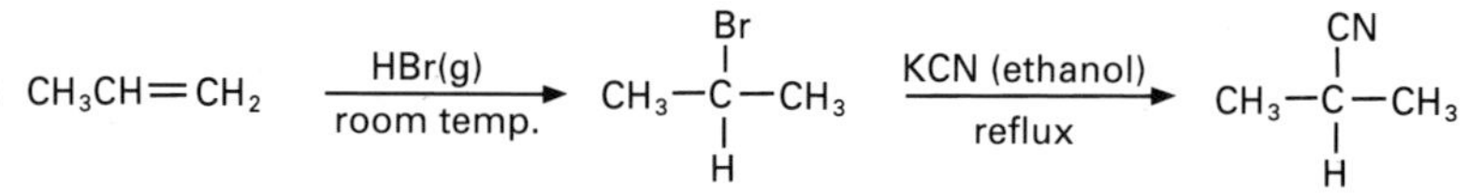

Note: *Markovnikov's Rule* is followed in step 1.

(d) $CH_3OH \xrightarrow[\text{reflux}]{P_{(red)} + I_2(s)} CH_3I \xrightarrow[\text{reflux}]{\text{KCN (ethanol)}} CH_3CN$

Activity 41.3

1 triphenylamine < phenylamine < ammonia < triethylamine < ethylamine
< diethylamine < tetraethylammonium hydroxide.
Since **quaternary ammonium hydroxides**, such as $(C_2H_5)_4N^+OH^-$, are ionic compounds, they ionise completely in aqueous solution. Hence, they are **strong bases**.

2 (a) $2C_2H_5NH_2(l) + H_2SO_4(aq) \rightarrow (C_2H_5\overset{+}{N}H_3)_2SO_4^{2-}(aq)$

(b) $\bigcirc\!\!-\overset{+}{N}H_3Cl^-\,(s) + (C_2H_5)_3N\,(l) \longrightarrow \bigcirc\!\!-NH_2\,(l) + \left[(C_2H_5)_3NH\right]^+Cl^-(s)$

stronger base   weaker base

(c) $[(C_2H_5)_3NH]^+Cl^-(s) +$ $NaOH(aq) \rightarrow (C_2H_5)_3N(aq) + Na^+Cl^-(aq) + H_2O(l)$
           stronger   weaker base
           base

3   Each of the amines slightly dissociates in aqueous solution:

$$N\!:\!(aq) + H_2O(l) \rightleftharpoons (\ N\!-\!H)^+(aq) + OH^-(aq)$$

Molarity at   0.01   constant   0   0
start

Molarity at $0.01 - x$ constant x x
equilibrium

Assuming very slight dissociation, $x << 0.01\,M$ and $0.01 - x \approx 0.1$. Thus, we can write down an expression for K_b:

$$K_b = \frac{[(\ N\!-\!H)^+(aq)]\,[OH^-(aq)]}{[\ N\!:\!(aq)]} = \frac{x^2}{0.01}$$

For methylamine, $K_b = 4.4 \times 10^{-4}\,M$. Thus,

$$4.4 \times 10^{-4} = \frac{x^2}{0.01}$$
$$4.4 \times 10^{-6} = x^2$$
$$2.1 \times 10^{-3} = x = [OH^-(aq)]$$
$$pOH = -\log_{10}[OH^-(aq)] = 2.7$$

Since $pH = 14 - pOH$, the pH of 0.01 M aqueous methylamine $= 14 - 2.7 = 11.3$.

Using an identical method, we find that 0.01 M aqueous solutions of dimethylamine and trimethylamine have pH values of 11.4 and 10.9, respectively.

Activity 41.4

1   (a) $[(C_2H_5)_2\overset{+}{N}H_2]_2SO_4^{2-}$ diethylammonium sulphate;
          $(C_2H_5)_2NH$, diethylamine is displaced by KOH, a strong base.

(b)

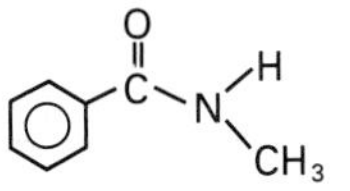

N–methylbenzamide

(c)

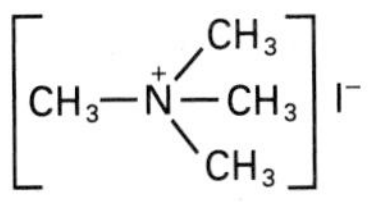

tetramethylammonium iodide, a quaternary ammonium salt

2

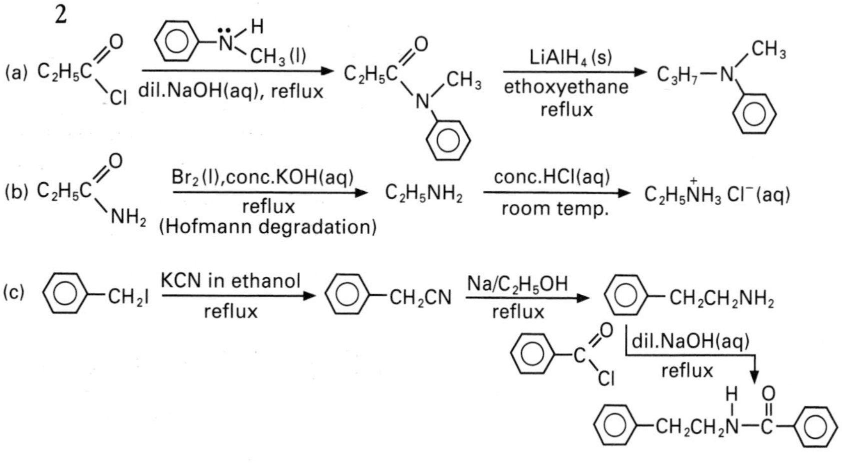

(a)

(b)

(c)

3   (i) With an acid chloride, e.g. ethanoyl chloride:

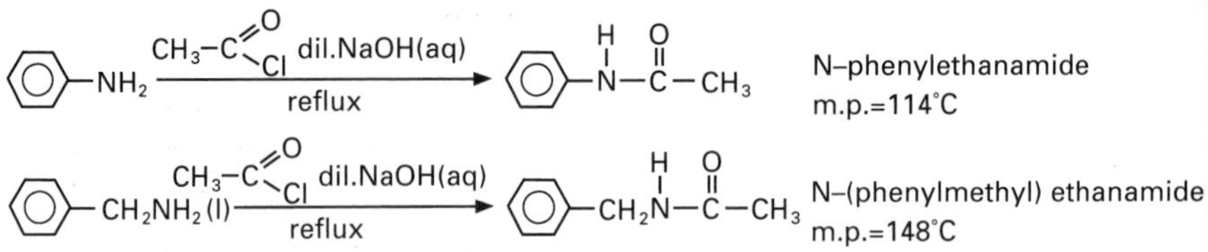

N–phenylethanamide
m.p.=114°C

N–(phenylmethyl) ethanamide
m.p.=148°C

As we saw in section 41.8 pure amides are crystalline solids which can be identified from their sharp melting points. Thus, we can distinguish between the amides and, hence, their parent amines.

(ii) With nitrous acid at 5°C:

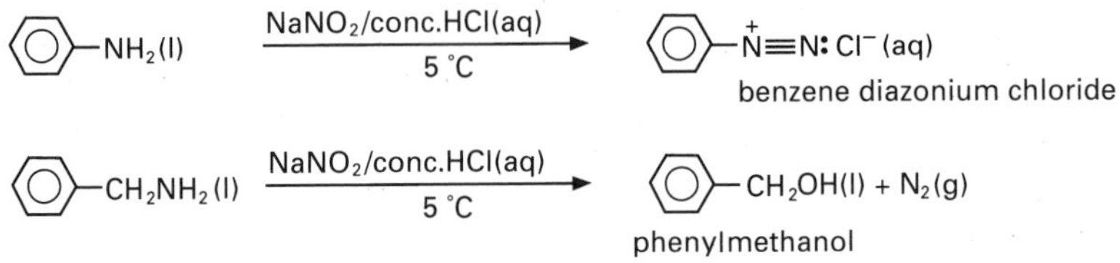

benzene diazonium chloride

phenylmethanol

Thus, bubbles of N_2 gas will only be seen in the reaction with phenylmethylamine.

41.13   Summary and revision plan

1   There are five main types of organic nitrogen compounds: **nitro compounds, nitriles, amines, amides** and **amino acids**.

2   The rules for naming these compounds are summarised in table 41.4.

Table 41.4   *Rules for naming organic nitrogen compounds*

Organic nitrogen compounds	general formula	how to name them
nitro-compounds	□—NO_2	Place the prefix **'nitro'** before the name of the parent hydrocarbon
nitriles	□—CN	Name the hydrocarbon with the same number of C atoms; then replace final **'e'** by **'onitrile'**.
amines	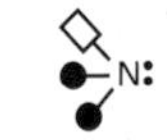 ◇•N:	Place the name of the alkyl, or phenyl, groups before the word **'amine'**; use the prefix **'N-'** to show a hydrocarbon skeleton joined to the N-atom
amides	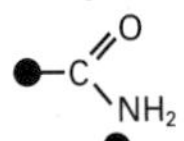 •—C(=O)NH_2	Name the parent acid and change **'oic acid'** to **'amide'**
amino acids	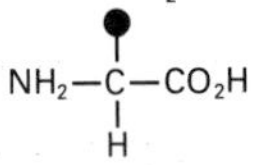 NH_2—C(H)—CO_2H	Place the prefix **'amino'** before the name of the parent carboxylic acid

3   Amines may be **primary (1°), secondary (2°)** or **tertiary (3°)** depending on whether their nitrogen atom is bonded to 1, 2 or 3 hydrocarbon skeletons, respectively.

4   The aliphatic members of each type of organic nitrogen compound form **homologous series**. As the chain length increases, the boiling points and $\Delta H_c^{\ominus}$ values rise steadily.

5   Due to the polarity of their functional groups, organic nitrogen compounds tend to form strong intermolecular **dipole-dipole attractions**. Hence, with the exception of 3° amines, they have higher boiling points than the hydrocarbons of similar molecular mass.

6   Figure 41.15 summarises the common ways of preparing organic nitrogen compounds and their important reactions.

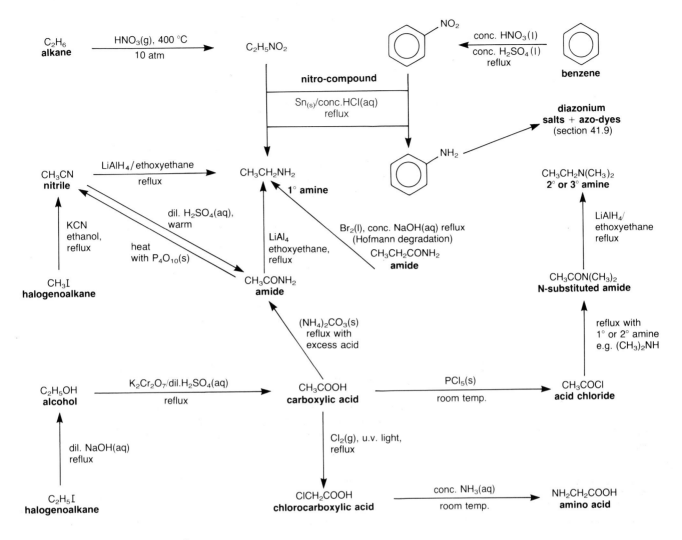

Figure 41.15 *Important synthetic routes for preparing organic nitrogen compounds*

7 Introducing a nitrile group into an organic molecule is an important step in adding a –CH_2– unit (section 41.3).

8 Amines are weak bases. Thus, they dissociate slightly in aqueous solution:

$$\underset{/}{\overset{\textstyle\diagdown}{\Rightarrow}}N: (aq) + H_2O(l) \rightleftharpoons [\underset{\Rightarrow}{\overset{\textstyle\diagdown}{}}N{-}H]^+(aq) + OH^-(aq)$$

The **base dissociation constant, K_b,** is given by

$$K_b = \frac{[(\overset{\diagdown}{\Rightarrow}N{-}H)^+]\,[OH^-(aq)]}{[\overset{\diagdown}{\Rightarrow}N{:}]}$$

Also, **$pK_b = -\log_{10}K_b$.** For stronger bases, K_b is *larger* and pK_b is *smaller*.

9 The K_b values reveal a pattern in amine basicity, namely,

increasing base strength ⟶

phenylamine ≪ ammonia < tertiary < primary < secondary

aliphatic

The basicity of an amine depends on (i) the availability of the lone pair on nitrogen for protonation and (ii) the stability of the resulting alkyl or alkylammonium ion. Since they have only a limited capacity for hydrogen bonding with water, tertiary alkylammonium ions, $[\overset{\diagdown}{\Rightarrow} N{-}H]^+(aq)$, are much less stable than primary or secondary alkylammonium ions. Thus, 3° amines are much weaker bases than other aliphatic amines.

Table 41.5 *Important reactions of amines*

Reagents/conditions	1° amines, e.g. $C_2H_5NH_2$	2° amines, e.g. $(C_2H_5)_2NH$	3° amines, e.g. $(C_2H_5)_3N$
strong acid (e.g. HCl(aq)), room temp.	**ionic salts** are formed $\rightarrow C_2H_5\overset{+}{N}H_3Cl^-$	$(C_2H_5)_2\overset{+}{N}H_2Cl^-$	$(C_2H_5)_3\overset{+}{N}H\,Cl^-$
acid chloride $CH_3C\overset{O}{\underset{Cl}{\diagup}}$ e.g.; room temp. *or* warming (base catalyst needed if aromatic amine used)	**N-substituted amides** formed $\rightarrow CH_3C\overset{O}{\underset{N\diagdown H}{\diagup}}{}^{C_2H_5}$	$CH_3C\overset{O}{\underset{N\diagdown C_2H_5}{\diagup}}{}^{C_2H_5}$	no reaction
halogenoalkane (e.g. CH_3I), heat in sealed vessel with excess amine	$\rightarrow$ **2° amine** $C_2H_5\diagdown \underset{H\diagup}{N}{-}CH_3$	$\rightarrow$ **3° amine** $C_2H_5\diagdown \underset{C_2H_5\diagup}{N}{-}CH_3$	$\rightarrow$ **quaternary ammonium salt** $\left[\begin{array}{c}C_2H_5\\C_2H_5{-}N{-}CH_3\\C_2H_5\end{array}\right]^+ I^-$
$NaNO_2$/dil. HCl(aq), (nitrous acid, HNO_2, *in situ*); 5 °C	aliphatic: $\rightarrow$ **alcohol** $+ N_2$(g) (C_2H_5OH) aromatic: $\rightarrow$ **diazonium salt** $\langle\!\bigcirc\!\rangle{-}\overset{+}{N}{\equiv}N\ Cl^-$ (aq)	a **nitrosoamine** e.g. $(C_2H_5)_2\,N{-}N{=}O$, a very poisonous oil.	aliphatic: $\rightarrow$ **nitrite salt** e.g. $(C_2H_5)_3\overset{+}{N}H\,NO^-$ aromatic: $\rightarrow$ **a nitroso salt**

How can making an amide help us to identify an amine or an acid chloride?

10 Due to the lone pair on nitrogen, amines react as bases and as nucleophiles. Their reactions are summarised in table 41.5.

11 The reaction of amines with **nitrous acid** is very important because:
▶ it allows us to classify an unknown amine as being 1°, 2° or 3°, aliphatic or aromatic; and
▶ 1° aromatic amines form **diazonium salts** (e.g. benzenediazonium chloride, $\langle\!\bigcirc\!\rangle{-}\underset{\sim}{N}{=}\overset{+}{\underset{\sim}{N}}Cl^-$, which are very valuable in organic synthesis).

12 Diazonium salts give two types of reaction:
▶ those in which N_2 **is evolved** and a nucleophilic group (e.g. $-I$, $-OH$) is attached to the benzene ring; and
▶ **coupling reactions** in which the nitrogen atoms remain as an **azo-group**, $-N{=}N-$. These are brightly coloured compounds, many of which are used as dyes.
Some important reactions of diazonium salts were given in section 41.9.

13 Although an amide contains the NH_2 group, the lone pairs of electrons on nitrogen is delocalised over the N—C—O σ bond framework. Thus, amides are extremely weak bases and very poor nucleophiles.

14 2-amino acids contain both $-NH_2$ and $-COOH$ groups. They are crystalline solids whose molecules exist as internal salts or **zwitterions**;

$$\overset{+}{N}H_3{-}\underset{H}{\overset{\bullet}{C}}{-}CO_2^-$$

Glycine apart, 2-amino acids are **optically active** (all laevoratatory). They show the typical chemical properties of amines and carboxylic acids.

15 A naturally occurring amino acid can be identified by measuring its **isoelectric point** (section 41.11).

16   Like the monomers of Nylon 66, amino acids form **condensation polymers**:

$$H_2N-\overset{\bullet}{\underset{H}{\overset{|}{C}}}-\overset{O}{\overset{||}{C}}-\left(\overset{H}{\underset{}{\overset{|}{N}}}-\overset{\bullet}{\underset{H}{\overset{|}{C}}}-\overset{O}{\overset{||}{C}}\right)_n-OH$$

In naturally occurring molecules, $\left(\overset{H}{\underset{H}{\overset{|}{N}}}-\overset{\bullet}{\underset{|}{\overset{|}{C}}}-\overset{O}{\overset{||}{C}}\right)$ can be one of about 22 different

groups. Each repeating unit, termed an amino acid residue, is joined to its neighbours via **peptide links**

$$\left(\overset{O}{\underset{}{\overset{||}{C}}}-\overset{H}{\underset{}{\overset{|}{N}}}\right)$$

In **proteins,** $n >$ about 50 residues.

17   About a sixth of our bodyweight is protein. **Fibrous** proteins have long straight-chain molecules which cross-link together to form materials of great strength and flexibility (e.g. skin and muscle). Molecules of a **globular** protein have a complex 3-dimensional structure. This enables them to perform highly specific biological functions (e.g. as enzymes and hormones).

18   Important reagents used in this chapter are listed in table 41.6.

Table 41.6   *Important reagents used in this chapter.*

Reagent/conditions	what it does
reagents in table 41.5	convert amines into various products
conc. $HNO_3(l)$, conc. $H_2SO_4(l)$, 55 °C	**nitrates** a benzene ring
Sn(s), conc. HCl(l) reflux	**reduces** an aromatic nitro-compound to a **primary amine**
KCN/ethanol, reflux	converts $\overset{}{\underset{}{>}}C-Hal \longrightarrow \overset{}{\underset{}{>}}C-CN$ thereby adding *another* C atom to the hydrocarbon skeleton
$LiAlH_4$/ethoxyethane, reflux	reducing agent; **nitrile → amine** $\overset{}{\underset{}{>}}C-CN \longrightarrow \overset{}{\underset{}{>}}C-CH_2NH_2$
$Br_2(l)$/conc. NaOH(aq), reflux	Hofmann degration: **amide → amine** having *one less* C atom
KI(aq), reflux	converts **diazonium salt** → iodobenzene
conc. HBr(aq), CuBr(s) reflux	→ bromobenzene
conc. HCl(aq) CuCl(s), reflux	→ chlorobenzene
NaCN(aq), CuCN(s), reflux	→ benzonitrile
$H_2O(l)$, boil	→ phenol
aromatic amine or phenol, 5 °C	converts **diazonium salt → azo-dyes**
PCl_5(s), room temp.	**halogenates** an amino acid, e.g. $NH_2CH_2CO_2H \longrightarrow NH_2CH_2C\overset{O}{\underset{Cl}{}}$
alcohol (e.g. $(CH_3OH(l))$), conc. $H_2SO_4(l)$, reflux	**esterification** of an amino acid, e.g. $NH_2CH_2CO_2H \longrightarrow NH_2CH_2C\overset{O}{\underset{OCH_3}{}}$

Index